# Licensing Intellectual Property in the Information Age

# Licensing Intellectual Property in the Information Age

SECOND EDITION

**Kenneth L. Port**
DIRECTOR OF INTELLECTUAL PROPERTY LAW STUDIES
WILLIAM MITCHELL COLLEGE OF LAW
ST. PAUL, MINNESOTA

**Jay Dratler, Jr.**
GOODYEAR PROFESSOR OF INTELLECTUAL PROPERTY
UNIVERSITY OF AKRON SCHOOL OF LAW
AKRON, OHIO

**Faye M. Hammersley, Esq.**
SCIENCE APPLICATIONS INTERNATIONAL CORPORATION
WASHINGTON, D.C.

**Terence P. McElwee**
INTELLECTUAL PROPERTY COUNSEL
UNIVERSITY OF ILLINOIS AT CHICAGO
CHICAGO, ILLINOIS

**Charles R. McManis**
WASHINGTON UNIVERSITY SCHOOL OF LAW
ST. LOUIS, MISSOURI

**Barbara A. Wrigley**
OPPENHEIMER, WOLFF AND DONNELLY, LLP
MINNEAPOLIS, MINNESOTA

CAROLINA ACADEMIC PRESS
Durham, North Carolina

ISBN 0-89089-890-1
LCCN 2005926966

CAROLINA ACADEMIC PRESS
700 Kent Street
Durham, North Carolina 27701
Telephone (919) 489-7486
Fax (919) 493-5668
www.cap-press.com

Printed in the United States of America

To Ellie, Emi and Paula
*K.L.P.*


To my wife, Aileen, whose steadfast love, patience, and
encouragement helped inspire me to make a contribution
to this book and to find the time to write it
*J.D.*


To Tom and Mary
*F.M.H.*


To Beth
*T.P.M.*


To my mother, Ruth
*C.R.M.*


To my parents, Bob and Frances, to whom I owe everything
*B.A.W.*

# Summary of Contents

# Contents

# Contents

# Preface to the Second Edition

In the short five years since the First Edition of this book was published, intellectual property licensing has grown even more significant than it was at that time. The global intellectual property licensing market now stands at more than $100 billion. Intellectual property assets today account for more than 40% of the net value of all corporations in America. *See* Kamil Idris, *Intellectual Property: A Power Tool For Economic Growth* 34 (2002). One simply cannot overstate the importance of intellectual property licensing to all American attorneys.

In recognition of the increased importance of licensing, we substantially revised the First Edition. So much has changed, in fact, that we decided to change the title of the book. It is no longer a "digital" age. Rather, we now, quite clearly, live in a more general "information" age. The new title is intended to capture that fact.

We have extensively modified and supplemented the material for wider coverage and better pedagogy. For example, there is a new chapter on licensing in the biotechnology field (Chapter 14). The introductory material in Chapter 1 has been completely redone to express our understanding that intellectual property licensing is truly an interdisciplinary field. Additionally, Chapter 2 on intellectual property in general has been completely revised to make it a better review and more accessible to students. Chapter 7 on common clauses in licensing agreements was redone to increase its scope and provide better explanation. Chapter 8 regarding software licenses was reworked to keep it as up to date as possible. Chapter 9 on antitrust was revised to add a section on misuse, provide better grounding in the basics and address the challenging issues posed by *United States v. Microsoft*. Many other changes were made.

We also decided that we could serve those adopting this book better if we moved the problems to a web site. Therefore, the problems were all deleted from the hard copy of this textbook. They can be found at www.caplaw.com/licensing. Making the problems web-based will allow us to update them and change them as this field continues to evolve. If you adopt this book, please refer to the web site often to keep track of these changes.

Also, in recognition of the growing complexity of intellectual property licensing, we found it extremely helpful to add two new co-authors to our efforts. Barbara Wrigley is a partner in the intellectual property practice group of Oppenheimer, Wolff and Donnelly LLP in Minneapolis, Minnesota, and has a substantial licensing practice. Her practice area requires her to be on the practical, front line of many of the issues presented in this book.

We also added Professor Jay Dratler, Jr., the Goodyear Professor of Intellectual Property at the University of Akron School of Law. For years, Professor Dratler has been a household name in the field of intellectual property licensing. In addition to his incredible depth of knowledge, he also brought an important eye for detail that has served this project well.

# Preface to the First Edition

Intellectual property is quickly becoming one of the most financially significant assets of corporations. The ability to recognize intellectual property which has value to others, select appropriate licensing partners, exploit that intellectual property for commercial gain, and police the quality of licensed properties significantly contributes to the net worth of any corporation engaged in such activity. Licensing intellectual property also plays a significant role in gaining market share.

Today, the retail sales of licensed consumer products worldwide alone exceeds $110 billion dollars per year. The United States Office of Technology Assessment estimates that the world trade in intellectual property directly affects 2.2% of the United States labor force and 5% of the gross national product. A full 25% by value of United States exports are in the form of licensed intellectual property. Any single industry that represents 25% of all United States exports clearly rises to the level of a national security issue.

However, a large portion of this market is being usurped via pirated intellectual property. Although no one is certain of the precise value of the pirated intellectual property, nor can commentators agree exactly on the impact it has on the United States economy as a whole, it is clear that for individual intellectual property owners the impact is substantial. Some industries, such as the compact disc industry, report that the size of their market would double but for international pirating. Whatever the actual size of the pirated market, it all represents potential licensing opportunities.

Therefore, it is crucial that well-trained American lawyers be familiar with the issues involved in the licensing of intellectual property. As intellectual property is involved in one quarter of our national exports, licensing clearly pervades much of the practice of law in any corporate/business setting.

This textbook is intended as an instructional tool to be used by law students at American law schools to understand the complex field of intellectual property licensing. There are many pitfalls that confront any entity attempting to become either a licensee or a licensor of intellectual property. A poorly drafted trademark license agreement, for example, will be null and void in the United States if quality control provisions are not included, and will likely result in a judicial finding of abandonment of the trademark itself. That is, without due care, a good faith attempt to license a trademark that was considered valuable enough to command a license royalty could result in the loss of the trademark right in its entirety.

First, this course book provides an introduction to the business and substantive law of intellectual property licensing. Next, the book methodically analyzes each area of legal concern raised by most intellectual property license agreements. Students should recognize that the subject of the book is about actually practicing intellectual property licensing. Because this practice consists largely of the art of negotiating and drafting license agreements, the book focuses on the license agreement as the targeted end product. Each chapter presents the relevant substantive law and commercial practice using cases, statutes or law review articles. The problem at the end of each chapter allows students to engage the subject, practice skills discussed in the substantive portion of each chapter, and actually "do" law rather than merely talk about it.

The term "intellectual property" as used herein means patents, trademarks, copyrights, trade secrets, and rights of publicity. For those students not familiar with one or more of these substantive areas of the law, Chapter 2 provides an overview. We begin, however, with a more detailed analysis of why owners of patents, trademarks, copyrights, trade secrets or rights of publicity should consider licensing as a business strategy.

# Acknowledgments

The authors would like to thank Mary Dicig, Howard Bremer, Mark Mersereau, Carl Christensen, and Jacie Sprtel. We also would like to express our appreciation to the various students at William Mitchell College of Law, Washington University, and the University of Akron who helped "test drive" various editions of this book. We are also deeply indebted to Meg Daniel and Cal Bonde, faculty support personnel at William Mitchell College of Law. Their dedication and encouragement are appreciated beyond words.

Jay Dratler, Jr. adds as follows:

I'd also like to acknowledge the help—sometimes unwitting—of students in my courses on licensing, copyright, computer law, and cyberlaw. They tested early versions of my contributions and helped me refine them. Without their help, I would not have understood what students of IP and licensing need to know most.

My contributions to this book are deeply indebted to my own legal education at Harvard Law School some thirty years ago. Wide-ranging courses in Accounting for Lawyers, Economics for Lawyers, Corporate Finance and Business Planning—not to mention what little IP was taught back then—instilled in me an interdisciplinary approach to the law. That approach guided me through eight years of practice and two decades of teaching and still helps me handle the subtle blend of law, business, economics, science and engineering that is licensing.

I'd also like to acknowledge help from two decades ago, during my practice in the heart of Silicon Valley. For four years, Fenwick and West gave me the opportunity to specialize almost exclusively in licensing. As I prepared to debark for academia, that firm provided moral and some financial support for a project that eventually became my treatises on licensing and IP. In the same vein, thanks are belatedly due to a former client, Micro Focus, and Paul Adams, its marketing executive some twenty years ago. While helping drive his firm to a successful public offering, Paul taught me more about the business of licensing—and the practical importance of slicing and dicing the field of use—than I've ever found in any book.

It has taken almost two decades for academia to catch up to practice and allow me to put what I learned back then into a full course on licensing that a law school could offer. My colleague Professor Jeffrey Samuels and my Dean and Associate Dean Richard Aynes and Elizabeth Reilly deserve credit for making it possible to offer a full course in licensing at the University of Akron. So do the rest of the faculty there, who wholeheartedly supported our nascent IP program from the very beginning.

Finally, I'd like to acknowledge our lead author, Ken Port. Without his initiative, leadership, patience, and persistence neither this book nor this improved Second Edition would exist. He made them happen.

Barbara A. Wrigley writes:

I would like to acknowledge various people who have fielded my constant questions during the past two years as I delved into many of the finer details that this text explores, especially Dena Van De Voort for her research assistance; Shirley Bock for her input on security interests; Jim Jorrisen for his expertise on the bankruptcy process; Barb Grahn for providing some pointers related to the practical aspects of licensing trademarks; and my assistants Kimberly Hayes, Pam Pederson and Brea Taken for getting the job done. If I have forgotten to mention any names it is merely my memory, not your lack of contribution or my appreciation of your input.

I would also like to acknowledge my co-authors, Ken, Jay, Chuck, Terry and Faye. I have learned much from each of you.

Without the support and understanding of my partners and colleagues at Oppenheimer Wolff & Donnelly, I would not have been able to devote the substantial amount of time that I did to writing, reviewing and editing the present text. Thank you.

I would also like to acknowledge the students in my Licensing Law classes. When Ken Port mentioned to me several years ago that William Mitchell College of Law was going to offer a class in Licensing Law and he was looking for an adjunct professor to teach it, I jumped at the opportunity. I remember my first day of class thinking how bright the students were. That sums up my experience at William Mitchell, a student body that is inquisitive, bright, and engaged. While there are too many names to mention, I thank each of you for having a great deal of patience and for providing your insight into the unfinished chapters and materials from which I taught. It has been my pleasure.

Lastly, I would like to acknowledge and thank the many clients I have represented and who, throughout my sixteen years of practice, have given me the opportunity to hone my "licensing law" skills in real time.

# Editorial Note

All deleted passages from excerpted articles and cases are indicated. Some footnotes have been deleted. Some have been renumbered.

# Licensing Intellectual Property
# in the Information Age

# Chapter 1

# What is Licensing?

## I. Introduction: The Importance of Licensing

A course on licensing is a "capstone" course in any intellectual property program. If you are a law student reading this book, you probably have taken a course in intellectual property. You may also have taken specialized courses in patents, trade secrets, copyright, or trademarks and unfair competition. No doubt you know something about intellectual property rights and how their owners enforce them in litigation. You also may know something about the remedies that an intellectual property owner whose rights are infringed can seek. What now? What can you do with that knowledge?

Generally speaking, intellectual property lawyers spend their time on three tasks: obtaining rights, litigating them, and transacting business in them. The usual law-school curriculum, however, deals in depth with one of the three alone: litigation. By the time you graduate from law school you will have read hundreds, if not thousands, of judicial opinions—usually of appellate courts—reporting the final results of litigation. Some of the cases you have read may have discussed obtaining and transacting rights indirectly, in the course of resolving a dispute. Some casebooks also may have brief descriptions of or notes on right-securing activity. Yet the emphasis on claims and defenses in litigation is overwhelming. So at this point you may know little about the two other major tasks on which intellectual property lawyers spend their days (and often their nights as well).

Logically speaking, the intellectual property lawyer's first task is to secure and perfect legal rights for clients. Patent lawyers draft and revise patent applications and "prosecute" them through the United States Patent and Trademark Office (PTO) until they are abandoned or patents issue. Trade-secret lawyers advise clients on trade-secrete protection programs, including security precautions, document marking, and contractual restraints. Copyright and trademark lawyers secure federal registrations. Sometimes trademark lawyers also help clients select trademarks that avoid conflicts with others' pre-existing rights and secure common-law rights. Intellectual property lawyers also draft relevant contracts, such as employment contracts, memoranda, and policy manuals.

Yet except for patent prosecution (on which some patent lawyers spend their whole careers), this work is hardly a full-time job. Today many firms employ legal assistants to draft and file applications for copyright and trademark registration, using lawyers only to review their work and handle problems that arise. If intellectual property lawyers had to depend upon securing rights to make a living, most of them (except patent lawyers) would starve.

Business transactions in intellectual property, however, are a whole different story. They are ubiquitous. Remember the contracts on which you click "I agree" (usually without reading them) while downloading computer software or installing it on your PC? Those are licenses. When you rent a movie on a DVD or VHS tape from your local video store, what gives you the right to play it? An *implied* license does—implied in the rental and its customary purpose. May you take your rental DVD or tape and show the movie to the public, charging an admission fee? No, because your implied license is limited to *private* performances. The copyright owner has the exclusive right to *public* performances, see 17 U.S.C. §106(4), and it usually reserves that right through (*inter alia*) a notice that appears on your screen as you play the movie.

As this last example shows, licensing is a complex business. Whether express or implied, a license may grant some rights while withholding others, and the entire structure of an industry may depend what rights it grants and withholds. Imagine, for example, what might happen to movie distribution if local video stores could authorize renters of DVDs and tapes to perform them publicly. The whole complex distribution network of the movie industry—which determines what theaters get to run what movies first—would collapse like a house of cards. The same is true of the software industry. How long would Microsoft, for example, stay in business if its shrinkwrap license allowed you to make unlimited copies of its operating systems and sell them to anyone?

These two simple examples, both from common experience, illustrate three important lessons of licensing. First, the *scope* of a license—what rights it grants and what it withholds, can make or break a business, even an industry. Second, licensing has a vast effect on our national economy. Without licensing as we know it, both the movie and the software industries might be very different and much smaller.

The third lesson is even more important—and crucial for this course. The terms of licensing agreements are often intimately bound up with the structure, operation and customs of a particular field of commerce or industry. Could you really understand the terms of your implied license to play a rented movie privately without knowing, at minimum, that the movie industry has a whole separate network of distributors—in place long before VHS tapes and DVDs were invented—for licensing public performances in theaters? Could you understand the typical end-user (software) license agreement without knowing that software vendors like Microsoft also have a separate network of distributors and want to give "end users" like you only a highly restricted rights to *use* their software, not to modify or distribute it, and then only in object-code form (a form that is difficult to read, understand, and modify)? As these examples illustrate, understanding the commercial and industrial context of a license is the key to understanding its terms. And as we will see, understanding context is also the key to drafting a license agreement that does the intended job, makes sense, and is likely to be enforced as the drafter intended.

It is also useful to recognize that licensing and other business transactions in intellectual property utterly dwarf litigation on any rational scale of economic importance. Lawsuits represent a failure of both the business deal and the legal system to specify rights clearly or fairly enough to avoid disputes. They are the friction in the well-oiled machine of our national economy. Yet that machine generally runs smoothly, day in and day out, as businesses form, operate, merge, consolidate, produce and sell products and services, and license other businesses to do the same—all without litigation. A Martian with economic training, on visiting Earth, might be surprised that students of intellectual property spend so much time studying the friction in the system and so little exploring its normal operation.

So it is to business, not friction, that this book is dedicated. Specifically, it is dedicated to the art, science and business of commercializing intellectual property. Of course, the "friction" of litigation employs large numbers of lawyers, and the risk of litigation is something that all transactional lawyers must keep in mind. But we begin with an emphasis on the positive: how licensing builds business and wealth in the information age. As we will see, that process can be as complex and intricate—and as fascinating—as the new global economy itself.

# II. Intellectual Property: An Odd Form of "Property" Indeed

Although we speak of intellectual *property*, a patent, trade secret, copyright, or trademark is very different from other forms of property (some claim it is not property at all). Unlike real or personal property, it is an invisible, intangible right. You cannot hold it, see it, touch it, weigh it, or use it directly to make anything of value. Without our entire legal system to enforce it, intellectual property would be utterly useless, for it has no intrinsic value at all.

This is not surprising, for intellectual property has one thing in common with other property rights: its essence is the right to exclude. Virtually every form of intellectual property reflects this fact, although the right to exclude is in some cases qualified or limited. For example, consider the following:

- A patent provides the right "to exclude others from making, using, offering for sale, or selling the [patented] invention throughout the United States or importing the invention into the United States, and, if the invention is a process,...the right to exclude others from using, offering for sale or selling throughout the United States, or importing into the United States, products made by that process...." 35 U.S.C. § 154(a)(1).

- A copyright provides "the exclusive rights to do and to authorize" any of six specified acts, namely: reproduction, preparation of derivative works (adaptation), distribution, public performance, public display, and digital audio transmission. 17 U.S.C. § 106. While the copyright act speaks of "exclusive rights" and not the right to exclude, it amounts to the same thing, for any unauthorized act within the copyright holder's exclusive rights can be enjoined. *See* 17 U.S.C. § 501(a) (defining infringement as violation of exclusive rights); 17 U.S.C. § 502 (prescribing injunctive relief as remedy).

- A legally protected trade secret provides the limited right to exclude others from acquiring the secret by improper means or using or disclosing a secret so acquired. *See* Uniform Trade Secrets Act § 1(1) (defining "misappropriation"); *id.*, § 1(2) (defining "improper means").

- Any trademark, even if not registered, provides only the right to exclude others from using it in a manner "likely to cause confusion, or to cause mistake, or to deceive as to the affiliation, connection, or association of [the user] with another person, or as to the origin, sponsorship, or approval of his or her goods, services or commercial activities by another person[.]" Lanham Act § 43(a)(1), 15 U.S.C. § 1125(a)(1). *See also*, Lanham Act § 32(1), 15 U.S.C. § 1114(1) (similar language for registered trademarks).

Thus, every form of intellectual property provides the owner with well-defined rights to exclude others from doing something that, in the absence of the legal system, they would be perfectly free to do.

What makes intellectual property a strange form of property is that it is quintessentially intangible.

All forms of property ultimately depend on intangible legal rights to exclude others. Yet traditional forms of property also refer to something tangible, which you can see, touch and feel. This point is obvious for tangible personal property, such as a car, a book or a cow. It also applies to real property, which you can see, touch, and enter. Indeed our forebears emphasized the tangible nature of real property by grabbing a fistful of earth in the ancient ceremony of "livery of seizin."

In contrast, intellectual property not only involves intangible legal rights; the very subject matter itself of intellectual property is intangible. A patent protects no single physical embodiment of an invention as such; rather, it controls the abstract information in the *invention*, as expressed in the patent's claims. *SRI International v. Matsushita Electric Corp.*, 775 F.2d 1107, 1121 (Fed. Cir. 1985) (*en banc*) ("if structural claims were to be limited to devices operated precisely as a specification-described embodiment is operated, there would be no need for claims"). The same is true of copyrights. A copyright in a book, for example, does not control commerce in the book, once lawfully made under the copyright owner's authority. *See* 17 U.S.C. § 109(a) (first-sale doctrine). Rather, the copyright controls only the tangible expression in the book, as distinguished from its ideas. *See* 17 U.S.C. § 102(b) (idea/expression dichotomy). Similarly, trademarks control abstract "devices" used to identify the source or origin of a good or service. Trade secrets a are abstract and intangible information. *See* Lanham Act § 45, 15 U.S.C. § 1127 (defining "trademark," in part, as "word, name, symbol or device, or combination thereof"); Uniform Trade Secrets Act § 1(4) (preamble) (defining trade secret as "information, including" certain examples). Thus, every form of intellectual property, in essence, controls a disembodied abstract idea.

This simple fact makes intellectual property, at the same time, both hard to grasp and hard to manage. Its subject matter is abstract information that has no physical substance. Furthermore, it depends upon the effective operation of the legal system to have any economic impact at all. In this respect also it is unlike physical property, which can be locked in a safe or surrounded by a fence. Furthermore, the *direct* impact of intellectual property is entirely negative: it prevents those who do not own it from doing things they otherwise might lawfully and productively do, normally without invading any anyone's tangible property.

The only thing that keeps intellectual property from being a perverse drag on economic advancement is its *indirect* impact. That indirect impact, however, is quite extraordinary. Among other things, it has made the United States arguably the most creative and innovative society in human history. The source of its beneficial effect is the economic paradox enshrined in the Constitution: only by "secur[ing] for limited Times to Authors and Inventors the exclusive Right to their respective Writings and Discoveries" can society "promote the Progress of Science and useful Arts[.]" U.S. Const., Art. I, § 8,

Cl. 8 ("Patent and Copyright Clause"). In patent law, for example, the economic paradox is as follows:

> Without patent protection, an innovating firm's rival could copy and market the innovator's successful [product]. Of course, the copyist would have to incur the cost of building and operating a manufacturing plant, but so does the innovator. Because the copyist can avoid the additional high cost of innovation, as well as much of the costs of marketing and promotion, it can afford to sell the [product] at a lower price than the innovator. Its entry into the market will either drive the innovator out or prevent the innovator from recovering its enormous development cost. As other firms learn these "rules of the game," they will channel their investment out of risky innovation and into safe copying. Only patent protection can make the innovator's substantial investment in development…economically rational and stem the "flight of capital" from innovation to copying.

Jay Dratler, Jr., *Alice in Wonderland Meets the U.S. Patent System*, 38 AKRON L. REV. 299, 314 (2005) (footnotes omitted). Patent law thus paradoxically advances innovation by preventing free copying of patented inventions from undermining the economic incentive to innovate.

Other fields of intellectual property have a similar rationale. As the Patent and Copyright Clause suggests, the rationale for copyright is quite close to that of patent law. *See Fox Film Corp. v. Doyal*, 286 U.S. 123, 127–28 (1932) ("The sole interest of the United States and the primary object in conferring the monopoly lie in the general benefits derived by the public from the labors of authors. A copyright, like a patent, is at once the equivalent given by the public for benefits bestowed by the genius and meditations and skill of individuals and the incentive to further efforts for the same important objects"). (internal quotation marks and citation omitted.) The rationale for trade-secret protection is similar, at least in part. *See Kewanee Oil Co. v. Bicron Corp.*, 416 U.S. 470, 484 ("Certainly the patent policy of encouraging invention is not disturbed by the existence of another form of incentive to invention"); *id.*, 416 U.S. at 485 ("Trade secret law will encourage invention in areas where patent law does not reach, and will prompt the independent innovator to proceed with the discovery and exploitation of his invention"). Although trademark protection is not based on incentives for *innovation*, it has an equally compelling economic rationale: promoting commerce by protecting a fluent consumer shorthand for identifying products and services in the marketplace and thereby avoiding confusion. *See Qualitex Co. v. Jacobson Product Co.*, 514 U.S. 159, 162–65 (1995) (discussing this rationale for trademark protection in context of color trademarks). The use of these identifiers of the source or origin of goods and services decreases the search costs consumers incur in finding the good or service they want. When search costs are reduced, the total costs of goods and services are reduced and consumers realize less total expense in acquiring the goods and services they want than would be the case if we did not recognize trademark protection at all.

Yet these solid economic rationales for protecting intellectual property does not make it any less odd. A right to exclude others from doing something they otherwise could and might do is no less abstract and ethereal because it performs a valuable economic function. Despite the intellectual property system's proven efficacy in encouraging innovation and creativity, those who create and use it must still come to grips with its lack of physical substance and total dependence on the legal system for any real value.

Since intellectual property has no direct and inherent use, its value appears only when it is sold, licensed, mortgaged or litigated. (An intellectual property owner does not, strictly speaking, *use* her right to exclude when she exploits intellectual property herself; she only uses it when she relaxes its strictures by selling, mortgaging or licensing it, or by suing to enforce it.) Thus, apart from litigation—which is not the focus of this book—the primary means of exploiting intellectual property are its sale, license and mortgage.

# III. Transactions in Intellectual Property: Sales, Licenses, and Mortgages

As we have seen, a right to exclude has no intrinsic value and depends entirely on enforcement to have any value or effect at all. This observation has real bite in certain developing economies, in which attention to intellectual property (and often to enforcing private legal rights generally) is weak and sporadic. Yet in industrially developed democracies, enforcement is generally good and therefore intellectual property, *qua* right to exclude, has real value.

In litigation, owners of intellectual property extract its value in the form of damages and other monetary relief, or in the form of monopoly rents that arise when legal injunctions crush economic competition. For a marvelous example of both of these effects, consider Polaroid's successful patent litigation against Kodak; it produced over $1billion of damages and an injunction forcing Kodak from the instant-camera business. *See Polaroid Corp. v. Eastman Kodak Co.*, 789 F.2d 1556, 1557, 1574 (Fed. Cir.), *cert. denied*, 479 U.S. 850 (1986) (affirming permanent injunction against Kodak's manufacture of infringing self-developing film and related cameras); "Instant Getaway: Kodak Loses a Patent Battle, *Time* at 43 (Jan. 20, 1986) (reporting damages as likely to exceed $1 billion and cost of complying with the injunction as $200 million for trading in infringing cameras and $100 million for closing plant).

Yet besides litigation, there are only three general ways to extract value from intellectual property. They are: (1) selling it; (2) licensing it; and (3) mortgaging it.

The third alternative—mortgaging—need not detain us now. Intellectual-property mortgages are common and becoming ever more widely used, but they differ little from other mortgages. First, like other mortgages, they are essentially financing vehicles and thus of as much interest to bankers as to people who make their living inventing or creating. Second, mortgages are by nature contingent: they have no effect as long as the underlying debt is paid or underlying obligation satisfied. Thus, apart from their assistance in financing innovative and creative ventures, intellectual property mortgages have little directly to do with the substance of innovative or creative activity. Chapter 13 *infra* lays out some of the basic rules for intellectual-property mortgages as part of a discussion of bankruptcy.

This leaves two basic alternatives to litigation for realizing economic value from a right to exclude others from using intellectual property: selling it and licensing it. In theory, these two alternatives are easy to distinguish. A "sale" of intellectual property involves a transfer of title to it, i.e., a transfer of *all* rights in it. Unless contingent, a sale is usually irrevocable. In contrast, a license, "[i]n its simplest form...means only leave to do a thing which the licensor otherwise would have a right to prevent." *Western Electric Co., Inc. v. Pacent Reproducer Corp.*, 42 F.2d 116, 118 (2d Cir. 1930). Thus, while a sale is a transfer of *all* the right to exclude, a license is only a partial relaxation or grant of the right to exclude, while reserving some other rights to the owner.

In practice, distinguishing a sale from a license of intellectual property is not always easy. There are three reasons. First, terminology is not always consistent. Documents may refer to a sale alternatively as an "assignment," "transfer," or "conveyance." Sometimes, however, they may refer to a *license* (if limited in territory) as a "grant." *See In re Cybernetics Services, Inc.*, 252 F.3d 1039, 1049–50 (9th Cir. 2001), provided in Chapter 13 *infra*. *See also*, 17 U.S.C. §§ 203(b)(1), 304(c)(6) ("derivative works exceptions" to author's statutory termination rights, using "grant" as general term for both assignments and licenses).

Second, a fully exclusive license—which both precludes further licenses by the same licensor and excludes the licensor itself from using the licensed subject matter—may be economically indistinguishable from a transfer. Copyright law recognizes this fact by defining a "transfer of copyright ownership" as including any "exclusive license." 17 U.S.C. § 101 (definition of "transfer of copyright ownership"). *See also*, 17 U.S.C. § 201(d)(2) (to same effect). Although patent law contains no precisely similar definition, exclusive patent licenses may approximate assignments for such purposes as a licensee's standing to sue for infringement. *See* Chapter 8 *infra*.

The final reason why it may be difficult to distinguish a sale from a license of intellectual property is that substance controls, not form. As the Supreme Court put it, "[w]hether a transfer of a particular right or interest under a patent is an assignment or a license does not depend upon the name by which it calls itself, but upon the legal effect of its provisions." *Waterman v. Mackenzie*, 138 U.S. 252, 256, 11 S. Ct. 334, 34 L. Ed. 923 (1891). A lawyer often cannot tell whether a particular document is an assignment or license without studying all of its provisions in the context of the transaction at issue.

As we will see, whether a particular grant is a sale or license of intellectual property has many legal and practical consequences. Among them are: the grantee's standing to sue for infringement (see Chapters 8, 13 *infra*), tax treatment (see Chapter 12 *infra*), and treatment in case of bankruptcy or insolvency (see Chapter 13 *infra*). By far the most important consequence, however, is the obvious one: a sale transfers all rights in the intellectual property, while a license usually reserves some of those rights to "sell" later.

From the owner's standpoint, nothing could be more vital. One of the chief advantages of intellectual property over tangible property is the flexibility that its abstract and intangible nature permits. An owner of tangible property may lawfully sell it only once. A owner and licensor of intellectual property, however, may quite lawfully license the same property over and over again, as long as he does so nonexclusively, or with respect to different rights.

A patent owner, for example, may license his patent nonexclusively to as many applicants as request licenses, and all may contribute to his income stream. Stanford Research Institute did exactly that when it licensed its Cohen-Boyer patent on revolutionary "gene-splicing" technology. It granted nonexclusive licenses to every applicant, thereby realizing a tremendous income stream. At the same time, its worldwide licensing strategy helped its patented technology become the foundation of the biotechnology industry today.

This sort of successful business strategy is not limited to nonexclusive licenses. An intellectual property owner can—perfectly lawfully—grant multiple *exclusive* licenses, thereby seeming to "sell" rights in the same thing again and again. A patentee can grant multiple exclusive licenses in different fields of use, in different territories, and at different times. For example, a medical patentee might license a diagnostic technique to three different firms for exclusive use, respectively, in diagnosing (1) cancer in humans, (2) other human diseases, and (3) diseases of animals. Or she might grant five exclusive licenses for use in diagnosis: (1) of humans; (2) of dogs; (3) of cats; (4) of other animals; and (5) in basic research. Similarly, a licensor of consumer software might license it exclusive for distribution by twenty different firms, one in the United States and nineteen in foreign countries. Or a movie producer might license a film for exclusive "first runs" by one distribution chain and later for exclusive "second runs" by another. (Granting multiple exclusive licenses may raise antitrust concern. *See* Chapter 9 *infra*. Generally speaking, however, exposure to antitrust liability decreases the more licensees there are and the more widely the licensed subject matter is exploited.)

The opportunities for an intellectual property owner to generate revenue from multiple licenses are virtually endless. The single pie of intellectual property rights can be sliced and diced into arbitrarily small portions, and each can be "sold" separately, by means of licensing, as long as there is demand. This is perhaps the most important reason why one should never confuse a license with a sale. A sale of intellectual property, if truly that, happens only once. With suitable preparation and strategy, however, licensing can go on forever. The consequences of the two transactions for the owner are as different as night and day.

# IV. The Dilemma of Licensing

As the foregoing discussion suggests, the abstract nature of intellectual property is a two-edged sword. On the one hand, intellectual property's intangible nature provides marvelous opportunities for "splitting the baby" without killing it—gleaning multiple streams of income from multiple licenses involving nonexclusive or different exclusive rights. Effective licensing strategies are therefore virtually unlimited. On the other hand, the abstract and intangible nature of intellectual property creates pitfalls for both the business person and the lawyer attempting to negotiate or document a business deal.

The best way to appreciate these pitfalls is to compare a contract for the sale of a patented machine with a license of the right to make and sell it. Suppose the machine is something large and highly complex, such as a high-speed photocopier-printer used by mass-market publishers. Both the contract of sale and the license of manufacturing rights will likely be complex documents. The sale contract will have to deal with such issues as warranties, supplies, parts, maintenance, and resale. The license will have to deal with such complex issues as technology transfer, technical support, sublicensing, rights to sue third parties for infringement, etc. (see Chapter 7 *infra*). But a drafter or enforcer of the contract for sale will always have one key advantage over the drafter of the license: tangible subject matter to use a reference point.

Unless the machine is the first of its kind, there will be prior exemplars to point to, or at least a prototype. If the buyer was shown a prototype or model, it may establish some parameters of the sale, such as size and performance features. *See* UCC § 2-313(c) ("Any sample or model which is made part of the basis of the bargain creates an express warranty that the whole of the goods shall conform to the sample or model"). When a dispute arises about the machine's operation, breakdown, service, parts, or the like, the tangible machine itself will always be there, providing mute testimony. Available for inspection and expert analysis, it can provide a tangible, real-world background in which to anchor the parties' dispute.

Not so the license. Although the license may *relate* to a tangible machine, the rights it conveys and its key terms have little to do with the machine's tangible reality. Rather, they relate to the inherently abstract and intangible protection of the governing intellectual property, here a patent. Who can make the machine? In what form? Where can it be made? What modifications can the licensee make? Who owns the modifications? Can rights to make the machine be sublicensed and, if so, to whom? Who has the right to sue infringers who make the machine without authorization, and under what circumstances? These are all abstract questions about the nature and extent of the intangible legal rights conveyed. Looking at the machine itself cannot answer any of them.

Whereas the terms of a sale contract relate directly to the tangible machine and its physical form, the terms of a license are intangible. This fact puts far more pressure on drafters of license agreements than on drafters of contracts for sale. In licensing, everything depends upon the precision of the drafter's pen because there is no tangible embodiment of the license rights. If, for example, the license does not state whether it is exclusive or nonexclusive, looking at the machine will not resolve that dispute. Similarly, a dispute over field of use (can the machine be used for magazine publishing only, or is book publishing permitted too?) will not usually yield to examination of the machine, although a course of performance may be relevant.

Thus, the nature of the subject matter of and rights conveyed by a license puts extraordinary pressure on both the deal planner and the contract drafter. A license agreement governs an "imaginary universe" of future possibilities. There often is little or nothing tangible on which to rely as one creates that imaginary universe on a word processor or yellow legal pad.

Moreover, as we will see, licensing is also a bit like ecology in that everything relates to everything else. Leave something out, and strange consequences may ensue. If the licensor does not warrant the machine for use under industrial conditions, why was that use not excluded in the granting clause? If the license allows manufacture and sale, in addition to internal use in the licensee's factory, why is there no provision for technical support or pass-through warranties? Litigants will often make such arguments if disputes arise, and they will not be frivolous, especially if grounded in common practice.

Such is the dilemma of licensing. Within very wide limits imposed by antitrust law and supervening federal policy (see Chapters 9 and 10, *infra*), freedom of contract allows the parties to construct licenses with almost unlimited flexibility. Yet that very flexibility can be a snare for the unwary. If drafters create a crooked universe, no simple recourse to a tangible product will allow them to straighten it out. Instead a court, with the aid of hindsight, will have to straighten it out as best it can. It may do so with the aid of parol evidence. Or it may assume—however counterfactual that assumption may be—that the parties drafted the contract as if they had thought about all the issues and left nothing important out.

The great flexibility of licensing has one overarching consequence, especially for beginners. Except under limited circumstances (such as end-user software licenses), drafting by modifying forms is dangerous and should be avoided. Do you want to live in someone else's imaginary universe? Does your client? Another imaginary universe may have been built for another deal, another technology, another business, or another industry entirely. Furthermore, unless you review that imaginary universe with all the care and diligence with which you should have built your own, you will never know whether it was a crooked universe even for the deal, technology, business, and industry for which it was drafted.

The point here is simple. Generally speaking, every license transaction is unique—far more so than the sale of any tangible item, no matter how complex. Forms may be useful for the ideas they contain, and individual clauses may be modified for particular purposes. But (apart from obvious exceptions like end-user software licenses) most license agreements require careful consideration of the entire "environment" of the imaginary universe—the deal, technology, business and industry involved. This is what makes licensing so fascinating, so different from other contractual enterprises, and so fraught with pitfalls for lawyer and client alike.

# V. Peeling the Onion of Licensing: A License's "Scope"

If you asked a typical licensor and licensee for the two most important terms of their license agreement, they would probably point to the so-called "granting clause" and the payment terms. The granting clause describes the rights being licensed, and the payment terms state the consideration.

We will discuss granting clauses and payment terms in much greater detail in Chapter 7. For now, however, two points are worth making. First, these two vital sets of terms illustrate the principle that licensing is like ecology in that everything relates to everything else.

It is hardly surprising that granting terms relate to payment provisions. After all, you get what you pay for. What may be surprising, however, is the minute level of detail on which this principle operates. Virtually every part of the granting clause influences payment, not only in amount, but in nature and timing as well.

To give just one quick example, an exclusive license not only generally commands higher royalties than a nonexclusive license; it often commands substantial up-front fees as well. Nonexclusive licenses, on the other hand, seldom command significant up-front payment; they are usually granted on a pay-as-you-go basis. Up-front payments compensate an exclusive licensor not only for exclusivity, but also for the risk that the licensee will fail or decline to commercialize the subject matter of the license

Even for a fully exclusive license, the magnitude of any up-front payment depends on the other parameters of the deal. For example, the more valuable the licensed property, the higher the up-front payments may be. Yet if the licensee will incur substantial start-up costs in commercializing the licensed matter (for example, in building a plant or training a large sales force) the licensor may reduce or forego up-front payments because the licensee's sunk expense itself serves as a sort of guarantee of diligent effort.

The second point worth making about granting clauses and payment terms is much more important. More than any others, these two sets of terms determine the parameters of the "imaginary universe" that is the licensing deal. Indeed, it is possible to say that these two terms, especially the granting clause, fix the structure of the imaginary universe.

The granting clause in a license is as important as the clause in a contract of sale that specifies what is being bought and sold. Both state what the deal is about and what payment is for. This comparison, however, does not do justice to the granting clause, for it neglects the incomparably greater difficulty posed by the abstract character, complexity, and flexibility of licensing.

In practice a granting clause in a license is less like a specification of goods and more like the layers of an onion. Each word and phrase of the granting clause fixes a parameter of the imaginary universe; each depends upon and supports the others; and together they determine the amount of payment that is reasonable.

The sum total of terms in the granting clause determines the "scope" of a license. The term "scope" of a license—what rights it conveys—includes several different concepts. Naturally, it first includes the subject matter of the license, i.e., the intellectual property itself. The license may specify this subject matter in legal terms. For example, it may refer to a particular patent application (by territory and serial number), issued patent (by territory and patent number), registered copyright (by country and registration number), registered trademark (by country and registration number), or the like. Or it may express the subject matter in business terms. For example, it may refer to the technology needed to make a certain product or a certain television show, described by name, title and/or format. Although either form of specification may create conceptual and practical difficulties, specifying the subject matter is usually the least problematic aspect of a license's scope.

The second aspect of scope is the nature of activities that the license authorizes. As discussed in Part II above, every form of intellectual property controls a specific list of activities from which the owner may exclude others. Patents grant a right to exclude others from making, using, selling, offering for sale, and importing patented products. *See* 35 U.S.C. § 154(a)(1). Copyright prohibits unauthorized reproducing, preparing derivative works (adapting), distributing, performing publicly, displaying publicly, or digital audio transmitting the copyrighted work. *See* 17 U.S.C. § 106. The granting clause must specify which of these activities is or are authorized, whether in the relevant statutory terms or in more general business terms. If the license includes more than one form of intellectual property, the specification of activities permitted may become complex.

The third aspect of scope is both less obvious and more important. This is the field of use. As noted above, a licensor can cut several different deals—even exclusive ones— with different fields of use, all without changing either the subject matter of a license or the activities it authorizes. A pharmaceutical research boutique, for example, can license a drug patent exclusively to three different pharmaceutical companies operating, respectively, in the fields of cancer diagnosis, Alzheimer's research, and animal health.

The practice of slicing and dicing fields of use in this way is one of the most important aspects of licensing. Not only does it create enormous and potentially lucrative business opportunities for any licensor. It is also economically good for everybody. It is good for the licensor because it multiplies the streams of revenue that the licensor can expect to receive for a single subject matter. It also reduces the licensor's risk of relying on any single licensee to commercialize and exploit the subject matter. Separating fields of use is good for licensees because all can work within their established fields of expertise, limit their payment (the narrower the field of use, the less they should have to pay for a license), and seek exclusivity to avoid competition within their narrow field of expertise. Field-of-use licensing may contribute to the public benefit as well by multiplying the chances of getting valuable new technologies to market. Moreover, *exclusive* field-of-use licensing has a special benefit: it provides an incentive for licensees to incur start-up costs and risks that may be necessary to bring the licensed subject matter to market. For these and other reasons, field-of-use restraints in licensing are subject to the rule of reason for antitrust purposes and are seldom challenged except in unusual circumstances. *See Transparent-Wrap Machine Corp. v. Stokes & Smith Co.*, 329 U.S. 637, 645 (1947); Chapter 9 *infra*.

Field-of-use restraints may satisfy simultaneously *both* a licensor's strategic-competitive interests *and* consumers' (society's) interests in wider exploitation of new technology. Suppose, for example, a medium-sized generic drug maker discovers and patents a cheap and effective cure for many forms of cancer. The patentee has experience in testing and marketing drugs to cure colon cancer, but has no experience with breast or lung cancer. Suppose further that much larger competitors in the drug market have substantial expertise in testing and marketing drugs in these fields. If the patentee's only option were to grant an exclusive worldwide license in all fields, or for all forms of cancer, the patentee might well refuse to license at all, hoping to keep the field of its expertise (colon cancer) to itself. Yet with field-of-use licensing, the patentee can keep that field to itself and license the other fields (breast and lung cancer) to other firms with better expertise, all without fear of losing its own exclusive right to the colon-cancer market. The result is a win-win-win situation, for the patentee, its putative rival drug makers, and society.

Although important, the licensed subject matter, the permitted activities and the field of use together still do not exhaust a license's scope. The next most important aspect of scope is exclusivity. If a license is fully exclusive, the licensee will avoid any competition with respect to the licensed subject matter, including competition from the licensor. Accordingly, exclusive licenses merit careful antitrust scrutiny, especially if they involve horizontal competitors or firms that dominate any relevant economic market. *See* Chapter 9 *infra*. Nonexclusive licenses tend to promote competition and therefore face less stringent antitrust scrutiny, but they generally garner lower royalty rates and little or no up-front payment.

The scope of a license may also include other matters. These include the territory and/or time period(s) in which the license operates (within the licensed field of use and with respect to the licensed subject matter and activities) and whether sublicensing is permitted. Because intellectual property law is territorial, licensing of counterpart intellectual property in several countries or regions (such as the European Union) sometimes occurs on a territorial basis. Territorial licensing requires antitrust scrutiny in the United States and Japan and special scrutiny in Europe, because an attempt to erase the economic consequences of national territories is one of the foundational principles of the European Union. Temporally restricted licensing still occurs in the field of copyright, as in the case of movie distribution to first-run and second-run theaters. Sublicensing is a common and increasingly important phenomenon, often at issue in negotiations, but it is too early to discuss it here. (*See* Chapter 7 *infra*.)

With this brief outline, the incomparable flexibility and complexity of licensing, as compared to sales of goods, becomes clearer. A sale of goods need only specify two things besides price: model number and quantity. In contrast, a license must specify at least seven aspects of scope: (1) subject matter; (2) activities permitted; (3) field of use; (4) exclusivity; (5) territory; (6) time; and (7) sublicensing. Moreover, each of these aspects of scope has its own dimensions, conceptual twists and peculiar relationship to payment terms. As a result, the parameters of licensing is incomparably more complex than the simple description involved in a sale of goods.

# VI. Strategic and Business Considerations

The flexibility enjoyed by licensors and licensees to customize their rights and obligations has many notable consequences. We have already discussed the close relationship between a license's scope and its payment terms, not only in overall amount but in timing and types of payment. Another equally important consequence of flexibility is its impact on the parties' business strategy.

Here again, licenses differ dramatically from simpler transactions like sales of goods. In general, a sale has straightforward and readily foreseeable strategic business consequences. The seller incurs the cost of goods sold, books revenue, delivers the product, and may have ongoing service and support obligations. The buyer pays the price, takes delivery, and may have supply and maintenance needs. Unless the buyer is a dealer or distributor, the seller usually knows where and how the goods will be used or (if the goods are commodities or simple or fungible products) does not care. The sale is most often a simple, "closed" transaction in which each party is satisfied with its limited role.

Licenses often have much broader and less foreseeable consequences. Moreover, the newer and more important the licensed subject matter, the more far-reaching and less foreseeable the consequences are likely to be. Sometimes license agreements involving new technologies may shape the destinies not only of the parties, but of whole industries. *[Business consequences]*

Two examples from the computer industry are relevant. In 1981, IBM made a stunning success entering the personal-computer market. It had had a virtual monopoly of the mainframe-computer market, but it had suffered severe competition in the market for smaller, less expensive "minicomputers." Along came the "microcomputer," now known as the PC (personal computer). Although IBM was slow to enter this new market, its highly successful 1981 entry gave it the chance to dominate this low-end market while it still dominated the high-end mainframe computer market. There was just one impediment. To secure rapid entry to market, IBM had licensed the operating system for its PC from Microsoft, rather than develop its own. *See* James Wallace and Jim Erickson, HARD DRIVE: BILL GATES AND THE MAKING OF THE MICROSOFT EMPIRE 188-206 (1992). As it later turned out, a common operating system (Microsoft's) and common processor chips (Intel's) were all that the industry needed to turn PCs into simple commodities that anyone could make and sell. IBM later tried to develop its own personal-computer operating system, called OS/2, but Microsoft's market lead was so great that IBM's rival operating system never caught on. In the end, the business of making PC hardware became a commodity business, dominated by the lowest-cost producer (Dell). Eventually IBM sold its personal-computer hardware business to the Chinese (Lenovo), and the mantle of computer-industry monopolist passed from IBM to Microsoft.

This entire history started with a simple license of the operating system "MS-DOS" from Microsoft to IBM, which apparently was nonexclusive. Had Microsoft granted an exclusive license, or had IBM insisted on writing its own competing operating system first, the entire PC industry might look very different today.

The second computer-industry case in which a license had dramatic strategic consequences involved Sun Microsystems and Microsoft. Sun had attempted to establish its Java programming language and Java cross-platform "middleware" technology as a limited alternative to Microsoft's monopoly operating systems. In 1996, Sun licensed Microsoft to use, modify and distribute these software technologies, apparently in an attempt to increase their popularity. Microsoft, however, adopted a business strategy of enhancing and modifying Sun's products so that they would operate only on Microsoft's platforms. *See Sun Microsystems, Inc. v. Microsoft Corp.*, 188 F.3d 1115 (9th Cir. 1999), reproduced in edited form in Chapter 10 *infra*. Sun complained that this strategy violated restrictions in the license agreement. The Ninth Circuit, however, dissolved a preliminary injunction, questioning whether the restraints at issue had been drafted as covenants or conditions of the license. On remand, the district court refused to reinstate the injunction, reasoning that the limitations were covenants, not conditions, precluding a copyright infringement action, and that other contractual limitations precluded injunctive relief for breach of contract. *See Sun Microsystems, Inc. v. Microsoft Corp.*, 81 F. Supp. 2d 1026, 1029, 1033 (N.D. Cal. 2000). Had Sun's lawyers drafted the license's limitations as both covenants and conditions, the recent history of Java technology and Sun's role as its originator might well have been quite different.

The purpose of these histories is not to second-guess hardworking lawyers, whose clients may have controlled their drafting and who worked under great pressure. *See id.*, 81 F.Supp. 2d at 1028 (noting that license agreement was concluding "in the early morning hours…after intense negotiation"). Yet these histories do show how the terms of licensing agreements—including such drafting details as whether limitations are conditions or covenants—can have dramatic consequences for a business or an entire industry. (Chapter 9 *infra* discusses Microsoft's antitrust liability for attempting to coopt Sun's Java products.)

What lawyers ought to do about this fact is a matter of some controversy. Some lawyers argue for a strict division of labor, in which clients handle business issues and lawyers handle the legal ones. Other lawyers argue that no licensing agreement can be properly understood without reference to its business context, and that a lawyer who drafts documents or advises clients in ignorance of that context is not providing full service.

Whatever the merits of these two positions, three things are clear. First, the extent to which a "purely legal" approach is viable depends upon the nature of the client. It is one thing for a lawyer to take marching orders from a large corporation that has business and technical managers along with in-house counsel to take responsibility for negotiations. It is quite another to expect a lone inventor or author, or even a small to medium size company unfamiliar with licensing, to take the same role. Such clients may not even know the range of terms that are possible or permissible in licensing. They may not know, for example, that field of use limitations are lawful, commonly used and a frequent source of increased revenue and reduced risk for licensors. Without instruction on these points, they may have no hope of understanding the terms of any license agreement. At either extreme, a lawyer who takes the trouble to understand the client's business and industry background can provide service of added value compared to one who does not.

Second, the line between "legal" and "business" issues is tenuous. As in ecology, everything in licensing relates to everything else. Strategic business considerations influence, if not determine, the scope of a license, including such key terms as subject matter, activities permitted and reserved, exclusivity, field of use, and territory. Those terms and limitations in turn affect, if not determine, what levels and types of payment are reasonable. As license negotiations proceed, conversation may shift abruptly among business issues, strategic industry concerns, monetary terms, legal limitations, likely remedies for breach or infringement, and the future of the relevant businesses and industries. A lawyer who knows nothing about the technologies, businesses or industries involved has little to add to these discussions, and the parties may fail to appreciate fully his pronouncements about "pure law" for lack of context.

Third and finally, because everything in a license agreement relates to everything else, an attempt to draft an agreement without some understanding of the real-world context may be inefficient. For example, purely "legal" terms like who has the right or obligation to sue third-party infringers, how the proceeds and costs of any such suit are allocated, and whether rights or obligations under the agreement may be assigned by agreement, merger or acquisition, directly affect strategic issues like the balance of technological power between the parties and how the relevant industry is likely to grow. A lawyer who does not understand the business will have to communicate specially with the client on every such issue—the more so if they are not explicitly raised in licensing discussions at which the lawyer is present. Not only is such repeated communication likely to be inefficient; it may kill the deal by raising important strategic issues late in the negotiation process when the parties are impatient with the lawyers or each other.

For all these reasons, this book takes the position that licensing lawyers, as quintessential *business* lawyers, must not be ostriches hiding their heads in the sand of legal abstraction. They should know something about business generally and something specifically about the businesses and industries in which their licensing clients engage. This assuredly does *not* mean that lawyers should second-guess their clients' business decisions or attempt to unduly influence business projections, valuations, etc. It does mean that licensing lawyers can draft better agreements, communicate better and more efficiently with clients, contribute better to rapid and amicable negotiation, and better anticipate and warn of pitfalls that have real-world importance if they take the trouble to learn how business people think and to understand key points of the technologies, businesses and industries in which their licensing clients engage.

To that end, this book contains chapters that may seem to some readers more about business than law. For example, Chapter 4 ( intellectual property audits), Chapter 5 (negotiation strategy) and Chapter 5 (valuation of intellectual property) are of this sort. The wise reader, however, will not take from these chapters the notion that lawyers should usurp accountants' audit functions, far less clients' control over business negotiations or business persons' "number crunching."

Rather, the reader may observe that all these functions are inherently cooperative and interdisciplinary. An accountant or business person cannot make an "audit" of intellectual property without knowing what that property is, what legal rights it entails, and what limitations, if any, on those rights exist. These are all legal questions. Therefore a lawyer must cooperate in or supervise an IP audit if its results are to make sense. A lawyer also may wish to supervise an IP audit for another, independent reason: embarrassing or legally damaging material discovered in the audit is far more likely to be covered by the attorney-client or work-product privilege if an attorney supervises it.

Similar considerations apply to negotiation. A lawyer sensitive to business and strategic issues may assist negotiation in many ways. First, she may defuse acrimonious business discussions with observations about controlling law. If, for example, a licensor insists on controlling the minimum prices at which a licensee sells its products, she may gently point out that vertical minimum price fixing is illegal *per se* and not advisable for either party. *See* Chapter 9 *infra*. Second, a lawyer with business savvy may notice strategic and business issues that a client misses, simply because lawyers are trained to focus on detail, think logically, and imagine consequences. Finally, by virtue of an analytical mind, a lawyer may help a client "pull together" the meaning and practical significance of business and legal terms. In none of these roles does the lawyer usurp the client's ultimate authority to make business and strategic decisions. Yet in every one the lawyer can provide substantial assistance to the client in reaching a fair and reasonable deal and understanding its meaning and consequences.

Helping with valuation may seem like the outer limits of a lawyer's competence. Lawyers are not generally trained in quantitative methods and numerical calculations. Indeed, many of us chose law over other professions out of aversion to numbers and mathematics. Yet the point of knowing something about valuation is not for lawyers to second-guess expert evaluators, far less to do the "number-crunching" themselves. When necessary, a good lawyer can hire competent experts for those jobs.

Rather, the point is that valuation, like many numerical and statistical exercises, is a product of the assumptions on which it is based. Change the underlying assumptions and you change the result—sometimes by factors of ten or more. Lawyers are trained to ferret out underlying assumptions, whether patent or hidden, and to put them to the test of reason. In the case of valuation, exercising this skill can provide a valuable service to clients, whether in the heat of negotiation or privately "on background." This is just one more way in which shaping a licensing deal can be a cooperative venture in which several minds, each with different training and expertise, are better than one.

Thus we hope the reader will take away three important lessons from the business-related chapters in this book. The first and most important is that a lawyer can add greater value to licensing by *cooperating actively* with others having different training and expertise, rather than attempting to throw disembodied legal advice "over the transom" like some Greek oracle. Second, in order to cooperate effectively, a lawyer must understand and appreciate the limits of his or her own training and expertise and communicate those limits effectively to the client and other experts. Such communication is not only a matter of effective cooperation, but an ethical responsibility as well. Finally, a lawyer should be flexible and adaptive in such interdisciplinary cooperation, stepping out of the "legal" role only when a client so requests or obviously needs assistance, and relying appropriately on others' expertise.

As mentioned above, the extent to which lawyers may feel obliged to step out of a more limited role will depend upon the nature and sophistication of their clients. Outside counsel supervising an IP audit conducted by in-house attorneys and accountants, who are assisted by experienced in-house research supervisors and technology managers, need do little but review their conclusions and reports and occasionally look over key documents. On the other hand, a lawyer engaged to conduct an IP audit by a start-up firm consisting of a bookkeeper and three doctors in computer science with no business experience may have to do the whole thing herself.

In making these decisions lawyers should remember the old saw that "a little knowledge is a dangerous thing." Yet at the same time, they should not allow excessive modesty to impair their service to their clients. Often a legally-trained mind can add value to a discussion of reasonable differing points of view. Cognizant of these two truths, a good lawyer should be able to recognize the differences between extremes, as well as shades of grey in the middle.

# Notes & Questions

1. *Licensing Strategy: Why Grant a License?* There a number of business or strategic reasons why an owner of technology or other intellectual property may wish to license it to others. These include:

   a.   Making money from royalties and/or license fees;
   b.   Using others' resources to bring the licensed subject matter to market;
   c.   Insuring rapid market entry;

d. Expanding into new markets involving new geographic regions, new products, or new fields;

e. Obtaining the right to use others' technology or intellectual property in return (cross-licensing and "pooling" of intellectual property);

f. Building a reputation as an innovator or creator; and

g. Controlling the direction of development and an industry or market sector.

Most of these reasons for licensing are straightforward and self-explanatory. A few, however, require explanation.

Point (b) through (d) are the licensing counterparts of a general rule of business—use "other people's money" when possible. Businesses often use other people's money by taking loans or by issuing stock, bonds, and other securities. Yet the fast pace of modern globalized business often requires pre-existing resources other than money. If a new product has substitutes or potential substitutes, its innovator may fear that serious competition may arise before the new product achieves substantial market entry. In that case, it may seek the assistance of others who have greater resources—such as a laboratory full of skilled researchers, a production plant, a trained sales force, or a broad distribution network—in further developing, distributing, producing or marketing the new product. For example, small biotechnology research firms often license their new technology to pharmaceutical giants that have the vast resources and expertise needed to take new drugs through the regulatory approval process and market them effectively. Similarly, patentees who have foreign counterparts to their U.S. patents may have no plants or distribution networks abroad and so may license their foreign counterpart patents to firms that do. The movie industry is rife with licensing of this sort: often film production companies use a bewildering variety of licensees to distribute their copyrighted properties to domestic theaters, to foreign theaters, in the form of VHS tapes and DVDs for home viewing, and eventually on broadcast and cable television.

The last point also requires brief explanation. Paradoxically, an owner of intellectual property often can better insure that it controls an industry by licensing it widely than be holding it "close to the chest." This is particularly true if the intellectual property has substitutes. Consider, for example, vibration-control technology for vehicles. There are many ways to control vibration, and many past and future discoveries in that field. A company that enjoys a minor "breakthrough" in the field might be better advised to license it broadly, so that everyone in the industry adopts its technology rather than try to "invent around" it, i.e., to develop non-infringing substitutes.

2. *Licensing strategy: why* not *grant a license?* Just as there are a number of reasons to grant licenses, there are a number of business and strategic reasons not to grant them. These include:

a. Losing control over a product or market as licensees develop their own versions of or improvements on the licensed subject matter;

b. Losing contact with the customers or "end users" (where served by licensees) and the ideas for innovation and improvement that customers provide;

c. Losing the incentive for expansion or vertical integration (for example, into distribution and marketing) because licensees are already doing it;

d. Depending on licensees for commercial exploitation of the licensed subject matter, and therefore for revenue;

e. Losing revenue or control over the licensed subject matter through piracy and unauthorized use; and

    f.   Forfeiting reputational benefits as downstream licensees enter the market and achieve fame and glory.

The story of Microsoft's enhancement of Sun Microsystems' Java technology, allegedly under license, illustrates many of these pitfalls. Microsoft tried to take the Java products away from Sun by modifying and improving them to run only on Microsoft's operating systems. In addition, because Microsoft was (and still is) far better known in the consumer and small business market than Sun, Microsoft's versions of the product enjoyed much wider customer contact and reputational benefits in that market.

Proper strategy in licensing, however, can ameliorate or eliminate many of these disadvantages. Can you think of a strategy or a license term that would help reduce the impact of each of the effects listed above?

3. *The licensee's decision: make or buy.* As the foregoing paragraphs suggest, an intellectual property owner's decision whether and how to grant others licenses is multidimensional and often complex. In contrast, the licensee's decision is usually much simpler. In general, a putative licensee seeks only the right to use or exploit something that it does not have the legal right to exploit. It then has a simple choice: (1) to develop the same or similar intellectual property (i.e., a reasonable substitute) itself or (2) to take the proffered license. This is known as the "make or buy" decision.

Of course the "make" alternative—developing a substitute for the subject matter of the prospective license—is easier for some forms of intellectual property and some types of subject matter than for others. Can you prioritize the list of major forms of intellectual property in order from the hardest to easiest for which to create substitutes? (If your knowledge of intellectual property is "rusty," you may wish to review the outlines of intellectual property at the beginning of Chapter 2 before making your list.) What effects do you think the "strength" of the various forms of intellectual property are likely to have on the "make or buy" decisions of prospective licensees? Are such decisions likely to be equally difficult if the subject matter is a new recombinant DNA technology or if it is a new situation comedy for television?

4. The importance of a "sense of the deal." As the substance of this chapter suggests, the structure and terms of a licensing arrangement are intimately related with the parties' business strategy. Indeed, in many cases it is impossible to separate strategy from the substance of important terms. That is why it is crucial for licensing lawyers to have a "sense of the deal" from a business and strategic perspective.

A "sense of the deal" is not only a matter of good client service. It is also a crucial part of the process of contract interpretation when the terms of a license are ambiguous or unclear. Judge Easterbrook of the Seventh Circuit perhaps said it best:

> To interpret a contract or other document, it is not enough to have a command of the grammar, syntax, and vocabulary of the language in which the document is written. One must know something about the practical as well as the purely verbal context of the language to be interpreted. In the case of a commercial contract, one must have a general acquaintance with commercial practices. This doesn't mean that judges should have an M.B.A. or have practiced corporate or commercial law, but merely that they be alert citizens of a market-oriented society so that they can recognize absurdity in a business context.

*Baldwin Piano, Inc. v. Deutsche Wurlitzer GmbH*, 392 F.3d 881, 883, 73 U.S.P.Q.2d (BNA) 1375 (7th Cir. 2004) (Easterbrook, J.) (internal quotation marks and citation omitted). In this case, Judge Easterbrook had to decide whether the termination clause in a trademark license should be interpreted as (1) allowing the licensor to terminate the license immediately or (2) requiring the licensee to be given time to cure an alleged breach. He noted that the license had arisen when the licensor had sold a subsidiary to the licensee. Since both parties recognized the trademark as a major asset of the subsidiary and its license as an important part of the entire transaction, Judge Easterbrook held that the sense of deal required the more lenient termination process. See id., 392 F.3d at 883 ("The [parent] decided to spin off the . . . jukebox business; to get a price reflecting this product line's going-concern value (as opposed to the physical value of the subsidiary's assets), the seller had to let the buyer use the [mark]").

5. *Strategic thinking.* For many law students (indeed, for many lawyers) strategic business thinking is a new and foreign discipline. Here are a few exercises in licensing strategy to help you "cut your teeth" is this important field:

**Exercise 1:** It is the early-1980s, at the dawn of the personal-computer industry. There are at least two dozen makers of various forms of personal computers (PCs), and several different manufacturers of the microprocessors and other chips used in them. Each PC producer has its own models of PCs, and each model uses a unique combination of circuits and chips, often of the producer's own manufacture. The industry is highly competitive, diverse and growing rapidly.

SCITRAN is a scientific programming language that has been used on mainframe computers for decades. Virtually all trained scientists and engineers now how to use it, and there is an enormous volume of pre-existing programs written in this language. Micro Science, a start-up company, has purchased from SCITRAN's developer all rights in SCITRAN for use on PCs. Micro Science plans to make a business of licensing those rights to PC manufacturers.

What would be the most productive licensing strategy for Micro Science? Should it "pick a winner" and license all worldwide rights in the PC version of SCITRAN to a single firm? Should it license all PC-makers in the industry nonexclusively? Or is there another strategy that might work better? As you consider these questions, think of the type of license that any licensee covets most and therefore will pay the most for. (This exercise is a modified version of an actual industry history.)

**Exercise 2.** Your client is a furniture manufacturer. Its industry is highly competitive, with easy entry and many strong players both at home and abroad. Consequently, every firm in the industry strives hard to maintain a competitive edge in style, production, variety, and quality.

Two years ago, your client developed a new form of paint that is easy and cheap to apply and extremely durable. The paint and the method of applying it are subject to pending patents.

Your client believes that the paint could be useful for vehicles of all kinds, including cars, trucks and boats. It has hired you to formulate a licensing strategy for the vehicle-production industry, in which your client has no interest in participating directly. Identify (in concept only, not contractual language) the major strategic points that should be included in every license that your client grants. Would you draft these strategic points as covenants (promises) of the licensee, conditions of the license, or both?

**Exercise 3.** Your client is a small biotechnology research boutique that has developed what appears to be a strikingly effective new antibiotic. Patents are pending in the U.S. and key foreign jurisdictions. Your client, however, has no expertise or resources for the complex and enormously expensive task of securing FDA approval for the drug, let alone for effective nationwide and international marketing.

Only three major drug firms have the money, experience, and expertise to secure FDA approval and market the new drug effectively. The first has competitive products and may seek to suppress or de-emphasize the new drug. The second is financially weak. It has experienced recent departures from its executive and professional ranks, but it has no competing products and is eager to license the new drug. The third has the largest number of new products in its "pipeline" of any pharmaceutical firm (but nothing directly competitive) and therefore may spread itself too thin in securing approval and marketing. All three firms want worldwide, exclusive licenses until the patents expire and will accept nothing else.

Your client has chosen to grant an exclusive, worldwide license to the second firm.

What are your client's remaining strategic concerns, and how might you deal with them in the terms of the license agreement?

**Exercise 4.** Your client is a "maverick" movie producer. For years it has produced movies that played only in "artsy" small theaters and occasionally in mainstream theaters on space-available basis. Your client's most recent film, however, has unexpectedly garnered considerable popularity. Several major newscasts have reported on it, and mainstream theater chains are beginning to request exhibition rights.

A movie distributor has approached your client and asked for "exclusive, worldwide" distribution rights. Neither you nor your client recognize the distributor's name, and neither you nor your client knows anything about it. Your client has asked you to begin discussions with the distributor on its behalf. What are your strategic concerns, what questions would you ask the distributor, and how might you respond to alternative answers?

# Chapter 2

# Overview of Intellectual Property Law

## I. Introduction

"Intellectual property law" refers to several areas of legal protection based on state common law, state and federal statutory prescriptions, and even the United States Constitution. Given the diverse sources and conceptual justifications for the legal protection of intellectual property, it becomes quickly apparent that the title "intellectual property law" is merely a convenient umbrella to describe certain intangible products of creativity that society has deemed worthy of protection, but that do not fit into the more traditional categories of real or personal property.

Intellectual property includes trademarks, copyrights, patents, and trade secrets. Each of these specific areas of intellectual property law and the scope of protection is summarized in the comparison outline below. The right of publicity and other *sui generis* forms of intellectual property are discussed in the notes at the end of the chapter. Students with some background in these areas of the law may simply read the comparison outline to refresh their recollection of the specific protections provided for each form of intellectual property law and test their own understanding by responding to the notes and the problem at the end of each sub-chapter. Students with little or no background may want to read the entire chapter to gain an overall understanding of each type of intellectual property.

---

## II. Comparison of Patents, Trademarks, Copyrights, and Trade Secrets

### A. Derivation of Rights

1. Patents and copyrights, and their corresponding federal statutes, are specifically derived from the Constitution, Article 1, section 8, clause 8.

2. Trademark rights are protectible under the Lanham Act, as amended, 15 U.S.C. §§ 1051–1141(n), and state common law of trademark law and unfair competition. The

Constitutional basis for federal trademark protection is the Commerce Clause, Article 1, section 8, clause 3.

3.    Trade secrets are governed by special state statutes (modeled on the Uniform Trade Secrets Act) or state common law. A federal statute, the Economic Espionage Act of 1996, criminalizes theft of trade secrets but provides no civil cause of action. 18 U.S.C. §§ 1831–1839.

## B.  Protectible Subject Matter

*3 types of patents*

1.    **Patents.** In the United States, there are three types of patents: <u>utility patents, plant patents, and design patents.</u>

(a) *Utility Patents.* Protection is afforded functional features of a process, machine, manufacture, composition of matter, or improvement thereof. 35 U.S.C. §§ 100, 101.

(b) *Plant Patents.* Protection is afforded for asexually reproduced varieties of plants. 35 U.S.C. §§ 161–164.

(c) *Design Patents.* Ornamental features of manufactured articles are protected. 35 U.S.C. §§ 171–173.

2.    **Trademarks, Service Marks, and Trade Dress.** Words, names, symbols or devices that indicate the source of goods or services may receive trademark or service mark protection. 15 U.S.C. §§ 1051–1054, 1125, 1127. Trade dress may consist of (i) product design or configuration or (ii) product packaging. In order to obtain trade dress protection, product packaging must be either inherently distinctive or have acquired secondary meaning. Product design can never be inherently distinctive and functions as trade dress only if it has acquired secondary meaning. Similarly, color can never be inherently distinctive. Color alone is protectible as a trademark so long as it is not a functional part of the item and secondary meaning is shown. Also, federally registrable are two specialized forms of trademarks and service marks — certification and collective marks. 15 U.S.C. § 1054.

3.    **Copyrights.** Works of original expression fixed in a tangible medium are copyrightable. 17 U.S.C. § 102(a). Ideas are not protectible, only the expression of the idea and then only when fixed in a tangible medium of expression. 17 U.S.C. § 102(b).

4.    **Trade Secrets.** Trade secret protection covers information used in a business that has independent economic value by virtue of not being generally known or readily ascertainable by others and with respect to which reasonable efforts have been made to avoid unauthorized disclosure. *See* Uniform Trade Secrets Act § 1(4).

## C.  Criteria for Protection

1.    **Patents**

a. *Utility Patents.* An invention must meet four criteria. It must consist of statutory subject matter and be useful, novel, and non-obvious. 35 U.S.C. §§ 101–102, 103. Utility patents are by far the most common and most important of the three types of patents.

b. *Plant Patents.* Plant patents protect an asexually reproduced plant variety that is new, distinct, and non-obvious. 35 U.S.C. §§ 103, 161.

c. *Design Patents.* An ornamental design must be novel, original, and non-obvious. Its form must be non-functional. 35 U.S.C. §§ 103, 171.

2. **Trademarks and Service Marks.** Marks must be used in a manner that identifies the source. In addition, trademarks and servicemarks must be distinctive or have acquired secondary meaning as discussed above. Trade dress and designs must also be nonfunctional.

3. **Copyrights.** The work must be original and fixed in a tangible medium of expression. For a three-dimensional design, the design must have a form that is not dictated by the article's function and is separable from the article's functional aspects.

4. **Trade Secrets.** Secrets must be protected with reasonable effort. Protection may be lost upon disclosure even if by someone other than the owner. Licensing subject to reasonable protection does not destroy secrecy.

# D.  Creation of Rights

1.   **Patents.** Patents are granted by the federal government after application and substantive examination. An issued utility or design patent gives the owner the right to exclude others from making, using, offering for sale, and selling the patented machine, process, manufacture, composition of matter, or design, or importing a patented product or design or a product of a patented process. 35 U.S.C. § 271. The same exclusive rights apply to plants actually asexually reproduced from patented plants.

2.   **Trademarks and Service Marks.** The creation of a trademark right derives from the "use" of the word, name, symbol, or device as a mark, not from the mere adoption of it. These rights are enhanced by federal registration. The owner of a trademark or service marks has the prima facie exclusive right to use the mark with covered goods or services. 15 U.S.C. § 1115. A mark becomes incontestable after five years of continuous use and submission to the U.S. Patent Trademark Office of Section 8 and 15 affidavits. 15 U.S.C. §§ 1058, 1065.

3.   **Copyrights.** Exclusive reproduction, adaptation, distribution, public performance, and public display rights are automatic upon creation and fixation of a work in a tangible medium of expression. 17 U.S.C. §§ 102, 106. However, in order to enforce the rights, federal registration of U.S. produced works is required. 17 U.S.C. §§ 408–412. To prevent the defense of "innocent infringer" a copyright notice, (c), along with the copyright owner's name and the year and date of first publication, is required under 17 U.S.C. § 401(d).

4.   **Trade secrets.** Information must be designated as trade secret and maintained in reasonable secrecy. Trade secret rights are non-exclusive. If a third party independently develops the same trade secret she also has the right to use it. There is no protection from independent derivation development or reverse engineering.

# E.  Duration of Rights

1.   **Patents**

a. *Utility Patents.* The term of a utility patent is twenty years from the earliest filing date, but possibly longer for applications filed on or after May 29, 2000, depending on certain circumstances (e.g., delays in prosecution by the PTO under 35 U.S.C. § 154(b) or, for medical devices and biologics, under 35 U.S.C. §§ 155–156). The term of a patent that issues from an application filed before June 8, 1995, is the longer of seventeen years from the date of issue or twenty years from the earliest filing date. For patents in force on June 8, 1995, the term is the longer of seventeen years from the date of grant or twenty years from the earliest filing date if the application from which the patent issued was pending for less than three years.

b. *Plant Patents.* The same basic term for utility patents applies.

c. *Design Patents.* The term is fourteen years from the date of the grant. 35 U.S.C. § 173.

2.    **Trademarks and Service marks.** Common law rights enure as long as the mark is in use; federal registration rights are granted for a ten-year renewable term for all registrations issued or renewed on or after November 16, 1989, provided that affidavits of continued use or excusable nonuse are filed under Section 8 of the Trademark Law Revision Act of 1988 between the fifth and sixth year following registration and the year prior to every renewal application. 15 U.S.C. §§ 1058, 1059. *See also,* 37 C.F.R. § 2.160(a) and TMEP § 1604.04. Registrations issued before November 16, 1989, remain in force for twenty years, subject to the filing of affidavits of continued use or excusable nonuse. 37 C.F.R. § 2.181(a)(1) and TMEP §§ 1604.

3.    **Copyrights.** For works created in or after 1978 the term of copyright is the life of the author plus 70 years; for works made for hire, the term of copyright is the earlier of 95 years from the date of publication or 120 years from creation. 17 U.S.C. § 302–305.

4.    **Trade Secrets.** Protection continues as long as the trade secrets are kept secret. If a trade secret is widely disclosed, even if it is disclosed by someone who misappropriated the trade secret, protection is lost.


# F.  Test for Infringement

1.    **Patents.**

a. *Utility Patents.* Making, using, selling, offering for sale, or importing anything embodying the claimed subject matter constitutes infringement. 35 U.S.C. § 271.

b. *Plant Patents.* The same rules apply as for utility patents, but only as to plants actually asexually reproduced from a patented plant.

c. *Design Patents.* The infringement standard is substantial similarity in the eyes of the ordinary observer.

2.    **Trademarks and Service Marks.** Likelihood of confusion, mistake, or deception is the United States standard for trademark and service mark infringement and related unfair competition. 15 U.S.C. §§ 1114, 1125(a). Dilution of famous marks requires "actual dilution" but not proof of economic harm. *See* 15 U.S.C. § 1125(c).

3.    **Copyrights.** Unless copying is admitted or proven by direct evidence, the infringement standard is circumstantial proof of (1) access and (2) substantial similarity. The unauthorized distribution, public performance, digital audio transmission or display of a work, or a work derived from the protected work is also infringement. 17 U.S.C. §§ 106, 501.

4. **Trade Secrets.** The proper term is "misappropriation," not infringement. The general standard of misappropriation is acquisition, use, or disclosure by "improper means," which includes breach of contract, breach of confidence, bribery, and industrial espionage. Uniform Trade Secrets Act § 1(1) and Comment. Independent development and reverse engineering are not misappropriation.

---

# III. Patents

## Foreword: Symposium on Intellectual Property Law
Kenneth L. Port
68 CHICAGO-KENT L. REV. 585, 590–94 (1993) (as revised 2004)

\* \* \*

Patents and copyrights trace their genesis to the Constitution. However, on the first level of analysis, patents and copyrights are conceptually quite distinct. Whereas copyrights protect creative works of authorship for a long period of time, patents protect inventions of useful machines, processes, or manufactures for a much shorter period of time—twenty years from the date of the first filing for most patents rather than life of the author plus seventy years for copyrights. Whereas copyrights subsist upon creation, patents only exist with express government recognition in the form of letters patent. Also, whereas copyright law does not protect against independent creation or development, patent law does.

The express purpose of granting greater rights to patentees than to other owners of intellectual property is to encourage invention and thereby benefit the development of the sciences. Although various theories justifying the granting of the patent monopoly exist, the generally accepted version is referred to as the "incentive theory." According to the incentive theory, the patent monopoly must be granted to inventors to compensate them for the time, money, and energy they invest in the invention and to assure them any monetary gain resulting from their invention. This will motivate inventors to invent more and, most importantly, to disclose their inventions to society so that society can put the inventions to use upon expiration of the patent grant.

The other justification for granting a patent monopoly to an inventor is more of a natural rights argument: an inventor should own title to the creations of his/her mind. A statute cannot grant or deny rights in one's own intellectual creations. Rather, an inventor has title in and to these inventions regardless of any statutory monopoly.

Patent law protects novel, non-obvious, and useful inventions generally embodied in machines, processes, or compositions of matter, i.e., chemical compositions. Patent rights do not exist independent of the express government grant of letters patent. Unlike copyright registration, patent registration is an expensive, time consuming task. Because the patent does not exist apart from the letters of patent, it is of primary importance to "claim" as broad coverage as possible. Many patentees have been greatly disappointed to have a minor technical mistake or shortcoming in drafting the claims invalidate their patent or preclude its enforcement. Therefore, patent registration is the first fundamental step in establishing patent rights.

The substantive requirements for obtaining a utility patent are as follows:

1. Statutory subject matter;
2. Novelty;
3. Utility;
4. Non-obviousness.

Statutory patentable subject matter includes "any new and useful process, machine, manufacture, or composition of matter, or any new and useful improvement thereof...." Although these parameters are quite broad, Section 103 of the Patent Act has been interpreted as not allowing patents on laws of nature or physical phenomena such as electromagnetism or gravity or radial flow. As with copyrights, patent protection is not available for an idea itself apart from some embodiment of that idea.

Inventions must also be useful to be granted patents. In practice, an invention need only be operable and capable of performing some function (actually useful or not) for humanity in order to satisfy the usefulness requirement. Inventions that directly conflict with known principles of physics or other sciences — such as a perpetual motion machine or inventions that are unreasonably dangerous — fail the utility test. So do processes whose products have no known, specific utility — a holding with potential applications to patents on genetic (DNA) sequences whose function is unknown.

Novelty is a more difficult hurdle to overcome. To determine if an invention is novel, what is known as the "single source" or "complete anticipation" rule applies. That is, if a single instance of prior art discloses each and every claimed element of an invention, that invention is "anticipated" by the reference. For example, if the prior art is a single magazine article that describes elements of a machine that processes hazardous waste into biodegradable garbage, a subsequent patent application on that machine by another would not be patentable because it is anticipated.

Most of the cases and literature concerning patents, however, deal with the concept of nonobviousness. The nonobviousness doctrine developed as a judicial construct to avoid granting a patent when public policy or other less articulable reasons dictated against granting a monopoly for an invention that satisfied the other statutory requirements.

Specifically, the nonobviousness requirement prevents patents from issuing when a person with ordinary skill in the art would have thought the invention "obvious" on the day the invention was made. The general test is stated in section 103 of the patent law and was applied by the Supreme Court in the seminal case *Graham v. John Deere Co*. In *Graham* the Supreme Court identified the criteria to determine whether an invention is obvious:

1. Identify the scope and content of the prior art;
2. Identify the difference between the prior art and the claims of the invention;
3. Determine what is the ordinary level of skill in the pertinent art; and
4. Look to "secondary considerations" or "objective factors," such as commercial success, long felt but unsolved needs, and failure of others.

Only when these technical requirements are satisfied can an inventor obtain a patent for the invention. However, once a patent does issue, the patentee is the exclusive owner of a comparatively strong monopoly. For most patents the duration is twenty years from the earliest filing date, and independent creation of the same invention is no defense to infringement.

* * *

# Graham v. John Deere

## 383 U.S. 1 (1966)

Mr. Justice Clark delivered the opinion of the Court.

After a lapse of 15 years, the Court again focuses its attention on the patentability of inventions under the standard of Art. I, §8, cl. 8, of the Constitution and under the conditions prescribed by the laws of the United States. Since our last expression on patent validity, *A. & P. Tea Co. v. Supermarket Corp.*, 340 U.S. 147 (1950), the Congress has for the first time expressly added a third statutory dimension to the two requirements of novelty and utility that had been the sole statutory test since the Patent Act of 1793. This is the test of obviousness, i. e., whether "the subject matter sought to be patented and the prior art are such that the subject matter as a whole would have been obvious at the time the invention was made to a person having ordinary skill in the art to which said subject matter pertains. Patentability shall not be negatived by the manner in which the invention was made." Sec. 103 of the Patent Act of 1952, 35 U.S.C. Sec. 103 (1964 ed.).

The questions, involved in each of the companion cases before us, are what effect the 1952 Act had upon traditional statutory and judicial tests of patentability and what definitive tests are now required. We have concluded that the 1952 Act was intended to codify judicial precedents embracing the principle long ago announced by this Court in *Hotchkiss v. Greenwood*, 11 How. 248 (1851), and that, while the clear language of Sec. 103 places emphasis on an inquiry into obviousness, the general level of innovation necessary to sustain patentability remains the same.

## II.

At the outset it must be remembered that the federal patent power stems from a specific constitutional provision which authorizes the Congress "To promote the Progress of...useful Arts, by securing for limited Times to...Inventors the exclusive Right to their...Discoveries." Art. I, §8, cl. 8. The clause is both a grant of power and a limitation. This qualified authority, unlike the power often exercised in the sixteenth and seventeenth centuries by the English Crown, is limited to the promotion of advances in the "useful arts." It was written against the backdrop of the practices—eventually curtailed by the Statute of Monopolies—of the Crown in granting monopolies to court favorites in goods or businesses which had long before been enjoyed by the public. *See* MEIN-HARDT, INVENTIONS, PATENTS AND MONOPOLY, pp. 30–35 (London, 1946). The Congress in the exercise of the patent power may not overreach the restraints imposed by the stated constitutional purpose. Nor may it enlarge the patent monopoly without regard to the innovation, advancement or social benefit gained thereby. Moreover, Congress may not authorize the issuance of patents whose effects are to remove existent knowledge from the public domain, or to restrict free access to materials already available. Innovation, advancement, and things which add to the sum of useful knowledge are inherent requisites in a patent system which by constitutional command must "promote the Progress of... useful Arts." This is the standard expressed in the Constitution and it may not be ignored. And it is in this light that patent validity "requires reference to a standard written into the Constitution." *A. & P. Tea Co. v. Supermarket Corp., supra*, at 154 (concurring opinion).

Within the limits of the constitutional grant, the Congress may, of course, implement the stated purpose of the Framers by selecting the policy, which in its judgment best effectuates the constitutional aim. This is but a corollary to the grant to Congress of any Article I power. *Gibbons v. Ogden*, 9 Wheat. 1. Within the scope established by the Constitution, Congress may set out conditions and tests for patentability. *McClurg v. Kingsland*, 1 How. 202, 206. It is the duty of the Commissioner of Patents and of the courts in the administration of the patent system to give effect to the constitutional standard by appropriate application, in each case, of the statutory scheme of the Congress.

Congress quickly responded to the bidding of the Constitution by enacting the Patent Act of 1790 during the second session of the First Congress. It created an agency in the Department of State headed by the Secretary of State, the Secretary of the Department of War and the Attorney General, any two of whom could issue a patent for a period not exceeding 14 years to any petitioner that "hath...invented or discovered any useful art, manufacture,...or device, or any improvement therein not before known or used" if the board found that "the invention or discovery [was] sufficiently useful and important...." 1 Stat. 110. This group, whose members administered the patent system along with their other public duties, was known by its own designation as "Commissioners for the Promotion of Useful Arts."

Thomas Jefferson, who as Secretary of State was a member of the group, was its moving spirit and might well be called the "first administrator of our patent system." *See* Federico, *Operation of the Patent Act of 1790*, 18 J. Pat. Off. Soc. 237, 238 (1936). He was not only an administrator of the patent system under the 1790 Act, but was also the author of the 1793 Patent Act. In addition, Jefferson was himself an inventor of great note. His unpatented improvements on plows, to mention but one line of his inventions, won acclaim and recognition on both sides of the Atlantic. Because of his active interest and influence in the early development of the patent system, Jefferson's views on the general nature of the limited patent monopoly under the Constitution, as well as his conclusions as to conditions for patentability under the statutory scheme, are worthy of note.

Jefferson, like other Americans, had an instinctive aversion to monopolies. It was a monopoly on tea that sparked the Revolution and Jefferson certainly did not favor an equivalent form of monopoly under the new government. His abhorrence of monopoly extended initially to patents as well. From France, he wrote to Madison (July 1788) urging a Bill of Rights provision restricting monopoly, and as against the argument that limited monopoly might serve to incite "ingenuity," he argued forcefully that "the benefit even of limited monopolies is too doubtful to be opposed to that of their general suppression," V Writings of Thomas Jefferson, at 47 (Ford ed., 1895).

His views ripened, however, and in another letter to Madison (Aug. 1789) after the drafting of the Bill of Rights, Jefferson stated that he would have been pleased by an express provision in this form:

> Art. 9. Monopolies may be allowed to persons for their own productions in literature & their own inventions in the arts, for a term not exceeding—years but for no longer term & no other purpose.

*Id.*, at 113.

And he later wrote:

> Certainly an inventor ought to be allowed a right to the benefit of his invention for some certain time....Nobody wishes more than I do that ingenuity should receive a liberal encouragement.

Letter to Oliver Evans (May 1807), V Writings of Thomas Jefferson, at 75–76 (Washington ed.).

Jefferson's philosophy on the nature and purpose of the patent monopoly is expressed in a letter to Isaac McPherson (Aug. 1813), a portion of which we set out in the margin. He rejected a natural-rights theory in intellectual property rights and clearly recognized the social and economic rationale of the patent system. The patent monopoly was not designed to secure to the inventor his natural right in his discoveries. Rather, it was a reward, an inducement, to bring forth new knowledge. The grant of an exclusive right to an invention was the creation of society—at odds with the inherent free nature of disclosed ideas—and was not to be freely given. Only inventions and discoveries which furthered human knowledge, and were new and useful, justified the special inducement of a limited private monopoly. Jefferson did not believe in granting patents for small details, obvious improvements, or frivolous devices. His writings evidence his insistence upon a high level of patentability.

As a member of the patent board for several years, Jefferson saw clearly the difficulty in "drawing a line between the things which are worth to the public the embarrassment of an exclusive patent, and those which are not." The board on which he served sought to draw such a line and formulated several rules, which are preserved in Jefferson's correspondence. Despite the board's efforts, Jefferson saw "with what slow progress a system of general rules could be matured." Because of the "abundance" of cases and the fact that the investigations occupied "more time of the members of the board than they could spare from higher duties, the whole was turned over to the judiciary, to be matured into a system, under which every one might know when his actions were safe and lawful." Letter to McPherson, *supra*, at 181, 182. Apparently Congress agreed with Jefferson and the board that the courts should develop additional conditions for patentability. Although the Patent Act was amended, revised or codified some 50 times between 1790 and 1950, Congress steered clear of a statutory set of requirements other than the bare novelty and utility tests reformulated in Jefferson's draft of the 1793 Patent Act.

## III.

The difficulty of formulating conditions for patentability was heightened by the generality of the constitutional grant and the statutes implementing it, together with the underlying policy of the patent system that "the things which are worth to the public the embarrassment of an exclusive patent," as Jefferson put it, must outweigh the restrictive effect of the limited patent monopoly. The inherent problem was to develop some means of weeding out those inventions which would not be disclosed or devised but for the inducement of a patent.

This Court formulated a general condition of patentability in 1851 in *Hotchkiss v. Greenwood*, 11 How. 248. The patent involved a mere substitution of materials—porcelain or clay for wood or metal in doorknobs—and the Court condemned it, holding:

> Unless more ingenuity and skill...were required...than were possessed by an ordinary mechanic acquainted with the business, there was an absence of that degree of skill and ingenuity which constitute essential elements of every invention. In other words, the improvement is the work of the skillful mechanic, not that of the inventor.

At p. 267.

*Hotchkiss*, by positing the condition that a patentable invention evidence more ingenuity and skill than that possessed by an ordinary mechanic acquainted with the business, merely distinguished between new and useful innovations that were capable of sustaining a patent and those that were not. The *Hotchkiss* test laid the cornerstone of the judicial evolution suggested by Jefferson and left to the courts by Congress. The language in the case, and in those which followed, gave birth to "invention" as a word of legal art signifying patentable inventions. Yet, as this Court has observed, "the truth is the word ['invention'] cannot be defined in such manner as to afford any substantial aid in determining whether a particular device involves an exercise of the inventive faculty or not." *McClain v. Ortmayer*, 141 U.S. 419, 427 (1891*); A. & P. Tea Co. v. Supermarket Corp., supra*, at 151. Its use as a label brought about a large variety of opinions as to its meaning both in the Patent Office, in the courts, and at the bar. The *Hotchkiss* formulation, however, lies not in any label, but in its functional approach to questions of patentability. In practice, *Hotchkiss* has required a comparison between the subject matter of the patent, or patent application, and the background skill of the calling. It has been from this comparison that patentability was in each case determined.

### IV.

The [1952 Patent] Act sets out the conditions of patentability in three sections. An analysis of the structure of these three sections indicates that patentability is dependent upon three explicit conditions: novelty and utility as articulated and defined in Sec. 101 and Sec. 102, and nonobviousness, the new statutory formulation, as set out in Sec. 103. The first two sections, which trace closely the 1874 codification, express the "new and useful" tests which have always existed in the statutory scheme and, for our purposes here, need no clarification. The pivotal section around which the present controversy centers is Sec.103. It provides:

> Sec. 103. Conditions for patentability; non-obvious subject matter.
>
> A patent may not be obtained though the invention is not identically disclosed or described as set forth in section 102 of this title, if the differences between the subject matter sought to be patented and the prior art are such that the subject matter as a whole would have been obvious at the time the invention was made to a person having ordinary skill in the art to which said subject matter pertains. Patentability shall not be negatived by the manner in which the invention was made.

The section is cast in relatively unambiguous terms. Patentability is to depend, in addition to novelty and utility, upon the "non-obvious" nature of the "subject matter sought to be patented" to a person having ordinary skill in the pertinent art.

* * *

It is undisputed that this section was, for the first time, a statutory expression of an additional requirement for patentability, originally expressed in *Hotchkiss*. It also seems apparent that Congress intended by the last sentence of Sec. 103 to abolish the test it believed this Court announced in the controversial phrase "flash of creative genius," used in *Cuno Corp. v. Automatic Devices Corp.*, 314 U.S. 84 (1941).

It is contended, however, by some of the parties and by several of the amici that the first sentence of Sec. 103 was intended to sweep away judicial precedents and to lower the level of patentability. Others contend that the Congress intended to codify the essential purpose reflected in existing judicial precedents—the rejection of insignificant variations and innovations of a commonplace sort—and also to focus inquiries under Sec. 103 upon nonobviousness, rather than upon "invention," as a means of achieving more stability and predictability in determining patentability and validity.

The Reviser's Note to this section, with apparent reference to *Hotchkiss*, recognizes that judicial requirements as to "lack of patentable novelty [have] been followed since at least as early as 1850." The note indicates that the section was inserted because it "may have some stabilizing effect, and also to serve as a basis for the addition at a later time of some criteria which may be worked out." To this same effect are the reports of both Houses, which state that the first sentence of the section "paraphrases language which has often been used in decisions of the courts, and the section is added to the statute for uniformity and definiteness."

We believe that this legislative history, as well as other sources, shows that the revision was not intended by Congress to change the general level of patentable invention. We conclude that the section was intended merely as a codification of judicial precedents embracing the *Hotchkiss* condition, with congressional directions that inquiries into the obviousness of the subject matter sought to be patented are a prerequisite to patentability.

V.

Approached in this light, the Sec. 103 additional condition, when followed realistically, will permit a more practical test of patentability. The emphasis on nonobviousness is one of inquiry, not quality, and, as such, comports with the constitutional strictures.

While the ultimate question of patent validity is one of law, *A. & P. Tea Co. v. Supermarket Corp., supra*, at 155, the Sec. 103 condition, which is but one of three conditions, each of which must be satisfied, lends itself to several basic factual inquiries. Under Sec. 103, the scope and content of the prior art are to be determined; differences between the prior art and the claims at issue are to be ascertained; and the level of ordinary skill in the pertinent art resolved. Against this background, the obviousness or nonobviousness of the subject matter is determined. Such secondary considerations as commercial success, long felt but unsolved needs, failure of others, etc., might be utilized to give light to the circumstances surrounding the origin of the subject matter sought to be patented. As indicia of obviousness or nonobviousness, these inquiries may have relevancy. *See* Note, *Subtests of "Nonobviousness": A Nontechnical Approach to Patent Validity*, 112 U. Pa. L. Rev. 1169 (1964).

This is not to say, however, that there will not be difficulties in applying the nonobviousness test. What is obvious is not a question upon which there is likely to be uniformity of thought in every given factual context. The difficulties, however, are comparable to those encountered daily by the courts in such frames of reference as negligence and scienter, and should be amendable to a case-by-case development. We believe that strict observance of the requirements laid down here will result in that uniformity and definiteness which Congress called for in the 1952 Act.

While we have focused attention on the appropriate standard to be applied by the courts, it must be remembered that the primary responsibility for sifting out unpatentable material lies in the Patent Office. To await litigation is—for all practical purposes—to debilitate the patent system. We have observed a notorious difference between the standards applied by the Patent Office and by the courts. While many reasons can be adduced to explain the discrepancy, one may well be the free rein often exercised by Examiners in their use of the concept of "invention." In this connection we note that the Patent Office is confronted with a most difficult task. Almost 100,000 applications for patents are filed each year. Of these, about 50,000 are granted and the backlog now runs well over 200,000. 1965 Annual Report of the Commissioner of Patents 13–14.

This is itself a compelling reason for the Commissioner to strictly adhere to the 1952 Act as interpreted here. This would, we believe, not only expedite disposition but bring about a closer concurrence between administrative and judicial precedent.

Although we conclude here that the inquiry which the Patent Office and the courts must make as to patentability must be beamed with greater intensity on the requirements of Sec. 103, it bears repeating that we find no change in the general strictness with which the overall test is to be applied. We have been urged to find in Sec. 103 a relaxed standard, supposedly a congressional reaction to the "increased standard" applied by this Court in its decisions over the last 20 or 30 years. The standard has remained invariable in this Court. Technology, however, has advanced—and with remarkable rapidity in the last 50 years. Moreover, the ambit of applicable art in given fields of science has widened by disciplines unheard of a half century ago. It is but an evenhanded application to require that those persons granted the benefit of a patent monopoly be charged with an awareness of these changed conditions. The same is true of the less technical, but still useful arts. He who seeks to build a better mousetrap today has a long path to tread before reaching the Patent Office.

\* \* \*

# Diamond v. Chakrabarty

## 447 U.S. 303 (1980)

Mr. Chief Justice Burger delivered the opinion of the Court.

We granted certiorari to determine whether a live, human-made micro-organism is patentable subject matter under 35 U. S. C. Sec. 101.

### I

In 1972, respondent Chakrabarty, a microbiologist, filed a patent application, assigned to the General Electric Co. The application asserted 36 claims related to Chakrabarty's invention of "a bacterium from the genus Pseudomonas containing therein at least two stable energy-generating plasmids, each of said plasmids providing a separate hydrocarbon degradative pathway." This human-made, genetically engineered bacterium is capable of breaking down multiple components of crude oil. Because of this property, which is possessed by no naturally occurring bacteria, Chakrabarty's invention is believed to have significant value for the treatment of oil spills.

Chakrabarty's patent claims were of three types: first, process claims for the method of producing the bacteria; second, claims for an inoculum comprised of a carrier material floating on water, such as straw, and the new bacteria; and third, claims to the bacteria themselves. The patent examiner allowed the claims falling into the first two categories, but rejected claims for the bacteria. His decision rested on two grounds: (1) that micro-organisms are "products of nature," and (2) that as living things they are not patentable subject matter under 35 U.S.C. Sec. 101.

Chakrabarty appealed the rejection of these claims to the Patent Office Board of Appeals, and the Board affirmed the examiner on the second ground. Relying on the legislative history of the 1930 Plant Patent Act, in which Congress extended patent protection to certain asexually reproduced plants, the Board concluded that Sec. 101 was not intended to cover living things such as these laboratory created micro-organisms.

The Court of Customs and Patent Appeals, by a divided vote, reversed on the authority of its prior decision in *In re Bergy*, 563 F.2d 1031, 1038 (1977), which held that "the fact that microorganisms...are alive...[is] without legal significance" for purposes of the patent law.

\* \* \*

II.

\* \* \*

[W]e must determine whether respondent's micro-organism constitutes a "manufacture" or "composition of matter" within the meaning of the statute.

III.

In cases of statutory construction we begin, of course, with the language of the statute. *Southeastern Community College v. Davis*, 442 U.S. 397, 405 (1979). And "unless otherwise defined, words will be interpreted as taking their ordinary, contemporary, common meaning." *Perrin v. United States*, 444 U.S. 37, 42 (1979). We have also cautioned that courts "should not read into the patent laws limitations and conditions which the legislature has not expressed." *United States v. Dubilier Condenser Corp.*, 289 U.S. 178, 199 (1933).

Guided by these canons of construction, this Court has read the term "manufacture" in § 101 in accordance with its dictionary definition to mean "the production of articles for use from raw or prepared materials by giving to these materials new forms, qualities, properties, or combinations, whether by hand-labor or by machinery." *American Fruit Growers, Inc. v. Brogdex Co.*, 283 U.S. 1, 11 (1931). Similarly, "composition of matter" has been construed consistent with its common usage to include "all compositions of two or more substances and...all composite articles, whether they be the results of chemical union, or of mechanical mixture, or whether they be gases, fluids, powders or solids." *Shell Development Co. v. Watson*, 149 F. Supp. 279, 280 (DC 1957) (citing 1 A. DELLER, WALKER ON PATENTS §14, p. 55 (1st ed. 1937)). In choosing such expansive terms as "manufacture" and "composition of matter," modified by the comprehensive "any," Congress plainly contemplated that the patent laws would be given wide scope.

The relevant legislative history also supports a broad construction. The Patent Act of 1793, authored by Thomas Jefferson, defined statutory subject matter as "any new and useful art, machine, manufacture, or composition of matter, or any new or useful improvement [thereof]." Act of Feb. 21, 1793, Sec. 1, 1 Stat. 319. The Act embodied Jefferson's philosophy that "ingenuity should receive a liberal encouragement." 5 Writings of Thomas Jefferson 75–76 (Washington ed. 1871). *See Graham v. John Deere Co.*, 383 U.S. 1, 7–10 (1966). Subsequent patent statutes in 1836, 1870, and 1874 employed this same broad language. In 1952, when the patent laws were recodified, Congress replaced the word "art" with "process," but otherwise left Jefferson's language intact. The Committee Reports accompanying the 1952 Act inform us that Congress intended statutory subject matter to "include anything under the sun that is made by man." S. Rep. No. 1979, 82d Cong., 2d Sess., 5 (1952); H. R. Rep. No. 1923, 82d Cong., 2d Sess., 6 (1952).

This is not to suggest that §101 has no limits or that it embraces every discovery. The laws of nature, physical phenomena, and abstract ideas have been held not patentable. *See Parker v. Flook*, 437 U.S. 584 (1978); *Gottschalk v. Benson*, 409 U.S. 63, 67 (1972); *Funk Brothers Seed Co. v. Kalo Inoculant Co.*, 333 U.S. 127, 130 (1948); *O'Reilly v. Morse*, 15 How. 62, 112–21 (1854); *Le Roy v. Tatham*, 14 How. 156, 175 (1853). Thus, a new mineral discovered in the earth or a new plant found in the wild is not patentable subject matter. Likewise, Einstein could not patent his celebrated law that $E=mc^2$; nor could Newton have patented the law of gravity. Such discoveries are "manifestations of…nature, free to all men and reserved exclusively to none." *Funk, supra*, at 130.

Judged in this light, respondent's micro-organism plainly qualifies as patentable subject matter. His claim is not to a hitherto unknown natural phenomenon, but to a non-naturally occurring manufacture or composition of matter—a product of human ingenuity "having a distinctive name, character [and] use." *Hartranft v. Wiegmann*, 121 U.S. 609, 615 (1887). The point is underscored dramatically by comparison of the invention here with that in *Funk*. There, the patentee had discovered that there existed in nature certain species of root-nodule bacteria which did not exert a mutually inhibitive effect on each other. He used that discovery to produce a mixed culture capable of inoculating the seeds of leguminous plants. Concluding that the patentee had discovered "only some of the handiwork of nature," the Court ruled the product non-patentable:

> Each of the species of root-nodule bacteria contained in the package infects the same group of leguminous plants which it always infected. No species acquires a different use. The combination of species produces no new bacteria, no change in the six species of bacteria, and no enlargement of the range of their utility. Each species has the same effect it always had. The bacteria perform in their natural way. Their use in combination does not improve in any way their natural functioning. They serve the ends nature originally provided and act quite independently of any effort of the patentee.

333 U.S., at 131.

Here, by contrast, the patentee has produced a new bacterium with markedly different characteristics from any found in nature and one having the potential for significant utility. His discovery is not nature's handiwork, but his own; accordingly it is patentable subject matter under § 101.

### IV

Two contrary arguments are advanced, neither of which we find persuasive.

### (A)

[The court first considered and rejected arguments that enactment of the Plant Patent Act of 1930 and the Plant Variety Protection Act of 1970 implied that Congress did not intend utility patents to cover living subject matter.]

\* \* \*

### (B)

The petitioner's second argument is that micro-organisms cannot qualify as patentable subject matter until Congress expressly authorizes such protection. His position rests on the fact that genetic technology was unforeseen when Congress enacted § 101. From this it is argued that resolution of the patentability of inventions such as respondent's should be left to Congress. The legislative process, the petitioner argues, is best equipped to weigh the competing economic, social, and scientific considerations involved, and to determine whether living organisms produced by genetic engineering should receive patent protection. In support of this position, the petitioner relies on our recent holding in *Parker v. Flook*, 437 U.S. 584 (1978), and the statement that the judiciary "must proceed cautiously when...asked to extend patent rights into areas wholly unforeseen by Congress." *Id.* at 596.

It is, of course, correct that Congress, not the courts, must define the limits of patentability; but it is equally true that once Congress has spoken it is "the province and duty of the judicial department to say what the law is." *Marbury v. Madison*, 1 Cranch 137, 177 (1803). Congress has performed its constitutional role in defining patentable subject matter in §101; we perform ours in construing the language Congress has employed. In so doing, our obligation is to take statutes as we find them, guided, if ambiguity appears, by the legislative history and statutory purpose. Here, we perceive no ambiguity. The subject-matter provisions of the patent law have been cast in broad terms to fulfill the constitutional and statutory goal of promoting "the Progress of Science and the useful Arts" with all that means for the social and economic benefits envisioned by Jefferson. Broad general language is not necessarily ambiguous when congressional objectives require broad terms.

Nothing in *Flook* is to the contrary. That case applied our prior precedents to determine that a "claim for an improved method of calculation, even when tied to a specific end use, is unpatentable subject matter under §101." 437 U.S. at 595, n. 18. The Court carefully scrutinized the claim at issue to determine whether it was precluded from patent protection under "the principles underlying the prohibition against patents for 'ideas' or phenomena of nature." *Id.*, at 593. We have done that here. *Flook* did not announce a new principle that inventions in areas not contemplated by Congress when the patent laws were enacted are unpatentable *per se*.

To read that concept into *Flook* would frustrate the purposes of the patent law. This Court frequently has observed that a statute is not to be confined to the "particular [applications]...contemplated by the legislators." *Barr v. United States*, 324 U.S. 83, 90 (1945). *Accord, Browder v. United States*, 312 U.S. 335, 339 (1941); *Puerto Rico v. Shell Co.*, 302 U.S. 253, 257 (1937). This is especially true in the field of patent law. A rule that unanticipated inventions are without protection would conflict with the core concept of the patent law that anticipation undermines patentability. *See Graham v. John Deere Co.*, 383 U.S. at 12–17. Mr. Justice Douglas reminded that the inventions most benefiting mankind are those that "push back the frontiers of chemistry, physics, and the like." *Great A. & P. Tea Co. v. Supermarket Corp.*, 340 U.S. 147, 154 (1950) (concurring opinion). Congress employed broad general language in drafting Sec. 101 precisely because such inventions are often unforeseeable.

\* \* \*

The grant or denial of patents on micro-organisms is not likely to put an end to genetic research or to its attendant risks. The large amount of research that has already occurred when no researcher had sure knowledge that patent protection would be available suggests that legislative or judicial fiat as to patentability will not deter the scientific mind from probing into the unknown any more than Canute could command the tides. Whether respondent's claims are patentable may determine whether research efforts are accelerated by the hope of reward or slowed by want of incentives, but that is all.

What is more important is that we are without competence to entertain these arguments—either to brush them aside as fantasies generated by fear of the unknown, or to act on them. The choice we are urged to make is a matter of high policy for resolution within the legislative process after the kind of investigation, examination, and study that legislative bodies can provide and courts cannot. That process involves the balancing of competing values and interests, which in our democratic system is the business of elected representatives. Whatever their validity, the contentions now pressed on us should be addressed to the political branches of the Government, the Congress and the Executive, and not to the courts.

We have emphasized in the recent past that "[our] individual appraisal of the wisdom or unwisdom of a particular [legislative] course...is to be put aside in the process of interpreting a statute." *TVA v. Hill*, 437 U.S., at 194. Our task, rather, is the narrow one of determining what Congress meant by the words it used in the statute; once that is done our powers are exhausted. Congress is free to amend Sec. 101 so as to exclude from patent protection organisms produced by genetic engineering. *Cf.* 42 U. S. C. §2181 (a), exempting from patent protection inventions "useful solely in the utilization of special nuclear material or atomic energy in an atomic weapon." Or it may choose to craft a statute specifically designed for such living things. But, until Congress takes such action, this Court must construe the language of §101 as it is. The language of that section fairly embraces respondent's invention.

Accordingly, the judgment of the Court of Customs and Patent Appeals is

*Affirmed.*

---

# State Street Bank & Trust Co. v. Signature Financial Group, Inc.

149 F.3d 1368 (Fed. Cir. 1998), *cert. denied*, 119 S. Ct. 851 (1999)

RICH, Circuit Judge.

Signature Financial Group, Inc. (Signature) appeals from the decision of the United States District Court for the District of Massachusetts granting a motion for summary judgment in favor of State Street Bank & Trust Co. (State Street), finding U.S. Patent No. 5,193,056 (the '056 patent) invalid on the ground that the claimed subject matter is not encompassed by 35 U.S.C. §101 (1994). *See State Street Bank & Trust Co. v. Signature Financial Group, Inc.*, 927 F. Supp. 502, 38 U.S.P.Q.2D (BNA) 1530 (D. Mass.1996). We reverse and remand because we conclude that the patent claims are directed to statutory subject matter.

## BACKGROUND

Signature is the assignee of the '056 patent which is entitled "Data Processing System for Hub and Spoke Financial Services Configuration." The '056 patent issued to Signature on 9 March 1993, naming R. Todd Boes as the inventor. The '056 patent is generally directed to a data processing system (the system) for implementing an investment structure which was developed for use in Signature's business as an administrator and accounting agent for mutual funds. In essence, the system, identified by the proprietary name Hub and Spoke (R), facilitates a structure whereby mutual funds (Spokes) pool their assets in an investment portfolio (Hub) organized as a partnership. This investment configuration provides the administrator of a mutual fund with the advantageous combination of economies of scale in administering investments coupled with the tax advantages of a partnership.

State Street and Signature are both in the business of acting as custodians and accounting agents for multi-tiered partnership fund financial services. State Street negotiated with Signature for a license to use its patented data processing system described and claimed in the '056 patent. When negotiations broke down, State Street brought a declaratory judgment action asserting invalidity, unenforceability, and noninfringement in Massachusetts district court, and then filed a motion for partial summary judgment of patent invalidity for failure to claim statutory subject matter under § 101. The motion was granted and this appeal followed.

## DISCUSSION

\* \* \*

The following facts pertinent to the statutory subject matter issue are either undisputed or represent the version alleged by the nonmovant. The patented invention relates generally to a system that allows an administrator to monitor and record the financial information flow and make all calculations necessary for maintaining a partner fund financial services configuration. As previously mentioned, a partner fund financial services configuration essentially allows several mutual funds, or "Spokes," to pool their investment funds into a single portfolio, or "Hub," allowing for consolidation of, *inter alia*, the costs of administering the fund combined with the tax advantages of a partnership. In particular, this system provides means for a daily allocation of assets for two or more Spokes that are invested in the same Hub. The system determines the percentage share that each Spoke maintains in the Hub, while taking into consideration daily changes both in the value of the Hub's investment securities and in the concomitant amount of each Spoke's assets.

In determining daily changes, the system also allows for the allocation among the Spokes of the Hub's daily income, expenses, and net realized and unrealized gain or loss, calculating each day's total investments based on the concept of a book capital account. This enables the determination of a true asset value of each Spoke and accurate calculation of allocation ratios between or among the Spokes.

The system additionally tracks all the relevant data determined on a daily basis for the Hub and each Spoke, so that aggregate year end income, expenses, and capital gain or loss can be determined for accounting and for tax purposes for the Hub and, as a result, for each publicly traded Spoke.

It is essential that these calculations are quickly and accurately performed. In large part this is required because each Spoke sells shares to the public and the price of those shares is substantially based on the Spoke's percentage interest in the portfolio. In some instances, a mutual fund administrator is required to calculate the value of the shares to the nearest penny within as little as an hour and a half after the market closes. Given the complexity of the calculations, a computer or equivalent device is a virtual necessity to perform the task.

The '056 patent application was filed 11 March 1991. It initially contained six "machine" claims, which incorporated means-plus-function clauses, and six method claims. According to Signature, during prosecution the examiner contemplated a § 101 rejection for failure to claim statutory subject matter. However, upon cancellation of the six method claims, the examiner issued a notice of allowance for the remaining present six claims on appeal. Only claim 1 is an independent claim.

The district court began its analysis by construing the claims to be directed to a process, with each "means" clause merely representing a step in that process. However, "machine" claims having "means" clauses may only be reasonably viewed as process claims if there is no supporting structure in the written description that corresponds to the claimed "means" elements. *See In re Alappat*, 33 F.3d 1526, 1540–41, 31 U.S.P.Q.2D (BNA) 1545, 1554 (Fed. Cir. 1994) (en banc). This is not the case now before us.

When independent claim 1 is properly construed in accordance with § 112, P 6, it is directed to a machine, as demonstrated below, where representative claim 1 is set forth, the subject matter in brackets stating the structure the written description discloses as corresponding to the respective "means" recited in the claims.

    1.   A data processing system for managing a financial services configuration of a portfolio established as a partnership, each partner being one of a plurality of funds, comprising:

(a) computer processor means [a personal computer including a CPU] for processing data; (b) storage means [a data disk] for storing data on a storage medium; (c) first means [an arithmetic logic circuit configured to prepare the data disk to magnetically store selected data] for initializing the storage medium; (d) second means [an arithmetic logic circuit configured to retrieve information from a specific file, calculate incremental increases or decreases based on specific input, allocate the results on a percentage basis, and store the output in a separate file] for processing data regarding assets in the portfolio and each of the funds from a previous day and data regarding increases or decreases in each of the funds, [sic, funds'] assets and for allocating the percentage share that each fund holds in the portfolio; (e) third means [an arithmetic logic circuit configured to retrieve information from a specific file, calculate incremental increases and decreases based on specific input, allocate the results on a percentage basis and store the output in a separate file] for processing data regarding daily incremental income, expenses, and net realized gain or loss for the portfolio and for allocating such data among each fund; (f) fourth means [an arithmetic logic circuit configured to retrieve information from a specific file, calculate incremental increases and decreases based on specific input, allocate the results on a percentage basis and store the output in a separate file] for processing data regarding daily net unrealized gain or loss for the portfolio and for allocating such data among each fund; and (g) fifth means [an arithmetic logic circuit configured to retrieve information from specific files, calculate that information on an aggregate basis and store the output in a separate file] for processing data regarding aggregate year-end income, expenses, and capital gain or loss for the portfolio and each of the funds.

Each claim component, recited as a "means" plus its function, is to be read, of course, pursuant to § 112, ¶ 6, as inclusive of the "equivalents" of the structures disclosed in the written description portion of the specification. Thus, claim 1, properly construed, claims a machine, namely, a data processing system for managing a financial services configuration of a portfolio established as a partnership, which machine is made up of, at the very least, the specific structures disclosed in the written description and corresponding to the means-plus-function elements (a)–(g) recited in the claim.

A "machine" is proper statutory subject matter under § 101. We note that, for the purposes of a § 101 analysis, it is of little relevance whether claim 1 is directed to a "machine" or a "process," as long as it falls within at least one of the four enumerated categories of patentable subject matter, "machine" and "process" being such categories.

This does not end our analysis, however, because the court concluded that the claimed subject matter fell into one of two alternative judicially-created exceptions to statutory subject matter. The court refers to the first exception as the "mathematical algorithm" exception and the second exception as the "business method" exception. Section 101 reads:

Whoever invents or discovers any new and useful process, machine, manufacture, or composition of matter, or any new and useful improvement thereof, may obtain a patent therefore, subject to the conditions and requirements of this title.

The plain and unambiguous meaning of § 101 is that any invention falling within one of the four stated categories of statutory subject matter may be patented, provided it meets the other requirements for patentability set forth in Title 35, i.e., those found in §§ 102, 103, and 112.

The repetitive use of the expansive term "any" in § 101 shows Congress's intent not to place any restrictions on the subject matter for which a patent may be obtained beyond those specifically recited in § 101. Indeed, the Supreme Court has acknowledged that Congress intended § 101 to extend to "anything under the sun that is made by man." *Diamond v. Chakrabarty*, 447 U.S. 303, 309, 65 L. Ed. 2d 144, 100 S. Ct. 2204 (1980); *see also Diamond v. Diehr*, 450 U.S. 175, 182, 67 L. Ed. 2d 155, 101 S. Ct. 1048 (1981). Thus, it is improper to read limitations into § 101 on the subject matter that may be patented where the legislative history indicates that Congress clearly did not intend such limitations. *See Chakrabarty*, 447 U.S. at 308 ("We have also cautioned that courts 'should not read into the patent laws limitations and conditions which the legislature has not expressed.'" (citations omitted)).

### The "Mathematical Algorithm" Exception

The Supreme Court has identified three categories of subject matter that are unpatentable, namely "laws of nature, natural phenomena, and abstract ideas." *Diehr*, 450 U.S. at 185. Of particular relevance to this case, the Court has held that mathematical algorithms are not patentable subject matter to the extent that they are merely abstract ideas. *See Diehr*, 450 U.S. 175, 67 L. Ed. 2d 155, 101 S. Ct. 1048, passim; *Parker v. Flook*, 437 U.S. 584, 57 L. Ed. 2d 451, 98 S. Ct. 2522 (1978); *Gottschalk v. Benson*, 409 U.S. 63, 34 L. Ed. 2d 273, 93 S. Ct. 253 (1972). In *Diehr*, the Court explained that certain types of mathematical subject matter, standing alone, represent nothing more than abstract ideas until reduced to some type of practical application, i.e., "a useful, concrete and tangible result." *Alappat*, 33 F.3d at 1544, 31 U.S.P.Q.2D (BNA) at 1557.

Unpatentable mathematical algorithms are identifiable by showing they are merely abstract ideas constituting disembodied concepts or truths that are not "useful." From a practical standpoint, this means that to be patentable an algorithm must be applied in a "useful" way. In *Alappat*, we held that data, transformed by a machine through a series of mathematical calculations to produce a smooth waveform display on a rasterizer monitor, constituted a practical application of an abstract idea (a mathematical algorithm, formula, or calculation), because it produced "a useful, concrete and tangible result"—the smooth waveform.

Similarly, in *Arrhythmia Research Technology Inc. v. Corazonix Corp.*, 958 F.2d 1053, 22 U.S.P.Q.2D (BNA) 1033 (Fed. Cir. 1992), we held that the transformation of electrocardiograph signals from a patient's heartbeat by a machine through a series of mathematical calculations constituted a practical application of an abstract idea (a mathematical algorithm, formula, or calculation), because it corresponded to a useful, concrete or tangible thing—the condition of a patient's heart.

Today, we hold that the transformation of data, representing discrete dollar amounts, by a machine through a series of mathematical calculations into a final share price, constitutes a practical application of a mathematical algorithm, formula, or calculation, because it produces "a useful, concrete and tangible result"—a final share price momentarily fixed for recording and reporting purposes and even accepted and relied upon by regulatory authorities and in subsequent trades. The district court erred by applying the *Freeman-Walter-Abele* test to determine whether the claimed subject matter was an unpatentable abstract idea. The *Freeman-Walter-Abele* test was designed by the Court of Customs and Patent Appeals, and subsequently adopted by this court, to extract and identify unpatentable mathematical algorithms in the aftermath of *Benson* and *Flook*. *See In re Freeman*, 573 F.2d 1237, 197 U.S.P.Q. (BNA) 464 (CCPA 1978) as modified by *In re Walter*, 618 F.2d 758, 205 U.S.P.Q. (BNA) 397 (CCPA 1980). The test has been thus articulated:

> First, the claim is analyzed to determine whether a mathematical algorithm is directly or indirectly recited. Next, if a mathematical algorithm is found, the claim as a whole is further analyzed to determine whether the algorithm is "applied in any manner to physical elements or process steps," and, if it is, it "passes muster under § 101."

*In re Pardo*, 684 F.2d 912, 915, 214 U.S.P.Q. (BNA) 673, 675–76 (CCPA 1982) (citing *In re Abele*, 684 F.2d 902, 214 U.S.P.Q. (BNA) 682 (CCPA 1982)) [footnotes omitted].

After *Diehr* and *Chakrabarty*, the *Freeman-Walter-Abele* test has little, if any, applicability to determining the presence of statutory subject matter. As we pointed out in *Alappat*, 33 F.3d at 1543, 31 U.S.P.Q.2D (BNA) at 1557, application of the test could be misleading, because a process, machine, manufacture, or composition of matter employing a law of nature, natural phenomenon, or abstract idea is patentable subject matter even though a law of nature, natural phenomenon, or abstract idea would not, by itself, be entitled to such protection. The test determines the presence of, for example, an algorithm. Under *Benson*, this may have been a sufficient indicium of nonstatutory subject matter.

However, after *Diehr* and *Alappat*, the mere fact that a claimed invention involves inputting numbers, calculating numbers, outputting numbers, and storing numbers, in and of itself, would not render it nonstatutory subject matter, unless, of course, its operation does not produce a "useful, concrete and tangible result." *Alappat*, 33 F.3d at 1544, 31 U.S.P.Q.2D (BNA) at 1557. After all, as we have repeatedly stated,

> every step-by-step process, be it electronic or chemical or mechanical, involves algorithm in the broad sense of the term. Since § 101 expressly includes processes as a category of inventions which may be patented and § 100(b) further defines the word "process" as meaning "process, art or method, and includes a new use of a known process, machine, manufacture, composition of matter, or material," it follows that it is no ground for holding a claim is directed to nonstatutory subject matter to say it includes or is directed to an algorithm. This is why the proscription against patenting has been limited to *mathematical* algorithms....

*In re Iwahashi*, 888 F.2d 1370, 1374, 12 U.S.P.Q.2D (BNA) 1908, 1911 (Fed. Cir. 1989) (emphasis in the original).

The question of whether a claim encompasses statutory subject matter should not focus on which of the four categories of subject matter a claim is directed to—process, machine, manufacture, or composition of matter—but rather on the essential characteristics of the subject matter, in particular, its practical utility. Section 101 specifies that statutory subject matter must also satisfy the other "conditions and requirements" of Title 35, including novelty, nonobviousness, and adequacy of disclosure and notice. *See*

*In re Warmerdam*, 33 F.3d 1354, 1359, 31 U.S.P.Q.2D (BNA) 1754, 1757–58 (Fed. Cir. 1994). For purpose of our analysis, as noted above, claim 1 is directed to a machine programmed with the Hub and Spoke software and admittedly produces a "useful, concrete, and tangible result." *Alappat*, 33 F.3d at 1544, 31 U.S.P.Q.2D (BNA) at 1557. This renders it statutory subject matter, even if the useful result is expressed in numbers, such as price, profit, percentage, cost, or loss.

### The Business Method Exception

As an alternative ground for invalidating the '056 patent under § 101, the court relied on the judicially-created, so-called "business method" exception to statutory subject matter. We take this opportunity to lay this ill-conceived exception to rest. Since its inception, the "business method" exception has merely represented the application of some general, but no longer applicable legal principle, perhaps arising out of the "requirement for invention"—which was eliminated by § 103. Since the 1952 Patent Act, business methods have been, and should have been, subject to the same legal requirements for patentability as applied to any other process or method.

The business method exception has never been invoked by this court, or the CCPA, to deem an invention unpatentable. Application of this particular exception has always been preceded by a ruling based on some clearer concept of Title 35 or, more commonly, application of the abstract idea exception based on finding a mathematical algorithm. Illustrative is the CCPA's analysis in *In re Howard*, 55 C.C.P.A. 1121, 394 F.2d 869, 157 U.S.P.Q. (BNA) 615 (CCPA 1968), wherein the court affirmed the Board of Appeals' rejection of the claims for lack of novelty and found it unnecessary to reach the Board's section 101 ground that a method of doing business is "inherently unpatentable." 394 F.2d at 872, 157 U.S.P.Q. (BNA) at 617 n.12.

State Street argues that we acknowledged the validity of the business method exception in *Alappat* when we discussed *Maucorps* and *Meyer*:

> *Maucorps* dealt with a business methodology for deciding how salesmen should best handle respective customers and *Meyer* involved a 'system' for aiding a neurologist in diagnosing patients. Clearly, neither of the alleged 'inventions' in those cases falls within any § 101 category.

*Alappat*, 33 F.3d at 1541, 31 U.S.P.Q.2D (BNA) at 1555.

However, closer scrutiny of these cases reveals that the claimed inventions in both *Maucorps* and *Meyer* were rejected as abstract ideas under the mathematical algorithm exception, not the business method exception. *See In re Maucorps*, 609 F.2d 481, 484, 203 U.S.P.Q. (BNA) 812, 816 (CCPA 1979); *In re Meyer*, 688 F.2d 789, 796, 215 U.S.P.Q. (BNA) 193, 199 (CCPA 1982).

Even the case frequently cited as establishing the business method exception to statutory subject matter, *Hotel Security Checking Co. v. Lorraine Co.*, 160 F. 467 (2d Cir. 1908), did not rely on the exception to strike the patent. In that case, the patent was found invalid for lack of novelty and "invention," not because it was improper subject matter for a patent. The court stated "the fundamental principle of the system is as old as the art of bookkeeping, i.e., charging the goods of the employer to the agent who takes them." *Id.* at 469. "If at the time of [the patent] application, there had been no system of bookkeeping of any kind in restaurants, we would be confronted with the question whether a new and useful system of cash registering and account checking is such an art as is patentable under the statute." *Id.* at 472.

This case is no exception. The district court announced the precepts of the business method exception as set forth in several treatises, but noted as its primary reason for finding the patent invalid under the business method exception as follows:

> If Signature's invention were patentable, any financial institution desirous of implementing a multi-tiered funding complex modeled [sic] on a Hub and Spoke configuration would be required to seek Signature's permission before embarking on such a project. *This is so because the '056 Patent is claimed [sic] sufficiently broadly to foreclose virtually any computer-implemented accounting method necessary to manage this type of financial structure.*

927 F. Supp. 502, 516, 38 U.S.P.Q.2D (BNA) 1530, 1542 (emphasis added).

Whether the patent's claims are too broad to be patentable is not to be judged under § 101, but rather under §§ 102, 103 and 112.

Assuming the above statement to be correct, it has nothing to do with whether what is claimed is statutory subject matter.

In view of this background, it comes as no surprise that in the most recent edition of the Manual of Patent Examining Procedures (MPEP) (1996), a paragraph of § 706.03(a) was deleted. In past editions it read:

> Though seemingly within the category of process or method, a method of doing business can be rejected as not being within the statutory classes. *See Hotel Security Checking Co. v. Lorraine Co.*, 160 F. 467 (2nd Cir. 1908) and *In re Wait*, 73 F.2d 982, 24 U.S.P.Q. (BNA) 88, 22 C.C.P.A. 822 (1934).

MPEP § 706.03(a) (1994).

This acknowledgment is buttressed by the U.S. Patent and Trademark 1996 Examination Guidelines for Computer Related Inventions, which now reads:

> Office personnel have had difficulty in properly treating claims directed to methods of doing business. Claims should not be categorized as methods of doing business. Instead such claims should be treated like any other process claims.

Examination Guidelines, 61 Fed. Reg. 7478, 7479 (1996).

We agree that this is precisely the manner in which this type of claim should be treated. Whether the claims are directed to subject matter within § 101 should not turn on whether the claimed subject matter does "business" instead of something else.

## CONCLUSION

The appealed decision is reversed and the case is remanded to the district court for further proceedings consistent with this opinion.

REVERSED and REMANDED.

---

# Notes on Patents

1. The Federal Circuit's rulings in *State Street* are controversial, especially among academic commentators. Those rulings raise fundamental questions regarding the scope of

patentable subject matter and how it relates to the nature of inventing and the purposes of the patent system. *Compare* Jay Dratler, Jr., *Does Lord Darcy Yet Live? The Case Against Software and Business-Method Patents*, 43 SANTA CLARA L. REV. 823 (2003), *and* John R. Thomas, *The Patenting of the Liberal Professions*, 40 B.C. L. REV. 1139 (1999), *with* Robert A. Kreiss, *Patent Protection for Computer Programs and Mathematical Algorithms: The Constitutional Limitations on Patentable Subject Matter*, 29 N.M L. REV. 31 (1999) (supporting trend in Federal Circuit's jurisprudence).

2. It is unclear whether *State Street* is consistent with the Supreme Court's views of computer-program-related inventions. The Supreme Court has reviewed only three such inventions. *See Diamond v. Diehr*, 450 U.S. 175 (1981); *Parker v. Flook*, 437 U.S. 584 (1978); *Gottschalk v. Benson*, 409 U.S. 63 (1972). It rejected patents on two of them—in *Benson* and *Flook*—holding them not patentable subject matter because patents would have monopolized a mathematical algorithm or formula. *See Flook*, 437 U.S. at 594–95; *Benson*, 409 U.S. at 71–72. Only in *Diehr* did the Court allow a patent, and it did so only because the invention (a process for curing rubber in a mold) involved physical systems and significant "post-solution" activity in addition to the computer program itself. *See Diehr*, 450 U.S. at 187, 191–92. As the Court described its reasoning:

> The respondents here do not seek to patent a mathematical formula. Instead, they seek patent protection for a process of curing synthetic rubber. Their process admittedly employs a well-known mathematical equation, but they do not seek to pre-empt the use of that equation. Rather, they seek only to foreclose from others the use of that equation in conjunction with all of the other steps in their claimed process. These include installing rubber in a press, closing the mold, constantly determining the temperature of the mold, constantly recalculating the appropriate cure time through the use of the formula and a digital computer, and automatically opening the press at the proper time.

*Id.* at 187. Is the Federal Circuit's decision in *State Street*, in which the Federal Circuit essentially allowed a patent to cover a type of *business* (hub and spoke investment partnerships using computerized accounting) because the patent applicant was first to write a computer program for such a business, consistent with these decisions?

3. No doubt some readers of this book have themselves written computer programs. If you have done so, did you think you were "inventing" at the time? Did you think that your writing your program would or should give you the exclusive right to write and use similar programs in a particular type of business? If so, did you think that that exclusive right should apply regardless of how the competing programs are written, i.e., what algorithms, programming techniques and computer code they use?

Suppose, for example, that you wrote the first specialized accounting program for a neighborhood bar. Did you think that your doing so entitled you to a patent covering all accounting systems for local alcoholic-beverage-service businesses? Wouldn't *State Street*'s holding support such a patent?

4. The rationales for limiting patentable subject matter, including the judge-made exceptions discussed in *State Street*, are among the most muddled in all of intellectual property law. In the absence of clear guiding principles, the Federal Circuit has veritably opened the floodgates to all sorts of patents. Consider Professor Thomas' lament:

> Among the more reviled Patent Office grants has been its 1968 patent on a method of swallowing a pill. Now we need scant imagination to envision patents on corporate ingestion of poison pills as well. With business and medical techniques firmly under wing, and patents on sports methods and proce-

dures of psychological analysis trickling out of the Patent Office, patents appropriating almost any sort of communicable practice seem easily attainable. Claims to methods within the disciplines of sociology, political science, economics and the law appear to present only the nearest frontier for the regime of patents. Under increasingly permissive Federal Circuit case law, techniques within such far-flung disciplines as language, the fine arts and theology also now appear to be within the realm of patentability.

John R. Thomas, *The Paternity of the Liberal Professions*, 40 B.C. L. Rev. 1139, 1163–64.

5. Like most of intellectual property law, patent law does not exist in a vacuum. The Supreme Court itself described the "backdrop" of patent law in a seminal patent-preemption decision, *Bonito Boats, Inc. v. Thunder Craft Boats, Inc.*, 489 U.S. 141, 144–45 (1989) (invalidating Fla. Stat. §559.94 (1987)), as pre-empted by federal patent law). There the Court said:

> The attractiveness of [a patent], and its effectiveness in inducing creative effort and disclosure of the results of that effort, depend almost entirely on a backdrop of free competition in the exploitation of unpatented designs and innovations. The novelty and nonobviousness requirements of patentability embody a congressional understanding, implicit in the Patent Clause itself, that free exploitation of ideas will be the rule, to which the protection of a federal patent is the exception.

*Id.*, 489 U.S. at 151.

6. The "backdrop of free competition" of which the *Bonito* Court spoke has been around for a long time. Indeed, it is the foundation of all of Anglo-American economic law.

Nearly four centuries ago, in 1623, the English Parliament adopted the Statute of Monopolies, which outlawed state-granted monopolies but provided an exception for patents. *See* An Act concerning Monopolies and Dispensations with penal Lawes and the Forefeyture thereof, 21 Jam., c. 3 § 1, 2, 6, 10 (1623).

Consider the following comparison between the English Statute of Monopolies and our Patent and Copyright Clause, combined with our Sherman Act:

> To the student of antitrust law, the English Statute of Monopolies... is startling in its modernity. Every major feature of modern antitrust law appears in it. Among other things, it has a general prohibition against monopoly, a reluctance to define the term too closely (lest a precise definition be circumvented), trust in common-law courts and juries to apply the prohibition, and awards of treble damages and costs to aggrieved parties. Reading the Statute of Monopolies today thus gives one the distinct impression that not much besides detail has changed in basic economic law in nearly four centuries.

> Yet the Statute of Monopolies differs from modern antitrust law in one important respect. It contains what we now know as intellectual property—patents and a precursor to copyrights—as explicit exceptions to its general prohibition on state-granted monopolies....

> It thus recognized explicitly, over 150 years earlier, what the Patent and Copyright Clause of the United States Constitution recognizes implicitly: monopolies on existing articles of commerce are bad, but temporary monopolies on innovations may be necessary to provide an incentive to create them.

* * *

It is odd that the Statute of Monopolies expresses far more directly than our Constitution the relationship of rule and exception between antitrust and intellectual property law. For the statute was no stranger to those who helped shape our Constitution. Thomas Jefferson was so opposed to monopolies that he wanted to include a prohibition against them in the Bill of Rights. As our Supreme Court has noted in [*Graham v. John Deere Co., supra*], Jefferson later approved the Patent and Copyright Clause, which granted Congress the power to enact temporary monopolies to encourage innovation and creativity, but he did so only after James Madison convinced him that 'ingenuity deserves liberal encouragement.' Given this history, it seems a mere quirk of fate that our Patent and Copyright Clause expresses the rule—that monopolies are bad—only by negative implication, while explicitly stating the exception to the rule—that patents and copyrights may be good. It took the United States yet another 100 years for the main principle of the Statute of Monopolies to appear as positive law in our Sherman [Antitrust] Act of 1890.

Jay Dratler Jr., *Does Lord Darcy Yet Live? The Case Against Software and Business-Method Patents*, 43 Santa Clara L. Rev. 823, 825–30 (2003).

7. If our patent law, our Constitution, and our antitrust laws embody the spirit of the Statute of Monopolies—that free competition is the rule and temporary patent and copyright monopolies the exception—doesn't that fact have implications for what types of alleged "inventions" should be eligible for patent protection?

Consider the following analysis:

Despite the misgivings of a reluctant and begrudging Supreme Court, the Federal Circuit has thrown the door wide open to patents on computer programs. At the same time, it has endorsed patents on new business methods, decreeing that a supposed prohibition against such patents never really existed. Then Congress, in an amendment to the patent statute ostensibly designed to limit such patents, has by implication endorsed them.

On its face, each of these developments appears to have shifted the delicate balance between free competition for business in general and temporary monopoly for genuine innovation, which the Statute of Monopolies decreed and the Patent and Copyright Clause continued. In modern industry, virtually every business uses computer programs in its operations. If computer programs are patentable, and if patent law (as it now appears to do) permits broad claims to computer programs performing specified business functions—without any limiting details as to how those functions are performed—a person can monopolize a particular line of business simply by being the first to write a computer program to perform the functions required in that line of business and broadly claiming the computer program in a patent. The same result can be achieved even more directly by patenting the essential features of the new line of business as a 'business method.' In either case, the result—monopolization of a line of business through development of related abstractions (software program or method)—does not obviously fall within a reasonable extrapolation of the exception to the prohibition against monopoly for 'new manufactures' that the Statute of Monopolies endorsed and American law continued.

Dratler, *supra* at 834–836 (2003).

8. Whatever you may think (or not think) about computer programs, consider Professor Thomas' list of potentially patentable items in Note 4 above. If all of those things are patentable, won't businesspeople eager to secure economically valuable (albeit temporary) monopolies patent them?

If they do so, what will happen to free competition? Will it survive, or will every business based upon a "new" twist, however general or abstract, enjoy a twenty-year monopoly and freedom from competition? Is that good or bad economic policy? Is it consistent with the spirit of the Statute of Monopolies and the letter of our Patent and Copyright Clause and our Sherman Act?

9. Now consider the requirement that an invention be "nonobvious" at the time it was made. When Thomas Jefferson said that some such criterion was required to avoid the "embarrassment of an exclusive patent," didn't he have in mind the negative economic consequences of an undeserved monopoly? If so, isn't there a direct relationship between the nonobviousness requirement and the question of subject matter; that is, what "new" inventions ought not to be eligible for patents?

10. Jefferson's original criterion for an invention (besides novelty) was that it be "*sufficiently* useful *and important*" (emphasis added). The *Hotchkiss* decision, cited in *Graham v. John Deere Co.*, *supra*, changed the criterion to something beyond the "skill of an ordinary mechanic." For nearly a century, the Courts interpreted *Hotchikiss* as requiring "invention," meaning some undefined quality of inventiveness. Finally, in 1952, Congress enacted the present nonobviousness requirement, intended, according to the *Graham* Court, to make no substantive change.

Which of these verbal formulations best expresses the underlying idea—that some inventions, although literally "new," do not deserve patents because granting them patents would conflict with the principles of free competition and free markets? Does "nonobviousness" focus too much on the inventor's ingenuity and the quality of her cognition? Are those things *economically* relevant? Was the *Graham* Court more incisive when it said that "[t]he inherent problem was to develop some means of weeding out those inventions which would not be disclosed or devised but for the inducement of a patent?" *Graham v. John Deere Co.*, 383 U.S. 1, 11 (1966). For a proposed answer to these questions, see Dratler, *supra* at 840–53.

11. These issues are fundamental to the nature of our, or any, patent system. They may take a long time to resolve. Although they are theoretical and abstract, they do have a direct relationship to licensing.

Most patents have multiple claims, arranged in an inverted pyramid. The claim at the top is often times the broadest. Successive claims are narrower and narrower, until the last may cover no more than the inventor's commercial or preferred embodiment.

Good patent lawyers usually draft claims in this fashion, hoping to achieve as broad coverage as possible while reserving narrower claims in case the broader ones are invalidated. For example, Samuel Morse's famous telegraph patent claimed every possible method of communicating with electromagnetic energy, in addition to the particular construction of the telegraph machine that Morse had invented. When the Supreme Court invalidated the general claim as too broad, Morse still could rely on the narrower ones. *O'Reilly v. Morse*, 56 U.S. 62 (1853).

When a patent contains such an inverted pyramid of increasingly narrow claims, how does a patentee know to whom to license the patent? Won't the patentee have to consider the likelihood that some of the claims might be invalidated as too broad? For example, consider the patent in *State Street*. Who would be potential licensees of that patent? Computer manufacturers? Computer programmers? Accountants? Investment advisors? Investment bankers? Stock brokers? Any business using brokerage-like accounting? All of the above? Doesn't the answer depend in part upon how broadly the law allows such an "invention" to be claimed?

12. The sample claim discussed in *State Street* says nothing about how the computer was programmed. Instead, it covers certain accounting *functions* performed for a certain type of business. Suppose, however, that narrower claims in the same patent *did* cover specific programming techniques, and nothing else, and that the Federal Circuit, instead of upholding it, had invalidated the broader claim? To whom might the patentee best license its patent then?

13. What do patents protect? Scientific principle? Abstract idea? A machine or process? What must an inventor do to get a patent? What legal process must she invoke? What requirements must an invention meet to merit a patent? What is the patent attorney's role? When a business applies for a patent, what are the risks the patent will not issue? That it will be a "weak" patent? When a business has technology but does not seek to patent it, what risks are incurred? That others will discover the technology independently or by reverse engineering the business' products? That others will steal the technology? That others will patent it and prevent the business from using its own technology?

---

# IV. Copyrights

## Foreword: Symposium on Intellectual Property Law
### Kenneth L. Port
### 68 Chicago-Kent L. Rev. 585, 587–90 (1993) (as revised 2005)

* * *

Copyrights, like patents, exist with express constitutional authorization. The Patent and Copyright Clause of the Constitution provides that copyrights, like patents, are to be granted "to promote the progress of science and useful arts, by securing for limited times to authors and inventors the exclusive right to their respective writings and discoveries." U.S. Const. Art. 1, sec. 8, cl. 8.

The generally accepted purpose of copyright law is to grant protection to specific authors to encourage all authors to create and disseminate their works. As a result, the public at large will have access to their original creations. The law assumes that, without such protection, authors would not create as much as they would with the protection; that without copyright protection ensuring exclusivity publishers would not publish as much as they would with protection; and that without copyright protection authors would be more inclined to sit on their ideas and choose not to make them public.

Copyright law generally protects works of original authorship that are fixed or expressed in a tangible medium of expression. Copyrightable subject matter includes literary works, musical works, dramatic works, pantomimes and choreographic works, pictorial, graphic and sculptural works, motion pictures and other audiovisual works, sound recordings, and architectural works. *See* 17 U.S.C. § 102(2).

Copyright protection subsists from the moment of creation regardless of registration or notice formalities and continues for the life of the author plus 70 years. Copyrights in anonymous works, pseudonymous works and "works made for hire" last for 95 years from the year of publication or 120 years from creation, whichever expires first.

Copyright grants the author of the work the exclusive right to reproduce the work, to prepare derivative works based upon the work, to distribute copies of the work for public sale or transfer ownership, to perform the work publicly, to display the work publicly, and to digitally transmit audio recordings.

There are three generally accepted limitations to the assertion of copyrights. First, unlike patent law, copyright only grants the holder the exclusive right to [exploit] the protected work. Independent development is a complete defense to an otherwise infringing act.

Secondly, copyright only protects the expression of an idea and not the underlying idea itself. *See* 17 U.S.C. § 102(b). This is generally referred to as the idea/expression dichotomy. Although a never-ending source of confusion by the courts and analysis by commentators, the idea/expression dichotomy is derived to prevent monopolies in ideas and encourage expression and publication of ideas.

Finally, copyright does not protect the underlying facts, systems, processes, or methods described in the work. Therefore, if I write a book about the Civil War, the words I choose as well as the organization and design should be copyrightable; however, the underlying facts upon which my book is based are not protected and anyone may use those facts even if my research to discover those facts was difficult and expensive.

Copyright litigation generally presents two issues. The first is the copyrightability of the work. The second is whether the copyrighted work was infringed. The infringement test is easy to state and difficult to apply: Copyrighted work A is infringed by subsequent work B if the author of work B was actually or arguably exposed to A (that is, had "access" to the work) and the resulting work B was substantially similar to A. In the words of Learned Hand, substantial similarity exists where the ordinary observer would look at two works and, not focusing on any dissimilarities, would overlook such dissimilarities and consider the two works aesthetically the same.

Below are summarized some of the underlying principles regarding copyrightability.

1.   Although copyright protection does not extend to underlying ideas or facts themselves, originality in organization is generally sufficient to warrant copyright protection; however, the work would only be protected to the extent the organization was original.

2.   Copyright protection is available only for the non-utilitarian aspect of a work. To the extent a work is useful it is not copyrightable. Similar principles apply to compilation of facts, such as databases. *See* 17 U.S.C. § 103.

3.   Copyright law also protects derivative works even when the underlying work is already in the public domain. If an author contributes enough originality, that author's contribution will result in a protected derivative work.

4.   The level of originality required for copyrightability is quite minimal. A work is original if it owes its origin to the author obtaining copyright ownership and has a modicum of creativity.

5. Copyright subsists from the moment the work is fixed in a tangible medium of expression. Nothing more need be done by an author to have a valid copyright in a work.

6. For works of U.S. origin, registration of copyrights is necessary prior to litigation. Timely registration is required to obtain statutory damages and attorney's fees. Formal notice requirements have also been relaxed since 1989.

\* \* \*

Condensed Ledger at Issue in *Baker v. Seldon*

| CONDENSED LEDGER. | | | | | | | | | | | | |

# Baker v. Selden

## 101 U.S. 99 (1879)

Mr. Justice Bradley delivered the opinion of the court.

Charles Selden, the testator of the complainant in this case, in the year 1859 took the requisite steps for obtaining the copyright of a book, entitled "Selden's Condensed Ledger, or Book-keeping Simplified," the object of which was to exhibit and explain a peculiar system of book-keeping. In 1860 and 1861, he took the copyright of several other books, containing additions to and improvements upon the said system. The bill of complaint was filed against the defendant, Baker, for an alleged infringement of these copyrights. The latter, in his answer, denied that Selden was the author or designer of the books, and denied the infringement charged, and contends on the argument that the matter alleged to be infringed is not a lawful subject of copyright.

The parties went into proofs, and the various books of the complainant, as well as those sold and used by the defendant, were exhibited before the examiner, and witnesses were examined on both sides. A decree was rendered for the complainant, and the defendant appealed.

The book or series of books of which the complainant claims the copyright consists of an introductory essay explaining the system of book-keeping referred to, to which are annexed certain forms or blanks, consisting of ruled lines, and headings, illustrating the system and showing how it is to be used and carried out in practice. This system effects the same results as book-keeping by double entry; but, by a peculiar arrangement of columns and headings, presents the entire operation, of a day, a week, or a month, on a single page, or on two pages facing each other, in an account-book. The defendant uses a similar plan so far as results are concerned; but makes a different arrangement of the columns, and uses different headings. If the complainant's testator had the exclusive right to the use of the system explained in his book, it would be difficult to contend that the defendant does not infringe it, notwithstanding the difference in his form of arrangement; but if it be assumed that the system is open to public use, it seems to be equally difficult to contend that the books made and sold by the defendant are a violation of the copyright of the complainant's book considered merely as a book explanatory of the system. Where the truths of a science or the methods of an art are the common property of the whole world, and author has the right to express the one, or explain and use the other, in his own way. As an author, Selden explained the system in a particular way. It may be conceded that Baker makes and uses account-books arranged on substantially the same system; but the proof fails to show that he has violated the copyright of Selden's book, regarding the latter merely as an explanatory work; or that he has infringed Selden's right in any way, unless the latter became entitled to an exclusive right in the system.

The evidence of the complainant is principally directed to the object of showing that Baker uses the same system as that which is explained and illustrated in Selden's books. It becomes important, therefore, to determine whether, in obtaining the copyright of his books, he secured the exclusive right to the use of the system or method of book-keeping which the said books are intended to illustrate and explain. It is contended that he has secured such exclusive right, because no one can use the system without using substantially the same ruled lines and headings which he has appended to his books in illustration of it. In other words, it is contended that the ruled lines and headings, given to illustrate the system, are a part of the book, and, as such, are secured by the copyright; and that no one can make or use similar ruled lines and headings, or ruled lines and headings made and arranged on substantially the same system, without violating the copyright. And this is really the question to be decided in this case. Stated in another form, the question is, whether the exclusive property in a system of book-keeping can be claimed, under the law of copyright, by means of a book in which that system is explained? The complainant's bill, and the case made under it, are based on the hypothesis that it can be.

It cannot be pretended, and indeed it is not seriously urged, that the ruled lines of the complainant's account-book can be claimed under any special class of objects, other than books, named in the law of copyright existing in 1859. The law then in force was that of 1831, and specified only books, maps, charts, musical compositions, prints, and engravings. An account-book, consisting of ruled lines and blank columns, cannot be called by any of these names unless by that of a book.

There is no doubt that a work on the subject of book-keeping, though only explanatory of well-known systems, may be the subject of a copyright; but, then, it is claimed only as a book. Such a book may be explanatory either of old systems, or of an entirely new system; and, considered as a book, as the work of an author, conveying information on the subject of book-keeping, and containing detailed explanations of the art, it may be a very valuable acquisition to the practical knowledge of the community. But there is a clear distinction between the book, as such, and the art which it is intended to illustrate. The mere statement of the proposition is so evident, that it requires hardly any argument to support it. The same distinction may be predicated of every other art as well as that of book-keeping. A treatise on the composition and use of medicines, be they old or new; on the construction and use of ploughs, or watches, or churns; or on the mixture and application of colors for painting or dyeing; or on the mode of drawing lines to produce the effect of perspective — would be the subject of copyright; but no one would contend that the copyright of the treatise would give the exclusive right to the art or manufacture described therein. The copyright of the book, if not pirated from other works, would be valid without regard to the novelty, or want of novelty, of its subject-matter. The novelty of the art or thing described or explained has nothing to do with the validity of the copyright. To give to the author of the book an exclusive property in the art described therein, when no examination of its novelty has ever been officially made, would be a surprise and a fraud upon the public. That is the province of letters-patent, not of copyright. The claim to an invention or discovery of an art or manufacture must be subjected to the examination of the Patent Office before an exclusive right therein can be obtained; and it can only be secured by a patent from the government.

The difference between the two things, letters-patent and copyright, may be illustrated by reference to the subjects just enumerated. Take the case of medicines. Certain mixtures are found to be of great value in the healing art. If the discoverer writes and publishes a book on the subject (as regular physicians generally do), he gains no exclusive right to the manufacture and sale of the medicine; he gives that to the public. If he desires to acquire such exclusive right, he must obtain a patent for the mixture as a new art, manufacture, or composition of matter. He may copyright his book, if he pleases; but that only secures to him the exclusive right of printing and publishing his book.

The copyright of a book on perspective, no matter how many drawings and illustrations it may contain, gives no exclusive right to the modes of drawing described, though they may never have been known or used before. By publishing the book, without getting a patent for the art, the latter is given to the public. The fact that the art described in the book by illustrations of lines and figures which are reproduced in practice in the application of the art, makes no difference. Those illustrations are the mere language employed by the author to convey his ideas more clearly. Had he used words of description instead of diagrams (which merely stand in the place of words), there could not be the slightest doubt that others, applying the art to practical use, might lawfully draw the lines and diagrams which were in the author's mind, and which he thus described by words in his book.

The copyright of a work on mathematical science cannot give to the author an exclusive right to the methods of operation which he propounds, or to the diagrams which he employs to explain them, so as to prevent an engineer from using them whenever occasion requires. The very object of publishing a book on science or the useful arts is to communicate to the world the useful knowledge which it contains. But this object would be frustrated if the knowledge could not be used without incurring the guilt of piracy of the book. And where the art it teaches cannot be used without employing the methods and diagrams used to illustrate the book, or such as are similar to them, such methods and diagrams are to be considered as necessary incidents to the art, and given therewith to the public; not given for the purpose of publication in other works explanatory of the art, but for the purpose of practical application.

Of course, these observations are not intended to apply to ornamental designs, or pictorial illustrations addressed to the taste. Of these it may be said, that their form is their essence, and their object, the production of pleasure in their contemplation. This is their final end. They are as much the product of genius and the result of composition, as are the lines of the poet or the historian's periods. On the other hand, the teachings of science and the rules and methods of useful art have their final end in application and use; and this application and use are what the public derive from the publication of a book which teaches them. But as embodied and taught in a literary composition or book, their essence consists only in their statement. This alone is what is secured by the copyright. The use by another of the same methods of statement, whether in words or illustrations, in a book published for teaching the art, would undoubtedly be an infringement of the copyright.

Recurring to the case before us, we observe that Charles Selden, by his books, explained and described a peculiar system of book-keeping, and illustrated his method by means of ruled lines and blank columns, with proper headings on a page, or on successive pages. Now, whilst no one has a right to print or publish his book, or any material part thereof, as a book intended to convey instruction in the art, any person may practice and use the art itself which he has described and illustrated therein. The use of the art is a totally different thing from a publication of the book explaining it. The copyright of a book on book-keeping cannot secure the exclusive right to make, sell, and use account-books prepared upon the plan set forth in such book. Whether the art might or might not have been patented, is a question which is not before us. It was not patented, and is open and free to the use of the public. And, of course, in using the art, the ruled lines and headings of accounts must necessarily be used as incident to it.

The plausibility of the claim put forward by the complainant in this case arises from a confusion of ideas produced by the peculiar nature of the art described in the books which have been made the subject of copyright. In describing the art, the illustrations and diagrams employed happen to correspond more closely than usual with the actual work performed by the operator who uses the art. Those illustrations and diagrams consist of ruled lines and headings of accounts; and it is similar ruled lines and headings of accounts which, in the application of the art, the book-keeper makes with his pen, or the stationer with his press; whilst in most other cases the diagrams and illustrations can only be represented in concrete forms of wood, metal, stone, or some other physical embodiment. But the principle is the same in all. The description of the art in a book, though entitled to the benefit of copyright, lays no foundation for an exclusive claim to the art itself. The object of the one is explanation; the object of the other is use. The former may be secured by copyright. The latter can only be secured, if it can be secured at all, by letters-patent.

\* \* \*

The conclusion to which we have come is, that blank account books are not the subject of copyright; and that the mere copyright of Selden's book did not confer upon him the exclusive right to make and use account-books, ruled and arranged as designated by him and described and illustrated in said book.

The decree of the Circuit Court must be reversed, and the cause remanded with instructions to dismiss the complainant's bill; and it is

*So ordered.*

\* \* \*

----

# Feist Publications, Inc. v. Rural Telephone Service Co., Inc.

## 499 U.S. 340 (1991)

Justice O'Connor delivered the opinion of the Court.

This case requires us to clarify the extent of copyright protection available to telephone directory white pages.

I

Rural Telephone Service Company, Inc., is a certified public utility that provides telephone service to several communities in northwest Kansas. It is subject to a state regulation that requires all telephone companies operating in Kansas to issue annually an updated telephone directory. Accordingly, as a condition of its monopoly franchise, Rural publishes a typical telephone directory, consisting of white pages and yellow pages. The white pages list in alphabetical order the names of Rural's subscribers, together with their towns and telephone numbers. The yellow pages list Rural's business subscribers alphabetically by category and feature classified advertisements of various sizes. Rural distributes its directory free of charge to its subscribers, but earns revenue by selling yellow pages advertisements.

Feist Publications, Inc., is a publishing company that specializes in area-wide telephone directories. Unlike a typical directory, which covers only a particular calling area, Feist's area-wide directories cover a much larger geographical range, reducing the need to call directory assistance or consult multiple directories. The Feist directory that is the subject of this litigation covers 11 different telephone service areas in 15 counties and contains 46,878 white pages listings — compared to Rural's approximately 7,700 listings. Like Rural's directory, Feist's is distributed free of charge and includes both white pages and yellow pages. Feist and Rural compete vigorously for yellow pages advertising.

As the sole provider of telephone service in its service area, Rural obtains subscriber information quite easily. Persons desiring telephone service must apply to Rural and provide their names and addresses; Rural then assigns them a telephone number. Feist is not a telephone company, let alone one with monopoly status, and therefore lacks independent access to any subscriber information. To obtain white pages listings for its area-wide directory, Feist approached each of the 11 telephone companies operating in northwest Kansas and offered to pay for the right to use its white pages listings.

Of the 11 telephone companies, only Rural refused to license its listings to Feist. Rural's refusal created a problem for Feist, as omitting these listings would have left a gaping hole in its area-wide directory, rendering it less attractive to potential yellow pages advertisers. In a decision subsequent to that which we review here, the District Court determined that this was precisely the reason Rural refused to license its listings. The refusal was motivated by an unlawful purpose "to extend its monopoly in telephone service to a monopoly in yellow pages advertising." *Rural Telephone Service Co. v. Feist Publications, Inc.*, 737 F. Supp. 610, 622 (Kan. 1990).

Unable to license Rural's white pages listings, Feist used them without Rural's consent. Feist began by removing several thousand listings that fell outside the geographic range of its area-wide directory, then hired personnel to investigate the 4,935 that remained. These employees verified the data reported by Rural and sought to obtain additional information.

As a result, a typical Feist listing includes the individual's street address; most of Rural's listings do not. Notwithstanding these additions, however, 1,309 of the 46,878 listings in Feist's 1983 directory were identical to listings in Rural's 1982–1983 white pages. App. 54 (P 15–16), 57. Four of these were fictitious listings that Rural had inserted into its directory to detect copying.

Rural sued for copyright infringement in the District Court for the District of Kansas taking the position that Feist, in compiling its own directory, could not use the information contained in Rural's white pages. Rural asserted that Feist's employees were obliged to travel door-to-door or conduct a telephone survey to discover the same information for themselves. Feist responded that such efforts were economically impractical and, in any event, unnecessary because the information copied was beyond the scope of copyright protection. The District Court granted summary judgment to Rural, explaining that "courts have consistently held that telephone directories are copyrightable" and citing a string of lower court decisions. 663 F. Supp. 214, 218 (1987). In an unpublished opinion, the Court of Appeals for the Tenth Circuit affirmed "for substantially the reasons given by the district court." App. to Pet. for Cert. 4a, judgt. order reported at 916 F.2d 718 (1990). We granted certiorari, 498 U.S. 808 (1990), to determine whether the copyright in Rural's directory protects the names, towns, and telephone numbers copied by Feist.

II

A

This case concerns the interaction of two well-established propositions. The first is that facts are not copyrightable; the other, that compilations of facts generally are. Each of these propositions possesses an impeccable pedigree. That there can be no valid copyright in facts is universally understood. The most fundamental axiom of copyright law is that "no author may copyright his ideas or the facts he narrates." *Harper & Row, Publishers, Inc. v. Nation Enterprises*, 471 U.S. 539, 556 (1985). Rural wisely concedes this point, noting in its brief that "facts and discoveries, of course, are not themselves subject to copyright protection." Brief for Respondent 24. At the same time, however, it is beyond dispute that compilations of facts are within the subject matter of copyright.

Compilations were expressly mentioned in the Copyright Act of 1909, and again in the Copyright Act of 1976.

There is an undeniable tension between these two propositions. Many compilations consist of nothing but raw data—i.e., wholly factual information not accompanied by any original written expression. On what basis may one claim a copyright in such a work? Common sense tells us that 100 uncopyrightable facts do not magically change their status when gathered together in one place. Yet copyright law seems to contemplate that compilations that consist exclusively of facts are potentially within its scope.

The key to resolving the tension lies in understanding why facts are not copyrightable. The *sine qua non* of copyright is originality. To qualify for copyright protection, a work must be original to the author. *See Harper & Row, supra,* at 547–549. Original, as the term is used in copyright, means only that the work was independently created by the author (as opposed to copied from other works), and that it possesses at least some minimal degree of creativity. 1 M. NIMMER & D. NIMMER, COPYRIGHT §§2.01[A], [B] (1990) (hereinafter NIMMER). To be sure, the requisite level of creativity is extremely low; even a slight amount will suffice. The vast majority of works make the grade quite easily, as they possess some creative spark, "no matter how crude, humble or obvious" it might be. *Id.* §1.08[C][1]. Originality does not signify novelty; a work may be original even though it closely resembles other works so long as the similarity is fortuitous, not the result of copying. To illustrate, assume that two poets, each ignorant of the other, compose identical poems. Neither work is novel, yet both are original and, hence, copyrightable. *See Sheldon v. Metro-Goldwyn Pictures Corp.,* 81 F.2d 49, 54 (CA2 1936).

Originality is a constitutional requirement. The source of Congress' power to enact copyright laws is Article I, Sec. 8, cl. 8, of the Constitution, which authorizes Congress to "secure for limited Times to Authors...the exclusive Right to their respective Writings." In two decisions from the late 19th century—*The Trade-Mark Cases,* 100 U.S. 82 (1879); and *Burrow-Giles Lithographic Co. v. Sarony,* 111 U.S. 53 (1884)—this Court defined the crucial terms "authors" and "writings." In so doing, the Court made it unmistakably clear that these terms presuppose a degree of originality.

In *The Trade-Mark Cases,* the Court addressed the constitutional scope of "writings." For a particular work to be classified "under the head of writings of authors," the Court determined, "originality is required." 100 U.S. at 94. The Court explained that originality requires independent creation plus a modicum of creativity: "While the word writings may be liberally construed, as it has been, to include original designs for engraving, prints, etc., it is only such as are original, and are founded in the creative powers of the mind. The writings which are to be protected are the fruits of intellectual labor, embodied in the form of books, prints, engravings, and the like." *Ibid.* (emphasis in original).

In *Burrow-Giles,* the Court distilled the same requirement from the Constitution's use of the word "authors." The Court defined "author," in a constitutional sense, to mean "he to whom anything owes its origin; originator; maker." 111 U.S., at 58 (internal quotation marks omitted). As in *The Trade-Mark Cases,* the Court emphasized the creative component of originality. It described copyright as being limited to "original intellectual conceptions of the author," 111 U.S. at 58, and stressed the importance of requiring an author who accuses another of infringement to prove "the existence of those facts of originality, of intellectual production, of thought, and conception." *Id.* at 59–60.

The originality requirement articulated in *The Trade-Mark Cases* and *Burrow-Giles* remains the touchstone of copyright protection today....It is this bedrock principle of copyright that mandates the law's seemingly disparate treatment of facts and factual compilations. No one may claim originality as to facts. This is because facts do not owe their origin to an act of authorship. The distinction is one between creation and discovery: The first person to find and report a particular fact has not created the fact; he or she has merely discovered its existence. To borrow from *Burrow-Giles*, one who discovers a fact is not its "maker" or "originator." 111 U.S. at 58. "The discoverer merely finds and records." NIMMER §2.03[E]. Census takers, for example, do not "create" the population figures that emerge from their efforts; in a sense, they copy these figures from the world around them....Census data therefore do not trigger copyright because these data are not "original" in the constitutional sense. NIMMER §2.03[E]. The same is true of all facts—scientific, historical, biographical, and news of the day. "They may not be copyrighted and are part of the public domain available to every person." *Miller v. Universal City Studios, Inc.*, 650 F.2d 1365, 1369 (CA5 1981).

Factual compilations, on the other hand, may possess the requisite originality. The compilation author typically chooses which facts to include, in what order to place them, and how to arrange the collected data so that they may be used effectively by readers. These choices as to selection and arrangement, so long as they are made independently by the compiler and entail a minimal degree of creativity, are sufficiently original that Congress may protect such compilations through the copyright laws.... Thus, even a directory that contains absolutely no protectible written expression, only facts, meets the constitutional minimum for copyright protection if it features an original selection or arrangement....

This protection is subject to an important limitation. The mere fact that a work is copyrighted does not mean that every element of the work may be protected. Originality remains the *sine qua non* of copyright; accordingly, copyright protection may extend only to those components of a work that are original to the author....Thus, if the compilation author clothes facts with an original collocation of words, he or she may be able to claim a copyright in this written expression. Others may copy the underlying facts from the publication, but not the precise words used to present them. In *Harper & Row*, for example, we explained that President Ford could not prevent others from copying bare historical facts from his autobiography, *See* 471 U.S. at 556–557, but that he could prevent others from copying his "subjective descriptions and portraits of public figures." *Id.* at 563. Where the compilation author adds no written expression but rather lets the facts speak for themselves, the expressive element is more elusive. The only conceivable expression is the manner in which the compiler has selected and arranged the facts. Thus, if the selection and arrangement are original, these elements of the work are eligible for copyright protection....No matter how original the format, however, the facts themselves do not become original through association....

This inevitably means that the copyright in a factual compilation is thin. Notwithstanding a valid copyright, a subsequent compiler remains free to use the facts contained in another's publication to aid in preparing a competing work, so long as the competing work does not feature the same selection and arrangement. As one commentator explains it: "No matter how much original authorship the work displays, the facts and ideas it exposes are free for the taking....The very same facts and ideas may be divorced from the context imposed by the author, and restated or reshuffled by second comers, even if the author was the first to discover the facts or to propose the ideas." Ginsburg, 1868. It may seem unfair that much of the fruit of the compiler's labor may be used by others without compensation. As Justice Brennan has correctly observed, however, this is not "some unforeseen byproduct of a statutory scheme." *Harper & Row*,

471 U.S. at 589 (dissenting opinion). It is, rather, "the essence of copyright," *ibid.*, and a constitutional requirement. The primary objective of copyright is not to reward the labor of authors, but "to promote the Progress of Science and useful Arts." Art. I, §8, cl. 8. *Accord, Twentieth Century Music Corp. v. Aiken*, 422 U.S. 151, 156 (1975). To this end, copyright assures authors the right to their original expression, but encourages others to build freely upon the ideas and information conveyed by a work. *Harper & Row, supra*, at 556–57. This principle, known as the idea/expression or fact/expression dichotomy, applies to all works of authorship. As applied to a factual compilation, assuming the absence of original written expression, only the compiler's selection and arrangement may be protected; the raw facts may be copied at will. This result is neither unfair nor unfortunate. It is the means by which copyright advances the progress of science and art.

This Court has long recognized that the fact/expression dichotomy limits severely the scope of protection in fact-based works. More than a century ago, the Court observed: "The very object of publishing a book on science or the useful arts is to communicate to the world the useful knowledge which it contains. But this object would be frustrated if the knowledge could not be used without incurring the guilt of piracy of the book." *Baker v. Selden*, 101 U.S. 99, 103 (1880). We reiterated this point in *Harper & Row*:

> No author may copyright facts or ideas. The copyright is limited to those aspects of the work—termed 'expression'—that display the stamp of the author's originality. "Copyright does not prevent subsequent users from copying from a prior author's work those constituent elements that are not original—for example...facts, or materials in the public domain—as long as such use does not unfairly appropriate the author's original contributions."

471 U.S. at 547–548 (citation omitted).

This, then, resolves the doctrinal tension: Copyright treats facts and factual compilations in a wholly consistent manner. Facts, whether alone or as part of a compilation, are not original and therefore may not be copyrighted. A factual compilation is eligible for copyright if it features an original selection or arrangement of facts, but the copyright is limited to the particular selection or arrangement. In no event may copyright extend to the facts themselves.

B

As we have explained, originality is a constitutionally mandated prerequisite for copyright protection. The Court's decisions announcing this rule predate the Copyright Act of 1909, but ambiguous language in the 1909 Act caused some lower courts temporarily to lose sight of this requirement.

The 1909 Act embodied the originality requirement, but not as clearly as it might have. *See* NIMMER §2.01. The subject matter of copyright was set out in §§3 and 4 of the Act. Section 4 stated that copyright was available to "all the writings of an author." 35 Stat. 1076. By using the words "writings" and "author"—the same words used in Article I, §8, of the Constitution and defined by the Court in *The Trade-Mark Cases* and *Burrow-Giles*—the statute necessarily incorporated the originality requirement articulated in the Court's decisions. It did so implicitly, however, thereby leaving room for error.

Section 3 was similarly ambiguous. It stated that the copyright in a work protected only "the copyrightable component parts of the work." It thus stated an important copyright principle, but failed to identify the specific characteristic—originality—that determined which component parts of a work were copyrightable and which were not.

Most courts construed the 1909 Act correctly, notwithstanding the less-than-perfect statutory language. They understood from this Court's decisions that there could be no copyright without originality. *See* Patterson & Joyce 760–61. As explained in the NIM-MER treatise: "The 1909 Act neither defined originality, nor even expressly required that a work be 'original' in order to command protection. However, the courts uniformly inferred the requirement from the fact that copyright protection may only be claimed by 'authors'.... It was reasoned that since an author is 'the...creator, originator' it follows that a work is not the product of an author unless the work is original." NIMMER §2.01 (footnotes omitted) (citing cases).

But some courts misunderstood the statute.... These courts ignored Secs. 3 and 4, focusing their attention instead on Sec. 5 of the Act. Section 5, however, was purely technical in nature: It provided that a person seeking to register a work should indicate on the application the type of work, and it listed 14 categories under which the work might fall. One of these categories was "books, including composite and cyclopaedic works, directories, gazetteers, and other compilations." Sec. 5(a). Section 5 did not purport to say that all compilations were automatically copyrightable. Indeed, it expressly disclaimed any such function, pointing out that "the subject-matter of copyright is defined in section four." Nevertheless, the fact that factual compilations were mentioned specifically in Sec. 5 led some courts to infer erroneously that directories and the like were copyrightable *per se*, "without any further or precise showing of original—personal—authorship." Jane C. Ginsburg, *Creation and Commercial Value; Copyright Protection of Works of Information*, 90 COLUM. L. REV. 1865, 1895 (1990).

Making matters worse, these courts developed a new theory to justify the protection of factual compilations. Known alternatively as "sweat of the brow" or "industrious collection," the underlying notion was that copyright was a reward for the hard work that went into compiling facts. The classic formulation of the doctrine appeared in *Jeweler's Circular Publishing Co.*, 281 F. at 88:

> The right to copyright a book upon which one has expended labor in its preparation does not depend upon whether the materials which he has collected consist or not of matters which are publici juris, or whether such materials show literary skill or originality, either in thought or in language, or anything more than industrious collection. The man who goes through the streets of a town and puts down the names of each of the inhabitants, with their occupations and their street number, acquires material of which he is the author.

The "sweat of the brow" doctrine had numerous flaws, the most glaring being that it extended copyright protection in a compilation beyond selection and arrangement—the compiler's original contributions—to the facts themselves. Under the doctrine, the only defense to infringement was independent creation. A subsequent compiler was "not entitled to take one word of information previously published," but rather had to "independently work out the matter for himself, so as to arrive at the same result from the same common sources of information." *Id.* at 88–89 (internal quotations omitted). "Sweat of the brow" courts thereby eschewed the most fundamental axiom of copyright law—that no one may copyright facts or ideas....

Decisions of this Court applying the 1909 Act make clear that the statute did not permit the "sweat of the brow" approach. The best example is *International News Service v. Associated Press*, 248 U.S. 215 (1918). In that decision, the Court stated unambiguously that the 1909 Act conferred copyright protection only on those elements of a work that were original to the author. International News Service had conceded taking news reported by Associated Press and publishing it in its own newspapers. Recognizing that section 5 of the Act specifically mentioned "'periodicals, including newspapers,'" section5(b), the Court acknowledged that news articles were copyrightable. *Id.* at 234. It flatly rejected, however, the notion that the copyright in an article extended to the factual information it contained: "The news element—the information respecting current events contained in the literary production—is not the creation of the writer, but is a report of matters that ordinarily are publici juris; it is the history of the day." *Ibid.*

Without a doubt, the "sweat of the brow" doctrine flouted basic copyright principles. Throughout history, copyright law has "recognized a greater need to disseminate factual works than works of fiction or fantasy." *Harper & Row*, 471 U.S. at 563. *Accord*, Gorman, *Fact or Fancy: The Implications for Copyright*, 29 J. COPYRIGHT SOC. 560, 563 (1982). But "sweat of the brow" courts took a contrary view; they handed out proprietary interests in facts and declared that authors are absolutely precluded from saving time and effort by relying upon the facts contained in prior works. In truth, "it is just such wasted effort that the proscription against the copyright of ideas and facts...[is] designed to prevent." *Rosemont Enterprises, Inc. v. Random House, Inc.*, 366 F. 2d 303, 310 (2nd. Cir. 1966), *cert. denied*, 385 U.S. 1009 (1967). "Protection for the fruits of such research...may in certain circumstances be available under a theory of unfair competition. But to accord copyright protection on this basis alone distorts basic copyright principles in that it creates a monopoly in public domain materials without the necessary justification of protecting and encouraging the creation of 'writings' by 'authors.'" NIMMER §3.04, p. 3–23 (footnote omitted).

## C

"Sweat of the brow" decisions did not escape the attention of the Copyright Office. When Congress decided to overhaul the copyright statute and asked the Copyright Office to study existing problems...the Copyright Office promptly recommended that Congress clear up the confusion in the lower courts as to the basic standards of copyrightability. The Register of Copyrights explained in his first report to Congress that "originality" was a "basic requisite" of copyright under the 1909 Act, but that "the absence of any reference to [originality] in the statute seems to have led to misconceptions as to what is copyrightable matter." Report of the Register of Copyrights on the General Revision of the U.S. Copyright Law, 87th Cong., 1st Sess., p. 9 (H. Judiciary Comm. Print 1961). The Register suggested making the originality requirement explicit. *Ibid.*

Congress took the Register's advice. In enacting the Copyright Act of 1976, Congress dropped the reference to "all the writings of an author" and replaced it with the phrase "original works of authorship." 17 U. S. C. Sec. 102(a). In making explicit the originality requirement, Congress announced that it was merely clarifying existing law: "The two fundamental criteria of copyright protection [are] originality and fixation in tangible form.... The phrase 'original works of authorship,' which is purposely left undefined, is intended to incorporate without change the standard of originality established by the courts under the present [1909] copyright statute." H. R. Rep. No. 94-1476, p. 51 (1976) (emphasis added) (hereinafter H. R. Rep.); S. Rep. No. 94-473, p. 50 (1975) (emphasis added) (hereinafter S. Rep.). This sentiment was echoed by the Copyright Office: "Our intention here is to maintain the established standards of originality...." Supplementary Report of the Register of Copyrights on the General Revision of U.S. Copyright Law, 89th Cong., 1st Sess., pt. 6, p. 3 (H. Judiciary Comm. Print 1965) (emphasis added).

To ensure that the mistakes of the "sweat of the brow" courts would not be repeated, Congress took additional measures. For example, Sec. 3 of the 1909 Act had stated that copyright protected only the "copyrightable component parts" of a work, but had not identified originality as the basis for distinguishing those component parts that were copyrightable from those that were not. The 1976 Act deleted this section and replaced it with Sec.102(b), which identifies specifically those elements of a work for which copyright is not available: "In no case does copyright protection for an original work of authorship extend to any idea, procedure, process, system, method of operation, concept, principle, or discovery, regardless of the form in which it is described, explained, illustrated, or embodied in such work." Section 102(b) is universally understood to prohibit any copyright in facts.... As with Sec. 102(a), Congress emphasized that Sec. 102(b) did not change the law, but merely clarified it: "Section 102(b) in no way enlarges or contracts the scope of copyright protection under the present law. Its purpose is to restate...that the basic dichotomy between expression and idea remains unchanged." H. R. Rep., at 57; S. Rep., at 54.

Congress took another step to minimize confusion by deleting the specific mention of "directories...and other compilations" in Sec. 5 of the 1909 Act. As mentioned, this section had led some courts to conclude that directories were copyrightable *per se* and that every element of a directory was protected. In its place, Congress enacted two new provisions. First, to make clear that compilations were not copyrightable *per se*, Congress provided a definition of the term "compilation." Second, to make clear that the copyright in a compilation did not extend to the facts themselves, Congress enacted Sec. 103.

The definition of "compilation" is found in Sec. 101 of the 1976 Act. It defines a "compilation" in the copyright sense as "a work formed by the collection and assembling of preexisting materials or of data that are selected, coordinated, or arranged in such a way that the resulting work as a whole constitutes an original work of authorship" (emphasis added).

The purpose of the statutory definition is to emphasize that collections of facts are not copyrightable *per se*. It conveys this message through its tripartite structure, as emphasized above by the italics. The statute identifies three distinct elements and requires each to be met for a work to qualify as a copyrightable compilation: (1) the collection and assembly of pre-existing material, facts, or data; (2) the selection, coordination, or arrangement of those materials; and (3) the creation, by virtue of the particular selection, coordination, or arrangement, of an "original" work of authorship. "This tripartite conjunctive structure is self-evident, and should be assumed to 'accurately express the legislative purpose.'" Patry, *Copyright in Compilations of Fact (or Why the "White Pages" Are Not Copyrightable)*, 12 COM. & LAW 37, 64 (Dec. 1990), 51, quoting *Mills Music*, 469 U.S. at 164.

At first glance, the first requirement does not seem to tell us much. It merely describes what one normally thinks of as a compilation—a collection of pre-existing material, facts, or data. What makes it significant is that it is not the sole requirement. It is not enough for copyright purposes that an author collects and assembles facts. To satisfy the statutory definition, the work must get over two additional hurdles. In this way, the plain language indicates that not every collection of facts receives copyright protection. Otherwise, there would be a period after "data."

The third requirement is also illuminating. It emphasizes that a compilation, like any other work, is copyrightable only if it satisfies the originality requirement ("an original work of authorship"). Although Sec. 102 states plainly that the originality requirement applies to all works, the point was emphasized with regard to compilations to ensure that courts would not repeat the mistake of the "sweat of the brow" courts by concluding that fact-based works are treated differently and measured by some other standard. As Congress explained it, the goal was to "make plain that the criteria of copyrightable subject matter stated in section 102 apply with full force to works...containing preexisting material." H. R. Rep., at 57; S. Rep., at 55.

The key to the statutory definition is the second requirement. It instructs courts that, in determining whether a fact-based work is an original work of authorship, they should focus on the manner in which the collected facts have been selected, coordinated, and arranged. This is a straight-forward application of the originality requirement. Facts are never original, so the compilation author can claim originality, if at all, only in the way the facts are presented. To that end, the statute dictates that the principal focus should be on whether the selection, coordination, and arrangement are sufficiently original to merit protection.

Not every selection, coordination, or arrangement will pass muster. This is plain from the statute. It states that, to merit protection, the facts must be selected, coordinated, or arranged "in such a way" as to render the work as a whole original. This implies that some "ways" will trigger copyright, but that others will not. See Patry, 57, and n. 76. Otherwise, the phrase "in such a way" is meaningless and Congress should have defined "compilation" simply as "a work formed by the collection and assembly of preexisting materials or data that are selected, coordinated, or arranged." That Congress did not do so is dispositive. In accordance with "the established principle that a court should give effect, if possible, to every clause and word of a statute," *Moskal v. United States*, 498 U.S. 103, 109–10 (1990) (internal quotation marks omitted), we conclude that the statute envisions that there will be some fact-based works in which the selection, coordination, and arrangement are not sufficiently original to trigger copyright protection.

As discussed earlier, however, the originality requirement is not particularly stringent. A compiler may settle upon a selection or arrangement that others have used; novelty is not required. Originality requires only that the author make the selection or arrangement independently (i.e., without copying that selection or arrangement from another work), and that it display some minimal level of creativity. Presumably, the vast majority of compilations will pass this test, but not all will. There remains a narrow category of works in which the creative spark is utterly lacking or so trivial as to be virtually nonexistent. *See generally Bleistein v. Donaldson Lithographing Co.*, 188 U.S. 239, 251 (1903) (referring to "the narrowest and most obvious limits"). Such works are incapable of sustaining a valid copyright. NIMMER Sec. 2.01[B].

Even if a work qualifies as a copyrightable compilation, it receives only limited protection. This is the point of Sec. 103 of the Act. Section 103 explains that "the subject matter of copyright...includes compilations," Sec. 103(a), but that copyright protects only the author's original contributions—not the facts or information conveyed:

> The copyright in a compilation...extends only to the material contributed by the author of such work, as distinguished from the preexisting material employed in the work, and does not imply any exclusive right in the preexisting material.

Sec. 103(b).

As Sec. 103 makes clear, copyright is not a tool by which a compilation author may keep others from using the facts or data he or she has collected. "The most important point here is one that is commonly misunderstood today: copyright...has no effect one

way or the other on the copyright or public domain status of the preexisting material."
H. R. Rep., at 57; S. Rep., at 55. The 1909 Act did not require, as "sweat of the brow"
courts mistakenly assumed, that each subsequent compiler must start from scratch and
is precluded from relying on research undertaken by another....Rather, the facts contained in existing works may be freely copied because copyright protects only the elements that owe their origin to the compiler—the selection, coordination, and arrangement of facts.

In summary, the 1976 revisions to the Copyright Act leave no doubt that originality,
not "sweat of the brow," is the touchstone of copyright protection in directories and
other fact-based works. Nor is there any doubt that the same was true under the 1909
Act. The 1976 revisions were a direct response to the Copyright Office's concern that
many lower courts had misconstrued this basic principle, and Congress emphasized repeatedly that the purpose of the revisions was to clarify, not change, existing law. The
revisions explain with painstaking clarity that copyright requires originality, § 102(a);
that facts are never original, §102(b); that the copyright in a compilation does not extend to the facts it contains, §103(b); and that a compilation is copyrightable only to
the extent that it features an original selection, coordination, or arrangement, Sec. 101.

The 1976 revisions have proven largely successful in steering courts in the right direction. A good example is *Miller v. Universal City Studios, Inc.*, 650 F. 2d, at
1369–1370: "A copyright in a directory...is properly viewed as resting on the originality of the selection and arrangement of the factual material, rather than on the industriousness of the efforts to develop the information. Copyright protection does
not extend to the facts themselves, and the mere use of information contained in a
directory without a substantial copying of the format does not constitute infringement" (citation omitted). Additionally, the Second Circuit, which almost 70 years
ago issued the classic formulation of the "sweat of the brow" doctrine in *Jeweler's
Circular Publishing Co.*, has now fully repudiated the reasoning of that decision....
Even those scholars who believe that "industrious collection" should be rewarded
seem to recognize that this is beyond the scope of existing copyright law. *See* Deni-
cola, *Copyright in Collections of Facts: A Theory for the Protection of Nonfiction Works*,
81 Colum. L. Rev. 516 (1981). ("The very vocabulary of copyright is ill suited to analyzing property rights in works of nonfiction"); *id.* at 520–521, 525; Ginsburg,
1867, 1870.

III

There is no doubt that Feist took from the white pages of Rural's directory a substantial amount of factual information. At a minimum, Feist copied the names,
towns, and telephone numbers of 1,309 of Rural's subscribers. Not all copying, however, is copyright infringement. To establish infringement, two elements must be
proven: (1) ownership of a valid copyright, and (2) copying of constituent elements
of the work that are original. *See Harper & Row*, 471 U.S. at 548. The first element is
not at issue here; Feist appears to concede that Rural's directory, considered as a
whole, is subject to a valid copyright because it contains some foreword text, as well
as original material in its yellow pages advertisements. *See* Brief for Petitioner 18; Pet.
for Cert. 9.

The question is whether Rural has proved the second element. In other words, did
Feist, by taking 1,309 names, towns, and telephone numbers from Rural's white pages,
copy anything that was "original" to Rural? Certainly, the raw data does not satisfy the
originality requirement. Rural may have been the first to discover and report the names,

towns, and telephone numbers of its subscribers, but this data does not "'owe its origin'" to Rural. *Burrow-Giles*, 111 U.S. at 58. Rather, these bits of information are uncopyrightable facts; they existed before Rural reported them and would have continued to exist if Rural had never published a telephone directory. The originality requirement "rules out protecting...names, addresses, and telephone numbers of which the plaintiff by no stretch of the imagination could be called the author." Patterson & Joyce, *Monopolizing the Law: The Scope of Copyright Protection for Law Reports and Statutory Compilations*, 36 UCLA L. Rev. 719 (1989).

Rural essentially concedes the point by referring to the names, towns, and telephone numbers as "preexisting material." Brief for Respondent 17. Section 103(b) states explicitly that the copyright in a compilation does not extend to "the preexisting material employed in the work."

The question that remains is whether Rural selected, coordinated, or arranged these uncopyrightable facts in an original way. As mentioned, originality is not a stringent standard; it does not require that facts be presented in an innovative or surprising way. It is equally true, however, that the selection and arrangement of facts cannot be so mechanical or routine as to require no creativity whatsoever. The standard of originality is low, but it does exist. *See* Patterson & Joyce 760, n. 144 ("While this requirement is sometimes characterized as modest, or a low threshold, it is not without effect") (internal quotation marks omitted; citations omitted). As this Court has explained, the Constitution mandates some minimal degree of creativity, *see The Trade-Mark Cases*, 100 U.S. at 94; and an author who claims infringement must prove "the existence of...intellectual production, of thought, and conception." *Burrow-Giles, supra,* at 59–60.

The selection, coordination, and arrangement of Rural's white pages do not satisfy the minimum constitutional standards for copyright protection. As mentioned at the outset, Rural's white pages are entirely typical. Persons desiring telephone service in Rural's service area fill out an application and Rural issues them a telephone number. In preparing its white pages, Rural simply takes the data provided by its subscribers and lists it alphabetically by surname. The end product is a garden-variety white pages directory, devoid of even the slightest trace of creativity.

Rural's selection of listings could not be more obvious: It publishes the most basic information — name, town, and telephone number — about each person who applies to it for telephone service. This is "selection" of a sort, but it lacks the modicum of creativity necessary to transform mere selection into copyrightable expression. Rural expended sufficient effort to make the white pages directory useful, but insufficient creativity to make it original.

We note in passing that the selection featured in Rural's white pages may also fail the originality requirement for another reason. Feist points out that Rural did not truly "select" to publish the names and telephone numbers of its subscribers; rather, it was required to do so by the Kansas Corporation Commission as part of its monopoly franchise. *See* 737 F. Supp. at 612. Accordingly, one could plausibly conclude that this selection was dictated by state law, not by Rural.

Nor can Rural claim originality in its coordination and arrangement of facts. The white pages do nothing more than list Rural's subscribers in alphabetical order. This arrangement may, technically speaking, owe its origin to Rural; no one disputes that Rural undertook the task of alphabetizing the names itself. But there is nothing remotely creative about arranging names alphabetically in a white pages directory. It is an age-old practice, firmly rooted in tradition and so commonplace that it has come to be expected as a matter of course. *See* Brief for Information Industry Association et al. at Amici Curiae 10 (alphabetical arrangement "is universally observed in directories published by local exchange telephone companies"). It is not only unoriginal, it is practically inevitable. This time-honored tradition does not possess the minimal creative spark required by the Copyright Act and the Constitution.

We conclude that the names, towns, and telephone numbers copied by Feist were not original to Rural and therefore were not protected by the copyright in Rural's combined white and yellow pages directory. As a constitutional matter, copyright protects only those constituent elements of a work that possess more than a de minimis quantum of creativity. Rural's white pages, limited to basic subscriber information and arranged alphabetically, fall short of the mark. As a statutory matter, 17 U.S.C. §101 does not afford protection from copying to a collection of facts that are selected, coordinated, and arranged in a way that utterly lacks originality. Given that some works must fail, we cannot imagine a more likely candidate. Indeed, were we to hold that Rural's white pages pass muster, it is hard to believe that any collection of facts could fail.

Because Rural's white pages lack the requisite originality, Feist's use of the listings cannot constitute infringement. This decision should not be construed as demeaning Rural's efforts in compiling its directory, but rather as making clear that copyright rewards originality, not effort. As this Court noted more than a century ago, "'great praise may be due to the plaintiffs for their industry and enterprise in publishing this paper, yet the law does not contemplate their being rewarded in this way.'" *Baker v. Selden*, 101 U.S. at 105.

The judgment of the Court of Appeals is

Reversed.

---

# Notes on Copyrights

1. Before the advent of computers and the Internet, copyright and patent lawyers had little in common. Copyright lawyers dealt largely with the publishing, entertainment, and education industries. Their primary purview was books, movies, plays, songs, pictures, poetry, and music, i.e., "arts and letters" broadly defined. Patent lawyers, on the other hand, dealt with such gritty things as engines, vehicles, electronics, plumbing, electricity, and weapons. Copyright and patent lawyers seemed as different as the poet or songwriter and the shop steward, and their clientele and cultures were worlds apart.

2. Today that divergence of cultures is a thing of the past. What brought the two cultures and two fields of law together was computers and computer programming. It is now blackletter law that computer programs are "literary works" within the meaning of copyright. *See* 17 U.S.C. §101 (definitions of "literary work" and "computer program"); *Computer Assocs. Int'l, Inc. v. Altai*, Inc., 982 F.2d 693, 702–703, 23 U.S.P.Q.2d (BNA) 1241 (2d Cir. 1992) (discussing definitions, their history and application). Thus, for purposes of copyright law there is little difference, in theory, between a computer program and a novel, although there is obviously a great difference in practice between the two works and the consequences of protecting their copyrights. Moreover, the fact that virtually every industry, from sewage disposal to the production of automobiles, requires computer programming for efficient operation makes using copyright law a necessity today for every industrialist.

3. More recently, the fields of copyright and patent became even closer as a result of the phenomenon known as the "convergence of media." *See* Note, *The Message in the Medium: The First Amendment on the Information Superhighway*, 107 HARVARD L. REV. 1062 (1994). Before the computer era, books, movies, and music were distinct industries, with distinct modes of producing, managing and distributing their products. Today, however, all creative works, from poems and fine art to movies and songs, can be reduced to the bits and bytes of digital records—and all can be prepared, edited, and distributed in the same manner, as digital files transmitted over the Internet. This convergence of media has made much of the differences among the publishing, entertainment and education industries, as well as those industries' collective differences with so-called "heavy" industry, as obsolete as the Model T Ford.

4. The World Wide Web gave the coup de grâce to the cultural separation of copyright and patent practitioners. Today virtually every business has a Website, whether or not it "publishes" anything in any other form. Copyright protects both the underlying HTML, XML, PHP or other code that generates the Web pages and the visual (and auditory!) content of the Web pages themselves. Add to that the protection provided for all the databases, spreadsheets, graphic presentations, and operating procedures that virtually every business today uses—not to mention the custom computer programs for accounting, projecting, planning and decision making—and you begin to see how virtually no business today can operate successfully without understanding and exploiting copyright protection.

5. Yet the "dead hand" of history has not entirely relaxed its grip. The divergent ways in which copyright and patent practitioners once treated their distinct subject matter still appear in modern licensing agreements. A music distribution agreement, for example, looks very different from a typical patent license, and both differ greatly from a typical book publishing agreement, even after the latter has been modified to cover distribution of the book as an "e-book," in databases, or over the Web. Some of the differences are largely a result of the differing histories of and customs in the industries involved, while others reflect past litigation or careful thought about the needs and consequences of differing modes of business operation. As time goes, the need for continued careful analysis in integrating older customs and procedures with new developments in the on-line world will only increase.

6. How do copyrights differ from patents and trademarks? What sorts of things does copyright protect? What are the substantive requirements for copyright protection? Are there requirements analogous to proper subject matter, novelty, utility, and nonobviousness in patent law? What are the "procedural" requirements for copyright protection, i.e., what steps must a copyright owner take to insure or perfect protection? What are the policies underlying copyright protection? What social/economic functions does copyright protection perform? Does copyright have anything in common with patents that trademarks do not?

---

# Metro-Goldwyn-Mayer Studios, Inc. v. Grokster Ltd.

### 380 F.3d 1154 (9th Cir. 2004)

THOMAS, CIRCUIT JUDGE:

This appeal presents the question of whether distributors of peer-to-peer file-sharing computer networking software may be held contributorily or vicariously liable for copyright infringements by users. Under the circumstances presented by this case, we conclude that the defendants are not liable for contributory and vicarious copyright infringement and affirm the district court's partial grant of summary judgment.

## I. Background

From the advent of the player piano, every new means of reproducing sound has struck a dissonant chord with musical copyright owners, often resulting in federal litigation. This appeal is the latest reprise of that recurring conflict, and one of a continuing series of lawsuits between the recording industry and distributors of file-sharing computer software.

The plaintiffs in the consolidated cases ("Copyright Owners") are songwriters, music publishers, and motion picture studios who, by their own description, "own or control the vast majority of copyrighted motion pictures and sound recordings in the United States."[1] Defendants Grokster Ltd. and StreamCast Networks, Inc. ("Software Distributors") are companies that freely distribute software that allows users to share computer files with each other, including digitized music and motion pictures. The Copyright Owners allege that over 90% of the files exchanged through use of the "peer-to-peer" file-sharing software offered by the Software Distributors involves copyrighted material, 70% of which is owned by the Copyright Owners. Thus, the Copyright Owners argue, the Software Distributors are liable for vicarious and contributory copyright infringement pursuant to 17 U.S.C. §§ 501-513, for which the Copyright Owners are entitled to monetary and injunctive relief. The district court granted the Software Distributors partial summary judgment as to liability arising from present activities and certified the resolved questions for appeal pursuant to Fed. R. Civ. P. 54(b).

To analyze the legal issues properly, a rudimentary under-standing of the peer-to-peer file-sharing software at issue is required—particularly because peer-to-peer file sharing differs from typical internet use. In a routine internet transaction, a user will connect via the internet with a website to obtain information or transact business. In computer terms, the personal computer used by the consumer is considered the "client" and the computer that hosts the web page is the "server." The client is obtaining information from a centralized source, namely the server.

In a peer-to-peer distribution network, the information available for access does not reside on a central server. No one computer contains all of the information that is available to all of the users. Rather, each computer makes information available to every other computer in the peer-to-peer network. In other words, in a peer-to-peer network, each computer is both a server and a client.

Because the information is decentralized in a peer-to-peer network, the software must provide some method of cataloguing the available information so that users may access it. The software operates by connecting, via the internet, to other users of the same or similar software. At any given moment, the network consists of other users of similar or the same software online at that time. Thus, an index of files available for sharing is a critical component of peer-to-peer file-sharing networks.

At present, there are three different methods of indexing: (1) a centralized indexing system, maintaining a list of available files on one or more centralized servers; (2) a completely decentralized indexing system, in which each computer maintains a list of

---

1. The plaintiffs in the Leiber case represent a certified class of over 27,000 songwriters and music publishers. The plaintiffs in the MGM case include most of the major motion picture studios and recording companies.

files available on that computer only; and (3) a "supernode" system, in which a select number of computers act as indexing servers.[2]

The first Napster system employed a proprietary centralized indexing software architecture in which a collective index of available files was maintained on servers it owned and operated. A user who was seeking to obtain a digital copy of a recording would transmit a search request to the Napster server, the software would conduct a text search of the centralized index for matching files, and the search results would be transmitted to the requesting user. If the results showed that another Napster user was logged on to the Napster server and offering to share the requested recording, the requesting user could then connect directly with the offering user and download the music file.

Under a decentralized index peer-to-peer file-sharing model, each user maintains an index of only those files that the user wishes to make available to other network users. Under this model, the software broadcasts a search request to all the computers on the network and a search of the individual index files is conducted, with the collective results routed back to the requesting computer. This model is employed by the Gnutella software system and is the type of architecture now used by defendant StreamCast. Gnutella is open-source software, meaning that the source code is either in the public domain or is copyrighted and distributed under an open-source license that allows modification of the software, subject to some restrictions.

The third type of peer-to-peer file-sharing network at present is the "supernode" model, in which a number of select computers on the network are designated as indexing servers. The user initiating a file search connects with the most easily accessible supernode, which conducts the search of its index and supplies the user with the results. Any computer on the network could function as a supernode if it met the technical requirements, such as processing speed. The "supernode" architecture was developed by KaZaa BV, a Dutch company, and licensed under the name of "FastTrack" technology.[3]

Both Grokster and StreamCast initially used the FastTrack technology. However, StreamCast had a licensing dispute with KaZaa, and now uses its own branded "Morpheus" version of the open-source Gnutella code. StreamCast users connect to other users of Gnutella-based peer-to-peer file-sharing software.[4] Both Grokster and StreamCast distribute their separate softwares free of charge. Once downloaded onto a user's computer, the software enables the user to participate in the respective peer-to-peer file-sharing networks over the internet.

---

2. This is an extremely simplistic overview of peer-to-peer file-sharing networks. There are a number of more complete descriptions available. *See, e.g.*, Yochai Benkler, *Coase's Penguin, or Linux and The Nature of the Firm*, 112 Yale L.J. 369, 396–400 (2002); Jesse M. Feder, *Is Betamax Obsolete?: Sony Corp. of America v. Universal City Studios, Inc. in the Age of Napster*, 37 Creighton L. Rev. 859, 862–68 (2004).

3. Since the litigation in this case began, control of the FastTrack software passed from KaZaa to Sharman Networks. KaZaa was named as a defendant in this action, but eventually ceased defending and default judgment was entered against it.

4. The owners of the FastTrack Software successfully prevented users of the StreamCast version of FastTrack from being able to connect to the Grokster and KaZaa users of FastTrack by using a software upgrade that was not sent to StreamCast users. Peer-to-peer file-sharing software upgrades can be coded in a way that prevents those who do not accept the upgrade from communicating with those who do, but those users who do not accept an upgrade may still be able to communicate with each other. The record indicates this has already occurred, with a number of non-upgraded users still being able to communicate and share files with each other.

Users of the software share digital audio, video, picture, and text files. Some of the files are copyrighted and shared without authorization, others are not copyrighted (such as public domain works), and still others are copyrighted, but the copyright owners have authorized software users in peer-to-peer file-sharing networks to distribute their work. The Copyright Owners assert, without serious contest by the Software Distributors, that the vast majority of the files are exchanged illegally in violation of copyright law.

## II. Analysis

The question of direct copyright infringement is not at issue in this case. Rather, the Copyright Owners contend that the Software Distributors are liable for the copyright infringement of the software users. The Copyright Owners rely on the two recognized theories of secondary copyright liability: contributory copyright infringement and vicarious copyright infringement. *Ellison v. Robertson*, 357 F.3d 1072, 1076 (9th Cir. 2004). We agree with the district court's well reasoned analysis that the Software Distributors' current activities do not give rise to liability under either theory.

### A. Contributory Copyright Infringement

The three elements required to prove a defendant liable under the theory of contributory copyright infringement are: (1) direct infringement by a primary infringer, (2) knowledge of the infringement, and (3) material contribution to the infringement. The element of direct infringement is undisputed in this case.

### 1. Knowledge

Any examination of contributory copyright infringement must be guided by the seminal case of *Sony Corp. of America v. Universal City Studios, Inc.*, 464 U.S. 417 (1984) ("*Sony- Betamax*"). In *Sony-Betamax*, the Supreme Court held that the sale of video tape recorders could not give rise to contributory copyright infringement liability even though the defendant knew the machines were being used to commit infringement. In analyzing the contours of contributory copyright infringement, the Supreme Court drew on the "staple article of commerce" doctrine from patent law. Under that doctrine, it would be sufficient to defeat a claim of contributory copyright infringement if the defendant showed that the product was "capable of substantial" or "commercially significant noninfringing uses." In applying this doctrine, the Court found that because Sony's Betamax video tape recorder was capable of commercially significant noninfringing uses, constructive knowledge of the infringing activity could not be imputed from the fact that Sony knew the recorders, as a general matter, could be used for infringement.

In *Napster I*, we construed *Sony-Betamax* to apply to the knowledge element of contributory copyright infringement. *Napster I* held that if a defendant could show that its product was capable of substantial or commercially significant noninfringing uses, then constructive knowledge of the infringement could not be imputed. Rather, if substantial non-infringing use was shown, the copyright owner would be required to show that the defendant had reasonable knowledge of specific infringing files.[5] *Napster*

---

5. In full, the test adopted in *Napster I* for defendants whose products are capable of substantial or commercially significant noninfringing uses is that "contributory liability may potentially be imposed only to the extent that the defendant (1) receives reasonable knowledge of specific infringing files...; (2) knows or should know that such files are available on the Napster system; and (3) fails to act to prevent viral distribution of the works." 239 F.3d at 1027. At this juncture, however, our focus is the standard of knowledge to be applied.

*I*, 239 F.3d at 1027; *see also A&M Records v. Napster*, 284 F.3d 1091, 1095-96 (9th Cir. 2002) (*"Napster II"*).[6]

Thus, in order to analyze the required element of knowledge of infringement, we must first determine what level of knowledge to require. If the product at issue is not capable of substantial or commercially significant noninfringing uses, then the copyright owner need only show that the defendant had constructive knowledge of the infringement. On the other hand, if the product at issue *is* capable of substantial or commercially significant noninfringing uses, then the copyright owner must demonstrate that the defendant had reasonable knowledge of specific infringing files and failed to act on that knowledge to prevent infringement. *See Napster I*, 239 F.3d at 1027.

In this case, the district court found it undisputed that the software distributed by each defendant was capable of substantial noninfringing uses. *Grokster I*, 259 F. Supp. 2d at 1035. A careful examination of the record indicates that there is no genuine issue of material fact as to noninfringing use. Indeed, the Software Distributors submitted numerous declarations by persons who permit their work to be distributed via the software, or who use the software to distribute public domain works. One striking example provided by the Software Distributors is the popular band Wilco, whose record company had declined to release one of its albums on the basis that it had no commercial potential. Wilco repurchased the work from the record company and made the album available for free downloading, both from its own web-site and through the software user networks. The result sparked widespread interest and, as a result, Wilco received another recording contract. Other recording artists have debuted their works through the user networks. Indeed, the record indicates that thousands of other musical groups have authorized free distribution of their music through the internet. In addition to music, the software has been used to share thousands of public domain literary works made available through Project Gutenberg as well as historic public domain films released by the Prelinger Archive. In short, from the evidence presented, the district court quite correctly concluded that the software was capable of substantial noninfringing uses and, therefore, that the *Sony-Betamax* doctrine applied.

The Copyright Owners submitted no evidence that could contradict these declarations. Rather, the Copyright Owners argue that the evidence establishes that the vast majority of the software use is for copyright infringement. This argument misapprehends the *Sony* standard as construed in *Napster I*, which emphasized that in order for limitations imposed by *Sony* to apply, a product need only be *capable* of substantial noninfringing uses. *Napster I*, 239 F.3d at 1021.[7] In this case, the Software Distributors

---

6. After *Napster I* was decided, the district court on remand required plaintiffs to give Napster notice of specific infringing files, and then required Napster to continually search its index and block all files containing the particular works at issue. *Napster II*, 284 F.3d at 1095–1096. The plaintiffs appealed, arguing that "Napster should be required to search for and to block all files containing any protected copyrighted works, not just those works with which plaintiffs have been able to provide a corresponding file name." *Id.* at 1096. We found that the district court had not "committed any error of law or abused its discretion," *id.*, and that "[t]he notice requirement abide[d]by our holding that plaintiffs bear the burden to provide notice to Napster of copyrighted works and files containing such works available on the Napster system before Napster has the duty to disable access to the offending content." (internal quotation marks omitted).

7. We are mindful that the Seventh Circuit has read *Sony's* substantial noninfringing use standard differently. *In re Aimster Copyright Litig.*, 334 F.3d 643, 651 (7th Cir. 2003). It determined that an important additional factor is how "probable" the noninfringing uses of a product are. The Copyright Owners urge us to adopt the *Aimster* rationale. However, *Aimster* is premised specifically on a fundamental disagreement with *Napster I's* reading of *Sony-Betamax*. We are not free to reject

have not only shown that their products are capable of substantial noninfringing uses,[8] but that the uses have commercial viability. Thus, applying *Napster I*, *Napster II*, and *Sony-Betamax* to the record, the district court correctly concluded that the Software Distributors had established that their products were capable of substantial or commercially significant noninfringing uses. Therefore, the district correctly reasoned, the Software Distributors could not be held liable for constructive knowledge of infringement, and the Copyright Owners were required to show that the Software Distributors had reasonable knowledge of specific infringement to satisfy the threshold knowledge requirement.

Having determined that the "reasonable knowledge of specific infringement" requirement applies here, we must then decide whether the Copyright Owners have raised sufficient genuine issues of material fact to satisfy that higher standard. As the district court correctly concluded, the time at which such knowledge is obtained is significant. Because contributory copyright infringement requires knowledge *and* material contribution, the Copyright Owners were required to establish that the Software Distributors had specific knowledge of infringement at a time at which they contributed to the infringement, and failed to act upon that information.... As the district court correctly observed, and as we explain further in our discussion of material contribution, "Plaintiffs' notices of infringing conduct are irrelevant," because "they arrive when Defendants do nothing to facilitate, and cannot do anything to stop, the alleged infringement" of specific copyrighted content. *See Napster II*, 284 F.3d at 1096 ("[P]laintiffs bear the burden to provide notice to Napster of copyrighted works and files containing such works available on the Napster system *before* Napster has the duty to disable access *to the offending content.*") (internal quotation marks omitted) (emphasis added).

In the context of this case, the software design is of great import. As we have discussed, the software at issue in *Napster I* and *Napster II* employed a centralized set of servers that maintained an index of available files. In contrast, under both StreamCast's decentralized, Gnutella-type network and Grokster's quasi-decentralized, supernode, KaZaa-type network, no central index is maintained. Indeed, at present, neither StreamCast nor Grokster maintains control over index files. As the district court observed, even if the Software Distributors "closed their doors and deactivated all computers within their control, users of their products could continue sharing files with little or no interruption."

Therefore, we agree with the district court that the Software Distributors were entitled to partial summary judgment on the element of knowledge.

## 2. Material Contribution

We also agree with the district court that with respect to their current software distribution and related activities, defendants do not materially contribute to copyright infringement.

---

our own Circuit's binding precedent.... Even if we were free to do so, we do not read *Sony-Betamax*'s holding as narrowly as does the Seventh Circuit. Regardless, it is not clear that application of the *Aimster* rationale would assist the Copyright Owners here. Implicit in the *Aimster* analysis is that a finding of substantial noninfringing use, including potential use, would be fatal to a contributory infringement claim, regardless of the level of knowledge possessed by the defendant. In *Aimster*, no evidence was tendered of any noninfringing product use.

8. Indeed, even at a 10% level of legitimate use, as contended by the Copyright Owners, the volume of use would indicate a minimum of hundreds of thousands of legitimate file exchanges.

In *Napster I*, we found material contribution after reciting the district court's factual finding that "Napster is an integrated service." 239 F.3d at 1022. We "agree[d] that Napster provides the site and facilities for direct infringement." We further cited the holding of *Netcom*, which found "substantial participation" based on Netcom's "failure to cancel a user's infringing message and thereby stop an infringing copy from being distributed worldwide." We have also found material contribution where a defendant operated a swap meet at which infringing products were sold and provided utilities, parking, and advertising. *Fonovisa, Inc. v. Cherry Auction, Inc.*, 76 F.3d 259, 261, 264 (9th Cir. 1996).

As indicated by the record, the Software Distributors do not provide the "site and facilities" for infringement, and do not otherwise materially contribute to direct infringement. Infringing messages or file indices do not reside on defendants' computers, nor do defendants have the ability to suspend user accounts.

While material contribution can be established through provision of site and facilities for infringement, followed by a failure to stop specific instances of infringement once knowledge of those infringements is acquired, the Software Distributors have not provided the site and facilities for infringement in the first place. If the Software Distributors were true access providers, failure to disable that access after acquiring specific knowledge of a user's infringement might be material contribution. *Netcom*, 907 F. Supp. at 1375. Or, if the Software Distributors stored files or indices, failure to delete the offending files or offending index listings might be material contribution. *Napster I*, 239 F.3d at 1022. However, the Software Distributors here are not access providers, and they do not provide file storage and index maintenance. Rather, it is the users of the software who, by connecting to each other over the internet, create the network and provide the access. "Failure" to alter software located on another's computer is simply not akin to the failure to delete a filename from one's own computer, to the failure to cancel the registration name and password of a particular user from one's user list, or to the failure to make modifications to software on one's own computer.

\* \* \*

While Grokster and StreamCast in particular may seek to be the "next Napster," the peer-to-peer file-sharing technology at issue is not simply a tool engineered to get around the holdings of *Napster I* and *Napster II*. The technology has numerous other uses, significantly reducing the distribution costs of public domain and permissively shared art and speech, as well as reducing the centralized control of that distribution. Especially in light of the fact that liability for contributory copyright infringement does not require proof of any direct financial gain from the infringement, we decline to expand contributory copyright liability in the manner that the Copyright Owners request.

## B. Vicarious Copyright Infringement

Three elements are required to prove a defendant vicariously liable for copyright infringement: (1) direct infringement by a primary party, (2) a direct financial benefit to the defendant, and (3) the right and ability to supervise the infringers. *Napster I*, 239 F.3d at 1022. "Vicarious copyright liability is an 'outgrowth' of respondeat superior," imposing liability on those with a sufficiently supervisory relationship to the direct infringer. In *Napster I*, we held that *Sony-Betamax* "has no application to...vicarious copyright infringement" because the issue of vicarious liability was "not before the Supreme Court" in that case.

*The elements of direct infringement and a direct financial benefit, via advertising revenue, are undisputed in this case.*

### 1. Right and Ability To Supervise

We agree with the district court that there is no issue of material fact as to whether defendants have the right and ability to supervise the direct infringers in this case. Allocation of liability in vicarious copyright liability cases has developed from a historical distinction between the paradigmatic "dance hall operator" and "landlord" defendants. *Cherry Auction*, 76 F.3d at 262. The dance hall operator is liable, while the landlord escapes liability, because the dance hall operator has the right and ability to supervise infringing conduct while the landlord does not. Thus, the "right and ability to supervise" describes a relationship between the defendant and the direct infringer.

A salient characteristic of that relationship often, though not always, is a formal licensing agreement between the defendant and the direct infringer. *See, e.g., Napster I*, 239 F.3d at 1023; *Cherry Auction*, 76 F.3d at 261; *Shapiro, Bernstein & Co. v. H.L. Green Co.*, 316 F.2d 304, 306 (2d Cir. 1963) (cited as the landmark case in *Cherry Auction*, 76 F.3d at 262). Indeed, *Napster I* found especially important the fact that Napster had an express policy reserving the right to block infringers' access for any reason. 239 F.3d at 1023 ("[A]bility to block infringers' access to a particular environment for any reason whatsoever is evidence of the right and ability to supervise.").

In *Cherry Auction*, we held that the right and ability to supervise existed where a swap meet operator reserved the right to terminate vendors for any reason, promoted the swap meet, controlled access by customers, patrolled the meet, and could control direct infringers through its rules and regulations. Similarly in *Napster I*, we found Napster had the right and ability to supervise Napster users because it controlled the central indices of files, users were required to register with Napster, and access to the system depended on the validity of a user's registration.

It does not appear from any of the evidence in the record that either of the defendants has the ability to block access to individual users. Grokster nominally reserves the right to terminate access, while StreamCast does not maintain a licensing agreement with persons who download Morpheus. However, given the lack of a registration and log-in process, even Grokster has no ability to actually terminate access to filesharing functions, absent a mandatory software upgrade to all users that the particular user refuses, or IP address-blocking attempts.[9] It is also clear that none of the communication between defendants and users provides a point of access for filtering or searching for infringing files, since infringing material and index information do not pass through defendants' computers.

In the case of StreamCast, shutting down its XML file altogether would not prevent anyone from using the Gnutella network. In the case of Grokster, its licensing agreement with KaZaa/Sharman does not give it the ability to mandate that root nodes be shut down. Moreover, the alleged ability to shut down operations altogether is more akin to the ability to close down an entire swap meet or stop distributing software altogether, rather than the ability to exclude individual participants, a practice of policing aisles, an ability to block individual users directly at the point of log-in, or an ability to delete individual filenames from one's own computer. *See Napster I*, 239 F.3d at 1023–24; *Cherry Auction*, 76 F.3d at 261–62. The sort of monitoring and supervisory relationship that has supported vicarious liability in the past is completely absent in this case.

---

9. IP address-blocking will not be effective against a user who, like most persons, does not have a permanent IP address, but is rather assigned one each time he connects to the Internet.

The district court here found that unlike Napster, Grokster and StreamCast do not operate and design an "integrated service," which they monitor and control. We agree. The nature of the relationship between Grokster and StreamCast and their users is significantly different from the nature of the relationship between a swap meet operator and its participants, or prior versions of Napster and its users, since Grokster and StreamCast are more truly decentralized, peer-to-peer file-sharing networks.

The district court correctly characterized the Copyright Owners' evidence of the right and ability to supervise as little more than a contention that "the software itself could be altered to prevent users from sharing copyrighted files." In arguing that this ability constitutes evidence of the right and ability to supervise, the Copyright Owners confuse the right and ability to supervise with the strong duty imposed on entities that have already been determined to be liable for vicarious copyright infringement; such entities have an obligation to exercise their policing powers to the fullest extent, which in Napster's case included implementation of new filtering mechanisms. *Napster II*, 284 F.3d at 1098 ("The tolerance standard announced *applies only to copyrighted works which Plaintiffs have properly noticed* as required by the modified preliminary injunction. That is, Napster must do everything feasible to block files from its system which contain noticed copyrighted works.") (emphasis added). But the potential duty a district court may place on a vicariously liable defendant is not the same as the "ability" contemplated by the "right and ability to supervise" test. Moreover, a duty to alter software and files located on one's own computer system is quite different in kind from a duty to alter software located on another person's computer. We agree with the district court that possibilities for upgrading software located on another person's computer are irrelevant to determining whether vicarious liability exists.

## C. Turning a "Blind Eye" to Infringement

The Copyright Owners finally argue that Grokster and StreamCast should not be able to escape vicarious liability by turning a "blind eye" to the infringement of their users, and that "[t]urning a blind eye to detectable acts of infringement for the sake of profit gives rise to liability." If the Software Distributors had a right and ability to control and supervise that they proactively refused to exercise, such refusal would not absolve them of liability. However, although that rhetoric has occasionally been employed in describing vicarious copyright infringement, there is no separate "blind eye" theory or element of vicarious liability that exists independently of the traditional elements of liability. Thus, this theory is subsumed into the Copyright Owners' claim for vicarious copyright infringement and necessarily fails for the same reasons.

## III.

Resolution of these issues does not end the case. As the district court clearly stated, its decision was limited to the specific software in use at the time of the district court decision. The Copyright Owners have also sought relief based on previous versions of the software, which contain significant—and perhaps crucial—differences from the software at issue. We express no opinion as to those issues.

As to the question at hand, the district court's grant of partial summary judgment to the Software Distributors is clearly dictated by applicable precedent. The Copyright Owners urge a re-examination of the law in the light of what they believe to be proper public policy, expanding exponentially the reach of the doctrines of contributory and vicarious copyright infringement. Not only would such a renovation conflict with binding precedent, it would be unwise. Doubtless, taking that step would satisfy the Copyright Owners' immediate economic aims. However, it would also alter general copyright law in profound ways with unknown ultimate consequences outside the present context. Further, as we have observed, we live in a quicksilver technological environment with courts ill-suited to fix the flow of internet innovation.... The introduction of new technology is always disruptive to old markets, and particularly to those copyright owners whose works are sold through well-established distribution mechanisms. Yet, history has shown that time and market forces often provide equilibrium in balancing interests, whether the new technology be a player piano, a copier, a tape recorder, a video recorder, a personal computer, a karaoke machine, or an MP3 player. Thus, it is prudent for courts to exercise caution before restructuring liability theories for the purpose of addressing specific market abuses, despite their apparent present magnitude.

Indeed, the Supreme Court has admonished us to leave such matters to Congress. In *Sony-Betamax*, the Court spoke quite clearly about the role of Congress in applying copyright law to new technologies. As the Supreme Court stated in that case, "The direction of Art. I is that *Congress* shall have the power to promote the progress of science and the useful arts. When, as here, the Constitution is permissive, the sign of how far Congress has chosen to go can come only from Congress." 464 U.S. at 456.

In this case, the district court correctly applied applicable law and properly declined the invitation to alter it. We affirm the district court, and remand for resolution of the remaining issues.

Affirmed.

---

# Notes and Questions on *Grokster*

1. The very same circuit, the Ninth Circuit, decided both *Napster I* and *Grokster*. Why did it find liability in *Napster I* and not in *Grokster*? Were the differences between the two decisions factual or legal? Try to articulate, as precisely and succinctly as possible, the reasons for the different results.

2. Ultimately the *Grokster* court, like the *Sony* Court, found no secondary liability. Can you analogize the two cases on their facts? How close is the analogy? Is it close enough for the Ninth Circuit to have decided the case by analogy only? Should the Ninth Circuit have decided the case on that basis?

3. In the *Aimster* decision, which the *Grokster* court explicitly refused to follow, the Seventh Circuit dealt with a Website much like Napster's. There were two salient differences, however. First, unlike Napster, Aimster actively encouraged infringement by providing tutorials involving infringing works and offering a "club" for $4.95 per month that touted file sharing for the top forty hits, nearly all of which were under copyright. *See In re Aimster Copyright Litigation*, 334 F.3d 643, 651-652, 67 U.S.P.Q.2d (BNA) 1233 (7th Cir. 2003) (Posner, J.), *cert. denied*, 124 S. Ct. 1069 (2004). Second, unlike Napster's, Aimster's peer-to-peer file-sharing software encrypted the files that users shared, so Aimster itself could not, even in theory, tell whether or not those files contained infringing material. *See id.*, 334 F.3d at 646.

Analogize or distinguish *Aimster* to/from *Grokster* on the facts. Could the *Grokster* court have distinguished *Aimster* on its facts, rather than refusing to follow it? If so how, and how convincing is the distinction?

In *Aimster* Judge Posner made short work of the defendant's argument that the encryption technology prevented it from having the knowledge of infringement necessary for contributory liability. Characterizing the lack of knowledge arising from encryption as "willful blindness," he implied it was merely a transparent ploy to avoid liability, which the law would not countenance. *See id.*, 334 F.3d at 650. In *Grokster*, the lack of a central directory or index of files also precluded the defendants there from having knowledge of what files their users shared. Was that feature a matter of "willful blindness," as in *Aimster*, or can *Aimster* be distinguished in this regard? Is the absence of a central index in *Grokster* a transparent ploy to avoid liability?

4. To say that the music and movie industries "went ballistic" after the Ninth Circuit's decision in *Grokster* would be an understatement. Both industries feared that massive infringement by file-sharing consumers, using technology like Grokster's, would undermine their business models, take the profit out of distributing songs and movies, and thereby kill the incentive to produce them. Practically *en masse*, both industries petitioned for *certiorari*, which the Supreme Court granted. The case will be decided some time during the spring of 2005, just as this book is going to press.

---

# Notes on the Digital Millennium Copyright Act

1. In 1998, implementing two international treaties, Congress accelerated the convergence of copyright and technology to warp speed by passing the Digital Millennium Copyright Act. For detailed discussion of this law, see JAY DRATLER, JR., CYBERLAW: INTELLECTUAL PROPERTY IN THE DIGITAL MILLENNIUM (2000).

2. The most important aspect of this law was a millennial shift in the focus of copyright protection from the act of copying itself to defeating technological measures that prevent copying. The law contains three new legal rules, all of which are virtually unprecedented in the 300-year history of Anglo-American copyright. First, an "anti-circumvention rule" prohibits defeating or circumventing technological measures (such as encryption and password-protection) that limit unauthorized access to copyrighted works. *See* 17 U.S.C. § 1201(a)(1)(A). Second, an "anti-trafficking rule" prohibits trafficking in and providing means to defeat such technological access-control measures. *See* 17 U.S.C. § 1201(a)(2), as applied in *Universal City Studios, Inc. v. Reimerdes*, 111 F. Supp. 2d 294, 1873 (S.D.N.Y. 2000), *aff'd sub nom. Universal City Studios, Inc. v. Corley*, 273 F.3d 429 (BNA) 1953 (2d Cir. 2001) (applying this rule to software for decrypting DVDs).

Third, a *second* anti-trafficking rule prohibits trafficking in and providing means to defeat technological measures that control the *uses* of copyrighted works, i.e., that permit some uses (such as streaming) while preventing others (such as downloading). *See* 17 U.S.C. § 1201(b), as applied in *RealNetworks, Inc. v. Streambox, Inc.*, 2000 U.S. Dist. LEXIS 1889 at *19 (W.D. Wash. Jan. 18, 2000). *See generally*, DRATLER, *supra* § 2.05[2] (distinguishing between access controls protected against trafficking in countermeasures under § 1201(a)(2) and use controls protected against trafficking in countermeasures under § 1201(b)). For the argument that the protection of computer software would be better served by a *sui generis* law, see Pamela Samuelson, et al., *A Manifesto Concerning the Legal Protection of Computer Programs*, 94 COLUM. L. REV. 2308 (1994).

3. Special civil and criminal sanctions, entirely separate from those for copyright infringement, enforce each of these three new rules. *See* 17 U.S.C. §§ 1203 (civil sanctions), 1204 (criminal penalties). Congress and the courts have made abundantly clear that these three new rules have little directly to do with copyright. *See* 17 U.S.C. § 1201(c)(1) (disclaiming any effect on copyright claims and defenses). Indeed, Congress codified these rules in a part of Title 17 of the United States Code that is not a part of the copyright statute. As a result, virtually all of the longstanding mechanisms for balance in copyright law, such as the doctrine of fair use, simply do not apply to claims under these new legal rules. *See* DRATLER, *supra*, § 2.10[2].

4. Nothing better illustrates the convergence of creative expression and technology in modern copyright law than the Millennium Act's unintended consequences. The Act was designed primarily to thwart digital piracy, especially on the Internet, by adding legal reinforcement to technological protection of copyrighted works such as digitized songs, movies, and books. Yet litigants soon realized that computer programs—including those embedded in printer-toner cartridges and garage-door openers—are copyrighted works, too. The result was a series of claims in which manufacturers of various devices sought to eliminate competition from rivals on the ground the rivals achieved product compatibility by trafficking in means (namely, their competing products) to circumvent controls on access to or use of computer programs embedded in the plaintiffs' products. *See Lexmark Intl., Inc. v. Static Control Components, Inc.*, 253 F. Supp.2d 943 (E.D. Ky. 2003) (upholding claim by summary judgment); *Chamberlain Group, Inc. v. Skylink Techs., Inc.*, 292 F. Supp. 2d 1040 (N.D. Ill. 2003) (rejecting claim by summary judgment, but only because industry custom authorized compatibility); *see also* DRATLER, § 2.05[1], [2] (analyzing such claims and suggesting inconsistencies with statutory scheme and intent).

5. The convergence of copyright and technology are epitomized by the rules of the Digital Millennium Copyright Act just discussed. Those rules encourage copyright lawyers to work more and more with engineers and product designers in order to give their clients the greatest benefit from the law. Patent lawyers already work closely with engineers, scientists, and other inventors to perfect patent applications—and even to suggest new lines of research so that additional patent applications may be filed! Now the opportunities offered by Section 1201 of the DMCA, in particular, suggest that copyright lawyers may have to consider similar cooperative effort.

---

# Other Notes & Questions

1. *Trade Secrets.* One other important area of intellectual property law is trade secrets. Trade secrets can be licensed just as any other type of intellectual property. The Uniform Trade Secrets Act, now adopted in 40 states, defines a trade secret as "information, including a formula, pattern, compilation, program, device, method, technique, or process that: (i) derives independent economic value, actual or potential, from not being generally known to, and not being readily ascertainable by proper means by, other persons who can obtain economic value from its disclosure or use; and (ii) is the

subject of efforts that are reasonable under the circumstances to maintain its secrecy." Uniform Trade Secrets Act, § 2(a), 14 U.L.A. 449 (1985). On the other hand, The Restatement (Third) of Unfair Competition, defines trade secrets as "any information that can be used in the operation of a business or other enterprise and that is sufficiently valuable and secret to the operation of a business or other enterprise to afford an actual or potential economic advantage over others." RESTATEMENT (THIRD) OF UNFAIR COMPETITION, § 39 (1995). Are there any substantial differences between these definitions of trade secret? Because the substance of trade secrets can be almost infinitely variable, it is important to include a precise definition of the term in the license agreement.

2. Why is trade secret law necessary? What gap is it intended to fill? Not only does trade secret law protect inventions for which the inventor has not, or cannot, obtain a patent, but also protects a wide variety of business information, such as customer lists, strategic plans, price lists, etc. Almost any body of information can be held as a trade secret. *See Nissan v. Motorola* in Chapter 4, *infra*. Although the Economic Espionage Act of 1996 criminalized the theft of trade secrets, *see* 18 U.S.C. §§ 1831-1839, there is no civil cause of action for misappropriation of trade secrets under federal law. Where should the line be drawn between federal patent law and state trade secret law? After all, if one fails to obtain a patent for an invention, it may still meet the definition of a trade secret and still be protected as such. Does this undermine the patent system? *See Kewanee Oil Co. v. Bicron Corp.*, 416 U.S. 470 (1974).

3. An important debate in trade secret law involves characterizing the protection. That is, it is unsettled whether a trade secret is property as such, or whether it is merely unlawful to acquire another's trade secret by tortious means, or use or disclose it in breach of an excess or implied contract of confidentiality. In *E.I. DuPont de Nemours Powder Co. v. Masland*, 244 U.S. 100 (1917), Justice Holmes characterized trade secret misappropriation as involving an abuse of confidential relationships rather than as a violation of a property right which would have been a far broader right than one rooted in tort or contract law. *See* 1 ROGER M. MILGRIM, MILGRIM ON TRADE SECRETS, § 2.01, at 2-2 (1996). This debate remains unresolved.

4. For a comprehensive discussion of the interface between trade secret and patent law, see *Kewanee Oil Co. v. Bicron Corp.*, 416 U.S. 470 (1974).

5. *The Right of Publicity*. Another emerging area of law also categorized as intellectual property is the right of publicity. The right of publicity is premised on the notion that every person possesses "the inherent right to control the commercial use of his or her identity." J. THOMAS MCCARTHY, THE RIGHTS OF PUBLICITY AND PRIVACY, 1.1, at 1-2 (1994). The Restatement of Unfair Competition (Third) Section 46 defines the right of publicity as follows: "One who appropriates the commercial value of a person's identity by using without consent the person's name, likeness, or other indicia of identity for purpose of trade is subject to liability...." That is, using another's identity without permission and for commercial gain is actionable. The right of publicity is intermingled with common law and statutory rights scattered across the states, each having different characteristics and attributes, creating an environment of unpredictability. *See* J. Thomas McCarthy, *The Human Persona as Commercial Property; The Right of Publicity*, 19 COLUM.-VLA J.L. & ARTS 129, 132 (1995). For a more detailed discussion of the right of publicity, see *Carson v. Here's Johnny Portable Toilets, Inc.*, 698 F.2d 831 (6th Cir. 1982); *Midler v. Ford Motor Co.*, 849 F.2d 460 (6th Cir. 1988); *White v. Samsung Elecs. Am., Inc.*, 971 F.2d 1395 (9th Cir. 1992).

6. *Other* Sui Generis *Forms of Protection*. A number of other specialized forms of federal intellectual property protection are recognized in the U.S. — namely plant variety pro-

tection, 7 U.S.C. §§ 2321-2382, semiconductor chip design protection, 17 U.S.C. §§ 901-014, and vessel hull design protection, 17 U.S.C. §§ 1301-1332. One theme illustrated by the cases in this chapter is that the boundaries of intellectual property have expanded over time and continue to do so. Practitioners in this field must take into account these fluid boundaries and future trends when drafting intellectual property licenses.

7. Of the four main types of intellectual property, name the different types of protection potentially afforded to each of the following: a polyamide polymer; a computer software program; a corporate logo; a method of implementing a first in, first out inventory system; the name of a Hollywood star; a training manual for new employees; the pattern on fabric used to make ties; an internet domain name; a photograph of the Eiffel Tower; a photograph of products advertised for sale in a magazine; the movie script for *Finding Nemo*; and the character Nemo.

There are many qualifications and exceptions that might limit intellectual property protection for a particular item. Name those qualifications and exceptions that might exist with respect to the items listed above.

# V. Trademarks

## Foreword: Symposium on Intellectual Property Law
Kenneth L. Port
68 CHICAGO-KENT L. REV. 594-601 (1993) (as revised 2004)

Trademark law is completely distinct from both patents and copyrights. Whereas patents and copyrights exist because of an express constitutional grant, trademarks do not enjoy such recognition. In fact, when confronted with the issue, the United States Supreme Court expressly held that the Patent and Copyright Clause of the Constitution did not envision protection of trademarks as well.

Rather than being based on the Patent and Copyright Clause, congressional authority to regulate trademarks is based on the Commerce Clause. This is why interstate commerce or "use" of a trademark is crucial for federal protection. Trademark protection is a common law concept that exists independent of any statute. In fact, the Lanham Act, the current trademark law, as originally enacted was said to be only a registration statute codifying common law.

The Supreme Court has reasoned that a trademark does not "depend upon novelty, invention, discovery, or any work of the brain. It requires no fancy or imagination, no genius, no laborious thought. Trademarks are simply founded on priority of appropriation."

Trademark jurisprudence has developed over centuries of time. The use of a mark to identify the source of a product actually began at least 3500 years ago when potters made scratchings on the bottom of their creations to identify source. The first judicial recognition of trademarks in a Common Law system did not come, however, until 1584 in what is known as "Sandforth's Case." From this rather inauspicious beginning where a mark owner was protected from economic loss due to the deceit of another, it soon became a well-accepted judicial notion in England that a mark deserved protection at common law to indicate source or origin of goods.

The American concept of trademark law followed this English common law notion. Today, the Lanham Act defines trademarks as any "word, name, symbol, or device or any combination thereof...used...to indicate the source of the goods...." Trademarks are generally categorized into one of four groups: generic, descriptive, suggestive, and arbitrary or fanciful.

The strongest mark is an arbitrary or fanciful one such as KODAK or EXXON. The weakest mark is a generic mark such as cellophane or aspirin. All marks fit somewhere on this continuum, although some courts have recognized that no clear lines separate these categories. The assignment of a specific trademark to one of these categories is not necessarily static. A mark can conceivably change status from one category to another based on the owner's use of the mark and the degree of consumer recognition developed in the mark.

Generic marks refer to the specific genus of which the particular product is a species. In other words, generic marks are terms for which no other descriptive word exists in the English language. A mark becomes generic when it ceases to denote source and instead starts to denote the product itself. Famous examples of marks that have become generic include "lite" for beer and "shredded wheat" for cereal. Generic marks are not registrable. The registrations for marks that become generic may be canceled at any time. The test for determining trademark genericism is whether the primary significance of the mark identifies the producer or the product. To the extent the primary significance of the mark is to identify the product, the mark has become generic.

The rationale for preventing trademark protection of generic marks is simple. Allowing a monopoly on the use of a commonly used term would be ludicrous. No individual should be able to appropriate existing terms in the language for their own commercial advantage when to do so would prevent competitors from using that term to describe their competing products. When a trademark stops denoting the source of a product but rather denotes the product itself, it becomes the victim of genericide and ceases to function as an indication of source or origin.

A descriptive mark merely describes the good or service on which it is used or an attribute of that good or service. In order to [make a mark] registrable and enforceable, the owner of a descriptive trademark must show that the mark has come to possess "secondary meaning." If a descriptive mark lacks secondary meaning, it is "merely descriptive" and therefore not registrable and not enforceable. Secondary meaning arises when a word is used long enough and enough money is spent promoting the mark that the consuming public associates the word with the product—that is, the word takes on a source-indicating significance.

Suggestive trademarks are those marks that, although not arbitrary or fanciful, require some amount of imagination to mark the association between the trademark and the goods or services. Suggestive marks therefore do not require a showing of secondary meaning to be validly registered and enforceable. Examples of suggestive marks include COPPERTONE for suntan lotion and HEARTWISE for vegetable protein meat substitute foods.

Arbitrary or fanciful marks are those that have no mark/product association whatsoever at conception. These marks are often referred to as "inherently distinctive" at least partially because they do not require secondary meaning in order to be registered or enforced.

Verbal trademarks that are inherently distinctive are protected without regard to secondary meaning. Trademarks that fall within the suggestive or arbitrary or fanciful categories are inherently distinctive and therefore need not possess secondary meaning. However, the owner of a descriptive mark must establish secondary meaning or courts will deny any recovery. The requirement that an otherwise descriptive mark have secondary meaning to be enforceable or registrable is justified as facilitating competition among producers. Granting protection from the moment of creation would amount to an obstacle to competition among producers of that product. The holder of one descriptive mark could block other competition from entering into a specific market merely by claiming trademark rights to the name or a descriptive feature of the product.

That is, the owner of a weak mark should not be able to protect or enforce that mark against others until that owner's rights have crystallized. Trademark rights in weak or descriptive marks crystallize when the consumers of goods associate a trademark with a producer of those goods. Unless the mark has secondary meaning, the mark is merely a word that other market participants would presumably need to adequately describe their products. Allowing trademark rights in a descriptive mark without secondary meaning essentially would be granting a monopoly on a word or words that competitors need to describe their goods.

Trademarks are subject to a wide range of restrictions not applicable to patents or copyrights. For example, trademarks are not assignable without the pertinent goodwill associated with the mark. An assignment in gross (transferring nothing but the mark itself) is invalid. Also, the test for infringement—likelihood of confusion of relevant purchasers—means that identical trademarks can be used on similar products as long as the relevant consumers would not be likely to be confused. Because of this restriction, many states and Congress, in 1996, have adopted anti-dilution laws prohibiting identical marks from being used on unrelated products (by definition a non-infringing act) in a manner that...dilute[s] the distinctiveness of the original mark.

\* \* \*

---

# Trade-Mark Cases: United States v. Steffens; United States v. Wittemann; United States v. Johnson
## 100 U.S. 82 (1887)

Mr. Justice Miller delivered the opinion of the court.

\* \* \*

The three cases whose titles stand at the head of this opinion [raise the same principal question:] namely, are the acts of Congress on the subject of trade-marks founded on any rightful authority in the Constitution of the United States?

The entire legislation of Congress in regard to trade-marks is of very recent origin. It is first seen in sects. 77 to 84, inclusive, of the act of July 8, 1870, entitled "An Act to revise, consolidate, and amend the statutes relating to patents and copyrights." 16 Stat. 198. The part of this act relating to trade-marks is embodied in chap. 2, tit. 60, sects. 4937 to 4947, of the Revised Statutes.

It is sufficient at present to say that they provide for the registration in the Patent Office of any device in the nature of a trade-mark to which any person has by usage established an exclusive right, or which the person so registering intends to appropriate by that act to his exclusive use; and they make the wrongful use of a trade-mark, so registered, by any other person, without the owner's permission, a cause of action in a civil suit for damages. Six years later we have the act of Aug. 14, 1876 (19 Stat. 141), punishing by fine and imprisonment the fraudulent use, sale, and counterfeiting of Trademarks registered in pursuance of the statutes of the United States, on which the informations and indictments are founded in the cases before us.

The right to adopt and use a symbol or a device to distinguish the goods or property made or sold by the person whose mark it is, to the exclusion of use by all other persons, has been long recognized by the common law and the chancery courts of England and of this country, and by the statutes of some of the States. It is a property right for the violation of which damages may be recovered in an action at law, and the continued violation of it will be enjoined by a court of equity, with compensation for past infringement. This exclusive right was not created by the act of Congress, and does not now depend upon it for its enforcement. The whole system of trade-mark property and the civil remedies for its protection existed long anterior to that act, and have remained in full force since its passage.

These propositions are so well understood as to require neither the citation of authorities nor an elaborate argument to prove them.

As the property in trade-marks and the right to their exclusive use rest on the laws of the States, and, like the great body of the rights of person and of property, depend on them for security and protection, the power of Congress to legislate on the subject, to establish the conditions on which these rights shall be enjoyed and exercised, the period of their duration, and the legal remedies for their enforcement, if such power exist at all, must be found in the Constitution of the United States, which is the source of all the powers that Congress can lawfully exercise.

In the argument of these cases this seems to be conceded, and the advocates for the validity of the acts of Congress on this subject point to two clauses of the Constitution, in one or in both of which, as they assert, sufficient warrant may be found for this legislation.

The first of these is the eighth clause of sect. 8 of the first article. That section, manifestly intended to be an enumeration of the powers expressly granted to Congress, and closing with the declaration of a rule for the ascertainment of such powers as are necessary by way of implication to carry into efficient operation those expressly given, authorizes Congress, by the clause referred to, "to promote the progress of science and useful arts, by securing for limited times, to authors and inventors, the exclusive right to their respective writings and discoveries."

As the first and only attempt by Congress to regulate the Right of trade-marks is to be found in the act of July 8, 1870, to which we have referred, entitled "An Act to revise, consolidate, and amend the statutes relating to Patents and Copyrights," terms which have long since become technical, as referring, the one to inventions and the other to the writings of authors, it is a reasonable inference that this part of the statute also was, in the opinion of Congress, an exercise of the power found in that clause of the Constitution. It may also be safely assumed that until a critical examination of the subject in the courts became necessary, it was mainly if not wholly to this clause that the advocates of the law looked for its support.

Any attempt, however, to identify the essential characteristics of a trade-mark with inventions and discoveries in the arts and sciences, or with the writings of authors, will show that the effort is surrounded with insurmountable difficulties.

The ordinary trade-mark has no necessary relation to invention or discovery. The trade-mark recognized by the common law is generally the growth of a considerable period of use, rather than a sudden invention.It is often the result of accident rather than design, and when under the act of Congress it is sought to establish it by registration, neither originality, invention, discovery, science, nor art is in any way essential to the right conferred by that act. If we should endeavor to classify it under the head of writings of authors, the objections are equally strong. In this, as in regard to inventions, originality is required. And while the word writings may be liberally construed, as it has been, to include original designs for engravings, prints, &c., it is only such as are original, and are founded in the creative powers of the mind. The writings which are to be protected are the fruits of intellectual labor, embodied in the form of books, prints, engravings and the like.

The trade-mark may be, and generally is, the adoption of something already in existence as the distinctive symbol of the party using it. At common law the exclusive right to it grows out of its use, and not its mere adoption. By the act of Congress this exclusive right attaches upon registration. But in neither case does it depend upon novelty, invention, discovery, or any work of the brain. It requires no fancy or imagination, no genius, no laborious thought. It is simply founded on priority of appropriation. We look in vain in the statute for any other qualification or condition. If the symbol, however plain, simple, old, or well-known, has been first appropriated by the claimant as his distinctive trade-mark, he may by registration secure the right to its exclusive use. While such legislation may be a judicious aid to the common law on the subject of trade-marks, and may be within the competency of legislatures whose general powers embrace that class of subjects, we are unable to see any such power in the constitutional provision concerning authors and inventors, and their writings and discoveries.

* * *

# Abercrombie & Fitch Company v. Hunting World, Incorporated
### 537 F.2d 4 (2d Cir. 1976)

FRIENDLY, Circuit Judge:

* * *

## II.

It will be useful at the outset to restate some basic principles of trademark law, which, although they should be familiar, tend to become lost in a welter of adjectives.

The cases, and in some instances the Lanham Act, identify four different categories of terms with respect to trademark protection. Arrayed in an ascending order which roughly reflects their eligibility to trademark status and the degree of protection accorded, these classes are (1) generic, (2) descriptive, (3) suggestive, and (4) arbitrary or fanciful. The lines of demarcation, however, are not always bright. Moreover, the difficulties are compounded because a term that is in one category for a particular product may be in quite a different one for another, because a term may shift from one category to another in light of differences in usage through time, because a term may have one meaning to one group of users and a different one to others, and because the same term may be put to different uses with respect to a single product. In various ways, all of these complications are involved in the instant case.

A generic term is one that refers, or has come to be understood as referring, to the genus of which the particular product is a species. At common law neither those terms which were generic nor those which were merely descriptive could become valid trademarks. *See Delaware & Hudson Canal Co. v. Clark*, 80 U.S. (13 Wall.) 311, 323, 20 L. Ed. 581 (1872) ("Nor can a generic name, or a name merely descriptive of an article or its qualities, ingredients, or characteristics, be employed as a trademark and the exclusive use of it be entitled to legal protection"). The same was true under the Trademark Act of 1905, *Standard Paint Co. v. Trinidad Asphalt Manufacturing Co.*, 220 U.S. 446, 55 L. Ed. 536, 31 S. Ct. 456 (1911), except for marks which had been the subject of exclusive use for ten years prior to its enactment, 33 Stat. 726. While, as we shall see, p. 10 *infra*, the Lanham Act makes an important exception with respect to those merely descriptive terms which have acquired secondary meaning, see § 2(f), 15 U.S.C. § 1052(f), it offers no such exception for generic marks. The Act provides for the cancellation of a registered mark if at any time it "becomes the common descriptive name [now, the "generic" name] of an article or substance," § 14(c). This means that even proof of secondary meaning, by virtue of which some "merely descriptive" marks may be registered, cannot transform a generic term into a subject for trademark. As explained in *J. Kohnstam, Ltd. v. Louis Mark and Company*, 47 C.C.P.A. 1080, 280 F.2d 437, 440 (C.C.P.A. 1960), no matter how much money and effort the user of a generic term has poured into promoting the sale of its merchandise and what success it has achieved in securing public identification, it cannot deprive competing manufacturers of the product of the right to call an article by its name.... We have recently had occasion to apply this doctrine of the impossibility of achieving trademark protection for a generic term, *CES Publishing Corp. v. St. Regis Publications, Inc.*, 531 F.2d 11 (1975). The pervasiveness of the principle is illustrated by a series of well known cases holding that when a suggestive or fanciful term has become generic as a result of a manufacturer's own advertising efforts, trademark protection will be denied save for those markets where the term still has not become generic and a secondary meaning has been shown to continue.... A term may thus be generic in one market and descriptive or suggestive or fanciful in another.

The term which is descriptive but not generic stands on a better basis. Although § 2(e) of the Lanham Act, 15 U.S.C. § 1052, forbids the registration of a mark which, when applied to the goods of the applicant, is "merely descriptive," § 2(f) removes a considerable part of the sting by providing that "except as expressly excluded in paragraphs (a)-(d) of this section, nothing in this chapter shall prevent the registration of a mark used by the applicant which has become distinctive of the applicant's goods in commerce" and that the Commissioner may accept, as prima facie evidence that the mark has become distinctive, proof of substantially exclusive and continuous use of the mark applied to the applicant's goods for five years preceding the application....

The category of "suggestive" marks was spawned by the felt need to accord protection to marks that were neither exactly descriptive on the one hand nor truly fanciful on the other—a need that was particularly acute because of the bar in the Trademark Act of 1905, 33 Stat. 724, 726, (with an exceedingly limited exception noted above) on the registration of merely descriptive marks regardless of proof of secondary meaning. *See Orange Crush Co. v. California Crushed Fruit Co.*, 54 App. D.C. 313, 297 F. 892 (1924). Having created the category the courts have had great difficulty in defining it. Judge Learned Hand made the not very helpful statement:

It is quite impossible to get any rule out of the cases beyond this: That the validity of the mark ends where suggestion ends and description begins.

*Franklin Knitting Mills, Inc. v. Fashionit Sweater Mills, Inc.*, 297 F. 247, 248 (S.D.N.Y.
1923), *aff'd per curiam*, 4 F.2d 1018 (2d Cir. 1925)—a statement amply confirmed by
comparing the list of terms held suggestive with those held merely descriptive in 3
CALLMANN, UNFAIR COMPETITION, TRADEMARKS AND MONOPOLIES § 71.2 (3d ed.).
Another court has observed, somewhat more usefully, that:

> A term is suggestive if it requires imagination, thought and perception to
> reach a conclusion as to the nature of goods. A term is descriptive if it forth-
> with conveys an immediate idea of the ingredients, qualities or characteristics
> of the goods.

*Stix Products, Inc. v. United Merchants & Manufacturers Inc.*, 295 F. Supp. 479, 488
(S.D.N.Y. 1968)....Also useful is the approach taken by this court in *Aluminum Fabricating Co. of Pittsburgh v. Season-All Window Corp.*, 259 F.2d 314 (2d Cir. 1958), that the
reason for restricting the protection accorded descriptive terms, namely the undesirability of preventing an entrant from using a descriptive term for his product, is much less
forceful when the trademark is a suggestive word since, as Judge Lumbard wrote, 259
F.2d at 317:

> The English language has a wealth of synonyms and related words with which
> to describe the qualities that manufacturers may wish to claim for their prod-
> ucts and the ingenuity of the public relations profession supplies new words
> and slogans as they are needed.

If a term is suggestive, it is entitled to registration without proof of secondary meaning. Moreover, as held in the *Season-All* case, the decision of the Patent Office to register a mark without requiring proof of secondary meaning affords a rebuttable presumption that the mark is suggestive or arbitrary or fanciful rather than merely
descriptive.

It need hardly be added that fanciful or arbitrary terms enjoy all the rights accorded
to suggestive terms as marks—without the need of debating whether the term is
"merely descriptive" and with ease of establishing infringement.

* * *

---

# Qualitex Co. v. Jacobson Products Co., Inc.
## 514 U.S. 159 (1995)

Justice Breyer delivered the opinion of the Court.

The question in this case is whether the Lanham Trademark Act of 1946 (Lanham
Act), 15 U.S.C. §§ 1051-1127 (1988 ed. and Supp. V), permits the registration of a
trademark that consists, purely and simply, of a color. We conclude that, sometimes, a
color will meet ordinary legal trademark requirements. And, when it does so, no special
legal rule prevents color alone from serving as a trademark.

I

The case before us grows out of petitioner Qualitex Company's use (since the 1950's)
of a special shade of green-gold color on the pads that it makes and sells to dry cleaning

firms for use on dry cleaning presses. In 1989 respondent Jacobson Products (a Qualitex rival) began to sell its own press pads to dry cleaning firms; and it colored those pads a similar green-gold. In 1991 Qualitex registered the special green-gold color on press pads with the Patent and Trademark Office as a trademark....Qualitex subsequently added a trademark infringement count, 15 U.S.C. § 1114(1), to an unfair competition claim, section 1125(a), in a lawsuit it had already filed challenging Jacobson's use of the green-gold color.

Qualitex won the lawsuit in the District Court. But, the Court of Appeals for the Ninth Circuit set aside the judgment in Qualitex's favor on the trademark infringement claim because, in that Circuit's view, the Lanham Act does not permit Qualitex, or anyone else, to register "color alone" as a trademark.

The courts of appeals have differed as to whether or not the law recognizes the use of color alone as a trademark. [Citations omitted.] Therefore, this Court granted certiorari. We now hold that there is no rule absolutely barring the use of color alone, and we reverse the judgment of the Ninth Circuit.

## II

The Lanham Act gives a seller or producer the exclusive right to "register" a trademark, 15 U.S.C. § 1052, and to prevent his or her competitors from using that trademark, section 1114(1). Both the language of the Act and the basic underlying principles of trademark law would seem to include color within the universe of things that can qualify as a trademark. The language of the Lanham Act describes that universe in the broadest of terms. It says that trademarks "include any word, name, symbol, or device, or any combination thereof." § 1127. Since human beings might use as a "symbol" or "device" almost anything at all that is capable of carrying meaning, this language, read literally, is not restrictive. The courts and the Patent and Trademark Office have authorized for use as a mark a particular shape (of a Coca-Cola bottle), a particular sound (of NBC's three chimes), and even a particular scent (of plumeria blossoms on sewing thread). If a shape, a sound, and a fragrance can act as symbols why, one might ask, can a color not do the same?

A color is also capable of satisfying the more important part of the statutory definition of a trademark, which requires that a person "use" or "intend to use" the mark:

> To identify and distinguish his or her goods, including a unique product, from those manufactured or sold by others and to indicate the source of the goods, even if that source is unknown.

15 U.S.C. § 1127.

True, a product's color is unlike "fanciful," "arbitrary," or "suggestive" words or designs, which almost automatically tell a customer that they refer to a brand.... The imaginary word "Suntost," or the words "Suntost Marmalade," on a jar of orange jam immediately would signal a brand or a product "source"; the jam's orange color does not do so. But, over time, customers may come to treat a particular color on a product or its packaging (say, a color that in context seems unusual, such as pink on a firm's insulating material or red on the head of a large industrial bolt) as signifying a brand. And, if so, that color would have come to identify and distinguish the goods—i.e. "to "indicate" their "source"—much in the way that descriptive words on a product (say, "Trim" on nail clippers or "Car-Freshner" on deodorizer) can come to indicate a product's origin....In this circumstance, trademark law says that the word (e.g., "Trim"), although not inherently distinctive, has developed "secondary meaning."...Again, one might ask, if trademark law permits a descriptive word with secondary meaning to act as a mark, why would it not permit a color, under similar circumstances, to do the same?

We cannot find in the basic objectives of trademark law any obvious theoretical objection to the use of color alone as a trademark, where that color has attained "secondary meaning" and therefore identifies and distinguishes a particular brand (and thus indicates its "source"). In principle, trademark law, by preventing others from copying a source-identifying mark, "reduces the customer's costs of shopping and making purchasing decisions," 1 J. McCarthy, McCarthy on Trademarks and Unfair Competition § 2.01[2], p. 2–3 (3d ed. 1994) (hereinafter McCarthy), for it quickly and easily assures a potential customer that this item—the item with this mark—is made by the same producer as other similarly marked items that he or she liked (or disliked) in the past. At the same time, the law helps assure a producer that it (and not an imitating competitor) will reap the financial, reputation-related rewards associated with a desirable product. The law thereby "encourages the production of quality products," *ibid.*, and simultaneously discourages those who hope to sell inferior products by capitalizing on a consumer's inability quickly to evaluate the quality of an item offered for sale....It is the source-distinguishing ability of a mark— not its ontological status as color, shape, fragrance, word, or sign—that permits it to serve these basic purposes. *See* Landes & Posner, *Trademark Law: An Economic Perspective*, 30 J. Law & Econ. 265, 290 (1987). And, for that reason, it is difficult to find, in basic trademark objectives, a reason to disqualify absolutely the use of a color as a mark.

Neither can we find a principled objection to the use of color as a mark in the important "functionality" doctrine of trademark law. The functionality doctrine prevents trademark law, which seeks to promote competition by protecting a firm's reputation, from instead inhibiting legitimate competition by allowing a producer to control a useful product feature. It is the province of patent law, not trademark law, to encourage invention by granting inventors a monopoly over new product designs or functions for a limited time, 35 U.S.C. §§ 154, 173, after which competitors are free to use the innovation. If a product's functional features could be used as trademarks, however, a monopoly over such features could be obtained without regard to whether they qualify as patents and could be extended forever (because trademarks may be renewed in perpetuity)....Functionality doctrine therefore would require, to take an imaginary example, that even if customers have come to identify the special illumination-enhancing shape of a new patented light bulb with a particular manufacturer, the manufacturer may not use that shape as a trademark, for doing so, after the patent had expired, would impede competition—not by protecting the reputation of the original bulb maker, but by frustrating competitors' legitimate efforts to produce an equivalent illumination-enhancing bulb....This Court consequently has explained that, "in general terms, a product feature is functional," and cannot serve as a trademark, "if it is essential to the use or purpose of the article or if it affects the cost or quality of the article," that is, if exclusive use of the feature would put competitors at a significant non-reputation-related disadvantage. *Inwood Laboratories, Inc.*, 456 U.S. at 850, n. 10. Although sometimes color plays an important role (unrelated to source identification) in making a product more desirable, sometimes it does not. And, this latter fact—the fact that sometimes color is not essential to a product's use or purpose and does not affect cost or quality—indicates that the doctrine of "functionality" does not create an absolute bar to the use of color alone as a mark. *See Owens-Corning*, 774 F.2d at 1123 (pink color of insulation in wall "performs no non-trademark function").

It would seem, then, that color alone, at least sometimes, can meet the basic legal requirements for use as a trademark. It can act as a symbol that distinguishes a firm's goods and identifies their source, without serving any other significant function....Indeed, the District Court, in this case, entered findings (accepted by the Ninth Circuit) that show Qualitex's green-gold press pad color has met these requirements. The green-gold color acts as a symbol. Having developed secondary meaning (for customers identified the green-gold color as Qualitex's), it identifies the press pads' source. And, the green-gold color serves no other function. (Although it is important to use some color on press pads to avoid noticeable stains, the court found "no competitive need in the press pad industry for the green-gold color, since other colors are equally usable." 21 U.S.P.Q.2D (BNA) at 1460. Accordingly, unless there is some special reason that convincingly militates against the use of color alone as a trademark, trademark law would protect Qualitex's use of the green-gold color on its press pads.

\* \* \*

## IV

Having determined that a color may sometimes meet the basic legal requirements for use as a trademark and that respondent Jacobson's arguments do not justify a special legal rule preventing color alone from serving as a trademark (and, in light of the District Court's here undisputed findings that Qualitex's use of the green-gold color on its press pads meets the basic trademark requirements), we conclude that the Ninth Circuit erred in barring Qualitex's use of color as a trademark. For these reasons, the judgment of the Ninth Circuit is

*Reversed.*

---

# Wal-Mart Stores, Inc., v. Samara Brothers, Inc.

## 529 U.S. 205 (2000)

SCALIA, J., delivered the opinion for a unanimous Court.

In this case, we decide under what circumstances a product's design is distinctive, and therefore protectible, in an action for infringement of unregistered trade dress under §43(a) of the Trademark Act of 1946 (Lanham Act)...15 U.S.C. §1125(a).

## I

Respondent Samara Brothers, Inc., designs and manufactures children's clothing. Its primary product is a line of spring/summer one-piece seersucker outfits decorated with appliqués of hearts, flowers, fruits, and the like. A number of chain stores, including JC Penney, sell this line of clothing under contract with Samara.

Petitioner Wal-Mart Stores, Inc., is one of the nation's best-known retailers, selling among other things children's clothing. In 1995, Wal-Mart contracted with one of its suppliers, Judy-Philippine, Inc., to manufacture a line of children's outfits for sale in the 1996 spring/summer season. Wal-Mart sent Judy-Philippine photographs of a number of garments from Samara's line, on which Judy-Philippine's garments were to be based; Judy-Philippine duly copied, with only minor modifications, 16 of Samara's garments, many of which contained copyrighted elements. In 1996, Wal-Mart briskly sold the so-called knockoffs, generating more than $ 1.15 million in gross profits.

\* \* \*

After sending cease-and-desist letters, Samara brought this action in the United States District Court for the Southern District of New York against Wal-Mart, Judy-

Philippine, [and others] for copyright infringement under federal law, consumer fraud and unfair competition under New York law, and—most relevant for our purposes—infringement of unregistered trade dress under § 43(a) of the Lanham Act.... All of the defendants except Wal-Mart settled before trial.

After a week long trial, the jury found in favor of Samara on all of its claims. Wal-Mart then renewed a motion for judgment as a matter of law, claiming, *inter alia*, that there was insufficient evidence to support a conclusion that Samara's clothing designs could be legally protected as distinctive trade dress for purposes of § 43(a). The District Court denied the motion.... The Second Circuit affirmed....

## II

The Lanham Act provides for the registration of trademarks, which it defines in § 45 to include "any word, name, symbol, or device, or any combination thereof [used or intended to be used] to identify and distinguish [a producer's] goods...from those manufactured or sold by others and to indicate the source of the goods...." 15 U.S.C. § 1127. Registration of a mark under § 2 of the Act, 15 U.S.C. § 1052, enables the owner to sue an infringer under § 32, 15 U.S.C. § 1114; it also entitles the owner to a presumption that its mark is valid, see § 7(b), 15 U.S.C. § 1057(b), and ordinarily renders the registered mark incontestable after five years of continuous use, see § 15, 15 U.S.C. § 1065. In addition to protecting registered marks, the Lanham Act, in § 43(a), gives a producer a cause of action for the use by any person of "any word, term, name, symbol, or device, or any combination thereof...which...is likely to cause confusion...as to the origin, sponsorship, or approval of his or her goods...." 15 U.S.C. § 1125(a). It is the latter provision that is at issue in this case.

The breadth of the definition of marks registrable under § 2, and of the confusion-producing elements recited as actionable by § 43(a), has been held to embrace not just word marks, such as "Nike," and symbol marks, such as Nike's "swoosh" symbol, but also "trade dress"—a category that originally included only the packaging, or "dressing," of a product, but in recent years has been expanded by many courts of appeals to encompass the design of a product.

The text of § 43(a) provides little guidance as to the circumstances under which unregistered trade dress may be protected. It does require that a producer show that the allegedly infringing feature is not "functional," see § 43(a)(3), and is likely to cause confusion with the product for which protection is sought, see § 43(a)(1)(A), 15 U.S.C. § 1125(a)(1)(A). Nothing in § 43(a) explicitly requires a producer to show that its trade dress is distinctive, but courts have universally imposed that requirement, since without distinctiveness the trade dress would not "cause confusion...as to the origin, sponsorship, or approval of [the] goods," as the section requires. Distinctiveness is, moreover, an explicit prerequisite for registration of trade dress under § 2, and "the general principles qualifying a mark for registration under § 2 of the Lanham Act are for the most part applicable in determining whether an unregistered mark is entitled to protection under § 43(a)." *Two Pesos, Inc. v. Taco Cabana, Inc.*, 505 U.S. 763, 768, 120 L. Ed. 2d 615, 112 S. Ct. 2753 (1992) (citations omitted).

In evaluating the distinctiveness of a mark under § 2 (and therefore, by analogy, under § 43(a)), courts have held that a mark can be distinctive in one of two ways. First, a mark is inherently distinctive if "[its] intrinsic nature serves to identify a particular source." *Ibid.* In the context of word marks, courts have applied the now-classic test originally formulated by Judge Friendly, in which word marks that are "arbitrary"

("Camel" cigarettes), "fanciful" ("Kodak" film), or "suggestive" ("Tide" laundry detergent) are held to be inherently distinctive. *See Abercrombie & Fitch Co. v. Hunting World, Inc.*, 537 F.2d 4, 10-11 (CA2 1976). Second, a mark has acquired distinctiveness, even if it is not inherently distinctive, if it has developed secondary meaning, which occurs when, "in the minds of the public, the primary significance of a [mark] is to identify the source of the product rather than the product itself." *Inwood Laboratories, Inc. v. Ives Laboratories, Inc.*, 456 U.S. 844, 851, n. 11, 72 L. Ed. 2d 606, 102 S. Ct. 2182 (1982).

The judicial differentiation between marks that are inherently distinctive and those that have developed secondary meaning has solid foundation in the statute itself. Section 2 requires that registration be granted to any trademark "by which the goods of the applicant may be distinguished from the goods of others"—subject to various limited exceptions. 15 U.S.C. § 1052. It also provides, again with limited exceptions, that "nothing in this chapter shall prevent the registration of a mark used by the applicant which has become distinctive of the applicant's goods in commerce"—that is, which is not inherently distinctive but has become so only through secondary meaning. § 2(f), 15 U.S.C. § 1052(f). Nothing in § 2, however, demands the conclusion that every category of mark necessarily includes some marks "by which the goods of the applicant may be distinguished from the goods of others" without secondary meaning—that in every category some marks are inherently distinctive.

Indeed, with respect to at least one category of mark—colors—we have held that no mark can ever be inherently distinctive. *See Qualitex*, 514 U.S. at 162-163. In *Qualitex*, petitioner manufactured and sold green-gold dry-cleaning press pads. After respondent began selling pads of a similar color, petitioner brought suit under § 43(a), and then added a claim under § 32 after obtaining registration for the color of its pads. We held that a color could be protected as a trademark, but only upon a showing of secondary meaning.

Reasoning by analogy to the *Abercrombie & Fitch* test developed for word marks, we noted that a product's color is unlike a "fanciful," "arbitrary," or "suggestive" mark, since it does not "almost automatically tell a customer that [it] refers to a brand," and does not "immediately...signal a brand or a product 'source,'" However, we noted that, "over time, customers may come to treat a particular color on a product or its packaging...as signifying a brand." Because a color, like a "descriptive" word mark, could eventually "come to indicate a product's origin," we concluded that it could be protected upon a showing of secondary meaning.

It seems to us that design, like color, is not inherently distinctive. The attribution of inherent distinctiveness to certain categories of word marks and product packaging derives from the fact that the very purpose of attaching a particular word to a product, or encasing it in a distinctive packaging, is most often to identify the source of the product. Although the words and packaging can serve subsidiary functions—a suggestive word mark (such as "Tide" for laundry detergent), for instance, may invoke positive connotations in the consumer's mind, and a garish form of packaging (such as Tide's squat, brightly decorated plastic bottles for its liquid laundry detergent) may attract an otherwise indifferent consumer's attention on a crowded store shelf—their predominant function remains source identification. Consumers are therefore predisposed to regard those symbols as indication of the producer, which is why such symbols "almost automatically tell a customer that they refer to a brand," 514 U.S. at 162-163, and "immediately...signal a brand or a product 'source,'" 514 U.S. at 163. And where it is not reasonable to assume consumer predisposition to take an affixed word or packaging as indication of source—where, for example, the affixed word is descriptive of the product ("Tasty" bread) or of a geographic origin ("Georgia" peaches)—inherent distinctiveness will not be found. That is why the statute generally excludes, from those word marks that can be registered as inherently distinctive, words that are "merely descriptive" of the goods, §2(e)(1), 15 U.S.C. §1052(e)(1), or "primarily geographically descriptive of them," see §2(e)(2), 15 U.S.C. §1052(e)(2). In the case of product design, as in the case of color, we think consumer predisposition to equate the feature with the source does not exist. Consumers are aware of the reality that, almost invariably, even the most unusual of product designs—such as a cocktail shaker shaped like a penguin—is intended not to identify the source, but to render the product itself more useful or more appealing.

The fact that product design almost invariably serves purposes other than source identification not only renders inherent distinctiveness problematic; it also renders application of an inherent-distinctiveness principle more harmful to other consumer interests. Consumers should not be deprived of the benefits of competition with regard to the utilitarian and esthetic purposes that product design ordinarily serves by a rule of law that facilitates plausible threats of suit against new entrants based upon alleged inherent distinctiveness. How easy it is to mount a plausible suit depends, of course, upon the clarity of the test for inherent distinctiveness, and where product design is concerned we have little confidence that a reasonably clear test can be devised. Respondent and the United States as amicus curiae urge us to adopt for product design relevant portions of the test formulated by the Court of Customs and Patent Appeals for product packaging in Seabrook Foods, Inc. v. Bar-Well Foods, Ltd., 568 F.2d 1342 (1977). That opinion, in determining the inherent distinctiveness of a product's packaging, considered, among other things, "whether it was a 'common' basic shape or design, whether it was unique or unusual in a particular field, [and] whether it was a mere refinement of a commonly-adopted and well-known form of ornamentation for a particular class of goods viewed by the public as a dress or ornamentation for the goods." Id. at 1344 (footnotes omitted). Such a test would rarely provide the basis for summary disposition of an anticompetitive strike suit. Indeed, at oral argument, counsel for the United States quite understandably would not give a definitive answer as to whether the test was met in this very case, saying only that "this is a very difficult case for that purpose."

It is true, of course, that the person seeking to exclude new entrants would have to establish the nonfunctionality of the design feature, see §43(a)(3), 15 U.S.C. A. §1125(a)(3) (Oct. 1999 Supp.)—a showing that may involve consideration of its esthetic appeal, see Qualitex, 514 U.S. at 170. Competition is deterred, however, not merely by successful suit but by the plausible threat of successful suit, and given the unlikelihood of inherently source-identifying design, the game of allowing suit based upon alleged inherent distinctiveness seems to us not worth the candle. That is especially so since the producer can ordinarily obtain protection for a design that is inherently source identifying (if any such exists), but that does not yet have secondary meaning, by securing a design patent or a copyright for the design—as, indeed, respondent did for certain elements of the designs in this case. The availability of these other protections greatly reduces any harm to the producer that might ensue from our conclusion that a product design cannot be protected under §43(a) without a showing of secondary meaning.

Respondent contends that our decision in Two Pesos forecloses a conclusion that product-design trade dress can never be inherently distinctive. In that case, we held that the trade dress of a chain of Mexican restaurants, which the plaintiff described as "a festive eating atmosphere having interior dining and patio areas decorated with artifacts, bright colors, paintings and murals," could be protected under §43(a) without a showing of secondary meaning.... *Two Pesos* unquestionably establishes the legal principle that trade dress can be inherently distinctive, but it does not establish that product-design trade dress can be. *Two Pesos* is inapposite to our holding here because the trade dress at issue, the decor of a restaurant, seems to us not to constitute product design. It was either product packaging—which, as we have discussed, normally is taken by the consumer to indicate origin—or else some tertium quid that is akin to product packaging and has no bearing on the present case.

Respondent replies that this manner of distinguishing *Two Pesos* will force courts to draw difficult lines between product-design and product-packaging trade dress. There will indeed be some hard cases at the margin: a classic glass Coca-Cola bottle, for instance, may constitute packaging for those consumers who drink the Coke and then discard the bottle, but may constitute the product itself for those consumers who are bottle collectors, or part of the product itself for those consumers who buy Coke in the classic glass bottle, rather than a can, because they think it more stylish to drink from the former. We believe, however, that the frequency and the difficulty of having to distinguish between product design and product packaging will be much less than the frequency and the difficulty of having to decide when a product design is inherently distinctive. To the extent there are close cases, we believe that courts should err on the side of caution and classify ambiguous trade dress as product design, thereby requiring secondary meaning. The very closeness will suggest the existence of relatively small utility in adopting an inherent-distinctiveness principle, and relatively great consumer benefit in requiring a demonstration of secondary meaning.

\* \* \*

We hold that, in an action for infringement of unregistered trade dress under § 43(a) of the Lanham Act, a product's design is distinctive, and therefore protectible, only upon a showing of secondary meaning. The judgment of the Second Circuit is reversed, and the case is remanded for further proceedings consistent with this opinion.

It is so ordered.

# Notes on Trademarks

1. Part of the role of the licensing lawyer and intellectual property manager is in determining what kinds of intellectual property are eligible for useful legal protection. In the field of trademarks, lawyers are often involved, for example, in helping a business *select* and clear trademarks for use with its products and services. By applying the rules that the foregoing decisions established or summarized, the lawyer can help a business choose marks that may be easier than others to register, protect, and defend against infringement.

2. The rules discussed in the foregoing cases are relatively easy to restate in the abstract. They might be summarized as follows:

a. *The "distinctiveness spectrum."* Verbal marks fall into four categories or "hues" of the so-called "distinctiveness spectrum": (i) arbitrary or fanciful (coined), (ii) suggestive, (iii) descriptive, and (iv) generic.

b. *Inherently distinctive marks.* Verbal marks in the first two categories, i.e., those that are arbitrary, fanciful, or suggestive, are inherently distinctive. They may be registered and can enjoy legal protection without a showing of secondary meaning.

c. *Descriptive and generic marks.* Verbal marks in the last two categories—descriptive and generic—are not inherently distinctive. Descriptive marks can acquire distinctiveness, i.e., secondary meaning, through use; once they have done so, they are eligible for registration and legal protection from unfair competition. Generic marks can never become distinctive, and so cannot be registered or protected as marks (although they may receive some minimal protection against blatant misuse under the law of unfair competition).

d. *Trade dress.* Nonverbal marks, including trade dress, fall into three possible categories: (i) product design, (ii) packaging, and (iii) "some *tertium quid* that is akin to product packaging," like the restaurant trade dress in *Two Pesos*. *Two Pesos, Inc. v. Taco Cabana, Inc.*, 505 U.S. 763 (1992). Product design, like verbal marks that are not inherently distinctive, requires a showing of acquired distinctiveness or secondary meaning for registration and protection. The other two categories may be inherently distinctive and therefore registrable and protectible *ab initio.* If not, they require secondary meaning just like product design.

e. *Functionality doctrine.* No mark or feature, however, can be registered or protected if it is "functional," i.e., if its use affects the cost or quality of the goods or services with which it is used. *See* 15 U.S.C. § 1052(e)(5), 1125(a)(3). The "functionality" doctrine applies most strongly to product features and aspects of product design, but the statutory language makes it applicable to verbal marks as well.

3. Part of the lawyer's role is to advise businesses on such matters as the distinctiveness spectrum and the functionality doctrine when they choose marks and symbols to serve as brand identifiers. Giving such advice, however, is not always as easy as it seems, because business goals may be in tension with legal doctrine. For example, lawyers almost always want their clients to pick marks near the "arbitrary/fanciful" end of the distinctiveness spectrum, so they can be protected immediately, without a showing of secondary meaning. But do marketers always feel the same way? Can you think of any reason why lawyers and marketers might disagree on marks and slogans to use as brand identifiers? Can you think of any examples of probable disagreement from our common commercial culture?

4. Another perennial difficulty in advising clients with regard to trademarks is the uncertainty of legal conclusions. The rules for trademark protection stated above are easy to state in outline form but not always easy to apply. If your client chose the following as brand identifiers for each of the stated products, into what categories would you place the identifier, and how easy do you think the identifier would be to protect as a trademark or trade dress? (For known marks, pretend that you are advising a client who is proposing to adopt that mark, as yet unused, for the first time.)

| Proposed Brand Identifier | Product or Service |
| --- | --- |
| a.  Chap-Stick | Lip balm preparation in a stick |
| b.  Q-Tips | Cotton swabs on small sticks |
| c.  Coppertone | Sun tan oil |
| d.  Beef & Brew | Restaurant services |
| e.  7-Eleven | Convenience store services |
| f.  Metallic cherry red color | Surf boards and surfing gear |

| | |
|---|---|
| g. Charlie | Perfume for women |
| h. Surgicenter | Outpatient surgical services |
| i. Bufferin | Buffered aspirin |
| j. Lite | Light (low calorie) beer |
| k. Vision Center | Optical clinic |
| l. Iridescent orange color | Foul weather gear for road repair crews |
| m. Old Crow | Whiskey |
| n. Xerox | Copying machines |
| o. Chicken of the Sea | Canned tuna |
| p. Opry | Country music concert services |
| r. Roach Motel | Cockroach trap |
| s. Micro | Balancing weights for car wheels |
| t. Maternally Yours | Maternity clothing store services |
| u. Chocolate Fudge | Diet soda with chocolate fudge flavor |
| v. Raisin Bran | Breakfast cereal with raisins and bran |
| w. Clorox | Household bleach |
| x. Pair of flexible springs for supports | Waist-high signs for gas stations |

5. Consider the following questions: How do trademarks differ from patents? What sorts of things are eligible for protection as trademarks or trade symbols? What are the substantive requirements for protecting a trade symbol? Are there requirements analogous to proper subject matter, novelty, utility, and nonobviousness in patent law? Are there requirements analogous to proper disclosure in a patent application? What are the "procedural" requirements for protecting a trademark, i.e., what steps must the owner take to insure or perfect protection? What are the policies underlying trademark protection? What social/economic functions does trademark protection perform?

6. How does "trade dress" differ from other trademarks and trade symbols? What doctrines of trade dress law avoid a collision between patent policy and trade dress protection? What types of trade dress raise the greatest risk of a collision — "service" trade dress (like the restaurant configuration in *Two Pesos*), packaging of products, or the configuration (shape) of products?

# Chapter 3

# Intellectual Property Audits

## I. Importance of an Audit

An intellectual property audit is a systematic identification and evaluation of the intellectual property assets held by a business. The audit process is sometimes known as "mapping," because it "maps" where in the business each intellectual property asset was created, where it currently resides, and how each relates to other intellectual property assets throughout the business. Undertaking such an audit requires a substantial commitment of time and resources. Dow Chemical's first audit of its intellectual property lasted a year, although today software tools can reduce the process to days. Dow's audit mapped 29,000 patents and assigned each to a business unit that would become financially responsible for its use.[1]

In a perfect world, an intellectual property audit would be a routine, recurring practice. The inventory would be valued (*see* Chapter 5 *infra*) using both proprietary tools (software, processes and business methods) and generally accepted accounting practices. The audit results would drive business strategy, helping the company to decide whether a technology should be (i) developed further into potential products, (ii) licensed out, (iii) donated to a university for the tax-writeoff, or (iv) abandoned.[2]

In the real world, most businesses do not conduct intellectual property audits at all. While gaining in popularity, the intellectual property audit remains an anomaly. Yet more and more businesses are beginning to recognize the importance of capturing the full value of intellectual property assets.[3]

Intellectual property audits are a particularly useful tool in developing a licensing strategy. The audit can identify the nature and value of intellectual properties, potential liabilities, and technology "gaps" in the portfolio that could be filled by licensing-in properties from third parties. Only by accurately assessing its strengths and weaknesses can a company profitably seek out the best license partners.

The audit also influences individual license negotiations, as a licensor that has mapped its intellectual property portfolio enters negotiations with clear objectives and desired terms already in hand. These licensors have a clear idea what their properties are

---

1. K. Rivette and D. Kline, Rembrandts in the Attic, Unlocking the Hidden Value of Patents 66 (2000).
2. *Id.*
3. *Id.*

worth and which companies make the most appropriate licensees. For the licensor, such negotiations are likely to be shorter, less expensive, and result in more favorable deals.

The licensee also benefits in that such licensors can accurately and completely define the intellectual properties being transferred, and provide assurance that *all* of the various properties necessary to achieve the licensee's desired end are included in that definition. The right to use a patented machine, without the complementary right to use the copyrighted software necessary to efficiently control the machine will be, if not useless, certainly worth significantly less. A prudent licensee will always conduct its own due diligence to confirm that the licensor's representations regarding the licensed property are accurate and complete. Due diligence will be much swifter and less expensive when the licensor can provide a well-documented paper trail.

After the license is executed, future intellectual property audits can provide the licensor with the data necessary to react intelligently (and profitably) to its current obligations and future options under that license. For instance, if the license grant includes rights to future improvements by the licensor on the originally-licensed technology, an audit by the licensor will identify what new developments, if any, may need to be disclosed to the licensee. The licensee will face a similar situation if the license agreement includes a grant-back provision covering its own developments.

Finally, intellectual property audits can lead to considerable cost savings, as patents and trademarks are identified that have no further value to the business, and on which maintenance fees and legal expenses no longer need be paid. Similarly, audits can also reveal expired or abandoned patents that have entered the public domain, disclosures of inventions that have entered the public domain and/or have become prior art, or trade secrets that have become publicly disclosed.

---

# II. Mapping Intellectual Properties

In addition to giving a licensor the basic information necessary to allow it to comply with its obligations under the agreement, an intellectual property audit also provides the knowledge necessary to make intelligent use of optional rights. For instance, if a licensee's intellectual property audit determines that one of its divisions has independently developed an alternate technology that will serve as an adequate substitute for technology that is currently licensed under an agreement having an automatic renewal clause, the licensee can promptly give notice of its desire to terminate that agreement at the next renewal.

Although an intellectual property audit's scope should include an entire company, with larger entities it is often impractical to conduct the audit simultaneously throughout the entire business. Often a company will audit its divisions one at a time. For the outside intellectual property audit consultant, this offers an opportunity to hone the audit strategy as the corporate culture becomes more familiar. Unfortunately, it also means many separate training sessions with key employees, since their assistance will be vital to the audit, and they cannot effectively contribute to the audit without a solid knowledge of what intellectual property will be created, maintained, and transferred.

While an intellectual property audit strategy can be systematized and standardized to some degree for use in different divisions of a particular company, it is difficult to take a "turn-key" audit package from one company and apply it to another. Intellectual property audits are likely to be more complete and dependable if tailored to the company at hand. However, there are some standard elements to almost all intellectual property audits. The material below describes some of the more typical elements of an intellectual property audit.

_____

## Intellectual Property—Licensing and Joint Venture Profit Strategies*

Gordon V. Smith & Russell L. Parr, pp. 432–52 (1998)

### MAPPING INTELLECTUAL PROPERTY

An inventory of intellectual property is a realistic goal but is complicated by the multifaceted nature of these intangible assets. Intellectual property cuts across many aspects of a business and often interplays with other intangible assets. When intellectual property does not cut across business boundaries, new questions arise, like: Why not?

The trademark of a company with various divisions and products, all using the same trademark banner, cannot be conveniently placed in an inventory account that is associated with one of the manufacturing plants or one of the divisions. But customer lists are often associated with a single business division. One business unit may be exclusively using a customer list that has potential for other divisions. Associating an exclusive list with one business unit is not recommended. Such a practice can psychologically block seeing the potential for broader application.

The process for taking an inventory of intellectual property is described as mapping. Intellectual property can stretch over many aspects of a corporation like a river that sustains life through entire regions of a country. It is not appropriate to identify a river with the inventory account of one U.S. state. Likewise, it is also inappropriate to identify many types of intellectual properties with one of the company plants, divisions, or subsidiaries. The process of mapping starts with a comprehensive list that identifies the various types of intellectual property. Then a mechanism is derived to show the many places where, in the organization, each of these assets is used. The map should be flexible, allowing the location of property use to be broadly defined, but also including identification of other applications. The usage location, defined as the primary activity or physical location of use, can be defined to run among products, divisions, or manufacturing locations. Different organizations will find that their own circumstances dictate how usage locations should be defined.

The questions to be answered in the mapping process are basic:

1. What intellectual property do we possess?
2. Where is it being used?

After these questions are answered, a great many new possibilities can be considered: Where else can we use the property? Can it he licensed? Is it being properly protected? Can it be contributed to a joint venture? Can it be traded to fill an intellectual property gap? Should an idle property be sold off for cash?

_____

* Reprinted with permission of the publisher, copyright 1993.

Once the basic questions are answered, new possibilities might appear for more fully exploiting these assets. Strategic planners that assess the profit centers and profit opportunities of large companies will find many aspects of mapping intellectual property familiar. However, the focus is shifted to intellectual property and away from business units.

Provided below is a brief outline of the steps needed to begin and complete the mapping process. The steps include:

1. Identification
2. Location
3. Coordination with strategic plans
4. Routing for internal exploitation
5. Identifying gaps
6. Routing for external application

This chapter will focus on providing guidance about what to look for and where to find intellectual property—identification and location.

## IDENTIFICATION

Keystone patents and flagship trademarks are easy to identify. But buried in the organization are many other gems just waiting to be discovered. Start with a list of all of the patents and trademarks of the company from the legal department. Then begin to think like a detective. But do not limit yourself to the list. Some very valuable intellectual property in the form of know-how can lurk unnoticed. Make inquiries throughout the company by interviewing managers from all divisions at all levels. It is important to get into the lower ranks of the organization because most of the best insights rise from the bottom to the top. Show everyone the complete list of patents and trademarks, and find out which are being used. Also find out why unused patents and trademarks are not being incorporated into activities. Ask everyone—employees, customers, suppliers—What *makes our product, company, or service special? Why are customers buying our goods?* Do not fall into the trap of only asking the marketing people why customers buy. They have prejudices, just like the engineering, customer service, and manufacturing people will. So ask everyone. The answers will range all over the place, but a few answers will lead to the discovery of unrecognized intellectual property. These are the intellectual property assets that can lead to new opportunities. These are the assets that a comprehensive inventory must discover. Examples include secret formulas, process procedures, quality control secrets, customer lists, incentive plans, databases, supplier agreements, employee training methods, and other intangible items never imagined.

> Xerox found that their internal training program was highly regarded by outsiders. They made an entire business by selling training programs to other companies.

The search must include line functions and staffing functions. Corporate databases can be just as valuable as keystone patents. Marketing plans can also be significantly valuable. They can also have great potential for application to other aspects of the business. The search must include extensive fieldwork, but cannot omit the all too familiar backyard of corporate headquarters.

> A Wisconsin power company spent millions to develop a new computer system that coordinated power production activities with customer utilization and billing. It was a sophisticated program, and other utilities could enjoy its bene-

fits without becoming a competitive threat. Wisconsin Power set up a subsidiary, and licensed the new company to market the computer program.

According to British Technology Group's chief executive Ian Harvey: "We believe that many corporations doing R&D use only 20 to 30% of the technology they have developed. The remainder lies unused for a variety of reasons." ("Global Technology-Asset Management: A New Survival Skill for the 1990s," by Jeffrey L. Staley, *Technology Transfer,* Fall 1991.) If Mr. Harvey is correct, this technology deserves to be found and exploited. If it is not useful for the present strategic plan, then sell it, license it, or form a joint venture with it. Do something with it.

Presented below is a list of intellectual property and intangible assets. Not all will possess the potential for further exploitation. Some will have mild potential; others could be great success stories. Each department of a corporation can be a treasure trove of exploitable property.

*Engineering*

   *Governmental approvals and acquisition expertise*

   Governmental regulation compliance

   Quality control testing procedures and equipment

   Design efficiencies

   Product defect statistics

   Assembled engineering workforce

*Research & Development*

   *Research programs*

   Patented technology applications

   Patented technology

   Prototypes

   Embryonic research

   Assembled research workforce

*Manufacturing*

   *Production practices*

   Knowledge about factors affecting quality

   Assembled manufacturing workforce

   Order backlog

   Spare parts annuity

   License agreements

   Process patents

   Material handling technology

   Vendor and supplier list

   Just-in-time raw materials delivery techniques

   Automated inspection procedures and equipment

*Distribution & Marketing*

Brands and trademarks

Advertising and media programs

Packaging research

Assembled sales staff and representatives

Retail accounts and shelf space

Statistics on loyal customer buying history

Competitor analysis

Copyrights on sales material

Distribution rights to other products

*Finance & Administration*

Management information systems

Long-term and favorable lease arrangements

Assembled workforce

Copyrights on computer software

Mortgage portfolios

Unique incentive programs

Here is a description of some of the intellectual property to be found from a mapping program. Not all of it will have the potential for enhanced exploitation, but some of it will. A few possibilities are discussed.

## ASSEMBLED WORKFORCE

In many businesses, the presence of a skilled workforce that is knowledgeable about company procedures and possesses expertise in certain fields is vital to continued profitability and growth. Access to some of these professionals can be used to leverage a company into a strategic alliance. It is common in the pharmaceutical industry for one partner to conduct product research and get government approvals, while the other partner is responsible for large-scale manufacturing and marketing. Expertise is needed in research, manufacturing, and marketing. A full assessment of the special skills of the entire workforce from all departments can be a unique proprietary asset. Successful corporations are very much like individuals. They develop areas of focused expertise, but are weak in other areas of life. Compounding the problem is that people of similar interests and expertise flock together. Managers with primary interests in research tend to like and hire people with similar strengths. In other companies, the dominant personality might be marketing. When this occurs, the company develops an unmatched expertise in an important business function. Instead of dooming the company because of its overspecialization, the dominant tendency attracts other companies possessing complementary specialties. Once a company recognizes its specialties, new possibilities can be discovered by looking for others that might like to joint venture.

## CAPTIVE SPARE PARTS ANNUITY

The continued purchase of replacement parts for capital equipment that have already been sold to customers can be an extraordinarily profitable portion of a business. If a company manufactures and sells complex capital equipment like aircraft, defense equipment, computer equipment, and other items requiring a substantial customer investment, then the customer purchasing the original item must continually return to the manufacturer for replacement parts and accessories. Typically, these items are sold at a healthy premium price contributing healthy profit margins. Premium pricing of these parts reflects the near monopoly position that the original equipment manufacturer possesses as the only source for these parts.

\* \* \*

The sale of spare parts, replacement parts, and accessories can be a substantial portion of a business. Some companies can estimate the amount of sales from this component of the business very accurately, and can therefore plan ahead to achieve the greatest amount of profitability. Sales of new equipment may be hurt during economic downturns, but replacement parts are usually very resilient.

\* \* \*

## COMPUTER SOFTWARE

Valuable computer software can be related to a company product or can represent internal controls that enhance the efficiency of operations. Microsoft Corporation has copyrighted products that serve as the foundation of their business. Federal Express has internal software and procedures that allow customers to ascertain the location of shipments in less than an hour. Federal Express uses this software to control operations, and also as a strong selling point to differentiate it from competitors.

Successful software products are usually a strong foundation from which to launch accessory software, products, and services. These can be handled internally or licensed out.

The Microsoft basic intellectual property, [its] operating system[s], [have] taken the company into a large product line of application programs, hardware accessories, programming books, and magazines.

## COPYRIGHTS

Copyrights are legally protected expressions of an idea, including films, books, articles, software, television programs, and other works. Decades of repeat sales are often possible. Copyrights are also excellent candidates for many forms of strategic alliances.

The movie industry has found great success in selling toys, T-shirts, and soundtracks to consumers during and after the run of a new motion picture. Dr. Seuss recently entered a license agreement associated with children's clothing. David Bowie has issued financial securities backed by the royalty income derived from his past albums. Martha Stewart has expanded her homemaking brand recognition into a life-style empire incorporating books, magazines, and television and radio programs.

## CUSTOMER LISTS

A list of established customer relationships comprised of individuals who repeatedly order from the company can have extraordinary value. The information contained in such lists usually includes the preferences of the customer, the buying patterns of the customer, and the history of purchases that have been received from the customer. In a sense, a list of loyal customers who regularly provide the company with sales is similar to the captive [sales of] parts. An opportunity exists by developing other products for sale to this loyal customer list. Also, the list can be a substantial asset for contributing to a joint venture. Loyal customers cost a lot to nurture, and creating a customer list from scratch takes time. Whenever a customer list exists, a valued piece of property exists for expanded exploitation.

## DISTRIBUTION NETWORKS

Many manufacturing companies do not possess an extensive staff of sales individuals. Instead, a network of independent distributors is used to find customers and get orders. These distributors receive a commission on each sale. They also can be a vital source of customer information. Many product enhancement ideas have come from customers through comments made to representatives of the distributor. Development of a distribution network can require an extensive amount of time as prospective distributors are identified, interviewed, qualified, and educated about the products that they will carry.

Lack of an established distribution network is many times the primary reason for product failure. New products from small companies often fail before the customer has a chance to vote on their commercial worthiness. If a new product cannot get to the shelves, the manufacturer will never realize any sales. Distribution networks are a strong bargaining chip when negotiating with a potential licensor, especially when the licensor does not have a similar means to reach consumers.

## TRADEMARKS

Identifying a trademark or brand most often is easily accomplished. For a short list of valuable names, look at the printing on the packaging of company products. Then, it is just a matter of determining, through consumer focus groups, the names and marks that can be exploited elsewhere, inside and outside of the company, without harming the core brand value.

## STRATEGIC PLAN AND GAP ANALYSIS

A well-defined strategic plan answers the questions: *"Where are we going, and how are we going to get there?"* Intellectual property is the vehicle that will take you to the future completion of your plan. With the map in one hand and the strategic plan in the other, you are ready to identify the missing pieces.

### (a) DuPont-Merck

Application of gap analysis by DuPont [Corporation] a few years ago indicated to the company that to be a winner in the pharmaceutical business in the future it had to address the core gaps—fundamental weaknesses—that existed in its drug-related business. While the company had a nearly full pipeline of research efforts, it realized that it lacked the important knowledge necessary to gain approval from the Food & Drug Administration for the drugs it hoped to bring to market. The company also realized that its marketing know-how and marketing network in the pharmaceutical industry was severely limited and almost nonexistent overseas. As DuPont considered the future it would face with its pharmaceutical division, it realized after critical analysis that the identified weaknesses could be filled by a strategic alliance with Merck.

Merck & Company, at about the same time, had a research pipeline that was less than robust. Still, Merck possessed extraordinarily important expertise in guiding new drug applications through the Food & Drug Administration approval process. Merck also possessed another strength that would solve another of DuPont's weaknesses—Merck had a well-established and respected marketing network in the United States and overseas. The resulting negotiations gave birth to the joint venture known as DuPont-Merck. DuPont brought the potential for development of new drug products to the alliance and Merck brought the regulatory and marketing expertise needed for commercialization.

## (b) Gap Analysis

Gap *analysis* is a forward-looking analysis that seeks to identify weaknesses that a company may have to deal with in the future. Gap analysis is also referred to as the *future-history approach,* as will be explained later. For now, think of the approach as studying the future as if it were the past. The approach can be especially useful for focusing on technological gaps that will exist and is a powerful way to help guide the licensing department as to the types of individual patent licenses and technology portfolio licenses that it should begin to develop. While the description of this analysis may sound simple, implementation is challenging. More importantly, the benefits of thoughtful application can be powerful.

Implementation of gap analysis requires four primary steps:

1.  Describe the future industry and economic conditions that will exist 10 to 15 years from now—Future Game.
2.  Describe the business characteristics of a hypothetical company that will dominate in the future scenario described in the first step—Future Winner.
3.  Access the current competencies and business characteristics of your company, as determined by mapping—Current Assessment.
4.  Compare your company to the Future Winner to find areas where important future competencies are lacking—Gap Identification.

* * *

## (c) Future Game

Step one in the process is to define the future game, where the game is defined as the economic and industry environment in which the company will compete. Part of the definition involves description of future products, customers, competitors, technologies, and manufacturing techniques as well as the future factors of production needed to play in the future game. This involves describing the business environment 10 to 15 years from now, but from the viewpoint of having just experienced the future being described. It involves describing the future in detail, as if it were already history—hence the secondary name for gap analysis: the future-history approach.

* * *

The resulting future game should include descriptions of the market that are expected to develop, the products that are expected to serve the market, the technologies that will be in your product, the competitive environment, the economic conditions, the people that will be needed to produce the product or service for the anticipated market, the facilities that will be required, the funding that will be needed, and the intellectual property in the form of trademarks and technology that will serve the anticipated future.

* * *

Accomplishing such a task can seem daunting, but it can be placed in a relatively simple framework by comparing the present situation to that which existed ten years ago. For each of the items just listed, describe the characteristics, in detail, for the different factors as they were ten years ago. Compare the nature of past factors as they are now.

The trends and shocking differences between the characteristics of ten years ago and today should be expected to continue. Comparison of the past with the present not only provides a practice session for defining the future game but the process will provide insights into the subtle and not-so-subtle changes that occurred in the past ten years.

\* \* \*

### (d) Future Winner

Step two of the gap analysis requires a description of the theoretical winner of the envisioned future game. For each of the characteristics that were previously defined, the competencies that are possessed by the winner of the future game should be described in detail. With the future game defined and broken into manageable pieces of markets, products, and production facilities, the theoretical winner of the future game can be described.

One way to start defining the theoretical winner is to study a respected competitor or group of competitors as is commonly done in benchmarking. An interesting aspect of benchmarking is to look at the competitive strategic alliance actions and licensing policies of competitors. If you look at what a competitor is doing with regard to the technology that it is licensing or the strategic alliances in which it is embarking, it is a very clear symbol of its plans, goals, and objectives and how it is positioning itself for the future game. Such an analysis can be instrumental in helping to focus your definition on the shape of the future game and also get a glimpse at what the competitors of the future game will possess in the way of the technology know-how, alliance strengths, and core competencies. The reason to focus on licenses, especially in the case of an exclusive license, is that the technology transfer represents a type of strategic alliance because the exclusive licensor has allied itself with the exclusive licensee.

Benchmarking should not dominate gap analysis. Care must be taken not to emulate the companies perceived to be setting the standards. In defining the future game and the future winner, no standards yet exist. Your implementation of steps one and two of the analysis are to set the standards. Benchmarking allows *others* to set the standards, and that is not the goal of gap analysis. Use benchmarking as a *tool* in helping to define the future winner, but not as the compass by which to guide your company.

### (e) Current Assessment

The third step in the process is to critically analyze your current situation at the present time with regard to all of the characteristics that will be important for winning the future game. The comparison between the core competencies that are possessed by the theoretical winner and those currently possessed today clearly identifies the gaps and identifies everything that must be done or obtained to fill the gaps in order to be the theoretical winner of the future gain.

### (f) Filling the Gaps

While the options for filling the gaps can be many, licensing of the technology that will be needed is certainly a key option. Licensing strategies dominate this book but other gap-filling methods are available. Additional options can include mergers and acquisitions, joint ventures, minority interests in third-party companies, strategic alliances, cross-licensing, hiring the technical people needed to develop the missing technology, consultants, and contractors.

### (i) Beyond Licensing

Some of the options for filling the gaps include:

- Direct licensing of the needed technology in exchange for a royalty payment
- Cross-licensing of patent portfolios to obtain the required technology
- Acquisition of companies possessing or likely to possess the technology will be needed in the future
- Strategic alliances
- Research grants and alliances with research institutions and universities
- Contracting for technology development with private companies
- Contracting for technology development with individuals as consultants
- Adding technical staff with the expertise needed to fill gaps
- Minority ownership interests in companies possessing the needed expertise

Regardless of how deficiencies are filled, gap analysis is a method for finding the intellectual property that will be needed in the future. The map shows what you have and the *gap* shows what you need. The entire process does not need to be completed before benefits are realized. Just defining the future game can yield important information about a company's future.

\* \* \*

---

# Maneuvering Through M & A*

Lawrence W. Sonsini, Michael Barclay, and David Berger
*Intellectual Property Magazine* (Spring 1995)
at www.ipmag.com/spring95.html

\* \* \*

One of the most important issues facing an acquirer looking to purchase technology is whether the target company owns or has exclusive rights to the technology being acquired. Resolving this issue can be accomplished by taking the following steps:

— *Trace the chain of title of each piece of intellectual property.* This involves a bit of detective work. First, ascertain the identity of all of the inventors and/or key developers of every product that will be acquired. Second, determine whether each inventor signed an employment, confidential information, and invention of assignment agreement. Such an agreement clarifies ownership of the employee's inventions by requiring the employee to disclose any prior inventions that the employee may have made before joining the target company, and obligates the employee to assign all inventions developed during the employment period to the company. If there is any gap in the chain of title between the invention of the intellectual property and the target company, the target company will need to take steps to have the inventor assign rights to the company. Third, examine whether the assignment of the intellectual property was properly recorded. This can include a patent and/or copyright search to ensure that the target owns the intellectual property that is being acquired. Finally, conduct a UCC search and review all key agreements to determine if any third parties have security interests in the intellectual property to be transferred. If any security interest is located, it may be necessary to obtain that party's consent to an assignment before or as part of an acquisition.

---

\* Reprinted with permission of the publisher, copyright 1995.

*—Obtain a list of all employees of the target company.* Ask whether those employees have signed an employment, confidential information, and invention-assignment agreement, and ask to review these agreements. While every employee may not be an inventor, every employee should have agreed that all information will remain confidential and that any inventions are the property of the employer.

The acquirer may find out after the deal has gone through that another employee had a hand in the creation of some piece of intellectual property and that employee may later try to make a claim against the company. In addition to analyzing the status of each of the inventors of the target company, it is also important to look at whether any employees have had any conflicts with former employers that could impact the employee's rights to assign his inventions to the present employer. The acquirer may also want specialized agreements concerning the technology at issue with the key developers from the target company.

＊ ＊ ＊

# III. The Role of Audits in Corporate Strategy

## The New Role of Intellectual Property in Commercial Transactions*

Melvin Simensky & Lanning G. Bryer, pp. 309–13 (1994)

＊ ＊ ＊

**Identifying and Protecting the Rights.** The intellectual property specialist first must identify the relevant intellectual property rights being used by the business to be transferred. To be as thorough as possible, it is helpful to have the complete cooperation of both parties, including their employees, who are often the most knowledgeable about the intellectual property rights at issue. This involves conducting an "intellectual property audit." The audit identifies all intellectual property rights being used by the business, ensuring that they are properly owned, registered, and licensed by the business, and that they are being used and protected properly. Proper use is particularly important for use-dependent rights in assets such as trademarks, tradenames, know-how, and confidential information, whose continued existence in law depends on proper procedures being followed to ensure protectability.

The specialist begins by preparing a list of questions to be asked of both parties in an attempt to elicit as much information about potential intellectual property rights as possible. The questions should be written in plain, everyday language to allow a full appreciation of the breadth of what is being sought.

＊ ＊ ＊

The purchaser's own information on the listed intellectual property rights may be a good starting point and, for some limited forms of transactions, may be all that is necessary. More likely, however, there will be a need for much greater detail, which can be obtained only from the vendor. It is best for the intellectual property specialist to visit

---

* Reprinted with permission of the publisher, copyright 1994.

the business premises and physically inspect the premises, plant, personnel, and products in order to gain a good understanding of the intellectual property rights involved in the business. The investigation begins at the front door, the specialist noting the trade name and any design used, and continues through all aspects of manufacturing, marketing, and distribution. The following is a generic list of some of the subject matter for inspection:

- Products and services
- Product components, ingredients and raw materials
- Manufacturing and packaging processes
- Manufacturing and packaging equipment
- Product design, components, shape, configuration
- Software (manufacturing and administrative)
- Packaging, containers, labeling
- Business and trade names, trademarks, trade dress
- Advertising and marketing materials
- Channels of trade: marketing, distribution and retailing relationships
- Business information, data, opportunities
- Research and development (product, process, packaging and marketing)
- Key employees in research, design, manufacturing, distribution and sales
- Employee relationships and agreements
- Third-party licenses, agreements, permissions, relationships
- Restrictions through financing and security
- Affiliated company interdependence (rights, technical support, licenses)
- Management and administrative support systems

**Ownership/Title.** A skeleton list of the intellectual property owned, registered, used, and licensed by the business can now be created. The blanks can be filled in through government searches and further inquiries with a view to creating a complete and accurate summary of the business's intellectual property portfolio. Investigations as to the title and/or codification of each identified right follow, along with searches to identify any security interests registered against the rights, contractual rights, and obligations affecting the rights and the existence and extent of any licenses, permissions, and entitlements. The unnerving aspect of this part of the transaction, for both lawyer and client, is the realization that despite the enormous cost of intellectual property, it is generally impossible to guarantee proper title and what, if any, encumbrances exist.

*(i)    Root of Title.* The root of title refers to the original legal and equitable basis upon which the right is owned. Whether the vendor has title to the right being sold, financed, or licensed is of paramount importance. Discovering the root of title is the goal of most intellectual property lawyers involved in a due diligence inquiry. To establish with any degree of certainty the root of title and to trace the proper assignment of the right to the vendor goes a long way toward assuring that proper title is being acquired by the purchasers.

Ascertaining the root of title with absolute certainty is a difficult task, which depends on the nature of intellectual property right involved. For example, copyright is solely a creature of statute in most countries around the world. However, in many countries registration of copyright is voluntary and protection arises automatically. In some countries, copyright assignments may be registered without the original right ever having been registered, creating a registered index that is misleading to those not in the know. It is important to identify the original author/creator of a copyright, as all rights belong to this person unless assigned in writing or by operation of law (employment). Even when the basic title to a copyright has been assigned to the vendor, not all ancillary rights may have been assigned. Some rights may have been retained by the original owner, or may never have been owned by the author, or have reverted back to the author by contract or operation of law. In many countries the author retains moral rights in a copyright that can never be assigned. These issues with respect to ownership are particularly difficult for copyright. Nevertheless, most other intellectual property rights have their own peculiarities with respect to ownership and title, which vary from country to country.

*(ii)   Assignments, Licenses, and Permissions.* Uncovering the root of title is only the first step. Next, the purchaser will require an assurance or proof that the right has been properly assigned to the vendor and that the vendor has not assigned or licensed part or some or all the right to third parties. Tracing effective assignments, licenses, and permissions of intellectual property rights is also a difficult task. There is no mandatory filing of assignments or licenses for any of the intellectual property rights in many countries, making it virtually impossible to ensure that the right in question has not already been assigned or licensed. As with ownership and title, the purchaser must ultimately rely on the representations and warranties of the vendor that the whole of the right is being transferred, unencumbered by any third-party rights or entitlements.

*(iii) Security Interests.* Intellectual property rights are today being pledged as security more than ever because of their increased importance and value to business. Unfortunately, in many jurisdictions the laws regarding security interests in intellectual property are as yet undeveloped, and there are still many concerns regarding pledging, registering, and enforcing such interests. Given the fundamental impact that a security agreement may have on the transfer of an intellectual property right, it is important when purchasing such property to conduct thorough searches for security interests. In some jurisdictions it is necessary to conduct searches under special financing and security interest legislation, as well as searches of the relevant intellectual property registers. A review of relevant financing and security interest agreements is also important. Ultimately, however, consultation with an expert in each jurisdiction is essential to determine the extent to which the vendor's intellectual property rights may be affected by security interests.

* * *

---

# Internal IP Audits Reveal Overlooked Possibilities: Audits Can Help Corporations Identify Which Inventions Would Be Most Profitable to Patent*

Arthur R. Whale<br>12 Nat'l L.J. (June 16, 1997) at C12

The Internal Revenue Service has given audits a bad name, but in the field of intellectual property, audits are more rewarding for the auditee. Nevertheless, these audits get surprisingly little attention. A test of need is whether a company, in the course of its business, originates or improves products, processes or methods of using products, knowledge of which would be of value to a competitor—or to a noncompetitor who might pay for access to the technology for other uses.

The intellectual property portion of a due diligence audit is usually associated with legal status and ownership of intellectual property in such transactions as acquisitions, mergers, joint ventures and technology transfers. But another audit that is useful to perform is that of internal corporate management of inventions. When competently and comprehensively done—usually by an outside attorney—it carries a high probability of uncovering overlooked opportunities for protecting investment in and proactively capitalizing on inventive efforts.

The nature and extent of periodic intellectual property audits depends in part on the magnitude of the company's developmental activities, competitive marketing environment and the existence or currency of its inventions management program. A starting premise is that all inventions of foreseeable importance to the company or its competitors should be considered for patenting, but not all patentable inventions should be patented. A key element of the audit is examination of procedures for maximizing enforceable protection of homegrown technology.

It is first important to examine or establish patenting policies. A company's interest in patenting may be primarily to permit it to use its own technology (defensive patenting). Alternatively, the company may seek broader patenting, either to pre-empt competitors from achieving the innovator's objectives by slightly different routes, or to provide an income flow through licensing (offensive patenting).

While narrow patents may serve today's purposes, a broader approach to patenting builds a larger foundation of protection that could provide more flexibility in addressing changing competitive conditions. The patenting policy should also anticipate the prospect of the company dropping interest in a discrete block of technology that, suitably covered by patents, could be attractive for selling, licensing or trading.

## Identifying Inventions to Patent

In the corporate context, identification of inventions for the inventions management inventory requires informed cooperation of the technical staffs. The differing nature of work emanating from research, development and production people should be recognized in designing details of their participation in harvesting inventions for consideration by the selection group. This is most efficiently accomplished by use of forms to facilitate disclosure and review of information necessary to the filing decision.

The costs of patenting may be difficult to predict, depending on the invention's complexity and its proximity to the prior art in the field. The cost of obtaining individual patents or even blanket coverage of a significant block of technology, however, usually pales in comparison with income prospects from a single, successful, protected product, process or use invention.

Depending on the corporate size and structure, a committee approach of members with diverse but relevant backgrounds can bring needed insights to value-based selection of inventions for patenting. Ideally, this group, meeting regularly, should include

---

* Reprinted with permission of the publisher, copyright 1997.

research, manufacturing, marketing and legal representatives and, as appropriate, the inventor, all forearmed with information and evaluations on agenda items. An audit affords an opportunity to assess the adequacy and efficiencies of these practices and to consider suggestions for improvement from the outside auditor.

Inventors start the engine of technology protection. It is vitally important that they and all others engaged in developing technology understand and follow rules for legally sufficient records of events, procedures performed and results of developmental work. These technologists may some day face challenges to the accuracy or adequacy of records and recollections in inventorship, infringement, validity or trade secret disputes.

Maintaining proper records is a high priority item for an audit. Under scrutiny would be notebooks of inventors and co-workers on projects and formalities for their maintenance, validation of entries, contemporaneity of their records and cross references to other records—all combining to create an unbroken paper trail often critical in patent prosecution and dispute resolution.

In order to protect technology against public disclosure that would bar patenting, it may be advisable to establish rules for review and possibly delay proposed publications. This review should include consideration not only of patenting but also of maintenance of the technology as a trade secret, for publication can erase the opportunity for both.

Finally, inherent in the decision to file patent applications is where to file them. The attorney should be prepared, as part of his or her contribution to the selection process, to advise on the timing and prospects for patenting in those countries where marketing factors suggest coverage would be desirable. The need for better information on costs, procedures and enforceability of foreign patents may surface in an audit.

\* \* \*

### Treatment of Trade Secrets

An audit can identify elements of an inventions management program that may be important in resolving or avoiding disputes with employees, former employees and consultants. Employee agreements are important to review to make sure they continue to be relevant, comply with the law and cover new employer-employee problems on the horizon. If there is no agreement, the advantages and disadvantages of instituting an agreement with current or future employees should be considered as part of an audit.

The most frequent provisions for debate are the obligations to refrain from subsequent competing employment and to maintain confidentiality of the company's trade secrets.

New employees should know they are expected to honor their obligations of confidence to former employers. State laws usually govern the duration of confidentiality and noncompete provisions.

Consulting agreements can raise the same problems but usually require different treatment. Consultants may have access to the company's trade secrets and also contribute information that is to be owned by the company. Consulting relationships can produce rights and obligations that should be anticipated and addressed before work begins.

The identification, protection and disposition of trade secrets, since they are intellectual property assets, should be included in a patent audit. The subject of trade secrets pervades many aspects of patenting, as seen above. Indeed, technology that is to be patented exists as a trade secret from its inception through the issuance of the patent; and, if no patent is granted, the application continues to be held in secrecy by the patent office. [An exception exists today: U.S. patent applications with foreign counterparts are published eighteen months after their priority dates. *See* 35 U.S.C. § 122(b).]

\* \* \*

An audit should examine the protection afforded trade secrets, the handling of trade secrets licensed or received from other parties and the physical measures for their protection. Among protective measures are provisions for access by authorized parties and making areas or equipment with visible trade secrets out of bounds for visitors and other unauthorized personnel.

\* \* \*

---

# The Intellectual Property Inventory: Why Do It?*
### Katherine C. Spelman & John J. Moss
### 429 PLI/PAT. 255, 257–59 (1996)

\* \* \*

An intellectual property inventory is not a uniform, off-the-shelf procedure, but comes in many varieties. Therefore, when considering an intellectual property inventory, a company must consider its particular needs and resources. One company's reasons and methods of conducting an intellectual property inventory may not be suitable for another.

An inventory should (1) address a specific set of purposes tailored to the company, and (2) provide the information required to achieve those purposes at the lowest possible cost. Designing such an inventory is best done as a joint effort among the employees who are best acquainted with the company's intellectual property assets, the employees responsible for the company's offensive and defensive strategy, and the intellectual property lawyers. This combined personnel effort results in simple efficiency. Managers of the company typically know the intellectual property assets best and can most effectively collect information. The intellectual property attorneys can assist in directing the collection and analysis of that information. Upper-level officers of the corporation are best suited to assess the offensive and defensive uses of the assets once quantified and categorized.

## Collecting Information

After the design of the intellectual property inventory is established, documents and information need to be collected. The documents include licenses, R&D, employee confidentiality, employee inventions, and independent contractor agreements, as well as patent, copyright, and trademark applications.

If a company has trade secrets, those secrets must be identified, quantified, and kept confidential. Any intellectual property inventory which includes a trade secret assessment should specify what information is meant to be kept secret and what secrecy measures are to be taken. It should include policies and procedures for maintaining secrecy and/or reevaluating regularly the need for secrecy.

---

* Reprinted with permission of the publisher, copyright 1996.

Trade secrets are often a company's most valuable, and most overlooked, intellectual property. Rights in trade secrets are easily lost if a company does not vigilantly enforce the secrecy of such information through clear policies and procedures.

Once all of the information on a company's intellectual property assets is collected, it should be entered into a database. A typical database resulting from an intellectual property inventory of applications, registrations, trade secrets, on a worldwide basis, usually includes:

- Client/owner of the asset;
- Title or name of the trademark, invention, copyright, or trademark;
- Particular country in which the asset is valid;
- Filing date/first use date or date of creation;
- Inventors, authors;
- Prior owner and how acquired (if any);
- Patent, trademark, or copyright registration number;
- Issue date;
- Renewal date; and
- Any other pending dates by which action must be taken (i.e., Office actions, annuity [and maintenance] payments).

In addition to this brief profile of each asset, the company should keep a separate paper or computer file containing documentation on the history of each asset, such as:

- Copies of all assignments or other transfer documents;
- In the case of trademarks, indicia of good will;
- In the case of patents, prior art statements;
- Foreign filing licenses;
- In the case of trademarks, registered user agreements; and
- Office actions, responses and prior art.

Having documented the existence and parameters of the assets with regard to each relevant country, the company should review each asset as it relates to the revenues from and anticipated growth of major product or service lines. For example, with regard to patents, this market-related analysis would include:

- A more detailed prior art analysis;
- Details about conception and reduction to practice;
- Review of the invention disclosure;
- A discussion of what elements were abandoned in prosecution and why;
- An evaluation as to the sufficiency of the full chain of title;
- Copies of all opinions of counsel relevant to that patent;
- A review of existing, pending, and attempted licenses;
- An in-depth review of all litigation;
- A discussion of the technology, history, and market position of the competitors;
- Copies of all infringement studies; and

- Discussions and projections of all existing commercial applications and usage at R&D facilities.

As can be seen, intellectual property inventories begin by focusing on the microcosm of the particular asset. The analysis then moves, on a country-by-country basis, to the macrocosm of the asset in relation to the corporation, the particular product/service line, and the larger market.

### Examining Larger Goals and Relationships with Other Companies

The most thorough intellectual property inventories include two further layers. The first is an evaluation of how the assets fit into the larger goals, policies, and procedures of the company. Intellectual properties are both "means" and "ends" in and of themselves. The earlier stage of the intellectual property inventory evaluated the assets themselves as an end, focusing on the strength and protection of each asset. This stage considers the assets in the context of the entire company.

One example is the role of employee hire and exit procedures (including training and continuing education) in substantiating trade secrets. A company creating a new product (e.g., an R&D facility), should ask whether systems are in place to clear conflicts, create proper lab notebooks and conduct trademark searches. Companies purchasing large quantities of customized and specifically ordered products should determine whether and how the third party involved is keeping the customizations and particular specifications secret.

Another analysis in this layer of the inventory should be how all intellectual property assets are identified and recognized. The nurturing of creativity is a fragile and unpredictable part of any company's business. A thorough intellectual property inventory should include measures by which the company reviews all burgeoning and extant assets to decide whether to pursue or abandon projects and assets, and whether to engage particular inventors.

The final layer of a thorough intellectual property inventory is a study of the company's relationships with others. For instance, if a company is considering a joint venture with another company, it is important to understand what assets exist before ideas and assets are shared. It will also be important to clarify how ownership of the assets created in the joint effort is to be handled.

Understanding competitors is also vital to an effective positioning of a company's assets. This layer of the analysis should consider the globalization and development of the company's technology in ways that maximize its ability to compete. Specific issues might include:

- Competitive developments;
- Projections about obsolescence, products going off patent, and alternative modes of protection;
- Foreign markets;
- How to address future obligations.

### Unique Issues to Consider

Every company will have unique issues that will need to be identified and addressed. An intellectual property inventory is analogous to a person's annual physical exam. It will differ for each company depending on its maturity and health.

The analysis of a company's intellectual property inventory can vary sharply with changes in the rules governing the protectability of particular intellectual property assets. For instance, in *Feist Publications v. Rural Telephone Service Co.*, 111 S. Ct. 1282 (1991), the U.S. Supreme Court held that "mere compilations of fact" were not copyrightable. This decision dramatically affected the assets of telephone companies, database service companies, university alumni organizations that sell mailing lists, companies that produce white pages and other directory listings, and companies whose business includes road maps or other factually related maps. Such companies have been forced to rethink their strategies for asset conception and protection.

Another dramatic example was a Supreme Court case clarifying the definition of "work made-for-hire" under the Copyright Act. In *Community for Creative Non-Violence v. Reid*, 490 U.S. 730 (1989), the Court held that independent consultants generally own all works created for the contracting company. Most companies, by contrast, expect to be the owners of works they commission whether those works are computer programs, manuals, or architectural designs. An audit can ensure that the company obtains copyright assignments from independent contractors, fulfilling the companies' expectations of total ownership.

A company may lose its intellectual property assets not only through changes in the law but also under current laws governing term and forfeiture. Rights may be lost through failure to pursue infringers. Trademarks may be lost through improper usage. Trademark registrations may be cancelled for failure to file specific affidavits between the fifth and sixth year after registration.

Intellectual property assets may also be lost by failing to comply with specific rules governing intellectual property contracts. A patent may become unenforceable if the royalty provisions of a patent license are improperly structured.

Recently, a company's contracts resulted in its copyright being held unenforceable. In the case of *Lasercomb America v. Reynolds*, 911 F.2d 970 (1990), the court held that a company improperly used its copyrights to extend its market power beyond the scope of the copyright. As a consequence, the court denied the company's efforts to enforce the copyright against infringers. The court said that the copyright could be enforced only after all the defective licenses had been redrafted. [For analysis of this and other decisions involving "copyright misuse," see JAY DRAFTER, JR. LICENSING OF INTELLECTUAL PROPERTY § 5.04[3], [5] (Law Journal Press 1994 & Supps.)]

## Conclusion

Once a comprehensive and thorough intellectual property inventory is performed, the costs of maintaining and updating it usually decline. Companies that engage in routine intellectual property inventories will ultimately save more resources than those which conduct inventories only upon capital infusions or transfers of corporate ownership. Moreover, whereas event-triggered intellectual property inventories tend to benefit only one aspect of a company, regular intellectual property inventories benefit the company's entire infrastructure.

An intellectual property inventory can also serve as an important tool in connection with an analysis of intracompany transfer pricing for income tax purposes. Although income tax transfer pricing issues concerning intellectual property are beyond the scope of this article, we note that there can be significant adverse U.S. tax consequences associated with the sharing of intellectual property on a non-arm's length basis among affiliated multinational corporations. In our experience, these types of tax problems can be reduced if multinational corporations identify the legal owner of valuable intellectual property and the extent to which intellectual property is assigned, licensed or otherwise shared within a multinational group. By carefully tracking such items, it is often easier to develop appropriate compensation arrangements within the multinational group in connection with the utilization of intellectual property.

Increasingly, intellectual property is the lifeblood of major corporations. Taking inventory of and tracking these intangible, but vital, assets are becoming an essential part of managing a large business.

\* \* \*

# IV. Results of the Audit

## Acquiring and Protecting Technology: The Intellectual Property Audit\*
David L. Hayes
8 COMPUTER LAW. 1 (1991)

\* \* \*

### Written Report of Results of the Audit

If the circumstances are such that a written report will be privileged and not discoverable, the results of an intellectual property audit should normally be memorialized in a report. The report should discuss the development history of the technology at issue, describe and evaluate intellectual property defects uncovered in the audit, propose and describe specific remedial action that needs to be taken or that has been taken, and respond to any other specific need for information the parties commissioning the audit may have.

If the audit was conducted in the context of an acquisition transaction, the report should provide the information necessary to decide whether the rights available are the rights required by the acquiring party, and should provide a basis for valuing the rights to be acquired. Necessary remedial action can be implemented either before the transaction is consummated or after the acquisition (with appropriate adjustments in the purchase price to reflect the risks or cost of the cure).

### Remedial Action

The audit may reveal the need for any of a number of forms of remedial action to cure deficiencies in intellectual property ownership or protection procedures:

### Federal and State Filings

The audit may uncover areas of intellectual property that have not been protected by appropriate federal filings, which should be made promptly. For example, patent protection may be available for certain aspects of the technology at issue, and the costs and

\* Reprinted with permission of the publisher, copyright 1991.

benefits of filing for such protection should be assessed. Copyright and trademark registration applications may need to be filed. Affidavits of continued use of trademarks may need to be filed, and payment of maintenance fees for issued patents may need to be made. Applications for renewal of copyright for works created before January 1, 1978 may need to be filed.

Recordation of transfers, exclusive licenses and other incidents of ownership may need to be filed with the appropriate federal and state offices. Security interests in intellectual property may not have been perfected properly, and the necessary state and federal filings may need to be done.

The audit may reveal the need to institute systematic procedures that ensure the appropriate federal filings are made as a matter of course in a timely manner as future products are created in which intellectual property rights may vest. A patent evaluation committee may need to be created to assess new technology for patentability and to decide in each instance whether patent applications should be filed based upon a cost/benefit analysis.

## Ownership Issues

Defects in title to intellectual property may have to be cured. Assignments of ownership from consultants may need to be secured and recorded with the appropriate federal agencies. Alternatively, quitclaim deeds may be obtained from an alleged author or inventor. In some instances an employee may have developed an invention incorporated into a company product on his or her own time, and rights to the invention may need to be secured.

The audit may reveal deficiencies in license rights from third parties to make derivative works that incorporate elements of works owned by such third parties. Absent sufficient license rights, there will be a cloud on the title of the derivative work the company has created.

The audit may reveal third parties who may be able to claim joint ownership with the company of the property and who, by virtue of such joint ownership, will be free to exploit the property themselves without the permission of the company. The joint owner's rights may need to be bought out. If the joint ownership concerns a copyright, the law will imply a duty of accounting of profits to the other joint owner from the exploitation of the joint work by the company. If the company does not desire to buy out the rights of the joint owner, a written agreement may be needed in which the joint owners agree that neither shall have a duty of accounting of profits to the other as a result of exploitation of the copyrighted work.

Potential defects discovered in patents may need to be remedied by additional disclosures to the patent office, requests for reexamination of a patent, filing a reissue application, amendments to pending applications, or a certificate of correction. Errors in copyright registration certificates may need to be corrected by filing supplementary copyright registrations. Errors in trademark applications may need to be similarly corrected.

The audit may reveal the need to cure omissions of copyright, trademark or patent notices. Systematic procedures may need to be set up to ensure that the proper proprietary rights notices—including notices required by the Federal Acquisition Regulations and the various supplements thereto to preserve rights vis-à-vis the federal government—are used in the future.

## Infringement Issues

If the audit reveals potential infringement of third party rights, licenses may be sought or the product at issue may be redesigned, if possible, to "invent around" a patent that covers the product, to remove technology that may be the trade secret of another, or to eliminate substantial similarity to the copyrighted work of another.

If it appears likely from the audit that consummation of a proposed acquisition will precipitate a lawsuit, it may be possible to obtain a partial or complete indemnification from the present owner or a third party. Purchaser control of any potential lawsuit might also be sought during the negotiations.

The audit may reveal areas of particular risk in which a "clean room" development should be used to develop a new product or portion thereof. Alternatively, if clean room procedures were used and the audit reveals defects in such procedures, portions of the product may need to be redeveloped, or a detailed examination of the resulting product may need to be made to determine whether there is substantial similarity to the product of another. Missing or inadequate affidavits from the clean room participants may need to be remedied.

## Other Issues

If the future value of a product depends heavily on retaining certain key personnel, some potential problems can be avoided by developing contractual or other incentives for such personnel to stay on. If the principals or key employees will not remain with the company after an acquisition, then consulting agreements, nondisclosure agreements or covenants not to compete (in states in which such covenants are enforceable) may lessen the severity of their departure. If there are important contracts preventing the assignment of key rights, it may be possible to secure the consent of all involved.

Prospective legal, marketing and R&D strategies can be designed to minimize the exposure from defects discovered in the audit. For instance, if an early version of a software product is in the public domain and cannot be copyrighted, future exposure may be reduced by immediately registering later versions. Key areas of technology for which patent protection might have been sought but was not can be bolstered by filing patents on improvements to such technology.

* * *

---

# Notes & Questions

1. *The Importance of Contracts.* Contracts are a critical source of information when evaluating a company's intellectual property. Key contracts include employee and third-party non-disclosure agreements, inventor assignments, copyright releases and permissions, licenses, R&D agreements, contracts with outside contractors and consultants, and supplier and distribution agreements. These may contain terms that affect rights in intellectual property.

All agreements should be carefully reviewed to insure that software developers, consultants, and suppliers have fully assigned their rights in any intellectual property developed and delivered under contract. Software and digital media can be especially troublesome to audit since they may have many individual authors (who may not even be employees of either party), and companies often mistakenly believe that they acquire title to software simply by having contracted and paid for it.

Expired or terminated contracts should be scrutinized. For example, an auditor should be wary of the following clauses: license grants, (non)exclusivity, (non)transferability, territory, term, confidentiality, ownership, warranty, indemnification, liability, escrow provisions, and equitable relief. *See* John F. Pinheiro, *Conducting the Intellectual Property Audit for Contractual Matters*, 429 PLI/PAT. 345 (1996).

3. *Auditing Trade Secrets.* As explained above, trade secrets include any information having economic value and for which the owner made "efforts which are reasonable under the circumstances to maintain secrecy." What does this mean to an auditor? At the very least, an auditor will have to become aware of customary practices in the company's industry. What is reasonable in the defense and semiconductor industries may be considered excessive and unnecessary in the office supply industry. What constitutes reasonable security? Is it contractual (e.g. employee or supplier non-disclosure agreements)? Physical (cameras and firewalls)? Documented policies and procedures? Can it be unwritten and cultural? An auditor must not only verify that security systems are in place and working, but also not compromise trade secrets in the process. *See* Jeffrey Anne Tatum & D. Peter Harvey, *Trade Secret Audits: Risks of Loss and Strategies for Protection*, 429 PLI/PAT. 383 (1996).

4. *Auditing Patents.* Auditing research and development operations and patent processes are crucial for any company whose business is built upon patented technology. Auditing can clarify inventorship, potential on-sale bar problems, and other matters affecting patent validity. Company policies and procedures should cover lab notebooks, confidentiality, and preparing invention disclosure forms. Schedules of all issued patents should be kept to ensure that maintenance and annuity fees are paid on time. Auditing also guards against duplication of other patents. For example, the company's patent record should be searched prior to filing a patent application. Finally, an audit can help determine a licensee's rights to continue using licensed technology in the event the licensor files for bankruptcy. *See, infra,* Chapter 13. Many companies have adopted an in-house patent committee to meet regularly to address these issues. *See* Don W. Martens, *Conducting the Intellectual Property Audit for Patents*, 429 PLI/PAT. 147 (1996).

5. *Auditing Trademarks.* While auditing trademarks may be one of the simplest tasks in the intellectual property audit, one must be careful not to overlook the obvious. For example, all trademarks should be docketed to ensure the foreign filings, Section 8 and 15 and renewal dates are met. Trademark licenses must have provisions allowing the trademark owner to control the quality of the product. As with patents, licensor indemnification agreements should be obtained before using a licensed trademark and searches should always be conducted prior to using new trademarks.

6. *Audits in Cyberspace.* The growth of e-business dictates that an intellectual property audit include the contents of web servers and workstations. Company web sites can contain hundreds of intellectual properties, including both proprietary and licensed software, video and audio clips, photos, graphics and images, text, trademarks, domain names, business methods, and databases. Software and methods of doing business may be patented or patentable. Source code behind a firewall may be protected by trade secret law. Digital copyright licensing is unsettled, as can be seen from three recent cases that have sent licensees scurrying to review older copyright licenses. *See Random House,*

*Inc., v. Rosetta Books, LLC*, 150 F. Supp. 2d 613 (S.D.N.Y. 2001) (exclusive right to distribute in "book form" does not extend to Internet publication); *New York Times Co., Inc. v. Tasini*, 533 U.S. 483, 121 S. Ct. 2381, 150 L. Ed. 2d 500, 69 USLW 4567 (2001) (authors may derive additional royalties from unlicensed electronic publication of their work); *The Rogers & Hammerstein Org. v. UMG Recordings, Inc.*, 60 U.S.P.Q.2d 1354 (S.D.N.Y. 2001) (standard mechanical rights license or compulsory license for public broadcasts does not include streaming over the Internet). *See* also Bruce P. Keller, *Conducting Intellectual Property Audits in Cyberspace*, 429 PLI/PAT. 483 (1996).

7. *Approaching the Client.* Consider how you would convince a client that it is worthwhile to spend $10,000 or more on a company-wide intellectual property audit.

8. *"IP Wasting" Liability.* Although no cases have yet been reported, a new potential cause of action has emerged known as "IP wasting." "IP wasting" occurs when corporate executives fail to maximize the value of their company's intellectual property portfolios. However, some claim that "IP wasting" is simply a scare tactic promoted by consulting firms trying to make inroads into the intellectual property audit business traditionally occupied by attorneys. Do directors have an affirmative duty to manage an intellectual property portfolio in the manner most likely to earn the highest return possible? What profession is most qualified to conduct the audit? Is there any role in an intellectual property audit for accounting firms? Most major accounting firms have intellectual property practices that focus on intellectual asset management (IAM) and IP auditing. *See* Deanna Hodgin, *Lawyers, CPAs Sparring over IP Audit 'Market,'* at www.ipmag.com/monthly/99-jan/hodgin.html.

9. *Further Reading.* For more information on intellectual property audits, see Schlossberg, *Conducting the Intellectual Property Audit for Contractual and Antitrust Matters*, 429 PLI/PAT. 263 (1996); Christopher P. Bussert & Robert A. Rosenbloom, *Conducting the Intellectual Property Audit for Copyright*, 429 PLI/PAT. 31 (1996); Kathleen F. Tranelli & Nancy A. Zoubek, *Conducting a Trademark Audit*, 429 PLI/PAT. 235 (1996); Katherine C. Spelman & John J. Moss, *The Intellectual Property Inventory: Why Do It?*, 429 PLI/PAT. 255 (1996); D. Peter Harvey, *Structuring Employment Relationships to Insure Ownership and Control of Intellectual Property*, 403 PLI/PAT. 35 (1995).

10. *Audit vs. Due Diligence.* A company performs an intellectual property audit to map and use its resources, to increase return on research and development expenditures, to analyze its portfolio for licensing opportunities, to look at defensive assets in case of litigation, to cut costs of maintaining unused assets, and to minimize exposure to infringement claims on those unused assets. Information collected in the IP audit analysis then may be employed in conducting the due diligence process. Companies perform due diligence in preparation for assignment (e.g., a sale or donation of a patent) or licensing of intellectual property assets. The assignor/licensor should perform diligence to ensure it owns the intellectual property it intends to sell or license. The assignor/licensor's diligence report will eventually become a schedule or exhibit for the assignment/license document. The assignee/licensee should perform diligence to ensure that it will receive the intellectual property rights that it is paying for. The assignee/licensee's diligence report will help determine the level of representations and warranties, indemnification, and insurance that the assignee/licensee requests from the assignor/licensor.

Any intellectual property transaction between two parties requires that the parties perform some level of intellectual property due diligence. The level of diligence requires a cost/benefit analysis that measures the level of risk that the transaction poses to the parties against the value of the intellectual property in the transaction. Types of transactions especially dependent upon sound IP due diligence are mergers, acquisitions, intellectual property and software licenses, software development, web development, technology development, and service agreements.

Both parties will benefit from a mutual non-disclosure agreement (NDA), which permits sharing of each other's confidential information without jeopardizing the patentability of non-patented technology or public disclosure of trade secrets relevant to the transaction. *See Nilssen v. Motorola, infra,* for what happens when NDAs are not carefully followed.

If the seller/licensor is performing due diligence, the checklist for the internal intellectual property diligence should arguably be as comprehensive as that of the assignee/licensee. Further, the seller/licensor will want to interview individual authors/inventors to confirm that the authors/inventors did not use any third party materials in creating the subject intellectual property (e.g., materials downloaded from the Internet, materials from another company, materials disclosed to seller/licensor under an NDA). Even if a seller/licensor is offering the intellectual property "as is" (with no representations, warranties, or intellectual property indemnification provisions), the seller/licensor will want to mitigate exposure to third party infringement claims. The seller/licensor will also want to confirm that every author/inventor has signed an employment agreement incorporating assignment of all intellectual property created by that employee during the course of employment (or a similar assignment document).

Below is a fairly comprehensive checklist for conducting intellectual property due diligence. The level of diligence depends on the type of transaction, the size and complexity of the intellectual property portfolio involved, the exposure presented by the deal, and the value of the portfolio. A company that buys or licenses all of the assets of another company will probably want to ask for everything on this list. A seller/licensor of software code may only need to pull information that is relevant to the company's development of the code (e.g., get a copy of the code, interview authors to confirm authorship of the code, and secure valid assignments from authors). It is worth repeating that the parties should agree up front—or at least before signing a letter of intent—on the intellectual property involved in the transaction. Otherwise, the intellectual property due diligence can last a very long time and hold up, or even kill, the proposed transaction.

In addition to the following list, the party conducting diligence may want to conduct an Internet investigation for all aspects of intellectual property covered by the transaction. At the end of the day, the materials obtained in this list will affect the representation, warranties, enforcement obligations, definitions, indemnity, and insurance sections of the agreement covering the proposed transaction.

## Intellectual Property Due Diligence Checklist

Non-disclosure agreements

Names of all authors/inventors

Name and contact information for intellectual property counsel

Employment agreements for all authors and inventors

Independent contractor agreements

Assignments of inventions

Software contracts

Litigation materials (pleadings, settlement agreements, insurance policies, orders)

Web development/hosting contracts

Outsourcing agreements

Service agreements

Intellectual property licenses (outgoing, incoming, software, oral, implied) and assignments

Reassignment databases for security interests taken

Loan agreements secured by intellectual property

Patent investigations should include: applications and registrations, laboratory notebooks, any materials available for pending patent applications (including, possibly, other patents in the field of technology, infringement studies, or patent availability studies), interviews with individual inventors, visits to the development site, and verification of patent inventory with the filing authority.

Trademark investigations should include: applications and registrations, files associated with each application and registration, corresponding trademark searches (including, possibly, infringement/availability opinions), file wrappers for all identified applications and registrations, lists of common law marks, UDRP (domain name arbitration) filings and orders, Trademark Trial and Appeal Board pleadings and orders, specimens, and Internet searches.

Copyright investigations should include: all issued copyright registrations and associated work, web site materials, all documentation and publications, all software code, all notice provisions, verification with Copyright Office files.

Trade secret investigations should include: all employee handbooks and other materials that may contain company trade secret policies, documents containing trade secrets, on-site treatment of trade secrets, and litigation materials pertaining to trade secrets. When trade secrets are particularly important, the acquiring party may wish to visit the seller/licensor's site and observe and document all practical measures taken to preserve secrecy.

11. For more information on intellectual property due diligence, see Michael B. Lachuk & James R. Myers, *IP Due Diligence in Business Transactions:* Develop Your Plan Now, ACCA Docket 21 (No.1) 44 (January 2003); GARY M. LAWRENCE, DUE DILIGENCE IN BUSINESS TRANSACTION § 13 (2002); Judith L. Church, *Intellectual Property Aspects of Corporate Acquisitions*, 14 ALI-ABA 323 (2001); Chynthia Kahn, *Strategic Issues in the Analysis of Computer Software Involved in Mergers, Acquisitions, and Strategic Alliances*, 559 PLI/PAT. 29 (1999).

––––––––––

# Chapter 4

# Negotiating the License

## I. Introduction

Negotiating and closing a licensing deal—from inception through courtship and culminating in the execution of the definitive licensing agreement—is a complex and challenging task for the licensing attorney. In some situations, the attorney may be called upon to put together the entire deal—identifying and contacting prospects, helping to assess technology value, negotiating the terms, and drafting the agreement. To recognize good licensing opportunities and put together successful licensing deals requires some practical understanding of two key characteristics of licensing as a business strategy.

First, the drive to license in or out is not an isolated phenomenon or a fad. It is just one expression of U.S. industry's move toward cooperative arrangements—joint ventures, strategic partnerships, alliances, and other organizational models—in an era of increased global competition and the accelerating pace of technological innovation. Peter Drucker calls the trend toward alliances of this sort, based on partnership not ownership, the greatest change in corporate structure and the way business is being conducted today. *See* PETER DRUCKER, MANAGING IN A TIME OF GREAT CHANGE (1995). As the rising costs and risks of new product development and the sheer size of global markets drive the creation of such alliances, companies struggle to better structure and capitalize on these relationships and avoid being manipulated or plundered by their partners in the process. Thus, to understand and implement licensing strategy requires that the practitioner understand the business environment in which one's clients operate.

Second, licensing is not just a transaction, it is a relationship. The licensing attorney who approaches a licensing opportunity from the perspective of a fight for the largest piece of a fixed pie does a great disservice to the client. The licensing "pie" is still "unbaked" when the agreement is negotiated. How large the pie could become remains unknown and at risk. The best agreement will be one that maximizes the shared and complementary interests of the parties and creates sufficient mutual gain such that both will contribute their energies toward commercial success ("the big pie").

Thus, the process of identifying suitable prospects and putting together licensing deals and similar strategic arrangements is often and appropriately compared to dating, courtship, and marriage. Trust, flexibility, industriousness, reliability, and prudence are virtues highly valued in both types of relationships. Like marriage, a successful licensing relationship can last a very long time. Patent licenses are usually granted for the life of the patents—twenty years from the date of first filing the application. The relationship can last even longer in situations where the license is signed before patent applications are filed, or when patented follow-on improvements extend the scope of the license. It can last much longer when licenses involve other forms of intellectual property, such as copyright, which can endure for more than a century.

Drafting an agreement that will launch a long-term relationship presents difficult challenges. The parties may be doing business long after the individuals who negotiated and best understood the intent of the agreement are gone, after one or both companies have been bought, sold, or changed business focus, or after the economic climate has radically changed. Disputes are to be expected and mechanisms for prompt resolution with minimal damage must be included. The interests of both parties at some future time may be served by a substantial modification or adjustment of the terms. Good draftsmanship will include planning for future contingencies and the vagaries of future contract interpretations.

# II. The Parties

No commercial or corporate law practice today can afford to be unfamiliar with intellectual property licensing. From off-the-shelf retail software to complex information technology products such as supply chain management, customer relations management, and e-commerce, all computer programs are licensed. This chapter will focus on the more specialized and intensive role of counsel where intellectual property is created and licensed under a negotiated agreement. While licensees seem to fit into one broad category—businesses seeking new sources of products that can generate revenue—licensors may be individuals, universities, government agencies, non-profit foundations, or research institutions, as well as other companies.

## A. Licensors

Licensors range from passive—licensing only when courted by others—to aggressive, for whom licensing represents a significant part of their mission or profit strategy. There are even reluctant licensors, who offer licenses to infringers in the hope of avoiding costly litigation.

In a proactive licensing strategy, intellectual property owners seek out licensees to build new revenue streams and to maximize their return on R&D investments by "spinning off" technologies into other industries or geographical territories that they are not prepared to exploit fully themselves. Pro-active licensors also include the public and nonprofit sectors—universities, nonprofit research institutions, and federal laboratories—who must license out not only to gain revenue, but also to meet institutional missions and to comply with legislative mandates that dictate rapid technology transfer of federally funded inventions. An aggressive strategy may include publicizing available technologies and trademarks via trade publications, direct mail, or posting to an online patent exchange.

The Internet has revolutionized intellectual property marketing by making technical and business information quickly and cheaply accessible to a worldwide audience. Vast resources of information about companies and technologies are available through searchable online databases and company web sites. Numerous resources are devoted specifically to the interests of licensors and licensees.

As a result, negotiating with a potential licensee on the other side of the world has become almost as easy as it is with one across town. While the proliferation of information about far-flung opportunities increases the number of potential business partners, licensing remains an exceedingly complex undertaking. As new advances in information technology continue to accelerate the speed of interaction among businesses, attorneys will have to develop new tools and ways of doing business to help their clients secure and maintain competitive advantage.

## B. Licensees

There is no common profile for companies that license-in intellectual property. Today, both new and established companies license for a variety of reasons. For the established company, the decision to license in may be driven by the need to solve technical problems, increase productivity, lower costs, add new products and product lines, or generally keep ahead of the competition. The early 1990s saw the widespread down-sizing or disappearance of large scale industrial R&D operations in many major U.S. corporations. Instead, R&D has become project-based and out-sourced on a flexible, as-needed basis. Companies increasingly look to research universities as sources for new technologies, and compete with each other to gain preferential access to university labs, especially in biotechnology.

# III. The Structure and Elements of a Deal

Every license is different—the industry, the nature of intellectual property rights being licensed, the business culture and setting, even the personalities of the principals and their lawyers. These differences make it difficult to generalize about the dynamic structure of licensing deals and how agreements are actually concluded. An outline of a hypothetical licensing negotiation is described below. While this suggests a chronology and simplicity that may not always (or ever) exist in reality, it may help to illuminate overall strategy.

## A. A Technology or Trademark Attracts Potential Licensees

The initial contact between licensor and licensee may result from a licensor sending out inquires to players in the same industry or from a licensee actively investigating different technologies to complement or supplement its own. Typically, the initial contact begins with an exchange of non-confidential information, primarily a description of the technology, but also perhaps a copy of a company's annual report, an issued patent, a published scientific article, even a conversation between the inventor and someone from the company's technical staff. These all help the parties to determine whether there is a potential opportunity that should be further evaluated.

---

**Modulation of Multidrug Resistance by New Tropane
Alkaloid Aromatic Esters from Erythroxylum pervillei**

**Field:** Human Therapeutics, Cancer chemotherapy,

**Key Words:** Multi-drug resistance, MDR1 gene, Hollow fiber test, Cancer chemotherapy, Erythroxylum pervillei, Pervilleines, Tropane Alkaloid Aromatic Esters, Verapamil

**Stage of Development:** Animal model completed, National Cancer Institute funding

**Patent Status:** US and PCT patent applications filed

**Status:** Seeking Licensing Partner, exclusive and worldwide

**Background**
University researchers have investigated several thousand plants collected mainly in tropical areas, in a project directed toward discovery of new anti-cancer agents of natural origin. Of all of the plants investigated, a chloroform-soluble extract of the Madagascan plant, Erythroxylum pervillei Baill. (Erythroxylaceae) gave the most pronounced selective inhibitory activity for a multidrug-resistant human cancer cell line (KB-V1), assessed in the presence of the antineoplastic drug, vinblastine (VLB). Chromatographic fractionation, using this cell line to monitor purification, led to the isolation and structural characterization of nine tropane aromatic ester alkaloids. Seven of these compounds are new (this fact has recently been substantiated using an electronic database) and have been assigned the names "pervilleines A-F" and "pervilleine A N-oxide."

**New Discovery**
The pervilleines have been tested: in vitro cytotoxicity of these compounds in a human tumor cell panel; multidrug resistance inhibition in an ovarian cancer cell line; and in vitro multidrug resistance modulation in some cell lines available at the National Cancer Institute. The basic conclusions from these experiments are: several of the pervilleines showed substantial selectivity for a multidrug-resistant cell line (KB, oral epidermoid) in the presence at vinblastine at UIC; pervilleines B and C reversed drug resistance in a multidrug-resistant human ovarian adenocarcinoma (SKVLB) cell line with potency comparable to the acridone carboxamide multidrug resistance (MDR) modulator GR120918; pervilleines B-D and F exhibited comparable potency to verapamil and cyclosporin A in increasing the cytotoxicity of the standard substance (DINIB).

**References:**
Mi, Q.; Cui, B.; et al, *Cancer Res.* 2001, 61, 4030-4037.
Silva, G. L.; Cui B.; et al, *Nat. Prod.* 2001, 64, 1514-1520.

**Contact:** Daniel F. Marselle, Director, Pharmacy Intellectual Property, 312-996-6187, marselle@uic.edu

---

Above is an example of how licensable intellectual properties are posted on the Internet. The disclosure describes a new compound with cancer inhibiting properties. *See* A. Douglas Kinghorn, Resistance of New Tropane Alkaloid Aromatic Esters from *Erythroxylum pervillei* (technology reference, University of Illinois at Chicago) at www.research.uic.edu/techtransfer/available-technologies/cu20.pdf. Thumbnail sketches like this are commonly found at university web sites and in commercial databases.

## B. The Non-Disclosure Agreement

Upon an expression of interest by the licensee showing a desire for more detailed information from the licensor, the parties will negotiate a non-disclosure agreement

("NDA"). This agreement allows the receiving party (licensee) to get sufficiently detailed information to evaluate the utility of the technology and the strength of the intellectual property rights, while protecting the disclosing party (licensor) from theft of its proprietary know-how, trade secrets, business strategy, and patent-enabling information. Usually such agreements are reciprocal so that the licensor can also obtain sensitive information from the licensee about its financial health, technical capabilities, and marketing expertise.

Any information, regardless of the format in which it is fixed, can be designated as confidential—strategic plans, financial data, customer lists, market reports, policy and procedure manuals, and information relating to any processes, discoveries, technologies, or concepts that are not generally available to the public. It will be noted that such information also fits the definition of a trade secret or know-how. The term know-how is used broadly to describe

> all industrial information and data, including trade secrets. Protectable know-how (trade secrets) includes formulas, unpatented inventions and techniques, business and marketing plans intended for internal use, and all other intellectual property, not protected in other ways, that is particular and essential to the operation of the business. Unprotectable know-how (also sometimes referred to as *show-how*) includes everything else, such as consulting and other assistance given to licensees during the transfer of technology.

ROBERT C. MEGANTZ, HOW TO LICENSE TECHNOLOGY, 26 (1996).

Know-how can be protected only by the vigilance of its owner and thus is disclosed only where necessary and always under a non-disclosure agreement. While it can be protected indefinitely, once disclosed it can be freely used by others and even patented by them but only if they invented it (and did not derive their invention from the trade secret owner's work), and then only if they can prove they invented it *first*. A misappropriation, however, can deprive the rightful owner of the ability to obtain a patent. *See Evans Cooling Sy. v. General Motors*, 125 F.3d 1448 (Fed. Cir. 1997), *cert. denied*, 525 U.S. 115 (1998) (pirated technology offered for sale by defendant triggers on-sale bar, defeating true owner's later patent application). Also, disclosure of trade secrets may destroy foreign patent rights immediately, while in the U.S. § 102(b) preserves patent rights for one year.

The non-disclosure agreement supplies the protection without which formation of a commercial relationship involving intellectual property would be impossible. It assures that information disclosed by the parties will not become "public," both literally and within the meaning of patent and trade secret law, for a stated term of years or forever. Specifically, the agreement binds the parties, their agents, and employees in three ways: i) to use the designated information for proper purposes (usually evaluation only) and to protect it from unauthorized use, publication or disclosure; ii) to abstain from using the information to unfairly compete or obtain unfair advantage vis a vis the disclosing party; and iii) to restrict access to confidential information to those who require such access to effectuate the licensing arrangement and who themselves are bound by a confidentiality agreement with one of the parties. The receiving party may also be required to comply with any other reasonable security measures requested in writing by the disclosing party, such as returning documents, devices, prototypes, software, etc., to the disclosing party within a certain period of time and not retaining copies of them. Finally, the NDA may state the parties' agreement that irreparable harm would occur upon unauthorized disclosure, so that injunctive relief would be available to an aggrieved party.

There are three commonly recognized situations in which a receiving party will not be bound by its prior agreement to keep trade secrets or know-how confidential:

- The information is, or later becomes, public knowledge other than by breach of the agreement
- The information is already in the possession of the receiving party prior to its receipt from the disclosing party
- The information is independently received by the receiving party from a third party who has no duty of non-disclosure

Variations of these three standard exceptions are common. They may, for example, permit independent development of the information if properly documented.

With the signing of the non-disclosure agreement, more complete disclosure of the licensable technology and assessment of legal rights therein can occur. The prospective licensee can then research market opportunities, determine internal capacity to exploit the licensed subject matter, and project potential profits. The licensor can assess the licensee's potential capacity to fully exploit the market to be licensed, both geographically and by product niche.

Obviously, neither superior draftsmanship nor timely injunctive relief can guarantee that the receiving party will use confidential information properly and avoid damaging the disclosing party. For that reason, even with a signed agreement, the information disclosed should be limited to the minimum necessary to facilitate further negotiations. When negotiations break down after confidential information has already been disclosed, litigation is often the result. Without exercising due care in the drafting process, unintended results can occur. Consider the following cases.

---

# Ole K. Nilssen v. Motorola, Inc.

### 963 F. Supp. 664 (N.D. Ill. 1997)

SHADUR, Senior District Judge.

Ole Nilssen ("Nilssen") has brought suit against Motorola, Inc. and its subsidiary Motorola Lighting, Inc....("Motorola") in connection with Motorola's alleged theft of Nilssen's trade secrets before Motorola's 1989 entry into the electronic ballast industry. Nilssen asserts claims for (1) breach of confidential relationship, (2) theft of trade secrets under the Illinois Trade Secrets Act ("Act" or "Illinois Act," 765 ILCS 1065/1 to /9) and (3) quantum meruit/implied contract/unjust enrichment.

Both sides have now filed summary judgment motions under Rule 56, with Nilssen seeking partial summary judgment only as to liability (and not as to damages) and with Motorola asking for a total victory as a matter of law....For the reasons stated in this memorandum opinion and order, Motorola's motion is granted in part and denied in part, while Nilssen's motion is denied.

\* \* \*

## Background

Motorola is a leading manufacturer of electronic components and devices. Robert Galvin ("Galvin") was its Chief Executive Officer from 1959 to 1990. Galvin first learned of electronic ballast technology in the 1960s—at a time when that technology was not yet mature—and looked into the possibility of developing electronic ballasts as a new Motorola business every few years thereafter.

Nilssen, a former Motorola employee who was fired in 1972, was president and owner of Innovation Center, Inc. at all times relevant to this dispute. In a July 12, 1982 letter to Galvin, Nilssen first approached Motorola about possible business opportunities in the electronic ballast business in which Nilssen and Motorola might join forces. Galvin, interested in evaluating whether Nilssen had developed a technology that might finally allow Motorola to enter that industry, forwarded Nilssen's letter to Levy Katzir ("Katzir")—then Vice President and General Manager of Motorola's New Enterprises Group. Katzir and Nilssen then met on October 25, 1982, but that meeting was unproductive and the parties took no further action on any of Nilssen's proposals.

On February 7, 1986 Nilssen made a second pitch to Motorola...to suggest that he had "available for exclusive licensing proprietary technology that permits the development of electronic ballasts of substantially reduced cost as compared with the least costly of presently available electronic ballasts."...Nilssen met with several Motorola representatives on March 18..., and on March 22 he followed up with a letter...reiterating several of the key issues discussed at the March 18 meeting. That letter disclosed (1) Nilssen's understanding of the key accounts in the electronic ballast industry, (2) a bill of materials for Nilssen's prototype ballast, (3) Nilssen's figures regarding the expected cost savings and profitability from use of his ballast and (4) Nilssen's analysis of the energy savings to result from his technology.

Nilssen and Motorola officials met several more times in 1986, but ultimately Motorola again decided not to pursue the electronic ballast business.

\* \* \*

In mid-1987 Motorola's Group began another review of Nilssen's technology...[and] gave Phil Gunderson ("Gunderson")—then a Group Vice-President—one of Nilssen's earlier communications about electronic ballasts and asked him to "look into it"....[O]n September 4, 1987 Nilssen and Motorola executed a Non-Disclosure Agreement (the "1987 Agreement") to establish the terms under which Nilssen would provide additional confidential information to Motorola....Essential provisions of the 1987 Agreement included these:

- "Confidential Information" was defined as "any device, graphics, written information or information in other tangible forms that is disclosed, for evaluation purposes, to Motorola by [Nilssen] relating to [electronic ballasts] and that is marked at the time of disclosure as being 'Confidential' or 'Proprietary.'"
- Information disclosed orally or visually and identified at the time of such disclosure as "Confidential" was to be considered as "Confidential Information" only if reduced to tangible form, marked "Confidential" and transmitted to Motorola within 30 days of such oral or visual disclosure.
- "Confidential Information" was explicitly defined to exclude "any information which: (a) Is or becomes publicly known through no wrongful act on Motorola's part; or (b) Is, at the time of disclosure under this Agreement, already known to Motorola without restriction on disclosure; or (c) Is, or subsequently becomes, rightfully and without breach of this Agreement, in Motorola's possession without an obligation restricting disclosure; or (d) Is independently developed by Motorola without breach of this Agreement; or (e) Is furnished to a third party by [Nilssen] without a similar restriction on the third party's rights; or (f) Is explicitly approved for release by written authorization of [Nilssen]."

- Motorola was not to "disclose the 'Confidential Information' to any third party" nor to "use the 'Confidential Information' for any purpose" other than "evaluation purposes, which evaluation is to be completed within two months from [September 1, 1987]."
  [NOTE: "Evaluation purposes" are not defined in the 1987 Agreement, which was drafted by Motorola...].

From September 1987 to May 1988...Nilssen "relayed a lot of information" to Motorola employees....on the subject of electronic ballasts in the form of both documents and oral discussions....That information comprised both business information—including projections of market size, potential marketing opportunities and estimated manufacturing costs—and technical information as to the design of Nilssen's electronic ballast....Among other disclosures Nilssen made in that second category, Nilssen provided Motorola with a prototype ballast containing many of his designs.

* * *

On May 6, 1988 Fred Tucker ("Tucker")—then Group's Vice-President and General Manager—decided that it still would not pursue that business....On May 20 Gunderson wrote to Nilssen to confirm that Group had decided not to enter the business, explaining that it would be "too great a departure from our core business plans"....Gunderson returned to Nilssen all documents that Nilssen had marked "confidential" pursuant to the 1987 Agreement....

In May 1988 Nilssen wrote to Galvin and again asked him to reconsider Group's decision. Galvin, Gunderson and other Motorola employees then proceeded with a series of meetings to discuss...the Nilssen technology.

* * *

After expressing concerns to Nilssen about his history of sending Motorola unsolicited material and as to his possible litigiousness, Motorola sought to modify the confidentiality agreement governing Nilssen's disclosures....On September 27, 1988 Nilssen, Gunderson (on behalf of Motorola) and Alling (as an outside consultant to Motorola) executed a new Non-Disclosure Agreement (the "1988 Agreement") that provided in pertinent part:

- Nilssen agreed to disclose to Ailing on a confidential basis his pending patent applications covering inventions embodied in the prototype ballasts that Nilssen sent to Motorola. All other information disclosed to Ailing was "on a non-confidential basis and without obligation of any kind."
- Any future confidential disclosures by Nilssen to Motorola were limited to pending patent applications, which Motorola agreed to receive in confidence. "Any other information" that Nilssen disclosed was to be "on a non-confidential basis and without obligation of any kind, unless Motorola agree[d], in writing to make an exception."
- Motorola had no obligation to maintain the confidentiality of any information that became publicly available.
- Motorola and Nilssen "agreed to discuss the confidentiality of information that Motorola has previously received from [Nilssen] in regard to electronic ballasts," the stated goal being "to more specifically identify what it is that should be treated as confidential."

Alling then completed a "Solid State Ballast Report" for Motorola on October 15, 1988. That report evaluated both technical and business issues involved in Motorola's possible entry into the electronic ballast business, and it concluded with a recommendation that Motorola should go forward with the business using Nilssen's technology....

Meanwhile, in September 1988 Nilssen met with Katzir, Gunderson and Motorola attorneys to discuss possible compensation for Nilssen's work. Katzir asked Nilssen to propose a royalty on a per ballast basis. When Nilssen refused to do so, Katzir warned that if the parties could not agree on compensation Motorola would "go ahead without [him]." Gunderson followed up on that meeting with an October 3 letter to Nilssen that outlined three possibilities for Motorola's entry into the electronic ballast industry: (1) entry without Nilssen's participation and without his technology, (2) entry using only a limited amount of Nilssen's technology or (3) entry with Nilssen's participation and using substantially all of his technology. Importantly, Gunderson's letter also confirmed the parties' agreement, based on a meeting that they had held the next day after signing the 1988 Agreement, as to identifying whether any of Nilssen's previous disclosures were to be treated as confidential:

> This is to confirm the various "to-do's" that resulted from our meeting with you last Wednesday, and also to confirm some of the conclusions we reached.
>
> Ole's [Nilssen's] "to-do's":
>
> * * *
>
> 2. Review your previously-submitted documents and determine whether any of them should have been stamped as "confidential." Our intent is to more specifically identify the information that you regard as confidential.

Neither party has cited to any part of the record indicating whether or to what extent Nilssen followed up on that "to-do"—but as the later discussion reflects, his action or inaction in that respect makes no difference to the analysis.

On October 18 Nilssen wrote to Galvin, criticizing Katzir's preference for an "arm's length relationship whereby Motorola would merely license from [Nilssen] a few specific patents." Nilssen argued that Katzir's position "effectively prevents the formation of what I believe would be by far the best arrangement for Motorola as well as myself: namely, the establishment of a partnership-like relationship...." On November 2 Galvin responded:

> While we have not yet completed our business evaluation, and we do not plan to decide prior to year end, it is important that I communicate to you at this time Motorola's position, so that we can jointly determine, as soon as possible, whether there is a good foundation for a mutually acceptable relationship, should we decide to pursue the Electronic Ballast business. It is important to make this determination at this time since it seems that there is a significant gap between our respective positions regarding the nature of the relationship, and the compensation level for your patents and know-how.

Galvin proposed a "framework" for "final negotiations" in which Nilssen's compensation would be a royalty of "around 0.5% on Sales" plus "a certain minimum" for technical assistance. Finally, Galvin offered to continue discussions "if there is a positive determination that a financial relationship with you appears doable"....

Nilssen responded...suggesting that Motorola's "compensation proposed" was "unreasonably low"....Nilssen's position was that he be paid "one third of the total value clearly attributable to [his] contribution...." In light of that "significant gap" between Nilssen and Motorola, Galvin sent Nilssen a November 22 letter terminating their discussions....

Once discussions with Nilssen were terminated, Alling recommended that Motorola communicate with Stevens about his electronic ballast technology....Motorola decided to enter the electronic ballast industry in February 1989....Lighting hired Stevens and executed a Licensing Agreement for the exclusive use of his electronic ballast technology on April 7, 1989. Stevens and other Motorola engineers participated in the improvement of electronic ballast design until December 1990, at which time Lighting completed its final design so that it could proceed to production.

## Nilssen's Illinois Act Claim

Nilssen's Illinois Act claim against Motorola for theft of trade secrets requires that he demonstrate (1) the existence of a protectable "trade secret" (as defined in Act 2(d)) and (2) Motorola's "misappropriation" (as defined in Act 2(b)) of that trade secret (*Mangren Research & Dev. Corp. v. National Chem. Co.*, 87 F.3d 937, 942–43 (7th Cir. 1996)). Nilssen suggests that he has proved each of those elements as a matter of law, while Motorola correspondingly argues that Nilssen's claim fails as a matter of law with respect to each element. This opinion addresses the two elements in turn.

## Existence of a "Trade Secret"

Act 2(d) defines a potentially actionable "trade secret" as:

Information, including but not limited to, technical or nontechnical data, a formula, pattern, compilation, program, device, method, technique, drawing, process, financial data, or list of actual or potential customers or suppliers, that:

(1) is sufficiently secret to derive economic value, actual or potential, from not being generally known to other persons who can obtain economic value from its disclosure or use; and

(2) is the subject of efforts that are reasonable under the circumstances to maintain its secrecy or confidentiality.

As a preliminary matter, Motorola suggests that Nilssen's failure to identify a *particular* trade secret is fatal to his claim. As *Composite Marine Propellers. Inc. v. Van Der Woude*, 962 F.2d 1263, 1266 (7th Cir. 1992) (per curiam) has warned:

It is not enough to point to broad areas of technology and assert that something there must have been secret and misappropriated. The plaintiff must show concrete secrets.

Hence Nilssen cannot state a claim for trade secret protection under the Act by simply "producing long lists of general areas of information which contain unidentified trade secrets" (*AMP Inc. v. Fleischhacker*, 823 F.2d 1199, 1203 (7th Cir. 1987)). Instead he must articulate protectable trade secrets with specificity or suffer dismissal of his claim....

Motorola's attack on that basis stems from interrogatory answers that Nilssen provided when asked to specify the precise scope of his alleged trade secrets. [H]e contended "that the information he provided Motorola in the 1987 and 1988 time period, and prior thereto, constituted a package of trade secret and confidential information." On that score this Court has spoken plainly of the legal insufficiency under *AMP* of such a "blunderbuss statement that 'Everything you got from us was a trade secret.' " (*qad. inc. v. ALN Assocs., Inc.*, No. 88 C 2246, 1990 WL 93362, at *3 (N.D. Ill. June 20, 1990)).

* * *

But other Nilssen submissions to Motorola and to this Court have more specifically identified his claimed trade secrets....In terms of technical information relating to the design of electronic ballasts, Nilssen suggests that he disclosed four key circuit elements to Motorola in confidence:

- A series resonant inverter driven by a half-bridge,
- Ballast output capable of driving more than two lamps in a series,
- Means for reducing the cathode heating voltage after lamp ignition, and
- A slow-down capacitor used across the inverter output.

And [certain exhibits] substantially narrow Nilssen's identification of nontechnical trade secret information...to a more articulable set. Relying primarily on the expert report of Horace DePodwin ("DePodwin"), Nilssen identified these items of nontechnical information that he claims were—along with Nilssen's technical knowledge of electronic ballast circuits—the "very basis for Motorola's decision to enter the business and its entry strategy":

- Information concerning the reliability, cost of manufacture and efficiency of Nilssen's ballast design, often in comparison to existing commercial electronic ballasts,
- Detailed information and analyses of the comparative performance of competitors' ballasts, based on tests Nilssen had conducted,
- Detailed information and analyses of competitive ballasts, including their relative economic advantages and disadvantages,
- Detailed analyses of potential channels for distributing electronic ballasts,
- Information concerning the size and structure of the electronic ballast market, including the prevailing methods of distribution and generally accepted product specifications,
- Estimates of electrical efficiencies that Motorola could expect to achieve with electronic ballast technology in the future, and
- Research and analysis concerning expected profitability following entry into the electronic ballast market and related markets.

This Court finds that level of specificity suffices to withstand Motorola's attack.... Decisions such as *Roton Barrier, Inc. v. Stanley Works*, 79 F.3d 1112, 1117–18 (Fed.Cir. 1996) (applying the Illinois Act) provide generally that a "trade secret" under that statute may include a compilation of confidential business and financial information. And Nilssen has documented each of those nontechnical items, at least to some extent, by referring to appropriate papers from the voluminous record in this case. Similarly, Nilssen's identification of his claimed technical trade secrets—the four key circuit elements of his electronic ballast—is quite specific. In sum, Nilssen's trade secrets as presently articulated are not so lacking in specificity as to require dismissal of his Illinois Act claim.

* * *

As their next battle line on the Illinois Act claim, the parties differ as to what "value" (if any) is to be attributed to Nilssen's trade secrets. Act 2(d)(1) limits trade secret protection to information that "is sufficiently secret to derive economic value, actual or potential, from not being generally known to other persons who can obtain economic value from its disclosure or use." So information that is generally known within an industry is not trade secret material....*Stampede Tool Warehouse. Inc. v. May*, 272 Ill.App.3d 580, 588, 209 Ill. Dec. 281, 287, 651 N.E.2d 209, 215 (1st Dist. 1995) (citation omitted) has further detailed the degree of secrecy necessary to impart "value" for a trade secret claim under the Act:

> In determining whether information is a trade secret, the focus of both the common law and the ITSA [the Act] is on the secrecy of the information sought to be protected. The key to secrecy is the ease with which information can be readily duplicated without involving considerable time, effort or expense.

Significantly, then, Motorola might prove that Nilssen's alleged trade secrets were without value by demonstrating that those secrets were easily duplicable through proper means....

To have any opportunity to prevail on his Illinois Act claim, then, Nilssen must first prove that his information was sufficiently secret — in the sense of not being duplicable without considerable time, effort or expense" — to constitute a "trade secret." Only then does the further "misappropriation" analysis become relevant.... *Hamer Holding Group. Inc. v. Elmore*, 202 Ill.App.3d 994, 1011–12, 148 Ill.Dec. 310, 321–22, 560 N.E.2d 907, 918–19 (1st Dist. 1990) (citations omitted) so held when it visited the issue as a matter of statutory construction:

* * *

> The key to "secrecy" is the ease with which information can be developed through other proper means: if the information can be readily duplicated without involving considerable time, effort or expense, then it is not secret. Conversely, information which can be duplicated only by an expensive and time-consuming method of reverse engineering, for instance, could be secret, and the ability to duplicate it would not constitute a defense....

In light of those standards, the existence of a trade secret under the Act is ordinarily a question of fact, for that inquiry necessarily involves the "factual question of whether the 'secrecy' of the information has been maintained and the ease or difficulty of obtaining the information from other sources" (2 GREGORY UPCHURCH, INTELLECTUAL PROPERTY LITIGATION GUIDE: PATENTS & TRADE SECRETS § 16.02, at 16–17 to 16–18 (1996)). What follows is a statement of the relevant facts supporting each party's motion for summary judgment on that basis, from which — when viewed through the alternate lenses required for such cross-motions — it becomes apparent that this Court cannot decide as a matter of law whether or not Nilssen's alleged trade secrets were of sufficient "secrecy" to be of "value" under the Act.

In the light most favorable to Motorola, each of the four technical elements of electronic ballasts that Nilssen now claims as a trade secret was either known in the industry or used in commercially available ballasts (or both) before Nilssen's 1988 disclosure to Motorola.

* * *

In the light most favorable to Nilssen, though, each of the four circuit elements was either unknown or underdeveloped and commercially infeasible at the time that Nilssen introduced them to Motorola.... Moreover, Nilssen urges that the combination of those four circuit elements (each of them little used — if at all — on an individual basis) was unknown in the field of electronic ballasts in 1988. Under Illinois law a trade secret may exist in the combination of a number of elements of information, even if each discrete element may be found in the public domain.... As *Syntex Ophthalmics, Inc. v. Tsuetaki*, 701 F.2d 677, 684 (7th Cir. 1983) has quoted from *Imperial Chem. Indus., Ltd. v. National Distillers & Chem. Corp.*, 342 F.2d 737, 742 (2d Cir. 1965):

[A] trade secret can exist in a combination of characteristics and components, each of which, by itself, is in the public domain, but the unified process, design and operation of which, in unique combination, affords a competitive advantage and is a protectable secret.

Thus the facts taken in a light most favorable to Nilssen suggest that his package of the four circuit elements was really of special "value," thus constituting a protectable trade secret. Not only does Clegg's report detail the generally-believed commercial impracticability in 1988 of each of Nilssen's four circuit elements, but Motorola's own documents include repeated references to the innovativeness and perceived profitability of Nilssen's ballast designs.... [One report] estimated a "Nilssen Design [Cost] Advantage" of $4.42 over the Triad-Utrad ballast—the key electronic ballast competitor—and therefore estimated that Nilssen's technology had an estimated net present value of approximately $50 million.

To return to a pro-Motorola view of the facts, however, in that light even Nilssen's "package" of the four identified circuit elements was not sufficiently secret to be of any value in the electronic ballast industry. Significantly three of those four elements... were disclosed to the public in Nilssen's United States Patent No. 4,677,345 issued June 30, 1987. Additionally, Motorola's expert Bruce Den Uyl ("Den Uyl") identifies a review... that found (1) that "Nilssen's ideas offered no competitive advantage" and (2) that other products on the market were "similar or identical" to ballasts produced using Nilssen's technology....

That same conclusion as to the inappropriateness of summary judgment on either side's motion applies to Nilssen's asserted nontechnical trade secrets.... In a light most favorable to Motorola, the facts reflect that Nilssen's cost, business and marketing information was both readily known in the industry and easily replicated.... And as for Motorola's ability to accumulate the relevant nontechnical information without Nilssen's assistance, Ailing concludes in his Report:

> Motorola had numerous employees who were familiar with the ballast industry and knew much or all of the information needed to enter the electronic ballast industry. Motorola, as a large user of lighting and ballasts in their own facilities, could have called on their own captive architects, engineers, or facility managers for information.... In short, Motorola had considerable expertise in-house regarding the lighting and ballast industry. In addition, at the appropriate time, it hired industry consultants and experts independent of Nilssen to obtain the appropriate information relative to the electronic ballast industry.

\* \* \*

[F]rom a pro-Nilssen stance it seems likely that at least some of his nontechnical information was secret and of value in the electronic ballast industry.... Nilssen's expert DePodwin opines that Nilssen's nontechnical information was both secret and proprietary, with each element fitting into one of three categories: (1) information that "originated and [was] held closely by Nilssen," (2) "information associated with judgments made by Nilssen over time" and (3) "some material which, while arguably public in certain constituent parts, when taken together, constituted proprietary property of value because of the way in which those components were combined and/or presented...." Further, on that same premise Nilssen's contribution of proprietary nontechnical information was critical for prompt entry into the electronic ballast industry—particularly for a firm entering the business as late into the product life cycle as was Motorola:

The information in question is of a kind that is both basic and critical to entry decisions in any industry setting, i.e., actual and/or projected production costs, performance, and market value of one's own proposed product line—or a product line essentially similar—as compared to the products with which it would have to compete.

\* \* \*

In summary, issues of fact now exist in both directions as to whether Nilssen's alleged technical and nontechnical trade secrets were sufficiently secret to have been of "value" to Motorola. That conclusion alone is sufficient for the conclusive defeat of Nilssen's motion for summary judgment.... But because the facts taken in a pro-Nilssen light at least presently create the reasonable inference that Nilssen did have protectable trade secrets of "value," summary judgment for Motorola on that basis is also inappropriate (at least for the time being).

### "Misappropriation" of a Trade Secret

This opinion now turns to Motorola's attack on the second essential component of Nilssen's Illinois Act claim: that Motorola "misappropriated" a protectable trade secret of Nilssen (Act 2(b);....For even if Nilssen held valuable trade secrets regarding the production of a marketable electronic ballast, Motorola would still be entitled to summary judgment if it could demonstrate as a matter of law that Motorola did not "misappropriate" any of those secrets in the statutory sense.

*American Antenna Corp. v. Amperex Elec. Corp.*, 190 Ill.App.3d 535, 538, 137 Ill.Dec. 417, 420, 546 N.E.2d 41, 44 (2d Dist. 1989) teaches:

A misappropriation of trade secrets occurs when a person acquires or discovers a trade secret by improper means or disclosures or uses a trade secret in breach of a duty of confidentiality imposed on him by the nature of his relationship with the owner of the trade secret or reposed in him by the owner in disclosing the information, and the owner of the trade secret is damaged by this improper acquisition, disclosure or use.

\* \* \*

While an express confidentiality agreement may certainly suffice to define the duty of confidentiality necessary for action under Act 2(b)(2)(B)(II), the existence of such an agreement is not a prerequisite to such an action....Rather a duty of confidentiality may be implied from the circumstances surrounding the parties' relationship (*Rockwell Graphic Sys., Inc. v. DEV Industries, Inc.*, 925 F.2d 174, 177 (7th Cir. 1991)).

Here the precise character of the relationship between Nilssen and Motorola changed several times during the 1986–88 period. Before September 4, 1987, when the parties executed the 1987 Agreement, they had no written understanding that Motorola would maintain the confidentiality of information that was relayed by Nilssen. Of course Nilssen first approached Motorola about opportunities in the electronic ballast industry in 1982, and he now contends that he conveyed proprietary information to Motorola before the 1987 Agreement....In addition, the 1987 Agreement provided that Motorola's "evaluation [was] to be completed within two months from the effective date of this Agreement" and Nilssen continued to provide Motorola with information well beyond that two-month period. It was not until September 27, 1988 that the parties entered into the 1988 Agreement.

Nilssen's position is that Motorola was under a duty to maintain the confidentiality of his disclosures—whenever made—at all times relevant to this litigation. As for his pre-1987-Agreement disclosures, Nilssen suggests that they were sufficiently limited and were communicated for the proper purpose (marketing his product) so as to fit into the category protected by a corresponding duty of confidentiality recognized in cases such as *Rockwell Graphic*, 925 F.2d at 177. Nilssen also points to additional circumstances surrounding his pre-1987-Agreement disclosures that might permit an inference that a confidential relationship then existed. For example, Nilssen's February 7, 1986 letter [stated]:

> I would like to meet…to discuss the possible participation by Motorola in the business of electronic ballasts. However, for me to be able to communicate effectively with you, it would be necessary for Motorola to accept my technical disclosures in confidence.

And Nilssen seeks to complete the picture by arguing that an implied duty of confidentiality persisted throughout the periods expressly covered by the 1987 and 1988 Agreements….

All of that, however, accords insufficient weight to the express contractual arrangements that ultimately governed the parties' relationship. It must be recognized that the Illinois Act does not purport to limit or override an express contractual arrangement governing the confidential exchange of proprietary information (*See* Act § 8(b)(1)). Instead, because a confidentiality agreement is a valid contract enforceable according to its terms…, Illinois law precludes the finding of "any implied duty of nondisclosure that would directly contradict the express agreement of the parties." Thus a contract that defines the degree of confidentiality among the parties also serves to establish—and to define—the duty of confidentiality required to underpin an Illinois Act claim (*Roton Barrier, Inc. v. Stanley Works*, 79 F.3d 1112, 1118 (Fed.Cir. 1996)).

In light of those standards, the terms of the 1987 and 1988 Agreements preclude a finding of any implied duty of confidentiality for Nilssen's disclosures not expressly reduced to writing and marked "confidential." As set out earlier, the 1987 Agreement established the exclusive mechanism by which Nilssen might establish his disclosures as confidential: He had to memorialize and transmit them in writing and mark them "confidential" or "proprietary…" And although the 1987 Agreement called for Motorola to evaluate Nilssen's technology for only a two-month period, the parties thereafter conducted themselves as if the terms of that agreement governed Nilssen's continuing 1987-to-1988 disclosures.

Then (and perhaps most critically) the 1988 Agreement unquestionably shows that the parties' contractual obligations—rather than any implied-at-law duties—governed the confidential relationship. That Agreement begins with this statement:

> This is to confirm the agreement we reached in regard to information you have disclosed, or will disclose, to Motorola….

It goes on to state:

> We also agreed to discuss the confidentiality of information that Motorola has previously received from you in regard to electronic ballasts. Our goal is to more specifically identify what it is that should be treated as confidential.

And the very next communication between the parties—Gunderson's October 3, 1988 letter to Nilssen—reflects precisely the agreement that emerged from that discussion…. [in which Nillssen agreed, as part of his "to-do's," to ] "review [his] previously-submitted documents and determine whether any of them should have been stamped as confidential."

Nothing in the record as spoken of by the litigants indicates the extent to which Nilssen did or did not implement that "to-do" by a post-1988-Agreement markup of his documents as "confidential." But that is not important—what is significant is that he was afforded the full opportunity to do so, and he cannot now contend that the trade secret concept extends to any implied duty stemming from his delivery to Motorola of any information (at any time during the parties' relationship) that he did not himself reduce to written form and stamp "confidential." In short, this Court holds, based on the 1987 and 1988 Agreements, including the parties' joint reading of the 1988 Agreement as reflected in the October 3 letter...just a few weeks later, that any disclosure that Nilssen believed to be proprietary—including *previous* disclosures that had not been so marked—had to be in written form and stamped "confidential."...This Court finds that Motorola was under no duty to maintain the confidentiality of any of Nilssen's disclosures (whenever made) that were not so marked.

With this opinion having thus fleshed out the potential scope of any duty on Motorola's part (or, more precisely, the standard for identifying that potential scope), it is time to turn to the "misappropriation" issue. In that respect, even on the premise of a possible duty under the Act not to use or to disclose Nilssen's trade secrets, Motorola further argues that it did not "misappropriate" any trade secret. To that end Motorola points to the terms of the 1987 Agreement, which specifically permitted Motorola's use of Nilssen's confidential information for "evaluation purposes...." Motorola urges that it did no more than to evaluate (and then to return) Nilssen's information.

But the required pro-Nilssen characterization on Motorola's Rule 56 motion could reasonably imply that Motorola's use of Nilssen's trade secrets went well beyond evaluation. Clegg's report details his opinion "that Motorola got [from Nilssen] the idea of and motivation for entering the electronic ballast business using" each of Nilssen's four circuit elements.

* * *

Similarly, DePodwin...attests that Nilssen's alleged nontechnical trade secrets were used in the implementation of Lighting's new business: "[m]uch of Motorola's entry strategy, concepts, and materials derive from Nilssen."

Motorola argues that it could not have misappropriated Nilssen's technical trade secrets because Lighting's ballast design team did not have access to Nilssen's information. In that respect Motorola says that Stevens and a group of Lighting engineers—none of whom had access to Nilssen's documents or designs—began work in the fall of 1989 based on a preliminary design of Stevens' Super Ballast....Motorola further says that Gunderson—the only Lighting employee to whom Nilssen had earlier delivered files—was given responsibility for testing Lighting's prototypes and competitors' ballasts, but that he had no role in selecting circuit configurations....

Again a view from Nilssen's perspective leads to the very different inference that Nilssen's designs were incorporated into Lighting's ballast. Nilssen disclosed to Motorola "a massive amount of proprietary information"...and Clegg's report details precisely which of those circuits he believes to have been incorporated into Motorola's design. Further, a reasonable jury might find that the Lighting decision makers who had access to Nilssen's designs incorporated those secrets into Lighting's ballast....The placement of key employees in a position where they might assimilate a trade secret permits an inference of misappropriation. Motorola admits that Katzir was centrally involved in the design of Lighting's ballast, and discovery has uncovered several of Nilssen's confidential disclosures in Katzir's files....Additionally it appears that Gunderson attended a series of meetings with Lighting's engineers at which its commercial ballast design was ultimately approved....

Importantly, it is not necessary to Nilssen's Illinois Act claim that Motorola have copied Nilssen's ballast design exactly. As *Mangren Research*, 87 F.3d at 944 quoted from *In re Innovative Constr. Sys., Inc.*, 793 F.2d 875, 887 (7th Cir. 1986):

> [T]he user of another's trade secret is liable even if he uses it with modifications or improvements upon it effected by his own efforts, so long as the substance of the process used by the actor is derived from the other's secret.

Indeed, Motorola might face liability for misappropriation under ITSA even if it used Nilssen's trade secrets "only to demonstrate what pitfalls to avoid" (*Affiliated Hosp. Prods.*, 57 Ill.App.3d at 807, 15 Ill.Dec. at 534, 373 N.E.2d at 1006).

In sum, the record demonstrates that a reasonable jury might find that Motorola misappropriated both technical and nontechnical trade secrets from Nilssen. Thus Motorola cannot prevail via summary judgment on Nilssen's Illinois Act claim.

\* \* \*

---

# Bell Helicopter Textron, Inc. v. Tridair Helicopters, Inc.
## 982 F. Supp. 318 (D. Del. 1997)

SCHWARTZ, Senior District Judge

\* \* \*

On January 22, 1993, Bell and Tridair executed a license agreement ("1993 Agreement") in which Tridair granted Bell certain rights to information relating to kits designed and manufactured by Tridair which can convert certain Bell single engine helicopters into twin engine helicopters. In exchange for these rights, Bell agreed to pay Tridair $60,000.00 for each new Bell helicopter manufactured using Tridair's conversion kit. According to the terms of the 1993 Agreement, Bell agreed and acknowledged that the technical data it received from Tridair was the proprietary information of Tridair and that Bell would maintain its confidentiality.

On December 20, 1994, Bell and Tridair entered into another licensing agreement ("1994 Agreement") whereby Tridair granted a license to Bell to utilize the technical data previously received to manufacture, have manufactured, use, sell and lease a twin engine Bell Model 407L(T) helicopter. Bell agreed to pay Tridair a royalty of $54,000.00 for each 407L(T) helicopter sold by Bell.

The parties agree conversion of Bells' single engine helicopter to twin engine helicopters was not a successful commercial venture. Moreover, Bell scrapped plans to manufacture and sell more of the Bell Model 407L(T) because of high costs and consequent lack of market demand. Instead, Bell began developing its own helicopter, allegedly using Tridair's technical data, in partnership with another company, Samsung. Tridair asserts Bell used the technical data revealed pursuant to the 1993 and 1994 Agreements in order to build this new helicopter in spite of lack of a license to do so. Tridair filed a lawsuit *inter alia* for trade secret misappropriation and Bell moved to dismiss the trade secret misappropriation claim. Although Bell and Tridair spent almost six months attempting to resolve this dispute pursuant to the provisions of the 1994 and 1993 Agreements, such attempts proved to be unsuccessful. This lawsuit followed.

\* \* \*

Bell contends that under *Cabot Corp. v. Fansteel, Inc.*, C.A. No. 10502, 1990 WL 181960, at 1 (Del. Ch. November 21, 1990), Tridair must specifically allege, "defendant has wrongfully gained access to the secret and has misappropriated it." However, reliance on *Cabot* is misplaced for three reasons.

First, the case at bar involved a factual scenario of a licensee who obtained a trade secret rightfully. In contrast, *Cabot* deals with the misappropriation of a trade secret by a competitor.

Second, if the "wrongfully gained access" pleading standard were applied strictly and literally, no current employee or licensee could ever "wrongfully gain access" to a trade secret because they would have gained access rightfully as an employee or licensee. Followed to its logical extreme, only those who were not an employee or licensee would be liable if a trade secret were misappropriated....

Third, the language of the statute itself does not support the "wrongfully gained access" pleading requirement.... It is concluded on the facts of this case that Tridair need not allege Bell wrongfully gained access to its trade secrets under DUTSA [the Delaware Uniform Trade Secrets Act].

### B. Duty to Maintain Secrecy and Limit Its Use

Bell next contended that it did not have a duty to maintain secrecy under the licensing agreement and therefore, could not have misappropriated Tridair's trade secrets. Not surprisingly, Tridair disagrees.

Under the Delaware Uniform Trade Secrets Act, misappropriation can occur in one of two manners: (1) acquisition by improper means, or (2) improper disclosure or use... Tridair relies on improper disclosure or use.

Under the "improper disclosure or use" branch of 6 DEL. CODE ANN. Tit. 6, sec. 2001(2)(b)(2) (B), one method of setting forth a trade secret misappropriation cause of action is by alleging that a person used a trade secret of another in circumstances where the person knew or had reason to know that the knowledge of the trade secret was acquired under circumstances where there was a duty to limit the use of the secret.

Delaware courts have not had an occasion to construe sec. 2001(2)(b)(2)(B). However, the "limit its use" language has been construed to apply to a scenario where a plaintiff, the owner of a trade secret, voluntarily disclosed it to a defendant under confidential circumstances and the defendant subsequently used the secret in breach of an agreement with the plaintiff. *See Pulsecard, Inc. v. Discover Card Services, Inc.*, 1996 WL 137819 (D. Kan. March 5, 1996). Tridair has alleged that, "Bell was provided access to and learned of [Tridair's] trade secrets in confidence."...

\* \* \*

The economic loss doctrine is a "judicially created doctrine that prohibits recovery in tort where a product has damaged only itself... and, the only losses suffered are economic in nature." *See Danforth v. Acorn Structures, Inc.*, 608 A.2d 1194, 1195 (Del. 1992). Bell contends that the economic loss doctrine applies to economic loss caused by trade secret misappropriation.

*  *  *

In the case *sub judice*, the misappropriation of trade secrets does not hurt the product itself, but rather, injures Tridair by increasing Tridair's competition and by causing Tridair to be deprived of the return of the money it expended in deriving the proprietary technical data. Further, to date, the economic loss doctrine has only been applied by Delaware courts where the "parties to the transaction have allocated the risk of product non-performance through the bargaining process." *See Danforth*, 608 A.2d at 1200. No such allocation of risk has occurred between Bell and Tridair. Tridair never bargained for Bell to allegedly misuse its trade secrets. It is therefore understandable that Bell could not cite any case in the country that has applied the economic loss doctrine to trade secret misappropriation.

*  *  *

# C.  Interests and Bargaining Positions

Negotiating a license involves not only reaching agreement about substantive rights and duties but also agreement about the bargaining process itself. Bargaining rules prescribe the rules of the "game" under which negotiations are conducted, and how the parties use certain tactics to their advantage (or not)—e.g., time and place, number of negotiators, control of drafts, presence of a decision-maker, "good-cop bad-cop," threats, repudiation of interim agreements—to reach more favorable outcomes. Each party has institutional interests (e.g., return on investment, minimizing risk) and specific bargaining positions (e.g., 5% royalties, zero up-front fees, rights to future improvements). Each brings to the table certain expectations, some reasonable and based upon personal and professional experience, others based on fears or unrealistic expectations. The licensor knows its intellectual property. The licensee knows its markets. Before negotiations begin, they may already have formed rigid positions on the terms each considers critical to the deal.

The impediments to a negotiated agreement take many forms. Certainly, differing assessment of the technology's value is a common problem. As will be seen in Chapter 5, there are no easily applied or generally accepted black-letter rules for valuing intellectual property. Especially troublesome are embryonic or early stage technologies that are not market-ready and thus present higher risks and more development costs for the licensee. Not all licensees are willing to assume such risks. Other stumbling blocks include: (i) uncertainty over how an individual technology will contribute to a final product; (ii) uncertainty over the costs of product development; (iii) different risk tolerance; and (iv) misunderstood or poorly-defined missions.

*  *  *

---

A comprehensive review of the literature of negotiation is beyond the scope of this book. However, perhaps the most famous and influential book written in the field of negotiation is Roger Fisher and William Ury's GETTING TO YES. In the excerpt below, the authors outline the paradigm shift that allows parties to move beyond traditional arm wrestling over positions to "interest-based bargaining."

*  *  *

---

# Getting To Yes*

## Roger Fisher & William Ury (1991)

* * *

Any method of negotiation may be fairly judged by three criteria: It should produce a wise agreement if agreement is possible. It should be efficient. And it should improve or at least not damage the relationship between the parties. (A wise agreement can be defined as one that meets the legitimate interests of each side to the extent possible, resolves conflicting interests fairly, is durable, and takes common interests into account.)

The most common form of negotiation...depends upon successively taking—and then giving up—a sequence of positions. Taking positions...serves some useful purposes in a negotiation; it tells the other side what you want; it provides an anchor in an uncertain and pressured situation; and it can eventually produce the terms of an acceptable agreement. But those purposes can be served in other ways. And positional bargaining fails to meet the basic criteria of producing a wise agreement, efficiently and amicably.

*Arguing over positions produces unwise agreements.* When negotiators bargain over positions, they tend to lock themselves into those positions. The more you clarify your position and defend it against attack, the more committed you become to it. The more you try to convince the other side of the impossibility of changing your opening position the more difficult it becomes to do so. Your ego becomes identified with your position. You now have a new interest in "saving face"—in reconciling future action with past positions—making it less and less likely that any agreement will wisely reconcile the parties' original interests.

The danger that positional bargaining will impede a negotiation was well illustrated by the breakdown of the talks under President Kennedy for a comprehensive ban on nuclear testing. A critical question arose: how many on-site inspections per year should the Soviet Union and the United States be permitted to make within the other's territory to investigate suspicious seismic events? The Soviet Union finally agreed to three inspections. The United States insisted on no less than ten. And there the talks broke down— over positions—despite the fact that no one understood whether an "inspection" would involve one person looking around for one day, or a hundred people prying indiscriminately for a month. The parties had made little attempt to design an inspection procedure that would reconcile the United States' interest in verification with the desire of both countries for minimal intrusion.

As more attention is paid to positions, less attention is devoted to meeting the underlying concerns of the parties. Agreement becomes less likely. Any agreement reached may reflect a mechanical splitting of the difference between final positions rather than a solution carefully crafted to meet the legitimate interests of the parties. The result is frequently an agreement less satisfactory to each side than it could have been.

*Arguing over positions is inefficient.* The standard method of negotiation may produce either agreement...or breakdown. In either event, the process takes a lot of time.

Bargaining over positions creates incentives that stall settlement. In positional bargaining you try to improve the chance that any settlement reached is favorable to you by starting with an extreme position, by stubbornly holding to it, by deceiving the other party as to your true views, and by making small concessions only as necessary to keep

---

* Reprinted with permission of the publisher, copyright 1991.

the negotiation going. The same is true for the other side. Each of those factors tends to interfere with reaching a settlement promptly. The more extreme the opening positions and the smaller the concessions, the more time and effort it will take to discover whether or not agreement is possible.

The standard minuet also requires a large number of individual decisions as each negotiator decides what to offer, what to reject, and how much of a concession to make. Decision-making is difficult and time-consuming at best. Where each decision not only involves yielding to the other side but will likely produce pressure to yield further, a negotiator has little incentive to move quickly. Dragging one's feet, threatening to walk out, stonewalling, and other such tactics become commonplace. They all increase the time and costs of reaching agreement as well as the risk that no agreement will be reached at all.

*Arguing over positions endangers an ongoing relationship.* Positional bargaining becomes a contest of will. Each negotiator asserts what he will and won't do. The task of jointly devising an acceptable solution tends to become a battle. Each side tries through sheer will power to force the other to change its position.... Anger and resentment often result as one side sees itself bending to the rigid will of the other while its own legitimate concerns go unaddressed. Positional bargaining thus strains and sometimes shatters the relationship between the parties.

\* \* \*

*Being nice is no answer.* Many people recognize the high costs of hard positional bargaining, particularly on the parties and their relationship. They hope to avoid them by following a more gentle style of negotiation. Instead of seeing the other side as adversaries, they prefer to see them as friends. Rather than emphasizing a goal of victory, they emphasize the necessity of reaching agreement. In a soft negotiating game the standard moves are to make offers and concessions, to trust the other side, to be friendly, and to yield as necessary to avoid confrontation....

The soft negotiating game emphasizes the importance of building and maintaining a relationship. Within families and among friends much negotiation takes place this way. The process tends to be efficient, at least to the extent of producing results quickly. As each party competes with the other in being more generous and more forthcoming, an agreement becomes highly likely. But it may not be a wise one. The results may not be as tragic as in the O. Henry story about an impoverished couple in which the loving wife sells her hair in order to buy a handsome chain for her husband's watch, and the unknowing husband sells his watch in order to buy beautiful combs for his wife's hair. However, any negotiation primarily concerned with the relationship runs the risk of producing a sloppy agreement.

More seriously, pursuing a soft and friendly form of positional bargaining makes you vulnerable to someone who plays a hard game of positional bargaining. In positional bargaining, a hard game dominates a soft one. If the hard bargainer insists on concessions and makes threats while the soft bargainer yields in order to avoid confrontation and insists on agreement, the negotiating game is biased in favor of the hard player. The process will produce an agreement, although it may not be a wise one. It will certainly be more favorable to the hard positional bargainer than to the soft one. If your response to sustained, hard positional bargaining is soft positional bargaining, you will probably lose your shirt.

\* \* \*

The answer to the question of whether to use soft positional bargaining or hard is "neither." Change the game. At the Harvard Negotiation Project we have been developing a method of negotiation explicitly designed to produce wise outcomes efficiently and amicably. This method, called *principled negotiation* or *negotiation on the merits*, can be boiled down to four basic points.

These four points define a straightforward method of negotiation that can be used under almost any circumstance. Each point deals with a basic element of negotiation, and suggests what you should do about it.

People:      Separate the people from the problem.

Interests:   Focus on interests, not positions.

Options:     Generate a variety of possibilities before deciding what to do.

Criteria:    Insist that the result be based on some objective standard.

The first point responds to the fact that human beings are not computers. We are creatures of strong emotions who often have radically different perceptions and have difficulty communicating clearly. Emotions typically become entangled with the objective merits of the problem. Taking positions just makes this worse because people's egos become identified with their positions. Hence, before working on the substantive problem, the "people problem" should be disentangled from it and dealt with separately. Figuratively if not literally, the participants should come to see themselves as working side by side, attacking the problem, not each other. Hence the first proposition: *Separate the people from the problem.*

The second point is designed to overcome the drawback of focusing on people's stated positions when the object of a negotiation is to satisfy their underlying interests. A negotiating position often obscures what you really want. Compromising between positions is not likely to produce an agreement which will effectively take care of the human needs that led people to adopt those positions. The second basic element of the method is: *Focus on interests, not positions.*

The third point responds to the difficulty of designing optimal solutions while under pressures. Trying to decide in the presence of an adversary narrows your vision. Having a lot at stake inhibits creativity. So does searching for the one right solution. You can offset these constraints by setting aside a designated time within which to think up a wide range of possible solutions that advance shared interests and creatively reconcile differing interests. Hence, the third basic point: *Before trying to reach agreement, invent options for mutual gain.*

Where interests are directly opposed, a negotiator may be able to obtain a favorable result simply by being stubborn. That method tends to reward intransigence and produce arbitrary results. However, you can counter such a negotiator by insisting that his single say-so is not enough and that an agreement must reflect some fair standard independent of the naked will of either side. This does not mean insisting that the terms be based on the standard you select, but only that some fair standard such as market value, expert opinion, custom, or law determine the outcome. By discussing such criteria rather than what the parties are willing or unwilling to do, neither party need give in to the other; both can defer to a fair solution. Hence the fourth basic point: *Insist on using objective criteria.*

* * *

To sum up, in contrast to positional bargaining the principled negotiation method of focusing on basic interests, mutually satisfying options, and fair standards typically results in a *wise* agreement. The method permits you to reach a gradual consensus on a joint decision efficiently without all the transactional costs of digging in to positions only to have to dig yourself out of them. And separating the people from the problem allows you to deal directly and emphatically with the other negotiator as a human being, thus making possible an amicable agreement.

\* \* \*

# Strategies for Exploiting Property Rights in Technology\*
William L. Respess
404 PLI/PAT. 179, 204–9 (1995)

\* \* \*

## Negotiating The Agreement

The best laid strategy for exploiting technology with a partner will come to nothing if an agreement cannot be reached. Negotiation is truly an art and like any artistic endeavor there are many styles and very different styles can be equally successful. The following are a few hints based on experience serving six CEOs.

1. *Be well prepared*. The negotiations easiest to conclude are those in which each party has a well thought out position. Those of us who have had the privilege, if not the pleasure, of negotiating with Japanese companies are always impressed with their preparation. If you are a small company negotiating with a large one, you can get pushed around a bit. One way to prepare for such negotiations, if the large company has a history of dealing with publicly traded small companies, is to obtain copies of its agreements with other small companies from the SEC and study them for insights they offer into what the large company is likely to find acceptable.

2. *Avoid "negotiating" with someone who cannot make the deal*. Early in the negotiations try to establish if your counterpart actually has deal-making authority. Once you concede a position in negotiations you usually cannot get it back. Therefore, if you and your counterpart appear to have struck a deal in which you have offered your most valuable compromises and he comes back with the message that his boss would not accept it unless changed in certain ways, you will find it difficult to condition giving on some or all of those points if your counterpart will give back in other areas. He will again have to take the deal back to the boss. Shuttle negotiating becomes the process in such a situation. It is slow and frustrating and often leads to a breakdown in negotiations. Negotiating with someone who cannot actually make the deal also can create false optimism. A large number of "deals" negotiated at great expense are not finally concluded because there really never was a deal that could be made on terms acceptable to both parties.

3. *A letter of intent almost always slows the process down*. Many businessmen favor entering into a letter of intent. However, there are several problems with them

---

beginning with whether or not they are meant to be binding. If one is drafted and actually signed, it should expressly state whether it is binding. A binding provision that the parties will negotiate exclusively for a defined period with each other can, however, usefully be made part of a letter of intent whose substantive provision are not binding. The main difficulty with a letter of intent is that the deal makers tend to go onto other things after the letter is drafted and leave resolution of remaining issues to others, usually their lawyers. Notwithstanding their best intentions, difficult points requiring substantial negotiation are often overlooked. When this is discovered, valuable momentum in the negotiating process has often been lost. In addition, when the areas of disagreement do surface, positions taken in the letter of intent tend to be looked at by one or the other party as set in concrete. An attempt to modify them in subsequent negotiations as a compromise to resolving other points will surely be looked upon as a bad faith negotiating play even if the letter of intent is not binding.

4. *The real deal maker should consider allowing another member of the negotiating team to negotiate particularly touchy points.* Most issues in negotiations are subject to compromise. Nevertheless, sometimes the negotiators see the movement required for compromise as a retreat from a valid position and take the retreat as a personal defeat. Once the deal makers are at odds with each other, the chances of concluding a negotiation successfully are greatly reduced. If, however, the CFO, director of research or the lawyer take the lead in delicate situations and personal feelings become a barrier to agreement, the CEO or other deal maker who has avoided such conflict with his counterpart can step in to rescue the negotiators.

5. *A third party participant may help negotiations.* In Japanese society confrontation is avoided. Thus American-style negotiations are not the rule. Negotiations in Japan are, therefore, traditionally facilitated by a third party known to both sides. When a difficult point is reached, the third party acts like a diplomat and shuttles back and forth between the parties to establish what each really wants and may suggest areas of compromise which can be reached outside the actual negotiations so that neither party loses face by advancing a position from which he must back away. Japanese trading companies traditionally play this kind of role. The author has several times participated in delicate negotiations between U.S. companies facilitated by investment bankers known to both even though actually retained by one of the parties. The banker is able to feel out the position of the other side and explore areas of compromise in a manner that the negotiators seem unable to achieve on their own.

*Mediator*

### Negotiating a Reasonable Royalty

Two elements of a license agreement loom larger than all the others in terms of importance. One is definition of the technology to be licensed and the other is how much is to be paid for it.

Determining the royalty to be paid is more of a process than each party proposing a royalty and compromising somewhere in between. Often one or the other of the parties' only justification for a royalty proposal is how it compares to the actual royalties in other agreements. While royalties in other agreements are relevant, always be prepared to justify the royalty proposed on as many other grounds as possible. Sophisticated economic models can be helpful but their usefulness depends upon the acceptability to the other side of the assumptions on which they are based. One useful reference against which to test a royalty proposal, whether arrived at by intuition or economic model, is the checklist of elements used by courts in determining a reasonable royalty as a measure of damages in patent litigation. *See Georgia-Pacific Corp. v. United States Plywood Corp.*, 318 F. Supp. 1116, 166 USPQ 235 (S.D.N.Y. 1970) *modified and aff'd* 446 F.2d 295, 170 USPQ 369 (2d.Cir. 1971). At least some of these elements are relevant to fashioning a royalty outside of the context of a determination of infringement.

In short, each party's royalty expectations should be evaluated in light of both factors external to the agreement, for example, market conditions affecting a patented product, and elements of the transaction itself which provide consideration in lieu of royalties or which limit the value of the license to the licensee.

* * *

# D.  Due Diligence

Due diligence simply describes the process undertaken by each party to ask and satisfactorily answer all critical factual and legal questions before signing the deal. "Transactional" due diligence is obviously more focused and limited in scope than the broader strategic examination that occurs in an intellectual property audit. (*See, infra,* Chapter 3.)

The following is a summary of the scientific, legal, and business issues to be resolved on both sides:

*Scientific Diligence*: Is the technology a good fit for the licensee? Or is there an alternative available? Are other component technologies from other sources required to develop the final product? What is the extent of additional development required to perfect the technology? If the technology has been tested only in the laboratory, or the device is only in prototype form, how much additional capital will be required to develop the final commercial product? Does the licensee have the in-house technical expertise to fully develop the technology?

*Legal Diligence*: Each patent and/or patent application is examined and the claims are analyzed. Have the requisite international rights been preserved? Are international rights needed? Have they already been protected? Does the patent offer a superior intellectual property position? Does the licensor own or have necessary rights in the relevant patents or patent applications? Depending on cost considerations, competitors' patents are also evaluated. For licenses that include nonpatented technology such as copyrights, trademarks, trade secrets, and possibly other intellectual property, questions must be asked and answered.

*Business Diligence*: The licensee's total costs are determined to the extent possible and compared to the cost of developing alternative technologies in-house. Included in the comparison are royalties and fees, assumption of future patent costs, if any, internal technology and product development costs, market analyses, customer surveys, and government regulatory approvals.

# E.  An Agreement Emerges As Key Terms Are Negotiated

## Licensing in International Strategy: A Guide for Planning and Negotiations*

Farok J. Contractor
(Quorum Books, 1985)

* * *

Caveats and Reminders for Writing Agreements

While conditions and requirements vary considerably from license to license, in my experience the following are some crucial items:

*What is Being Transferred?* The agreement must define the technology exactly, and as narrowly as possible from the licensor's perspective. How do we define a "future improvement"? Will it be passed on to the licensee free of charge, or will there be additional payment? If so, how much or how will it be negotiated?

*Types of Compensation.* Some governments try to limit or scrutinize some categories of payment. Not all categories of payment may be deductible for taxes to the licensee, nor will the tax treatment be identical for the licensor. As a rule it is useful to be aware of alternative forms of payment and agree with the licensee on more than one or two channels of payment:

- Lump-sum fee (paid at signing, start-up, or later?)
- "Running" royalty
- Plant design and commissioning
- Technical assistance fee
- Per diem charges for technicians/personnel loaned [(excluding their expenses?)]
- Patent royalty (if treated separately)
- Trademark royalty (if treated separately)
- Management consultancy fee
- Sale of plant and equipment
- Sale of components
- Purchase of product from licensee
- Shares in licensee company stock and dividends thereon

With such a comprehensive list, if the licensee wants the technology seriously and will cooperate, there are always means to compensate the technology supplier adequately, even in the more restrictive LDCs (Less-Developed Countries) and Socialist-bloc nations. An up-front fee is desirable because it may cover the licensor's transfer costs and is definitive proof of the licensee's intention to go into production. Too large an amount, however, may be too large an early burden on the licensee (unless the lump-sum is financed by a bank). "Running royalties," by contrast, means a "pay as you earn" situation for the licensee. Sometimes, the lump-sum amount is applied as a credit against future royalties.

Royalties are usually a flat percentage of sales (or a flat amount related to physical output, tons, square feet, gallons, etc.). However, royalties may decrease with vol-

---

ume—the licensor having taken a share of the earnings now leaves more of the future gains of expansion to the licensee. Or royalties may in rare cases increase with volume of output—the rationale here would be that this enables the licensor to share with the licensee in the cost economies of a large scale production, if achieved....Licensors should try to avoid mention of industry royalty norms or "most favored licensee" clauses that would tend to reduce compensation toward that paid by the lowest-paying licensee. (Licensees will, for these very reasons, try to mention these factors in negotiations and try to find out what other licensees are paying for the technology.)

\* \* \*

[C]ompensation is related to several benchmarks of cost and market value. The list below provides further detail and demonstrates the uniqueness of each situation. The + or - sign indicates whether the total licensing agreement compensation increases or decreases as a function of the following variables:

- Size of market or territory (+)
- Competition faced by licensee in the product market (-)
- Transfer costs (+)
- Opportunity costs to licensor (+)
- Exclusivity granted to licensee (+)
- Years since the patent was registered (-)
- Age of technology in general (-)
- Exportability of product by licensee (+)
- Number of alternative sources for similar technology (-)
- Commercial proof of production viability, as opposed to pilot plant or unproven method (+)
- Strength of patent and its defensibility (+)
- Inclusion of internationally known trademark (+)
- Ubiquitous licensing of standardized process to many licensees (-)
- Agreement includes present and future technologies developed by licensor (+)
- Inclusion of performance guarantees (+)
- Agreement includes other income source for licensor, such as supply of components (-)

*Payment Definitions.* Most royalties are linked to the licensee's "sales," but how are "sales" defined? "FOB less returns less excise duties," for example? Are royalties to be paid monthly, quarterly, or annually? In the agreement, a licensor should prefer the words "payments received" versus "payments made." For example, a license may make the payment, but the remitting bank may fail (such a thing has happened); or the funds may be deemed inconvertible. In such cases the licensee has "made" the payment, but the licensor has not "received" them. If the agreement merely says "payment made," the licensee is absolved of legal responsibility.

The question of foreign exchange risk is linked to the issue of indexation. Many agreements make no mention of this, on the assumption that a devaluation of the licensee's currency will (in the long run, through Purchasing Power Parity theory) be offset by inflationary increases in local currency sales of the licensed product to which the royalties are pegged. Since this economic adjustment occurs relatively freely in nations with floating currencies, this need not be a large worry in such countries. Nor is it a worry in countries where the government "manages" the foreign exchange rate; the overwhelming tendency is to "support" their currency, to prevent or forestall its devaluation, thus "overvaluing" it, despite domestic inflation. This benefits the licensor.

When then are these foreign exchange factors of major concern? In two scenarios: (1) in the cases where the government is alleged to "undervalue" its currency, notably the Japanese yen; and (2) when the royalty is not expressed as a percentage of sales value, but linked to other criteria such as physical output measures. In such cases, from the licensor's viewpoint, it is necessary to write specific escalator clauses linking royalties with a price index....

*Defining the Territory.* Since one of the critical factors in determining compensation is the size of the market, defining the limits of the licensee's territory is important. Limiting territory is also crucial because the licensor may be doing business in neighboring countries or may wish to establish licensees there. This issue is a legal minefield because both U.S. antitrust law and the recipient country's regulations apply. Attorneys will want to concern themselves with whether it is legally permissible to specify a place of manufacture and/or sales territory.

While of definite concern in industrial nations, particularly the European Economic Community (EEC) [now the European Union (EU)], it is easy to overdo this point in other nations and hurt the negotiations process needlessly. As a practical matter, many licensees have their hands full with their own country's market and the propensity to export is usually very low (although this is a matter to be carefully assessed by the licensor). At any rate, when an explicit prohibition cannot be written, the licensor may, with feigned generosity, offer themselves as the international marketing channel. That way, there may be some control (and a chance to earn additional profit).

The last territorial issue concerns sub-license rights. Should the licensee be given those rights and under what conditions?

*Trademark Licensing....* A well-known trademark may have great economic value to the licensee (which incidentally will be shared with the licensor). However, it may also be tarnished by a poor quality item made by the licensee. More likely, with a widely licensed brand name there may arise a doubt in the minds of the consumers as to whether the item is superior or "elite."

A critical issue with trademarks is what happens on termination of an agreement. Extensive use of the trademark by the licensee is tantamount to them locking their company into its use. The wider the mark's recognition among consumers, the more the licensee becomes dependent on its continued use. When an agreement is to be renewed, this may reduce their bargaining leverage vis-a-vis the licensor if the latter still holds the rights to the trademark. Do the country's laws permit the licensor this privilege? [U.S. laws generally do so, saving a trademark owner great leverage in renewal.]

*Cancellation of License.* It is important for both parties to agree in advance on the conditions under which the agreement may be [terminated or] canceled. ["Termination" is the more common term in the United States.] Three principal licensor concerns are:

1.  [The licensee's f]ailure to develop or sell the licensed product or to use the licensed process. This can be handled by specifying either a minimum annual

royalty or minimum turnover, failing which the agreement is void. (Of course, it is clear that when a licensee is making a large capital investment incorporating the technology, their intention of making a commercial success of the venture is strong. In such a case it may be overzealous to insist on such a clause.)

2. Maintenance of quality standards, especially if trademark is licensed. Besides the threat of cancellation as a last resort, the licensor may reserve the right of periodic inspection.

3. Inconvertibility of royalty payments from licensee currency to hard currencies. It may be worth it, to make inconvertibility a reason for agreement cancellation.

* * *

# F. The Most Basic Terms of a License: The "Scope" of the License

The terms that specify exactly what is licensed and for what purposes are by far the most important terms of any licensing agreement. They are even more important than the payment terms, for they tell what payment is for. Without knowing what payments are *for*, neither the parties nor a court can determine whether payments are fair, reasonable, and appropriate.

The provisions of a license that control what is licensed and for what purposes are often referred to under the general heading of "scope" or "scope of the license." They include the nature of the intellectual property licensed, the particular rights granted and reserved, the exclusivity (if any) of the grant, the permitted fields of use, the licensed territory, and any explicit limitations on the foregoing. Each of these terms has profound significance for the value of the license in business, its effect (or lack thereof) on unlicensed competition, the type and size of payment that is appropriate, and the law's treatment of the parties in the event of a dispute.

Given their importance from both business and legal perspectives, it is surprising how often, in the real world, these vital terms are incompletely specified, ambiguous, or unclear. Few businesspeople would sell a car (for example) without specifying its make, model and year, the size of its engine, and its accessories. Yet the federal reporters are filled with cases in which licensing terms that answer the basic question "what is the deal?" are missing, ambiguous, unclear, or poorly thought through.

Brief reflection, however, reveals the cause of these all-too-frequent lapses. Goods such as cars are tangible things. They are capable of being inspected, weighed, and measured. If a seller makes only a single line of cars, specifying which of them is to be sold is hardly a difficult matter. Even if a legal description is incomplete or inaccurate, the actual sale of the first item may reveal the nature of the deal, because a tangible object intrinsically contains its own description.

The rights conveyed by licenses, however, are a different thing altogether. They are entirely intangible. Unlike a car or other tangible good, they do not intrinsically contain their own description. The only thing that determines them is the wording of the license itself. Indeed, except for prototypes and samples (whose sale is not rare, but is also not common, in licensing), there is seldom any tangible embodiment or description of the rights conveyed except the license itself. This fact puts extraordinary pressure on both licensee—to describe precisely what rights it is buying—and licensor—to specify what rights, if any, it holds in reserve.

The terms in the "scope" of a license generally fall into six categories: (1) the intellectual property licensed; (2) the nature of the rights granted; (3) the exclusivity, if any, of the grant; (4) the field of use; (5) the licensed territory; and (6) any limitations. Each of these terms is sufficiently complex, and sufficiently fraught with both peril and opportunity, to merit separate discussion.

**1. The subject matter of the license: the intellectual property involved.** The first step in specifying the scope of a license is to lay out what intellectual property it covers. In what property is the license supposed to convey rights? Is the subject matter patents, trade secrets, copyrights, trademarks, some other intellectual property, or a combination of the foregoing? Are rights in the intellectual property inchoate—a patent *application*, an unregistered copyright, an unregistered common-law trademark—or have the rights been perfected by an appropriate governmental filing and the issuance of a patent or registration certificate?

Other provisions of the license may depend upon the answers to these questions. For example, if the rights are inchoate, the license agreement should specify who is to perfect them, and who is to pay the cost of doing so.

Although specifying the property at issue may seem simple, that simplicity is often deceptive. The job may seem quick enough if the license covers only a single patent or a single version of computer software covered by a single copyright registration certificate. Why not just specify the title of the invention or software, list the number of the patent or copyright registration certificate (or attach a copy to the license) and be done with it?

The answer is clear but troubling for lawyers. The bare legal rights appurtenant to a single form of intellectual property may not, in themselves, be useful in business. A patent licensee, for example, may need the licensor's auxiliary trade secrets and know-how, which are not disclosed in the patent, in order to make commercial use of the patented technology. For example, in a well-known decision, the Federal Circuit held that the patent on the M-16 rifle was not invalid for failure to disclose how to make its parts interchangeable and to mass produce the weapon, because the claims of the patent had nothing to do with interchangeability or mass production. *See Christianson v. Colt Indus. Operating Corp.*, 822 F.2d 1544, 1562–64 (Fed. Cir. 1987), *vacated and remanded on jurisdictional grounds*, 86 U.S. 800 (1988). Thus a licensee seeking the technology for mass production would have required more than just a bare patent license. Similarly, a software licensee may need more than a bare license to "run" software; it may need to modify and adapt the software and, for that purpose, may have to have access to secret source code or so-called "application programming interfaces" (APIs). Without such "auxiliary technology" or "auxiliary rights," otherwise valuable rights in the bare intellectual property (patent or copyright) may be as worthless as a car without an engine.

This fact of life is and should be sobering for licensing lawyers, especially those just beginning their careers. It implies that licensing anything is perilous without some knowledge of the subject matter of the license and its business application. Of course lawyers are not expected to be product marketers, far less engineers or scientists. Yet neither can lawyers hide behind the "ostrich credo," saying "I'm a *lawyer*; I don't know anything about business, and I don't give business or technical advice." Strict adherence to the ostrich credo may produce a fine piece of legal work that has little or no commercial value.

Partly to avoid paying lawyers' high fees for just such marginally useful work, business people often insist on describing the subject matter of a license in business, not legal, terms. (For more on this point, see JAY DRATLER, JR., LICENSING OF INTELLECTUAL PROPERTY § 1.05 (Law Journal Press 1994 & supps. (LEXIS, LJLIP). For example, a firm seeking a license from Colt to mass produce the M-16 rifle might describe the subject matter of the license simply as "the M-16 Technology" and define that term as including the product (weapon) and the process of its production (including parts interchangeability and mass production). Then the lawyers—or a court later, in the event of a dispute—would have to sort out (perhaps with the help of engineers) what patents and other intellectual property (such as trade secrets) were covered. There are advantages and disadvantages to this approach, but the lawyer who wishes to maintain good relationships with her clients should learn to accommodate it, for example, by carefully scrutinizing the key definitions and, if appropriate, attaching a schedule of licensed patents, patent applications and trade secrets as part of the definition.

**2. The rights conveyed and reserved.** Once the subject matter of the license—the intellectual property it covers—is specified, the next step is enumerating the rights in it that the license grants and withholds. To a certain extent, the rights available for grant depend upon the type of intellectual property covered. Once the parties have described the intellectual property, they can look up the rights available (for example, in the governing federal statute) and negotiate which ones are to be granted and which reserved to the licensor. As in specifying the intellectual property, however, the apparent simplicity of this process is deceptive, for determining what rights a licensee will need often involves peering into the future. Each of these processes is worthy of discussion.

For federally protected intellectual property, the governing federal statute specifies what rights are available for license. Patent law gives a patentee the right to exclude others from making, using, selling, offering for sale, or importing a patented product, and from using, selling, offering for sale, or importing products made by a patented process. *See* 35 U.S.C. §§ 154(a)(1). Copyright law gives the copyright owner the six exclusive rights to (1) reproduce, (2) prepare derivative works from, (3) distribute, (4) publicly perform, (5) publicly display, and (6) digitally audio transmit the copyrighted work. *See* 17 U.S.C. § 106 (specifying also which rights apply to which kinds of works). While the federal trademark statute does not specify rights as precisely, its "related company" provisions do require that a licensee's use of a licensed mark be limited to goods or services whose "nature and quality" are controlled by the licensor. *See* 15 U.S.C. § 1055 (discussing use and first use of mark by related company); Lanham Act § 45, 15 U.S.C. § 1127 (defining "related company" as one whose use of mark is controlled with respect to nature and quality of goods or services). *See generally* DRATLER, *supra*, § 11.03 (discussing legal requirement for control of nature and quality of goods and services on which licensed marks are used).

So far so good. Is specifying licensed rights then simply a matter of dividing the statutory list of rights between licensee (for those granted) and licensor (for those reserved)? Unfortunately, the process is hardly that simple, for two reasons. First, under longstanding patent doctrine and the doctrine of "divisibility of copyright" the statutory rights are infinitely divisible. Among other things, license agreements can parse them in terms of territory and field of use (see Points 4 and 5 below). Second, and equally important, a license that slavishly divides the rights along the lines of the discrete statutory terms ("make, use, and sell," etc.) would, in most cases, make little commercial sense. For example, a patent licensee that wishes to make patented products for its own internal use, as well as for sale to others, would need the rights to make, use, sell, and offer them for sale, if not to import them. As in the case of specifying the intellectual property described above, a well-drafted license agreement must parse rights to accommodate business needs, lest it produce the proverbial car without an engine.

What makes this process difficult is that license agreements are usually concluded before production and marketing of *anything* begins. Changes in business conditions, new technology, or general economic conditions may motivate or require the licensee's use of rights not originally contemplated, or (from the licensor's side) the assertion of restrictions or reservations that are not clear.

Two examples are worth noting. The first—familiar to most copyright students—is the rights of publishers with respect to the work of freelance authors who contribute to a particular issue of a magazine or newspaper. When electronic databases such as LEXIS/NEXIS came along, the publishers would have liked to include the freelancers' independently copyrighted contributions in the material from their periodicals that they licensed for republication in the electronic databases. The Supreme Court, however, ruled that publishers had no statutory right to do so. *See New York Times Co. v. Tasini*, 533 U.S. 483, 498–99 (2001). In the absence of appropriate contractual licenses or assignments, the publishers had to modify their contracts to obtain those rights from freelance authors.

A second case, from the field of software, demonstrates the importance of reservations of rights. Sun Microsystems, a computer hardware maker, developed a computer programming language, called "Java," designed especially for use on the Internet. Sun licensed the software to Microsoft, no doubt in order to expand its usage and appeal. Microsoft, however, developed its own proprietary version of Java, intending (according to Sun) to "migrate" customers to its proprietary version and eventually take the product away from Sun. *See Sun Microsystems, Inc. v. Microsoft Corp.* (In re *Microsoft Corp. Antitrust Litigation*), 333 F.3d 517, 522–24 (4th Cir. 2003). After Sun sued Microsoft for antitrust violations and copyright infringement, Sun and Microsoft entered into a settlement agreement, which contained a limited license of Java to Microsoft. Microsoft later developed further proprietary versions of Sun's Java technology, and Sun sued again. Although the appeals court ultimately denied Sun a preliminary injunction on antitrust grounds, it granted such an injunction on the ground of copyright infringement, holding that Microsoft's use of Java had exceeded limitations in the settlement license. *See id.*, 333 F.3d at 534–36.

Both of these examples illustrate the importance of considering future developments in licensing. Had newspaper and magazine publishers included rights to republish freelancers' articles in electronic databases earlier, the *Tasini* litigation might not have been necessary. Sun's prescience in including appropriate limitations in its Java settlement license to Microsoft (if not in the original license) may well have prevented Microsoft from taking Sun's software product market away entirely.

Of course no one—least of all lawyers—owns a crystal ball that can predict developments in technology and business with complete accuracy. Yet these two examples, in different ways, illustrate the value, not only of making the effort, but of cooperating with engineers, product developers, marketers, and other executives in doing so. Only by putting all of their heads together can people in these different lines of work hope to anticipate what rights their firms may need (or for licensors, what reservations of rights they might wish they had) years in the future. The accelerating rate of change in business, economics and technology, coupled with the relatively long life of intellectual property—twenty years for patents, a century or more for copyrights, and potentially forever for trademarks and trade secrets—makes such cooperation imperative in "parsing" rights granted and rights reserved.

One other point with respect to rights is worth making. When courts have to fill in silent contracts, they normally rule that rights not expressly granted are reserved. *See* DRATLER, *supra*, § 1.06[1]. That rule is not invariable, however. Courts can impose rights by implication where it makes sense to do so. *See id.* The moral of the story is that good lawyers do not leave important questions to the vagaries of implication in litigation. Licensees should make sure that all rights they need are stated expressly in the license, and licensors should make sure that all reservations of rights on which they later might wish to rely are also so stated. Licensors may rely on a general statement that all rights not expressly granted are reserved, but such boilerplate, which merely restates the common law, is far less effective than explicit reservations of important rights.

**3. Exclusivity.** Apart from the intellectual property covered and the rights conveyed and reserved, the exclusivity (*vel non*) of a license is probably its most important term. Exclusivity may not seem that important to lawyers. After all, lawyers deal in words, and resolving this issue may take just one word: "exclusive" or "nonexclusive." Yet for the business person, that one word makes all the difference between the quiet life of monopoly and the hurly burly of no-holds-barred competition.

The exclusivity of a license agreement also implicates a whole host of related terms. If the license is *fully* exclusive, i.e., if the license excludes even the licensor, then the licensor will depend wholly upon the licensee for commercial exploitation of the subject matter of the license. To the extent the license is a major source of revenue, the licensor may depend upon it for revenue as well. Accordingly, licensors often demand up-front payments or substantial investment in commercial exploitation of the licensed subject matter as recompense for an exclusive license. While not unheard of, up-front payments and requirements for substantial investment in nonexclusive licenses are rare.

Exclusivity also may influence the terms of license agreement relating to defense of intellectual property against third-party infringers. An exclusive licensee may insist on having rights to sue infringers and to keep all or part of the proceeds of any recovery. If a license is nonexclusive, the licensor usually will insist on keeping those rights, particularly if there is to be more than one nonexclusive license, because dividing those rights among multiple nonexclusive licensees would only dilute the incentive and motivation to exercise them.

Another important effect of exclusivity relates to antitrust and competition law. Exclusive licenses often require close scrutiny under the these laws, especially when they have the purpose or effect of entrenching a monopoly or dominant position with respect to the licensed subject matter. Nonexclusive licenses, however, require much less antitrust scrutiny, especially when there are several nonexclusive licensees of the same subject matter. Antitrust and competition law seek to promote competition, and nonexclusive licenses generally do that, especially when they encourage multiple nonexclusive licensees to compete among themselves in commercially exploiting the common subject matter of their licenses. *See generally*, DRATLER, *supra*, §§ 6.05[2], 7.08.

By now it should be clear that exclusive and nonexclusive licenses are (except when nonexclusivity is a sham without business substance) completely different animals. In many respects, exclusive licenses, within their possibly limited scope, have an economic effect more like assignments than licenses. Copyright law explicitly recognizes this point by defining an exclusive license, within its purview, as a "transfer of copyright ownership." *See* 17 U.S.C. § 101 (definition of "transfer of copyright ownership"). In addition, exclusivity: (1) affects the licensee's standing to sue infringers on its own, *see* DRATLER, *supra*, § 8.06; (2) imposes implied duties of good faith and diligence on the licensee, *see id.*, § 8.07; and (3) may require the license to be recorded in order to receive protection against intervening bona-fide purchasers of rights. *See id.*, § 8.02.

Because of these important differences, no lawyer should sit down to draft a license agreement without knowing whether the parties intend it to be exclusive or nonexclusive. Furthermore, if the license is to be exclusive, the lawyer should enquire whether it will exclude the licensor (a fully exclusive license) or not (a "co-exclusive" license). Whatever the answer, the license should so state explicitly, in order to avoid any misunderstanding.

4. **Field of use.** In discussing rights granted and reserved (see Point 2 above), we noted that most statutory rights can be subdivided into infinitely small bundles. One of the most important ways in which they can be subdivided is by field of use. Indeed, it exaggerates little to say that, from a licensor's standpoint, field-of-use limitations are one of the most important ways to make money from a single licensed property.

An example best illustrates this point. Suppose that Firm X develops an accurate blood test for cancer at the microscopic level, before it becomes clinically significant. Firm X applies for several patents covering this test and related technology. The test works with both humans and animals and has considerable accuracy in both. Firm X, however, is a small research boutique, without the personnel, skill, or resources to take the test through clinical testing and governmental approval, let alone to manufacture and market test kits.

Firm X, however, has proposals from two firms that wish to in-license its testing technology. Firm A is a multinational pharmaceutical firm with vast resources and a large pipeline of human drugs and test procedures in every phase of clinical testing, production, and marketing. Firm B is a much smaller American firm, specializing in veterinary medicine, which has had great recent success in obtaining regulatory approval for, producing, and marketing medical tests for animals.

Both firms have requested exclusive licenses of Firm X's technology, and both have refused to make any up-front payment for a license until after regulatory approval for a licensed product is received. Firm X's managers estimate that the human market for the tests is ten times the animal market. They also predict that test kits for humans will sell for $150 each, while those for animals will command no more than $40. Finally, they think that clinical testing and governmental approval for the human market will take five years, while the same process for the animal market will take no more than eighteen months.

Firm X is low on cash, and it needs an infusion of funds now. What should it do? If it licenses Firm A exclusively, its long-term prospects are much greater, but it may have to wait a long time for substantial, if any, returns. If it licenses Firm B exclusively, it may see returns more quickly, but it might forego the lucrative human market, since Firm B has no expertise or interest in human health care.

The best answer is for Firm X to offer *each* of Firm A and Firm B an exclusive license, with each license limited to the respective licensee's particular field of use. That is, Firm X would license the test technology to Firm A exclusively in the field of human testing, and to Firm B exclusively within the field of animal testing. Both Firms A and B would likely accept this offer, as the two markets are distinct and require distinct expertise to enter, and each of the two firms who not have to suffer competition in its own market.

Who would win with such a strategy? Just about everybody. Firm X would win because it could license its technology into both of its principal potential markets and receive two revenue streams instead of one. Firm A and Firm B would both win, because their exclusive licenses would protect their respective markets from competition, thereby encouraging them to invest substantially in exploiting those markets.

What about the public? It would win also, because Firm X's exploitation of both markets would amortize its cost of research more quickly. Furthermore, the fact that Firm X could license both firms might cause it to accept a lower royalty from Firm A than it would otherwise (because it could get additional revenue from Firm B). The lower royalty paid by Firm A might ultimately result in lower prices for test kits to the public. Economists call this phenomenon "price discrimination": by addressing a second (animal) market at a lower price per kit, Firm X could "subsidize" its research in the human health field, resulting in lower costs of production in that field and potentially lower prices. Thus everyone—licensor, licensees, and the public—potentially can win from field-of-use licensing.

Exclusive field-of-use licensing is particularly important in the field of computer software. Today, there are only a few major vendors of personal computer hardware. Rather than giving each only a nonexclusive license, a software vendor can offer each an exclusive license, limited to its particular brand of computer hardware. In this way, the software vendor can allow each manufacturer to control how distributors and dealers within its distribution chain use the licensed software on its own hardware. That control makes the software licenses more valuable to each hardware maker, thereby justifying a larger return to the software vendor. At the same time, each hardware maker (and its distribution chain) competes with the other hardware makers (and their respective distribution chains) to market the licensed software. The result is almost the same as a series of nonexclusive licenses, but the exclusivity (within each hardware maker's distribution chain) provides for greater vertical control, which may both justify a higher return to the software vendor and increase competition in the use of the software as between the major hardware brands.

Because of these potentially beneficial effects, field-of-use restraints are governed by the rule of reason for antitrust purposes and are generally upheld as lawful. *See General Talking Pictures Corp. v. General Elec. Co.*, 304 U.S. 175, (1938), *aff'd on rehearing* 205 U.S. 124, 127 (1938); DRATLER, *supra*, §7.04. In copyright licensing, field-of-use limitations in exclusive licenses are routine and expected, because every exclusive license is a slice of copyright ownership. Territorial restrictions might also be considered field-of-use restraints, but they require more probing antitrust analysis and therefore are considered separately.

**5. Territorial limitations.** Another common limitation on the scope of a license is a limitation to particular territory. Such a limitation allows the licensee to exploit the licensed subject matter, but only inside a specified territory.

Territorial limitations may appear in both exclusive and nonexclusive licenses, but their economic effect may be the same whether or not the licenses are exclusive. If the licensee, for example, only grants one license within each of several disjoint territories, it does not matter whether the licenses are nominally exclusive or not. Even if they purport to be nonexclusive, the fact that the territories are disjoint makes them exclusive in effect.

Territorial limitations usually have one of two business purposes. First, they may simply reflect the reality of licensees' businesses. For example, if a licensee has facilities and does business only in Illinois, it may make sense to limit its license to that state, so that the licensor can retain the right to grant exclusive licenses elsewhere. (Presumably the exclusive licenses elsewhere would command a higher price than nonexclusive ones.)

The second common rationale for territorially exclusive licensing is start-up costs. A licensee may have to make a substantial investment in plant, equipment, hiring, training, or production in order to exploit newly licensed subject matter. If it does, the licensor can encourage and reward that investment by granting the license exclusivity within its territory, either directly by granting it an exclusive territorial license, or indirectly by promising not to grant others licenses in the exclusive territory. In either case, the license arrangement gives the licensee "breathing room"—in the form of effective freedom from competition—within its territory.

Although territorial limitations might be analogized to limitations on field of use, they require greater antitrust scrutiny because of their potential negative impact on competition. Exclusive territories can hurt competition even more than price fixing because, if strictly enforced, they preclude *any* competition whatsoever, even competition on nonprice terms that price-fixing might allow.

In the United States, the validity of exclusive territories depends mostly upon whether they are "horizontal" or "vertical" in effect. If they have a horizontal effect, i.e., if they limit competition between what otherwise would be direct, primary competitors, they are illegal *per se. See United States v. Topco Assocs, Inc.*, 405 U.S. 596, 609–12 (1972) (where independent sofa manufacturers formed holding company to own jointly-used trademark and to grant ostensible trademark licenses with effective exclusive territories, scheme was essentially one to divide territory among independent horizontal competitors and therefore was illegal *per se*).

Yet territorial restraints imposed *vertically,* for example, by a licensor on licensees within a vertical licensing pyramid, are governed by the rule of reason that applies generally to nonprice vertical restraints, at least if that pyramid competes with rivals offering similar products or services using other technology. *See Cont'l T.V., Inc. v. GTE Sylvania Inc.*, 433 U.S. 36, 58–59 (1977) (holding that nonprice vertical restraints are governed generally by the rule of reason). The more strongly the vertical, *intra*brand territorial restraints assist *inter*brand competition between independent licensing pyramids, the more likely they are to be lawful. *See* DRATLER, *supra*, § 7.11[1]. Yet where there is no interbrand competition, for example, because the licensing pyramid at issue has market power in a defined market, even vertically imposed territorial restraints may be unlawful.

Outside the United States, territorial restraint rules are more strict. The European Union generally disapproves of exclusive territories, except for limited periods, because they conflict with one of its most basic principles: the free movement of goods, services, and people among its member states. *See* DRATLER, *supra*, § 7.11[2]. Japan allows exclusive territories and export limitations for licensed technology, but only with respect to exports to territory in which the licensor owns patents and is exploiting them. *See* DRATLER, *supra*, § 7.11[3].

**6. Other limitations on scope.** The foregoing aspects of a license's scope—intellectual property covered, rights conveyed and reserved, exclusivity, field of use, and territory—are, no doubt, the most common and generally the most important aspects of scope. But they are not the only ones; nor are they necessarily the most important in every licensing deal. Terms that may have business importance are as varied as the industries that engage in licensing and the transactions that they enter.

Additional common terms of scope may relate to follow-on technology. For example, if the licensor agrees or offers to include its own improvements in the license, it may *insist* that the licensee use the offered improvements, rather than the originally licensed technology. Such terms are common, for example, in software licensing. A software licensor may want licensees to use only the latest version of the licensed software, in order to minimize the cost and effort involved in maintenance and training. A software license for such a purpose, for example, might terminate the license for replaced technology a specified time after replacement technology is included in the license and accepted by the licensee. In such a case, the "scope" of the license would depend on both the improvement technology developed by the licensor and the passage of time.

This is just one example, among many, of how the "scope" of a license may change in ways that are not easily categorized. The important point is that all such descriptions and limitations of scope be stated as clearly and explicitly as possible, for the use of licensed subject matter beyond the scope of a license generally constitutes infringement of the licensed intellectual property. *See* DRATLER, *supra*, § 1.06[1].

---

# G. The Final Agreement Is Drafted and Signed

Drafting is an arduous process that usually continues throughout the negotiations. Licensors find it strategically beneficial to control the drafts in order to exert maximum influence on the language used.

Pride of authorship has no place in this setting. This is not a work of literature but rather the road map for a dynamic relationship. If the other party disagrees over terminology or wants what appears to be an irrelevant clause it may be wise to humor it. Chapter 7, *infra*, will introduce the standard clauses appearing in most license agreements.

---

# H. Transfer of Technology and Technical Assistance

Licensees will want the scope of the actual technology transfer to be carefully spelled out in the agreement. More than intellectual property rights may be needed for successful commercialization. A patent license, for instance, may not disclose much of the licensor's valuable know-how. Also, the licensor's research may have continued after the patent was issued, creating a gap between the licensed technology and the licensor's technology. In addition, there are tangible property rights to be considered. For example, software licensees may need the source code and documentation. Or to understand the technology's genesis or evolution, licensees of devices may want older prototypes. In the case of method patents, manufacturing techniques and experimental data would be valuable. Biotech licensees will want biological materials, for example, stem cells, antibodies, genes, or other organisms that have been cultured by the licensor. All these are examples of tangible materials that would be valuable to the licensee. In addition, the inventor may have a wealth of technical information that was earned the hard way: through trial and error.

One solution for the licensee is to obtain the services of the inventor to provide technical assistance for a time after the license is executed. For example, the agreement may specify that the inventor will work on site at the licensee's plant to teach the technology. It is in the licensor's interest that the licensee have whatever assistance or know-how may be required to help develop a successful royalty-bearing product. On the other hand, should technical assistance not be available, the licensor may intentionally choose a licensee with high technical capabilities in a very similar business so that little assistance from the licensor is expected or required.

## I.   Monitoring

Because licenses involve a continuing relationship, vigilance is required. Vigilance may take many forms and adds real costs to the deal for the licensor. Vigilance can include (i) monitoring infringement by third parties, or even the licensee, in the case of a limited field of use or a territorially-restricted license; (ii) periodic review of royalty statements to insure payment accuracy, and when necessary, ordering outside audits of the licensee's books; and (iii) threatening termination of the license if the licensee's performance violates the agreement, e.g., royalty-bearing products fail to reach the market within the time specified or fail to reach required sales minimums.

# IV. Licensing in More Complex Arrangements

The opening remarks of this chapter touched on the current business trend toward collaborative arrangements. The myriad forms these partnerships can take are beyond the scope of this text; however, one model in which licensing plays a key role involves a substantial contribution of products, technology, and/or research and development by at least one party (typically the smaller one) and some sort of investment (equity, debt or R&D funding) and/or services by the other party (typically the larger party). Such an arrangement risks that the larger entity may, in effect, plunder the smaller, especially if negotiations are halted or, after signing, the relationship breaks down.

### Form, Function, and Fairness: Structuring
### the Technology Joint Venture*

Scott Killingsworth
15 (No. 3) COMPUTER LAW. 1 (March 1998)

Technology based joint ventures are a powerful way for companies with complementary strengths to enter new markets more quickly and effectively than either venturer could manage alone. Because both technology itself and markets for technology products change rapidly, an equally rapid market entry and swift capture of significant market share are often critical to long-term success. But due to the combined effects of constant technological change and the trend towards corporate specialization, it is increasingly unlikely that any given company will possess all the necessary ingre-

---

\* Reprinted with permission of the publisher, copyright 1998.

dients for rapid and effective entry into a new market. In this environment, competitive advantage belongs to the company that can quickly identify, and combine forces with, a partner who has what that company needs, and who needs what that company has.

\* \* \*

### Technology Venture Paradigms

The term "joint venture" is used here in the broad sense of a strategic alliance of two or more separate business entities, sharing assets and risks in joint pursuit of a discrete market. Its legal structure may fall anywhere along the continuum between a bare license and a merger. The classic joint venture is a new entity—a partnership, limited liability company, or corporation—to which each joint venturer has contributed assets in exchange for an equity interest in the venture; but similar principles apply to contractual joint ventures, strategic partnerships, and even some distribution and manufacturing agreements. For purposes of issues related to technology transfer, the distinctions among these forms are often less significant than what they have in common.

Most joint ventures are characterized by asymmetry in the strengths or assets that each partner contributes to the venture. If both partners contribute essentially the same things, the only advantage of the venture is size, but if each partner has strength the other lacks, important synergies are possible. A joint venture allows each venturer not only to avoid the expense and risk involved in directly acquiring the particular asset it needs (whether capital, brand recognition, a distribution channel, a technology, or a factory), but also, importantly, to save the time required to do so. At the same time, this natural lack of symmetry in the parties' contributions also produces structural tensions for the venture, since inevitably comparisons must be drawn between apples and oranges. Deals are made when the added value from synergy is perceived as outweighing both the uncertainties about the relative value of the parties' contributions and the dilutive effect of sharing the wealth with one's partner.

Another characteristic feature is that the venture exists to pursue a market somehow distinct from those already occupied by the venture partners; this distinction may be defined by technology, by geography, by vertical market or end-use, or by marketing or distribution channel. Such an incremental market offers an attractive risk-reward picture because, whatever assets must be placed at risk to enter it, the venturer's core business is not among them. The particular market involved can influence the choice of venture structure: for example, the more unstable or unpredictable the market, the looser and more easily dismantled the venture will likely be.

Recurring paradigms for technology joint ventures include the following:

Two venturers contribute complementary technologies which are used together to create a new product. The joint venture is dedicated to manufacturing, marketing and distributing that product and creates an infrastructure for doing so independent of either venture partner. Each partner gains access to a new product niche.

\* \* \*

A start-up company that has promising intellectual property and little else allies with an "industry player" with access to capital, manufacturing capacity, and a distribution network. The "player" gains the benefit of the technology company's innovation, and possibly a new breakthrough product, and the start-up gains everything it needs to commercialize its invention and enter the market before others emulate or leapfrog the technology.

## Structural Goals

What goals should one aim for in designing a joint venture, aside from synergy in the achievement of the venture's business purpose (at one end of the spectrum) and protection of the venturers' separate interests (at the other)? Flexibility, fairness, and simplicity should be near the top of the list. By definition, a joint venture envisions a continuing relationship between the venturers, which, whether or not lawyers like to admit it, will entail unanticipated developments, negotiations and adjustments over time. Add to this the inherent uncertainties of technology markets and it becomes evident that the venture's governing documents will serve no one well if they resemble a crystal lattice: highly structured, internally interdependent at every point, and brittle.

Flexibility means greater emphasis on creating processes for resolving business issues when they arise than on attempting to resolve all possible issues in advance. Fairness creates a collaborative atmosphere conducive to resolving conflicts, and simplicity makes it easier to understand the issues and to document and administer their resolution. A flexible structure also tends to simplicity, since it is much less complicated to create reasonable methods of adapting to unanticipated developments than to try to anticipate the entire universe of problems that could arise and to negotiate solutions for each.

In many cases, flexibility, simplicity, and fairness can all be promoted by giving the parties *choices* if certain events occur, as opposed to merely dictating obligations and relying, implicitly, on contract remedies if those obligations are not fulfilled. Technology ventures are especially amenable to this technique in connection with concepts such as exclusivity, obligation to exploit technology, sales or royalty *minima*, field of use, and the like.

Consider a hypothetical venture that has licensed technology from a venturer on an exclusive basis, with an obligation to exploit expressed in terms of minimum royalties. Under a straight-contract-obligation structure, the consequences of failure to exploit might simply be to pay the minimum royalty or to risk either termination of the license, or dissolution of the venture. But in the joint venture context, termination or dissolution is seldom an attractive prospect for anyone, and it is also unlikely that the licensor-venturer would really be happy with mere receipt of the minimum royalty, particularly when half of it indirectly comes out of the venturer's own pocket and drains the venture's capital. What that venturer wants is effective commercialization of its technology.

To achieve this, we might think in terms of choices rather than obligations: if sales of the licensed products do not generate the minimum royalty, the licensor-venturer might be given options to license others in the market or require the venture to do so, to sell directly into the market for a limited period, to promote the product at its own expense as a capital contribution to the venture, to add the amount of the royalty shortfall to its capital account in the venture, or even to take voting control of the venture. Options such as these can motivate the parties to seek the true cause of the failure to meet *minima* and to select a remedy appropriate to the problem.

Suppose the exclusive remedy for failure to meet *minima* is revocation of the venture's exclusivity in the market. If the problem is with the venture's ineffective marketing or distribution, revocation of exclusivity may be a reasonably good solution; and the threat of revocation should strongly motivate the venture to market as effectively as possible. But if the problem is *not* the marketing but the product itself, revocation of exclusivity could be self-defeating—merely accelerating commoditization and price competition as to a product that is already in trouble. No one has an interest in forcing the venture to throw good marketing money after bad on a flawed product.

\* \* \*

---

# Licensing in International Strategy:
## A Guide for Planning and Negotiations*
Farok J. Contractor
(Quorum Books, 1985)

\* \* \*

### The Narrowest Definition: Transfer of Patent Rights and Trademarks

In the narrowest definition, a license is merely permission given to another firm to engage in an activity otherwise legally forbidden to it. The concept flows from the fact that patents and trademarks are legally sanctioned monopolies on rights, proprietary to a company. These production and market rights are transferred to a licensee under an agreement for a consideration. A simple transfer of only a patent or a trademark to the licensee presumes, however, that the licensee is independently capable and merely awaits the conferral of the right to proceed on its own. Studies show that this is true only in a small minority of cases. In an analysis of some 3,500 agreements registered at the European Economic Community (EEC) Commission's office in 1976, patents were included in 56 percent of them, together with 'know-how' (which is unpatented but proprietary information in production, administration, and marketing) and other agreement provisions calling for training of licensee personnel or similar services. However, pure patent licenses were found in only a quarter of agreements and trademarks alone in only 4 percent. Similarly, in my earlier study of 102 international agreements made by U.S.-based firms, patents were included in 63 percent, but were deemed crucial in only a tiny minority. A 1982 survey of 259 companies by the Licensing Executive Society...support[ed] the view that, in an all-industry sense, while patents might well be part of many agreements, in a majority of cases know-how is of greater value to the licensee or technology recipient. Pure patent licensing occurs overall in about one of twenty agreements. (In specific industries like pharmaceuticals or chemicals, however, patents assume greater importance....)

### A Broader Definition: The Transfer of Technology

The transfer of technology is the transfer of a capability in production, administration, or marketing. It includes (a) rights to the use of patented information and trademarks in certain territories abdicated by agreement in favor of the licensee; (b) information that is proprietary but not patented, commonly called know-how (this may take the form of specifications, models, drawings, manuals, forms, layouts, checklists, charts, computer programs and so on); and (c) services such as equipment installation, start-up, testing, training, recruitment, management development, etc. Most international licensing agreements...are in fact technology transfers in a fuller sense.

Licensors properly view the process as not merely the one-time act of transferring patent rights, but as a relationship with the other enterprise over time. Some agree-

---

ments specifically provide for the transfer of new models, technical changes and updates, or more efficient procedures as long as the agreement remains valid, foreseeing the licensee's need for a continuing liaison with the licensor firm. *Business International* relates instances in the early 1970s where East European firms, having purchased only patent rights from British companies, could not convert them into effective production and had to call back the technology suppliers for further assistance and training.

\* \* \*

### The Broadest Perspective: Licensing as the Core of a Larger Contractual Package

Just as most international technology licensing agreements comprise considerably more than the conveyance of intellectual property rights to the licensee, the past decade has seen the growth of even more broadly defined contractual or "non-equity" agreements, where the technical license might constitute only the nucleus or catalyst of the whole arrangement....

While typically including a technology license on which front-end fees and royalties are paid, a broader package might include any of the following elements: turnkey plant, supply of components to the licensee, contract assembly or production for third countries, guaranteed "off-take" or "buy-back" in lieu of cash, management service, marketing assistance, advertising support, and cross-licensing of technologies. An illuminating taxonomy is used by the French in describing agreements as "clef en main," "product en main," or "march-e en main." The first is "key in hand" or turnkey, where the technology supplier's obligations cease after plant erection. In the second case, the technology supplier is required also to ensure effective production, through training or on-site personnel under a production management contract. In the "march-e en main" or market-in-hand case, they are also required to market the product under a general management service agreement that renders marketing assistance or in the extreme by guaranteeing purchase of some fraction of output.

The use of a broader contractual package wrapped around a technology licensing core is one of the basic strategy recommendations.... Two of the principal objections to licensing can be thereby overcome, namely, inadequate compensation and the danger of possible loss of the technology and the creation of competition.

\* \* \*

# Quantitative Methods of Valuing Intellectual Property*
### Russell L. Parr & Gordon V. Smith, *in* The New Role
#### of Intellectual Property in Commercial Transactions (1994)

\* \* \*

1.4    Factors That Drive Strategic Alliances: Time, Cost, Risk

Companies typically seek to expand product lines, increase market share, minimize new product development costs, expand market opportunities internationally, and reduce business risks. They seek to create corporate value for investors.

---

* Reprinted with the permission of the publisher, copyright 1994.

*Too Expensive on Your Own.* Even the largest companies cannot fund all the intellectual property programs that they may desire. Research programs can run into hundreds of millions of dollars annually, and trademark costs can reach billions of dollars. A major force behind the desire to form strategic alliances is the high level of investment needed to create new intellectual properties. The following list gives an indication of the amounts required to create, acquire, or protect keystone intellectual property:

- Pharmaceutical companies spend almost $250 million to develop and commercialize a new drug. [More recent studies put this figure as high as $800 million, at least if the cost of failed efforts is included.]
- Hoffman LaRoche paid $300 million to Cetus Corporation for the polymerase chain reaction technology.
- Philip Morris spends more than $2 billion annually on advertising programs to support the continuing recognition of its portfolio of brand names.
- A film producer paid $9 million for the television rights to the new book *Scarlet.*

One of the first major joint ventures of the 1990s was the combination of pharmaceutical product lines from DuPont with the distribution network of Merck & Company. The new joint venture company, DuPont-Merck, is equally owned by the two companies. DuPont had a product line of drugs but needed help with international distribution. The time and cost required to create its own network of sales staff was a formidable obstacle to fast growth and return on the research effort that DuPont had in the new drug line. Part of DuPont's worries included the remaining patent life associated with some of their drug products. By the time a self-created distribution network could be established, some of the valuable products would be off-patent. Full exploitation of patents required that sales be maximized during the premium price years before generic products hit the market. DuPont needed a way to tap its full market potential—fast.

Merck has annual sales of more than $6.5 billion. It also has one of the largest research and development budgets in the world. Even so, Merck has limitations as to the number of new drugs it can discover, investigate, develop, and commercialize. Access to a new line of already commercialized products was a great attraction for Merck.

The DuPont-Merck joint venture saved DuPont both time and money. It gave this company immediate access…to an international distribution network. Simultaneously, Merck gained immediate access to a whole new product line that would have cost enormous amounts of time and money to develop. This joint venture is a classic case of how the factors of time and cost drive strategic alliances founded on access to intellectual property. It also illustrates how strategic combinations of key intellectual property can reduce the investment risk associated with new ventures. If DuPont had attempted to build its own international distribution network, the cost would have been high, the time needed long, and there was no assurance that the company would successfully construct a network that could move the goods. Merck enjoyed a reduction in investment risk by gaining access to the profits associated with the DuPont product line. If Merck had embarked on its own plan to duplicate the DuPont product line, there was no assurance that it would have been completely successful. Furthermore, there was the risk that the Merck product line could have ultimately infringed on the DuPont product line. The two companies saved research funds, gained immediate access to commercialized intellectual property, and reduced business risk. Judy Lewent, chief financial officer at Merck & Company, told The Wall Street Journal that the Merck-DuPont deal "added about a third to our research capacity."

\* \* \*

# V. Government License Rights Regulations and Proprietary Technical Data and Software

The United States federal government ("government") licenses technical data and computer software under a variety of regulations. For example, most civilian agencies adhere to Federal Acquisition Regulations (FAR), while military agencies adhere to Department of Defense FAR Supplement (DFARS). Some civilian agencies, like NASA and the Department of Energy, have their own regulations. When considering these issues, one should carefully review the applicable procurement regulations and consult secondary sources, as most procurement regulations are confusing and may seem internally inconsistent. Because coverage of all the complexities of government data rights issues would likely double the size of this text, included below is a summary of issues relating to the delivery to the government of proprietary technical data and software, which does not address in detail the government's license in intellectual property created in performance of a government contract.

---

## A. Licensing Proprietary Non-Commercial Software to the USG

Proprietary software may be delivered to the government with a restricted license. "Non-commercial" or "proprietary" software generally means privately funded, operable software that has not yet been offered to commercial customers. Once software qualifies as non-commercial under particular procurement regulations, contractors may provide the software to the government with certain restrictions on the government's rights (a "restricted rights" license). Successfully delivering non-commercial software to a government agency with these restricted rights is a complex process that contains many traps for the unwary. Failing to meet the requirements for delivering software to a government agency with restricted rights carries the risk that the government agency will later assert an essentially unlimited license in the privately funded software.

One should first carefully review the applicable procurement regulations to determine that restricted rights delivery is permitted and that the software qualifies for delivery with restricted rights. To qualify, the software must have been "developed" before delivery. "Developed" generally means that software is workable and there has been analysis or testing sufficient to demonstrate to reasonable people that the software will likely operate as intended. *See* FAR 52.227-14(a); DFARS 252.227-7014(a)(6)(Jun. 1995). The software must also be segregable from the remainder of the deliverable and must not be modified in performance of the contract, because intermingling with government-funded software may result in the government asserting greater rights in the software.

If the software meets these requirements, it can be provided to the government with a "restricted rights" license. Delivery of the software with "restricted rights" places certain limitations on the government's use of the software, namely, the government may: (1) use the software on one computer at one time, to be accessed by only one terminal or central processing unit unless otherwise contractually permitted; (2) transfer the above license to another government agency; (3) make archival and backup copies; and (4) modify the software, subject to the restrictions in (1)–(3). The government is prohibited from using the software for competitive procurement and from disclosing to others. FAR 52.227-19. That being said, the government still takes an unlimited license in some exempted portions of the restricted rights software, discussed in more detail below.

When protecting one's rights in proprietary, non-commercial software, the three most important things to remember are notice, notice, and notice. First, the software owner must explicitly identify the software in the bid and any proposed statement of work. The statement of work should explicitly identify software that is subject to restricted rights, and should clearly prohibit any modification to the software in performance of the contract. Second, the software must be identified in both the contract and final statement of work. The format for the contract is the same as for the bid. Finally, any software included in deliverables must bear the legend required by the applicable government regulations. It is hard to overstate the importance of satisfying these notice requirements because, as explained in Note 16 below, a contractor's failure to meet the notice requirements will result in the government's assertion of an essentially unlimited license in the software.

---

# B. Licensing Commercial Software to the Government

Procurement regulations generally define "commercial" software as privately funded software that has been offered to commercial (non-government) customers, although different regulations contain subtle definitional differences and should therefore be reviewed carefully to determine if a particular software product qualifies as "commercial" under a particular regulation.

The general rule is that commercial software, licensed by contractors or subcontractors at any tier, is likewise licensed to the government with the same terms and conditions as the commercial license accompanying the software. *See* FAR 12.212 12.502; DFARS 227.7202-1(a), 7202-3(a); 7103-3(b) (Jun. 1995); FAR Subpart 27.4. However, this general rule has the condition that the government cannot agree to any terms of a standard license that are inconsistent with the federal procurement law or that does not meet with the procuring agency's requirements. FAR 27.405(b)(2)(ii). This condition permits the procuring agency to use a standard contract clause in lieu of abiding by the contractor's standard commercial license. Thus a government agency may choose to negotiate its rights under a commercial license by stating that the commercial license is inconsistent with the law, or that the commercial license does not meet the agency's requirement (under FAR 27.404(e) or 52.227-19).

This can create problems for contractors who procure commercial software for the government under contracts containing FAR 52.227-19. Specifically, FAR 52.227-19 contains certain exemptions that provide the government with unlimited rights in some portions of restricted rights software. The exemptions apply to (1) form, fit, and function data; (2) manuals or instructional and training material for installation, operation, or routine maintenance and repair; and (3) (for defense agencies) studies, analyses, test data, or similar data produced for the contract. The government takes "unlimited rights" in the software that falls within these exemptions. This essentially means that the federal government can use, and permit others to use, for any purpose, those portions of the software subject to FAR 52.227-19 exemptions.

These exemptions may be inconsistent with the software owner's standard commercial license accompanying the software. The government could argue that the commercial license is either inconsistent with the procurement law or that it does not meet the agency's requirements, so the agency is allowed to use a standard contract clause—in this case FAR 52.227-19—in lieu of more restrictive commercial license terms. Therefore, the government may argue that incorporation of FAR 52.227-19 in a solicitation or contract renders the software's standard commercial license accompanying the software entirely irrelevant. At minimum, the government would obtain the minimum restricted rights, regardless of the terms contained in the commercial license.

The government's assertion of these broader rights may be unacceptable to a contractor or subcontractor commercial licensor. Worse, a contractor may now risk exposure of both a breach of contract claim (by the commercial software vendor) and possible indemnification obligations to the government (depending upon the terms of the prime contract). For example, a contractor procures the software from a third party vendor with the expectation of delivering it to the government, only to find that the government asserts greater rights than are permitted by the commercial software license (under FAR 52.227-19).

Thus, one rule of thumb for reviewing government proposals that anticipate the delivery of commercial software is to look for FAR 52.227-19 and request its deletion. You can then address a particular commercial license's failure to meet government's needs during the bidding or negotiation for that contract and avoid dispute during contract administration. If commercial software is a deliverable, make sure that commercial licenses are directly between the government and the commercial software vendor, but be sure that the license grant permits the prime contractor to use the software on behalf of the government. That way, the contractor is out of the "chain of title" should a dispute arise between the government and the commercial software vendor. Another important tip is to ensure that the prime contract does not require any modifications to the commercial software using government funds, to avoid providing the government the opportunity to argue that it has greater rights in the commercial software.

To attempt to preempt these ambiguities, commercial owners should address the issue in the standard commercial license terms and affix notices on the software. First, software owners should draft their commercial licenses to expressly address the rights the government is entitled to in the commercial software. For example, the commercial license should contain a standard clause addressing purchases by or for the government. At minimum, this clause should: (1) expressly state that the government agrees to treat the software as commercial under the applicable regulations; (2) that the commercial provisions supercede contrary terms in other contract documents; and (3) require the government to contact the software owner if the government finds any term of the commercial license unacceptable.

A software owner should also place proprietary legends (identifying the product as "commercial computer software") on the software in multiple conspicuous places on software products. This includes legends on both tangible and electronic copies of the software, related documentation, the source code, and packing materials.

# C. Providing Technical Data to the Government with Limited Rights

Certain technical data may also be delivered to the government with restrictions on the government's use of that data, known as "limited rights." Technical data that usually qualifies for delivery to the government with limited rights is data developed solely at private expense that is either: (1) confidential financial or commercial information, or (2) trade secrets pertaining to an item, component, or process developed. FAR 52.227-14(a); DFARS 252.227-7013(b)(3).

Although each regulation has its own definition, "limited rights" restrictions generally forbid the government's use or disclosure of technical data outside the government or for competitive procurement, except for emergency repair or overhaul, or disclosure to or use by a foreign government for evaluation purpose (where the owner of the data is notified and the recipient may not make further use or disclosure of the data). FAR 52.227-14 (*Alternate II*); DFARS 252.227-7013(a)(13).

Delivery procedures for limited rights data differ between the military and civilian regulations, although some general rules apply. First, the limited rights data must be explicitly identified in the bid and any proposed statement of work. The statement of work should explicitly state that limited rights data will not be modified in performance of the contract. Second, the limited rights data must be identified in both the contract and final statement of work. The format for the contract is the same as for the bid. Finally, any limited rights data included in deliverables must bear the legend as required by the applicable government regulations. It is hard to overstate the importance of satisfying these notice requirements because, as stated above, failure to meet the notice requirements will likely result in the government customer asserting an essentially unlimited license in the data.

Note that even if a contractor successfully asserts that the government has limited rights in contractor data, the FAR provides exceptions to the government's restrictions. Specifically, the FAR provides a list of examples of specific purposes for which the government might desire to disclose limited rights data to third parties. FAR 27.404(d)(1)(i)–(iv).

---

# Notes & Questions

1. *What Do Nondisclosure Agreements Do?* Duties to preserve confidences often arise even in arm's-length business transactions. Under appropriate circumstances (far short of an explicit agreement), courts may find that one firm receiving confidential information from another has a legal duty to avoid betraying the confidences of, and otherwise "ripping off," the provider of the confidential information. *See, e.g., Smith v. Dravo Corp.*, 203 F.2d 369, 376–77 (7th Cir.1953); *Forest Labs., Inc. v. Formulations, Inc.*, 299 F. Supp. 202, 208–10 (E.D. Wis. 1969), *aff'd in part and rev'd in part on other ground*, 452 F.2d 621 (7th Cir. 1971). *Cf. Metallurgical Indus., Inc. v. Fourtek, Inc.*, 790 F.2d 1195, 1204 (5th Cir. 1986) (arm's-length customer may be "on notice" of supplier's misappropriation of third party's trade secret).

Thus, a nondisclosure agreement is not always necessary to protect trade secrets; courts may step in to avoid injustice. What economic or social purpose does their doing so serve? Would it be better if courts simply required explicit agreements and allowed others to steal the ideas of anyone stupid enough to disclose them without written assurances?

2. If agreements are not always necessary, and if courts generally protect good-faith disclosers of confidential matter against evident "rip offs," why bother with a nondisclosure agreement? What purposes does it serve, especially in confidential business negotiations in which the courts are likely to protect trade secrets anyway? How would you answer your client if she asks you "why bother"?

3. Lawyers drafting nondisclosure agreements try to accomplish the following: First, they try to establish the existence of a confidential relationship. Second, they try to define the scope of that relationship, including the matter to be held in confidence. Third, they set limits on the scope of the relationship and matter subject to it. These limits often include explicit exceptions to the confidential relationship, defined either generally or with specific reference to named or described technology or other intellectual property. To whom are these limits important, the discloser, disclosee, or both? Fourth, lawyers fix the term or duration of the relationship (i.e., how long the disclosed information must be held in confidence). Fifth, they may specify what the disclosee must, can, and cannot do with the disclosed information (and with tangible records containing it) during the relationship. Sixth, they often specify what the disclosee can or must do with tangible records at the end of the confidential relationship. Finally, lawyers drafting nondisclosure agreements often try to specify legal remedies for violating the contractual obligations. (For example, they may specify injunctive relief as a "standard," rather than an "extraordinary" remedy, or they may require the losing party in any dispute to pay the winner's attorneys' fees.)

4. Many of these same points would be foci of contention in any trade-secret litigation. For example, Uniform Trade Secrets Act § 4 provides for attorneys' fee recoveries under certain circumstances. What additional benefits, if any, derive from attempting to specify these things as a matter of contract in nondisclosure agreements? Are agreements of this sort just the usual lawyer's "belt and suspenders," or is there real value in having them?

5. Nondisclosure provisions of this sort appear not only in stand-alone agreements, such as those signed at the outset of business discussions. They also appear in many, if not most, license agreements involving trade-secret technology, know-how, or confidential business or financial information. Indeed, nondisclosure provisions can be considered a sort of trade secret "license," describing what is licensed, what the license can and cannot do with it, and for how long. (Normally the "licensee" can do *something* with the confidential information, if only evaluate it; otherwise there would be no need for disclosure.)

Most technology licenses contain nondisclosure provisions at least as long and detailed as those contained in stand-alone nondisclosure agreements. Therefore knowing how to draft effective and appropriate nondisclosure agreements is an essential part of every licensing lawyer's "bag of tricks."

6. Practical considerations often loom as large as legal ones in deciding how to draft nondisclosure language. This is especially true for stand-alone nondisclosure agreements.

Typically those agreements come at the outset of a business relationship, when the parties are just getting to know one another. Whatever is said in the business meetings, a fourteen-page nondisclosure agreement with lots of fine print may say even louder,

"We don't trust you!" That kind of approach may cause lawyers to be too intimately involved too early in the deal and may ultimately "kill the deal." Was this what happened in the *Nilssen* case, or was it Motorola's intent on either getting the Nilssen technology for a lowball price or else circumventing it? What term was critical to Motorola's avoiding summary judgment against it in the *Nilssen* case? What term was critical for Tridair in the *Bell Helicopter Textron* case?

7. Another important practical consideration is the legitimate fear that large companies have of overbroad nondisclosure covenants. Suppose that you are general counsel of a large, multinational corporation with five research and development laboratories in different states and in foreign countries, working in eighteen different fields of technology. Your client's business manager is interested in exploring the possibility of a strategic partnership with a small and highly entrepreneurial start-up firm. She sends you a proposed nondisclosure agreement that she would like to sign on behalf of the corporation. In it, the start-up company asks your client to treat as confidential "any and all disclosures made in business meetings, whether written or oral."

What concerns do you have and how might you advise your client? Your client's business manager is intensely interested in the start-up's technology and wants to begin discussions as soon as possible. Should you advise her to sign the agreement as is? Why or why not? What terms do you think big companies like General Motors, IBM, and Microsoft might insist on having before they would agree to sign a nondisclosure agreement with a smaller company, in order to get a look at its technology? What terms do you think should or might be standard in any nondisclosure agreement?

8. In the long term, the most important practical consideration for nondisclosure agreements is the same as for licensing generally: the agreement, if successful, is not the end, but the beginning of a cooperative business relationship. The analogy to dating and marriage made for licenses, *supra*, is just as apt for nondisclosure agreements.

Indeed, for stand-alone nondisclosure agreements, the analogy can be taken a step further. Nondisclosure agreements at the outset of business negotiations are a bit like blind dates. Each party wants to discover the other's qualities, capabilities, and intentions, and each party wants to protect itself against undesired intentions or actions on the other's part. At the same time, neither party wants to give the impression of being so self-protective or paranoid as to doom the chance of a successful relationship at the onset.

Thus, drafting and negotiating a successful nondisclosure agreement requires careful balancing, weighing both self-protection and accommodation, with an eye on circumstances and the parties' respective strategic goals. Most nondisclosure agreements are similarly broad, and many contain familiar "boilerplate" (particularly with regard to exceptions). Yet no two are exactly alike, and each requires careful tailoring to the actual business circumstances and the parties' needs and expectations.

9. *Ethical Issues in Negotiating.* The struggle for commercial advantage in licensing negotiations can involve ethical problems that are neither well addressed by Codes of Professional Conduct nor well understood by many practitioners. For two excellent and comprehensive analyses of this topic, see Eleanor Holmes Norton, *Bargaining and the Ethic of Process,* 64 N.Y.U. L. REV. 493 (1989); James White, *Machiavelli and the Bar: Limitations on Lying in Negotiation,* 1980 AM. B. FOUND. RESEARCH J. 926. White notes that "negotiation is non-public behavior," and consequently in negotiation "ethical norms can probably be violated with greater confidence that there will be no discovery and punishment.... [thus] the standard becomes even more difficult for the honest lawyer to follow, for by doing so he may be forfeiting a significant advantage for his client to others who do not follow the rules."

Consider the ABA MODEL RULES OF PROFESSIONAL CONDUCT (1983):

Rule 4.1, Truthfulness in Statements to Others:

In the course of representing a client a lawyer shall not knowingly:

(a) make a false statement of material fact or law to a third person; or

(b) fail to disclose a material fact to a third person when disclosure is necessary to avoid assisting a criminal or fraudulent act by a client, unless disclosure is prohibited by Rule 1.6 [dealing with lawyer-client confidentiality].

*Misrepresentation.* A lawyer is required to be truthful when dealing with others on a client's behalf, but generally has no affirmative duty to inform an opposing party of relevant facts. A misrepresentation can occur if the lawyer incorporates or affirms a statement of another person that the lawyer knows is false. Misrepresentations can also occur by failure to act.

*Statements of Fact.* This Rule refers to statements of fact. Whether a particular statement should be regarded as one of fact can depend on the circumstances. Under generally accepted conventions in negotiation, certain types of statements ordinarily are not taken as statements of material fact. Estimates of price or value placed on the subject of a transaction and a party's intentions as to an acceptable settlement of a claim are in this category, and so is the existence of an undisclosed principal except where non-disclosure of the principal would constitute fraud.

*Fraud by Client.* Paragraph (b) recognizes that a lawyer may be required to disclose certain information to avoid being deemed to have assisted the client's crime or fraud. The requirement of disclosure created by this paragraph is, however, subject to the obligations created by Rule 1.6.

10. What would you do in each of the following common negotiation situations? Does Rule 4.1 provide any guidance?

(a) As attorney for the licensee, your client wants you to tell the licensor that the licensee has the technical expertise to successfully commercialize a technology. Your client has previously told you otherwise.

(b) As attorney for the licensor, your client tells you to insist that the licensee have each of its 500 employees individually sign a highly restrictive confidentiality agreement. You believe this is a nuisance issue designed solely to throw your opponent off balance and to create additional bargaining "currency."

(c) Your client has instructed you to accept any royalty offer of 2% or higher. Later, opposing counsel says, "I think 2% will settle this case, will your client accept 2%?" You believe that, given more time and some hard bargaining, the licensee will pay 3% or more.

Do you see any ethical dilemmas? In the last setting a truthful answer ends any possibility of negotiating a higher royalty rate, while a negative response is a lie. How would you distinguish cases where truthfulness is a professional obligation and where it is not?

11. *Licensing to Competitors.* In many technology-based industries, patentees license their inventions to companies with whom they compete. There are many possible motivations for this behavior, including cross-licensing of extensive intellectual property portfolios, settlement of infringement litigation, and the need—increasingly in the present business environment—for competitors to use each others' complementary inputs. That is, if one entity refuses to license to others, it may have difficulty getting access through licenses to other companies' innovations.

12. The most noteworthy examples of competitor licensing can be found in the semiconductor manufacturing industry. In the last twenty-five years, the U.S. Patent and Trademark Office has issued more that 80,000 semiconductor patents. Cross-licensing is a ubiquitous industry practice, driven by the extraordinarily rapid pace of innovation and technological change. *See* Roy Weinstein & Shanbe Huang, *Valuing Patents and Intangible Assets in the Semiconductor Industry,* THE LICENSING JOURNAL, Vol. 19, No. 2, February 1999. The licenses generally include not only patents currently owned or controlled by the parties, but also all patents that will be applied for during the term of the agreement. Weinstein and Huang note that, in effect, licenses are a commodity:

> [L]icensees pay for technology that they may already be using, technology that they may want to use in the future, and technology in which they do not and will never have any interest. They do so because the benefits associated with access to technology that enhances the value of their own intellectual property outweigh the costs of paying for technology that... is useless.

*Id.* at 9.

Texas Instruments, owner of one of the largest semiconductor patent portfolios, earns royalties in excess of $500 million per year from cross-licensing with its smaller competitors. Given that the construction of a new chip manufacturing plant can reach $1 billion and that Moore's Law of chip innovation is still holding true (the number of transistors per square inch on integrated circuits doubles every eighteen months and will continue to do so for at least another two decades), is it any wonder that manufacturers look for ways to spread or "lay-off" the risk and cost of innovation with their competitors? One of the largest and most ambitious technology joint ventures is Sematech, a non-profit R&D consortium comprised of eleven major manufactures. Sematech partners with government laboratories and research universities to develop new semiconductor technologies. Sematech's patents are licensed to the member companies. Is cross-licensing in this environment inefficient? Or incredibly innovative?

Some experts in antitrust matters—the "other side of the coin" of intellectual property—suggest that widespread cross-licensing in the semiconductor industry results from too many patents being granted for too little innovation. Rampant cross-licensing of a myriad patents on minor incremental improvements, they think, is economically inefficient. *See To Promote Innovation: The Proper Balance of Competition and Patent Law and Policy,* Report by the Federal Trade Commission, Ch. 3, at 30–41 (October 2003), available *at* www.ftc.gov/reports/index.htm (visited April 27, 2004) (hereinafter "FTC 2003 Innovation Report") (discussing whether "patent thickets" in industry, used both offensively and defensively, in which hundreds of patents can cover single product and licensing royalties, purposely fixed at less than probable cost of litigation to discourage testing of patent validity, ultimately hurt consumers and impede both competition and innovation). Is the same analysis likely to apply to all industries? Is it likely to apply to the pharmaceutical industry, for example? To the computer software industry? Where this analysis applies what is the most attractive solution: (1) to change the law of licensing, or (2) to adjust the patent system to require more robust and pioneering innovation before patents are granted? For extensive discussion of these points, see FTC 2003 Innovation Report, *supra.*

13. *Further Ethical Issues in Negotiating and Drafting IP Licenses: The Lawyer Becomes the Witness.* A lawyer may be disqualified from further representing a client if called to testify as a witness because he or she negotiated the disputed license. *Supreme Beef Processors, Inc. v. American Consumer Indus., Inc.,* 441 F. Supp. 1064, 1069 (N.D. Tex. 1977). Under what cir-

cumstances a lawyer must testify is unclear. Some courts have stated that the lawyer who drafts an ambiguous document should testify on behalf of his or her client; however, others have found otherwise. *Compare Paretti v. Cavalier Label Co.*, 722 F. Supp. 985, 986 (S.D.N.Y. 1989) (lawyer must be disqualified even if the only witness capable of explaining clause or if lawyer negotiates, executed, and administers a contract and is therefore a key witness), *with Motown Record Corp. v. Mary Jane Girls, Inc.*, 118 F.R.D. 35, 38 (S.D.N.Y. 1987) (no disqualification even though lawyer was involved in the negotiations between the parties). At what point do you believe it is a lawyer's duty to disqualify himself and testify?

Rule 1.1 of the American Bar Association's Model Rules of Professional Conduct states that a lawyer shall provide competent representation to a client. Competent representation requires the legal knowledge, skill, thoroughness, and preparation reasonably necessary for the representation. Now consider whether an attorney drafting the IP licensing agreement is obligated to seek a specialist. For example, suppose a general practice lawyer who drafts a software license for the licensee fails to include permission to create derivative works (modify the software) or sublicense to customers. Or suppose such a lawyer fails to include such business terms as testing procedures. Does the failure to seek a specialist in software licenses violate Model Rule 1.1? *See* Larry M. Zanger, *Ethics in Licensing*, 534 PLI/PAT. 571, 574 (1998).

14. *Patent Licensing in E-Commerce: Business Model or Fad?* Hoping to transform intellectual property licensing into an "e-business," more than forty intellectual property "exchanges" have been created in the hope of creating an online market of technology sellers and buyers. These companies offer access to searchable databases of licensable technologies, along with various matchmaking services and other features to attract potential licensors and licensees. Significant hurdles to a viable business-to-business intellectual property market include the lack of valuable proprietary content to spark revenues, the absence of unpatented university early-stage technologies, and the inherent difficulties of conducting technology valuation and due diligence from the desktop. Early front runners include yet2.com <yet2.com>, Delphion <delphion.com>, an IBM joint venture, the Patent and License Exchange <pl-x.com>, University Ventures <uventures.com>, and others catering to niche markets <biostreet.com>, <pharmalicensing.com>, and <techex.com>.

For students of intellectual property licensing, the Internet also offers access to an increasing number of both free and pay sites devoted to tracking and posting deals and actual license agreements. Although proprietary business terms are deleted, these provide fascinating insight into drafting strategies.

15. *Judicial Interpretation of Data Rights Clause.* A recent Court of Federal Claims case emphasizes the importance of notice when providing privately-funded data and software to the government. In *Ervin and Associates, Inc. v. United States*, 59 Fed. Cl. 267 (Fed. Cl. 2004), the U.S. Court of Federal Claims confirmed that the government's ability to broadly assert the scope of FAR 52.227-14. At issue was the interpretation of a 1994 contract between Ervin and the U.S. Department of Housing and Urban Development (HUD) under which Ervin was to collect and review audited annual financial statements submitted by owners of HUD-related loans. Ervin then provided allegedly private "data" to HUD, requesting that HUD refrain from providing it to other agencies ("Data," as defined by the FAR, may include software). HUD then made the data available to other agencies and third parties, including competitors of Ervin.

Ervin brought suit under the Contract Disputes Act, alleging HUD's breach of the contract by provision of the data to Ervin's competitors. At issue was whether Ervin had successfully established that HUD should obtain less-than-unlimited rights under FAR

52.227-14. The court held that HUD had obtained unlimited rights in the data because Ervin's data did not qualify for less than unlimited rights (i.e., limited or restricted rights). First, Ervin had failed to establish that the data had been developed at private expense, as the court found that Ervin created the data in performance of the contract. Second, even where the data might qualify as less-than-unlimited rights data, Ervin did not withhold it or provide the data with the required notices.

Thus, *Ervin* stands for the general rule that contractors must "mark it or lose it." *See also Gen. Atronics Corp.* 2002 WL 450441, ASBCA No. 49196 (ASBCA 2002) (a contractor's failure to precisely follow the procurement regulations requiring that a contractor mark software with appropriate legends before delivery to the government resulted in the government obtaining unlimited rights in that software).

16. *The Government's Breach of Restricted Rights License.* Although rare, intellectual property owners do sometimes sue the government for breach of a license agreement and prevail. In *Ship Analytics Int'l Inc.*, 2001 WL 66653 (ASBCA 2001) (page numbers unavailable), 2001 WL 520820 (ASBCA 2001), the Armed Services Board of Contract Appeals (ASBCA) found that the government (Navy) breached its contract by providing Ship Analytics' privately-funded source code (previously furnished to the Navy under the contract) to a third party to upgrade ship-handling simulators. In 1986, the Naval Training Systems Center issued a request for proposals (RFP) for a "computer-based simulator system for teaching ship-handling skills to naval students." The trainer had four simulated bridges, which could operate independently or together, and a problem control center. The trainer simulated ship control cues, internal and external communication, and radar/sonar displays, but it specifically did not provide any "out-the-window or real world visual setting" for the students.

Ship Analytics responded to the RFP and proposed using its Pilotship 2000 software for the trainer. Pilotship 2000 had been developed solely with private funds. Ship Analytics' proposal indicated that use of the Pilotship 2000 software was conditioned "upon execution of a software license agreement granting the Government restricted rights to the software." Because source code was a contract deliverable, the Navy asked Ship Analytics for clarification concerning whether it would be disclosing its source code. In a 1989 meeting between the parties, the Navy indicated that it needed the source code to maintain and support the Pilotship 2000 software over the life of the trainer. Ship Analytics responded that it did not want the source code to get turned over to a competitor or to anyone for other than maintenance and support. Ship Analytics later submitted a revised proposal that "authorized third party access to the licensed software to perform 'services' on or with the software" for the Navy "with the restriction that it not be used, duplicated or disclosed [by the third party] except in direct performance of the services."

In 1993–94 the Navy sought to obtain an upgraded trainer that would provide an "out the window" simulation experience from Small Business Administration sole-source contract to Enzian Technology, Inc. (Enzian). Ship Analytics learned of the proposed upgrade and notified the government that Ship Analytics believed the action to be a breach of its contract and license agreement. In 1995 the Navy awarded the contract to Enzian and Ship Analytics terminated the license for breach and the appeal followed. The Navy contended it had unlimited rights in the source code. The Board rejected this contention, finding that Ship Analytics' interpretation of the government's rights in the code had been clearly conveyed to the Navy and the Navy did nothing to object to or change this interpretation.

*Suggested Reading for Additional Information on Government Data Rights in Software and Technical Data*: Matthew S. Simchak, *Protecting Rights in Technical Data and Com-*

*puter Software: Applying the Ten Practical Rules and Their Corollaries,* 33 Pub. Con. L. J. 139 (Fall 2003); Matthew S. Simchak & David A. Vogel, Simchak & Vogel on Data Rights (Fed. Pub. Seminars 1999); Lionel M. Lavenue, *Technical Data Rights in Government Procurement: Intellectual Property Rights in Computer Software and the Indicia of Information Systems and Information Technology,* 32 USFLR 1 (Fall 1997); and Lionel M. Lavenue, *Database Rights and Technical Data Rights: The Expansion of Intellectual Property for the Protection of Databases,* 38 SANCLR 1 (1997).

17. *Providing Commercial Software to the Government Under General Services Administration Contracts.* The United States government often obtains commercial software under General Services Administration (GSA) Multiple Awards contracts as permitted under FAR Part 12. The GSA negotiates and administers contracts through which federal agencies can acquire products and services, including commercial computer software. The GSA purchases software subject to the Federal Acquisition Regulations governing "commercial computer software" discussed above.

A commercial software owner recently sued the GSA for breach of contract, or in the alternative, a "taking" under the Fifth Amendment, based on the government's use of the commercial software outside the scope of the commercial license and the terms of the additional terms included in the GSA contract (the "utilization limitations"). In *Data Enterprises of the Northwest,* 2004 WL 323922, GSBCA No. 15,607 (GSBCA Feb. 4, 2004) (page numbers unavailable), the General Services Board of Contract Appeals (GSBCA) ordered the government to pay damages to a software manufacturer after the Navy used the manufacturer's documentation and data dictionary to help develop new functions in, and then migrate data to, a competing software program.

The plaintiff, Data Enterprises of the Northwest ("Data Enterprises") created ATICTS asset management software with private funds. Data Enterprises entered into a GSA contract that granted federal agencies (including the Department of Defense) a license to the use of ATICTS software. In 1999, the Navy considered combining the ATICTS software with software owned by one of Data Enterprises' competitors. The Navy then used the ATICTS documentation to help augment the competitor's asset management software. The Navy also used an ATICTS tool to exchange data from the ATICTS software to the new program.

As stated above, the GSA contract contained a "utilizations limitations" clause, which specifically prohibited the Navy from copying or otherwise disclosing the software and documentation. The GSBCA found that in "purchasing a license to use the ATICTS software, Government agencies gain restricted rights to use the software." The GSBCA then held that the Navy had breached the scope of the "utilization limitations" in the GSA contract by using Data Enterprises' software and documentation to create the new program. The GSBCA based the damages on the lost profits that Data Enterprises would have made on the sales of the ACICTS software had the breach not occurred. These damages would cease in December 2006, the GSBCA reasoned, because by that date the Navy would have been able to develop new software not based on Data Enterprises software and documentation.

Practically speaking, because FAR Part 27.405(b)(2)(i) specifically provides that the government must obtain rights "sufficient for the Government to fulfill the need for which the software is being acquired" and "[s]uch rights may be negotiated" per the restricted rights clauses (FAR Part 27.405(e) & FAR 52.227-19), shouldn't an owner of privately-funded commercial software always presume the government takes a "restricted rights" license in this software, regardless of the terms of the contract? Because the "utilization limitations" in most GSA contracts mirror the restricted rights license contained in the FAR, doesn't the same hold true for commercial software delivered to the government under GSA contracts?

———————

# Chapter 5

# Valuation of Intellectual Property

## I. Introduction

### Valuation of Assets: The Basics

"Valuation" is the process of determining the economic or business value of an asset. That process is by no means unique to intellectual property. On the contrary, it is an essential part of practically every business venture.

In a fundamental way, valuation is the essence of business. In free-market transactions, an asset is sold at a single, stated price. The price the seller receives is the same as the price the buyer pays. Yet buyer and seller usually value the asset differently. Their different perceptions of value are what drive the transaction and make the business world revolve.

If you purchase a car, for example, you and the car dealer value the car differently. The car dealer is most concerned with the profit made from the sale. That is, she wants to maximize the difference between what she paid the manufacturer for the car (plus her cost of holding, maintaining, and selling it) and what you pay her to buy it. If the price you are willing to pay is below these costs, the dealer will make no profit from the sale, and the sale ordinarily will not take place. You, on the other hand, value the car based on its use in transportation, its aesthetics, and its emotional appeal. If you like red, for example, you might be willing to pay several hundred dollars more for a cherry red car than one painted "government-issue green," even though there is no difference in the cost of applying the two different colors of paint. The difference between the two methods of valuing the transactions—profit for the dealer and your personal preferences for you—are what drive the transaction and make business possible.

As this simple example illustrates, valuation is part art and part science. For the car dealer, it is mostly science. If the car dealer knows her business well, she will be able to compute to the nearest penny the profit that she will make from selling you the car at any given price. For you, on the other hand, valuation is a matter of preference and judgment. How much more are you willing to pay for the cherry red roadster than for the pedestrian green sedan? That is a matter of judgment that no science yet devised can predict.

Valuation is often a matter of judgment even regardless of personal preference. There are two reasons for this. First, in real business, many variables affect valuation. It may be impossible to calculate or even to estimate all of them. Second—and most important—valuation in business usually involves a guess about the future. Will consumer demand for a new product increase or decrease? Will interest rates rise or fall? Will the planned new highway go right by the property for sale or will it be built in the other direction? Questions like these, to which there is often no concrete answer, may profoundly affect the value of an asset. Smart buyers "win" in business by predicting the future better than sellers who do not see the increased value that unforeseen future events may give an asset.

For example, consider a piece of vacant farmland. Suppose a buyer knows or suspects that a planned new highway will run right next to it. He may purchase the farmland at a low price and sell it later at a much higher price for commercial or residential property development. The land does not change; it is the very same piece of property. Yet its valuation changes based upon its use and surrounding circumstances (i.e., the highway). By anticipating new uses and recognizing the value inherent in them, the land speculator can make a fortune.

The precise nature of the asset does not matter. It may be a plot of vacant land, a house, a car, a truckload of commodities, an ongoing business, a patent, or a copyright license. The basic question remains the same: what is its monetary "value" and how might that value depend upon future circumstances? Yet valuation of intellectual property is often more difficult than valuation of so-called "hard" assets both because intellectual property is intangible and because there may be no established market for the asset (or even assets of the same type). That is, intellectual property assets, more so than many hard assets, may be "unique." A nonexistent market or a "thin" market— one in which similar transactions are rare—always makes it harder to value an asset.

Whatever the nature of the asset, however, the basic approaches to valuation remain the same. There are three fundamental methods for valuing any asset: the cost method, the market method, and the income method. Virtually every other method of valuing assets is a variation or combination of these three.

**1. Basic terminology.** The three methods of valuation—cost, market, and income— are part of the basic training of accountants and are taught assiduously in business schools. Unfortunately, they are not generally a part of the legal curriculum. As a result, law students usually require some conceptual background in order to understand and apply the three methods. If you have had no training or experience in accounting or business, you should begin by reading and assimilating the basic terms defined in Appendix A to this chapter.

With regard to terminology, it is critically important to understand the differences among three related terms: price, cost, and value. The "price" is what a seller demands for an asset. The initial price is also called the "asking price," or (in real-property transactions) the "listing price." This price exists whether or not there is ever a sale, i.e., whether or not the seller ever finds a buyer willing to purchase the asset at the stated price.

Once a sale closes at a given price (the "selling price," which may be different from the asking price), that price becomes the buyer's cost. That is, the "selling price" that the buyer pays to purchase the asset becomes the buyer's "cost" for that asset. If the buyer seeks to make a quick profit by reselling the asset to someone else, the buyer's profit will be the difference between the buyer's cost and the new selling price to the new buyer.

Value, however, is entirely different in concept from both price and cost. For example, consider that vacant piece of farmland again. Suppose that a major highway is to be built next to the property, but neither buyer nor seller knows that fact. The parties then may agree on a selling price for the property (which, on closing of the sale, becomes the buyer's "cost"), that is much lower than the value which the free market will put on the property once the highway project is generally known.

Thus "value" is in general a much more slippery term than either price or cost. Price is usually known to the penny, either as a stated asking price or as a price paid at closing. Cost is also generally known, or it can be calculated from known payments disbursed in the past. Value, however, is a somewhat metaphysical concept that depends on estimation, guesswork, and projections, taking into account possible future use, economic conditions, and unknown developments. (Consider, for example, how the "value" of a plant producing telegraph machines might have changed upon the invention and introduction of the telephone.)

**2. The cost method.** The simplest method of valuation is based upon cost. According to this method, the "value" of an asset is what it costs.

There are two chief variants of the cost method of valuation. The first relies on historical cost, i.e., the actual cost paid for an asset. Under this method, the value of the asset in a particular holder's hands is what that holder paid for it. The second method relies on replacement cost, i.e., what it would cost to rebuild or replace the asset with current techniques and at current cost. These two variants of the cost method of valuation differ in simplicity, currency, and effect.

This "historical cost" method of valuation has the virtue of simplicity. It is easy to calculate, particularly for the buyer; the buyer of the asset only has to remember what she paid for it. The historical cost method, however, has obvious flaws, for it fails to take into account how economic conditions and other circumstances may change with time.

Perhaps the most obvious change in the circumstances of an asset is its deterioration with time. Buildings and other structures are the classic example. If left alone, they weather, decay, or suffer deterioration from use. Constant maintenance, with constant expense, is required to keep them in good condition. Even with regular maintenance, virtually every building eventually requires replacement or substantial remodeling.

Accountants and business people recognize the inevitable need for replacing and remodeling buildings and similar assets using the concept of "depreciation" in value. When new, a building may be worth all of the cost required to build it. Yet every building has a projected "lifetime," after which rebuilding or substantial remodeling is expected. As the end of that projected lifetime approaches, the expected expense of rebuilding or remodeling threatens, and the economic value of the building declines. In accounting terms, the building is said to "depreciate" with time.

There are many formulas and methods for calculating depreciation. The simplest is the most obvious: so-called "straight-line" depreciation. This method assumes that the building or other depreciable asset will have to be replaced completely at end of its projected lifetime and so will then have a value of zero. The depreciated value at any time before the end of the projected lifetime is therefore computed on a "straight-line" basis, i.e., by assuming equal depreciation for every unit of time. For example, if the lifetime of a building were assumed to be 40 years, the annual decrease in value would be assumed to be one-fortieth, or 2.5%, of its initial value, which is often assumed to be its cost.

After ten years, for example, a building that cost $100,000 to build would have depreciated 25% and therefore would have a depreciated value of $75,000. Such a value is often called "depreciated cost" in order to distinguish it from its "historical cost," which would remain at $100,000—the actual historical price paid for the construction.

Like much of the process of valuation, computing depreciation is part art, part science. Projecting the lifetime of an asset requires judgment and guesswork about the future. Moreover, some assets do not depreciate at all. Land, for example, does not depreciate because land, unlike the buildings on it, does not deteriorate. On the contrary, land often appreciates in value with increasing population density and therefore increasing demand. As the humorist Will Rogers famously put it, "They ain't makin' any more land." Thus, if a single asset includes a building and the land it stands on, only the building, not the land, should be depreciated.

A moment's thought suggests that similar problems attend valuing intellectual property. As an intangible, intellectual property does not really "depreciate," at least not like a physical structure. Certain forms of intellectual property, such as patents and copyrights, have a finite lifetime fixed by statute, but the analogy to physical structures is incomplete. For one thing, patents and copyrights do not necessarily decrease in value toward the end of their terms. A patented pharmaceutical, or a copyrighted novel, or painting may have its greatest economic value toward the end of the term of protection. More important, technology may become obsolete or be replaced by better substitutes long before the end of a patent's term. If it does, the resulting depreciation hardly occurs on a "straight line" basis.

As a result of these and other difficulties, attempts to "depreciate" intellectual-property assets are far more art and less science than attempts to depreciate buildings. These difficulties often make the cost method of valuation unreliable, although it is perhaps the easiest to apply.

Even more generally, the cost method is often the least reliable method of valuation. The whole point of valuation is to determine what an asset is worth now. Historical cost measures only what one person (the buyer) thought it was worth in the past; and attempts to adjust historical cost through depreciation not only are inaccurate, but also neglect many important economic circumstances, including possible appreciation. As a result, most business people use the cost method only as a rough guide to current value, unless the cost was incurred quite recently.

The second variant of the cost method—replacement-cost valuation—avoids some of the difficulties of the historical cost method but lacks its simplicity. By focusing on what it would cost to replace the asset under current conditions, this method avoids the use of "stale" historical data and keeps valuation fresh. By focusing on current conditions, it allows current development in techniques and technology to be considered in calculating replacement cost. Yet because replacement cost is a hypothetical construct (calculated in the absence of any real replacement) it involves more than just mere historical memory. Instead, it requires hypothetical calculation of what it would cost to replace an asset under current conditions if the holder of the asset decided to replace it. It therefore invites speculation and guesswork regarding the costs of labor and materials and the appropriateness of different techniques and technologies that were developed after the asset was actually created. For these reasons, replacement-cost valuation is more difficult and uncertain, and involves more art and less science, that valuation based upon historical cost.

**3. The market method.** In a free-market system, the most reliable method of valuation is the "market price," or the price that the market will bear. In theory, and sometimes in practice, this price derives from numerous transactions in which willing buyers and willing sellers actually trade the asset in question, or assets of the same kind. The more numerous are the transactions—i.e., the broader and more robust the market—the more reliable is the valuation set by the collective market price.

The market method of valuation works marvelously for some assets. The classic example is stock, i.e., securities of public companies traded on public securities exchanges. Nationwide markets like the New York Stock Exchange or NASDAQ facilitate hundreds and sometimes thousands of daily sales transactions in each listed stock. More important, they report the price of each sale immediately. The prices of these many transactions collectively determine the market value of each exchange-traded stock.

Because stock markets like these involve so many transactions so quickly reported, economists consider them "efficient" markets. That is, they react quickly to news of changing economic conditions and the changing fortunes of each company whose stock is traded. The stock markets' response to changing stock valuation is so rapid that many stock traders pay extra to receive "real-time" stock quotations, rather than wait a mere twenty minutes for delayed quotations available at a lower price.

Stock markets also illustrate the danger of using cost as a method of valuation in a changing market. Suppose you buy 100 shares of Acme Computers on Monday at $50 per share. If you use the cost method of valuation, your assessed value of each share is $50. But suppose on Tuesday Acme announces a new patent on computer technology that gives it a substantial advantage over its competitors. As a result of that announcement alone, the market price of an Acme share might rise to $70, making your cost valuation obsolete overnight. If Acme's competitor made such an announcement, the market value of your stock might fall to $35 per share, making your cost valuation an overestimate.

The primary difficulty with market valuation is that very few assets enjoy markets as broad and "efficient" as the nationwide markets for common stock. Some assets do not trade regularly. Unlike shares of a single company's stock, some assets are not fungible. If assets do not trade regularly, then a market valuation may become "stale," i.e., inapplicable in light of changing economic conditions and circumstances. If assets are not fungible, and if each asset is to some extent unique, then a market price determined for one asset may not apply to a different one of the same kind.

Unfortunately, intellectual property shares both of these characteristics. There is no "stock exchange" or established market for patents and copyrights (or licenses under them). Transactions involving these assets occur only irregularly, and many are secret, with no public price reported. Furthermore, every patented invention and every copyrighted work is unique, so a price for one does not necessarily apply to another. When one adds to this complexity the multiple possibilities of differing license scope (term, breadth of license, exclusivity and field of use), the difficulty of using a market price for one license to value another becomes apparent.

These complexities, however, do not render attempts at market valuation totally futile. Similar problems attend market valuation in one of the most common assets, real property. Sales of homes, like intellectual property licenses, are irregular and sporadic. Each home is, by law and in practice, unique. Yet the real-property industry routinely uses an appraised "market" value of homes as a basis for pricing real property and financing its purchase.

Market valuation for homes (usually by appraisal) relies on two tricks. First, the evaluator searches for "comparables," i.e., sales of homes that appear to be comparable to the home to be valued. In order to be "comparable," a sale must be not too remote in time (so as not to be "stale"); it must involve a property in the same or a similar general location; and it must involve a home with similar features. Second, the evaluator "adjusts" the sale prices of the comparable homes to account for obvious differences between the "comparable" homes sold and the home to be valued. For example, the evaluator takes account of differences in home size by adjusting the sale price of each "comparable" home using an average dollar-per-square-foot figure appropriate for the neighborhood. Similarly, the valuator can account for such things as swimming pools or attractive views by applying an average figure by which such features increase the value of a home in the given neighborhood. By adjusting in this way the actual sales prices of a number of "comparable" homes (typically a half-dozen or so), an appraiser can arrive at a reasonable estimate of what the current market price of the home to be valued should be.

The same two-step valuation process—finding "comparable" market transactions and adjusting their prices for differences—can be applied to transactions involving intellectual property. Suppose, for example, that the subject property is an exclusive license of a patent on an improvement in automobile transmissions. The evaluator will look for exclusive licenses of patents on similar improvements in the automobile industry (or, in the absence of similar patents, similar trade-secret technology) and then will attempt to adjust their "prices" (usually royalty rates) to take into account relevant differences in the technology, the automobile market, and the terms of the licenses. If the property is a license of a copyrighted situation comedy for television production, the evaluator will look for similar licenses of similar situation comedies and attempt to compare prices and terms.

Even more than in the case of home appraisals, however, this sort of valuation of intellectual property is more art than science. The evaluator will generally encounter at least three difficulties. First, he often will have trouble finding comparable transactions at all. There may be no recent "comparable" transaction involving similar technology or copyrighted materials and similar terms. Second, unlike real-property sales and stock-market transactions, intellectual-property transactions are generally not publicly reported. Therefore the evaluator may have trouble obtaining accurate information about the price and terms of "comparable" intellectual property transactions even if he knows or suspects that they exist. Finally, "comparable" intellectual-property transactions will seldom be identical or even substantially similar to the one to be evaluated, so the evaluator may have to be quite clever and imaginative in making adjustments to render the "comparable" transactions meaningful. For all these reasons, market valuation of intellectual property is, in the general case, an uncertain business requiring a great deal of educated judgment and plain guesswork.

This does not mean, however, that market valuation is useless or futile for intellectual property. Its utility depends in large measure upon the nature of the transaction to be valued. Just as one tract home in a single subdivision may be much like another, so simple nonexclusive licenses of pedestrian improvements in a given field may have many "comparable" transactions that can be appropriately adjusted and used in valuation. On the other hand, just as a million-dollar home on the top of the only developed hill in town may have no "comparables," so a pioneering patent may have no really "comparable" intellectual property to provide a market value. Which of these extreme cases applies, how to select "comparable" transactions, and how to adjust them to make the comparisons relevant are always matters of judgment and "art." There is no simple formula or mechanical solution to arriving at a "market" value for intellectual property or licenses under it.

**4. The income method.** The third and final general method for valuing assets generally is the "income method." As its name suggests, this method is best applied when the asset is used in a business or is itself a going business. It values the asset by asking a simple question: "how much can the asset earn?"

The classic example is real property used in a business. Consider, for example, a rental apartment building. A landlord who buys such a building in order to rent apartments to tenants can value her building in three ways. If she paid $500,000 to buy the building, that is her historical cost. This is the building's valuation under the "cost" method. If she paid a fair "market" price for the building, her cost may be a good estimate of its value, at least for a while.

After a few years pass, however, or after she improves the property by remodeling all the apartments, her historical cost may no longer be an appropriate measure of valuation. Then she might use the "market" method of valuation. She might be looking for more recent sales of similar apartment properties in the same general location and adjust them for evident differences.

The third method of valuation takes into account the fact that the apartment building is part of a business, namely, the owner's apartment-rental business. It values the asset first by determining how much annual income the asset will earn. That is, it first determines the net profit (revenue less expenses, *see* Appendix A) that the building has earned in the past or is expected to earn in normal operation. Then this method converts the annual earnings or profit figure into a capital asset valuation by multiplying the annual earnings by some multiplier, typically in the range from 4 to 25. Determining what multiplier to use to convert annual earnings into putative value is, of course, the essence of this method of valuation, comprising much of the valuation "art."

In our example, suppose the apartment building contains ten apartments, each of which the landlord rents out at an average rent of $1,100 per month. Suppose her expenses of operation (maintenance, insurance, legal fees, accounting fees, advertising) are $100 per month per apartment. Then her monthly net profit per apartment is $1,000, her total monthly earnings are $10,000, and her annual earnings are $120,000. To evaluate the apartment building, she must now select a multiple that properly reflects what "comparable" assets might earn the same $120,000 per year.

Instead of searching for such comparable assets, the evaluator might simply calculate the present value of a stream of earnings of $120,000 per year, stretching into the indefinite future. (*See* Appendix B, *infra*, A Note on Present Value.) Mathematically, that would be one way of evaluating the putative future stream of income and therefore the asset that generates it. Such an approach, however, would neglect that actual nature of the asset producing the earnings, including the risk that, at some point, the stream of earnings might cease. Searching for comparable assets that produce the same stream of earnings is more realistic and, as we will see, better accounts for the actual risk of producing (or not producing) those earnings with the aid of the particular asset at issue.

One asset that might earn $120,000 per year is an investment in United States Treasury Notes. If the Notes pay interest at 4% per year, our hypothetical apartment-building owner could earn the same $120,000 by investing 25 times that amount (1 divided by 0.04), or $3 million, in treasury notes.

Does this mean that the apartment building is worth $3 million? Probably not. The reason is risk. An investment in treasury notes of the United States government is one of the most risk-free investments known in finance. A person who invested $3 million in them could sleep soundly at night, knowing that he would receive $120,000 per year reliably, without fail, unless the Republic crumbled.

Our hypothetical apartment-building owner, however, is not so lucky. She has to worry about many things. Fire, hail, lightning or other natural disaster might destroy her building, and her insurance might not cover the damage. Her tenants might refuse to pay rent, and she might have to incur legal expense, plus lost rent, to evict them. Angry evicted tenants might trash her apartments on the way out. Her property might decline in rental or resale value if the neighborhood deteriorates due, for example, to polluting industries locating nearby. With all these risks, no one in her right mind would invest $3 million in the apartment building just to earn $120,000 per year, when she could earn the same amount, entirely risk free, by investing in treasury notes.

The evaluator of this hypothetical apartment-rental business therefore must adjust her earnings multiple for risk. That is, she must adjust the multiplier or "valuation factor" downward from 25 to take account of many real risks of the apartment-rental business. For example, the evaluator might choose a lower multiplier of ten, giving our owner's business a valuation of ten times annual earnings of $120,000, or $1.2 million.

As this example shows, the devil of income valuation is in the multiplier. Calculating the historical or potential earnings of an asset is relatively straightforward, especially if the asset, like our hypothetical apartment building, has been used in business before. Determining an appropriate multiplier to get to valuation, however, is as much art as science.

As a rule of thumb, business asset evaluators often use a multiplier of ten, corresponding to an interest rate of 10%. (This "standard" 10% rate is quite ancient; the Bible mentions it.) But a multiplier like that is just a rough "guesstimate." For more accurate evaluation, the multiplier must be based upon two factors: prevailing interest rates and risk. Prevailing interest rates (ultimately fixed by the Federal Reserve Board) vary with time, from lows in the single digits to highs (in times of great inflation) approaching twenty percent. Since the rate of interest paid by treasury notes depends upon generally prevailing interest rates, those rates must be considered in setting any income valuation multiplier. Moreover, since the risk of a particular business or asset is normally independent of generally prevailing interest rates, it, too, must be considered, as discussed above. The multiplier used for income valuation therefore depends upon a careful and often artful assessment of generally prevailing interest rates and the many risks involved in exploiting the particular asset at issue.

Evaluating the risk component of the multiplier is no simple matter. Risks in business arise from a bewildering variety of circumstances. Often there are insufficient data to quantify a single source of risk, let alone to determine appropriate numerical weights for assessing the combined numerical impact of multiple sources of risk.

Rather than attempt to evaluate and weigh numerous practical sources of risk on an a priori basis, evaluators often use a hybrid income-market approach to valuation. First, they calculate or estimate the annual earnings expected to be produced by the asset in question. Then, in order to calculate the valuation multiple, they computer similar multiples for similar assets believed to be comparable.

For example, suppose a dry-cleaning business is the asset to be evaluated. After calculating the historical or projected earnings of that business, one might attempt to determine the risk-adjusted multiple by separately assessing all the myriad risks to which such a business is subject—a formidable task! Alternatively, since sales of dry-cleaning businesses are not uncommon, the evaluator might simply examine recent sales of such businesses. Then he could calculate the multiple by which each sales price exceeded the relevant earnings and use the average multiple so determined as the multiple for evaluating the business in question. In this way, the evaluator could let the marketplace determine a specific multiple adjusted both for general interest rates and for the peculiar risks of the dry-cleaning business.

Of course this hybrid method is fraught with the same difficulties as market valuation generally. There may be few or no sales of comparable businesses to use. Even if comparable sales exist, their details may be secret. Determining the sale price, let alone the earnings figure necessary to arrive at a comparable multiple, therefore may be practically impossible. Finally, if the comparable sales are not recent in time or involve business of differing scope and character, then their multiples may have to be adjusted, through calculations that may be tantamount to guesswork, in order to take account of the differences.

All of these difficulties of course attend valuation of intellectual property and licenses under it. Indeed, these assets exacerbate the difficulties just discussed, as they are normally less common and less public than sales of dry-cleaning businesses. Nevertheless, information on comparable transactions may be available in textbooks, public reports of public companies, governmental or other statistical reports, or other public documents. To the extent relevant information is publicly available, earnings multiples derived from actual market transactions provide a powerful and generally reliable method of evaluating an asset whose primary purpose is generating income.

---

Valuations methods are many and varied. They depend upon the precise nature of the asset, its purpose or use, the relevant business and industry, and even general economic conditions. Virtually every method of valuation used in business, however, is a variant or combination of the three discussed above — cost, market, and income. Even the more accurate approach to income valuation discussed above involves a variant of the income approach, using market-based "comparable" sales to calculate the relevant earnings multiple. Because virtually all methods of valuation are variants of these three, understanding the theory of and deficiencies in the three basic methods should give the lawyer a basis for understanding, supporting and challenging any method of valuation that the accounting profession or business people may dream up.

# II. Valuation Methodologies

The new "Information Economy" that emerged in the 1990s turned the valuation of corporate assets upside down. In 1982 physical assets of industrial corporations comprised 62.3% of companies' market value. Ten years later, they made up only 37.9%. *See* THOMAS A. STEWART, INTELLECTUAL CAPITAL, THE NEW WEALTH OF ORGANIZATIONS (1997). Among non-industrial companies the ratio is even more striking — Microsoft's physical assets comprise only about 1% of its total market value. Truly, companies like Microsoft derive almost their entire shareholder value from intangible assets, especially intellectual property. Because intellectual property is so readily transferable, cooperative arrangements and joint ventures have proliferated, forcing businesses to search for new and more sophisticated tools for determining the value of intellectual property. Despite this sea change, the basic accounting methods for asset valuation have changed little.

The following articles introduce and examine quantitative asset valuation methods. They illustrate how traditional cost concepts do not relate well to intellectual property valuation when using the cost method. Licensing negotiations commonly use the other two methods, the market and income/economic models. More sophisticated analyses are discussed in Section III.

---

# A New Method To Value Intellectual Property*
Ted Hagelin
30 A.I.P.L.A. Q. J. 353 (2002)

## 1. INTRODUCTION

The value of intangible assets relative to the value of physical and financial assets has continuously increased since the early 1980s. One measure of this increase is the market-to-book (M/B) value for the S&P 500 companies. During the 1970s, the M/B ratio for the S&P 500 companies hovered around one; by 2000, the M/B ratio was over six. This means that in 2000 for every $6 of market value less than $1 was comprised of physical and financial assets while the remaining $5 (83.3%) was comprised of intangible assets. For many companies, the ratio of intangible assets to physical and financial assets is considerably higher. Smith and Parr have calculated the following percentages of intangible assets for the following companies: Johnson & Johnson (87.9%); Proctor & Gamble (88.5%); Merck (93.5%); Microsoft (97.8%); and Yahoo! (98.9%).

The importance of intangible assets has created an urgent need to value these assets in many contexts including intellectual property management, acquisitions, sales, joint ventures, and licensing. In the context of intellectual property management, intangible asset valuation is necessary to establish performance measures and evaluate business strategies. In the context of acquisitions, sales, and joint ventures, intangible asset valuation is necessary to determine the value of a company to a buyer or seller and the value of partners' contributions to collaborative undertakings. In licensing, intangible asset valuation is necessary to determine the value of a license to the licensor and licensee. Other areas where intangible asset valuation is important include filing of foreign patents, payment of patent maintenance fees, intellectual property audits, inter-company transfers of intellectual property, charitable contributions of intellectual property, and collateralization and securitization of intellectual property.

There are two types of intangible assets. One type of intangible asset is a true asset in the sense that the owner has a legally enforceable right to appropriate the benefits derived from the asset. This type includes patents, copyrights, trade secrets, and trademarks. I will refer to this type of intangible asset as an intellectual property asset. The second type of intangible asset is not a true asset because the owner has no legally enforceable rights in the asset. This type includes assembled workforce, employee training, management skill, and customer patronage. I will refer to this type of intangible asset as an intangible advantage. Another difference between an intellectual property asset and an intangible advantage is that an intellectual property asset can be transferred separately from a transfer of the company while an intangible advantage cannot be transferred separately from the company. Although intangible advantages contribute

---

greatly to the value of a firm, the focus of this article will be intellectual property assets, specifically patents.

Valuation of intellectual property assets is more difficult than valuation of tangible assets for four primary reasons. First, the public trading markets that exist for financial and physical assets do not exist for intellectual property assets. Although exchanges of intellectual property assets occur every day in every industry, these exchanges are sporadic and specialized, motivated by strategic advantages unique to the firms involved. Second, the terms and conditions of intellectual property transfers vary widely. Lawyers and licensing professionals negotiate and craft agreements to suit the special needs of their clients, and rarely are two agreements identical. Third, intellectual property assets are inherently dissimilar, and the dissimilarity is sometimes required by law. For example, patents must be novel and nonobvious compared to prior art; copyrights must be original works of authorship; and trademarks must be distinctive. Fourth, and most important, the details of intellectual property transfers are rarely made available to the public. Again, the principal motivation for intellectual property asset exchanges is strategic advantage, and firms will not publicize exchange details which could reveal strategy objectives.

There are a few circumstances, however, in which an intellectual property asset can be easily valued. If an intellectual property asset has been determined to be invalid, or if legal protection has expired or lapsed, the intellectual property asset has zero value. The discussion of valuation methods in this article assumes that the intellectual property asset is valid and that rights in the asset are enforceable.

* * *

## II. VALUATION METHODS DEVELOPED FOR INTELLECTUAL PROPERTY

### 1. The 25 Percent Rule

The 25 percent rule is a widely discussed valuation rule of thumb. Although there are many variations on the 25 percent rule, the most often given definition is that the licensor should receive 25 percent of the licensee's gross profit from the licensed technology. This statement of the rule makes clear that its purpose is not the valuation of a technology *per se*, but rather the apportionment of a technology's value between the licensor and licensee. Discussions of the 25 percent rule generally provide that the percentage split between the licensor and licensee should be adjusted upwards or downwards to take into account the parties' respective investment and risk in the licensed technology.

There is some disagreement over the usefulness of the 25 percent rule. Smith and Parr, for example, find the rule useful only as a crude guideline for an order of magnitude royalty rate. Smith and Parr note that the 25 percent rule cannot quantify the adjustments necessary for varying degrees of investment and risk on the part of licensors and licensees, and that the use of gross profits for the royalty base ignores differences in marketing, advertising, and selling expenses for different technologies. Stiroh and Rapp find the 25 percent rule even less useful. They point out that the rule fails to consider the number and utility of alternative technologies and that it is at odds with empirical surveys that indicate that a majority of licensees would be unwilling to pay more than 10% of gross profits in royalties.

On the other hand, Razgaitis finds the 25 percent rule more useful because it is consistent with two other generally accepted rules of thumb and conforms to general patterns of research and development spending. Razgaitis cites two rules of thumb as consistent with the 25 percent rule: (i) buyers need to be convinced that they will benefit three times the cost of obtaining the benefit before committing to a purchase and (ii) developing a new technology is one-quarter of the way to producing a commercial product. In addition, Razgaitis cites statistics that indicate that technology companies spend about 33% of their gross profit on discretionary research and development as also generally consistent with the 25 percent rule. The reasoning is that a company would be willing to pay an external organization (licensor) approximately the same amount for technology as it cost the company (licensee) to create the technology internally.

The 25 percent rule is more easily used in the case of process technology than product technology. In the case of process technology, the 25 percent rule can be applied directly to the manufacturing cost savings attributable to the new technology. However, new product technology is generally associated with only a component portion of a product's total functionality. In this case, the 25 percent rule should be applied only to the additional profit (increased unit sales or higher unit prices), which can be attributed to the enhanced functionality. Associating sales or prices with different aspects of a product's functionality is difficult, but necessary. If the 25 percent rule is applied to profits that are not attributable to the licensed technology, the licensor would receive a royalty windfall and the licensee would be deprived of a fair return on investment.

Despite difficulties in application and disagreements over usefulness, all commentators seem to agree that the 25 percent rule is the most simple, flexible, and often referenced valuation method.

### 2. Industry Standards

Valuation of intellectual property by industry standards is another popular valuation method. The industry standards method, also referred to as the market or comparable technology method, attempts to value an intellectual property asset by reference to royalty rates in similar past transactions. Although some writers view the industry standards method as completely distinct from the 25 percent rule, in fact they share much in common. Similar to the 25 percent rule, the industry standards method does not attempt to value an intellectual property asset *per se*, but rather it apportions the value of the intellectual property asset between the licensor and licensee. Also similar to the 25 percent rule, the industry standards method is based on past experience. The difference between the 25 percent rule and the industry standards method is the greater degree of specificity generally associated with the industry standards method. Whereas the 25 percent rule is applied across all industries and to all technologies, the industry standards method is specific to a given industry and given technology.

One version of the industry standards method (the 3 to 5 percent rule) and one version of the 25 percent rule (25% of the licensee's net profits) can produce highly comparable results. The 3 to 5 percent rule states "[w]hen licensing important technologies (as opposed to minor improvements) royalty rates [ranging] from 3 percent to 5 percent of the manufacturer's selling price are common in many industries." If the licensee's net profit margin is between 12% and 20%, not an uncommon range for many industries, the 25 percent rule and the 3 to 5 percent rule produce substantially similar results.

More specific versions of the industry standards method report royalties based on the industry, the technology, and the degree of innovation. Megantz, for example, cites the following royalty ranges for various industries (all royalty rates discussed in this section are based on net sales):

- Computing. 1%–5% for hardware and as high as 25% for software.

- Biotechnology. 8%–12% depending on factors such as stage of development and intellectual property strength; usually including large initial payments up to tens of millions of dollars.
- Automotive. Below 5% for licensed in technologies, with the majority below 2% with slightly higher rates for licensed-out technology.
- Health Care. License in rates between 2% and 10%; license out rates between 5% and 10%.
- Consumer Electronics. Less than 1% for higher priced items; around 3% for lower priced items; and as much as 50% for game software.

Megantz also notes that licensing out royalty rates are generally higher than licensing in royalty rates.

Razgaitis provides an example of royalties based on specific technologies within the medical industry: reagents and processes (1%–3%), reagent kits (2%–10%), diagnostics in vitro (2%–6%), diagnostics in vivo (3%–8%), therapeutics (4%–12%), and medical instruments (4%–10%). This example also includes information on up-front payments and minimum payments.

Finally, a survey of royalty rates published in les Nouvelles provides an example of royalty rates linked to innovation. The authors designed a three-level "innovativeness scale": (i) revolutionary (satisfies a long-felt need or creates a whole new industry); (ii) major improvement (significantly enhances superiority of an existing product, process, or service); and (iii) minor improvement (creates an incremental improvement in an existing product or service). The median royalty range for licensing out was between 5% and 10% for revolutionary technology; between 4% and 8% for major improvements; and between 2% and 5% for minor improvements.

Information on royalty rates is available from a number of different sources. Articles on royalty rates and licensing terms are regularly published in les Nouvelles (published by the Licensing Executive Society) and the Journal of the Association of University Technology Managers (published by the Association of University Technology Managers). There is also a publication dedicated solely to the financial aspects of licensing, Licensing Economics Review (published by AUS Consultants). Information on royalty rates and licensing terms can also be found in business articles, price lists, contracts filed with the Securities and Exchange Commission, and court decisions in infringement cases. All licensing information, however, must be carefully assessed for accuracy and relevance.

The industry standards method of valuation is subject to a number of limitations. Some of these limitations relate to the comparability of transactions discussed above in connection with the market method of valuation. Intellectual property is inherently dissimilar, and intellectual property exchanges are motivated by unique strategic considerations. In addition, published royalty rates are often based on broad industry classifications and provided in terms of wide percentage ranges. There may be significant differences in royalty rates within an industry, and the wide percentage ranges may provide little guidance on an appropriate royalty rate for the intellectual property asset being valued. Finally, focusing on royalty rates in the abstract without considering a host of other factors, such as the presence of license fees, minimum royalties, cross-licenses, whether the licenses are exclusive or nonexclusive, the relationships between the parties and their relative bargaining power, the stage of development of the technology, and changes in market demand, results in the worst of both worlds—subjective royalty rates masked by an objective methodology.

## 3. Ranking

The ranking method of valuation compares the intellectual property asset to be valued to comparable intellectual property assets on a subjective or objective scale. The ranking method is often used in conjunction with the industry standards method to determine a more precise royalty rate within an industry royalty rate range. There are five components to a ranking method: (i) scoring criteria, (ii) scoring system, (iii) scoring scale, (iv) weighting factors, and (v) decision table. Scoring criteria are factors that can be used to compare intellectual property assets, for example potential market size, scope of protection, and stage of development. Scoring systems are values assigned to scoring criteria, such as a 1–5 or 1–10 point system or a high/medium/low system. Scoring scales (methods) are the means of applying the scoring system. Subjective scaling generally utilizes a panel of experts whereas objective scaling is based on measurable past experience. Weighting factors are used to differentiate the importance of the scoring criteria. The decision table combines the scoring criteria, criteria values, and criteria weights to calculate a composite score, which can then be compared to the average score for a comparable intellectual property asset.

As with the other valuation methods discussed above, selection of the comparable intellectual property asset transactions is key to using the ranking method. In addition, the ranking method requires selection of appropriate comparative criteria and criteria weights. One of the most often cited set of comparative criteria is the *Georgia-Pacific* criteria used to determine reasonable royalty rates for patent infringement damages. The *Georgia-Pacific* case sets forth fifteen factors to be considered in determining a reasonable royalty rate, including past royalties received by the patentee, past royalties paid by licensees, the nature and scope of past licenses, the portion of profit or selling price customary as royalty rates in the industry, and the advantages of the patented technology over older products or processes.

Surveys have indicated that the four most important *Georgia-Pacific* factors are: (i) nature of protection, (ii) utility over older methods, (iii) scope of exclusivity, and (iv) commercial success. Razgaitis has identified five criteria as most important: (i) estimated attainable market size and overall product profit margins (key factors in determining the earnings attributable to an intellectual property asset); (ii) strength of intellectual property protection (patents, trade secrets, copyrights, and trademarks); (iii) breadth of intellectual property protection (how easy it is to operate outside the boundaries of the intellectual property without performance or price penalties); (iv) stage of development (amount of additional investment, development risk, and time to profitability); and (v) market environment (market growth or decline, strong or weak competitors, available or unavailable infrastructures).

Relying on the surveys mentioned above, Razgaitis finds the least important factors to be advice of experts, convoyed sales (additional sales associated with patented technology), and whether the license is foreign or domestic.

The ranking method of valuation has many advantages. It forces selection of criteria that affect the value of intellectual property assets as well as consideration of comparative scoring on these criteria. It provides a common basis for negotiation discussions among licensing experts while also being understandable to non-experts. Accumulated experience with the ranking method leads over time to more quantitative applications.

The three major disadvantages of the ranking method of valuation are the identification of comparable (benchmark) intellectual property asset transactions; the subjectivity in selection, weighting, and scoring of criteria; and the translation of a decision table composite score into a royalty rate or dollar adjustment. Comparability is as much of a challenge in the ranking method as it is in the other methods for the same reasons. Although there appears to be some agreement on general criteria that most affect intellectual property value, selecting criteria for a specific intellectual property asset is more difficult. For example, how would one compare novel features of a new intellectual property asset to older substitute products or processes? Weighting and scoring pose similar subjectivity problems. How would one weight the strength of intellectual property protection against the stage of technology development? How would a score be assigned to protection strength and to stage of development, and how would the two scoring systems relate to one another? Finally, regardless of how a composite score is calculated for an intellectual property asset, its translation into an adjustment to the comparable (average) royalty rate or payment is subject to further subjectivity. For example, if the composite score for the intellectual property asset being valued is 4 and a comparable average intellectual property asset has a composite score of 3, does that mean that the intellectual property asset being valued should command a 33% higher royalty rate or licensee fee?

Despite the disadvantages of the ranking method, its widespread use attests to its widely perceived usefulness.

### 4. Surrogate Measures

Surrogate measures have been developed to value patents. Surrogate measures do not value patents by reference to profits, industry standards, or rankings, but by reference to the patents themselves. The three most common types of surrogate measures are the number of patents issued to a company, payment of patent maintenance fees, and prior art citations. These measures have been shown to correlate, on average, with a firm's market value, suggesting that investors use these measures explicitly or implicitly in making investment decisions.

The number of patents issued to a company (patent count) is an indicator of the level of research and development expenditures and the number of product/process innovations, both of which are independently associated with market value. The payment of patent maintenance fees is an indicator of the quality of a patent portfolio (the more patents renewed, the higher the quality; the more patents lapsed, the lower the quality). There are two types of prior art citation measures: forward citations and backward citations. The forward citation measure counts the number of citations to a patent as prior art in subsequently issued patents. The greater the number of citations, the greater the importance [value] of a patent. The backward citation measure counts the number of scientific papers cited in a patent. The backward citation measure is an indicator of the level of basic science research underlying a patent. Citation weighted patent counts have been shown to be associated with firms' market values. Citation-based measures have also been shown to be predictive of future stock returns and the market-to-book values of public companies.

Citation-based valuation measures have moved from the realm of academic research to commercial application. CHI Research, a leading provider of citation based research, claims that over a ten-year test period, its method of selecting a stock portfolio based on patent citation measures generated an average annual gain of 38% compared to the S&P 500 Index average annual gain of 16% and the NASDAQ average annual gain of 25%. The widely read and highly regarded patent scorecard published annually by Technology Review uses CHI's methodology to rank companies' patent portfolios in a number of different industries. Technology Review ranks a company's patent portfolio based on the number of patents in the company's portfolio, the number of citations to the company's patents from the previous five years as prior art in the current year's issued patents, the number of science references listed in the company's patent portfolio, and the median age of patents cited as prior art in the company's patent portfolio.

Royalty income has also been used to value patents. Studies of royalty income indicate that investors value a dollar of patent royalties 2–3 times higher than a dollar of ordinary income. One explanation for the higher valuation of royalty income is that it is more stable because patents are usually licensed for several years whereas other sources of income are more transitory. Another explanation for the higher valuation of royalty income is that the profit margin on royalty income is significantly higher than the profit margin on other sources of income.

Other patent-based measures include technology cycle time (defined as the median age of the patents in a patent portfolio), the number of products covered by patents, the number of patents commercialized in products, the number of outstanding patent applications, the annual percentage growth rate in issued patents, and the number of patents issued per research and development employee.

Research and development measures ("R&D") are also used to value patents. Research and development measures include annual R&D expenditures as a percentage of sales or operating earnings, percentage of R&D employees, R&D employees' average seniority and education level, expenditures on R&D employee training, R&D incentives, and percentage of sales attributable to new products. Although these other patent-based and R&D measures have not been studied empirically, many valuation professionals believe they are useful.

Surrogate measures, especially patent-based measures, have become widely accepted valuation methods. The utility of surrogate measures, however, is limited in three respects. First, the measures themselves can be inherently misleading. For example, a patent count ignores the well-documented disparity in patent values. A portfolio with a few broad patents might be far more valuable than a portfolio with many narrow patents. Similarly, a large number of citations to a patent might not be because the patent has current commercial value, but because the patent is based on basic research that could be a long way from practical application. Second, the measures can be manipulated. Firms can inflate the value of their patent portfolios by filing more, but relatively minor, improvement patents or by citing more, but relatively less important, scientific papers as prior art. Third, surrogate measures can only be used to value patent portfolios. Valuation of patent portfolios is very useful to investors and financial analysts. Intellectual property managers and licensing professionals, however, need to value individual, or related groups of, patents. Surrogate measures are far less useful in these valuation tasks.

## 5. Disaggregation Methods

There are two basic types of disaggregation methods: value disaggregation and income disaggregation. Value disaggregation seeks to apportion some fraction of total value to intellectual property assets whereas income disaggregation seeks to apportion some fraction of total income to intellectual property assets.

The simplest form of value disaggregation first calculates the market value of a firm, either from the price of its outstanding common stock, in the case of a public company, or from substitute measures such as price-earnings ratios or net cash flows, in the case of a private company. The value of the firm's monetary assets (e.g., securities, working capital receivables) and tangible assets (e.g., land, buildings, equipment) are subtracted from the market value of the firm to determine the value of the intangible assets. This form of disaggregation is useful to provide perspective on the importance of intangible assets to a firm but cannot be used to value different types of intangible assets or to value individual, or related groups of, intangible assets.

A more sophisticated value disaggregation method divides the value of a firm among its business divisions and the value of the business divisions among the products sold by the divisions. The value of a given product is then apportioned among the monetary, tangible, intangible, and brand assets (trademarks, brand names) associated with the product. The monetary, tangible, and intangible assets associated with the product can be based on the ratio calculated for the firm as a whole, and the value of the brand assets can be based on the difference between the value of products incorporating the brand assets and the value of generic substitute products. This method of valuation has the benefit of associating intangible assets with specific products, albeit in an undifferentiated fashion. It also has the benefit of separating out the value of brand assets from other intangible assets. This method, however, cannot value intellectual property assets (e.g., patents, copyrights, trade secrets) separately from intangible advantages (e.g., assembled work force, employee training) nor can it value individual or related groups of, intellectual property assets.

A macro-economic model of value disaggregation has recently been proposed. This method attempts to apportion a country's Gross Domestic Product ("GDP") among all enforceable patents in the country. The method begins by dividing GDP into economic sectors defined by the Standard Industrial Codes ("SICs") and associating all enforceable patents with the economic sectors by associating the SICs with the United States Patent and Trademark Office ("PTO") patent classification code. The value of each economic sector is then apportioned among the enforceable patents associated with that sector based on a set of measures, including the number of claims, the number of independent claims, the length of the independent claims, the length of the specification, the number of figures, and the number of prior art references cited. The advantage of the macro-economic model is that it allows an inexpensive automated valuation of a large number of patents at a time. The disadvantage is that the valuation is very coarse.

Income disaggregation calculates the earnings of a firm or business unit and apportions a fraction of these earnings to intellectual property assets based upon various factors. One form of income disaggregation, developed for Dow Chemical Company by Arthur D. Little, is the Tech Factor Method. The Tech Factor Method quantifies the monetary contribution of each patent as a percentage of the business' total net present revenue. The Tech Factor Method utilizes a cross-functional team of internal and/or external experts to evaluate the commercial, technical, and legal aspects of a technology. Tech Factor valuation begins with a determination of the net present value of the incremental cash flow of a business unit attributable to the technology being valued. Next, a technology factor range (low, medium, or high quality assessment) is assigned to the technology based on its utility and competitive advantage attributes. Finally, the net present value of the incremental cash flow is multiplied by the technology factor to calculate the value of the technology. The advantage of the Tech Factor Method is that it provides a structured, easily understood process for valuing technology. The disadvantage of the Tech Factor Method is that it requires assembly of a large multi-functional team possessing detailed knowledge of the competitive environment and business and marketing plans. The Tech Factor Method also does not provide a quantitative means for determining the incremental cash flow attributable to a technology or for determining the exact technology factor within a technology factor range.

Another income disaggregation method is the Knowledge Capital Scorecard developed by Professor Baruch Lev. The Knowledge Capital Scorecard first subtracts from a firm's annual normalized earnings the earnings from tangible and financial assets. The remainder of the earnings, which are generated by knowledge assets, is divided by a knowledge capital discount rate to calculate the value of knowledge assets. The advantage of the Knowledge Capital Scorecard is that it associates intangible assets with measurable earnings and calculates a realistic present value for intangible assets. The disadvantages of the Knowledge Capital Scorecard are that it cannot separate the different types of intangible assets and cannot value individual, or related groups of, intangible assets.

### 6. Monte Carlo Method

The Monte Carlo method of valuing intellectual property assets is primarily used as a refinement of the income method discussed earlier. Whereas the income method assigns a single value to the variables used in calculating the net present value ("NPV") of an asset, the Monte Carlo method assigns a range of values to the variables. For example, two revenue variables used to determine the NPV of an intellectual property asset are the price premium and additional unit sales attributable to the asset, and two expense variables are the cost of goods sold ("COGS") and sales, general, and administrative expenses ("SG&A") associated with the increased sales revenue. The income method would assign a single value to each of these variables. For example, the price premium might be $1,000, the additional sales might be 10,000 units, the COGS might be 60% of sales revenue, and SG&A might be 25% of sales revenue. The Monte Carlo method would assign a range of values to each of these variables. For example, the price premium might be between $800 and $1,200, the additional unit sales might be between 9,000 and 11,000, the COGS might be between 55% and 65%, and the SG&A might be between 15% and 35%.

In addition to assigning a range of values to each variable, the Monte Carlo method requires that a probability be assigned to the individual values within a range. There are four basic types of probability distribution: uniform, triangular, normal, and log-normal. Uniform distribution assigns the same probability to each value within a range; triangular distribution assigns the highest probability to a single value and decreases the probability of values below and above the highest probable value by a straight line; normal distribution (bell curve) decreases the probability of values below and above the highest probable value by a symmetric curve which gradually approaches zero probability at both ends; and log-normal distribution decreases the probability of values below and above the highest value by an asymmetric curve reflecting the uneven distribution of values over the range of values.

The Monte Carlo method works by calculating the NPV of an intellectual property asset typically between 500 and 1,000 times based upon a random selection of the probability weighted values that have been determined for each variable. Each calculation, or iteration, yields a single NPV. The multiple NPVs are then plotted by the frequency of their occurrence. This provides an indication of the most likely NPV as well as the probability of an NPV being above or below the most likely value by a given amount.

The most likely NPV calculated by the Monte Carlo method should not differ from the NPV calculated by the income method. Presumably, the single values assigned to each variable in the income method are the most probable values, so a random selection from a range of probability weighted values would select these single values most often. The benefit of the Monte Carlo method is that it can calculate minimum and maximum NPVs and can associate intermediate NPVs with the probability of their real-ization. For example, the Monte Carlo method might calculate the minimum NPV to be $300,000 and the maximum NPV to be $600,000 (there is zero probability that the NPV will be below the minimum or above the maximum). Similarly, the Monte Carlo method might calculate that there is a 80% probability that the NPV will be above $400,000 and a 20% probability that the NPV will be above $500,000. Such information is useful in licensing negotiations because it provides the parties perspective on the pos-sible outcomes of the exchange. The Monte Carlo method is also useful to determine how different variables affect the uncertainty of the NPV calculation. For example, the Monte Carlo method can be used to determine whether the revenue or expense vari-ables most contribute to NPV uncertainty. This information is also useful in licensing negotiations because it directs the parties' attention to monitoring and measuring the most critical variables.

Although the Monte Carlo method is based on sophisticated mathematics, this is not a barrier to its use. There are user-friendly software products available to implement the Monte Carlo method. Two such products are Crystal Ball(r) developed by Decisioneer-ing, Inc. and @Risk developed by Palisade Corporation. Both companies provide prod-uct support and user training. The challenge in implementing the Monte Carlo method is obtaining the necessary information. The accuracy of the NPV calculations yielded by the Monte Carlo method are totally dependent on the accuracy of the value ranges and the probabilities assigned to individual values. Extensive databases are required to pro-vide this information.

### 7. Option Methods

Option methods of valuing intellectual property assets are based on a widely used method for valuing stock options, known throughout the financial industry as the Black-Scholes formula. The Black-Scholes formula values a stock option as a function of five variables: (i) the price at which the option can be exercised (the strike price); (ii) the current market price of the stock; (iii) the amount of time remaining before the option expires; (iv) the volatility of the stock price; and (v) a risk-free rate of re-turn. Even if the strike price is higher than the current market price, the option still has value if the option period is sufficiently long and the price volatility is sufficiently great. The longer the option period and the greater the price volatility, the higher the probability that the strike price will be below the market price at some point. Under the Black-Scholes formula, the essence of a stock option's value lies in the right to wait and see what happens to a stock's price and to exercise or not exercise the option accordingly.

The adaptation of stock option valuation to intellectual property valuation is based on the same "wait and see" methodology. Option valuation of intellectual property views an investment in intellectual property as an option to develop the intellectual property further or to abandon the intellectual property, depending upon future tech-nical and market information. Option valuation is most useful for intellectual property investments that have long-term returns and high risks. The income method often un-dervalues these types of investments because of the compounding effect of risk over long periods of time. Option valuation compensates for this discounting effect. Option valuation recognizes that the risk of the intellectual property investment is not uniform over time but decreases as additional technical and market information is obtained, and that the owner of the intellectual property has the choice to continue to invest in the in-tellectual property or to abandon it at any time.

An ingenious adaptation of the Black-Scholes formula to the valuation of patents was developed by The Patent & License Exchange ("pl-x"). The pl-x method, named Technology Risk and Reward Unit Metrics or TRRU(r), substitutes a set of patent analog variables for the Black-Scholes stock option variables. The variables used in the Black-Scholes formula and their TRRU(r) equivalents are as follows: (i) the strike price equivalent is the remaining development cost required to commercialize the intellectual property; (ii) the current stock price equivalent is the mean market value of products which incorporate similar patents; (iii) the option exercise period equivalent is the remaining length of time until commercial utilization; (iv) the stock price volatility equivalent is product value volatility; and (v) the risk-free rate of return is the same in Black-Scholes and TRRU(r). In addition to the Black-Scholes analogs, TRRU(r) also includes a patent expiration variable to account for the decline in an intellectual property asset's value over its lifetime. The mean market value of products incorporating similar patents and the value volatility of these products are determined by daily tracking of the stock prices of small companies in approximately 370 niche technology sectors.

The advantages of the TRRU(r) method are that it utilizes quantitative parameters to measure value and can value individual patents. The disadvantage of the TRRU(r) method is that it does not distinguish between major and minor advances over prior art in calculating a patent's value and it relies on complex mathematics.

Software is available for users who want to develop the internal capability to implement option valuation. One such software program is FlexAble, developed by Real Options Software. Real Options Software also provides training and consulting services. Numerous articles, books, and websites devoted to real options are also available. Many of these are referenced at real-options.com, an information exchange on real options.

The advantages of option valuation are that it avoids exaggerating the risk of investing in intellectual property assets and provides an objective, repeatable means for calculating intellectual property value. The disadvantages of option valuation are its complex mathematics and its requirement of extensive information databases.

## IV. COMPETITIVE ADVANTAGE VALUATION® SOFTWARE

Competitive Advantage Valuation® ("CAV") is a new method to value intellectual property assets. The CAV method was developed over a number of years through a series of research projects undertaken in the Technology Transfer Research Center at Syracuse University on behalf of a variety of client organizations. These research projects assessed the commercial potential of many different types of early-stage technologies by analyzing the engineering, marketing, licensing, and intellectual property advantages and disadvantages associated with these technologies. When presented with the final research findings, the question most often asked by client organizations was, "So, what's the invention worth?" CAV was developed to answer this question in a simple and direct way.

### 1. Unique Features of the CAV Method

In comparison to other valuation methods, the CAV method combines a number of unique features. Most importantly, the CAV method is specific. It can be used to value individual intellectual property assets relative to prior art and to determine differences in value within a group of related intellectual property assets. The more specific a valuation method, the more useful it is in managing intellectual property assets. In addition to specificity, the CAV has other unique features.

The CAV method is understandable to the broad cross-section of professionals practicing in the fields of licensing and intellectual property management. The easier a valuation method is to understand, the lower the transaction costs of negotiation and the quicker the parties can know whether an agreement can be reached.

The CAV method is repeatable and not dependent upon the subjective choices of individuals or groups. The more repeatable a valuation method, the easier it is for parties to focus their attention on the variables and value inputs on which they agree or disagree.

The CAV method is affordable in terms of the time and cost of obtaining necessary information and performing the valuation analysis. The more affordable a valuation method, the more broadly it will be adopted and the more likely it will be standardized.

The CAV method is flexible and can be used to value any type of intellectual property as well as licenses, prospective research and development investments, and pre-market products. The more flexible a valuation method, the more it can be shared across business divisions and used as a common benchmark.

Finally, the CAV method is scalable. A simple CAV analysis can be performed using built-in default formulas to calculate values and more advanced CAV analyses can be performed using statistical software tools to calculate values. The more scalable a valuation method, the greater the user's ability to choose the trade-off between the time and cost of the valuation, and the desired degree of accuracy of the result.

## 2. Overview of the CAV Method

The major premise of the CAV method is that intellectual property assets have no inherent value; the value of intellectual property assets resides entirely in the value of the tangible assets that incorporate them. The minor premise of the CAV method is that the value of a given intellectual property asset can best be measured by the competitive advantage which that asset contributes to a product, process, or service. For the purpose of explanation, I will discuss the CAV method with respect to an existing product.

The CAV method is a novel combination of the income and disaggregation approaches to valuation. In its most general form, the CAV method consists of six basic steps:

(1) The intellectual property asset to be valued ("IPA") is associated with a product and the product's net present value is calculated.

(2) The product's net present value is apportioned among tangible assets, intangible advantages, and intellectual property assets. There are three groups of intellectual property assets: technical (utility patents, functional software copyrights, and technical trade secrets); reputational (trademarks, service marks, and brand names); and operational (business method patents and proprietary business processes).

(3) The product is associated with competition parameters, which can be used to compare the product to substitute products, and competition parameter weights are calculated. There are three groups of competition parameters: technical (price and performance), reputational (recognition and impression), and operational (cost and efficiency). Weights are calculated for each parameter group and for individual parameters within each group.

(4) The IPA is associated with an individual competition parameter and the IPA's competitive advantage relative to substitute intellectual property assets is calculated. Substitute intellectual property assets are assets that are incorpo-

rated in substitute products and associated with the same competition parameter as the IPA.

(5) The IPA is associated with complementary intellectual property assets and the IPA's competitive advantage relative to complementary intellectual property assets is calculated. Complementary intellectual property assets are assets that are incorporated in the same product and associated with the same parameter group as the IPA.

(6) The value of the IPA is calculated by apportioning a share of the product's intellectual property asset value to the IPA based upon the IPA's competitive advantage contribution relative to substitute and complementary intellectual property assets.

If the IPA is associated with multiple products, the IPA's relative competitive advantage contribution to each product is calculated and these contributions are summed to calculate the total value of the IPA. If the IPA is associated with multiple parameters, the IPA's relative competitive advantage contribution for each parameter is calculated and these contributions are summed to calculate the total value of the IPA.

As noted above, the CAV method is easy to use. The information required is obtainable from public domain sources, and the calculations are based on simple algebra. In addition, the CAV method provides an intuitively logical association among the valuation elements. An intellectual property asset is associated with a product, the product is associated with a set of competition parameters, and the intellectual property asset is associated with one of these parameters. Finally, the CAV method provides a set of default formulas for calculating the portion of a product's net present value attributable to intellectual property assets, the weights for competition parameter groups, and the weights for individual parameters within the parameter groups.

### 3. Other Applications of the CAV Method

In addition to valuing intellectual property assets, the CAV method can also be used to value intellectual property licenses, prospective research and development investments, and pre-market products.

When valuing intellectual property licenses the CAV method is used to calculate a minimum license value to the licensor, a maximum license value to the licensee, and a division of the net license value between the licensor and licensee. The minimum license value to the licensor represents the licensor's loss in competitive advantage and market share due to the license. Because the licensor's investment in an intellectual property asset is a sunk cost, it is only necessary to calculate the minimum value of a license to the licensor when the licensor is licensing an intellectual property asset that is currently being used and the licensee is a competitor firm. If the intellectual property asset is not currently being used or the licensee is not a competitor firm, the minimum value of the license to the licensor is zero. The maximum value of the license to the licensee represents the licensee's gain in competitive advantage and market share due to the license. The net value of the license is divided between the licensor and licensee by a formula that provides the licensor and licensee an equal rate of return on their respective investments in the license. If the licensor and licensee assume unequal levels of risk, the rate of return is adjusted to reflect this. The CAV method can be used to compare alternative licensors and licensees and alternative license terms.

When valuing prospective research and development investments the CAV method is used to calculate the gain in competitive advantage and market share that a prospective research and development investment could potentially yield. The gain in competitive advantage and market share is calculated by comparing an existing product to an improved product incorporating the new research and development. The value of the gain in competitive advantage and market share is adjusted for technical, market, and intellectual property risks. The CAV method can be used to compare alternative research and development investments and to determine which investments provide the highest rates of return.

When valuing pre-market products the CAV method is used to calculate the net present value of the product market, the relative competitive advantage of the pre-market product in comparison to an average substitute product, and the pre-market product's predicted market share. The calculation of the net present value of a product market is similar to the calculation of the net present value of a product. The only difference is that in the former case the calculation is based on all the products in a market while in the latter case it is based on a single product. The calculation of the pre-market product's relative competitive advantage consists of calculating the competitive advantage of an average substitute product, calculating the competitive advantage of the pre-market product, and calculating the difference between the two. The pre-market product's predicted market share is calculated from its relative competitive advantage. The value of the pre-market product is adjusted for technical market, and intellectual property risks. The CAV method can be used to compare alternative product features, prices, and performance levels to determine which product configurations would capture the highest potential market shares.

## CONCLUSION

The valuation of intellectual property assets is a multi-trillion dollar challenge in today's economy. The success of companies, and indeed the welfare of society, increasingly depends on intellectual property. Intellectual property assets cannot be effectively managed or efficiently transferred without adequate means to value them. Fortunately, a number of new methods to value intellectual property have been developed in recent years. Although each of these methods has limitations, together they provide intellectual property managers with a set of very useful decision-making tools.

No single valuation method is ever definitive. In the realm of tangible assets, the cost, market, and income methods are often combined in valuing plant and equipment. Likewise with intellectual property assets, multiple valuation methods are often employed to reach a final determination of value. Different valuation methods provide different perspectives on an asset's value. Research on valuation methodologies is also never finished.

\* \* \*

---

# How To License Technology\*
### Robert C. Megantz
### (John Wiley & Sons 1996)

\* \* \*

### Economic Analysis

The preferred way to value technology is to estimate the future income attributable to its use. This is done by economic analysis, a standard business technique and exactly the same method used to value tangible assets. Substantial effort and market knowledge is required to value technology using economic analysis, usually by both the licensor and licensee. However, the information and strategies generated can be extremely useful in understanding the potential risks and rewards of both parties and in determining appropriate license terms. Most importantly, the use of economic analysis assures full valuation of the technology. Both the licensor and licensee should conduct the economic analysis from their perspectives, and ideally the results of both analyses will be similar.

The economic benefit provided by a technology can be estimated using several different approaches, including the following:

1. Determine the excess earnings generated through use of the technology. Projected earnings are compared to required returns on all other tangible and intangible assets, which are based on the risk associated with each asset. The difference between projected earnings and required returns represents the value of the technology.
2. Estimate the royalty income that could be earned by licensing the technology. After adjusting the amount to take into account the licensees' shares of profits, the total represents the technology's value.
3. Estimate all business assets and subtract the value of all tangible assets and other intangible assets, with the remainder representing the value of the technology.
4. Combine the above methods or use other techniques developed for specific situations.

An appropriate discount rate is applied to the value estimates to account for risk. All these methods require a detailed analysis of the technology being valued. The first step is to determine as accurately as possible the benefits offered by the technology. Determination of benefits could include answering the following questions:

Is the licensed technology an essential and primary feature of the product being considered (for example, a "standard" technology needed to compete in the market) or a nonessential improvement?

Does the technology provide improvement in performance? If so, what competitive advantage will be obtained by marketing licensed products (can a higher price be justified, will market share increase or a new market be created, and so forth)?

Are there other licensees? If so, what has their experience been with the technology?

Does the technology lower the cost of sales, operating expenses, and so on? If so, by how much?

What is the useful life of the technology?

What capital investment would be needed to utilize the technology? What alternatives are available? How do they compare to the licensed technology, both technologically and in terms of their potential economic benefit?

What is the size of the market?

To what stage has the licensed technology been developed? Basic research represents the first stage of development, where the technology concept is invented and proven. Most university-based licensing occurs at this phase. Next, the technology is developed into a usable form (for example, a marketable product) and product and market testing is conducted. Then, the pilot production stage proves that the technology can be mass-produced while meeting quality, safety, and regulatory requirements. The final stage is when the technology or product has been fully commercialized and proven. The investment in and value of the technology increases as each stage is successfully completed.

Can the technology be used in other markets? If so, an analysis of the technology's prospects in all other potential markets should be undertaken, including the probability of successful exploitation, size of the opportunity, ability of the licensee to exploit the market, and so on.

Will use of the licensed technology result in increased revenues from other products? In many cases introducing a new or improved product will increase sales of other products, and the economic benefit of these potential related sales should not be overlooked.

Next, the components of the technology being valued should be examined.

1. The patent portfolio. Are the patents fundamental or improvements? Have patents been applied for or issued in all important markets? Is it possible to engineer around the patents? Have the patents been litigated? Will future patents be included in the license?

2. The trademarks. How well known are the trademarks in the markets in which licensed products will be sold? Have they been protected and policed adequately? What types of trademark promotion have been done in the past, and what (if anything) is the licensor offering in the agreement?

3. The know-how. Is the know-how important in manufacturing and selling licensed products? Who will pay for technology transfer? What part of know-how is trade secrets, and what part is show-how?

4. The copyrighted works. How easy would it be to rewrite the copyrighted works? If computer software or firmware, how efficient is the code being supplied, and will it work without modification in the application envisioned?

Personnel from manufacturing, finance, R&D, and marketing should work together to develop quantitative answers to these questions. Manufacturing personnel can determine what new equipment, material, and labor costs would be associated with the production of products incorporating the new technology, and whether sufficient capacity exists in current facilities. The finance department can determine what capital expenditures would be required to implement and run the manufacturing facility and what production levels would be required to ensure profitability. R&D personnel can assess the technology and various alternatives and determine what additional development would be required to ready the technology for production. The marketing department can identify competitive products and assess the market prospects and potential selling price of the new product. Product sales estimates are often based on a product-life-cycle model, in which growth is slow during the introduction phase, rapid during an intermediate phase, levels off once the product has achieved maturity, and then declines. The span and timing of the life cycle depends on the market and product. Legal counsel can, if required, research the intellectual property history.

At this point projected cash flow over the life of the technology can be estimated, and one or more of the analysis approaches can be employed. Cash inflow to the licensor will include initial payments, running royalties, and any other payments stipulated in the agreement. Licensor's cash outflows will include the costs of transferring the technology to the licensee, further technology development, license administration, intellectual property costs, and so forth. Licensee's cash inflows will include revenues from licensed and related-product sales, whereas outflows will consist of royalty payments, product development and marketing expenses, capital investments, and so forth.

In all analyses certain information and outcomes will not be known. Techniques have been developed to allow the incorporation of unknown outcomes into analyses. One such method is decision tree analysis, where various chains of events are envisioned and their probabilities and potential outcomes determined. Alternatives examined can include licensing or not licensing the technology, different license terms, targeting or not targeting certain markets, capital investment, and so forth. Based on the probabilities of each scenario and the economic outcome, the risk and potential for market success for a number of alternatives can be estimated.

* * *

## Discounted Cash Flow

License agreements can require that periodic payments be made or that running royalties be paid on products manufactured or sold in a defined period of time (such as a calendar quarter or year). Other agreements might call for a single up-front payment. When negotiating terms it is helpful to know the present value of an anticipated future revenue stream, both to value the overall agreement and to determine the most advantageous strategy. Different strategies can be compared based on their present values, and the most attractive alternative (the one with the highest present value) chosen.

Discounting future cash flow to obtain its present value is the method used to obtain this information. In this calculation cash flow is defined as net cash flow, that is, the difference between cash inflow and cash outflow. The data required to calculate present value includes net revenue amounts, timing of payments, and risk.

### Net Revenue Amounts

This would include any initial payments made and the estimated future royalty stream, minus the costs associated with administering the agreements, transferring the technology, providing support, and so forth. Projected revenues can be developed using economic analysis, and costs should be estimated based on the terms of the agreement. The accuracy and utility of the present value calculation will depend greatly on the accuracy of these estimates; market research and the resulting projected sales figures must be of high quality.

### Timing of Payments

Initial payments will obviously have a higher present value than future royalty payments that, projected farther and farther into the future, will have less and less present value.

### Risk

The likelihood of the payments being made must be estimated. From this estimation a discount rate is chosen depending on the degree of risk. Factors affecting risk include the reliability of the cash flow estimates and their underlying assumptions, the viability of the licensee, and so on. Very low-risk investments, such as US government treasury bills, might carry a discount rate of 6 percent; the higher the risk the higher the discount rate applied. Once these three pieces of information are known, calculating the present value is straightforward.

———————

# III. Valuing Early Stage Technologies

## A. University Research as a Source of Licensable Technology

The valuation of university research and technology presents special problems. Defining and valuing licensable subject matter in a university setting can be a bewildering experience. Researchers often describe such technology as "early stage" or "embryonic" because, even if patented, it may exist only in very raw form—databases, software, bench prototypes, specialized know-how, lab notebooks, research data, and the like. Obtaining the rights to such technologies and turning them into commercial products can involve additional, substantial risks not found in wholly industrial licensing settings. As noted in Chapter 4, differences in licensing philosophies among companies and universities and federal mandates can also contribute to valuation difficulties that can inhibit negotiations.

The following article describes a successful approach to valuation of early stage technology at Research Corporation Technologies (RCT). RCT is a successful independent technology management company. It specializes in evaluating university technologies for commercial potential, obtains the rights to patent and develop these technologies, and then licenses them to third parties with generous royalties realized by the institutions and inventors. The company maintains a permanent staff of scientists, engineers, and intellectual property attorneys and reviews hundreds of invention disclosures from non-profit research institutions every year.

\* \* \*

———————

## Appraising Inventions: The Key to Technology Management\*

John T. Perchorowicz
J. Assoc. University Tech. Mgrs. (1995)

\* \* \*

When an organization seeks to maximize the value of an invention through development or licensing, the commercialization process begins with an appraisal that includes analysis of technology, patentability, and marketability, as well as calculation of the expected value through the term of the patent. Technology managers allocate limited human and financial resources to inventions in their portfolios on the basis of rational assessments of factors such as anticipated risk, cost, time, and revenue.

———————

The hypothetical case in this article presents a greatly simplified example of RCT's approach to technology appraisal.

## TECHNICAL ASSESSMENT

The technical assessment defines the inventive concept, its theoretical basis and scope, as well as potential commercial applications and technical value.

A broad, objective review of fields in which the invention may have an impact requires unbiased research by an individual who understands the technology from a scientific perspective.

Resources available to the assessor include the inventors, their academic and industrial contacts, and searches of published technical articles and patents. Inventors often recognize their colleagues' technical publications but they rarely investigate patents. Often, industrial contacts provide useful information despite their biases and potential conflicts.

A vision of potential products results from an understanding of the invention's technical limitations. The assessor must identify other technologies required for commercialization, unprecedented products or markets, potential for circumvention of the patent, difficulty of detecting infringement, potential users of the technology and their motivations, and the costs and benefits of adopting the technology in comparison to available or anticipated functional equivalents.

## PATENTABILITY ASSESSMENT

An assessment of patentability provides a basis for formulation of patent strategy and an understanding of the strategy's strengths and weaknesses in relation to potential markets for defined products. An initial investigation reveals any bars to patent rights due to publications or failure to meet requirements for utility and enablement. Licensable [patent] claims must adequately cover the envisioned products.

A monopoly advantage enables the seller to induce and protect investments in product development. If a monopoly is unavailable, then a dominant patent position yields more value than a subservient position. The ability to either dominate follow-on technology or block current technology will provide value and leverage in licensing.

Geographic breadth of patents in countries where the invention will be practiced protects both licensee and licensor in their efforts to exclude competition for a time and maximize return.

Practicality and economic feasibility determine the capacity to enforce patents. Consider, for example, a new, unapproved use for a drug that is currently marketed for an approved use. Physicians could infringe patent claims for the new use by writing prescriptions for the unapproved use of the drug. Such infringements prove difficult to detect and costly to prosecute case by case.

Finally, infringements of patent claims to a process [by] making a product obtainable by other means may prove difficult to detect, unless the product bears traces of the claimed process. Alternatively, an unpatented process may circumvent the contemplated patent. Consideration of all these factors permits a determination of a patent's value to the licensee.

## MARKET ASSESSMENT

The goals in market assessment include determination of the technology's expected value in marketable products, identification of potential licensees, and development of a commercialization strategy. After identification of optimum and secondary commercialization paths, the licensor can estimate appropriate royalty rates. While royalty rates bear directly on value, we need not repeat here the many published techniques for their determination. Rates and calculation theories vary among industries and technologies, based in part on their impact upon the final product's value.

Other factors that may require consideration include exclusivity, developmental investments, start-up companies, marketing costs and environment, competing technologies or products, and the target industry's receptivity to new ideas and willingness to invest in them.

## FINANCIAL ANALYSIS

A financial analysis estimates the present value of a technology, an important value for planning decisions such as whether to allocate resources to commercializing the invention, and how to structure and value investments. While technical, market, and patentability factors impact analyses, true value determinations also consider risk factors, costs, time, and revenue.

A naive analysis would set the present value of an incremental improvement to a technology—say, a cure for a disease—based on the erroneous assumption that the market equals current expenditures for treatment of the disease.

The more sophisticated analysis modeled below values a product for the interdiction or treatment of septic shock. Septic shock results when patients with systemic bacterial infection experience circulatory collapse, a severe drop in blood pressure with its associated complications. This blood pressure drop generally occurs rapidly, does not respond well to the usual pressor agents, and often leads to death within 24 hours. Each year in the United States and Europe, one million people develop sepsis and 35% die of the disease.

Rather than an intervention in the infectious cause of septic shock, this technology merely allows maintenance of blood pressure, prolonging the period during which the bacterial infection can be treated. The data in this example offer only an illustration rather than an exhaustive analysis.

The analysis begins with the patent's filing date, in this case of a GATT patent that will expire 20 years from that date. This determines the period of time during which revenue can accrue.

Next the appraiser determines the number of septic shock patients that could benefit from the treatment, how many will be treated, and how that number might change with time based on the expected date of product marketing and the percentage of market that would be captured if this were the sole available treatment. A treatment price provides the basis for an approximate calculation of sales and income, assuming a royalty rate reasonable to the industry.

Table 5.1 shows a financial analysis that employs these factors to calculate a present value for the royalty stream of about $23 million, calculated at a discount rate of 12%. Costs of patenting, development, and marketing are excluded in this table.

The model assumes that the invention occurred in 1994, no divulgation created a patent bar, and a provisional patent application was filed in 1995 to gain a year toward a formal filing and start of the clock toward patent expiration. For simplicity, this example assumes that one worldwide patent application was filed and that all patent actions occurred on the first day of the year. The patent therefore expires at the end of 2015, together with the right to collect royalties.

Table 5.1   Market for Septic Shock Treatment

| Year | Patients Sepsis | Shock | Market Penetration (%) | Treatment Market ($K) | Royalty at 5% ($K) |
|------|------|------|------|------|------|
| 1995 | 1,000 | 500 | 0 | 0 | 0 |
| 1996 | 1,010 | 505 | 0 | 0 | 0 |
| 1997 | 1,020 | 510 | 0 | 0 | 0 |
| 1998 | 1,030 | 515 | 0 | 0 | 0 |
| 1999 | 1,041 | 520 | 0 | 0 | 0 |
| 2000 | 1,051 | 526 | 0 | 0 | 0 |
| 2001 | 1,062 | 531 | 30 | 47,768 | 2,388 |
| 2002 | 1,072 | 536 | 65 | 104,533 | 5,227 |
| 2003 | 1,083 | 541 | 80 | 129,943 | 6,497 |
| 2004 | 1,094 | 547 | 90 | 147,648 | 7,382 |
| 2005 | 1,105 | 552 | 90 | 149,124 | 7,456 |
| 2006 | 1,116 | 558 | 90 | 150,615 | 7,531 |
| 2007 | 1,127 | 563 | 90 | 152,121 | 7,606 |
| 2008 | 1,138 | 569 | 90 | 153,643 | 7,682 |
| 2009 | 1,149 | 575 | 90 | 155,179 | 7,759 |
| 2010 | 1,161 | 580 | 90 | 156,731 | 7,837 |
| 2011 | 1,173 | 586 | 90 | 58,298 | 7,915 |
| 2012 | 1,184 | 592 | 90 | 59,881 | 7,994 |
| 2013 | 1,196 | 598 | 90 | 161,480 | 8,074 |
| 2014 | 1,208 | 604 | 90 | 163,095 | 8,155 |
| 2015 | 1,220 | 610 | 90 | 164,726 | 8,236 |
| Present Value at 12% | | | | | 22,736 |

We also assume that one million people in regions covered by patents will contract sepsis in 1995. Estimating conservatively, the patient population increases 1% per year. Half will experience septic shock, including the symptoms of circulatory collapse de-

**Table 5.2   Impact of Risk Factors on Present Value**

| Risk Factor | Risk-Adjusted Probability | Present Value |
| --- | --- | --- |
| Patent issues in strength and geographic breadth desired | 80% | $18,189,000 |
| Patent survives future legal challenges | 90% | $16,370,000 |
| Company licenses projects in current state of development | 10% | $1,637,000 |
| Regulators grant final approval | 1% | $164,000 |
| Public accepts product | 100% | $164,000 |
| Public prefers product | 60% | $98,000 |

scribed above for which the product is appropriate. Nearly all patients who experience shock will be treated. The cost of the treatment is set at $300.

The model further assumes that a product will achieve development, FDA approval, and marketing by 2001. During that first year of product life, the treatment will capture 30% of the potential market, ramping up to 90% over three years and maintaining that level for the life of the patent.

We can now calculate the market size and the royalty return based on a royalty rate of 5%. Calculating a present value at a discount rate of 12% yields $22.7 million.

The large present value of the royalty stream predicted by this best-case scenario seems to call for commercialization of the invention. However, this model does not account for the risks associated with developing the product and bringing it to market. The present value falls to $98,000 after adjustment for the risk factors summarized in Table 5.2.

Selection and quantification of appropriate risk factors results from extensive experience, research, and debate. These numbers, while inexact, provide a framework for rigorous critical analysis of a project's value, traceable over time as the probabilities of factors change.

At the time of most technology appraisals, the patent has not been filed. Additionally, despite the inventor's knowledge about his scientific competitors, the appraiser must conduct adequate industrial research to gain a sense of the anticipated patent's ability to dominate competing technologies. This perspective permits prospective licensees or investors to gauge potential returns.

The geographic breadth of patents also directly influences the ability to collect royalties. We could further assign a probability of patents issuing in each geographic region of importance and include a factor for each patent's strength. All of these risk factors change fluidly as additional information becomes available.

If we multiply the probability of obtaining a patent, set at 80%, by the probability of its surviving legal challenges, set at 90%, the overall probability of patent success falls to 72% at present. Because anticipated patents issue in all important areas, the 80% probability of issuance rises to 100% and ceases to negatively impact value, while the probability of surviving legal challenges may also change.

Similarly, each stage of technical development merits assignment of a degree of risk. University-derived technologies rarely permit easy assessment of the value of final products. Usually years of high-cost research precede product definition, development, and introduction.

The non-risk-adjusted value in the model assumed an existing product. Realistic risk factors include the project's attractiveness at its current state of development to a prospective licensee. This factor is influenced by performance of additional research to reduce the risk perceived by the licensee.

A more difficult assessment to control, the ability of a licensee to produce a marketable product, varies according to intensity of motivation, availability of capital, and influence of a product champion in driving the development process.

Recently, several products designed to interrupt the physiological progression in sepsis leading to circulatory collapse failed to gain regulatory approval following clinical trials. In light of this experience, we estimate the probability of licensing success for the product in its current state of development at only 10%. The potential licensee might view this as the probability of successfully obtaining regulatory approval. This probability would increase as additional data demonstrate the safety and efficacy of the treatment.

The likelihood of final regulatory approval might not exceed 1% based on industry experience with technologies at an equally early stage. If the compound proves effective in acute-care settings when administered for short time periods, long-term toxicity and safety issues may not arise. If these issues became significant, the estimate of probability of success would decrease. The compound must complete pre-clinical trials and Phases I, II, and III clinical trials. In this case, investigators can easily measure the uncomplicated end points for clinical trials: blood pressure or mortality. We anticipate low toxicity based on available information. At any point in the regulatory process, failure will drive the probability of success to zero along with the present value of the technology. Conversely, this probability increases upon achievement of regulatory milestones.

Public acceptance generally follows approval by regulatory authorities. In this case we define the consumer as the prescribing physician. In Table 1, a market penetration of 90% represents knowledge of the need for intervention and recognition of a particular treatment. We assume a probability of acceptance by physicians of 100%. Note that this factor differs from market share as discussed below.

* * *

Although we have identified no competitors so far, some probably will appear eventually. The risk factor for competition depends on how users view this technology's differential utility, such as decreased side effects or increased benefits.

The model assumes that the product will reach the market first, capturing significant market share and recognition as an effective treatment. Assuming that competing products reduce this preference by 40%, we set the factor for product differentiation at 60%.

We calculate the probability of achieving success by multiplying together all of the assigned probabilities. For our example, this probability approximates 0.04% or 1 in 2,000. Based upon past experience with technologies at a similar stage of development and risk profile, this probability proves sufficient to attract investment interest compared to most university-derived technologies.

Alternatively, to value an investment in the technology or to sell it outright, we could multiply the probability of achieving the present value derived in Table 1 by the probability of attaining successful introduction (the product of all of the probabilities in Table 2). This yields a value of about $100,000 for the invention at its present state of development.

This estimated value should achieve accuracy within an order of magnitude if it employs reasonably accurate risk factors. Frequently, errors arise from inclusion of the same risk in more than one factor or from over- or under-estimating requirements for commercializing the invention. Naturally the accuracy of estimates increases as a product approaches realization.

\* \* \*

# IV. Valuation of Trademarks

## Quantitative Methods of Valuing Intellectual Property
Russell L. Parr & Gordon V. Smith, THE NEW ROLE
OF INTELLECTUAL PROPERTY IN COMMERCIAL TRANSACTIONS\*
(John Wiley & Sons, Inc., New York, 1994)

\* \* \*

Do well-known trademarks contribute to stock performance? The answer is definitely yes. Philip Morris recently provided a strong example of how brand names and stock prices intermingle. Many of the leveraged buy-outs of the 1980s involved companies that possessed the most widely known brands. The huge prices paid for these companies ($25 billion for RJR Nabisco) were partially justified by a belief that the acquired brands could be managed more aggressively, meaning that product prices could be raised faster. This tactic worked for a while; however, consumers will only pay so much, and not pay a penny more, to keep an "old friend" brand product around the house. A modest premium is tolerable, but the price ceiling can quickly be reached when alternative products of equal utility are available. Enter quality generics and house brands.

In an attempt to thwart market share advances of discount cigarettes, Philip Morris recently announced a 20% price cut of its premier Marlboro brand cigarettes. Discount cigarettes have demonstrated tremendous growth, currently at 36% of the market from a standing-still start in 1981, with some analysts predicting a 50% market share by the end of the decade. The price difference for a pack of cigarettes is substantial. House brands are priced at $1.00, whereas premium brands such as Marlboro were priced at $2.40 a pack. The price cut by Philip Morris is expected to reduce pretax tobacco profits by $2 billion from the $5.2 billion it earned last year. In response to the announcement investors pushed the stock downward by 23% in one day, and Philip Morris lost nearly $13 billion of value—all of which is considered to be a reduction in the value of the brand name. The Marlboro brand will still sell at a premium over discount cigarettes and will surely retain a large number of brand-loyal consumers. However, an upper boundary for the price that consumers are willing to pay for mystique and image

---

\* Reprinted with permission of the publisher, copyright 1994.

has apparently been found. Jack Trout, a marketing consultant, told The Wall Street Journal, "This shows that even the biggest and strongest brands in the world are vulnerable." The stock price of Philip Morris continues to reflect the strength of the Marlboro brand.

# V. Judicial Valuation

In addition to receiving expert opinions from accountants, appraisers, and other professionals, the intellectual property practitioner can gain insight into the valuation of intellectual property from cases where the Federal Courts have set royalties as damages in patent infringement and eminent domain cases. In the cases below, note how the courts evaluated the trial records, including the prior dealings of the parties and expert opinions and reports, to arrive at royalties.

One possible method for valuing intellectual property is to calculate the profits lost when someone infringes it. That loss is also a measure of the damages that courts may award for the infringement.

Whether valuing intellectual property or assessing the cost of infringement, it is important to distinguish between the intellectual property owner's loss of its own profits and any illicit profits that the infringer made from the infringement. The former is a measure of the intellectual property owner's damages from the infringement, while the latter is a measure of the infringer's unjust enrichment. Virtually every form of intellectual property law allows the property owner to recover its own lost profits as a measure of damages. Common-law restitution, in general, also allows a property owner to recover biased on another's unjust enrichment from using the property without permission.

Yet not every form of statutory intellectual property recognizes a restitutionary remedy. Utility and plant patents are exceptions to the general rule; they have no provision for recovering an infringer's profits as such. *See General Motors Corp. v. Devex Corp.*, 461 U.S. 648, 651–53 (BNA) 1185 (1983) (explaining history and rationale of statutory amendments that eliminated recoveries of infringer's profits in utility and plant patent litigation). However, other forms of intellectual property do recognize a restitutionary remedy. See 35 U.S.C. §289 (allowing recovery of infringer's profits in design patent cases); 17 U.S.C. §504(a) (b) (allowing recovery of infringer's profits in copyright cases); Lanham Act §35(a)(1), codified as amended 15 U.S.C. §1117(a)(1) (allowing recovery of defendant's profits in trademark-infringement cases federal unfair competition cases); Uniform Trade Secrets Act §3 (allowing recovery of "the unjust enrichment caused by misappropriation"); 17 U.S.C. §911(b) (allowing recovery of infringer's profits in semiconductor chip protection cases). In part because an infringer's profits cannot be recovered in utility and plant patent cases, patent law puts special emphasis on the patent owner's lost profits as a measure of damages.

The basic monetary remedy for infringement of utility and plant patents is "damages adequate to compensate for the infringement, but in no event less than a reasonable royalty for the use made of the invention by the infringer, together with interest and costs as fixed by the court." 35 U.S.C. §284. Courts have long held that a patent owner's lost profits are a legitimate measure of damages, but the general rule of causation imposes limitations in calculating lost profits. The following seminal case sets forth the most basic causal limits on damages recoveries measured by the patent owner's lost profits in utility and plant patent cases.

---

# A. Lost Profits

## Panduit Corp. v. Stahlin Bros. Fibre Works
### 575 F.2d 1152 (6th Cir. 1978)

\* \* \*

MARKEY, Chief Judge.

### Lost Profits Due To Lost Sales

To obtain as damages the profits on sales he would have made absent the infringement, i.e., the sales made by the infringer, a patent owner must prove: (1) demand for the patented product, (2) absence of acceptable noninfringing substitutes, (3) his manufacturing and marketing capability to exploit the demand, and (4) the amount of the profit he would have made....When actual damages, e.g., lost profits, cannot be proved, the patent owner is entitled to a reasonable royalty. A reasonable royalty is an amount, "which a person, desiring to manufacture and sell a patented article, as a business proposition, would be willing to pay as a royalty and yet be able to make and sell the patented article, in the market, at a reasonable profit." [Citations omitted].

\* \* \*

---

# B. Reasonable Royalty

## Georgia-Pacific Corp. v. United States Plywood Corp.
### 318 F. Supp. 1116 (S.D.N.Y. 1970)

TENNEY, District Judge.

By opinion dated October 26, 1956, entered in an action by Georgia-Pacific Corporation (hereinafter referred to as 'GP') for a declaratory judgment of invalidity and non-infringement of three patents held by United States Plywood Corporation (hereinafter referred to as 'USP') and upon a counterclaim by USP for patent infringement and unfair competition, my late brother Judge Herlands found USP's three patents (one Deskey and two Bailey patents) invalid for lack of invention, not infringed by GP's product and further, that there was no proof that GP engaged in acts of unfair competition. 148 F. Supp. 846 (S.D.N.Y.1956). The Court of Appeals reversed and remanded in 1958, holding that Claim 1 of USP's Deskey Patent No. 2,286,068 covering 'Weldtex' striated fir plywood valid and infringed by GP. 258 F.2d 124 (2d Cir.), *cert. denied*, 358 U.S. 884, 79 S. Ct. 124, 3 L. Ed.2d 112 (1958).

Following the decision of the Court of Appeals, the case was referred to a special master to determine the amount of damages to be awarded to USP under 35 U.S.C. section 284 (1952), which provides for 'damages adequate to compensate for the infringement.' The master, computing damages upon the basis of GP's profits derived from the sale of the infringing article, awarded $685,837.00 to USP. Judge Herlands, on exception to the Master's Report, concluded that under the instant circumstances and controlling statute GP's profits did not constitute the proper measure of recovery, and that the award to USP should have been computed on the basis of a reasonable royalty.

\* \* \*

Following the submission of this cause to Judge Herlands as set forth above, Judge Herlands on August 28, 1969 died without having made such determination, it being understood, however, that at time time of his death, Judge Herlands had prepared a draft of his opinion herein together with notes or other memoranda relating thereto.

\* \* \*

Based upon this stipulation, and after a careful review of the entire record, the Court has accepted and adopted, with minor amendment, the reasoned opinion of Judge Herlands, which follows.

\* \* \*

While the parties agree upon the doctrinal criteria of a reasonable royalty, they differ sharply in their application of those principles to the hard specifics of the evidence. The extreme divergence of the parties is reflected in the difference between GP's submission that the reasonable royalty herein should be fixed at a figure somewhere between a dollar and one-half to three dollars per thousand square feet and USP's claim that the minimum reasonable royalty should be the rate of fifty dollars per thousand square feet.

A comprehensive list of evidentiary facts relevant, in general, to the determination of the amount of a reasonable royalty for a patent license may be drawn from a conspectus of the leading cases. The following are some of the factors mutatis mutandis seemingly more pertinent to the issue herein:

1. The royalties received by the patentee for the licensing of the patent in suit, proving or tending to prove an established royalty.
2. The rates paid by the licensee for the use of other patents comparable to the patent in suit.
3. The nature and scope of the license, as exclusive or non-exclusive; or as restricted or non-restricted in terms of territory or with respect to whom the manufactured product may be sold.
4. The licensor's established policy and marketing program to maintain his patent monopoly by not licensing others to use the invention or by granting licenses under special conditions designed to preserve that monopoly.
5. The commercial relationship between the licensor and licensee, such as, whether they are competitors in the same territory in the same line of business; or whether they are inventor and promoter.
6. The effect of selling the patented specialty in promoting sales of other products of the licensee; th[e] existing value of the invention to the licensor as a generator of sales of his non-patented items; and the extent of such derivative or convoyed sales.
7. The duration of the patent and the term of the license.
8. The established profitability of the product made under the patent; its commercial success; and its current popularity.
9. The utility and advantages of the patent property over the old modes or devices, if any, that had been used for working out similar results.

10. The nature of the patented invention; the character of the commercial embodiment of it as owned and produced by the licensor; and the benefits to those who have used the invention.

11. The extent to which the infringer has made use of the invention; and any evidence probative of the value of that use.

12. The portion of the profit or of the selling price that may be customary in the particular business or in comparable businesses to allow for the use of the invention or analogous inventions.

13. The portion of the realizable profit that should be credited to the invention as distinguished from non-patented elements, the manufacturing process, business risks, or significant features or improvements added by the infringer.

14. The opinion testimony of qualified experts.

15. The amount that a licensor (such as the patentee) and a licensee (such as the infringer) would have agreed upon (at the time the infringement began) if both had been reasonably and voluntarily trying to reach an agreement; that is, the amount which a prudent licensee—who desired, as a business proposition, to obtain a license to manufacture and sell a particular article embodying the patented invention—would have been willing to pay as a royalty and yet be able to make a reasonable profit and which amount would have been acceptable by a prudent patentee who was willing to grant a license.

The drawing of proper conclusions from conflicting evidence concerning the amount of a reasonable royalty has been said to call "for the exercise of judicial discretion by the District Court." *General Motors Corp. v. Dailey*, 93 F.2d 938, 942 (6th Cir. 1937). Both sides agree that this Court has a broad range of judgment in evaluating the relevant factors.

In the present case there is a multiplicity of inter-penetrating factors bearing upon the amount of a reasonable royalty. But there is no formula by which these factors can be rated precisely in the order of their relative importance or by which their economic significance can be automatically transduced into their pecuniary equivalent. In discharging its responsibility as fact finder, the Court has attempted to exercise a discriminating judgment reflecting its ultimate appraisal of all pertinent factors in the context of the credible evidence.

The parties agree that there was no "established" royalty for USP's Weldtex or GP striated. Consequently, it is necessary to resort to a broad spectrum of other evidentiary facts probative of a "reasonable" royalty.

Two of the earlier and typical cases relied upon by both parties are *Dowagiac Mfg. Co. v. Minnesota Moline Plow Co.*, 235 U.S. 641, 35 S. Ct. 221, 59 L. Ed. 398 (1915) and *United States Frumentum Co. v. Lauhoff*, 216 F. 610 (6th Cir. 1914). In *Dowagiac Mfg. Co.*, *supra*, 235 U.S. at 648, 35 S. Ct. at 224, the Supreme Court said that, where a patentee could not prove lost profits, infringer's profits or an established royalty, the patentee could "show the value by proving what would have been a reasonable royalty, considering the nature of the invention, its utility and advantages, and the extent of the use involved." In *United States Frumentum Co.*, *supra*, 216 F. at 617, the court referred to the following elements as relevant to the determination of a reasonable royalty: the nature of plaintiff's patent property; the extent to which defendant took it; and its utility and commercial value as evidenced by its advantages over other devices, by the extent of its use, and by the profits and savings that could be made upon its sale or adoption.

The parties rely upon the traditional array of facts probative of a reasonable royalty. But, in addition, USP places heavy reliance upon a later formulation called "the willing buyer and willing seller" rule.

The rule is pronounced in *Horvath v. McCord Radiator & Mfg. Co.*, 100 F.2d 326, 335 (6th Cir. 1938), *cert. denied, Carrier Engineering Corporation v. Horvath*, 308 U.S. 581, 60 S. Ct. 101, 84 L. Ed. 486, *rehearing denied*, 308 U.S. 636, 60 S. Ct. 171, 84 L. Ed. 529 (1939), in these terms:

> In fixing damages on a royalty basis against an infringer, the sum allowed should be reasonable and that which would be accepted by a prudent licensee who wished to obtain a license but was not so compelled and a prudent patentee, who wished to grant a license but was not so compelled.

A variant phrasing set forth in *Faulkner v. Gibbs*, 199 F.2d 635, 639 (9th Cir. 1952) reads:

> The primary inquiry, often complicated by secondary ones, is what the parties would have agreed upon, if both were reasonably trying to reach an agreement.

The rule is more a statement of approach than a tool of analysis. It requires consideration not only of the amount that a willing licensee would have paid for the patent license but also of the amount that a willing licensor would have accepted. What a willing licensor and a willing licensee would have agreed upon in a suppositious negotiation for a reasonable royalty would entail consideration of the specific factors previously mentioned, to the extent of their relevance. Where a willing licensor and a willing licensee are negotiating for a royalty, the hypothetical negotiations would not occur in a vacuum of pure logic. They would involve a market place confrontation of the parties, the outcome of which would depend upon such factors as their relative bargaining strength; the anticipated amount of profits that the prospective licensor reasonably thinks he would lose as a result of licensing the patent as compared to the anticipated royalty income; the anticipated amount of net profits that the prospective licensee reasonably thinks he will make; the commercial past performance of the invention in terms of public acceptance and profits; the market to be tapped; and any other economic factor that normally prudent businessmen would, under similar circumstances, take into consideration in negotiating the hypothetical license.

As pointed out in an earlier decision herein by this court (243 F. Supp. at 539), the very definition of a reasonable royalty assumes that, after payment, "the infringer will be left with a profit." It is necessary to consider, as an element in determining the amount of the reasonable royalty, the fact that GP would be willing hypothetically to pay a royalty which would produce "a reasonable profit" for GP. *See Faulkner v. Gibbs*, 199 F.2d 635, 639 (9th Cir. 1952).

It is evident, therefore, that the formulation called the willing seller and willing buyer rule represents an attempt to colligate diverse evidentiary facts of potential relevance. In applying the formulation, the Court must take into account the realities of the bargaining table and subject the proofs to a dissective scrutiny.

\* \* \*

There is some confusion in GP's analysis arising out of the circumstance that USP was unable to prove before the master the amount of its lost profits as damages. GP argues that the same deficiencies of proof which resulted in the master's finding—that USP proved the fact of damage but not the quantum of such damage—similarly vitiate USP's present effort to use, as one of the primary factors for evaluating a reasonable royalty, the profits that it would have reasonably anticipated it would make at the time when a royalty would have been negotiated hypothetically with GP. Similarly, GP is in error when it argues that, because this court rejected the master's use of GP's infringing profits as the legal measure of damages, evidence of GP's reasonably anticipated profits as of 1955 is irrelevant to the present inquiry.

Certain basic statistics are not in dispute. GP's sales of the infringing striated plywood totaled 15,899,000 square feet and amounted to sales proceeds to GP of $2,547,393. The period of the infringement was March 1955 through September 1958.

The manufacturing part of the infringement began in February 1955. As pointed out by the Court of Appeals (258 F.2d at 127):

The plaintiff, Georgia-Pacific Corporation, first manufactured its accused panels in February 1955 and in March delivered a sample to defendant's manager in Newark.

The hypothetical negotiations are, therefore, time-placed in February 1955 and the relevant factors are viewed in that frame of time-reference.

* * *

In the hypothetical negotiations, USP would have been reasonable in taking the position that it would not accept a royalty significantly less than the profit it was making by its policy of licensing no one to sell striated fir plywood in the United States.

In searching for and considering the available evidence of Weldtex's profitability— evidence claimed by USP to exist but whose existence in the record is denied by GP— it is necessary to distinguish sharply that inquiry from the entirely separate issue of the amount of USP's damages in the form of lost profits attributable to GP's infringing sales. That latter issue of lost profits as the measure of damages had been litigated before the special master who found (and this Court affirmed that finding, 243 F. Supp. at 510) that USP had failed to prove that it had sustained a measurable amount of lost profits caused by GP's infringing sales after February 1955 although USP had proved the fact of such damages as distinguished from its quantum. 243 F. Supp. at 512–13.

What must be considered now is the fixation of a reasonable royalty—a determination prescribed by the statute and made necessary for the very reason that USP was unable to prove the quantum of its damages in the form of lost profits. What must be considered now as one of the elements, *inter alia*, relevant to the determination of the amount of a reasonable royalty, is the rate of profits that USP was making on Weldtex at the time GP began its infringement, and not the amount of profits that USP lost as the result of GP's infringing sales—profits that USP made and was making on and before February 1955 and that it reasonably anticipated it would continue to make, not the profits that it actually lost after February 1955. The statute created the recovery of a reasonable royalty for the very purpose of affording fair compensation in cases such as this, where the victimized patentee is unable to prove that he lost a measurable amount of profits as the result of the infringement.

It is clear, then, that under the statute a reasonable royalty is an alternative way of recovering general compensatory damages and that it is not equitable or commensurable with actual damages computed in terms of demonstrably proved lost profits. This distinction must be emphasized because GP has obfuscated the issue by coalescing the two different concepts. Still another preliminary clarification of the issue is needed. GP makes the dual argument that "the proofs of 'profitability' of Weldtex are so unsubstantial, or are so unrelated to Deskey value that the backlash is proof that there is no Deskey value." The foregoing statement, phrased as it is in the disjunctive, embraces two independent points; (1) that USP has failed to prove the profitability of Weldtex and (2) that USP's evidence of Weldtex's profitability is "unrelated to Deskey value" — the latter contention being one that poses the issue of apportionment and that will be discussed separately herein in terms of the value of the Deskey invention.

In this juncture, we are considering the issue of the profitability of Weldtex and the record evidence bearing upon that issue.

\* \* \*

During the years 1952 to 1958, Weldtex was manufactured to two sources: the contract mills where approximately 80 per cent of USP's total Weldtex was produced and sold to USP by said mills; and USP's own Seattle plant where approximately 20 per cent of the Weldtex was produced. On an incremental or differential cost accounting basis (as distinguished from an absorption-cost accounting basis), USP made an average profit of $54.25 per thousand square feet with respect to the Weldtex produced by USP from the contract mills; and USP made an average profit of $86.16 per thousand square feet with respect to the Weldtex produced at USP's Seattle plant. When these two profit figures are weighed on the basis of the 80 per cent to 20 per cent production ratio, the ultimate result is $60.63 as the average rate of profit per thousand square feet earned by USP on all its Weldtex sales at the time of the infringement, computed on an incremental cost accounting basis.

Incremental cost accounting, however, is not considered by the court as appropriate in determining the actual profitability of Weldtex during the years prior to and up to February 1955. Arguably, that method of cost accounting might be appropriate in evaluating the factor of suppositious profit on additional hypothetical sales that USP would anticipate and preserve for itself by not licensing GP. But the absorption cost-basis is more reliable and pertinent to a determination of the historical profitability of Weldtex during the years prior to and up to February 1955.

Computed by the absorption method, USP's average rate of profit on its Weldtex sales was $48.64 per thousand square feet at the time of the infringement.

USP argues that, independently of USP Exhibit 5B, the Antoville and Heilpern testimony establishes that $60.63 is the rate of profit per thousand square feet of Weldtex sold, and that that figure is "conservative." The Court has considered the Antoville testimony—which is the predicate for USP's contention that the overall profit on Weldtex was approximately $68.00 per thousand square feet—and the Heilpern testimony—which is the predicate for USP's contention that the overall profit on Weldtex ranged from $52.00 to $60.00 per thousand square feet. That testimony does not impress the Court as sufficiently persuasive to warrant a finding other than that USP's average actual profit on Weldtex sales was approximately $48.00 per thousand square feet; and the Court so finds.

\* \* \*

## CONCLUSION

The amount of the reasonable royalty fixed by the Court has been derived from a close factual analysis of the total record. The reasonable-royalty case law analysis, based on all the reasonable-royalty decisions in this circuit and the most pertinent decisions elsewhere, has furnished general guidelines in the form of the applicable criteria of legal principles and operative facts. To the extent that there is precedential guidance, that factor has been subjected to the qualifications and modifications required by a realistic comparison of the particular facts and individual circumstances in the prior decisions and those in the case at bar.

The Court finds and concludes that $50.00 per thousand square feet of the patented product, striated fir plywood, made and sold by GP, represents a fair reasonable royalty that should be paid by GP. This amounts to $800,000, which is hereby awarded to USP, together with interest on the said award computed from the date of the last infringement, September 1, 1958, to the date of payment of the award, at the rate of 6 per cent per annum....

———————

# Georgia-Pacific Corporation v.
# U.S. Plywood-Champion Papers, Inc.
### 446 F.2d 295, 298–300 (2d Cir. 1971),
### *cert. denied*, 404 U.S. 870 (1971)

FIENBURG, Circuit Judge

\* \* \*

### IV.

GP's last, and most substantial, challenge concerns its profits on striated plywood after payment of the suppositious royalty. GP asserts, and the court below appears to have accepted, the proposition that under the willing buyer-willing seller rule a reasonable "royalty must be fixed so as to leave the infringer, or suppositious licensee, a reasonable profit." *See* 318 F. Supp. at 1122. The trial court's award appears to acknowledge this standard:

> [A] royalty of $50.00 per thousand square feet payable by GP to USP would have enabled GP to realize a reasonable profit...GP's average realization on all its striated fir plywood sales throughout the infringement period was $159.41 per one thousand square feet...(and) after paying $50.00 per one thousand square feet to USP, the remainder of about $109.41 would enable GP to make a substantial profit.

*Id.* at 1143.

Yet we cannot square this result with the trial court's finding that GP would reasonably have expected to earn profits approximating USP's, $48.65 per thousand square feet. *Id.* at 1131. Even if a small degree of profit is added for collateral sales in order to justify the court's subsequent finding that "GP's reasonably expected rate of profit on the sale of striated fir plywood would have been $50.00 per thousand square feet," id at 1141, the royalty imposed still gobbles up all of GP's expected profit. We also note that the trial court's $800,000 award more than encompasses the $685,837 that the Master found to be GP's actual profits.

Thus, although we affirm the other findings we feel that, despite the trial court's professed intention to do so, it did not allow GP a reasonable profit after paying the suppositious royalty. This is a basic error that should be corrected. We would, in fact, be inclined to remand for reconsideration were it not for the extraordinary length of time this litigation has already lingered and the willingness of the party ultimately paying the damages to have us dispose of the case. Accordingly, we turn to a redetermination of the award on the basis of the record before us.

Since the error was to leave GP no profit at all after payment of the suppositious reasonable royalty of $50 per thousand square feet, we must first determine what would be a reasonable profit for GP after payment of the royalty. We note that the Master found, on the basis of GP's annual reports, that GP's average net profit on sales of all products during the period of infringement was slightly over nine per cent of sales. It follows that GP would have been willing to pay a royalty which, after payment of its other costs, would leave it nine per cent profit on sales of the licensed item. Since the trial court found that GP's "average realization" on those sales was $159,41, such a profit would be $14.35 per thousand square feet in the present case. The remainder is arithmetic:

|  | $ Per Thousand Square Feet |
|---|---|
| GP's Expected Profit on Item | $ 50.00 |
| -9% Profit on Sales | -14.35 |
| Assumed Reasonable Royalty | $ 35.65 |

The district court apparently used a rounded-off figure of 16,000,000 square feet for GP's total sales of the infringing item. Using that figure and multiplying it by the reduced reasonable royalty of $35.65 per thousand square feet, we arrive at a rounded-off total award of $570,000. We realize that no one can be sure what the parties would have done had they actually negotiated. But determination of an assumed reasonable royalty is in essence a device for retroactively reaching a just result, and we feel that a reasonable royalty of $35.65 per thousand square feet is a fair one on the basis of the record before us. Accordingly, we modify the lower court's award of a reasonable royalty of $50.00 per thousand square feet to $35.65 per thousand square feet and determine that GP is liable in the amount of $570,000 before interest.

\* \* \*

# Hughes Aircraft Company v. The United States
## 86 F.3d 1566 (Fed. Cir. 1996)

ARCHER, Chief Judge.

Hughes Aircraft Company (Hughes) appeals the judgment of the United States Court of Federal Claims awarding Hughes compensation based on a 1% royalty rate with respect to spacecraft manufactured and used by or for the United States, which embody the invention of Hughes' United States Patent No. 3,758,051 (the Williams patent). *Hughes Aircraft Co. v. United States*, 31 Fed. Cl. 481, 35 U.S.P.Q.2d 1243 (1994) (*Hughes XII*). Hughes argues that the 1% royalty rate is too low. The United States cross-appeals contending that certain spacecraft were incorrectly included in the royalty base and that the interest rates used to calculate Hughes' delay damages were too high. We affirm.

## BACKGROUND

A. The Williams patent relates to an apparatus for controlling the orientation of the spin axis of spin-stabilized space vehicles such as satellites positioned in orbit around the earth. The patent was issued to Donald Williams on September 11, 1973. To correct orbital deviations, the Williams apparatus applies a reactive force to the satellite by firing a jet so as to "precess," or tip, the satellite into the proper position. Although this technique was known in the prior art, the Williams apparatus was the first to maintain its spin axis with reference to a fixed external coordinate system. *Hughes Aircraft Co. v. United States*, 717 F.2d 1351, 1360, 219 U.S.P.Q. 473, 479 (Fed. Cir. 1983) (Hughes VII).

The present suit began in 1973 when Hughes brought a claim under 28 U.S.C. §1498 against the United States for just compensation stemming from the use and manufacture by or for the government of spacecraft embodying the invention claimed in the Williams patent. During the course of the protracted litigation that followed, it was determined by the Court of Federal Claims that Hughes is entitled to just compensation with respect to 81 spacecraft. *Hughes Aircraft Co. v. United States*, 29 Fed. Cl. 197, 243–48, 29 U.S.P.Q.2d 1974, 2010 (1993) (*Hughes X*)....The Court of Federal Claims then found the value of the compensation base for calculating Hughes' award to be $3.577 billion, which was arrived at by using "total spacecraft cost," i.e., the total procurement cost, including payload costs, to the government of the 81 spacecraft. *Hughes Aircraft Co. v. United States*, 31 Fed. Cl. 464, 468 n.5, 477 (1994) (*Hughes XI*).

In *Hughes XII*, the Court of Federal Claims considered only the calculation of the amount of Hughes' award. The court first determined what royalty rate to apply to the compensation base to provide Hughes a reasonable royalty for the government's use of the patented invention. The court then considered the amount of pre-judgment interest (sometimes called "delay damages"), which together with the reasonable royalty would provide "reasonable and entire compensation." Because an established royalty rate did not exist for licensing the Williams patent, the court determined the royalty rate using the "willing buyer/willing seller" rule. Under this rule, a reasonable royalty is set at the rate that the court determines a "willing licensor and licensee would bargain for at hypothetical negotiations on the date infringement started." *State Indus. v. Mor-Flo Indus.*, 883 F.2d 1573, 1580, 12 U.S.P.Q.2d 1026, 1031 (Fed. Cir. 1989).

The court's royalty rate analysis focused initially on three letters containing acceptable license terms that Hughes had sent to other aerospace companies during the period from 1974 to 1978, none of which resulted in a licensing agreement. The first was a July 1974 letter from Hughes to the Philco-Ford Corporation (Philco-Ford) offering to license the Williams patent and the McLean patent together for 5%, or separately for 3%, of "the sales price of the satellite calculated at the time it is delivered to the launch pad." Although Hughes' letter was sent while a suit was pending against Philco-Ford in which Hughes accused Philco-Ford of infringing the Williams patent, the court found nothing in the letter to suggest that the offer was part of a proposed settlement of the litigation and found that the letter was sent by Hughes merely in response to earlier requests by Philco-Ford for terms at which any licenses had been offered to parties unrelated to the suit.

The second letter relied on by the court was sent by Hughes to TRW, Inc. (TRW) in September of 1974 and offered a license at the identical rate described in the letter to Philco-Ford. The court noted that there had never been any litigation or threat of litigation between Hughes and TRW relating to the Williams patent With regard to the TRW and Philco-Ford letters, the court found it significant that the anticipated royalty base underlying those offers was smaller than the royalty base in this case.

The third letter was sent by Hughes to Messerschmitt-Bolkow-Blohm (MBB), a German corporation, as part of a series of letters regarding settlement of claims by Hughes against MBB. As such, the court recognized that this letter could not fairly be considered an ordinary proposal of licensing terms. The court instead relied on language in the letter in which Hughes stated that its "normal royalty rate" for licensing the Williams and McLean patents together was 5% of the "full contact price" for a commercial spacecraft or 2% of the "full contract price" for a scientific or experimental spacecraft, with the provision that the cost of scientific or experimental spacecraft did not include the cost of scientific or experimental payloads provided to MBB by others The court found that all of the 81 spacecraft in the royalty base were "scientific or experimental vehicles." As Hughes had done in its Ford-Philco and TRW letters, the court reduced the 2% rate quoted in the MBB letter for both the Williams and McLean patents by a factor of 40% to arrive at a 1.2% rate for licensing only the Williams patent for scientific or experimental vehicles.

Based on the three offers, the Court of Federal Claims reasoned that negotiations would start at a rate of something less than 1.2% and that the negotiated rates would not fall below the 1% rate the government conceded would result in just compensation. According to the court, the royalty rate would "quickly settle on one percent." As additional support for the 1% royalty rate, the court pointed to the large size of the royalty base in this case. The court said that "[i]t is axiomatic that the larger the potential compensation base to which a royalty rate will be applied, the lower will be the rate." The court also noted that Williams was not a "pioneer" invention, that the license taken by the government was non-exclusive and unaccompanied by know-how, that the Hughes license offers to the aerospace companies were not accepted, and that Hughes had an incentive to discourage the development of alternative technology and encourage the use of the Williams invention. As to this last factor the court found that alternatives to the Williams invention existed in 1973 or were soon after developed. Based on all of these factors, the court determined that a royalty rate of 1% would be reasonable.

B.     In this appeal Hughes puts forth several grounds for reversing the Court of Federal Claims' decision that its compensation should be limited to a 1% royalty rate. Hughes argues that the court erred as a matter of law by treating the rates contained in the letters to Ford-Philco, TRW and MBB as a ceiling on the royalty rate. Also, Hughes asserts that the rates contained in the letters were artificially low due to widespread infringement of the Williams patent and due to the settlement context in which two of them were sent. Hughes further contends that reliance on the letters was improper because this conflicts with the policy behind Federal Rule of Evidence 408, which in certain circumstances requires the exclusion of evidence of offers made attempting to compromise a disputed claim. Finally, Hughes argues that the determination of the 1% royalty award was based upon three clearly erroneous factual findings. Specifically, Hughes takes issue with the findings that all of the 81 spacecraft determined to be compensable were "scientific or experimental" as that designation was used in the MBB letter, that the royalty base contemplated in the three letters was relatively smaller than the royalty base at issue here, and that during the term of the Williams patent non-infringing substitutes were available. Although it sought a 15% royalty rate before the Court of Federal Claims, Hughes now argues that it is entitled to at least a 3% royalty rate, which it derives from the proffered royalty rate for license of the Williams patent as set forth in two of the letters to the aerospace companies. The government's unlicensed use of a patented invention is properly viewed as a taking of property under the Fifth Amendment through the government's exercise of its power of eminent domain and the patent holder's remedy for such use is prescribed by 28 U.S.C. § 1498(a). Under section 1498(a), the patent owner is entitled to its "reasonable and entire compensation for such use and manufacture." Because recovery is based on eminent domain, the proper measure is "what the owner has lost, not what the taker has gained." *Leesona*, 599 F.2d at 969, 202 U.S.P.Q. at 435. Generally, the preferred manner of reasonably and entirely compensating the patent owner is to require the government to pay a reasonable royalty for its license as well as damages for its delay in paying the royalty.... The parties do not dispute that this is the proper form of compensation; rather, they disagree as to the amount of compensation due and the manner in which it was determined.

Valuation determinations for purposes of eminent domain are reviewed for clear error as are determinations of what constitutes a reasonable royalty.... We will reverse a finding as clearly erroneous only if on the entire evidence we "are left with the definite and firm conviction that a mistake has been committed."... In determining what constitutes a reasonable royalty, the court has discretion to make certain subsidiary decisions, such as what methodology to use to arrive at a reasonable royalty, and those decisions are reviewed for an abuse of discretion....

Hughes asserts that the Court of Federal Claims held as a matter of law that the rates contained in the letters to Ford-Philco, TRW and MBB established a ceiling to the royalty rate. It contends that this was a legal conclusion, not a factual finding, and that the court's conclusion is erroneous. The court, however, did not hold as a matter of law that a reasonable royalty can never go above the amount specified in a license offer. Rather, the court analyzed the three letters at issue, as well as other factors, and found that in this case the rates quoted in the letters had the effect of placing a ceiling on the royalty rate. *See Unisplay*, 69 F.3d at 519, 36 U.S.P.Q.2d at 1545–46 (holding that a reasonable royalty larger than that contained in license proposals and agreements was not supported by the evidence). Thus, while trying to cast its argument as one attacking a legal conclusion, Hughes is in essence challenging the court's factual findings based on its weighing of the evidence. That, however, is the special province of the trial court and we review such factual findings for clear error....

Both parties rely on the Court of Claims decision in *Pitcairn* to support their respective positions on whether offers to license a patented invention should or should not be viewed as a ceiling to the reasonable royalty. *Pitcairn*, however, provides no hard and fast rule. Pitcairn illustrates that the circumstances surrounding the industry as a whole as well as other relevant factors should be considered to determine what weight to afford an offer to license an invention. The facts of a particular case may call for a reasonable royalty that is more, less or the same as the offered royalty. *See Pitcairn*, 547 F.2d at 1118, 192 U.S.P.Q. at 618–19 (finding it appropriate under the facts of that case to take into account offers to license a patent when determining a reasonable royalty). The Court of Federal Claims, as is appropriate, looked at the relevant facts and circumstances at the time when infringement began. As set forth above, the court relied on numerous factors in addition to the Hughes license offers as supporting its finding that hypothetical negotiators would not have agreed to a license at a rate greater than 1.2%. Based on the evidence we are not convinced that the court clearly erred in determining that the ceiling royalty rate in a hypothetical negotiation would be 1.2%.

Hughes also contends that the court clearly erred by failing to take into account the consequence of widespread infringement of the Williams patent. We discern no such failing and are not convinced that any upward adjustment of the court's royalty determination is required for this reason.

The cases cited by Hughes do not, as it argues, support the broad proposition that the court must reject or give very little weight to offers made when there is widespread infringement. Rather these cases stand for the proposition that the entirety of the circumstances should be considered and that the court can consider the effects of infringement.

While we agree that it is appropriate to look at what effect infringement has had on the value of a patent, the court need not consider that in a vacuum. It should take into account other evidence as was done in this case. The court expressly found that at the time of issuance of the Williams patent in 1973 "the space industry was a booming one with prospects for exponential growth" and that "[t]his was the context of Hughes' contacts with three major aerospace firms over the period from 1974 to 1978 in an effort to license the Williams patent." The court also considered the context in which the offers were made. It noted that one was made while litigation was pending but as a continuation of earlier licensing negotiations and not in settlement of that claim, that one was made in settlement of claims but contained an indication of "normal" royalty rates and that the other was made while no litigation was pending. In addition, apart from its conclusory statements that infringement must have lowered the rates offered, Hughes has pointed to no evidence showing that the offers in the letters were actually reduced because of widespread infringement. While Hughes points to certain instances of infringement, it does not show that the license offers were affected by these infringements. In contrast, the court found that one of the letters expressly stated that the proffered royalty rate was Hughes' "normal" rate, not a low rate it was willing to accept because of infringement, thus belying on its face Hughes' contention that the royalty rate was depressed by infringement.

Finally, the court did not clearly err in supporting its determination of the royalty rate with the finding that the potential royalty base of the competitors receiving the royalty offers was smaller than the royalty base in this case, which included all spacecraft costs and payload costs, and with the finding that there were acceptable non-infringing alternatives. Hughes' evidence and arguments are insufficient to overturn these findings. Furthermore, these findings were just two out of many that the court used to support its royalty rate determination and Hughes has failed to show that any error associated with these findings would be anything but harmless.

Because the Court of Federal Claims did not clearly err or abuse its discretion in its determination of a reasonable royalty rate, we affirm the 1% royalty rate.

———————

# Minco, Inc. v. Combustion Engineering, Inc.
## 95 F.3d 1109 (Fed. Cir. 1996)

Per Curiam

In this patent infringement case, Combustion Engineering, Inc. (CE) appeals and Minco, Inc. cross-appeals a final decision of the United States District Court for the Eastern District of Tennessee. The patent at issue, 4,217,462 (the '462 patent), claims a rotary furnace for fusing minerals. The district court found CE willfully infringed claims 3 and 4 of the '462 patent. The court also found that these claims were neither invalid nor unenforceable and that laches did not apply. The court awarded damages of $3,455,329 and a reasonable royalty of $7,408,179.40. Because the infringement was willful, the court doubled the damages for an overall award of $21,727,016.80 plus attorneys fees and pre-judgment interest. Because the record supports the district court's findings and conclusions, this court affirms.

\* \* \*

## Damages

The Patent Act provides for "damages adequate to compensate for the infringement but in no event less than a reasonable royalty for the use made of the invention by the infringer." 35 U.S.C. § 284 (1994). This court has clarified that adequate damages can include lost profits due to diverted sales, price erosion, and increased expenditures caused by infringement. *Lam, Inc. v. Johns-Manville Corp.*, 718 F.2d 1056, 1065, 219 U.S.P.Q. 670, 675 (Fed. Cir. 1983). Because fashioning an adequate damages award depends on the unique economic circumstances of each case, the trial court has discretion to make important subsidiary determinations in the damages trial, such as choosing a methodology to calculate damages. *SmithKline Diagnostics, Inc. v. Helena Lab. Corp.*, 926 F.2d 1161, 1164, 17 U.S.P.Q.2d 1922, 1925 (Fed. Cir. 1991); *King Instruments Corp. v. Otari Corp.*, 767 F.2d 853, 863, 226 U.S.P.Q. 402, 409 (Fed. Cir. 1985).

## Reasonable Royalty

The Patent Act permits damages awards to encompass both lost profits and a reasonable royalty on that portion of an infringer's sales not included in the lost profit calculation. *State Indus., Inc. v. Mor-Flo Indus., Inc.*, 883 F.2d 1573, 1577, 12 U.S.P.Q.2d 1026, 1028 (Fed. Cir. 1989), *cert. denied*, 493 U.S. 1022 (1990). A segment of the infringer's sales may not warrant a lost profits award because the patentee cannot establish causation for that segment. *Perego*, 65 F.3d at 952–53. For instance, a patent owner may not operate in the specific geographical area covered by the infringer or may not have had the manufacturing or marketing capacity to make the infringer's sales. However, the patentee would still be entitled to a reasonable royalty on each of those sales. 35 U.S.C. § 284 (1994).

In this case, the district court awarded a reasonable royalty on CE sales beyond 95% of Minco's manufacturing capacity from May 1988 through July 1990. Minco also received a reasonable royalty on CE sales from 1986 through April 1988, during which CE produced a blended fused silica. In total, the district court awarded a reasonable royalty on approximately 122,329,000 pounds of fused silica.

A district court may calculate a reasonable royalty by postulating a hypothetical negotiation between a willing licensor and licensee at the time infringement commenced. This hypothetical construct seeks the percentage of sales or profit likely to have induced the hypothetical negotiators to license use of the invention. In this case, the district court awarded Minco a royalty rate of 20% on the gross value of CE's applicable sales. The district court based this relatively high royalty on a number of findings. First, Minco and CE competed head-to-head. Second, at the time of infringement, CE had an inferior product. Third, the market contained no non-infringing alternatives. Fourth, CE itself regarded the invention as a significant advance. Fifth, the industry enjoyed high rates of profit. The trial court found that CE realized earnings before interest and taxes rate of 22.4% of sales under the jumbo kiln technology. Sixth, CE's earnings before taxes increased substantially after its use of the accused furnaces.

In addition to the court's other findings, because the industry enjoyed high profitability and the invention produced higher quality fused silica, this court detects no clear error in the district court's royalty award. The economic evidence on this point supports the finding that these hypothetical negotiators might have entered a license calculated at 20% of sales.

* * *

# Notes & Questions

1. *Royalties and Valuation.* A royalty represents an agreed allocation of future profits between the licensee and the licensor. ROBERT C. MEGANTZ, HOW TO LICENSE TECHNOLOGY 55 (John Wiley & Sons 1996). Many licensing professionals have suggested that licensing is the last remaining domain in the civilized world of business where old-fashioned bargaining occurs. To the uninitiated, the process of setting royalties has been described as "shrouded in mystery." T. WILLEY, ROYALTIES, VALUATION, FINANCIAL CONSIDERATION, V. 11-3.1 Autm Tech. Transfer Practice Manual 1 (1994). Clearly, there are no "right" or "wrong" royalty rates, and no absolutes in negotiating. Determining the appropriate measure of profit used for purposes of calculating royalties can be difficult. To overcome potential difficulties, the agreement may fix royalties as a percentage of net sales or as some other more easily quantified measure, such as a certain dollar amount per unit sold, even though this may not represent the exact share of the negotiated profits. Estimating the profit margin of the licensed products can convert a share of profits to a percentage of sales. Alternatively, profit sharing coupled with performance requirements to ensure that the licensee will actively exploit the technology.

Megantz, *supra*, suggests a variety of objective standards to determine royalty rates, including a rule of thumb of three percent to five percent of the manufacture's selling price, industry sector standards developed from royalty surveys, and auctions. The data in the survey tables below illustrates that rates vary widely by industry.

Although typically one thinks of licensing compensation in terms of "running" royalties, i.e., rates of compensation payable over time and dependent upon extrinsic factors (such as the amount of net sales or profits), running royalties are only part of a wide variety of compensation schemes that can be adapted by the skillful practitioner to achieve a successful agreement. The full range of methods for compensating licensors include the following:

- Lump sum licensing fees due up-front when the agreement is entered.
- Annual "milestone" payments that constitute minimum royalties to be paid whether a product is on the market or not, designed to force the licensee to commercialize as quickly as possible.
- Technical assistance, management, and other consulting fees for helping to insure that the licensee implements the new product or technology successfully.
- Patent royalties payable only on products covered by claims of existing patents or pending patent applications.

### Licensing-Out Royalty Rates, Survey Data © 1993 Battelle
### Royalty Rate Category

| Primary Industry | 0–2% | 2–5% | 5–10% | 10–15% | 15–20% | 20–25% | Over 25% |
|---|---|---|---|---|---|---|---|
| Aerospace | | 40.0% | 55.0% | 5.0% | | | |
| Automotive | 35.0% | 45.0% | 20.0% | | | | |
| Chemical | 18.0% | 57.4% | 23.9% | 0.5% | | | 0.1% |
| Computer | 42.5% | 57.5% | | | | | |
| Electronics | | 50.0% | 45.0% | 5.0% | | | |
| Energy | | 50.0% | 15.0% | 10.0% | | 25.0% | |
| Food consumer | 12.5% | 62.5% | 25.0% | | | | |
| General mfg. | 21.3% | 51.5% | 20.3% | 2.6% | 0.8% | 0.8% | 2.6% |
| Govt./University | 7.9% | 38.9% | 36.4% | 16.2% | 0.4% | 0.6% | |
| Healthcare equip. | 10.0% | 10.0% | 80.0% | | | | |
| Pharmaceutical | 1.3% | 20.7% | 67.0% | 8.7% | 1.3% | 0.7% | 0.3% |
| Telecommunication | | | | 100.0% | | | |
| Other | 11.2% | 41.2% | 28.7% | 16.2% | 0.9% | 0.9% | 0.9% |

- Trademark royalties.
- Know-how royalties, if treated separately, are paid for trade secrets and unpatented processes, methods, techniques that contribute significantly to licensed products, but may either be unpatentable or more valuable if held secret.
- Sale of plant or equipment to make licensed products.
- Sale of components to be incorporated into licensed products.
- Purchase of products from licensee.
- Equity in the licensee company, an especially useful consideration when the licensee is a start-up company and has no demonstrated ability to successfully commercialize.

2. *Intellectual Property Valuation and Bankruptcy.* Valuation assumes critical importance in a bankruptcy setting. The debtor may seek maximum value for its intellectual property while creditors prefer the lowest valuation. Thus, the method of valuation employed can affect the results of the bankruptcy proceeding. Some factors that affect valuation in the bankruptcy setting are as follows:

- A liquidated or moved asset may fetch a lower value.
- An asset created for a particular purpose may have no value when removed from that arena.
- Intellectual properties have higher risk factors than those of tangible assets.
- Intellectual property values fluctuate over time.

WILLIAM L. NORTON, JR., NORTON BANKR. L. & PRACTICE 2D § 151:18 (1997–98). In one well-known case, a bankruptcy auditor established the value of Macy's name and brands in order to obtain royalty rates for use of these assets. The Macy's corporate name, brands, and trademarks were valued at over $400 million. Weston Anson, *Valuing Trademarks, Patents, and Other Intangibles in a Bankruptcy Environment*, 15 Am. Bankr. Inst. J. 29 (1996). Which valuation method might most favor the debtor? Why?

3. *Judicial Finding of "Reasonable Royalties."* Note that in patent infringement cases, it is common to bifurcate decisions on liability and damages because district courts' discretion under 35 U.S.C. § 284 (1994): "upon finding for the claimant the court shall award the claimant damages adequate to compensate for the infringement, but in no event less than a reasonable royalty for the use made of the invention by the infringer...." Courts often cite the "willing seller/willing buyer" rule, outlined in Georgia-Pacific Corp. v. United States Plywood Corp., 318 F. Supp. 1116 (S.D.N.Y. 1970), affirmed 446 F.2d 295 (2d. Cir. 1971), and applied by the court in the Minco case, supra. The court in Georgia-Pacific described this as "[t]he amount that the licensor (such as the patentee) and a licensee (such as the infringer) would have agreed upon (at the time the infringement began) if both had been reasonable and voluntarily trying to reach an agreement...." Is this a legal standard, a ride, a process, or a starting point for analysis? Does it make sense when the patentee has refused to license the infringer and the latter has deliberately infringed?

Imagining hypothetical negotiations among "reasonable" parties appears to be an enigmatic concept at best, yet the court in Hughes did not shy away from describing hypothetical negotiations that started at a rate of something less than 1.2% and then "would quickly settle on one percent." Hughes Aircraft Co. v. United States, 86 F.3d 1566 (Fed. Cir. 1996). Considering the complexity of valuation, are there more desirable alternatives for fixing royalties? Should it be done by arbitration? Perhaps the court should appoint a special master with the single obligation of setting royalty rates.

4. *Compensation Base.* In addition to determining a royalty rate, courts also must determine a compensation base that necessarily takes into account the unique economic circumstances of each case. Compare the award in Hughes, supra—1% royalty on the retail price of a product—with the award in Minco, supra—20% of gross profits. The key factors taken into consideration by the lower courts in setting reasonable royalty rates are among the following:

- whether the patent was for a "pioneer" invention (*Hughes*) or a "significant advance" (*Minco*);
- whether the infringer was a direct competitor of the patent holder and thus likely to be liable for lost profits (*Minco*);
- the commercial impact of infringement on the market (*Hughes*);
- the size of the compensation base (*Hughes*);
- customary profit margins in the industry (*Minco*);
- the existence of non-infringing alternative technologies available to potential licensees (*Hughes, Minco*).

Are the factors weighed by the court in those cases likely to be persuasive in an arm's length negotiation between willing seller and willing buyer? Do you recognize any of the same factors used by Parr and Smith, supra?

5. *Royalties in Eminent Domain Cases.* The government's power to secure the unlicensed use of a patented invention for its contractors, Hughes, supra, leaves the patent holder with only one remedy—a reasonable royalty plus the damages caused by delay in pay-

ment. See 28 U.S.C. § 1498(a); *Leesona Corp. v. United States*, 599 F.2d 958, 973 (Ct. Cl. 1979). Thus, the government can secure what is, in effect, a compulsory license of any patent for the government's own use. See Chapter 4, *supra* note 9, Compulsory Licensing. Note that the statute allows the government to delegate its eminent domain power over patents to its contractors. Doesn't the government's power to take a patent license through eminent domain, coupled with 28 U.S.C. § 1498(a), confer extraordinary economic power on the contractor licensee? Usually included in research and development contracts, this significant power relieves the licensee from any liability for patent infringement. The licensee, therefore, can freely divert the revenue stream of the patent owner with full indemnification from the government. Is there a potential for abuse? Why shouldn't the patent owner be able to recover lost profits from the contractor if they can be adequately proved?

In *Brunswick Corporation v. the United States*, 36 Fed. Cl. 204 (Fed. Cl. 1998), involving the government's purchase of camouflage screens, some of which were held to infringe on Brunswick's patent, the court said that Congress directed the Army to "expand its industrial base for the production of camouflage screens in order to maintain a reliable industrial mobilization capacity," and further noted that "[t]his type of outside policy-making and political influence is peculiar to the federal government and is properly taken into account when considering whether a reasonable royalty would adequately compensate an aggrieved patentee." The court found that the number of units purchased by the government was greater than would have been the case in the absence of the compulsory license, and that this supported a lower amount of compensation than that (lost profits) sought by Brunswick. *See also Gargoyles, Inc. v. United States*, 113 F.3d 1572 (Fed. Cl. 1997).

6. In *Hughes, supra*, the court said that "[i]t is axiomatic that the larger the potential compensation base to which a royalty rate will be applied, the lower will be the rate." *Hughes Aircraft Co. v. United*, 86 F.3d 1566, 1570 (Fed. Cir. 1996). How does this rule fit with the preferred income analysis approach to valuation described by Smith and Parr and Megantz? Does such a rule have anything to do with valuation at all? Doesn't the proper valuation of a patent lie in the invention's utility to users? Isn't that utility independent of the size of the compensation base? Does this supposed rule unfairly penalize the licensor? Could it be that the multibillion-dollar compensation base at issue here influenced the court?

7. *Analytical Approach.* The Federal Circuit in *TWM Mfg. Co. v. Dura Corp.*, 789 F.2d 895 (Fed. Cir. 1986), used another judicial approach to royalty determination, the "analytical" approach. This analytical approach determines an infringer's anticipated net profit from the sales of the infringing products and subtracts the infringer's usual or acceptable net profits to determine the reasonable royalty. Which approach is easier for a plaintiff to prove? Why are courts unable to settle on one uniform royalty calculation for all circumstances?

8. *Valuation as Pre-Litigation Strategy.* Knowing the value of a potential adversary's intellectual property is sometimes as important as knowing the value of your client's intellectual property. An attorney should complete a cost/benefit analysis before motion and discovery deadlines. David A. Hass & James E. Malackowski, *Prelitigation Damages and Techniques: Patents and More*, 2 (No.6) INTELL. PROP. STRATEGIST 1 (1996); *see also*, GREGORY J. BATTERSBY & CHARLES W. GRIMES, AN INSIDER'S GUIDE TO ROYALTY RATES (1998–99).

9. *Compulsory Licenses.* Problems in valuing intellectual property can sometimes motivate the government or private organizations (with the government's approval) to form

a collective rights organization. This type of organization may "promulgate rules and procedures for placing a monetary value on members' property rights." Robert P. Merges, Contracting into Liability Rules: Intellectual Property Rights and Collective Rights Organizations, 84 Calif. L. Rev. 1293, 1294 (1998). One current controversy is whether Congress should legislate a compulsory license for digital information needed by the multimedia industry. Merges, supra, argues it should not. What affect might compulsory licensing have on the valuation of intellectual properties?

10. *Questions.* What are the pros and cons of the market, cost, and income approaches to valuation? What different factors should an attorney consider when valuing patents, trademarks, or copyrights? Should she use the same royalty calculation regardless of the intellectual property at issue? Does the contribution margin necessarily equal the royalty rate? What are the dangers in this?

11. *The 25 Percent Rule.* The 3 to 5 Percent Rule was noted, supra, to show that this is a common way to conceptualize the range of royalties in many industries. One calculates the royalty as 3 to 5 percent of the manufacturer's selling price. Another common starting point is the "25 Percent Rule," under which one calculates the royalty at 25 percent of the company's gross profit driven by or touching upon the subject intellectual property. *See* GORDON V. SMITH & RUSSELL L. PARR, VALUATION OF INTELLECTUAL PROPERTY AND INTANGIBLE ASSETS 375 (2d ed., 1994). In the end, how does this differ from the 3 to 5 percent rule? Which one would you, as an auditor, want to use for your client? What factors should you consider in determining which approach to use?

12. *Unexpected Forums.* Valuation of intellectual property can arise even in divorce proceedings. For example, courts in New York and New Jersey have held that "one's status as a celebrity.... [is] a form of marital property subject to distribution to the extent that the other spouse's contribution and efforts led to an increase in the value of the celebrity's career." Elliot H. Gourvitz & Laurence J. Cutler, *Distribution of Contingent Property Interests*, 14 No. 9 FAIR$HAIR 10 (1994) (citing *Elkus v. Elkus*, 572 N.Y.S.2d 901 (App. Div. 1991)). Previously, in *O'Brien v. O'Brien*, 66 N.Y.2d 576 (1985), the court held that a medical license was subject to "distribution like other intangible assets including a law degree, an accounting degree, the licensing and certification of a physician's assistant" to a name a few. Gourvitz & Cutler, *supra*, at 11 (emphasis added). *See also*, Debra Perrotta, ESTATE PLANNING FOR OWNERS OF PATENTS AND COPYRIGHTS, 21 EST. PLAN. 94 (1994) (valuation of intellectual property arising in an estate planning setting).

13. *Factors to Consider.* Factors that can affect the discount rate are inflation, liquidity, real interest rates, a risk premium, and the possibility of the intellectual property extending into new markets. What factors should be considered important in determining the discount rate when a trademark is used in a new market? What factors would raise the discount rate? What factors would lower it?

14. *Trademark Valuation and Takeovers.* A trademark can be a company's most valuable asset. Its value may be critical in corporate takeovers:

> Despite all of the evils attributed to corporate raiders, a primary benefit [of takeovers] is a revitalized attitude among managers toward corporate value... Some of the most popular takeover targets are the owners of well-known trademarks. Developing a world-class trademark can take many years and ultimately require a billion dollars. Instead, corporate raiders are currently buying established trademarks at less than the amount required to develop a new one. This intellectual property is being recognized as a vital corporate asset.

Many acquisitions are based upon the perception that additional opportunities exist for extension of trademarks into related and sometimes unrelated fields. Incremental exploitation of this intellectual property can be achieved separately from its original utilization. A trademark that has captured the trust and loyalty of consumers usually commands premium pricing....Application of this valuable characteristic to other product and service ventures can generate new sources of earning power from the same asset. Corporations that are not pursuing such opportunities find themselves acquisition targets of those that can recognize the possibilities.

Corporations that already possess strong trademarks are purchasing organizations that can produce new products upon which the name can be placed. As a defense, joint ventures and licensing are actively being investigated as opportunities for enhanced utilization of intellectual property. The goal is to assure full exploitation of the intellectual property that is owned and forestall takeover attempts.

Parr, *supra* at 233.

Is this a fair representation of the value of trademarks in corporate takeovers?

15. *Option Analysis at Merck.* An alternative method of calculating the value of intellectual property is "option analysis" apparently used at Merck. *See* Gary L. Sender, Harvard Bus. Rev. 92 (Jan.–Feb. 1994). In the pharmaceutical industry, it may be entirely unrealistic to use net-present-value techniques in calculating the value of intellectual property, such as patents on drugs, while the asset is still under development. Especially in the early stages of research projects, which may or may not turn into marketable drugs, predicting the cash flow and market conditions in the future would be nearly impossible. In many long-term pharmaceutical research projects, option analysis may be more appropriate.

In option analysis, the license is structured so that the larger pharmaceutical company makes an up-front payment to the outside entity conducting the research. This up-front payment is followed by a series of progress payments depending upon the status of the research. If the research is progressing, the larger pharmaceutical company financing the research reserves the right to continue the payments in exchange for exclusive access to the results, but it has no obligation to do so. The series of payments constitute an attempt to revalue the intellectual property asset at every important stage in the development process, including clinical and regulatory testing. The right to stop progress or "option" payments allows the company financing the project to limit its long-term exposure.

# Appendix A

You may have trouble reading the different valuation methods covered by this chapter if you have had no previous exposure to accounting and economic concepts. Here are brief, nonpedantic definitions of some basic accounting concepts that may help you. These definitions are for conceptual understanding only. They may not be entirely accurate at a level of detail required, for example, for the accounting profession. The definitions are in conceptual, rather than alphabetical, order.

**Price:** what someone pays for something. This term may refer to an asking or offered price but most commonly refers to an amount actually paid by a willing party in a voluntary market transaction.

**Cost:** an expense, i.e., what was paid for something in the past. The seller's price, once received, is the buyer's cost.

Cost may be an historical price paid or a computed cost. For example, one way of determining the "cost" of IP is to add up all the expenses paid for the research and development that produced the IP. This sort of "cost" often includes many separate items of expense, such as the salaries of the R&D workers, the rent for the building they worked in, the cost of materials and supplies that they used in the R&D, the cost of electricity and other utilities, and the cost of licensing ("inward") any others' technology needed in the R&D.

**Value:** the theoretical economic worth of something, usually in the absence of a single transaction that fixes its price or cost.

For example, if Contair were a publicly traded company, one measure of its value might be the total market value of its outstanding stock, i.e., the market value per share, multiplied by the total number of shares outstanding.

This number is not the same as price or cost. It's not a price because no one has ever actually bought the whole company, and no one has ever paid this (or any other) price. The actual price that someone might pay for the whole company might be less or (more commonly) more than this computed value.

Value is also not necessarily the same as cost. For example, one might try to compute the "cost" of Contair by adding up the amounts that Contair paid for all its tangible and intangible assets. Even if accurately computed, this sum of expenses is not necessarily what someone would pay to buy Contair. Among other things, it neglects the value of Contair's "good will," or business reputation, for which Contair never paid any separately identifiable amount, but which may be worth millions.

**Revenue:** the money a business firm receives from its operations. Normally "revenue" means "gross revenue," i.e., the money received without any deductions for expenses. For example, if a firm makes a single type of product at a uniform price, its annual revenue would be the number of items sold during the year, multiplied by the single price customers paid for each of them.

**Profit:** the money a business firm makes in its operations, i.e., its revenue less its costs. Although related, profit and revenue are very different things. A firm may have huge revenue but, if its costs are high, may have negative profit, i.e., it may lose money. Profit is the thing most important to businesses because, generally speaking, it is what business owners put in their pocket.

**Gross Profit:** revenue less direct or "above the line" costs, usually the costs of labor and materials ("costs of goods sold"). This number reflects the profitability of operations directly associated with production, neglecting the general costs of the business as a whole.

**Gross Profit Margin:** gross profit divided by revenue, expressed as a percentage. This is a measure of profitability of the firm's production operations. The higher the percentage (i.e., the closer profit is to revenue), the more successful the firm. Most firms have gross profit margins of about 50%. Microsoft has reported gross profit margins over 80%. (Can you think of any reason for the difference?)

**Net Profit (also called "earnings"):** gross profit less additional expenses of the business, including marketing, advertising, distribution, and general and administrative expenses (i.e., "overhead"). A lower figure than gross profit, this figure reflects the money really made after all business expenses are paid. This is what public companies may pay their shareholders in dividends (or keep to invest in their operations), and what owners of private companies may take home.

**Net profit margin, also called just "profit margin":** net profit divided by revenue, expressed as a percentage. This is just the percentage that revenue less total expenses bears to revenue. The higher the better.

Net profit margins vary widely, depending upon the type and scale of business. Supermarkets typically have low net profit margins of 4% or less. Other business' profit margins vary widely, typically in the range of 10% to 25%.

**Method of valuation:** a method of calculating or estimating the value of a thing, in the absence of a recent, comparable market transaction at a specified price, from which value could be directly inferred.

In the absence of a recent, comparable market price on which to estimate value, there may be numerous competing methods to do so. No one method is necessarily "right," and each may have its advantages and disadvantages. Serious business people often use several different methods and compare them, assessing the assumptions on which each is based, in order to estimate the "real" value of a thing.

For example, we can estimate Contair's value in a sale of the whole business by adding the cost of all Contair's assets, as described above. As noted above, however, this method neglects the value of Contair's good will, for which it paid nothing specific. If Contair's reputation is strong and valuable (as appears to be the case here), the "cost" method of valuation may underestimate Contair's value as a going concern.

We might also estimate Contair's value as a going concern by the income method, which has several variations. One common variation simply multiplies a firm's net profit, in dollars, by ten to estimate the total value. This method, however, is more a "rule of thumb" than a serious valuation method. Why? Because the ratio of value to earnings depends upon many things, including prevailing interest rates and risk.

For example, interest rates on certain treasury notes are now about 4%. These notes are among the most secure and risk-free investments known to finance. This means that today one can, with virtually no risk, expect to receive $4 per year on a $100 investment—a value/earnings ratio of 25 to 1, not the 10 to 1 under the rule of thumb.

The lower valuation (10 times earnings) for businesses reflects the risk of doing business. The treasury notes are valued at 25 times their earnings because they are very secure. Most businesses have much greater risk (both of losing money and of failing completely) than these treasury notes. Accordingly, the market values them at a lower multiple (10 to 1 versus 25 to 1) because of the greater risk of loss.

If used properly, the "income" valuation method must take account of both of these variables: (1) prevailing interest rates, which determine how much earnings investors expect from a given investment with little or no risk and (2) the risk of the particular business at issue—the higher the risk, the lower the multiple of earnings.

**Back to Supermarkets.** "What about supermarkets?" you might ask. Earlier we said supermarkets typically earn net profit margins, or "earnings," of about 4%, about the

same as treasury notes today! Why would anyone in his or her right mind invest in supermarkets when he·or she could make the same earnings, with lower risk, by investing
in treasury notes?

That's a very good question, which may have many answers. First, investments in supermarkets aren't very liquid (it's not easy to sell a supermarket chain for cash), and the
investments today may reflect better relative supermarket-investing conditions in the
past. Second, supermarkets themselves are not very risky businesses (everyone needs
food!), and so it is not entirely surprising that the market values them not too differently from treasury notes. Third, present conditions may represent a relatively short-
term phenomenon. If present conditions persist in the long term, investment may leave
the field of supermarkets, leading, in turn, to fewer outlets, less competition, higher
prices, and therefore higher returns to investors in that field.

This (oversimplified) picture explains conceptually how free markets for investments
are self-adjusting. If returns in an industry are too low, investment will flee, competition will suffer, prices will rise, and earnings will increase. If returns are too high, they
will attract new investment, which will increase competition, lower prices and thereby
lower earnings, eventually causing investment to flee.

All these effects, however, take time. Rates of return have both short-term and
long-term variations. The variation in rates of return to follow prevailing interest
rates, with a risk adjustment, reflects long-term trends. In the short term, a number of
things can cause the rate of return of a business or industry to rise or fall. One of these
things may be responsible for the fact that supermarkets now appear to offer about the
same rate of return as treasury notes. In the long run, however, just as in gambling,
"The House always wins, and a low rate of return eventually will reduce investment in
a given field."

---

# Appendix B

Virtually any valuation method based on income, including income methods for
valuing intellectual property, depends on the notion of "present value." In essence,
"present value" is just the value today of a payment to be made at some specified time in
the future. In general, the present value of a future payment is less than the face value of
the future payment because of the "time value of money," i.e., the fact that money earns
interest. A simple example illustrates this principle.

1. **Compound interest.** Suppose you have $100. You can earn interest on that
money—virtually risk free—by depositing it in a federally insured savings account. If
the saving account pays interest on your deposit at 2% per year, you will have $102 at
the end of the first year.

As the years go by, your deposit will earn additional interest. If the interest paid is
"simple" interest, only your initial deposit, and not the interest on it, will earn additional interest. For example, a simple-interest account would give you $104 at the end
of the second year, $106 at the end of the third, and so on.

Yet nearly all investments today earn so-called "compound" interest, that is, they
earn interest on both the principal and all accrued interest. Under a compound-interest

guess is very important, because of the strong exponential effect of interest rates, which causes small changes in the assumed rate to make big differences in calculated outcomes.

Moreover, estimating a single "average" interest rate over the time period of interest is only the beginning. You may recall that the interest rate assumed in our example, 2%, was the rate of return for a virtually risk-free investment (in a federally insured bank account). Any real business venture—especially one involving an untried new technology eligible for patenting—necessarily involves greater risk.

A basic principle of economics and investing states that investors demand a higher return for undertaking greater risk. According to this risk/return principle, investors will demand a so-called "risk premium" for investing in our hypothetical, untried patentable technology. That is, they will demand a rate of return several points higher than the interest rate on federally insured bank accounts. Without such a premium, they would be silly to invest in the new risky technology when they could earn money at the same rate through a bank account and sleep much better at night.

So the risk-adjusted rate of return—and therefore the risk-adjusted rate for discounting to present value—will be much higher in a venture involving untried new technology than in our simple example of a risk-free bank account. Determining how much higher is a matter of educated guesswork, just as is determining what "average" future interest rates are likely to be over a long future time period, even in a risk-free environment.

Finally, there are multiple additional sources of uncertainty in any real present-value calculation. Estimates of the probable royalty rate, the selling price of the patented products, and the number of products to be sold each year are all attempts to predict the unknowable future. Therefore they are all additional sources of uncertainty and possible contention. Each of these figures derives from an educated guess, which business people call a "projection," and which is more art than science. Each depends upon a number of assumptions about the future, some of which may be implicit or unstated.

Therefore the hard part of present-value calculations is not the mathematics of calculating present value. The hard part is the guesswork and research into products, markets, and competition—not to mention future interest rates and appropriate risk premiums—that goes into the underlying revenue projections from which present values are calculated.

The role of the lawyer includes clarifying and (where appropriate) questioning this guesswork and the research and assumptions that underlie it. Computers or competent assistants can do the mathematics without much trouble and usually without error. But no computer yet developed can uncover and evaluate the validity of hidden assumptions and guesswork behind the numbers used as input. As an old computer user's slogan advises, "Garbage in, garbage out." The lawyer's role in reviewing present-value calculations is largely confined to determining whether this slogan applies to the assumptions, hidden or revealed, that underlie the numbers.

---

regime, at the end of the second year, you would have earned 2% interest on the entire amount accumulated at the end of the first year, or $102. So your total deposit at the end of Year 2 would be $102 (the amount at the end of the first year) plus 0.02 x $102, or $104.04.

The extra four cents do not sound like much, but the effect of compounding grows rapidly as time goes on, according to the laws of "exponential growth rates" in mathematics. For example, here's a table showing how your deposit would grow for the first twenty years, at an interest rate of 2% per year, using both simple and compound interest.

| End of Year | Simple Interest | Compound Interest |
| --- | --- | --- |
| 1 | 102 | 102 |
| 2 | 104 | 104.04 |
| 3 | 106 | 106.12 |
| 4 | 108 | 108.24 |
| 5 | 110 | 110.40 |
| 6 | 112 | 112.61 |
| 7 | 114 | 114.86 |
| 8 | 116 | 117.17 |
| 9 | 118 | 119.51 |
| 10 | 120 | 121.90 |
| 11 | 122 | 124.34 |
| 12 | 124 | 126.82 |
| 13 | 126 | 129.36 |
| 14 | 128 | 131.95 |
| 15 | 130 | 134.59 |
| 16 | 132 | 137.28 |
| 17 | 134 | 140.02 |
| 18 | 136 | 142.82 |
| 19 | 138 | 145.68 |
| 20 | 140 | 148.59 |

The "exponential" effect of compounding depends strongly on both the interest rate and the elapsed time. At a higher rate of interest of 15%, for example, compounding would more than double your money in five years, whereas simple interest would give you only a 75% return.

**2. Present value as the inverse of compounding.** As you can see from the foregoing example, compound interest makes money grow with time, at an even faster rate than would simple interest. At the end of twenty years, your $100 would grow to $148.59, even at the low rate of 2%. What that means is that—assuming interest rates stay stable—your $100 will be worth $148.59 in twenty years, without your doing anything and with virtually no risk (remember, your deposit was in a federally insured account!).

Now suppose someone promised to give you some money in twenty years, but not before. What would that promise be worth now? If the promise was to give you

$148.59 in twenty years, it would be worth only $100 today, because $100 invested today would be worth the promised amount in twenty years. Therefore no rational person would buy a note promising to pay $148.59 in twenty years for any more than $100 today. In economic terms, the "present value" of the future payment of $148.59 in twenty years is $100.

**3. A general formula.** Based on this simple example, we can calculate a formula to determine what any future payment would be worth today, i.e., the present value (PV) of any future payment (FP). To do that, we first calculate what an amount PV would be worth in n years. After year 1, compounding would make the future value

$$FP(Y1) = (1 + i) * PV$$

where i is just the interest rate, expressed as a decimal instead of a percentage. In our example above, i = 2% = 0.02, so the future payment after one year is (1 + 0.02) x $100, or (1.02) * $100, or $102, as shown above.

To calculate the future payment after two years, we just multiple the future payment after one year by the same "compounding factor" (1 + i):

$$FP(Y2) = (1 + i) * (1 + i) * PV = (1 + i)^2 * PV$$

By what mathematicians call "induction," i.e., by repeating the same process again and again, we can see that the future payment that would be equivalent to PV at the end of any arbitrary future Year n is just

$$FP(Yn) = (1 + i)^n * PV$$

That is, the future payment at the end of year n is just the present value PV, multiplied n times by the compounding factor (1 + i), which was 1.02 in our example.

Now to find the present value PV from the future payment FP, we just work backwards. We divide both sides of the equation by $(1 + i)^n$, and we get:

$$PV = FP(Yn) / (1 + i)^n$$

This is the basic formula for present value. It is quite general. It works for any time period and for any number of periods n, as long as you remember that i is the interest rate for that time period. For example, to calculate the present value of a future payment of $100 made after 180 months, just use the formula

$$PV = FP(M180) / (1+i)^{180}$$

where i is the monthly rate of interest expressed as a decimal. In our example, i would be 2% /12, or 0.001666667.

**4. Multiple future payments.** In valuing intellectual property, or indeed any property, there is rarely just a single future payment. Usually there is a stream of future payments whose present value must be calculated.

For example, suppose you have a patentable technology. You think the patent application will be ready for filing in two years, and the technology will be ready for commercial production in five years. If you file the patent application in two years, the patent will expire twenty years later, or in 22 years. *See* 35 U.S.C. § 154. Your royalty stream, however, probably won't begin to run until commercial production starts in five years. Therefore, you would expect the royalty stream under the patent to run from year 5 through year 22, for a total of 18 years.

To calculate the present value of this eighteen-year future royalty stream, you would first estimate the amount of royalties that you would receive from licensing during each of the years 5 through 22. Each estimate would require a whole host of assumptions and

subsidiary estimates. For example, you might estimate the selling , product, the royalty rate to which a licensee would agree, and th products to be sold during each year. Then, with the estimate of each turns in hand, you would calculate the present value of each year's esti using the formula that we just derived. Finally, you would add up that pres all of the eighteen years 5 through 22, as follows:

$$PV(Y5) = (Estimated\ royalties\ for\ year\ 5) / (1 + i)^5$$

$$+$$

$$PV(Y6) = (Estimated\ royalties\ for\ year\ 6) / (1 + i)^6$$

$$\cdot$$

$$\cdot$$

$$\cdot$$

$$+$$

$$PV(Y22) = (Estimated\ royalties\ for\ year\ 22) / (1 + i)^{22}$$

where i is the annual interest rate (expressed as a decimal) used for discounting to present value. Expressed in a single formula, the present value of the total eighteen-year royalty stream would be

$$PV\ (whole\ stream) = \sum_{n=5}^{n=22} (Estimated\ royalties\ for\ year\ n) / (1 + i)^n$$

This formula may look complicated, but modern technology makes calculating it simple Most business and many general-purpose advanced calculators allow you to calculate th present value of a single future payment at the touch of a button, simply by plugging the number of years and the interest or discount rate. So do some Web sites. See How Finance Works, moneychimp website *at* www.moneychimp.com/articles/ works/fmpresval.htm (visited April 29, 2004). Some calculators will even calculat present value of a sum of future payments, in accordance with the last formula abo

**5. The hard part.** Believe it or not, the hard part of a complete present-value c tion is not the math. Modern calculators or computers, or a good assistant with background, make the calculations easy. If the math is done right, there shou uncertainty or error. What is hard is not the math, but the assumptions and that lie behind the calculations.

You may have noticed that all our examples above assumed a single, cons rate for as much as twenty-two years in the future. Yet every adult knows f experience that interest rates do not stay fixed; they fluctuate yearly, if not may vary by wide margins, for example, from the high teens in the early 1 low single digits in 2004. Any estimate of a single "average" interest rate o decade or more is therefore no more than an educated guess. Yet the pr

# Chapter 6

# Copyright: Multimedia and Entertainment Licensing

## I. Introduction

The majority of licenses in today's business world involve more than one licensed intellectual property right. Licenses granting rights in multiple properties are common in the media and entertainment industries, where all types of intellectual property can play a simultaneous part in the creation of a single product. The end result could be anything from an e-commerce website, to an Andrew Lloyd Webber musical, a Tom Cruise movie, Metallica CD, or a university distance-education course.

Licensing of digital works is changing rapidly. Likely, it will be years before the powers that be resolve the political struggles over modernizing copyright law. Meanwhile, new technologies will continue to find ways to circumvent copyright protection of music, movies, and software. Authors, artists and consumers on the one side, and publishers, the recording industry, and the media on the other, continue to struggle over the proper scope of copyright and fair use. The following materials illustrate the difficulties of obtaining license rights to pre-existing content for new uses.

## Multimedia Licensing: The Basics

Before discussing practical aspects of multimedia licensing, it may be useful to have some basic background. What is "multimedia"? What branches of intellectual property law most often apply to it? What recent developments in the law are most relevant to multimedia licensing, and how has the law sought to adapt itself to this new technology?

Answers to these questions are still a work in progress, but a few partial answers and some apparent trends are evident. Students who have had a course in copyright law, Internet law, or cyberlaw may find this material a useful review. Those who have had no such courses should study it intensely, for these partial answers, although highly conceptual, serve as basic building blocks for both current understanding and future developments.

**1. What Does "Multimedia" Mean?** The word "multimedia" is a much overused and potentially misleading term. Literally defined, it refers to a work involving more than one medium or mode of expression. In this sense, "multimedia" productions are nothing new. Movies, for example, have included both video (frames photographed on celluloid) and audio (on a synchronized sound track) since "talkies" first appeared in the 1920s. Television similarly has combined audio and video portions since its advent in the 1940s.

The real meaning of the term "multimedia," as well as the term's current importance, derives from modern computer technology and the so-called "convergence of media" that it fostered. Today's general-purpose digital computers can record, reproduce, and play traditional media—text, sound, pictures, audio, audiovisual works, animation, etc.—in exactly the same form: a sequence of digital ones and zeros. The various media "converge" in recording, storage, and playback as standardized digital files.

This does not mean, however, that modern computers handle all media in exactly the same way. Each traditional form of medium enjoys several alternative formats for computer handling and storage, and the formats vary from medium to medium. Text, for example, generally uses the "ASCII" code, which stands for "American Standard Code for Information Interchange." In this code, each letter, number, and other textual character is assigned a unique numerical value. Other coding schemes are also available, especially for foreign languages using non-Roman characters. Audio also has several alternative formats, each of which uses a particular method to compress the digital numbers representing the volume of sound waves at particular instants of time. (Because sound waves change rapidly, their proper recording requires up to 50,000 digital "samples" per second, and efficient handling with current technology requires the resulting voluminous data to be compressed for transmission and storage.) The popular MPEG3 or "MP3" format represents only one particular compromise between data compression and audio quality, but there are several others, including WAV. Similarly, alternative still-picture formats, such as JPG, GIF, PNG, and audiovisual formats, such as MPEG-1, MPEG-2 and MPEG-4, make different trade-offs between data compression and quality.

As the existence of these various formats suggests, it is a misconception to think that the convergence of media has not eliminated all differences among technologies for handling different media. Media convergence has allowed all media to operate with similar or compatible *hardware*—typically a general-purpose or special-purpose computer—which accommodates the differences between different media and different formats through software. Because software is more adaptable than hardware, this accommodation has important consequences for the efficiency of both use and development of media technology.

Regardless of their particular format, digital files reflecting various media are stored and handled in much the same way, as series of digital bits (ones or zeroes) recorded on various storage media. The very same hardware, typically a general-purpose computer using standard storage media (such as a hard drive, CD-ROM, or DVD) can store, play, reproduce, and manage all of these files as long as it has the appropriate software for the particular format of interest. It is in this sense that all these media "converge." Handling different media no longer requires distinct and specialized equipment (such as magnetic tape or vinyl disks for sound and celluloid film projectors for video); only the software need change. As a result, with the right software a single digital file will record, store, display, and perform text, sound, video and animation.

Such a file truly deserves the moniker "multimedia" because it manages a variety of traditionally different media using the very same computer equipment, albeit with spe-

regime, at the end of the second year, you would have earned 2% interest on the entire amount accumulated at the end of the first year, or $102. So your total deposit at the end of Year 2 would be $102 (the amount at the end of the first year) plus 0.02 x $102, or $104.04.

The extra four cents do not sound like much, but the effect of compounding grows rapidly as time goes on, according to the laws of "exponential growth rates" in mathematics. For example, here's a table showing how your deposit would grow for the first twenty years, at an interest rate of 2% per year, using both simple and compound interest.

| End of Year | Simple Interest | Compound Interest |
| --- | --- | --- |
| 1 | 102 | 102 |
| 2 | 104 | 104.04 |
| 3 | 106 | 106.12 |
| 4 | 108 | 108.24 |
| 5 | 110 | 110.40 |
| 6 | 112 | 112.61 |
| 7 | 114 | 114.86 |
| 8 | 116 | 117.17 |
| 9 | 118 | 119.51 |
| 10 | 120 | 121.90 |
| 11 | 122 | 124.34 |
| 12 | 124 | 126.82 |
| 13 | 126 | 129.36 |
| 14 | 128 | 131.95 |
| 15 | 130 | 134.59 |
| 16 | 132 | 137.28 |
| 17 | 134 | 140.02 |
| 18 | 136 | 142.82 |
| 19 | 138 | 145.68 |
| 20 | 140 | 148.59 |

The "exponential" effect of compounding depends strongly on both the interest rate and the elapsed time. At a higher rate of interest of 15%, for example, compounding would more than double your money in five years, whereas simple interest would give you only a 75% return.

**2. Present value as the inverse of compounding.** As you can see from the foregoing example, compound interest makes money grow with time, at an even faster rate than would simple interest. At the end of twenty years, your $100 would grow to $148.59, even at the low rate of 2%. What that means is that—assuming interest rates stay stable—your $100 will be worth $148.59 in twenty years, without your doing anything and with virtually no risk (remember, your deposit was in a federally insured account!).

Now suppose someone promised to give you some money in twenty years, but not before. What would that promise be worth now? If the promise was to give you

$148.59 in twenty years, it would be worth only $100 today, because $100 invested today would be worth the promised amount in twenty years. Therefore no rational person would buy a note promising to pay $148.59 in twenty years for any more than $100 today. In economic terms, the "present value" of the future payment of $148.59 in twenty years is $100.

**3. A general formula.** Based on this simple example, we can calculate a formula to determine what any future payment would be worth today, i.e., the present value (PV) of any future payment (FP). To do that, we first calculate what an amount PV would be worth in n years. After year 1, compounding would make the future value

$$FP(Y1) = (1 + i) * PV$$

where i is just the interest rate, expressed as a decimal instead of a percentage. In our example above, i = 2% = 0.02, so the future payment after one year is (1 + 0.02) x $100, or (1.02) * $100, or $102, as shown above.

To calculate the future payment after two years, we just multiple the future payment after one year by the same "compounding factor" (1 + i):

$$FP(Y2) = (1 + i) * (1 + i) * PV = (1 + i)2 * PV$$

By what mathematicians call "induction," i.e., by repeating the same process again and again, we can see that the future payment that would be equivalent to PV at the end of any arbitrary future Year n is just

$$FP(Yn) = (1 + i)n * PV$$

That is, the future payment at the end of year n is just the present value PV, multiplied n times by the compounding factor (1 + i), which was 1.02 in our example.

Now to find the present value PV from the future payment FP, we just work backwards. We divide both sides of the equation by (1 + i)n, and we get:

$$PV = FP(Yn) / (1 + i)n$$

This is the basic formula for present value. It is quite general. It works for any time period and for any number of periods n, as long as you remember that i is the interest rate for that time period. For example, to calculate the present value of a future payment of $100 made after 180 months, just use the formula

$$PV = FP(M180) / (1+i)180$$

where i is the monthly rate of interest expressed as a decimal. In our example, i would be 2% /12, or 0.001666667.

**4. Multiple future payments.** In valuing intellectual property, or indeed any property, there is rarely just a single future payment. Usually there is a stream of future payments whose present value must be calculated.

For example, suppose you have a patentable technology. You think the patent application will be ready for filing in two years, and the technology will be ready for commercial production in five years. If you file the patent application in two years, the patent will expire twenty years later, or in 22 years. *See* 35 U.S.C. § 154. Your royalty stream, however, probably won't begin to run until commercial production starts in five years. Therefore, you would expect the royalty stream under the patent to run from year 5 through year 22, for a total of 18 years.

To calculate the present value of this eighteen-year future royalty stream, you would first estimate the amount of royalties that you would receive from licensing during each of the years 5 through 22. Each estimate would require a whole host of assumptions and subsidiary estimates. For example, you might estimate the selling price of the patented product, the royalty rate to which a licensee would agree, and the likely number of products to be sold during each year. Then, with the estimate of each year's royalty returns in hand, you would calculate the present value of each year's estimated returns, using the formula that we just derived. Finally, you would add up that present value for all of the eighteen years 5 through 22, as follows:

$$PV(Y5) = (\text{Estimated royalties for year 5}) / (1 + i)5$$

$$+$$

$$PV(Y6) = (\text{Estimated royalties for year 6}) / (1 + i)6$$

$$.$$

$$.$$

$$.$$

$$+$$

$$PV(Y22) = (\text{Estimated royalties for year 22}) / (1 + i)22$$

where i is the annual interest rate (expressed as a decimal) used for discounting to present value. Expressed in a single formula, the present value of the total eighteen-year royalty stream would be

$$n=22$$

$$PV \text{ (whole stream)} = \Sigma \text{ (Estimated royalties for year n)} / (1 + i)n$$

$$n=5$$

This formula may look complicated, but modern technology makes calculating it simple. Most business and many general-purpose advanced calculators allow you to calculate the present value of a single future payment at the touch of a button, simply by plugging in the number of years and the interest or discount rate. So do some Web sites. See e.g., How Finance Works, moneychimp website *at* www.moneychimp.com/articles/finworks/fmpresval.htm (visited April 29, 2004). Some calculators will even calculate the present value of a sum of future payments, in accordance with the last formula above.

**5. The hard part.** Believe it or not, the hard part of a complete present-value calculation is not the math. Modern calculators or computers, or a good assistant with a math background, make the calculations easy. If the math is done right, there should be no uncertainty or error. What is hard is not the math, but the assumptions and estimates that lie behind the calculations.

You may have noticed that all our examples above assumed a single, constant interest rate for as much as twenty-two years in the future. Yet every adult knows from personal experience that interest rates do not stay fixed; they fluctuate yearly, if not monthly. They may vary by wide margins, for example, from the high teens in the early 1980s to the very low single digits in 2004. Any estimate of a single "average" interest rate over a period of a decade or more is therefore no more than an educated guess. Yet the precise value of the guess is very important, because of the strong exponential effect of interest rates, which causes small changes in the assumed rate to make big differences in calculated outcomes.

Moreover, estimating a single "average" interest rate over the time period of interest is only the beginning. You may recall that the interest rate assumed in our example, 2%, was the rate of return for a virtually risk-free investment (in a federally insured bank account). Any real business venture—especially one involving an untried new technology eligible for patenting—necessarily involves greater risk.

A basic principle of economics and investing states that investors demand a higher return for undertaking greater risk. According to this risk/return principle, investors will demand a so-called "risk premium" for investing in our hypothetical, untried patentable technology. That is, they will demand a rate of return several points higher than the interest rate on federally insured bank accounts. Without such a premium, they would be silly to invest in the new risky technology when they could earn money at the same rate through a bank account and sleep much better at night.

So the risk-adjusted rate of return—and therefore the risk-adjusted rate for discounting to present value—will be much higher in a venture involving untried new technology than in our simple example of a risk-free bank account. Determining how much higher is a matter of educated guesswork, just as is determining what "average" future interest rates are likely to be over a long future time period, even in a risk-free environment.

Finally, there are multiple additional sources of uncertainty in any real present-value calculation. Estimates of the probable royalty rate, the selling price of the patented products, and the number of products to be sold each year are all attempts to predict the unknowable future. Therefore they are all additional sources of uncertainty and possible contention. Each of these figures derives from an educated guess, which business people call a "projection," and which is more art than science. Each depends upon a number of assumptions about the future, some of which may be implicit or unstated.

Therefore the hard part of present-value calculations is not the mathematics of calculating present value. The hard part is the guesswork and research into products, markets, and competition—not to mention future interest rates and appropriate risk premiums—that goes into the underlying revenue projections from which present values are calculated.

The role of the lawyer includes clarifying and (where appropriate) questioning this guesswork and the research and assumptions that underlie it. Computers or competent assistants can do the mathematics without much trouble and usually without error. But no computer yet developed can uncover and evaluate the validity of hidden assumptions and guesswork behind the numbers used as input. As an old computer user's slogan advises, "Garbage in, garbage out." The lawyer's role in reviewing present-value calculations is largely confined to determining whether this slogan applies to the assumptions, hidden or revealed, that underlie the numbers.

———————

# Chapter 6

# Copyright: Multimedia and Entertainment Licensing

## I. Introduction

The majority of licenses in today's business world involve more than one licensed intellectual property right. Licenses granting rights in multiple properties are common in the media and entertainment industries, where all types of intellectual property can play a simultaneous part in the creation of a single product. The end result could be anything from an e-commerce website, to an Andrew Lloyd Webber musical, a Tom Cruise movie, Metallica CD, or a university distance-education course.

Licensing of digital works is changing rapidly. Likely, it will be years before the powers that be resolve the political struggles over modernizing copyright law. Meanwhile, new technologies will continue to find ways to circumvent copyright protection of music, movies, and software. Authors, artists and consumers on the one side, and publishers, the recording industry, and the media on the other, continue to struggle over the proper scope of copyright and fair use. The following materials illustrate the difficulties of obtaining license rights to pre-existing content for new uses.

## Multimedia Licensing: The Basics

Before discussing practical aspects of multimedia licensing, it may be useful to have some basic background. What is "multimedia"? What branches of intellectual property law most often apply to it? What recent developments in the law are most relevant to multimedia licensing, and how has the law sought to adapt itself to this new technology?

Answers to these questions are still a work in progress, but a few partial answers and some apparent trends are evident. Students who have had a course in copyright law, Internet law, or cyberlaw may find this material a useful review. Those who have had no such courses should study it intensely, for these partial answers, although highly conceptual, serve as basic building blocks for both current understanding and future developments.

**1. What Does "Multimedia" Mean?** The word "multimedia" is a much overused and potentially misleading term. Literally defined, it refers to a work involving more than one medium or mode of expression. In this sense, "multimedia" productions are nothing new. Movies, for example, have included both video (frames photographed on celluloid) and audio (on a synchronized sound track) since "talkies" first appeared in the 1920s. Television similarly has combined audio and video portions since its advent in the 1940s.

The real meaning of the term "multimedia," as well as the term's current importance, derives from modern computer technology and the so-called "convergence of media" that it fostered. Today's general-purpose digital computers can record, reproduce, and play traditional media—text, sound, pictures, audio, audiovisual works, animation, etc.—in exactly the same form: a sequence of digital ones and zeros. The various media "converge" in recording, storage, and playback as standardized digital files.

This does not mean, however, that modern computers handle all media in exactly the same way. Each traditional form of medium enjoys several alternative formats for computer handling and storage, and the formats vary from medium to medium. Text, for example, generally uses the "ASCII" code, which stands for "American Standard Code for Information Interchange." In this code, each letter, number, and other textual character is assigned a unique numerical value. Other coding schemes are also available, especially for foreign languages using non-Roman characters. Audio also has several alternative formats, each of which uses a particular method to compress the digital numbers representing the volume of sound waves at particular instants of time. (Because sound waves change rapidly, their proper recording requires up to 50,000 digital "samples" per second, and efficient handling with current technology requires the resulting voluminous data to be compressed for transmission and storage.) The popular MPEG3 or "MP3" format represents only one particular compromise between data compression and audio quality, but there are several others, including WAV. Similarly, alternative still-picture formats, such as JPG, GIF, PNG, and audiovisual formats, such as MPEG-1, MPEG-2 and MPEG-4, make different trade-offs between data compression and quality.

As the existence of these various formats suggests, it is a misconception to think that the convergence of media has not eliminated all differences among technologies for handling different media. Media convergence has allowed all media to operate with similar or compatible *hardware*—typically a general-purpose or special-purpose computer—which accommodates the differences between different media and different formats through software. Because software is more adaptable than hardware, this accommodation has important consequences for the efficiency of both use and development of media technology.

Regardless of their particular format, digital files reflecting various media are stored and handled in much the same way, as series of digital bits (ones or zeroes) recorded on various storage media. The very same hardware, typically a general-purpose computer using standard storage media (such as a hard drive, CD-ROM, or DVD) can store, play, reproduce, and manage all of these files as long as it has the appropriate software for the particular format of interest. It is in this sense that all these media "converge." Handling different media no longer requires distinct and specialized equipment (such as magnetic tape or vinyl disks for sound and celluloid film projectors for video); only the software need change. As a result, with the right software a single digital file will record, store, display, and perform text, sound, video and animation.

Such a file truly deserves the moniker "multimedia" because it manages a variety of traditionally different media using the very same computer equipment, albeit with specialized software. Since the different software needed to handle the various formats is hidden inside the computer and therefore is generally "transparent" to the user, all the average user sees is a machine playing the various media—text, still pictures, sound, and video—all at once.

2. **Multimedia's Legal Significance.** As the foregoing discussion suggests, the primary significance of the term "multimedia" is the combination, using single hardware technology (computers), of works of authorship or artistry that, in the past, required different equipment for their recording, storage, and use. The transformation from multiple hardware technologies to a single one is largely of historical interest. As the years pass, few will remember or care that songs were once recorded using grooved vinyl disks and played back with needles traversing those grooves, or that movies were once recorded as photographic images on celluloid, spinning through a light beam and projected on a screen.

As a matter of law, however, the separate technological origins of the various media will have continuing importance for a long time to come. Many existing works of literature, music, drama, and film were created for use with specialized hardware and were separately copyrighted as such. Their copyrights may last for well over a century.[1] Notwithstanding the convergence of media, anyone who wants to use properties developed for separate media and lawfully copyrighted as separate works will have to get permission from the author, artist, or copyright owner until the copyright expires.

Of course the chief practical advantage of multimedia technology is that is allows works in many media to be combined simply and easily. For example, a modern multimedia file might contain the text of a famous poem, the sounds of that poem put to music, a visual image of an artist's oil painting, and clips of sounds from popular songs and of audiovisual excerpts from popular movies. As long at these works are still under separate copyright, the producer of the multimedia work must get permission from the copyright owner or an appropriate licensee of each work in order to use them lawfully in the multimedia production. In addition, the multimedia producer must consider the rights of publicity of individual actors and artists, as well as the possible role of union and guild contracts relating to the underlying works. As a result, the task of "clearing" permission to use all the previously copyrighted components of a new multimedia production may be formidable.

3. **The Importance of Copyright.** If one considers both the content of a multimedia production and the technology for its playback, multimedia works may run the entire gamut of intellectual property protection. Patents may—and often do—cover the technology for recording and playback. For example, patents may cover the method and apparatus for using lasers to record digital data on CDs or DVDs and for playing the data back with portable lasers. With increasing numbers of patents being granted for software and algorithms, patents also may cover the software and algorithms used for data compression, recording and playback.[2] To the extent unpatented aspects of these technologies are not disclosed to the public, they may be protected as trade secrets.[3] In

---

1. Copyrights in anonymous works and works made for hire (typically, corporate works) last for 95 years after their first publication or 120 years after their creation, whichever expires first. *See* 17 U.S.C. § 302(c). Copyright in works by known individual authors lasts for 70 years after their death. *See* 17 U.S.C. § 302(a). If, for example, a young girl writes a song when she is fifteen and lives to the age of 95, her copyright will last for 150 years.

2. Patents of this kind are not without controversy. *See supra* Chapter 2.

3. For example, aspects of recording or playback software distributed only in object-code form under covenants against reverse-engineering may be protected as trade secrets.

addition, the computers or other hardware used for recording and playing back multimedia productions may include specialized chips whose "mask works" or physical layouts are protected under the Semiconductor Chip Protection Act of 1984.[4] Copyright of course covers the content of any multimedia production. To the extent the content depicts individuals or uses their names, likenesses or personalities, it may infringe individuals' rights of publicity.[5] Finally, the law of trademarks or unfair competition may protect trademarks and trade names used for the recording devices, the recordings, their particular content, or a particular producer of content. Thus virtually every form of intellectual property known to the law may play a role in multimedia productions.

From a licensing perspective, however, the situation is not normally as complicated as these facts might suggest. In practice, the technology for producing, recording and playing multimedia productions (including patents, trade secrets, semiconductor chip protection, and copyrights on formatting and other software) is usually licensed separately from the content of the multimedia productions whose distribution uses that technology. The production, recording and playback technology can be applied to a myriad of different multimedia productions by different producers, authors and artists. Normally, rights in the technology are held by persons other than those who hold rights in the content; inventors develop the technology, while producers, authors, composes and artists create the content. Moreover, those who hold rights in the technology have an incentive (unless they manufacture the relevant equipment and blank media themselves and wish to exclude competition) to license that technology as widely as possible, both to insure against the failure of a single manufacturer and to encourage the use of the licensed technology as a "standard" for similar equipment and media worldwide. In contrast, holders of rights in content often grant exclusive licenses to a single distributor in order to encourage maximum concentration of marketing and promotion of the particular content. A producer of CDs or DVDs may hold licenses of both the relevant technology and the recorded content, but the technology and content licenses will ordinarily be separate agreements governing separate rights in vastly different intellectual property held by separate persons.

As a result, it is possible to make a generally valid conceptual distinction between technology and content licensing in the multimedia world. Licenses of technology (patents, trade secrets, protected semiconductor chip designs, and possibly related trademarks), whether to produce protected equipment or blank media, or to record on protected blank media, are much like similar technology licenses in any industry involved in widespread distribution of consumer products. They fall under the general heading of patent or technology licensing, and they present no special problems.

Content licensing, however, is another matter entirely. The term "multimedia licensing," as a distinct field of legal or business practice, usually refers to the licensing of *content* because it is there that the special problems of multimedia most often arise. The difficulty is that, by its nature, multimedia encourage the production of creative works that include or combine previous works of all kinds. As noted above, these separate works, if still under copyright, require separate licensing for inclusion in the multime-

---

4. 17 U.S.C. §§ 901–914, discussed in JAY DRATLER, JR., INTELLECTUAL PROPERTY LAW: COMMERCIAL, CREATIVE, AND INDUSTRIAL PROPERTY, Ch. 8 (Law Journal Press 1991 & Supps.) (LEXIS, LJLIP).

5. *See White v. Samsung Electronics America, Inc.*, 971 F.2d 1395, 1397–99, 23 U.S.P.Q.2d (BNA) 1583 (9th Cir. 1992) (allowing trial on claim that television advertisement showing robot in wig, dress and circumstances similar to those of Vanna White in her role as hostess of television show "Wheel of Fortune" infringed her right of publicity under common law of California).

dia production, and they may also implicate additional rights in included content, including rights of publicity and rights in trademarks, service marks, or trade names. It is these aspects of multimedia licensing, relating to *content* drawn from various sources, that give the multimedia field its special character and create unusual difficulty for both the licensing attorney and the producer.

Insofar as creative works are concerned, the primary field of intellectual property is copyright. Virtually every form of creative work, whether a poem, song, piece of instrumental music, work of fine art, photograph, sculpture, architectural work, film, television production, or multimedia work, is protected by copyright. As a result, others' rights under copyright are the chief concern of a multimedia producer who seeks to combine or include previously-created works in a new way. "Clearing" rights in all previously-created works to be used, i.e., getting appropriate permission to use them, is the central challenge of the multimedia producer and the lawyer who represents him. As a result, copyright plays the central role in multimedia production, although the lawyer must also consider rights of publicity, trademarks and unfair competition, and contractual rights of unions and guilds.

**4. Some Basic Principles of Copyright.** In order to appreciate the central role that copyright plays in multimedia licensing, it is useful to review some relevant principles of copyright protection. These include: the exclusive rights of copyright holders, the divisibility of copyright, the effect of the first-sale doctrine, the rule of *MAI Systems Corp. v. Peak Computer, Inc.*,\* and the important role of secondary liability in the computer and Internet age.

**a. The exclusive rights of copyright holders.** Section 106 of the Copyright Act of 1976, as amended,[6] gives copyright owners six exclusive rights. These are the rights to: (1) to reproduce or copy the copyrighted work; (2) to prepare derivative works based upon it (i.e., to adapt or transform it); (3) to distribute the work in tangible form; (4) to publicly perform the work directly or indirectly through electronic or mechanical devices; (5) to publicly display the work; and (6) to perform a sound recording by means of a digital audio transmission. Under Section 106, the copyright holder has the exclusive right not only to do, but to *authorize*, these activities.

Normally a multimedia production that includes all or part of a pre-existing work implicates one or more of these exclusive rights. The mere act of incorporating a pre-existing work into a new one implicates either the reproduction right (if the copy is exact) or the derivative-work right (if the pre-existing work is modified or transformed during its incorporation). If the multimedia production is distributed in tangible form, for example, on CDs or DVDs, the distribution right also is implicated.

Electronic transmission over the Internet, may not implicate the distribution right, for the question whether intangible transmission constitutes "distribution" is still unresolved. However, transmission over the Internet ordinarily *will* implicate one or more of the other exclusive rights. Distribution by "streaming" to multiple unrelated parties normally constitutes a *public* performance by virtue of the second clause of the definition of "publicly." This clause covers "communicat[ing] a performance or display...to the public, by means of any device or process, whether the members of the public capable of receiving the performance or display receive it in the same place or in separate places and at the same time or at different times."[7] If the transmission over the Internet

---

\* *MAI Systems Corp. v. Peak Computer, Inc.*, 991 F.2d 511 (9th Cir. 1993).

6. 17 U.S.C. § 106.

7. 17 U.S.C. § 101 (definition of performing or displaying a work "publicly," clause (2)).

allows the recipient to download a copy of the work, the downloaded copy must be authorized, or the right of reproduction will have been violated. As this brief discussion shows, the six exclusive rights that copyright holders have are sufficiently comprehensive to preclude most, if not all, commercial exploitation of pre-existing works in multimedia productions without permission.

**b. The doctrine of "divisibility of copyright."** Under the doctrine of "divisibility of copyright," each of the six exclusive rights of copyright holders is like a separate copyright. It may be owned, assigned, licensed, or withheld separately.[8] As a result, a grant under one exclusive right does not imply a grant of another. Indeed, the rule for copyright law is to the contrary: any rights not explicitly conveyed are deemed reserved.[9]

Not only is every one of the six exclusive rights potentially like a separate copyright. In addition, each of the those rights may be subdivided into an infinite number of infinitely small bundles of rights—in scope, time, territory and field of use—each of which can be transferred and licensed separately.[10] Thus, for example, an exclusive license to broadcast a particular song once only, on a specified frequency in Dubuque, Iowa, at precisely 12 noon on January 15, 2006, is a right that, insofar as assignment and transfer are concerned, is economically tantamount to ownership of a slice of copyright in the song.[11]

Because of the doctrine of divisibility of copyright—and the conceptual separation of each of the six exclusive rights comprised in a copyright—a multimedia producer must be sure to have "clearance" or permission under all the rights that she intends to use. If, for example, the producer wishes to incorporate a copyrighted popular song in her multimedia production and to transmit that production to the public over the Internet, she will require a license not only to reproduce the song in the course of incorporating it but also to publicly perform the song (and probably to distribute it as well). She may also require a license of the digital audio transmission right, unless her proposed use falls within the statutory exceptions set forth in 17 U.S.C. § 114(d). Every producer of multimedia works must likewise consider carefully what rights he or she will need in every copyrighted work to be used.

**c. The first-sale doctrine and its limitations.** The first-sale doctrine in copyright law is a potential source of confusion in determining what permission is needed in order to use pre-existing works in multimedia productions. Under this doctrine, a "first sale" of a tangible object embodying a copyrighted work, if legitimately made under the authority of the copyright owner, relaxes certain aspects of the copyright *with respect to that particular object only. See* 17 U.S.C. § 109. Thus, for example, if you buy a legitimate

---

8. The 1976 Act says as much:
> Any of the exclusive rights comprised in a copyright, including any subdivision of any of the rights specified by section 106, may be transferred...and owned separately. The owner of any particular exclusive right is entitled, to the extent of that right, to all of the protection and remedies accorded to the copyright owner by this title.

17 U.S.C. § 201(d)(2).

9. *See* JAY DRATLER, JR., LICENSING OF INTELLECTUAL PROPERTY, § 1.06[1] (Law Journal Press 1994 & Supps.).

10. The divisible rights include "any subdivision of any of the rights specified by section 106." 17 U.S.C. § 201(d)(2). *See also supra* note 8.

11. *See also* 17 U.S.C. § 101 (definition of "transfer of copyright ownership") (emphasis added.):
> A 'transfer of copyright ownership' is an assignment, mortgage, *exclusive license,* or any other conveyance, alienation, or hypothecation of a copyright *or of any of the exclusive rights comprised in a copyright,* whether or not it is limited in time or place of effect, but not including a nonexclusive license.

(not pirate) copy of a book, you may "distribute" *that copy* by sale, loan, lease, or gift without infringing any right of the copyright holder. *See* 17 U.S.C. § 109(a). This rule facilitates trade in tangible objects embodying copyrighted works and avoids having to research the copyright "pedigree" of such tangible objects as books and records before, for example, selling used ones in a garage or yard sale.

The first-sale doctrine, however, is subject to two important limitations, which preclude its general use in lieu of permission for multimedia productions. First, the first-sale doctrine applies only to the particular copy or phonorecord sold. It does not permit making additional copies or phonorecords from that copy, i.e., it does not relax the most basic right of the copyright holder — the exclusive right to manufacture copies or phonorecords. (Simple logic corroborates this result; if the first-sale doctrine relaxed the reproduction right, then any purchaser of a book could become a legally authorized publisher of it, and copyright would be worthless.)

The second important limitation of the first sale doctrine is that it generally relaxes only two of the six exclusive rights of the copyright holder, namely, the distribution right (*see* 17 U.S.C. § 109(a)) and the public display right (*see* 17 U.S.C.§ 109(c)).[12] Moreover, it relaxes even those rights only in limited ways. Its relaxation of the display right allows, for example, the owner of a painting to display it in a gallery, but only directly or by projection of a single image in the same place. Its relaxation of the distribution right does not permit commercial lending or rental or sound recordings or computer programs. *See* 17 U.S.C. § 109(b).

Most important for multimedia producers, it is well established that the first-sale doctrine in copyright law does *not* relax the reproduction right, the derivative-work right,[13] or the public performance right.[14] Thus, even if a multimedia producer has purchased a legitimate copy or phonorecord embodying a pre-existing work, that purchase does not give the producer the right to incorporate the pre-existing work into a new multimedia production, with or without modification, or the right to perform the resulting production publicly, for example, by transmission over the Internet. Notwithstanding the first-sale doctrine, the copyright holder's permission is still required for all those activities.

**d. The rule of *MAI Systems Corp. v. Peak Computer, Inc.*** One of the most important copyright decisions for the computer and Internet age was *MAI Systems Corp. v. Peak Computer, Inc.*[15] In that case, the Ninth Circuit ruled that digital data representing a copyrighted work, once stored in the random-access memory or "RAM" of a digital computer, constitute a "copy" of that work, notwithstanding the fact that storage in RAM is "volatile" in the sense that it disappears when the computer is turned off.[16]

---

12. There is also a limited relaxation of the public performance right, but it applies only to "an electronic audiovisual game intended for use in coin operated equipment" and relaxes the public performance right only to permit playing on such equipment. 17 U.S.C. § 109(e).

13. *See, e.g., Mirage Editions, Inc. v. Albuquerque A.R.T. Co.*, 856 F.2d 1341, 1344, 8 U.S.P.Q.2d (BNA) 1171 (9th Cir. 1988); *Lee v. A.R.T. Co.*, 125 F.3d 580, 581, 44 U.S.P.Q.2d (BNA) 1153 (7th Cir. 1997) (assuming same principle but finding no derivative work under circumstances).

14. *See, e.g., Columbia Pictures Industries, Inc. v. Aveco, Inc.*, 800 F.2d 59, 64, 230 U.S.P.Q. (BNA) 869 (3d Cir. 1986) ("The rights protected by copyright are divisible and the waiver of one does not necessarily waive any of the others.") (citation omitted); *Columbia Pictures Industries, Inc. v. Redd Horne, Inc.*, 749 F.2d 154, 159–60, 224 U.S.P.Q. (BNA) 641 (3d Cir. 1984).

15. 991 F.2d 511 (9th Cir. 1993), *cert. denied*, 510 U.S. 1033 (1994).

16. *See id.*, 991 F.2d at 518–19.

The rationale for this decision was sound. The definitions of "copies" and "fixed" in 17 U.S.C. § 101 require that a "copy" be "sufficiently permanent or stable to permit it to be perceived, reproduced, or otherwise communicated for a period of more than transitory duration."[17] In other words, something is a "copy" under copyright law if it lasts long enough to permit its perception, transmission, or the generation of further copies. Who can doubt that today, when the Internet allows further copies not only to be made from data in RAM, but to be flashed around the world in milliseconds, at the click of a mouse, such data satisfy this criterion in both letter and spirit? For this reason, every court that has addressed the issue has agreed with the *MAI* court that content in RAM constitutes "copies."[18]

A 1998 amendment to the copyright statute[19] reversed one narrow result of the *MAI* decision: that third-party maintenance personnel, which had no license to use a copyrighted operating system, infringed the copyright in that system by turning on a computer device in order to maintain it, thereby causing the copyrighted operating system to be loaded into RAM.[20] The statutory amendment, however, only provided a narrow exception to copyright liability for the purpose of allowing third-party maintenance and repair. It did not affect the basic holding of *MAI* and its progeny, that matter in RAM is a "copy" which requires the copyright holder's authorization.[21]

The importance of the rule of *MAI* for multimedia production is hard to overstate. Consider, for example, a multimedia producer who would like to incorporate a clip from a previously copyrighted work in his production. If he has no permission to do so, his copying the clip into his computer's memory in order to manipulate or incorporate it infringes the copyright, at least in the absence of a fair use defense. The "loading" of the clip inro RAM, for "playing" or other software purposes, also infringes the copyright. Likewise a consumer's playing the clip as part of the multimedia production stored on a CD would infringe, because playing the CD would require loading the data at least temporarily into RAM. In other words, by virtue of the *MAI* decision, the producer's preparation of the multimedia production and its use by consumers, whether by "playing" a tangible recording or by streaming or downloading under Internet transmission, would infringe the copyright owner's reproduction right in the clip, unless the circumstances are such that these activities constitute fair use.

---

17. 17 U.S.C. § 101 (definition of "fixed," in part). *See also id.*, (definition of "copies," with similar language).

18. *Triad Systems Corp. v. Southeastern Express Co.*, 64 F.3d 1330, 1333, 1335 (9th Cir. 1995), *cert. denied*, 516 U.S. 1145 (1996); *NLFC, Inc. v. Devcom Mid-America*, 45 F.3d 231, 234 (7th Cir. 1995) ("Neither party disputes that loading software into a computer constitutes the creation of a copy under the Copyright Act."); *Vault Corp. v. Quaid Software Ltd.*, 847 F.2d 255, 260 (5th Cir. 1988) (stating dictum that: "the act of loading a program from a medium of storage into a computer's memory creates a copy of the program").

*Cf., DSC Communications Corp. v. DGI Technologies, Inc.*, 81 F.3d 597, 600–1 (5th Cir. 1996) (declining to decide "whether booting up a…microprocessor card constitutes impermissible copying" because defendant's substantial likelihood of prevailing on copyright misuse defense prevented broadening of preliminary injunction as plaintiff requested).

19. *See* 17 U.S.C. § 117(c), (d), as amended by Title III, "Computer Maintenance Competition Assurance Act," of the Digital Millennium Copyright Act, Pub. L. No. 105-304, § 302(3), 112 Stat. 2860, 2887 (Oct. 28, 1998).

20. *See MAI Systems Corp. v. Peak Computer, Inc.*, 991 F.2d 511, 513, 517, 519 (9th Cir. 1993), *cert. dismissed*, 510 U.S. 1033 (1994).

21. For further discussion of this point, see JAY DRATLER, JR., INTELLECTUAL PROPERTY LAW: COMMERCIAL, CREATIVE, AND INDUSTRIAL PROPERTY § 6.01[1][c] (Law Journal Press 1991 & Supps.) (LEXIS, LJIPCP).

"Streaming," however, has an indeterminate character insofar as copyright infringement is concerned. As a technological matter, streaming may not involve loading an entire "streamed" work into RAM all at once. Often streaming uses a "buffer," or limited series of locations in RAM, to load portions of a digital work for real-time "playing" in succession shortly after receipt. Once played, these successive portions of the work are digitally shifted out of the buffer or overwritten by new ones. As a result, a work "streamed" using a buffer is never entirely in RAM at one time. Buffer technology is almost invariably used for longer works, such as movies, or "works" of indeterminate length, such as "webcasting."

As a legal matter, it is unclear whether downloading successive portions of a work into a buffer in this manner constitutes making a "copy" of anything. Even if it does, making such successive partial copies for real-time "playing," without being able to download or keep a complete copy, may constitute fair use under certain circumstances. Thus streaming is one of many cases in which the rule of *MAI* complicates copyright law, making it depend upon exactly how modern technology works—a fact that often turns copyright hearings into graduate seminars in computer and digital engineering.

The defense of fair use under Section 107 only adds to this complexity. Except in extreme cases, a determination of "fair use" is one of the most uncertain and risky in all of copyright law. Therefore, as a matter of practice and prudence, the rule of *MAI* requires permission for incorporating most, if not all, previously existing works into multimedia productions, whether in whole or in part.[22]

**e. The importance of secondary liability.** Copyright law recognizes two, and perhaps three, types of secondary liability. The first type—vicarious liability—is an application of the notion of *respondeat superior* in tort. It has two elements: (1) the right and ability to control the infringing activity; and (2) a direct financial benefit from it.[23] The second—contributory infringement—is an offshoot of the doctrine of enterprise liability. It has also two elements: (1) actual or constructive knowledge of the infringement; and (2) inducing, causing or materially contributing to it.[24] Copyright law also recognizes a special type of contributory infringement: the manufacture and sale or general-purpose recording or copying technology constitutes contributory infringement only if: (1) the purveyor of that technology has actual or constructive knowledge that it is used for infringing purposes; and (2) the technology has no substantial noninfringing use.[25]

---

22. Minimal "sampling" of individual sounds, or their video equivalent, may be sufficiently *de minimis* to avoid a finding of infringement, but determining when this is so is a risky and uncertain business. *See Newton v. Diamond*, 349 F.3d 591, 595–97 (9th Cir. 2003) (affirming judgment that digital "sample" of plaintiff's work, consisting of six-second, three-note segment, was *de minimis* and therefore not infringement, even though defendant "looped" sample to create multiple repetitions in his allegedly infringing work).

23. *See, e.g., A&M Records v. Napster, Inc.*, 239 F.3d 1004, 1022–24 (9th Cir. 2001); *Fonovisa, Inc. v. Cherry Auction, Inc.*, 76 F.3d 259, 262 (9th Cir. 1996); *Gershwin Publ'g Corp. v. Columbia Artists Mgmt., Inc.*, 443 F.2d 1159, 1162 (2d Cir. 1971); *Shapiro Bernstein and Co. v. H. L. Green Co.*, 316 F.2d 304, 308 (2d Cir. 1963).

24. *See, e.g., A&M Records, Inc. v. Napster, Inc.*, 239 F.3d 1004, 1019 (9th Cir. 2001); *Casella v. Morris*, 820 F.2d 362, 365 (11th Cir. 1987); *Fonovisa, Inc. v. Cherry Auction, Inc.*, 76 F.3d 259, 264 (9th Cir. 1996); *Gershwin Publishing Corp. v. Columbia Artists Management, Inc.*, 443 F.2d 1159, 1162 (2d Cir. 1971) (seminal case, stating definition of contributory infringement).

25. *See Sony Corp. of America v. Universal City Studios, Inc.*, 464 U.S. 417, 425, 428, 451 (1984) (assuming knowledge on defendant's part, then borrowing contributory infringement standard from patent law and holding that maker of general-purpose copying equipment is not liable for contributing to infringement of copyright by users of that equipment if the equipment is "capable of substantial noninfringing uses").

All these doctrines of secondary liability have existed since at least the 1980s, but their importance increased dramatically with the advent of the Internet. The reason is simple: infringement by millions of consumers on the Internet is often hard to police or curtail. Therefore copyright owners often seek to hold responsible the purveyors of technology that assists or induces infringement. The classic case was *Napster*, in which the Ninth Circuit held an Internet "peer-to-peer" file-sharing service responsible for the acts of numerous consumers who "shared" copyrighted musical files without authorization.[26] As the *Napster* decision suggested, the doctrines of secondary liability offer copyright holders the promise of both efficiency and effectiveness in litigation by allowing them to shut down infringing activities at their source.

The doctrines of secondary liability are important in copyright licensing for two reasons. First, they allow copyright owners, by prohibiting secondary infringement, to control activities that do not directly infringe their copyrights but assist others in infringing. Second, these doctrines may make it necessary for purveyors of multimedia or Internet technology—like Napster—to obtain licenses for their activities from copyright owners, even though their activities do not directly infringe any copyright. Napster, for example, did not infringe any copyright directly, since the peer-to-peer Internet transfer technology that if facilitated allowed users of its service to send musical files to each other directly, without passing through Napster's system. The Ninth Circuit's decision that contributory and vicarious infringement were both likely under the circumstances, however, required Napster to get a license from the major musical studios in order to continue its business.

**f. The Digital Millennium Copyright Act.** Owners and licensors of multimedia productions also need to be conscious of one of the most revolutionary statutes in the 300-year history of copyright law: the Digital Millennium Copyright Act.[27] Among other things, this statute made it easier to protect copyrighted works from unauthorized access and use by outlawing both circumventing protective technological measures and providing the means to do so. Under Section 1201 of this statute, it is both a civil[28] and criminal[29] offense to defeat such things as encryption and password protection to gain unauthorized access to copyrighted works.[30] It is also a civil and criminal offense to provide others with means to defeat such protection,[31] or to defeat technological use-control measures,[32] such as those that allow streaming but prevent downloading of copyrighted works.[33]

In order to take advantage of these protective legal provisions, however, purveyors of multimedia productions must use technological measures, either to protect them

---

26. *See A&M Records v. Napster, Inc.*, 284 F.3d 1091, 1097–99 (9th Cir. 2002) (upholding, as not abuse of discretion, modified preliminary injunction, based on liability for both contributory and vicarious infringement, that required music-file sharing service to shut down if it could not demonstrate that it could effectively control users' sharing of infringing musical files by finding and removing references to them in its central file-sharing directory).

27. Digital Millennium Copyright Act, Pub. L. No. 105-304, § 1, 112 Stat. 2860, 2860 (Oct. 28, 1998), codified in scattered sections of Title 17 U.S.C.

28. *See* 17 U.S.C. § 1203 (civil remedies).

29. *See* 17 U.S.C. § 1204 (criminal penalties). Criminal liability requires that the civil offenses be done "willfully and for purposes of commercial advantage or private financial gain." 17 U.S.C. § 1204(a) (preamble).

30. *See* 17 U.S.C. § 1201(a)(1(A).

31. *See* 17 U.S.C. § 1201(a)(2).

32. *See* 17 U.S.C. § 1201(b)(1).

33. *See RealNetworks, Inc. v. Streambox, Inc.*, 2000 U.S. Dist. LEXIS 1889 at *19, 21–23 (W.D. Wash., Jan. 18, 2000).

from unauthorized access or to permit some uses of them (such as streaming) and deny others (such as downloading). Multimedia licenses, especially to distributors, broadcasters, and Internet transmitters, therefore ought to specify when such technological measures are required as a conditions of further dissemination of multimedia works. They may also specify the nature of the technological measures required (e.g., encryption or password protection) and perhaps specify important technological details. As distinguished from access-control measures,[34] disseminators may apply use-control measures[35] lower in the licensing chain, but the copyright owner also may wish to control such voluntary measures, whether for the sake of uniformity or for other business reasons.

One other aspect of the Digital Millennium Copyright Act may be relevant to multimedia licensing involving the Internet. Section 512 of the Copyright Act of 1976, adopted as part of the Digital Millennium Copyright Act, protects Internet service provides against certain kinds of copyright liability, both direct and secondary, when they act as mere conduits for others' infringing material and do not participate in creating or modifying it. In order to qualify for this protection, Internet service providers must satisfy a series of exceedingly complex statutory conditions. In addition, service providers wishing to take advantage of Section 512's protection must meet some general preliminary conditions, including establishing, announcing, and implementing reasonable policies for terminating repeat infringers, accommodating standard technological measures, and designating and announcing agents to receive notices of infringement.

* * *

As the foregoing discussion suggests, there is a lot of law — much of it relatively new — that a multimedia licensing attorney much know. Much of the work of multimedia licensing, however, and a large share of its frustration, does not involve dealing with new and uncertain law. Rather, it involves obtaining permission to use all of the protected properties that a creative multimedia author, artist or producer may wish, for creative reasons, to use freely.

Multimedia by its nature lends itself to new and creative uses of pre-existing works of music, literature, art, and film. Much of the material that creative souls may wish to use may be freely available on the Internet, the broadcast media, or other readily available sources. The fact that this material is available, however, does not mean that it is lawful to incorporate it into another work for widespread reproduction, transmission, distribution, and sale. A creative person who thinks the contrary, or who relies on an exuberant nonlegal interpretation of "fair use," may find himself or herself the subject of numerous copy-

---

34. *See* 17 U.S.C. § 1201(a)(3)(A), (B) (statutory definitions relating to technological measures to control access, both of which require "the authority of the copyright owner").

35. *See* 17 U.S.C. § 1201(b)(2)(A), (B) (similar definitions relating to technological measures for controlling use, neither of which refer to copyright owner's authorization).
There is an apparent practical reason for this difference. While a copyright owner may want a technological measure to control access to a work (for example, encryption) to be absolute and uniform, others further down in the chain of licensing may have reasons for imposing their own use controls. For example, consider an Internet distributor of multimedia files from many sources. If *some* of its suppliers want to permit only streaming, and not downloading of the multimedia files, the distributor may wish to apply that same restriction to *all* of its files, regardless of source, for reasons on uniformity and technological simplicity. Section 1201(b)(2)(B), which describes *use-control* technological measures, permits the distributor to do so on its own initiative by omitting the requirement of Section 1201(a)(3)(B) for *access-control* technological measures that they be installed "with the authority of the copyright owner."

right infringement lawsuits and an attractive creative frolic turned into a nightmare of litigation. It is up to the creative person's attorney to avoid this frustrating result by slogging through the tedious work of obtaining necessary permission to use each of the pre-existing creative properties that the artist or producer incorporates into a multimedia work. The following articles illustrate just how much legwork obtaining that permission may involve.

---

# Evolution of the Multimedia Species Developers Eager for Easy Access to Other People's Product May Interact Differently Once They Become Owners*

James M. Kennedy
*at* www.ipmag.com/kennedy.html

There has been much discussion recently about the difficulties in licensing content from traditional entertainment media for use in consumer software products. As software developers and publishers have sought to use excerpts from still photographs or from existing film or television properties, they have been stymied by numerous hurdles: required permission from copyright holders, principal talent, guilds and unions—all of whom have an interest in how and when a clip of an existing audio/visual work is used.

Creation of audio/visual works directly for multimedia productions will eventually make these obstacles less important. However, there will always be some desire on the part of software developers to use existing content in new products. In an effort to facilitate use of these properties, several developers have relied heavily upon the "fair use" exception under the copyright laws, arguing that their use is so incidental that no permission is required. Others have called for a compulsory license to use film and television clips in software products, and for the creation of a central database from which such clips can be extracted by developers.

Not surprisingly, chief among the proponents of compulsory licensing and database schemes are companies that have developed the technology to create and administer the necessary massive accounting and database systems. Underlying these arguments and proposals is an assumption—largely unquestioned—that reducing the cost of and the obstacles to using existing content is a good thing. Substantial changes to the existing rules of content licensing are neither necessary nor desirable, however; the existing rules, cumbersome and frustrating as they are, work exactly as intended and should be preserved in the multimedia area.

## THE TRADITION OF LICENSING

To appreciate the current content licensing process, it is helpful to understand the place clip licensing holds in the traditional entertainment community. For most copyright holders, licensing of portions of existing films and television programs is an incremental revenue source that is often more trouble than it is worth.

Although a film studio may hold exclusive distribution rights or even the copyright to a property, it is not the only party that needs to consent to use of a clip in a new and different medium. Other parties may have an ownership interest in the copyright and a contractual right to consent to clip licenses. Principal talent appearing in the desired

---

clip, as well as guild and union talent appearing or involved in the clip, also have an interest in how their work is used. If the clip includes music, the publisher, composer, recording artist and musicians also need to be considered.

Responding to clip license requests is time-consuming and distracting for the licensor. The flow of requests is constant, each prospective licensee needs an immediate answer, and no one wants the exact same clip. Even the largest copyright holders—the film and television studios—have neither the time nor the resources to identify all of the creative elements whose permission or approval may be required in each requested clip. The fees a licensor can charge for this ancillary use of its property do not justify either extensive research into each clip or giving the licensee representations, warranties and indemnities. The only commercially reasonable course for a licensor is to make a determination of whether it approves of the prospective use and, if so, document its permission and provide a copy of the clip. The licensee is therefore left to identify for itself what other approvals are necessary and to secure those permissions.

The need to obtain permission for uses other than as part of the original work derives from a variety of sources. Copyright law grants the owner of a creative work the right to determine how and when that work will be reproduced and distributed to the public, and what new works can be derived from the original. Not only does copyright law apply to the overall audio/visual work from which a clip is taken, but also to any creative works incorporated into the clip (e.g., a popular recording used as background music, or a famous work of art included in a scene) that may be protected by a separate copyright held by a different person.

For example, the producer of the film *Stand By Me* would have had to secure permission to include that song in the movie, and a new license would probably be required for any use of a clip from that movie that includes a portion of that song. If the film or television product were originally produced under guild jurisdiction (Screen Actors Guild, Writers Guild, Directors Guild, etc.), the guild members will have rights under collective bargaining agreements to approve new uses of clips incorporating their work. Star talent often have contractual approval rights in addition to those provided in guild agreements.

Even if an audio/visual work is not subject to guild or union rules, many states recognize statutory or common-law rights of publicity and rights of privacy, which require permission before using the name, voice or likeness of any living person or any deceased personality. A clip from the movie *Casablanca* in a soft drink commercial, for example, may therefore require permission from the estate of Humphrey Bogart in addition to a license from the owner of the copyright of the film.

If a clip is used without obtaining the requisite permissions from individuals and owners of protectable elements within the clip, the owner of the clip will be the party held liable in the first instance. For that reason, the clip license agreement authorizing the license to use the clip will specifically state that the licensee is responsible for obtaining all necessary permissions and must indemnify the licensor for any liability arising from the licensee's failure to obtain those permissions. Many clip licenses make the securing of all necessary licenses and approvals a condition precedent to use of the clip; if the licensee does not obtain the necessary rights, it must not only indemnify the licensor against any damages, but must also discontinue use of the clip.

The right to consent to use of a clip in a manner other than as part of the original production has been hard fought over years of guild negotiations, copyright suits, congressional action and individual negotiation. The current array of rights reflects a consensus that the creative talents who contribute to an audio/visual work have an interest in determining whether and when their work will be used in ways not originally contemplated, and should be compensated for such additional use. It reflects an understanding that a clip is more than a tangible piece of videotape or film—a piece of film or tape represents a collaboration between creative talents that has resulted in a new and unique asset. Moreover, it reflects an acknowledgment that that new and unique asset is the product of risk, which should be rewarded—financial risk by the production company or other financier that funded the production, and professional risk by talent that has chosen to contribute to the production.

* * *

### CHOOSING CONTENT OVER TECHNOLOGY

The argument for compulsory licensing and centralized databases might be more compelling to licensors if there were an overwhelming public demand for the new and unique uses of technology for creative purposes. However, to date the pace of technological development has far outpaced the desire for products using that technology. Telephone companies, cable companies, investment bankers and even content providers have pursued technology alliances with all the enthusiasm of a puppy chasing a speeding car. Unfortunately, most of the results of such alliances have been just about as productive.

One glaring failure of most of these ventures and alliances is that they have been focused primarily on the technology, rather than considering whether they are providing a product or service [that] consumers want to buy. Regardless of how "cool" the underlying technology may be, what drives success in the entertainment market is ultimately content: the characters and the story, and creation of compelling and engaging content is not an easy task.

This fundamental misunderstanding underlies much of the failure of ill-advised marriages of content and technology. The ability to find the right combination of script, actors, directing and other creative elements is a unique and special skill, and is valuable because it is so rare. Left to our own devices, most of us would create stories that are predictable, unimaginative and dull. That is one reason why interactive movies, for example, have thus far failed to catch fire with mass audiences.

I, for one, have little desire to see a movie where I, with all the imagination of a corporate lawyer, get to choose the ending or make plot decisions. In my sports fantasy movie, the ball never goes through Bill Buckner's legs and the Red Sox always win the World Series; in my interactive movie, *Forrest Gump* gets hit by a bus. And if I don't want to see a movie I would create, I certainly have no interest in sitting through a film whose plot is determined by the majority vote of a group of people whose only qualifications are that they had $7 and nothing better to do than sit in a dark theatre.

Creativity is something special, and as such deserves to be rewarded. A software developer desires to use particular existing film or video clips because they are unique, or convey a certain feeling or message, or have become popular among potential customers of the producer's software product.

It is fair and appropriate that the software producer should have to seek permission for such use, and pay a fee to the persons who created or control that work. Otherwise, the software producer will receive a "free ride" on someone else's creativity. The price of the software title will be artificially low, because it will not represent the cost of creating the content that comprises the product.

In addition, permitting use of clips from existing content without requiring approval of the original creators, in the multimedia area as much as any other, can result in uses that negatively impact the value of the original creation and the reputations of those associated with it. Moreover, requiring those who seek to use existing works to obtain permission and pay a negotiated fee arguably fosters creativity; if simply using existing content is not an easy option, more software developers will have incentives to create their own original audio/visual works rather than "borrow" from someone else.

* * *

---

# II. Problems in Licensing Multimedia

## Negotiating Multimedia Agreements: Issues Associated With Acquiring Multiple Rights From Multiple Parties*

John C. Yates
631 PLI/PAT. 935 (2001)

### I. INTRODUCTION

Multimedia transactions often present unique issues for negotiation. Because multimedia involves the merging of software technology with content from divergent sources, a single deal may require negotiating rights with persons representing the software, entertainment, publishing and art industries. Traditional methods of allocating rights in each industry are different. Thus, the technology attorney representing a client in a multimedia deal potentially is faced with a wider range of issues than normally presented in a single software transaction.

### II. TYPES OF MULTIMEDIA DEALS

#### A. Parties.

Multimedia negotiations generally implicate four parties: a content owner, a developer, a publisher and a distributor. One party may also play two or more roles. For example, the publisher may also be the distributor.

#### B. Transactions.

Multimedia transactions generally fall into three types:

*1. Specific Users.* The first involves the development of a multimedia product for a specific user contracting for the product's development—typically a business-to-business transaction.

*2. General Consumers.* The second primary form of multimedia transaction involves the development of a work for and distribution to the general consumer.

---

* Reproduced by permission of the author, copyright 2001.

*3. Internet Distribution.* The third type may fall within one of the previously described categories but adds the unique aspect of being distributed or used through the Internet.

For each transaction type, understanding the rights involved and negotiating the acquisition of such rights up front is critical. Rights negotiated later in a product's life are often more costly—both financially and to the success of the deal.

## III. DEVELOPMENT OF MULTIMEDIA WORKS FOR A SPECIFIC USER

### A. Introduction.

1. Business-to-business multimedia transactions usually involve a developer and a company (the "Company") contracting for the specific development of the work, often a training or marketing title. The parties should develop a plan with budget projections and a time line for completion of each deliverable to be created under the project.

2. The agreement between the parties should incorporate this plan, as well as set forth the specific development process and define each party's role. Moreover, the agreement should describe the components of the work and the parties' rights and obligations with respect to those components.

### B. The Development Process.

The agreement between the developer and the Company should act as a roadmap for the parties to follow during the development process. The following issues should be addressed:

- What resources will be included in the work?
- Who will provide the resources?
- If third party resources are required, who will bear the cost? Will the developer acquire the rights and sublicense or transfer such rights to the Company?
- What will be delivered to the Company for review?
- What will be the review process?
- Will the Company have approval over the deliverables? If so, what will be the standard for such approvals? What is the process if the Company does not approve a component submitted for review?
- What if the Company requests a design change? Will the developer be obligated to perform the change? Who will bear the cost? How will such change affect the development schedule?
- How will the developer be paid? Will payments be based upon each progressive deliverable approved?
- Can the agreement be terminated prior to the work being completed? If so, who will own the partially created work? Will the Company have the right to contract another party to finish the work?

### C. Ownership by the Company.

While the developer will want to keep all rights in any new property created for the product, the Company will likely be putting up a substantial sum of money and may demand owning all the work product, including any preexisting works incorporated into the final product.

\* \* \*

### D. Content and Other Resources Provided by the Company.

To rightfully use third-party works in the development process, the developer must obtain appropriate licenses. These rights should be obtained directly from the Company with respect to any materials provided by the Company.

*1. Content.*

- The developer should request a license for the right to use the materials provided by the Company for purposes of developing the work.
- The developer should also require the Company to warrant that any Company materials may be used by the developer without infringing any third party rights.

\* \* \*

*2. Warranties.* In light of the *MAI* decision and its progeny, if the developer will be using any computer or software resources of the Company, the developer should negotiate a warranty by the Company that its use of such resources will not infringe any third party rights.

\* \* \*

### E. Ownership by Developer.

The Software Engine. In developing multimedia products, developers usually place the software executable files in separate files from the audiovisual content and data. The programming elements (the "Engine") drive the multimedia product by "calling" the content from the separate files to create the outputs and screen displays. The Engine can be used to create numerous multimedia titles relatively inexpensively and quickly by merely using new content. Thus, retaining ownership to the Engine is highly valuable to the developer and should be negotiated where possible.

\* \* \*

### F. Release.

*1. From The Developer.* In the event the developer is an individual and includes his own voice or other characteristics in the work, the Company should negotiate a release for any claims by the developer associated with the Company's use of such characteristics.

*2. From Third Parties.* If the developer is using any characteristics of third parties (or is an entity using the characteristics of employees), the developer should be required to obtain similar releases from such parties for the benefit of the Company.

\* \* \*

### IV. DEVELOPMENT OF MULTIMEDIA WORKS FOR DISTRIBUTION TO GENERAL CONSUMERS

### A. Introduction.

1. When creating a multimedia work for distribution to the general public, the developer will likely use third-party material. The material may come from several different sources and include pre-existing works or original works developed specifically for the project.

2. Whatever the source, the developer must obtain sufficient rights to such material to allow for its intended use and distribution of the work.

## B. Acquisition of Rights to Pre-existing Works

Some of the most commonly used pre-existing works and the type of rights the developer must negotiate are as follows:

*1. Text.* Pre-existing literary works and other forms of text are likely to be protected by copyright. Thus, the developer will need to acquire the right to use such works from the copyright owner.

In negotiating such rights, the developer must be careful that the person it is negotiating with actually owns the rights to be granted. For example, a publisher of a book may appear to be the copyright owner of the text therein. However, the book publishers may be the copyright holder of the book as a whole only, whereas the individual components such as the text and pictures are separately copyrighted by other parties. The publisher in this case is likely to be a mere licensee of the text and not authorized to sublicense any rights to the developer.

[Section 201(c) of the Copyright Act gives owners of copyright in "collective works" a statutory privilege to publish individually copyrighted contributions in their collective words, as well as in versions and "later collective work[s] in the same series." This privilege, however, is narrowly construed, so it is usually better to have an explicit agreement on using such contributions. See *infra* Note on Collective Works.]

*2. Music.* Musical works have two elements to them, and each is separately protected by copyright. The first copyrightable element is the songwriter's underlying composed music (and lyrics), while the other element is the actual sound recording made of that musical composition by a recording artist.

a) Musical Compositions.

(1) Mechanical License. A recording artist must obtain a mechanical license to use a songwriter's musical composition on a record.

Compulsory Mechanical Licenses. [Section 115 of t]he Copyright Act provides for a compulsory mechanical license where the copyright owner has already authorized one recording of the work and [that recording has been publicly distributed in the United States.] A compulsory mechanical license permit the licensee to record, reproduce and distribute the work in a phonorecord. Distribution, however, must be limited to the public for private use. Moreover, a compulsory license does not permit reproduction of the music with still images or motion pictures.

Contractual Licenses. Although the Copyright Act provides for a compulsory mechanical license, because of stringent payment and accounting procedures mandated by the Act, it is simpler to obtain the license through the music publisher or its agent, [usually] the Harry Fox Agency.

(2) Synchronization License. Developers will need one if they will use the music in connection with visual images. A synchronization license normally permits distribution in connection with public performance of the work. This type of license is appropriate for a developer intending to [perform or] display the work through [movies,] interactive television or another type of public vehicle. A synchronization license may be obtained through the Harry Fox Agency in some cases, and in others must be negotiated with the music publisher or author. The Copyright Act does not provide a compulsory synchronization license, so granting such rights are within the copyright owner's discretion. To distribute the multimedia work (containing

music synchronized with visual images) to the public for private use, the developer will need to obtain a type of synchronization license called a "videogram license."

(3) Performance Rights. If a work is going to be shown to audiences, the developer will also need to negotiate "public performance rights" [under section 106(4).] Songwriters usually permit performing arts societies like ASCAP, SESAC or BMI to license their public performance rights. Like a synchronization license, the songwriter has discretion whether to grant public performance rights of their underlying musical compositions.

b) Sound Recordings. If a particular recording of an underlying song is to be used by the developer, it is necessary to obtain a license to use that particular recording in addition to acquiring the rights to use the underlying song. [The reason is that the sound recording and the song—lyrics and music—are separate works with separate copyrights, which may belong to different owners. *See* 17 U.S.C. §§ 101 (Definition of "Sound recordings"), 114(a)-(c)]. A] sound recording copyright encompasses the creative input of the recording artist and includes both the performers' and the producers' creative contributions to the sound recording.

Note: if the recording is synchronized with audiovisuals, then the recording is a component of that overall work and not considered a "sound recording". [*See* 17 U.S.C. § 101.]

In addition to obtaining a sound recording license, the developer may have to negotiate use fees with the American Federation of Musicians (the "AF of M") if the recording includes performances by AF of M members. These fees are negotiated by the AF of M on a case by case basis.

*3. Databases.* Facts included in a database are not copyrightable. However, if the facts have been selected, coordinated and arranged in such a way as to be deemed "original", the database as a whole may be copyrightable and thus, the developer will need to acquire sufficient rights to use the information. [*See generally, Feist Publ'ns Inc. v. Rural Tel. Serv. Co.*, 499 U.S. 430 (1991).] In obtaining rights to databases, the developer should negotiate proper warranties with the licensor. Where the information is critical to the accuracy of the final work, the licensor should warrant the correctness of the information. If the data contains personal information on certain people, the licensor should warrant that the information is not libelous and does not violate any rights of privacy.

*4. Characters.*

a) Copyright Issues. Preexisting characters used in multimedia works may [be protected] in graphic form, as described in the text of a story or as represented in a performance. All such forms may be copyrighted. If the developer uses a copyrighted character without the permission of the copyright owner, he will infringe the copyright regardless of the context in which the character is used. Thus, negotiated rights to use pre-existing characters will likely be necessary.

b) Trademark and Dilution Issues. Characters (most often "graphic characters") may also be protected by trademark because of their association with certain goods or services. To avoid accusations of passing off the work as distributed by the character's trademark owner, the developer should negotiate the right to use the character with its appropriate owner.

*5. Photographs and Still Images.* Copyright protection in a photograph originally vests in the photographer. Thus, to use a photograph, regardless of its form, the developer must obtain licensing rights from the photographer or the photographer's assignee(s). If the photograph includes a person, the developer may also need to consider right of [publicity and] privacy issues.

*6. Film Clips.* The multimedia developer must acquire the right to use the entire clip as a whole, usually from the producer of the footage. It also may have to secure rights to individual components within the clip, such as the musical compositions, an underlying script or pre-existing works of art. Additionally, if people appear in the clip, the developer will need to obtain clearances from such persons and consider rights of publicity and rights of privacy.

a) News Clips. News organizations will generally negotiate a license to their footage based upon a per second basis. However, they do not have the right to authorize the developer's use of [footage of] the persons appearing in the licensed news footage. These rights must be negotiated with such individuals [because the news organization's release normally does not cover the individual's right of publicity, and the fair-use exception for news reporting may not cover further commercial use of the clip, especially if that use is not solely for news reporting purposes.] News commentators are generally members of unions [e.g. the Screen Actors Guild ("SAG") or the American Federation of Television and Radio Artists ("AFTRA")] which require that such persons appearing in news footage consent to the distribution of the footage and/or receive a negotiated payment from the licensee.

b) Film and Television Clips. The production company financing a film or program will usually own the copyright to the film or program and be authorized to license extracted footage. These licenses are usually based on a per-cut and per-minute basis, and the rates will vary depending upon the term and territory for the license. The copyright license granted by the [production] company will [probably not] include other clearances and consents which may be required from the performers appearing in the footage.

(1) Feature Film: SAG (Screen Actors Guild). If the clip is from a feature film (such as a movie or television drama), television situation comedy or primetime drama, the developer will have to negotiate payments to all actors appearing in the clip who are members of SAG. As of January 1, 1996, the minimum fee paid to each such actor is $522.00 plus 13.3 percent for contribution to SAG's pension and welfare fund.

(2) Television Taping: AFTRA (American Federation of Television and Radio Artists). If the clip is from a television variety show, soap opera or similar taped program, the developer will have to negotiate payments with each AFTRA member appearing in the clip. Like SAG, AFTRA mandates minimum payments, however, they are variable depending upon the length of the program from which the clip is extracted.

(3) Minimum Fees. The fees set by the unions are minimum fees which must be paid to the actors. Where the actor is well known the fees will be considerably higher.

(4) Negotiating with Actors. When negotiating payments with actors, the developer will likely deal with the actor's agent. The unions prevent the agents from taking a commission out of the actors' payments received through licensing film clips, and thus the agent has little incentive to ne-

gotiate a deal. One author suggests that the developer offer an additional fee to the agent as inducement.

(5) Writers and Directors: WGA and DGA. The developer may have to negotiate rights to any film or television clip with the Directors Guild of America ("DGA") and the Writers Guild of America ("WGA"). These unions negotiate and receive payment on behalf of their members. The DGA rates are based upon the length of the clip and whether it derives from television or a feature film. The WGA charges a flat two percent of the license fees received by the developer from entities exploiting the multimedia work incorporating the writer's work.

7. *Scope of License.* The developer should consider obtaining rights to use the content for other purposes and in other forms of media, both known and unknown. However,[the desire to cover all contingencies] must be balanced with the expense involved and the risk of paying for unnecessary rights. If the developer believes it may require additional rights in the future, the developer may want to negotiate an option for such rights to be exercised within a specified period. Issues that the developer should consider in negotiating the scope of the license to third-party content received are as follows:

- What is the content? The content licensed should be defined in the agreement with particularity. Where possible, copies of the content should be attached to the agreement.
- How much of the content will be used? Does the developer need rights to the whole work, or just portions?

The [license] must address the developer's rights of use with particularity. Since technology is changing at such a rapid speed, it is important to the developer that the licensing language specifically state that the developer's scope of license includes the right to exploit the work by any means or methods now or hereafter [developed.] In the event such language is absent, the developer may be prevented from using the content in a type of medium invented after the execution of the agreement. This [developer should consider demanding] the following rights:

- to use the content for any and all purposes
- to use the content in any and all embodiments or formats to incorporate and use the content in, and in connection with, any and all technologies, now known or hereafter [developed]
- to reproduce, adapt, digitize, modify, alter, enhance, translate or otherwise exploit the content to publicly perform and display, exhibit, transfer, transmit, broadcast or otherwise distribute the content, by any and all means or as a part of any and all embodiments or formats, now known or hereafter to [developed]

The third-party content owner will likely wish to limit the developer's rights to a specific project, thereby requiring that the developer pay additional licensing fees to further exploit the content. The content owner should also propose a reservation-of-rights clause which clarifies that any rights not specifically granted to the developer will be retained by the content owner. Without such a provision, however, general contract law will likely provide that the content owner retains such rights. If the content owner is concerned about the integrity of his content, the content owner may negotiate the right to approve the final work incorporating his content.

Will the developer need the content for purposes other than incorporation in the multimedia work? For example, will the developer want to use the content in marketing, advertising or packaging materials? If so, such rights should be included in the scope of the license. If the content being licensed is a story or similar type of work, the developer may desire negotiating "sequel" rights.

Will the developer's rights be exclusive or nonexclusive? If the developer's rights are exclusive, the content owner may want [to obligate] the developer to use the content and exploit the final product. Will the developer be modifying the work? If the work is a "work of visual art," the developer should negotiate a waiver by the owner of his moral rights.

The developer will want to investigate whether the content owner has granted any prior licenses to the content. Specifically, the developer will want to ensure that any prior licenses do not conflict with the rights desired by the developer. Depending upon the scope of the license granted to the developer, the developer will want to include in its agreement with the content owner some or all of the following representations and warranties: [that] the content owner has not licensed, assigned, transferred, encumbered or conveyed his right, title or interest in the content to any other third party; [that] the content owner has all right, title and interest to the content; and [that] the content owner has full right, power and authority to enter into the license, and grant all of the rights, title and interest granted therein.

* * *

# Notes & Questions

The use of motion picture footage subject to copyright or contractual protection raises a host of complicated [issues] that must be considered when drafting a license agreement for multimedia works. In addition to obtaining a license from the copyright holder to the final movie, the following must be taken into consideration:

1. *Unions or Other Representative Groups.* Motion picture footage is sometimes subject to collective bargaining agreements between the unions and the movie studios. The person drafting a license to use motion picture footage must verify whether reuse of such footage requires a royalty payment to a union or representative group.

2. *Merchandising Payments.* More and more often, actors require a percentage of the proceeds generated by the sale of three dimensional dolls or other toys based on the character they portray in the motion picture. The person drafting a merchandising license must verify whether the contracts with the actors require such payment. Use of movie footage in a multimedia setting may trigger a claim that such use is, in fact, a merchandising use even though it may not be in three-dimensional form.

3. *Geographic Locations.* Use of some famous locations in the original motion picture may have been subject to negotiation by the producers of the original footage. Reuse of such scenes may or may not be the subject of the original agreement. If it is, the reuse may be subject to the terms and conditions of that prior agreement; if not, a new release may have to be negotiated.

4. *Product Placement.* Products are placed in motion pictures in a rather intentional manner. Doing so may require a release from the owner of the trademark as it may imply some sort of sponsorship of the movie. Therefore, reuse of such footage also may require the release and/or payment of royalties to the trademark owner.

5. *Recycling.* Reusing stock footage where the actors are not recognizable and the scenes or products included are not recognizable will usually not require any type of special license or release except for one by the copyright holder to the footage itself.

6. *Out-takes.* Using out-takes (footage shot but edited out of the final film for various reasons) in multimedia requires the same releases from the Union, actors, etc. as using footage that is included in the final form of the movie. The royalty rate due may be somewhat lower, or out-takes may specifically be excluded from some contracts with the original producer; but that should not be taken for granted and must be verified.

7. *Music.* Today, most motion pictures include an original sound track that raises separate licensing and merchandising issues. Any excerpted music from the original sound track requires a release and, most likely, a royalty payment to the composer of the original music.

The concern with music does not end there. In addition to obtaining a license from the composer or other copyright holder, one must obtain a license to synchronize (if necessary) the music in the multimedia work to different images than those in the original motion picture. Although the Copyright Act does not give the performer of a "sound recording" an exclusive copyright in the performance, reuse of a musical performance in a multimedia work may trigger either the compulsory license provisions of Section 115 or a claim to a right of publicity by the performer. Therefore, to reuse music in a multimedia work, one must obtain releases from the owners of the copyrights to the footage, the musical composition, the performers regarding their right to publicity, and perhaps a compulsory license fee. *See* 17 U.S.C. Sec. 114.

Further releases also may be necessary.

8. *Derivative works and underlying works.* The copyright act defines a "derivative work" in part as "a work based upon one or more pre-existing works, such as a translation, musical arrangement, dramatization, fictionalization, motion picture version, sound recording, art reproduction...or any other form in which a work may be recast, transformed or adapted." 17 U.S.C. § 101 (definition of "derivative work"). The work on which a derivative work is based, or from which it is derived, is usually called the "underlying work," rather than the "original work," in order to avoid confusion with the requirement of originality for copyright protection.

Motion pictures and similar audiovisual productions are often classic derivative works, for they are usually based upon an underlying book, play, story, or song. The existence of such an underlying work may complicate the task of "clearing" use of a clip or excerpt from a film or other audiovisual work because the clip is covered by at least two copyrights. First, there is the copyright in the film or audiovisual work itself, from which the clip is taken. Second, there is the copyright in the underlying book, play, story or song on which the film or audiovisual work is based.

There may be more than one underlying work that requires consideration. For example, consider a film of a performance of an opera, in which the opera is based upon a (nonmusical) dramatic play derived from a novel. The play is a derivative work based upon the novel; the opera is a derivative work of *both* the play and the novel; and the film would be a derivative work of all three. *See G. Ricordi & Co. v. Paramount Pictures,*

*Inc.*, 189 F.2d 469 (2d Cir. 1951). As a result, a multimedia producer who wished to use a clip from the film would require permission from owners of copyright (if unexpired) in the film, opera, play, and novel—at least to the extent that the desired clip used original material from each. That is, the multimedia producer would require four consents, likely from four different copyright owners, to use one clip.

9. *Renewal and Termination Rights.* Renewal and termination rights can make "clearing" derivative works especially complicated. Renewal rights arise out of the two separate terms 28-year terms of copyright—the initial and renewal terms—that existed before the Copyright Act of 1976 came into effect on January 1, 1978. Termination rights for post-1977 works have similar purpose and effect. Both renewal and termination rights can give authors and their statutory successors a "new estate" in copyright, allowing them to abrogate grants of assignments and licenses and, if they wish, negotiate new ones with the same or different grantees.

Works copyrighted before 1978 may have *both* renewal rights and termination rights. Although renewal is now automatic, renewal rights still arise upon expiration of the first copyright term. *See* 17 U.S.C. § 304(a)(1), (2). The last renewal rights of this sort will arise on January 1, 2006 (1978 plus 28). If a grant of an assignment or license for such a work was made *before* 1978, then termination rights arise during a five-year "window" beginning 56 years after first publication of the work with copyright notice. *See* 17 U.S.C. § 304(c)(3). Many of these termination "windows" are already open; some have passed. If the grant was made *after* 1977, the five-year window opens 35 years after execution of the grant or (if the grant covers publication) on the later of 35 years after publication or 40 years after execution of the grant. *See* 17 U.S.C. § 203(a)(3). The first of these termination windows will open on January 1, 2013 (1978 plus 35).

For works created after 1977, the rules are simpler. There are no renewal rights because there is only a single term of copyright for post-1977 works. *See* 17 U.S.C. § 302. Termination is governed by the same rules as for post-1977 grants with respect to pre-1978 copyrights. That is, the five-year termination window opens 35 years after execution of the grant or (if the grant covers publication) on the later of 35 years after publication or 40 years after execution of the grant. *See* 17 U.S.C. § 203(a)(3).

There are two important statutory exceptions to termination rights. First, they do not apply to works made for hire. *See* 17 U.S.C. §§ 203(a) (preamble), 304(c) (preamble). This is one of the things that makes a work's status as made for hire *vel non* so important. A copyright may be assigned or transferred to the employer or hiring party whether or not it is statutorily a work made for hire. Works that are not made for hire, however, are always subject to the termination rights of their authors and their authors' families. Second, termination rights to do apply to grants of assignments and licenses made by will. *See* 17 U.S.C. §§ 203(a) (preamble), 304(c) (preamble). This is one reason among many why estate planners for creative people should be familiar with the laws governing copyright, as well as their interaction with state probate and inheritance laws and federal estate and income tax laws.

The purpose of the statutory provisions for renewal and termination of copyright is the same: to protect starving authors and artists, who sell their work for low prices when they are unknown, by allowing them to participate in later appreciation in their work's value with time. The method is also the same: by renewing the copyright and thereby gaining a "new estate," or by terminating existing grants, authors, artists and their families can renegotiate contracts for better remuneration. *See generally, Stewart v. Abend*, 495 U.S. 207, 217–20, 224–30 (1990).

Renewal and termination provisions, however, can cause great trouble and hardship for assignees and licensees. For example, renewal rights in works underlying a movie can stop commercial exploitation of the movie dead in its tracks. *See id.*, at 229–30. An exception in the 1976 Act prevents *termination* from stopping the exploitation of *pre-termination* derivative works such as movies, see 17 U.S.C. § 203(b)(1), but the exception does not apply to renewals of copyright in pre-1978 works. *See Stuart, supra*, at 222–27.

10. *"Moral Rights."* The "moral rights" of authors and artists are the rights to prevent distortion or mutilation of their works and mis-attribution of authorship. These rights comes from Europe, particularly France, from which the idea of *"droit morale"* spread, through the Berne Convention, to most of the developed world. Article 6*bis*(1) of the Berne Convention, to which the United States is a party, reads as follows:

> Independently of the author's economic rights, and even after the transfer of the said rights, the author shall have the right to claim authorship of the work and to object to any distortion, mutilation or other modification of, or other derogatory action in relation to, the said work, which would be prejudicial to his honor or reputation.

Moral rights, for example, prohibited a buyer from disassembling a famous three-dimensional "mobile" of Picasso's, showing birds in flight, and selling each bird separately.

Despite its accession to the Berne Convention, the United States has always been suspicious of moral rights. The reason is not that Americans fail to respect the genius and honor of authors and artists. Rather, American copyright experts fear the effect of the existence and assertion of moral rights on the free exercise of, and commerce in, the *economic* rights in copyright. Imagine how much more confusing licensing transactions in copyrighted computer programs might be if every computer programmer who ever worked, for example, for Microsoft had the right to claim that recent modifications or updates had "distorted" or "mutilated" his or her original computer program!

The United States is not alone in these concerns. Russia's copyright statute, for example, although generally recognizing moral rights, explicitly excludes computer programs and databases from them.

The United States, however, has for over a century lead worldwide resistance to the expansion of moral rights, primarily on grounds of economic certainty and efficiency. Even for two years after acceding to the Berne Convention, the United States took the position that its own common-law rules of contract and unfair competition, as codified federally in Section 43(a) of the Lanham Act, provided sufficient protection of authors' moral rights that no changes in its copyright law were necessary. Finally, under pressure from other Berne Convention members, particularly in the European Union, the United States adopted the first explicit recognition of moral rights in its own copyright law with the Visual Artists Rights Act of 1990. *See* 17 U.S.C. § 101 (definition of "work of visual art"); 17 U.S.C. § 106A (rights of attribution and integrity for authors of works of visual art).

This statute, called "VARA," has extremely limited scope. It applies only to "still" images or sculptures, i.e., paintings, drawings, prints, photographs and sculptures, that are one of a kind or part of a limited edition of 200 copies or fewer. *See* 17 U.S.C. § 101 (definition of "work of visual art," clauses (1) and (2)). Its key definition explicitly excludes, *inter alia*, any "motion picture of other audiovisual work" and any "book, magazine, newspaper, periodical, data base, electronic information service, electronic publication, or similar publication." *Id.* (exception at end of definition). As these limitations show, the statute was drafted explicitly to preclude moral rights from interfering with the transfer and exploitation of economic rights (under copyright) in audio-visual, multimedia, and computerized works.

Because moral rights in the United States are so limited, they generally do not require special attention with respect to multimedia productions under United States law, unless a protected work of visual art is featured or shown (other than in passing) in the multimedia production. The difficulty with this conclusion, however, is that the United States is not an island. The market for multimedia productions today is generally a global market, especially if the Internet is used as a medium for distribution. Since moral rights are generally much stronger elsewhere than in the United States, a producer or licensee of multimedia productions for worldwide distribution would be unwise to ignore them, especially in Europe.

Consideration of moral rights abroad may require four steps. First, since moral rights vary considerably among nations, a producer or licensee must determine which nations and regions are its principal geographic markets. Second, it must determine which jurisdictions' laws, if any, are likely to cause difficulties with respect to moral rights. Third, if an analysis of relevant laws suggests the necessity, it must locate the individual authors and artists whose moral rights are in question and determine whether they have sufficient "honor and reputation" to enjoy moral rights. Not every author or artists enjoys the necessary level of public recognition. Finally, the producer or licensee must secure the consent of protected authors and artists for what it wishes to do. Thus, in jurisdictions like France with strong moral rights, these non-economic rights may require an entirely separate layer of "clearance" for licensing.

11. *Four "Clearance" Tasks.* The moral of this long and rather the complex story is that producers and licensees of multimedia works must undertake five research tasks, particularly for works expected to have a long commercial lifetime. First, for each derivative work that they use, they must discover on what, if any, underlying works the derivative work is based. Second, they must identify the owners of copyright not only in the derivative works that they use, but also in the underlying works on which those derivative works are based. Third, they must seek a license for their activities from the owner of copyright in the derivative work and from the owner of copyright in each underlying work from which original material is included in the portion of the derivative work that they wish to use.

Fourth, those wishing to "clear" the derivative work must consider the dates of creation and publication of all relevant works, as well as the dates on which the underlying-work owners licensed the creation of each relevant derivative work, and decide whether renewal or termination rights are sufficiently imminent or valuable to consider. If so, they then must locate the owners of the renewal or termination rights and consider how to deal with them. An author could pre-assign his or her renewal right, but the pre-assignment is valid only if the author lives to see the renewal. *See Stuart, supra,* at 220–21. Termination rights, however, cannot generally be pre-assigned. *See* 17 U.S.C. §203(b)(4). As a result, a firm wishing to "clear" rights in a work based upon a grant that is nearing termination may wish to postpone substantial investment in the new work until the termination window opens and negotiate with the owners of the termination interests, usually the author's or artist's family.

Finally, producers of multimedia works must consider the moral rights of authors and artists, as discussed above. If a multimedia work includes "still" images or sculpture protected by VARA, the producer must consider the moral rights of their authors or artists. If the multimedia work is to be distributed abroad, or if it contains foreign material (such as similar images or even "clips" of audiovisual works), then producers must consider the impact of foreign moral rights law and, where necessary, secure consent of domestic or foreign authors or artists. Performing all these tasks with sufficient diligence to avoid substantial liability—let alone to avoid lawsuits—can be a demanding, painstaking, and tedious task.

\* \* \*

# III. Licensing "Publicity" in Multimedia Settings

## Licensing Celebrity Rights of Publicity in Multimedia Products*

Jeffrey P. Weingart
3 NO. 1 MULTIMEDIA STRATEGIST 1 (1996)

\* \* \*

The proliferation of entertainment-related interactive multimedia products has created new challenges in the area of celebrity rights licensing. As the use of a celebrity's name or image may add value to an interactive product, the right to use a celebrity's persona has become a valuable commodity in the interactive marketplace.

The right of publicity protects the celebrity's right to control this valuable commodity. Obtaining consent to use a celebrity's likeness in a new media application is a matter of negotiation. A carefully drafted license will protect the publicity rights of a celebrity and also protect a developer against claims of infringement. Existing licenses and consents negotiated during pre-CD-ROM and pre-Internet days often do not contain language sufficient to convey licenses to use elements of celebrity personas on such new media. An understanding of strategies and techniques for negotiating publicity rights licenses, including how to secure consents for use of a name or likeness, can be crucial for the product development process.

\* \* \*

### Strategies for Negotiating Right of Publicity Licenses

Whoever wishes to use one or more elements of a person's persona in connection with promoting a product or service may do so by first obtaining that person's consent. In some cases, a person whose name, likeness or voice appears in content may have given consent for the commercial use of these features in certain contexts. For instance, in their employment contracts, professional athletes often give their consent for the league in which they play to broadcast their pictures and use their names and related information for promotional purposes.

The comments to section 46 of the Restatement of Law 3d Unfair Competition provide that "[c]onsent can be communicated through a formal agreement such as a license or assignment. In the absence of an applicable statute requiring consent in writing, consent can also be implied from conduct or inaction reasonably interpreted as manifesting consent."

---

* Reprinted with permission of the publisher, copyright 1996.

A person's ability to license or transfer the commercial value of one's identity is rooted in the case law that has treated the right of publicity as a property right. It is also generally agreed that the right of publicity is in the nature of an intellectual property right. The Restatement provides that the right of publicity may be assigned or licensed. The assignability of rights of publicity are distinguished from rights of privacy, which courts continue to label as personal, and therefore non-assignable.

Moreover, the Restatement provides and courts have held that the right to grant the exclusive privilege of publishing one's picture, for instance, may validly be made "in gross," i.e., "without an accompanying transfer of a business or of anything else." Significantly, as noted in the Restatement, the right of publicity, as distinct from rights in a trademark, "is not dependent upon a public association of the identity with a particular source of goods or services, and publicity rights may thus be assigned in gross without the transfer of any accompanying business or goodwill."

In contrast to an assignment by which an assignor can transfer to a third-party ownership "in gross" of the right to commercially exploit elements of one's persona, a license generally grants to a licensee limited rights to make use of certain components of one's persona for specific purposes [and in specific] contexts and territories over a defined period of time. Thus, in many instances, it would be preferable for an entity such as a publisher to receive an assignment of a right to commercially exploit a celebrity's likeness rather than a license to do so.

The reality, however, is that the economics of an assignment are often not attractive to either side in a negotiation. Even in situations in which famous individuals have apparently consented to the commercial use of their likenesses in some contexts, it may be that such consent was limited.

Note: A licensee of the right to commercially exploit someone's likeness should always insist on obtaining a release and waiver that releases the licensee from claims such as infringement of rights of publicity that the licensor could have brought against the licensee but for the license.

### Securing Rights From Celebrities

Securing rights of publicity from celebrities can often be difficult. Initially, most celebrities are represented solely through agents. This alone can make a negotiation more time-consuming and costly than it otherwise might have been. Second, celebrities tend to be busy people. Accordingly, their agents often seek to build flexibility into their schedules, perhaps at the expense of potential licensees. Accommodating a celebrity's schedule can create obstacles to an orderly product development or endorsement schedule that requires recording or filming time on behalf of the celebrity.

At the same time, a celebrity will seek to guarantee as much income from a given license/product endorsement as possible. The result is often a license agreement that holds the celebrity to few actual time or schedule commitments, but which obligates the licensee to pay the celebrity fees sooner rather than later and according to a strict schedule. A licensing agreement could contain clauses seeking to hold the celebrity to a reasonable schedule with respect to content delivery and public appearances.

Payment terms in celebrity licenses can also become a challenging issue. Celebrities who license all or portions of their personas for commercial purposes often seek guaranteed payments, regardless of how products associated with their likenesses fare in the marketplace.

Note: It is important to be clear in a celebrity licensing agreement as to whether the licensee has an obligation to exploit the licensed likeness. For instance, if a licensee elects to drop a product line, will it still be required to make guaranteed payments to the celebrity? And if the agreement includes a stream of royalty payments to the celebrity, does the licensee have an implied or express obligation to make a good-faith attempt to sell the subject goods?

In contrast, licensees would prefer to tie payments to the success of a product line being endorsed by the celebrity. In many cases, a combination of annual, guaranteed payments applied against royalties, in conjunction with a deferred royalty stream tied to percentages of net revenue actually received by the licensee, may be appropriate. Such an arrangement has the effect of lowering a licensee's initial expenditure while at the same time providing financial incentive to the celebrity to do everything he or she can to ensure that the product is successful in the marketplace.

Other issues fall into the personal rather than the legal category. For example, standard licensee-oriented celebrity agreements often contain language permitting a licensee to terminate the agreement upon the occurrence of an event that decreases the commercial value of the celebrity's likeness, such as: the celebrity's death or disability (inability of the celebrity to perform his duties and obligations for licensee); the celebrity's refusal to follow the directions of the licensee in connection with providing content; the celebrity's arrest, indictment or conviction for the commission of a crime; or any other conduct, public or private, involving moral turpitude or which has or may reasonably be expected to have an adverse effect on the licensee's business, reputation or interests.

While a celebrity may be sensitive to seeing provisions governing conduct in his or her license agreement, the need for such a provision from the licensee's viewpoint has been confirmed repeatedly. In an era when scandals involving celebrities seem to erupt in the press almost daily, licensees must protect themselves by being able to exit a celebrity relationship. The need for such a termination provision is especially acute when a celebrity has sought and received guaranteed minimum payments over the term of the agreement. Under such circumstances, a licensee may be locked into making guaranteed payments to a celebrity who has, for instance, run afoul of the law. By applying the strategies and techniques for negotiating publicity rights licenses discussed in this article, the attorney will be equipped to meet the contractual challenges in the development of new multimedia products.

* * *

# IV. Title Searches and Licenses

## Searching for the Right Stuff*

Fran Smallson
LEGAL TIMES, May 15, 1995, at 55

The growth of multimedia, touted as the single most promising technological innovation in decades for fields as varied as entertainment, health care, and the automotive

---

* Reprinted with permission from the publisher, copyright 1995.

industry, has one major obstacle: the maze surrounding obtaining rights to use content supplied by others. The most difficult questions in that maze are not just how to license the content once it has been identified, but rather which content needs to be licensed and where one will find the potential licensor.

The closest analogy to this process is a title search when purchasing real property. Unlike the real property search, however, when a client chooses to license someone else's pre-existing works rather than create original content, the owners of the pre-existing works are often numerous, difficult to identify and hard to locate.

* * *

Acquiring a license to use a film clip presents the developer with perhaps the most complicated licensing challenge, as it involves the most numerous set of potential licensors....

Although a motion picture may be protected as a single "work," it is often composed of many other protected works. The following categories are potential rights that the developer may need to acquire separately:

- The film clip itself.
- The screenplay and any literary rights upon which it is based, such as a novel. (The rights to the characters and title may need to be acquire separately).
- Pre-existing works included in the motion picture, such as: visual works of art (statues, paintings, photographs, etc.), architecture, and portions of other motion pictures or videos that may be contained within the film clip.
- Works created for use in the motion picture such as: special effects (including sound), animation (including drawings, script and voices), and choreography.
- Music rights (including composition, lyrics and performances).
- Actors' images and voices.

These rights fall into two basic categories: "intrinsic" and "extrinsic." Generally, intrinsic rights include the script and any works created by motion picture studio employees for use in the film. These rights are usually considered the property of the studio and thus are most likely included in a license granted by the studio to use the clip.

Extrinsic rights are those retained by other parties, such as performers, musicians or composers, and must be licensed separately. Generally, pre-existing works fall within this category and include, among others, music rights and any literary work upon which the screenplay is based.

Although these right-holders may have licensed their work for use in the film, the [film producer] may not have the authority to allow others to use the works in a new multimedia production. For this reason it is important to check, whenever possible, the agreements surrounding the creation of the motion picture, including collective bargaining agreements with various unions, and to obtain warranties that the licensor of the motion picture clip actually has the authority to grant the relevant related rights.

## COPYRIGHT SEARCHES

To determine whether a work and its related rights are protected by a registered copyright you may wish to consider a copyright search through United States Copyright Office records. The Copyright Office charges $20 for each hour or fraction of an hour searched. A copyright (and trademark) search may be performed online using DIALOG. Such a copyright search, however, will only reveal copyrights registered in the United States, and even if works are not registered they may still be protected by copyright law.

Other leads for locating right-holders include film archives, such as those at the University of California at Los Angeles and University of Southern California. At UCLA, searches may be performed online to locate information on the films archived there. In addition, the Library of Congress, the American Film Institute and the Academy of Motion Picture Arts and Sciences are useful resources in tracking ownership of motion picture-related rights.

In addition, various online services are beginning to address, in part, the needs associated with multimedia licensing. One such service is being developed by the USC Entertainment Technology Center—ETC—which is sponsored by a mix of high-technology and entertainment companies including Apple Computer, Viacom, Pacific Bell and Warner Brothers. The ETC has developed HollyNet, which is an online marketplace for film producers to locate everything needed to make a film, including the location of actors, stock footage and music.

If the motion picture to be used is based upon a pre-existing work such as a novel, the multimedia developer must generally obtain permission to use that work. Since the novel will most likely be protected under copyright law, a U.S. Copyright Office search as described above should be considered. Contacting the publisher of the novel is also a good way to begin negotiations to acquire the necessary rights.

Although the script is usually considered an intrinsic part of a motion picture and the rights to use it often accompany the rights to use the motion picture, the screenwriter may have retained rights under what is known as the "separation of rights." This includes such rights as publication, sequel and merchandising rights. If the writer must be located, one option is to contact the Writers Guild of America.

The characters in a motion picture may be based upon an underlying literary work and protected by copyright. Titles, although not protectable by copyright, may be registered with the Motion Picture Association (which will only perform searches for their members). In addition to risking copyright infringement for the unauthorized use of characters, use of a well-known title or character without permission may result in liability for unfair competition or a violation of a person's right of publicity. Thompson & Thompson, a database search service, will perform character and title searches to assist in determining whether the use might potentially infringe on others' rights.

Privacy and rights of publicity are other issues of concern when using characters since use of a character may infringe on a right to privacy or publicity if the character is similar to or actually based upon an existing person. The right to prevent others from commercially exploiting [celebrities'] performances and persona is generally known as the right of publicity. A performer, and any other individual for that matter, has a protectable identity that may be represented by his or her name, nickname, picture, voice, physical attributes or performing style; individually or together they form a "persona."

The right of publicity is protected by many states and is also protected by the agreements between the performers' unions and most motion picture studios. Unless a performer has specifically assigned the rights to use his or her image, persona and voice to the studio for use in other productions, the multimedia developer must obtain permission from that performer to avoid potential liability for defamation, violation of the performer's right to privacy or publicity and possibly unfair competition. This rule also applies to the use of famous stunts performed by recognizable stuntpersons.

Even if a film is within the public domain, the developer may still be required to obtain clearance from the performers. The performers' rights are distinct from any copyright in the film itself and may survive the actor and will be passed along to the performer's heirs even after the copyright expires.

Most actors will be identified in the film credits. However, there may be smaller, non-speaking parts not contained in the credits but that may still require clearance. In such cases, the performers may sometimes be identified by referring to the American Film Institute's catalog of films, through the directories of the Academy of Motion Pictures Arts and Sciences or by using HollyNet as described above. Once the performer has been identified, he or she may be located through the organizations mentioned above or through the appropriate union (the Screen Actors Guild or the American Federation of Television and Radio Artists). Generally, when obtaining rights from union performers, the developers may also be required to compensate the unions to which the performer belongs.

## OTHER WORKS OF ART

If the desired clip contains pre-existing works of art, such as a painting or statue, a separate release may be required. Generally, the test is whether or not the art is background. Simply put, if the piece of art is one of the main focal points in the scene, it is not considered background and permission of the owner is necessary to use it. If it is barely noticeable and not mentioned, then it can most likely be re-used without any special permission. When in doubt, however, it is best to obtain a clearance or remove the artwork from the clip, if possible.

An animation clip included in a film clip has many protectable components, including the script, voice-overs and characters. In addition to copyright, animated characters may be protected by trademark law. The Screen Cartoonist Union may help you locate artists involved in the actual screen production. If the animation is based upon a pre-existing comic strip, that material must be considered also. To determine ownership of the previously published work, you may also contact the publisher or the Graphic Artists Guild.

## MUSIC LICENSES

Copyright protection extends to two separate aspects of music: (1) the musical composition, which also may be divisible into two aspects, the music itself and the lyrics; and (2) the embodiment of the music, that is, the sound recording. Licenses may need to be obtained for each aspect. The appropriate license will depend on how the multimedia product will incorporate the music. There are seven distinct types of music licenses:

- Synchronization (when musical compositions are used in "timed-relation" with audiovisual works).
- Mechanical (music without any synchronized or visual accompaniment).
- Public performance (performed to the public).
- Master recording (reproduction of a musical composition of a particular artist).
- Adaptation (when alterations or modifications are to be made to a particular work).
- New media (for distribution on new media including CD-ROM).
- Print licenses.

Although the music industry is slowly adapting to the various new uses for its products, the original licensing categories were not initially created with multimedia products in mind and do not necessarily cover the seemingly infinite possibilities created by multimedia. Since the intended use of licensed music may not fall squarely within any of these categories, it is important that rights, whatever the named category, be clearly set forth in the license agreement.

The distinction between whether your client wishes to license the music itself or the sound recording of the music is a very important issue in a licensing matter, particularly where music has fallen into the public domain. Although a work such as Beethoven's Symphony No. 9 is now within the public domain, the specific music recording of a given performance, say by the New York Philharmonic, may be copyrighted. Moreover, there may be several individual copyright-holders who have copyright interests in the sound recording. They might include the conductor, orchestra and choral group.

The process of locating copyright holders in a particular piece of music can be very complicated. The first step should naturally be to look at a copy of the work for such details as a copyright notice, when and where the work was published and the identity of the author and publisher. Unfortunately, this is not always the most reliable way to find copyright-holders, because music jackets may not properly identify all of the copyright-holders to a particular work, and they may not provide an address or other means to contact the record producer.

If the music is an audio recording and a synchronization license is needed for a multimedia production, the best place to begin is the Harry Fox Agency in New York or Copyright Management Inc. in Nashville. These companies license synchronization rights on behalf of the vast majority of music publishers. If these companies do not represent the copyright-holder, they may know who does. In addition, the Clearing House in Los Angeles also performs clearing services for music rights.

Another good source for locating copyright holders is performing-rights societies. You can call the "index" department of ASCAP (American Society of Composers, Authors & Publishers), BMI (Broadcast Music Inc.) or SESAC (formerly Society of European State Authors and Composers, now just SESAC), and ask for the names and telephone numbers of the music publishers who own the songs you want to use.

Public-performance licenses may also be obtained from these societies; however, they do not generally grant the other licenses that likely will be necessary for use with a multimedia product. With the growth of multimedia, practices are changing, and new departments are currently being developed at these societies to meet the emerging needs. Finally, other organizations such as TRF Music Libraries provide a more full range of music licensing that includes rights relating to multimedia productions.

## MUSIC VIDEOS

One aspect of music licensing that may need special attention is the area of rock or music videos. As with a film clip, it is important to obtain the full range of rights in addition to the video rights, such as performance rights of the musicians, actors and/or models, and the music rights discussed above. Unfortunately, there is no uniform means of obtaining such clearances.

In some cases, it is sufficient to negotiate with the band or its representatives (which may be the record company) to obtain all the music, visual and performance rights of the band members. In other instances, it may be necessary to obtain a release from each individual band member who performs in the video, as well as releases from the record company, unions, video producers and other performers.

Other less obvious areas include trademark releases. For instance, if the video or film clip contains trademarks of companies that may be promoting the concert or simply T-shirts worn by the band members that bear the logos of shoe companies, for instance, the developer may need to obtain releases from those companies as well.

Unfortunately, there is no standardized way to obtain the rights necessary to use most motion picture clips in a multimedia production. There are several means, however, to protect the developer in the process of locating and obtaining the required consent of each necessary right-holder.

When negotiating with a party who claims to have title to all rights in a clip, check other sources whenever possible and obtain a warranty of title and right to license and indemnification. A warranty or indemnity is only good if the licensor has sufficient financial resources to back up such assurances. Thus, the developer should also consider obtaining an errors-and-omissions insurance policy, requiring that a due-diligence search be conducted. This will help protect the developer in the event the developer somehow innocently infringes on someone else's rights.

Finally, be aware that just because the developer obtains the rights to use a work, the developer does not necessarily have the right to alter the work without specific permission to do so. The concept of "moral rights" allows the author of a work to maintain some control over its manipulation and may limit the multimedia producer's ability to change, modify or enhance the work, despite receiving permission to reproduce it in a multimedia work.

The legal concept of "moral rights" in copyrighted works is fairly new in the United States but exists with wide application in various foreign countries. Moral rights have now limited recognition in the United States for works of visual art, which includes, with limitations, paintings, drawings, prints, sculptures and still photographs. It does not include applied art, motion pictures or other audio-visual works, books, periodicals, data bases, electronic information services or publications. [*See* 17 U.S.C. §§ 101 (definition of "work of visual art"), 106A.]

The entertainment and software industries are slowly adjusting to licensing practices that will be more suitable for multimedia. It will be some time, however, before obtaining rights to many pre-existing works can be described as anything but arduous.

---

# Notes and Questions

1. *Copyright Ownership: Get it in Writing!* More often than most other works, multimedia productions involve the contributions of several or many creative people. Artists, writers, composers, musicians, film-makers, and animators may collaborate to produce them. Producers may, without collaboration, use pre-existing copyrighted works, such as clips, "samples," songs, or images. Whether or not there is collaboration, the use of the creative output of many people nearly always puts copyright ownership in doubt. One of the most common practical pitfalls in all of copyright law is failure to specify in writing who owns the copyright in the results.

When the creative output of two or more individuals ends up in a single work, copyright ownership may depend upon as many as four different copyright doctrines, as follows.

> a. *Derivative work.* If the producer modifies and transforms a pre-existing copyrighted work without collaboration, the multimedia production will likely be a derivative work. *See* 17 U.S.C. § 101 (definition of "derivative work"). The principal consequence of its characterization as a derivative work

is that the owner of copyright in the underlying work will, in the absence of agreement to the contrary, have the right to control exploitation of the multimedia production. *See* 17 U.S.C. § 106(1); *Stewart v. Abend*, 495 U.S. 207, 222–27 (1990); *G. Ricordi & Co. v. Paramount Pictures, Inc.*, 189 F.2d 469 (2d Cir. 1951). Even if a license or consent is granted to use the underlying work in the multimedia production, the scope of the license or permission may inhibit use, performance of distribution of the multimedia production. For this reason, thoughtfully drafted licenses to use underlying works are essential.

b. *Joint work*. The 1976 Act defines "joint work" as "work prepared by two or more authors with the intention that their contributions be merged into inseparable or interdependent parts of a unitary whole." Case law parses this definition into two key elements: (1) mutual contributions; and (2) mutual intent, which need not be contemporaneous.

A work is joint if two or more persons contribute to it and each, at some relevant time, intends his or her contribution to be merged into the whole. For example, a writer may supply lyrics to a song after the composer has created the melody, and the two need not even know each other, as long as both intend the combination. *See Edward B. Marks Music Corp. v. Jerry Vogel Music Co.*, 140 F.2d 266, 267 (2d Cir. 1944). Collaboration, in the sense of working together at the same place or time, is not required for a joint work. On the other hand, a change in one joint author's intent can make her latest modification of a series of admittedly joint works a derivative work of the previous joint work, owned exclusively by her. *See Weissmann v. Freeman, supra*, at 1223. In any event, the better view requires each joint owner's contribution to be copyrightable; it cannot consist of mere original uncopyrightable ideas and concepts or mere editorial suggestions that have *de minimis* content. *See Erickson v. Trinity Theatre, supra*, at 1069–71.

The legal consequences of joint ownership are often surprising even to the joint owners themselves. Joint ownership is co-ownership as *tenants in common*. *See* 17 U.S.C. § 201(a). Each joint owner has an independent, nonexclusive right to exploit the copyrighted work, subject to a duty to account for and share profits with the other joint owners. In the absence of agreement to the contrary, the split of profits is presumed to be equal, *regardless of the joint owners' relative creative contributions*. *See Erickson, supra*, at 1069–71. As a result of these rules, a minor contributor to a multimedia production may have an independent right to exploit the production commercially as well as an equal share of the profits from other owners' exploitation in the absence of a written agreement allocating ownership and/or joint-ownership shares.

c. *Work made for hire*. The "work made for hire" doctrine is perhaps the most important doctrine of copyright law governing copyright ownership. If a work is a "work made for hire," the employer or other hiring party for whom the work is made is deemed the author of the work and owns the copyright *ab initio*, without the need for a copyright assignment. *See* 17 U.S.C. § 201(b). Works made for hire, moreover, are excepted from the statutory termination rights of authors and their families. As a result, it is extremely important for hiring parties to be sure that works for whose creation they pay are indeed works made for hire under the statute. If they are not, those parties must obtain a copyright assignment from the people they hire if the wish to own copyright in the works they create.

There are two categories of works made for hire. The first covers works "prepared by an employee within the scope of his or her employment." 17 U.S.C. § 101 (definition of "work made for hire" ("Clause (1)"). In a seminal decision with which every student of copyright law should be familiar, the Supreme Court held that who is an "employee" under this definition, as distinguished from an independent contractor or "freelancer," depends upon the application of the federal common-law of agency, using a multifactor test outlined in the RE-STATEMENT (SECOND) OF AGENCY § 220(2) (1958). *See Community for Creative Non-Violence v. Reid*, 490 U.S. 730, 739–40, 751–52 (1989). As the Supreme Court defined it, the factors in this test are diverse and various and include:

> [T]he hiring party's right to control the manner and means by which the product is accomplished . . . the skill required; the source of the instrumentalities and tools; the location of the work; the duration of the relationship between the parties; whether the hiring party has the right to assign additional projects to the hired party; the extent of the hired party's discretion over when and how long to work; the method of payment; the hired party's role in hiring and paying assistants; whether the work is part of the regular business of the hiring party; whether the hiring party is in business; the provision of employee benefits; and the tax treatment of the hired party. . . . No one of these factors is determinative.

*Id.* at 751–52 (citations omitted). The large number of factors and the need to weigh and balance them to determine whether the hired party is an employee or independent contractor often makes this multifactor test uncertain in outcome.

The second category of works made for hire consists of those that fall within one or more of nine statutorily specified categories of works *and* for which there is a written agreement explicitly imposing the "work made for hire" categorization. *See* 17 U.S.C. § 101 (definition of "work made for hire" ("Clause (2)"). Although this clause is often inapplicable to other types of works, it can apply to multimedia works because the list of nine categories includes works used "as part of a motion picture or other audiovisual work." *Id.* Thus a contribution to a motion picture of other multimedia production is a classic example of a work that may be a work made for hire under Clause (2), *but only if there is a written agreement expressly saying so.*

This latter proviso again gives the use of written agreements paramount importance. If the type of agreement required by Clause (2) exists, a contribution to a multimedia production properly characterized as a "motion picture of other audiovisual work" will be a work made for hire. The multimedia producer will own its copyright from the outset, and the authors or artists who created it (and their families) will have no termination rights. Otherwise, the contribution may be a joint work, giving its author the rights to exploit it independently and to share equally in the production firm's profits; or it may be an underlying work, giving the production firm the Hobson's choice of eliminating it or having exploitation of the entire production controlled by the author of the contribution. Even if the production firm resolves the issues by requiring an assignment of copyright, the contribution, if not a "work made for hire," will be subject to termination rights.

d. *Contributions to collective works.* Another doctrine affects copyright ownership by controlling contributions to collective works. A "collective work" is "a work, such as a periodical issue, anthology, or encyclopedia, in which a number of contributions, constituting separate and independent works in themselves, are assembled into a collective whole." 17 U.S.C. § 101 (definition of "collective work"). As a species of compilation, a collective work must have some originality in its selection, arrangement, and coordination of the separate contributions in order to merit separate copyright protection. *See* 17 U.S.C. § 101 (definition of compilation). If it has, it enjoys a separate copyright that protects only the collective-work author's originality. *See* 17 U.S.C. §§ 103(b), 201(c).

The notion of such a separate copyright in a collective work is practically important for two reasons. First, the collective-work owner's copyright notice protects all the separate contribution copyrights. *See* 17 U.S.C. § 404. Since the United States' accession to the Berne Convention, however, this point is no longer so important, because copyright notice is now optional, and its omission can never forfeit copyright protection. *See* 17 U.S.C. §§ 401, 402. The second point is more important: the collective-work owner, even in the absence of an agreement or license, has a "privilege" to publish the individual copyrighted contributions to the collective work. *See* 17 U.S.C. § 201(c).

This privilege of a collective-work owner to publish individual contributions to the collective work is not limited to publication of the initial collective work alone. The statute gives the collective-work owner the privilege of "reproducing and distributing the contribution as part of that collective work, any revision of that collective work, and any later collective work in the same series." *Id*. The Supreme Court, however, has interpreted the words "as part of...a revision" in this privilege narrowly. *See N.Y. Times Co. v. Tasini*, 533 U.S. 483 (2001). Applying a "context" test, the Court concluded that stripping out graphics, formatting, captions and adjacent articles (underinclusive context) and dumping individual contributions into large databases with many new articles (overinclusive context) prevented electronic databases such as LEXIS from being classified as "revisions" of original collective works such as newspaper or magazine issues. *See id.*, at 499–504. As a result, the statutory privilege does not allow magazine and newspaper publishers to include or authorize the inclusion of separately copyrighted feature articles as individually retrievable entries in electronic databases. *See id.*, at 506.

These limitations may have only rare application to multimedia productions, since the statutory provisions governing "collective works" seem to focus primarily on print media. They do, however, re-emphasize the importance of making sure that written agreements provide permission of every use of copyrighted works that is currently contemplated and even reasonably foreseeable. Because their standard agreements had not licensed contributed feature articles for use in electronic databases, the *Tasini* decision required newspaper and magazine publishers to renegotiate contracts for pre-existing features and to revise their standard agreements to provide this right. Similar difficulties attend the use of pre-existing movies, songs and other works for distribution over the Internet, in multimedia productions or otherwise.

2. *Copyright Ownership and Licensing.* The four copyright-ownership doctrines addressed in Note 1 above come into play most prominently when a multimedia producer seeks to determine who has ownership of copyright in the resulting production. Ideally, the producer would like to make sure that it and it alone owns the copyright, at least if cost of doing so is not prohibitive. If the producer is careless and does not have neces-

sary written agreements with its contributors and collaborators, they may own the copyright jointly with the producer, or their contributions may be underlying works of which the production is derivative. In either case, the cost to the producer could be both unexpected and staggering.

To avoid this unfortunate result, producers should strive to maintain copyright ownership of all contributions to their productions, whether made in collaboration or otherwise. If the contributions are made by independent contractors or "freelancers," so that they are not works made for hire under 17 U.S.C. § 101 ("Clause (1)"), the producer should put in place written agreements that (i) invoke Clause (2) by expressly stating that the works are works made for hire, (ii) transfer and assign the copyright to the producer, and/or agree to transfer and assign it in the future, or (iii) do both. Assignment agreements are particularly important if the only basis for "work made for hire status" is Clause (1) because the multifactor test for "employees" may have an uncertain outcome. Even if Clause (2) seems to apply, "backup" assignments may be helpful in case someone challenges the contribution's status as part of a motion picture or audiovisual work. In other words, if the producer has paid for ownership of the copyright, the lawyer drafting the agreement should use every redundant form of "belt and suspenders" to insure that the producer acquires the rights she paid for, notwithstanding any uncertainty surrounding application of the "work made for hire" doctrine.

There are, however, circumstances in which the ownership approach may be inappropriate. These fall generally into two categories. First, a collaborator or contributor who has a credible or persuasive case of "independent contractor" status may insist on retaining ownership of her creative contribution, and the producer may be unwilling to pay the price or meet the terms necessary to obtain ownership. Second, the producer may want to use *pre-existing* creative material having nothing to do with collaboration in, contribution to, or production of the current production. (This latter situation is the subject of much of the reading in this chapter.)

In either of these instances, cost or practical difficulties may prevent the producer from obtaining copyright ownership of all the materials to be included in the multimedia production. In that case the producer will have to obtain the necessary permission to use those materials without obtaining ownership of copyright in them. Whether called "consent," "permission," "acquiescence," "waiver," or "license," such permission is, in essence, a license under copyright (and possibly other rights) in the underlying material and should be treated as such.

In particular, the multimedia producer should give careful attention to the *scope* of any such license. How can the producer use the licensed material? In what way and in what types of productions? How can those productions be produced and distributed or transmitted? In what way and using what media? Is Internet transmission permissible? May the producer set up a website and include the licensed material in matter that consumer may download automatically at their discretion? How long does the license last? Is it exclusive, either in general, or for a particular type of multimedia production, defined, for example, by subject matter, medium of distribution, or audience? Answers to these questions will determine the price of the license, its usefulness in actual business, and whether the producer will have to "go back to the well" for additional permission if the production is successful and the producer desires additional uses or wider distribution.

3. *New Uses and New Media.* Among the most difficult questions in multimedia licensing—indeed in virtually all copyright licensing today!—are those of new media and new technology. The case of popular music illustrates the problem. During the twenti-

eth century alone, there were at least eight generations of different technology used to record and distribute musical performances: (1) waxed cylinders; (2) vinyl disks; (3) wire recordings; (4) tape recordings; (5) tape cassettes; (6) CDs; (7) DVDs; and (8) digital computer files in MP3 and other formats. Even this list neglects variations on these technological themes, such as the three speeds of vinyl records (78, 45, and 33 RPM) used successively during the heyday of analog "platters."

Toward the end of the twentieth century, the pace of technology change greatly accelerated. For example, the last four of the media for music listed above arrived during the last thirty years of the twentieth century. That constitutes an average of one new medium every 7.5 years. If that pace of technological progress continues, let alone further accelerates, a copyright lasting about a century would see between twelve and thirteen changes in media or recording technology.

The drafters of the Copyright Act of 1976 were well aware of this problem. They attempted to resolve it by making the copyright statute technology independent. Specifically, they made copyright cover all "original works of authorship fixed in any tangible medium of expression, *now known or later developed*." 17 U.S.C. § 102(a) (emphasis added). The also put the same phrase, "now known or later developed," in several key definitions. *See* 17 U.S.C. § 101 (definitions of "copies," "device, machine or process," "phonorecords," and "proprietor"). The intent of these words was to make copyright general and to avoid having to amend the statute each time a new technology of recording or disseminating creative expression arose.

Congress' effort to keep the statute independent of technology appears to have stumbled considerably with the advent of the Internet and the convergence of technology under the influence of computers. The Audio Home Recording Act of 1992, for example, was originally intended to meet the "threat" of digital audio tape recording (DAT) technology by allowing consumers to copy music for noncommercial purposes but imposing a statutory royalty on recording equipment and media and requiring equipment to contain technology to prevent serial copying (making perfect digital copies from copies). *See* 17 U.S.C. §§ 1001–1008, discussed in JAY DRATLER, JR., INTELLECTUAL PROPERTY LAW: COMMERCIAL, CREATIVE, AND INDUSTRIAL PROPERTY § 6.01[5][f] (Law Journal Press 1991 & Supps.). This law, however, suffered a statutory meltdown when it confronted the distribution of music in the form of digital MP3 files over the Internet. The courts determined that the statute simply did not apply to that technology. Moreover, the legislative history suggested that exclusion was indeed Congress' intent, in part due to the lobbying efforts of the computer industry. Similar technology dependence is explicit in provisions governing the statutory digital audio transmission right. *See* 17 U.S.C. § 114(d)–(i), a putative "safe harbor" from unwarranted infringement liability for Internet service providers; 17 U.S.C. § 512, especially (b) and (c), and satellite transmissions; 17 U.S.C. §§ 119, 122.

If the copyright statute itself is slowly sliding off the ladder of technology independence, the situation with licensing is even more uncertain. The traditional rule for copyright licensing has been that all rights not explicitly granted are reserved. Based on this rule, several courts have held that a licensee's failure to anticipate new technology and provide for it in the license agreement is fatal to its claim that the license permits use of the new technology. *See Rey v. Lafferty*, 990 F.2d 1379, 1390–91 (1st Cir. 1993) (license to portray character in animations for "television viewing" did not cover videocassette release); *Cohen v. Paramount Pictures Corp.*, 845 F.2d 851, 854 (9th Cir. 1988) (license, made before invention of videocassettes, to record and copy motion picture and exhibit it "by means of television" did not include right to distribute it in videocassette form); *cf. Apple Computer, Inc. v. Microsoft Corp.*, 759 F. Supp. 1444, 1447–48, 1451 (N.D. Cal. 1991) (settlement license permitting use and sublicensing of visual displays in certain of licensee's application programs did not permit visual displays generated by calls to licensor's copyrighted operating system).

The Second Circuit appears to be trying to develop a doctrine to ameliorate these difficulties. *See Boosey & Hawkes Music Publishers, Inc. v. Walt Disney Co.*, 145 F.3d 481 (2d Cir. 1998) (holding video channels of distribution included as they were foreseeable at the time of contracting based upon unrefuted evidence that "a nascent market for home viewing of feature films existed by 1939," when the license was made); *Bartsch v. Metro-Goldwyn-Mayer, Inc.*, 391 F.2d 150, 155 (2d Cir. 1968) ("licensees may properly pursue any uses which may reasonably be said to fall within the medium as described in the license"). Whether it will continue in this same direction, and whether other circuits will adopt its liberal approach, is still uncertain.

4. *Drafting Licenses in a Time of Accelerating Technological Change.* What is the appropriate role of courts in these circumstances? Should they interpret copyright licenses as technology independent, as the Second Circuit appears to be trying to do? Whom would this approach generally favor, producers of creative material or their disseminators? Is it consistent with the economic policies underlying the copyright statute? Does it provide balanced incentives for both creation and dissemination of original expressive material?

Should the approach depend on the terms of the license agreement? Is a broad interpretation of a license's scope more appropriate in a paid-up license for a lump sum, or in a license with a running royalty, which gives the copyright owner a specified percentage of the licensee's profits from exploiting the copyrighted work?

How can/should the licensing attorney deal with these issues? Is "boilerplate" enough to avoid an adverse judicial decision? Can a copyright owner-licensor gain the upper hand simply by inserting a clause stating that all uses not explicitly permitted are excluded? Can a licensee gain the upper hand by inserting a clause saying that all uses not prohibited are permitted? *See Boosey & Hawkes, supra*, 145 F.3d at 488.

Is it better to list exhaustively all uses permitted? all uses prohibited? Should a court enforce broad language of scope that permits, for example, "performance by any means now known or hereafter developed?" Should a court enforce such language if the license recites that the licensee paid extra for these broad rights? if the license is a paid-up license for a lump sum? if the license is exclusive? Do your answers to these questions suggest that courts are likely to interpret licenses provision by provision, or considered as a whole? Are general rules of interpretation possible? desirable?

5. *Automated Rights Management.* A possible future method of dealing with multimedia and multi-party licenses is through Automated Rights Management ("ARM"). *See* Tom Bell, *Fair Use v. Fared-Use: The Impact of Automated Rights Management on Copyright's Fair Use Doctrine*, 76 N.C.L. Rev. 557 (1998). ARM provides electronic means by which permissions and royalties can be registered and paid. These may be in many forms, including "firewalls and passwords to limit access to information, digital watermarks and stenography to identify electronic documents, micro-payments, and embedded applications to ensure that users pay for protected information." *Id.* at 559 n.8.

ARM appeals to information providers because it stands to give them the power to accomplish two things that hitherto seemed impossible in digital intermedia. First, ARM will make it possible and cost-effective for information providers to enforce standard copyright or trade secret claims. Second, ARM will empower them to enforce contracts that define different or additional rights. Additionally, ARM promises to perform these functions cleanly and effectively, without resort to uncertain and wasteful litigation.

*Id.* at 564.

The Digital Millennium Copyright Act included statutory provisions facilitating ARM. Section 1202 of the Copyright Act defines "copyright management information" ("CMI") and prohibits unauthorized persons from falsifying, removing, altering or otherwise tampering with it. *See* 17 U.S.C. §§ 1202–1204 (CMI rules and civil and criminal sanctions for violating them).

In essence, CMI is a glorified and potentially much expanded form of the "copyright notice" that the statute used to require before the United States' accession to the Berne Convention. *Cf.* 17 U.S.C. §§ 401 (copyright notice for copies), 401 (copyright notice for phonorecords). The definition of CMI permits copyright owners to include information concerning the creators and owners of copyrighted material, such as authors, directors, and performers. *See* 17 U.S.C. § 1202(c) (definition of CMI). More important, it allows copyright owners to include the "[t]erms and conditions for use of the work," and it allows any permitted information to be referenced by "[i]dentifying numbers or symbols referring to such information or links to such information." *Id.*, ¶¶ (6) and (7). Thus, for example, a link or computer code referring to standard terms or conditions for using a work could be "copyright management information," which the statute protects from unauthorized falsification, alteration or removal by civil and criminal sanctions. Congress' obvious purpose in adopting these provisions was to encourage and protect from tampering means to automate the process of licensing and "clearing" permission for the use of copyrighted works.

Do you believe ARM will actually allow for the easier exchange of creative expression? Greater or lesser fair use? or more control for copyright owners?

Given the statutory protection now afforded ARM by the Digital Millenium Copyright Act, §§ 1201 and 1202, *supra* Chapter 2, note 7, and the willingness of computer hackers to continue defying protective technologies, perhaps the battle has only intensified. Does the automated rights management approach to digital works (including copyrighted works on the Internet) obviate the need for copyright law in digital works? Some case law suggests that courts may prefer licenses over fair use. *See Am. Geophysical Union v. Texaco Inc.*, 60 F.3d 913 (2d Cir. 1994), *cert. dismissed*, 516 U.S. 1005 (1995) (systematic copying of articles from technical journals is not fair use when licensing and payment opportunities exist); *Princeton Univ. Press v. Michigan Document Serv., Inc.*, 99 F.3d 1381 (6th Cir. 1996) (*en banc*), *cert. denied*, 520 U.S. 1156 (1997) (agreeing with *Am. Geophysical*). For more information on automated rights management alternatives, see Bell, *supra*, at 564–67. Do you believe the fair use exception may be phased out by technological advances? Should it be? For a thought-provoking discussion of the issues and implications, see LAWRENCE LESSIG, THE FUTURE OF IDEAS (Random House New York 2001).

6. *Web Site Creation.* Is a license required to use the copyrighted content of another on a web site? Although the obvious answer is yes, what about content that only appears via hyperlink to another site? In that case, unique copyright concerns may arise due to the architecture of websites and the nature of hyperlinks.

When a link on one page refers to the "home page" of another web site, the link is called a "surface link." Links to other pages *within* the linked site are known as "deep links." Surface links generally do not require a license, unless the surface link is displayed as a trademark, and is likely to mislead consumers as to an affiliation, sponsorship, or other connection between the sites and/or their contents. In such a case, the trademark owner could demand a license or force removal of the mark.

In *Ticketmaster Corp. v. Microsoft* (No. CV 97-3055 RAP (C.D. Cal. filed April 28, 1997), Microsoft used a "deeplink" to bypass the Ticketmaster home page and advertising, and take visitors directly to the ticket purchasing pages, which arguably benefited Ticketmaster. Nonetheless, Ticketmaster sought to bar the deep link, claiming that the practice infringed on Ticketmaster's trademark, diluted the mark's value and violated state and federal laws concerning unfair competition. Unfortunately, this issue remains unsettled because the parties settled before trial.

Microsoft did drop its deep link. The lesson appears to be this: if one is going to make a deep link to another page, it would be wise to obtain a license from the owner of the linked web site.

---

# Appendix C: Sources for Licensing Releases

## 1. MUSIC LICENSING SERVICES

ASCAP
(Performing-rights society representing music copyright owners; grants public-performance licenses.)
American Society of Composers, Authors & Publishers
1 Lincoln Plaza
New York, N.Y. 10023
(212) 595-3050

BMI
(Performing-rights society and licensing organization representing over 160,000 music copyright owners; grants public-performance licenses to over 3 million musical works.)
320 W. 57th St.
New York, NY 10019
(212) 586-2000

SESAC
(Performing-rights society and licensing organization representing over 200,000 copyrighted compositions; grants public-performance licenses; maintains agreements with over 45 foreign performing-rights societies.)
55 Music Square East
Nashville, TN 37203
(615) 320-0055

TRF Music Inc.
(Source for all types of music licensing for television, radio, film and multimedia con-

taining over 50,000 selections.)
747 Chestnut Ridge Road
Chestnut Ridge, NY 10977
(914) 356-0800

## 2. MULTIMEDIA LICENSING

TOTAL CLEARANCE, Inc.
(Provides extensive worldwide clearance services for all types of multimedia, including film, video, television, text, music, photographs, etc. Has a staff fluent in eight languages.)
P.O. Box 836
Mill Valley, CA 94942
(415) 389-1531
Fax: (415) 380-9542
<footage.net>


The Clearing House Ltd.
(Specializes in music clearances for television, film producers and interactive multimedia products.)
849 S. Broadway, Seventh floor
Los Angeles, CA 90014
(213) 624-3947


BZ/Rights & Permissions Inc.
(Clearing service for various rights including music, film, literature, and television.)
121 W. 27th St. #901
New York, N.Y. 10001
Phone:(212) 924-3000
Fax: (212) 924-2525
<bzrights.com>

## 3. UNIONS AND GUILDS

AFTRA
(Union representing over 75,000 members in the fields of radio, television, recordings and interactive media; provides resources to locate individuals in these fields. AFTRA does not provide clearing services.)
American Federation of Television and Radio Artists
260 Madison Ave.
New York, N.Y. 10016
(212) 532-0800


Graphic Artists Guild
(Labor union of graphic artists; provides some assistance to locate member graphic artists or their publishers. GAG does not provide clearing services.)
11 W. 20th St., Eighth floor
New York, NY 10011
(212) 463-7730

Screen Actors Guild
(Union representing over 78,000 professional actors and performing artists; provides resources for locating actors and artists. SAG does not provide clearing services.)
5757 Wilshire Blvd., Eighth Floor
Los Angeles, CA 90036
(213) 954-1600


The Songwriters Guild of America
(Association of songwriters; provides resources for locating songwriters but does not provide clearing services.)
6430 Sunset Blvd., Suite 1002
Hollywood, CA 90028
(213) 462-1108


## 4. RESEARCH FACILITIES AND SEARCH SERVICES

Academy of Motion Pictures Arts and Sciences
(The Academy's Margaret Herrick Library serves as a central source of information on all facets of motion pictures and includes, films, books, periodicals, files of clippings, still photographs and screenplays.)
333 S. La Cienega Blvd.
Beverly Hills, CA 90211
(310) 247-3000


The American Film Institute
(Nonprofit organization dedicated to preserving film, television and video with extensive library of books, films, scripts, television programming, etc. Library is open to the public.)
2021 N. Western Ave.
Los Angeles, CA 90027
(213) 856-7600


DIALOG Information Services Inc.
(Online data-base information service for general information in multiple fields.)
3460 Hillview Ave.
Palo Alto, CA 94304
(800) 334-2564


Thompson & Thompson
(Search service used for determining U.S. availability and registerablity of trademarks, copyrights, titles, designs and characters, film and TV titles, characters and designs. Will research chain of title of all copyrighted works.)
550 Victory Road
North Quincy, MA 02171-1545
(617) 479-1600

UCLA Film and Television Archive
(Contains the largest university-held collection of motion pictures and broadcast programming. The archive's collection can be found through ORION2, UCLA's online information system, or its successor after July 7, 2004. The archive's commercial services
division makes its newsreel collection accessible to media producers to include vintage
footage in production.)
Archive Research and Study Center
(temporarily located in 160 Powell Library)
46 Powell Library
405 Hilgrad Ave.
Los Angeles, CA 90024-1517
(310) 206-5388
<library.ucla.edu/new-orion>


University of Southern California School of Cinema & Television
(University research facility with online marketplace to help filmmakers and multime-
dia developers locate actors, footage and other materials necessary for filmmaking.)
The Integrated Studio Project
Los Angeles, CA 90089-2211
(213) 740-6207


U.S. Copyright Office
Register of Copyrights
Library of Congress
Washington, D.C. 20559
(202) 707-3000

# Chapter 7

# Key Provisions in License Agreements and Special Types of License Agreements

## I. Introduction

The material in this chapter introduces the key provisions in the license agreement itself and the more general provisions found in most commercial contracts. Among the common terms found in a license agreement are the preamble or heading; recitals; definitions; grant including the scope of the license; consideration or royalty payments; most favored licensee provisions; right to inspect and audit; confidentiality; term, termination, and post-termination rights and obligations; third party infringement, standing to sue and control of litigation; representations, warranties, and indemnity; and notice-patent marking. Other clauses such as transferability and force majeure are often referred to as "boilerplate," but as we will see are "not so boiler plate." Still other clauses are common terms that govern the risks of adverse consequences, for example arbitration/litigation and choice of law. Some clauses are subject specific in that they might be important in a trademark license, but not applicable in a patent or copyright license.

Additionally special types of license arrangements will be discussed. More and more frequently, a company will enter into a strategic alliance with another company to supplement its weaknesses or complement its strengths. For example, one company may be strong in research and development but weak in marketing or distribution. Another company may have strong manufacturing skills but no R&D. Strategic alliances usually include some collaboration in the development of new products with an allocation of rights to make and sell. One issue that frequently arises and is often the subject of tense negotiations between the parties is ownership of the resulting intellectual property.

---

## II. Key Provisions

The most important thing to remember when drafting a license agreement is that each transaction is fact specific and, therefore, the provisions of the license agreement will vary from transaction to transaction. Consequently, the best practice to employ when drafting a license agreement is to consider all of the implications that each clause raises. If you do not address these implications, a court may do so for you, often with unanticipated consequences.

Samples of the various clauses identified above are set forth in italics in the paragraphs that follow. The clauses are followed by a short commentary highlighting differences among the clauses presented, common pitfalls associated with the clauses, and questions that may arise.

## A.  Heading

*THIS AGREEMENT is made this 1st day of February 2002 (the "Effective Date") by and between Contair Corporation, a Pennsylvania corporation having offices at 1122 Spruce Street, Havertown, Pennsylvania 66211, ("Licensor") and GNN Corporation, a corporation organized under the laws of Belgium having offices at 12645 Rue de Livourne 8, B1, Brussels ("Licensee").*

Mostly out of custom (although the custom has some intuitive sense), virtually every license agreement starts out with language that defines the parties. The purpose is not only to name the parties, but also to provide third parties (i.e., those who are not presently involved in the transaction but subsequently become involved such as an aquiror-assignee) with information regarding where the parties can be found or where they are incorporated. This is especially true in the case where one of the parties is a foreign corporation. Parties may intend to stay in one location and in touch with licensees or licensors; however, corporate reality dictates that it is rather difficult to predict where and in what form any given corporate entity will be ten years after the execution of a license agreement. To address this issue, the identification of the parties should include the official corporate name, the state in which it is incorporated, and the principal address of the corporation.

Another important function of the Heading is to identify the Effective Date. Remember, under general contract principles a contract is effective as of the date the last party executes the agreement. If the parties for some reason would like the contract to have effect as of another date, (i.e. the beginning of the licensee's fiscal year)  identifying that date in the Heading as the "Effective Date" easily accomplishes the goal

## B.  Recitals

*WHEREAS, Licensor manufactures, distributes and sells luxury automobiles in the United States and many foreign countries; and*

*WHEREAS, Licensor, by prior use and registration, has established rights in and to the trademark ESTRELLA (the "Trademark") for use on automobiles, parts, and accessories; and*

*WHEREAS, Licensee manufactures, distributes and sells luxury watercraft namely yachts; and*

*WHEREAS, Licensor is the owner of all right, title and interest in and to U.S. Pat. No. 9,999,999 to Smyth et al. entitled Voice Activated Locking Mechanism issued on February 9, 1999 (as more particularly set forth below) (the "Licensed Patents"); and*

*WHEREAS, Licensee desires to obtain a license to (i) use the Trademark on or in connection with the sale of its luxury yachts; and (ii) manufacture and sell luxury yachts that incorporate the voice recognition technology covered by the Patents and Licensor desires to grant a license to Licensee for the foregoing purposes only on the following terms and conditions.*

*NOW, THEREFORE, in consideration of the mutual promises and covenants set forth herein, and other good and valuable consideration, the sufficiency and receipt of which is hereby acknowledged, the parties hereto hereby agree as follows.*

Recitals or "whereas" clauses are anachronisms in modern contracts; however, they should not be treated lightly. These clauses can perform a number of useful functions.

First, Recitals acquaint the reader with the background of the transaction. For example, the parties may be settling litigation between them, or one party may be interested in licensing technology to enter a new market. Whatever the reason, the Recitals set forth the parties' intent for entering into the license agreement. Recitals often provide the background necessary for a party who is asked years later to read, understand, and interpret the contract, for example a judge.

Second, clients actually like reading and understanding their "deal." Many licensors of intellectual property are not multinational corporations. Many licensors are individuals. Even if the licensor is a large corporation, individuals make up the corporation and make decisions regarding intellectual property. Oftentimes, the subject matter of the license agreement may be an individual's life work. He may not understand much of any license agreement, but he will understand and appreciate reading the background that led up to the agreement.

The Recitals should provide general background information about the parties, identify the patents or know-how being licensed, the dispute being settled, if any, and any other agreements that may be referenced or superseded.

Notice the last clause of the Recitals above. All licenses, indeed all contracts, need consideration to be validly formed. The last recital specifically identifies the consideration and waives either party's right to challenge the sufficiency of that consideration in the future.

Lastly, while the Recitals provide the background information as to the parties' intent to enter into the license, they are not necessarily legally binding. Consequently, any provision to which the drafter wants one or both parties to be bound should be drafted (or repeated) in the body of the agreement.

-----

# C.  Definitions

*"Affiliate" shall mean any entity that directly or indirectly controls, is controlled by, or is under common control with Licensee and for such purpose "control" shall mean the possession, direct or indirect, of the power to direct or cause the direction of the management and policies of the entity, whether through the ownership of voting securities, by contract or otherwise.*

*"Contract Year" shall mean the 12-month period commencing on the Effective Date and each subsequent 12-month period during the term of this Agreement and the partial 12-month period, if any, expiring upon the termination or expiration of this Agreement.*

*"Confidential Information" shall mean all data, discoveries, inventions, documents, reports, source code, and all information embodied in written, graphical, digital, oral or other tangible form related to Inventions that is disclosed to Licensee. Confidential Information also includes the existing and potential intellectual property rights in the Technology, and all business and legal arrangements between the parties under this Agreement. Confidential Information shall not include any information that, at the time of disclosure, was: (i) previously and legally in the possession of, or independently developed by, Licensee; (ii) generally available to the public other than by an unauthorized act or omission of Licensee; (iii) disclosed to Licensee by a third party having no obligation of confidentiality with respect thereto; or (iv) required to be disclosed by law.*

*"Field of Use" shall mean field of luxury yachts.*

*"Improvements" shall mean all discoveries or inventions that fall within the claims of the Licensed Patent, whether or not patentable, and all patentable and non-patentable discoveries, inventions, or modifications of, and enhancements to Confidential Information or Technology related to the manufacture or use of Licensed Products developed or obtained by any means by either party during the term of this Agreement.*

*"Licensed Product" shall mean a product which absent this license, when sold, transferred, otherwise disposed of, or placed into use by or for Licensee: (a) infringes or induces contributory infringement of one or more (i) claims of any one of the Licensed Patents, or (ii) copyrights of any part of the Licensed Documentation; (b) performs a Licensed Process; or (c) includes a component that would render the product inoperative for its intended purpose if separated from the product and which either (i) infringes or induces contributory infringement of one or more (1) claims of any one of the Licensed Patent Applications or (2) copyrights of any part of the Licensed Documentation or (ii) performs a Licensed Process.*

*"Net Sales" shall mean the actual invoice price at which Licensed Products shall be sold by Licensee, but shall not include taxes or assessments which are normally billed separately, cash discounts allowed for prompt payment, transportation costs, and amounts refunded, allowed or credited in connection with defective, damaged or returned items.*

*"Licensed Patents" shall mean U.S. Pat. No. 9,999,999 to Smyth et al., entitled Voice Activated Locking Mechanism, issued on February 9, 1999, all continuations, continuations-in-part, divisions, reissues, reexaminations, renewals and extensions thereof, all applications claiming priority thereto and all patens issuing thereon, and all foreign counterparts.*

*Royalty Amount" shall have the meaning ascribed thereto in Section 3.1.*

*"Technology" shall mean all patented and unpatented inventions, Confidential Information, and know-how relating to the design, construction, and manufacture (including equipment or machinery) of voice-activated technology.*

*"Territory" shall mean all the countries of North America.*

*"Trademark" shall mean the mark ESTRELLA.*

License agreements, as well as other contracts, typically use "definitions" to precisely define vague terms, or create a short-hand reference to a term or phraseology that is used frequently throughout the agreement, or both. If the use of definitions is extensive a separate section entitled "Definitions" usually appears at the beginning of the agreement. If the license agreement is rather simple, definitions may be found in the body of the agreement close to the source of the term or phraseology that it is defining. Most typically, the drafting attorney uses a combination of both methods. As you will notice in the Heading section above, we have identified "Licensor" and "Licensee" close to the source of the term we were identifying, as well as the Effective Date. Similarly, we have identified the "Licensed Patents" and "Trademark" that we are licensing in the Recitals, close to the source of the term. While certainly not necessary, and some attorneys would argue that it is redundant, we have also defined both terms again in the Definitions section above. In that regard, care should be taken not to draft conflicting terms.

Another technique of drafting attorneys is to include a defined term in the definitions section but reference where it may be found in the agreement. This is typically done when it makes more sense to define the term close to the source but the definition takes several sentences to explain. An example of this is the "Royalty Amount" section above.

Definitions can be arranged within the definitions section hierarchically, or, in other words in the order, that the reader will come across them in the agreement, or alphabetically. While it is common practice to "number" definitions, as 1.1, 1.2, 1.3, etc., practically speaking it is much more convenient not to number them at all because as various definitions are added and deleted throughout the drafting process more time will be spent on renumbering than on anything else.

The definition for affiliates above is derived from the language of Rule 12b-2 promulgated under the 1934 Securities Exchange Act and is just one of the many versions of what may constitute an affiliate. Other popular versions include the percentage ownership by the parent of the entity to be defined as an "Affiliate." Under what circumstances might a licensee want to include a definition of licensee affiliates? Under what circumstances might a licensor want to include a definition of licensee affiliates?

The parties may want to define "contract year" if one party maintains its books on a fiscal year basis while the other party maintains its books on a calendar year basis and the parties desire to reconcile the two systems. Similarly, when the royalty payment cycle is not a calendar year basis, the contract year may be defined.

If in addition to licensing patents, know-how, or confidential information to be exchanged, a definition of confidential information is usually included. If the parties have already entered into a non-disclosure agreement (NDA) as part of the initial process of negotiating (*see* Chapter 4) then it is important to ensure that the confidentiality provisions of the license agreement do not conflict with the provisions of the NDA, or alternatively that the terms of the license agreement supersede the terms of the NDA.

"Field of Use" may also be termed "licensed field" or "product field" or simply "field" and may be drafted for a particular market, as above, or for a particular application or use.

One of the most hotly negotiated definitions is the definition of "Improvements." In negotiating rights to improvements, consider whether the licensee should grant back its improvements to the licensor, and/or whether the licensor's improvements will be covered in this or a separate agreement. Should this clause even cover after-acquired technology? Should the clause cover technology that is "licensed in" as contrasted with technology developed internally? Should the clause only cover improvements necessarily related to the licensed technology? Improvements are usually defined as anything that would infringe the claims of the licensed patent, anything that performs the same function as the licensed subject matter in a better or more economical way, anything that affects the "form, fit, or function" of the licensed product (when the product is a medical device), or any modification of or enhancement to the licensed product (or process) that provides economic value. When drafting the definition of improvements consider time limits. Should the licensor or licensee grant back improvements that are developed within one year of the effective date? Five years? More? Also, consider providing for notice to the other party regarding development of the improvement. Lastly, consider joint ownership issues with respect to the development of improvements if the parties intend to collaborate using the term of the agreement.

When defining the licensed, royalty-bearing product, determine whether the licensed technology may include both patented inventions and unpatented or unpatentable know-how and trade secrets, in which case a definition of "Technology" that includes both know-how and patents may be desirable.

The definition of "Net Sales" is typical of definitions found in many license agreements and forms the royalty base: the base upon which the royalty amount is calculated. "Gross profit" and "Gross sales" are other definitions that are frequently used as the royalty base.

The definition of "Licensed Products" is an example of the interdependence on definitions of other defined terms (not shown).

---

## D. Grant Clause

*Licensor hereby grants to Licensee the exclusive right and license under the Licensed Patents and Technology to make, use, sell, offer for sale and import Licensed Products in the Territory for use in the Field of Use during the term of this Agreement. Licensee shall not have the right to sublicense, in whole or in part, the Licensed Patent or the Technology, but shall have the right to subcontract with third party manufacturers who are bound by confidentiality terms at least as strict as stated in this Agreement. The license granted hereunder shall be transferable only in accordance with the provisions in Section 14.1 [i.e., assignment provisions].*

*Licensor also grants to Licensee the exclusive right and license to use the Trademark on the Licensed Products in connection with advertising, promoting, and selling the Licensed Products in the Territory, only within the Field of Use, during the term of this Agreement.*

Every license agreement requires a grant clause. That is, there needs to be language specifically stating, "I license to you the use of patent X and trademark Y." However, the grant clause has many dimensions. It should identify the licensed intellectual property, the scope and character of the grant, its duration, and how the licensee will use the intellectual property. The grant clause answers the question "What rights is the Licensor granting?" Rights associated with patented technology include the separable rights to make, use, sell, and import. The right "to make" typically implies the right to use or sell, or both.

In the case of a license to a new company or joint venture, the Licensor may want the license to be contingent upon whether the licensee obtains a certain amount of financing or investment. If so, the parties should expressly state the amount and type (e.g., debt or equity) along with any provisions necessary for unwinding the transaction if the licensee fails to obtain financing.

Will the license be non-exclusive or exclusive? As will be seen later, the character of the license may have substantial tax implications (*see infra* Chapter 12). If the license is exclusive, does the licensor want to reserve any rights to itself or will working the invention by the licensor constitute a breach of the agreement? Intellectual property licenses may include both types (exclusive and non-exclusive) in a single license. For example, the licensor could grant an exclusive license for a specific technology, and a non-exclusive license to a "background" technology, the rights to which may be required to practice the licensed rights. If the grant clause is silent regarding its character, courts will interpret it as a non-exclusive license. Another type of grant is a "co-exclusive" license in which two parties have similar rights.

Exclusive licenses are frequently "restricted" as to geographical scope and permitted fields of use. What will the territory for the license be? The world? Just North America? Most licensees have local or regional—not worldwide—abilities to sell products. Therefore, a licensor may want to grant multiple "exclusive" licenses for maximum exploitation of any given intellectual property. Do territorial restrictions apply to the entire distribution chain (and end user locations) or only to the initial sale? If territories are divided, the parties may consider a joint marketing arrangement where each party is obligated to turn over opportunities in the other party's market.

The licensor should expressly grant or prohibit the licensee's right to sublicense the intellectual property rights, and if granted, the right should be carefully delineated. The exclusive right "to make" may imply the right to grant sublicenses. If the grant is silent, in an exclusive license the license will imply the right to grant sublicenses. Conversely, a non-exclusive licensee does not have the right to grant sublicenses unless the right is expressly granted. Therefore, it is critical that the grant deal explicitly with sublicensing rights whether the grant is exclusive or non-exclusive.

Under what circumstances should the licensee be allowed to grant sublicenses? Under what circumstances should the grant merely include the right to subcontract the manufacture of the licensed product? Licensees prefer flexibility in running their business and most likely will always want the right to sublicense. The licensor, on the other hand, will perceive itself "losing control" over the technology if it grants sublicensing rights. However, the right to grant sublicenses will extend the market and the revenue derived by the licensor. If the grant includes the right to sublicense, the licensor will likely want to capture a portion of the royalties earned by the licensee by virtue of the sublicense. How would you draft such a provision into the grant clause? In addition, if the right to grant sublicenses is granted, the licensor may desire to restrict further sublicensing by sublicensees. The parties must also consider the effect of the termination of the license on any sublicenses. Are the sublicenses terminated or do they survive? Does the licensor assume control of those sublicenses? If so, how does the licensor contact the sublicensees? Do you think it is preferable to include a notice obligation in the license agreement each time the licensee grants a sublicense? If so, should the notice include the name, address and material terms of the sublicense agreement? Should the license agreement contain a term stating that each sublicense agreement must include a clause that in the event of breach royalties will be paid directly to the licensor?

A grant of "have made" rights to the licensee is interpreted as the right to have a licensed product manufactured for it by a third party. As we will see in Chapter 8, under certain circumstances "have made" right offers some protection to the third party from an infringement charge by creating an implied license. Before granting "have made" rights, the drafting attorney would be well-advised to consult with its client about possible unintended results.

In the case of licensing software to end users, the licensor will want the right to approve the licensee's end user license agreement (EULA) to ensure that it has sufficient limitations on warranties and indemnification for the licensor.

Lastly, beware of incomplete or vague grants. Consider the following grant for a copyrighted software program:

*Licensor hereby grants to Licensee an exclusive, non-transferable, except in accordance with the provisions of Section 14.1, royalty-bearing, license under the Technology during the term of this Agreement to use the Licensed Software.*

What does "use" mean? Is it covered by any of the exclusive rights set forth in 17 U.S.C. § 106? If not, do we know what the licensee has the right to do? Can the licensee make copies? Modify the software program? Create derivative works? Sell and distribute copies of the software program? A well-drafted grant that mimics the statutory language will ensure that a total stranger reading the agreement will know what rights the licensor intended to grant.

---

# E.  Forms of Consideration

*In consideration for the license granted hereunder, Licensee shall pay to Licensor, concurrently upon execution of this Agreement, a non-refundable, lump sum payment in the amount of $150,000, which shall be creditable toward royalties payable in respect of Licensed Product. In addition, Licensee shall pay to Licensor, as hereinafter provided, during the term of this Agreement, the following Royalty Amount:*

*(a) a royalty of 2% on the aggregate of all Net Sales for Trademark Rights; and*

*(b) a royalty of 15% on all sublicensing revenue.*

*Licensee shall pay the Royalty Amount within thirty (30) days after the end of each calendar quarter. The Royalty Amount shall accrue upon receipt by Licensee of payment for Licensed Product.*

The royalty clause is the heart of the license agreement, comprising the sum bargain of the parties in a description of what is conveyed and what is paid in return. In Chapters 4 and 5, the valuation and negotiation of royalties were considered at length. When reducing valuation negotiations to writing, the licensor seeks to maximize return on investment by not overlooking any possible form of compensation. In the definitions clause, the licensor will seek to define the royalty triggering event, i.e., a sale, a performance, a display, or use, etc., as broadly as possible, shifting as much risk of loss as possible to the licensee, while requiring that the licensee provide adequate assurances that royalties will be correctly calculated. Similarly, the licensee will want the royalty-triggering event defined as narrowly and simply as possible, not only to minimize royalties, but also to decrease the risk of error and to minimize the accounting costs of tracking and reporting royalties.

Royalty structure raises many questions. Are the royalties based on a percent of sales, per unit, or a combined basis? Does the rate decrease or increase with increasing sales or is it a flat sum?

If the royalty is structured as a percentage of net sales, what counts as a "net sale"? Do sales to affiliates count in the computation of net sales? What about sales by affiliates? Are sales to the licensor counted? What about sales to sublicensees? Note: Licensors should consider this issue carefully, as licensees could otherwise sublicense for a small royalty rate in return for an equity share, no part of which would ever be enjoyed by the licensor. What amounts are excluded? (E.g., taxes, duties, shipping and insurance expenses, etc.) Are there allowances for returns? Are demonstration and promotional units excluded?

The parties may need to adjust royalties for products that include both licensed and unlicensed components or technologies. An interesting drafting problem is presented when the licensed product is not a product at all but a component of a product. Consider the following clause:

*Licensee agrees to pay a royalty on net sales of the sensor as follows:*

*(a) 3% on net sales of the sensor with signal processing electronics attached; and*

*(b) 4% on net sales of the sensor with both signal processing and conditioning electronics attached.*

When using "net sales" as the royalty base consider revenue recognition issues. The licensor will want to accelerate payment of royalties. Try to avoid using "the date the Licensed Product is sold" as the trigger for royalty accrual because "sold" is itself a vague term. A better solution is to define what "sold" means, e.g., "Sold shall mean the earlier of the date the product is invoiced or the date the product is shipped." The licensee, on the other hand, will want to delay revenue recognition. A royalty that accrues on the date the licensee receives payment for the licensed product is a licensee-favorable revenue recognition clause.

If the royalty clause contains a provision for an up-front payment, consider whether the parties intend to credit up-front payments against future royalties as in the clause above. Or is the up-front payment in exchange for the transfer of know-how? Is it refundable if the license is terminated or if the licensee does not successfully develop or market the licensed products? Does your answer change if the licensed technology becomes obsolete making the sales of licensed products difficult?

Should a minimum guaranteed royalty be included in the agreement? Consider the following minimum guaranteed royalty clause:

*Licensee shall pay to Licensor a royalty of three percent (3%) of Net Sales for Licensed Products used, sold or otherwise disposed of in the Licensed Territory. Notwithstanding the foregoing, if the total royalties payable to Licensor hereunder for any Contract Year during the term of this Agreement is less than U.S. $500,000 (the "Minimum Guaranteed Royalty"), Licensee shall pay to Licensor, within 45 days after December 31st of such Contract Year, the difference between the Minimum Guaranteed Royalty and the total of all royalties payable to Licensor under this Agreement for such Contract Year (the "Delinquent Amount").*

How should minimum royalties be calculated? Minimum royalties may be considered onerous by the licensee, unless the market is already proven. If minimum royalties are not achieved, what are the consequences? Is this an actionable breach on the part of the licensor a basis for termination or a conversion from an exclusive to a non-exclusive license? Must the licensee achieve actual sales, or can the licensee make up the difference out-of-pocket?

Consider other types of royalties such as a capped royalty or periodic lump sum payments:

*Licensee shall pay to Licensor a royalty of three percent (3%) of Net Sales of Licensed Product made, used, sold, or otherwise disposed of in the Licensed Territory during the term of this Agreement, until such time as the total sum of all royalties paid by Licensee equals*

*U.S. five million dollars (U.S. $5,000,000), whereby this License Agreement shall automatically convert to a fully-paid up license."*

*In consideration of the license granted herein, Licensee shall pay to Licensor the sum of one hundred thousand dollars (U.S. $100,000) per year until the Licensed Patent expires.*

Is a royalty structured as a capped royalty or a periodic payment favorable to a licensor or licensee? Or is it neutral in effect, favoring neither licensor nor licensee? Would your answer change if the technology were mature technology? If the technology were new?

Then there are "licensed processes," such as manufacturing process improvements that reduce costs or increase productivity. Such a royalty provision might be structured as "x" dollars for each 1% reduction in scrap resulting from use of the Licensed Technology.

Royalty clauses are negotiated and drafted by lawyers and interpreted and carried out by accountants. A poorly drafted royalty clause can be an excessive burden on a licensee's business operation: it may impose burdensome accounting, tracking, and reporting requirements.

---

## F.  Delivery of Tangible Property

*Within 30 days after execution of this agreement, Licensor shall deliver to Licensee's business place the ESTRELLA logo and mark in the form of die cuts, electronic images, photographs, molds, and other media, as particularly described in Exhibit D. For the first 12 months of this agreement, Licensor's graphic designer, John Jones, shall spend 10 hours per month at a place of business designated by Licensee to work on integrating the ESTRELLA logo and mark into Licensee's marketing programs.*

This clause determines exactly how the transfer, if any, of tangible property takes place. This ranges from the clear-cut and obvious—delivery of source code, manuals, and documentation in the case of computer software—to the arcane and complex—delivery and installation of equipment and a six-month training program conducted by designated personnel in the case of a complex manufacturing technology. Because it is seldom, if ever, in the licensor's best interest that the licensee fail, both parties will want to accurately describe how the licensed rights will be transferred.

---

## G.  Improvements

*The Licensor shall promptly disclose to Licensee in writing all Improvements that may be discovered, developed, invented, or acquired by Licensor during the term of this Agreement in sufficient detail to enable Licensee to consider licensing such Improvement ("Notice"). In consideration of the Option Fee, Licensor grants to Licensee an irrevocable option to obtain an exclusive license to Improvements at a royalty rate, and upon terms, mutually agreeable to the Parties (the "Option"). The Option shall expire 90 days after Notice is delivered to Licensee.*

"Improvement" should always be explicitly defined (*see* Definitions, *supra* Part C). An improvement can be a modification or enhancement to the licensed intellectual property invented by either party after the license is executed. In each case, the question is whether improvements must be shared. The improvement clause is especially important in software licenses where the licensee knows that the licensor will continue creating new versions of the software code. The licensee will want to be protected from having to compete in the future with the licensor or another licensee who has obtained a newer version of the licensed software.

In the case of jointly-owned improvements (e.g., inventors employed by the licensor and licensee), will there be an obligation of accounting for use and/or licensing profits? How do the parties determine who will file the patent applications? Share filing and maintenance costs? What about potential bankruptcy and abandonment problems? The implications of jointly-owned technology are discussed infra.

## H.  Most Favored Licensee

*If during the term of the Agreement the Licensor grants to any third party a license to the Licensed Patent at a royalty rate that is less than the royalty rate granted herein, then Licensor shall promptly notify Licensee of such license, and this Agreement shall automatically be amended to provide for such more favorable rate.*

There is no general rule of law that requires a licensor to provide for identical royalty rates to all licensees. While licensees typically negotiate for the inclusion of a "most favored licensee" clause, licensors typically resist. If the parties decided to include such a clause in their agreement, whether the clause has retroactive effect or not, only prospective effect must be addressed. Naturally licensors will not want to refund received royalties, and licensees will want a clause to be retroactive. Licensors should also provide notice if the change is prospective. In addition, a licensor would be wise to offer such a clause only if the economic terms of the two agreements are the same. In this regard the licensor should consider all terms: royalties, minimum guaranteed royalties, up-front licensing fees, support fees, pre-payments, guaranteed marketing expenditures, *et cetera*. The licensee, on the other hand, should consider the situation where the consideration is not a royalty rate at all, but rather equity in the company or other non-cash consideration. In such a case does the licensee derive a false sense of security in having the most favored licensee clause in the agreement?

## I.  Right to Inspect and Audit Books and Records

*Books and Records. Licensee shall make and keep substantially full and complete business records and books showing the quantity of Licensed Product sold by Licensee. Such records shall be in reasonably sufficient detail to enable Licensor to determine the Royalty Amount payable to it. Licensee shall maintain such records and books for a period of three years from the making thereof.*

*Report. Within thirty (30) days after the end of each calendar quarter during the term of this Agreement, beginning with the first such quarter in which Licensed Product is sold by Licensee, Licensee shall prepare a substantially true and accurate written report, certified by an officer of Licensee, that shows the quantity of Licensed Product sold by Licensee and its Affiliates during the calendar quarter immediately preceding, and will deliver a copy thereof to Licensor with the Royalty Amount due under Section 3.1 for the same period.*

*Audit. (a) Licensee shall permit, upon request by Licensor and at Licensor's sole cost and expense, an independent, outside auditor chosen by Licensor (the "Auditor") to have access, no more than once in each calendar year during the term of this Agreement during reasonable business hours and upon at least ten (10) business days written notice, to Licensee's books and records applicable only to the Licensed Products for the purpose of verifying the fees payable as provided for in this Agreement (an "Audit"). Any engagement letter executed between Licensor and the Auditor shall provide that the Auditor shall disclose to Licensor only information relating solely to the accuracy of the Royalty Payment and the amount of the shortfall, if any. The Auditor shall be required as a condition to conducting the Audit to agree that no copies of such records will be made or retained by it except for the Auditor's notes made during the audit.*

*(b) If Licensee disputes the results of any Audit conducted pursuant to Section (a) above (a "Disputed Audit") it shall provide written notice to Licensor within 10 business days of receiving the results of the Audit conducted pursuant to Section (a) and then an additional Audit shall be conducted by a firm of independent public accountants (the "Neutral Auditor") selected jointly by Licensee and Licensor. Such firm shall be selected by the parties within thirty (30) days following Licensor's notice to Licensee of the results of the Disputed Audit. The Neutral Auditor shall not have provided accounting services for either party within the previous thirty-six (36) month period. Licensor and Licensee shall execute a reasonable engagement letter. Any engagement letter executed between Licensor and the Neutral Auditor shall provide that the Neutral Auditor shall disclose to Licensor and Licensee only information relating solely to the accuracy of the Royalty Payment and the amount of the shortfall, if any. The Neutral Auditor shall be required as a condition to conducting the Audit to agree that no copies of such records will be made or retained by it excepting the Neutral Auditor's notes made during the audit. The Neutral Auditor's determination shall be made within thirty (30) days of its selection; shall be set forth in a written statement delivered to Licensee and Licensor; and shall be final and binding on Licensee and Licensor. Except as provided by Section (c) the fees, costs, and expenses relating to any Audit conducted pursuant to this Section (b) shall be borne by Licensor.*

*(c) If it has been determined pursuant to Section (a) or, if applicable, Section (b) that Licensee has failed to pay at least 95% of the royalties due and owning Licensor for the period of time the Audit encompasses, then Licensor shall, in addition to any other remedies available to it, recover from Licensee the fees, costs, and expenses incurred by Licensor to its outside auditors in conducting any such Audit under Section (a) or (b), which revealed the shortfall.*

The licensee usually agrees to keep accurate records, to supply a copy to the licensor on a periodic basis, and to pay royalties in a specific fashion and by a specified time if not covered by the Royalty clause. The license typically limits the right to inspect and audit to twice per year. It is important to draft in a mechanism to resolve disputes over payment of royalties including seeking resolution through a respected accounting firm. The licensor usually bears the expense of the audit because the licensor controls (up to a certain extent) how frequently it wishes to audit the licensee's books and how extensive the audit will be. For example, although the license agreement may provide for three audits per year, the licensor may elect to audit only once per year during the first few years, and if a discrepancy is found, more frequently thereafter. If the audit discloses a shortfall in royalty payment, the licensee typically bears the cost of the audit is provided that a dispute mechanism is included.

———————

# J.  Representations and Warranties

*To the best of Licensor's knowledge, the manufacture of the Licensed Product when manufactured in accordance with the Technology does not infringe or misappropriate the intellectual property rights of any third party. Except as otherwise expressly set forth in this Agreement, Licensor makes no representations and extends no warranties of any kind, either express or implied, including but not limited to warranties of merchantability, fitness for a particular purpose, and validity of patent claims, issued or pending.*

Although many lawyers use the term "representation" and "warranty" interchangeably, each term may receive different treatment under the law. A licensee may rely on a licensor's representation and, if unsatisfied, claim that the licensor's representation constituted fraud in the inducement. The damages for such fraud (e.g., the amount paid under the license minus any benefits obtained) may be different from those under a breach of warranty claim (e.g., a reduction in price). Thus, in order to "save" this license, a licensor should only make warranties and avoid making representations. Alternatively, as in the clause above, the actual knowledge of the licensor "qualifies" the representation. In cases where the technology is mature, is it fair for the licensor to offer a representation with a "knowledge qualifier"? Is it more fair to include a knowledge qualifier when the licensor has not yet developed the technology.

The licensor will try to avoid making any warranties regarding the licensed subject matter beyond warranting the licensor's own title and right of ownership in the property. In the case of universities and other non-profits, even a warranty of title may not be available. In any event, licensees will conduct their own due diligence, and may demand copies of written opinions from the licensor's counsel (be aware of potential waiver of privilege issues) or consultant's reports to determine title.

Under section 2-316 of the UCC, a licensor can disclaim all warranties except those expressly made in the license agreement. Otherwise, the licensor is potentially liable for implied warranties, such as merchantability or fitness for a particular purpose. These disclaimers must be conspicuous. Similarly, the licensor will try to avoid making express warranties, simply because, once the subject matter of the license is transferred, the licensee becomes its custodian and is in a superior position to protect against liability risks. As always, the parties can qualify and bargain for such risks. For some types of technology, such as computer software, the length of a warranty should be an element determining the price of the license.

---

# K.  Confidentiality

*Obligations and Exceptions. Licensee shall maintain Licensor Confidential Information confidential and shall not use any Licensor Confidential Information except as provided in this Agreement. Licensee shall take or shall cause to be taken all precautions reasonably necessary to safeguard Licensor Confidential Information. Such precautions shall be to a degree not less protective than Customer uses in safeguarding its own confidential information. Licensee shall disclose Licensor Confidential Information received hereunder only to Licensee's employees, and then only to the extent necessary to manufacture or sell Licensed Intermediate Product or Licensed Final Product. Licensee shall advise each of its employees who ob-*

*tains or has access to Licensor Confidential Information of Licensee's obligations to Licensor hereunder and shall execute a confidentiality agreement on behalf of each such employee naming Licensor as a third party beneficiary.*

***Surviving Obligation.** If this Agreement is terminated by either party pursuant to Section 13.3 or expires pursuant to Section 14.1, then the obligation of Licensee to protect against the unauthorized disclosure of Licensor Confidential Information shall survive such termination or expiration of this Agreement.*

***Injunctive Relief.** Licensee acknowledges that its failure to keep Licensor Confidential Information confidential will result in immediate and irreparable damage to Licensor. Licensee also acknowledges that any remedy ultimately awarded or granted under Article 10 may be meaningless in the absence of such equitable relief as any court of competent jurisdiction may deem proper. Consequently, Licensor shall be entitled, pending arbitration, to such equitable relief as any court of competent jurisdiction may deem proper to enforce the provisions of Section 9.1.*

***Return.** Upon the termination of this Agreement by Licensor or by Licensee for any reason prior to the expiration of the term, or upon expiration of the term of this Agreement, Licensee shall promptly discontinue the use of, and return to Licensor or its designee, all copies of Licensor Confidential Information which were furnished to or otherwise came into the possession of Licensee during the term hereof, and all notes, summaries, and other documents or material containing Licensor Confidential Information.*

Both parties should remain attentive to confidentiality issues that may arise during the term of the license agreement, which differ from those addressed in the non-disclosure agreement executed prior to the beginning of negotiations (*see* Chapter 4). After all, the parties are not merely exploring a potential business opportunity; they are getting full access to the technology. If there is particularly valuable unpatented technology, perhaps there should be a longer term of protection for trade secrets.

If the license agreement includes the transfer of know-how, a section regarding the obligations of the licensee to maintain confidential information is essential. The parties should take care to ensure that the license agreement provisions do not conflict with any previous non-disclosure agreements or, alternatively, that the prior non-disclosure agreements terminate upon execution of the license agreement.

In situations where the license agreement contains a grant to patented and non-patented technology, it is prudent to remember that the patent's disclosure is in the public domain; know-how transferred to the licensee is not public. The licensor should consider including restrictions of the non-patented technology to third-parties and employees who do not need the technology to implement the license agreement. The licensor will want to include a provision enabling it to compel the licensee to enforce the provision against the licensee's employees for breach and to provide for the return or destruction of the confidential information upon expiration or termination of the agreement. The licensee will want to consider whether post-termination residual rights are necessary. Consider the following carve-out:

*Licensee shall not be required to purge electronic backup and archival copies of License information made in the ordinary course of business, which may contain Licensor Confidential Information.*

If the licensee insists on such a provision is there something the licensor can negotiate for in return?

See the definition of confidentiality in Definitions, *supra*. Note that it only protects the licensor. Should such a term be mutual? What is the standard of protection for confidential information? The standard could be to "hold in confidence" or to impose the same measures as the recipient uses to protect its own information. Is the recipient liable for inadvertent or accidental disclosure? What is the duration of the covenant? Note: Sublicensees should only be allowed access to confidential and proprietary information upon signing covenants at least as restrictive as those in the main agreement.

---

## L. Indemnification

*Licensee's Indemnification.* Licensee shall indemnify and hold Licensor harmless from and against any and all actual expenses, damages, costs and liabilities incurred by Licensor arising out of or relating to: (i) Licensee's, or any of its agent's, vendor's, or employee's, negligent or reckless manufacture of Licensed Product; (ii) Licensee's, or any of its agent's, vendor's, or employee's, negligent or reckless use or sale of Licensed Product; (iii) Licensee's, or any of its agent's, vendor's, or employee's, use, installation, or maintenance of the equipment used in connection with the Licensed Process; (iv) any Event of Default under this Agreement on the part of Licensee; (v) any loss, damage, or expense incurred by Licensor as a result of any advertising claim or any other representation or warranty made by Licensee, or any of its agents, vendors, or employees, that Licensed Product may have any capability or characteristic beyond that set forth in Licensor's own advertising literature with respect to Licensed Product; and (vi) any and all claims, actions, suits, proceedings, demands, assessments, penalties, obligations, judgments, costs, and reasonable legal and other expenses incident to any of the foregoing or incurred in investigating, defending or attempting to avoid the same, opposing the imposition thereof or in enforcing this indemnity.

*Licensor's Indemnification.* Licensor shall indemnify and hold Licensee harmless from and against any and all actual expenses, damages, costs and liabilities incurred by Licensee arising out of or relating to (i) any inaccurate representation or breach of warranty by Licensor under Section XX; (ii) any Event of Default under this Agreement on the part of Licensor; (iii) Licensee's manufacture or use of any Licensed Product or proper manufacture, use, or sale of any Licensed Product or Licensee's use of the Licensed Patent, the Licensor Confidential Information, or the Licensed Process, including any claim for property damage, personal injury, or patent infringement made against Licensee, arising out of or relating to any of the foregoing (which indemnity is not available if any of the foregoing are attributable to an Event of Default by Licensee or Licensee's, or any of its agent's, vendor's, or employee's negligence, recklessness, or willful misconduct); and (iv) any and all claims, actions, suits, proceedings, demands, assessments, penalties, obligations, judgments, costs and reasonable legal and other expenses incident to any of the foregoing or incurred in investigating, defending or attempting to avoid the same, opposing the imposition thereof, or in enforcing this indemnity.

*Insurance.* Notwithstanding anything to the contrary contained herein, and without in any manner limiting or relieving Licensor from its obligations pursuant to Section XXX hereof, Licensor shall obtain and maintain in full force and effect for the duration of this Agreement, general liability insurance in the minimum amount of $1,000,000 per occurrence in order to protect Licensee against any and all damages, losses, obligations and liabilities against which Licensee is indemnified pursuant to Section XXX above.

An indemnification clause shifts the risk of third-party claims from one party to another. The principle behind an indemnification clause is that the party most able to protect against such potential liability should be responsible for all resultant losses.

Depending on the structure of the deal and the relative bargaining power of the parties, most intellectual property licenses will include some sort of intellectual property indemnification clause. For software licenses, the licensee will usually demand indemnification. For further development of new technology, the licensor is more likely to demand indemnification from licensee. If both parties are providing materials for a collaborative effort, the parties may want mutual indemnifications. Is the indemnification limited to a specific type of intellectual property (e.g. patent)? Is it limited to "willful" patent infringement? Is it subject to the limitation of liability cap, or does it include time limitations? Is it limited to claims arising in the U.S. or worldwide? Are there exclusions from indemnity? Examples of this include unauthorized use by the licensee or failure of the licensee to use the latest version of the intellectual property.

The indemnitee should be required to provide prompt notice to the indemnitor of any claim the indemnitee becomes aware of. Who controls the defense and settlement? Are costs reimbursed as they are incurred or only after "final" resolution of the dispute? What are the indemnitor's obligations regarding finding replacements for the infringed technology? Is the indemnitor allowed to choose between finding a replacement, making the product non-infringing, or providing functionally equivalent technology? Alternatively, the indemnitor may choose to merely refund the license fee to the indemnitee upon notice of a claim or cancel the contract. The indemnitor may want to refrain from offering indemnification for foreign transactions until the indemnitor conducts due diligence in the product market of that particular foreign country.

Also either party may consider adding an insurance clause in the agreement to ensure that the other party carries insurance so that it can fulfill its obligations to indemnify.

----

# M. Quality Control (Trademark)

*Goodwill and Ownership. Licensee recognizes the value of the goodwill associated with the Trademark, and acknowledges that the Trademark and all rights therein and the goodwill appurtenant thereto and which accrues during the Term of this License Agreement belong exclusively to Licensor, and Licensee shall not acquire any rights in the Trademark other than as explicitly granted herein. Licensor retains the right to use and to license the use of the Trademark for any and all goods or services except as expressly set forth herein.*

*Quality Of Goods. The quality of the Licensed Product sold during the Term of this License Agreement as well as the manner and style in which the Trademark is used by Licensee shall be at least as high as the quality standards maintained by Licensor prior to the Effective Date.*

*Quality Control. Licensee may not use, offer for sale, sell, advertise, ship, or distribute any Licensed Product bearing the Trademark until Licensee has provided Licensor with a sample of the use of the Trademark on Licensed Product and has received written approval from Licensor for such use and sale during the Term. After Licensor approves the samples, Licensee shall not deviate therefrom in any respect without first obtaining the prior written approval of Licensor, which approval shall not be unreasonably withheld.*

Under United States trademark law, a licensor must either assert quality control over the products manufactured under the licensed trademark or be able to do so. If there are no quality control provisions in a trademark license agreement and/or the licensor cannot assert quality control over the finished product, courts will deem the license invalid and the trademark usually abandoned by the licensor.

The best way to avoid these dire consequences is to ensure that adequate quality control provisions are included in any trademark license agreement. These clauses are sometimes very long and complicated, requiring the licensee to provide the licensor with product samples and wait for the licensor's approval prior to marketing the products. Sometimes they are very brief, allowing the licensor simply to observe and reject products bearing the trademark. At a minimum, the language should clarify the licensor's right to inspect the manufacturing facility, the minimum standards for the relevant products, and consequences of the licensee's failure to adhere to the license agreement.

Also under United States trademark law, use is necessary to maintain rights in or to a trademark. Use by a licensee inures to the licensor; however, if the licensee licenses a mark and does not use it for three years, a rebuttable presumption arises that the mark has been abandoned. Therefore, the license agreement should contain a clause requiring the licensee to use the mark and notify the licensor if it ceases using the mark.

---

# N. Exploitation by Licensee

*Licensee shall use commercially reasonable efforts consistent with the efforts made by Licensee with respect to Licensee's other products during the five-year period preceding the Effective Date to develop and commercially launch the Licensed Product within three years of the Effective Date. After launching the Licensed Product, Licensee shall, at its own expense, use its best efforts to market, advertise, distribute, sell and promote the sale and use of the Licensed Product in the Territory, including attendance at the industry meetings, conventions and trade fairs set forth in Article VI. Licensee shall fully develop and exploit the market for the Licensed Product throughout the Territory and shall spend a minimum of $750,000 per year on such marketing efforts, excluding overhead. Notwithstanding the foregoing, Licensee shall not be required to undertake any activity contemplated herein if such activity would not generate a profit that is, in Licensee's reasonable judgment, sufficient to justify the efforts involved.*

The licensor will want to insure that the licensee uses its "best efforts" to develop and sell a royalty-bearing product, while the licensee will want to promise a good deal less, since the unpredictable vagaries of business may make some license obligations impractical. The exploitation clause is a key part of any exclusive license because the licensor will depend entirely upon a single licensee (at least in a particular field and territory) to secure a return on its investment. The licensor will want to insure that the exclusive licensee does not fail, whether intentionally or otherwise, to make the licensed product a commercial success.

Courts have come to generally interpret "best efforts" as "reasonable efforts," a tepid standard to be sure. While courts will presume a best efforts clause in license agreements, including the clause permits a licensor to sue for breach of contract and obtain damages in the amount of a reasonable royalty had the licensee put the intellectual property to its reasonable use.

The preferred approach to enforcing best efforts from a licensee is to include in the clause a list of very specific obligations coupled with the right to terminate the license for noncompliance. Such performance requirements might include, for example, a minimum number of annual sales contacts per year and submission of marketing plans, budgets, milestone data requirements, and quarterly sales activity reports. In the case of biotechnology and new drug development, licensors may insist upon a timetable for commercialization with milestone payments due at certain stages of development:

*Licensee shall obtain all government permits and approvals necessary to commercialize Licensed Products within 24 months of the date of this Agreement. Upon securing such approvals, Licensee shall pay to Licensor $750,000.*

The parties should consider the consequences of the licensee's failure to meet its obligations. Can the licensor terminate the contract? Is the failure to meet such obligations defined as a material breach of the agreement? How often should the licensee report on its progress to the licensor? In the exploitation clause above, does the last sentence excuse the licensee from using "commercially reasonable efforts" to exploit? Which party does the clause protect?

---

## O.  Third Party Infringement, Standing to Sue, and Control of Litigation

**Action by Licensor.** *With respect to the Licensed Rights only, when information comes to the attention of Licensor or Licensee to the effect that any of the Licensed Rights in the Field of Use have been or are threatened to be infringed by a third party, Licensor or Licensee, as the case may be, shall notify the other party in writing of any such infringement or threatened infringement of which it becomes aware. Licensor shall have the initial right but not the obligation to take any action to stop such infringement or otherwise enforce Licensee's rights and Licensee shall, at Licensor's expense, cooperate with Licensor in any such action. If Licensor determines that it is necessary or desirable for Licensee to join any such suit, action or proceeding, Licensee shall, at Licensor's expense, execute all documents and perform such other acts as may be reasonably required. If Licensor initiates suit hereunder it shall have the exclusive right to employ counsel of its own selection and to direct and control the litigation or any settlement thereof (subject to the penultimate sentence hereof) and shall be entitled to first reimburse itself out of any sums recovered in such suit or in settlement thereof for all costs and expenses, including reasonable attorneys' fees, necessarily involved in the prosecution of such suit, and any funds that shall remain from said recovery shall be distributed to Licensor and Licensee in proportion to the loss incurred by each of them. In any such action, Licensee shall, at it own expense, have the right to non-controlling participation through counsel of its own selection. If Licensor desires to settle such claim or suit, it shall first give Licensee written notice of the terms of the proposed settlement and Licensee shall have the right to approve or reject such proposal. The failure of Licensee to respond to a notice of settlement within ten (10) business days following the giving of such notice by Lumen shall automatically constitute an approval of the terms of the proposed settlement contained therein.*

**Action by Licensee.** *In the event Licensor takes no action to stop such infringement within ninety (90) days of receipt of notice from Licensee or within ninety (90) days of it*

*otherwise becoming aware of such infringement, Licensee shall have the right to com-*
*mence an action against such infringement, at its own expense and in its own name and*
*shall have the right to join Licensor as a party plaintiff and Licensor shall join in any*
*such action. Licensor shall execute all documents and take all other actions, at Licensee's*
*expense, including giving testimony, which may reasonably be required in connection*
*with such suit, action or proceeding. In any action instituted by Licensee under this Sec-*
*tion 6(c)(ii), Licensee shall have the exclusive right to employ counsel of its own selection*
*and to direct and control the litigation or any settlement thereof (subject to the penulti-*
*mate sentence hereof) and shall be entitled to first reimburse itself out of any sums recov-*
*ered in such suit or in settlement thereof for all costs and expenses, including reasonable*
*attorneys' fees, necessarily involved in the prosecution of such suit, and any funds that*
*shall remain from said recovery shall be distributed to Licensor and Licensee in propor-*
*tion to the loss incurred by each of Licensor and Licensee. Licensor shall, at it own ex-*
*pense, have the right to non-controlling participation through counsel of its own selec-*
*tion. If Licensee desires to settle such claim or suit, it shall first give Licensor written*
*notice of the terms of the proposed settlement and Licensor shall have the right to ap-*
*prove or reject such proposal. The failure of Licensor to respond to a notice of settlement*
*within ten (10) business days following the giving of such notice by Licensee shall auto-*
*matically constitute an approval of the terms of the proposed settlement contained*
*therein.*

When negotiating infringement litigation clauses, consider the downside of exposing the parties to risks of litigation over inconsequential infringements. Might there
be reasonable market thresholds to be met? Which party makes the determination as
to what is infringing activity? Is there some neutral standard that can be incorporated
into the agreement such as an independent opinion of third party counsel? Consider
who should have the right to recover damages. The parties will want to provide reciprocal duties to cooperate in favor of the party bringing the infringement action. The
license should include responsibility for costs of litigation and distribution of the
proceeds. Aren't such settlements in the nature of royalties and thus payable to the licensor?

---

## P. Term, Termination and Post-Termination Rights and Obligations

*Term. This Agreement shall commence as of the Effective Date and shall expire upon*
*expiration of the Licensed Patent unless earlier terminated in accordance with a provi-*
*sion of this Agreement. Expiration as used herein shall mean the expiration of the Li-*
*censed Patent at the end of its statutory term; expiration for failure to pay fees when due,*
*which failure is not remedied within the time provided for by 37 C.F.R. § 1.362; or with*
*respect to the Licensed Patent, a final judgment of patent invalidity or unenforceability*
*by a court or administrative agency of competent jurisdiction from which no appeal is or*
*can be taken.*

*Termination. Either party may terminate this Agreement upon ninety- (90-) days' writ-*
*ten notice for any material breach or default of the other party hereto. Such notice shall be-*
*come effective at the end of the ninety-day period unless during such ninety-day period the*
*party in breach shall cure such breach or default or, if such breach is incapable of being*

*cured within such ninety-day period, the party in breach begins substantial efforts to cure such breach or default.*

*Upon termination of this Agreement for any reason:*

    (i)  *Licensor's right to receive all payments accrued and unpaid on the effective date of such termination shall survive the termination or expiration of this Agreement until fully discharged.*

    (ii)  *All manufacture of the Licensed Products shall cease. Licensee may sell, offer to sell, advertise and promote its existing inventory of Licensed Products on a non-exclusive basis for a period not to exceed sixty (60) days post-termination (the "Post-Termination Period"); provided, however, that the Royalty Amount shall be due and payable on all Post-Termination sales within forty-five (45) days after the Post-Termination Period and shall be accompanied by the report required in Section 6.1. Licensee may continue to use its Labeling and Promotional Literature during the Post-Termination Period only in conjunction with the activities set forth in the preceding sentence. Upon the expiration of the Post-Termination Period, all use of the Trademark and Labeling and Promotional Literature shall cease; all sales and offers to sell, advertising and promotion of the Licensed Products shall immediately cease; and all remaining Labeling and Promotional Literature shall be destroyed and its destruction certified by an officer of Licensee.*

    (iii)  *Any other remedies which either party may then or thereafter have hereunder or otherwise shall survive.*

The agreement should contain clear provisions for the term of the agreement, termination upon default or breach of either party, and voluntary termination.

If the licensed intellectual property includes multiple patents, a clause stating that the agreement does not terminate until all the licensed patents expire may be included. Consider also whether royalties should abate if several of the licensed patents expire while the others do not. If the license is a license of patents, and the term is silent, the court will construe "the term of the agreement" to mean the life of the licensed patent. If the licensed property is a trademark, the term of the agreement, and some post-expiration period to sell inventory, is the appropriate term. Other "terms" should be considered and discussed with the client. For example, in some cases the term of the agreement may be more appropriately expressed as the life cycle of a product, if shorter than the life of the licensed patent, or upon market obsolescence.

In the event of termination by either party, the parties should address the consequences in each circumstance: (i) what rights continue or terminate; (ii) penalties for termination; (iii) whether termination is the sole remedy for certain failures; (iv) the fate of downstream licensees; and (v) support and maintenance of the installed base in the case of copyright/software licenses.

Consider the following questions. Upon termination, does the licensee have the right to liquidate its inventory of a licensed product? If so, during what period of time? Can the licensee complete its manufacture of work-in-process? What happens to outstanding purchase orders? Should the licensee return or destroy any licensed information or information disclosed under a non-disclosure agreement? Does the licensor have a right to use licensee's data and, if so, under what terms? Do any terms of the agreement survive termination? If so, those surviving terms must be expressly listed.

# Q. "Not So Boilerplate" Provisions

1. **Force Majeure Events.** Consider the following two force majeure clauses:

*A. Neither party shall be liable to the other for any failure to perform as required by this Agreement, to the extent such failure to perform is caused by any of the following: labor disturbances or disputes of any kind, accidents, failure to obtain any required governmental approval, civil disorders, acts of aggression, acts of God, strikes, fires, floods, embargoes, war, energy or other conservation measure, failure of utilities, mechanical breakdowns, material shortages, disease, or similar occurrences.*

*B. Neither party shall be liable to the other for any failure to perform as required by this Agreement, to the extent such failure to perform is caused by any of the following: civil disorders, acts of aggression, acts of God, floods, earthquakes, riots, embargoes, war, or any similar cause beyond the control of, or occurring without the fault of the party whose performance is excused under this Section (the "Excused Party") and which could not have been avoided by the exercise of due care. The Excused Party shall give notice to the other party detailing the force majeure event that the Excused Party claims excuses performance hereunder and the time period during which the Excused Party desires to have its performance excused. As soon as possible after cessation of the force majeure event upon which the Excused Party is relying, the Excused Party shall once again be obligated to perform in accordance with the terms and conditions of this Agreement.*

As anyone who has ever litigated a force majeure clause will testify, they are not just boilerplate. Parties typically include the force majeure clause to be able to cancel their respective obligations if wars, riots, acts of terrorism, foreign government intervention, *et cetera.* make the performance of the contract impossible. The legal definition of force majeure is a force outside the control of the parties and which cannot be avoided by the exercise of due care. BLACK'S LAW DICTIONARY, 673 (8th ed. 2004). So the failure to include such a clause may require the licensee to make minimum royalty payments even though intervening events have made performance impossible. However, proposed force majeure clauses must be examined to insure that the acts identified as force majeure events are truly outside the control of the party who is seeking to have performance excused. Alternatively, a clause may be drafted specifically stating events are force majeure only if they are outside the control of the party seeking to have its performance excused.

Consider Clause A above. Are strikes, labor unrest, fires, and material shortages outside the control of the parties? What if low wages or inhospitable working conditions were the cause of the strike or labor unrest? Is that outside the control of the licensee? What exactly is "labor unrest"? Is a fire a force majeure event when the party seeking to have performance excused left paint close to machinery that was producing sparks and caused ignition? Is a shortage of raw materials a force majeure event? Can't the licensee go out into the "spot" market and procure a supply of raw materials to make the licensed product? Is an accident ever a force majeure event? If Johnny Jones is injured on the line should the licensee be excused from paying royalties? Is a "failure of utilities" a force majeure event? What if the licensee failed to pay its electric bill? Consider the situation where the licensed product is a medical device that required it be cleared for marketing by the Food and Drug Administration. Under what circumstances can a "failure to obtain any required governmental approval" be considered a force majeure event? When is failure to procure governmental approval not a force majeure event? After numerous submissions to FDA or only after one submission? The parties must take care in drafting the force majeure clause. Unfortunately, parties do not take care in drafting force majeure clauses: these clauses are often cut and pasted from document to document, frequently with unintended results.

Consider the force majeure Clause B above. The clause is limited to acts beyond the control of the parties and which could not have been avoided by the exercise of due care. By including this type of language, the force majeure clause will cover acts that are not listed if the party seeking to have performance excused can demonstrate that the act in question meets the required terminology. However, the clause also goes further by excusing performance only, during the duration of that force majeure event. As soon as the event terminates, the excused party is obligated once again to perform. Should the drafting attorney also include a further sentence that failure to perform after cessation of the force majeure event is cause for termination? Or can this be considered a material breach, which in most contracts is always cause for termination?

2. **Assignment and Transferability.**

Consider the following Assignment clauses:

- *This Agreement may not be assigned by Licensee without the prior written approval of Licensor. For the purposes of this section, a change in the persons or entities who control 50% or more of the equity securities or voting interest of Licensee shall be considered an assignment of Licensee's rights.*

- *Licensee may assign this Agreement to any person to whom it transfers all or substantially all of its proprietary rights in the Product provided that such person is not a competitor of Licensor. Otherwise, neither party may assign, voluntarily, by operation of law, or otherwise, any rights or delegate any duties under this Agreement (other than the right to receive payments) without Licensee's prior written consent, and any attempt to do so without that consent will be void. This Agreement will bind and inure to the benefit of the parties and their respective successors and permitted assigns.*

- *This Agreement is not assignable by licensee, voluntarily or by operation of law or otherwise, without the prior written consent of the Licensor. Licensee may not assign this Agreement except to a successor to substantially the entire business of Licensee, without the prior written consent of Licensor. The terms of this Agreement shall be binding upon and inure to the benefit of and be enforceable by the permitted respective successors and assigns of the parties hereto.*

Assignment clauses are typically considered "boiler-plate" with little thought being given to what type of clause should be included in the agreement. When a licensee-corporation is acquired, the licensor may find that valuable intellectual property rights are not only in the possession of one of its competitors but now the competitor also has a license to practice those rights; this is an eye-opening experience for any licensor. How do the three assignment clauses above differ? What are the differences trying to accomplish? Does it really matter?

With these three clauses in mind, consider the following article, which introduces the effect of corporate law on unwitting licensors and licensees of intellectual property. After reading the article, consider the effect on a licensor who agreed to any one of the assignment clauses drafted above. Which assignment clause would best protect the licensor?

# Will Intellectual Property Rights Survive a Merger?*

Jon Dettmann & Mike Stanchfield

15 J. Proprietary Rts. 9 (2003)

A company acquires a multimillion-dollar company with a license to technology that is critical to the strategic future of the acquiror's business. The transaction took nearly a year to complete and thousands of hours to finalize. The structure, a "forward-triangular" merger in which the target corporation merges out of existence into a newly created shell subsidiary, is complicated, but it defers taxation for the target corporation's shareholders. It is a good deal for all concerned.

But the acquiror should not break out the champagne yet. Imagine that the next phone call is from an arch-competitor making a startling claim. He says that it turns out that the competitor licensed this critical technology years earlier to the company that was just acquired. And, because of the way that the acquiror structured its merger deal, the license was improperly transferred and is now void . . . and he also mentions that the price to re-license the technology just went up. A lot.

\* \* \*

[T]he next day the competitor files a complaint in federal court, alleging breach of the license agreement and infringement of the underlying patent. A year later, after a painful and expensive discovery period, the court grants the competitor's motion for summary judgment and renders the license void. . . .

## License Voided

Licensors of intellectual property may argue that a merger in which a licensee does not "survive" as a separate corporate entity may void the license, even if the license agreement contained no prohibition against merger, acquisition, or transfer.

This argument is based on an arcane line of federal cases holding that "patent licenses are not assignable unless expressly made so." More recently, some federal courts have extended this rule in ways that affect corporate mergers and have found, in effect, that certain mergers can constitute transfers that void patent licenses. . . .

## How Mergers Work

Does a merger involve a transfer of assets? Most statutes say no.

The corporation laws of most states . . . provide that, in the event of a merger, the merging corporation ceases to exist as a separate legal entity and all of its assets [vest] in the surviving corporation. . . . Originally, most state statutes said either "transferred to" or "transferred to and vested in." This language . . . has been eliminated from most (but not all) merger statutes, specifically to avoid any "transfer" of assets resulting from the transaction. . . . If mergers did create an express transfer of assets from a merging to a surviving corporation, then none of the non-transferable assets of the merging corporation would survive the transaction.

## Three Structures

There are three principal ways that mergers are generally structured:

---

* Reprinted by permission of the authors and their law firm, Faegre & Benson LLP, Minneapolis MN, copyright 2003.

1.    A "direct" merger merges the target into the acquirer, with the target ceasing to exist.

2.    A "forward-triangular" merger merges the target into a shell subsidiary of the acquirer, with the target ceasing to exist.

3.    A "reverse subsidiary" merger merges the shell subsidiary into the target, with the target surviving.

\* \* \*

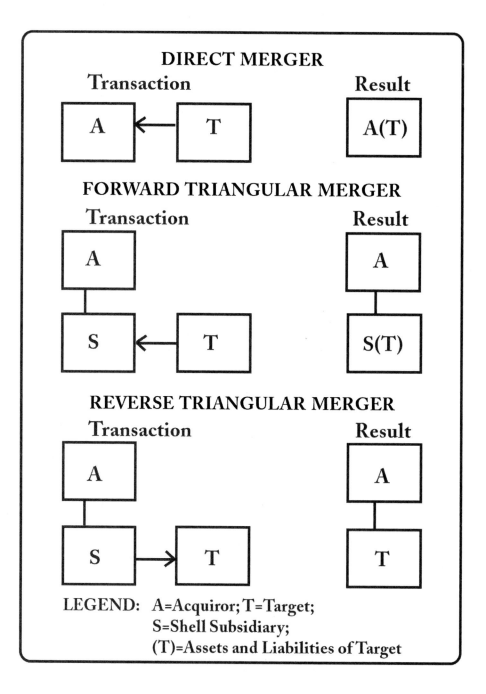

One of the most advantageous transactional forms for...beneficial tax deferment is the forward triangular merger, in which the target does not survive. Other than to the IRS, however, there is no significance in this choice to any outside party, such as a patent licensor, and no basis for any rule on assignability of assets that runs contrary to state corporation statutes. To any third party, the effect of the transaction is exactly the same. So why are IP rights potentially at risk? The answer comes from a rare and nearly extinct branch of the law known as federal general common law.

## An *Erie* Problem

To trace the roots of this issue, one has to go all the way back to 1852. In the case of *Troy Iron & Nail Factory v. Corning,* the U.S. Supreme Court alluded to a supposed rule that patent licenses were not assignable unless the contract explicitly said so. In other words, if a patent license said nothing about its assignability, then the license was not assignable, and a licensee could not transfer the license without the licensor's consent. Although this rule was contrary to the standard doctrine that contracts are assignable absent a provision to the contrary, the Supreme Court subsequently recognized it as a federal general common law rule, a judicially created federal rule, in several of its other decisions that century.

The Supreme Court has never recognized this rule in modern times, and in 1938, the Supreme Court discarded altogether the notion of federal general common law in the landmark case *Erie R.R. v. Tompkins* when it held, "There is no federal general common law." But the Supreme Court never struck down the purported rule on assignability, and even since *Erie,* several federal circuit courts, including the Sixth, Seventh, and Ninth Circuits, have continued to recognize the rule.

## The *PPG Industries* Case

In the context of a corporate merger, the most important of these cases is *PPG Industries, Inc. v. Guardian Industries Corp.,* a 1979 case out of the Sixth Circuit. *PPG* presented a problem similar to the one described above: A licensee merged into a competitor of the licensor; the license was expressly not transferable; and the licensor cried foul. In voiding the license, the Sixth Circuit recognized the purported federal rule and found that the applicable state merger laws did create a transfer of assets (even though one of them, Delaware, used only the "vested in" language). The court held that it was up to the licensee to negotiate a provision allowing it to merge, which the licensee had failed to do.

The main difference between *PPG* and the situation described above is that in *PPG* the licensee merged directly into its competitor. In the hypothetical, the licensee merged into a shell corporation, with no assets or liabilities of its own, created for the single purpose of effecting the acquisition. At least some federal district courts have distinguished similar situations as an exception to the federal rule because the only result of the transaction is a transformation in the licensee's corporate form.

In other words, in the eyes of the licensor, the licensee looks exactly the same as it did prior to the transaction, as opposed to a direct merger, in which the ultimate result may be a much larger entity. As recently as last year, however, a federal district court in the Eastern District of Missouri reviewed a forward-triangular merger and found that "federal law governs the issue of transferability of [a patent license] and that the [forward triangular] merger constituted a transfer." After 150 years, federal courts are still applying the rule.

Nevertheless, there are substantial flaws in this doctrine. First, the structure of the merger, which is usually chosen primarily for tax purposes, cannot matter to the licensor. The acquiring company could accomplish the same result by reverse-triangular merger, or even by a simple direct stock purchase or tender offer, without triggering the federal general common law rule. There is no reason such a rule should apply to some mergers and acquisitions but not to others when the ultimate result is the same.

Second, this federal common law doctrine would not seem able to survive the *Erie* decision. In order for federal courts to create federal general common law, there must be some significant conflict between state law and some federal policy or interest. But the federal patent laws are silent on patent licenses, and in fact, the Supreme Court has repeatedly recognized that patent licenses, like all other contracts, are governed by state law. Federal general common law cannot be used for the mere purpose of shifting a contracting burden. Yet that is all this purported rule does. It shifts the burden from the licensor to the licensee to obtain express provisions regarding transferability and merger.

### Avoiding the Problem

The easiest way to avoid this problem is to negotiate around it in advance. The doctrine applies only if there is no merger-related provision in the licensing agreement, so parties can avoid any dispute by negotiating terms in a license related to a possible merger of the licensee. Although such terms may make the license more expensive, the increase in price will pale in comparison to the expense of foregoing significant tax benefits or having to renegotiate a favorable license. Importantly, choosing the law of a particular state to govern the contract may not be enough to avoid application of the federal doctrine. Some courts have done so anyway.

If the license already exists, however, and a merger transaction is on the horizon, then it is important to understand the possible impact of this doctrine during the initial stages of the deal. During due diligence, the buyer should conduct a thorough review of all intellectual property licenses. If a potential problem is uncovered, the parties may want to consider alternative structures to get the deal done. If it is possible to obtain tax deferment through a reverse subsidiary merger, for example, then this may be a preferable form. For those acquisitions that cannot qualify for tax deferment under this form, there is one other option, called a "double dummy" or "double wing" merger, which is more complicated, but which may offer the same tax benefits with the licensee still surviving as a legal entity.

If the transaction is already too far along, then the company may decide—in fact, may need—to damn the torpedoes and accept the litigation risk. Recent Supreme Court decisions indicate that the court continues to be skeptical of federal general common law.

Moreover, some lower federal courts have recognized that the rule does not apply to mere changes in corporate form, suggesting that some courts would accept forward-triangular mergers as an exception to the rule.

The fact is, however, that acquirers can still get caught in the unfortunate position of having to renegotiate valuable license agreements or to surrender them altogether. Knowing and understanding this rule in advance may prevent a company from having a merger celebration cut short.

---

## R.  General Provisions

**1. Patent Marking.** A licensor should include a provision that obligates the licensee to mark licensed products for any approved use or distribution. *See* U.S.C. § 287.

**2. Governing Law and Dispute Resolution.** What law governs the agreement? Obviously, most parties strongly prefer to be governed by the forum and laws of their own jurisdiction. Distinguish between governing law and jurisdiction. The parties might provide that governing law is a neutral jurisdiction where neither party resides but which has ample case law on the subject. For example, New York and California might be suitable choices for governing law in a copyright license. Forum is a different matter. While there never seems to be a problem when both parties reside in one state, what is the result when the parties reside in different states? Consider providing a disincentive to litigation. In other words, if the licensor brings suit she will do so in the licensee's jurisdiction and if the licensee brings suit, he will do so in the licensor's jurisdiction. What if licensor and licenses are in different countries? Arbitration clauses are common in license agreements and can be tailored to the needs of the parties, including the preservation of rights to seek injunctive relief at any time in the process. For a detailed discussion about alternative dispute resolution in licensing, see Chapter 10.

**3. Notice.** Be sure to provide for personal delivery, electronic transmission and facsimile transmission if the parties desire. If one of the parties resides in a foreign jurisdiction, be sure to provide for service that actually exists in that jurisdiction. For example, many foreign jurisdictions do not have "registered" or "certified" mail and the U.S. Postal Service may not offer that type of service in a particular foreign jurisdiction.

**4. Controlling Language.** If one party to a license agreement is a foreign corporation, the controlling language should be specified especially when arbitration has been provided. If no controlling language is provided, consider the affect a translation into French might have on the interpretation of the agreement.

**5. Export Control.** This clause should apply to exports and re-exports and to the provision of information to foreign nationals even in the United States. Export issues are subject to the Export Administration Regulations (EAR). The parties must look to the EAR to determine whether an export license is needed.

---

# III. Strategic Alliances and Special Considerations

Strategic alliances were born in the early 1980s when cash-strapped biotech companies looked for assistance from Big Pharma partners to fund their R&D efforts. The small biotech company usually retained ownership of the resulting intellectual property and Big Pharma gained an equity position in the company. Since that time strategic alliances have become a household word. Although they have many forms, everyone has heard of them and has their own idea of what they are. Most strategic alliances, however, have certain things in common. In some instances, one party's technology will be leveraged with another party's marketing savvy, distribution channels and/or marketing capabilities, or knowledge of regulatory hurdles. There is typically a substantial contribution of technology and/or R&D efforts by one party with funding by the other. In exchange for an on-going royalty or other consideration, one company may obtain the manufacturing or distribution rights, or both, to the developed technology. The following articles introduce the subject of joint ownership of intellectual property resulting from a strategic alliance or joint development program and the different types of issues that may arise when the parties are not diligent about reducing their agreement to writing.

---

# Joint Ownership of Intellectual Property Issues and Approaches in Strategic Alliances

Gary H. Moore*
4 Internet Law & Bus. 749 (2003)

## I. INTRODUCTION

Strategic alliances often include collaboration in research or development. Indeed, the potential for collaborative development may be one of the key factors in the establishment of the alliance. The ownership status of joint development efforts, and the parties' respective rights and obligations with respect to them, both during the alliance and afterwards, are often important issues in structuring the relationship.

One solution that is frequently proposed is that intellectual property developed in the course of this collaboration should be "jointly owned" by both parties. With truly collaborative development efforts, it may be difficult to separate the contributions of each party. Employees from each party may jointly develop different aspects or modules of strategic technology or software, and may even be co-inventors on patentable inventions. Pre-existing technology or proprietary content of the parties may be combined into an integrated product or solution. Moreover, joint ownership may in fact arise, by default, from some joint development activities, unless the parties explicitly provide to the contrary.

In these settings, joint ownership may seem like a fair and symmetrical solution. The parties may also believe that joint ownership is simpler than trying to allocate ownership to one party or the other. But joint ownership of intellectual property is anything but simple. Joint ownership creates numerous complexities. To make matters worse, the rights and duties of joint owners are poorly understood by many business people, vary between the different forms of intellectual property, and also vary from country to country. Joint ownership, therefore, has the potential for serious unintended consequences, if not carefully considered and structured. Because of this, many lawyers have a justifiable reluctance to provide for joint ownership, and it is often wise to avoid it if other structures can be used to achieve the parties' objectives. Despite its complexities, however, joint ownership may be an appropriate solution in some cases. Or, whether or not appropriate, it may be insisted upon by one or both of the parties.

\* \* \*

## II. JOINT OWNERSHIP IS POSSIBLE

### A. Patents and Copyrights

Patents and copyrights are personal property, and it is clearly established that multiple owners may own joint undivided interests in them. If multiple persons are co-inven-

---

tors of a patentable invention or co-authors of a joint work of authorship, joint owner-ship may arise by operation of law in the absence of an agreement to the contrary. Joint ownership can also be created by a sole owner conveying an undivided interest in the patent or copyright to one or more third parties.

Under both patent and copyright law, assignments must be in writing. Both patent and copyright law also provide for recordation of assignments. An unrecorded assign-ment is valid as between the two parties, but will be void against a subsequent transferee who takes an assignment in good faith for a valuable consideration without notice of the prior assignment. Thus, if the parties are relying on an assignment of copyrights or patents to achieve joint ownership, they should record the assignment. Note that the re-quirement of recordation applies to assignments (and some exclusive licenses), but does not apply to non-exclusive licenses, which survive a subsequent assignment of the patent or copyright whether or not the subsequent assignee had notice of the non-ex-clusive license. Thus, if the parties merely grant each other non-exclusive licenses in their relevant solely-owned intellectual property, recordation is not necessary.

There is a well-developed body of U.S. law concerning the respective rights of co-owners of patents and copyrights. But for reasons that will be discussed below, it is best not to rely upon on these default rules, which can yield conflicting and unintended re-sults. Joint ownership of patents and copyrights is also recognized in most foreign juris-dictions. However, the rights of the joint ownership may be significantly different than under U.S. law, which can also create traps for the unwary.

### B. Trade Secrets

In contrast to patents and copyrights, there is limited law on the subject of joint ownership of trade secrets. But joint ownership of trade secrets has also been recog-nized, at least in a few cases. Although trade secrets are treated as personal property for many purposes, a trade secret's "proprietary" nature derives not from the knowledge it-self, but from its secrecy. In view of this attribute, the Fourth Circuit recently concluded that "the inherent nature of a trade secret limits the usefulness of an analogy to prop-erty in determining the elements of a trade-secret misappropriation claim," observing that "[w]hile the information forming the basis of a trade secret can be transferred, as with personal property, its continuing secrecy provides the value...." The peculiar na-ture of trade secrets needs to be taken into account in deciding what it means for trade secrets to be jointly "owned" by the parties and in defining the relationship between the parties calling for joint ownership.

### C. Trademarks

Joint ownership of trademarks is also possible, but only in limited circumstances. In most settings, the notion of two different parties owning a trademark runs counter to the fundamental purpose of a trademark, which is to serve as a designation of origin from a single, or at least singly controlled, source. As a result, joint ownership of trademarks is viable only in circumstances where the co-owners have in place a struc-ture to assure joint control over the nature and quality of goods or services to be sold under the mark.

It is worth noting that the legal obstacles to joint ownership of a *trademark* present no obstacles to joint ownership of an *entity* owning a trademark. If joint ownership of rights to a trademark is essential to a strategic alliance, the parties should in most cases consider forming a jointly-owned separate entity (joint venture, LLC, etc.) to own the mark and use or license it for the benefit of the owners. Because of the limited circumstances where joint ownership of trademarks would be appropriate, we will focus the remainder of this paper on other forms of intellectual property, i.e., patents, copyright and trade secrets.

## III. JOINT OWNERSHIP MAY ARISE WITHOUT EXPRESS AGREEMENT

In deciding whether and how to address joint ownership in a strategic alliance, the parties should bear in mind that joint ownership of patents and copyright can arise by operation of patent and copyright, without express agreement between the parties for such joint ownership. Thus, an agreement providing, for example, that each party will own the technology it develops in the course of the collaboration may be overly simplistic in cases where joint development may take place.

### A. Patents: Co-Inventors

If a patentable invention is made by two or more co-inventors, each co-inventor presumptively owns an undivided interest in the patent. As the Federal Circuit has observed, "where inventors choose to cooperate in the inventive process, their joint inventions may become joint property without some express agreement to the contrary."[1] Moreover, each co-inventor presumptively owns an undivided interest in the *entire* patent, even if a particular co-inventor contributed to the subject matter of only some of the claims in the patent.

In most corporate settings, each employee engaged in research and development will have signed a proprietary rights agreement, assigning rights in his or her inventions to the employer, with the result that the employer is the owner of the inventions and resulting patents. In collaborative development efforts between *two* companies, joint ownership of patentable inventions may arise by operation of law, if at least one employee of each company is a co-inventor. In that case, each company will presumptively be a co-owner of the patent (by assignment from its respective inventor-employees), unless there is some express agreement to the contrary.

It is not necessary that joint inventors physically work together or at the same time. Nor is it necessary that they each make the same type or amount of contribution, or contribute to the invention of every claim in a patent. What is necessary is that each co-inventor contributes, in some significant manner, to the "conception" of the invention. Conception occurs when there is a "definite and permanent idea of the complete invention" such that only ordinary skill would be necessary to reduce the invention to practice without extensive research or experimentation. On the other hand, a collaborator does not become a co-inventor merely by assisting the original inventor in explaining the current state of the art or assisting in reduction of the invention to practice using ordinary skill in the art. As the Federal Circuit has noted, the determination of whether a person is a joint inventor is "fact specific, and no bright-line standard will suffice in every case."

Whether employees of two companies are *inventors* of a patent is a matter of patent law, regardless of what the agreement between the parties may provide. Whether the two companies will be *co-owners* of the patents, on the other hand, is something that can be specified by agreement and is therefore within their control. If the parties wish to avoid joint ownership, their agreement can negate co-ownership by allocating sole ownership to one of the parties of inventions and resulting patents. To be completely clear on the point, the agreement should include an assignment of the other party's interest

---

1. *Ethicon Inc. v. United States Surgical Corp.*, 135 F.3d 1456, 1466 (Fed. Cir. 1998).

in such joint inventions. If the parties are silent on the subject of joint ownership, they may find themselves as joint owners by operation of law—with all the consequences of joint ownership discussed below, which may or may not match the parties' interests or expectations.

## B. Copyrights: Co-Authors

The Copyright Act expressly provides that authors of a "joint work" are co-owners of the copyright in the work. A "joint work" is a "work prepared by two or more authors with the intention that their contributions be merged into inseparable or interdependent parts of a unitary whole." Just as co-inventors of a patentable invention are presumptively co-owners of the patent, co-authors of a "joint work" are presumptively co-owners of the copyright in the joint work. Moreover, as with co-inventors of a patented invention, a co-author of a joint work owns an undivided interest in the joint work *as a whole*, even though he or she may have contributed to only a portion of it.

As with co-inventors, it is not necessary that co-authors work together physically or make their contributions at the same time. They may be complete strangers. Nor is there any requirement that the contributions of each co-author be equal in quantity or quality. However, beyond these similarities, the tests for determining co-authorship are quite distinct from the tests for determining co-inventor of an invention.

The first requirement for co-authorship, according to the majority rule, is that each co-author's contribution must itself be copyrightable subject matter. The Ninth Circuit's decision in *Ashton-Tate Corp. v. Ross*, [916 F.2d 516 (9th Cir. 1990)] illustrates the operation of this requirement. Two software developers decided to collaborate on development of a spreadsheet program for the Apple Macintosh. One worked on the "engine," while the other worked on the user interface. Later the two parted. The user interface developer went to work for Ashton-Tate, a software publisher, where he combined the user interface he had developed with a different "engine" to create a spreadsheet program called "Full Impact." The other developer claimed that he had an ownership interest in the copyright in Full Impact on the grounds that he was a co-author of the co-developer's user interface because he had contributed ideas and guidance to the development of the user interface and a handwritten sheet listing the commands the user interface should support. However, the Ninth Circuit held that the engine developer was not a co-author of the user interface because his contributions to it were not themselves copyrightable subject matter.

The second requirement for co-authorship relates to the intent of the parties or their respective control over the creation of the work, or both. This requirement is articulated differently in different circuits. The Second and Seventh Circuits focus on the intent of the parties. To be co-authors, both (or all if more than two) authors must *intend*, at the time of creation of their contribution, not only that their contributions "be merged into inseparable or interdependent parts of a unitary whole," but also that they will be co-authors of the resulting merged work. The Ninth Circuit, on the other hand, applies a multi-factor test to determine whether a contributor of copyright subject matter is a co-author of a joint work. The Ninth Circuit considers not only (a) whether the co-authors "objectively manifested" a "shared intent to be authors," but also (b) whether a putative co-author exercised "control" over the creation of the work, and (c) the "audience appeal" of the respective contributions.[2] Of these, according to the Ninth

---

2. *Aalmuhammed v. Lee*, 202 F.3d 1227, 1234 (9th Cir. 1999).

Circuit, "control in many cases will be most important" in the absence of any contract between the parties.

There is no requirement that the parties' mutual intent (or respective rights of control) be contained in any "collaboration agreement" or other writing. Indeed, there is no requirement that the parties have explicitly discussed the subject of co-authorship. However, a written agreement between the parties is the best "objective manifestation" of whether the parties intended to be or not to be co-authors of a joint work, and will probably fe dispositive in most cases.

It is important to distinguish a "joint work" from a "derivative work." Each of the co-authors of a joint work is a co-owner of the copyright in the joint work. However, the copyright in a derivative work belongs to the author of a derivative work, not the author of the work on which the derivative work is based. Thus, where one of two co-authors subsequently makes a derivative work based on the joint work, the other co-author's joint authorship in the prior joint work is insufficient to make him or her a joint author of the derivative work. Since it is possible for co-authors of a joint work to make their contributions at different times, what distinguishes a "joint work" in which both contributors are co-authors, from a "derivative work" in which they are not? The answer is the mutual intent of the co-authors to be, or not to be, co-authors, and, in the Ninth Circuit, whether they both exercised creative control over the work.

Unlike co-inventors of a patentable invention, parties collaborating to produce copyrightable works have some control over whether or not their work product will be considered a "joint work." Each individual's status as "co-inventor" of a patentable invention arises regardless of the terms of any agreement between them. Whether two parties are or are not co-authors of a joint work, on the other hand, depends upon (among other things) their intent. Thus, if parties do not want their collaborative efforts to be considered a joint work, they can effectively prevent that result by expressly providing in their agreement that they do not intend their respective contributions to be considered contributions to a joint work. Such an objective manifestation of mutual intent not to be co-authors of a joint work should be dispositive in most cases.

If they wish to have work product be considered a joint work, the collaboration agreement should so provide and unequivocally satisfy that element of co-authorship. However, under the majority rule such shared intent (and even shared creative control) is not sufficient to constitute contributors co-authors of a joint work, since to qualify as a co-author each contributor must in fact contribute copyrightable subject matter. If it is not clear that this latter requirement will be satisfied, but the parties nonetheless wish (despite the complications to be discussed in following sections) to have the resulting product be jointly owned, their agreement should contain an express assignment by each of an undivided interest in the copyright to the other party.

## IV. THE SUBJECT MATTER OF JOINT OWNERSHIP SHOULD BE CLEARLY DEFINED

As discussed above, silence on the subject of joint ownership may not prevent joint ownership from arising by operation of law. If the parties do not wish to be joint owners, they should take care to consider this possibility in drafting their agreement. For example, they may specify that one collaborator shall be the sole owner of any intellectual property in a specified subject matter, regardless of whether developed by it alone or jointly with the other party, and include an assignment by the non-owning party of its intellectual property rights than may otherwise accrue to it.

If the parties wish (or are willing) to be joint owners of intellectual property result-ing from their collaboration, they should define clearly the subject matter that is to be jointly owned. A general provision that intellectual property that may be "jointly devel-oped" during the course of a collaboration is to be jointly owned may not be clear enough for these purposes. For example, do "jointly developed" patents include only those for which for the parties' employees would qualify as co-inventors under the patents laws or is it to be judged by some other standard? If so, what standard? Do "jointly developed" works of authorship include only those to which both parties con-tribute copyrightable subject matter or are they to be judged by a different standard? If so, what standard?

One approach to defining the subject matter of joint ownership, particularly patents, is expressly to adopt the criteria of co-inventorship under the patent law. The parties may stipulate that the parties will jointly own any patent on which at least one employee from each company is deemed, as a matter of patent law, to be a co-inventor. In effect, the agreement does not change what would be jointly owned in the absence of the agreement, but serves to provide ground rules for the treatment of that which would be jointly owned if the agreement were silent. This approach has several advantages: (1) it leverages the es-tablished body of law on co-inventorship; (2) in the course of applying for the patent, the patent attorneys will in any event have to go through this exercise, since each co-inventor must be named in the patent as matter of patent law; and (3) it relates to subject matter that the parties in many cases may not be willing to allocate solely to the other party.

A similar approach is possible with respect to copyrights, but raises more issues. In the case of copyright, the parties are in a position to specify whether or not they wish to be co-authors, and a clear contract provision on point will probably be dispositive on that point. If the parties wish to be treated as co-owners of jointly developed copyright subject matter, they should consider and provides that joint ownership will require each party to have contributed copyrightable subject, to avoid uncertainty on that issue.

In other cases, the parties may wish to provide for joint ownership regardless of whether they would technically qualify as co-inventors or co-authors under patent or copyright. Examples of approaches to defining the subject of joint ownership include:

(i) Any inventions, improvements, works of authorship and other innovations made, conceived, developed or reduced to practice by either party, whether alone or jointly with the other party, *in the course of the agreement*, and all patents, copyrights, trade secrets and other intellectual property rights therein.

(ii) Any inventions, improvements, works of authorship and other innovations relating to [a defined subject matter] developed by either party, whether alone or jointly with the other party, during the course of the agreement, and all patents, copyrights, trade secrets and other intellectual property rights therein.

(iii) Any modifications or improvements to, or derivative works based upon [Party A's licensed intellectual property] developed by [Party B] during the course of the agreement.

(iv) [A defined product] and any intellectual property rights therein.

## V. EXPLOITING AND LICENSING JOINTLY OWNED INTELLECTUAL PROPERTY

One of the complexities of joint ownership of patents and copyrights is that the rules that apply in the absence of explicit agreement between the co-owners differ between patents and copyrights and may or may not reflect the parties' expectations, as described in the following discussion. Thus, in most cases, the parties should expressly provide for and define their respective rights and obligations by agreement, and not rely on these default rules.

## A. Patents

### 1. Default Rules

In absence of agreement to the contrary, each joint owner of a patent may make, use, offer to sell, sell and import the patented invention without the consent of the other joint owners and without accounting to the other joint owners for any share of the profits. Each co-owner's rights also carry with them the right to license others under any of those rights, also without the consent of the other co-owner or any obligation to account. As a corollary of the fact that each co-owner has the right to use and license the patented invention, no co-owner, acting alone, has the power to grant a truly exclusive license.

The right to grant licenses has been described as putting each co-owner "at the mercy" of the other co-owner. One decision summed this up as follows:

> In its essence all that the Government confers by the patent is the right to exclude others from making, using or vending the invention [citation omitted], aid as to this essential attribute of the property each joint owner is in a very real sense at the mercy of any other . . . [Each joint owner's] unlimited right to license others may, for all practical purposes, destroy the monopoly and so amount to an appropriation of the whole value of the patent.[3]

Just how much each co-owner is "at the mercy" of the other co-owners is illustrated by the Federal Circuit's decision in *Ethicon, Inc v. U.S. Surgical Corp.*, 135 F.3d 1456 (Fed. Cir. 1998). Ethicon, as assignee of the only named inventor (Yoon), brought an infringement suit against an infringer. After suit was tiled, the defendant became aware that there was a second unnamed co-inventor (Choi). The defendant contacted Choi and obtained a license under the patent from him, agreeing to pay him a contingent fee if it was successful in defending against the suit brought by Ethicon. The defendant then successfully asserted the license from Choi as a defense against Ethicon's suit. Since the defendant had a license from one co-owner, Ethicon, as assignee of the other co-owner of the patent, had no claim of infringement, and the case was dismissed. Choi also purported to grant the defendant a retroactive license, but the court held that the license was not effective to extinguish past claims of infringement by Ethicon that arose before the license was granted. However, as will discussed below, all co-owners must join in a suit for infringement, and since Choi refused to join in the suit, Ethicon had no remedy past infringement and therefore that part of its case was dismissed as well. The net result was that Ethicon could recover nothing on the patent.

These are the rules in the United States. The default rules applicable to jointly owned patents are quite different in many foreign countries. In Canada and the U.K., for example, in the absence of an agreement to the contrary, a joint owner of a patent, while having the right to itself exploit the patented invention, has right to license a third party

---

3. *Talbot v. Quaker State Oil Refining Co.*, 104 F.2d 967, 968 (3d Cir 1939).

(or convey anything other than its entire ownership interest to a third party) without the consent of the other joint owner.

### 2. Effect of Agreement Between Co-Owners

The foregoing are the default rules in the absence of agreement between the co-owners. The co-owners are generally free to vary their respective rights, subject to the constraints of the antitrust laws and public policy. Thus, for example, one co-owner can grant the other co-owner the exclusive right to use the patented invention, negating the first owner's right to use the invention. Conversely, the co-owners can agree that, while each of them will have the right to use the patented invention, only one of them will have the exclusive right to grant licenses to third parties.

Even where the default rules may seem consistent with the parties' intent, it is still advisable to define the parties' rights explicitly by agreement. Explicit agreement will minimize surprises or unintended results. Moreover, as will be discussed below, the default rules with respect to copyright are different than those governing patents. Particularly where the parties' collaboration may involve both patentable and copyrightable subject matter (e.g. computer software), the default rules may lead to conflicting or ambiguous results. Explicit agreement on ground rules (and choice of law) is also important where there may be jointly owned intellectual property rights in multiple countries, since the default rules differ from country to country.

To be effective, agreements curtailing the default rights of each co-owner with respect to the jointly owned patent should be explicit and complete in defining the parties' rights. The default rule may intrude if the parties fail to make the ground rules clear. The Federal Circuit's decision in *Schering* [*Corp. v. Roussel-UCLAF SA*, 104 F.3d 341 (Fed. Cir. 1997)] illustrates the pitfalls of joint ownership even when the parties have an express agreement on the subject. Co-owners of a pharmaceutical patent (Schering and Roussel), agreed that if one co-owner wished to bring an infringement action against a third party and the other co-owner did not wish to join in the suit, the non-joining co-owner "shall render all reasonable assistance to said other party in connection therewith." One co-owner (Roussel) entered license negotiations under the patent with a third party. While these negotiations were proceeding, the other co-owner (Schering) requested Roussel's assistance in bringing an infringement suit against that third party. Roussel responded that it was engaged in licensing negotiations with the third party. Whereupon Schering filed an infringement suit against the third party and notified Roussel that it was invoking its rights to assistance under the terms of the co-ownership agreement. Despite the suit, Roussel and the third party completed their license negotiations and Roussel granted the third party a license. The third party then asserted its license from Roussel as a defense in Schering's infringement suit. The Federal Circuit upheld this defense. The Court started from the principle that each co-owner was entitled to license others without the consent of the other owner, unless it had given up that right through an "agreement to the contrary." Schering argued that an agreement giving each co-owner the right to bring infringement suit unilaterally and requiring the other co-owner to render "reasonable assistance" was such an agreement to the contrary. The Federal Circuit disagreed, concluding that the "reasonable assistance" referred to *litigation* assistance and was also not intended to limit the non-suing co-owner's right to *license* the defendant.

Another potential pitfall to consider: While agreements limiting or allocating the rights of co-owners of a patent are binding on the co-owners, they may not be binding on third parties without notice of them. The parties could seek to overcome this limitation by recording their co-ownership agreement with the U.S. Patent and Trademark Office. Recording an assignment of a joint interest gives the assignee record title to an undivided interest and constitutes constructive notice. However, the recording of a co-ownership agreement allocating or restricting rights between the co-owners may not be sufficient to create constructive notice of those allocations or restrictions.

\* \* \*

## B. Copyrights

### 1. Default Rules

In the absence of an agreement to the contrary, under U.S. copyright law each co-owner of a copyright has an independent right, without obtaining the consent of the other co-owners, to exploit the copyright. Thus, each co-owner is free to copy, distribute, prepare derivative works based on the joint work and exercise the other exclusive rights of a copyright. Further, each co-owner is entitled to grant non-exclusive licenses under any of these rights to third parties. These principles apply whether or not the co-owners are co-authors or acquired their joint ownership interest in the copyright by other means.

The rights of co-owners of a copyright under U.S. copyright law to exploit the copyright are generally similar to the rights of co-owners of patents, with a major difference. A co-owner of a copyright must account to the owner for a ratable share of any profits earned from using or licensing the copyright. The duty to account is said not to derive from the copyright law itself, but from "equitable doctrines relating to unjust enrichment and general principles of law governing the rights of co-owners." However, Congress expressly acknowledged this rule in adopting the Copyright Act. The right to an accounting is generally held to be governed solely by state law, although one decision held that a co-owner's right to share in the profits derived from a joint work arises under the Copyright Act and preempted any claim under state law for unjust enrichment.

The obligation to account for profits represents, of course, an entirely different regime than that applicable to co-ownership of patents, and a potential trap for the unwary. Whereas joint owners of patents are (absent some other agreement) essentially free to use and license the patent without regard to the other co-owner, co-owners of copyrighted subject matter remain economically joined at the hip.

The duty to account applies to a transferee of a co-owner's ownership in the copyright. Each co-owner is entitled to transfer his interest in the joint work to a third party, without the consent of the other owners. But the transferee, as co-owner, is subject to (and also the beneficiary of) the duty to account between co-owners. Because the transferee remains subject to the duty to account, it appears that the transferor does not have to account to his co-owners for profits realized upon transfer of his ownership interest.

Parties considering joint ownership should bear in mind that the rules governing the rights of co-owners are different in many foreign countries from those in the U.S. In many foreign jurisdictions, all co-owners must join in licensing the copyright to a third party. Under English law, the joint owner of a copyright may not even exploit the copyright himself (e.g., distribute copies of the work) without the consent of the other co-owners. Thus absent an agreement among the co-owners, the co-owner of the copyright under English copyright law would have far fewer unilateral rights than under U.S. law. As with patents, therefore, parties contemplating co-ownership of copyrights should provide expressly concerning their respective rights to exploit and license the copyrightable subject matter and pay close attention to choice of law provisions.

### 2. Effect of Agreement Between Co-Owners

Like co-owners of a patent, co-owners of a copyright are free to agree to a different allocation of rights among themselves than the foregoing default rules. They may agree, for example, that neither of them will have the right to license the work to third parties without the consent of the other co-owner. They are free to override the duty to account, or to reapportion profit sharing among themselves, as they see fit.

A re-allocation of rights among co-owners may be considered a "transfer of copyright ownership" under Section 204(a) of the Copyright Act, and therefore valid only if it is in writing and signed by the owner of the rights conveyed. This requirement may apply to any agreement that varies any of the rights a co-owner of a copyright would enjoy in the absence of agreement. One court also noted that "while it is not required that the writing explicitly mention 'copyright' or 'exclusive right'. . . the better practice is that it should."

Restrictive agreements among co-owners (for example, an agreement that neither will license third parties without the approval of the other co-owner) are probably binding on third parties with notice. As with agreements between patent co-owners, however, it is doubtful that agreements restricting the rights of co-owners to grant licenses to third parties will be binding on third parties without notice. The Copyright Act permits any "transfer of copyright ownership or other document pertaining to a copyright" to be recorded in the Copyright Office. Recordation gives all persons constructive notice of the facts stated in the recorded document (if the document identifies the work and the work has been registered). Thus, recordation of the restrictive agreement may provide constructive notice.

### C. Trade Secrets

There is scant precedent on the rights of joint owners of a trade secret to exploit or license others to exploit the trade secret, or whether they have any duty to account to the other co-owner for any profits derived from exploitation of the trade secret. The few reported cases support the conclusion that in the absence of an agreement to the contrary, each co-owner is entitled to use a joint trade secret in it business. These cases do not suggest that the exploiting co-owners have any duty to account for profits to the other co-owners. Nevertheless, it would seem at least arguable that the same "equitable doctrines" relating to the rights of co-owners that require co-owners of copyright to account to each other would also apply to co-owners of trade secrets.

Of particular importance in the case of trade secrets are what obligations, if any, a co-owner may have, in the absence of express agreement, to prevent disclosure of the trade secrets, and, conversely, what rights each co-owner has to license or disclose the trade secret to third parties. The skimpy authority suggests that a co-owner owes a duty to the other co-owner to protect the trade secret against "unlawful and unreasonable disclosure." Thus, in one case, the court concluded that a co-owner of a trade secret could be enjoined by the other co-owner from "unreasonably" disclosing trade secrets in a patent application.

Given the scarcity of precedent, co-owners of a trade secret should specify their respective rights by express agreement. The co-ownership agreement should provide, among other things, to what extent each party has the right to use the trade secrets, and to license others to use it, whether or not the consent of the other co-owners is required, and whether there is or is not any duty to account to the other co-owners for profits from the use or licensing of the trade secret. In addition, in the case of trade secrets, the parties should specify whether they do or do not have any duty to the other co-owner to protect the trade secret from disclosure, and whether they may or may not disclose it to third parties. Of course, if one or the other party is free to disclose generally the jointly owned trade secrets, it effectively has the right to destroy the value of the trade secret. If this is not consistent with the parties' intent, they may provide that each co-owner may only license the trade secret to a third party under a license requiring the third party to protect its secrecy.

\* \* \*

## VII. ENFORCEMENT AGAINST THIRD PARTIES

Patents and other intellectual property rights are essentially simply the right to enforce the legal rights to exclude others from using the intellectual property. Thus, their value derives from the ability to enforce those rights against third parties. Joint ownership, particularly joint ownership of patents, complicates the ability to bring enforcement proceedings. Potential enforcement issues should be carefully considered before agreeing to joint ownership.

### A. Patents

As a matter of substantive patent law, all co-owners of a patent must join as plaintiffs in an infringement suit against a third party. Thus, absent some agreement to the contrary, each co-owner of a patent can effectively block the other co-owner(s) from bringing infringement suits. This is precisely what occurred in the *Ethicon* decision discussed above in Part III, where one co-owner (Ethicon) was left with no ability to maintain an infringement suit because the other co-owner (Choi) refused to join as a plaintiff.

The requirement that all co-owners join as plaintiffs rests on three primary considerations. First, it is a corollary of the right of each co-owner to license third parties. Second, it protects the interest of a co-owner in avoiding the estoppel effect of a judgment declaring the patent invalid in which he or she did not participate. Third, it protects the interests of a defendant in avoiding multiple suits concerning infringement of the same patent. . . .

The co-owners can overcome [the requirement that all co-owners join as plaintiffs] by agreement. The co-owners may agree by contract that one co-owner (or each co-owner) will have the unilateral right to sue infringers in its sole discretion, and obligate the other co-owners to join in the suit. . . ."A co-owner who grants another owner a right to bring litigation in his 'sole discretion' should not be allowed to argue later than such litigation should be precluded on the ground that it is detrimental to his interests in the patent."

Merely eliminating the veto of the other co-owners over infringement suits may not be enough to permit a co-owner to bring suit. What would happen if the dissenting co-owner who had granted the other co-owner the unilateral right to sue infringers is not subject to the personal jurisdiction of the court and therefore cannot be joined under Rule 19(a)? There is authority that an infringement action by one co-owner can proceed without joining the other co-owner where the suing co-owners have the *exclusive* right to bring infringement suits.

\* \* \*

[M]erely providing by agreement that each co-owner has a unilateral right to sue infringers of the patent may not be sufficient to enable each co-owner to exercise that right.

Parties entering co-ownership agreement relating to patents should take this into account. A provision requiring the non-suing co-owner to join as party, or consenting to being named as a party, in a suit brought by the other co-owner, if necessary to maintain the suit, might be considered. However, one or both parties may be unwilling to give the other co-owner the right to drag it into litigation, particularly since the unilateral right to sue will most likely be invoked in cases where the parties have disagreed on whether to bring suit.

The co-owners should also consider the interplay between their respective rights to sue and their respective rights to license third parties. As the *Schering* case richly illustrates, the right of a co-owner to bring suit against infringers can effectively be defeated by the other co-owner choosing to license the defendant. In some cases, an approach to this interplay may be for the parties to agree that neither co-owner will license a third party who is a defendant in a pending infringement suit brought by the other co-owner, so long as the suit is pending. This at least avoids the embarrassment and futility of having the rug pulled out from under a pending suit. But it does not completely address the issue and raises other issues that will need to be considered, including: Will the suing co-owner in effect gain exclusive licensing rights as to a defendant by bringing suit? Should a co-owner be required to give advance notice to the other co-owner prior to bringing suit, and if so how does such a notice affect the right of the other co-owner to license the target? How should the proceeds from a judgment or settlement of the suit be allocated?

## B. Copyrights

Under Section 501 (b) of the Copyright Act, "[t]he legal or beneficial owner of an exclusive right under a copyright is entitled . . . to institute an action for any infringement of that particular right committed while he or she is the owner of it." Unlike co-owners of patents, one co-owner of a copyright cannot block the other co-owner from suing for infringement by simply refusing to join in the suit. Rather, under Section 501(b), the court "may require the joinder, and shall permit the intervention, of any person having or claiming an interest in the copyright."

The Second Circuit held in *Edward B. Marks Corp. v. Jerry Vogel Music Co.*, [140 F.2d 268 (2d Cir. 1944)] that a co-owner of a copyright had standing to bring a suit for infringement in its own name without the joinder (or consent) of the other co-owner. It concluded that the co-owners are not indispensable, because their rights "can be reserved in the judgment." If the absent co-owner cannot be served, the action can nevertheless be decided as to the plaintiff co-owner. The plaintiff co-owner cannot, however, recover all the statutory damages or all of the defendant's profits. Rather its recovery is limited to recovering "plaintiff's own part; that is to say, to its own actual damages, to its proper share of any statutory damages, and to its proper share of the profits."

[F]or avoidance of doubt, parties contemplating joint ownership of a copyright who wish to maintain the independent right to sue should agree in advance whether each will have unilateral right to sue, and if so, provide that the other party will join, if necessary, as a party in the suit. And clearly, if co-owners of copyright do not wish to permit each co-owner to be able to bring suits against infringers unilaterally, they should expressly so provide in their agreement.

## C. Trade Secrets

Each co-owner of a trade secret probably has standing to sue for misappropriation without the consent, and without joining the other co-owners. In *DTM Research, L.L.C. v. AT&T Corp.*, [58 USPQ2d 1236 (4th Cir. 2001)], the Fourth Circuit recently held that the plaintiff in an action for misappropriation of a trade secret did not need to establish "fee simple ownership" of the secret and could maintain a claim even if other parties also possessed the same trade secret. The court reasoned that the nature of a trade secret made "ownership" a poor analogy. While a trade secret plaintiff under the Uniform Trade Secret Act must prove that the information qualifies as a trade secret, the misappropriation rests on proving that the defendant acquired the trade secret by improper means. Although co-ownership was not involved, the same reasoning would appear to support the right of a co-owner to maintain an action

## VIII. CONCLUSION

Joint ownership of intellectual property introduces both complexities and the potential for significant unintended consequences. If joint ownership is proposed, one is well advised to examine critically what objectives the parties seek to accomplish by joint ownership and consider whether those objectives cannot be accomplished more simply by sole ownership by one party, accompanied by a license of applicable rights to the other party. If the parties do structure their relationship to include joint ownership of intellectual property (or if their collaboration is such that joint ownership may arise by operation of law), they should take care to think through and explicitly agree upon the ground rules.

---

# Addressing Intellectual Property Ownership When Drafting Joint Development Agreements*

Sharon L. Tasman
8 (No. 7) INTELL. PROP. STRATEGIST (April 2002)

Parties entering into joint development and other collaborative agreements often are most concerned about what services each of them will perform as part of the collaborative effort. As a result, they often neglect to address the one issue they are quickest to litigate: who owns the intellectual property rights created as a result of the collaboration. The parties' attorneys can help them to avoid litigation related to this issue by making sure that the collaboration agreement competently allocates intellectual property ownership and responsibility for its protection and defense.

## Apportioning Ownership

To avoid potential disputes among the parties, collaborative agreements should outline three major areas of intellectual property: (1) that which each party brings to the transaction (i.e., that which each party has developed prior to and/or outside the scope of the collaborative agreement—contributed IP); (2) that which the parties create as a result of the collaborative effort (joint IP); and (3) that which consists of modifications to or derivatives of a party's contributed IP.

Of these three categories, the easiest to define clearly is each party's contributed IP. The parties to the agreement can identify their respective contributed IP, either in the body of the agreement or in schedules. The list would include not only patents, trademarks and copyrighted materials, but also any trade secrets or other intellectual property that will be disclosed and used as part of the collaborative effort.

---

\* Reprinted by permission of the author and the publisher, copyright 2002.

With regard to the joint IP, the parties first should define clearly what they expect to come of the collaborative effort: research reports, patentable technology or an actual product. Once the parties have defined the expected joint IP, they can decide how to apportion its ownership. When doing so, it is important to carefully consider the purposes of the collaborative relationship, as well as each party's respective needs.

There are many means by which joint IP can be apportioned so as to ensure that both parties' goals are accomplished. The most straightforward method is for the parties to agree that any joint IP created as a result of the collaboration shall be truly jointly owned by the parties. This would be an appropriate structure if all parties to the agreement are willing to allow the unrestricted use of the joint IP by one another. In the case of a two-party agreement, each party would have an undivided one-half interest in the whole of the joint IP and the agreement should specify whether the parties are obligated to account to each other for profits resulting from the use of the joint IP.

If, however, due to the parties' business or technical concerns, there need to be restrictions on one or both party's use of the joint IP, this can be accomplished in a number of ways. One option would be for all the intellectual property rights to be assigned to one of the parties, which then would grant a license, limited as dictated by the business concerns, to the other party.

Alternatively, both parties can be considered joint owners of all the joint IP, with each party agreeing to certain restrictive conditions on their use or disclosure of it. This situation often arises when a party wants to prohibit the disclosure of the joint IP to one or more competitors.

An additional concern arises when one of the parties—often an educational institution—receives government funding. In such a case, the government may have rights to use intellectual property (and possibly any underlying contributed IP) created as a result of the government funding. The parties must ensure that intellectual property created with government funding will be available without overly burdensome restrictions, taking into account any requirements that apply to particular intellectual property because of government funding.

Because the joint IP often will contain some of the parties' contributed IP, each party needs to be cognizant of the potential downstream exposure of its contributed IP-regardless of how the rights to the joint IP are apportioned. For example, even if the contract provides for true joint ownership of the joint IP, it may be appropriate to include: (1) a limitation in the contract providing that neither party may sever the other party's underlying intellectual property in a manner that permits use of that property independently of the joint development; and (2) a corresponding requirement that any downstream contracts obligate any potential sublicensees or other third parties that may come in contact with the joint IP to abide by such limitations.

The third and final category of intellectual property rights—modifications or derivatives of either party's contributed IP—often can be the most difficult to address. First, there is often a fine line between a modification or derivative of a party's previously existing intellectual property and the joint development effort that is the fundamental purpose of the collaborative relationship. This distinction can be made clearer by including in the contract a careful and specific description of the joint IP expected to be created as a result of the effort. This consideration is important because each party to a collaborative effort typically wants to retain the unfettered right to continue to use its individual contributed IP, including any modifications or derivatives, without restriction.

This situation often arises in the computer software arena. While a party that has developed a complex computer program may be willing to allow a "plug in" module to be jointly owned, the party is likely to want to own any modifications to the original program that may be made to accommodate the plug-in module. If the parties agree that modifications to each party's contributed IP are not intended to fall within the definition of the joint IP but shall be owned by the "contributing" party, it will be important to include express assignments from each party to the other of any modifications to or derivative versions of a party's contributed IP. To ensure that such express assignments are effective, it is important that only employees and consultants of each party who have signed appropriate assignment of invention and assignment of copyright agreements perform work under the collaborative agreement.

### Handling Patent Prosecution and Infringement Claims

Related to the determination of ownership of intellectual property rights is the manner in which any patent prosecution and third-party infringement claims will be handled with respect to the joint IP. It is helpful to address in the collaborative agreement which party or parties will: (1) decide whether to protect joint IP through patent or to maintain it through trade secret; (2) be responsible for filing and prosecuting patent applications and maintaining the resulting patents; and (3) pay for patent prosecution and maintenance expenses.

This type of provision also should clearly provide that, if the party charged with filing the patent application and prosecuting and maintaining the patent either expressly elects not to make the filing or is not handling its responsibilities in a timely manner, the other party is entitled to file the application or take whatever steps are necessary to protect the patent rights. It is particularly helpful to include an express power-of-attorney provision to enable the other party to take the necessary actions more easily when deadlines are looming. In addition, it is worthwhile considering whether the party who takes over the patent prosecution should be entitled to become the sole owner of the patent application and the underlying intellectual property rights regardless of how the parties had previously agreed to apportion the joint IP. Although it isn't common, this provision is more or less desirable depending on which party you are representing.

In addition, the collaborative agreement should specify which party or parties are responsible for defending, and paying any expenses and damages in connection with, claims that the joint IP infringes third parties' intellectual property rights. It is common to include language stating that if the real cause of the infringement claim is one party's underlying contributed IP, the party who contributed such infringing intellectual property will bear the burden of the infringement claim.

Finally, the agreement should address the converse situation: a third party's infringement of the joint IP. Once again, the collaborative agreement should specify which party or parties have the responsibility for prosecuting the third-party infringer. It also should require the parties' cooperation in any prosecution and establish how any awards would be split.

An agreement that includes the foregoing provisions will avoid many disputes that might otherwise arise between the parties.

[This article first appeared in the April 2002 issue of THE INTELLECTUAL PROPERTY STRATEGIST. Eds.]

---

# Notes and Questions

1. *Ownership Structure of Intellectual Property Created as a Result of a Service Development Agreement.* Parties enter into development agreements for a variety of reasons. One common reason is that a company might not have development resources or its development resources are stretched on other products but the company has ample money to contract with a third party to perform the development. These agreements usually anticipate the creation of intellectual property (IP) and the ownership and/or license clause may be structured in many ways. (Note that a development provider will almost always create something in performance of the contract that would qualify as IP.) Some options for structuring such an IP clause are detailed below with (1) being the most "pro-customer" (meaning that the customer receives the most rights in vendor-created IP) and (8) being the most "pro-vendor" (meaning that the vendor receives the most rights in vendor-created IP):

(1) Customer takes sole ownership of all IP embodied in deliverables, with no grant-back license to vendor and no "residuals clause." This would be close to a "work for hire" type contract, but vendor cannot perform similar work in future.

(2) Customer takes sole ownership of all IP embodied in deliverables (both newly created and pre-existing) and grants back to Vendor (i) a broad (unfettered) license, (ii) a limited license expressly limited in some fashion, or (iii) residuals clause.

(3) Customer takes sole ownership of all *newly created* IP embodied in deliverables, with no grant-back license to the vendor and some form of residuals clause included for protection of vendor. Vendor retains sole ownership of pre-existing works with (i) a limited license to customer for pre-existing works or (ii) a broad license to customer for pre-existing works.

(4) Customer takes sole ownership of all *newly created* IP embodied in deliverables and grants back to vendor a limited license expressly limited in some fashion. Vendor retains sole ownership of pre-existing works with (i) a limited license to customer for pre-existing works or (ii) a broad license to customer for pre-existing works.

(5) Customer takes sole ownership of all *newly created* IP embodied in deliverables and grants back to vendor a broad (unfettered) license. Vendor retains sole ownership of pre-existing works with (i) a limited license to customer for pre-existing works or (ii) a broad license to customer for pre-existing works.

(6) Vendor and customer each share "undivided one-half ownership" in all *newly created* IP in deliverables. Vendor retains sole ownership of pre-existing works with (i) a limited license to customer for pre-existing works or (ii) a broad license to customer for pre-existing works.

(7) Vendor retains sole ownership of all IP in deliverables and grants customer a "broad" (unfettered) type license to customer. (Common when pre-existing work modified for customer's use.)

(8) Vendor retains sole ownership of all IP in deliverables and grants customer a limited "internal use only" type license to customer. This is similar to a typical software end user type license agreement ("EULA").

2. *Questions to Be Considered.* As a lawyer drafting the service development agreement the following are questions that should be considered:

- Is the intellectual property an integral part of your client's business?
- Is the intellectual property intended to guarantee revenue for your client in terms of subsequent sales/licenses to third parties?
- If the customer wins the ownership battle will it lose the war (i.e., will vendor put its "B-team" on the project?)?
- Why does the customer "have" to own the intellectual property? Will a license-back approach meet the customer's business goals?
- Can the vendor segregate what is delivered/assigned in the statement of work?
- Can the vendor identify pre-existing vendor intellectual property?

3. *General Note Regarding Deliverables.* Assignment or license of IP in deliverables can apply to different types of IP, i.e., patent, copyright, or trade secret. Assignment or license of IP can be further divided into categories of pre-existing, modified pre-existing, or new.

4. *Residuals Clauses.* A residuals clause is not a license to IP. It does not convey any right to use documentation, tools or other materials or information that can be identified as IP. The purpose of a residuals clause is to provide the vendor with some comfort that the customer will not challenge use of information retained in the unaided memory of vendor personnel. Personnel can merely continue to work for a vendor (which is the purpose of a residuals clause). One should not rely on residuals clauses. To obtain sufficient rights for a vendor, the drafting attorney should determine what the vendor intends to do in the future and (i) retain rights or (ii) obtain an express license from the customer. This will require consideration of the statement of work and analysis of future business opportunities. An example of a residuals clause is as follows:

> *Nothing in this Agreement precludes the parties from using Residual Knowledge of the other party. "Residual Knowledge" means ideas, concepts, know-how or techniques related to Disclosing Party's technology that are retained in the unaided memories of the other's employees who have had access to confidential information consistent with the terms of this Agreement. An employee's memory is unaided if the employee has not intentionally memorized the Information for the Purpose of retaining and subsequently using or disclosing it. Each party's use of Residual Knowledge is subject to any valid patent, copyright, and semiconductor mask work rights of Disclosing Party.*

5. *Vendor Retains All Rights/Limited License to Customer.* Here the license to a customer is limited to "internal use only." Many vendors use this type of IP clause for the "standard" service agreement. An attempt to limit the license to vendor pre-existing material embodied in a deliverable may not be practical where the customer has broader rights in the remaining, unsegregable portions of the deliverable.

6. *Vendor Retains All Rights/Unlimited License to Customer.* Under this scenario, the customer has no restrictions. A customer will have the ability to provide a license to a competitor or actually become a competitor. Consider excluding the right to use vendor pre-existing intellectual property that the deliverable embodies by carving out pre-existing vendor IP and subjecting it to a limited license, or by not incorporating vendor pre-existing IP into any deliverable.

7. *Assignment of All Rights to Customer.* The assignor should threat an assignment of rights just like the sale of any "hard" asset. Therefore, it should identify and inventory anything subject to assignment. It could set out what is delivered/assigned in the statement of work and identify pre-existing vendor IP (e.g., ideas, concepts, methods, soft-

ware, documentation). The vendor should conduct such an inventory even if it will receive a license-back, so that the vendor can track what rights and obligations it has for those deliverables.

(i) *Assignment of Rights to Customer—Copyright.* Assignment of copyright covers any "expression of ideas fixed in a tangible form" but not the ideas themselves. This applies to software, documentation, reports, analyses, descriptions, *et cetera.* (anything "written" during performance of the contract). The practical effect of a copyright assignment clause is that the vendor cannot reuse these assigned materials, whether modified or not, without permission from the customer. To administer this obligation, the vendor must identify and segregate materials belonging to customer (these may also be subject to NDA or confidentiality obligations). The vendor should destroy all but one archival copy at the end of performance (to resist the strong urge to reuse materials). If only assigning copyright, a vendor can re-write copyrighted materials from "scratch," but this does not include modifications to any deliverables.

(ii) *Assignment of Rights to Customer—Copyright and Patent.* This is an assignment of copyright plus "inventions for which patent protection is sought." In addition to restrictions on use of copyrighted materials, the vendor cannot provide or offer services covered by the patent during the patent term without permission of the customer. The vendor should obtain an obligation from the customer to notify the vendor if any patent applications are filed. If patents are not specifically licensed back then the vendor should avoid providing or offering the same services for at least one year post-performance (the deadline for filing patent applications) thus avoiding the risk of infringing or turning subsequent customers into infringers.

(iii) *Assignment of Rights to Customer—Inventions.* This is language that assigns "inventions" or "inventions, patented or unpatented." This type of assignment is not limited to a patent term or to "patent worthy" developments. This approach can be highly unfavorable to vendors, as the vendor will need to avoid contamination of others with customer-owned information. This requires that a vendor segregate the work facility for that contract from other work facilities. Vendor personnel should be limited to one project at a time, as development of IP should be tied to the contract. The vendor should limit access to project information only to project personnel and, essentially, treat all customer-owned developments as confidential.

(iv) *Additional Considerations When Assigning IP.* Assignment of intellectual property raises problems for the vendor as far as establishing independent development if customer-owned information is propagated throughout the vendor's company. As stated above, all customer-owned developments should be treated as CONFIDENTIAL and the vendor bears the administrative burdens that such treatment entails. The parties should use the assignment clause to set up an audit trail of what "stays" and what "goes" and should be able to answer that question for every piece of IP upon contract closeout. The vendor should destroy all but one copy of everything that "goes."

8. *License Back to Vendor—Limited in Scope.* This approach is broader than a residuals clause. In the license-back, the parties must articulate what the vendor needs or wants to do with the IP. The vendor must obtain a license for re-use of any assigned

IP. Therefore, the vendor must determine the necessary scope of the license and realize it will have limitations on further license or assignment of that IP. Any IP that is subject to a limited license should be marked with the subject limitations, as this IP may have to be identified/carved out of subsequent projects. The vendor will no longer have exclusive rights and therefore the vendor cannot challenge third party use of such IP.

9. *License Back to Vendor—Unlimited.* Consider that the vendor will no longer have exclusive rights in the IP. Therefore, the vendor cannot restrict competitors' use of this IP because the vendor does not own the IP. Also be sure that the license is really "unlimited"—look for restrictions that may not meet the vendor's business goals and note that courts interpret the term "use" narrowly, such that a license-back for an "unlimited right to use" IP embodied in a deliverable may not be sufficiently broad to meet the vendor's need for specific "uses," such as the ability to display the deliverable publicly. Therefore, be sure to expressly list all desired future "uses" within the license-back. *See, e.g, Mendler v. Winterland Prod., Ltd.,* 207 F.3d 1119 (9th Cir. 2000) (court reversed judgment of non-infringement of plaintiff's copyrighted photograph of two ships in America's Cup yacht race holding that defendant infringed plaintiff's copyright and exceeded scope of license to use photographs as "guides, models, and examples, for illustrations" by altering them and affixing them to t-shirts).

10. *Vendor Owns Pre-Existing and Derivative Assignment to Customer New Works.* Make sure that the parties can identify what they believe to be "new" works within the statement of work.

---

# Chapter 8

# Contract Law Issues in Intellectual Property Licensing

## I. Introduction

Licensing presents mixed issues of federal intellectual property law and state contract law. Federal law governs the definition, scope, and validity of most intellectual property rights, while state law determines the duties of the parties to each other under the agreement itself. Tension can arise between the two spheres when the parties seek to do by contract that which is forbidden by intellectual property law, as with licensor patent or copyright misuse.

In this chapter, we consider some of the many important issues that arise under contract law:

- Does a licensee have the right to sue infringers?
- Can a license be implied in law, even if not expressly granted?
- Are shrink-wrap and online license agreements the new contracts of adhesion?
- What approaches help make online licenses enforceable?
- Do intellectual property law exclusions preempt license agreement prohibitions?
- What happens to intellectual property rights when the free market accepts various types of open source and freeware licenses?

---

## II. Scope of Exclusive Licenses and Standing to Sue

### Western Electric Co., Inc. v. Pacent Reproducer Corp.
42 F.2d 116 (2d Cir. 1930)

SWAN, Circuit Judge.

\* \* \*

It is conceded that a bare license to practice a patented invention gives the licensee no right to join as plaintiff in a suit against an infringer. In its simplest form, a license means only leave to do a thing which the licensor would otherwise have a right to prevent. Such a license grants to the licensee merely a privilege that protects him from a claim of infringement by the owner of the patent monopoly. *Heaton, etc., Co. v. Eureka Specialty Co.* (C.C.A. 6) 77 F. 288, 290, 35 L.R.A. 728; *De Forest, etc., Co. v. Radio Corp.* (D.C. Del.) 9 F.(2d) 150, 151. He has no property interest in the monopoly of the patent, nor any contract with the patent owner that others shall not practice the invention. Hence the patent owner may freely license others, or may tolerate infringers, and in either case no right of the patent licensee is violated. Practice of the invention by others may indeed cause him pecuniary loss, but it does him no legal injury. Compare the analogous situation where the author of a copyrighted play grants a license to produce it, reserving moving picture rights, discussed in *Tully v. Triangle Film Corp.* (D.C.S.D.N.Y.) 229 F. 297, 298. Infringement of the patent can no more be a legal injury to a bare licensee than a trespass upon Blackacre could be an injury to one having a nonexclusive right of way across Blackacre. Therefore it is obvious that a bare licensee can neither sue alone, nor join with the patent owner, in an infringement suit. *See Blair v. Lippincott Glass Co.* (C.C. Ind.) 52 F. 226; *Brookfield v. Novelty Glass Mfg. Co.* (C.C.A. 1) 170 F. 960, 962....

But a license to practice the invention may be accompanied by the patent owner's promise that others shall be excluded from practicing it within the field of use wherein the licensee is given leave. It is not disputed that an "exclusive licensee" has the right of joinder with the patent owner in an infringement suit. The dispute is as to the meaning of "exclusive licensee" within this rule. In *Heap v. Hartley*, 42 Ch. Div. 461, 470, Lord Justice Fry defined an exclusive license as "leave to do a thing, and a contract not to give leave to anybody else to do the same thing." A patent licensee having such a contract is obviously prejudiced by an infringement of the patent, for the patentee's sufferance of an unauthorized practice of an invention is as harmful to his promisee as would be the grant of a license in direct violation of the contract. To make effective such a contract, the licensee must have the right to compel the patentee to assert his monopoly for the benefit of his licensee; that is, the latter must have the right of joinder in a suit to restrain infringement, or of suing in the patentee's name if the patentee refuses to join in the litigation. In speaking of exclusive licenses in *Independent Wireless Co. v. Radio Corp.*, 269 U.S. 459, at page 469, 46 S. Ct. 166, 170, 70 L. Ed. 357, Chief Justice Taft said:

> Such exclusive licenses frequently contain express covenants by the patent owner and licensor to sue infringers that expressly cast upon the former the affirmative duty of initiating and bearing the expense of the litigation. But, without such express covenants, the implied obligation of the licensor to allow the use of his name is indispensable to the enjoyment by the licensee of the monopoly which by personal contract the licensor has given.

If the licensee is granted not only leave to make, use, and vend the invention, but also the right to exclude from the licensed field every one else, including the patent owner himself, the grant may amount to an assignment of an interest in the patent, entitling the licensee (assignee) to sue an infringer in his own name; if it is less inclusive, it remains a license.

\* \* \*

The definition of an exclusive license, quoted above from the English case, might be thought to imply that an "exclusive licensee" is a sole licensee. But we do not so understand it. A bare license might be outstanding in one when the patent owner grants a license to another accompanied by the promise that the grantor will give no further licenses. In such a case, the second licensee needs the protection of the right of joinder in a suit against infringers as much as though he were the sole licensee. We see no reason why he should not have it, and we think the authorities recognize his right. See *Radio Corp. v. Emerson* (C.C.A. 2) 296 F. 51, where there were apparently outstanding nonexclusive license rights in the De Forest Company; *Gayler v. Wilder*, 10 How. 481, 13 L. Ed. 504, where the patentee retained the privilege of practicing the invention within the licensed territory, paying the licensee a royalty. Nor do the defendants challenge this view, if we correctly understand their position, for their brief asserts that the distinguishing characteristic of an exclusive license is a promise, express or implied, by the licensor, that he will not thereafter license others. The real issue between the parties is whether the agreement of May 7th contains such a promise, the appellants asserting, and the appellees denying, that it does. To that issue we shall now direct attention.

Both parties concede that the agreement contains nothing to prevent prior licensees of the grantor if there be any, from practicing the invention. Possibly also the grantor itself may do so, for it is not clear that the words of the grant, "all the rights which it now has or may hereafter have (under the patents) to exclude others," would include the patent owner's privilege of using the invention itself. But we cannot doubt that such a grant precludes the patent owner from thereafter granting new licenses to others. It has "assigned" all its existing rights to exclude from the patent monopoly in the specified field, and only one having the right to exclude can grant a license to enjoy. It is urged by the defendants that the attempted assignment is only an assignment of remedies against infringers and is inoperative to convey any "title" or "interest" in the patents; reliance being placed upon *Crown Die & Tool Co. v. Nye Tool & Machine Works*, 261 U.S. 24, 43 S. Ct. 254, 67 L. Ed. 516, as authority for this assertion. Let it be assumed that no "title" or "interest" in the patent is transferred even when the grantee of the right to exclude enjoys a license under the patent, which he did not in the *Crown* case, nevertheless the attempted assignment must surely import an implied promise by the grantor to do nothing to defeat the rights that he purports to convey. The granting of new licenses ad libitum would completely defeat the rights of exclusion that he has purported to transfer for a consideration to his grantee.

Hence an obligation that the grantor will not thereafter grant any similar license is, we think, clearly to be implied. But the defendants contend that the final portion of the agreement reciting the "intention" of the instrument shows that the grantor meant to retain the power to give additional licenses. Reliance is placed upon the limitation of the assigned rights to rights against "infringers," and on the concluding recital that "nothing herein contained shall in any way affect or alter the rights" of the grantor "against others than infringers within the aforesaid field." The defendants' construction of the language of the "intention" clause seems to us completely to destroy the granting clause, both as an assignment of the grantor's rights to exclude and as an implied covenant to grant no similar license to others. The instrument must be interpreted, if possible, so as to give meaning to all its terms. We think this is possible. The reservation of the grantor's rights "against others than infringers within the aforesaid field" may refer, not only to its rights against infringers in other fields, but also to its rights against prior licensees, if such there be, within the limited field, and to rights against those who may commit a tort other than infringement, such as slander of title of the patents. To reserve the power to grant licenses by such a phrase as "rights against others than infringers" puts a strained construction upon the phrase. It should not be adopted when the result would be to contradict the granting portion of the agreement.

The question, therefore, is whether a license agreement which reserves to the licensor, and to possible prior licensees, the privilege of practicing the invention, but contains an implied promise that the licensor will give no further license within the specified field of use, entitles the promisees to join with the licensor in an infringement suit. Under the principles already discussed, we think it does. They are as directly prejudiced by an infringement as they would be if sole licensees, and under the assignment they are beneficially interested in the fruits of any recovery in the suit. Upon recognized principles of equity, they should be permitted to join as coplaintiffs with the patent owner.

* * *

---

# License Agreement at Issue in *Western Electric Co., Inc. v. Pacent Reproducer Corp.*

Whereas, the undersigned American Telephone and Telegraph Company, a New York corporation, is the owner of certain United States patents, and rights to and under patents, relating or applicable to systems and apparatus for recording sound and to systems and apparatus for the reproduction of sound from records thereof, including the patents listed in the schedule hereto attached and marked Schedule A; and

Whereas, Western Electric Company, Incorporated, a New York corporation, and Electrical Research Products, Inc., a Delaware corporation, are now engaged in making, selling, leasing, installing, and using apparatus for recording sound and apparatus for reproducing sound from records thereof, by virtue of licenses from said American Telephone and Telegraph Company under said patents for certain uses or fields of business and desire to continue such business and to exclude infringers of the said patents from said field of business.

Now, therefore, in consideration of One Dollar and other good and valuable consideration, receipt of which is hereby acknowledged, and of the royalties heretofore paid and agreed to be paid under the aforesaid licenses, the American Telephone and Telegraph Company hereby confirms the aforesaid licenses to Western Electric Company, Incorporated, and Electrical Research Products, Inc., and does hereby assign and set over to said Western Electric Company, Incorporated, and Electrical Research Products, Inc., all the rights which it now has or may hereafter have under or arising from said patents or any of them (specifically including without excluding others each and all of the patents listed in said Schedule A) to exclude others from the manufacture, sale, lease, installation and/or use of apparatus, devices, systems or methods

(1)   for the recording of sound for the production of sound records:

    (a)      for sale to the public as phonograph records, or

    (b)      for use in connection with the exhibition of pictures, except in the home;

(2)   for the reproduction of sound from sound records:

    (a)      as a public performance, or

(b)        in connection with the exhibition of pictures, except in the home;

and for the same consideration the American Telephone and Telegraph Company assigns and sets over to said Western Electric Company, Incorporated, and said Electrical Research Products, Inc., all claims recoverable in law or in equity, whether damages, profits, savings, or of any other kind or description which the American Telephone and Telegraph Company now has or may hereafter have arising out of the infringement of the aforesaid patents within said field; the intention being that in so far as concerns the exclusion of infringers of said patents from the aforesaid field of business, Western Electric Company, Incorporated, and Electrical Research Products, Inc., shall be vested with full rights in the premises as American Telephone and Telegraph Company would have had this assignment not been made, including the right for their own benefit, to bring suit on said patents or any of them, either at law or in equity, against infringers in said field of business to exclude such infringers from practicing the inventions of said patents, and for their own use and benefit to collect damages which may arise by reason of the future infringement of said patents by infringers within said field of business, but nothing herein contained shall in any way affect or alter the rights of American Telephone and Telegraph Company against others than infringers within the aforesaid field.

# Notes

1. In *Western Electric, supra,* the court found that a "bare licensee" has no standing to sue for infringement. What must appear in a license agreement to give a licensee standing to sue? *See* JAY DRATLER, JR., LICENSING OF INTELLECTUAL PROPERTY § 8.06 (1994) (discussing standing issue and related legal doctrines for various forms of intellectual property).

2. *Exclusive Copyright Licensee Needs Licensor's Consent to Transfer Rights.* In *Gardner v. Nike Inc.,* 279 F.3d 774 (9th Cir. 2002), Nike Inc. granted Sony Music an exclusive, perpetual, worldwide license to use a character called "MC Teach." The agreement was silent regarding Sony's right to assign its rights under the exclusive license. Sony later assigned all its rights in the license to Gardner in exchange for royalties based on proceeds from use of the character. When Nike threatened legal action, Gardner filed a declaratory judgment action on the validity of the transfer of Sony's rights. The U.S. District Court for the Central District of California found that the 1976 Copyright Act required that Sony obtain Nike's consent to transfer its rights and granted Nike summary judgment. Gardner appealed. *Id.* at 777.

On appeal, the Ninth Circuit noted that the question of transferability of an exclusive license under the 1976 Act was a matter of first impression. Under the 1909 Act, an assignee was entitled to transfer its rights without consent while a copyright licensee was not, based on the doctrine of indivisibility. This doctrine provides that a copyright owner possesses a "bundle" of rights and any grant of rights less than assignment is considered a license. Thus, only a copyright owner had standing to sue for infringement, so alleged infringers did not have to face successive lawsuits. *Id.* at 778.

As applied to exclusive licenses, the 1976 Act removed much this "indivisibility doctrine" because the definition of "transfer of copyright" includes an exclusive license.

Further, the Act authorizes the transfer of copyright ownership in whole or in part where the contract does not require licensor's consent. *Id*. at 779.

Regardless, the Ninth Circuit held that the 1976 Copyright Act does not permit a licensee to transfer its exclusive rights without consent of the licensor and that the plain language of the statute limits the rights afforded to exclusive licensees under in the 1976 Act. Specifically, the court reasoned that the law under the 1909 Act remained unchanged because the exclusive licensee rights language of the 1976 Act was limited to "protections and remedies," and Congress did not expressly address the issue of an exclusive licensee's right to transfer. Thus, the language in the 1976 Act limiting an exclusive licensee's rights (§ 201(d)(2)) takes precedence over the language discussing the transfer of copyright ownership (§§ 101 and 201(d)(1)). The court also stated that in order to assure the licensor can monitor the copyright, the burden should be on the licensee to obtain express consent to transfer the licensee's exclusive rights. *Id*. at 779–81.

The Ninth Circuit's approach to interpreting the 1976 Act is arguably counter to a plain reading of the applicable sections. Do you believe that the language granting owners of certain rights in copyright all "protections and remedies" accorded to a copyright owner is not sufficient to create an exception to the general policy to allow transferability of rights? One lesson from this case is that parties should expressly include important terms and avoid relying on default rules in the absence of such terms. Note that this prohibition on assignment may also raise issues should a licensee file for bankruptcy, as discussed in Chapter 13.

---

# III. Implied Licenses

Express contract language is not necessary to establish a licensor/licensee relationship. Courts will find an implied license if the terms of documents, letters between the parties, a course of conduct, or any combination of these indicate that the parties intended to create a license. As one court stated, "like any other implied contract, an implied license arises out of the objective conduct of the parties, which a reasonable man would regard as indicating that an agreement has been reached." *Medeco Security Locks, Inc. v. Lock Techn. Corp.*, 199 U.S.P.Q. 519, 524 (S.D.N.Y. 1976).

The rules for implying licenses in the various intellectual property law fields differ. See the notes at the end of this chapter for information on implied licenses in trademark and copyright matters. This subsection addresses implied licensing of patents.

---

## De Forest Radio Telephone & Telegraph Co. v. United States
### 273 U.S. 236 (1927)

TAFT, C.J.

\* \* \*

The De Forest Radio Telephone & Telegraph Company filed its petition in the Court of Claims against the United States, seeking to recover for an alleged unlawful use by the government of certain patented vacuum tubes or audions used in radio communication. The suit was brought under the Act of June 25, 1910, c. 423 (36 Stat. 851), as amended by the Act of July 1, 1918, c. 114 (40 Stat. 704, 705). The Act of 1910 provided that whenever an invention described in and covered by a patent of the United States should thereafter be used by the government without license of the owner or lawful right to use it, the owner could recover reasonable compensation for the use in the Court of Claims, provided that the United States could avail itself of all defenses, general or special, which might be pleaded by any other defendant charged with infringement. The amending act of 1918 enlarged the scope of the act by providing that the recovery by the owner should include compensation for patented inventions used or made by or for the United States.

The petition showed that the two patents involved in the suit were granted to De Forest, and by him were duly assigned to the appellant, the company bearing his name; that that company executed and delivered to the Western Electric Company a written instrument conveying certain rights in the patents, which were subsequently conveyed to the American Telephone & Telegraph Company. This contract was set out in the petition. In consideration of $1 and other good and valuable considerations it granted a license to make, use, install, operate, and lease, and to sell or otherwise dispose of to others for sale, installation, and operation, apparatus and systems embodying or made or operating in accordance with the invention. It purported to give this license for the full terms of the patents and for all transferable rights of the De Forest Company in the inventions, except such as were expressly reserved by that company. The reservations included nonassignable rights for the purpose of making the articles in question for, and selling them to, the United States government for its use. The instrument further provided that the Western Company and the De Forest Company might respectively institute and conduct suits against others for any of the patents within the fields in which each respectively possessed rights, but that all such suits should be conducted at the expense of the party bringing them, that party to retain any judgment recovered in any such suits.

Paragraph 12 of the instrument provided that the Western Company might transfer to others, in whole or in part, the rights granted by the instrument, and might assign rights thereunder or grant licenses to various persons, firms, or corporations for the several uses to which the inventions were applicable. The petition further alleges that the United states, being engaged in war, informed the American Telephone & Telegraph Company that it desired to have large numbers of the audions made promptly for it by the General Electric Company and others; that the American Telephone & Telegraph Company replied by writing to the Chief Signal Officer of the Army that it would not do anything to interfere with the immediate manufacture of the audions, provided it were understood and agreed that the Telephone & Telegraph Company "waived none of its claims under any patents or patent rights owned by it on account of said manufacture, and that all claims under patent rights and all patent questions be reserved and later investigated, adjusted, and settled by the United States." The plan was accepted by the United States, and the orders for said audions were thereafter given by the United States to said General Electric Company and said Moorhead Laboratories. Inc., who made them and delivered them to the government, which used them.

The petition further alleged that, for the purpose of assisting the United States to obtain said audions promptly pursuant to the orders given, the American Telephone &

Telegraph Company furnished information, drawings, and blueprints to the General Electric Company, and permitted representatives and experts of the United States and of said General Electric Company to witness and study the manufacture of said audions by the Telephone & Telegraph Company, all to the end that the audions might be the more promptly made and delivered to the United States for use in the war in which it was then engaged.

After the filing of the petition in the suit, it was amended by an averment that, after the audions were made and used by the United States, negotiations were carried on between it and the American Telephone Company, and that the latter company executed a release to the United States and all manufacturers acting under its orders of "all claims for compensation for the making and use of the audions, and that the release included all claims which had arisen or might thereafter arise for royalties, damages, profits, or compensation for infringement of any or all letters patent owned or controlled by the Telephone & Telegraph Company, whether expressly recited therein or not, for the manufacture or use prior thereto, and for use by the United States occurring thereafter."

The petition was demurred to, the demurrer was sustained, and the petition dismissed. It is conceded by the parties that on the face of the petition, with the contracts which were made exhibits, the De Forest Company and the American Telephone & Telegraph Company had each the right to license to the United States the making and use of these audions, and that, if either did so license them, it would be a complete defense to a claim for damages for the tort of infringement by the other.

The sole question, therefore, which the Court of Claims considered and decided against the appellant was whether, on the facts recited in the petition, the American Telephone & Telegraph Company had in fact given a license to the United States to have made and use these audions covered by the patents. In other words, was the claim that the American Telephone & Telegraph Company had against the United States, for the manufacture and use of the audions, based on a contract, or was it based on a tort? If it were the former, it was a full defense to any claim by the De Forest Company. If it were the latter, the De Forest Company was entitled to recover under the act of 1918.

The appellant says that the necessary effect of the allegations of his petition is that the Telephone Company said to the United States, in answer to the United States' notice that it wished to make and use the audions, "You will be infringing my rights; I shall not stop you, but I notify you that I shall hold you for such infringement;" and therefore that the subsequent acts of the United States and its manufacturers were torts. We think a different construction should be given the allegations. The agreement by the Telephone Company that it would not do anything to interfere with the immediate making of the audions for the United States, interpreted in the light of its subsequent action in assisting the United States to a prompt making of the audions for its use, in furnishing the needed information and drawings and blueprints for such manufacture, and in giving to the experts of the United States and its manufacturers the opportunity to witness and study the manufacture of audions by the Telephone Company, to the end that the audions might be more promptly manufactured and delivered to the United States for use in the war, made such conduct clearly a consent to their manufacture and use, and a license, and this without any regard to the effect of the subsequent release by the Telephone & Telegraph Company of compensation for such manufacture and use.

No formal granting of a license is necessary in order to give it effect. Any language used by the owner of the patent or any conduct on his part exhibited to another, from

which that other may properly infer that the owner consents to his use of the patent in making or using it, or selling it, upon which the other acts, constitutes a license, and a defense to an action for a tort. Whether this constitutes a gratuitous license, or one for a reasonable compensation, must, of course, depend upon the circumstances; but the relation between the parties thereafter in respect of any suit brought must be held to be contractual, and not an unlawful invasion of the rights of the owner. Concede that, if the owner had said, "If you go on and infringe my patent, I shall not attempt to enjoin you, but I shall subsequently sue you for infringement," the tort would not be waived; that is not this case. Here the circumstances show clearly that what the company was doing was not only fully consenting to the making and using by the United States of the patent, but was aiding such making and using, and in doing so was licensing it, only postponing to subsequent settlement what reasonable compensation, if any, it might claim for its license.The case of *Henry v. Dick,* 224 U.S. 1, in its main point was overruled in the *Motion Picture Patents Company v. Universal Film Company,* 243 U.S. 502; but that does not shake the authority of the language of the Court in the following passage (p. 24):

> "If a licensee be sued, he can escape liability to the patentee for the use of his invention by showing that the use is within his license; but, if his use be one prohibited by the license, the latter is of no avail as a defense. As a license passes no interest in the monopoly, it has been described as a mere waiver of the right to sue by the patentee," *citing* ROBINSON ON PATENTS, §§ 806 and 808.

In this case the language used certainly indicated the purpose of the Telephone Company not to seek an injunction against infringement, and not to sue for damages therefor, but only to sue or seek for an amicable settlement by payment of just compensation. Such action by the Telephone Company was a license, and constituted a complete defense against a suit for infringement by the De Forest Company.

Judgment affirmed.

\* \* \*

---

# Implied License: An Emerging Threat to Contributory Infringement Protection\*
Michael J. Swope
68 TEMP. L. REV. 281 (1995)

\* \* \*

### II. Substantive Implied License Patent Law

To show an implied license, the courts have evaluated any combination of the following three tests: (1) patent exhaustion; (2) infringement estoppel; and (3) the noninfringing use test—commonly referred to as the *Bandag* test. Patent exhaustion relieves the purchaser of infringement for using a product following an authorized sale. Under patent exhaustion theory, the purchaser of a product acquires an implied license to patent claims that cover the product and may also acquire an implied license to incident patent claims. Courts have applied infringement estoppel to establish an implied license

---

to patent claims when the purchaser successfully proves reliance on the actions of the patent owner. More recently, courts have applied a kind of noninfringing use test when no patent claims cover the product, but the purchaser seeks to acquire an implied license to incident claims.

### A. Development of the Patent Exhaustion Doctrine

Implied patent license analysis first developed over 120 years ago under a patent exhaustion theory. Under patent exhaustion, the patent owner loses patent rights in an individual product following an authorized sale. In the seminal decision of *Adams v. Burke*, the United States Supreme Court held that the purchaser of a coffin "acquired the right to use that coffin for the purpose for which all coffins are used." In *Adams*, the patentee gave exclusive rights to an assignee to make, use, and sell coffin lids within a ten-mile radius of Boston. The patentee then gave a second assignee the exclusive rights to make, use, and sell coffin lids outside the ten-mile radius. The first assignee sold a coffin using this lid to Burke, a Boston-area undertaker. Burke used the lid outside of the allowed ten-mile radius.

When the second assignee tried to resurrect patent rights against Burke, the Court held that the patent owner's control of the lid "perishes in the first use of it."

\* \* \*

The *Adams* Court's application of patent exhaustion narrowly encompassed only claims that directly covered the product sold. In *United States v. Univis Lens Co.*, decided nearly seventy years after *Adams*, the United States Supreme Court considered whether, under patent exhaustion theory, the purchaser of a product acquired an implied license to incident patent claims. In this case, the patent owner, Univis Lens, had several patent claims for the process of making a multi-focal eyeglass lens. The claims, for example, covered the method of producing, grinding, and polishing lens blanks. Univis Lens used a subset of the patent claims to manufacture lens blanks. Thereafter, it licensed and sold those blanks to wholesalers and retailers. After purchasing the Univis Lens blanks, these wholesalers and retailers, by practicing other Univis Lens patent claims, finished various stages of a lens. Thus, the issue before the Court was whether a patent owner could exclude a purchaser from practicing claimed inventions necessary to finish an incomplete product.

In addressing the patent owner's rights after the sale, the *Univis Lens* Court held that the "sale of a lens blank by the patentee or by his licensee is…in itself both a complete transfer of ownership of the blank, which is within the protection of the patent law, and a license to practice the final stage of the patent procedure." The Court reasoned that only one patent covered the process of making a multi-focal lens. Furthermore, the patent was not "fully practiced" until the lens blank was ground and polished. The *Univis Lens* Court determined that the sale of the unfinished product gave the purchaser an implied license to the claims embodied in the product, as well as incident claims necessary to finish the product.

To support its holding that the sale exhausted the patent owner's rights, the Court noted that the policy of patent laws is to promote the progress of the useful arts by granting exclusionary rights to the inventor. The *Univis Lens* Court reasoned that allowing the patent owner to collect a reasonable royalty for the sale of a product that embodies the patent owner's invention serves this policy. The sale price of the lens blanks, however, had included a royalty for practicing the patented invention required to finish the product. Because the patent owner had already received compensation for a completed product, collection of additional royalties for the use of other claimed inventions arising from the same patent would exceed the compensation intended by the patent system and give the patent owner double compensation.

Conventionally, patent exhaustion occurred after a sale. In a recent decision, *Intel Corp. v. ULSI System Technology, Inc.*, the United States Court of Appeals for the Federal Circuit applied patent exhaustion theory in a case in which the putative infringer did not buy anything from the patentee. In this case, the putative infringer, ULSI System Technology, designed a math co-processor that was covered by Intel patent claims. To overcome infringement liability, ULSI successfully exploited a cross-licensing agreement between Intel and Hewlett-Packard ("HP").

The terms of the Intel-HP agreement granted HP a license to make and sell math co-processors covered by Intel patent claims. Under an independent agreement between HP and ULSI, however, HP also manufactured math co-processors according to ULSI's chip design. ULSI then resold the HP-manufactured chips in competition with Intel. When Intel sued ULSI for infringement, ULSI argued that it had purchased the chips from HP, and that the sale by HP exhausted Intel's patent rights. Intel, on the other hand, argued that because HP merely had provided fabrication services, no patent rights were exhausted. The court characterized the transaction between HP and ULSI as a "contract for manufacture and sale of chips." Thus, the sale of HP-manufactured chips to ULSI exhausted Intel's patent rights to those chips. Even though the Intel patent included both method and apparatus claims that covered the chips, Intel had exhausted its patent rights.

In addition to expansion of the definition of "sale" preceding patent exhaustion, what constitutes a completed product for purposes of patent exhaustion may also be expanding. Even where the product is complete, incident claims necessary to make the product commercially viable may be included in an implied license. In *Cyrix Corp. v. Intel Corp.*, the United States District Court for the Eastern District of Texas expanded the *Univis Lens* holding to include an implied license to incident patent claims needed to make a complete product commercially viable. In *Cyrix*, a cross-licensing agreement between Texas Instruments and Intel allowed Texas Instruments to make, use, and sell microprocessors covered by Intel patent claims. In a separate transaction, Texas Instruments fabricated microprocessors for Cyrix, the putative infringer. Intel sued Cyrix for infringement and contributory infringement. However, Cyrix successfully argued that its implied license to those Intel claims that directly covered the Cyrix microprocessor chip also implied a license to incident claims necessary for the intended use of the chip. Similar to the *ULSI System Technology* court's conclusion, the *Cyrix* court concluded that Texas Instruments sold the chips to Cyrix, and that patent exhaustion precluded infringement. Unlike *ULSI System Technology*, however, the chips in *Cyrix* could not be used for any commercially viable purpose without infringement of other Intel claims. Specifically, the finished microprocessor could not be used for its intended purpose without external memory. Thus, Cyrix risked liability as a contributory infringer.

Despite the factual differences between the two cases, the *Cyrix* court determined that the *Univis Lens* rationale controlled. The court reasoned that commercial necessity created an implied license to the other related patent claims. Relying on a drawing in the patent specification that showed a connection between the microprocessor and external memory, and statements made by Intel to the Patent and Trademark Office, the court reasoned that the microprocessor was "intended to be used with external memory." Thus, the *Cyrix* court expanded patent exhaustion to create an implied license to use incident claims if necessary to accomplish a product's intended purpose. In contrast, the *Univis Lens* court expanded patent exhaustion to include only unfinished products. Furthermore, the *Cyrix* court broadly defined "necessity" to include the "ability to sell a device at a profit and to afford the development and continuation of an ongoing business."

In summary, under patent exhaustion theory, the authorized sale of a product embodying an invention creates an implied license to use and resell the product free from liability for patent infringement. A patent owner has been properly compensated for the use of that invention once the product that embodies the claimed invention is sold. Upon such sale, the patent owner waives exclusionary rights with respect to that product.

Finding an implied license to claimed inventions not embodied in, but incident to, products that embody other inventions is more complicated. However, courts will find such a license under patent exhaustion when the patent owner sells an incomplete product. In that situation, the scope of the implied license expands to include incident claims, regardless of their method or apparatus nature. Furthermore, the patent owner's waiver applies to any incident patent claims that are necessary to finish the product or use the product for its intended purpose. The intended purpose may include the purchaser's ability to sell the product profitably.

## B. Implied License by Infringement Estoppel

In addition to patent exhaustion analysis, courts have found an implied license under infringement estoppel analysis. Under estoppel, the focus of the analysis shifts from the product to the conduct of the patent owner. If that conduct causes a purchaser to act, a license may be implied.

The seminal case for implied license by estoppel is *De Forest Radio Telephone & Telegraph Co. v. United States*. In that case, the plaintiff, De Forest Radio Telephone & Telegraph Company, had a licensing agreement with the American Telephone & Telegraph Company ("AT&T") by which each company licensed its patent rights to the other, and each company had the right to sublicense. In this exchange, De Forest gave AT&T a license to make a vacuum tube embodying a De Forest invention. A short time later, AT&T received a letter from the United States government that expressed the government's desire to have the vacuum tubes manufactured by General Electric for governmental consumption. AT&T responded by indicating that it would not do anything to interfere with the immediate manufacture of the [vacuum tubes], provided it were understood and agreed that [AT&T] "waived none of its claims under any patents or patent rights owned by it on account of said manufacture, and reserved the right to investigate the patent rights involved for later adjustment." Thereafter, through a series of blueprints, AT&T showed representatives from General Electric how to make the vacuum tubes. When De Forest discovered that the government had used the De Forest vacuum tube invention, De Forest sued the government for patent infringement.

To resolve the dispute, the parties asked the court to determine whether AT&T's conduct had granted to the United States a sublicense to the De Forest patent. Such a sublicense would allow the United States to rely on the cross-licensing agreement between De Forest and AT&T as a defense to De Forest's suit for patent infringement. If AT&T's conduct did not rise to the level of a sublicense, then the United States would be liable to De Forest for patent infringement. The *De Forest* Court found that the conduct of the authorized licensee, AT&T, did amount to a license. The Court reasoned that "[n]o formal granting of a license is necessary in order to give it effect." Moreover, the Court stated that any language or conduct exhibited by the patent owner that leads to a reasonable inference of consent to the use of the patent owner's invention constitutes a license. Such a license is a defense to patent infringement. Here, the *De Forest* Court found that the United States' inference based on AT&T's conduct was reasonable. Thus, the United States could use AT&T's conduct to show the existence of an implied license and thereby relieve itself of liability for patent infringement.

The *De Forest* Court established the rule of law in implied license by estoppel. The estoppel doctrine also has been used as a defense to patent infringement when the circumstances surrounding a sale rise to the level of an implied license. For example, in *St. Joseph Iron Works v. Farmers Manufacturing Co* ., the United States Court of Appeals for the Fourth Circuit found that the plaintiff's conduct granted the defendant an implied license to a method claim. In that case, St. Joseph entered into a contract with Farmers Manufacturing that gave Farmers Manufacturing the right to use St. Joseph's basket weaving method claims to manufacture baskets. The terms of the contract provided that Farmers Manufacturing would "automatically become entitled" to any more favorable license terms granted by St. Joseph to any other parties.

St. Joseph then equipped a second company with appliances that allowed that company to practice the claimed method. Based on these actions, the *St. Joseph* court determined that St. Joseph granted the second company a royalty-free implied license. Moreover, since St. Joseph granted the second company a royalty-free license, the court found that Farmers Manufacturing was also entitled to practice the method royalty-free. *St. Joseph* set the outer limits of when the circumstances surrounding a sale rise to the level of creating an implied license. The facts here clearly pointed to an implied license: when a patent owner sets up a purchaser's equipment in a way that obviously infringes the patent owner's invention, the patent owner's conduct amounts to an implied license.

While the circumstances of a sale could create an implied license, the outcome is less certain when the facts are not as clear as those in *St. Joseph*. In *Stickle v. Heublein, Inc.*, the United States Court of Appeals for the Federal Circuit, addressing implied license estoppel for the first time, found that the unilateral expectations of the purchaser are not enough to create an implied license. In that case, Stickle had a variety of patents comprising both apparatus and method claims for the automated manufacture of taco shells. Under a contract, Stickle manufactured taco shell-making machines, according to the patents, and agreed to sell several of the machines to Heublein. After delivery of the first machine, two problems developed: (1) the machine did not operate according to specification; and (2) Stickle became ill and could not complete the delivery of additional machines. Heublein then had the remaining machines manufactured by a third party and resisted further payments to Stickle. After Stickle's subsequent death, his estate sued Heublein for patent infringement.

In arguing that the course of conduct between the parties amounted to an implied license, Heublein asserted that Stickle had "encouraged Heublein 'to do whatever was necessary to keep the project on track.'" The court distinguished this comment from AT&T's conduct in *De Forest* because the new fryers were only in the design stage, that is, they had not yet fully included the Stickle inventions. Moreover, ongoing contractual discussions were underway at the time. The parties were negotiating an agreement that required Heublein to pay royalties for each machine manufactured. The court rejected Heublein's argument and noted:

> One common thread in cases in which equitable estoppel applies is that the actor committed himself to act, and indeed acted, as a direct consequence of another's conduct. Thus, an implied license cannot arise out of the unilateral expectations or even reasonable hopes of one party. One must have been led to take actions by the conduct of the other party. Here, the court held that Stickle's conduct did not rise to the level of granting Heublein an implied license.

To summarize, the implied license by estoppel defense shifts the focus of whether an implied license arose away from the product itself and toward the circumstances of the transaction between the parties. Conversely, in patent exhaustion the implied license arises when the product necessarily implies the right to use it in a particular way. When the product itself cannot satisfy the grant of an implied license, a putative infringer may use estoppel to argue that the conduct of the patent owner created an implied license. If the purchaser reasonably relies on the conduct of the patent owner or authorized seller, an implied license may arise. However, if the relationship is governed by an ongoing contractual relationship, as in *Stickle*, the license should be controlled by contract. As a result, the purchaser would be less likely to obtain an implied license if the contract did not grant the purchaser an express license.

### C. Implied License by the Noninfringing Use Test

For well over a century, courts used either patent exhaustion or estoppel analysis to determine whether an implied license was created in a purchaser. The primary test was patent exhaustion, but in a few instances implied license arose by estoppel. Patent exhaustion generally applied to cases in which a product embodied patent claims. Estoppel applied when the purchaser reasonably relied on the patent owner's conduct. However, cases arose where neither of these analyses satisfactorily applied. In this third category, the mere sale of a non-patented product useful in practicing a claimed invention did not imply a license to practice that invention when the product had other uses. To apply this rule consistently, the courts eventually adopted a test that borrowed features of both patent exhaustion and estoppel.

This third category of implied license arises when the product sold does not embody an apparatus claim, but could be used to practice a method claim. One example of this kind of situation is the United States Supreme Court's decision in *Lawther v. Hamilton*. The case does not announce any new analyses useful in the more complex modern cases to follow, but it does clearly highlight the non-patented product dilemma. Here, the product could be used to practice a method invention although the product did not embody any patent claims. In *Lawther*, the plaintiff patented a process for extracting linseed oil from linseeds. The claimed invention was an improvement over older methods because it extracted more oil in fewer steps. The plaintiff patent owner also sold equipment for extracting linseed oil. The equipment could be used in the old as well as the new extraction methods. The defendant purchased linseed oil extraction equipment from the plaintiff and used the equipment to practice the plaintiff's improved method. Subsequently, the plaintiff sued the defendant for infringement. In response, the defendant argued that the equipment could be used to practice the plaintiff's method invention. For that reason, argued the defendant, an implied license arose from the plaintiff's sale of the equipment, protecting the defendant purchaser from infringement liability. The Court disagreed, holding that no implied license arose because the equipment could be used to practice other methods of linseed oil extraction. Thus, according to the Court, when the plaintiff patent owner sold the equipment he did not implicitly grant a license to use the patented extraction method.

\* \* \*

In summary, after the authorized sale of a product that does not embody a claimed invention, the *Bandag* test is used to determine whether the purchaser has an implied license to use the product to practice incident patent claims. Under the *Bandag* test, an implied license arises where the purchaser establishes: (1) the product cannot be used for any purpose without infringing the patent owner's claims; and (2) the circumstances of the sale plainly indicate that a license should be inferred. *Met-Coil* expands upon the *Bandag* test by allowing an implied licensee to substitute any consumable component of a combination where that component does not itself embody a claimed invention.

---

# The Impact of the Patent Exhaustion and Implied License Doctrines on License Negotiations*

Christopher D. Joslyn

10 INTELL. PROP. STRATEGIST 3 (Oct. 2003)

Nothing should be left to chance when drafting patent licenses. Indeed, the parties on both sides of the transaction have a keen interest in eliminating ambiguities. This is particularly true with respect to the scope of the license grant. The licensor must be reasonably assured that it has not inadvertently given away more than what was bargained for. On the other side, the licensee must be reasonably assured that it may use the patent as it intended without being sued for infringement.

Beyond the language of the grant, a key consideration for both parties is the impact of the patent exhaustion and implied license doctrines. Both doctrines operate similarly. In essence, they limit the licensor's right to claim infringement against downstream users of its patent or sellers of devices that embody the patent. Although these doctrines are often applied with indistinguishable results, the requirements for each are different. Moreover, these doctrines also differ in scope.

Patent exhaustion results from an authorized, unconditional sale or license of a patented device. Subsequent sales and uses cannot infringe the patent covering the device. If the device had only been licensed for use in a particular product, however, the licensor would have a cause of action for any subsequent sale or use of the device apart from the product. An implied license arises when the licensor sells or licenses articles that have no reasonable, non-infringing uses, other than practicing the patent, and the circumstances plainly indicate that the grant of a license should be inferred. Significantly, it should be recognized that the scope of the implied license doctrine is somewhat broader than what is permissible under the patent exhaustion doctrine because the licensee would also have the right to make the patented article.

Nonetheless, there is some discrepancy among the courts over which doctrine controls the disposition of any particular case. In *Anton/Bauer, Inc. v. PAG Ltd.*, 329 F.3d 1343 (Fed. Cir. 2003), the Federal Circuit held that an implied license permitted consumers to practice a claimed invention with no liability for infringement. The patent involved a battery pack connection, composed of a patented female and unpatented male plate, used in conjunction with video cameras. Anton/Bauer sold the female plates directly to video camera manufacturers, who sold the cameras to consumers with the female plate incorporated into the camera. When the defendant began selling compatible battery packs fitted with the male plate, Anton/Bauer sued for contributory infringement on the grounds that PAG had induced consumers to violate its rights in the patented combination. The court held that there was no underlying infringement because the female plate had been sold without restriction and was useful only in performing the claimed combination. Thus, Anton/Bauer had granted an implied license.

---

* Reprinted by permission of the author and the publisher, copyright 2003.

By contrast, the Northern District of California has taken a slightly different tack under a similar fact pattern. In *LG Electronics v. Asustek,* 248 F. Supp.2d 912 (N.D. Cal. 2003), the defendants had purchased microprocessors and chipsets from a licensee of LG and installed them in computers. LG claimed that the combination of these items infringed its patents. However, the court found that LG's patent rights in the combination were exhausted by the unconditional sale of the microprocessors and chipsets. Based on a synthesis of Supreme Court and Federal Circuit cases, the court held that the patent exhaustion doctrine also applied to the unrestricted sale of the essential components comprising a patented article. Since the microprocessors and chipsets were essential components of LG's patented combination, and these components would have been inoperable unless used in the combination, LG had exhausted its patent rights in the combination.

Although these cases are similar in outcome, they also highlight some key issues for licensors. First and foremost, the licensor must determine whether the nature of the patent poses risks for licensing arrangements. In the *Anton/Bauer* case, the licensor could not prevent others from making compatible battery packs because the patented aspects of the locking mechanism resided solely on the female plate. Anton/Bauer might have protected its patented combination had the patented aspects of the locking mechanism been divided among the female and male plates. Likewise, Anton/Bauer might have placed restrictions on the use of the plates or otherwise taken steps to negate the inference of a license.

Second, the licensor must determine whether the sale or license of separately patented components has implications for patented combinations. In the *LG Electronics* case, the licensor was not able to prevent computer manufacturers from combining microprocessors and chipsets purchased from LG's licensee because the components had no reasonable non-infringing uses on their own. Had LG placed conditions on the sale and use of these components, through its licensee, downstream purchasers would have been required to seek a license from LG in order to combine the components.

However, licensors are not the only parties that need to calculate the impact of these doctrines. One important limitation of both doctrines is the concept of unrestricted sale or license. In the exhaustion context, this is particularly critical for those who take licenses from a licensee. Unless the grant from the patentee to the licensee is unrestricted with respect to subsequent sales and uses of articles or combinations thereof, the restrictions will flow downstream. Similarly, since most agreements disclaim all licenses not expressly granted, the implied license defense will be unavailable to the licensee.

Licensees should also be aware of licensing arrangements that involve method patents because the patent exhaustion doctrine may not be applicable. As the *LG Electronics* court held, the sale of a device does not exhaust the licensor's rights under a separate method patent. Thus, even if the licensor sells equipment that practices a patented method for accomplishing a specific function, the licensee is not free under the exhaustion doctrine to practice that method without a license. Although the licensee could argue that the circumstances indicate that the sale of the equipment gives rise to an implied license, most agreements disclaim all licenses not expressly granted. Under these circumstances, the implied license doctrine [may be] inapplicable. Therefore, the key issue for licensees is to make sure that any method claims are expressly included in the license grant. Moreover, the grant should also include the right for the licensees' customers to practice the method patent.

Although the patent exhaustion and implied license doctrines add complexity to the drafting process, both sides of the transaction can easily avoid disputes later on in the relationship. Actively contemplating the nature of the patents, the structure of the li-

censing arrangement and the portfolio of intellectual property necessary for the transaction will help the licensor and the licensee select appropriate express grants and limitations. And both parties will get what they bargained for.

---

# "Have Made" Rights—A Trap for the Unwary*
### Michael P. Bregenzer
### 10 Intell. Prop. Today 13 (July 2003)

Many patent licenses grant the licensee a "have made" right. In general, a "have
made" right, which is derived from the term "to make" set forth in 35 U.S.C. § 271(a),
permits a licensee to have an unlicensed third party make a licensed product for the licensee. There are no magic words to grant a licensee "have made" rights. For example, a
license that grants the right "to make, to have made, to use, to sell (either directly or indirectly), to lease and to otherwise dispose of Licensed Products," conveys "have made"
rights.

In addition to permitting the licensee to have a licensed product manufactured for it
by a third party, a "have made" right also offers limited protection from an infringement charge for the third party manufacturer. Specifically, to the extent an unlicensed
third party manufactures a licensed product for a licensee with "have made" rights, the
unlicensed third party cannot be liable for infringement to the licensor/patent owner.
Thus, the effect of granting "have made" rights is to provide a limited license to third
parties. Inasmuch as a license is an absolute defense to a charge of patent infringement,
by granting "have made" rights to a licensee, the licensor may be unintentionally providing a defense to a patent infringement suit to a third-party under an implied license
theory.

The case of *Intel Corp. v. Broadcom*, 173 F. Supp.2d 201 (D. Del. 2001), is instructive
in this regard. In that case, Intel filed suit against Broadcom charging infringement of
five U.S. patents. One of the affirmative defenses raised by Broadcom was that to the extent certain of the allegedly infringing products were made for or sold to licensees of
Intel with "have made" rights included in their licenses, Broadcom's manufacture of
those products was shielded from infringement. For example, in that ease, Broadcom
sold allegedly infringing products to Sony. Sony had a license from Intel that allowed
them to "have made" certain products.

Ultimately, both Intel and Broadcom moved for summary judgment on Broadcom's
license defense. The key issue the court needed to decide in order to resolve the summary judgment motions was:

> [W]hether Broadcom *made* the products pursuant to a request from the li-
> censee, in which case the making and selling would be authorized to the extent
> that licensee's license allows it to be, or whether Broadcom simply *sold* allegedly
> infringing off-the-shelf products to parties that happened to be licensees.

In reaching the conclusion that this was the key issue, the court stated that,

---

"[a]n unlicensed third party in the position of Broadcom only is afforded the protections of a license if those protections are conveyed by the licensee to the third party as an exercise of the licensed party's 'have made' rights. Broadcom cannot lay claim to those protections if they were never conveyed to Broadcom."

The court noted that it had come to the exact same conclusion when it had addressed the issue of whether "have made" rights confer protections to manufacturers of "off the shelf" parts in *Thorn EMI North America, Inc. v. Hyundai Elec. Indus. Co.*[CA 94-332-RRM, 1996 U.S. Dist. LEXIS 21170 (Dist. Del. 1996)]. In that case, the court found that, "a foundry commissioned by IBM to manufacture HEI products would have the protection of the license agreement, [but that] a manufacturer of 'off the shelf' products is not a foundry...[and] therefore, whether or not it sold the products to IBM, would not be protected by the agreement."

The court ultimately denied summary judgment to both Intel and Broadcom, finding that, "it is unclear whether Broadcom made the products pursuant to a request from the licensee." The court went on to conclude that the:

[G]ranting of "have made" rights to licensees does not, however, give the licensee the inherent right to in some way immunize prior acts of infringement through its subsequent purchase of off the shelf goods. To the extent that the "have made" right allows the licensee to purchase the licensed products off of the shelf of an unlicensed third party, that right may shield the licensee from subsequent liability for using or selling that product. However, the "have made" right in that situation does not immunize the unlicensed third party.

The license defense arose again at trial. In that regard, the jury was instructed regarding Broadcom's license defense as follows:

An accused infringer may be protected from infringement liability if the accused infringer makes products for the use or sale of a licensee under a patent in suit. In order to take advantage of such "have made" rights, the accused infringer must prove the following factors:

First, the accused infringer must prove that the party for whom it produces the accused product was a licensee under the patent in suit at the time of the accused sales.

Second, the accused infringement must prove that the licensee has valid "have made" rights under its license to the patent in suit. For the licensee to have valid "have made" rights, the license agreement must authorize that licensee to have the patented product, or a portion of the patented product, made for it by an outside source like the accused infringer.

Third, the accused infringer must prove that the products it makes are "licensed products" as defined under the licensee.

Fourth, the accused infringer must prove that it made products pursuant to a request from the licensee. If the accused infringer sells "off the shelf" or stock products, the accused infringer would not be protected from infringement liability under "have made" rights.

Because Broadcom did not introduce any evidence concerning the license defense, the court vacated the jury verdict finding that Broadcom's sales to twelve separate licensees did not constitute infringement, and granted Intel's motion for a new trial.

The importance of this case can be seen in the test set forth in the foregoing jury my obstruction. More specifically; in order to avail itself of an implied license defense under a "have made" rights clause, a third-party manufacturer must establish the following four facts:

1. That the party for whom it produces the accused product was a licensee under the patent in suit at the time of the accused sales.
2. That the licensee has valid "have made" rights under its license to the patent in suit.
3. That the products it makes are "licensed products" as defined under the license.
4. That it made products pursuant to a request from the licensee.

Notably, with respect to the fourth element, the court specifically stated that if a third-party manufacturer sells "off the shelf" or stock products, that party would not be able to establish this factor, and would not be protected from infringement liability.

Based on this case, it is foreseeable that manufacturers, when negotiating sales of a potentially infringing product, could include language in the purchase/sales agreement providing that the manufacturer is making the product at the specific request of the customer/licensee, in an attempt to shield those sales from a future charge of infringement. While it may be difficult for the manufacturer to establish that it is making the product pursuant to the request of a licensee if the manufacturer is making the product prior to its sale to the licensee, it still remains a viable defense that will, at a minimum, unnecessarily increase the costs associated with bringing an infringement action. While there are some favorable eases limiting the scope of "have made" rights when it comes to "off the shelf" components, a company takes a significant risk in relying on this law rather than carefully drafting its licenses. For example, in the *Intel v. Broadcom* case, the jury found that Broadcom's sales to twelve customers that were Intel's licensees were immunized from infringement based on those licensees' "have made" rights. While the court ultimately granted Intel a new trial on this issue, it is clearly a significant concern.

This problem can be easily addressed before litigation, by limiting the scope of the "have made" rights at the time of the license grant. There are obviously many ways to address this issue. For example, to avoid the situation addressed in *Intel v. Broadcom,* a licensor can restrict the "have made" rights to exclude "off the shelf" products. Another alternative would be to restrict the "have made" rights to products designed by the licensee. A third alternative would be to limit the "have made" rights so as to exclude products sold by the third-party manufacturer to others.

The key to avoiding the implied license issue under a "have made" license provision is to carefully draft the license, because courts are often less than sympathetic to a party claiming that the scope of its license should be interpreted in some way other than the plain language of the license.

* * *

In conclusion, the law is clear that "have made" rights can extend to third party manufacturers, resulting in an implied license. In certain circumstances, this implied license can have unintended consequences, such as waiving a charge of infringement against a third-party manufacturer. Thus, it is important to consider the issue of "have made" rights at the time a license is granted and decide whether certain limitations on the "have made" rights should be included so as to avoid an argument at some later date that a third-party does not infringe because it makes the infringing products under a licensees' "have made" rights.

# Notes

1. *Implied Licenses of Copyrighted Works.* Implied licenses of copyrighted works can be found in a variety of circumstances. *See Foad Consulting Group, Inc. v. Musil Govan Azzalino*, 270 F.3d 821 (9th Cir. 2001) (implied nonexclusive license to use and adapt copyrighted plans for specified project found in the absence of express development contract language to the contrary). However, where a written license agreement exits, courts will generally refuse to infer additional terms. *See Arp Films, Inc. v. Marvel Entm't Group, Inc.*, 952 F.2d 643, 650 (2d Cir. 1991). If a right is not expressly granted in the license, the presumption is that the copyright holder retained that right: "licenses are assumed to prohibit any use not authorized." *S.O.S. v. Payday, Inc.*, 886 F.2d 1081, 1088 (9th Cir. 1989).

2. *Implied Licenses of Trademarks.* A basic principle of trademark law is that any license of a trademark without adequate quality control provisions governing the use of the mark is invalid. This is referred to as "naked licensing." A naked license can also lead to a finding of abandonment of the mark by the licensor. *See Dawn Donut Co. v. Hart's Food Stores, Inc.*, 267 F.2d 358 (2d Cir. 1959). An implied trademark license conflicts with this basic principle. Therefore, the only setting in which a court is likely to find an implied trademark license is under "an existing contract or longstanding business relationship for imposing such control obligations." J. DRATLER, LICENSING OF INTELLECTUAL PROPERTY, § 3.04[8][d] (Law Journal Press 1994).

3. *Implied License to Sublicense and Assign in Patents.* A non-exclusive license is neither divisible nor sublicenseable unless such rights are expressly authorized. *Ozyagcilar v. Davis*, 221 U.S.P.Q. 1064, 1070–71 (D.S.C. (1983); *E.I. du Pont de Nemours and Co., Inc., v. Shell Oil Co.*, 498 A.2d 1108, 1114 (S. Ct. Del. 1985) ("A nonexclusive patent license conveys certain indivisible rights under the patent, which are personal to the licensee. As such these rights are not susceptible to sublicensing, unless specific permission is given."); *Federal Labs., Inc. v. Comm'r of Internal Revenue*, 73 USPQ 453 (T.C. 1947) ("A sub-license can be granted only where the license expressly authorizes, and the main licensee is the agent of the licensor in negotiating a sub-license"); Steven Z. Szczepanski, *Contract Law Aspects of Licensing, in* ECKSTROMS LICENSING IN FOREIGN AND DOMESTIC OPERATIONS, at § 2.04 (2004) (when a non-exclusive license agreement is silent as to licensee's right to divide or sublicense, the licensed rights are neither divisible nor sublicenseable); H. EINHORN, PATENT LICENSING TRANSACTIONS § 2.04 at 29 (2002) ("It has generally been held that rights arising under parent licenses are not divisible, and that a licensee may not grant sublicenses unless he is authorized to do so by the terms of the license.") The right to sublicense may not be implied from the language of the grant and courts have held that a nonexclusive patent license carries with it an implied prohibition on sublicensing. *E.I. du Pont de Nemours, supra*, at 1114. Similarly, the grant language does not include the ability to transfer or assign the license to a third party. The mere granting of a license to make, use or sell a patented article does not confer upon the licensee the right to transfer his license unless the patentee has consented thereto. *Rock-Ola Mfg. Corp. v. Fiben Mfg. Co.*, 168 F.2d 919 (8th Cir. 1948).

4. *Other License Scope Issues.* Licensees must ensure that the scope of the license they are obtaining is sufficiently broad to meet the needs of their business model. For example, if the grant of the license of source code specifies a particular version of software, use of the licensed source code in conjunction with another program probably

exceeds the scope of the license grant. *See PlayMedia Sys., Inc. v. Am. Online, Inc.*, 171 F. Supp.2d 1094 (C.D. Cal. 2001) (the court applied principles of contract interpretation to interpret the license agreement and find that AOL's use of PlayMedia's source code with AOL's AOL Media Player was outside AOL's license to use the source code in conjunction with PlayMedia's WINAMP program). Licensors must be sure not to license more intellectual property than they have a right to.

5. *Effective IP Assignment Language for To-Be-Created Intellectual Property.* In *Speedplay, Inc. v. Bebop Inc.*, the Federal Circuit distinguished between enforceable intellectual property assignments and unenforceable "agreements to assign" intellectual property. At issue was the enforceability of intellectual property assignment language in a "Confidentiality and Inventions Agreement" (CIA). The CIA defined "Inventions" as any intellectual property conceived or developed by the inventor within the scope of his employment. The assignment language stated that all inventions covered by the CIA " 'shall belong exclusively to [assignee] and [inventor] hereby conveys, transfers and assigns to [assignee]…all right, title and interest in and to Inventions.' " 211 F.3d 1245, 1253 (Fed. Cir. 2000).

> Bebop challenges Speedplay's rights in the '894 patent on two grounds. First, Bebop contends that the CIA is merely a "promise to assign a future invention." That contention invokes this court's decision in *Arachnid, Inc. v. Merit Industries, Inc.*, 939 F.2d 1574, 1576, 19 USPQ2d 1513, 1514 (Fed.Cir.1991) in which a contractor agreed that any inventions it conceived " 'shall be the property of [the client], and all rights thereto *will be assigned* ' " by the contractor to the client. Holding that the client could not bring an infringement action based on that contractual language, the Arachnid court characterized the promise as "an *agreement to assign,* not an assignment." *Id.* at 1580, 1580–81, 19 USPQ2d at 1518, 1518–19. The language in the CIA, however, differs significantly from the language at issue in *Arachnid.* It provides that inventions "shall belong" to Speedplay, and that Bryne "hereby conveys, transfers and assigns" the inventions to Speedplay. Therefore, this case is not controlled by *Arachnid,* but by *Filmtec Corp. v. Allied-Signal Inc.*, 939 F.2d 1568, 1570, 19 USPQ2d 1508, 1509 (Fed.Cir.1991), in which the contractor agreed " 'to grant and does hereby grant' " to the client the rights and title to any invention, whether patentable or not. In *Filmtec* this court stated that "no further act would be required once an invention came into being; the transfer of title would occur by operation of law. *Id.* at 1573, 939 F.2d 1568, 19 USPQ2d at 1512.

*Id.* at 1253 (Fed. Cir. 2000). Thus, to be effective, employee invention assignment agreements—or any agreement anticipating the assignment of IP not yet created—must contain "current" language assigning to-be-created intellectual property (e.g., "to grant and hereby does grant" or "hereby conveys, transfers, and assigns") and must avoid mere promises of assignment.

7. *Can a License Avoid the On-Sale Bar?* The Patent Act prohibits the patenting of an invention that has been "on sale" for more than one year prior to filing date of the patent application. In *Pfaff v. Wells Elecs., Inc.*, 525 U.S. 55 (1998), the Supreme Court established a two-part test for determining the sale of an invention: (1) whether the invention is "ready for patenting;" and (2) whether the patented technology has been commercially offered for sale. The Supreme Court's opinion did not define what it meant by a "commercial" offer for sale.

In *Group One Ltd. v. Hallmark Cards, Inc.*, the Federal Circuit specifically addressed the issue of a "commercial offer for sale." 254 F.3d 1041 (Fed. Cir. 2001), *cert.*

*denied*, 534 U.S. 1127 (2002). Group One sued Hallmark for patent infringement based on a machine and method for creating shredded and curled ribbon for packaging. The district court found that communications between the parties constituted an offer for sale to start the time period for the on-sale bar, even though the communications did not constitute a contractual offer for sale.

First, the Federal Circuit held that an offer must "meet the level of an offer for sale in the contract sense..." for that offer to start the time period for the on-sale bar. In this case, the Federal Circuit held that the parties' correspondence did not result in a commercial offer for sale based on Uniform Commercial Code definitions. In addition, advertising and promotion may be only invitations for offers. *Id.* at 1047–48. Second, the Federal Circuit considered the issue of whether an offer to license raised the on-sale bar. Two of the judges concluded that the Federal Circuit did not need to address this issue, because the court had already held that the parties' communications did not qualify as commercial activity sufficient to start the time period for the on-sale bar. *Id.* at 1049.

The third judge on the panel, Judge Alan Lourie, filed additional remarks stating that an offer to license does not automatically raise the on-sale bar. Specifically, Judge Lourie stated that although there would be instances where a license rose to the equivalent of a sale (such as a click-wrap license for commercial software), that was not always the case:

> We have held in *Mas-Hamilton* that providing a machine to a potential customer with an offer to convey "production rights" or the "right to market the invention" does not constitute an offer to sell the invention that violates the on-sale bar. *Mas-Hamilton Group v. LaGardl Inc.*, 156 F.3d 1206, 1217, 48 USPQ2d 1010, 1019 (Fed.Cir. 1998). That is because a license under a patent is not usually a sale of the patented product, and the statute bars a sale, not a license. A license is analogous to granting or waiving rights under *the patent*, which is distinct from selling *the machine* covered by the patent.
>
> A patent license, if it is non-exclusive, is an agreement to forbear from suit. If the license is exclusive, it may be tantamount to an assignment of the patent. In neither case is the invention of the patent necessarily on sale when the license is executed. In fact, if a license were equivalent to a sale for purposes of the on-sale bar, many patents would be invalidated long before the invention itself is put on sale because the grant of licenses often long precedes commercialization by sale of the invention. The law does not start the on-sale bar clock running when a license to an invention is executed.
>
> The on-sale bar is intended to limit the time for an inventor to commercialize an invention before filing a patent application. The statute refers to a patented invention itself being on sale, not to an agreement with another party concerning the commercialization of the invention at some future time, following which the invention would then be placed on sale. An important consequence of the distinction between the sale and the license of a patented machine is thus the time at which the on-sale clock starts running. With a license, the licensee of a machine would not normally be able to immediately begin commercialization of the invention, whereas if the machine had been sold, the sale itself is the commercialization that starts the on-sale clock running. How long Hallmark, the potential licensee in this case, would have taken before it could have put the invention into commercial use is not known. But it would not have been immediate, whereas the sale of the machine, had it occurred, would have been immediate.

*Id.* at 1052–53 (Additional Remarks, Circuit Judge Lourie, emphasis in original).

---

# IV. Shrink-Wrap and Click-Wrap Licenses

In the early 1980s, personal computers and the software that runs on them became mass-market commodities. Vendors of the software, including the all-important operating system, protected their products primarily by copyright and, to a lesser extent, by the law of trade secrets. To guard their commercial interests and their intellectual property, vendors decided to license their software subject to contractual restrictions, rather than to sell copies outright and rely on the same statutory framework on which booksellers rely. The result was the first widespread attempt to license, not sell, a mass-market product used by consumers for nonbusiness purposes.

Some vendors relied on technological measures in addition to licensing. Their technological copy-protection schemes were effective against all but expert and determined "hackers," but they made using the software difficult and cumbersome. One scheme, for example, required the original floppy diskette for the software to remain in the disk drive in order for the software to operate. If the user's computer had only one floppy disk drive—as many computers did—using the software rendered that drive unusable for other purposes, even if the user had transferred the software to the hard drive beforehand. Because these "copy-protection" schemes made computers and software harder to use, they were universally panned by reviewers, disliked by consumers, and ultimately rejected by the marketplace.

The market's rejection of these early technological copy-protection schemes left only one means to protect vendor's intellectual property and business interests: mass-market licensing. The licenses were standard forms of some length and complexity. Consideration of marketing, aesthetics and readability precluded placing them on the outside of cartons for software and computers. Accordingly, many vendors began placing them directly under the plastic "shrink-wrap" that covered the box, or inside the box itself, with a prominent notice on the license or the box directing the buyer's attention to the license. These licenses became known as "shrink-wrap" or "tear me open" licenses, because they purported to come into force by the consumer's act of tearing open the shrink-wrap or using the software. The vendors relied on the age-old notion that an offer could specify how a contract was formed, in this case the user's act of opening the package, using the software, or failing to return the software to the vendor within a specified time.

Several variants of this "acceptance by action" procedure arose later. In some, the software itself, before it would do anything useful, contained a screen referring the user to the license and requiring the user to indicate acceptance by pressing a key or keys indicating assent. In others, the software displayed the entire license on screen before asking for assent. As the Internet developed, on-line distributors of software used similar means to require assent from users before allowing software to be downloaded. Many vendors required the user to "click here" or check a "yes" box indicating assent to the license terms. By analogy to the "shrink-wrap" licenses for software marketed in boxes, these on-line licenses became known by the incongruous name of "click-wrap" licenses.

Detailed terms for mass-market purchases are nothing new, as anyone who has bought a car or major appliance knows. These precise mechanisms of indicating assent, however, were new. Because they did not involve a manual, written signature, and because they could raise questions regarding the consumer's actual awareness of the terms, they troubled many users and led to legal speculation as to their enforceability.

Over a decade passed before the courts provided any definitive answer. As the decisions below suggest, the answer was simple in concept but sometimes not easy to apply. Whatever their physical or technological form, mass-market licenses are contracts like any others and obey the same rules. The common law or relevant statutes like the Uniform Commercial Code (if applicable) determines whether and when a contract is formed. The same rules for offer, acceptance, consideration, and mutual assent to terms apply to shrink-wrap, click-wrap and other on-line agreements as to contracts in general. Under these rules, most mass-market licenses are valid, but a vendor that does not pay attention to detail can find the courts unwilling to enforce its licenses.

# A. The Validity of Shrink-Wrap and Click-Wrap Licenses

## ProCD, Inc. v. Zeidenberg
### 86 F.3d 1447 (7th Cir. 1996)

EASTERBROOK, Circuit Judge.

Must buyers of computer software obey the terms of shrink-wrap licenses? The district court held not, for two reasons: first, they are not contracts because the licenses are inside the box rather than printed on the outside; second, federal law forbids enforcement even if the licenses are contracts. 908 F. Supp. 640 (W.D. Wis. 1996)....  Shrink-wrap licenses are enforceable unless their terms are objectionable on grounds applicable to contracts in general (for example, if they violate a rule of positive law, or if they are unconscionable). Because no one argues that the terms of the license at issue here are troublesome, we remand with instructions to enter judgment for the plaintiff.

I

ProCD, the plaintiff, has compiled information more than 3,000 telephone directories into a computer database. We may assume that this database cannot be copyrighted, although it is more complex, contains more information (nine-digit zip codes and census industrial codes), is organized differently, and therefore is more original than the single alphabetical directory at issue in *Feist Publications, Inc. v. Rural Telephone Service Co.*, 499 U.S. 340, 111 S. Ct. 1282, 113 L. Ed.2d 358 (1991). *See* Paul J. Heald, *The Vices of Originality*, 1991 Sup. Ct. Rev. 143, 160–68. ProCD sells a version of the database, called SelectPhone (trademark), on CD-ROM discs....A proprietary method of compressing the data serves as effective encryption too. Customers decrypt and use the data with the aid of an application program that ProCD has written. This program, which is copyrighted, searches the database in response to users' criteria (such as "find all people named Tatum in Tennessee, plus all firms with 'Door Systems' in the corporate name").

The resulting lists (or, as ProCD prefers, "listings") can be read and manipulated by other software, such as word processing programs.

The database in SelectPhone (trademark) cost more than $10 million to compile and is expensive to keep current. It is much more valuable to some users than to others. The combination of names, addresses, and SIC codes enables manufacturers to compile lists of potential customers. Manufacturers and retailers pay high prices to specialized information intermediaries for such mailing lists; ProCD offers a potentially cheaper alternative. People with nothing to sell could use the database as a substitute for calling long distance information, or as a way to look up old friends who have moved to unknown towns, or just as an electronic substitute for the local phone book. ProCD decided to engage in price discrimination, selling its database to the general public for personal use at a low price (approximately $150 for the set of five discs) while selling information to the trade for a higher price. It has adopted some intermediate strategies too: access to the SelectPhone (trademark) database is available via the America Online service for the price America Online charges to its clients (approximately $3 per hour), but this service has been tailored to be useful only to the general public.

If ProCD had to recover all of its costs and make a profit by charging a single price—that is, if it could not charge more to commercial users than to the general public—it would have to raise the price substantially over $150. The ensuing reduction in sales would harm consumers who value the information at, say, $200. They get consumer surplus of $50 under the current arrangement but would cease to buy if the price rose substantially. If because of high elasticity of demand in the consumer segment of the market the only way to make a profit turned out to be a price attractive to commercial users alone, then all consumers would lose out—and so would the commercial clients, who would have to pay more for the listings because ProCD could not obtain any contribution toward costs from the consumer market.

To make price discrimination work, however, the seller must be able to control arbitrage. An air carrier sells tickets for less to vacationers than to business travelers, using advance purchase and Saturday-night-stay requirements to distinguish the categories. A producer of movies segments the market by time, releasing first to theaters, then to pay-per-view services, next to the videotape and laserdisc market, and finally to cable and commercial TV. Vendors of computer software have a harder task. Anyone can walk into a retail store and buy a box. Customers do not wear tags saying "commercial user" or "consumer user." Anyway, even a commercial-user-detector at the door would not work, because a consumer could buy the software and resell to a commercial user. That arbitrage would break down the price discrimination and drive up the minimum price at which ProCD would sell to anyone.

Instead of tinkering with the product and letting users sort themselves—for example, furnishing current data at a high price that would be attractive only to commercial customers, and two-year-old data at a low price—ProCD turned to the institution of contract. Every box containing its consumer product declares that the software comes with restrictions stated in an enclosed license. This license, which is encoded on the CD-ROM disks as well as printed in the manual, and which appears on a user's screen every time the software runs, limits use of the application program and listings to non-commercial purposes.

Matthew Zeidenberg bought a consumer package of SelectPhone (trademark) in 1994 from a retail outlet in Madison, Wisconsin, but decided to ignore the license. He formed Silken Mountain Web Services, Inc., to resell the information in the Select-

Phone (trademark) database. The corporation makes the database available on the Internet to anyone willing to pay its price—which, needless to say, is less than ProCD charges its commercial customers. Zeidenberg has purchased two additional Select-Phone (trademark) packages, each with an updated version of the database, and made the latest information available over the World Wide Web, for a price, through his corporation. ProCD filed this suit seeking an injunction against further dissemination that exceeds the rights specified in the licenses (identical in each of the three packages Zeidenberg purchased). The district court held the licenses ineffectual because their terms do not appear on the outside of the packages. The court added that the second and third licenses stand no different from the first, even though they are identical, because they might have been different, and a purchase does not agree to—and cannot be bound by—terms that were secret at the time of purchase. 908 F. Supp. at 654.

## II

Following the district court, we treat the licenses as ordinary contracts accompanying the sale of products, and therefore as governed by the common law of contracts and the Uniform Commercial Code. Whether there are legal differences between "contracts" and "licenses" (which may matter under the copyright doctrine of first sale) is a subject for another day. See Microsoft Corp. v. Harmony Computers & Electronics, Inc., 846 F. Supp. 208 (E.D.N.Y. 1994). Zeidenberg does not argue that Silken Mountain Web Services is free of any restrictions that apply to Zeidenberg himself, because any effort to treat the two parties as distinct would put Silken Mountain behind the eight ball on ProCD's argument that copying the application program onto its hard disk violates the copyright laws. Zeidenberg does argue, and the district court held, that placing the package of software on the shelf is an "offer," which the customer "accepts" by paying the asking price and leaving the store with the goods. Peeters v. State, 154 Wis. 111, 142 N.W. 181 (Wis. 1913). In Wisconsin, as elsewhere, a contract includes only the terms on which the parties have agreed. One cannot agree to hidden terms, the judge concluded. So far, so good—but one of the terms to which Zeidenberg agreed by purchasing the software is that the transaction was subject to a license. Zeidenberg's position therefore must be that the printed terms on the outside of a box are the parties' contract—except for printed terms that refer to or incorporate other terms. But why would Wisconsin fetter the parties' choice in this way? Vendors can put the entire terms of a contract on the outside of a box only by using microscopic type, removing other information that buyers might find more useful (such as what the software does, and on which computers it works), or both. The "Read Me" file included with most software, describing system requirements and potential incompatibilities, may be equivalent to ten pages of type; warranties and license restrictions take still more space. Notice on the outside, terms on the inside, and a right to return the software for a refund if the terms are unacceptable (a right that the license expressly extends), may be a means of doing business valuable to buyers and sellers alike. See E. ALLAN FARNSWORTH, 1 FARNSWORTH ON CONTRACTS § 4.26 (1990); RESTATEMENT (2D) OF CONTRACTS § 211 comment a (1981) ("Standardization of agreements serves many of the same functions as standardization of goods and services; both are essential to a system of mass production and distribution. Scarce and costly time and skill can be devoted to a class of transactions rather than the details of individual transactions.") Doubtless a state could forbid the use of standard contracts in the software business, but we do not think that Wisconsin has done so.

Transactions in which the exchange of money precedes the communication of detailed terms are common. Consider the purchase of insurance. The buyer goes to an agent, who explains the essentials (amount of coverage, number of years) and remits the premium to the home office, which sends back a policy. On the district judge's understanding, the terms of the policy are irrelevant because the insured paid before receiving them. Yet the device of payment, often with a "binder" (so that the insurance takes effect immediately even though the home office reserves the right to withdraw coverage later), in advance of the policy, serves buyers' interests by accelerating effectiveness and reducing transactions costs. Or consider the purchase of an airline ticket. The traveler calls the carrier or an agent, is quoted a price, reserves a seat, pays, and gets a ticket, in that order. The ticket contains elaborate terms, which the traveler can reject by canceling the reservation. To use the ticket is to accept the terms, even terms that in retrospect are disadvantageous. *See Carnival Cruise Lines, Inc. v. Shute*, 499 U.S. 585, 111 S. Ct. 1522, 113 L. Ed. 2d 622 (1991); *see also Vimar Seguros y Reaseguros, S.A. v. M/V Sky Reefer*, ___ U.S. ___, 115 S. Ct. 2322, 132 L. Ed. 2d 462 (1995) (bills of lading). Just so with a ticket to a concert. The back of the ticket states that the patron promises not to record the concert; to attend is to agree. A theater that detects a violation will confiscate the tape and escort the violator to the exit. One could arrange things so that every concertgoer signs this promise before forking over the money, but that cumbersome way of doing things not only would lengthen queues and raise prices but also would scotch the sale of tickets by phone or electronic data service.

Consumer goods work the same way. Someone who wants to buy a radio set visits a store, pays, and walks out with a box. Inside the box is a leaflet containing some terms, the most important of which usually is the warranty, read for the first time in the comfort of home. By Zeidenberg's lights, the warranty in the box is irrelevant; every consumer gets the standard warranty implied by the U.C.C. in the event the contract is silent; yet so far as we are aware no state disregards warranties furnished with consumer products. Drugs come with a list of ingredients on the outside and an elaborate package insert on the inside. The package insert describes drug interactions, contraindications, and other vital information—but, if Zeidenberg is right, the purchaser need not read the package insert, because it is not part of the contract.

Next consider the software industry itself. Only a minority of sales take place over the counter, where there are boxes to peruse. A customer may place an order by phone in response to a line item in a catalog or a review in a magazine. Much software is ordered over the Internet by purchasers who have never seen a box. Increasingly software arrives by wire. There is no box; there is only a stream of electrons, a collection of information that includes data, an application program, instructions, many limitations ("MegaPixel 3.14159 cannot be used with BytePusher 2.718"), and the terms of sale. The user purchases a serial number, which activates the software's features. On Zeidenberg's arguments, these unboxed sales are unfettered by terms—so the seller has made a broad warranty and must pay consequential damages for any shortfalls in performance, two "promises" that if taken seriously would drive prices through the ceiling or return transactions to the horse-and-buggy age.

According to the district court, the U.C.C. does not countenance the sequence of money now, terms later. (Wisconsin's version of the U.C.C. does not differ from the Official Version in any material respect, so we use the regular numbering system. Wis. Stat. § 402.201 corresponds to U.C.C. § 2-201, and other citations are easy to derive.) One of the court's reasons—that by proposing as part of the draft Article 2B a new U.C.C. § 2-2203 that would explicitly validate standard-form user licenses, the American Law Institute and the National Conference of Commissioners on Uniform Laws have conceded the invalidity of shrink-wrap licenses under current law, see 908 F. Supp. at 655–56—

depends on a faulty inference. To propose a change in a law's text is not necessarily to propose a change in the law's effect. New words may be designed to fortify the current rule with a more precise text that curtails uncertainty. To judge by the flux of law review articles discussing shrink-wrap licenses, uncertainty is much in need of reduction—although businesses seem to feel less uncertainty than do scholars, for only three cases (other than ours) touch on the subject, and none directly addresses it. See *Step-Saver Data Systems, Inc. v. Wyse Technology*, 939 F. 2d 91 (3d Cir. 1991); *Vault Corp. v. Quaid Software Ltd.*, 847 F.2d 255, 268–70 (5th Cir. 1988); *Arizona Retail Systems, Inc. v. Software Link, Inc.*, 831 F. Supp. 759 (D. Ariz. 1993). As their titles suggest, these are not consumer transactions. *Step-Saver* is a battle-of-the-forms case, in which the parties exchange incompatible forms and a court must decide which prevails. [Citations omitted]. Our case has only one form; U.C.C. § 2-207 is irrelevant. *Vault* holds that Louisiana's special shrink-wrap-license statute is preempted by federal law, a question to which we return. And *Arizona Retail Systems* did not reach the question, because the court found that the buyer knew the terms of the license before purchasing the software.

What then does the current version of the U.C.C. have to say? We think that the place to start is § 2-204(1): "A contract for sale of goods may be made in any manner sufficient to show agreement, including conduct by both parties which recognizes the existence of such a contract." A vendor, as master of the offer, may invite acceptance by conduct, and may propose limitations on the kind of conduct that constitutes acceptance. A buyer may accept by performing the acts the vendor proposes to treat as acceptance. And that is what happened. ProCD proposed a contract that a buyer would accept by using the software after having an opportunity to read the license at leisure. This Zeidenberg did. He had no choice, because the software splashed the license on the screen and would not let him proceed without indicating acceptance. So although the district judge was right to say that a contract can be, and often is, formed simply by paying the price and walking out of the store, the U.C.C. permits contracts to be formed in other ways. ProCD proposed such a different way, and without protest Zeidenberg agreed. Ours is not a case in which a consumer opens a package to find an insert saying "you owe us an extra $10,000" and the seller files suit to collect. Any buyer finding such a demand can prevent formation of the contract by returning the package, as can any consumer who concludes that the terms of the license make the software worth less than the purchase price. Nothing in the U.C.C. requires a seller to maximize the buyer's net gains.

Section 2-606, which defines "acceptance of goods," reinforces this understanding. A buyer accepts goods under § 2-606(1)(b) when, after an opportunity to inspect, he fails to make an effective rejection under § 2-602(1). ProCD extended an opportunity to reject if a buyer should find the license terms unsatisfactory; Zeidenberg inspected the package, tried out the software, learned of the license, and did not reject the goods. We refer to § 2-606 only to show that the opportunity to return goods can be important; acceptance of an offer differs from acceptance of goods after delivery, see *Gillen v. Atlanta Systems, Inc.*, 997 F.2d 280, 284 n. 1 (7th Cir. 1993); but the U.C.C. consistently permits the parties to structure their relations so that the buyer has a chance to make a final decision after a detailed review.

Some portions of the U.C.C. impose additional requirements on the way parties agree on terms. A disclaimer of the implied warranty of merchantability must be "conspicuous." U.C.C. § 2-316(2), incorporating U.C.C. § 1-201(10). Promises to make firm offers, or to negate oral modifications, must be "separately signed." U.C.C. §§ 2-205, 2-209(2). These special provisos reinforce the impression that, so far as the U.C.C. is concerned, other terms may be as inconspicuous as the forum-selection clause on the back of the cruise ship ticket in *Carnival Lines*. Zeidenberg has not located any Wisconsin case—for that matter, any case in any state—holding that under the U.C.C. the ordinary terms found in shrink-wrap licenses require any special prominence, or otherwise are to be undercut rather than enforced. In the end, the terms of the license are conceptually identical to the contents of the package. Just as no court would dream of saying that SelectPhone (trademark) must contain 3,100 phone books rather than 3,000, or must have data no more than 30 days old, or must sell for $100 rather than $150—although any of these changes would be welcomed by the customer, if all other things were held constant—so, we believe, Wisconsin would not let the buyer pick and choose among terms. Terms of use are no less a part of "the product" than are the size of the database and the speed with which the software compiles listings. Competition among vendors, not judicial revision of a package's contents, is how consumers are protected in a market economy. *Digital Equipment Corp. v. Uniq Digital Technologies, Inc.*, 73 F.3d 756 (7th Cir. 1996). ProCD has rivals, which may elect to compete by offering superior software, monthly updates, improved terms of use, lower price, or a better compromise among these elements. As we stressed above, adjusting terms in buyers' favor might help Matthew Zeidenberg today (he already has the software) but would lead to a response, such as a higher price, that might make consumers as a whole worse off.

III

The district court held that, even if Wisconsin treats shrink-wrap licenses as contracts, §301(a) of the Copyright Act, 17 U.S.C. §301(a), prevents their enforcement. 908 F. Supp. at 656–59. The relevant part of §301(a) preempts any "legal or equitable rights [under state law] that are equivalent to any of the exclusive rights within the general scope of copyright as specified by section 106 in works of authorship that are fixed in a tangible medium of expression and come within the subject matter of copyright as specified by sections 102 and 103." ProCD's software and data are "fixed in a tangible medium of expression," and the district judge held that they are "within the subject matter of copyright." The latter conclusion is plainly right for the copyrighted application program, and the judge thought that the data likewise are "within the subject matter of copyright" even if, after *Feist*, they are not sufficiently original to be copyrighted. 908 F. Supp. at 656–57. [Citations Omitted] One function of §301(a) is to prevent states from giving special protection to works of authorship that Congress has decided should be in the public domain, which it can accomplish only if "subject matter of copyright" includes all works of a type covered by §§ 102 and 103, even if federal law does not afford protection to them.

But are rights created by contract "equivalent to any of the exclusive rights within the general scope of copyright"? Three courts of appeals have answered "no." *National Car Rental System, Inc. v. Computer Associates International, Inc.*, 991 F.2d 426, 433 (8th Cir. 1993); *Taquino v. Teledyne Monarch Rubber*, 893 F.2d 1488, 1501 (5th Cir. 1990); *Acorn Structures, Inc. v. Swantz*, 846 F.2d 923, 926 (4th Cir. 1988). The district court disagreed with these decisions, 908 F. Supp. at 658, but we think them sound. Rights "equivalent to any of the exclusive rights within the general scope of copyright" are rights established by law—rights that restrict the options of persons who are strangers to the author. Copyright law forbids duplication, public performance, and so on, unless the person wishing to copy or perform the work gets permission; silence means a ban on copying. A copyright is a right against the world. Contracts, by contrast, generally affect only their parties; strangers may do as they please, so contracts do not create "exclusive rights." Someone who found a copy of SelectPhone (trademark) on the street would not be affected by the shrink-wrap license—though the federal copyright laws of their own force would limit the finder's ability to copy or transmit the application program.

Think for a moment about trade secrets. One common trade secret is a customer list. After *Feist*, a simple alphabetical list of a firm's customers, with address and telephone numbers, could not be protected by copyright. Yet *Kewanee Oil Co. v. Bicron Corp.*, 416 U.S. 470, 94 S. Ct. 1879, 40 L. Ed.2d 315 (1974), holds that contracts about trade secrets may be enforced—precisely because they do not affect strangers' ability to discover and use the information independently. If the amendment of § 301(a) in 1976 overruled *Kewanee* and abolished consensual protection of those trade secrets that cannot be copyrighted, no one has noticed—though abolition is a logical consequence of the district court's approach. Think, too, about everyday transactions in intellectual property. A customer visits a video store and rents a copy of *Night of the Lepus*. The customer's contract with the store limits use of the tape to home viewing and requires its return in two days. May the customer keep the tape, on the ground that § 301(a) makes the promise unenforceable?

A law student obtaining public-domain documents, under a contract limiting the results to educational endeavors; may the student resell his access to this database to a law firm from which LEXIS seeks to collect a much higher hourly rate? Suppose ProCD hires a firm to scour the nation for telephone directories, promising to pay $100 for each that ProCD does not already have. The firm locates 100 new directories, which it sends to ProCD with an invoice for $10,000. ProCD incorporates the directories into its database; does it have to pay the bill? Surely yes; *Aronson v. Quick Point Pencil Co.*, 440 U.S. 257, 99 S. Ct. 1096, 59 L. Ed.2d 296 (1979), holds that promises to pay for intellectual property may be enforced even though federal law (in *Aronson*, the patent law) offers no protection against third-party uses of that property. *See also Kennedy v. Wright*, 851 F.2d 963 (7th Cir. 1988). But these illustrations are what our case is about. ProCD offers software and data for two prices: one for personal use, a higher price for commercial use. Zeidenberg wants to use the data without paying the seller's price; if the law student and Quick Point Pencil Co. could not do that, neither can Zeidenberg.

\* \* \*

*Aronson* emphasized that enforcement of the contract between Aronson and Quick Point Pencil Company would not withdraw any information from the public domain. That is equally true of the contract between ProCD and Zeidenberg. Everyone remains free to copy and disseminate all 3,000 telephone books that have been incorporated into ProCD's database. Anyone can add SIC codes and zip codes. ProCD's rivals have done so. Enforcement of the shrink-wrap license may even make information more readily available, by reducing the price ProCD charges to consumer buyers. To the extent licenses facilitate distribution of object code while concealing the source code (the point of a clause forbidding disassembly), they serve the same procompetitive functions as does the law of trade secrets. *Rockwell Graphic Systems, Inc. v. DEV Industries, Inc.*, 925 F.2d 174, 180 (7th Cir.1991). Licenses may have other benefits for consumers: many licenses permit users to make extra copies, to use the software on multiple computers, even to incorporate the software into the user's products. But whether a particular license is generous or restrictive, a simple two-party contract is not "equivalent to any of the exclusive rights within the general scope of copyright" and therefore may be enforced.

REVERSED AND REMANDED.

# Hill v. Gateway 2000, Inc.

105 F.3d 1147 (7th Cir. 1997), *cert. denied*, 118 S. Ct. 47 (1997)

EASTERBROOK, J.

A customer picks up the phone, orders a computer, and gives a credit card number. Presently a box arrives, containing the computer and a list of terms, said to govern unless the customer returns the computer within 30 days. Are these terms effective as the parties' contract, or is the contract term-free because the order-taker did not read any terms over the phone and elicit the customer's assent?

One of the terms in the box containing a Gateway 2000 system was an arbitration clause. Rich and Enza Hill, the customers, kept the computer more than 30 days before complaining about its components and performance. They filed suit in federal court arguing, among other things, that the product's shortcomings make Gateway a racketeer (mail and wire fraud are said to be the predicate offenses), leading to treble damages under RICO for the Hills and a class of all other purchasers. Gateway asked the district court to enforce the arbitration clause; the judge refused, writing that "the present record is insufficient to support a finding of a valid arbitration agreement between the parties or that the plaintiffs were given adequate notice of the arbitration clause." Gateway took an immediate appeal, as is its right. 9 U.S.C. § 16(a)(1)(A).

The Hills say that the arbitration clause did not stand out: they concede noticing the statement of terms but deny reading it closely enough to discover the agreement to arbitrate, and they ask us to conclude that they therefore may go to court. Yet an agreement to arbitrate must be enforced "save upon such grounds as exist at law or in equity for the revocation of any contract." 9 U.S.C. § 2; *Doctor's Associates, Inc. v. Casarotto*, 134 L. Ed. 2d 902, 116 S. Ct. 1652 (1996), holds that this provision of the Federal Arbitration Act is inconsistent with any requirement that an arbitration clause be prominent. A contract need not be read to be effective; people who accept take the risk that the unread terms may in retrospect prove unwelcome. *Carr v. CIGNA Securities, Inc.*, 95 F.3d 544, 547 (7th Cir. 1996); *Chicago Pacific Corp. v. Canada Life Assurance Co.*, 850 F.2d 334 (7th Cir. 1988). Terms inside Gateway's box stand or fall together. If they constitute the parties' contract because the Hills had an opportunity to return the computer after reading them, then all must be enforced.

*ProCD, Inc. v. Zeidenberg*, 86 F.3d 1447 (7th Cir. 1996), holds that terms inside a box of software bind consumers who use the software after an opportunity to read the terms and to reject them by returning the product. Likewise, *Carnival Cruise Lines, Inc. v. Shute*, 499 U.S. 585, 113 L. Ed.2d 622, 111 S. Ct. 1522 (1991), enforces a forum-selection clause that was included among three pages of terms attached to a cruise ship ticket. *ProCD* and *Carnival Cruise Lines* exemplify the many commercial transactions in which people pay for products with terms to follow; *ProCD* discusses others. 86 F.3d at 1451–52. The district court concluded in *ProCD* that the contract is formed when the consumer pays for the software; as a result, the court held, only terms known to the consumer at that moment are part of the contract, and provisos inside the box do not count. Although this is one way a contract could be formed, it is not the only way: "A vendor, as master of the offer, may invite acceptance by conduct, and may propose limitations on the kind of conduct that constitutes acceptance. A buyer may accept by performing the acts the vendor proposes to treat as acceptance." *Id.* at 1452. Gateway shipped computers with the same sort of accept-or-return offer ProCD made to users of its software. ProCD relied on the Uniform Commercial Code rather than any peculiarities of Wisconsin law; both Illinois and South Dakota, the two states whose law might govern relations between Gateway and the Hills, have adopted the U.C.C.; neither side has pointed us to any atypical doctrines in those states that might be pertinent; *ProCD* therefore applies to this dispute.

Plaintiffs ask us to limit *ProCD* to software, but where's the sense in that? *ProCD* is about the law of contract, not the law of software. Payment preceding the revelation of full terms is common for air transportation, insurance, and many other endeavors. Practical considerations support allowing vendors to enclose the full legal terms with their products. Cashiers cannot be expected to read legal documents to customers before ringing up sales. If the staff at the other end of the phone for direct-sales operations such as Gateway's had to read the four-page statement of terms before taking the buyer's credit card number, the droning voice would anesthetize rather than enlighten many potential buyers. Others would hang up in a rage over the waste of their time. And oral recitation would not avoid customers' assertions (whether true or feigned) that the clerk did not read term X to them, or that they did not remember or understand it. Writing provides benefits for both sides of commercial transactions. Customers as a group are better off when vendors skip costly and ineffectual steps such as telephonic recitation, and use instead a simple approve-or-return device. Competent adults are bound by such documents, read or unread. For what little it is worth, we add that the box from Gateway was crammed with software. The computer came with an operating system, without which it was useful only as a boat anchor. *See Digital Equipment Corp. v. Uniq Digital Technologies, Inc.*, 73 F.3d 756, 761 (7th Cir. 1996). Gateway also included many application programs. So the Hills' effort to limit *ProCD* to software would not avail them factually, even if it were sound legally—which it is not.

For their second sally, the Hills contend that *ProCD* should be limited to executory contracts (to licenses in particular), and therefore does not apply because both parties' performance of this contract was complete when the box arrived at their home. This is legally and factually wrong: legally because the question at hand concerns the formation of the contract rather than its performance, and factually because both contracts were incompletely performed. *ProCD* did not depend on the fact that the seller characterized the transaction as a license rather than as a contract; we treated it as a contract for the sale of goods and reserved the question whether for other purposes a "license" characterization might be preferable. 86 F.3d at 1450. All debates about characterization to one side, the transaction in *ProCD* was no more executory than the one here: Zeidenberg paid for the software and walked out of the store with a box under his arm, so if arrival of the box with the product ends the time for revelation of contractual terms, then the time ended in *ProCD* before Zeidenberg opened the box. But of course ProCD had not completed performance with delivery of the box, and neither had Gateway. One element of the transaction was the warranty, which obliges sellers to fix defects in their products. The Hills have invoked Gateway's warranty and are not satisfied with its response, so they are not well positioned to say that Gateway's obligations were fulfilled when the motor carrier unloaded the box. What is more, both ProCD and Gateway promised to help customers to use their products. Long-term service and information obligations are common in the computer business, on both hardware and software sides. Gateway offers "lifetime service" and has a round-the-clock telephone hotline to fulfill this promise. Some vendors spend more money helping customers use their products than on developing and manufacturing them. The document in Gateway's box includes promises of future performance that some consumers value highly; these promises bind Gateway just as the arbitration clause binds the Hills.

Next the Hills insist that *ProCD* is irrelevant because Zeidenberg was a "merchant" and they are not. Section 2-207(2) of the U.C.C., the infamous battle-of-the-forms section, states that "additional terms [following acceptance of an offer] are to be construed as proposals for addition to a contract. Between merchants such terms become part of the contract unless...." Plaintiffs tell us that *ProCD* came out as it did only because Zeidenberg was a "merchant" and the terms inside ProCD's box were not excluded by the "unless" clause. This argument pays scant attention to the opinion in *ProCD*, which concluded that, when there is only one form, "sec. 2-207 is irrelevant." 86 F.3d at 1452. The question in *ProCD* was not whether terms were added to a contract after its formation, but how and when the contract was formed—in particular, whether a vendor may propose that a contract of sale be formed, not in the store (or over the phone) with the payment of money or a general "send me the product," but after the customer has had a chance to inspect both the item and the terms. *ProCD* answers "yes," for merchants and consumers alike. Yet again, for what little it is worth we observe that the Hills misunderstand the setting of *ProCD*. A "merchant" under the U.C.C. "means a person who deals in goods of the kind or otherwise by his occupation holds himself out as having knowledge or skill peculiar to the practices or goods involved in the transaction." § 2-104(1). Zeidenberg bought the product at a retail store, an uncommon place for merchants to acquire inventory. His corporation put ProCD's database on the Internet for anyone to browse, which led to the litigation but did not make Zeidenberg a software merchant.

At oral argument the Hills propounded still another distinction: the box containing ProCD's software displayed a notice that additional terms were within, while the box containing Gateway's computer did not. The difference is functional, not legal. Consumers browsing the aisles of a store can look at the box, and if they are unwilling to deal with the prospect of additional terms can leave the box alone, avoiding the transactions costs of returning the package after reviewing its contents. Gateway's box, by contrast, is just a shipping carton; it is not on display anywhere. Its function is to protect the product during transit, and the information on its sides is for the use of handlers ("Fragile!" "This Side Up!") rather than would-be purchasers.

Perhaps the Hills would have had a better argument if they were first alerted to the bundling of hardware and legal-ware after opening the box and wanted to return the computer in order to avoid disagreeable terms, but were dissuaded by the expense of shipping. What the remedy would be in such a case—could it exceed the shipping charges?—is an interesting question, but one that need not detain us because the Hills knew before they ordered the computer that the carton would include some important terms, and they did not seek to discover these in advance. Gateway's ads state that their products come with limited warranties and lifetime support. How limited was the warranty—30 days, with service contingent on shipping the computer back, or five years, with free on-site service? What sort of support was offered? Shoppers have three principal ways to discover these things. First, they can ask the vendor to send a copy before deciding whether to buy. The Magnuson-Moss Warranty Act requires firms to distribute their warranty terms on request, 15 U.S.C. §2302(b)(1)(A); the Hills do not contend that Gateway would have refused to enclose the remaining terms too. Concealment would be bad for business, scaring some customers away and leading to excess returns from others. Second, shoppers can consult public sources (computer magazines, the Web sites of vendors) that may contain this information. Third, they may inspect the documents after the product's delivery. Like Zeidenberg, the Hills took the third option. By keeping the computer beyond 30 days, the Hills accepted Gateway's offer, including the arbitration clause.

The Hills' remaining arguments, including a contention that the arbitration clause is unenforceable as part of a scheme to defraud, do not require more than a citation to

*Prima Paint Corp. v. Flood & Conklin Mfg. Co.*, 388 U.S. 395, 18 L. Ed. 2d 1270, 87 S. Ct. 1801 (1967). Whatever may be said pro and con about the cost and efficacy of arbitration (which the Hills disparage) is for Congress and the contracting parties to consider. Claims based on RICO are no less arbitrable than those founded on the contract or the law of torts. *Shearson/American Express, Inc. v. McMahon*, 482 U.S. 220, 238–42, 96 L. Ed. 2d 185, 107 S. Ct. 2332 (1987). The decision of the district court is vacated, and this case is remanded with instructions to compel the Hills to submit their dispute to arbitration.

---

## Specht v. Netscape Communications Corp.
### 306 F.3d 17 (2d Cir. 2002)

SOTOMAYOR, Circuit Judge.

This is an appeal from a judgment of the Southern District of New York denying a motion by defendants-appellants Netscape Communications Corporation and its corporate parent, America Online, Inc. (collectively, "defendants" or "Netscape"), to compel arbitration and to stay court proceedings. In order to resolve the central question of arbitrability presented here, we must address issues of contract formation in cyberspace. Principally, we are asked to determine whether plaintiffs-appellees ("plaintiffs"), by acting upon defendants' invitation to download free software made available on defendants' webpage, agreed to be bound by the software's license terms (which included the arbitration clause at issue), even though plaintiffs could not have learned of the existence of those terms unless, prior to executing the download, they had scrolled down the webpage to a screen located below the download button. We agree with the district court that a reasonably prudent Internet user in circumstances such as these would not have known or learned of the existence of the license terms before responding to defendants' invitation to download the free software, and that defendants therefore did not provide reasonable notice of the license terms. In consequence, plaintiffs' bare act of downloading the software did not unambiguously manifest assent to the arbitration provision contained in the license terms.

We also agree with the district court that plaintiffs' claims relating to the software at issue—a "plug-in" program entitled SmartDownload ("SmartDownload" or "the plug-in program"), offered by Netscape to enhance the functioning of the separate browser program called Netscape Communicator ("Communicator" or "the browser program")—are not subject to an arbitration agreement contained in the license terms governing the use of Communicator. Finally, we conclude that the district court properly rejected defendants' argument that plaintiff website owner Christopher Specht, though not a party to any Netscape license agreement, is nevertheless required to arbitrate his claims concerning SmartDownload because he allegedly benefited directly under SmartDownload's license agreement. Defendants' theory that Specht benefited whenever visitors employing SmartDownload downloaded certain files made available on his website is simply too tenuous and speculative to justify application of the legal doctrine that requires a nonparty to an arbitration agreement to arbitrate if he or she has received a direct benefit under a contract containing the arbitration agreement.

We therefore affirm the district court's denial of defendants' motion to compel arbitration and to stay court proceedings.

## BACKGROUND

### I. Facts

In three related putative class actions, plaintiffs alleged that, unknown to them, their use of SmartDownload transmitted to defendants private information about plaintiffs' downloading of files from the Internet, thereby effecting an electronic surveillance of their online activities in violation of two federal statutes, the Electronic Communications Privacy Act, 18 U.S.C. §§ 2510 *et seq.,* and the Computer Fraud and Abuse Act, 18 U.S.C. § 1030.

Specifically, plaintiffs alleged that when they first used Netscape's Communicator—a software program that permits Internet browsing—the program created and stored on each of their computer hard drives a small text file known as a "cookie" that functioned "as a kind of electronic identification tag for future communications" between their computers and Netscape. Plaintiffs further alleged that when they installed SmartDownload—a separate software "plug-in" that served to enhance Communicator's browsing capabilities—SmartDownload created and stored on their computer hard drives another string of characters, known as a "Key," which similarly functioned as an identification tag in future communications with Netscape. According to the complaints in this case, each time a computer user employed Communicator to download a file from the Internet, SmartDownload "assume[d] from Communicator the task of downloading" the file and transmitted to Netscape the address of the file being downloaded together with the cookie created by Communicator and the Key created by SmartDownload. These processes, plaintiffs claim, constituted unlawful "eavesdropping" on users of Netscape's software products as well as on Internet websites from which users employing SmartDownload downloaded files.

In the time period relevant to this litigation, Netscape offered on its website various software programs, including Communicator and SmartDownload, which visitors to the site were invited to obtain free of charge. It is undisputed that five of the six named plaintiffs—Michael Fagan, John Gibson, Mark Gruber, Sean Kelly, and Sherry Weindorf—downloaded Communicator from the Netscape website. These plaintiffs acknowledge that when they proceeded to initiate installation of Communicator, they were automatically shown a scrollable text of that program's license agreement and were not permitted to complete the installation until they had clicked on a "Yes" button to indicate that they accepted all the license terms. If a user attempted to install Communicator without clicking "Yes," the installation would be aborted. All five named user plaintiffs expressly agreed to Communicator's license terms by clicking "Yes." The Communicator license agreement that these plaintiffs saw made no mention of SmartDownload or other plug-in programs, and stated that "[t]hese terms apply to Netscape Communicator and Netscape Navigator" and that "all disputes relating to this Agreement (excepting any dispute relating to intellectual property rights)" are subject to "binding arbitration in Santa Clara County, California."

Although Communicator could be obtained independently of SmartDownload, all the named user plaintiffs, except Fagan, downloaded and installed Communicator in connection with downloading SmartDownload. Each of these plaintiffs allegedly arrived at a Netscape webpage captioned "SmartDownload Communicator" that urged them to "Download With Confidence Using SmartDownload!" At or near the bottom of the screen facing plaintiffs was the prompt "Start Download" and a tinted button labeled "Download." By clicking on the button, plaintiffs initiated the download of SmartDownload.

Once that process was complete, SmartDownload, as its first plug-in task, permitted plaintiffs to proceed with downloading and installing Communicator, an operation that was accompanied by the click-wrap display of Communicator's license terms described above.

The signal difference between downloading Communicator and downloading SmartDownload was that no click-wrap presentation accompanied the latter operation. Instead, once plaintiffs Gibson, Gruber, Kelly, and Weindorf had clicked on the "Download" button located at or near the bottom of their screen, and the downloading of SmartDownload was complete, these plaintiffs encountered no further information about the plug-in program or the existence of license terms governing its use. The sole reference to SmartDownload's license terms on the "SmartDownload Communicator" webpage was located in text that would have become visible to plaintiffs only if they had scrolled down to the next screen.

Had plaintiffs scrolled down instead of acting on defendants' invitation to click on the "Download" button, they would have encountered the following invitation: "Please review and agree to the terms of the Netscape SmartDownload software license agreement before downloading and using the software." Plaintiffs Gibson, Gruber, Kelly, and Weindorf averred in their affidavits that they never saw this reference to the Smart-Download license agreement when they clicked on the "Download" button. They also testified during depositions that they saw no reference to license terms when they clicked to download SmartDownload, although under questioning by defendants' counsel, some plaintiffs added that they could not "remember" or be "sure" whether the screen shots of the SmartDownload page attached to their affidavits reflected precisely what they had seen on their computer screens when they downloaded SmartDownload.

In sum, plaintiffs Gibson, Gruber, Kelly, and Weindorf allege that the process of obtaining SmartDownload contrasted sharply with that of obtaining Communicator. Having selected SmartDownload, they were required neither to express unambiguous assent to that program's license agreement nor even to view the license terms or become aware of their existence before proceeding with the invited download of the free plug-in program. Moreover, once these plaintiffs had initiated the download, the existence of SmartDownload's license terms was not mentioned while the software was running or at any later point in plaintiffs' experience of the product.

Even for a user who, unlike plaintiffs, did happen to scroll down past the download button, SmartDownload's license terms would not have been immediately displayed in the manner of Communicator's click-wrapped terms. Instead, if such a user had seen the notice of SmartDownload's terms and then clicked on the underlined invitation to review and agree to the terms, a hypertext link would have taken the user to a separate webpage entitled "License & Support Agreements." The first paragraph on this page read, in pertinent part:

> The use of each Netscape software product is governed by a license agreement. You must read and agree to the license agreement terms BEFORE acquiring a product. Please click on the appropriate link below to review the current license agreement for the product of interest to you before acquisition. For products available for download, you must read and agree to the license agreement terms BEFORE you install the software. If you do not agree to the license terms, do not download, install or use the software.

Below this paragraph appeared a list of license agreements, the first of which was "*License Agreement for Netscape Navigator and Netscape Communicator Product Family* (Netscape Navigator, Netscape Communicator and Netscape SmartDownload)." If the user clicked on that link, he or she would be taken to yet another webpage that contained the full text of a license agreement that was identical in every respect to the Communicator license agreement except that it stated that its "terms apply to Netscape Communicator, Netscape Navigator, and Netscape SmartDownload." The license agreement granted the user a nonexclusive license to use and reproduce the software, subject to certain terms:

> BY CLICKING THE ACCEPTANCE BUTTON OR INSTALLING OR USING NETSCAPE COMMUNICATOR, NETSCAPE NAVIGATOR, OR NETSCAPE SMARTDOWNLOAD SOFTWARE (THE "PRODUCT"), THE INDIVIDUAL OR ENTITY LICENSING THE PRODUCT ("LICENSEE") IS CONSENTING TO BE BOUND BY AND IS BECOMING A PARTY TO THIS AGREEMENT. IF LICENSEE DOES NOT AGREE TO ALL OF THE TERMS OF THIS AGREEMENT, THE BUTTON INDICATING NON-ACCEPTANCE MUST BE SELECTED, AND LICENSEE MUST NOT INSTALL OR USE THE SOFTWARE.

Among the license terms was a provision requiring virtually all disputes relating to the agreement to be submitted to arbitration:

> Unless otherwise agreed in writing, all disputes relating to this Agreement (excepting any dispute relating to intellectual property rights) shall be subject to final and binding arbitration in Santa Clara County, California, under the auspices of JAMS/EndDispute, with the losing party paying all costs of arbitration.

Unlike the four named user plaintiffs who downloaded SmartDownload from the Netscape website, the fifth named plaintiff, Michael Fagan, claims to have downloaded the plug-in program from a "shareware" website operated by ZDNet, an entity unrelated to Netscape. Shareware sites are websites, maintained by companies or individuals, that contain libraries of free, publicly available software. The pages that a user would have seen while downloading SmartDownload from ZDNet differed from those that he or she would have encountered while downloading SmartDownload from the Netscape website. Notably, instead of any kind of notice of the SmartDownload license agreement, the ZDNet pages offered only a hypertext link to "more information" about SmartDownload, which, if clicked on, took the user to a Netscape webpage that, in turn, contained a link to the license agreement. Thus, a visitor to the ZDNet website could have obtained SmartDownload, as Fagan avers he did, without ever seeing a reference to that program's license terms, even if he or she had scrolled through all of ZDNet's webpages.

The sixth named plaintiff, Christopher Specht, never obtained or used SmartDownload, but instead operated a website from which visitors could download certain electronic files that permitted them to create an account with an internet service provider called WhyWeb. Specht alleges that every time a user who had previously installed SmartDownload visited his website and downloaded WhyWeb-related files, defendants intercepted this information. Defendants allege that Specht would receive a representative's commission from WhyWeb every time a user who obtained a WhyWeb file from his website subsequently subscribed to the WhyWeb service. Thus, argue defendants, because the "Netscape license agreement…conferred on each user the right to download and use both Communicator and SmartDownload software," Specht received a benefit under that license agreement in that SmartDownload "assisted in obtaining the WhyWeb file and increased the likelihood of success in the download process." This benefit, defendants claim, was direct enough to require Specht to arbitrate his claims pursuant to Netscape's license terms. Specht, however, maintains that he never received any commissions based on the WhyWeb files available on his website.

## DISCUSSION

### I. Standard of Review and Applicable Law

\* \* \*

The FAA provides that a "written provision in any…contract evidencing a transaction involving commerce to settle by arbitration a controversy thereafter arising out of such contract or transaction…shall be valid, irrevocable, and enforceable, save upon such grounds as exist at law or in equity for the revocation of any contract." 9 U.S.C. §2. It is well settled that a court may not compel arbitration until it has resolved "the question of the very existence" of the contract embodying the arbitration clause. *Interocean Shipping Co. v. Nat'l Shipping & Trading Corp.*, 462 F.2d 673, 676 (2d Cir.1972). "[A]rbitration is a matter of contract and a party cannot be required to submit to arbitration any dispute which he has not agreed so to submit." *AT & T Techs., Inc. v. Communications Workers of Am.*, 475 U.S. 643, 648, 106 S. Ct. 1415, 89 L. Ed. 2d 648 (1986) (quotation marks omitted). Unless the parties clearly provide otherwise, "the question of arbitrability—whether a[n]…agreement creates a duty for the parties to arbitrate the particular grievance—is undeniably an issue for judicial determination." *Id.* at 649, 106 S. Ct. 1415.

The district court properly concluded that in deciding whether parties agreed to arbitrate a certain matter, a court should generally apply state-law principles to the issue of contract formation. *Mehler v. Terminix Int'l Co.*, 205 F.3d 44, 48 (2d Cir.2000); *see also Perry v. Thomas*, 482 U.S. 483, 492 n. 9, 107 S. Ct. 2520, 96 L. Ed. 2d 426 (1987) ("[S]tate law, whether of legislative or judicial origin, is applicable [to the determination of whether the parties agreed to arbitrate] if that law arose to govern issues concerning the validity, revocability, and enforceability of contracts generally."). Therefore, state law governs the question of whether the parties in the present case entered into an agreement to arbitrate disputes relating to the SmartDownload license agreement. The district court further held that California law governs the question of contract formation here; the parties do not appeal that determination.

### II. Whether This Court Should Remand for a Trial on Contract Formation

Defendants argue on appeal that the district court erred in deciding the question of contract formation as a matter of law. A central issue in dispute, according to defendants, is whether the user plaintiffs actually saw the notice of SmartDownload's license terms when they downloaded the plug-in program. Although plaintiffs in their affidavits and depositions generally swore that they never saw the notice of terms on Netscape's webpage, defendants point to deposition testimony in which some plaintiffs, under repeated questioning by defendants' counsel, responded that they could not "remember" or be entirely "sure" whether the link to SmartDownload's license terms was visible on their computer screens. Defendants argue that on some computers, depending on the configuration of the monitor and browser, SmartDownload's license link "appears on the first screen, without any need for the user to scroll at all." Thus, according to defendants, "a trial on the factual issues that Defendants raised about each and every Plaintiffs' [sic ] downloading experience" is required on remand to remedy the district court's "error" in denying defendants' motion as a matter of law.

Section 4 of the FAA provides, in relevant part, that "[i]f the making of the arbitration agreement...be in issue, the court shall proceed summarily to the trial thereof." 9 U.S.C. §4. We conclude for two reasons, however, that defendants are not entitled to a remand for a full trial. First, during oral argument in the district court on the arbitrability of the five user plaintiffs' claims, defendants' counsel repeatedly insisted that the district court could decide "as a matter of law based on the uncontroverted facts in this case" whether "a reasonably prudent person could or should have known of the [license] terms by which acceptance would be signified." "I don't want you to try the facts," defendants' counsel told the court. "I think that the evidence in this case upon which this court can make a determination [of whether a contract existed] as a matter of law is uncontroverted." Accordingly, the district court decided the issue of reasonable notice and objective manifestation of assent as a matter of law. "[I]t is a well-established general rule that an appellate court will not consider an issue raised for the first time on appeal." *Greene v. United States*, 13 F.3d 577, 586 (2d Cir.1994); *see also Gurary v. Winehouse*, 190 F.3d 37, 44 (2d Cir.1999) ("Having failed to make the present argument to the district court, plaintiff will not be heard to advance it here."). Nor would it cause injustice in this case for us to decline to accept defendants' invitation to consider an issue that defendants did not advance below.

Second, after conducting weeks of discovery on defendants' motion to compel arbitration, the parties placed before the district court an ample record consisting of affidavits and extensive deposition testimony by each named plaintiff; numerous declarations by counsel and witnesses for the parties; dozens of exhibits, including computer screen shots and other visual evidence concerning the user plaintiffs' experience of the Netscape webpage; oral argument supplemented by a computer demonstration; and additional briefs following oral argument. This well-developed record contrasts sharply with the meager records that on occasion have caused this Court to remand for trial on the issue of contract formation pursuant to 9 U.S.C. §4. *See, e.g., Interbras Cayman Co. v. Orient Victory Shipping Co., S.A.*, 663 F.2d 4, 5 (2d Cir.1981) (record consisted of affidavits and other papers); *Interocean Shipping*, 462 F.2d at 676 (record consisted of pleadings, affidavits, and documentary attachments). We are satisfied that the unusually full record before the district court in this case constituted "a hearing where evidence is received." *Interocean Shipping*, 462 F.2d at 677. Moreover, upon the record assembled, a fact-finder could not reasonably find that defendants prevailed in showing that any of the user plaintiffs had entered into an agreement on defendants' license terms.

In sum, we conclude that the district court properly decided the question of reasonable notice and objective manifestation of assent as a matter of law on the record before it, and we decline defendants' request to remand for a full trial on that question.

### III. Whether the User Plaintiffs Had Reasonable Notice of and Manifested Assent to the SmartDownload License Agreement

Whether governed by the common law or by Article 2 of the Uniform Commercial Code ("UCC"), a transaction, in order to be a contract, requires a manifestation of agreement between the parties. *See Windsor Mills, Inc. v. Collins & Aikman Corp.*, 25 Cal. App. 3d 987, 991, 101 Cal. Rptr. 347, 350 (1972) ("[C]onsent to, or acceptance of, the arbitration provision [is] necessary to create an agreement to arbitrate."); *see also* Cal. Com.Code §2204(1) ("A contract for sale of goods may be made in any manner sufficient to show agreement, including conduct by both parties which recognizes the existence of such a contract."). Mutual manifestation of assent, whether by written or spoken word or by conduct, is the touchstone of contract. *Binder v. Aetna Life Ins.*

*Co.,* 75 Cal. App. 4th 832, 848, 89 Cal. Rptr. 2d 540, 551 (Cal. Ct. App. 1999); *cf.* Re-
STATEMENT (SECOND) OF CONTRACTS § 19(2) (1981) ("The conduct of a party is not
effective as a manifestation of his assent unless he intends to engage in the conduct
and knows or has reason to know that the other party may infer from his conduct that
he assents."). Although an onlooker observing the disputed transactions in this case
would have seen each of the user plaintiffs click on the SmartDownload "Download"
button, *see Cedars Sinai Med. Ctr. v. Mid-West Nat'l Life Ins. Co.,* 118 F. Supp. 2d 1002,
1008 (C.D. Cal. 2000) ("In California, a party's intent to contract is judged objectively,
by the party's outward manifestation of consent."), a consumer's clicking on a download button does not communicate assent to contractual terms if the offer did not
make clear to the consumer that clicking on the download button would signify assent
to those terms; *see also Windsor Mills,* 25 Cal. App. 3d at 992, 101 Cal. Rptr. at 351
("[W]hen the offeree does not know that a proposal has been made to him this objective standard does not apply."). California's common law is clear that "an offeree, regardless of apparent manifestation of his consent, is not bound by inconspicuous contractual provisions of which he is unaware, contained in a document whose
contractual nature is not obvious." *Id.; see also Marin Storage & Trucking, Inc. v. Benco
Contracting & Eng'g, Inc.,* 89 Cal. App. 4th 1042, 1049, 107 Cal. Rptr. 2d 645, 651 (Cal.
Ct. App. 2001) (same).

Arbitration agreements are no exception to the requirement of manifestation of assent. "This principle of knowing consent applies with particular force to provisions
for arbitration." *Windsor Mills,* 101 Cal. Rptr. at 351. Clarity and conspicuousness of
arbitration terms are important in securing informed assent. "If a party wishes to
bind in writing another to an agreement to arbitrate future disputes, such purpose
should be accomplished in a way that each party to the arrangement will fully and
clearly comprehend that the agreement to arbitrate exists and binds the parties
thereto." *Commercial Factors Corp. v. Kurtzman Bros.,* 131 Cal. App. 2d 133, 134–35,
280 P.2d 146, 147–48 (1955) (internal quotation marks omitted). Thus, California
contract law measures assent by an objective standard that takes into account both
what the offeree said, wrote, or did and the transactional context in which the offeree
verbalized or acted.

### A. The Reasonably Prudent Offeree of Downloadable Software

Defendants argue that plaintiffs must be held to a standard of reasonable prudence
and that, because notice of the existence of SmartDownload license terms was on the
next scrollable screen, plaintiffs were on "inquiry notice" of those terms. We disagree
with the proposition that a reasonably prudent offeree in plaintiffs' position would necessarily have known or learned of the existence of the SmartDownload license agreement prior to acting, so that plaintiffs may be held to have assented to that agreement
with constructive notice of its terms. *See* Cal. Civ. Code § 1589 ("A voluntary acceptance
of the benefit of a transaction is equivalent to a consent to all the obligations arising
from it, so far as the facts are known, or ought to be known, to the person accepting.").
It is true that "[a] party cannot avoid the terms of a contract on the ground that he or
she failed to read it before signing." *Marin Storage & Trucking,* 89 Cal. App. 4th at 1049,
107 Cal. Rptr. 2d at 651. But courts are quick to add: "An exception to this general rule
exists when the writing does not appear to be a contract and the terms are not called to
the attention of the recipient. In such a case, no contract is formed with respect to the
undisclosed term." *Id.; cf. Cory v. Golden State Bank,* 95 Cal. App. 3d 360, 364, 157 Cal.
Rptr. 538, 541 (Cal. Ct. App. 1979) ("[T]he provision in question is effectively hidden

from the view of money order purchasers until after the transactions are completed.... Under these circumstances, it must be concluded that the Bank's money order purchasers are not chargeable with either actual or constructive notice of the service charge provision, and therefore cannot be deemed to have consented to the provision as part of their transaction with the Bank.").

Most of the cases cited by defendants in support of their inquiry-notice argument are drawn from the world of paper contracting.

As the foregoing cases suggest, receipt of a physical document containing contract terms or notice thereof is frequently deemed, in the world of paper transactions, a sufficient circumstance to place the offeree on inquiry notice of those terms. "Every person who has actual notice of circumstances sufficient to put a prudent man upon inquiry as to a particular fact, has constructive notice of the fact itself in all cases in which, by prosecuting such inquiry, he might have learned such fact." Cal. Civ.Code § 19. These principles apply equally to the emergent world of online product delivery, pop-up screens, hyperlinked pages, click-wrap licensing, scrollable documents, and urgent admonitions to "Download Now!" What plaintiffs saw when they were being invited by defendants to download this fast, free plug-in called SmartDownload was a screen containing praise for the product and, at the very bottom of the screen, a "Download" button. Defendants argue that under the principles set forth in the cases cited above, a "fair and prudent person using ordinary care" would have been on inquiry notice of SmartDownload's license terms. *Shacket,* 651 F. Supp. at 690.

We are not persuaded that a reasonably prudent offeree in these circumstances would have known of the existence of license terms. Plaintiffs were responding to an offer that did not carry an immediately visible notice of the existence of license terms or require unambiguous manifestation of assent to those terms. Thus, plaintiffs' "apparent manifestation of...consent" was to terms "contained in a document whose contractual nature [was] not obvious." *Windsor Mills,* 25 Cal. App. 3d at 992, 101 Cal. Rptr. at 351. Moreover, the fact that, given the position of the scroll bar on their computer screens, plaintiffs may have been aware that an unexplored portion of the Netscape webpage remained below the download button does not mean that they reasonably should have concluded that this portion contained a notice of license terms. In their deposition testimony, plaintiffs variously stated that they used the scroll bar "[o]nly if there is something that I feel I need to see that is on—that is off the page," or that the elevated position of the scroll bar suggested the presence of "mere[ ] formalities, standard lower banner links" or "that the page is bigger than what I can see." Plaintiffs testified, and defendants did not refute, that plaintiffs were in fact unaware that defendants intended to attach license terms to the use of SmartDownload.

We conclude that in circumstances such as these, where consumers are urged to download free software at the immediate click of a button, a reference to the existence of license terms on a submerged screen is not sufficient to place consumers on inquiry or constructive notice of those terms. The SmartDownload webpage screen was "printed in such a manner that it tended to conceal the fact that it was an express acceptance of [Netscape's] rules and regulations." *Larrus,* 266 P.2d at 147. Internet users may have, as defendants put it, "as much time as they need[ ]" to scroll through multiple screens on a webpage, but there is no reason to assume that viewers will scroll down to subsequent screens simply because screens are there. When products are "free" and users are invited to download them in the absence of reasonably conspicuous notice that they are about to bind themselves to contract terms, the transactional circumstances cannot be fully analogized to those in the paper world of arm's-length bargaining. In the next two sections, we discuss case law and other legal authorities that have addressed the circumstances of computer sales, software licensing, and online transacting. Those authorities tend strongly to support our conclusion that plaintiffs did not manifest assent to SmartDownload's license terms.

## B. Shrink-wrap Licensing and Related Practices

Defendants cite certain well-known cases involving shrink-wrap licensing and related commercial practices in support of their contention that plaintiffs became bound by the SmartDownload license terms by virtue of inquiry notice. For example, in *Hill v. Gateway 2000, Inc.*, 105 F.3d 1147 (7th Cir.1997), the Seventh Circuit held that where a purchaser had ordered a computer over the telephone, received the order in a shipped box containing the computer along with printed contract terms, and did not return the computer within the thirty days required by the terms, the purchaser was bound by the contract. *Id.* at 1148–49. In *ProCD, Inc. v. Zeidenberg*, the same court held that where an individual purchased software in a box containing license terms which were displayed on the computer screen every time the user executed the software program, the user had sufficient opportunity to review the terms and to return the software, and so was contractually bound after retaining the product. *ProCD*, 86 F.3d at 1452; *cf. Moore v. Microsoft Corp.*, 293 A.D.2d 587, 587, 741 N.Y.S.2d 91, 92 (2d Dep't 2002) (software user was bound by license agreement where terms were prominently displayed on computer screen before software could be installed and where user was required to indicate assent by clicking "I agree"); *Brower v. Gateway 2000, Inc.*, 246 A.D.2d 246, 251, 676 N.Y.S.2d 569, 572 (1st Dep't 1998) (buyer assented to arbitration clause shipped inside box with computer and software by retaining items beyond date specified by license terms); *M.A. Mortenson Co. v. Timberline Software Corp.*, 93 Wash.App. 819, 970 P.2d 803, 809 (1999) (buyer manifested assent to software license terms by installing and using software), *aff'd*, 140 Wash.2d 568, 998 P.2d 305 (2000); *see also I.Lan Sys.*, 183 F. Supp. 2d at 338 (business entity "explicitly accepted the click-wrap license agreement [contained in purchased software] when it clicked on the box stating 'I agree'").

These cases do not help defendants. To the extent that they hold that the purchaser of a computer or tangible software is contractually bound after failing to object to printed license terms provided with the product, *Hill* and *Brower* do not differ markedly from the cases involving traditional paper contracting discussed in the previous section. Insofar as the purchaser in *ProCD* was confronted with conspicuous, mandatory license terms every time he ran the software on his computer, that case actually undermines defendants' contention that downloading in the absence of conspicuous terms is an act that binds plaintiffs to those terms. In *Mortenson*, the full text of license terms was printed on each sealed diskette envelope inside the software box, printed again on the inside cover of the user manual, and notice of the terms appeared on the computer screen every time the purchaser executed the program. *Mortenson*, 970 P.2d at 806. In sum, the foregoing cases are clearly distinguishable from the facts of the present action.

## C. Online Transactions

Cases in which courts have found contracts arising from Internet use do not assist defendants, because in those circumstances there was much clearer notice than in the present case that a user's act would manifest assent to contract terms.

After reviewing the California common law and other relevant legal authority, we conclude that under the circumstances here, plaintiffs' downloading of SmartDownload did not constitute acceptance of defendants' license terms. Reasonably conspicuous notice of the existence of contract terms and unambiguous manifestation of assent to those terms by consumers are essential if electronic bargaining is to have integrity and credibility. We hold that a reasonably prudent offeree in plaintiffs' position would not have known or learned, prior to acting on the invitation to download, of the reference to SmartDownload's license terms hidden below the "Download" button on the next screen. We affirm the district court's conclusion that the user plaintiffs, including Fagan, are not bound by the arbitration clause contained in those terms.

[The Court concluded that there was no duty to arbitrate.]

* * *

## CONCLUSION

For the foregoing reasons, we affirm the district court's denial of defendants' motion to compel arbitration and to stay court proceedings.

---

# Notes and Questions

1. The last decision, *Netscape,* is virtually unique in holding a mass-market software license unenforceable. Did the court hold that online agreements are generally invalid? If not, precisely what did it hold? Is that holding consistent with the rules for contract formation generally? What steps would you advise Netscape to take in order to increase the chances of its online agreements being enforced? How difficult would those steps be to implement, and how effective would they be?

2. The *Hill* decision addressed an interesting question regarding contract formation: what happens if the steps that the offeror requires to avoid accepting the offered terms are onerous or expensive? The product there was a whole personal-computer system, which has some weight and heft. Returning it to the seller for a refund could be inconvenient, expensive, or both. Is a contract formed if the offeror's terms require the user to bear the inconvenience or expense of returning a heavy piece of merchandise in order to avoid acceptance? The *Hill* court said yes, at least in the case where the user had the opportunity to learn about the contract terms before taking delivery and did not do so. Is that a satisfactory answer? from the viewpoint of economic efficiency in the marketplace? From the viewpoint of the buyer's inferrable assent? From the viewpoint of fairness?

In any event, how far does the *Hill* rationale go? Suppose you buy a car online from a website and the terms of the online agreement require you to drive or ship the car across the country for warranty service. Is that term valid? Does/should the answer depend upon whether you had the chance to learn of the term before clicking on "Purchase"? Or does/should it depend upon other doctrines of contract law?

---

# B. Approaches to Making Online Licenses Enforceable

Despite the practical, common-sense approach of decisions like *ProCD* and *Hill*, many lawyers have been and remain anxious about the general status of electronic contracts, including electronic licenses. Their anxiety motivated the development of a model statute, the Uniform Electronic Transactions Act, or UETA. This statute's principal purpose was to state what should have been obvious: that an otherwise valid agreement does not fail to form a contract just because electronic means were used in communicating or reflecting the agreement. UETA is not limited to license agreements but addresses electronic transactions generally.

Perhaps because of its modest purpose and scope, UETA enjoyed rapid adoption in the several states. As of 2003, at least forty-one states had enacted versions of UETA into law.

UETA's basic purpose was to make electronic transactions as valid (and as invalid) as those transactions using paper. In other words, it was designed to render the medium of transaction—paper or electrons—irrelevant for legal purposes. In so doing, it helped "level the playing field" for electronic contracts, thereby encouraging both the private sector and state governments to invest money in technological means for making, communicating, and storing electronic transactions.

Although this was UETA's primary purpose, it is not the statute's only effect. UETA also contains provisions regarding the proper way to give notice (for example, of offers, acceptance, and assent to terms), authentication and attribution of electronic messages, the desirability of electronic systems that allow users to print or store electronic documents, electronic transactions by state governments, and other matters. It even contains provisions for transferrable electronic documents, which might ultimately replace checks and other negotiable instruments.

---

## Uniform Electronic Transactions Act

The following consists of excerpts from the Uniform Electronic Transactions Act. Many states have now adopted these, or similar, provisions.

---

§2 - DEFINITIONS

In this [Act]:

(1) "Agreement" means the bargain of the parties in fact, as found in their language or inferred from other circumstances and from rules, regulations, and procedures given the effect of agreements under laws otherwise applicable to a particular transaction.

(2) "Automated transaction" means a transaction conducted or performed, in whole or in part, by electronic means or electronic records, in which the acts or records of one or both parties are not reviewed by an individual in the ordinary course in forming a

contract, performing under an existing contract, or fulfilling an obligation required by the transaction.

(3) "Computer program" means a set of statements or instructions to be used directly or indirectly in an information processing system in order to bring about a certain result.

(4) "Contract" means the total legal obligation resulting from the parties' agreement as affected by this [Act] and other applicable law.

(5) "Electronic" means relating to technology having electrical, digital, magnetic, wireless, optical, electromagnetic, or similar capabilities.

(6) "Electronic agent" means a computer program or an electronic or other automated means used independently to initiate an action or respond to electronic records or performances in whole or in part, without review or action by an individual.

(7) "Electronic record" means a record created, generated, sent, communicated, received, or stored by electronic means.

(8) "Electronic signature" means an electronic sound, symbol, or process attached to or logically associated with a record and executed or adopted by a person with the intent to sign the record.

(9) "Governmental agency" means an executive, legislative, or judicial agency, department, board, commission, authority, institution, or instrumentality of the federal government or of a State or of a county, municipality, or other political subdivision of a State.

(10) "Information" means data, text, images, sounds, codes, computer programs, software, databases, or the like.

(11) "Information processing system" means an electronic system for creating, generating, sending, receiving, storing, displaying, or processing information.

(12) "Person" means an individual, corporation, business trust, estate, trust, partnership, limited liability company, association, joint venture, governmental agency, public corporation, or any other legal or commercial entity.

(13) "Record" means information that is inscribed on a tangible medium or that is stored in an electronic or other medium and is retrievable in perceivable form.

(14) "Security procedure" means a procedure employed for the purpose of verifying that an electronic signature, record, or performance is that of a specific person or for detecting changes or errors in the information in an electronic record. The term includes a procedure that requires the use of algorithms or other codes, identifying words or numbers, encryption, or callback or other acknowledgment procedures.

(15) "State" means a State of the United States, the District of Columbia, Puerto Rico, the United States Virgin Islands, or any territory or insular possession subject to the ju-

risdiction of the United States. The term includes an Indian tribe or band, or Alaskan native village, which is recognized by federal law or formally acknowledged by a State.

(16) "Transaction" means an action or set of actions occurring between two or more persons relating to the conduct of business, commercial, or governmental affairs.

* * *

## §5 - USE OF ELECTRONIC RECORDS AND ELECTRONIC SIGNATURES; VARIATION BY AGREEMENT

(a) This [Act] does not require a record or signature to be created, generated, sent, communicated, received, stored, or otherwise processed or used by electronic means or in electronic form.

(b) This [Act] applies only to transactions between parties each of which has agreed to conduct transactions by electronic means. Whether the parties agree to conduct a transaction by electronic means is determined from the context and surrounding circumstances, including the parties' conduct.

(c) A party that agrees to conduct a transaction by electronic means may refuse to conduct other transactions by electronic means. The right granted by this subsection may not be waived by agreement.

(d) Except as otherwise provided in this [Act], the effect of any of its provisions may be varied by agreement. The presence in certain provisions of this [Act] of the words "unless otherwise agreed," or words of similar import, does not imply that the effect of other provisions may not be varied by agreement.

(e) Whether an electronic record or electronic signature has legal consequences is determined by this [Act] and other applicable law.

* * *

## §7 - LEGAL RECOGNITION OF ELECTRONIC RECORDS, ELECTRONIC SIGNATURES, AND ELECTRONIC CONTRACTS

(a) A record or signature may not be denied legal effect or enforceability solely because it is in electronic form.

(b) A contract may not be denied legal effect or enforceability solely because an electronic record was used in its formation.

(c) If a law requires a record to be in writing, an electronic record satisfies the law.

(d) If a law requires a signature, an electronic signature satisfies the law.

## §8 - PROVISION OF INFORMATION IN WRITING; PRESENTATION OF RECORDS

(a) If parties have agreed to conduct a transaction by electronic means and a law requires a person to provide, send, or deliver information in writing to another person, the requirement is satisfied if the information is provided, sent, or delivered, as the case may be, in an electronic record capable of retention by the recipient at the time of receipt. An electronic record is not capable of retention by the recipient if the sender or its information processing system inhibits the ability of the recipient to print or store the electronic record.

(b) If a law other than this [Act] requires a record (i) to be posted or displayed in a certain manner, (ii) to be sent, communicated, or transmitted by a specified method, or (iii) to contain information that is formatted in a certain manner, the following rules apply:

(1) The record must be posted or displayed in the manner specified in the other law.

(2) Except as otherwise provided in subsection (d)(2), the record must be sent, communicated, or transmitted by the method specified in the other law.

(3) The record must contain the information formatted in the manner specified in the other law.

(c) If a sender inhibits the ability of a recipient to store or print an electronic record, the electronic record is not enforceable against the recipient.

(d) The requirements of this section may not be varied by agreement, but:

(1) to the extent a law other than this [Act] requires information to be provided, sent, or delivered in writing but permits that requirement to be varied by agreement, the requirement under subsection (a) that the information be in the form of an electronic record capable of retention may also be varied by agreement; and

(2) a requirement under a law other than this [Act] to send, communicate, or transmit a record by [first-class mail, postage prepaid] [regular United States mail], may be varied by agreement to the extent permitted by the other law.

## § 9 - ATTRIBUTION AND EFFECT OF ELECTRONIC RECORD AND ELECTRONIC SIGNATURE

(a) An electronic record or electronic signature is attributable to a person if it was the act of the person. The act of the person may be shown in any manner, including a showing of the efficacy of any security procedure applied to determine the person to which the electronic record or electronic signature was attributable.

(b) The effect of an electronic record or electronic signature attributed to a person under subsection (a) is determined from the context and surrounding circumstances at the time of its creation, execution, or adoption, including the parties' agreement, if any, and otherwise as provided by law.

\* \* \*

## § 12 - RETENTION OF ELECTRONIC RECORDS; ORIGINALS

(a) If a law requires that a record be retained, the requirement is satisfied by retaining an electronic record of the information in the record which:

(1) accurately reflects the information set forth in the record after it was first generated in its final form as an electronic record or otherwise; and

(2) remains accessible for later reference.

(b) A requirement to retain a record in accordance with subsection (a) does not apply to any information the sole purpose of which is to enable the record to be sent, communicated, or received.

(c) A person may satisfy subsection (a) by using the services of another person if the requirements of that subsection are satisfied.

(d) If a law requires a record to be presented or retained in its original form, or provides consequences if the record is not presented or retained in its original form, that law is satisfied by an electronic record retained in accordance with subsection (a).

(e) If a law requires retention of a check, that requirement is satisfied by retention of an electronic record of the information on the front and back of the check in accordance with subsection (a).

(f) A record retained as an electronic record in accordance with subsection (a) satisfies a law requiring a person to retain a record for evidentiary, audit, or like purposes, unless a law enacted after the effective date of this [Act] specifically prohibits the use of an electronic record for the specified purpose.

(g) This section does not preclude a governmental agency of this State from specifying additional requirements for the retention of a record subject to the agency's jurisdiction.

* * *

§ 14 - AUTOMATED TRANSACTION

In an automated transaction, the following rules apply:

(1) A contract may be formed by the interaction of electronic agents of the parties, even if no individual was aware of or reviewed the electronic agents' actions or the resulting terms and agreements.

(2) A contract may be formed by the interaction of an electronic agent and an individual, acting on the individual's own behalf or for another person, including by an interaction in which the individual performs actions that the individual is free to refuse to perform and which the individual knows or has reason to know will cause the electronic agent to complete the transaction or performance.

(3) The terms of the contract are determined by the substantive law applicable to it.

---

# Notes and Questions on UETA and Other Statutes

1. *Update on Click-Wrap and Browse-Wrap Cases.* Litigation continues over these types of agreements as plaintiffs seek to avoid onerous contract terms. While courts may find

for a contract's formation, they are hesitant to enforce some of the more burdensome terms. As seen above in *Specht*, where a person downloads software from the Internet without clicking-or being required to click-acceptance of the licensing agreement, that person will not be held to those terms.

In *I.LAN Systems Inc. v. NetScout Service Level Corp.*, 183. F. Supp. 2d 328 (D. Mass. 2002), the court ruled that under Massachusetts law, click-though license agreements filled voids to the extent that preexisting agreements were silent. However, the majority of case law suggests, as in *Specht*, that courts are hesitant to uphold these types of license terms or similar terms of service. *See, e.g., Am. Online, Inc. v. Superior Court of Alameda County*, 90 Cal. App. 4th, 1 (Cal. Ct. App. 2001) (venue selection clause in terms of service agreement held unenforceable because it denies California consumers rights under California consumer law and is contrary to California public policy); *Williams v. Am. Online, Inc.*, 2001 Mass. Super. LEXIS 11 (Mass. 2001) (exclusive jurisdiction and forum selection clause in terms of service not binding where injury occurred prior to clicking "I agree"); *Am. Online, Inc. v. Booker*, 781 So. 2d 423 (Fla. Dist. Ct. App. 2001) (forum selection clause in terms of service contract not enforced in Florida even where class action procedures in state courts not available in Virginia); *Matthew Bender & Co. v. Jurisline.com, L.L.C.*, 91 F. Supp. 2d 677 (S.D.N.Y. 2000) (shrink-wrap agreement terms apply to uncopyrightable portion of database); *Caspi v. Microsoft Network, L.L.C.*, 323 NJ Super. 118 (N.J. Super. Ct. App. Div. 1999) (forum selection clause enforced in click-wrap agreement); *M.A. Mortenson Co., Inc. v. Timberline Software Corp.*, 970 P.2d 803 (Wash. Ct. App. 1999), *aff'd* 998 P.2d 305 (Wash. 2000) (limitation on liability in shrink-wrap license agreement enforced).

Will *respondeat superior* apply to these types of agreements? Can a company become legally bound to a shrink-wrap or click-wrap licensor by the assent of an employee? Electronic transactions have eliminated the opportunities parties formerly had to identify each other and assess apparent authority. What do you think of a click-wrap term stating that, if the licensee is a corporation, the licensee's clicked assent constitutes a warranty of valid authority to bind the employer or principal?

2. *Full Text of UETA.* The official 1999 Final Act of UETA, complete with extensive commentary on each section, is available online (as of Nov. 30, 2004) at

www.law.upenn.edu/bll/ulc/fnact99/1990s/ueta99.htm

The official comments are a valuable source of interpretive guidance and "must reading" for any lawyer who wishes to apply UETA, especially in litigation.

Of course, any lawyer applying UETA in a particular state should rely only on the text of the law (and any legislative history) as adopted in that state. For a list of states that have adopted UETA and citations to their enactments, see Jay Dratler, Jr., Licensing of Intellectual Property § 1.06[1] n. 17.43 (Law Journal Press, 1994).

3. *Sources of UETA.* The primary reason for the success and rapid adoption of UETA was its modest approach to electronic transactions, which its drafters themselves described as "minimalist." According to the official comments:

> The Act's treatment of records and signatures demonstrates best the minimalist approach that has been adopted. Whether a record is attributed to a person is left to law outside this Act. Whether an electronic signature has any effect is left to the surrounding circumstances and other law. These provisions are salutary directives to assure that records and signatures will be treated in the same manner, under currently existing law, as written records and manual signatures.

National Conference of Commissioners on Uniform State Laws (NCCUSL), 1999 Final Act of UETA, Prefatory Note, Comment B. As this comment suggests, UETA does not attempt to modify or re-invent contract law. Rather, it merely defines the circumstances under which electronic communications and records have the same legal effect as if they had been on paper. The basic rules of contract formation are left to operate as they otherwise would. As a result, determining whether a contract exists nearly always requires resort to other law—the common law, the Uniform Commercial Code, or other statutes—in addition to UETA.

4. *UCITA.* A much less successful model statute took a far more invasive approach to its legal surgery. The Uniform Computer Information Transactions Act (UCITA) was an ambitious attempt to prescribe "default rules" (i.e., baseline rules that, for the most part, either conctracting party can modify or avoid), as well as a few invariable rules, for a wide range of licensing agreements in a wide range of industries. *See* National Conference of Commissioners on Uniform State Laws (NCCUSL), 2002 Final Act, Uniform Computer Information Transactions Act, available online (as of Nov. 30, 2004) at

www.law.upenn.edu/bll/ulc/ucita/2002final.htm

UCITA is a lengthy, highly complex statute; it has sixty-six definitions of terms, plus eleven borrowed from the Uniform Commercial Code. *See* UCITA 2002, *supra*, § 102. Its table of contents alone runs three pages; the definitions and their official commentary occupy over twenty pages; and the whole statute, including commentary, is 262 pages long. Its scope provisions alone (*see id.*, § 103) run three and one-half pages, have seven exceptions, three special definitions, and require nine pages of commentary to elucidate. As a result, in the general case it takes considerable study and analysis just to decide whether the statute, by its own terms, applies to a particular transaction. Digesting the statute at the level of detail required for accurate legal analysis and application is therefore a major undertaking.

Only two states, Virginia and Maryland, have adopted UCITA. *See* Md. Commercial Law Code Ann. §§ 22-101 through 22-816; Va. Code Ann. §§ 59.1-501.1 through 59.1-509.2. One reason may be the statute's length, complexity, and ambitious coverage. Unlike UETA, UCITA *does* purport to modify and re-invent a number of traditional rules of contract law. As a result, controversy has dogged it from the beginning. For an overview of the history and nature of the controversy, including the American Law Institute's decision to abandon what started as a joint project with the National Conference of Commissioners on Uniform State Law, see Brian D. McDonald, *The Uniform Computer Information Transactions Act*, 16 BERKELEY TECH. L.J. 461 (2001).

Fortunately for lawyers who don't want to digest over 250 pages of dense legal prose in order to draft an occasional license agreement, UCITA is mostly optional. UCITA's choice-of-law rules allow parties in other states (or even those in adopting states) to "opt out" of UCITA by choosing another state's law. *See* UCITA 2002, § 109(a). Under UCITA itself, that choice of law is enforceable except that, in consumer contracts, it cannot vary a legal principle that would apply invariably (i.e., a mandatory, "nondefault" rule) in the absence of agreement. *See id.*, § 109(a), (b). Thus, loosely speaking, parties both inside and outside of Maryland and Virginia can "opt out" of UCITA except to the extent that their doing so would obviate mandatory consumer-protection provisions in force in those states. Many practitioners routinely "opt out" of UCITA in this manner, if only to avoid the lengthy and uncertain analysis of how the book-length statute and commentary might affect their agreements.

UCITA, and before that a move to add intellectual property licenses to a new Article 2B of the UCC, have been criticized as attempting to replace intellectual property rules with contract rights. *See* Mark A. Lemly, *Beyond Preemption: The Law and Policy of Intellectual Property Licensing*, 87 CALIF. L. REV. 111 (1999). Would so doing provide more or less predictability?

5. *E-SIGN.* A federal statute called the Electronic Signatures in Global and National Commerce Act (E-SIGN) has much the same purpose and effect as UETA. *See* Pub. L. No. 106-229, Title I, 114 Stat. 464 (June 30, 2000), codified in 15 U.S.C. §§ 7001-7006. Its first provision decrees:

> Notwithstanding any statute, regulation, or other rule of law (other than [15 U.S.C. §§ 7001-7021], with respect to any transaction in or affecting interstate or foreign commerce—
>
> (1) a signature, contract, or other record relating to such transaction may not be denied legal effect, validity, or enforceability solely because it is in electronic form; and
>
> (2) a contract relating to such transaction may not be denied legal effect, validity, or enforceability solely because an electronic signature or electronic record was used in its formation.

15 U.S.C. § 7001(a). E-SIGN contains definitions of terms and detailed provisions regarding the format and timing of consumer disclosures in electronic transactions and how statutory requirements for verification or acknowledgment work in an electronic world. *See* 15 U.S.C. § 7006; *see also* 15 U.S.C. § 7001(b).

E-SIGN does not pre-empt UETA in states that have adopted UETA's 1999 Final Act. Indeed, duly adopted provisions of the 1999 UETA may "modify, limit, or supersede the provisions" of E-SIGN, with certain limitations. 15 U.S.C. § 7002(a). Therefore, UETA provides the basic rules for electronic transactions in states that have adopted its 1999 version. E-SIGN provides supplementary rules in those states and basic rules for electronic commerce in the eleven states and territories that have adopted UETA. E-SIGN's detailed provisions on pre-emption, however, merit scrutiny in states that have adopted the 1999 UETA but have included nonstandard provisions or exceptions. *See* 15 U.S.C. § 7002(a).

6. *Prior to UETA.* Before the advent of UETA, a few states tried to dispel the anxiety surrounding shrink-wrap licenses by drafting statutes that purport to make them enforceable. Only one of these statutes is still on the books: the Louisiana Software License Enforcement Act, La. Rev. Stat. Ann. §§ 51:1961-51:1966. Its survival no doubt reflects the unique position of Louisiana as a "code" state, whose legal traditions derive not from English common law, but from French civil law.

The Louisiana law contains a list of specific provisions in software licenses agreements that it purports to render enforceable. *See id.*, § 51:1964.

Among them are covenants against reverse engineering and disassembly of object code for computer software (the form in which software is usually distributed to consumers). *See id.*, § 51:1964(3). The Fifth Circuit, however, has held that this provision is pre-empted by Section 117 of the Copyright Act of 1976, as amended. 17 U.S.C. § 117. *See Vault Corp. v. Quaid Software Ltd.*, 847 F.2d 255, 269–70, 7 U.S.P.Q.2d (BNA) 1281 (5th Cir. 1988). The issue of pre-emption is discussed in the next section.

7. *Comparing UETA and UCITA.* Although both deal with computers and modern information systems, UETA (the "Uniform Electronic Transactions Act") and UCITA (the

"Uniform Computer Information Transactions Act") are vastly different model statutes. UETA is a relatively simple statute with relatively modest goals. Its Section 2 contains sixteen definitions, and it runs only forty-seven pages, including its official comments.

In contrast, UCITA is an ambitious and highly complex statute, designed to cover a wide range of licensing transactions involving "computer information" and computer programs. For an additional overview of the history and nature of the controversy, including the American Law Institute's decision to abandon what started as a joint project with the National Conference of Commissioners on Uniform State Law, see Brian D. McDonald, *The Uniform Computer Information Transactions Act*, 16 BERKELEY TECH. L.J. 461 (2001).

As a result of these differences in complexity and legal acceptance, the two model statutes have fared differently in the state legislatures. As stated in Note 4, only two states, Maryland and Virginia, have adopted UCITA. In contrast, forty-one states had adopted UETA as of October 2002. (Ohio's version of UETA appears at Ohio Rev. Code Ann. §§ 1306.01-1306.23.) Thus, while UCITA may crop up in contracts in other states by virtue of choice-of-law provisions and agreements to "opt in" to UCITA's provisions, business lawyers practicing outside of Maryland and Virginia are much more likely to encounter UETA than UCITA.

8. *Additional Issues Arising From UETA*

a. *Purpose.* What is the main purpose of UETA as a whole? Is it to provide uniform rules for electronic contracting, including contract formation, remedies, warranties, etc.? Or is its purpose much narrower?

b. *Scope.* What is UETA's scope, i.e., to what does it apply? What basic definition governs the scope of UETA's coverage? Is this definition broad or narrow? Does the statute's application depend upon the intent of parties to a deal? Does UETA apply retroactively to deals done before its was adopted?

c. *Effect on Substantive Contract Law.* Does UETA change the substantive law of contracts? Does it determine invariably when electronic records create a binding contract? Does it generally create invariable rules or "default" rules, which apply in the absence of agreement to the contrary? If UETA does not provide rules of substantive contact law, then precisely what does it do? Does it validate automated transactions that are otherwise lawful under applicable substantive law?

d. *"Click-Wrap" Contracts.* How does UETA treat "click-wrap" contracts? Are they invariably valid and unenforceable, or does UETA impose preconditions for their enforcement? If there are preconditions, what are they, and under what circumstances do they arise? Do "click-wrap" contracts eliminate the sources of legal and practical uncertainty identified in such cases as *ProCD* and *Hill v. Gateway 2000, Inc.*?

e. *Electronic Signatures.* Under UETA, what determines whether an electronic signature is valid? Does an electronic form provide any advantage in terms of validation? Under UETA, can a mouse click be a signature? Can an e-mail? Does the statute validate oral transactions? Do agreed security procedures provide any presumption of validity? In general, what determines whether there was an agreement to use electronic means?

f. *Conditions on Enforcement.* Are there any general conditions on the enforcement of an electronic record? What if some bug in or unusual characteristic of a person's system prevents an electronic record from being stored? What if another law requires a message to be posted, displayed, sent, communicated, transmitted, or formatted in a particular way? Does UETA overturn that other law?

g. *Attribution*. Does UETA prescribe a specific rule for attribution of electronic records? What determines whether a signature was the act of a particular person? Do UETA's rules for attribution alter existing law? Once an electronic record is attributed to a person, is the record automatically enforceable against that person, or do the usual legal excuses apply? Is a signature required for attribution of a record? Is a security procedure required? is it best? What determines the effect of an attribution? Does a statutory notarization requirement preclude use of electronic means to consummate a transaction?

h. *Effect of Change or Error*. Is a party to an electronic transaction bound despite unintended changes and errors? Can a business avoid a transaction by claiming an electronic error? What are the conditions for avoiding a transaction based upon an electronic error? If this "out" is not available, what law governs electronic error? Can the provisions for electronic error be varied by agreement? Does a person have to show that an error was caused by electronic mistake, such as a computer "glitch," in order to take advantage of this section? What law applies if an electronic agent makes an error? Do the statute's provisions for electronic error provide an incentive for makers of electronic agents to build systems that minimize errors? Can an individual who receives software or text information in error avoid the transaction?

i. *Record Retention*. Must records of transactions be retained in paper form? What are the requirements for record retention in electronic form? Can records fail to meet the statutory standard if their storage technology becomes obsolete? On the other hand, can paper records be destroyed once electronic counterparts have been prepared and are maintained with non-obsolete technology? Are transmission headers and such considered parts of electronic records which must be retained? Does the best evidence rule still require a paper "original"?

j. *Automated Transactions*. Does UETA permit and validate automated transactions? Can a valid automated transaction involve two electronic agents, i.e., can it be completely automated? Can it involve an electronic agent and an individual? Which kinds of transactions are now more common? What law governs automated transactions? Does validation of electronic transactions violate the usual contract principle that intention much accompany assent in order to form a contract? Can electronic agent transactions satisfy signature requirements?

k. *Sending and Receiving Electronic Records*. When is an electronic record sent? When is it received? Need an individual be aware of receipt in order for it to occur? Are these rules invariable? Do these rules determine an electronic record's legal effect? Do they provide for general broadcast messages? Does UETA determine the effect of a sender trying to "pull back" or retrieve a message? Can a recipient avoid receipt under UETA by leaving e-mail messages on the server? Can a person designate different addresses for different purposes? Can a person designate the place of sending or receipt unilaterally?

9. *Special UETA Problems*. Consider the following problems under UETA.

a. While at the Law School, Patty offers to sell her 1999 Toyota Camry to Dave for $7,000. Dave says he is interested but will get back to Patty by e-mail. At 4:00 p.m., Dave sends, and Patty receives and reads, an e-mail in which Dave agrees to purchase the car for $7,000. At 5:00 p.m., Patty receives an e-mail offer from Betty to purchase the same car for $8,000; Patty declines Betty's offer, saying in her e-mail response that she already sold the car to Dave. At 8:00 p.m., Patty receives a second e-mail from Dave saying he changed his mind and won't purchase the car after all. Does Dave have a binding contract to buy the car for $7,000? (Assume these events all take place in Ohio, and note that under Ohio Revised Code §1302.04(a)—Ohio's version of UCC §2-201(a)—a contract for the sale of goods for $500 or more must be in writing.)

b. Polly opens a checking account in person at the First National Bank. When she opens the account she receives a packet of documents totaling about fifty pages. Included in the packet is a small brochure entitled "Account Agreement," consisting of twelve pages of fine print in nineteen numbered paragraphs. Paragraph 18, entitled "Account and Fee Changes," contains fourteen sentences of complex legal prose, the eighth of which reads as follows:

> Bank shall have the right to change the account terms, including any fee for services, by posting a notice of change on the Bank's Website at www.eighth-second.com; you agree that any such posting shall give you notice of the change, and your use of the account after any such posting shall constitute your agreement to be bound by the change.

A single, full-color sheet in Polly's account-opening packet, entitled "Account Fees," lists a "bounced check charge" as $15. Two months after Polly opens her account, the bank posts a notice on its website stating that, effective immediately, this fee is increased to $35. Polly never sees the notice; in fact, Polly has no PC and does not know how to "surf the web." Polly continues to use the account. Due to her own mistake in balancing her checkbook, she later bounces ten checks. Is Polly liable for ten times the difference between the old and new fees, i.e., $200? What difference would it make if: (a) Polly has a PC and knows how to surf the web, but never visits the bank's website; or (b) Polly regularly uses the bank's website for "on-line banking"?

c. Duncan is a registered customer of Amazing.com's website. In the past, he provided his name, address, and credit-card information to Amazing.com's secure server, so that he could use its patented "one-click shopping" technology. This technology allows him, once he finds a book he wants, to buy a selected quantity of that book by filling in the quantity and clicking only once on the proper icon. Duncan is an avid Harry Potter fan. Every day, he searches Amazing.com's website for the long-awaited latest Harry Potter episode. When he finally finds it, he is so excited that he presses the "one" key extra hard, unintentionally filling the "quantity" box with the number "111" instead of the number "1." So intent is Duncan on completing his order that he doesn't notice this. No human being inside Amazing.com reviews the order, and in due course it is filled automatically.

A few days later, the friendly UPS man arrives at Duncan's house with a large box. On opening it, Duncan discovers 111 identical copies of the latest Harry Potter book. Is he obliged to pay for them? (Be sure to consider both contract formation and possible defenses.) Would it make a difference if Amazing.com's website had allowed Duncan to print out the order? If it had required Duncan to review and submit the order a second time, including quantity, before consummating the purchase, but did not allow him to print it out? If it had both required Duncan to review and resubmit the order and allowed him to print it out? Would it make a difference if Duncan had been ordering the books as purchasing agent on behalf of a large corporation?

d. Microsell is a major vendor of computer software and hardware, which prides itself on its "cool technology." Microsell offers "electronic agent" software that will "crawl the Web" to find and purchase items specified by the user. For example, if a user wants to buy a portable CD player, she need only enter into the software the type, features, and price range she wants, and the agent is supposed to find the lowest-priced item that meets her requirements and purchase it for her automatically. Microsell calls this software the "BuyAgent" and advertises it as a "low price finder."

Penelope Purchaser buys a license for the software from Microsell for $395. As her first trial, she asks the software to buy her a "boom box." She specifies all the parameters for her boom box, including size, weight, wattage, battery life, and other features, and she specifies a price range of $200 to $500. Penelope invokes the BuyAgent to "crawl the web" and to make her purchase on her behalf while she goes out for dinner. When Penelope returns, she find that the BuyAgent has bought a boom box meeting her requirements from Microsell for $499. In a few minutes surfing the Web, however, she find that several other vendors also offer boom boxes meeting her requirements for prices ranging from $249 to $387. Can Penelope avoid or rescind the transaction? If so, how? If not, does she have any action against Microsell? Would she if the "BuyAgent" had been a human being employed by Microsell, to whom she had given the same instructions?

----

# C.  License Agreement Prohibitions and Preemption

The Supremacy Clause of the United States Constitution, Article VI, Clause 2, decrees that federal statutes and treaties are "the supreme Law of the Land" and bind judges, "any Thing in the Constitution or Laws of any State to the Contrary notwithstanding." Therefore where a federal statute conflicts with state law, including state law governing contracts, the state law must fall. The state law, or enforcement of the offending contract, is said to be "pre-empted" by federal law.

There are three general types of federal pre-emption. The first occurs when a state law conflicts irreconcilably with federal law. The second occurs when a federal statute itself explicitly prescribes pre-emption, as does Section 301 of the Copyright Act of 1976, 17 U.S.C. § 301, discussed in the case below. The third occurs where a federal statute is so comprehensive and complete that it "occupies the field" of relevant law and leaves no room for the operation of state law.

----

## Bowers v. Baystate Technologies, Inc.
### 320 F.3d 1317 (Fed. Cir. 2003), *cert. denied*, 539 U.S. 928 (2003)

RADER, Circuit Judge.

Following trial in the United States District Court for the District of Massachusetts, the jury returned a verdict for Harold L. Bowers on his patent infringement, copyright infringement, and breach of contract claims, while rejecting Baystate Technologies, Inc.'s claim for patent invalidity. The jury awarded Mr. Bowers separate damages on each of his claims. The district court, however, omitted the copyright damages as duplicative of the contract damages. Because substantial evidence supports the jury's verdict that Baystate breached the contract, this court affirms that verdict. This court holds also that the district court did not abuse its discretion in modifying the damages award. Nevertheless, because no reasonable jury could find that Baystate infringes claim 1 as properly construed, this court reverses the patent infringement verdict.

I.

Harold L. Bowers (Bowers) created a template to improve computer aided design (CAD) software, such as the CADKEY tool of Cadkey, Inc. Mr. Bowers filed a patent application for his template on February 27, 1989. On June 12, 1990, United States Patent No. 4,933,514 ('514 patent) issued from that application.

\* \* \*

Mr. Bowers commercialized the '514 patent template as Cadjet for use with CADKEY.

n February 1, 1993, Mr. Bowers requested reexamination of the '514 patent in view of prior art, namely the Keymaster template. Like the '514 patent template, the Keymaster template provides a unified visual representation of many CAD commands. Like the preferred embodiment of the '514 patent, the Keymaster template operates with CAD-KEY software. Following examiner rejections, the Board of Patent Appeals and Interferences ultimately found some amended claims of the '514 patent patentable. The PTO issued a reexamination certificate on December 9, 1997. U.S. Patent No. B1- 4,933,514.

Since the early 1980s, CAD programs have assisted engineers to draft and design on a computer screen. George W. Ford, III, a development engineer and supervisor of quality control at Heinemann Electric, envisioned a way to improve Mr. Bowers' template and CAD software. Specifically, Mr. Ford designed Geodraft, a DOS-based add-on program to operate with CAD. Geodraft allows an engineer to insert technical tolerances for features of the computer-generated design. These tolerances comply with the geometric dimensioning and tolerancing (GD & T) requirements in ANSI Y14.5M, a standard promulgated by the American National Standards Institute (ANSI). Geodraft works in conjunction with the CAD system to ensure that the design complies with ANSI Y14.5M-a task previously error-prone due to the standard's complexity. Geodraft automatically includes symbols specifying the correct GD & T parameters. Mr. Ford obtained a registered copyright, TX 2-939-672, covering Geodraft.

In 1989, Mr. Ford offered Mr. Bowers an exclusive license to his Geodraft software. Mr. Bowers accepted that offer and bundled Geodraft and Cadjet together as the Designer's Toolkit. Mr. Bowers sold the Designer's Toolkit with a shrink-wrap license that, *inter alia*, prohibited any reverse engineering.

In 1989, Baystate also developed and marketed other tools for CADKEY. One of those tools, Draft-Pak version 1 and 2, featured a template and GD & T software. In 1988 and 1989, Mr. Bowers offered to establish a formal relationship with Baystate, including bundling his template with Draft-Pak. Baystate rejected that offer, however, telling Mr. Bowers that it believed it had "the in-house capability to develop the type of products you have proposed."

In 1990, Mr. Bowers released Designer's Toolkit. By January 1991, Baystate had obtained copies of that product. Three months later, Baystate introduced the substantially revised Draft-Pak version 3, incorporating many of the features of Designer's Toolkit. Although Draft-Pak version 3 operated in the DOS environment, Baystate later upgraded it to operate with Microsoft Windows®.

Baystate's introduction of Draft-Pak version 3 induced intense price competition between Mr. Bowers and Baystate. To gain market share over Baystate, Mr. Bowers negotiated with Cadkey, Inc., to provide the Designer's Toolkit free with CADKEY. Mr. Bowers planned to recoup his profits by selling software upgrades to the users that he hoped to lure to his products. Following pressure from Baystate, however, Cadkey, Inc., repudiated its distribution agreement with Mr. Bowers. Eventually, Baystate purchased Cadkey, Inc., and eliminated Mr. Bowers from the CADKEY network—effectively preventing him from developing and marketing the Designer's Toolkit for that program.

On May 16, 1991, Baystate sued Mr. Bowers for declaratory judgment that 1) Baystate's products do not infringe the '514 patent, 2) the '514 patent is invalid, and 3) the '514 patent is unenforceable. Mr. Bowers filed counterclaims for copyright infringement, patent infringement, and breach of contract.

Following trial, the jury found for Mr. Bowers and awarded $1,948,869 for copyright infringement, $3,831,025 for breach of contract, and $232,977 for patent infringement. The district court, however, set aside the copyright damages as duplicative of the contract damages and entered judgment for $5,270,142 (including pre-judgment interest). Baystate filed timely motions for judgment as a matter of law (JMOL), or for a new trial, on all of Mr. Bowers' claims. Baystate appeals the district court's denial of its motions for JMOL or a new trial, while Mr. Bowers appeals the district court's denial of copyright damages. This court has jurisdiction under 28 U.S.C. §1295(a)(1) (2000).

II.

Baystate raises a number of issues that are not unique to the jurisdiction of this court. On those issues, this court applies the law of the circuit from which the appeal is taken, here the First Circuit.

* * *

A.

Baystate contends that the Copyright Act preempts the prohibition of reverse engineering embodied in Mr. Bowers' shrink-wrap license agreements. Swayed by this argument, the district court considered Mr. Bowers' contract and copyright claims coextensive. The district court instructed the jury that "reverse engineering violates the license agreement only if Baystate's product that resulted from reverse engineering infringes Bowers' copyright because it copies protectable expression." Mr. Bowers lodged a timely objection to this instruction. This court holds that, under First Circuit law, the Copyright Act does not preempt or narrow the scope of Mr. Bowers' contract claim.

Courts respect freedom of contract and do not lightly set aside freely-entered agreements. The Copyright Act provides that "all legal or equitable rights that are equivalent to any of the exclusive rights within the general scope of copyright...are governed exclusively by this title." 17 U.S.C. §301(a) (2000). The First Circuit does not interpret this language to require preemption as long as "a state cause of action requires an extra element, beyond mere copying, preparation of derivative works, performance, distribution or display." *Data Gen. Corp. v. Grumman Sys. Support Corp.*, 36 F.3d 1147, 1164, 32 USPQ2d 1385, 1397 (1st Cir. 1994) (quoting *Gates Rubber Co. v. Bando Chem. Indus.*, 9 F.3d 823, 847, 28 USPQ2d 1503, 1520 (10th Cir. 1993)).

In *Data General*, Data General alleged that Grumman misappropriated its trade secret software. 36 F.3d at 1155. Grumman obtained that software from Data General's customers and former employees who were bound by confidentiality agreements to refrain from disclosing the software. *Id.* at 1154–55. In defense, Grumman argued that the Copyright Act preempted Data General's trade secret claim. *Id.* at 1158, 1165. The First Circuit held that the Copyright Act did not preempt the state law trade secret claim. *Id.* at 1165. Beyond mere copying, that state law claim required proof of a trade secret and breach of a duty of confidentiality. *Id.* These additional elements of proof, according to the First Circuit, made the trade secret claim qualitatively different from a copyright claim. *Id.* In contrast, the First Circuit noted that claims might be preempted whose extra elements are illusory, being "mere label[s] attached to the same odious business conduct." *Id.* at 1165 (quoting *Mayer v. Josiah Wedgwood & Sons, Ltd.,* 601 F. Supp. 1523, 1535, 225 USPQ 776, 784 (S.D.N.Y. 1985)). For example, the First Circuit observed that "a state law misappropriation claim will not escape preemption...simply because a plaintiff must prove that copying was not only unauthorized but also commercially immoral." *Id.*

The First Circuit has not addressed expressly whether the Copyright Act preempts a state law contract claim that restrains copying. This court perceives, however, that *Data General's* rationale would lead to a judgment that the Copyright Act does not preempt the state contract action in this case. Indeed, most courts to examine this issue have found that the Copyright Act does not preempt contractual constraints on copyrighted articles.

In *ProCD*, for example, the court found that the mutual assent and consideration required by a contract claim render that claim qualitatively different from copyright infringement. 86 F.3d at 1454. Consistent with *Data General's* reliance on a contract element, the court in *ProCD* reasoned: "A copyright is a right against the world. Contracts, by contrast, generally affect only their parties; strangers may do as they please, so contracts do not create 'exclusive rights.'" *Id.* Indeed, the Supreme Court recently noted "[i]t goes without saying that a contract cannot bind a nonparty." *EEOC v. Waffle House, Inc.,* 534 U.S. 279, 122 S. Ct. 754, 764, 151 L. Ed. 2d 755 (2002). This court believes that the First Circuit would follow the reasoning of *ProCD* and the majority of other courts to consider this issue. This court, therefore, holds that the Copyright Act does not preempt Mr. Bowers' contract claims.

In making this determination, this court has left untouched the conclusions reached in *Atari Games v. Nintendo* regarding reverse engineering as a statutory fair use exception to copyright infringement. *Atari Games Corp. v. Nintendo of America, Inc.,* 975 F.2d 832, 24 USPQ2d 1015 (Fed. Cir. 1992). In *Atari,* this court stated that, with respect to 17 U.S.C. § 107 (fair use section of the Copyright Act), "[t]he legislative history of section 107 suggests that courts should adapt the fair use exception to accommodate new technological innovations." *Atari,* 975 F.2d at 843. This court noted "[a] prohibition on all copying whatsoever would stifle the free flow of ideas without serving any legitimate interest of the copyright holder." *Id.* Therefore, this court held "reverse engineering object code to discern the unprotectable ideas in a computer program is a fair use." *Id.* Application of the First Circuit's view distinguishing a state law contract claim having additional elements of proof from a copyright claim does not alter the findings of *Atari.* Likewise, this claim distinction does not conflict with the expressly defined circumstances in which reverse engineering is not copyright infringement under 17 U.S.C. § 1201(f) (section of the Digital Millennium Copyright Act) and 17 U.S.C. § 906 (section directed to mask works).

* * *

This court now considers the scope of Mr. Bowers' contract protection. Without objection to the choice of law, the district court applied Massachusetts contract law. Accordingly, contract terms receive "the sense and meaning of the words which the parties have used; and if clear and free from ambiguity the words are to be taken and understood in their natural, usual and ordinary sense." *Farber v. Mutual Life Ins. Co.,* 250

Mass. 250, 253, 145 N.E. 535 (Mass. 1924); *see also Kelly v. Marx,* 428 Mass. 877, 881, 705 N.E.2d 1114 (Mass. 1999) ("The proper course is to enforce contracts according to their plain meaning and not to undertake to be wiser than the parties.") (quoting *Guerin v. Stacy,* 175 Mass. 595, 597, 56 N.E. 892 (1900) (Holmes, C.J.)).

In this case, the contract unambiguously prohibits "reverse engineering." That term means ordinarily "to study or analyze (a device, as a microchip for computers) in order to learn details of design, construction, and operation, perhaps to produce a copy or an improved version." *Random House Unabridged Dictionary* (1993); *see also* THE FREE ON-LINE DICTIONARY OF COMPUTING (2001), *at* wombat.doc.ic.ac.uk/foldoc/foldoc. cgi?reverse+engineering (last visited Jul. 17, 2002). Thus, the contract in this case broadly prohibits any "reverse engineering" of the subject matter covered by the shrink-wrap agreement.

The record amply supports the jury's finding of a breach of that agreement. As discussed above, the district court erred in instructing the jury that copyright law limited the scope of Mr. Bowers' contract protection. Notwithstanding that error, this court may affirm the jury's breach of contract verdict if substantial record evidence would permit a reasonable jury to find in favor of Mr. Bowers based on a correct understanding of the law. *Larch v. Mansfield Mun. Elec. Dept.,* 272 F.3d 63, 69 (1st Cir. 2001). The shrink-wrap agreements in this case are far broader than the protection afforded by copyright law. Even setting aside copyright violations, the record supports a finding of breach of the agreement between the parties. In view of the breadth of Mr. Bowers' contracts, this court perceives that substantial evidence supports the jury's breach of contract verdict relating to both the DOS and Windows versions of Draft-Pak.

The record indicates, for example, that Baystate scheduled two weeks in Draft-Pak's development schedule to analyze the Designer's Toolkit. Indeed, Robert Bean, Baystate's president and CEO, testified that Baystate generally analyzed competitor's products to duplicate their functionality.

The record also contains evidence of extensive and unusual similarities between Geodraft and the accused Draft-Pak—further evidence of reverse engineering. James Spencer, head of mechanical engineering and integration at the Space and Naval Warfare Systems Center, testified that he examined the relevant software programs to determine "the overall structure of the operating program" such as "how the operating programs actually executed the task of walking a user through creating a [GD&T] symbol." Mr. Spencer concluded: "In the process of taking the [ANSI Y14.5M] standard and breaking it down into its component parts to actually create a step-by-step process for a user using the software, both Geodraft and Draft-Pak [for DOS] use almost the identical process of breaking down that task into its individual pieces, and it's organized essentially identically." This evidence supports the jury's verdict of a contract breach based on reverse engineering.

Mr. Ford also testified that he had compared Geodraft and Draft-Pak. When asked to describe the Draft-Pak interface, Mr. Ford responded: "It looked like I was looking at my own program [i.e., Geodraft]." Both Mr. Spencer and Mr. Ford explained in detail similarities between Geodraft and the accused Draft-Pak. Those similarities included the interrelationships between program screens, the manner in which parameter selection causes program branching, and the manner in which the GD&T symbols are drawn.

Both witnesses also testified that those similarities extended beyond structure and design to include many idiosyncratic design choices and inadvertent design flaws. For example, both Geodraft and Draft-Pak offer "straightness tolerance" menu choices of "flat" and "cylindric," unusual in view of the use by ANSI Y14.5M of the terms "linear" and "circular," respectively. As another example, neither program requires the user to provide "angularity tolerance" secondary datum to create a feature control frame—a technical oversight that causes creation of an incomplete symbol. In sum, Mr. Spencer testified: "Based on my summary analysis of how the programs function, their errors from the standard and their similar nomenclatures reflecting nonstandard items, I would say that the Draft-Pak [for DOS] is a derivative copy of a Geodraft product."

Mr. Ford and others also demonstrated to the jury the operation of Geodraft and both the DOS and Windows versions of the accused Draft-Pak. Those software demonstrations undoubtedly conveyed information to the jury that the paper record on appeal cannot easily replicate. This court, therefore, is especially reluctant to substitute its judgment for that of the jury on the sufficiency and interpretation of that evidence. In any event, the record fully supports the jury's verdict that Baystate breached its contract with Mr. Bowers.

Baystate does not contest the contract damages amount on appeal. Thus, this court sustains the district court's award of contract damages. Mr. Bowers, however, argues that the district court abused its discretion by dropping copyright damages from the combined damage award. To the contrary, this court perceives no abuse of discretion.

The shrink-wrap license agreement prohibited, *inter alia,* all reverse engineering of Mr. Bowers' software, protection encompassing but more extensive than copyright protection, which prohibits only certain copying. Mr.Bowers' copyright and contract claims both rest on Baystate's copying of Mr. Bowers' software. Following the district court's instructions, the jury considered and awarded damages on each separately. This was entirely appropriate. The law is clear that the jury may award separate damages for each claim, "leaving it to the judge to make appropriate adjustments to avoid double recovery." *Britton v. Maloney,* 196 F.3d 24, 32 (1st Cir. 1999) (*citing Spectrum Sports, Inc. v. McQuillan,* 506 U.S. 447, 451 n. 3, 113 S. Ct. 884, 122 L. Ed. 2d 247 (1993)); *see also Data Gen. Corp. v. Grumman Sys. Support Corp.,* 825 F. Supp. 340, 346 (D.Mass. 1993) ("So long as a plaintiff is not twice compensated for a single injury, a judgment may be comprised of elements drawn from separate…remedies."), *aff'd in relevant part,* 36 F.3d 1147 (1st Cir. 1994). In this case, the breach of contract damages arose from the same copying and included the same lost sales that form the basis for the copyright damages. The district court, therefore, did not abuse its discretion by omitting from the final damage award the duplicative copyright damages. Because this court affirms the district court's omission of the copyright damages, this court need not reach the merits of Mr. Bowers' copyright infringement claim.

\* \* \*

## CONCLUSION

Because substantial evidence supports the jury's verdict that Baystate breached its contract with Mr. Bowers, this court affirms that verdict. This court holds also that the district court did not abuse its discretion in omitting as duplicative copyright damages from the damage award.

\* \* \*

DYK, Circuit Judge, concurring in part and dissenting in part.

I join the majority opinion except insofar as it holds that the contract claim is not preempted by federal law. Based on the petition for rehearing and the opposition, I have concluded that our original decision on the preemption issue, reaffirmed in today's revision of the majority opinion, was not correct. By holding that shrink-wrap licenses that override the fair use defense are not preempted by the Copyright Act, 17 U.S.C. §§ 101 *et seq.*, the majority has rendered a decision in conflict with the only other federal court of appeals decision that has addressed the issue—the Fifth Circuit decision in *Vault Corp. v. Quaid Software Ltd.*, 847 F.2d 255 (5th Cir. 1988). The majority's approach permits state law to eviscerate an important federal copyright policy reflected in the fair use defense, and the majority's logic threatens other federal copyright policies as well. I respectfully dissent.

* * *

## II

The fair use defense is an important limitation on copyright. Indeed, the Supreme Court has said that "[f]rom the infancy of copyright protection, some opportunity for fair use of copyrighted materials has been thought necessary to fulfill copyright's very purpose, '[t]o promote the Progress of Science and useful Arts....' U.S. Const., Art. I, § 8, cl.8." *Campbell v. Acuff-Rose Music, Inc.*, 510 U.S. 569, 575, 114 S. Ct. 1164, 127 L. Ed. 2d 500 (1994). The protective nature of the fair use defense was recently emphasized by the Court in the *Eldred* case, in which the Court noted that "copyright law contains built-in accommodations," including "the 'fair use' defense [which] allows the public to use not only facts an ideas contained in the copyrighted work, but also expression itself in certain circumstances." *Id.* at 123 S. Ct. 769.

We correctly held in *Atari Games Corp. v. Nintendo of America, Inc.*, 975 F.2d 832, 843 (Fed.Cir. 1992), that reverse engineering constitutes a fair use under the Copyright Act. The Ninth and Eleventh Circuits have also ruled that reverse engineering constitutes fair use. *Bateman v. Mnemonics, Inc.*, 79 F.3d 1532, 1539 n. 18 (11th Cir. 1996); *Sega Enters. Ltd. v. Accolade, Inc.*, 977 F.2d 1510, 1527–28 (9th Cir. 1992). No other federal court of appeals has disagreed.

We emphasized in *Atari* that an author cannot achieve protection for an idea simply by embodying it in a computer program. "An author cannot acquire patent-like protection by putting an idea, process, or method of operation in an unintelligible format and asserting copyright infringement against those who try to understand that idea, process, or method of operation." 975 F.2d at 842. Thus, the fair use defense for reverse engineering is necessary so that copyright protection does not "extend to any idea, procedure, process, system, method of operation, concept, principle, or discovery, regardless of the form in which it is described, explained, illustrated, or embodied in such work," as proscribed by the Copyright Act. 17 U.S.C. § 102(b) (2000).

## III

A state is not free to eliminate the fair use defense. Enforcement of a total ban on reverse engineering would conflict with the Copyright Act itself by protecting otherwise unprotectable material. If state law provided that a copyright holder could bar fair use of the copyrighted material by placing a black dot on each copy of the work offered for sale, there would be no question but that the state law would be preempted. A state law that allowed a copyright holder to simply label its products so as to eliminate a fair use defense would "substantially impede" the public's right to fair use and allow the copyright holder, through state law, to protect material that the Congress has determined must be free to all under the Copyright Act. *See Bonito Boats*, 489 U.S. at 157, 109 S. Ct. 971.

I nonetheless agree with the majority opinion that a state can permit parties to contract away a fair use defense or to agree not to engage in uses of copyrighted material that are permitted by the copyright law, if the contract is freely negotiated. A freely negotiated agreement represents the "extra element" that prevents preemption of a state law claim that would otherwise be identical to the infringement claim barred by the fair use defense of reverse engineering. *See Data Gen.,* 36 F.3d at 1164–65.

However, state law giving effect to shrink-wrap licenses is no different in substance from a hypothetical black dot law. Like any other contract of adhesion, the only choice offered to the purchaser is to avoid making the purchase in the first place. *See Fuentes v. Shevin,* 407 U.S. 67, 95, 92 S. Ct. 1983, 32 L. Ed. 2d 556 (1972). State law thus gives the copyright holder the ability to eliminate the fair use defense in each and every instance at its option. In doing so, as the majority concedes, it authorizes "shrink-wrap agreements... [that] are far broader than the protection afforded by copyright law." *Ante* at 1326.

## IV

There is, moreover, no logical stopping point to the majority's reasoning. The amici rightly question whether under our original opinion the first sale doctrine and a host of other limitations on copyright protection might be eliminated by shrink-wrap licenses in just this fashion. *See* Brief for Electric Frontier Foundation et al. as *Amici Curiae* 10. If by printing a few words on the outside of its product a party can eliminate the fair use defense, then it can also, by the same means, restrict a purchaser from asserting the "first sale" defense, embodied in 17 U.S.C. § 109(a), or any other of the protections Congress has afforded the public in the Copyright Act. That means that, under the majority's reasoning, state law could extensively undermine the protections of the Copyright Act.

## V

The Fifth Circuit's decision in *Vault* directly supports preemption of the shrink-wrap limitation. The majority states that *Vault* held that "a state law prohibiting all copying of a computer program is preempted by the federal Copyright Act" and then states that "no evidence suggests the First Circuit would extend this concept to include private contractual agreements supported by mutual assent and consideration." *Ante* at 1325. But, in fact, the Fifth Circuit held that the specific provision of state law that authorized contracts prohibiting reverse engineering, decompilation, or disassembly of computer programs was preempted by federal law because it conflicted with a portion of the Copyright Act and because it "'touche[d] upon an area' of federal copyright law." 847 F.2d at 269–70 (quoting *Sears, Roebuck,* 376 U.S. at 229, 84 S. Ct. 784). From a preemption standpoint, there is no distinction between a state law that explicitly validates a contract that restricts reverse engineering (*Vault*) and general common law that permits such a restriction (as here). On the contrary, the preemption clause of the Copyright Act makes clear that it covers "any such right or equivalent right in any such work *under the common law or statutes of any State.*" 17 U.S.C. § 301(a) (2000) (emphasis added).

I do not read *ProCD, Inc. v. Zeidenberg,* 86 F.3d 1447 (7th Cir. 1996), the only other court of appeals shrink-wrap case, as being to the contrary, even though it contains broad language stating that "a simple two-party contract is not 'equivalent to any of the exclusive rights within the general scope of copyright.'" *Id.* at 1455. In *ProCD,* the Seventh Circuit validated a shrink-wrap license that restricted the use of a CD-ROM to non-commercial purposes, which the defendant had violated by charging users a fee to access the CD-ROM over the Internet. The court held that the restriction to non-commercial use of the program was not equivalent to any rights protected by the Copyright

Act. Rather, the "contract reflect[ed] private ordering, essential to efficient functioning of markets." *Id.* at 1455. The court saw the licensor as legitimately seeking to distinguish between personal and commercial use. "ProCD offers software and data for two prices: one for personal use, a higher prices for commercial use," the court said. The defendant "wants to use the data without paying the seller's price." *Id.* at 1454. The court also emphasized that the license "would not withdraw any information from the public domain" because all of the information on the CD-ROM was publicly available. *Id.* at 1455.

The case before us is different from *ProCD*. The Copyright Act does not confer a right to pay the same amount for commercial and personal use. It does, however, confer a right to fair use, 17 U.S.C. § 107, which we have held encompasses reverse engineering.

*ProCD* and the other contract cases are also careful not to create a blanket rule that all contracts will escape preemption. The court in that case emphasized that "we think it prudent to refrain from adopting a rule that anything with the label 'contract' is necessarily outside the preemption clause." 86 F.3d at 1455. It also noted with approval another court's "recogni[tion of] the possibility that some applications of the law of contract could interfere with the attainment of national objectives and therefore come within the domain" of the Copyright Act. *Id.* The Eighth Circuit too cautioned in *National Car Rental* that a contractual restriction could impermissibly "protect rights equivalent to the exclusive copyright rights." 991 F.2d at 432.

I conclude that *Vault* states the correct rule; that state law authorizing shrink-wrap licenses that prohibit reverse engineering is preempted; and that the First Circuit would so hold because the extra element here "merely concerns *the extent to which* authors and their licensees can prohibit unauthorized copying by third parties." *Data Gen.*, 36 F.3d at 1165 (emphasis in original). I respectfully dissent.

----------

# Notes and Questions

1. *Section 117.* The decision of the Fifth Circuit in *Vault Corp.*, discussed in *Bowers*, did not depend upon the details or drafting of the Louisiana statute or of the underlying agreement that it purported to enforce. Rather, the analysis addressed a basic question: whether vendors of software can "opt out" by contract of federal statutory rules that, like § 117, appear to be mandatory. (Section 117(a) gives owners of copies of computer programs the right to use and adapt those copies to run computers and to make backup copies.)

What made the question difficult is that the relevant portion of § 117 by its terms applies only to "the owner of a copy of a computer program." 17 U.S.C. § 117(a) (preamble). Most form software license agreements purport to deny the licensee the status of "owner of a copy," in part in order to render § 117 inapplicable.

The word "owner" of a copy of a computer program in the current § 117 evolved from the word "possessor" during the legislative process. There is little legislative history explaining why the change was made. Why might it have been made? Did Congress intend to allow software vendors to deny users their statutory rights by contractually denying them the status of "owners"? Or might Congress have had a simpler motive:

denying statutory rights to borrowers of software as distinguished from legitimate licensees? Can you think of any other motives that Congress might have had, besides allowing vendors to obviate the statute by form contracts?

2. *Fair Use.* Both the majority and dissent in *Bowers* discuss the issue of fair use. The cases they both cite hold that it is fair use, and not copyright infringement, to copy a computer program for the purpose of reverse- engineering it, i.e., for the purpose of extracting the uncopyrightable ideas, techniques, and processes that make it work, *if* there is no other practical way of getting at those ideas, techniques, and processes.

The fair use doctrine in copyright law of course has much broader application than reverse engineering of computer programs. *See* 17 U.S.C. § 107 (prescribing nonexclusive four-factor test for assessing whether use of *any* copyrighted work is fair and therefore not infringing). The reverse-engineering application, however, is an important one for the conceptual coherence of copyright law. If a computer-program copyright owner could use her copyright to preclude reverse engineering, she could, in effect, extend her copyright to cover the ideas, techniques and processes underlying her program, couldn't she? Wouldn't her doing so conflict with the fundamental principle that copyright does not extend to ideas, techniques, and processes? *See* 17 U.S.C. § 102(b); *Baker v. Selden,* 101 U.S. 99, 103, 25 L. Ed. 841 (1880).

3. *Further Consideration of Bowers Dissent.* There may be another path to the dissenting conclusion. Section 117(a) gives "the owner of a copy of a computer program" the right, *inter alia,* to make a copy or adaptation "as an essential step in the utilization of a computer program in conjunction with a machine." 17 U.S.C. § 117(a)(1). This statute may contemplate reverse engineering as such a "utilization," but we must answer two questions before reaching that conclusion. First, is copying or adapting a copy for purposes of reverse engineering the type of "utilization" that Congress contemplated? Second, if so, can the software vendor deprive a licensee of the benefit of these statutory rights by contract, either by denying the licensee the status of copy "owner" that is a threshold condition of applying § 117(a), or by narrowing the type of "utilization" permitted to exclude reverse engineering?

If a license contract could limit the type of "utilization" permissible under § 117(a)(1) to that permitted or contemplated by the licensor, the statutory rights wouldn't be worth much, would they? Wouldn't they then simply be redundant, duplicating the terms of the license agreement? The Fifth Circuit has interpreted the "archival copy" permission in § 117(a)(2) liberally, but it did not specifically address the "utilization" permission now in § 117(a)(1). *See Vault Corp. v. Quaid Software Ltd.,* 847 F.2d 255, 266–67 (5th Cir. 1988). Does either the majority or dissent in *Bowers* address the statutory scope of that permission?

The second question is whether a licensor can render § 117(a) inapplicable by saying (usually in a form agreement) that the licensee is not an "owner of a copy" as § 117(a) requires. Does either the majority or dissent in *Bowers* answer this question?

Does the majority in *Bowers* adequately address the impact of § 117(a) on licensees' rights? Has § 117(a) become a virtual dead letter because no one knows who "an owner of a copy" is and what "utilization" means? Or is § 117 a sleeping charter of users' rights just waiting to awaken for judicial vindication?

4. *Pre-emption and the First Sale Doctrine.* Can intellectual property owners use standard click-wrap license terms to nullify statutory limitations on the rights of copyright owners the Copyright Act? For example, can the first sale doctrine (codified in 17 U.S.C. § 109(a)) contract terms circumvent, as Judge Dyk explains in his principal example in

*Baystate?* By licensing the use of copies of software, rather than selling the software, owners attempt to avoid the restrictions of § 109(a) and prohibit the transfer of copies. In *Softman Products, LLC v. Adobe Systems, Inc.*, 171 F. Supp. 2d 1075 (C.D. Cal. 2001), the court rejected the defendant's characterization of the transaction as a "license" and looked to the facts surrounding the transaction to conclude that the transaction was actually a "sale." Therefore, the court held that the software license term prohibiting the transfer of copies did not apply to downstream transfers under the first sale doctrine. Do you agree with the court's characterization of the transaction?

# V. Other Issues in Online Contracting

## Online Contracting*

Gary Hood & Ben Foster
*in* 9 Business Law & the Internet (IICLE 2002)

* * *

### III. SATISFYING "WRITING" AND "SIGNATURE" REQUIREMENTS

Aside from the offer and acceptance requirements for contract formation, other potential barriers to electronic contracting are the various statutory "writing" and "signature" requirements imposed on certain types of contracts (collectively referred to as the statute of frauds). A strict interpretation of the statute of frauds would indicate that the "writing requirement" is not satisfied, for example, if parties negotiate an agreement via e-mail or instant messaging. *See CompuServe, Inc. v. Patterson*, 89 F.3d 1257, 1260–61 (6th Cir. 1996) (involving contract negotiations by e-mail between software developer and Internet subscriber service). Unless the final terms are printed out, the contract would exist only in computer memory and would not contain an ink signature of either party.

#### A. Judicial Uncertainty

Prior to the passage of electronic signature legislation, courts struggled to broadly construe "writing" requirements to avoid the strict application of the statute of frauds to invalidate electronic contracts. While the Ninth Circuit has held that loading software from a disk into a computer's memory constitutes "fixation in a tangible medium" for intellectual property purposes (*see MAI Systems Corp. v. Peak Computer, Inc.*, 991 F.2d 511, 518–19 (9th Cir. 1993)), this reasoning was not extended to apply to the statute of frauds. In *In re RealNetworks, Inc.*, Privacy Litigation, No. 00 C 1366, 2000 WL 631341 at *3 (N.D. Ill. May 8, 2000), the district court ruled that the click-through online software license agreement satisfied the writing requirement and adopted a case-by-case approach to future cases, reasoning as follows:

> Because electronic communications can be letters or characters formed on the screen to record or communicate ideas by visible signs and can be legible characters that represent words and letters as well as form the conveyance of meaning, it would seem that the plain meaning of the word "written" does

---

* Reprinted with permission of the authors and the publisher, copyright 2002.

not exclude all electronic communications. That being said, the Court does not now find that all electronic communications may be considered "written." Rather, the Court examines the contract at issue in this action and finds that its easily printable and storable nature is sufficient to render it "written."

## B. Legislative Responses

In response to the uncertainty in court decisions and pressure from the business community, many states and more recently the federal government have enacted legislation that has largely removed the statute of frauds as a significant legal barrier to e-commerce. The states have taken three general approaches to electronic contracting legislation.

A small minority of states enacted laws that guarantee enforceability of electronic contracts only if the electronic communications are created and transmitted using a public key infrastructure (PKI) based encryption and authentication technology. PKI is the leading standards-based digital signature technology, involving the use of two mathematically related cryptographic keys, referred to as a "private key" and a "public key." The private key is kept secret by the key holder and is used to encrypt information, which can be decrypted only with that key holder's public key. The PKI-encrypted message is considered "digitally signed" by the private key holder. Because the private key is unique to a specific key holder, digital signatures reduce the chance of unauthorized or forged electronic communications.

Other states adopted a technology-neutral approach ultimately incorporated into the Uniform Electronic Transactions Act (UETA) (see below), which merely equates electronically stored documents with written documents and provides that the intent to authenticate a document is the key element of a "signature," regardless of whether such intent was manifested electronically or otherwise.

A third group of states, led by Illinois (see the Electronic Commerce Security Act (ECSA), 5 ILCS 175/1-101, et seq.), adopted a blended approach that is technologically neutral as to the elimination of the statute of frauds barrier but provides a set of (mostly rebuttable) evidentiary presumptions afforded only to electronic contracts created and transmitted using a PKI-based technology. In light of UETA (which is currently under consideration in Illinois) and the federal E-SIGN legislation (see below), this chapter does not discuss the ECSA in detail. For a thorough discussion of the ECSA, see R. J. Robertson, Jr., and Thomas J. Smedinghoff, *Illinois Law Enters Cyberspace: The Electronic Commerce Security Act*, 87 Ill. B.J. 308 (June 1999).

This lack of uniformity among the states conflicted with the need for certainty in e-commerce laws and resulted in the preparation of UETA and, ultimately, the enactment of federal E-SIGN legislation. UETA is a model act drafted and approved by the National Conference of Commissioners on Uniform State Laws, which provides that a record or a signature "may not be denied legal effect or enforceability solely because it is in electronic form." UETA § 7(a). UETA is technology neutral in that a signature can be "an electronic sound, symbol, or process attached to or logically associated with a record and executed or adopted by a person with the intent to sign the record." UETA § 2(7). Finally, UETA leaves contracting parties free to require more secure types of authentication or particular technologies when they mutually agree to do so.

Although 37 states and the District of Columbia have adopted UETA in some form, many states moved slowly in the process. Others, like Illinois, are presently considering the uniform legislation. In 2000, Congress passed legislation to bring down the barriers to e-commerce in interstate commerce and ensure that slow-moving states would not continue to delay the process. Effective October 1, 2000, the Electronic Signatures in Global and National Commerce Act (E-SIGN), 15 U.S.C. §7001, et seq., confirms that electronic contracts satisfy "writing" and "signature" requirements while retaining other evidentiary requirements applicable to standard contracts. E-SIGN is drafted to work in conjunction with UETA or alternative state statutes that are consistent with E-SIGN such as the ECSA. In order to encourage consistency between E-SIGN and the various state laws, E-SIGN preempts state laws that are not either (1) enactments of UETA or (2) consistent with E-SIGN and not technology specific (i.e., that do not accord greater legal status to various forms of digital signatures). In light of this provision, the states that adopted legislation directed solely at PKI-based digitally signed documents are clearly preempted. It is debatable, however, whether Illinois' ECSA evidentiary presumptions in favor of PKI-based digital signatures render the ECSA "technology specific" for purposes of § 101 of E-SIGN (15 U.S.C. § 7001) as that section relates only to the enforceability of electronic contracts and not evidentiary concerns. Nevertheless, after the enactment of E-SIGN, the Illinois legislature has introduced UETA for consideration.

Like UETA, E-SIGN gives electronic contracts the same legal standing as traditional paper documents while retaining the formal writing and/or signature requirements for certain sensitive documents such as wills, eviction notices, court orders, notices of suspension of utilities, product recall notices, and documents pertaining to hazardous materials. Consumers must give prior consent to receiving online documents and must have the right to opt out of using electronic contracting and receive agreements in paper form at any time. Furthermore, firms seeking to restrict transactions to an "electronic-only" format are required to "reasonably demonstrate" that customers have the computer equipment to receive documents electronically. Companies must disclose to consumers their right to receive information in nonelectronic form.

## IV. EVIDENTIARY CONCERNS

In addition to the traditional requirements of offer and acceptance and the potential legal barrier imposed by the statute of frauds, the party seeking to enforce an electronic contract must be prepared to prove the existence of the online contract, the date it was agreed on, and the identity of the other contracting party. Without an appropriate technology solution for capturing, retaining, time-stamping, authenticating, and accessing both the text of the contract and the facts surrounding its assent by the contracting party, it may be impossible for a party seeking to enforce such an agreement to meet its burden of proof. In circumstances in which the likelihood and/or consequences of fraud are high, the use of a digital signature or comparable technology solution should be considered. Although aside from Illinois' ECSA and a few similar state statutes (which may be preempted by E-SIGN, as discussed in § 9.11 above) there are no statutory evidentiary presumptions that result from using such technology, the evidentiary burden with such technologies would be much more easily satisfied and practically uncontestable.

## V. CONCLUSIONS AND SUGGESTIONS FOR PRACTITIONERS

Electronic contracts are becoming a standard course of dealing in some industries and are likely to achieve widespread commercial acceptance in most areas of commerce.

Recently, the law has begun to catch up to this business reality and has removed many of the potential legal barriers to electronic contracting. That said, practitioners must pay special attention to the application of traditional contract principles to electronic contracts and recommend approaches that balance the level of risk to the client with the commercial reality of the need for readable and relatively unobtrusive but enforceable online agreements.

## PRACTICE POINTERS

In light of the principles discussed in this chapter, practitioners should consider making the following recommendations when structuring and/or advising clients on the enforceability of electronic contracts.

If technologically and commercially feasible, use a click-through mechanism...that requires users to scroll through the text of an online agreement and to click on a box that says "I Agree" (or similar words) in order to manifest assent to those terms.

Verify that no industry-specific laws or regulations impose unique requirements on your client's online agreements (such as in the health care industry).

Review the contract language as it appears online in order to ensure that any provisions that must be conspicuous (e.g., warranty disclaimers, consent to exclusive venue and jurisdiction, etc.) appear appropriately capitalized and/or otherwise highlighted so as to stand out from the other terms of the contract.

Include an option for users to print the agreement and access it online after their initial click-through.

Ensure that the links to such online agreements and other legal notices are prominently and logically displayed within the site, preferably placed "above the fold" (i.e., without the need to scroll).

Verify that your client uses technology to capture and store information about when, how, and by whom each user's assent to the contract(s) occurred.

When security is of paramount concern, consider using an encryption/authentication solution such as PKI digital signature technology to authenticate users and protect the integrity of information.

* * *

---

# VI. The Open Code Movement

## Open Source Software Licensing:
## Using Copyright Law to Encourage Free Use*
Natasha T. Horne
17 Ga. St. U.L. Rev. 863 (2001)

Introduction.

The open source movement is gaining widespread attention due to a number of recent developments in the computer software industry. With these recent developments, it is no wonder that the term "open source software," or "free software," has become one of the hottest buzz words in the computer industry. The computer industry continues to evolve at amazing and unprecedented speed. The Internet has, in a very short amount of time, gone mainstream. But with this fast-paced development and with the increased use and acceptance of computers, the software industry struggles to meet the demands of its users. Users seek rapid releases, easy customization, and quick bug fixes. Some critics believe that today's software industry cannot survive in this fast-paced marketplace without making some revolutionary changes. Their answer? Open Source Software. Part I of this Note reviews the history and philosophies of the open source movement. Part II discusses the roles copyright and software licensing play in open source software development. Part III examines the licensing terms of several popular open source licenses used today. Part IV provides a few pointers for selecting a license. Finally, Part V suggests that the open source movement may be disproving the need for financial incentives under copyright law.

## I. What Is the Open Source Movement?

### A.What Is "Open Source"?

Unknown to most, the open source movement has been around for decades since the beginning of the development of the UNIX platform. However, only recently has the term gained attention through the growing popularity of several open source projects and through the increasing popularity of the Internet. The open source movement revolves around the notion of making software "open source," or in other words, making source code freely available to anyone. The word "open" refers to making source code freely available to other developers so that they can enhance the software, modify the code, or fix software bugs and glitches. The word "source" refers to source code. Source code consists of statements written by a software programmer in a programming language, such as C, C++, Pascal, Fortran, Java, or Basic. These statements instruct the computer as to what commands to process. Software tools convert source code into object code. It is actually the object code that the computer executes and understands. However, it is very difficult for humans to read or modify this code. Historically, companies have made software available to third parties only in object code form. Companies view their source code as intellectual property, or as a trade secret, and therefore, rarely release it to third parties. In the event a company does decide to release the source code, it releases it under very strict licensing terms. The Open Source Movement hopes to change this proprietary way of thinking.

### B. What Is the Open Source Movement?

The open source movement comprises a community consisting primarily of developers and organizations interested in revolutionizing the software industry. The movement believes that in order for the software industry to meet the demands of this rapidly changing marketplace efficiently, developers must make source code freely, or openly, available. The open source development model suggests several advantages. First, allowing everyone to view and modify the source code results in higher quality software and rapid innovation. Users from around the world can easily participate in the development and testing of a software product via the Internet or e-mail. The community places great value in the high level of expertise possessed by the developers who

---

* Reprinted with permission of the publisher, copyright 2001

write, modify, and enhance the code. Further, through this collaboration, the product will develop quickly and efficiently. In contrast to a proprietary development model, no schedules govern development under the open source model. For example, as the need for increased functionality arises, any developer can implement code from around the world at any time without prior permission from the owner of the code. Also, by making source code open for the world to use, modify, and reuse, developers can use any other developer's enhancements and modifications to the code when they have a need for similar functionality. On the other hand, the open source development model has several shortcomings. First, no one entity maintains control over common development issues, such as compatibility. This commonly leads to fragmentation, also called "forking." Fragmentation results when multiple varying versions of a software package emerge in the marketplace. These varying versions can easily confuse consumers. Further, there is no organization responsible for the product. This could present problems when software bugs are too difficult for the user to fix and too low a priority for anyone else to fix. Also, development under this model can be "chaotic and undirected." Development depends solely on the interest of the developers and is rarely managed by one organization or individual. Finally, in an open source model, "there are limited financial incentives for improvements and innovations." Often, the developers volunteer their time and participate only in their spare time. It is noteworthy, however, that there are differing theories on how "open" open source should be. For example, should a developer who has modified or enhanced open source software be required to give these modifications or enhancements back to the open source community? Should proprietary code that has been combined with open source code fall under the open source licensing terms? When developing software under an open source development model, it is essential to select a license that corresponds with one's theory of open source development.

## II. Open Source Software Licensing.

Because software is very easy to copy but very "difficult and expensive to create," it is important to protect software through copyright law. The Copyright Act of 1976 (hereinafter "the Act") allows a software developer to retain control over the use of his work, and it protects his software code from unlawful copying and distribution. Copyright offers "an inexpensive means of protecting... software from unauthorized copying and misappropriation." In 1980, Congress amended the Act to include copyright protection for computer programs. Under the Act, computer programs are considered "literary works" and are protected from unauthorized copying. The legislative history of section 102(b) makes clear that the "expression" adopted by the programmer is the copyrightable element in a computer program; the actual processes or methods embodied in the program are not within the protectable scope of copyright law. Copyright protects all forms of computer code and may also extend to program design documentation, including schematics and flowcharts; user manuals and software documentation; the structure, sequencing, and organization of the code; and the program's user interface. Copyright also extends to new material that the author adds to a previously existing work. For example, a derivative work may include an updated version of an existing program or a translation of a program to another language platform. Once a work is copyrighted, the author has secured a bundle of exclusive rights. Under section 106, these rights include the right to reproduce the work; the right to create "derivative works" based on the work; the right to distribute copies of the work to the public by sale, license, or lease; the right to perform the work publicly; and the right to display the work publicly. Although registration of a copyright is not required, it is beneficial. Once registered, an author is "presumed the owner of the copyright in the material deposited with the registration." The information submitted with the copyright registration form is presumed to be true in the absence of proof to the contrary. If the author registers his work before infringement or within three months of publishing, and the author prevails in an infringement suit, he receives two additional benefits. First, in the event of litigation, the court can order the infringer to pay attorney's fees and court costs. Second, the author may elect to have the court award statutory damages up to $100,000 per infringement without having to establish damages actually suffered. Infringement occurs when someone "exploits one or more of the... owner's exclusive rights without...permission." This usually involves the unauthorized reproduction or distribution of the work, or the unauthorized creation of derivative works based on it.

## A. Licensing Generally.

When an owner of a work "decides to transfer to one or more people the use and enjoyment of part or all of his 'bundle of legal rights,'" yet wishes to retain ownership of these rights, he uses a license. The license "defines the nature and extent of [the granted] permission." Normally, the original owner of the bundle of rights grants the license. Sometimes, however, a license allows a licensee to grant sub-licenses.

## B. Proprietary Software Licensing.

In a proprietary software development model, code is first copyrighted and then distributed under a license agreement that gives its users special rights. Proprietary licenses usually restrict software to execute-only format and limit the number of installations allowed per copy of software. Generally, only those users who have [licensed] the software can use it. Further, as mentioned above, a developer or a developing organization rarely makes its source code available. When it is made available by the software developer, it is usually at an extra charge, and it is only made available for limited purposes. Licensing agreements in a proprietary market help the owners preserve their market share, obtain the maximum return on each transaction, and safeguard intellectual property rights.

## C. Open Source Software Licensing.

Ironically, licensing and copyright law are central to the open source movement, as well. Licensing is essential in allowing the original developer to maintain control over the future free use of his source code and to license away rights normally protected by copyright law. Once an open source developer has copyrighted his code, thereby establishing property rights in the code, he will use licensing terms that carry out his desired open source development model.

## D. Open Source Licensing Terms.

As mentioned above, licensing terms will vary depending on a developer's theory on how "open" his open source software should be. Developers should thoroughly review the terms in the licensing agreement before they begin working on an open source project or before they select a license to govern their work. The following paragraphs highlight a few common licensing terms used in various open source development models.

### 1. Code Cannot Be Used in Proprietary or Commercial Software.

Some licenses may restrict the use of open source code in proprietary or commercial software. Developers who voluntarily release code to the general public without having received financial return may want to use a license to keep companies or individuals from reaping the financial benefits of their efforts.

### 2. Author's Attribution and Integrity.

Many developers who work on open source projects volunteer their work in exchange for the recognition and reputation well-written code gives them within the development community. Therefore, developers often seek licensing terms that require future licensees to acknowledge them in derived works that use their code. Licensees may be able to meet this requirement by retaining copyright notices on the code as they pass it on or modify it. The license may also require that the licensee label the derivative work with a different version number, or that he distribute the source code unmodified along with a mechanism that combines the code with any future modifications when the software is compiled for use by the computer. This way, the original code remains intact, and future licensees do not attribute later modifications to the original developer. Licenses may also prohibit the use of the name of the author of given code to endorse or promote products derived from that code.

### 3. Forced Distribution.

Licenses often contain terms that require future developers who modify or enhance open source code to return their modifications and enhancements to the open source community. Allowing a licensee to modify the source code or fix bugs without returning the modifications or enhancements to the public is often thought to counter several of the advantages of developing code under an open source model, such as the benefit of rapid product enhancement through collaboration.

### 4. Forced Use of the Same License.

Some licenses require that works derived from the source code be subject to the same licensing terms of the original license. The Open Source Movement [uses this approach] to protect the openness of the source code and to keep the original author's licensing wishes intact.

### 5. Distribution of Source Code.

Open access to the source code is fundamental to the Open Source Movement because it allows for easy repair and modification of a program. Thus, some licenses require that the licensee distribute software with its source code. If a developer cannot distribute a product with its source code, then usually the license requires that the developer give a well-known (or well-advertised) means of obtaining the source code without additional charge (excluding non-content-based distribution fees).

### 6. Unencumbered Redistribution of Derivative Works.

At the heart of the Open Source Movement is the notion that licensees should be freely able to view, modify, and reuse the original source code. Thus, licenses usually explicitly grant licensees the right to create derivative works without first acquiring permission or paying royalties. Further, the license usually explicitly permits the licensee to distribute the software built from modified or derivative source code. However, licenses differ on whether the developer must make the source code of derivative works available.

### 7. No Warranties.

Most open source licenses require that licensees accept the software "as is." This shifts the risk away from the code developer to the user. If open source developers were required to assume liability for defects in their code, they would be less willing to contribute code voluntarily or without cost. The need to deflect risk may lead to the incorporation of additional contractual terms to standard open source licenses. For example, choice of law and choice of venue clauses may become more important as certain jurisdictions make it more difficult to disclaim warranties, limit liability, or enforce standard-form agreements.

### 8. Self-Perpetuating License Terms.

Licenses often require that the licensing terms apply to everyone to whom the software is redistributed. They also require that licensees pass on the licensing terms unaltered to subsequent licensees. This keeps the licensing terms (and the intent of the original developer) intact.

### 9. Non-Discrimination and Non-Contamination.

Some open source licenses require that the licensee not discriminate against any individual or group, and that it not restrict the use of the software in a particular field or endeavor. Further, they often require that the license not place restrictions on or apply to separate software programs, such as proprietary software, that has been distributed along with the open source code.

## III. Open Source Licenses.

Several examples of open source software licenses exist on the Internet. Before selecting a license or contributing to an open source project, it is important that the developer understand the licensing terms and restrictions of the agreement. The following sections compare and contrast the most popular open source licenses that are available on the Internet.

### A.    The GNU General Public License (GPL).

The fundamental goal of the Free Software Foundation (hereinafter "FSF") is to keep free software "free" or, in other words, to allow anyone to use, modify, and distribute original software code and any derived versions thereof freely. In order to accomplish this, the FSF has developed a licensing theory called "copyleft" (which is a pun on copyright). Under this theory, the GPL allows a user to copy, modify, and distribute GPL'd code, so long as the user agrees to pass on to other users these licensing rights unimpaired with all derivative versions of the code. Therefore, anyone who develops software based on code licensed under the GPL must grant the public free use, modification, and distribution of the derived work. Thus, if the developer uses GPL'd code in a proprietary program containing proprietary source code, then the developer must make available the proprietary source code under the terms of the GPL, unless the sections not derived from the GPL'd code can be reasonably considered, and are distributable, as independent and separate works. This "tainting effect" may pose problems for commercial entities, such as Netscape, that are considering converting proprietary software into an open source product that includes either a third party technology or that shares source code with other products that they are not converting to open source.

In addition to agreeing not to establish proprietary rights in the software itself, or in subsequent versions thereof, and to pass on changes and modifications to the software, users must agree to provide the source code to anyone [to whom] they give the object code. Therefore, developers must ensure that anyone who receives the software from them in object code form has unconditional access to the source code. A developer can meet this requirement by distributing the software with the source code or by providing instructions on how to access the source code. Further, developers must include notices of the GPL in the software. Thus, all source files must show notice of the application of the GPL to the code and any derived works. Any modified and distributed version of the software must also indicate that it is not the original and must provide the above notices on the computer screen during program execution. Finally, licensees must accept the software without warranties of any kind. A licensee accepts the terms of the license by modifying or distributing the program's source code (or the source code of a derived work). Additionally, any attempt to copy, distribute, or sub-license the code under terms not expressly provided for in the GPL will automatically terminate one's rights under the license.

B.    The Berkeley Software Distribution License (BSD).

The BSD license, first used for the Berkeley Software Distribution of Unix, is known to be the least restrictive of the open source licenses available today. The license is unlike the GPL in many ways. The BSD license grants unlimited rights to use and distribute modified or unmodified source and binary code, provided that the licensee has met a number of conditions. First, licensees must agree to keep intact the copyright notices, licensing terms, and disclaimer of warranties with each distribution of the source code. Similarly, when distributing the code in binary form, licensees must reproduce the copyright notices, licensing terms, and disclaimer of warranties in the documentation and other materials distributed with the code. Lastly, the BSD license restricts licensees from using the name of the university, or the names of its contributors, to endorse or promote derivative works without prior permission. Unlike the GPL and most other open source licenses, the BSD license does not require that any modifications or enhancements of the original code be contributed back to the open source community. Similarly, the BSD license does not contain any provisions that keep licensees from making the code proprietary. Though many open source advocates prefer licenses that require licensees to provide source code of derivative works back to the open source community, the BSD license may be an appropriate option for commercial entities because it avoids the "tainting effect" of the GPL and provides licensees the option of making their enhancements and modifications proprietary.

C.    The Aladdin License.

The Aladdin license resembles the GPL but provides additional restrictions. First, the license explicitly prohibits a commercial organization from accepting money for the software, except in limited circumstances to cover the costs of distribution of the code. Second, licensees may not distribute a "free" version of the software in a distribution medium containing paid-for software. As long as the licensee complies with the restrictions of the Aladdin license and distributes an unmodified copy of the license with the code (though license modifications may include a description of the licensed work and the law of the country where the work was created), the licensee may freely copy and distribute literal copies, modified copies, or derived versions of the software's source code throughout the world, in any medium. As mentioned above, the Aladdin license explicitly restricts distribution of the program or any derivative works by a commercial organization to a third party if it receives payment in connection with the distribution. The license allows distribution fees as long as the fees are not content-dependent. Also, the software must be distributed independent of any other product or service and may not be distributed in a medium containing paid-for software.

D.    The Mozilla Public License (MPL) and the Netscape Public License (NPL).

In March 1998, Netscape announced its plan to release its source code for the Netscape Communicator and to implement an open source strategy. Specifically, Netscape announced two reasons for releasing the Communicator source code. First, using an open source development model will result in a higher quality, more full-featured product due to increased scrutiny of the code and the expansion of the developer community. Second, releasing the source code will encourage other developers to use Netscape technology in their own products, perhaps resulting in more user accessibility and broader platform support. The MPL and the NPL, authored by Netscape Communications, strike a balance between the BSD license and the GPL. In developing these licenses, Netscape attempted "to strike a middle ground between promoting free source development by commercial enterprises and protecting free source developers." These licenses were implemented in order to ensure that developers return their modifications to the open source community, and they assist Netscape in retaining specific rights that allow it to continue proprietary development of other packages and maintain existing contracts with third parties. These licenses serve as a good model for any commercial company looking to develop an open source product, to convert a proprietary product to open source, or to make open source extensions or additions to proprietary products.

1. MPL.

Similar to the GPL, the MPL requires that licensees make modified or new files freely and publicly available in source code form. Unlike the GPL, however, one interesting aspect of the MPL is that it allows developers to distribute their own files with "covered files" (any software or code that is covered by the MPL) under any licensing terms, provided that the developer has not modified the actual covered files. Thus, the licensee need not make the source code for a proprietary work available even if the work contains unmodified MPL'd code. However, if the licensee has modified the covered files, then the developer must distribute the derived work under the open source MPL terms. Modifications to the software include: (1) changing anything within one of the files contained in the source code, (2) placing excerpts of source code from one of the files into a new file, or (3) renaming a file or combining two or more files contained in the source code. However, adding a new file that does not contain any of the original source code or subsequent modified code is not a modification and does not fall under the terms of the MPL. This is true even if the new file is referenced by changes made in the source code, although those changes constitute a modification. However, the licensee must make changes to the MPL-covered source code freely available. Additionally, the MPL contains several terms that protect the project and its developers against patent issues surrounding code that has been contributed to the project. It basically requires that all contributors release all patent rights that may be exposed by the code. This prevents people from contributing patented code to the project and then later attempting to collect patent fees for the use of the code. Note, however, that this does not prevent anyone from contributing code for which someone else owns a patent. One commentator has criticized this waiver clause because it requires the waiver of patent claims to the entire Mozilla code, not just to the specific code that has been contributed by the developer. Another interesting addition to this license is the legal.txt file that must accompany all distributions. The text file covers several issues, including liability, arbitration, and included code under dispute, under a patent, or under another limiting license. Netscape decided that these issues should be clearly disclosed so that each developer can understand the issues surrounding the code to the greatest extent possible.

### 2. NPL.

The NPL, a variation of the MPL, is used specifically with the Netscape Communicator source code. Netscape needed a separate license for the Communicator source code to protect existing contracts still in force that govern shared source code with other proprietary products, and that govern the licensing of source code to third parties. Thus, the NPL comprises the terms of the MPL but grants Netscape two additional rights. First, the license grants Netscape the right to use code licensed under the NPL in other products without having those products fall under the NPL. Second, the license grants Netscape the right to re-license source code that falls under the NPL, including any additions made by non-Netscape developers, to third parties under terms other than those in the NPL.

### E. Sun's Community Source License (SCSL).

Sun has distinguished its license from other open source licenses by calling it a "community source" license. The community source development model differs from the open source development model in two significant ways. First, Sun requires and enforces compatibility among released versions of the software, and second, Sun allows proprietary modifications and extensions to the software. Sun created community source development principles to blend the best aspects of the proprietary and open source license models. Its primary goal in implementing this model is to balance the need of an organization to innovate rapidly while maintaining proprietary advantages. Sun recognizes several advantages in using this model. First, it protects a developer's intellectual property rights in his software. While a developer must give "error corrections...back to the community, [his] other modifications can remain proprietary...." Further, unlike under a pure open source model, a single organization is responsible for the original code base. Therefore, the "infrastructure...of the original code and the upgrades to it are owned by the developing organization" and are shared. However, the community may contribute its modifications and grant rights to the community for use of the modifications. By keeping control over the source code, Sun ensures compatibility among the varying versions of software. All internally distributed code must pass test suites. The license requires commercial distributors "to use relatively recent upgraded code" and to pass the test suites. For extensions to the code, the license requires the community members to supply their specifications and test suites. However, like the open source model, no central organization sets development schedules and priorities. Further, innovation and releases are not subject to a schedule, though the code must first pass a conformance suite. In order to implement this model, Sun has established two different levels of licenses: the Research Use license and the Commercial Use license.

The Research Use license is a click-wrap license available on the Internet, while the Commercial Use license must actually be signed and executed by both the developer and Sun. The actual licensing terms are likely to vary for each technology or product. Therefore, for the purpose of this Note, the following paragraphs will discuss generally the terms of the Sun Community Source License Version 3.0 JINI Technology Specific

Attachment v. 1.0 (hereinafter "Jini license"). The Research Use license primarily grants all licensees the royalty-free rights to use, reproduce, and modify the original and upgraded source code for research; to distribute copies to other licensees and students; and to use test kits to develop and test code. Error corrections must be returned to the community, must carry notices that the code is subject to the terms of SCSL, and must be distributed with a file that documents the changes made. Other modifications, such as performance enhancements, adaptations, and extensions, may remain proprietary. However, interfaces to these modifications must be open and specified. Once the technology has been evaluated and adopted by the community under the Research Use license, the code can be released internally (within the licensee's business or organization) or externally under the Commercial Use license.

The Commercial Use license grants the licensee the right to reproduce and distribute compliant code that passes certain test suites and conforms to certain specifications. Depending on the technology licensed, some models require that royalties, trademark fees, or both, be paid to Sun under the Commercial Use license. Before commercial distribution, the license must be signed and executed by Sun and the licensee, and the product must pass certain compatibility tests. In some cases, products distributed under this license must carry the appropriate Sun logo, requiring the execution of a separate trademark licensing agreement with Sun. Similar to the open source licenses discussed above, the SCSL provides a disclaimer of warranties and a limitation of liability clause. Further, it also includes terms that prohibit the licensee from challenging Sun's ownership or use of Sun trademarks, from attempting to register any Sun trademarks, and from incorporating any Sun trademarks into his own trademarks, product names, service marks, company names, or domain names.

Sun's implementation of its community source model has received mixed reviews from the open source community. However, the license provides an interesting example of how commercial entities can take advantage of the benefits of developing under an open source model while still maintaining proprietary advantages.

## IV. Selecting a License.

A developer should carefully review licensing terms before selecting a license to govern his code or before contributing code to an open source project. At a minimum, a license should include a disclaimer of warranties to protect open source contributors from liability. The absence of such a disclaimer would potentially discourage open source developers from contributing code because of the risk of liability. Further, in order to ensure that all derivations of the code will fall under the same licensing terms, the developer will need self-perpetuating licensing terms in the license. A developer must also ensure that the license is carefully drafted to grant him the rights to use, copy, modify, and distribute the original code, rights normally protected by copyright law. Then, the developer should review the license to ensure that it reflects his open source development model. Questions regarding whether future contributors must give their modifications back to the open source community, whether fees can be charged for the distribution of the code, and whether copyright notices must be prominently displayed should guide the developer in making this decision and must be answered before the appropriate license can be selected.

## V. The Open Source Movement-Tipping the Balance in Favor of Free Use?

The fundamental goal of the United States' intellectual property regime is to balance free access to information...on the one hand, and the encouragement of investment in innovation through the exclusive rights of...copyright...laws on the other hand.

Nonetheless, copyright law effectively gives authors a monopoly in their work. However, some scholars have reasoned that society would still develop socially useful works in the absence of financial incentives. They argue that simple personal satisfaction, the quest for respect and esteem, and the power of convention also induce society to create. Critics also question whether awarding rights in a work for the life of the author plus seventy years provides any additional incentive to create. The Open Source Movement appears to dispel the need for such financial incentives to encourage creativity. By making the source code available to anyone to use, modify, enhance, and redistribute, the movement is effectively encouraging productivity. Developers from around the world collaborate to create a more reliable, robust product. Moreover, open source software development is more in tune with the needs of society. Most importantly, anyone can reuse code to create additional beneficial products. Nonetheless, the Open Source Movement must rely on copyright protection and software licensing to effect its development model. Without protection, developers would not have control over the future free use and dissemination of their code.

Conclusion

Though many theories exist on how "open" open source software should be, one thing is certain: copyright protection and software licensing are essential in implementing any open source development model. Developers and commercial entities should thoroughly review licensing terms before contributing to any open source project or selecting an open source license for their work. These terms will dictate, for example, to what extent licensees are encouraged or required to return enhancements and modifications to the open source community, to what extent derived works are governed by the license, whether prior contributors must be acknowledged in works using their code, and whether open source code may be combined or distributed with proprietary software. Further, depending on its terms, an open source license can be an effective means of taking advantage of the benefits of developing under an open source model, while at the same time attending to commercial business needs (such as the development of proprietary products in addition to open source products) or retaining certain rights in the code.

---

# Linux Users Risk Infringement*

Bradley C. Wright

13 INTELL. PROP. & TECH. L.J. 1 (2001)

Companies have for many years relied on commercially available operating systems to power their computers and computer-related products. Most computers are sold with pit-installed operating systems that allow the computers to be used immediately after opening the box. The cost of the operating system is generally included in the cost of the computer. Users who want to upgrade to a different or newer version of the operating system generally must purchase the upgraded or different operating system as a separate product. Examples of commercially available operating systems include Solaris (Sun Microsystems), Windows (Microsoft), Mac OS (Apple Computer), UNIX (various companies), OS/2 (IBM), and others.

---

Regardless of whether the operating system was purchased with the computer or was installed by the user, the features and capabilities of the operating system are determined by the company that developed the operating system. Although the user can install new application programs on the computer, there is generally no easy way for the user to modify the operating system itself.

In recent years, the Linux operating system has started competing with commercially available operating systems. Originally developed by Linus Torvalds in the early 1990s, Linux is referred to as "open source" software because its source code (*i.e.,* human-readable computer instructions) is freely available and can be modified to suit a particular user's needs. Linux has been gradually modified over the years by hundreds of independent programmers, each of whom contributed one or more improvements to the original computer code. Although it can be downloaded over the Internet for free, some companies sell prepackaged versions of Linux, including documentation, for a small fee that is still generally less than the cost of buying a commercially available operating system.

Because of its appeal as a "free" operating system, an increasing number of companies, including computer manufacturers IBM and Dell, have begun using and selling computers that incorporate Linux. Proponents believe that Linux is cost-effective because there are no licensing fees and because Linux can be modified to suit a particular user's needs. Although many people refer to Linux as being "free" there are a number of legal strings attached to its use. Because computer software is protected by copyright law, any copying, modification, or further distribution of Linux must be done only with permission of the copyright owners.

As explained in more detail subsequently, the supposedly "free" Linux is restricted by a license that allows users to use it only if the users make the source code (including any modifications) available to others. Although this seems simple and fair enough, the fine print in the license may also obligate users who distribute Linux in combination with their own software to give away their rights to copyrights and patents in that software. Failure to follow the license provisions exactly also may subject a company to a claim of copyright infringement by any of the hundreds of programmers who contributed to Linux. By using Linux, a company could inadvertently grant licenses to others to freely use software that has been separately developed, copyrighted, or even patented by the company.

## Who Owns Linux?

Because Linus Torvalds created the initial version of Linux (major portions of which remain in today's widely distributed Linux) he owns the copyright to at least parts of Linux. Many different computer programmers also have modified Linux with the intention that their contribution be merged into and distributed with the ever-changing software. Consequently, many of these programmers also have a copyright [interest] in various parts of the Linux operating system. Under principles of copyright law, each of these copyright owners could potentially assert a claim for copyright infringement against anyone who copies, modifies, or further distributes Linux. All of these programmers will be referred to as "upstream contributors" and their rights in their contributions as "upstream rights." These rights may include copyrights and patent rights.

A company that copies, uses, or modifies Linux will be referred to as being "downstream" of all those who made contributions to the particular version of Linux before them. The company will be "upstream" of any later users or contributors who use the company's modified version of Linux. For example, if a computer manufacturer modifies Linux to operate on its computers, it will distribute a modified version of Linux when it sells the computers with the modified Linux. Keeping track of all the potential copyright owners and their respective rights is a seemingly impossible undertaking. Even more troublesome is determining what, if any, copyright infringement damages might be available to a particular copyright owner, given that Linux is generally distributed free of charge (*i.e.*, no lost profits), and given that statutory infringement damages and attorney fees are not available unless the copyright owners register their copyright before infringement begins.

### Open Source Licenses

Richard Stallman, a harsh critic of patenting computer software, started the Free Software Foundation in the 1980s to promote the idea that all software should be free for all to use without restrictions, especially restrictions involving copyrights or patents. (The word "free" in this context refers to the freedom to modify and further distribute the software, rather than nonpecuniary distribution.) One of his earliest projects was to develop a clone of the UNIX operating system that was to be free for all to use. Known as GNU, a recursive acronym for "GNU's Not UNIX," Stallman's software was distributed for others to copy, modify, and distribute.

Although critical of legal restrictions on software, Stallman ironically needed to rely on such restrictions to ensure that his software was freely distributed. This is because under US copyright law, programmers who modify Stallman's software automatically obtain a copyright in the improvements, and further releases of the modified software could subject downstream users to a charge of copyright infringement by those programmers. Assuming that the improvements also were patentable, those programmers might also obtain patent rights in their improvements, subjecting downstream users to patent infringement.

Stallman ensured that his software could continue to be improved and distributed without restriction by distributing it subject to a software license. The license is embedded in the source code released by Stallman, such that anyone reading the code will see it. Referred to as the GNU General Public License or GPL, this license essentially releases downstream users from charges of copyright infringement as long as they agree that their additions and modifications to the software will be made free from any restrictions. The GPL asserts that free programming "is threatened constantly by software patents" and that the license requires that "any patent must be licensed for everyone's free use or not licensed at all."

The GPL, which has been widely incorporated into a multitude of software over the years, can be found at *uiww.gnu.or~q/copyIefl/gpl.html.* A slimmed down variant of this license, known as the GNU Lesser General Public License or Lesser License, is intended for use with special types of software known as libraries. Unfortunately, both licenses are fraught with ambiguities, probably reflecting the fact that a non-lawyer drafted them. More problematically, different variants of so-called open source licenses have cropped up over the years, as different programmers and entities sought to craft their own special restrictions on software. The GNU project's Web site lists dozens of such licenses, some with bizarre names such as "The License of Zope," and attempts to categorize them according to whether they are compatible with GPL.

Much of Linux has been distributed subject to the GPL. Stallman asserts that there are millions of "Linux-based variants of the GNU system" and argues that people should refer to them not as Linux but as "GNU/Linux." According to the Free Software Foundation, the GPL is intended to permit programmers and companies to use the software freely and to modify it, subject to various conditions and obligations. There are, however, many upstream contributors, each of whom may have contributed modifications to any particular version of Linux. This makes it difficult to evaluate whether a particular version of Linux is subject to potentially different and conflicting licenses. Moreover, some upstream contributors may have incorporated another's software into Linux without the right to do so.

Thus, there is a risk that Linux software obtained from any particular source, such as Red Hat Software, may not be fully covered by the GPL license. There is always the possibility that an upstream contributor incorporated modifications that it had no right to incorporate, and had no right to license, or will assert that it had rejected the GPL license terms. Either situation could result in a copyright infringement claim based on parts of Linux that were not licensed. Some third-party vendors, such as Debian, apparently try to ensure that all of their software is licensed under GPL.

The GPL contains a number of clumsily worded terms and conditions that purportedly grant a license to copy, distribute, and modify the software to which it pertains, in this case, Linux. The license imposes a number of duties on the licensee, such as providing notice of any modifications made by the licensee; providing a written offer to distribute a machine-readable copy of the source code; and publishing a copy of the GPL with the code.

Most ominously, the GPL obligates the licensee to automatically grant a no-cost license to the entire world in any new software that is distributed or published by the licensee, if it "in whole or in part contains or is derived from [Linux] or any part thereof." This provision, when read in conjunction with other ambiguous portions of the GPL, could form the basis for quite a bit of mischief. In particular, companies that use, modify, or further distribute Linux may unwittingly give away copyrights and patent rights to other software that "contains or is derived from" any part of Linux. For example, if a company develops a complex computer program that analyzes seismic data for oil exploration purposes that uses a very small utility from a Linux library, the entire computer program apparently will become free for the entire world to use, even if the company had patented or copyrighted that program. This provision of the license gives it an almost virus-like quality—once it attaches to a piece of software, it propagates to any further variations, improvements, or "derived" software.

The GPL contains a confusing definition of "derived" software, on the one hand seemingly equating it with the legal definition of derivative works under copyright law, but on the other hand including any software "containing the Program [Linux] or a portion of it, either verbatim or with modifications and/or translated into another language." Even more confusingly [it includes] software that "in whole or in part contains or is derived from the Program [Linux]." Yet another provision of the license states that "But when you distribute the same sections as part of a whole that is a work based on the Program, the distribution of the whole must be on the terms of this License, whose permissions for other licensees extend to the entire whole, and thus to each and every part regardless of who wrote it." Even a lawyer could not have written a more ambiguous clause. How a court will sort out all these circular and inconsistent definitions is unknown; in the meantime, companies are using Linux and potentially subjecting themselves to these ambiguities. What this means is that a company may not be able to determine with certainty what rights it is giving up if it uses, modifies, or further distributes Linux.

## Avoiding the GPL

Assuming for the moment that the GPL is enforceable in a court of law, one might wonder whether it is possible to avoid its effect by taking certain actions or by inaction.

As most software licenses, the GPL is a contract that is interpreted pursuant to state law. Nevertheless, an essential feature of any contract, including any license, is that a party to a license must manifest assent to the terms of the license. What if a company rejects the terms of the GPL license and uses Linux anyway? For those who merely want to install Linux on a computer and use it without modifying it in any way, there may be a way around the restrictive license provisions, at least as to copyright infringement.

US copyright law allows a copyright owner to prohibit others from: (1) copying the work; (2) preparing derivative works; and (3) distributing copies of the work to the public. Other rights are not directly implicated with respect to computer software. These rights are subject to various limitations, such as the limitation in 17 U.S.C. section 117 that permits the owner of a copy of a computer program to make another copy and to adapt the computer program if the copying or adaptation is essential to using the program in conjunction with a machine. This limitation might benefit a company (*e.g.*, a computer manufacturer) if it were to purchase all of its copies of Linux from another source, such as Red Hat Software. If the sale from Red Hat (or other source) is deemed to make the company the legal owner of each of the copies of the Linux software, then the company could use those legally obtained copies under the provisions of section 117, as long as each individual copy were loaded onto one machine.

The adaptation right in section 117 is subject to the limitation, however, that any adaptations may be transferred to another person or company only with the authorization of the copyright holder. In other words, the right to transfer the legally obtained copy does not the company could not adapt Linux to operate on a particular machine and then transfer the modified Linux to customers under this provision. However, the customers might be able to configure the machines to adapt Linux in a particular manner without running afoul of section 117. There are few court decisions addressing this provision under the copyright statute, thus leading to some uncertainty in its application. Moreover, the provisions of section 117 do not provide a defense to a claim of patent infringement if an upstream contributor has patented an improvement that found its way into Linux.

Nevertheless, it may be possible for a company to reject the GPL and to copy and distribute Linux in the limited manner described without being subjected to a claim of copyright infringement. In that case, many of the risks and obligations under the GPL, discussed subsequently, will be avoided.

### Validity of the GPL Generally

Is the GPL a valid contract that can be enforced against one who violates its provisions or who raises it as a defense in an infringement lawsuit brought by one of the many copyright owners of Linux? No reported court decisions have addressed the validity or effect of this license. Although section 5 of the GPL asserts that merely modifying or distributing software that is subject to the license indicates acceptance of the GPL, a court is not likely to agree with this assertion. The GPL is in the nature of a unilateral contract, because the offer of a license by each "upstream" copyright holder, that is, by each prior contributor to the Linux software, can be accepted by performance under the contract-manifesting acceptance. Merely copying and modifying the software is consistent with acceptance of the GPL, but it is equally consistent with rejection of the GPL by a party intending to infringe or believing that there are no enforceable rights in the software.

A court probably will conclude that both the GPL and the Lesser License are unilateral contracts that can be validly accepted under certain conditions. However, in order to invoke the provisions of the license, a user will need to manifest its assent to one of the licenses by an *affirmative act (e.g.,* by further distributing the Linux software including a notice that the software is covered by one of these licenses). The mere act of copying or using the Linux software, without more, is indistinguishable from an act of copyright infringement and does not constitute acceptance of the license terms.

Conversely, a company could affirmatively reject the GPL by including with any distributed software an affirmative statement that any software modified or further distributed by the company is not subject to the licenses, and that no further license is granted to the modified or further distributed software. (Of course, rejecting the GPL carries its own risks, because it could subject the company to copyright infringement.) Including a notice that the software is distributed under the GPL likely will be considered a manifestation of acceptance of the GPL. Similarly, making source code available in accordance with the terms of the GPL likely will be taken as manifestation of acceptance of the contract.

### Linking Linux Libraries with Application Programs

The Linux software distributed by various vendors includes not only the Linux kernel, but so-called libraries of functions that can be linked and used by application programs. The Lesser License is, apparently intended to cover such situations.

The Lesser License asserts that linking and using the Linux libraries constitutes copyright infringement because it allegedly creates a "derivative work" based on the library. It is doubtful that this definition of "derivative work" will be accepted by a court, particularly because it seems to ignore the provisions of 17 U.S.C. section 117. As explained, the legal owner of a copy of a computer program is entitled to make one copy of that program in order to operate it on the computer. Therefore, assuming that a company owns a legal copy *(i.e.,* it purchases each copy separately) of Linux for each computer that it intends to provide to customers, it seems that the company could link its software to such Linux libraries (which essentially "copies" the linked library routines) without departing from the protections of 17 U.S.C. section 117, and such linked applications could be transferred to customers under 17 U.S.C. section 117(b).

Although there are no reported court decisions on this specific point, it seems that merely linking library subroutines into an application program, even if computer instructions in those library subroutines are modified to operate together with the application program, should not constitute creation of a derivative work.

### Obligations under the GPL

The GPL states that it applies to "most of the Free Software Foundation's software and to any other program whose authors commit to using it?" The following table briefly summarizes the rights granted by the license; the obligations of the licensee; and (as interpreted by this author), the action that will be necessary to constitute an acceptance of the license.

| Rights Granted by license | Obligations of Licensee | Action Necessary to Accept License |
|---|---|---|
| Copy and distribute source code without changes. | Publish on each copy a copyright notice; disclaimer of warranty; GPL notice; and copy of the GPL license. See end of GPL for examples. | Distribute source code including copyright notice; disclaimer of warranty; GPL notice; and copy of the GPL license. |
| Modify code, and copy and distribute modified code. | All of the above, and:<br>1. Place notice in all modified files, indicating change and date of change.<br>2. Must license any new code you distribute that contains or is derived from the original code without charge under terms of GPL.<br>3. If modified code normally prints announcements, must print or display copyright notice, disclaimer of warranty, redistribution rights, and instructions for viewing GPL license.<br>4. Exception: Above duties do not apply to identifiable sections that are not derived from the original code, and that are distributed separately from the original code. | MI of the above, and:<br>1. Distribute modified code with notice indicating change and date of change;<br>2. Indicate that modified code is subject to GPL license; and<br>3. Print or display copyright notice, disclaimer of warranty, redistribution rights, and instructions for viewing GPL, unless code is not interactive. |
| Copy and distribute object or executable code (including unchanged and modified). | All of the above, and any one of the following:<br>1. Distribute machine-readable source code corresponding to the modified object or executable code on a medium; OR<br>2. Distribute written offer, valid for 3 years, to give any third party a machine-readable copy of the corresponding source code; OR<br>3. Distribute offer that you received with the original code to obtain source code (not allowed for commercial distribution). | All of the above, and any one of the following:<br>1. Distribute machine-readable source code corresponding to the modified object or executable code; OR<br>2. Distribute written offer, valid for 3 years, to give any third party a machine-readable copy of the corresponding source code; OR<br>3. Distribute offer that you received with the original code to obtain source code. |

## Obligations under the Lesser License

The Lesser License states that it is intended for use with specially designed software packages, such as libraries, and permits linking of such libraries with non-free programs. The term "library" is defined as a collection of software functions and/or data prepared so as to be conveniently linked with application programs to form executables. The Lesser License also states that a computer program that merely links to libraries is not a "derivative work" of the library, and thus falls outside the scope of the Lesser License. However, according to the Lesser License, when a computer program is linked with the library, it will become an executable that is a derivative of the library, and thus is covered by the license. The table on the following page briefly summarizes the provisions of the Lesser License.

## Risks of Using, Modifying, or Distributing Linux

Many of the ambiguities and potential traps inherent in the GPL and Lesser License have been mentioned. The following describes some of the risks that companies might incur in using, modifying, or redistributing Linux.

First and foremost, a company runs the risk of being sued for copyright infringement for copying, modifying, or further distributing copies of Linux or its constituent parts. This flows naturally from section 106 of the copyright statute, which provides copyright owners with the exclusive right to copy, prepare derivative works, or further distribute copyrighted software. Any of the many originators or contributors of the Linux kernel or libraries could potentially assert a claim for copyright infringement. Although this decidedly is not in the spirit of the "free software" movement, a big enough target that invoked the ire of a group of computer programmers could subject itself to such a lawsuit. Many of these programmers belong to organizations that openly deride and taunt large companies that have software patents or that don't agree with their views. Except for the strategy of using a single purchased copy of Linux on each computer without modification (as discussed supra), the company must rely on the GPL for defense. If the company failed to abide by the GPL provisions exactly, or violated one of the explicit prohibitions in the license that negates the license, the license defense could be completely compromised.

Second, assuming that a company scrupulously abided by the GPL provisions and modified Linux for its use, the company might unwittingly give away its copyrights and patent rights to any of its software that becomes intermingled with Linux or parts of Linux. This flows from the GPL provisions mandating that any modified versions of Linux (and any other computer software that is "derived from" or "contains parts of" Linux), and from the ambiguous nature defining what is "derived from" Linux.

Consequently, a programmer working for the company might unwittingly incorporate a part of "free" Linux software into one of the company's flagship software products, thus unknowingly forfeiting any copyrights or patent rights that the company might have in such products. Some commentators have suggested that this provision could be circumvented by building a wall around the Linux-based programs, such that the company's products do not directly interface with Linux.

Third, a company that abides entirely by the GPL might nevertheless be sued by a copyright owner whose works were improperly incorporated into Linux by an upstream contributor. For example, if a rogue programmer took a copyrighted library function from a third party and incorporated that function into part of Linux, that third party could still come after all Linux users for copyright infringement. In that case, the GPL is of no effect, because that copyright owner never assented to having the copyrighted function incorporated into Linux. In this respect, every downstream user must rely on

| Rights Granted by License | Obligations of Licensee | Action Necessary to Accept License |
|---|---|---|
| Copy and distribute library source code (same as GPL). | Same as GPL, except applies to libraries only. | Same as GPL (see Figure 1), except refers to Lesser License instead of GPL. |
| Modify library code, and copy and distribute modified library code. | All of the above, *and*:<br><br>1. Must only modify library in such a way that it remains a library.<br><br>2. Place notice in all modified files, indicating change and date of change.<br><br>3. Modified library must be licensed at no charge to all third parties under terms of Lesser License.<br><br>4. If a library function refers to an application program for data or function, the library function must still function in the event the application does not supply the data or function. | All of the above, *and*:<br><br>1. Place notice in modified library files, indicating change and date of change.<br><br>2. Indicate that modified library code is subject to Lesser License. |
| Copy and distribute object or executable library code (including unchanged and modified). | All of the above, *and*:<br>Must accompany code with corresponding machine-readable source code on a medium. | All of the above, *and*:<br>Distribute machine-readable source code corresponding to object or executable code. |
| Link application programs with library code and distribute the executable. | All of the following:<br><br>1. Must permit modification of application for customer's own use, and reverse engineering for debugging purposes.<br><br>2. Must give prominent notice with application program that library is used and that library is covered by Lesser License.<br><br>3. Supply copy of Lesser License.<br><br>4. If application displays copyright notices, include copyright notice for the library.<br><br>5. Do one of the following:<br><br>a. Provide machine-readable source code for the library (including any changes) and source or object code of the application, so that user can modify the library and relink to produce modified executable.<br><br>b. Use a shared library mechanism for linking with the library,<br><br>c. Provide written offer with application valid for 3 years to give items in (a).<br><br>d. Offer access to copy items in (a) from a designated place.<br><br>e. Verify that user has already received items in (a). | All of the following:<br><br>1. Give prominent notice with application program that the library is covered by Lesser License.<br><br>2. Supply copy of Lesser License.<br><br>3. If application displays copyright notices, include copyright notice for library.<br><br>4. Do one of the following:<br><br>a. Provide machine-readable source code for the library (including any changes) and source or object code of the application, so that user can modify the library and relink to produce modified executable.<br><br>b. Use a shared library mechanism for linking with the library.<br><br>c. Provide written offer with application valid for 3 years to give items in (a).<br><br>d. Offer access to copy items in (a) from a designated place.<br><br>e. Verify that user has already received items in (a). |

the good faith and licensed activities of all upstream contributors. Any break in the chain can prove disastrous for all downstream users. The Free Software Foundation appears to recognize this problem, but it does not propose a solution.

Fourth, a company that distributes its software bundled together with Linux, even if its software does not incorporate parts of Linux, and even if Linux is not modified, might unintentionally grant a license to its software (*i.e.*, free from any copyright or patent restrictions), due to the vague and confusing definitions provided in the GPL. This flows from the clause in the license that "when you distribute the same sections as part of a whole…the distribution of the whole must be on the terms of this License."

Finally, as set forth in Figures 1 and 2, accepting the CPL or Lesser License incurs numerous obligations, such as distributing software to third parties or maintaining an offer for three years to supply a machine-readable copy of the software to any third party. These duties may impose various costs on a company.

Many companies are using and modifying Linux for their own use and for computers that are then sold to customers. Such uses carry the risk that the company's copyrights and patent rights in computer software bundled with the Linux code will be automatically licensed to anyone that uses Linux. Those companies may also be subject to a copyright infringement claim by any of the programmers who have contributed to Linux, or by a third party whose software was illegally incorporated into Linux. The GPL and its cousins have not yet been interpreted or applied by a court, leaving substantial risks that this ambiguous legal document will have unintended consequences.

---

# Enforcing the GNU GPL*

Eben Moglen
September 10, 2001
*at* www.gnu.org/philosophy/enforcing-gpl.html

Microsoft's anti-GPL offensive this summer has sparked renewed speculation about whether the GPL is "enforceable." This particular example of "FUD" (fear, uncertainty and doubt) is always a little amusing to me. I'm the only lawyer on earth who can say this, I suppose, but it makes me wonder what everyone's wondering about: enforcing the GPL is something that I do all the time.

Because free software is an unorthodox concept in contemporary society, people tend to assume that such an atypical goal must be pursued using unusually ingenious, and therefore fragile, legal machinery. But the assumption is faulty. The goal of the Free Software Foundation in designing and publishing the GPL, is unfortunately unusual: we're reshaping how programs are made in order to give everyone the right to understand, repair, improve, and redistribute the best-quality software on earth. This is a transformative enterprise; it shows how in the new, networked society traditional ways of doing business can be displaced by completely different models of production and distribution. But the GPL, the legal device that makes everything else possible, is a very robust machine precisely because it is made of the simplest working parts.

---

The essence of copyright law, like other systems of property rules, is the power to exclude. The copyright holder is legally empowered to exclude all others from copying, distributing, and making derivative works.

This right to exclude implies an equally large power to license—that is, to grant permission to do what would otherwise be forbidden. Licenses are not contracts: the work's user is obliged to remain within the bounds of the license not because she voluntarily promised, but because she doesn't have any right to act at all except as the license permits.

But most proprietary software companies want more power than copyright alone gives them. These companies say their software is "licensed" to consumers, but the license contains obligations that copyright law knows nothing about. Software you're not allowed to understand, for example, often requires you to agree not to decompile it. Copyright law doesn't prohibit decompilation, the prohibition is just a contract term you agree to as a condition of getting the software when you buy the product under shrink-wrap in a store, or accept a "click-wrap license" on line. Copyright is just leverage for taking even more away from users.

The GPL, on the other hand, subtracts from copyright rather than adding to it. The license doesn't have to be complicated, because we try to control users as little as possible. Copyright grants publishers power to forbid users to exercise rights to copy, modify, and distribute that we believe all users should have; the GPL thus relaxes almost all the restrictions of the copyright system. The only thing we absolutely require is that anyone distributing GPL'd works or works made from GPL'd works distribute in turn under GPL. That condition is a very minor restriction, from the copyright point of view. Much more restrictive licenses are routinely held enforceable: every license involved in every single copyright lawsuit is more restrictive than the GPL.

Because there's nothing complex or controversial about the license's substantive provisions, I have never even seen a serious argument that the GPL exceeds a licensor's powers. But it is sometimes said that the GPL can't be enforced because users haven't "accepted" it.

This claim is based on a misunderstanding. The license does not require anyone to accept it in order to acquire, install, use, inspect, or even experimentally modify GPL'd software. All of those activities are either forbidden or controlled by proprietary software firms, so they require you to accept a license, including contractual provisions outside the reach of copyright, before you can use their works. The free software movement thinks all those activities are rights, which all users ought to have; we don't even want to cover those activities by license. Almost everyone who uses GPL'd software from day to day needs no license, and accepts none. The GPL only obliges you if you distribute software made from GPL'd code, and only needs to be accepted when redistribution occurs. And because no one can ever redistribute without a license, we can safely presume that anyone redistributing GPL'd software intended to accept the GPL. After all, the GPL requires each copy of covered software to include the license text, so everyone is fully informed.

Despite the FUD, as a copyright license the GPL is absolutely solid. That's why I've been able to enforce it dozens of times over nearly ten years, without ever going to court.

Meanwhile, much murmuring has been going on in recent months to the supposed effect that the absence of judicial enforcement, in U.S or other courts, somehow demonstrates that there is something wrong with the GPL, that its unusual policy goal is implemented in a technically indefensible way, or that the Free Software Foundation, which authors the license, is afraid of testing it in court. Precisely the reverse is true. We do not find ourselves taking the GPL to court because no one has yet been willing to risk contesting it with us there.

So what happens when the GPL is violated? With software for which the Free Software Foundation holds the copyright (either because we wrote the programs in the first place, or because free software authors have assigned us the copyright, in order to take advantage of our expertise in protecting their software's freedom), the first step is a report, usually received by e-mail to <license-violation@gnu.org>. We ask the reporters of violations to help us establish necessary facts, and then we conduct whatever further investigation is required.

We reach this stage dozens of times a year. A quiet initial contact is usually sufficient to resolve the problem. Parties thought they were complying with GPL, and are pleased to follow advice on the correction of an error. Sometimes, however, we believe that confidence-building measures will be required, because the scale of the violation or its persistence in time makes mere voluntary compliance insufficient. In such situations we work with organizations to establish GPL-compliance programs within their enterprises, led by senior managers who report to us, and directly to their enterprises' managing boards, regularly. In particularly complex cases, we have sometimes insisted upon measures that would make subsequent judicial enforcement simple and rapid in the event of future violation.

In approximately a decade of enforcing the GPL, I have never insisted on payment of damages to the Foundation for violation of the license, and I have rarely required public admission of wrongdoing. Our position has always been that compliance with the license, and security for future good behavior, are the most important goals. We have done everything to make it easy for violators to comply, and we have offered oblivion with respect to past faults.

In the early years of the free software movement, this was probably the only strategy available. Expensive and burdensome litigation might have destroyed the FSF, or at least prevented it from doing what we knew was necessary to make the free software movement the permanent force in reshaping the software industry that it has now become. Over time, however, we persisted in our approach to license enforcement not because we had to, but because it worked. An entire industry grew up around free software, all of whose participants understood the overwhelming importance of the GPL—no one wanted to be seen as the villain who stole free software, and no one wanted to be the customer, business partner, or even employee of such a bad actor. Faced with a choice between compliance without publicity or a campaign of bad publicity and a litigation battle they could not win, violators chose not to play it the hard way.

We have even, once or twice, faced enterprises which, under US copyright law, were engaged in deliberate, criminal copyright infringement: taking the source code of GPL'd software, recompiling it with an attempt to conceal its origin, and offering it for sale as a proprietary product. I have assisted free software developers other than the FSF to deal with such problems, which we have resolved—since the criminal infringer would not voluntarily desist and, in the cases I have in mind, legal technicalities prevented actual criminal prosecution of the violators—by talking to redistributors and potential customers. "Why would you want to pay serious money," we have asked, "for software that infringes our license and will bog you down in complex legal problems, when you can have the real thing for free?" Customers have never failed to see the pertinence of the question. The stealing of free software is one place where, indeed, crime doesn't pay.

But perhaps we have succeeded too well. If I had used the courts to enforce the GPL years ago, Microsoft's whispering would now be falling on deaf ears. Just this month I have been working on a couple of moderately sticky situations. "Look," I say, "at how many people all over the world are pressuring me to enforce the GPL in court, just to prove I can. I really need to make an example of someone. Would you like to volunteer?"

Someday someone will. But that someone's customers are going to go elsewhere, talented technologists who don't want their own reputations associated with such an enterprise will quit, and bad publicity will smother them. And that's all before we even walk into court. The first person who tries it will certainly wish he hadn't. Our way of doing law has been as unusual as our way of doing software, but that's just the point. Free software matters because it turns out that the different way is the right way after all.

---

# Notes & Questions

1. SCO v. IBM *and "Upstream" Exposure.* A recent lawsuit by The SCO Group (SCO) highlights the risks associated with use of open source code. As explained above, promoters of Linux software claim that the use of software is governed by the terms of the GNU General Public License (GPL). However, SCO has recently challenged that assumption. On March 6, 2003, SCO filed a lawsuit against IBM based on the intellectual property rights in the UNIX code acquired by SCO from Novell. SCO has alleged that after IBM licensed the UNIX code from SCO's predecessors, IBM then misappropriated SCO trade secrets and infringed SCO copyrights in the UNIX for use in IBM's Linux. Plaintiff's Amended Complaint, *SCO Group, Inc. v. Int'l Bus. Machs.*, No. 2:03cv0294 (D. Utah, filed June 16, 2003) *available at* www.thescogroup.com/scosource/complaint3.06.03.html.

At issue is a 1995 asset purchase agreement, under which SCO argues that it acquired from Novell the copyright and trade secret embodied in the UNIX source code. IBM has filed several counterclaims, including claims that SCO's UNIX code infringes several IBM patents. IBM also claims that SCO violated the GPL by distributing Linu for several years under the GPL license. Defendant IBM's Answer to the Amended Complaint and Counterclaim (*SCO Group, Inc. v. Int'l Bus. Machs. Corp.*, No. 2:03cv0294 (D. Utah, filed Aug. 6, 2003) *available at* www.thescogroup.com/ibmlawsuit/ibm_counterclaims.pdf; and Defendant IBM's Amended Counterclaims Against SCO *SCO Group, Inc. v. Int'l. Bus. Machs. Corp.* (D. Utah, filed September 25, 2003) *available at* www.thescogroup .com/ibmlawsuit/ibmamendedcounterclaims.pdf.

SCO clearly also intends to hold GPL/Linux licensees accountable for the alleged infringement of UNIX. On May 12, 2003, SCO sent letters to 1,500 of the world's largest companies notifying them of SCO's alleged IP rights in UNIX, its suit against IBM, and an assertion that IBM's Linux is an "unauthorized derivative of UNIX." A copy of the letter can be found at http://linuxfromscratch.org/pipermail/lfs-chat/2003-May/013682. html. SCO has since sued AutoZone and Daimler Chysler for infringement of SCO's UNIX copyrights, based on each company's use of Linux. Steven Shankland, *SCO Suits Target Two Big Linux Users*, CNET News.com, March 3, 2004, *at* news.com.com/2100-1014-5168921.html?tag=nl. SCO has also recently threatened legal action against two federal supercomputer users, the Lawrence Livermore National Laboratory and the National Energy Research Scientific Computing Center. Stephen Shankland, *SCO Targets Federal Supercomputer Users*, CNET News.com, March 19, 2004, news.com.com/2100-7344-5176308.html. Several companies have since entered into UNIX licensing agreements with SCO in an effort to avoid litigation. Stephen Shankland, *Computer Associates, Others Sign SCO Licenses*, CNET News.com, March 4, 2004, news.com.com/2100-7344-5170310.html.

IBM customers Red Hat and Novell are also engaged in separate lawsuits with SCO and SCO has stated that it intends to sue more people in the future. *See* Plaintiff's Complaint, *Red Hat, Inc. v. SCO Group, Inc.*, No. 1:03cv00772 (D. Del., filed August 4, 2003); Plaintiff's Complaint, *SCO Group, Inc. v. Novell, Inc.*, No. 2:04cv00139 (D. Utah, filed February 6, 2004).

*Suggested Additional* SCO v. IBM *Reading*. George Taulbee & Todd S. McClelland, *Open Source Basics and a Snap-Shot of the SCO Litigation*, 8 ELEC. BANKING L. & COM. REP. 5 (February 2004); Lothar Determann & Andrew Coan, *Spoiled Code?*: SCO v. Linux, 8 CYBERSPACE LAW. 8 (January, 2004); and James A. Harvey & Todd S. McClelland, SCO v. IBM: *The Open Source Benefits and Risks Are Real*, 20 COMP. & INT. LAW. (2003).

2. *Enforcement of the GPL.* As of the date of this printing, there are still no court decisions that directly address the GPL. One contract dispute looked to be the first case for enforcement of the GPL, where the plaintiff alleged that the defendant had violated the GPL by distributing a program based on GPL-governed source code without complying with the GPL license. The court declined to enter a preliminary injunction and did not rule on the GPL compliance issue. *Progress Software Corp. v. MySQL AB*, 195 F. Supp. 2d 328 (D. Mass. 2002). The parties later settled their differences before the issue could be addressed. ComputerWire, *MySQL, NuSphere Settle GPL Contract Dispute*, The Register (November 11, 2002) *at* www.theregister.co.uk/content/4/28021.html. One possible reason for the nonexistence of any such suit is the issue of standing: who gets to sue, and who must be joined as the plaintiff? If 1,000 programmers have all contributed to Linux, must they all be joined as owners of the copyrighted work?

3. *Considerations When Implementing Open Source.* Assume you are in-house counsel for a software company. Your developers are eager to commercialize a certain software tool they have developed. While conducting your diligence, you realize that your developers have incorporated GPL-licensed source code within their tool (your developers had reviewed the GPL license and interpreted it to mean that the developers were free to use it). What do you do? If the proposed customer is sophisticated, you may be able to have your developers remove those portions of the code that are open source and require that the customer directly obtain this code. What about a novice end user? Technical arguments have been made that developers can create code that "dips into" the functionality of open source code without invoking an open source license, however, no one has yet tested these arguments in court. *See* Michael Trachtman, *Can CORBA Sidestep Open-Source Licensing?* (Web Techniques, April 2001) *at* www.newarchitectmag.com/archives/2001/04/trachtman/. Should you disclose this open source code in your license agreement? Are you providing a defense for future infringers? If you do not disclose the existence of the open source code, you risk a suit from the sponsors of the GPL; however, to date this organization has not enforced the GPL license in the courts.

4. Some have argued that the collaborative integrity of open-source software is akin the the notion of moral rights in Civ Law jurisdictions. That is, "Moral rights seek to protect the creator's personality as embodied in the work. The open-source approach similarly protects the transparency necessary to show the programmer's personality in contributing to a project." Greg R. Vetter, *The Collaborative Integrity of Open-Source Software*, 2004 UTAH L. REV. 563, 699–700. Do you agree?

# Chapter 9

# Antitrust and Misuse Issues in Licensing

## I. Introduction

This chapter explores two related field of law—antitrust law and misuse doctrine—as applied to licensing. Although these two fields of law are not easy to study, they are vital to the preservation and advancement of our economic system. They insure the survival of free markets and the vitality of competition against interference by private parties acting in their own narrow self-interest. They are thus part of the essential economic "checks and balances" that keep markets in a free society free.

When working effectively, antitrust law and misuse doctrine secure important benefits to our society. By prohibiting private interference with the competitive process, they promote free markets. Free and competitive markets, in turn, provide consumers with lower prices, higher output, and increased product variety and choice, as compared to monopolies. By forcing sometimes reluctant business firms to compete, these laws insure that innovation and licensing for the benefit of the many will not be stifled to serve the interests of the few.

Many today know the horror stories of production snafus and inefficiencies in the former Soviet Union. There were frequent shortages of basic consumer products, such as groceries and toilet paper. There were occasionally grand fiascoes, such as the production of tens of thousands of left shoes with no right shoes to match. In the end, Communism left whole industries stagnant and outdated by decades. Monopoly—in the form of centralized state control of production—was the primary practical mechanism by which Communism did all this economic damage. Communism failed in large measure because it made state monopoly, rather than free markets, a central organizing principle of the economies that it touched.

Today, all the world's advanced economies recognize the importance of free markets and competition and the desirability of avoiding private monopoly through appropriate legal restraint. The names of the relevant laws differ. In Japan and Russia, the name is "anti-monopoly law." In the European Union, it is "competition law," and in the United States "antitrust law." But all of these laws have the same purpose and effect—preserving competition and free markets against private restraint—and all use much the same means. For example, Articles 85 and 86 of the Treaty of Rome, which established the European Economic Community that later became the European Union, are modified and updated counterparts of Sherman Act Sections 1 and 2, respectively, in the United

States. *See* JAY DRATLER, JR., LICENSING OF INTELLECTUAL PROPERTY § 5.03[1], [2] (Law Journal Press 1994 & Supps.), LEXIS, LJLIP.

Competition law, however, may be even more important in the United States than in the rest of the industrialized world. The reason is freedom of expression. The United States has no government-owned or operated broadcasting system like the British Broadcasting Company or the "First Channel" in Russia. (The Public Broadcasting Corporation, which runs the Public Broadcasting System, is by law a nongovernmental corporation independently operated, and its local affiliates are all privately and independently run.) Instead, virtually all means of communication in the United States, whether involving broadcasting, cable or telephone lines, or the Internet, are owned and operated by private parties. Therefore the First Amendment, our principal means of securing free expression, does not apply to any of them, for by its terms it restrains only government or "state action."

What, then, prevents a single private firm, or a single individual, from "cornering the market" in means of expression inside the United States? What prevents a Gates or Rupert Murdoch from acquiring ownership of the Internet's backbone or of all radio and television stations (including cable) serving particular markets? Attempts of the Chinese to control communication over the Internet inside the People's Republic of China, although only partly successful, suggest that technology alone is not the answer. Inside the United States, nothing else provides an answer — nothing, that is, except antitrust law and incorporation of its principles into other laws, such as the Communications Act of 1934. *See, e.g.,* 47 U.S.C. §§ 160, 314. For elaboration of this point, see Jay Dratler, Jr., *Why Antitrust Matters in Cyberspace: A Brief Essay, at* http://gozips.uakron.edu/~dratler/2005cyberlaw/materials/whyantitrust.htm (last visited February 15, 2005).

In other countries, competition law is largely a matter of government surveillance and enforcement. *See* Dratler, LICENSING, *supra,* § 5.01 (Japan and EU), 5.03[3] (EU). This is partly true in the United States. The United States government sometimes undertakes "major" antitrust litigation, such as the famous case brought against IBM in the seventies and the case against Microsoft in the nineties, which is excerpted and discussed below. Yet government antitrust enforcement is only a small part of the picture in the United States. *See id.,* §§ 5.01, 5.02[4][a].

Unlike most other countries, the United States has a robust and widely used system for *private* enforcement of the antitrust laws. Section 4(a) of the Clayton Act, 15 U.S.C. § 15(a), permits private parties to sue for injury sustained as a result of violations of the antitrust laws and to recover treble damages and their attorneys' fees if they win. Sherman Act § 4, 15 U.S.C. § 4, and Clayton Act § 16, 15 U.S.C. § 26, provide for injunctive relief. Congress intended these provisions — especially the "carrot" of treble damages — to motivate private parties to serve as "private attorneys general" in enforcing the antitrust laws, and they have admirably served that purpose. There are literally hundreds of private antitrust cases on the books and hundreds more adjudicating antitrust counterclaims in intellectual property infringement cases. Thus, in the United States, neither the development of antitrust law nor its use to protect competition in the marketplace is hostage to federal government policy.

Another unique aspect of United States' law — misuse doctrine — also helps to preserve competition against private restraint. This doctrine is a shield, not a sword: it provides a defense to intellectual-property infringement claims. Where it applies, however, it renders otherwise valid intellectual property unenforceable until its owner has "purged" the misuse. It is thus a vital doctrine for licensors and licensees of intellectual property, as well as owners.

Misuse doctrine, however, is far less precise than antitrust law, for it depends on general notions of equity and "public policy," rather than the precise, economically-based principles of antitrust law that we will study. Congress cut back misuse doctrine as applied to patents with the Patent Misuse Amendments Act of 1988. Yet those amendments did not resolve all questions about misuse even in the patent field, and they said nothing about copyright. As a consequence, the doctrine of "copyright misuse" has been a sort of "loose cannon" in the field of copyright licensing, threatening to render otherwise valid copyrights unenforceable unless their licensing is done carefully with competition in mind.

Both antitrust law and misuse are complex fields of law, based in part upon principles of competition and therefore economics. Antitrust law alone requires a full semester's study just to scratch the surface. Therefore a one-chapter introduction in a licensing course can hardly do justice to these complex subjects.

This chapter has three limited goals. The first is to introduce the general concept of competition law and to demonstrate how it promotes competition and free markets, and, through them, consumer welfare. The second is to explore fundamental concepts of antitrust analysis, including market definition, market power, the distinction between interbrand competition and intrabrand competition, the related distinction between horizontal and vertical effects, and the basis antitrust offenses. Finally, this chapter uses the much-discussed case of *United States v. Microsoft* to illustrate how these principles operate in the context of licensing, namely, the licensing of copyrighted commercial computer software.

---

# II. A "Drinking from a Fire Hose" Introduction to Antitrust

Antitrust law is one of the most conceptually difficult and challenging fields in all of Anglo-American law. The reason is easy to state but difficult to appreciate fully, especially for students new to the field. More than almost every other field of law, antitrust is interdisciplinary at its very core. Its understanding requires habits of thought and "mindsets" characteristic not only of lawyers, but of economists and business people as well.

In order to understand antitrust decisions, let alone predict future trends in the field, you must be able to assimilate and apply basic economic principles. In addition, appreciating particular decisions may require understanding the business dynamics and/or technology of particular industries, which are often only dimly and incompletely described in the text of judicial opinions themselves. Therefore, to a significant degree, antitrust law is not just another field of law, but an entirely distinct discipline.

That is the major reason for taking a course in antitrust law while in law school. Usually, busy practicing lawyers can "pick up" new fields of law by attending CLE courses or through self study. Doing so with antitrust, although possible in theory, is in practice incomparably more difficult. The best way to assimilate antitrust law is to devote a significant and concentrated amount of time to its study, either in a law-school course or in a postgraduate course of similar length and depth. Truly assimilating antitrust requires developing new mindsets, which, for most lawyers, are just as new and challenging as learning to "think like a lawyer" was to most first-year law students. In order to know and apply antitrust, your must learn not only to think like a lawyer, but to think like an economist and a business person as well. As the Supreme Court stated in what is undoubtedly its most important antitrust decision in the last quarter of the twentieth century: antitrust analysis "must be based upon demonstrable economic effect rather than…formalistic line drawing." *Continental T.V., Inc. v. GTE Sylvania Inc.*, 433 U.S. 36, 58–59 (1977).

**1. Economic purpose: competition.** The first thing to understand about antitrust law is that it has a generally recognized primary economic purpose: to protect free markets and free competition from interference by private forces acting in their own self-interest. If you had to describe the purpose of antitrust law in one word, that word would be "competition."

**2. The Sherman Act: a quasi-constitutional statute.** Although other statutes comprise part of antitrust law, by far the most important statute is the Sherman Act of 1890. Its penal, remedial, and procedural provisions have undergone amendment over the years, but its basic substantive provisions are virtually unchanged since its enactment over a century ago.

One reason for this constancy is the statute's generality. "As a charter of [economic] freedom, the [Sherman] Act has a generality and adaptability comparable to that found to be desirable in constitutional provisions." *Appalachian Coals, Inc. v. United States*, 288 U.S. 344, 359–60 (1933). The substantive portions of the Sherman Act's two basic provisions, which are set forth below, comfortably fit on half a page, yet the judicial decisions and commentary that give them shape fill volumes. The principal consequence of this generality is that real antitrust law, i.e., law with sufficient specificity and generality to apply with confidence and precision, is almost entirely judge-made. Hundreds of judicial decisions—principally those of the United States Supreme Court—constitute the sum and substance of antitrust law.

**3. Antitrust and the Bill of Rights.** If antitrust law resembles constitutional law in this respect, the likeness is no accident. Thomas Jefferson originally wanted to include a prohibition against monopolies, like that in the old English Statute of Monopolies, in our Bill of Rights. *See Graham v. John Deere Co.*, 383 U.S. 1, 7–9 (1966) (discussing Jefferson's key role in founding our intellectual-property system). Eventually, he accepted the argument that "ingenuity should receive a liberal encouragement[.]" *Id.*, 383 U.S. at 8, quoting Letter to Oliver Evans (May 1807), V *Writings of Thomas Jefferson*, at 75–76 (Washington ed.). He therefore endorsed our Constitution's Patent and Copyright Clause (Art. I, § 8, cl. 8). With its limitations of time and purpose, that Clause strongly suggests that free competition is the rule of our national economy and state-granted monopolies like patents and copyrights the exception. The fact that the general rule appears only by negative implication in our Constitution is largely an accident of history. *See* Jay Dratler, Jr., *Does Lord Darcy Yet Live? The Case against Software and Business-Method Patents*, 43 Santa Clara L. Rev. 823, 823–30 (2003).

In any event, the pregnant negative in the Patent and Copyright Clause gave birth to the Sherman Act a century later. Today there is little doubt that the Sherman Act is as fundamental to our nation's economic constitution as the Bill of Rights is to our political constitution. As Justice Thurgood Marshall so eloquently put it:

> Antitrust laws in general, and the Sherman Act in particular, are the Magna Carta of free enterprise. They are as important to the preservation of economic

freedom and our free-enterprise system as the Bill of Rights is to the protection of our fundamental personal freedoms. And the freedom guaranteed each and every business, no matter how small, is the freedom to compete—to assert with vigor, imagination, devotion, and ingenuity whatever economic muscle it can muster.

*United States v. Topco Assocs., Inc.*, 405 U.S. 596, 610, 92 S. Ct. 1126, 31 L. Ed. 2d 515 (1972).

Thus, antitrust law resembles the Constitution in three respects. First, it is vital to the very structure of our society, in particular, to the operation of our national economy. Second, its basic provisions are general and require interpretation by the courts. Third, because the courts (absent action by Congress) give antitrust law its form and detail, the nine philosopher kings and queens who sit on the Supreme Court largely control its substance. Although this state of affairs may seem strange in a democracy, it does have its advantages. The courts are often less susceptible to lobbying and political pressure, and more amenable to impartial reason (including new economic learning), than the Congress might be.

**4. The Two Basic Rules.** The Sherman Act has two basic provisions. Section 1 (15 U.S.C. § 1) outlaws contracts, combinations, and conspiracies in restraint of trade. As its subject suggests, it focuses on concerted or collective action by which private parties attempt to suppress competition through private agreement. Classic examples of illegal agreements under Section 1 are agreements by which competing producers fix the prices at which they will sell their products ("price fixing"), or by which competing construction firms agree which among themselves which will submit the low bid for a public works projects ("bid rigging"). Although it is seldom widely reported in the mass media, almost every year individuals go to prison for bid rigging, usually in connection with public contracts with municipalities.

In contrast to Section 1, Section 2 deals primarily with unilateral action by a single firm in unlawfully obtaining, extending, maintaining, or attempting to obtain a monopoly of a defined market. Section 2 does not outlaw merely *having* a monopoly, *if* it was achieved by lawful means, such as winning in hard competition. Section 2 does, however, outlaw gaining, maintaining or extending a monopoly (even one property achieved) by improper means, i.e., conduct designed to crush, rather than promote, competition. The European phrase for the same offense—"abuse of dominant position"—much better describes the essence of the offense than any term common in American practice.

One fact about Section 2 is important to understand at the outset. Conduct constituting a Section 2 offense need not be unlawful in itself, whether under the antitrust laws or otherwise. Conduct that is perfectly lawful for a smaller firm may be unlawful for a monopolist or near-monopolist if it is directed toward suppressing competition rather than competing. One of the conceptual difficulties of Section 2 cases is that anticompetitive conduct may come in a bewildering profusion of varieties, limited only by the fertile imaginations of business people wishing to escape the rigors of competition.

**5. Civil and Criminal Offenses.** The basic substantive text of the key Sherman-Act provisions is set forth below. It is rather simple. As the text states, the basic prohibitions are criminal in nature. Section 4 of the Clayton Act, 15 U.S.C. § 16, provides corresponding civil causes of action, with the well-known mandatory remedies of treble damages and attorneys' fees for successful plaintiffs. Thus, violations of either Section 1 or Section 2 are both civil offenses and (if the requisite state of mind exists) felonies.

Even in times of relatively lax antitrust enforcement by the federal government, defendants caught in flagrant antitrust violations such as price fixing and bid rigging serve jail time.

**6. The *per-se* "rule."** Two basic modes of analysis apply in antitrust law. Certain types of conduct are deemed "illegal *per se*," i.e., illegal in themselves. In order to condemn these types of conduct, one need, in theory, only identify them, that is, verify that they fall within a defined category of prohibited conduct. The rationale for categorical prohibition is that certain types of conduct are so invariably anticompetitive that the cost of identifying the rare cases in which they might have a neutral or positive effect on competition is not worth the effort. As the Supreme Court put it:

> [T]here are certain agreements or practices which because of their pernicious effect on competition and lack of any redeeming virtue are conclusively presumed to be unreasonable and therefore illegal without elaborate inquiry as to the precise harm they have caused or the business excuse for their use. This principle of *per se* unreasonableness not only makes the type of restraints which are proscribed by the Sherman Act more certain to the benefit of everyone concerned, but it also avoids the necessity for an incredibly complicated and prolonged economic investigation into the entire history of the industry involved, as well as related industries, in an effort to determine at large whether a particular restraint has been unreasonable—an inquiry so often wholly fruitless when undertaken.

*N. Pac. Ry. Co. v. United States*, 356 U.S. 1, 5 (1958).

Today *per-se* analysis is not applied as strictly or as widely as it once was. Certain so-called "*per-se*" rules, like the rule against tying, now require more than simple categorization of behavior; they also require limited inquiry into market structure and performance, including market power. *See Jefferson Parish Hospital District No. 2 v. Hyde*, 466 U.S. 2, 16–19, 26 (1984) ("*per-se*" rule for tying depends, *inter alia*, on whether defendant has sufficient market power in tying product to coerce purchase of tied product). Today only a few types of conduct are generally recognized as illegal *per se*: (1) horizontal division of markets or customers among competitors; (2) price fixing; (3) tying with market power; and (4) boycotts by groups with market power. See Dratler, *supra* § 5.02[2][a][iii] (Law Journal Press 1994 & Supps.).

**7. The "rule of reason."** The second type of analysis used in antitrust law is called the "rule of reason." The focus of this mode of analysis is on determining whether the challenged behavior unreasonably restrains competition.

Unlike analysis under the *per-se* "rule," analysis under the rule of reason is usually plenary. Normally it requires a complex examination of the relevant industries, their performance and structure, relevant geographic, product and service markets, relevant market conditions (including barriers to entry), the positions of the litigants and others in those markets, and the effect of the challenged behavior on competition. *See id.*, § 5.02[2][a][ii]. The classic judicial description of the rule of reason is as follows:

> [T]he legality of an agreement or regulation cannot be determined by so simple a test, as whether it restrains competition. Every agreement concerning trade, every regulation of trade, restrains. To bind, to restrain, is of their very essence. The true test of legality is whether the restraint imposed is such as merely regulates and perhaps thereby promotes competition or whether it is such as may suppress or even destroy competition. To determine that question the court must ordinarily consider the facts peculiar to the business to which

the restraint is applied; its condition before and after the restraint was imposed; the nature of the restraint and its effect, actual or probable. The history of the restraint, the evil believed to exist, the reason for adopting the particular remedy, the purpose or end sought to be attained, are all relevant facts. This is not because a good intention will save an otherwise objectionable regulation or the reverse; but because knowledge of intent may help the court to interpret facts and to predict consequences.

*Board of Trade v. United States*, 246 U.S. 231, 238 (1918).

**8. When the rule of reason applies.** Three practical facts about the rule of reason are worth mentioning. First, the rule of reason is the exclusive mode of analysis for claims under Sherman Act §2. There is no such thing as a *"per-se* illegal" act of monopolization or attempt to monopolize, by a single actor. *Per-se* analysis developed under Section 1, for concerted action among two or more parties, because concerted action was thought to create a more potent threat to competition than unilateral action by a single party, no matter how powerful. *See Copperweld Corp. v. Independence Tube Corp.*, 467 U.S. 752, 768, 768–69 (1984) (finding that "single-firm activity is unlike concerted activity covered by §1, which 'inherently is fraught with anticompetitive risk'") (citation and internal quotation marks omitted).

The second important fact about the rule of reason is that its application is difficult, time-consuming, and expensive. In essence, the rule requires a real-world investigation of all economic, technological, industrial and business circumstances that are relevant to assessing the effect on competition of the challenged behavior in the relevant geographic, product and service markets. In other words, the rule requires proof in a courtroom (albeit with the help of expert testimony!), of all the facts and circumstances that an economist might use to prove or disprove an anticompetitive effect. Applying the rule of reason therefore makes antitrust litigation complex, expensive, and time-consuming.

Finally, in Section 1 cases in which *per-se* analysis might apply, the battle over whether to apply *per-se* or rule-of-reason analysis is often the entire war. If the plaintiff succeeds in convincing the court that a *per-se* rule should apply, the plaintiff nearly always wins. In contrast, if a defendant in a Section 1 case convinces the court to apply the rule of reason, the defendant usually wins or can force a favorable settlement.

This latter conclusion is not invariable, however. Sometimes courts apply an abbreviated analysis under the rule of reason, taking only a "quick look" to be sure that the effect of the challenged behavior is as anticompetitive as it first appears. *See* DRATLER, *supra*, § 5.02[2][a][ii]. In general, however, in a Section 1 case determining which mode of analysis to apply is a key part of the litigation. These observations do not apply, of course, to Section 2 cases because those cases use only one mode of analysis: the rule of reason.

\* \* \*

As you read the statute and the cases that follow, consider the following questions. How does a court define "competition"? in what markets, i.e., industries and geographic areas? What specific conduct of the defendants allegedly impaired competition, and how? How did that conduct differ from normal *competitive* business conduct, which seeks to exploit or heighten competition in order to gain customers and make money? As you consider these questions in each case, try to put yourself in the shoes of the business people involved. Then try to put yourself in the shoes of an economist looking at the performance of the markets addressed in terms of efficiency and consumer welfare. Does the defendant's conduct hurt competition and consumers and, if so, how?

---

# III. The Fundamentals of Modern Antitrust: *Per Se* Illegality and the Rule of Reason

## The Antitrust Laws

### Sherman Act § 1, 15 U.S.C. § 1.

Every contract, combination in the form of trust or otherwise, or conspiracy, in restraint of trade or commerce among the several States, or with foreign nations, is hereby declared to be illegal. Every person who shall make any contract or engage in any combination or conspiracy hereby declared to be illegal shall be deemed guilty of a felony, and, on conviction thereof, shall be punished by fine not exceeding $ 10,000,000 if a corporation, or, if any other person, $ 350,000, or by imprisonment not exceeding three years, or by both said punishments, in the discretion of the court.

### Sherman Act § 2, 15 U.S.C. § 2.

Every person who shall monopolize, or attempt to monopolize, or combine or conspire with any other person or persons, to monopolize any part of the trade or commerce among the several States, or with foreign nations, shall be deemed guilty of a felony, and, on conviction thereof, shall be punished by fine not exceeding $ 10,000,000 if a corporation, or, if any other person, $ 350,000, or by imprisonment not exceeding three years, or by both said punishments, in the discretion of the court.

### Clayton Act § 4, 15 U.S.C. § 15(a).

(a) Amount of recovery; prejudgment interest. Except as provided in subsection (b), any person who shall be injured in his business or property by reason of anything forbidden in the antitrust laws may sue therefor in any district court of the United States in the district in which the defendant resides or is found or has an agent, without respect to the amount in controversy, and shall recover threefold the damages by him sustained, and the cost of suit, including a reasonable attorney's fee. The court may award under this section, pursuant to a motion by such person promptly made, simple interest on actual damages for the period beginning on the date of service of such person's pleading setting forth a claim under the antitrust laws and ending on the date of judgment, or for any shorter period therein, if the court finds that the award of such interest for such period is just in the circumstances.

[Subsection (b) limits damages recoverable by foreign states and their instrumentalities to single damages, rather than treble damages, under specified circumstances.]

---

# United States v. Socony-Vacuum Oil Co.
## 310 U.S. 150 (1940)

*[This case involved criminal charges against 27 corporations and 56 individuals for violating Sherman Act § 1. After dismissals, a jury found 16 corporations and 30 individuals guilty, but the judge granted new trials and JNOV to some defendants. The court fined the remaining 12 corporations $5,000 each, and the remaining 5 individuals $1,000 each. All appealed. The court of appeals granted new trials, but the Supreme Court reversed.*

*The indictment alleged that the defendants: (1) had "combined and conspired together for the purpose of artificially raising and fixing the tank car prices of gasoline" in the "spot markets" in the East Texas and Mid-Continent fields; (2) "ha[d] artificially raised and fixed said spot market tank car prices of gasoline and ha[d] maintained said prices at artificially high and non-competitive levels, and at levels agreed upon among them and ha[d] thereby intentionally increased and fixed the tank car prices of gasoline contracted to be sold and sold in interstate commerce...;" (3) had "arbitrarily," by reason of the provisions of the prevailing form of jobber contracts that made the price to the jobber dependent on the average spot market price, "exacted large sums of money from thousands of jobbers with whom they ha[d] had such contracts in said Mid-Western area"; and (4) "in turn have intentionally raised the general level of retail prices prevailing in said Mid-Western area."*

*The essence of the indictment was that the defendants—primarily major, vertically integrated oil companies—had conspired to manipulate gasoline prices on the "spot" market through coordinated purchases of gasoline from independent refiners. (The "spot" market is the market for spontaneous purchases not controlled by pre-existing contracts, i.e., the current market for current purchases of uncommitted supplies.) The indictment alleged that the defendants, through a trade association, had purchased more than half of all gasoline produced by independent refiners, and had allocated and sold it to themselves, in excess of the amounts that they would have purchased without their coordinated program. It also alleged that some defendants had procured independent refiners to curtail their production.*

*The indictment named certain independent refiners as co-conspirators, but not as defendants. It also named certain trade publications as defendants, which allegedly published falsely high prices at other defendants' request, on which the independent refiners allegedly relied to assess prices on the spot market.*

*An important part of the alleged conspiracy involved the distribution of gasoline by the major defendants to retail gas stations. Over 4,000 independent "jobbers" distributed more than half of all the gasoline that the major defendants sold to retail gas stations in the subject area. The majors, however, set the price at which they sold gasoline to the "jobbers" according to a formula based upon the spot market price. When the spot market price went up, the wholesale price for the major oil companies' sales at wholesale to the jobbers went up, and hence the retail price of gasoline went up. The indictment thus alleged that, by manipulating the spot price of gasoline sold by independent refiners, which was an important part of the formula used to calculate the price for sales by the major oil companies to jobbers, the major oil companies, in effect, had manipulated the retail price for gasoline to jobbers and retail customers in the affected region. The spot market price, the indictment alleged, was particularly susceptible to manipulation, since sales by independent refiners on which it was based amounted to less then 5% of all gasoline marketed in the affected region.]*

MR. JUSTICE DOUGLAS delivered the opinion of the Court.

\* \* \*

### III. *The Alleged Conspiracy.*

The alleged conspiracy is not to be found in any formal contract or agreement. It is to be pieced together from the testimony of many witnesses and the contents of over 1,000 exhibits, extending through the 3,900 printed pages of the record. What follows is based almost entirely on unequivocal testimony or undisputed contents of exhibits, only occasionally on the irresistible inferences from those facts.

\* \* \*

It was estimated that there would be between 600 and 700 tank cars of distress gasoline produced in the Mid-Continent oil field every month by about 17 independent refiners. These refiners, not having regular outlets for the gasoline, would be unable to dispose of it except at distress prices. Accordingly, it was proposed and decided that certain major companies (including the corporate respondents) would purchase gasoline from these refiners. The Committee would assemble each month information as to the quantity and location of this distress gasoline. Each of the major companies was to select one (or more) of the independent refiners having distress gasoline as its "dancing partner," and would assume responsibility for purchasing its distress supply. In this manner buying power would be coordinated, purchases would be effectively placed, and the results would be much superior to the previous haphazard purchasing. There were to be no formal contractual commitments to purchase this gasoline, either between the major companies or between the majors and the independents. Rather it was an informal gentlemen's agreement or understanding whereby each undertook to perform his share of the joint undertaking. Purchases were to be made at the "fair going market price."

\* \* \*

[Later the independent refiners] divided up the major companies; each communicated with those on his list, advised them that the program was launched, and suggested that they get in touch with their respective "dancing partners." Before the month was out all companies alleged to have participated in the program (except one or two) made purchases; 757 tank cars were bought from all but three of the independent refiners who were named in the indictment as sellers.

\* \* \*

The defendant companies sold about 83% of all gasoline sold in the Mid-Western area during 1935. As we have noted, major companies, such as most of the defendants, are those whose operations are fully integrated — producing crude oil, having pipe lines for shipment of the crude to its refineries, refining crude oil, and marketing gasoline at retail and at wholesale. During the greater part of the indictment period the defendant companies owned and operated many retail service stations through which they sold about 20% of their Mid-Western gasoline in 1935 and about 12% during the first seven months of 1936. Standard Oil Company (Indiana) was known during this period as the price leader or market leader throughout the Mid-Western area. It was customary for retail distributors, whether independent or owned or controlled by major companies, to follow Standard's posted retail prices. Its posted retail price in any given place in the Mid-Western area was determined by computing the Mid-Continent spot market price and adding thereto the tank car freight rate from the Mid-Continent field, taxes and 5 cents. The 5 cents was the equivalent of the customary 2 cents jobber margin and 3 cents service station margin. In this manner the retail price structure throughout the Mid-Western area during the indictment period was based in the main on Mid-Continent spot market quotations, or, as stated by one of the witnesses for the defendants, the spot market was a "peg to hang the price structure on."

About 24% of defendant companies' sales in the Mid-Western area in 1935 were to jobbers, who perform the function of middlemen or wholesalers. Since 1925 jobbers were purchasing less of their gasoline on the spot tank car markets and more under long term supply contracts from major companies and independent refiners. These contracts usually ran for a year or more and covered all of the jobber's gasoline requirements during the period. The price which the jobber was to pay over the life of the contract was not fixed; but a formula for its computation was included. About 80% or more of defendant companies' jobber contracts provided that the price of gasoline sold thereunder should be the Mid-Continent spot market price on the date of shipment. This spot market price was to be determined by averaging the high and low spot market quotations reported in the *Chicago Journal of Commerce* and *Platt's Oilgram* or by averaging the high and low quotations reported in the *Journal* alone. The contracts also gave the jobber a wholly or partially guaranteed margin between the price he had to pay for the gasoline and the normal price to service stations — customarily a 2 cents margin.[1]

There is no central exchange or market place for spot market transactions. Each sale is the result of individual bargaining between a refiner and his customers, sales under long-term contracts not being included. It is a "spot" market because shipment is to be made in the immediate future — usually within ten or fifteen days. Sales on the spot tank car markets are either sales to jobbers or consumers, sales by one refiner to another not being included.[2] The prices paid by jobbers and consumers in the various spot markets are published daily in the trade journals, *Platt's Oilgram* and *Chicago Journal of Commerce*.

\* \* \*

*[The Court reviewed statistical evidence that the wholesale and retail prices of certain grades of gasoline had increased slowly but steadily after the defendants' program went into effect.]*

There was also ample evidence that the spot market prices substantially affected the retail prices in the Mid-Western area during the indictment period. As we have seen, Standard of Indiana was known during this period as the price or market leader throughout this area. It was customary for the retailers to follow Standard's posted retail prices, which had as their original base the Mid-Continent spot market price. Standard's policy was to make changes in its posted retail price only when the spot market base went up or down at least 3/10 cents a gallon and maintained that change for a period of 7 days or more. Standard's net reduction in posted prices for the 6 months pre-

---

1. The following is illustrative: The spot market price (computed as indicated) was to govern when that price plus freight, plus $5^1/_2$ ¢ per gallon did not exceed the posted service station price, exclusive of tax, at destination on date of shipment. In case that aggregate figure exceeded the service station price, then the price to the jobber would be reduced by an amount equal to one-half of the excess. In some cases the major companies assumed the full amount of the difference. The margin of $5^1/_2$ ¢ was based on the seller's discount of $3^1/_2$ ¢ to jobbers. Hence if the seller increased or decreased that discount generally then the margin of $5^1/_2$ ¢ would be increased or decreased by an equal or like amount. The wording of the various contracts varied but there was great uniformity in principle.

2. For this reason "spot open market" is frequently used, "open" market referring to sales which are not made on contract nor based on future publications.

ceding March 1935 was 1.9 cents per gallon. From March 1935 to June 1935 its posted retail prices were advanced 3/10 cents four times.

Retail prices in the Mid-Western area kept close step with Mid-Continent spot market prices during 1935 and 1936, though there was a short lag between advances in the spot market prices and the consequent rises in retail prices. This was true in general both of the subnormal and normal retail prices. To be sure, when the tank car spot market leveled out on a plateau from June to the end of 1935, there was not quite the same evenness in the higher plateau of the average retail prices. For there were during the period in question large numbers of retail price cuts in various parts of the Mid-Western area, though they diminished substantially during the spring and summer of 1935. Yet the average service station price (less tax) having reached 13.26 cents by the middle of April (from 12.56 cents near the first of March) never once fell below that amount; advanced regularly to 13.83 cents by the middle of June; declined to 13.44 cents in August; and after an increase to 13.60 cents during the last of the summer remained at 13.41 cents during the balance of 1935 except for a minor intermediate drop. In sum, the contours of the retail prices conformed in general to those of the tank car spot markets.

\* \* \*

## V. *Application of the Sherman Act.*

### A. CHARGE TO THE JURY

The court charged the jury that it was a violation of the Sherman Act for a group of individuals or corporations to act together to raise the prices to be charged for the commodity which they manufactured where they controlled a substantial part of the interstate trade and commerce in that commodity. The court stated that where the members of a combination had the power to raise prices and acted together for that purpose, the combination was illegal; and that it was immaterial how reasonable or unreasonable those prices were or to what extent they had been affected by the combination. It further charged that if such illegal combination existed, it did not matter that there may also have been other factors which contributed to the raising of the prices. In that connection, it referred specifically to the economic factors...which respondents contended were primarily responsible for the price rise and the spot markets' stability in 1935 and 1936.... The court then charged that, unless the jury found beyond a reasonable doubt that the price rise and its continuance were "caused" by the combination and not caused by those other factors, verdicts of "not guilty" should be returned.

\* \* \*

The Circuit Court of Appeals held this charge to be reversible error, since it was based upon the theory that such a combination was illegal *per se*. In its view respondents' activities were not unlawful unless they constituted an unreasonable restraint of trade. Hence, since that issue had not been submitted to the jury and since evidence bearing on it had been excluded, that court reversed and remanded for a new trial so that the character of those activities and their effect on competition could be determined. In answer to the government's petition respondents here contend that the judgment of the Circuit Court of Appeals was correct, since there was evidence that they had affected prices only in the sense that the removal of the competitive evil of distress gasoline by the buying programs had permitted prices to rise to a normal competitive level; that their activities promoted rather than impaired fair competitive opportunities; and therefore that their activities had not unduly or unreasonably restrained trade.

\* \* \*

In *United States v. Trenton Potteries Co.*, 273 U.S. 392, this Court sustained a conviction under the Sherman Act where the jury was charged that an agreement on the part of the members of a combination, controlling a substantial part of an industry, upon the prices which the members are to charge for their commodity is in itself an unreasonable restraint of trade without regard to the reasonableness of the prices or the good intentions of the combining units. There the combination was composed of those who controlled some 82 per cent of the business of manufacturing and distributing in the United States vitreous pottery. Their object was to fix the prices for the sale of that commodity. In that case the trial court refused various requests to charge that the agreement to fix prices did not itself constitute a violation of law unless the jury also found that it unreasonably restrained interstate commerce. This Court reviewed the various price-fixing cases under the Sherman Act beginning with *United States v. Trans-Missouri Freight Assn.*, 166 U.S. 290, and *United States v. Joint Traffic Assn.*, 171 U.S. 505, and said " . . . it has since often been decided and always assumed that uniform price-fixing by those controlling in any substantial manner a trade or business in interstate commerce is prohibited by the Sherman Law, despite the reasonableness of the particular prices agreed upon." (p. 398.). This Court pointed out that the so-called "rule of reason" announced in *Standard Oil Co. v. United States*, 221 U.S. 1, and in *United States v. American Tobacco Co.*, 221 U.S. 106, had not affected this view of the illegality of price-fixing agreements. And in holding that agreements "to fix or maintain prices" are not reasonable restraints of trade under the statute merely because the prices themselves are reasonable, it said (pp. 397–98):

> The aim and result of every price-fixing agreement, if effective, is the elimination of one form of competition. The power to fix prices, whether reasonably exercised or not, involves power to control the market and to fix arbitrary and unreasonable prices. The reasonable price fixed today may through economic and business changes become the unreasonable price of tomorrow. Once established, it may be maintained unchanged because of the absence of competition secured by the agreement for a price reasonable when fixed. Agreements which create such potential power may well be held to be in themselves unreasonable or unlawful restraints, without the necessity of minute inquiry whether a particular price is reasonable or unreasonable as fixed and without placing on the government in enforcing the Sherman Law the burden of ascertaining from day to day whether it has become unreasonable through the mere variation of economic conditions Moreover, in the absence of express legislation requiring it, we should hesitate to adopt a construction making the difference between legal and illegal conduct in the field of business relations depend upon so uncertain a test as whether prices are reasonable—a determination which can be satisfactorily made only after a complete survey of our economic organization and a choice between rival philosophies.

\* \* \*

*[The Court next discussed the case of* Appalachian Coals, Inc. v. United States, *288 U.S. 344 (1933), in which the Supreme Court had applied the rule of reason to activities very similar to those in this case. Both were depression-era cases. Both involved producers of commodities (coal and oil) who had suffered from dramatically reduced demand for their products, which had threatened drastically reduced prices—often below the cost of produc-*

tion — and therefore *bankruptcy.* In both cases, industry participants had set up joint agencies with the goals of avoiding "distress" sales and price wars, and thereby avoiding massive bankruptcy and dislocation in the industry. In Appalachian Coals, the joint agency was a joint seller (very much like a cartel) with the power to stabilize prices by selling the defendants' coal jointly. Here the joint agency was a joint buyer attempting to stabilize prices by joint purchases on the spot market (an intermediate wholesale market), which affected retail pricing through the major companies' jobber-pricing formulas. The key difference, however, appears to have been that, in Appalachian Coals, the government had not carefully documented the effect of the defendants' behavior on prices as it had done in this case.]

Thus in reality the only essential thing in common between the instant case and the *Appalachian Coals* case is the presence in each of so-called demoralizing or injurious practices. The methods of dealing with them were quite divergent. In the instant case there were buying programs of distress gasoline which had as their direct purpose and aim the raising and maintenance of spot market prices and of prices to jobbers and consumers in the Mid-Western area, by the elimination of distress gasoline as a market factor. The increase in the spot market prices was to be accomplished by a well organized buying program on that market: regular ascertainment of the amounts of surplus gasoline; assignment of sellers among the buyers; regular purchases at prices which would place and keep a floor under the market. Unlike the plan in the instant case, the plan in the *Appalachian Coals* case was not designed to operate vis-a-vis the general consuming market and to fix the prices on that market. Furthermore, the effect, if any, of that plan on prices was not only wholly incidental but also highly conjectural. For the plan had not then been put into operation. Hence this Court expressly reserved jurisdiction in the District Court to take further proceedings if, *inter alia*, in "actual operation" the plan proved to be "an undue restraint upon interstate commerce." And as we have seen it would *per se* constitute such a restraint if price-fixing were involved.

[*After reviewing several other precedential decisions, the Court concluded that the* per se *rule of* Trenton Potteries *was still good law.*]

* * *

Therefore the sole remaining question on this phase of the case is the applicability of the rule of the *Trenton Potteries* case to these facts.

Respondents seek to distinguish the *Trenton Potteries* case from the instant one. They assert that in that case the parties substituted an agreed-on price for one determined by competition; that the defendants there had the power and purpose to suppress the play of competition in the determination of the market price; and therefore that the controlling factor in that decision was the destruction of market competition, not whether prices were higher or lower, reasonable or unreasonable. Respondents contend that in the instant case there was no elimination in the spot tank car market of competition which prevented the prices in that market from being made by the play of competition in sales between independent refiners and their jobber and consumer customers; that during the buying programs those prices were in fact determined by such competition; that the purchases under those programs were closely related to or dependent on the spot market prices; that there was no evidence that the purchases of distress gasoline under those programs had any effect on the competitive market price beyond that flowing from the removal of a competitive evil; and that if respondents had tried to do more than free competition from the effect of distress gasoline and to set an arbitrary non-competitive price through their purchases, they would have been without power to do so.

But we do not deem those distinctions material.

In the first place, there was abundant evidence that the combination had the purpose to raise prices. And likewise, there was ample evidence that the buying programs at least contributed to the price rise and the stability of the spot markets, and to increases in the price of gasoline sold in the Mid-Western area during the indictment period. That other factors also may have contributed to that rise and stability of the markets is immaterial. For in any such market movement, forces other than the purchasing power of the buyers normally would contribute to the price rise and the market stability. So far as cause and effect are concerned it is sufficient in this type of case if the buying programs of the combination resulted in a price rise and market stability which but for them would not have happened. For this reason the charge to the jury that the buying programs must have "caused" the price rise and its continuance was more favorable to respondents than they could have required. Proof that there was a conspiracy, that its purpose was to raise prices, and that it caused or contributed to a price rise is proof of the actual consummation or execution of a conspiracy under § 1 of the Sherman Act.

Secondly, the fact that sales on the spot markets were still governed by some competition is of no consequence. For it is indisputable that that competition was restricted through the removal by respondents of a part of the supply which but for the buying programs would have been a factor in determining the going prices on those markets. But the vice of the conspiracy was not merely the restriction of supply of gasoline by removal of a surplus. As we have said, this was a well organized program. The timing and strategic placement of the buying orders for distress gasoline played an important and significant role. Buying orders were carefully placed so as to remove the distress gasoline from weak hands. Purchases were timed. Sellers were assigned to the buyers so that regular outlets for distress gasoline would be available. The whole scheme was carefully planned and executed to the end that distress gasoline would not overhang the markets and depress them at any time. And as a result of the payment of fair going market prices a floor was placed and kept under the spot markets. Prices rose and jobbers and consumers in the Mid-Western area paid more for their gasoline than they would have paid but for the conspiracy. Competition was not eliminated from the markets; but it was clearly curtailed, since restriction of the supply of gasoline, the timing and placement of the purchases under the buying programs and the placing of a floor under the spot markets obviously reduced the play of the forces of supply and demand.

The elimination of so-called competitive evils is no legal justification for such buying programs. The elimination of such conditions was sought primarily for its effect on the price structures. Fairer competitive prices, it is claimed, resulted when distress gasoline was removed from the market. But such defense is typical of the protestations usually made in price-fixing cases. Ruinous competition, financial disaster, evils of price cutting and the like appear throughout our history as ostensible justifications for price-fixing. If the so-called competitive abuses were to be appraised here, the reasonableness of prices would necessarily become an issue in every price-fixing case. In that event the Sherman Act would soon be emasculated; its philosophy would be supplanted by one which is wholly alien to a system of free competition; it would not be the charter of freedom which its framers intended.

The reasonableness of prices has no constancy due to the dynamic quality of business facts underlying price structures. Those who fixed reasonable prices today would perpetuate unreasonable prices tomorrow, since those prices would not be subject to continuous administrative supervision and readjustment in light of changed conditions. Those who controlled the prices would control or effectively dominate the market. And those who were in that strategic position would have it in their power to destroy or drastically impair the competitive system. But the thrust of the rule is deeper and reaches more than monopoly power. Any combination which tampers with price structures is engaged in an unlawful activity. Even though the members of the price-fixing group were in no position to control the market, to the extent that they raised, lowered, or stabilized prices they would be directly interfering with the free play of market forces. The [Sherman] Act places all such schemes beyond the pale and protects that vital part of our economy against any degree of interference. Congress has not left with us the determination of whether or not particular price-fixing schemes are wise or unwise, healthy or destructive. It has not permitted the age-old cry of ruinous competition and competitive evils to be a defense to price-fixing conspiracies. It has no more allowed genuine or fancied competitive abuses as a legal justification for such schemes than it has the good intentions of the members of the combination. If such a shift is to be made, it must be done by the Congress. Certainly Congress has not left us with any such choice. Nor has the Act created or authorized the creation of any special exception in favor of the oil industry. Whatever may be its peculiar problems and characteristics, the Sherman Act, so far as price-fixing agreements are concerned, establishes one uniform rule applicable to all industries alike. There was accordingly no error in the refusal to charge that in order to convict the jury must find that the resultant prices were raised and maintained at "high, arbitrary and noncompetitive levels." The charge in the indictment to that effect was surplusage.

Nor is it important that the prices paid by the combination were not fixed in the sense that they were uniform and inflexible. Price-fixing as used in the *Trenton Potteries* case has no such limited meaning. An agreement to pay or charge rigid, uniform prices would be an illegal agreement under the Sherman Act. But so would agreements to raise or lower prices whatever machinery for price-fixing was used. That price-fixing includes more than the mere establishment of uniform prices is clearly evident from the *Trenton Potteries* case itself, where this Court noted with approval *Swift & Co. v. United States*, 196 U.S. 375, in which a decree was affirmed which restrained a combination from "raising or lowering prices or fixing uniform prices" at which meats will be sold. Hence, prices are fixed within the meaning of the *Trenton Potteries* case if the range within which purchases or sales will be made is agreed upon, if the prices paid or charged are to be at a certain level or on ascending or descending scales, if they are to be uniform, or if by various formulae they are related to the market prices. They are fixed because they are agreed upon. And the fact that, as here, they are fixed at the fair going market price is immaterial. For purchases at or under the market are one species of price-fixing. In this case, the result was to place a floor under the market—a floor which served the function of increasing the stability and firmness of market prices. That was repeatedly characterized in this case as stabilization. But in terms of market operations stabilization is but one form of manipulation. And market manipulation in its various manifestations is implicitly an artificial stimulus applied to (or at times a brake on) market prices, a force which distorts those prices, a factor which prevents the determination of those prices by free competition alone.

* * *

As we have indicated, the machinery employed by a combination for price-fixing is immaterial.

Under the Sherman Act a combination formed for the purpose and with the effect of raising, depressing, fixing, pegging, or stabilizing the price of a commodity in interstate or foreign commerce is illegal *per se*. Where the machinery for price-fixing is an agreement on the prices to be charged or paid for the commodity in the interstate or foreign channels of trade, the power to fix prices exists if the combination has control of a substantial part of the commerce in that commodity. Where the means for price-fixing are purchases or sales of the commodity in a market operation or, as here, purchases of a part of the supply of the commodity for the purpose of keeping it from having a depressive effect on the markets, such power may be found to exist though the combination does not control a substantial part of the commodity. In such a case that power may be established if as a result of market conditions, the resources available to the combinations, the timing and the strategic placement of orders and the like, effective means are at hand to accomplish the desired objective. But there may be effective influence over the market though the group in question does not control it. Price-fixing agreements may have utility to members of the group though the power possessed or exerted falls far short of domination and control. Monopoly power ( *United States v. Patten*, 226 U.S. 525) is not the only power which the Act strikes down, as we have said. Proof that a combination was formed for the purpose of fixing prices and that it caused them to be fixed or contributed to that result is proof of the completion of a price-fixing conspiracy under § 1 of the Act.[3] The indictment in this case charged that this combination had that purpose

---

3. Under this indictment proof that prices in the Mid-Western area were raised as a result of the activities of the combination was essential, since sales of gasoline by respondents at the increased prices in that area were necessary in order to establish jurisdiction in the Western District of Wisconsin. Hence we have necessarily treated the case as one where exertion of the power to fix prices (i. e. the actual fixing of prices) was an ingredient of the offense. But that does not mean that both a purpose and a power to fix prices are necessary for the establishment of a conspiracy under § 1 of the Sherman Act. That would be true if power or ability to commit an offense was necessary in order to convict a person of conspiring to commit it. But it is well established that a person may be guilty of conspiring although incapable of committing the objective offense.... And it is likewise well settled that conspiracies under the Sherman Act are not dependent on any overt act other than the act of conspiring.... It is the "contract, combination... or conspiracy in restraint of trade or commerce" which § 1 of the Act strikes down, whether the concerted activity be wholly nascent or abortive on the one hand, or successful on the other. *See United States* v. *Trenton Potteries Co.*, 273 U.S. 392, 402 (1927).

In view of these considerations a conspiracy to fix prices violates § 1 of the Act though no overt act is shown, though it is not established that the conspirators had the means available for accomplishment of their objective, and though the conspiracy embraced but a part of the interstate or foreign commerce in the commodity. Whatever may have been the status of price-fixing agreements at common law... the Sherman Act has a broader application to them than the common law prohibitions or sanctions. *See United States* v. *Trans-Missouri Freight Assn.*, 166 U.S. 290, 328 (1897). Price-fixing agreements may or may not be aimed at complete elimination of price competition. The group making those agreements may or may not have power to control the market. But the fact that the group cannot control the market prices does not necessarily mean that the agreement as to prices has no utility to the members of the combination. The effectiveness of price-fixing agreements is dependent on many factors, such as competitive tactics, position in the industry, the formula underlying price policies. Whatever economic justification particular price-fixing agreements may be thought to have, the law does not permit an inquiry into their reasonableness. They are all banned because of their actual or potential threat to the central nervous system of the economy.

The existence or exertion of power to accomplish the desired objective... becomes important only in cases where the offense charged is the actual monopolizing of any part of trade or commerce in violation of § 2 of the Act. An intent and a power to produce the result which the law condemns are then necessary. As stated in *Swift & Co.* v. *United States*, 196 U.S. 375, 396 (1905), "[W]hen that intent and the consequent dangerous probability exist, this statute, like many others and like the

and effect. And there was abundant evidence to support it. Hence the existence of power on the part of members of the combination to fix prices was but a conclusion from the finding that the buying programs caused or contributed to the rise and stability of prices.

* * *

---

# Continental T.V., Inc. v. GTE Sylvania Inc.
## 433 U.S. 36 (1977)

MR. JUSTICE POWELL delivered the opinion of the Court.

Franchise agreements between manufacturers and retailers frequently include provisions barring the retailers from selling franchised products from locations other than those specified in the agreements. This case presents important questions concerning the appropriate antitrust analysis of these restrictions under §1 of the Sherman Act, and the Court's decision in *United States v. Arnold, Schwinn & Co.*, 388 U.S. 365 (1967).

I

Respondent GTE Sylvania Inc. (Sylvania) manufactures and sells television sets through its Home Entertainment Products Division. Prior to 1962, like most other television manufacturers, Sylvania sold its televisions to independent or company-owned distributors who in turn resold to a large and diverse group of retailers. Prompted by a decline in its market share to a relatively insignificant 1% to 2% of national television sales,[4] Sylvania conducted an intensive reassessment of its marketing strategy, and in 1962 adopted the franchise plan challenged here. Sylvania phased out its wholesale distributors and began to sell its televisions directly to a smaller and more select group of franchised retailers. An acknowledged purpose of the change was to decrease the number of competing Sylvania retailers in the hope of attracting the more aggressive and competent retailers thought necessary to the improvement of the company's market position.[5] To this end, Sylvania limited the number of franchises granted for any given area and required each franchisee to sell his Sylvania products only from the location or locations at which he was franchised.[6] A franchise did not constitute an exclusive territory, and Sylvania retained sole discretion to increase the number of retailers in an area in light of the success or failure of existing retailers in developing their market. The revised marketing strategy appears to have been successful during the period at issue here, for by 1965 Sylvania's share of national television sales had increased to approximately 5%, and the company ranked as the Nation's eighth largest manufacturer of color television sets.

---

common law in some cases, directs itself against that dangerous probability as well as against the completed result." But the crime under §1 is legally distinct from that under §2 though the two sections overlap in the sense that a monopoly under §2 is a species of restraint of trade under §1. Only a confusion between the nature of the offenses under those two sections would lead to the conclusion that power to fix prices was necessary for proof of a price-fixing conspiracy under §1.

4. RCA at that time was the dominant firm with as much as 60% to 70% of national television sales in an industry with more than 100 manufacturers.

5. The number of retailers selling Sylvania products declined significantly as a result of the change, but in 1965 there were at least two franchised Sylvania retailers in each.

6. Sylvania imposed no restrictions on the right of the franchisee to sell the products of competing manufacturers.

This suit is the result of the rupture of a franchiser-franchisee relationship that had previously prospered under the revised Sylvania plan. Dissatisfied with its sales in the city of San Francisco,[7] Sylvania decided in the spring of 1965 to franchise Young Brothers, an established San Francisco retailer of televisions, as an additional San Francisco retailer. The proposed location of the new franchise was approximately a mile from a retail outlet operated by petitioner Continental T. V., Inc. (Continental), one of the most successful Sylvania franchisees. Continental protested that the location of the new franchise violated Sylvania's marketing policy, but Sylvania persisted in its plans. Continental then canceled a large Sylvania order and placed a large order with Phillips, one of Sylvania's competitors.

During this same period, Continental expressed a desire to open a store in Sacramento, Cal., a desire Sylvania attributed at least in part to Continental's displeasure over the Young Brothers decision. Sylvania believed that the Sacramento market was adequately served by the existing Sylvania retailers and denied the request.[8] In the face of this denial, Continental advised Sylvania in early September 1965, that it was in the process of moving Sylvania merchandise from its San Jose, Cal., warehouse to a new retail location that it had leased in Sacramento. Two weeks later, allegedly for unrelated reasons, Sylvania's credit department reduced Continental's credit line from $ 300,000 to $ 50,000.[9] In response to the reduction in credit and the generally deteriorating relations with Sylvania, Continental withheld all payments owed to John P. Maguire & Co., Inc. (Maguire), the finance company that handled the credit arrangements between Sylvania and its retailers. Shortly thereafter, Sylvania terminated Continental's franchises, and Maguire filed this diversity action in the United States District Court for the Northern District of California seeking recovery of money owed and of secured merchandise held by Continental.

The antitrust issues before us originated in cross-claims brought by Continental against Sylvania and Maguire. Most important for our purposes was the claim that Sylvania had violated § 1 of the Sherman Act by entering into and enforcing franchise agreements that prohibited the sale of Sylvania products other than from specified locations.[10] At the close of evidence in the jury trial of Continental's claims, Sylvania requested the District Court to instruct the jury that its location restriction was illegal only if it unreasonably restrained or suppressed competition. Relying on this Court's decision in *United States v. Arnold, Schwinn & Co., supra*, the District Court rejected the proffered instruction in favor of the following one:

> Therefore, if you find by a preponderance of the evidence that Sylvania entered into a contract, combination or conspiracy with one or more of its dealers pursuant to which Sylvania exercised dominion or control over the products sold to the dealer, after having parted with title and risk to the products, you must

---

7. Sylvania's market share in San Francisco was approximately 2.5% — half its national and northern California average.

8. Sylvania had achieved exceptional results in Sacramento, where its market share exceeded 15% in 1965.

9. In its findings of fact made in conjunction with Continental's plea for injunctive relief, the District Court rejected Sylvania's claim that its actions were prompted by independent concerns over Continental's credit. The jury's verdict is ambiguous on this point. In any event, we do not consider it relevant to the issue before us.

10. Although Sylvania contended in the District Court that its policy was unilaterally enforced, it now concedes that its location restriction involved understandings or agreements with the retailers.

find any effort thereafter to restrict outlets or store locations from which its dealers resold the merchandise which they had purchased from Sylvania to be a violation of Section 1 of the Sherman Act, regardless of the reasonableness of the location restrictions.

In answers to special interrogatories, the jury found that Sylvania had engaged "in a contract, combination or conspiracy in restraint of trade in violation of the antitrust laws with respect to location restrictions alone," and assessed Continental's damages at $ 591,505, which was trebled pursuant to 15 U.S.C. § 15 to produce an award of $ 1,774,515.[11]

On appeal, the Court of Appeals for the Ninth Circuit, sitting *en banc*, reversed by a divided vote. The court acknowledged that there is language in *Schwinn* that could be read to support the District Court's instruction but concluded that *Schwinn* was distinguishable on several grounds. Contrasting the nature of the restrictions, their competitive impact, and the market shares of the franchisers in the two cases, the court concluded that Sylvania's location restriction had less potential for competitive harm than the restrictions invalidated in *Schwinn* and thus should be judged under the "rule of reason" rather than the *per se* rule stated in *Schwinn*. The court found support for its position in the policies of the Sherman Act and in the decisions of other federal courts involving nonprice vertical restrictions.[12]

We granted Continental's petition for certiorari to resolve this important question of antitrust law.

## II

### A

We turn first to Continental's contention that Sylvania's restriction on retail locations is a *per se* violation of § 1 of the Sherman Act as interpreted in *Schwinn*. The restrictions at issue in *Schwinn* were part of a three-tier distribution system comprising, in addition to Arnold, Schwinn & Co. (Schwinn), 22 intermediate distributors and a network of franchised retailers. Each distributor had a defined geographic area in which it had the exclusive right to supply franchised retailers. Sales to the public were made only through franchised retailers, who were authorized to sell Schwinn bicycles only from specified locations. In support of this limitation, Schwinn prohibited both distributors and retailers from selling Schwinn bicycles to nonfranchised retailers. At the retail level, therefore, Schwinn was able to control the number of retailers of its bicycles in any given area according to its view of the needs of that market.

As of 1967 approximately 75% of Schwinn's total sales were made under the "Schwinn Plan." Acting essentially as a manufacturer's representative or sales agent, a distributor participating in this plan forwarded orders from retailers to the factory.

---

11. The jury also found that Maguire had not conspired with Sylvania with respect to this violation. Other claims made by Continental were either rejected by the jury or withdrawn by Continental. Most important was the jury's rejection of the allegation that the location restriction was part of a larger scheme to fix prices.

12. There were two major dissenting opinions. Judge Kilkenny argued that the present case is indistinguishable from *Schwinn* and that the jury had been correctly instructed. Agreeing with Judge Kilkenny's interpretation of *Schwinn*, Judge Browning stated that he found the interpretation responsive to and justified by the need to protect "individual traders from unnecessary restrictions upon their freedom of action."

Schwinn then shipped the ordered bicycles directly to the retailer, billed the retailer, bore the credit risk, and paid the distributor a commission on the sale. Under the Schwinn Plan, the distributor never had title to or possession of the bicycles. The remainder of the bicycles moved to the retailers through the hands of the distributors. For the most part, the distributors functioned as traditional wholesalers with respect to these sales, stocking an inventory of bicycles owned by them to supply retailers with emergency and "fill-in" requirements. A smaller part of the bicycles that were physically distributed by the distributors were covered by consignment and agency arrangements that had been developed to deal with particular problems of certain distributors. Distributors acquired title only to those bicycles that they purchased as wholesalers; retailers, of course, acquired title to all of the bicycles ordered by them.

In the District Court, the United States charged a continuing conspiracy by Schwinn and other alleged co-conspirators to fix prices, allocate exclusive territories to distributors, and confine Schwinn bicycles to franchised retailers.... [T]he Government argued that the nonprice restrictions were *per se* illegal as part of a scheme for fixing the retail prices of Schwinn bicycles. The District Court rejected the price-fixing allegation because of a failure of proof and held that Schwinn's limitation of retail bicycle sales to franchised retailers was permissible under § 1. The court found a § 1 violation, however, in "a conspiracy to divide certain borderline or overlapping counties in the territories served by four Midwestern cycle distributors."

* * *

Schwinn came to this Court on appeal by the United States from the District Court's decision. Abandoning its *per se* theories, the Government argued that Schwinn's prohibition against distributors' and retailers' selling Schwinn bicycles to nonfranchised retailers was unreasonable under § 1 and that the District Court's injunction against exclusive distributor territories should extend to all such restrictions regardless of the form of the transaction. The Government did not challenge the District Court's decision on price fixing, and Schwinn did not challenge the decision on exclusive distributor territories.

The Court acknowledged the Government's abandonment of its *per se* theories and stated that the resolution of the case would require an examination of "the specifics of the challenged practices and their impact upon the marketplace in order to make a judgment as to whether the restraint is or is not 'reasonable' in the special sense in which § 1 of the Sherman Act must be read for purposes of this type of inquiry." Despite this description of its task, the Court proceeded to articulate the following "bright line" *per se* rule of illegality for vertical restrictions: "Under the Sherman Act, it is unreasonable without more for a manufacturer to seek to restrict and confine areas or persons with whom an article may be traded after the manufacturer has parted with dominion over it." But the Court expressly stated that the rule of reason governs when "the manufacturer retains title, dominion, and risk with respect to the product and the position and function of the dealer in question are, in fact, indistinguishable from those of an agent or salesman of the manufacturer."

Application of these principles to the facts of *Schwinn* produced sharply contrasting results depending upon the role played by the distributor in the distribution system. With respect to that portion of Schwinn's sales for which the distributors acted as ordinary wholesalers, buying and reselling Schwinn bicycles, the Court held that the territorial and customer restrictions challenged by the Government were *per se* illegal. But, with respect to that larger portion of Schwinn's sales in which the distributors functioned under the Schwinn Plan and under the less common consignment and agency arrangements, the Court held that the same restrictions should be judged under the rule of reason. The only retail restriction challenged by the Government prevented franchised retailers from supplying nonfranchised retailers. The Court apparently perceived no material distinction between the restrictions on distributors and retailers, for it held:

> The principle is, of course, equally applicable to sales to retailers, and the decree should similarly enjoin the making of any sales to retailers upon any condition, agreement or understanding limiting the retailer's freedom as to where and to whom it will resell the products.

Applying the rule of reason to the restrictions that were not imposed in conjunction with the sale of bicycles, the Court had little difficulty finding them all reasonable in light of the competitive situation in "the product market as a whole."

### B

In the present case, it is undisputed that title to the television sets passed from Sylvania to Continental. Thus, the *Schwinn per se* rule applies unless Sylvania's restriction on locations falls outside Schwinn's prohibition against a manufacturer's attempting to restrict a "retailer's freedom as to where and to whom it will resell the products." As the Court of Appeals conceded, the language of *Schwinn* is clearly broad enough to apply to the present case. Unlike the Court of Appeals, however, we are unable to find a principled basis for distinguishing *Schwinn* from the case now before us.

Both Schwinn and Sylvania sought to reduce but not to eliminate competition among their respective retailers through the adoption of a franchise system. Although it was not one of the issues addressed by the District Court or presented on appeal by the Government, the Schwinn franchise plan included a location restriction similar to the one challenged here. These restrictions allowed Schwinn and Sylvania to regulate the amount of competition among their retailers by preventing a franchisee from selling franchised products from outlets other than the one covered by the franchise agreement. To exactly the same end, the Schwinn franchise plan included a companion restriction, apparently not found in the Sylvania plan, that prohibited franchised retailers from selling Schwinn products to nonfranchised retailers. In *Schwinn* the Court expressly held that this restriction was impermissible under the broad principle stated there. In intent and competitive impact, the retail-customer restriction in *Schwinn* is indistinguishable from the location restriction in the present case. In both cases the restrictions limited the freedom of the retailer to dispose of the purchased products as he desired. The fact that one restriction was addressed to territory and the other to customers is irrelevant to functional antitrust analysis and, indeed, to the language and broad thrust of the opinion in Schwinn. As Mr. Chief Justice Hughes stated in *Appalachian Coals, Inc. v. United States*, 288 U.S. 344, 360, 377 (1933): "Realities must dominate the judgment.... The Anti-Trust Act aims at substance."

### III

Sylvania argues that if *Schwinn* cannot be distinguished, it should be reconsidered. Although *Schwinn* is supported by the principle of stare decisis...we are convinced that the need for clarification of the law in this area justifies reconsideration. *Schwinn* itself was an abrupt and largely unexplained departure from *White Motor Co. v. United States*, 372 U.S. 253 (1963), where only four years earlier the Court had refused to endorse a *per se* rule for vertical restrictions. Since its announcement, *Schwinn* has been the subject of continuing controversy and confusion, both in the scholarly journals and in the federal courts. The great weight of scholarly opinion has been critical of the decision,[13] and a number of the federal courts confronted with analogous vertical restrictions have sought to limit its reach.[14] In our view, the experience of the past 10 years should be brought to bear on this subject of considerable commercial importance.

The traditional framework of analysis under § 1 of the Sherman Act is familiar and does not require extended discussion. Section 1 prohibits "[e]very contract, combination.... or conspiracy, in restraint of trade or commerce." Since the early years of this century a judicial gloss on this statutory language has established the "rule of reason" as the prevailing standard of analysis. *Standard Oil Co. v. United States*, 221 U.S. 1 (1911).

Under this rule, the fact-finding weighs all of the circumstances of a case in deciding whether a restrictive practice should be prohibited as imposing an unreasonable restraint on competition.[15] *Per se* rules of illegality are appropriate only when they relate to conduct that is manifestly anticompetitive. As the Court explained in *Northern Pac. R. Co. v. United States*, 356 U.S. 1, 5 (1958), "there are certain agreements or practices which because of their pernicious effect on competition and lack of any redeeming virtue are conclusively presumed to be unreasonable and therefore illegal without elaborate inquiry as to the precise harm they have caused or the business excuse for their use."[16]

In essence, the issue before us is whether *Schwinn's per se* rule can be justified under the demanding standards of *Northern Pac. R. Co.* The Court's refusal to endorse a *per se*

---

13. A former Assistant Attorney General in charge of the Antitrust Division has described Schwinn as "an exercise in barren formalism" that is "artificial and unresponsive to the competitive needs of the real world." Baker, *Vertical Restraints in Times of Change: From White to Schwinn to Where?*, 44 ANTITRUST L.J. 537 (1975). [The Court cites seven articles criticizing *Schwinn*, including Posner, *Antitrust Policy and the Supreme Court: An Analysis of the Restricted Distribution, Horizontal Merger and Potential Competition Decisions*, 75 COLUM. L. REV. 282 (1975), and two to the contrary.]

14. Indeed, as one commentator has observed, many courts "have struggled to distinguish or limit *Schwinn* in ways that are a tribute to judicial ingenuity." Robinson, *Recent Antitrust Developments: 1974*, 75 COLUM. L. REV. 243, 272 (1975).

15. One of the most frequently cited statements of the rule of reason is that of Mr. Justice Brandeis in *Chicago Bd. of Trade v. United States*, 246 U.S. 231, 238 (1918):

> The true test of legality is whether the restraint imposed is such as merely regulates and perhaps thereby promotes competition or whether it is such as may suppress or even destroy competition. To determine that question the court must ordinarily consider the facts peculiar to the business to which the restraint is applied; its condition before and after the restraint was imposed; the nature of the restraint and its effect, actual or probable. The history of the restraint, the evil believed to exist, the reason for adopting the particular remedy, the purpose or end sought to be attained, are all relevant facts. This is not because a good intention will save an otherwise objectionable regulation or the reverse; but because knowledge of intent may help the court to interpret facts and to predict consequences.

16. *Per se* rules thus require the Court to make broad generalizations about the social utility of particular commercial practices. The probability that anticompetitive consequences will result from a practice and the severity of those consequences must be balanced against its procompetitive consequences. Cases that do not fit the generalization may arise, but a *per se* rule reflects the judgment that such cases are not sufficiently common or important to justify the time and expense necessary to identify them. Once established, *per se* rules tend to provide guidance to the business community and to minimize the burdens on litigants and the judicial system of the more complex rule-of-reason trials, *see Northern Pac. R. Co. v. United States*, 356 U.S. 1, 5; *United States v. Topco Associates, Inc.*, 405 U.S. 596, 609–10 (1972), but those advantages are not sufficient in themselves to justify the creation of *per se* rules. If it were otherwise, all of antitrust law would be reduced to *per se* rules, thus introducing an unintended and undesirable rigidity in the law.

rule in *White Motor Co.* was based on its uncertainty as to whether vertical restrictions satisfied those standards. Addressing this question for the first time, the Court stated:

> We need to know more than we do about the actual impact of these arrangements on competition to decide whether they have such a 'pernicious effect on competition and lack...any redeeming virtue'...(*Northern Pac. R. Co. v. United States, supra,* p. 5) and therefore should be classified as *per se* violations of the Sherman Act.

Only four years later the Court in *Schwinn* announced its sweeping *per se* rule without even a reference to *Northern Pac. R. Co.* and with no explanation of its sudden change in position. We turn now to consider *Schwinn* in light of *Northern Pac. R. Co.*

The market impact of vertical restrictions[17] is complex because of their potential for a simultaneous reduction of intrabrand competition and stimulation of interbrand competition.[18] Significantly, the Court in *Schwinn* did not distinguish among the challenged restrictions on the basis of their individual potential for intrabrand harm or interbrand benefit. Restrictions that completely eliminated intrabrand competition among Schwinn distributors were analyzed no differently from those that merely moderated intrabrand competition among retailers. The pivotal factor was the passage of title: All restrictions were held to be *per se* illegal where title had passed, and all were evaluated and sustained under the rule of reason where it had not. The location restriction at issue here would be subject to the same pattern of analysis under *Schwinn.*

It appears that this distinction between sale and nonsale transactions resulted from the Court's effort to accommodate the perceived intrabrand harm and interbrand benefit of vertical restrictions. The *per se* rule for sale transactions reflected the view that vertical restrictions are "so obviously destructive" of intrabrand competition[19] that their use would "open the door to exclusivity of outlets and limitation of territory further than prudence permits."[20] Conversely, the continued adherence to the traditional rule of

---

17. As in *Schwinn,* we are concerned here only with nonprice vertical restrictions. The *per se* illegality of price restrictions has been established firmly for many years and involves significantly different questions of analysis and policy.

18. Interbrand competition is the competition among the manufacturers of the same generic product—television sets in this case—and is the primary concern of antitrust law. The extreme example of a deficiency of interbrand competition is monopoly, where there is only one manufacturer. In contrast, intrabrand competition is the competition between the distributors—wholesale or retail—of the product of a particular manufacturer.

The degree of intrabrand competition is wholly independent of the level of interbrand competition confronting the manufacturer. Thus, there may be fierce intrabrand competition among the distributors of a product produced by a monopolist and no intrabrand competition among the distributors of a product produced by a firm in a highly competitive industry. But when interbrand competition exists, as it does among television manufacturers, it provides a significant check on the exploitation of intrabrand market power because of the ability of consumers to substitute a different brand of the same product.

19. The Court did not specifically refer to intrabrand competition, but this meaning is clear from the context.

20. The Court also stated that to impose vertical restrictions in sale transactions would "violate the ancient rule against restraints on alienation." This isolated reference has provoked sharp criticism from virtually all of the commentators on the decision, most of whom have regarded the Court's apparent reliance on the "ancient rule" as both a misreading of legal history and a perversion of antitrust analysis. "We quite agree with MR. JUSTICE STEWART's dissenting comment in *Schwinn* that 'the state of the common law 400 or even 100 years ago is irrelevant to the issue before us: the effect of the antitrust laws upon vertical distributional restraints in the American economy today.'" 388 U.S., at 392.

We are similarly unable to accept Judge Browning's interpretation of *Schwinn.* In his dissent

reason for nonsale transactions reflected the view that the restrictions have too great a potential for the promotion of interbrand competition to justify complete prohibition.[21] The Court's opinion provides no analytical support for these contrasting positions. Nor is there even an assertion in the opinion that the competitive impact of vertical restrictions is significantly affected by the form of the transaction. Nonsale transactions appear to be excluded from the *per se* rule, not because of a greater danger of intrabrand harm or a greater promise of interbrand benefit, but rather because of the Court's unexplained belief that a complete *per se* prohibition would be too inflexible.

Vertical restrictions reduce intrabrand competition by limiting the number of sellers of a particular product competing for the business of a given group of buyers. Location restrictions have this effect because of practical constraints on the effective marketing area of retail outlets. Although intrabrand competition may be reduced, the ability of retailers to exploit the resulting market may be limited both by the ability of consumers to travel to other franchised locations and, perhaps more importantly, to purchase the competing products of other manufacturers. None of these key variables, however, is affected by the form of the transaction by which a manufacturer conveys his products to the retailers.

Vertical restrictions promote interbrand competition by allowing the manufacturer to achieve certain efficiencies in the distribution of his products. These "redeeming virtues" are implicit in every decision sustaining vertical restrictions under the rule of reason. Economists have identified a number of ways in which manufacturers can use such restrictions to compete more effectively against other manufacturers. *See, e.g., Preston, Restrictive Distribution Arrangements: Economic Analysis and Public Policy Standards*, 30 LAW & CONTEMP. PROB. 506, 511 (1965).[22] For example, new manufacturers

---

below he argued that the decision reflects the view that the Sherman Act was intended to prohibit restrictions on the autonomy of independent businessmen even though they have no impact on price, quality, and quantity of goods and services. This view is certainly not explicit in *Schwinn*,which purports to be based on an examination of the "impact [of the restrictions] upon the marketplace." 388 U.S., at 374. Competitive economies have social and political as well as economic advantages, see e.g., *Northern Pac. R. Co. v. United States*, 356 U.S., at 4, but an antitrust policy divorced from market considerations would lack any objective benchmarks.

21. In that regard, the Court specifically stated that a more complete prohibition "might severely hamper smaller enterprises resorting to reasonable methods of meeting the competition of giants and of merchandising through independent dealers." 388 U.S., at 380. The Court also broadly hinted that it would recognize additional exceptions to the *per se* rule for new entrants in an industry and for failing firms, both of which were mentioned in *White Motor* as candidates for such exceptions. The Court might have limited the exceptions to the *per se* rule to these situations, which present the strongest arguments for the sacrifice of intrabrand competition for interbrand competition. Significantly, it chose instead to create the more extensive exception for nonsale transactions which is available to all businesses, regardless of their size, financial health, or market share. This broader exception demonstrates even more clearly the Court's awareness of the "redeeming virtues" of vertical restrictions.

22. Marketing efficiency is not the only legitimate reason for a manufacturer's desire to exert control over the manner in which his products are sold and serviced. As a result of statutory and common-law developments, society increasingly demands that manufacturers assume direct responsibility for the safety and quality of their products. For example, at the federal level, apart from more specialized requirements, manufacturers of consumer products have safety responsibilities under the Consumer Product Safety Act, 15 U.S.C. § 2051 *et seq.* (1970 ed., Supp. V), and obligations for warranties under the Consumer Product Warranties Act, 15 U.S.C. § 2301 *et seq.* (1970 ed., Supp. V). Similar obligations are imposed by state law. *See, e.g.,* Cal. Civ. Code § 1790 *et seq.* (West 1973). The legitimacy of these concerns has been recognized in cases involving vertical restrictions. *See, e.g., Tripoli Co. v. Wella Corp.*, 425 F.2d 932 (CA3 1970).

and manufacturers entering new markets can use the restrictions in order to induce competent and aggressive retailers to make the kind of investment of capital and labor that is often required in the distribution of products unknown to the consumer. Established manufacturers can use them to induce retailers to engage in promotional activities or to provide service and repair facilities necessary to the efficient marketing of their products. Service and repair are vital for many products, such as automobiles and major household appliances. The availability and quality of such services affect a manufacturer's goodwill and the competitiveness of his product. Because of market imperfections such as the so-called "free rider" effect, these services might not be provided by retailers in a purely competitive situation, despite the fact that each retailer's benefit would be greater if all provided the services than if none did....

Economists also have argued that manufacturers have an economic interest in maintaining as much intrabrand competition as is consistent with the efficient distribution of their products. Bork, *The Rule of Reason and the Per Se Concept: Price Fixing and Market Division [II]*, 75 YALE L. J. 373, 403 (1966); Posner, *supra*, n. 13, at 283, 287–88.[23] Although the view that the manufacturer's interest necessarily corresponds with that of the public is not universally shared, even the leading critic of vertical restrictions concedes that *Schwinn's* distinction between sale and nonsale transactions is essentially unrelated to any relevant economic impact. Comanor, *Vertical Territorial and Customer Restrictions: White Motor and Its Aftermath*, 81 HARV. L. REV. 1419, 1422 (1968).[24] Indeed, to the extent that the form of the transaction is related to interbrand benefits, the Court's distinction is inconsistent with its articulated concern for the ability of smaller firms to compete effectively with larger ones. Capital requirements and administrative expenses may prevent smaller firms from using the exception for nonsale transactions.......[25]

We conclude that the distinction drawn in *Schwinn* between sale and nonsale transactions is not sufficient to justify the application of a *per se* rule in one situation and a rule of reason in the other. The question remains whether the *per se* rule stated in *Schwinn* should be expanded to include nonsale transactions or abandoned in favor of a return to the rule of reason. We have found no persuasive support for expanding the *per se* rule. As noted above, the *Schwinn* Court recognized the undesirability of "prohibit[ing] all vertical restrictions of territory and all franchising...." 388 U.S., at 379–80.[26] And even Continental does not urge us to hold that all such restrictions are *per se* illegal.

---

23. "Generally a manufacturer would prefer the lowest retail price possible, once its price to dealers has been set, because a lower retail price means increased sales and higher manufacturer revenues." *Note*, 88 HARV. L. REV. 636, 641 (1975). In this context, a manufacturer is likely to view the difference between the price at which it sells to its retailers and their price to the consumer as its "cost of distribution," which it would prefer to minimize. Posner, *supra*, n. 13, at 283.

24. Professor Comanor argues that the promotional activities encouraged by vertical restrictions result in product differentiation and, therefore, a decrease in interbrand competition. This argument is flawed by its necessary assumption that a large part of the promotional efforts resulting from vertical restrictions will not convey socially desirable information about product availability, price, quality, and services. Nor is it clear that a *per se* rule would result in anything more than a shift to less efficient methods of obtaining the same promotional effects.

25. We also note that *per se* rules in this area may work to the ultimate detriment of the small businessmen who operate as franchisees. To the extent that a *per se* rule prevents a firm from using the franchise system to achieve efficiencies that it perceives as important to its successful operation, the rule creates an incentive for vertical integration into the distribution system, thereby eliminating to that extent the role of independent businessmen.

26. Continental's contention that balancing intrabrand and interbrand competitive effects of vertical restrictions is not a "proper part of the judicial function"...is refuted by *Schwinn* itself.

We revert to the standard articulated in *Northern Pac. R. Co.*, and reiterated in *White Motor*, for determining whether vertical restrictions must be "conclusively presumed to be unreasonable and therefore illegal without elaborate inquiry as to the precise harm they have caused or the business excuse for their use." Such restrictions, in varying forms, are widely used in our free market economy. As indicated above, there is substantial scholarly and judicial authority supporting their economic utility. There is relatively little authority to the contrary.[27] Certainly, there has been no showing in this case, either generally or with respect to Sylvania's agreements, that vertical restrictions have or are likely to have a "pernicious effect on competition" or that they "lack...any redeeming virtue."[28] Accordingly, we conclude that the *per se* rule stated in *Schwinn* must be overruled.[29] In so holding we do not foreclose the possibility that particular applications of vertical restrictions might justify *per se* prohibition under *Northern Pac. R. Co.* But we do make clear that departure from the rule-of-reason standard must be based upon demonstrable economic effect rather than—as in *Schwinn*—upon formalistic line drawing.

In sum, we conclude that the appropriate decision is to return to the rule of reason that governed vertical restrictions prior to *Schwinn*. When anticompetitive effects are shown to result from particular vertical restrictions they can be adequately policed under the rule of reason, the standard traditionally applied for the majority of anticompetitive practices challenged under § 1 of the Act. Accordingly, the decision of the Court of Appeals is

*Affirmed.*

---

# Notes & Questions on *Per Se* Illegality and the Rule of Reason

1. *Socony-Vacuum Oil* and *GTE Sylvania* are two of the most important decisions in modern antitrust law. *Socony* reconfirmed the *per se* rule for price fixing. *GTE Sylvania*

---

*United States v. Topco Associates, Inc.*, 405 U.S., at 608, is not to the contrary, for it involved a horizontal restriction among ostensible competitors.

27. There may be occasional problems in differentiating vertical restrictions from horizontal restrictions originating in agreements among the retailers. There is no doubt that restrictions in the latter category would be illegal *per se*, see, e.g., *United States v. General Motors Corp.*, 384 U.S. 127 (1966); *United States v. Topco Associates, Inc.*, *supra*, but we do not regard the problems of proof as sufficiently great to justify a *per se* rule.

28. The location restriction used by Sylvania was neither the least nor the most restrictive provision that it could have used. But we agree with the implicit judgment in *Schwinn* that a *per se* rule based on the nature of the restriction is, in general, undesirable. Although distinctions can be drawn among the frequently used restrictions, we are inclined to view them as differences of degree and form....We are unable to perceive significant social gain from channeling transactions into one form or another. Finally, we agree with the Court in *Schwinn* that the advantages of vertical restrictions should not be limited to the categories of new entrants and failing firms. Sylvania was faltering, if not failing, and we think it would be unduly artificial to deny it the use of valuable competitive tools.

29. The importance of stare decisis is, of course, unquestioned, but as Mr. Justice Frankfurter stated in *Helvering v. Hallock*, 309 U.S. 106, 119 (1940), "Stare decisis is a principle of policy and not a mechanical formula of adherence to the latest decision, however recent and questionable, when such adherence involves collision with a prior doctrine more embracing in its scope, intrinsically sounder, and verified by experience."

established the rule of reason as the appropriate mode of analysis for vertical nonprice restraints in product distribution. Both cases are still good law, and both have many progeny. Although both cases established important legal principles that are still viable, both are equally important for their analysis of the antitrust issues before them. Is that analysis based on verbal formalism, or on actual economic effect? Is it more "legal" or more "economic"? Is the answer appropriate to the kind of law that antitrust is and the kinds of things it governs?

2. Try to describe, as succinctly as you can, exactly what the defendants in each of these two cases did. In *Socony*, did the defendants actually agree on what the prices of gasoline would be? Was their conduct the same as that of crooked contractors who "rig bids" on government contracts by deciding who will make the low bid, and for how much? What precisely was wrong with their conduct, and why did Justice Douglas declare it an assault on the "central nervous system" of our economy?

3. In *Socony*, why didn't the Court care whether the price of gasoline was reasonable? What were the economic reasons? What were the institutional reasons? Was the Court being too harsh in not even permitting the defendants to justify the prices that resulted from their conduct? Should the defendants have been given a chance to demonstrate that the price trends reported by the government were due in whole or part to changes in general economic conditions? Why or why not?

4. How broad or narrow is the *per se* rule of *Socony*? Would/should it apply to competitors who agree on only a *component* of price? on discounts or rebates, or whether to provide them?

5. Both *Socony* and *Appalachian Coals*, to which the *Socony* Court refers, involved responses to drastic decreases in consumer demand as a result of the Great Depression. In *Socony*, oil producers complained that, due to low demand and price wars, prices for gasoline were insufficient to justify running and maintaining many wells. For technical reasons, they said, wells that stopped production even temporarily would be spoiled, i.e., rendered useless for future production, thereby forfeiting all the capital investment in drilling them and preparing their infrastructure. *Appalachian Coals* involved similar claims that low prices would drive coal producers into bankruptcy, but there was no claim that temporary cessation of mining would spoil the mines. If the *Socony* Court rejected these Depression-era justifications for trying to control prices by collective action, is there any justification that is likely to succeed today?

6. *GTE Sylvania* is perhaps the most important antitrust decision in the last thirty years. Like a number of important antitrust decisions, it overruled a decision to the contrary—in this case one only four years old. What precisely did the defendant in *GTE Sylvania* do? What economic justification was there for its conduct? What possible economic harm might that conduct have caused?

7. Exactly how did the defendants' conduct in *Socony* differ from the defendant's conduct in *GTE Sylvania*? In footnote 14 (the Court's footnote 18), the Court describes the focus of *GTE Sylvania* as "nonprice vertical restrictions." What does this mean? Can you describe precisely what each word in that phrase means and why it is important from an economic perspective? Why should price restraints be illegal *per se*, and nonprice restraints only subject to the rule of reason? What about the vertical/horizontal distinction? Can you explain it? Which type of restraint—vertical or horizontal—is more likely to affect competition adversely?

8. The *GTE Sylvania* Court also emphasizes the distinction between interbrand and intrabrand competition. Can you explain that distinction? Can you give a concrete ex-

ample of each kind of competition, preferably from your own personal experience? The *GTE Sylvania* Court also states that *inter*brand competition is the primary focus of antitrust law. Do you agree? Why or why not?

9. How did the restraints imposed by the defendant in *GTE Sylvania* affect both interbrand and intrabrand competition? Was the net effect procompetitive or anticompetitive? How did GTE Sylvania's market position (i.e., market dominance or lack of it) affect the analysis and conclusion? If GTE Sylvania had had an 85% share of the market for color televisions, would/should the Court have reached the same result? Is it better to consider such factors as market share under a *per se* rule or the rule of reason?

---

# IV. The Evolution of Antitrust Law and Licensing

## State Oil Co. v. Khan
### 522 U.S. 3 (1997)

JUSTICE O'CONNOR delivered the opinion of the Court.

Under § 1 of the Sherman Act, "every contract, combination..., or conspiracy, in restraint of trade" is illegal. In *Albrecht v. Herald Co.*, 390 U.S. 145, 88 S. Ct. 869, 19 L. Ed. 2d 998 (1968), this Court held that vertical maximum price fixing is a *per se* violation of that statute. In this case, we are asked to reconsider that decision in light of subsequent decisions of this Court. We conclude that *Albrecht* should be overruled.

I

Respondents, Barkat U. Khan and his corporation, entered into an agreement with petitioner, State Oil Company, to lease and operate a gas station and convenience store owned by State Oil. The agreement provided that respondents would obtain the station's gasoline supply from State Oil at a price equal to a suggested retail price set by State Oil, less a margin of 3.25 cents per gallon. Under the agreement, respondents could charge any amount for gasoline sold to the station's customers, but if the price charged was higher than State Oil's suggested retail price, the excess was to be rebated to State Oil. Respondents could sell gasoline for less than State Oil's suggested retail price, but any such decrease would reduce their 3.25 cents-per-gallon margin.

About a year after respondents began operating the gas station, they fell behind in lease payments. State Oil then gave notice of its intent to terminate the agreement and commenced a state court proceeding to evict respondents. At State Oil's request, the state court appointed a receiver to operate the gas station. The receiver operated the station for several months without being subject to the price restraints in respondents' agreement with State Oil. According to respondents, the receiver obtained an overall profit margin in excess of 3.25 cents per gallon by lowering the price of regular-grade gasoline and raising the price of premium grades.

Respondents sued State Oil in the United States District Court for the Northern District of Illinois, alleging in part that State Oil had engaged in price fixing in violation of

§ 1 of the Sherman Act by preventing respondents from raising or lowering retail gas prices. According to the complaint, but for the agreement with State Oil, respondents could have charged different prices based on the grades of gasoline, in the same way that the receiver had, thereby achieving increased sales and profits. State Oil responded that the agreement did not actually prevent respondents from setting gasoline prices, and that, in substance, respondents did not allege a violation of antitrust laws by their claim that State Oil's suggested retail price was not optimal.

The District Court found that the allegations in the complaint did not state a *per se* violation of the Sherman Act because they did not establish the sort of "manifestly anti-competitive implications or pernicious effect on competition" that would justify *per se* prohibition of State Oil's conduct.... The District Court held that respondents had not shown that a difference in gasoline pricing would have increased the station's sales; nor had they shown that State Oil had market power or that its pricing provisions affected competition in a relevant market.

Accordingly, the District Court entered summary judgment for State Oil on respondents' Sherman Act claim.

The Court of Appeals for the Seventh Circuit reversed. The court first noted that the agreement between respondents and State Oil did indeed fix maximum gasoline prices by making it "worthless" for respondents to exceed the suggested retail prices. After reviewing legal and economic aspects of price fixing, the court concluded that State Oil's pricing scheme was a *per se* antitrust violation under *Albrecht v. Herald Co.*, *supra*. Although the Court of Appeals characterized *Albrecht* as "unsound when decided" and "inconsistent with later decisions" of this Court, it felt constrained to follow that decision. In light of *Albrecht* and *Atlantic Richfield Co. v. USA Petroleum Co.*, 495 U.S. 328, 110 S. Ct. 1884, 109 L. Ed. 2d 333 (1990) (*ARCO*), the court found that respondents could have suffered antitrust injury from not being able to adjust gasoline prices.

We granted certiorari to consider two questions, whether State Oil's conduct constitutes a *per se* violation of the Sherman Act and whether respondents are entitled to recover damages based on that conduct.

II

A

Although the Sherman Act, by its terms, prohibits every agreement "in restraint of trade," this Court has long recognized that Congress intended to outlaw only unreasonable restraints. As a consequence, most antitrust claims are analyzed under a "rule of reason," according to which the finder of fact must decide whether the questioned practice imposes an unreasonable restraint on competition, taking into account a variety of factors, including specific information about the relevant business, its condition before and after the restraint was imposed, and the restraint's history, nature, and effect. Some types of restraints, however, have such predictable and pernicious anticompetitive effect, and such limited potential for procompetitive benefit, that they are deemed unlawful *per se*. *Northern Pacific R. Co. v. United States*, 356 U.S. 1, 5, 78 S. Ct. 514, 2 L. Ed. 2d 545 (1958).

*Per se* treatment is appropriate "once experience with a particular kind of restraint enables the Court to predict with confidence that the rule of reason will condemn it." *Maricopa County, supra,* at 344; *see also Broadcast Music, Inc. v. Columbia Broadcasting*

*System, Inc.*, 441 U.S. 1, 19, n. 33, 99 S. Ct. 1551, 60 L. Ed. 2d 1 (1979). Thus, we have expressed reluctance to adopt *per se* rules with regard to "restraints imposed in the context of business relationships where the economic impact of certain practices is not immediately obvious." *FTC* v. *Indiana Federation of Dentists*, 476 U.S. 447, 458–59, 106 S. Ct. 2009, 90 L. Ed. 2d 445 (1986).

A review of this Court's decisions leading up to and beyond *Albrecht* is relevant to our assessment of the continuing validity of the *per se* rule established in *Albrecht*. Beginning with *Dr. Miles Medical Co. v. John D. Park & Sons Co.*, 220 U.S. 373, 31 S. Ct. 376, 55 L. Ed. 502 (1911), the Court recognized the illegality of agreements under which manufacturers or suppliers set the minimum resale prices to be charged by their distributors. By 1940, the Court broadly declared all business combinations "formed for the purpose and with the effect of raising, depressing, fixing, pegging, or stabilizing the price of a commodity in interstate or foreign commerce" illegal *per se*. *United States v. Socony-Vacuum Oil Co.*, 310 U.S. 150, 223, 60 S. Ct. 811, 84 L. Ed. 1129 (1940).

Accordingly, the Court condemned an agreement between two affiliated liquor distillers to limit the maximum price charged by retailers in *Kiefer-Stewart Co. v. Joseph E. Seagram & Sons, Inc.*, 340 U.S. 211, 71 S. Ct. 259, 95 L. Ed. 219 (1951), noting that agreements to fix maximum prices, "no less than those to fix minimum prices, cripple the freedom of traders and thereby restrain their ability to sell in accordance with their own judgment."

In subsequent cases, the Court's attention turned to arrangements through which suppliers imposed restrictions on dealers with respect to matters other than resale price. In *White Motor Co. v. United States*, 372 U.S. 253, 83 S. Ct. 696, 9 L. Ed. d 738 (1963), the Court considered the validity of a manufacturer's assignment of exclusive territories to its distributors and dealers.

The Court determined that too little was known about the competitive impact of such vertical limitations to warrant treating them as *per se* unlawful. Four years later, in *United States v. Arnold, Schwinn & Co.*, 388 U.S. 365, 87 S. Ct. 1856, 18 L. Ed. 2d 1249 (1967), the Court reconsidered the status of exclusive dealer territories and held that, upon the transfer of title to goods to a distributor, a supplier's imposition of territorial restrictions on the distributor was "so obviously destructive of competition" as to constitute a *per se* violation of the Sherman Act.

In *Schwinn*, the Court acknowledged that some vertical restrictions, such as the conferral of territorial rights or franchises, could have procompetitive benefits by allowing smaller enterprises to compete, and that such restrictions might avert vertical integration in the distribution process. The Court drew the line, however, at permitting manufacturers to control product marketing once dominion over the goods had passed to dealers.

*Albrecht*, decided the following Term, involved a newspaper publisher who had granted exclusive territories to independent carriers subject to their adherence to a maximum price on resale of the newspapers to the public. Influenced by its decisions in *Socony-Vacuum*, *Kiefer-Stewart*, and *Schwinn*, the Court concluded that it was *per se* unlawful for the publisher to fix the maximum resale price of its newspapers. 390 U.S. at 152–54. The Court acknowledged that "maximum and minimum price fixing may have different consequences in many situations," but nonetheless condemned maximum price fixing for "substituting the perhaps erroneous judgment of a seller for the forces of the competitive market."

*Albrecht* was animated in part by the fear that vertical maximum price fixing could allow suppliers to discriminate against certain dealers, restrict the services that dealers could afford to offer customers, or disguise minimum price fixing schemes. The Court rejected the notion (both on the record of that case and in the abstract) that, because the newspaper publisher "granted exclusive territories, a price ceiling was necessary to protect the public from price gouging by dealers who had monopoly power in their own territories."

In a vigorous dissent, Justice Harlan asserted that the majority had erred in equating the effects of maximum and minimum price fixing. *Id.*, at 156–68 (Harlan, J., dissenting). Justice Harlan pointed out that, because the majority was establishing a *per se* rule, the proper inquiry was "not whether dictation of maximum prices is *ever* illegal, but whether it is *always* illegal." He also faulted the majority for conclusively listing "certain unfortunate consequences that maximum price dictation might have in other cases," even as it rejected evidence that the publisher's practice of fixing maximum prices counteracted potentially anticompetitive actions by its distributors. Justice Stewart also dissented, asserting that the publisher's maximum price fixing scheme should be properly viewed as promoting competition, because it protected consumers from dealers such as Albrecht, who, as "the only person who could sell for home delivery the city's only daily morning newspaper," was "a monopolist within his own territory." *Id.*, at 168 (Stewart, J., dissenting).

Nine years later, in *Continental T. V., Inc. v. GTE Sylvania Inc.*, 433 U.S. 36, 97 S. Ct. 2549, 53 L. Ed. 2d 568 (1977), the Court overruled *Schwinn*, thereby rejecting application of a *per se* rule in the context of vertical nonprice restrictions. The Court acknowledged the principle of *stare decisis*, but explained that the need for clarification in the law justified reconsideration of *Schwinn*:

> Since its announcement, *Schwinn* has been the subject of continuing controversy and confusion, both in the scholarly journals and in the federal courts. The great weight of scholarly opinion has been critical of the decision, and a number of the federal courts confronted with analogous vertical restrictions have sought to limit its reach. In our view, the experience of the past 10 years should be brought to bear on this subject of considerable commercial importance.

433 U.S. at 47–49 (footnotes omitted). The Court considered the historical context of *Schwinn*, noting that *Schwinn's per se* rule against vertical nonprice restrictions came only four years after the Court had refused to endorse a similar rule in *White Motor Co.*, and that the decision neither explained the "sudden change in position," nor referred to the accepted requirements for *per se* violations set forth in *Northern Pacific R. Co.* The Court then reviewed scholarly works supporting the economic utility of vertical nonprice restraints. *See id.*, at 54–57 (citing, *e.g.*, Posner, *Antitrust Policy and the Supreme Court: An Analysis of the Restricted Distribution, Horizontal Merger and Potential Competition Decisions*, 75 COLUM. L. REV. 282 (1975); Preston, *Restrictive Distribution Arrangements: Economic Analysis and Public Policy Standards*, 30 LAW & CONTEMP. PROB. 506 (1965)). The Court concluded that, because "departure from the rule-of-reason standard must be based upon demonstrable economic effect rather than—as in *Schwinn*—upon formalistic line drawing," the appropriate course would be "to return to the rule of reason that governed vertical restrictions prior to *Schwinn.*" *GTE Sylvania, supra*, at 58–59.

In *GTE Sylvania*, the Court declined to comment on *Albrecht's per se* treatment of vertical maximum price restrictions, noting that the issue "involved significantly different questions of analysis and policy." Subsequent decisions of the Court, however, have hinted that the analytical underpinnings of *Albrecht* were substantially weakened by *GTE Sylvania*. We noted in *Maricopa County* that vertical restraints are generally more defensible than horizontal restraints. And we explained in *324 Liquor Corp. v. Duffy*, 479 U.S. 335, 341–42, 107 S. Ct. 720, 93 L. Ed. 2d 667 (1987), that decisions such as *GTE Sylvania* "recognize the possibility that a vertical restraint imposed by a *single* manufacturer or wholesaler may stimulate interbrand competition even as it reduces intrabrand competition."

Most recently, in *ARCO*, 495 U.S. 328, 110 S. Ct. 1884, 109 L. Ed. 2d 333 (1990), although *Albrecht's* continuing validity was not squarely before the Court, some disfavor with that decision was signaled by our statement that we would "assume, *arguendo*, that *Albrecht* correctly held that vertical, maximum price fixing is subject to the *per se* rule." 495 U.S. at 335, n. 5. More significantly, we specifically ceiling acknowledged that vertical maximum price fixing "may have procompetitive interbrand effects," and pointed out that, in the wake of *GTE Sylvania*, "the procompetitive potential of a vertical maximum price restraint is more evident…than it was when *Albrecht* was decided, because exclusive territorial arrangements and other nonprice restrictions were unlawful *per se* in 1968." 495 U.S. at 343, n. 13 (citing several commentators identifying procompetitive effects of vertical maximum price fixing, including, *e.g.*, P. AREEDA & H. HOVENKAMP, ANTITRUST LAW ¶ 340.30b, p. 378, n. 24 (1988 Supp.); Blair & Harrison, *Rethinking Antitrust Injury*, 42 VAND. L. REV. 1539, 1553 (1989); Easterbrook, *Maximum Price Fixing*, 48 U. CHI. L. REV. 886, 887–90 (1981)).

## B

Thus, our reconsideration of *Albrecht's* continuing validity is informed by several of our decisions, as well as a considerable body of scholarship discussing the effects of vertical restraints. Our analysis is also guided by our general view that the primary purpose of the antitrust laws is to protect interbrand competition. "Low prices," we have explained, "benefit consumers regardless of how those prices are set, and so long as they are above predatory levels, they do not threaten competition." *ARCO, supra,* at 340. Our interpretation of the Sherman Act also incorporates the notion that condemnation of practices resulting in lower prices to consumers is "especially costly" because "cutting prices in order to increase business often is the very essence of competition." *Matsushita Elec. Industrial Co. v. Zenith Radio Corp.*, 475 U.S. 574, 594, 106 S. Ct. 1348, 89 L. Ed. 2d 538 (1986).

So informed, we find it difficult to maintain that vertically-imposed maximum prices could harm consumers or competition to the extent necessary to justify their *per se* invalidation. As Chief Judge Posner wrote for the Court of Appeals in this case:

> As for maximum resale price fixing, unless the supplier is a monopsonist he cannot squeeze his dealers' margins below a competitive level; the attempt to do so would just drive the dealers into the arms of a competing supplier. A supplier might, however, fix a maximum resale price in order to prevent his dealers from exploiting a monopoly position.…Suppose that State Oil, perhaps to encourage…dealer services…has spaced its dealers sufficiently far apart to limit competition among them (or even given each of them an exclusive territory); and suppose further that Union 76 is a sufficiently distinctive and popular brand to give the dealers in it at least a modicum of monopoly power. Then State Oil might want to place a ceiling on the dealers' resale prices in order to prevent them from exploiting that monopoly power fully. It would

do this not out of disinterested malice, but in its commercial self-interest. The higher the price at which gasoline is resold, the smaller the volume sold, and so the lower the profit to the supplier if the higher profit per gallon at the higher price is being snared by the dealer.

93 F.3d at 1362. *See also* R. Bork, The Antitrust Paradox 281–82 (1978) ("There could, of course, be no anticonsumer effect from [the type of price fixing considered in *Albrecht*], and one suspects that the paper has a legitimate interest in keeping subscriber prices down in order to increase circulation and maximize revenues from advertising.").

We recognize that the *Albrecht* decision presented a number of theoretical justifications for a *per se* rule against vertical maximum price fixing. But criticism of those premises abounds. The *Albrecht* decision was grounded in the fear that maximum price fixing by suppliers could interfere with dealer freedom. In response, as one commentator has pointed out, "the ban on maximum resale price limitations declared in *Albrecht* in the name of 'dealer freedom' has actually prompted many suppliers to integrate forward into distribution, thus eliminating the very independent trader for whom *Albrecht* professed solicitude." P. Areeda [& H. Hovenkamp], Antitrust Law, ¶ 1635, p. 395 (1989). For example, integration in the newspaper industry since *Albrecht* has given rise to litigation between independent distributors and publishers. *See* P. Areeda & H. Hovenkamp, Antitrust Law ¶ 729.7, pp. 599–614 (1996 Supp.).

The *Albrecht* Court also expressed the concern that maximum prices may be set too low for dealers to offer consumers essential or desired services. But such conduct, by driving away customers, would seem likely to harm manufacturers as well as dealers and consumers, making it unlikely that a supplier would set such a price as a matter of business judgment. In addition, *Albrecht* noted that vertical maximum price fixing could effectively channel distribution through large or specially-advantaged dealers. It is unclear, however, that a supplier would profit from limiting its market by excluding potential dealers. Further, although vertical maximum price fixing might limit the viability of inefficient dealers, that consequence is not necessarily harmful to competition and consumers.

Finally, *Albrecht* reflected the Court's fear that maximum price fixing could be used to disguise arrangements to fix minimum prices, which remain illegal *per se*. Although we have acknowledged the possibility that maximum pricing might mask minimum pricing, see *Maricopa County*, 457 U.S. at 348, we believe that such conduct—as with the other concerns articulated in *Albrecht*—can be appropriately recognized and punished under the rule of reason.

Not only are the potential injuries cited in *Albrecht* less serious than the Court imagined, the *per se* rule established therein could in fact exacerbate problems related to the unrestrained exercise of market power by monopolist-dealers. Indeed, both courts and antitrust scholars have noted that *Albrecht's* rule may actually harm consumers and manufacturers. Other commentators have also explained that *Albrecht's per se* rule has even more potential for deleterious effect on competition after our decision in *GTE Sylvania*, because, now that vertical nonprice restrictions are not unlawful *per se*, the likelihood of dealer monopoly power is increased. We do not intend to suggest that dealers generally possess sufficient market power to exploit a monopoly situation. Such retail market power may in fact be uncommon. Nor do we hold that a ban on vertical maximum price fixing inevitably has anticompetitive consequences in the exclusive dealer context.

After reconsidering *Albrecht's* rationale and the substantial criticism the decision has received, however, we conclude that there is insufficient economic justification for *per se* invalidation of vertical maximum price fixing. That is so not only because it is difficult to accept the assumptions underlying *Albrecht*, but also because *Albrecht* has little or no relevance to ongoing enforcement of the Sherman Act. *See Copperweld Corp. v. Independence Tube Corp.*, 467 U.S. 752, 777 & n.25, 104 S. Ct. 2731, 81 L. Ed. 2d 628 (1984). Moreover, neither the parties nor any of the *amici curiae* have called our attention to any cases in which enforcement efforts have been directed solely against the conduct encompassed by *Albrecht's per se* rule.

Respondents argue that reconsideration of *Albrecht* should require "persuasive, expert testimony establishing that the *per se* rule has distorted the market." Their reasoning ignores the fact that *Albrecht* itself relied solely upon hypothetical effects of vertical maximum price fixing. Further, *Albrecht's* dire predictions have not been borne out, even though manufacturers and suppliers appear to have fashioned schemes to get around the *per se* rule against vertical maximum price fixing. In these circumstances, it is the retention of the rule of *Albrecht*, and not, as respondents would have it, the rule's elimination, that lacks adequate justification.

* * *

C

Despite what Chief Judge Posner aptly described as *Albrecht's* "infirmities, [and] its increasingly wobbly, moth-eaten foundations," 93 F.3d at 1363, there remains the question whether *Albrecht* deserves continuing respect under the doctrine of *stare decisis*. The Court of Appeals was correct in applying that principle despite disagreement with *Albrecht*, for it is this Court's prerogative alone to overrule one of its precedents.

We approach the reconsideration of decisions of this Court with the utmost caution. *Stare decisis* reflects "a policy judgment that in most matters it is more important that the applicable rule of law be settled than that it be settled right." *Agostini v. Felton*, 1997 U.S. LEXIS 4000, *58, 117 S. Ct. 1997, 138 L. Ed. 2d 391 (1997) [internal citation omitted]. It is the preferred course because it promotes the evenhanded, predictable, and consistent development of legal principles, fosters reliance on judicial decisions, and contributes to the actual and perceived integrity of the judicial process. This Court has expressed its reluctance to overrule decisions involving statutory interpretation, *see, e.g.*, *Illinois Brick Co. v. Illinois*, 431 U.S. 720, 736, 97 S. Ct. 2061, 52 L. Ed. 2d 707 (1977), and has acknowledged that *stare decisis* concerns are at their acme in cases involving property and contract rights.... Both of those concerns are arguably relevant in this case.

But *stare decisis* is not an inexorable command. In the area of antitrust law, there is a competing interest, well-represented in this Court's decisions, in recognizing and adapting to changed circumstances and the lessons of accumulated experience. Thus, the general presumption that legislative changes should be left to Congress has less force with respect to the Sherman Act in light of the accepted view that Congress "expected the courts to give shape to the statute's broad mandate by drawing on common-law tradition." *National Soc. of Professional Engineers v. United States*, 435 U.S. 679, 688, 98 S. Ct. 1355, 55 L. Ed. 2d 637 (1978). As we have explained, the term "restraint of trade," as used in § 1, also "invokes the common law itself, and not merely the static content that the common law had assigned to the term in 1890." *Business Electronics*, 485 U.S. at 732; *see also GTE Sylvania*, 433 U.S. at 53, n. 21.... Accordingly, this Court has reconsidered its decisions construing the Sherman Act when the theoretical underpinnings of those decisions are called into serious question.

Although we do not "lightly assume that the economic realities underlying earlier decisions have changed, or that earlier judicial perceptions of those realities were in error," we have noted that "different sorts of agreements" may amount to restraints of trade "in varying times and circumstances," and "it would make no sense to create out of the single term 'restraint of trade' a chronologically schizoid statute, in which a 'rule of reason' evolves with new circumstances and new wisdom, but a line of *per se* illegality remains forever fixed where it was." *Business Electronics, supra,* at 731–32. Just as *Schwinn* was "the subject of continuing controversy and confusion" under the "great weight" of scholarly criticism, *GTE Sylvania, supra,* at 47–48, *Albrecht* has been widely criticized since its inception. With the views underlying *Albrecht* eroded by this Court's precedent, there is not much of that decision to salvage.

* * *

Although the rule of *Albrecht* has been in effect for some time, the inquiry we must undertake requires considering "'the effect of the antitrust laws upon vertical distributional restraints in the American economy today.'" *GTE Sylvania, supra,* at 53, n.21 (quoting *Schwinn,* 388 U.S. at 392 (Stewart, J., concurring in part and dissenting in part)). As the Court noted in *ARCO,* 495 U.S. at 336, n. 6, there has not been another case since *Albrecht* in which this Court has "confronted an unadulterated vertical, maximum-price-fixing arrangement." Now that we confront *Albrecht* directly, we find its conceptual foundations gravely weakened.

In overruling *Albrecht,* we of course do not hold that all vertical maximum price fixing is *per se* lawful. Instead, vertical maximum price fixing, like the majority of commercial arrangements subject to the antitrust laws, should be evaluated under the rule of reason. In our view, rule-of-reason analysis will effectively identify those situations in which vertical maximum price fixing amounts to anticompetitive conduct.

There remains the question whether respondents are entitled to recover damages based on State Oil's conduct. Although the Court of Appeals noted that "the district judge was right to conclude that if the rule of reason is applicable, Khan loses," its consideration of this case was necessarily premised on *Albrecht's per se* rule. Under the circumstances, the matter should be reviewed by the Court of Appeals in the first instance. We therefore vacate the judgment of the Court of Appeals and remand the case for further proceedings consistent with this opinion.

*It is so ordered.*

─────────

# Notes on *Khan* and the Evolution of Antitrust Law

1. Like *GTE Sylvania,* the *Khan* decision marks another reversal in direction by the Supreme Court. Do you agree with the Court that getting it right is more important than following precedent in the field of antitrust? What arguments can you make for getting it right, and what arguments for stability?

2. Are *Socony* and *Khan* consistent? Did the conduct of the defendant in *Khan* (and in *Albrecht,* discussed in *Khan*) differ from the conduct of the defendant in *Socony*? If so, precisely what was the difference, and what economic effect would it be expected to have?

3. *GTE Sylvania* stands for the general proposition that vertical nonprice restraints in product distribution are governed by the rule of reason. Thus, if a restraint is vertical in character and doesn't involve price, it should be lawful if reasonable. Was the restraint in *Khan* vertical? Did it involve price? Do the rule and result in *Khan* suggest that one out of two is good enough?

4. The rationale for *Khan* is perhaps easier to see by looking at the facts of *Albrecht*. Precisely what did the defendant in *Albrecht* do? What were the probable purpose and economic effect of its conduct? Was the *Khan* Court right in overruling *Albrecht* and refusing to treat such conduct as illegal *per se*? What mode of analysis—*per se* illegality or the rule of reason—applies to vertical *minimum* price restraints in product distribution after *Khan*?

5. *GTE Sylvania* introduced the notion of interbrand competition as a key purpose of antitrust law. Can you justify the result in *Khan* based on the primacy of interbrand competition? How might a manufacturer's setting distributors' *maximum* resale prices help one brand compete against another? How might its doing so hurt interbrand competition? Is it obvious in general whether the effects of such a restraint will be procompetitive or anticompetitive? If not, was the Court right to reject the *per se* rule?

6. Which of these three antitrust cases, *Socony*, *GTE Sylvania*, or *Khan*, is more likely to apply to contractual restraints in licensing and why? Are licensing agreements generally horizontal or vertical? Do restraints in licensing generally involve price or other terms? When they involve price, will they normally involve vertical or horizontal restraints? minimum or maximum prices? Are the federal government's *Antitrust Guidelines for the Licensing of Intellectual Property*, *infra* p. 478, right when they say that licensing restraints generally fall under the rule of reason?

---

# United States v. Topco Associates, Inc.

### 405 U.S. 596 (1972)

MR. JUSTICE MARSHALL delivered the opinion of the Court.

The United States brought this action for injunctive relief against alleged violation by Topco Associates, Inc. (Topco), of § 1 of the Sherman Act....Following a trial on the merits, the United States District Court for the Northern District of Illinois entered judgment for Topco,...and the United States appealed directly to this Court pursuant to § 2 of the Expediting Act....We noted probable jurisdiction, and we now reverse the judgment of the District Court.

I

Topco is a cooperative association of approximately 25 small and medium-sized regional supermarket chains that operate stores in some 33 States. Each of the member chains operates independently; there is no pooling of earnings, profits, capital, management, or advertising resources. No grocery business is conducted under the Topco name. Its basic function is to serve as a purchasing agent for its members.[1] In this ca-

---

1. In addition to purchasing various items for its members, Topco performs other related functions: e.g., it insures that there is adequate quality control on the products that it purchases; it assists members in developing specifications on certain types of products (e.g., equipment and supplies); and it also aids the members in purchasing goods through other sources.

pacity, it procures and distributes to the members more than 1,000 different food and related nonfood items, most of which are distributed under brand names owned by Topco. The association does not itself own any manufacturing, processing, or warehousing facilities, and the items that it procures for members are usually shipped directly from the packer or manufacturer to the members. Payment is made either to Topco or directly to the manufacturer at a cost that is virtually the same for the members as for Topco itself.

All of the stock in Topco is owned by the members, with the common stock, the only stock having voting rights, being equally distributed. The board of directors, which controls the operation of the association, is drawn from the members and is normally composed of high-ranking executive officers of member chains. It is the board that elects the association's officers and appoints committee members, and it is from the board that the principal executive officers of Topco must be drawn. Restrictions on the alienation of stock and the procedure for selecting all important officials of the association from within the ranks of its members give the members complete and unfettered control over the operations of the association.

Topco was founded in the 1940's by a group of small, local grocery chains, independently owned and operated, that desired to cooperate to obtain high quality merchandise under private labels in order to compete more effectively with larger national and regional chains.[2] With a line of canned, dairy, and other products, the association began. It added frozen foods in 1950, fresh produce in 1958, more general merchandise equipment and supplies in 1960, and a branded bacon and carcass beef selection program in 1966. By 1964, Topco's members had combined retail sales of more than $2 billion; by 1967, their sales totaled more than $2.3 billion, a figure exceeded by only three national grocery chains [A&P, Safeway, and Kroger].

Members of the association vary in the degree of market share that they possess in their respective areas. The range is from 1.5% to 16%, with the average being approximately 6%. While it is difficult to compare these figures with the market shares of larger regional and national chains because of the absence in the record of accurate statistics for these chains, there is much evidence in the record that Topco members are frequently in as strong a competitive position in their respective areas as any other chain. The strength of this competitive position is due, in some measure, to the success of

---

2. The founding members of Topco were having difficulty competing with larger chains. This difficulty was attributable in some degree to the fact that the larger chains were capable of developing their own private-label programs.

Private-label products differ from other brand-name products in that they are sold at a limited number of easily ascertainable stores. A&P, for example, was a pioneer in developing a series of products that were sold under an A&P label and that were only available in A&P stores. It is obvious that by using private-label products, a chain can achieve significant cost economies in purchasing, transportation, warehousing, promotion, and advertising. These economies may afford the chain opportunities for offering private-label products at lower prices than other brand-name products. This, in turn, provides many advantages of which some of the more important are: a store can offer national-brand products at the same price as other stores, while simultaneously offering a desirable, lower priced alternative; or, if the profit margin is sufficiently high on private-brand goods, national-brand products may be sold at reduced price. Other advantages include: enabling a chain to bargain more favorably with national-brand manufacturers by creating a broader supply base of manufacturers, thereby decreasing dependence on a few, large national-brand manufacturers; enabling a chain to create a "price-mix" whereby prices on special items can be lowered to attract customers while profits are maintained on other items; and creation of general goodwill by offering lower priced, higher quality goods.

Topco-brand products. Although only 10% of the total goods sold by Topco members bear the association's brand names, the profit on these goods is substantial and their very existence has improved the competitive potential of Topco members with respect to other large and powerful chains.

It is apparent that from meager beginnings approximately a quarter of a century ago, Topco has developed into a purchasing association wholly owned and operated by member chains, which possess much economic muscle, individually as well as cooperatively.

II

Section 1 of the Sherman Act provides, in relevant part:

> "Every contract, combination in the form of trust or otherwise, or conspiracy, in restraint of trade or commerce among the several States, or with foreign nations, is declared to be illegal...."

The United States charged that, beginning at least as early as 1960 and continuing up to the time that the complaint was filed, Topco had combined and conspired with its members to violate § 1 in two respects. First, the Government alleged that there existed: "a continuing agreement, understanding and concert of action among the co-conspirator member firms acting through Topco, the substantial terms of which have been and are that each co-conspirator member firm will sell Topco-controlled brands only within the marketing territory allocated to it, and will refrain from selling Topco-controlled brands outside such marketing territory." The division of marketing territories to which the complaint refers consists of a number of practices by the association.

Article IX, § 2, of the Topco bylaws establishes three categories of territorial licenses that members may secure from the association:

> "(a) *Exclusive*—An exclusive territory is one in which the member is licensed to sell all products bearing specified trademarks of the Association, to the exclusion of all other persons."

> "(b) *Non-exclusive*—A non-exclusive territory is one in which a member is licensed to sell all products bearing specified trademarks of the Association, but not to the exclusion of others who may also be licensed to sell products bearing the same trademarks of the Association in the same territory."

> "(c) *Coextensive*—A coextensive territory is one in which two (2) or more members are licensed to sell all products bearing specified trademarks of the Association to the exclusion of all other persons...."

When applying for membership, a chain must designate the type of license that it desires. Membership must first be approved by the board of directors, and thereafter by an affirmative vote of 75% of the association's members. If, however, the member whose operations are closest to those of the applicant, or any member whose operations are located within 100 miles of the applicant, votes against approval, an affirmative vote of 85% of the members is required for approval. Bylaws, Art. I, § 5. Because, as indicated by the record, members cooperate in accommodating each other's wishes, the procedure for approval provides, in essence, that members have a veto of sorts over actual or potential competition in the territorial areas in which they are concerned.

Following approval, each new member signs an agreement with Topco designating the territory in which that member may sell Topco-brand products. No member may sell these products outside the territory in which it is licensed. Most licenses are exclusive, and even those denominated "coextensive" or "non-exclusive" prove to be *de facto* exclusive. Exclusive territorial areas are often allocated to members who do no actual business in those areas on the theory that they may wish to expand at some indefinite future time and that expansion would likely be in the direction of the allocated territory. When combined with each member's veto power over new members, provisions for exclusivity work effectively to insulate members from competition in Topco-brand goods. Should a member violate its license agreement and sell in areas other than those in which it is licensed, its membership can be terminated under Art. IV, §§ 2 (a) and 2 (b) of the bylaws. Once a territory is classified as exclusive, either formally or *de facto*, it is extremely unlikely that the classification will ever be changed. *See* Bylaws, Art. IX.

The Government maintains that this scheme of dividing markets violates the Sherman Act because it operates to prohibit competition in Topco-brand products among grocery chains engaged in retail operations. The Government also makes a subsidiary challenge to Topco's practices regarding licensing members to sell at wholesale. Under the bylaws, members are not permitted to sell any products supplied by the association at wholesale, whether trademarked or not, without first applying for and receiving special permission from the association to do so.[3] Before permission is granted, other licensees (usually retailers), whose interests may potentially be affected by wholesale operations, are consulted as to their wishes in the matter. If permission is obtained, the member must agree to restrict the sale of Topco products to a specific geographic area and to sell under any conditions imposed by the association. Permission to wholesale has often been sought by members, only to be denied by the association. The Government contends that this amounts not only to a territorial restriction violative of the Sherman Act, but also to a restriction on customers that in itself is violative of the Act.

From the inception of this lawsuit, Topco accepted as true most of the Government's allegations regarding territorial divisions and restrictions on wholesaling, although it differed greatly with the Government on the conclusions, both factual and legal, to be drawn from these facts.

---

3. Article IX, § 8, of the bylaws provides, in relevant part:
"Unless a member's membership and licensing agreement provides that such member may sell at wholesale, a member may not wholesale products supplied by the Association. If a membership and licensing agreement permits a member to sell at wholesale, such member shall control the resale of products bearing trademarks of the Association so that such sales are confined to the territories granted to the member, and the method of selling shall conform in all respects with the Association's policies."
Shortly before trial, Topco amended this bylaw with an addition that permitted any member to wholesale in the exclusive territories in which it retailed. But the restriction remained the same in all other cases.
It is apparent that this bylaw on its face applies whether or not the products sold are trademarked by Topco. Despite the fact that Topco's general manager testified at trial that, in practice, the restriction is confined to Topco-branded products, the District Court found that the bylaw is applied as written. We find nothing clearly erroneous in this finding. Assuming, *arguendo*, however, that the restriction is confined to products trademarked by Topco, the result in this case would not change.

* * *

III

On its face, §1 of the Sherman Act appears to bar any combination of entrepreneurs so long as it is "in restraint of trade." Theoretically, all manufacturers, distributors, merchants, sellers, and buyers could be considered as potential competitors of each other. Were §1 to be read in the narrowest possible way, any commercial contract could be deemed to violate it. *Chicago Board of Trade v. United States*, 246 U.S. 231, 238 (1918) (Brandeis, J.). The history underlying the formulation of the antitrust laws led this Court to conclude, however, that Congress did not intend to prohibit all contracts, nor even all contracts that might in some insignificant degree or attenuated sense restrain trade or competition. In lieu of the narrowest possible reading of §1, the Court adopted a "rule of reason" analysis for determining whether most business combinations or contracts violate the prohibitions of the Sherman Act.... An analysis of the reasonableness of particular restraints includes consideration of the facts peculiar to the business in which the restraint is applied, the nature of the restraint and its effects, and the history of the restraint and the reasons for its adoption. *Chicago Board of Trade v. United States, supra*, at 238.

While the Court has utilized the "rule of reason" in evaluating the legality of most restraints alleged to be violative of the Sherman Act, it has also developed the doctrine that certain business relationships are *per se* violations of the Act without regard to a consideration of their reasonableness. In *Northern Pacific R. Co. v. United States*, 356 U.S. 1, 5 (1958), Mr. Justice Black explained the appropriateness of, and the need for, *per se* rules:

> There are certain agreements or practices which because of their pernicious effect on competition and lack of any redeeming virtue are conclusively presumed to be unreasonable and therefore illegal without elaborate inquiry as to the precise harm they have caused or the business excuse for their use. This principle of *per se* unreasonableness not only makes the type of restraints which are proscribed by the Sherman Act more certain to the benefit of everyone concerned, but it also avoids the necessity for an incredibly complicated and prolonged economic investigation into the entire history of the industry involved, as well as related industries, in an effort to determine at large whether a particular restraint has been unreasonable—an inquiry so often wholly fruitless when undertaken.

It is only after considerable experience with certain business relationships that courts classify them as *per se* violations of the Sherman Act.... One of the classic examples of a *per se* violation of §1 is an agreement between competitors at the same level of the market structure to allocate territories in order to minimize competition. Such concerted action is usually termed a "horizontal" restraint, in contradistinction to combinations of persons at different levels of the market structure, e.g., manufacturers and distributors, which are termed "vertical" restraints. This Court has reiterated time and time again that "horizontal territorial limitations...are naked restraints of trade with no purpose except stifling of competition." *White Motor Co. v. United States*, 372 U.S. 253, 263 (1963). Such limitations are *per se* violations of the Sherman Act. *See Addyston Pipe & Steel Co. v. United States*, 175 U.S. 211 (1899), aff'g 85 F. 271 (CA6 1898) (Taft, J.); *United States v. National Lead Co.*, 332 U.S. 319 (1947); *Timken Roller Bearing Co. v. United States*, 341 U.S. 593 (1951); *Northern Pacific R. Co. v. United States, supra; Citizen Publishing Co. v. United States*, 394 U.S. 131 (1969); *United States v. Sealy, Inc.*, 388 U.S. 350 (1967); *United States v. Arnold, Schwinn & Co.*, 388 U.S. 365, 390 (1967) (STEWART, J., concurring in part and dissenting in part); *Serta Associates, Inc. v. United States*, 393 U.S. 534 (1969), aff'g 296 F. Supp. 1121, 1128 (ND Ill. 1968).

We think that it is clear that the restraint in this case is a horizontal one, and, therefore, a *per se* violation of § 1. The District Court failed to make any determination as to whether there were *per se* horizontal territorial restraints in this case and simply applied a rule of reason in reaching its conclusions that the restraints were not illegal.... In so doing, the District Court erred.

*United States v. Sealy, Inc., supra,* is, in fact, on all fours with this case. Sealy licensed manufacturers of mattresses and bedding to make and sell products using the Sealy trademark. Like Topco, Sealy was a corporation owned almost entirely by its licensees, who elected the Board of Directors and controlled the business. Just as in this case, Sealy agreed with the licensees not to license other manufacturers or sellers to sell Sealy-brand products in a designated territory in exchange for the promise of the licensee who sold in that territory not to expand its sales beyond the area demarcated by Sealy. The Court held that this was a horizontal territorial restraint, which was *per se* violative of the Sherman Act.[4]

Whether or not we would decide this case the same way under the rule of reason used by the District Court is irrelevant to the issue before us. The fact is that courts are of limited utility in examining difficult economic problems.[5] Our inability to weigh, in any meaningful sense, destruction of competition in one sector of the economy against promotion of competition in another sector is one important reason we have formulated *per se* rules.

In applying these rigid rules, the Court has consistently rejected the notion that naked restraints of trade are to be tolerated because they are well intended or because they are allegedly developed to increase competition. *E. g., United States v. General Motors Corp.,* 384 U.S. 127, 146–47 (1966); *United States v. Masonite Corp.,* 316 U.S. 265 (1942); *Fashion Originators' Guild v. FTC,* 312 U.S. 457 (1941). Antitrust laws in general, and the Sherman Act in particular, are the Magna Carta of free enterprise. They are as important to the preservation of economic freedom and our free-enterprise system as the Bill of Rights is to the protection of our fundamental personal freedoms. And the freedom guaranteed each and every business, no matter how small, is the freedom to compete— to assert with vigor, imagination, devotion, and ingenuity whatever economic muscle it can muster. Implicit in such freedom is the notion that it cannot be foreclosed with respect to one sector of the economy because certain private citizens or groups believe that such foreclosure might promote greater competition in a more important sector of the economy. *Cf. United States v. Philadelphia National Bank,* 374 U.S. 321, 371 (1963).

The District Court determined that by limiting the freedom of its individual members to compete with each other, Topco was doing a greater good by fostering competition between members and other large supermarket chains. But, the fallacy in this is that Topco has no authority under the Sherman Act to determine the respective values of competition in various sectors of the economy. On the contrary, the Sherman Act gives to each Topco member and to each prospective member the right to ascertain for itself whether or not competition with other supermarket chains is more desirable than

---

4. It is true that in *Sealy* the Court dealt with price fixing as well as territorial restrictions. To the extent that *Sealy* casts doubt on whether horizontal territorial limitations, unaccompanied by price fixing, are *per se* violations of the Sherman Act, we remove that doubt today.

5. There has been much recent commentary on the wisdom of *per se* rules.... Without the *per se* rules, businessmen would be left with little to aid them in predicting in any particular case what courts will find to be legal and illegal under the Sherman Act. Should Congress ultimately determine that predictability is unimportant in this area of the law, it can, of course, make *per se* rules inapplicable in some or all cases, and leave courts free to ramble through the wilds of economic theory in order to maintain a flexible approach.

competition in the sale of Topco-brand products. Without territorial restrictions, Topco members may indeed "[cut] each other's throats." *Cf. White Motor Co., supra,* at 278 (Clark, J., dissenting). But, we have never found this possibility sufficient to warrant condoning horizontal restraints of trade.

The Court has previously noted with respect to price fixing, another *per se* violation of the Sherman Act, that: "The reasonable price fixed today may through economic and business changes become the unreasonable price of tomorrow. Once established, it may be maintained unchanged because of the absence of competition secured by the agreement for a price reasonable when fixed." *United States v. Trenton Potteries Co.,* 273 U.S. 392, 397 (1927). A similar observation can be made with regard to territorial limitations. *White Motor Co., supra,* at 265 n. 2 (BRENNAN, J., concurring). There have been tremendous departures from the notion of a free-enterprise system as it was originally conceived in this country. These departures have been the product of congressional action and the will of the people. If a decision is to be made to sacrifice competition in one portion of the economy for greater competition in another portion, this too is a decision that must be made by Congress and not by private forces or by the courts. Private forces are too keenly aware of their own interests in making such decisions and courts are ill-equipped and ill-situated for such decisionmaking. To analyze, interpret, and evaluate the myriad of competing interests and the endless data that would surely be brought to bear on such decisions, and to make the delicate judgment on the relative values to society of competitive areas of the economy, the judgment of the elected representatives of the people is required.

Just as the territorial restrictions on retailing Topco-brand products must fall, so must the territorial restrictions on wholesaling. The considerations are the same, and the Sherman Act requires identical results. We also strike down Topco's other restrictions on the right of its members to wholesale goods. These restrictions amount to regulation of the customers to whom members of Topco may sell Topco-brand goods. Like territorial restrictions, limitations on customers are intended to limit intra-brand competition and to promote inter-brand competition. For the reasons previously discussed, the arena in which Topco members compete must be left to their unfettered choice absent a contrary congressional determination....

We reverse the judgment of the District Court and remand the case for entry of an appropriate decree.

*It is so ordered.*

R. Justice Blackmun, concurring in the result.

The conclusion the Court reaches has its anomalous aspects, for surely, as the District Court's findings make clear, today's decision in the Government's favor will tend to stultify Topco members' competition with the great and larger chains. The bigs, therefore, should find it easier to get bigger and, as a consequence, reality seems at odds with the public interest. The *per se* rule, however, now appears to be so firmly established by the Court that, at this late date, I could not oppose it. Relief, if any is to be forthcoming, apparently must be by way of legislation.

MR. CHIEF JUSTICE BURGER, dissenting.

This case does not involve restraints on interbrand competition or an allocation of markets by an association with monopoly or near-monopoly control of the sources of supply of one or more varieties of staple goods. Rather, we have here an agreement among several small grocery chains to join in a cooperative endeavor that, in my view, has an unquestionably lawful principal purpose; in pursuit of that purpose they have mutually agreed to certain minimal ancillary restraints that are fully reasonable in view of the principal purpose and that have never before today been held by this Court to be *per se* violations of the Sherman Act.

In joining in this cooperative endeavor, these small chains did not agree to the restraints here at issue in order to make it possible for them to exploit an already established line of products through noncompetitive pricing. There was no such thing as a Topco line of products until this cooperative was formed. The restraints to which the cooperative's members have agreed deal only with the marketing of the products in the Topco line, and the only function of those restraints is to permit each member chain to establish, within its own geographical area and through its own local advertising and marketing efforts, a local consumer awareness of the trademarked family of products as that member's "private label" line. The goal sought was the enhancement of the individual members' abilities to compete, albeit to a modest degree, with the large national chains which had been successfully marketing private-label lines for several years. The sole reason for a cooperative endeavor was to make economically feasible such things as quality control, large quantity purchases at bulk prices, the development of attractively printed labels, and the ability to offer a number of different lines of trademarked products. All these things, of course, are feasible for the large national chains operating individually, but they are beyond the reach of the small operators proceeding alone.

I

*[Justice Burger exhaustively reviews the precedent cited by the majority and concludes that each cited case is inapposite, because it dealt primarily with price-fixing, because it involved vertical and not horizontal restraint, or for other reasons.]*

* * *

II

The foregoing analysis of the cases relied upon by the majority indicates to me that the Court is not merely following prior holdings; on the contrary, it is establishing a new *per se* rule. In the face of the District Court's well supported findings that the effects of such a rule in this case will be adverse to the public welfare, the Court lays down that rule without regard to the impact that the condemned practices may have on competition. In doing so, the Court virtually invites Congress to undertake to determine that impact. I question whether the Court is fulfilling the role assigned to it under the statute when it declines to make this determination; in any event, if the Court is unwilling on this record to assess the economic impact, it surely should not proceed to make a new rule to govern the economic activity.

* * *

Like the rule of reason, t]he *per se* rules that have been developed are similarly directed to the protection of the public welfare; they are complementary to, and in no way inconsistent with, the rule of reason. The principal advantages that flow from their use are, first, that enforcement and predictability are enhanced and, second, that unnecessary judicial investigation is avoided in those cases where practices falling within the scope of such rules are found. As the Court explained in *Northern Pacific R. Co. v. United States,* "There are certain agreements or practices which because of their pernicious effect on competition and lack of any redeeming virtue are conclusively presumed to be unreasonable and therefore illegal without elaborate inquiry as to the precise harm they have caused or the business excuse for their use." In formulating a new *per se* rule today, the Court does not tell us what "pernicious effect on competition" the practices here outlawed are perceived to have; nor does it attempt to show that those practices "lack…any redeeming virtue." Rather, it emphasizes only the importance of predictability, asserting that "courts are of limited utility in examining difficult economic problems" and have not yet been left free by Congress to "ramble through the wilds of economic theory in order to maintain a flexible approach."

* * *

Although it might well be desirable in a proper case for this Court to formulate a *per se* rule dealing with horizontal territorial limitations, it would not necessarily be appropriate for such a rule to amount to a blanket prohibition against all such limitations. More specifically, it is far from clear to me why such a rule should cover those division-of-market agreements that involve no price fixing and which are concerned only with trademarked products that are not in a monopoly or near-monopoly position with respect to competing brands. The instant case presents such an agreement; I would not decide it upon the basis of a *per se* rule.[6]

The District Court specifically found that the horizontal restraints involved here tend positively to promote competition in the supermarket field and to produce lower costs for the consumer. The Court seems implicitly to accept this determination, but says that the Sherman Act does not give Topco the authority to determine for itself "whether or not competition with other supermarket chains is more desirable than competition in the sale of Topco-brand products." But the majority overlooks a further specific determination of the District Court, namely, that the invalidation of the restraints here at issue "would not increase competition in Topco private label brands." Indeed, the District Court seemed to believe that it would, on the contrary, lead to the likely demise of those brands in time. And the evidence before the District Court would appear to justify that conclusion. There is no national demand for Topco brands, nor has there ever been any national advertising of those brands. It would be impracticable for Topco, with its limited financial resources, to convert itself into a national brand distributor in competition with distributors of existing national brands. Furthermore, without the right to grant exclusive licenses, it could not attract and hold new members as replacements for those of its present members who, following the pattern of the past, eventually grow sufficiently in size to be able to leave the cooperative organization and develop their own individual private-label brands. Moreover, Topco's present members, once today's decision has had its full impact over the course of time, will have no more reason to promote Topco products through local advertising and merchandising efforts than they will have such reason to promote any other generally available brands.

---

6. The national chains market their own private-label products, and these products are available nowhere else than in the stores of those chains. The stores of any one chain, of course, do not engage in price competition with each other with respect to their chain's private-label brands, and no serious suggestion could be made that the Sherman Act requires otherwise. I fail to see any difference whatsoever in the economic effect of the Topco arrangement for the marketing of Topco-brand products and the methods used by the national chains in marketing their private-label brands. True, the Topco arrangement involves a "combination," while each of the national chains is a single integrated corporation. The controlling consideration, however, should be that in neither case is the policy of the Sherman Act offended, for the practices in both cases work to the benefit, and not to the detriment, of the consuming public.

The issues presented by the antitrust cases reaching this Court are rarely simple to resolve under the rule of reason; they do indeed frequently require us to make difficult economic determinations. We should not for that reason alone, however, be overly zealous in formulating new *per se* rules, for an excess of zeal in that regard is both contrary to the policy of the Sherman Act and detrimental to the welfare of consumers generally. Indeed, the economic effect of the new rule laid down by the Court today seems clear: unless Congress intervenes, grocery staples marketed under private-label brands with their lower consumer prices will soon be available only to those who patronize the large national chains.

---

# Notes on *Topco*, Antitrust Arithmetic, and the Antitrust Rules Matrix

1. Notwithstanding Chief Justice Burger's arguments in dissent, *Topco's per se* rule against horizontal territorial and customer restraints remains rock solid. *See, e.g., Palmer v. BRG of Georgia, Inc.*, 498 U.S. 46, 49–50 (1990) (agreements among competitors to divide territory are illegal *per se* "regardless of whether the parties split a market within which both do business or whether they merely reserve one market for one and another for the other"). The *Palmer* case is one in which law students had a direct and personal interest as consumers: it involved an agreement by two bar-review companies not to offer their competing bar-study courses in each other's territories.

2. What policy justifies a strong *per se* rule against competitors dividing up territory or customers? How does such horizontal division compare, for example, to horizontal price fixing? If two makers of washing machines agree to price their similar models the same, is all competition foreclosed? They can still compete on such things as pre-sale and post-sale service and warranties, can't they? Can they still compete on such "non-price" items if they agree among themselves that "you sell only to Customer A, and I'll sell only to Customer B"? If they agree that "you sell only in Territory A, and I'll sell only in Territory B"? How would you prioritize horizontal price fixing, horizontal territorial division, and horizontal customer division, in light of their respective probable negative impact on competition and consumer welfare?

3. Do/should changes in business and technology affect these conclusions? For example, does the advent of Internet selling affect the economic impact of horizontal territorial division? Does it affect the economic impact of an agreement among competitors not to establish retail outlets within 100 miles of each others' locations? If so, would it have the same effect for all products, or would the effect differ, for example, as between washing machines and hand-held calculators?

4. The territorial restraint in *Topco* was similar to the territorial restraint in *GTE Sylvania*, yet *Topco* applied a *per se* rule and *GTE Sylvania* the rule of reason. Can you articulate why? Did *GTE Sylvania*, the later case, overrule *Topco*?

5. As Chief Justice Burger's dissent suggests, the result in *Topco* turned on two key points of legal theory: (1) the majority's characterization of the restraints as horizontal; and (2) the majority's refusal to weigh one type of competition (among large supermarket chains) against another type of competition (among the smaller chains that made up Topco). On the first point, the majority saw the restraints as a horizontal division of

territory among competitors, namely, the individual supermarket chains selling Topco-branded goods. Chief Justice Burger, however, saw the restraints as more vertical, akin to those imposed by a hypothetical single manufacturers of Topco products among its regional distributors.

Which characterization is *economically* more realistic in this context? Marshal the factual arguments and analogies for both sides and draw a conclusion. How important is Chief Justice Burger's observation that the Topco brand would not exist but for all the small "Topco" chains acting together? Which way does that observation cut?

6. *Topco*'s second point of legal theory is perhaps even more important. The majority in *Topco* unambiguously refuses to weigh one type of competition against another. It doesn't matter, they say, that Topco's restraints might allow the smaller supermarket chains collectively to compete better against the large national chains with their own private-label goods. What matters is that the restraints obviously impair competition among the smaller chains selling Topco-branded goods. Trying to weigh one type of competition against another, the majority says, would require the courts to "ramble through the wilds of economic theory."

7. From the standpoint of pure logic, this approach leaves much to be desired. Economics is a *quantitative* science, which antitrust law is supposed to track. The *Topco* defendants wanted the Court only to perform the very *simplest* of arithmetical operations: comparing one effect to another, or subtracting one from the other to see if the net result is positive or negative. If the courts cannot countenance even such a minimal introduction of arithmetic, how can they ever hope to keep antitrust law consistent with economic learning? Does it make sense to rule, as the *Topco* Court seemingly did, that *any* negative effect on competition merits *per se* exclusion, even if it produces a larger positive effect on competition and consumer welfare?

8. Although the *Topco* Court's "no comparison" approach may seem downright silly to an economist, it did have a foundation in law and precedent. In *Philadelphia National Bank*, which the *Topco* majority cited for this approach, the U.S. government challenged a proposed merger between "the second and third largest of the 42 commercial banks with head offices in the Philadelphia metropolitan area." 374 U.S. at 330. After detailed quantitative analysis of the effect of the merger on competition in the relevant market, the Court concluded that the proposed merger would be anticompetitive. 374 U.S. at 356, 361 (defining relevant market as commercial banking in four-county Philadelphia metropolitan area); 374 U.S. at 364–66 (concluding merger would be anticompetitive because it would give combined firm "at least" a 30% market share and would increase share held by two top firms by 33%). The Court utterly rejected as an "affirmative justification" the argument that the merger would increase competition between Philadephia's banks and New York's generally much larger "money-center banks." Said the Court:

> We reject this application of the concept of "countervailing power." ... If anti-competitive effects in one market could be justified by procompetitive consequences in another, the logical upshot would be that every firm in an industry could, without violating [Clayton Act] §7, embark on a series of mergers that would make it in the end as large as the industry leader. For if all the commercial banks in the Philadelphia area merged into one, it would be smaller than the largest bank in New York City. This is not a case, plainly, where two small firms in a market propose to merge in order to be able to compete more successfully with the leading firms in that market.

Doesn't this passage suggest that, while it may be permissible to balance procompetitive and anticompetitive effects in a single market, it is not permissible to compare procompetitive and anticompetitive effects in *different* markets? Although borrowing from Clayton Act §7 merger jurisprudence, the *Topco* Court did no more than transplant this principle into the jurisprudence of Sherman Act §1.

9. The textual statutory basis for this transplantation, however, is not immediately apparent. Sherman Act §2 does outlaw monopolization of "any part of the trade or commerce among the several States." 15 U.S.C. §2 (in part). And the Supreme Court has held that the words "any part" connote a defined geographic and product market, just as do the words "in any line of commerce or in any activity affecting commerce in any section of the country," which appear in Clayton Act §7, 15 U.S.C. §18. *See Brown Shoe Co. v. United States*, 370 U.S. 294, 324 (1962) ("The area of effective competition must be determined by reference to a product market (the 'line of commerce') and a geographic market (the 'section of the country')."); *United States v. Grinnell Corp.*, 384 U.S. 563, 572 (1966) (same rules for market definition apply under Sherman Act §2 and Clayton Act §3); 384 U.S. at 573 ("We see no reason to differentiate between 'line' of commerce in the context of the Clayton Act and 'part of commerce for purposes of the Sherman Act."). But there is no similar word in §1. Neither the word "line" nor the word "part" appears there.

10. Insofar as precedent is concerned, isn't the entire theoretical basis of *GTE Sylvania* a comparison of the effects on interbrand and intrabrand competition? Aren't those two different markets? If the *GTE Sylvania* Court allowed a comparison between the obviously negative effects of vertical nonprice restraints on intrabrand competition and their potentially positive effects on interbrand competition, then did *GTE Sylvania* overrule *Topco* on this point *sub silentio*?

11. Whatever abstract infirmities inhere in the continued co-existence of *Topco* and *GTE Sylvania,* it is abundantly clear that an important line falls between vertical and horizontal contractual restraints. *Topco* is still good law, and *GTE Sylvania* has so many progeny that its rule can hardly be doubted.

With this in mind, make a four-box antitrust "matrix." Label the two columns "horizontal" and "vertical" and the two rows "price" and "nonprice." Now, in each of the resulting four squares, fill in the blanks with the applicable rule endorsed by the cases you have studied. In the "vertical-price" square, does a single rule apply, or does the rule depend on a further variable? If so, what? When you are finished, you should have a useful template to guide your analysis of most antitrust issues involving contractual restraints.

12. As you refine and use your matrix, remember that the dividing lines between the rows and columns may not always be as clear in practice as they might seem in theory. Can you think of cases in which an ostensibly "nonprice" restraint might be recharacterized as one involving price? Can you think of cases in which an ostensibly "vertical" restraint might be recharacterized as "horizontal"? Might *Topco* itself have been such a case?

13. In general, where on your matrix would/should most contractual restraints in licensing fall? Are the most common contractual restraints in licensing vertical or horizontal? Do most of them control price or other matters? What general rule—the rule of reason or the *per se* rule—would you expect to apply to most contractual restraints in licensing? Might the answer depend in part upon whether the license is exclusive and on the number of licensees?

# V. Licensing Restrictions and Antitrust Guidelines

## Clinton Administration Expresses More Than Intellectual Curiosity in Antitrust Issues Raised by Intellectual Property Licensing*

Ilene Knable Gotts & Howard W. Fogt, Jr.

22 A.I.P.L.A.Q.J. 1 (1994)

\* \* \*

### I. FEDERAL ANTITRUST JURISDICTION IS FAR-REACHING

#### A.Pre-Acquisition Reporting and Related Investigations

Both the FTC and DOJ have the power under federal antitrust laws to investigate anticompetitive conduct and to challenge such conduct in judicial or administrative proceedings. Because federal law requires parties to notify both the FTC and the DOJ of most proposed acquisitions or exclusive licensing arrangements exceeding certain size thresholds, the FTC and DOJ can investigate and challenge such proposed arrangements prior to consummation. A full investigation by either agency can delay a...licensing arrangement for several months and subject parties to hundreds of thousands of dollars in legal costs as well as the inconvenience of responding to extensive discovery requests. These costs escalate sharply when a foreign company is involved (directly or indirectly) in an acquisition since, as part of the investigation, the company may be required to provide English translations of all relevant documents. Either federal enforcement agency's interest in investigating and blocking a transaction often is influenced by complaints from competitors or customers who can help the agency to understand the relevant market while convincing the agency that the transaction is anticompetitive. In reviewing transactions subject to preacquisition reporting, the enforcement agencies use their ability to block consummation as a powerful tool for coercing parties to modify proposed deals or even to abandon them altogether.

#### B.Investigation of Unreported Transactions and Non-Merger Related Conduct

The FTC and DOJ also have authority to investigate unreported transactions and non-merger related conduct which may be anticompetitive in nature or effect. The two agencies can order companies suspected of anticompetitive conduct to provide information and documents relating to their operations and activities. In addition, the agencies can demand information and documents from competitors and customers of the targeted company. The agencies can start an investigation either of their own initia-

---

\* Reprinted with permission of the publisher, copyright 1994.

tive or as a result of a complaint by a third party (once again, perhaps a disgruntled competitor or customer). Under the rules of procedure of each agency, the provision of information by third parties in an investigation is not disclosed except in a civil litigation, and then usually under seal of court. Furthermore, at the completion of an investigation, the agency may institute a legal proceeding challenging conduct which the agency believes violated or continues to violate the antitrust laws. The FTC may commence administrative or civil proceedings, while the DOJ can additionally institute a criminal action.

## II. INTERPLAY BETWEEN U.S. INTELLECTUAL PROPERTY ANTITRUST LAWS AND EVOLUTION OF FEDERAL ENFORCEMENT

A fundamental tension exists between antitrust laws and intellectual property laws in the United States. The purpose of antitrust laws is to promote consumer welfare by preserving the free competitive market place and promoting vigorous market competition. Competition laws specifically prohibit conduct which results in or has the realistic probability of establishing monopolies [or] restraining competition. In the United States, these antitrust laws stem, at least in part, from the Constitutional prohibition against restraints on interstate commerce. In order to accomplish these goals, the antitrust laws prohibit certain types of business conduct that are considered to restrain trade unreasonably. On the other hand, the U.S. Constitution specifically provides that in order to promote the "progress of service and useful arts," the intellectual property laws provide inventors with a lawful "limited" monopoly for a prescribed number of years. The right bestowed upon a patentee by the grant of a patent, for instance, is the power to exclude others from making, using or selling [are now also importing or offering for sale] the invention during the patent term. In many respects, the grant of a patent is analogous to a statutory or common law exemption from the antitrust laws. The function of this "exemption" is to provide proper incentives to inventors to disclose voluntarily the invention and how it works.

This conflict between antitrust law proscriptions against restrictive practices and intellectual property rights to exclusion and exclusivity has ebbed and flowed over time, often moving in cycles, depending to some extent upon the philosophies of the incumbent policy-makers. Nevertheless, federal antitrust agency enforcement treatment of intellectual property has shifted dramatically during the last 30–40 years and has been characterized by a gradual movement away from prohibitionist per se rules to a more market-focused enforcement.

Basically, there appear to be three distinct periods in U.S. antitrust enforcement policy during the twentieth century. The first period occurred roughly from 1914 to 1940. This was generally a period of benign antitrust enforcement. It was marked by a relative tolerance of restrictive practices whether in the form of cartels or patent pools. There was no substantial interest in the competitive consequences of licensing practices. It is useful to remember that during the depression of the 1930s the U.S. Government encouraged, through the National Recovery Act, the formation of industry "cartels" and that the U.S. Supreme Court in the *Appalachian Coal* case sanctioned what would be called in European or Japanese parlance a "crisis cartel" among Eastern coal producers.

After the Second World War, antitrust enforcement attained much greater vigor (harkening back to the initial "trust-busting" days of the late 19th century under President Teddy Roosevelt). In the post World War II modernization and economic expansion environment, cartels were vigorously attacked and antitrust principles were applied, increasingly across the board, in a rigid and *per se* fashion. This second or so-called "traditional" period viewed the conduct of holders of intellectual property rights suspiciously and severely restricted the lawful extension and application of those rights. There was little or no concern for the "market" relevance of their enforcement policies. The high point of the "traditional" period was the commencement of major investigations and civil actions challenging the licensing and marketing practices of companies and the adoption of the "Nine No-No's" by the DOJ.

During this time period, the DOJ and the courts generally viewed certain patent licensing practices as *per se* illegal. These prohibited licensing restrictions, colloquially referred to as the "Nine No-No's," were as follows:

- tying the purchase of unpatented materials to the grant of a license;

- requiring the licensee to assign back to the licensor subsequent patents;

- restricting the right of the purchaser of the product in the resale of the product;

- restricting the licensee's ability to deal in products outside the scope of the patent;

- a licensor's agreement not to grant further licenses;

- mandatory package licenses;

- royalty provisions not reasonably related to the licensee's sales;

- restrictions on a licensee's use of a product made by a patented process; and

- minimum resale price provisions for the licensed products.

Clearly, as demonstrated by the "Nine No-No's," federal enforcement agents viewed licensing arrangements with great suspicion during the pre-Reagan era. Patents, during this traditional period, were assumed to be monopolies and the only way to minimize their anticompetitive effects was to construe the rights of the patentee as narrowly as possible. The monopoly granted under the patent law was not under any circumstances to be viewed as carte blanche in matters relating to the use of such rights.

The third phase commenced in approximately 1980 and reached its peak during the Reagan and [first] Bush Administrations. The shift in federal enforcement scrutiny began with the official DOJ abandonment of the Nine No-Nos in 1981. During this period, while not returning in any sense to the *laissez faire* enforcement attitudes predating World War II, theories promoted by the "Chicago School of Economics" played a critical role in "modernizing" antitrust policy. Both the DOJ and the courts became much more willing to evaluate licensing provisions under a rule of reason analysis and to permit those restrictions which, on balance, maximize the legitimate economic benefits, especially market efficiency, and promote innovation to flow from patent licenses. One of the primary reasons for this shift is the focus of the patent relationship as vertical in nature (e.g., between a supplier and customer) rather than horizontal (e.g., between two competing manufacturers) and the change in the treatment of vertical relationships by the enforcement agencies.

The epitome of this more relaxed period of scrutiny occurred in 1988 with the release of the new [Antitrust Guidelines for International Operations[s]]. The Guidelines delineate a four-part "rule of reason" test to determine the permissibility of licensing arrangements:

---

s. *Authors' note: Antitrust Division, Department of Justice, Antitrust Guidelines for International Operations, 53 Fed. Reg. 21584 (June 8, 1988). DOJ adopted these Guidelines during the last year of the Reagan Administration. The first Bush Administration left them intact. In 1994, the Clinton Administration proposed and vetted for comment substantially revised guidelines. See Request for Comments on Draft Antitrust Enforcement Guidelines for International Operations, 59 Fed. Reg. 52810, 52810 (Oct. 19, 1994). The revised guidelines were adopted in 1995 and superseded the 1988 guidelines. See United*

1. Does the license restrain competition between the licensor and licensees in a relevant market for technology, and, if so, is it likely that the agreement will create, enhance, or facilitate the exercise of market power?

2. Does the license expressly or implicitly restrain competition in any other market in which the licensor and licensee do or would compete in the absence of the license (i.e., "spill-over effects")?

3. To the extent that there are vertical restraints in the license: (i) does the license result in anticompetitive exclusion beyond the exclusion provided by the intellectual property rights themselves; and (ii) does the license facilitate collusion?

4. Assuming that under the above three criteria there is a determination that the license creates a significant risk of anticompetitive effects, then the Department will consider whether the risks of anticompetitive effects are outweighed by pro-competitive efficiency benefits from the license and its restriction.

During this...period, very few matters involving intellectual property transfers were scrutinized by the federal enforcement agencies. The DOJ and courts alike appeared to believe that patents rarely, if ever, bestowed market power. Although some courts appear to have followed this shift in policy, it is also important to note that there were few court opinions decided during this time frame and many of the older decisions remained as the latest statement of the law. These older decisions take a less lenient approach to restrictions that go beyond what is inherent in the patent itself.

\* \* \*

*[The 1988 Antitrust Guidelines for International Operations were a product of the Reagan Administration. Not surprisingly, they represented a "relaxation" of antitrust enforcement. It would be a mistake, however, to think of the 1988 Guidelines as returning to the unprincipled laissez faire philosophy of the early twentieth century. Rather, they represented an attempt to collect, codify, and systematize then-current academic and judicial learning regarding antitrust and competition policy.*

*The 1988 Guidelines made an important contribution to the policy debate. The two previous eras of policy making had simply emphasized one side of the equation or the other. In the early twentieth century, judicial and administrative enforcement had emphasized the value of innovation and intellectual property in promoting competition and economic growth, paying little attention to possible economic harm caused by the abuse of intellectual property rights. In contrast, the post-War period had emphasized the harm that might arise from abuse, paying little attention to how contractual restraints in licensing intellectual property might promote the goals of innovation and competition. Based in large measure on studies and commentary by followers of the so-called "Chicago School" of economics, the 1988 Guidelines began the difficult process of balancing these two goals — encouraging innovation by enforcing intellectual property rights and yet protecting competition from abuse of those rights.*

*The 1988 Guidelines abjured blanket prohibitions against restraints based upon simplistic analysis and formal distinctions. Instead, they focused, as the GTE Sylvania Court had demanded, on substantial economic effect. Reflecting the deregulatory and free-market predilections of the Reagan Administration, however, the 1988 Guidelines tended to give the benefit of the doubt to restrictive behavior in the absence of clear proof of economic harm*

---

*States Department of Justice and Federal Trade Commission, Antitrust Enforcement Guidelines for International Operations (April 1995), LEXIS, DOJANT.*

*from abuse. The first Bush Administration left the 1988 Guidelines intact but offered no new guidance on the difficult interface between antitrust and intellectual property.*

*The Clinton Administration continued the work begun in the Reagan Administration in two ways. First, it proposed and, after comment, adopted a special set of guidelines for intellectual property licensing. See United States Department of Justice and Federal Trade Commission, Antitrust Guidelines for the Licensing of Intellectual Property, reprinted in 49 PAT. TRADEMARK & COPYRIGHT J. (BNA) 714 (April 13, 1995). Finalized in 1995, the Licensing Guidelines also avoided simplistic analysis and formal distinctions. Instead, they proposed several methods of analysis—each involving substantial quantitative aspects—for balancing the likely economic benefit and likely economic harm of contractual restrictions in licensing. Second, the Clinton Administration proposed and, after comment, adopted a substantial revision of the 1988 international guidelines, which also addressed certain aspects of licensing. See United States Department of Justice and Federal Trade Commission, Antitrust Enforcement Guidelines for International Operations (April 1995), available on LEXIS at following path Legal: Area of Law—By Topic: Antitrust & Trade: Administrative Materials & Regulations (visited June 8, 2004).*

*Like the Reagan Administration's 1988 Guidelines, the Clinton Administration's two sets of 1995 guidelines bear the earmarks of the policy predilections of the administration that developed them. The Clinton Administration's Guidelines reveal a greater concern for possible abuse of intellectual property rights and a greater willingness to analyze the effect of alleged abuse. In an apparent attempt to discourage private firms from "cornering the market" in emerging technologies, the 1995 Licensing Guidelines attempt to define "markets" in "technology" and "innovation," as distinguished from the traditional subjects of market definition, namely existing products and services. For an analysis and critique of these legal innovations, see JAY DRATLER, JR., LICENSING OF INTELLECTUAL PROPERTY § 5.02[2][b][i][C] (Law Journal Press 1994 & Supps.).*

*The most important point that emerges from review of the 1988 and 1995 guidelines, however, is not their differences, but their similarities. Both sets of guidelines begin where the GTE Sylvania Court suggested: with substantial economic effect, rather than barren formalism. Both recognize the importance of neutral, non-ideological analysis of real-world economic effect. Both suggest and sometimes require a significant quantitative component of economic analysis, particularly in defining markets and assessing firms' market power in them.*

*The importance of these similarities is hard to overestimate. The Reagan Administration was one of self-described "revolutionary" conservatives. The Clinton Administration had a center-left economic ideology that others sometimes described as "liberal." Yet despite the ideological gulf that divided the two administrations, both recognized the value of neutral, non-ideological economic analysis, guided by untainted reason and informed by mathematics, in balancing the goals of robust competition and robust intellectual property protection. It may be too early to suggest that political authorities will leave economic analysis of competition and innovation to neutral experts, as they largely (and successfully!) have done with the management of the nation's central banking system. Nevertheless, the days when the direction of antitrust enforcement whipped back and forth in the political winds like a weathervane caught in a gale appear to be largely behind us.*

*This does not mean, however, that politics and ideology no longer play a part in antitrust policy and enforcement. There is still room for ideology where economic analysis is uncertain or controversial, where the process of analysis is well-established but the facts and evidence are incomplete or ambiguous, and where new problems arise that existing economic analysis has not yet mastered. Private attempts to control markets in emerging or future technologies, be-*

*fore those markets create recognizable products and services may fall into the latter category, as the 1995 Licensing Guidelines appeared to assume. Yet the advance of rational economic analysis has slowly and inexorably narrowed the "knowledge" gap in which the lack of a reasoned approach gives sway to unfettered ideology and political bias. The similar guidelines produced by two very different administrations in the last years of the twentieth century, as well as the consistent approach of the Supreme Court beginning with* GTE Sylvania *all suggest that the gap available for raw political whim will get smaller and smaller as time goes by.]*

## III. OVERVIEW OF FEDERAL ANTITRUST LAWS

The federal antitrust laws are set forth in several federal statutes, including the Sherman Act and the Clayton Act. Individual states also have similar statutes, which are not addressed in this Article. The U.S. antitrust laws apply to conduct which has a not insubstantial effect on U.S. foreign and interstate commerce. Sections 1 and 2 of the Sherman Act constitute the primary federal antitrust provisions under which intellectual property transfers—including licensing and marketing arrangements and acquisitions—are evaluated by the federal enforcement agencies. Section 1 of the Sherman Act prohibits agreements between parties that restrain trade unreasonably. In contrast, Section 2 of the Sherman Act prohibits monopolization and attempts to monopolize the market (i.e., unilateral conduct) as well as conspiracies to do the same (i.e., concerted activity). The Sherman Act can result in both civil and criminal liability. The DOJ seeks criminal relief for "hard core" anticompetitive conduct, including jail terms and fines. In civil actions, both the DOJ and FTC seek injunctive relief, and, where appropriate, damages.

Section 7 of the Clayton Act proscribes stock and assets acquisitions whose effect "may be substantially to lessen competition, or to tend to create a monopoly." The grant of an exclusive basis or transfer of patent or name may be evaluated under Clayton section 7 by "asset transfers." Unlike Sherman Section 2, the Clayton Act seeks to address possible restraints upon competition at the "incipiency" stage.

Generally, antitrust laws fall into two categories: (1) prohibited conduct involving two or more companies; and (2) prohibited conduct where only one company is involved.

### A. Concerted Conduct

To determine whether an agreement unreasonably restricts competition under Sherman Section 1, courts use one of two methods of analysis—a "*per se*" rule or a "rule of reason." A court's selection of which one of these approaches to employ often determines the outcome. Under the *per se* approach, proof of the conduct is sufficient to establish the violation without examination of its context or consequences. Under this approach, the court will not consider any arguments or evidence that the particular agreement is procompetitive. In contrast, the rule of reason approach typically requires another lengthy and complex inquiry into the relative competitive benefits and threats of a particular arrangement. The plaintiff has a heavy burden to establish that a particular practice is an unreasonable restraint of trade. Given these differences, the Fifth Circuit has aptly stated that "[t]he *per se* rule is the trump card of antitrust law. When an antitrust plaintiff successfully plays it, he needs only tally his score."

Relatively few business practices are automatically accorded *per se* treatment. The *per se* rule flatly prohibits "agreements" whose nature and necessary effect are so plainly anticompetitive that no elaborate study of the industry is needed to establish "legality." To be "plainly anticompetitive," the agreement must have a "pernicious effect on competition and lack of any redeeming virtue." Such "*per se*" treatment is appropriate only in situations where "the practice facially appears to be one that would always or almost always tend to restrict competition and decrease output." The categories of conduct that are particularly likely to be accorded *per se* treatment include price-fixing, tying arrangements and market divisions. Therefore, licensing arrangements which contain these types of provisions—either expressly or implicitly—should be avoided whenever possible.

\* \* \*

## B. Unilateral Conduct

The principles of Sherman Section 2 are unchanged when intermeshed with intellectual property law. Unilateral conduct is impermissible under Section 2 of the Sherman Act if monopoly power is used to exclude or discourage competition. Monopoly power is the power to raise prices without a significant loss of market share to competitors who can respond to the increase in price with a corresponding increase in product output. By definition, monopolists usually have significant market position with respect to any given market. Size or power, in and of itself, does not, however, violate the Sherman Act. Indeed, it is permissible to acquire monopoly power through patents or through ability, initiative or efficiencies. It is only the use of such patents to maintain or extend the power inherent in the patent beyond the terms of the patent that raises concern.

There are several types of conduct that violate Section 2: (1) monopolization; (2) attempted monopolization; and (3) conspiracy to monopolize. [The first two] claims are similar since both require threshold showings of intent and market power. While intellectual property rights can provide the holder with an advantage in the market place, the grant of such property rights does not automatically bestow market power. Section 2 is concerned with the unlawful attainment of market power.

Monopoly is "the power to control prices or exclude competition." There is no bright line between those market shares that constitute monopoly power and those that do not. While market shares in the 65% to 70% or higher range typically support a finding of "market power," shares below 50% generally will not. In contrast, Judge Learned Hand in an oft-cited case, *United States v. Aluminum Co. of America*, wrote that "it is doubtful whether sixty or sixty-four percent would be enough; and certainly thirty-three percent is not." [148 F.2d 416, 424 (2d Cir. 1945).]

In an attempted monopolization claim, market shares not reaching the level required for actual monopolization may be sufficient to establish a "dangerous probability of success" in attaining a monopoly if other factors, such as barriers to entry or weak competition, exist. For instance, market shares between 60 and 69% have consistently been considered sufficient; most courts have found market shares of 50% adequate; and shares as low as 35%–40% have been enough when [buttressed by] other relevant market conditions.

The critical starting point for any Sherman Section 2 or Clayton Section 7 analysis is the definition of the relevant market affected by the patentee's conduct. The relevant market is generally defined as "the area of [effective] competition" within which the defendant operates. Typically, the relevant product market is identified as those products reasonably interchangeable by consumers for the same purposes; the relevant geographic market is that geographic area in which trade of these products occurs (or is likely to occur). Economic concepts, such as cross elasticities of demand, are used to determine the relevant market. Some courts also have considered relevant cross elasticity of supply.

A patent provides the legal right to exclude others from making, using, [importing, offering for sale,] or selling the product or process covered by the patent. Historically, courts characterized a patentee's power to exclude others from producing the claimed invention as a "monopoly." In the last decade, however, a number of lower court decisions and the International Guidelines recognized that even a patent does not necessarily confer [economic] monopoly or market power in a relevant market. Therefore, the legality of any intellectual property related arrangement depends upon an assessment of the patent's exclusionary power in the relevant market. This, in turn, requires an assessment of market conditions and the extent to which there are economically feasible and functional substitutes for the patented product such that any attempts by the licensor and licensee to exercise market power would be defeated.

One interesting area of patent licensing and exclusive marketing arrangements which can raise questions under Section 2 of the Sherman Act and/or Section 7 of the Clayton Act is patent accumulation. Although generally the accumulation of internally developed patents is not, in and of itself, a violation of the antitrust laws, patent accumulation, under certain circumstances can violate Section 2 of the Sherman Act and, where acquisitions are involved, Section 7 of the Clayton Act. For instance, filing trivial patents primarily as a means of creating an impediment to market entry by others may create antitrust liability under Section 2.

It is doubtful that a patent accumulation case based solely on internally produced patents would under ordinary circumstances succeed. A case may exist, however, where there is a multitude of internally developed patents along with the purchase of several related patents. It may also be necessary to establish that the patent purchaser had market power (and the relevant market existed) before the acquisitions took place. Moreover, certain acquisitions of patents by a company with monopoly power (or perhaps the potential of gaining monopoly power) may violate Sherman Section 2 and/or Clayton Section 7.

* * *

# Antitrust Guidelines of the Department of Justice and Federal Trade Commission
## Antitrust Guidelines for the Licensing of Intellectual Property
(April 6, 1995)
*Reprinted in* 4 TRADE REG. REP. (CCH) P. 13,132 (1995)

### 1. Intellectual property protection and the antitrust laws

1.0    These Guidelines state the antitrust enforcement policy of the U.S. Department of Justice and the Federal Trade Commission (individually, "the Agency," and collectively, "the Agencies") with respect to the licensing of intellectual property protected by patent, copyright, and trade secret law, and of know-how.[30] By stating their general pol-

---

30. These Guidelines do not cover the antitrust treatment of trademarks. Although the same general antitrust principles that apply to other forms of intellectual property apply to trademarks as well, these Guidelines deal with technology transfer and innovation-related issues that typically arise with respect to patents, copyrights, trade secrets, and know-how agreements, rather than with product differentiation issues that typically arise with respect to trademarks.

icy, the Agencies hope to assist those who need to predict whether the Agencies will challenge a practice as anti-competitive. However, these Guidelines cannot remove judgment and discretion in antitrust law enforcement. Moreover, the standards set forth in these Guidelines must be applied in unforeseeable circumstances. Each case will be evaluated in light of its own facts, and these Guidelines will be applied reasonably and flexibly.[31]

* * *

## 2. General principles

2.0 These Guidelines embody three general principles: (a) for the purpose of antitrust analysis, the Agencies regard intellectual property as being essentially comparable to any other form of property; (b) the Agencies do not presume that intellectual property creates market power in the antitrust context; and (c) the Agencies recognize that intellectual property licensing allows firms to combine complementary factors of production and is generally pro-competitive.

### 2.1 Standard antitrust analysis applies to intellectual property

The Agencies apply the same general antitrust principles to conduct involving intellectual property that they apply to conduct involving any other form of tangible or intangible property. That is not to say that intellectual property is in all respects the same as any other form of property. Intellectual property has important characteristics, such as ease of misappropriation, that distinguish it from many other forms of property. These characteristics can be taken into account by standard antitrust analysis, however, and do not require the application of fundamentally different principles.

Although there are clear and important differences in the purpose, extent, and duration of protection provided under the intellectual property regimes of patent, copyright, and trade secret, the governing antitrust principles are the same. Antitrust analysis takes differences among these forms of intellectual property into account in evaluating the specific market circumstances in which transactions occur, just as it does with other particular market circumstances.

Intellectual property law bestows on the owners of intellectual property certain rights to exclude others. These rights help the owners to profit from the use of their property. An intellectual property owner's rights to exclude are similar to the rights enjoyed by owners of other forms of private property. As with other forms of private property, certain types of conduct with respect to intellectual property may have anti-competitive effects against which the antitrust laws can and do protect. Intellectual property is thus neither particularly free from scrutiny under the antitrust laws, nor particularly suspect under them.

* * *

The Agencies recognize that the licensing of intellectual property is often international. The principles of antitrust analysis described in these Guidelines apply equally to domestic and international licensing arrangements. However, as described in the 1995

---

31. As is the case with all guidelines, users should rely on qualified counsel to assist them in evaluating the antitrust risk associated with any contemplated transaction or activity. No set of guidelines can possibly indicate how the Agencies will assess the particular facts of every case. Parties who wish to know the Agencies' specific enforcement intentions with respect to any particular transaction should consider seeking a Department of Justice business review letter pursuant to 28 C.F.R. § 50.6 or a Federal Trade Commission Advisory Opinion pursuant to 16 C.F.R. §§ 1.1-1.4.

Department of Justice and Federal Trade Commission Antitrust Enforcement Guidelines for International Operations, considerations particular to international operations, such as jurisdiction and comity, may affect enforcement decisions when the arrangement is in an international context.

## 2.2 Intellectual property and market power

Market power is the ability profitably to maintain prices above, or output below, competitive levels for a significant period of time. The Agencies will not presume that a patent, copyright, or trade secret necessarily confers market power upon its owner. Although the intellectual property right confers the power to exclude with respect to the specific product, process, or work in question, there will often be sufficient actual or potential close substitutes for such product, process, or work to prevent the exercise of market power. If a patent or other form of intellectual property does confer market power, that market power does not by itself offend the antitrust laws. As with any other tangible or intangible asset that enables its owner to obtain significant supra-competitive profits, market power (or even a monopoly) that is solely "a consequence of a superior product, business acumen, or historic accident" does not violate the antitrust laws. Nor does such market power impose on the intellectual property owner an obligation to license the use of that property to others. As in other antitrust contexts, however, market power could be illegally acquired or maintained, or, even if lawfully acquired and maintained, would be relevant to the ability of an intellectual property owner to harm competition through unreasonable conduct in connection with such property.

## 2.3 Pro-competitive benefits of licensing

Intellectual property typically is one component among many in a production process and derives value from its combination with complementary factors. Complementary factors of production include manufacturing and distribution facilities, workforces, and other items of intellectual property. The owner of intellectual property has to arrange for its combination with other necessary factors to realize its commercial value. Often, the owner finds it most efficient to contract with others for these factors, to sell rights to the intellectual property, or to enter into a joint venture arrangement for its development, rather than supplying these complementary factors itself.

Licensing, cross-licensing, or otherwise transferring intellectual property (hereinafter "licensing") can facilitate integration of the licensed property with complementary factors of production. This integration can lead to more efficient exploitation of the intellectual property, benefiting consumers through the reduction of costs and the introduction of new products. Such arrangements increase the value of intellectual property to consumers and to the developers of the technology. By potentially increasing the expected returns from intellectual property, licensing also can increase the incentive for its creation and thus promote greater investment in research and development.

Sometimes the use of one item of intellectual property requires access to another. An item of intellectual property "blocks" another when the second cannot be practiced without using the first. For example, an improvement on a patented machine can be blocked by the patent on the machine. Licensing may promote the coordinated development of technologies that are in a blocking relationship.

Field-of-use, territorial, and other limitations on intellectual property licenses may serve procompetitive ends by allowing the licensor to exploit its property as efficiently and effectively as possible. These various forms of exclusivity can be used to give a licensee an incentive to invest in the commercialization and distribution of products embodying the licensed intellectual property and to develop additional applications for the licensed property. The restrictions may do so, for example, by protecting the licensee against free-riding on the licensee's investments by other licensees or by the licensor. They may also increase the licensor's incentive to license, for example, by protecting the licensor from competition in the licensor's own technology in a market niche that it prefers to keep to itself. These benefits of licensing restrictions apply to patent, copyright, and trade secret licenses, and to know-how agreements.

---

## Example 1[32]

*Situation:* ComputerCo develops a new, copyrighted software program for inventory management. The program has wide application in the health field. ComputerCo licenses the program in an arrangement that imposes both field of use and territorial limitations. Some of ComputerCo's licenses permit use only in hospitals; others permit use only in group medical practices. ComputerCo charges different royalties for the different uses. All of ComputerCo's licenses permit use only in specified portions of the United States and in specified foreign countries.[33] The licenses contain no provisions that would prevent or discourage licensees from developing, using, or selling any other program, or from competing in any other good or service other than in the use of the licensed program. None of the licensees are actual or likely potential competitors of ComputerCo in the sale of inventory management programs.

*Discussion:* The key competitive issue raised by the licensing arrangement is whether it harms competition among entities that would have been actual or likely potential competitors in the absence of the arrangement. Such harm could occur if, for example, the licenses anticompetitively foreclose access to competing technologies (in this case, most likely competing computer programs), prevent licensees from developing their own competing technologies (again, in this case, most likely computer programs), or facilitate market allocation or price-fixing for any product or service supplied by the licensees. (*See* section 3.1.) If the license agreements contained such provisions, the Agency evaluating the arrangement would analyze its likely competitive effects as described in parts 3–5 of these Guidelines. In this hypothetical, there are no such provisions and thus the arrangement is merely a subdivision of the licensor's intellectual property among different fields of use and territories. The licensing arrangement does not appear likely to harm competition among entities that would have been actual or likely potential competitors if ComputerCo had chosen not to license the software program. The Agency therefore would be unlikely to object to this arrangement. Based on these facts, the result of the antitrust analysis would be the same whether the technology was protected by patent, copyright, or trade secret. The Agency's conclusion as to likely competitive effects could differ if, for example, the license barred licensees from using any other inventory management program.

---

## 3. Antitrust concerns and modes of analysis

### 3.1 Nature of the concerns

While intellectual property licensing arrangements are typically welfare-enhancing and procompetitive, antitrust concerns may nonetheless arise. For example, a licensing arrangement could include restraints that adversely affect competition in goods markets

---

32. The examples in these Guidelines are hypothetical and do not represent judgments about, or analysis of, any actual market circumstances of the named industries.

33. These Guidelines do not address the possible application of the antitrust laws of other countries to restraints such as territorial restrictions in international licensing arrangements.

by dividing the markets among firms that would have competed using different technologies....An arrangement that effectively merges the research and development activities of two of only a few entities that could plausibly engage in research and development in the relevant field might harm competition for development of new goods and
services....An acquisition of intellectual property may lessen competition in a relevant
antitrust market....The Agencies will focus on the actual effects of an arrangement, not
on its formal terms.

The Agencies will not require the owner of intellectual property to create competition
in its own technology. However, antitrust concerns may arise when a licensing arrangement harms competition among entities that would have been actual or likely potential
competitors[34] in a relevant market in the absence of the license (entities in a "horizontal
relationship"). A restraint in a licensing arrangement may harm such competition, for example, if it facilitates market division or price-fixing. In addition, license restrictions with
respect to one market may harm such competition in another market by anticompetitively foreclosing access to, or significantly raising the price of, an important input, or by
facilitating coordination to increase price or reduce output. When it appears that such
competition may be adversely affected, the Agencies will follow the analysis set forth
below....

### 3.2 Markets affected by licensing arrangements

Licensing arrangements raise concerns under the antitrust laws if they are likely to
affect adversely the prices, quantities, qualities, or varieties of goods and services[35] either currently or potentially available. The competitive effects of licensing arrangements often can be adequately assessed within the relevant markets for the goods affected by the arrangements. In such instances, the Agencies will delineate and analyze
only goods markets. In other cases, however, the analysis may require the delineation
of markets for technology or markets for research and development (innovation
markets).

### 3.2.1 Goods markets

A number of different goods markets may be relevant to evaluating the effects of a licensing arrangement. A restraint in a licensing arrangement may have competitive effects
in markets for final or intermediate goods made using the intellectual property, or it may
have effects upstream, in markets for goods that are used as inputs, along with the intellectual property, to the production of other goods. In general, for goods markets affected by a
licensing arrangement, the Agencies will approach the delineation of relevant market and
the measurement of market share in the intellectual property area as in section 1 of the U.S.
Department of Justice and Federal Trade Commission Horizontal Merger Guidelines.[36]

---

34. A firm will be treated as a likely potential competitor if there is evidence that entry by that
firm is reasonably probable in the absence of the licensing arrangement.

35. Hereinafter, the term "goods" also includes services.

36. U.S. Department of Justice and Federal Trade Commission, *Horizontal Merger Guidelines*
(April 17, 1992) (hereinafter "*1992 Horizontal Merger Guidelines*"). As stated in section 1.41 of the
*1992 Horizontal Merger Guidelines*, market shares for goods markets "can be expressed either in dollar terms through measurement of sales, shipments, or production, or in physical terms through
measurement of sales, shipments, production, capacity or reserves."

[*Authors' note*: The *Horizontal Merger Guidelines* were revised in limited respects in 1997. *See Revision to the Horizontal Merger Guidelines* Issued by the U.S. Department of Justice and the Federal
Trade Commission, 1997 FTC LEXIS 283 (April 8, 1997). The revision addressed efficiencies that
may result from mergers and did not disturb the earlier Guidelines' basic antitrust analysis, for example, their quantitative rules for determining market definition and market share.]

### 3.2.2 Technology markets

Technology markets consist of the intellectual property that is licensed (the "licensed technology") and its close substitutes—that is, the technologies or goods that are close enough substitutes significantly to constrain the exercise of market power with respect to the intellectual property that is licensed.[37] When rights to intellectual property are marketed separately from the products in which they are used,[38] the Agencies may rely on technology markets to analyze the competitive effects of a licensing arrangement.

To identify a technology's close substitutes and thus to delineate the relevant technology market, the Agencies will, if the data permit, identify the smallest group of technologies and goods over which a hypothetical monopolist of those technologies and goods likely would exercise market power—for example, by imposing a small but significant and nontransitory price increase. The Agencies recognize that technology often is licensed in ways that are not readily quantifiable in monetary terms.[39] In such circumstances, the Agencies will delineate the relevant market by identifying other technologies and goods which buyers would substitute at a cost comparable to that of using the licensed technology.

In assessing the competitive significance of current and likely potential participants in a technology market, the Agencies will take into account all relevant evidence. When market share data are available and accurately reflect the competitive significance of market participants, the Agencies will include market share data in this assessment. The Agencies also will seek evidence of buyers' and market participants' assessments of the competitive significance of technology market participants. Such evidence is particularly important when market share data are unavailable, or do not accurately represent the competitive significance of market participants. When market share data or other indicia of market power are not available, and it appears that competing technologies are comparably efficient, the Agencies will assign each technology the same market share. For new technologies, the Agencies generally will use the best available information to estimate market acceptance over a two-year period, beginning with commercial introduction.

### 3.2.3 Research and development: innovation markets

If a licensing arrangement may adversely affect competition to develop new or improved goods or processes, the Agencies will analyze such an impact either as a separate competitive effect in relevant goods or technology markets, or as a competitive effect in a separate innovation market. A licensing arrangement may have competitive effects in a separate innovation market. A licensing arrangement may have competitive effects on innovation that cannot be adequately addressed through the analysis of goods or technology markets. For example, the arrangement may affect the development of goods that do not yet exist. Alternatively, the arrangement may affect the development of new

---

37. For example, the owner of a process for producing a particular good may be constrained in its conduct with respect to that process not only by other processes for making that good, but also by other goods that compete with the downstream good and by the processes used to produce those other goods.

38. Intellectual property is often licensed, sold, or transferred as an integral part of a marketed good. An example is a patented product marketed with an implied license permitting its use. In such circumstances, there is no need for a separate analysis of technology markets to capture relevant competitive effects.

39. For example, technology may be licensed royalty-free in exchange for the right to use other technology, or it may be licensed as part of a package license.

or improved goods or processes in geographic markets where there is no actual or likely potential competition in the relevant goods.

An innovation market consists of the research and development directed to particular new or improved goods or processes, and the close substitutes for that research and development. The close substitutes are research and development efforts, technologies, and goods that significantly constrain the exercise of market power with respect to the relevant research and development, for example by limiting the ability and incentive of a hypothetical monopolist to retard the pace of research and development. The Agencies will delineate an innovation market only when the capabilities to engage in the relevant research and development can be associated with specialized assets or characteristics of specific firms.

In assessing the competitive significance of current and likely potential participants in an innovation market, the Agencies will take into account all relevant evidence. When market share data are available and accurately reflect the competitive significance of market participants, the Agencies will include market share data in this assessment. The Agencies also will seek evidence of buyers' and market participants' assessments of the competitive significance of innovation market participants. Such evidence is particularly important when market share data are unavailable or do not accurately represent the competitive significance of market participants. The Agencies may base the market shares of participants in an innovation market on their shares of identifiable assets or characteristics upon which innovation depends, on shares of research and development expenditures, or on shares of a related product. When entities have comparable capabilities and incentives to pursue research and development that is a close substitute for the research and development activities of the parties to a licensing arrangement, the Agencies may assign equal market shares to such entities.

\* \* \*

### 3.3 Horizontal and vertical relationships

As with other property transfers, antitrust analysis of intellectual property licensing arrangements examines whether the relationship among the parties to the arrangement is primarily horizontal or vertical in nature, or whether it has substantial aspects of both. A licensing arrangement has a vertical component when it affects activities that are in a complementary relationship, as is typically the case in a licensing arrangement. For example, the licensor's primary line of business may be in research and development, and the licensees, as manufacturers, may be buying the rights to use technology developed by the licensor. Alternatively, the licensor may be a component manufacturer owning intellectual property rights in a product that the licensee manufactures by combining the component with other inputs, or the licensor may manufacture the product, and the licensees may operate primarily in distribution and marketing.

In addition to this vertical component, the licensor and its licensees may also have a horizontal relationship. For analytical purposes, the Agencies ordinarily will treat a relationship between a licensor and its licensees, or between licensees, as horizontal when they would have been actual or likely potential competitors in a relevant market in the absence of the license.

The existence of a horizontal relationship between a licensor and its licensees does not, in itself, indicate that the arrangement is anti-competitive. Identification of such relationships is merely an aid in determining whether there may be anti-competitive effects arising from a licensing arrangement. Such a relationship need not give rise to an anti-competitive effect, nor does a purely vertical relationship assure that there are no anti-competitive effects.

The following examples illustrate different competitive relationships among a licensor and its licensees.

## Example 5

*Situation:* AgCo, a manufacturer of farm equipment, develops a new, patented emission control technology for its tractor engines and licenses it to FarmCo, another farm equipment manufacturer. AgCo's emission control technology is far superior to the technology currently owned and used by FarmCo, so much so that FarmCo's technology does not significantly constrain the prices that AgCo could charge for its technology. AgCo's emission control patent has a broad scope. It is likely that any improved emissions control technology that FarmCo could develop in the foreseeable future would infringe AgCo's patent.

*Discussion:* Because FarmCo's emission control technology does not significantly constrain AgCo's competitive conduct with respect to its emission control technology, AgCo's and FarmCo's emission control technologies are not close substitutes for each other. FarmCo is a consumer of AgCo's technology and is not an actual competitor of AgCo in the relevant market for superior emission control technology of the kind licensed by AgCo. Furthermore, FarmCo is not a likely potential competitor of AgCo in the relevant market because, even if FarmCo could develop an improved emission control technology, it is likely that it would infringe AgCo's patent. This means that the relationship between AgCo and FarmCo with regard to the supply and use of emissions control technology is vertical. Assuming that AgCo and FarmCo are actual or likely potential competitors in sales of farm equipment products, their relationship is horizontal in the relevant markets for farm equipment.

## Example 6

*Situation:* FarmCo develops a new valve technology for its engines and enters into a cross-licensing arrangement with AgCo, whereby AgCo licenses its emission control technology to FarmCo and FarmCo licenses its valve technology to AgCo. AgCo already owns an alternative valve technology that can be used to achieve engine performance similar to that using FarmCo's valve technology and at a comparable cost to consumers. Before adopting FarmCo's technology, AgCo was using its own valve technology in its production of engines and was licensing (and continues to license) that technology for use by others. As in Example 5, FarmCo does not own or control an emission control technology that is a close substitute for the technology licensed from AgCo. Furthermore, as in Example 5, FarmCo is not likely to develop an improved emission control technology that would be a close substitute for AgCo's technology, because of AgCo's blocking patent.

*Discussion:* FarmCo is a consumer and not a competitor of AgCo's emission control technology. As in Example 5, their relationship is vertical with regard to this technology. The relationship between AgCo and FarmCo in the relevant market that includes engine valve technology is vertical in part and horizontal in part. It is vertical in part because AgCo and FarmCo stand in a complementary relationship, in which AgCo is a consumer of a technology supplied by FarmCo. However, the relationship between AgCo and FarmCo in the relevant market that includes engine valve technology is also horizontal in part, because FarmCo and AgCo are actual competitors in the licensing of valve technology that can be used to achieve similar engine performance at a comparable cost. Whether the firms license their valve technologies to others is not important for the conclusion that the firms have a horizontal relationship in this relevant market.

Even if AgCo's use of its valve technology were solely captive to its own production, the fact that the two valve technologies are substitutable at comparable cost means that the two firms have a horizontal relationship.

As in Example 5, the relationship between AgCo and FarmCo is horizontal in the relevant markets for farm equipment.

### 3.4 Framework for evaluating licensing restraints

In the vast majority of cases, restraints in intellectual property licensing arrangements are evaluated under the rule of reason. The Agencies' general approach in analyzing a licensing restraint under the rule of reason is to inquire whether the restraint is likely to have anticompetitive effects and, if so, whether the restraint is reasonably necessary to achieve procompetitive benefits that outweigh those anticompetitive effects. *See Federal Trade Commission v. Indiana Federation of Dentists*, 476 U.S. 447 (1986); *NCAA v. Board of Regents of the University of Oklahoma*, 468 U.S. 85 (1984); *Broadcast Music, Inc. v. Columbia Broadcasting System, Inc.*, 441 U.S. 1 (1979); 7 Phillip E. Areeda, Antitrust Law § 1502 (1986).

In some cases, however, the courts conclude that a restraint's "nature and necessary effect are so plainly anticompetitive" that it should be treated as unlawful *per se*, without an elaborate inquiry into the restraint's likely competitive effect. *Federal Trade Commission v. Superior Court Trial Lawyers Association*, 493 U.S. 411, 433 (1990); *National Society of Professional Engineers v. United States*, 435 U.S. 679, 692 (1978). Among the restraints that have been held *per se* unlawful are naked price-fixing, output restraints, and market division among horizontal competitors, as well as certain group boycotts and resale price maintenance.

To determine whether a particular restraint in a licensing arrangement is given *per se* or rule of reason treatment, the Agencies will assess whether the restraint in question can be expected to contribute to an efficiency-enhancing integration of economic activity. *See Broadcast Music*, 441 U.S. at 16–24. In general, licensing arrangements promote such integration because they facilitate the combination of the licensor's intellectual property with complementary factors of production owned by the licensee. A restraint in a licensing arrangement may further such integration by, for example, aligning the incentives of the licensor and the licensees to promote the development and marketing of the licensed technology, or by substantially reducing transactions costs. If there is no efficiency-enhancing integration of economic activity and if the type of restraint is one that has been accorded *per se* treatment, the Agencies will challenge the restraint under the *per se* rule. Otherwise, the Agencies will apply a rule of reason analysis.

Application of the rule of reason generally requires a comprehensive inquiry into market conditions. (*See* sections 4.1–4.3.) However, that inquiry may be truncated in certain circumstances. If the Agencies conclude that a restraint has no likely anticompetitive effects, they will treat it as reasonable, without an elaborate analysis of market power or the justifications for the restraint. Similarly, if a restraint facially appears to be of a kind that would always or almost always tend to reduce output or increase prices,[40] and the restraint is not reasonably related to efficiencies, the Agen-

---

40. Details about the Federal Trade Commission's approach are set forth in *Massachusetts Board of Registration in Optometry*, 110 F.T.C. 549, 604 (1988). In applying its truncated rule of reason inquiry, the FTC uses the analytical category of "inherently suspect" restraints to denote facially anticompetitive restraints that would always or almost always tend to decrease output or increase prices, but that may be relatively unfamiliar or may not fit neatly into traditional *per se* categories.

cies will likely challenge the restraint without an elaborate analysis of particular industry circumstances. *See Indiana Federation of Dentists* 476 U.S. at 459–60; *NCAA,* 468 U.S. at 109.

**Example 7**

*Situation:* Gamma, which manufactures Product X using its patented process, offers a license for its process technology to every other manufacturer of Product X, each of which competes world-wide with Gamma in the manufacture and sale of X. The process technology does not represent an economic improvement over the available existing technologies. Indeed, although most manufacturers accept licenses from Gamma, none of the licensees actually uses the licensed technology. The licenses provide that each manufacturer has an exclusive right to sell Product X manufactured using the licensed technology in a designated geographic area and that no manufacturer may sell Product X, however manufactured, outside the designated territory.

*Discussion:* The manufacturers of Product X are in a horizontal relationship in the goods market for Product X. Any manufacturers of Product X that control technologies that are substitutable at comparable cost for Gamma's process are also horizontal competitors of Gamma in the relevant technology market. The licensees of Gamma's process technology are technically in a vertical relationship, although that is not significant in this example because they do not actually use Gamma's technology.

The licensing arrangement restricts competition in the relevant goods market among manufacturers of Product X by requiring each manufacturer to limit its sales to an exclusive territory. Thus, competition among entities that would be actual competitors in the absence of the licensing arrangement is restricted. Based on the facts set forth above, the licensing arrangement does not involve a useful transfer of technology, and thus it is unlikely that the restraint on sales outside the designated territories contributes to an efficiency-enhancing integration of economic activity. Consequently, the evaluating Agency would be likely to challenge the arrangement under the *per se* rule as a horizontal territorial market allocation scheme and to view the intellectual property aspects of the arrangement as a sham intended to cloak its true nature.

If the licensing arrangement could be expected to contribute to an efficiency-enhancing integration of economic activity, as might be the case if the licensed technology were an advance over existing processes and used by the licensees, the Agency would analyze the arrangement under the rule of reason applying the analytical framework described in this section.

In this example, the competitive implications do not generally depend on whether the licensed technology is protected by patent, is a trade secret or other know-how, or is a computer program protected by copyright; nor do the competitive implications generally depend on whether the allocation of markets is territorial, as in this example, or functional, based on fields of use.

### 4. General principles concerning the Agencies' evaluation of licensing arrangements under the rule of reason

#### 4.1 Analysis of anti-competitive effects

The existence of anti-competitive effects resulting from a restraint in a licensing arrangement will be evaluated on the basis of the analysis described in this section.

#### 4.1.1 Market structure, coordination, and foreclosure

When a licensing arrangement affects parties in a horizontal relationship, a restraint in that arrangement may increase the risk of coordinated pricing, output restrictions, or the acquisition or maintenance of market power. Harm to competition also may occur if the arrangement poses a significant risk of retarding or restricting the development of new or improved goods or processes. The potential for competitive harm depends in part on the degree of concentration in, the difficulty of entry into, and the responsiveness of supply and demand to changes in price in the relevant markets. *Cf. 1992 Horizontal Merger Guidelines* §§ 1.5, 3.

When the licensor and licensees are in a vertical relationship, the Agencies will analyze whether the licensing arrangement may harm competition among entities in a horizontal relationship at either the level of the licensor or the licensees, or possibly in another relevant market. Harm to competition from a restraint may occur if it anticompetitively forecloses access to, or increases competitors' costs of obtaining, important inputs, or facilitates coordination to raise price or restrict output. The risk of anticompetitively foreclosing access or increasing competitors' costs is related to the proportion of the markets affected by the licensing restraint; other characteristics of the relevant markets, such as concentration, difficulty of entry, and the responsiveness of supply and demand to changes in price in the relevant markets; and the duration of the restraint. A licensing arrangement does not foreclose competition merely because some or all of the potential licensees in an industry choose to use the licensed technology to the exclusion of other technologies. Exclusive use may be an efficient consequence of the licensed technology having the lowest cost or highest value.

Harm to competition from a restraint in a vertical licensing arrangement also may occur if a licensing restraint facilitates coordination among entities in a horizontal relationship to raise prices or reduce output in a relevant market. For example, if owners of competing technologies impose similar restraints on their licensees, the licensors may find it easier to coordinate their pricing. Similarly, licensees that are competitors may find it easier to coordinate their pricing if they are subject to common restraints in licenses with a common licensor or competing licensors. The risk of anticompetitive coordination is increased when the relevant markets are concentrated and difficult to enter. The use of similar restraints may be common and procompetitive in an industry, however, because they contribute to efficient exploitation of the licensed property.

### 4.1.2 Licensing arrangements involving exclusivity

A licensing arrangement may involve exclusivity in two distinct respects. First, the licensor may grant one or more *exclusive licenses*, which restrict the right of the licensor to license others and possibly also to use the technology itself. Generally, an exclusive license may raise antitrust concerns only if the licensees themselves, or the licensor and its licensees, are in a horizontal relationship. Examples of arrangements involving exclusive licensing that may give rise to antitrust concerns include cross-licensing by parties collectively possessing market power (*see* section 5.5), grantbacks (*see* section 5.6), and acquisitions of intellectual property rights (*see* section 5.7).

A non-exclusive license of intellectual property that does not contain any restraints on the competitive conduct of the licensor or the licensee generally does not present antitrust concerns even if the parties to the license are in a horizontal relationship, because the non-exclusive license normally does not diminish competition that would occur in its absence.

A second form of exclusivity, *exclusive dealing*, arises when a license prevents or restrains the licensee from licensing, selling, distributing, or using competing technologies. *See* section 5.4. Exclusivity may be achieved by an explicit exclusive dealing term in the license or by other provisions such as compensation terms or other economic incentives. Such restraints may anticompetitively foreclose access to, or increase competitors' costs of obtaining, important inputs, or facilitate coordination to raise price or reduce output, but they also may have procompetitive effects. For example, a licensing arrangement that prevents the licensee from dealing in other technologies may encourage the licensee to develop and market the licensed technology or specialized applications of that technology....

The antitrust principles that apply to a licensor's grant of various forms of exclusivity to and among its licensees are similar to those that apply to comparable vertical restraints outside the licensing context, such as exclusive territories and exclusive dealing. However, the fact that intellectual property may in some cases be misappropriated more easily than other forms of property may justify the use of some restrictions that might be anticompetitive in other contexts.

As noted earlier, the Agencies will focus on the actual practice and its effects, not on the formal terms of the arrangement. A license denominated as non-exclusive (either in the sense of exclusive licensing or in the sense of exclusive dealing) may nonetheless give rise to the same concerns posed by formal exclusivity. A non-exclusive license may have the effect of exclusive licensing if it is structured so that the licensor is unlikely to license others or to practice the technology itself. A license that does not explicitly require exclusive dealing may have the effect of exclusive dealing if it is structured to increase significantly a licensee's cost when it uses competing technologies. However, a licensing arrangement will not automatically raise these concerns merely because a party chooses to deal with a single licensee or licensor, or confines his activity to a single field of use or location, or because only a single licensee has chosen to take a license.

---

### Example 8

*Situation:* NewCo, the inventor and manufacturer of a new flat panel display technology, lacking the capability to bring a flat panel display product to market, grants BigCo an exclusive license to sell a product embodying NewCo's technology. BigCo does not currently sell, and is not developing (or likely to develop), a product that would compete with the product embodying the new technology and does not control rights to another display technology. Several firms offer competing displays, BigCo accounts for only a small proportion of the outlets for distribution of display products, and entry into the manufacture and distribution of display products is relatively easy. Demand for the new technology is uncertain and successful market penetration will require considerable promotional effort. The license contains an exclusive dealing restriction preventing BigCo from selling products that compete with the product embodying the licensed technology.

*Discussion:* This example illustrates both types of exclusivity in a licensing arrangement. The license is exclusive in that it restricts the right of the licensor to grant other licenses. In addition, the license has an exclusive dealing component in that it restricts the licensee from selling competing products.

The inventor of the display technology and its licensee are in a vertical relationship and are not actual or likely potential competitors in the manufacture or sale of display products or in the sale or development of technology. Hence, the grant of an exclusive license does not affect competition between the licensor and the licensee. The exclusive license may promote competition in the manufacturing and sale of display prod-

ucts by encouraging BigCo to develop and promote the new product in the face of uncertain demand by rewarding BigCo for its efforts if they lead to large sales. Although
the license bars the licensee from selling competing products, this exclusive dealing aspect is unlikely in this example to harm competition by anticompetitively foreclosing
access, raising competitors' costs of inputs, or facilitating anticompetitive pricing because the relevant product market is unconcentrated, the exclusive dealing restraint
affects only a small proportion of the outlets for distribution of display products, and
entry is easy. On these facts, the evaluating Agency would be unlikely to challenge the
arrangement.

### 4.2 Efficiencies and justifications

If the Agencies conclude, upon an evaluation of the market factors described in section 4.1, that a restraint in a licensing arrangement is unlikely to have an anticompetitive
effect, they will not challenge the restraint. If the Agencies conclude that the restraint has,
or is likely to have, an anticompetitive effect, they will consider whether the restraint is
reasonably necessary to achieve procompetitive efficiencies. If the restraint is reasonably
necessary, the Agencies will balance the procompetitive efficiencies and the anticompetitive effects to determine the probable net effect on competition in each relevant market.

The Agencies' comparison of anticompetitive harms and procompetitive efficiencies
is necessarily a qualitative one. The risk of anticompetitive effects in a particular case
may be insignificant compared to the expected efficiencies, or vice versa. As the expected anticompetitive effects in a particular licensing arrangement increase, the Agencies will require evidence establishing a greater level of expected efficiencies.

The existence of practical and significantly less restrictive alternatives is relevant to a determination of whether a restraint is reasonably necessary. If it is clear that the parties
could have achieved similar efficiencies by means that are significantly less restrictive, then
the Agencies will not give weight to the parties' efficiency claim. In making this assessment,
however, the Agencies will not engage in a search for a theoretically least restrictive alternative that is not realistic in the practical prospective business situation faced by the parties.

When a restraint has, or is likely to have, an anticompetitive effect, the duration of
that restraint can be an important factor in determining whether it is reasonably necessary to achieve the putative procompetitive efficiency. The effective duration of a restraint may depend on a number of factors, including the option of the affected party to
terminate the arrangement unilaterally and the presence of contract terms (e.g., unpaid
balances on minimum purchase commitments) that encourage the licensee to renew a
license arrangement. Consistent with their approach to less restrictive alternative analysis generally, the Agencies will not attempt to draw fine distinctions regarding duration;
rather, their focus will be on situations in which the duration clearly exceeds the period
needed to achieve the procompetitive efficiency.

The evaluation of procompetitive efficiencies, of the reasonable necessity of a restraint to achieve them, and of the duration of the restraint, may depend on the market
context. A restraint that may be justified by the needs of a new entrant, for example,
may not have a procompetitive efficiency justification in different market circumstances. *Cf. United States v. Jerrold Electronics Corp.*, 187 F. Supp. 545 (E.D. Pa. 1960),
*aff'd per curiam*, 365 U.S. 567 (1961).

### 4.3 Antitrust "safety zone"

Because licensing arrangements often promote innovation and enhance competition, the Agencies believe that an antitrust "safety zone" is useful in order to provide

some degree of certainty and thus to encourage such activity.[41] Absent extraordinary circumstances, the Agencies will not challenge a restraint in an intellectual property licensing arrangement if (1) the restraint is not facially anticompetitive[42] and (2) the licensor and its licensees collectively account for no more than twenty percent of each relevant market significantly affected by the restraint. This "safety zone" does not apply to those transfers of intellectual property rights to which a merger analysis is applied....

Whether a restraint falls within the safety zone will be determined by reference only to goods markets unless the analysis of goods markets alone would inadequately address the effects of the licensing arrangement on competition among technologies or in research and development.

If an examination of the effects on competition among technologies or in research development is required, and if market share data are unavailable or do not accurately represent competitive significance, the following safety zone criteria will apply. Absent extraordinary circumstances, the Agencies will not challenge a restraint in an intellectual property licensing arrangement that may affect competition in a technology market if (1) the restraint is not facially anticompetitive and (2) there are four or more independently controlled technologies in addition to the technologies controlled by the parties to the licensing arrangement that may be substitutable for the licensed technology at a comparable cost to the user. Absent extraordinary circumstances, the Agencies will not challenge a restraint in an intellectual property licensing arrangement that may affect competition in an innovation market if (1) the restraint is not facially anticompetitive and (2) four or more independently controlled entities in addition to the parties to the licensing arrangement possess the required specialized assets or characteristics and the incentive to engage in research and development that is a close substitute of the research and development activities of the parties to the licensing agreement.

The Agencies emphasize that licensing arrangements are not anticompetitive merely because they do not fall within the scope of the safety zone. Indeed, it is likely that the great majority of licenses falling outside the safety zone are lawful and procompetitive. The safety zone is designed to provide owners of intellectual property with a degree of certainty in those situations in which anticompetitive effects are so unlikely that the arrangements may be presumed not to be anticompetitive without an inquiry into particular industry circumstances. It is not intended to suggest that parties should conform to the safety zone or to discourage parties falling outside the safety zone from adopting restrictions in their license arrangements that are reasonably necessary to achieve an efficiency-enhancing integration of economic activity. The Agencies will analyze arrangements falling outside the safety zone based on the considerations outlined in parts 3–5.

The status of a licensing arrangement with respect to the safety zone may change over time. A determination by the Agencies that a restraint in a licensing arrangement qualifies for inclusion in the safety zone is based on the factual circumstances prevailing at the time of the conduct at issue.

---

41. The antitrust "safety zone" does not apply to restraints that are not in a licensing arrangement, or to restraints that are in a licensing arrangement but are unrelated to the use of the licensed intellectual property.

42. "Facially anticompetitive" refers to restraints that normally warrant per se treatment, as well as other restraints of a kind that would always or almost always tend to reduce output or increase prices. *See* section 3.4.

## 5. Application of general principles

5.0 This section illustrates the application of the general principles discussed above to particular licensing restraints and to arrangements that involve the cross-licensing, pooling, or acquisition of intellectual property. The restraints and arrangements identified are typical of those that are likely to receive antitrust scrutiny; however, they are not intended as an exhaustive list of practices that could raise competitive concerns.

### 5.1 Horizontal restraints

The existence of a restraint in a licensing arrangement that affects parties in a horizontal relationship (a "horizontal restraint") does not necessarily cause the arrangement to be anticompetitive. As in the case of joint ventures among horizontal competitors, licensing arrangements among such competitors may promote rather than hinder competition if they result in integrative efficiencies. Such efficiencies may arise, for example, from the realization of economies of scale and the integration of complementary research and development, production, and marketing capabilities.

Following the general principles outlined in section 3.4, horizontal restraints often will be evaluated under the rule of reason. In some circumstances, however, that analysis may be truncated; additionally, some restraints may merit *per se* treatment, including price fixing, allocation of markets or customers, agreements to reduce output, and certain group boycotts.

---

### Example 9

*Situation:* Two of the leading manufacturers of a consumer electronic product hold patents that cover alternative circuit designs for the product. The manufacturers assign their patents to a separate corporation wholly owned by the two firms. That corporation licenses the right to use the circuit designs to other consumer product manufacturers and establishes the license royalties. None of the patents is blocking; that is, each of the patents can be used without infringing a patent owned by the other firm. The different circuit designs are substitutable in that each permits the manufacture at comparable cost to consumers of products that consumers consider to be interchangeable. One of the Agencies is analyzing the licensing arrangement.

*Discussion:* In this example, the manufacturers are horizontal competitors in the goods market for the consumer product and in the related technology markets. The competitive issue with regard to a joint assignment of patent rights is whether the assignment has an adverse impact on competition in technology and goods markets that is not outweighed by procompetitive efficiencies, such as benefits in the use or dissemination of the technology. Each of the patent owners has a right to exclude others from using its patent. That right does not extend, however, to the agreement to assign rights jointly. To the extent that the patent rights cover technologies that are close substitutes, the joint determination of royalties likely would result in higher royalties and higher goods prices than would result if the owners licensed or used their technologies independently. In the absence of evidence establishing efficiency-enhancing integration from the joint assignment of patent rights, the Agency may conclude that the joint marketing of competing patent rights constitutes horizontal price fixing and could be challenged as a *per se* unlawful horizontal restraint of trade. If the joint marketing arrangement results in an efficiency-enhancing integration, the Agency would evaluate the arrangement under the rule of reason. However, the Agency may conclude that the anticompetitive effects are sufficiently apparent, and the claimed integrative efficiencies are sufficiently weak or not reasonably related to the restraints, to warrant challenge of the arrangement without an elaborate analysis of particular industry circumstances (*see* section 3.4).

## 5.2 Resale price maintenance

Resale price maintenance is illegal when "commodities have passed into the channels of trade and are owned by dealers." *Dr. Miles Medical Co. v. John D. Park & Sons Co.*, 220 U.S. 373, 408 (1911). It has been held *per se* illegal for a licensor of an intellectual property right in a product to fix a licensee's resale price of that product. *United States v. Univis Lens Co.*, 316 U.S. 241 (1942); *Ethyl Gasoline Corp. v. United States*, 309 U.S. 436 (1940).[43] Consistent with the principles set forth in section 3.4, the Agencies will enforce the *per se* rule against resale price maintenance in the intellectual property context.

## 5.3 Tying arrangements

A "tying" or "tie-in" or "tied sale" arrangement has been defined as "an agreement by a party to sell one product...on the condition that the buyer also purchases a different (or tied) product, or at least agrees that he will not purchase that [tied] product from any other supplier." *Eastman Kodak Co. v. Image Technical Services, Inc.*, 112 S. Ct. 2072, 2079 (1992). Conditioning the ability of a licensee to license one or more items of intellectual property on the licensee's purchase of another item of intellectual property or a good or a service has been held in some cases to constitute illegal tying.[44] Although tying arrangements may result in anticompetitive effects, such arrangements can also result in significant efficiencies and procompetitive benefits. In the exercise of their prosecutorial discretion, the Agencies will consider both the anticompetitive effects and the efficiencies attributable to a tie-in. The Agencies would be likely to challenge a tying arrangement if: (1) the seller has market power in the tying product; (2) the arrangement has an adverse effect on competition in the relevant market for the tied product; and (3) efficiency justifications for the arrangement do not outweigh the anticompetitive effects. The Agencies will not presume that a patent, copyright, or trade secret necessarily confers market power upon its owner.

Package licensing—the licensing of multiple items of intellectual property in a single license or in a group of related licenses—may be a form of tying arrangement if the licensing of one product is conditioned upon the acceptance of a license of another, separate product. Package licensing can be efficiency enhancing under some circumstances. When multiple licenses are needed to use any single item of intellectual property, for example, a package license may promote such efficiencies. If a package license constitutes a tying arrangement, the Agencies will evaluate its competitive effects under the same principles they apply to other tying arrangements.

* * *

---

43. *But cf. United States v. General Electric Co.*, 272 U.S. 476 (1926) (holding that an owner of a product patent may condition a license to manufacture the product on the fixing of the first sale price of the patented product). Subsequent lower court decisions have distinguished the *GE* decision in various contexts. *See, e.g., Royal Indus. v. St. Regis Paper Co.*, 420 F.2d 449, 452 (9th Cir. 1969) (observing that *GE* involved a restriction by a patentee who also manufactured the patented product and leaving open the question whether a nonmanufacturing patentee may fix the price of the patented product); *Newburgh Moire Co. v. Superior Moire Co.*, 237 F.2d 283, 293–94 (3rd Cir. 1956) (grant of multiple licenses each containing price restrictions does not come within the *GE* doctrine); *Cummer-Graham Co. v. Straight Side Basket Corp.*, 142 F.2d 646, 647 (5th Cir.) (owner of an intellectual property right in a process to manufacture an unpatented product may not fix the sale price of that product), *cert. denied*, 323 U.S. 726 (1944); *Barber-Colman Co. v. National Tool Co.*, 136 F.2d 339, 343–44 (6th Cir. 1943).

44. *See, e.g., United States v. Paramount Pictures, Inc.*, 334 U.S. 131, 156–58 (1948) (copyrights); *International Salt Co. v. United States*, 332 U.S. 392 (1947) (patent and related product).

### 5.4 Exclusive dealing

In the intellectual property context, exclusive dealing occurs when a license prevents the licensee from licensing, selling, distributing, or using competing technologies. Exclusive dealing arrangements are evaluated under the rule of reason. *See Tampa Electric Co. v. Nashville Coal Co.*, 365 U.S. 320 (1961) (evaluating legality of exclusive dealing under section 1 of the Sherman Act and section 3 of the Clayton Act); *Beltone Electronics Corp.*, 100 F.T.C. 68 (1982) (evaluating legality of exclusive dealing under section 5 of the Federal Trade Commission Act)...In determining whether an exclusive dealing arrangement is likely to reduce competition in a relevant market, the Agencies will take into account the extent to which the arrangement (1) promotes the exploitation and development of the licensor's technology and (2) anticompetitively forecloses the exploitation and development of, or otherwise constrains competition among, competing technologies.

The likelihood that exclusive dealing may have anticompetitive effects is related, *inter alia*, to the degree of foreclosure in the relevant market, the duration of the exclusive dealing arrangement, and other characteristics of the input and output markets, such as concentration, difficulty of entry, and the responsiveness of supply and demand to changes in price in the relevant markets. (*See* sections 4.1.1 and 4.1.2.) If the Agencies determine that a particular exclusive dealing arrangement may have an anticompetitive effect, they will evaluate the extent to which the restraint encourages licensees to develop and market the licensed technology (or specialized applications of that technology), increases licensors' incentives to develop or refine the licensed technology, or otherwise increases competition and enhances output in a relevant market....

### 5.5 Cross-licensing and pooling arrangements

Cross-licensing and pooling arrangements are agreements of two or more owners of different items of intellectual property to license one another or third parties. These arrangements may provide procompetitive benefits by integrating complementary technologies, reducing transaction costs, clearing blocking positions, and avoiding costly infringement litigation. By promoting the dissemination of technology, cross-licensing and pooling arrangements are often procompetitive.

Cross-licensing and pooling arrangements can have anticompetitive effects in certain circumstances. For example, collective price or output restraints in pooling arrangements, such as the joint marketing of pooled intellectual property rights with collective price setting or coordinated output restrictions, may be deemed unlawful if they do not contribute to an efficiency-enhancing integration of economic activity among the participants. Compare *NCAA* 468 U.S. at 114 (output restriction on college football broadcasting held unlawful because it was not reasonably related to any purported justification) with *Broadcast Music*, 441 U.S. at 23 (blanket license for music copyrights found not *per se* illegal because the cooperative price was necessary to the creation of a new product). When cross-licensing or pooling arrangements are mechanisms to accomplish naked price fixing or market division, they are subject to challenge under the *per se* rule. *See United States v. New Wrinkle, Inc.*, 342 U.S. 371 (1952) (price fixing).

Settlements involving the cross-licensing of intellectual property rights can be an efficient means to avoid litigation and, in general, courts favor such settlements. When such cross-licensing involves horizontal competitors, however, the Agencies will consider whether the effect of the settlement is to diminish competition among entities that would have been actual or likely potential competitors in a relevant market in the absence of the cross-license. In the absence of offsetting efficiencies, such settlements may be challenged as unlawful restraints of trade. *Cf. United States v. Singer Manufacturing*

*Co.*, 374 U.S. 174 (1963) (cross-license agreement was part of broader combination to exclude competitors).

Pooling arrangements generally need not be open to all who would like to join. However, exclusion from cross-licensing and pooling arrangements among parties that collectively possess market power may, under some circumstances, harm competition. *Cf. Northwest Wholesale Stationers, Inc. v. Pacific Stationery & Printing Co.*, 472 U.S. 284 (1985) (exclusion of a competitor from a purchasing cooperative not *per se* unlawful absent a showing of market power)...In general, exclusion from a pooling or cross-licensing arrangement among competing technologies is unlikely to have anticompetitive effects unless (1) excluded firms cannot effectively compete in the relevant market for the good incorporating the licensed technologies and (2) the pool participants collectively possess market power in the relevant market. If these circumstances exist, the Agencies will evaluate whether the arrangement's limitations on participation are reasonably related to the efficient development and exploitation of the pooled technologies and will assess the net effect of those limitations in the relevant market. *See* section 4.2.

Another possible anticompetitive effect of pooling arrangements may occur if the arrangement deters or discourages participants from engaging in research and development, thus retarding innovation. For example, a pooling arrangement that requires members to grant licenses to each other for current and future technology at minimal cost may reduce the incentives of its members to engage in research and development because members of the pool have to share their successful research and development and each of the members can free ride on the accomplishments of other pool members....However, such an arrangement can have procompetitive benefits, for example, by exploiting economies of scale and integrating complementary capabilities of the pool members, (including the clearing of blocking positions), and is likely to cause competitive problems only when the arrangement includes a large fraction of the potential research and development in an innovation market....

## Example 10

*Situation:* As in Example 9, two of the leading manufacturers of a consumer electronic product hold patents that cover alternative circuit designs for the product. The manufacturers assign several of their patents to a separate corporation wholly owned by the two firms. That corporation licenses the right to use the circuit designs to other consumer product manufacturers and establishes the license royalties. In this example, however, the manufacturers assign to the separate corporation only patents that are blocking. None of the patents assigned to the corporation can be used without infringing a patent owned by the other firm.

*Discussion:* Unlike the previous example, the joint assignment of patent rights to the wholly owned corporation in this example does not adversely affect competition in the licensed technology among entities that would have been actual or likely potential competitors in the absence of the licensing arrangement. Moreover, the licensing arrangement is likely to have procompetitive benefits in the use of the technology. Because the manufacturers' patents are blocking, the manufacturers are not in a horizontal relationship with respect to those patents. None of the patents can be used without the right to a patent owned by the other firm, so the patents are not substitutable. As in Example 9, the firms are horizontal competitors in the relevant goods market. In the absence of collateral restraints that would likely raise price or reduce output in the relevant goods market or in any other relevant antitrust market and that are not reasonably related to an efficiency-enhancing integration of economic activity, the evaluating Agency would be unlikely to challenge this arrangement.

## 5.6 Grantbacks

A grantback is an arrangement under which a licensee agrees to extend to the licensor of intellectual property the right to use the licensee's improvements to the licensed technology. Grantbacks can have procompetitive effects, especially if they are nonexclusive. Such arrangements provide a means for the licensee and the licensor to share risks and reward the licensor for making possible further innovation based on or informed by the licensed technology, and both promote innovation in the first place and promote the subsequent licensing of the results of the innovation. Grantbacks may adversely affect competition, however, if they substantially reduce the licensee's incentives to engage in research and development and thereby limit rivalry in innovation markets.

A non-exclusive grantback allows the licensee to practice its technology and license it to others. Such a grantback provision may be necessary to ensure that the licensor is not prevented from effectively competing because it is denied access to improvements developed with the aid of its own technology. Compared with an exclusive grantback, a nonexclusive grantback, which leaves the licensee free to license improvements technology to others, is less likely to have anticompetitive effects.

The Agencies will evaluate a grantback provision under the rule of reason, see generally *Transparent-Wrap Machine Corp. v. Stokes & Smith Co.*, 329 U.S. 637, 645–48 (1947) (grantback provision in technology license is not *per se* unlawful)... considering its likely effects in light of the overall structure of the licensing arrangement and conditions in the relevant markets. An important factor in the Agencies' analysis of a grantback will be whether the licensor has market power in a relevant technology or innovation market. If the Agencies determine that a particular grantback provision is likely to reduce significantly licensees' incentives to invest in improving the licensed technology, the Agencies will consider the extent to which the grantback provision has offsetting procompetitive effects, such as: (1) promoting dissemination of licensees' improvements to the licensed technology; (2) increasing the licensors' incentives to disseminate the licensed technology; or (3) otherwise increasing competition and output in a relevant technology or innovation market. *See* section 4.2. In addition, the Agencies will consider the extent to which grantback provisions in the relevant markets generally increase licensors' incentives to innovate in the first place.

## 5.7 Acquisition of intellectual property rights

Certain transfers of intellectual property rights are most appropriately analyzed by applying the principles and standards used to analyze mergers, particularly those in the 1992 Horizontal Merger Guidelines. The Agencies will apply a merger analysis to an outright sale by an intellectual property owner of all of its rights to that intellectual property and to a transaction in which a person obtains through grant, sale, or other transfer an exclusive license for intellectual property (i.e., a license that precludes all other persons, including the licensor, from using the licensed intellectual property).[45] Such transactions may be assessed under section 7 of the Clayton Act, Sections 1 and 2 of the Sherman Act, and section 5 of the Federal Trade Commission Act.

---

45. The safety zone of section 4.3 does not apply to transfers of intellectual property such as those described in this section.

**Example 11**

*Situation:* Omega develops a new, patented pharmaceutical for the treatment of a particular disease. The only drug on the market approved for the treatment of this disease is sold by Delta. Omega's patented drug has almost completed regulatory approval by the Food and Drug Administration. Omega has invested considerable sums in product development and market testing, and initial results show that Omega's drug would be a significant competitor to Delta's. However, rather than enter the market as a direct competitor of Delta, Omega licenses to Delta the right to manufacture and sell Omega's patented drug. The license agreement with Delta is nominally nonexclusive. However, Omega has rejected all requests by other firms to obtain a license to manufacture and sell Omega's patented drug, despite offers by those firms of terms that are reasonable in relation to those in Delta's license.

*Discussion:* Although Omega's license to Delta is nominally nonexclusive, the circumstances indicate that it is exclusive in fact because Omega has rejected all reasonable offers by other firms for licenses to manufacture and sell Omega's patented drug. The facts of this example indicate that Omega would be a likely potential competitor of Delta in the absence of the licensing arrangement, and thus they are in a horizontal relationship in the relevant goods market that includes drugs for the treatment of this particular disease. The evaluating Agency would apply a merger analysis to this transaction, since it involves an acquisition of a likely potential competitor.

### 6. Enforcement of invalid intellectual property rights

The Agencies may challenge the enforcement of invalid intellectual property rights as antitrust violations. Enforcement or attempted enforcement of a patent obtained by fraud on the Patent and Trademark Office or the Copyright Office may violate Section 2 of the Sherman Act, if all the elements otherwise necessary to establish a Section 2 charge are proved, or [a violation of] section 5 of the Federal Trade Commission Act. *Walker Process Equipment, Inc. v. Food Machinery & Chemical Corp.*, 382 U.S. 172 (1965) (patents); *American Cyanamid Co.*, 72 F.T.C. 623, 684–85 (1967), *aff 'd sub. nom.*, *Charles Pfizer & Co.*, 401 F.2d 574 (6th Cir. 1968), *cert. denied*, 394 U.S. 920 (1969) (patents); *Michael Anthony Jewelers, Inc. v. Peacock Jewelry, Inc.*, 795 F. Supp. 639, 647 (S.D.N.Y. 1992) (copyrights)... Inequitable conduct before the Patent and Trademark Office will not be the basis of a Section 2 claim unless the conduct also involves knowing and willful fraud and the other elements of a Section 2 claim are present....Actual or attempted enforcement of patents obtained by inequitable conduct that falls short of fraud under some circumstances may violate Section 5 of the Federal Trade Commission Act....Objectively baseless litigation to enforce invalid intellectual property rights may also constitute an element of a violation of the Sherman Act.

---

# Notes and Questions on the 1995 Guidelines

1. Recall the four-box matrix of antitrust law that you made at the end of Section III of this Chapter. It had two columns referring to contractual restraints, labeled "horizontal" and "vertical." It also had two rows labeled "price" and "non-price." How does that matrix apply to licensing? In each box in your matrix, insert the relevant section(s) of

the 1995 Guidelines (and the numbers of relevant examples) that apply to the contractual restraints in that box. Is the matrix still a useful tool? Is it consistent with the 1995 Guidelines as set forth above?

2. As you can see from the 1995 Guidelines and its examples, antitrust analysis is hardly a mechanical or formulaic process. A patent pooling and cross-licensing arrangement may be virtually risk-free (in terms of antitrust exposure) or quite risky, depending on such things as the nature and relationships of the cross-licensees and whether the patents at issue involve substitute or blocking technology. Similarly, a license arrangement that is "non-exclusive" on paper may warrant stringent antitrust scrutiny if the licensor in fact never grants any other licenses. This fact-dependence is consistent with the Supreme Court's approach in *GTE Sylvania* and its progeny, under which courts are supposed to examine substantial economic effect, not barren formalism.

3. As a practical matter, what the search for economic effect means is that courts try to examine the real world to determine whether a license restriction is likely to have a procompetitive or anticompetitive effect. If the purpose and effect is to fix prices or divide markets horizontally among firms that otherwise might compete vigorously, it is likely to be illegal *per se*. If the license restraint seems to enhance and encourage competition, or to provide substantial consumer benefits, it is likely to pass muster under the rule of reason.

One good—although hardly infallible—rule of thumb is a client's motivation. If a client seems to want a particular contractual restraint in licensing in order to avoid or crush competition, that restraint may well be anticompetitive and raise serious antitrust concern. After all, clients know their business best. If they think a restraint will minimize competition, they may well be right. That's why courts also look at motivation, not because intent is an element of any antitrust violation (it isn't!) but because intentions, especially those of sophisticated business executives, may well reflect economic reality.

4. The "safety zone" described in Section 4.3 of the 1995 Guidelines is sometimes called the "five company" rule. It provides a limited safe harbor if a firm engaged in a licensing restraint is one of five or more firms exploiting the same defined market, and the other firms in the same market are not so restrained. The 20%-market-share rule is just the "flip side" of the five-company rule.

The five-company rule is only a guide to the two federal agencies' enforcement intentions, not to substantive antitrust law. Some restraints—particularly horizontal ones— may create antitrust exposure even when the five-company rule is satisfied. For example, would you advise your client to agree with horizontal competitors to fix the price of its products or licensed technology, or to divide geographic territory among them, even if all the parties to the agreement together had less than a 20% share of relevant markets?

5. Section 4.2 of the 1995 Guidelines discusses "less restrictive alternative" analysis of contractual and other restraints. In making this analysis, however, it says that the federal agencies "will not engage in a search for a theoretically least restrictive alternative that is not realistic in the practical prospective business situation faced by the parties."

What does this mean? Does it mean that, if a firm tries to justify an apparently anticompetitive restraint by asserting a legitimate business goal, that the justification will fail if there is a practical, real-world alternative way of reaching the same business goal without the restraint?

6. One common restraint that business people often seek is control over the price at which licensees sell licensed products. For example, suppose that a licensor with a prod-

uct patent licenses the patent non-exclusively to several manufacturers, in exchange for a royalty of 10% of the price at which they sell their patented products. The licensor may fear that some (or even all) of licensees will sell their products at very low prices, thereby producing a very low royalty (at 10% of each price).

This fear may be legitimate. For example, if the licensee-manufacturers have multiple product lines, they might sell the patented products at very low prices as "loss leaders" to promote their other products. Or they might discover new methods of producing the products, allowing them to lower substantially their cost of manufacture, and therefore their sales price.

One way of handling this problem is for the licensor to try to control the prices at which its licensees sell the licensed (patented) products. For example, the license might contain a clause under which each licensee agrees not to sell any licensed product for a price less than $10 per unit.

Would such a clause raise any antitrust concern? If so, how would you analyze it? Is the clause likely to be approved under the rule of reason or condemned as illegal *per se*? Can you think of any realistic alternative way to solve the problem of "loss leaders" and insure the licensor a reasonable royalty on each sale by licensees?

7. In 2002, the Federal Trade Commission and the Department of Justice conducted a number of hearings to highlight the intersection of antitrust and intellectual property law and policy. *See* Press Release, Federal Trade Commission, FTC/DOJ Hearings to Highlight the Intersection of Antitrust and Intellectual Property Law and Policy (Apr. 10, 2002), *available at* www.ftc.gov/opa/2002/04/iplaw2.htm. These hearings intend to address a number of issues, including patent pools, cross licensing, and standard setting. On March 5, 2002, the Federal Trade Commission and the Department of Justice announced new clearance procedures for antitrust matters. This Memorandum of Agreement amends the clearance process and formally allocates primary areas of responsibility (between the FTC and the DOJ) on an industry-wide basis, but does not purport to limit the jurisdiction of either agency. A copy of the Agreement is located at Memorandum of Agreement Between the Federal Trade Commission and The Antitrust Division of the United States Department of Justice Concerning Clearance Procedures for Investigations (Feb. 27, 2002), *available at* www.ftc.gov/opa/2002/02/clearance/ftcdojagree.pdf. For example, the Agreement allocates the areas of media and entertainment to the DOJ (both the FTC and the DOJ have experience in these areas). A summary of the terms of the Agreement is located at Press Release, Federal Trade Commission, FTC and DOJ Announce New Clearance Procedures for Antitrust Matters (Mar. 5, 2002), *available at* www.ftc.gov/opa/2002/03/clearance. htm.

---

# VI. Copyright and Other Misuse

Near the middle of the last century, the defense of "misuse" of intellectual property arose. It appeared first in patent cases, in which a patent owner tried to tie the sale of unpatented goods to the sale or lease of patented ones. Courts disfavored tying of this sort, seeing it as an attempt to extend the economic power of the patent beyond its proper bounds. They ruled it an offense against equity, rendering the relevant patents unenforceable, at least temporarily. Courts refrained from *invalidating* patents on this ground. Rather, they held the patents *unenforceable* until the patent owner could "purge" the misuse and its effects, for example, by eliminating both the tie and its economic effects.

All this was judge-made law. Courts founded the misuse defense on broad notions of equity and public policy. They saw no need to coordinate misuse doctrine with antitrust law because misuse was a *defense*, while antitrust law provided causes of action. Moreover, in tying cases the defense then seemed to jibe well with antitrust law, for antitrust courts at that time viewed tying as invariably illegal *per se*, without analyzing whether or not the patent really provided market power in any "tying" product. Like the antitrust courts of the time, courts adjudicating patent-infringement cases applied the nascent misuse doctrine through simple categorization of behavior, without analyzing market definition, market power, or substantial economic effect.

Eventually the patent bar rebelled. It saw the broad, unprincipled approach to tying—declaring it misuse with little or no substantive analysis—as eroding the value of patents. In particular, the patent bar viewed refusal to allow contractual limitations on how patented products might be used as undermining the exclusive "use" right that patent law granted explicitly. In addition, the misuse doctrine had been applied inconsistently, and the patent bar saw it as imposing substantial uncertainty on patent-related businesses.

In the Patent Act of 1952, the patent bar proposed, and Congress adopted, provisions to preserve the broad "use" right of patentees. Those provisions were codified in Section 271(d)(1)–(3) of the patent act. The Supreme Court upheld them in its seminal decision in *Dawson Chemical Co. v. Rohm & Haas Co.*, 448 U.S. 176, 100 S. Ct. 2601, 65 L. Ed. 2d 696 (1980), which allowed a process patentee to control the use of an unpatented chemical by licensing the process of using that chemical as an herbicide.

Those 1952 provisions, however, did not specifically address the issue of tying, so the patent bar had to return to Congress again. In the Patent Misuse Amendments of 1988, Congress added Section 271(d)(4) and (5) which precluded misuse defenses based on a patentee's mere refusal to license, or based on tying absent a showing of market power in the tying product.

With these amendments, Congress coordinated the misuse defense with antitrust law and, at the same time, substantially cut back the growth of misuse in the field of patents. Yet neither the 1952 provisions nor the 1988 patent misuse amendments applied to fields of intellectual property other than patents. Less than two years after the patent misuse amendments, the federal courts of appeals began to extend the doctrine of misuse to copyright.

---

# Lasercomb America, Inc. v. Reynolds
### 911 F.2d 970 (4th Cir. 1990)

SPROUSE, Circuit Judge.

Appellants Larry Holliday and Job Reynolds appeal from a district court judgment holding them liable to appellee Lasercomb America, Inc., for copyright infringement and for fraud, based on appellants' unauthorized copying and marketing of appellee's software. We affirm in part, reverse in part, and remand for recomputation of damages.

I

### Facts and Proceedings Below

Appellants and defendants below are Larry Holliday, president and sole shareholder of Holiday Steel Rule Die Corporation (Holiday Steel), and Job Reynolds, a computer programmer for that company. Appellee is Lasercomb America, Inc. (Lasercomb), the plaintiff below. Holiday Steel and Lasercomb were competitors in the manufacture of steel rule dies that are used to cut and score paper and cardboard for folding into boxes and cartons. Lasercomb developed a software program, Interact, which is the object of the dispute between the parties. Using this program, a designer creates a template of a cardboard cutout on a computer screen and the software directs the mechanized creation of the conforming steel rule die.

In 1983, before Lasercomb was ready to market its Interact program generally, it licensed four prerelease copies to Holiday Steel which paid $ 35,000 for the first copy, $ 17,500 each for the next two copies, and $ 2,000 for the fourth copy. Lasercomb informed Holiday Steel that it would charge $ 2,000 for each additional copy Holiday Steel cared to purchase. Apparently ambitious to create for itself an even better deal, Holiday Steel circumvented the protective devices Lasercomb had provided with the software and made three unauthorized copies of Interact which it used on its computer systems. Perhaps buoyed by its success in copying, Holiday Steel then created a software program called "PDS-1000," which was almost entirely a direct copy of Interact, and marketed it as its own CAD/CAM die-making software. These infringing activities were accomplished by Job Reynolds at the direction of Larry Holliday.

There is no question that defendants engaged in unauthorized copying, and the purposefulness of their unlawful action is manifest from their deceptive practices. For example, Lasercomb had asked Holiday Steel to use devices called "chronoguards" to prevent unauthorized access to Interact. Although defendants had deduced how to circumvent the chronoguards and had removed them from their computers, they represented to Lasercomb that the chronoguards were in use. Another example of subterfuge is Reynolds' attempt to modify the PDS-1000 program output so it would present a different appearance than the output from Interact.

When Lasercomb discovered Holiday Steel's activities, it registered its copyright in Interact and filed this action against Holiday Steel, Holliday, and Reynolds on March 7, 1986. Lasercomb claimed copyright infringement, breach of contract, misappropriation of trade secret, false designation of origin, unfair competition, and fraud. Defendants filed a number of counterclaims. On March 24, 1986, the district court entered a preliminary injunction, enjoining defendants from marketing the PDS-1000 software.

\* \* \*

[U]ltimately, all of the counterclaims were dismissed; Lasercomb's claims of misappropriation of trade secret, false designation of origin, and unfair competition were dismissed as preempted by the Copyright Act; the court found the defendants liable to Lasercomb for copyright infringement, rejecting their affirmative defenses of misuse of copyright and lack of statutory copyright notice; and the court held for Lasercomb on its claims of breach of contract and fraud.

The district court awarded Lasercomb $ 105,000 in actual damages for copyright infringement and for fraud—with Holiday Steel, Holliday, and Reynolds jointly and severally liable—plus $ 10,000 against Holliday and $ 5,000 against Reynolds as punitive damages on the fraud claim. All defendants were permanently enjoined from publishing and marketing the PDS-1000 software.

Holliday and Reynolds raise several issues on appeal. They do not dispute that they copied Interact, but they contend that Lasercomb is barred from recovery for infringement by its concomitant culpability. They assert that, assuming Lasercomb had a perfected copyright, it impermissibly abused it. This assertion of the "misuse of copyright" defense is based on language in Lasercomb's standard licensing agreement, restricting licensees from creating any of their own CAD/CAM die-making software.

\* \* \*

## II

### Misuse of Copyright Defense

A successful defense of misuse of copyright bars a culpable plaintiff from prevailing on an action for infringement of the misused copyright. Here, appellants claim Lasercomb has misused its copyright by including in its standard licensing agreement clauses which prevent the licensee from participating in any manner in the creation of computer-assisted die-making software. The offending paragraphs read:

> D. Licensee agrees during the term of this Agreement that it will not permit or suffer its directors, officers and employees, directly or indirectly, to write, develop, produce or sell computer assisted die making software.

> E. Licensee agrees during the term of this Agreement and for one (1) year after the termination of this Agreement, that it will not write, develop, produce or sell or assist others in the writing, developing, producing or selling computer assisted die making software, directly or indirectly without Lasercomb's prior written consent. Any such activity undertaken without Lasercomb's written consent shall nullify any warranties or agreements of Lasercomb set forth herein.

The "term of this Agreement" referred to in these clauses is ninety-nine years. Defendants were not themselves bound by the standard licensing agreement. Lasercomb had sent the agreement to Holiday Steel with a request that it be signed and returned. Larry Holliday, however, decided not to sign the document, and Lasercomb apparently overlooked the fact that the document had not been returned. Although defendants were not party to the restrictions of which they complain, they proved at trial that at least one Interact licensee had entered into the standard agreement, including the anticompetitive language.

The district court rejected the copyright misuse defense for three reasons. First, it noted that defendants had not explicitly agreed to the contract clauses alleged to constitute copyright misuse. Second, it found "such a clause is reasonable in light of the delicate and sensitive area of computer software." And, third, it questioned whether such a defense exists. We consider the district court's reasoning in reverse order.

### A. Does a "Misuse of Copyright" Defense Exist?

We agree with the district court that much uncertainty engulfs the "misuse of copyright" defense. We are persuaded, however, that a misuse of copyright defense is inherent in the law of copyright just as a misuse of patent defense is inherent in patent law.

The misuse of a patent is a potential defense to suit for its infringement, and both the existence and parameters of that body of law are well established. *E.g., United States Gypsum Co. v. National Gypsum Co.*, 352 U.S. 457, 465, 1 L. Ed. 2d 465, 77 S. Ct. 490 (1957).... Although there is little case law on the subject, courts from time to time have intimated that the similarity of rationales underlying the law of patents and the law of copyrights argues for a defense to an infringement of copyright based on misuse of the copyright. *E.g., United States v. Loew's, Inc.*, 371 U.S. 38, 44–51, 9 L. Ed. 2d 11, 83 S. Ct. 97 (1962); *United States v. Paramount Pictures, Inc.*, 334 U.S. 131, 157–59, 92 L. Ed. 1260, 68 S. Ct. 915 (1948); *Mitchell Bros. Film Group v. Cinema Adult Theater*, 604 F.2d 852, 865 & n.27 (5th Cir. 1979), *cert. denied*, 445 U.S. 917, 63 L. Ed. 2d 601, 100 S. Ct. 1277 (1980). The origins of patent and copyright law in England, the treatment of these two aspects of intellectual property by the framers of our Constitution, and the later statutory and judicial development of patent and copyright law in this country persuade us that parallel public policies underlie the protection of both types of intellectual property rights. We think these parallel policies call for application of the misuse defense to copyright as well as patent law.

### 1. Overview

Because of the paucity of precedent in the copyright misuse area, some historical perspective of the elements underlying intellectual property law is helpful to our inquiry....

During the sixteenth century, it became common for the English Crown to grant "letters patent," which gave individuals exclusive rights to produce, import and/or sell given items within the kingdom.... These monopolies were granted for such commonplace items as salt, vinegar, and calfskins, to name but a few. The practice of granting monopolies led to widespread abuses, such as shortages and inflated prices for items that would otherwise be easily and cheaply available. Consequently, Parliament passed the Statute of Monopolies (1623–24), prohibiting the creation of such monopolies by the Crown. An exception was made, however, to permit a patent to be granted for a period of fourteen years to the creator of a new invention. 21 Jac., ch. 3, §6.

The rationale for allowing patents for new inventions was and is to encourage their creation for the benefit of society.... The monopolies granted by the Crown had been odious because they restrained trade in articles that had previously been a part of the public domain. An invention, however, does not withdraw anything from public traffic; rather, it introduces something new. To encourage and reward inventors for increasing the inventory of useful objects, the government grants them, for a limited time, the right to exclude others from making and selling their inventions.... *United States v. Dubilier Condenser Corp.*, 289 U.S. 178, 186, 77 L. Ed. 1114, 53 S. Ct. 554 (1933).

The development of copyright law in England likewise grew out of a differentiation by Parliament between a monopoly that restricts publication of works and a limited copyright that encourages the efforts of authors. In sixteenth-century England, the Crown granted to the Stationers' Company the exclusive right to publish and print all published works (apparently to enable censorship of Protestant materials). In the early 1700s, the Stationer's Company petitioned Parliament to recognize that these rights inured to it in perpetuity. Instead, Parliament passed the Statute of Anne (1709–10), the first known copyright legislation. A. LATMAN, THE COPYRIGHT LAW: HOWELL'S COPYRIGHT LAW REVISED AND THE 1976 ACT 2–3 (5th ed. 1979) [hereinafter HOWELL'S COPYRIGHT LAW].... That statute gave authors the sole right of publication for up to twenty-eight years. Thus, the English statutory treatment of copyright was similar to that of patent in that it granted the creator a monopoly for a limited time only.

It is significant, we think, that the framers of our Constitution continued the English development of intellectual property law and considered in tandem those property rights protectable by copyrights and those protectable by patents. In giving Congress the power to create copyright and patent laws, the framers combined the two concepts in one clause, stating a unitary purpose—to promote progress. Article I, section 8, clause 8 of the United States Constitution provides:

> [The Congress shall have power] To promote the Progress of Science and use-ful Arts, by securing for limited Times to Authors and Inventors the exclusive Right to their respective Writings and Discoveries.

This clause was adopted without debate, and material explaining the intention of the framers is limited. However, a comment in *The Federalist* papers indicates the public policy behind the grant of copyright and patent powers is essentially the same:

> The utility of this power will scarcely be questioned. The copyright of authors has been solemnly adjudged, in Great Britain, to be a right of common law. The right to useful inventions seems with equal reason to belong to the inventors. The public good fully coincides in both cases with the claims of individuals.

*The Federalist*, No. 43 at 279 (J. Madison) (Mod. Lib. ed. 1941). Supreme Court comment has likewise equated the public policies of copyright and patent. For example, in *Mazer v. Stein*, 347 U.S. 201, 219, 98 L. Ed. 630, 74 S. Ct. 460 (1953), the Supreme Court stated:

> The economic philosophy behind the clause empowering Congress to grant *patents and copyrights* is the conviction that encouragement of individual effort by personal gain is the best way to advance public welfare through the talents of au-thors and inventors in "Science and useful Arts." Sacrificial days devoted to such creative activities deserve rewards commensurate with the services rendered.

(Emphasis added.) *See also Loew's*, 371 U.S. at 44–51; *Paramount Pictures*, 334 U.S. at 154–59. The philosophy behind copyright, parallel to that discussed above for patent, is that the public benefits from the efforts of authors to introduce new ideas and knowl-edge into the public domain. To encourage such efforts, society grants authors exclusive rights in their works for a limited time.

## 2. The Misuse of Patent Defense

Although a patent misuse defense was recognized by the courts as early as 1917, most commentators point to *Morton Salt Co. v. G. S. Suppiger*, 314 U.S. 488, 86 L. Ed. 363, 62 S. Ct. 402 (1942), as the foundational patent misuse case. In that case, the plaintiff Morton Salt brought suit on the basis that the defendant had infringed Morton's patent in a salt-depositing machine. The salt tablets were not themselves a patented item, but Morton's patent license required that licensees use only salt tablets produced by Morton. Morton was thereby using its patent to restrain competition in the sale of an item which was not within the scope of the patent's privilege. The Supreme Court held that, as a court of equity, it would not aid Morton in protecting its patent when Morton was using that patent in a manner contrary to public policy. The Court stated:

> The grant to the inventor of the special privilege of a patent monopoly carries out a public policy adopted by the Constitution and laws of the United States, "to promote the Progress of Science and useful Arts, by securing for limited

Times to...Inventors the exclusive Right..." to their "new and useful" inventions. United States Constitution, Art. I, §8, cl. 8, 35 U.S.C. §31. But the public policy which includes inventions within the granted monopoly excludes from it all that is not embraced in the invention. It equally forbids the use of the patent to secure an exclusive right or limited monopoly not granted by the Patent Office and which it is contrary to public policy to grant.

*Id.* at 492. Thus, the Supreme Court endorsed "misuse of patent" as an equitable defense to a suit for infringement of that patent.

Since *Morton Salt*, the courts have recognized patent misuse as a valid defense and have applied it in a number of cases in which patent owners have attempted to use their patents for price fixing, tie-ins, territorial restrictions, and so forth.... The patent misuse defense also has been acknowledged by Congress in the 1988 Patent Misuse Reform Act, Pub. L. No. 100-703, 102 Stat. 4676 (1988) (codified at 35 U.S.C. §271(d)(4) & (5)), which limited but did not eliminate the defense.

### 3. The "Misuse of Copyright" Defense

Although the patent misuse defense has been generally recognized since *Morton Salt*, it has been much less certain whether an analogous copyright misuse defense exists. This uncertainty persists because no United States Supreme Court decision has firmly established a copyright misuse defense in a manner analogous to the establishment of the patent misuse defense by *Morton Salt*. The few courts considering the issue have split on whether the defense should be recognized, and we have discovered only one case which has actually applied copyright misuse to bar an action for infringement. *M. Witmark & Sons v. Jensen*, 80 F. Supp. 843 (D. Minn. 1948), *appeal dismissed*, 177 F.2d 515 (8th Cir. 1949).

We are of the view, however, that since copyright and patent law serve parallel public interests, a "misuse" defense should apply to infringement actions brought to vindicate either right. As discussed above, the similarity of the policies underlying patent and copyright is great and historically has been consistently recognized. Both patent law and copyright law seek to increase the store of human knowledge and arts by rewarding inventors and authors with the exclusive rights to their works for a limited time. At the same time, the granted monopoly power does not extend to property not covered by the patent or copyright. *Morton Salt*, 314 U.S. at 492; *Paramount Pictures*, 334 U.S. at 156–58; *cf. Baker v. Selden*, 101 U.S. 99, 101–4, 25 L. Ed. 841 (1880).

Thus, we are persuaded that the rationale of *Morton Salt* in establishing the misuse defense applies to copyrights. In the passage from *Morton Salt* quoted above, the phraseology adapts easily to a copyright context:

The grant to the [author] of the special privilege of a [copyright] carries out a public policy adopted by the Constitution and laws of the United States, 'to promote the Progress of Science and useful Arts, by securing for limited Times to [Authors]...the exclusive Right...' to their ['original' works]. United States Constitution, Art. I, §8, cl. 8, [ 17 U.S.C.A. §102]. But the public policy which includes [original works] within the granted monopoly excludes from it all that is not embraced in the [original expression]. It equally forbids the use of the [copyright] to secure an exclusive right or limited monopoly not granted by the [Copyright] Office and which it is contrary to public policy to grant.

*Cf. Morton Salt*, 314 U.S. at 492. Having determined that "misuse of copyright" is a valid defense, analogous to the misuse of patent defense, our next task is to determine whether the defense should have been applied by the district court to bar Lasercomb's infringement action against the defendants in this case.

### B. The District Court's Finding that the Anticompetitive Clauses Are Reasonable

In declining to recognize a misuse of copyright defense, the district court found "reasonable" Lasercomb's attempt to protect its software copyright by using anticompetitive clauses in their licensing agreement. In briefly expressing its reasoning, the court referred to the "delicate and sensitive" nature of software. It also observed that Lasercomb's president had testified that the noncompete language was negotiable.

If, as it appears, the district court analogized from the "rule of reason" concept of antitrust law, we think its reliance on that principle was misplaced. Such reliance is, however, understandable. Both the presentation by appellants and the literature tend to intermingle antitrust and misuse defenses.... A patent or copyright is often regarded as a limited monopoly—an exception to the general public policy against restraints of trade. Since antitrust law is the statutory embodiment of that public policy, there is an understandable association of antitrust law with the misuse defense. Certainly, an entity which uses its patent as the means of violating antitrust law is subject to a misuse of patent defense. However, *Morton Salt* held that it is not necessary to prove an antitrust violation in order to successfully assert patent misuse:

> It is unnecessary to decide whether respondent has violated the Clayton Act, for we conclude that in any event the maintenance of the present suit to restrain petitioner's manufacture or sale of the alleged infringing machines is contrary to public policy and that the district court rightly dismissed the complaint for want of equity.

314 U.S. at 494. *See also Hensley Equip. Co. v. Esco Corp.*, 383 F.2d 252, 261 & n. 19, *amended on reh'g*, 386 F.2d 442 (5th Cir. 1967)....

So while it is true that the attempted use of a copyright to violate antitrust law probably would give rise to a misuse of copyright defense, the converse is not necessarily true—a misuse need not be a violation of antitrust law in order to comprise an equitable defense to an infringement action. The question is not whether the copyright is being used in a manner violative of antitrust law (such as whether the licensing agreement is "reasonable"), but whether the copyright is being used in a manner violative of the public policy embodied in the grant of a copyright.

Lasercomb undoubtedly has the right to protect against copying of the Interact code. Its standard licensing agreement, however, goes much further and essentially attempts to suppress any attempt by the licensee to independently implement the idea which Interact expresses. The agreement forbids the licensee to develop or assist in developing *any* kind of computer-assisted die-making software. If the licensee is a business, it is to prevent all its directors, officers and employees from assisting in any manner to develop computer-assisted die-making software. Although one or another licensee might succeed in negotiating out the noncompete provisions, this does not negate the fact that Lasercomb is attempting to use its copyright in a manner adverse to the public policy embodied in copyright law, and that it has succeeded in doing so with at least one licensee....

The language employed in the Lasercomb agreement is extremely broad. Each time Lasercomb sells its Interact program to a company and obtains that company's agreement to the noncompete language, the company is required to forego utilization of the

creative abilities of all its officers, directors and employees in the area of CAD/CAM die-making software. Of yet greater concern, these creative abilities are withdrawn from the public. The period for which this anticompetitive restraint exists is ninety-nine years, which could be longer than the life of the copyright itself.

We previously have considered the effect of anticompetitive language in a licensing agreement in the context of patent misuse. *Compton v. Metal Products, Inc.*, 453 F.2d 38 (4th Cir. 1971), *cert. denied*, 406 U.S. 968, 32 L. Ed. 2d 667, 92 S. Ct. 2414 (1972). Compton had invented and patented coal auguring equipment. He granted an exclusive license in the patents to Joy Manufacturing, and the license agreement included a provision that Compton would not "engage in any business or activity relating to the manufacture or sale of equipment of the type licensed hereunder" for as long as he was due royalties under the patents. Suit for infringement of the Compton patents was brought against Metal Products, and the district court granted injunctive relief and damages. On appeal we held that relief for the infringement was barred by the misuse defense, stating:

> The need of Joy to protect its investment does not outweigh the public's right under our system to expect competition and the benefits which flow therefrom, and the total withdrawal of Compton from the mining machine business... everywhere in the world for a period of 20 years unreasonably lessens the competition which the public has a right to expect, and constitutes misuse of the patents.

*Id.* at 45. *Cf. Berlenbach, supra* (applying misuse doctrine where license to sell patented ski bindings prohibited licensee from manufacturing or selling any competing ski binding).

We think the anticompetitive language in Lasercomb's licensing agreement is at least as egregious as that which led us to bar the infringement action in *Compton*, and therefore amounts to misuse of its copyright. Again, the analysis necessary to a finding of misuse is similar to but separate from the analysis necessary to a finding of antitrust violation. The misuse arises from Lasercomb's attempt to use its copyright in a particular expression, the Interact software, to control competition in an area outside the copyright, *i.e.*, the idea of computer-assisted die manufacture, regardless of whether such conduct amounts to an antitrust violation.

### C. The Effect of Appellants Not Being Party to the Anticompetitive Contract

In its rejection of the copyright misuse defense, the district court emphasized that Holiday Steel was not explicitly party to a licensing agreement containing the offending language. However, again analogizing to patent misuse, the defense of copyright misuse is available even if the defendants themselves have not been injured by the misuse. In *Morton Salt*, the defendant was not a party to the license requirement that only Morton-produced salt tablets be used with Morton's salt-depositing machine. Nevertheless, suit against defendant for infringement of Morton's patent was barred on public policy grounds. Similarly, in *Compton*, even though the defendant Metal Products was not a party to the license agreement that restrained competition by Compton, suit against Metal Products was barred because of the public interest in free competition. *See also Hensley Equip. Co.*, 383 F.2d at 261; *cf. Berlenbach*, 329 F.2d at 784–85.

Therefore, the fact that appellants here were not parties to one of Lasercomb's standard license agreements is inapposite to their copyright misuse defense. The question is whether Lasercomb is using its copyright in a manner contrary to public policy, which question we have answered in the affirmative.

In sum, we find that misuse of copyright is a valid defense, that Lasercomb's anticompetitive clauses in its standard licensing agreement constitute misuse of copyright, and that the defense is available to appellants even though they were not parties to the standard licensing agreement. Holding that Lasercomb should have been barred by the defense of copyright misuse from suing for infringement of its copyright in the Interact program, we reverse the injunction and the award of damages for copyright infringement.

Because of this holding, we do not reach the other defenses to copyright infringement advanced by appellants.

Although we find misuse of copyright, we reject the contention of appellants—that they should recover attorney fees from Lasercomb under 17 U.S.C. § 505 because Lasercomb brought this action in bad faith. Given the conduct of defendants and the obscurity of their defenses, we find such a position completely untenable.

## III

### Finding of Fraud

The complaint alleged that defendants committed fraud "at the time they sought to purchase a license to use the software at the Holiday plant" by representing to Lasercomb that they would preserve Lasercomb's copyright and proprietary rights in Interact. The district court found Lasercomb had established fraud by showing that defendants made various false representations on which Lasercomb reasonably relied in continuing its relationship with Holiday Steel, thereby giving defendants the opportunity to make the unlawful copies.... [W]e affirm the district court's finding of fraud.

\* \* \*

## IV

### Calculation of Damages

\* \* \*

[*The court remanded for recalculation of damages on the fraud count, while not disturbing the award of punitive damages, which had not been appealed.*]

*Affirmed in part, reversed in part, and remanded*

# Notes and Questions on Misuse

1. To understand the breadth of the holding in *Lasercomb*, it is important to focus on the facts of the case. What was the reason the court held the plaintiff's copyright unenforceable? It had something to do with a license agreement, didn't it? Were the defendants themselves parties to this license agreement? If not, who was?

2. Did the court invalidate the plaintiff's copyright? Except for the misuse defense, wasn't the copyright infringement claim in the case straightforward and valid? Try to articulate, as precisely as possible, why the court refused to uphold a claim for apparently willful copyright infringement. Whom did the alleged misuse threaten or hurt? The de-

fendant? Third parties? The public? What was the precise nature of the harm that justi-fied refusing to enforce a valid copyright?

3. Is the court concerned with the possible effect of the plaintiff's standard form of li-cense agreement on competition? If so, what particular clause of the license agreement raised the concern? Did the court analyze its effect on competition? Did the court scru-tinize, in the words of the *GTE Sylvania* Court, "substantial economic effect," as an-titrust law requires, or did it resort to "barren formalism"?

4. One hundred years is a long time, but not longer than the life of a copyright. When *Lasercomb* was decided, copyright in unpublished corporate "works made for hire" lasted 100 years from their creation, a term now extended to 120 years. *See* 17 U.S.C. § 302(c). Can you think of any legitimate business reason why the plaintiff licensor might have wanted to preclude licensees from developing competing software during the life of the copyright? If a licensee did develop such competing software during the term of the copyright, what might the licensor suspect? How would those suspicions be resolved?

5. Here are the statutory provisions by which Congress, in the 1952 patent act and the Patent Misuse Amendments of 1988, cut back the misuse defense in patent law:

> No patent owner otherwise entitled to relief for infringement or contributory infringement of a patent shall be denied relief or deemed guilty of misuse or il-legal extension of the patent right by reason of his having done one or more of the following: (1) derived revenue from acts which if performed by another without his consent would constitute contributory infringement of the patent; (2) licensed or authorized another to perform acts which if performed without his consent would constitute contributory infringement of the patent; (3) sought to enforce his patent rights against infringement or contributory in-fringement; (4) refused to license or use any rights to the patent; or (5) condi-tioned the license of any rights to the patent or the sale of the patented product on the acquisition of a license to rights in another patent or purchase of a sep-arate product, unless, in view of the circumstances, the patent owner has mar-ket power in the relevant market for the patent or patented product on which the license or sale is conditioned.

35 U.S.C. § 271(d). If Congress had used the words "patent or copyright" wherever the word "patent" appears in this statute, would it have made a difference in the outcome of the *Lasercomb* case? If not, could a case much like *Lasercomb* also occur in the patent field? What practical risks might such a possibility present to a patentee and her license attorneys?

6. *Lasercomb* is hardly one of a kind. Besides the Fourth Circuit, two other federal cir-cuit courts of appeals—the Fifth Circuit and the Ninth Circuit—have upheld a copy-right misuse defense. *See Alcatel USA, Inc. v. DGI Tech., Inc.*, 166 F.3d 772, 777, 783, 793–94 (5th Cir. 1999) (reversing injunctive relief for copyright infringement based on copyright misuse, while dismissing copyright infringement defendant's antitrust claim on merits); *DSC Communications Corp. v. DGI Tech., Inc.*, 81 F.3d 597, 601 (5th Cir. 1996) (accepting defense for purposes of framing preliminary injunction in same case); *Practice Mgmt. Info. Corp. v. Am. Med. Assoc.*, 121 F.3d 516, 521 (9th Cir. 1997); *see also, Supermarket of Homes, Inc. v. San Fernando Valley Bd. of Realtors*, 786 F.2d 1400, 1408 (9th Cir. 1986). Another two circuits—the Seventh and Eleventh—have recognized the defense in *dictum*. *See Assessment Tech., of WI, LLC v. WIREdata, Inc.*, 350 F.3d 640, 647 (7th Cir. 2003); *F.E.L. Pub'ns, Ltd. v. Catholic Bishop of Chicago*, 214 U.S.P.Q. (BNA)

409, 413 n.9 (7th Cir. 1982); *Bellsouth Adver. & Publ'g Corp. v. Donnelley Info. Publ'g, Inc.*, 933 F.2d 952, 961 (11th Cir. 1991), *rev'd on other grounds* 999 F.2d 1436, 1439 n.5 (11th Cir. 1993) (en banc), *cert. denied* 510 U.S. 1101 (1994) ("Although the patent misuse defense closely fits the copyright law situation and may someday be extended to discipline those who abuse their copyrights, we decline to extend the application in the context before us because there is no antitrust violation."). Finally, the Eighth Circuit has assumed its existence *arguendo*. *See United Tel. Co. of Missouri v. Johnson Publ'g Co.*, 855 F.2d 604, 612 (8th Cir. 1988) ("On the assumption that judicial authority teaches that the patent misuse doctrine may be applied or asserted as a defense to copyright infringement, the stipulated facts in this case do not support" the defense.).

7. Perhaps the most interesting "take" on copyright misuse is that of the Seventh Circuit, which includes two of the foremost antitrust and economic experts on the federal bench, Judges Posner and Easterbrook. In 1982, Judge Posner, writing for the court, disparaged the notion of copyright misuse as potentially conflicting with antitrust law. "Our law is not rich in alternative concepts of monopolistic abuse," he wrote, "and it is rather late in the day to try to develop one without in the process subjecting the rights of patent holders to debilitating uncertainty." *USM Corp. v. SPS Tech., Inc.*, 694 F.3d 505, 512 (7th Cir. 1982), *cert. denied* 462 U.S. 1107 (1983) (citation omitted). A few years later, he expressed additional skepticism regarding copyright misuse, noting that copyright, which does not control facts or ideas and allows independent development of the same subject matter, contains intrinsic safeguards against economic monopolies. *See Saturday Evening Post Co. v. Rumbleseat Press, Inc.*, 816 F.2d 1191, 1198–99 (7th Cir. 1987). He therefore concluded that "[i]f any monopolies harmful to the public have even been built on invalid copyrights, we have not heard of them." *Id.*, 816 F.2d at 1199.

Yet in 2004, Judge Posner came very close to recognizing the copyright misuse defense, brandishing it as a club to bludgeon copyright holders who might try to overstep the legitimate bounds of their intellectual property rights. *See Assessment Tech. of WI, LLC v. WIREdata, Inc.*, 350 F.3d 640, 646–47 (7th Cir. 2003). The occasion for this near-conversion was a case in which a copyright holder had attempted, by threats and bluster, to extend the protection of its copyright to raw data, including data that it itself had not even developed. *See id.* at 642–43. Although recognizing that his earlier opinions "had intimated skepticism" about copyright misuse, Judge Posner opined as follows:

> Cases such as *Lasercomb*…cut misuse free from antitrust, pointing out that the cognate doctrine of patent misuse is not so limited, though a difference is that patents tend to confer greater market power on their owners than copyrights do, since patents protect ideas and copyrights, as we have noted, do not. The argument for applying copyright misuse beyond the bounds of antitrust, besides the fact that confined to antitrust the doctrine would be redundant, is that for a copyright owner to use an infringement suit to obtain property protection, here in data, that copyright law clearly does not confer, hoping to force a settlement or even achieve an outright victory over an opponent that may lack the resources or the legal sophistication to resist effectively, is an abuse of process.

*Id.* at 646–47 (7th Cir. 2003) (citations omitted).

8. This last passage of Judge Posner's deserves careful scrutiny. What does Judge Posner mean by saying "confined to antitrust the [misuse] doctrine would be redundant"? The antitrust laws provide causes of action to remedy harm caused by anticompetitive con-

duct. Misuse doctrine provides a defense to claims for infringement of intellectual property. Is that redundant?

Moreover, is misuse doctrine confined to antitrust law? That is, does misuse doctrine provide a defense to infringement claims if and only if an antitrust counterclaim is viable? Was that the case in *Lasercomb*? Or is misuse doctrine based upon public policy and notions of equity that are completely independent of antitrust? Is that what Judge Posner means when he says that *Lasercomb* cut misuse free from antitrust?

Finally, does the law really need another way to fight abuse of process? The old tort still exists, although the more modern term for it is "wrongful civil proceedings." *See* RESTATEMENT (SECOND) OF TORTS § 674 (1977). Should the law provide, as an adjunct to state tort remedies, escape from liability for clear infringement, as in *Lasercomb*?

9. Antitrust law balances on a knife edge. Condemn too little, and the law will allow private parties to suppress competition and distort the economy to their benefit. Condemn too much, and the law may suppress the motive forces of competition itself. This is why the law weighs intent little in deciding whether antitrust liability exists: too much emphasis on intent may ultimately crush competitive zeal itself.

Perhaps the best statement of this principle from Judge Easterbrook in *A.A. Poultry Farms, Inc. v. Rose Acre Farms, Inc.*, 881 F.2d 1396, 1402 (7th Cir. 1989), *cert. denied*, 494 U.S. 1019 (1990):

> Intent does not help to separate competition from attempted monopolization and invites juries to penalize hard competition. It also complicates litigation. Lawyers rummage through business records seeking to discover tidbits that will sound impressive (or aggressive) when read to a jury. Traipsing through the warehouses of business in search of misleading evidence both increases the costs of litigation and reduces the accuracy of decisions. Stripping intent away brings the real economic questions to the fore at the same time as it streamlines antitrust litigation.

If antitrust law is balanced on a knife-edge, then what would be the effect of a misuse defense based ostensibly on threats to competition, but lacking all the checks and balances of antitrust analysis? Won't it tip the balance?

As you ponder this point, consider the practical effects of a robust copyright misuse defense "cut loose" (in Judge Posner's words) from antitrust law. Except for gross violations like *per se* illegal price fixing or horizontal division of customers or markets, licensors who have small shares of all relevant product and service markets don't have to worry too much about licensing restrictions. Indeed, the 1995 Licensing Guidelines' "safety zone" provides substantial comfort unless market shares exceed 20%. That is a nice rule of thumb that helps lend some certainty to the very uncertain and complex world of antitrust.

Yet what good would that rule of thumb be if a court could render valid copyrights unenforceable on the basis of broad notions of public policy and equity? Indeed, what good would the 1995 Licensing Guidelines be? Wouldn't a misuse doctrine allowing such broad defenses cause licensing attorneys to worry again, regardless of how small their clients' market shares might be?

10. In the general case, antitrust analysis is complex and time consuming. Yet the human (and judicial!) impulse to do good without having to think much about how is strong and universal. There is even talk of extending the doctrine of misuse to cover abuse of the Digital Millennium Copyright Act.

Recall from Chapter 6, *supra*, that § 1201 of the Copyright Act (17 U.S.C. § 1201), as added by the Digital Millennium Copyright Act, prohibits circumvention of technological measures to protect copyrighted works and trafficking in the means of circumvention. The original intent of § 1201 was to reinforce technological measures that copyright owners use to protect their creative works from piracy. Yet clever plaintiffs have sought to use it to control the unauthorized refilling of toner cartridges and to prevent rival manufacturers from selling compatible transmitters for remote garage-door openers. *See Lexmark Int'l, Inc. v. Static Control Components, Inc.*, 253 F. Supp.2d 943, 956–58 (E.D. Ky. 2003) (using Section 1201 to enforce contractual restraint against re-using certain toner cartridges); *Chamberlain Group, Inc. v. Skylink Tech., Inc.*, 68 U.S.P.Q.2d (BNA) 1009 (N.D. Ill. 2003) (*Skylink I*) (denying summary judgment to plaintiff, who made garage-door openers, for various reasons). *But see Chamberlain Group, Inc. v. Skylink Tech., Inc.*, 292 F. Supp.2d 1040 (N.D. Ill. 2003) (*Skylink II*) (granting *defendant* summary judgment on § 1201(a)(2) claim on ground its customers had implied authorization to circumvent, if any circumvention had occurred).

Cases like these are part of the so-called "Aftermarket Wars," in which manufacturers of specialized products attempt to control the aftermarkets for related compatible components, spare parts, and service. The essence of all these cases is the legal right to control related markets; it therefore quintessentially involves antitrust.

The Aftermarket Wars are relatively new antitrust conflicts, now being fought against the background of over a century of antitrust jurisprudence. Should the courts cut the Gordian knot of all that antitrust complexity, at least in § 1201 cases, by introducing the notion of Millennium Act abuse? Or would it be preferable for Congress to amend § 1201 to restrict it to its original intent — protecting creative works from piracy — and exclude the Aftermarket Wars from the literal scope of § 1201? *See* Jay Dratler, Jr., Cyberlaw: Intellectual Property Law in the Digital Millennium § 2.05[1] (Law Journal Press 2002 & Supps.)

---

# Notes on Antitrust and Misuse Generally

1. For in-depth coverage of antitrust issues as they apply to in the licensing of intellectual property, see Intellectual Property Antitrust 1995 (D. Bender, ed. 1995); J. Dratler, Licensing of Intellectual Property §§ 5, 6 (2003); R. Milgrim, Milgrim on Licensing, § 2 (1997); Sheila J. McCartney, 7 (No. 6) J. Proprietary Rts. 10 (1995).

2. What purpose(s) do the antitrust laws serve? If you could reduce their goal to a single word, what would that word be? Was Justice Marshall's *dictum* comparing the importance of the antitrust laws to that of the Magna Carta hyperbole or a rhetorical flourish, or was he on to something? Can the antitrust laws or their underlying purposes help explain the difference between the economies of the United States and the former Soviet Union?

3. Most antitrust issues in licensing arise under Sherman Act § 1 (or equivalent prohibitions of §§ 2 and 3 of the Clayton Act). The reason is simple: § 1 governs contracts, combinations, and conspiracies in restraint of trade, i.e., collective or concerted action

by more than one actor. A license by definition involves more than a single party. Therefore, contractual restraints in licensing must be evaluated to determine whether they are in restraint of trade, i.e., whether they violate the rule of reason or fall into one of the few remaining categories of activity that is illegal *per se*. Today those categories include minimum price fixing (horizontal or vertical), horizontal maximum price fixing, horizontal division of markets (for example, by geographic territory, customers, or subject matter), horizontal restriction of output, and group boycotts against rivals by groups with market power or access to an essential facility. *See* DRATLER, *supra*, § 5.02[2][a][iii].

4. Sherman Act § 2, however, can come into play when one or more of the parties to the licensing arrangement dominate or nearly dominate a relevant market. If actual dominance exists, there may be a claim under Sherman Act § 2 for "monopolization." If dominance is not actual, but merely threatened, there may be a claim for attempting to monopolize.

A claim for monopolization has three elements: (1) the definition of a relevant market; (2) a showing of monopoly power in that market (i.e., the power to raise prices or exclude competition), and (3) conduct that tends to extend, maintain, or entrench the monopoly power in a way that smothers competition, rather than fostering or constituting competition. *See id.*, § 5.02[2][b][ii].

A claim for attempting to monopolize also has three elements: (1) market definition; (2) a showing of near dominance in the relevant market; and (3) conduct that demonstrates a dangerous probability of success in monopolizing the defined market. *See id.*, § 5.02[2][b][iii].

Both types of claims require proof of market definition, in terms of both geography and a relevant product or service, using economic and practical indicia. *See id.*, § 5.02[2][b][i]. Market definition is one of the most difficult hurdles for antitrust plaintiffs to clear, and many antitrust plaintiffs stumble over it and never recover.

5. Even where market domination seems obvious, it may be difficult to prove. Once market dominance (i.e., monopoly power) is proven, however, a monopolist's conduct that is not otherwise unlawful may support a cause of action under Sherman Act § 2. The conduct need not be unlawful, let alone illegal under Sherman Act § 1; conduct that is entirely lawful for a firm in a nondominant position may support a claim under Sherman Act § 2 against a monopolist or near-monopolist. *See id.*, § 5.02[2][b][ii].

6. Identifying conduct that supports a monopolization claim is not always easy. Conduct that is honestly industrial or part of competition itself can never be the basis of a Sherman Act § 2 claim. If it could be, the Sherman Act would penalize competition, rather than trying to promote it.

Thus the trick for plaintiffs and for courts is to distinguish hard competition (which also may hurt economic rivals) from acts that use a monopolist's or near-monopolist's dominance or near-dominance to crush competition without actually competing on the merits. One way of doing this is to look for the absence of any short-term commercial advantage arising out of the challenged conduct. If there is no evident short-term commercial advantage, and the benefits of the challenged conduct appear only to promise long-term benefit from crushing competition, then the conduct may well be anticompetitive and therefore unlawful under Sherman Act § 2.

7. *Internet-related Antitrust Litigation.* How do you define the relevant market for Internet-related services? A district court in Pennsylvania refused to find that AOL monopo-

lized the market for advertising via its clients' e-mail accounts. *Cyber Promotions, Inc. v. America Online, Inc.*, 948 F. Supp. 456 (E.D. Pa. 1996). The court rejected Cyber Promotions' argument that AOL had "refused to deal" in violation of the Sherman Act's § 2. The court refused to adopt Cyber Promotions' definition of the relevant market as "the market for providing direct marketing advertising material via electronic transmission to AOL's subscribers." The court noted that Cyber Promotions and AOL are not direct competitors and antitrust law does not forbid a private company such as AOL "from excluding from its system advertisers like Cyber [Promotions] who refuse to pay AOL any fee (as opposed to those advertisers who do pay a fee) for their advertising on Aol's system." *Id.* at 462, *citing Monsanto Co. v. Spray-Rite Service Corp.*, 465 U.S. 752, 761 (1984).

Do you think it matters that AOL and Cyber Promotions are not direct competitors? Are you convinced they are not? Do you believe that alternative methods of advertising were comparable? Finally, do you agree with Cyber Promotions' definition of the relevant market? Do you have a better one?

8. *Compulsory Licensing as an Antitrust Remedy.* Compulsory licensing can be a powerful remedy in antitrust actions. For example, in 1998, Monsanto agreed to a compulsory license, at the behest of the U.S. Department of Justice, as a condition of the proposed combination of Monsanto and DeKalb. Monsanto agreed to license corn germ plasm to more than 150 seed companies for use in creating corn hybrids with transgenic improvements. Similarly, in a 1997 Decision and Order from the Federal Trade Commission regarding the merger between Ciba-Geigy Ltd. and Sondoz Ltd. into Vovartis AG, Ciba-Geigy and Sandoz were required to license a patent portfolio, data, and know-how relating to hemophilia gene rights and other products to Rhone-Poulenc Rorer. The newly merged entity was also required to grant non-exclusive licenses to all requesters for patent and other rights to some products, with royalties capped at no greater than 3% of the net sales price. *See also United States v. S.C. Johnson & Son*, 1994 U.S. Dist. Lexis 20797 (N.D. Ill. 1994) (enjoining S.C. Johnson from entering into an exclusive license with Bayer A.G. regarding certain active ingredients in insecticides for household use). Do such licenses make effective market correcting tools?

9. *Relevant Product Markets.* In *AD/SAT v. Associated Press*, 181 F.3d 216 (2d Cir. 1999), Associated Press ("AP") owned and operated a satellite network. AD/SAT delivered advertisements to newspapers over that network. AP launched its own service that delivered advertisements to newspapers over its own network. AD/SAT challenged AP's entrance into the market. AD/SAT alleged that AP engineered an antitrust conspiracy to boycott AD/SAT and monopolize the market for electronic transmission of advertisements to newspapers. The Second Circuit affirmed the district court's ruling that the relevant product market was not the electronic delivery of advertisements to newspapers but the delivery of advertisements to newspapers *by any means*. *Id.* at 229. The court stated that "[t]he relevant market for purposes of antitrust litigation is the 'area of effective competition' within which the defendant operates." *Id.* at 227 (citing *Tampa Elec. Co. v. Nashville Coal Co.*, 365 U.S. 320, 327–28 (1961)). Thus court thus defined the relevant market rather broadly. The court concluded that AP's service enjoyed only a small share of that market and within that market there was sufficient competition. The court also noted that new technology for data transmission and the low cost of entry into the market implies that competition will increase. *Id.* at 230. Was the court justified in considering the number of competitors in future markets?

# VII. Sherman Act §2 and the Microsoft Litigation

As the foregoing material suggests, §1 of the Sherman Act is the section most relevant to licensing. It outlaws unreasonably anticompetitive contracts, and license agreements are but one species of contract. Therefore the lens of §1, bifurcated as it is into "*per se*" and "rule of reason" prisms, is the one most often used to examine restrictive provisions in licenses.

Yet Sherman Act §2 is hardly irrelevant to licensing. It may come into play whenever any party to a license agreement has monopoly or near-monopoly power in any defined market. Because it requires actual or incipient economic dominance, claims under it do not arise as often as claims under §1. Yet cases involving §2 are often extremely important precisely because they involve dominant players in the economy. Often they raise issues that affect not only a narrow industry, but an entire sector of the national economy.

*Microsoft III*, the D.C. Circuit's 2001 decision in the federal government's antitrust action against the software giant, was such a case. Although involving difficult law and economic theory and exceedingly complex facts, the case is worth assiduous study for three reasons. First, it was the most recent of three decisions in the latter third of the twentieth century—all ultimately settled—in which the federal government sought to restore free competition in a vital national industry. (The other two involved IBM and AT&T.) Second, it is the first major government antitrust case involving the so-called "new economy," i.e., the information industries, as distinguished from traditional manufacturing. It therefore raises unique issues of law and economics and addresses unique and creative economic theories. At a fundamental level, *Microsoft III* raises the question whether the "new economy" is really so new after all.

Finally, because of the economic importance of the industries involved—computers and software—*Microsoft III* implicates fundamental issues of national economic policy. Will antitrust law continue to ensure that small and independent firms have the right to compete as it has in the past? Will it continue to guarantee consumers a free choice between competing products and services? These questions are no less important in the twenty-first century than they were in the twentieth. The Supreme Court has said that "competition is our fundamental national economic policy." *United States v. Philadelphia Nat'l Bank*, 374 U.S. 321, 372 (1963). Cases like *Microsoft III* will determine how well that policy works.

From the perspective of licensing, we study *Microsoft III* for four pedagogic reasons. First, it provides an excellent introduction to the §2 offense of monopolizing a defined market, with all the nuance and complexity of modern industry. Second, it introduces the offense of *attempting* to monopolize a defined market, also a §2 offense, and it illustrates that judicial reluctance to impose antitrust sanctions when monopolization is not complete. Third, it explores the concepts of market definition and market power, which are central not only to §2 claims, but to many §1 claims as well. Finally, it strengthens understanding of the nature and elements of the §1 tying offense, which can invoke either the *per se* rule or the rule of reason. This offense is of critical importance in our modern economy, in which the convergence of media and convergence of technologies dictates that firms compete—and attempt to exclude competition—by combining products and technologies together in marketable bundles. In this regard, *Microsoft III* addresses to what extent a firm that has gained a legitimate monopoly in one product can extend the scope of that monopoly by integrating other products or additional functions into that product.

However, there is no getting away from the fact that *Microsoft III* is a difficult case. Everything about it is difficult. The industry at issue is exceedingly complex, with many different, independent players at many levels. Although the basic technological elements—Microsoft's "Windows" operating systems and web browsers—are familiar to virtually everyone, the technological and economic interactions between an operating system and a web browser may not be. Additionally, many do not apprehend how their design affects the multifarious players in the industry. The law is complex (and new to many students in this course), and several aspects of the D.C. Circuit application are controversial. Finally, the economic theory addressed in the case is modern and highly sophisticated and not brilliantly illuminated in the court's opinion.

The very complexity of the case, however, is itself worthy of study, for it raises two questions, both vital to the future of antitrust law. First, might the very complexity of the law and theory allow clever lawyers, backed up by clever expert witnesses, to pull the wool over judges' eyes? Second, does the confluence of complex technologies, complex law, and complex economic theory run the risk of outpacing the limits of human decision making, especially by generalists? (For more on both of these issues, see the Note at the end of this section.)

---

# United States v. Microsoft Corp.
## 253 F.3d 34 (D.C. Cir. 2001) ("*Microsoft III*")

PER CURIAM.

\* \* \*

Microsoft Corporation appeals from judgments of the District Court finding the company in violation of §§ 1 and 2 of the Sherman Act and ordering various remedies.

The action against Microsoft arose pursuant to a complaint filed by the United States and separate complaints filed by individual States. The District Court determined that Microsoft had maintained a monopoly in the market for Intel compatible PC operating systems in violation of § 2; attempted to gain a monopoly in the market for internet browsers in violation of § 2; and illegally tied two purportedly separate products, Windows and Internet Explorer ("IE"), in violation of § 1.... To remedy the Sherman Act violations, the District Court issued a Final Judgment requiring Microsoft to submit a proposed plan of divestiture, with the company to be split into an operating systems business and an applications business.... The District Court's remedial order also contains a number of interim restrictions on Microsoft's conduct.

\* \* \*

Microsoft's appeal contests both the legal conclusions and the resulting remedial order. There are three principal aspects of this appeal. First, Microsoft challenges the District Court's legal conclusions as to all three alleged antitrust violations and also a number of the procedural and factual foundations on which they rest. Second, Microsoft argues that the remedial order must be set aside, because the District Court failed to afford the company an evidentiary hearing on disputed facts and, also, because the substantive provisions of the order are flawed. Finally, Microsoft asserts that the trial judge committed ethical violations by engaging in impermissible *ex parte* contacts and making inappropriate public comments on the merits of the case while it was pending. Microsoft argues that these ethical violations compromised the District Judge's appearance of impartiality, thereby necessitating his disqualification and vacatur of his Findings of Fact, Conclusions of Law, and Final Judgment.

\* \* \*

[W]e find that some but not all of Microsoft's liability challenges have merit. Accordingly, we affirm in part and reverse in part the District Court's judgment that Microsoft violated § 2 of the Sherman Act by employing anticompetitive means to maintain a monopoly in the operating system market; we reverse the District Court's determination that Microsoft violated § 2 of the Sherman Act by illegally attempting to monopolize the internet browser market; and we remand the District Court's finding that Microsoft violated § 1 of the Sherman Act by unlawfully tying its browser to its operating system.

\* \* \*

We vacate in full the Final Judgment embodying the remedial order and remand the case to a different trial judge for further proceedings consistent with this opinion.

## I. INTRODUCTION

### A. Background

In July 1994, officials at the Department of Justice ("DOJ"), on behalf of the United States, filed suit against Microsoft, charging the company with, among other things, unlawfully maintaining a monopoly in the operating system market through anticompetitive terms in its licensing and software developer agreements. The parties subsequently entered into a consent decree, thus avoiding a trial on the merits. *See United States v. Microsoft Corp.*, 312 U.S. App. D.C. 378, 56 F.3d 1448 (D.C. Cir. 1995) ("*Microsoft I*"). Three years later, the Justice Department filed a civil contempt action against Microsoft for allegedly violating one of the decree's provisions. On appeal from a grant of a preliminary injunction, this court held that Microsoft's technological bundling of IE 3.0 and 4.0 with Windows 95 did not violate the relevant provision of the consent decree. *United States v. Microsoft Corp.*, 331 U.S. App. D.C. 121, 147 F.3d 935 (D.C. Cir. 1998) ("*Microsoft II*"). We expressly reserved the question whether such bundling might independently violate §§ 1 or 2 of the Sherman Act.

\* \* \*

On May 18, 1998, shortly before issuance of the *Microsoft II* decision, the United States and a group of State plaintiffs filed separate (and soon thereafter consolidated) complaints, asserting antitrust violations by Microsoft and seeking preliminary and permanent injunctions against the company's allegedly unlawful conduct.... Relying almost exclusively on Microsoft's varied efforts to unseat Netscape Navigator as the preeminent internet browser, plaintiffs charged four distinct violations of the Sherman Act....

The District Court scheduled the case on a "fast track."

\* \* \*

After a 76-day bench trial, the District Court issued its Findings of Fact. *United States v. Microsoft Corp.*, 84 F. Supp. 2d 9 (D.D.C. 1999) ("*Findings of Fact*")....[T]he District Court referred the case to mediation to afford the parties an opportunity to settle their differences. The Honorable Richard A. Posner, Chief Judge of the United States Court of Appeals for the Seventh Circuit, was appointed to serve as mediator. The parties concurred in the referral to mediation and in the choice of mediator.

Mediation failed after nearly four months of settlement talks between the parties. On April 3, 2000, with the parties' briefs having been submitted and considered, the District Court issued its conclusions of law [holding Microsoft liable on all claims except for attempting to monopolize].

\* \* \*

### B. Overview

Before turning to the merits of Microsoft's various arguments, we pause to reflect briefly on two matters of note, one practical and one theoretical.

The practical matter relates to the temporal dimension of this case. The litigation timeline in this case is hardly problematic. Indeed, it is noteworthy that a case of this magnitude and complexity has proceeded from the filing of complaints through trial to appellate decision in a mere three years.

What is somewhat problematic, however, is that just over six years have passed since Microsoft engaged in the first conduct plaintiffs allege to be anticompetitive. As the record in this case indicates, six years seems like an eternity in the computer industry. By the time a court can assess liability, firms, products, and the marketplace are likely to have changed dramatically. This, in turn, threatens enormous practical difficulties for courts considering the appropriate measure of relief in equitable enforcement actions, both in crafting injunctive remedies in the first instance and reviewing those remedies in the second. Conduct remedies may be unavailing in such cases, because innovation to a large degree has already rendered the anticompetitive conduct obsolete (although by no means harmless). And broader structural remedies present their own set of problems, including how a court goes about restoring competition to a dramatically changed, and constantly changing, marketplace. That is just one reason why we find the District Court's refusal in the present case to hold an evidentiary hearing on remedies—to update and flesh out the available information before seriously entertaining the possibility of dramatic structural relief—so problematic.

We do not mean to say that enforcement actions will no longer play an important role in curbing infringements of the antitrust laws in technologically dynamic markets, nor do we assume this in assessing the merits of this case. Even in those cases where forward-looking remedies appear limited, the Government will continue to have an interest in defining the contours of the antitrust laws so that law-abiding firms will have a clear sense of what is permissible and what is not. And the threat of private damage actions will remain to deter those firms inclined to test the limits of the law.

The second matter of note is more theoretical in nature. We decide this case against a backdrop of significant debate amongst academics and practitioners over the extent to which "old economy" § 2 monopolization doctrines should apply to firms competing in dynamic technological markets characterized by network effects. In markets characterized by network effects, one product or standard tends towards dominance, because "the utility that a user derives from consumption of the good increases with the number of other agents consuming the good." Michael L. Katz & Carl Shapiro, *Network Externalities, Competition, and Compatibility*, 75 Am. Econ. Rev. 424, 424 (1985). For example, "an individual consumer's demand to use (and hence her benefit from) the telephone network…increases with the number of other users on the network whom she can call or from whom she can receive calls." Howard A. Shelanski & J. Gregory Sidak, *Antitrust Divestiture in Network Industries*, 68 U. Chi. L. Rev. 1, 8 (2001). Once a product or standard achieves wide acceptance, it becomes more or less entrenched. Competition in such industries is "for the field" rather than "within the field." *See* Harold Demsetz, *Why Regulate Utilities?*, 11 J.L. & Econ. 55, 57 & n.7 (1968) (emphasis omitted).

In technologically dynamic markets, however, such entrenchment may be temporary, because innovation may alter the field altogether. *See* Joseph A. Schumpeter, Capitalism, Socialism And Democracy 81–90 (Harper Perennial 1976). Rapid technological change leads to markets in which "firms compete through innovation for temporary market dominance, from which they may be displaced by the next wave of product advancements." Shelanski & Sidak, at 11–12 (discussing Schumpeterian competition, which proceeds "sequentially over time rather than simultaneously across a market"). Microsoft argues that the operating system market is just such a market.

Whether or not Microsoft's characterization of the operating system market is correct does not appreciably alter our mission in assessing the alleged antitrust violations in the present case. As an initial matter, we note that there is no consensus among commentators on the question of whether, and to what extent, current monopolization doctrine should be amended to account for competition in technologically dynamic markets characterized by network effects.…Indeed, there is some suggestion that the economic consequences of network effects and technological dynamism act to offset one another, thereby making it difficult to formulate categorical antitrust rules absent a particularized analysis of a given market.…

Moreover, it should be clear that Microsoft makes no claim that anticompetitive conduct should be assessed differently in technologically dynamic markets. It claims only that the measure of monopoly power should be different. For reasons fully discussed below, we reject Microsoft's monopoly power argument.

With this backdrop in mind, we turn to the specific challenges raised in Microsoft's appeal.

## II. MONOPOLIZATION

Section 2 of the Sherman Act makes it unlawful for a firm to "monopolize." 15 U.S.C. §2. The offense of monopolization has two elements: "(1) the possession of monopoly power in the relevant market and (2) the willful acquisition or maintenance of that power as distinguished from growth or development as a consequence of a superior product, business acumen, or historic accident." *United States v. Grinnell Corp.*, 384 U.S. 563, 570–71, 16 L. Ed. 2d 778, 86 S. Ct. 1698 (1966). The District Court applied this test and found that Microsoft possesses monopoly power in the market for Intel-compatible PC operating systems. Focusing primarily on Microsoft's efforts to suppress Netscape Navigator's threat to its operating system monopoly, the court also found that Microsoft maintained its power not through competition on the merits, but through unlawful means. Microsoft challenges both conclusions. We defer to the District Court's findings of fact, setting them aside only if clearly erroneous. Fed. R. Civ. P. 52(a). We review legal questions *de novo*.

\* \* \*

## A. Monopoly Power

While merely possessing monopoly power is not itself an antitrust violation,...it is a necessary element of a monopolization charge....The Supreme Court defines monopoly power as "the power to control prices or exclude competition." *United States v. E.I. du Pont de Nemours & Co.*, 351 U.S. 377, 391, 100 L. Ed. 1264, 76 S. Ct. 994 (1956). More precisely, a firm is a monopolist if it can profitably raise prices substantially above the competitive level....Where evidence indicates that a firm has in fact profitably done so, the existence of monopoly power is clear. See Rebel Oil Co. v. Atl. Richfield Co., 51 F.3d 1421, 1434 (9th Cir. 1995); *see also FTC v. Indiana Fed'n of Dentists*, 476 U.S. 447, 460–61, 90 L. Ed. 2d 445, 106 S. Ct. 2009 (1986) (using direct proof to show market power in Sherman Act § 1 unreasonable restraint of trade action). Because such direct proof is only rarely available, courts more typically examine market structure in search of circumstantial evidence of monopoly power....Under this structural approach, monopoly power may be inferred from a firm's possession of a dominant share of a relevant market that is protected by entry barriers. *See Rebel Oil*, 51 F.3d at 1434. "Entry barriers" are factors (such as certain regulatory requirements) that prevent new rivals from timely responding to an increase in price above the competitive level....

The District Court considered these structural factors and concluded that Microsoft possesses monopoly power in a relevant market. Defining the market as Intel-compatible PC operating systems, the District Court found that Microsoft has a greater than 95% share. It also found the company's market position protected by a substantial entry barrier.

\* \* \*

### 1. Market Structure

#### a. Market definition

"Because the ability of consumers to turn to other suppliers restrains a firm from raising prices above the competitive level," *Rothery Storage & Van Co. v. Atlas Van Lines, Inc.*, 253 U.S. App. D.C. 142, 792 F.2d 210, 218 (D.C. Cir. 1986), the relevant market must include all products "reasonably interchangeable by consumers for the same purposes." *du Pont*, 351 U.S. at 395. In this case, the District Court defined the market as "the licensing of all Intel-compatible PC operating systems worldwide," finding that there are "currently no products—and...there are not likely to be any in the near future—that a significant percentage of computer users worldwide could substitute for [these operating systems] without incurring substantial costs."...Calling this market definition "far too narrow," Microsoft argues that the District Court improperly excluded three types of products: non-Intel compatible operating systems (primarily Apple's Macintosh operating system, Mac OS), operating systems for non-PC devices (such as handheld computers and portal websites), and "middleware" products, which are not operating systems at all.

We begin with Mac OS. Microsoft's argument that Mac OS should have been included in the relevant market suffers from a flaw that infects many of the company's monopoly power claims: the company fails to challenge the District Court's factual findings, or to argue that these findings do not support the court's conclusions. The District Court found that consumers would not switch from Windows to Mac OS in response to a substantial price increase because of the costs of acquiring the new hardware needed to run Mac OS (an Apple computer and peripherals) and compatible software applications, as well as because of the effort involved in learning the new system and transferring files to its format.... The court also found the Apple system less appealing to consumers because it costs considerably more and supports fewer applications.... Microsoft neither points to evidence contradicting the District Court's findings nor alleges that supporting record evidence is insufficient.

* * *

Microsoft's challenge to the District Court's exclusion of non-PC based competitors, such as information appliances (handheld devices, etc.) and portal websites that host server based software applications, suffers from the same defect: the company fails to challenge the District Court's key factual findings. In particular, the District Court found that because information appliances fall far short of performing all of the functions of a PC, most consumers will buy them only as a supplement to their PCs.... The District Court also found that portal websites do not presently host enough applications to induce consumers to switch, nor are they likely to do so in the near future.... Again, because Microsoft does not argue that the District Court's findings do not support its conclusion that information appliances and portal websites are outside the relevant market, we adhere to that conclusion.

This brings us to Microsoft's main challenge to the District Court's market definition: the exclusion of middleware. Because of the importance of middleware to this case, we pause to explain what it is and how it relates to the issue before us.

Operating systems perform many functions, including allocating computer memory and controlling peripherals such as printers and keyboards.... Operating systems also function as platforms for software applications. They do this by "exposing"—*i.e.*, making available to software developers—routines or protocols that perform certain widely-used functions. These are known as Application Programming Interfaces, or "APIs."... For example, Windows contains an API that enables users to draw a box on the screen.... Software developers wishing to include that function in an application need not duplicate it in their own code. Instead, they can "call"—*i.e.*, use—the Windows API.... Windows contains thousands of APIs, controlling everything from data storage to font display....

Every operating system has different APIs. Accordingly, a developer who writes an application for one operating system and wishes to sell the application to users of another must modify, or "port," the application to the second operating system.... This process is both time consuming and expensive.

"Middleware" refers to software products that expose their own APIs.... Because of this, a middleware product written for Windows could take over some or all of Windows's valuable platform functions—that is, developers might begin to rely upon APIs exposed by the middleware for basic routines rather than relying upon the API set included in Windows. If middleware were written for multiple operating systems, its impact could be even greater. The more developers could rely upon APIs exposed by such middleware, the less expensive porting to different operating systems would be. Ultimately, if developers could write applications relying exclusively on APIs exposed by middleware, their applications would run on any operating system on which the middleware was also present.... Netscape Navigator and Java—both at issue in this case—are middleware products written for multiple operating systems....

Microsoft argues that, because middleware could usurp the operating system's platform function and might eventually take over other operating system functions (for instance, by controlling peripherals), the District Court erred in excluding Navigator and

Java from the relevant market. The District Court found, however, that neither Navigator, Java, nor any other middleware product could now, or would soon, expose enough APIs to serve as a platform for popular applications, much less take over all operating system functions.... Again, Microsoft fails to challenge these findings, instead simply asserting middleware's "potential" as a competitor... The test of reasonable interchangeability, however, required the District Court to consider only substitutes that constrain pricing in the reasonably foreseeable future, and only products that can enter the market in a relatively short time can perform this function.... Whatever middleware's ultimate potential, the District Court found that consumers could not now abandon their operating systems and switch to middleware in response to a sustained price for Windows above the competitive level.... Nor is middleware likely to overtake the operating system as the primary platform for software development any time in the near future.

Alternatively, Microsoft argues that the District Court should not have excluded middleware from the relevant market because the primary focus of the plaintiffs' § 2 charge is on Microsoft's attempts to suppress middleware's threat to its operating system monopoly. According to Microsoft, it is "contradictory," to define the relevant market to exclude the "very competitive threats that gave rise" to the action.... The purported contradiction lies between plaintiffs' § 2 theory, under which Microsoft preserved its monopoly against middleware technologies that threatened to become viable substitutes for Windows, and its theory of the relevant market, under which middleware is not presently a viable substitute for Windows. Because middleware's threat is only nascent, however, no contradiction exists. Nothing in § 2 of the Sherman Act limits its prohibition to actions taken against threats that are already well-developed enough to serve as present substitutes. Because market definition is meant to identify products "reasonably interchangeable by consumers," *du Pont*, 351 U.S. at 395, and because middleware is not now interchangeable with Windows, the District Court had good reason for excluding middleware from the relevant market.

### b. Market power

Having thus properly defined the relevant market, the District Court found that Windows accounts for a greater than 95% share.... The court also found that even if Mac OS were included, Microsoft's share would exceed 80%.... Microsoft challenges neither finding, nor does it argue that such a market share is not predominant. *Cf. Grinnell*, 384 U.S. at 571 (87% is predominant); *Eastman Kodak Co. v. Image Technical Servs., Inc.*, 504 U.S. 451, 481, 119 L. Ed. 2d 265, 112 S. Ct. 2072 (1992) (80%); *du Pont*, 351 U.S. at 379, 391 (75%).

Instead, Microsoft claims that even a predominant market share does not by itself indicate monopoly power. Although the "existence of [monopoly] power ordinarily may be inferred from the predominant share of the market," *Grinnell*, 384 U.S. at 571, we agree with Microsoft that because of the possibility of competition from new entrants,... looking to current market share alone can be "misleading." *Hunt-Wesson Foods, Inc. v. Ragu Foods, Inc.*, 627 F.2d 919, 924 (9th Cir. 1980).... In this case, however, the District Court was not misled. Considering the possibility of new rivals, the court focused not only on Microsoft's present market share, but also on the structural barrier that protects the company's future position.... That barrier — the "applications barrier to entry" — stems from two characteristics of the software market: (1) most consumers prefer operating systems for which a large number of applications have already been written; and (2) most developers prefer to write for operating systems that already have a substantial consumer base.... This "chicken-and-egg" situation ensures that applications will continue to be written for the already dominant Windows, which in turn ensures that consumers will continue to prefer it over other operating systems.

Challenging the existence of the applications barrier to entry, Microsoft observes that software developers do write applications for other operating systems, pointing out that at its peak IBM's OS/2 supported approximately 2,500 applications....This misses the point. That some developers write applications for other operating systems is not at all inconsistent with the finding that the applications barrier to entry discourages many from writing for these less popular platforms. Indeed, the District Court found that IBM's difficulty in attracting a larger number of software developers to write for its platform seriously impeded OS/2's success.

Microsoft does not dispute that Windows supports many more applications than any other operating system. It argues instead that "it defies common sense" to suggest that an operating system must support as many applications as Windows does (more than 70,000, according to the District Court) to be competitive....Consumers, Microsoft points out, can only use a very small percentage of these applications. As the District Court explained, however, the applications barrier to entry gives consumers reason to prefer the dominant operating system even if they have no need to use all applications written for it:

> The consumer wants an operating system that runs not only types of applications that he knows he will want to use, but also those types in which he might develop an interest later. Also, the consumer knows that if he chooses an operating system with enough demand to support multiple applications in each product category, he will be less likely to find himself straitened later by having to use an application whose features disappoint him. Finally, the average user knows that, generally speaking, applications improve through successive versions. He thus wants an operating system for which successive generations of his favorite applications will be released—promptly at that. The fact that a vastly larger number of applications are written for Windows than for other PC operating systems attracts consumers to Windows, because it reassures them that their interests will be met as long as they use Microsoft's product.

*Findings of Fact* ¶ 37. Thus, despite the limited success of its rivals, Microsoft benefits from the applications barrier to entry.

Of course, were middleware to succeed, it would erode the applications barrier to entry. Because applications written for multiple operating systems could run on any operating system on which the middleware product was present with little, if any, porting, the operating system market would become competitive....But as the District Court found, middleware will not expose a sufficient number of APIs to erode the applications barrier to entry in the foreseeable future.

Microsoft next argues that the applications barrier to entry is not an entry barrier at all, but a reflection of Windows' popularity. It is certainly true that Windows may have gained its initial dominance in the operating system market competitively—through superior foresight or quality. But this case is not about Microsoft's initial acquisition of monopoly power. It is about Microsoft's efforts to maintain this position through means other than competition on the merits. Because the applications barrier to entry protects a dominant operating system irrespective of quality, it gives Microsoft power to stave off even superior new rivals. The barrier is thus a characteristic of the operating system market, not of Microsoft's popularity, or, as asserted by a Microsoft witness, the company's efficiency....

Finally, Microsoft argues that the District Court should not have considered the applications barrier to entry because it reflects not a cost borne disproportionately by new entrants, but one borne by all participants in the operating system market. According to Microsoft, it had to make major investments to convince software developers to write for its new operating system, and it continues to "evangelize" the Windows platform today. Whether costs borne by all market participants should be considered entry barriers is the subject of much debate.... We need not resolve this issue, however, for even under the more narrow definition it is clear that there are barriers. When Microsoft entered the operating system market with MS-DOS and the first version of Windows, it did not confront a dominant rival operating system with as massive an installed base and as vast an existing array of applications as the Windows operating systems have since enjoyed.... Moreover, when Microsoft introduced Windows 95 and 98, it was able to bypass the applications barrier to entry that protected the incumbent Windows by including APIs from the earlier version in the new operating systems. This made porting existing Windows applications to the new version of Windows much less costly than porting them to the operating systems of other entrants who could not freely include APIs from the incumbent Windows with their own.

## 2. Direct Proof

\* \* \*

*[The court rejected Microsoft's argument that, because the computer-software industry is particularly "dynamic," §2 claims addressing that industry should require direct proof of market power, i.e., power to sustain price increases despite competition. Microsoft argued that its large investments in research and development and the low prices for its operating systems demonstrated an absence of market power.]*

\* \* \*

Even if we were to require direct proof, moreover, Microsoft's behavior may well be sufficient to show the existence of monopoly power. Certainly, none of the conduct Microsoft points to—its investment in R&D and the relatively low price of Windows—is inconsistent with the possession of such power.... The R&D expenditures Microsoft points to are not simply for Windows, but for its entire company, which most likely does not possess a monopoly for all of its products. Moreover, because innovation can increase an already dominant market share and further delay the emergence of competition, even monopolists have reason to invest in R&D.... Microsoft's pricing behavior is similarly equivocal. The company claims only that it never charged the short-term profit-maximizing price for Windows. Faced with conflicting expert testimony, the District Court found that it could not accurately determine what this price would be.... In any event, the court found, a price lower than the short-term profit-maximizing price is not inconsistent with possession or improper use of monopoly power.... Cf. *Berkey Photo, Inc. v. Eastman Kodak Co.*, 603 F.2d 263, 274 (2d Cir. 1979) ("If monopoly power has been acquired or maintained through improper means, the fact that the power has not been used to extract [a monopoly price] provides no succor to the monopolist.").

\* \* \*

More telling, the District Court found that some aspects of Microsoft's behavior are difficult to explain unless Windows is a monopoly product. For instance, according to the District Court, the company set the price of Windows without considering rivals' prices…something a firm without a monopoly would have been unable to do. The District Court also found that Microsoft's pattern of exclusionary conduct could only be rational "if the firm knew that it possessed monopoly power."…It is to that conduct that we now turn.

## B. Anticompetitive Conduct

As discussed above, having a monopoly does not by itself violate §2. A firm violates §2 only when it acquires or maintains, or attempts to acquire or maintain, a monopoly by engaging in exclusionary conduct "as distinguished from growth or development as a consequence of a superior product, business acumen, or historic accident." *Grinnell*, 384 U.S. at 571; *see also United States v. Aluminum Co. of Am.*, 148 F.2d 416, 430 (2d Cir. 1945) (Hand, J.) ("The successful competitor, having been urged to compete, must not be turned upon when he wins.").

In this case, after concluding that Microsoft had monopoly power, the District Court held that Microsoft had violated §2 by engaging in a variety of exclusionary acts (not including predatory pricing), to maintain its monopoly by preventing the effective distribution and use of products that might threaten that monopoly. Specifically, the District Court held Microsoft liable for: (1) the way in which it integrated IE into Windows; (2) its various dealings with Original Equipment Manufacturers ("OEMs"), Internet Access Providers ("IAPs"), Internet Content Providers ("ICPs"), Independent Software Vendors ("ISVs"), and Apple Computer; (3) its efforts to contain and to subvert Java technologies; and (4) its course of conduct as a whole. Upon appeal, Microsoft argues that it did not engage in any exclusionary conduct.

Whether any particular act of a monopolist is exclusionary, rather than merely a form of vigorous competition, can be difficult to discern: the means of illicit exclusion, like the means of legitimate competition, are myriad. The challenge for an antitrust court lies in stating a general rule for distinguishing between exclusionary acts, which reduce social welfare, and competitive acts, which increase it.

From a century of case law on monopolization under §2, however, several principles do emerge. First, to be condemned as exclusionary, a monopolist's act must have an "anticompetitive effect." That is, it must harm the competitive *process* and thereby harm consumers. In contrast, harm to one or more *competitors* will not suffice. "The [Sherman Act] directs itself not against conduct which is competitive, even severely so, but against conduct which unfairly tends to destroy competition itself." *Spectrum Sports, Inc. v. McQuillan*, 506 U.S. 447, 458, 122 L. Ed. 2d 247, 113 S. Ct. 884 (1993); *see also Brooke Group Ltd. v. Brown & Williamson Tobacco Corp.*, 509 U.S. 209, 225, 125 L. Ed. 2d 168, 113 S. Ct. 2578 (1993) ("Even an act of pure malice by one business competitor against another does not, without more, state a claim under the federal antitrust laws.…").

Second, the plaintiff, on whom the burden of proof of course rests…must demonstrate that the monopolist's conduct indeed has the requisite anticompetitive effect.

\* \* \*

Third, if a plaintiff successfully establishes a *prima facie* case under §2 by demonstrating anticompetitive effect, then the monopolist may proffer a "procompetitive justification" for its conduct. *See Eastman Kodak*, 504 U.S. at 483. If the monopolist asserts a procompetitive justification—a nonpretextual claim that its conduct is indeed a form of competition on the merits because it involves, for example, greater efficiency or enhanced consumer appeal—then the burden shifts back to the plaintiff to rebut that claim....

Fourth, if the monopolist's procompetitive justification stands unrebutted, then the plaintiff must demonstrate that the anticompetitive harm of the conduct outweighs the procompetitive benefit.

\* \* \*

Finally, in considering whether the monopolist's conduct on balance harms competition and is therefore condemned as exclusionary for purposes of § 2, our focus is upon the effect of that conduct, not upon the intent behind it. Evidence of the intent behind the conduct of a monopolist is relevant only to the extent it helps us understand the likely effect of the monopolist's conduct....

With these principles in mind, we now consider Microsoft's objections to the District Court's holding that Microsoft violated § 2 of the Sherman Act in a variety of ways.

### 1. Licenses Issued to Original Equipment Manufacturers

The District Court condemned a number of provisions in Microsoft's agreements licensing Windows to OEMs, because it found that Microsoft's imposition of those provisions (like many of Microsoft's other actions at issue in this case) serves to reduce usage share of Netscape's browser and, hence, protect Microsoft's operating system monopoly. The reason market share in the browser market affects market power in the operating system market is complex, and warrants some explanation.

Browser usage share is important because a browser (or any middleware product, for that matter) must have a critical mass of users in order to attract software developers to write applications relying upon the APIs it exposes, and away from the APIs exposed by Windows. Applications written to a particular browser's APIs, however, would run on any computer with that browser, regardless of the underlying operating system. "The overwhelming majority of consumers will only use a PC operating system for which there already exists a large and varied set of...applications, and for which it seems relatively certain that new types of applications and new versions of existing applications will continue to be marketed...." *Findings of Fact* ¶ 30. If a consumer could have access to the applications he desired—regardless of the operating system he uses—simply by installing a particular browser on his computer, then he would no longer feel compelled to select Windows in order to have access to those applications; he could select an operating system other than Windows based solely upon its quality and price. In other words, the market for operating systems would be competitive.

Therefore, Microsoft's efforts to gain market share in one market (browsers) served to meet the threat to Microsoft's monopoly in another market (operating systems) by keeping rival browsers from gaining the critical mass of users necessary to attract developer attention away from Windows as the platform for software development.

\* \* \*

In evaluating the restrictions in Microsoft's agreements licensing Windows to OEMs, we first consider whether plaintiffs have made out a *prima facie* case by demonstrating that the restrictions have an anticompetitive effect. In the next subsection, we conclude that plaintiffs have met this burden as to all the restrictions. We then consider Microsoft's proffered justifications for the restrictions and, for the most part, hold those justifications insufficient.

### a. Anticompetitive effect of the license restrictions

The restrictions Microsoft places upon Original Equipment are of particular importance in determining browser usage share because having an OEM pre-install a browser on a computer is one of the two most cost-effective methods by far of distributing browsing software. (The other is bundling the browser with internet access software distributed by an IAP.) *Findings of Fact* ¶ 145. The District Court found that the restrictions Microsoft imposed in licensing Windows to OEMs prevented many OEMs from distributing browsers other than IE.... In particular, the District Court condemned the license provisions prohibiting the OEMs from: (1) removing any desktop icons, folders, or "Start" menu entries; (2) altering the initial boot sequence; and (3) otherwise altering the appearance of the Windows desktop....

The District Court concluded that the first license restriction—the prohibition upon the removal of desktop icons, folders, and Start menu entries—thwarts the distribution of a rival browser by preventing OEMs from removing visible means of user access to IE. The OEMs cannot practically install a second browser in addition to IE, the court found, in part because "pre-installing more than one product in a given category...can significantly increase an OEM's support costs, for the redundancy can lead to confusion among novice users."...That is, a certain number of novice computer users, seeing two browser icons, will wonder which to use when and will call the OEM's support line. Support calls are extremely expensive and, in the highly competitive original equipment market, firms have a strong incentive to minimize costs.

\* \* \*

As noted above, the OEM channel is one of the two primary channels for distribution of browsers. By preventing OEMs from removing visible means of user access to IE, the license restriction prevents many OEMs from pre-installing a rival browser and, therefore, protects Microsoft's monopoly from the competition that middleware might otherwise present. Therefore, we conclude that the license restriction at issue is anticompetitive....

The second license provision at issue prohibits OEMs from modifying the initial boot sequence—the process that occurs the first time a consumer turns on the computer. Prior to the imposition of that restriction, "among the programs that many OEMs inserted into the boot sequence were Internet sign-up procedures that encouraged users to choose from a list of IAPs assembled by the OEM." *Findings of Fact* ¶ 210. Microsoft's prohibition on any alteration of the boot sequence thus prevents OEMs from using that process to promote the services of IAPs, many of which—at least at the time Microsoft imposed the restriction—used Navigator rather than IE in their internet access software....Microsoft does not deny that the prohibition on modifying the boot sequence has the effect of decreasing competition against IE by preventing OEMs from promoting rivals' browsers. Because this prohibition has a substantial effect in protecting Microsoft's market power, and does so through a means other than competition on the merits, it is anticompetitive....

Finally, Microsoft imposes several additional provisions that, like the prohibition on removal of icons, prevent OEMs from making various alterations to the desktop: Microsoft prohibits OEMs from causing any user interface other than the Windows desktop to launch automatically, from adding icons or folders different in size or shape from those supplied by Microsoft, and from using the "Active Desktop" feature to promote third-party brands. These restrictions impose significant costs upon the OEMs; prior to Microsoft's prohibiting the practice, many OEMs would change the appearance of the desktop in ways they found beneficial.

The dissatisfaction of the OEM customers does not, of course, mean the restrictions are anticompetitive. The anticompetitive effect of the license restrictions is, as Microsoft itself recognizes, that OEMs are not able to promote rival browsers, which keeps developers focused upon the APIs in Windows. *Findings of Fact* ¶ 212 (quoting Microsoft's Gates as writing, "winning Internet browser share is a very very important goal for us," and emphasizing the need to prevent OEMs from promoting both rival browsers and IAPs that might use rivals' browsers)...This kind of promotion is not a zero-sum game; but for the restrictions in their licenses to use Windows, OEMs could promote multiple IAPs and browsers. By preventing the OEMs from doing so, this type of license restriction, like the first two restrictions, is anticompetitive: Microsoft reduced rival browsers' usage share not by improving its own product but, rather, by preventing OEMs from taking actions that could increase rivals' share of usage.

### b. Microsoft's justifications for the license restrictions

Microsoft argues that the license restrictions are legally justified because, in imposing them, Microsoft is simply "exercising its rights as the holder of valid copyrights."...Microsoft also argues that the licenses "do not unduly restrict the opportunities of Netscape to distribute Navigator in any event."

Microsoft's primary copyright argument borders upon the frivolous. The company claims an absolute and unfettered right to use its intellectual property as it wishes: "If intellectual property rights have been lawfully acquired," it says, then "their subsequent exercise cannot give rise to antitrust liability."...That is no more correct than the proposition that use of one's personal property, such as a baseball bat, cannot give rise to tort liability. As the Federal Circuit succinctly stated: "Intellectual property rights do not confer a privilege to violate the antitrust laws." *In re Indep. Serv. Orgs. Antitrust Litig.*, 203 F.3d 1322, 1325 (Fed. Cir. 2000).

\* \* \*

*[Microsoft next argued that its copyright gave it the right to prevent unauthorized alteration of its software.]*

The only license restriction Microsoft seriously defends as necessary to prevent a "substantial alteration" of its copyrighted work is the prohibition on OEMs automatically launching a substitute user interface upon completion of the boot process. *See Findings of Fact* ¶ 211 ("[A]few large OEMs developed programs that ran automatically at the conclusion of a new PC system's first boot sequence. These programs replaced the Windows desktop either with a user interface designed by the OEM or with Navigator's user interface."). We agree that a shell that automatically prevents the Windows desktop from ever being seen by the user is a drastic alteration of Microsoft's copyrighted work, and outweighs the marginal anticompetitive effect of prohibiting the OEMs from substituting a different interface automatically upon completion of the initial boot process. We therefore hold that this particular restriction is not an exclusionary practice that violates § 2 of the Sherman Act.

In a second variation upon its copyright defense, Microsoft argues that the license restrictions merely prevent OEMs from taking actions that would reduce substantially the value of Microsoft's copyrighted work: that is, Microsoft claims each license restriction in question is necessary to prevent OEMs from so altering Windows as to undermine "the principal value of Windows as a stable and consistent platform that supports a broad range of applications and that is familiar to users." Microsoft, however, never substantiates this claim, and, because an OEM's altering the appearance of the desktop or promoting programs in the boot sequence does not affect the code already in the product, the practice does not self-evidently affect either the "stability" or the "consistency" of the platform.... Therefore, we conclude Microsoft has not shown that the OEMs' liberality reduces the value of Windows except in the sense that their promotion of rival browsers undermines Microsoft's monopoly—and that is not a permissible justification for the license restrictions.

* * *

In sum, we hold that with the exception of the one restriction prohibiting automatically launched alternative interfaces, all the OEM license restrictions at issue represent uses of Microsoft's market power to protect its monopoly, unredeemed by any legitimate justification. The restrictions therefore violate §2 of the Sherman Act.

### 2. Integration of IE and Windows

Although Microsoft's license restrictions have a significant effect in closing rival browsers out of one of the two primary channels of distribution, the District Court found that "Microsoft's executives believed...its contractual restrictions placed on OEMs would not be sufficient in themselves to reverse the direction of Navigator's usage share. Consequently, in late 1995 or early 1996, Microsoft set out to bind [IE] more tightly to Windows 95 as a technical matter." *Findings of Fact* ¶ 160.

Technologically binding IE to Windows, the District Court found, both prevented OEMs from pre-installing other browsers and deterred consumers from using them. In particular, having the IE software code as an irremovable part of Windows meant that pre-installing a second browser would "increase an OEM's product testing costs," because an OEM must test and train its support staff to answer calls related to every software product preinstalled on the machine; moreover, pre-installing a browser in addition to IE would to many OEMs be "a questionable use of the scarce and valuable space on a PC's hard drive." *Id.* ¶ 159.

* * *

### a. Anticompetitive effect of integration

As a general rule, courts are properly very skeptical about claims that competition has been harmed by a dominant firm's product design changes. In a competitive market, firms routinely innovate in the hope of appealing to consumers, sometimes in the process making their products incompatible with those of rivals; the imposition of liability when a monopolist does the same thing will inevitably deter a certain amount of innovation. This is all the more true in a market, such as this one, in which the product itself is rapidly changing.... Judicial deference to product innovation, however, does not mean that a monopolist's product design decisions are *per se* lawful. *See Foremost Pro Color*, 703 F.2d at 545; *see also Cal. Computer Prods.*, 613 F.2d at 739, 744; *In re IBM Peripheral EDP Devices Antitrust Litig.*, 481 F. Supp. 965, 1007–8 (N.D. Cal. 1979).

The District Court first condemned as anticompetitive Microsoft's decision to exclude IE from the "Add/Remove Programs" utility in Windows 98. *Findings of Fact* ¶ 170. Microsoft had included IE in the Add/Remove Programs utility in Windows 95...but when it modified Windows 95 to produce Windows 98, it took IE out of the Add/Remove Programs utility. This change reduces the usage share of rival browsers not by making Microsoft's own browser more attractive to consumers but, rather, by discouraging OEMs from distributing rival products. Because Microsoft's conduct, through something other than competition on the merits, has the effect of significantly reducing usage of rivals' products and hence protecting its own operating system monopoly, it is anticompetitive....

Second, the District Court found that Microsoft designed Windows 98 "so that using Navigator on Windows 98 would have unpleasant consequences for users" by, in some circumstances, overriding the user's choice of a browser other than IE as his or her default browser....Because the override reduces rivals' usage share and protects Microsoft's monopoly, it too is anticompetitive.

Finally, the District Court condemned Microsoft's decision to bind IE to Windows 98 "by placing code specific to Web browsing in the same files as code that provided operating system functions."...Putting code supplying browsing functionality into a file with code supplying operating system functionality "ensures that the deletion of any file containing browsing-specific routines would also delete vital operating system routines and thus cripple Windows...." As noted above, preventing an OEM from removing IE deters it from installing a second browser because doing so increases the OEM's product testing and support costs; by contrast, had OEMs been able to remove IE, they might have chosen to pre-install Navigator alone.

* * *

[W]e conclude that such commingling has an anticompetitive effect; as noted above, the commingling deters OEMs from pre-installing rival browsers, thereby reducing the rivals' usage share and, hence, developers' interest in rivals' APIs as an alternative to the API set exposed by Microsoft's operating system.

### b. Microsoft's justifications for integration

Microsoft proffers no justification for two of the three challenged actions that it took in integrating IE into Windows—excluding IE from the Add/Remove Programs utility and commingling browser and operating system code. Although Microsoft does make some general claims regarding the benefits of integrating the browser and the operating system, it neither specifies nor substantiates those claims. Nor does it argue that either excluding IE from the Add/Remove Programs utility or commingling code achieves any integrative benefit. Plaintiffs plainly made out a prima facie case of harm to competition in the operating system market by demonstrating that Microsoft's actions increased its browser usage share and thus protected its operating system monopoly from a middleware threat and, for its part, Microsoft failed to meet its burden of showing that its conduct serves a purpose other than protecting its operating system monopoly. Accordingly, we hold that Microsoft's exclusion of IE from the Add/Remove Programs utility and its commingling of browser and operating system code constitute exclusionary conduct, in violation of § 2.

As for the other challenged act that Microsoft took in integrating IE into Windows—causing Windows to override the user's choice of a default browser in certain circumstances—Microsoft argues that it has "valid technical reasons." Specifically, Microsoft claims that it was necessary to design Windows to override the user's preferences when he or she invokes one of "a few" out "of the nearly 30 means of accessing the Internet."...According to Microsoft:

> The Windows 98 Help system and Windows Update feature depend on ActiveX controls not supported by Navigator, and the now-discontinued Channel Bar utilized Microsoft's Channel Definition Format, which Navigator also did not support. Lastly, Windows 98 does not invoke Navigator if a user accesses the Internet through 'My Computer' or 'Windows Explorer' because

doing so would defeat one of the purposes of those features—enabling users to move seamlessly from local storage devices to the Web *in the same browsing window.*

*Id.* (internal citations omitted). The plaintiff bears the burden not only of rebutting a proffered justification but also of demonstrating that the anticompetitive effect of the challenged action outweighs it. In the District Court, plaintiffs appear to have done neither, let alone both; in any event, upon appeal, plaintiffs offer no rebuttal whatsoever. Accordingly, Microsoft may not be held liable for this aspect of its product design.

### 3. Agreements with Internet Access Providers

The District Court also condemned as exclusionary Microsoft's agreements with various IAPs. The IAPs include both Internet Service Providers, which offer consumers internet access, and Online Services ("OLSs") such as America Online ("AOL"), which offer proprietary content in addition to internet access and other services. *Findings of Fact* ¶ 15.

\* \* \*

The District Court condemned Microsoft's actions....

*[The condemned actions fell into two categories. First, Microsoft had offered IAPs promotional inducements to use IE, including free copies of IE, bonuses for signing up customers to use IE, and free kits (called IE Access Kits) to help IAPs customize how their Websites appeared on IE. Second, "Microsoft agreed to provide easy access to IAPs' services from the Windows desktop in return for the IAPs' agreement to promote IE exclusively and to keep shipments of internet access software using Navigator under a specific percentage, typically 25%."]*

\* \* \*

The rare case of price predation aside [which plaintiffs did not press upon appeal], the antitrust laws do not condemn even a monopolist for offering its product at an attractive price, and we therefore have no warrant to condemn Microsoft for offering either IE or the IEAK free of charge or even at a negative price. Likewise, as we said above, a monopolist does not violate the Sherman Act simply by developing an attractive product. *See Grinnell*, 384 U.S. at 571 ("Growth or development as a consequence of a superior product [or] business acumen" is no violation.). Therefore, Microsoft's development of the IEAK does not violate the Sherman Act.

We turn now to Microsoft's deals with IAPs concerning desktop placement.... Under [its AOL] agreement Microsoft puts the AOL icon in the OLS folder on the Windows desktop and AOL does not promote any non-Microsoft browser, nor provide software using any non-Microsoft browser except at the customer's request, and even then AOL will not supply more than 15% of its subscribers with a browser other than IE.

The Supreme Court most recently considered an antitrust challenge to an exclusive contract in *Tampa Electric Co. v. Nashville Coal Co.*, 365 U.S. 320, 5 L. Ed. 2d 580, 81 S. Ct. 623 (1961). That case, involved a challenge to a requirements contract, was brought under § 3 of the Clayton Act and §§ 1 and 2 of the Sherman Act. The Court held that an exclusive contract does not violate the Clayton Act unless its probable effect is to "foreclose competition in a substantial share of the line of commerce affected." *Id.* at 327. The share of the market foreclosed is important because, for the contract to have an adverse effect upon competition, "the opportunities for other traders to enter into or remain in that market must be significantly limited." *Id.* at 328. Although "neither the Court of Appeals nor the District Court [had] considered in detail the question of the relevant market," *id.* at 330, the Court in *Tampa Electric* examined the record and, after defining the relevant market, determined that the contract affected less than one percent of that market. After concluding, under the Clayton Act, that this share was "conservatively speaking, quite insubstantial," the Court went on summarily to reject the Sherman Act claims. *Id.* at 335 ("If [the contract] does not fall within the broader prescription of §3 of the Clayton Act it follows that it is not forbidden by those of the [Sherman Act].").

Following *Tampa Electric*, courts considering antitrust challenges to exclusive contracts have taken care to identify the share of the market foreclosed. Some courts have indicated that §3 of the Clayton Act and §1 of the Sherman Act require an equal degree of foreclosure before prohibiting exclusive contracts.... Other courts, however, have held that a higher market share must be foreclosed in order to establish a violation of the Sherman Act as compared to the Clayton Act....

Though what is "significant" may vary depending upon the antitrust provision under which an exclusive deal is challenged, it is clear that in all cases the plaintiff must both define the relevant market and prove the degree of foreclosure. This is a prudential requirement; exclusivity provisions in contracts may serve many useful purposes.... Permitting an antitrust action to proceed any time a firm enters into an exclusive deal would both discourage a presumptively legitimate business practice and encourage costly antitrust actions. Because an exclusive deal affecting a small fraction of a market clearly cannot have the requisite harmful effect upon competition, the requirement of a significant degree of foreclosure serves a useful screening function....

*[This district court rejected plaintiffs' exclusive-dealing claim under §1, and plaintiffs did not appeal that ruling.]*

Turning to §2, the [district] court stated: "the fact that Microsoft's arrangements with various [IAPs and other] firms did not foreclose enough of the relevant market to constitute a §1 violation in no way detracts from the Court's assignment of liability for the same arrangements under §2.... All of Microsoft's agreements, including the non-exclusive ones, severely restricted Netscape's access to those distribution channels leading most efficiently to the acquisition of browser usage share." *Conclusions of Law*, at 53.

On appeal Microsoft argues that "courts have applied the same standard to alleged exclusive dealing agreements under both Section 1 *and* Section 2," and it argues that the District Court's holding of no liability under §1 necessarily precludes holding it liable under §2.

* * *

The basic prudential concerns relevant to §§1 and 2 are admittedly the same: exclusive contracts are commonplace—particularly in the field of distribution—in our competitive, market economy, and imposing upon a firm with market power the risk of an antitrust suit every time it enters into such a contract, no matter how small the effect, would create an unacceptable and unjustified burden upon any such firm. At the same time, however, we agree with plaintiffs that a monopolist's use of exclusive contracts, in certain circumstances, may give rise to a §2 violation even though the contracts foreclose less than the roughly 40% or 50% share usually required in order to establish a §1 violation....

In this case, plaintiffs allege that, by closing to rivals a substantial percentage of the available opportunities for browser distribution, Microsoft managed to preserve its monopoly in the market for operating systems. The IAPs constitute one of the two major channels by which browsers can be distributed. *Findings of Fact* ¶ 242. Microsoft has exclusive deals with "fourteen of the top fifteen access providers in North America[, which] account for a large majority of all Internet access subscriptions in this part of the world." *Id.* ¶ 308. By ensuring that the "majority" of all IAP subscribers are offered IE either as the default browser or as the only browser, Microsoft's deals with the IAPs clearly have a significant effect in preserving its monopoly; they help keep usage of Navigator below the critical level necessary for Navigator or any other rival to pose a real threat to Microsoft's monopoly....

Plaintiffs having demonstrated a harm to competition, the burden falls upon Microsoft to defend its exclusive dealing contracts with IAPs by providing a procompetitive justification for them. Significantly, Microsoft's only explanation for its exclusive dealing is that it wants to keep developers focused upon its APIs—which is to say, it wants to preserve its power in the operating system market....That is not an unlawful end, but neither is it a procompetitive justification for the specific means here in question, namely exclusive dealing contracts with IAPs. Accordingly, we affirm the District Court's decision holding that Microsoft's exclusive contracts with IAPs are exclusionary devices, in violation of § 2 of the Sherman Act.

4. Dealings with Internet Content Providers, Independent Software Vendors, and Apple Computer

> *[The court next addressed Microsoft's promotional and exclusive deals with ICPs (independent content providers, who develop Websites), ISV's (independent software vendors, who develop and market applications that interoperate with Microsoft's operating systems, and Apple Computer). It first rejected, for lack of substantial evidence, the claim that Microsoft's deals with ICPs were anticompetitive. It upheld, however, the claim that Microsoft's exclusive deals with independent software vendors, under which they agreed to use and promote IE exclusively, were anticompetitive and, in the absence of justification, violated Section 2. The reasoning was similar to that applied to the exclusive deals with IAPs above. The court then turn to Microsoft's behavior vis-à-vis Apple Computer.]*

* * *

Finally, the District Court held that Microsoft's dealings with Apple violated the Sherman Act. *See Conclusions of Law*, at 42–43. Apple is vertically integrated: it makes both software (including an operating system, Mac OS), and hardware (the Macintosh line of computers). Microsoft primarily makes software, including, in addition to its operating system, a number of popular applications. One, called "Office," is a suite of business productivity applications that Microsoft has ported to Mac OS. The District Court found that "ninety percent of Mac OS users running a suite of office productivity applications [use] Microsoft's Mac Office." *Findings of Fact* ¶ 344. Further, the District Court found that:

> In 1997, Apple's business was in steep decline, and many doubted that the company would survive much longer....Many ISVs questioned the wisdom of continuing to spend time and money developing applications for the Mac OS. Had Microsoft announced in the midst of this atmosphere that it was ceasing to develop new versions of Mac Office, a great number of ISVs, customers, developers, and investors would have interpreted the announcement as Apple's death notice.

*Id.* ¶ 344. Microsoft recognized the importance to Apple of its continued support of Mac Office. *See id.* ¶ 347 (quoting internal Microsoft e-mail) ("[We] need a way to push these guys[, *i.e.*, Apple] and [threatening to cancel Mac Office] is the only one that seems to make them move."); *see also id.* ("[Microsoft Chairman Bill] Gates asked whether Microsoft could conceal from Apple in the coming month the fact that Microsoft was almost finished developing Mac Office 97."); *id.* at ¶ 354 ("I think…Apple should be using [IE] everywhere and if they don't do it, then we can use Office as a club.").

In June 1997 Microsoft Chairman Bill Gates determined that the company's negotiations with Apple " 'have not been going well at all.…Apple let us down on the browser by making Netscape the standard install.' Gates then reported that he had already called Apple's CEO…to ask 'how we should announce the cancellation of Mac Office.…'" *Id.* at ¶ 349. The District Court further found that, within a month of Gates' call, Apple and Microsoft had reached an agreement pursuant to which [Microsoft agreed to continue updating Mac Office for five years and Apple agreed to bundle IE with the Mac operating system and make it the default browser and exclusive desktop browser icon.]…The agreement also prohibits Apple from encouraging users to substitute another browser for IE, and states that Apple will "encourage its employees to use [IE]."

This exclusive deal between Microsoft and Apple has a substantial effect upon the distribution of rival browsers. If a browser developer ports its product to a second operating system, such as the Mac OS, it can continue to display a common set of APIs. Thus, usage share, not the underlying operating system, is the primary determinant of the platform challenge a browser may pose. Pre-installation of a browser (which can be accomplished either by including the browser with the operating system or by the OEM installing browser) is one of the two most important methods of browser distribution, and Apple had a not insignificant share of worldwide sales of operating systems. *See id.* ¶ 35 (Microsoft has 95% of the market not counting Apple and "well above" 80% with Apple included in the relevant market). Because Microsoft's exclusive contract with Apple has a substantial effect in restricting distribution of rival browsers, and because (as we have described several times above) reducing usage share of rival browsers serves to protect Microsoft's monopoly, its deal with Apple must be regarded as anticompetitive.…

Microsoft offers no procompetitive justification for the exclusive dealing arrangement.…Accordingly, we hold that the exclusive deal with Apple is exclusionary, in violation of § 2 of the Sherman Act.

### 5. Java

Java, a set of technologies developed by Sun Microsystems, is another type of middleware posing a potential threat to Windows' position as the ubiquitous platform for software development. *Findings of Fact* ¶ 28. [The Java product, or "Java runtime environment," included several components, one of which was a "Java virtual machine" (JVM), which translated Java programs into instructions for the operating system. The idea of JVM was to provide a "portable" Java environment that could be adapted or "ported" to different operating systems. Once so "ported," it would provide the same programming environment on all of them.]

In May 1995 Netscape agreed with Sun to distribute a copy of the Java runtime environment with every copy of Navigator, and "Navigator quickly became the principal vehicle by which Sun placed copies of its Java runtime environment on the PC systems of Windows users." *Id.* ¶ 76. Microsoft, too, agreed to promote the Java technologies—or so it seemed. For at the same time, Microsoft took steps "to maximize the difficulty with which applications written in Java could be ported from Windows to other platforms, and vice versa." *Conclusions of Law,* at 43. Specifically, the District Court found that Microsoft took four steps to exclude Java from developing as a viable cross-platform threat: (a) designing a JVM incompatible with the one developed by Sun; (b) entering into contracts, the so-called "First Wave Agreements," requiring major ISVs to promote Microsoft's JVM exclusively; (c) deceiving Java developers about the Windows-specific nature of the tools it distributed to them; and (d) coercing Intel to stop aiding Sun in improving the Java technologies.

### a. The incompatible JVM

The District Court held that Microsoft engaged in exclusionary conduct by developing and promoting its own JVM. *Conclusions of Law,* at 43–44. Sun had already developed a JVM for the Windows operating system when Microsoft began work on its version. The JVM developed by Microsoft allows Java applications to run faster on Windows than does Sun's JVM, *Findings of Fact* ¶ 389, but a Java application designed to work with Microsoft's JVM does not work with Sun's JVM and vice versa.

\* \* \*

[A] monopolist does not violate the antitrust laws simply by developing a product that is incompatible with those of its rivals....In order to violate the antitrust laws, the incompatible product must have an anticompetitive effect that outweighs any procompetitive justification for the design. Microsoft's JVM is not only incompatible with Sun's, it allows Java applications to run faster on Windows than does Sun's JVM. Microsoft's faster JVM lured Java developers into using Microsoft's developer tools, and Microsoft offered those tools deceptively, as we discuss below. The JVM, however, does allow applications to run more swiftly and does not itself have any anticompetitive effect. Therefore, we reverse the District Court's imposition of liability for Microsoft's development and promotion of its JVM.

### b. The First Wave Agreements

The District Court also found that Microsoft entered into First Wave Agreements with dozens of ISVs to use Microsoft's JVM. *See Findings of Fact* ¶ 401 ("In exchange for costly technical support and other blandishments, Microsoft induced dozens of important ISVs to make their Java applications reliant on Windows-specific technologies and to refrain from distributing to Windows users JVMs that complied with Sun's standards."). Again, we reject the District Court's condemnation of low but non-predatory pricing by Microsoft.

To the extent Microsoft's First Wave Agreements with the ISVs conditioned receipt of Windows technical information upon the ISVs' agreement to promote Microsoft's JVM exclusively, they raise a different competitive concern. The District Court found that, although not literally exclusive, the deals were exclusive in practice because they required developers to make Microsoft's JVM the default in the software they developed.

While the District Court did not enter precise findings as to the effect of the First Wave Agreements upon the overall distribution of rival JVMs, the record indicates that Microsoft's deals with the major ISVs had a significant effect upon JVM promotion. As discussed above, the products of First Wave ISVs reached millions of consumers....Moreover, Microsoft's exclusive deals with the leading ISVs took place against a backdrop of foreclosure: the District Court found that "when Netscape announced in May 1995 [prior to Microsoft's execution of the First Wave Agreements] that it would include with every copy of Navigator a copy of a Windows JVM that complied with Sun's standards, it appeared that Sun's Java implementation would achieve the necessary ubiquity on Windows." *Findings of Fact* ¶394. As discussed above, however, Microsoft undertook a number of anticompetitive actions that seriously reduced the distribution of Navigator, and the District Court found that those actions thereby seriously impeded distribution of Sun's JVM. *Conclusions of Law*, at 43–44. Because Microsoft's agreements foreclosed a substantial portion of the field for JVM distribution and because, in so doing, they protected Microsoft's monopoly from a middleware threat, they are anticompetitive.

Microsoft offered no procompetitive justification for the default clause that made the First Wave Agreements exclusive as a practical matter. *See Findings of Fact* ¶401. Because the cumulative effect of the deals is anticompetitive and because Microsoft has no procompetitive justification for them, we hold that the provisions in the First Wave Agreements requiring use of Microsoft's JVM as the default are exclusionary, in violation of the Sherman Act.

### c. Deception of Java developers

Microsoft's "Java implementation" included, in addition to a JVM, a set of software development tools it created to assist ISVs in designing Java applications. The District Court found that, not only were these tools incompatible with Sun's cross-platform aspirations for Java — no violation, to be sure — but Microsoft deceived Java developers regarding the Windows-specific nature of the tools.... That is, developers who relied upon Microsoft's public commitment to cooperate with Sun and who used Microsoft's tools to develop what Microsoft led them to believe were cross-platform applications ended up producing applications that would run only on the Windows operating system.

When specifically accused by a *PC Week* reporter of fragmenting Java standards so as to prevent cross-platform uses, Microsoft denied the accusation and indicated it was only "adding rich platform support" to what remained a crossplatform implementation. An e-mail message internal to Microsoft, written shortly after the conversation with the reporter, shows otherwise:

> [The reporter] accused us of being schizo with this vs. our java approach, i said he misunderstood [ — ]that [with Java] we are merely trying to add rich platform support to an interop layer....this plays well....at this point its [*sic*] not good to create MORE noise around our win32 java classes. instead we should just quietly grow j [(Microsoft's development tools)] share and assume that people will take more advantage of our classes without ever realizing they are building win 32-only java apps.

Finally, other Microsoft documents confirm that Microsoft intended to deceive Java developers, and predicted that the effect of its actions would be to generate Windows-dependent Java applications that their developers believed would be cross-platform; these documents also indicate that Microsoft's ultimate objective was to thwart Java's threat to Microsoft's monopoly in the market for operating systems. One Microsoft document, for example, states as a strategic goal: "Kill cross-platform Java by growing the polluted Java market." [It also notes that "[c]ross-platform capability is by far *the* number one reason for choosing/using Java." (emphasis in original)].

Microsoft's conduct related to its Java developer tools served to protect its monopoly of the operating system in a manner not attributable either to the superiority of the operating system or to the acumen of its makers, and therefore was anticompetitive. Unsurprisingly, Microsoft offers no procompetitive explanation for its campaign to deceive developers. Accordingly, we conclude this conduct is exclusionary, in violation of §2 of the Sherman Act.

## d. The threat to Intel

The District Court held that Microsoft also acted unlawfully with respect to Java by using its "monopoly power to prevent firms such as Intel from aiding in the creation of cross-platform interfaces." *Conclusions of Law,* at 43. In 1995 Intel was in the process of developing a high performance, Windows-compatible JVM. Microsoft wanted Intel to abandon that effort because a fast, cross-platform JVM would threaten Microsoft's monopoly in the operating system market. At an August 1995 meeting, Microsoft's Gates told Intel that its "cooperation with Sun and Netscape to develop a Java runtime environment...was one of the issues threatening to undermine cooperation between Intel and Microsoft." *Findings of Fact* ¶ 396. Three months later, "Microsoft's Paul Maritz told a senior Intel executive that Intel's [adaptation of its multimedia software to comply with] Sun's Java standards was as inimical to Microsoft as Microsoft's support for non-Intel microprocessors would be to Intel." *Id.* ¶ 405.

Intel nonetheless continued to undertake initiatives related to Java.

\* \* \*

Intel finally capitulated in 1997, after Microsoft delivered the *coup de grace.*

One of Intel's competitors, called AMD, solicited support from Microsoft for its "3DX" technology.... Microsoft's Allchin asked Gates whether Microsoft should support 3DX, despite the fact that Intel would oppose it. Gates responded: "If Intel has a real problem with us supporting this then they will have to stop supporting Java Multimedia the way they are. I would gladly give up supporting this if they would back off from their work on JAVA." *Id.* ¶ 406.

Microsoft's internal documents and deposition testimony confirm both the anticompetitive effect and intent of its actions.

\* \* \*

Microsoft does not deny the facts found by the District Court, nor does it offer any procompetitive justification for pressuring Intel not to support cross-platform Java. Microsoft lamely characterizes its threat to Intel as "advice." The District Court, however, found that Microsoft's "advice" to Intel to stop aiding cross-platform Java was backed by the threat of retaliation, and this conclusion is supported by the evidence cited above. Therefore we affirm the conclusion that Microsoft's threats to Intel were exclusionary, in violation of § 2 of the Sherman Act.

## 6. Course of Conduct

The District Court held that, apart from Microsoft's specific acts, Microsoft was liable under § 2 based upon its general "course of conduct."

\* \* \*

[T]he District Court did not point to any series of acts, each of which harms competition only slightly but the cumulative effect of which is significant enough to form an independent basis for liability. The "course of conduct" section of the District Court's opinion contains, with one exception, only broad, summarizing conclusions. The only specific acts to which the court refers are Microsoft's expenditures in promoting its browser...which we have explained are not in themselves unlawful. Because the District Court identifies no other specific acts as a basis for "course of conduct" liability, we reverse its conclusion that Microsoft's course of conduct separately violates § 2 of the Sherman Act.

## C. Causation

As a final parry, Microsoft urges this court to reverse on the monopoly mainte-nance claim, because plaintiffs never established a causal link between Microsoft's an-ticompetitive conduct, in particular its foreclosure of Netscape's and Java's distribu-tion channels, and the maintenance of Microsoft's operating system monopoly. *See Findings of Fact* ¶ 411 ("There is insufficient evidence to find that, absent Microsoft's actions, Navigator and Java already would have ignited genuine competition in the market for Intel-compatible PC operating systems."). This is the flip side of Mi-crosoft's earlier argument that the District Court should have included middleware in the relevant market. According to Microsoft, the District Court cannot simultane-ously find that middleware is not a reasonable substitute *and* that Microsoft's exclu-sionary conduct contributed to the maintenance of monopoly power in the operating system market. Microsoft claims that the first finding depended on the court's view that middleware does not pose a serious threat to Windows... while the second find-ing required the court to find that Navigator and Java would have developed into seri-ous enough cross-platform threats to erode the applications barrier to entry. We dis-agree.

Microsoft points to no case, and we can find none, standing for the proposition that, as to § 2 *liability* in an equitable enforcement action, plaintiffs must present direct proof that a defendant's continued monopoly power is precisely attributable to its anticom-petitive conduct.

* * *

To require that § 2 liability turn on a plaintiff's ability or inability to reconstruct the hypothetical marketplace absent a defendant's anticompetitive conduct would only en-courage monopolists to take more and earlier anticompetitive action.

We may infer causation when exclusionary conduct is aimed at producers of nascent competitive technologies as well as when it is aimed at producers of estab-lished substitutes. Admittedly, in the former case there is added uncertainty, inas-much as nascent threats are merely *potential* substitutes. But the underlying proof problem is the same — neither plaintiffs nor the court can confidently reconstruct a product's hypothetical technological development in a world absent the defendant's exclusionary conduct. To some degree, "the defendant is made to suffer the uncertain consequences of its own undesirable conduct." 3 AREEDA & HOVENKAMP, ANTITRUST LAW ¶ 651c, at 78.

Given this rather edentulous test for causation, the question in this case is not whether Java or Navigator would actually have developed into viable platform substi-tutes, but (1) whether as a general matter the exclusion of nascent threats is the type of conduct that is reasonably capable of contributing significantly to a defendant's contin-ued monopoly power and (2) whether Java and Navigator reasonably constituted nascent threats at the time Microsoft engaged in the anticompetitive conduct at issue. As to the first, suffice it to say that it would be inimical to the purpose of the Sherman Act to allow monopolists free reign to squash nascent, albeit unproven, competitors at will — particularly in industries marked by rapid technological advance and frequent paradigm shifts. *Findings of Fact* ¶¶ 59–60. As to the second, the District Court made ample findings that both Navigator and Java showed potential as middleware platform threats. *Findings of Fact* ¶¶ 68–77. Counsel for Microsoft admitted as much at oral argu-ment. ("There are no constraints on output. Marginal costs are essentially zero. And there are to some extent network effects. So a company like Netscape founded in 1994 can be by the middle of 1995 clearly a potentially lethal competitor to Windows because it can supplant its position in the market because of the characteristics of these markets.").

Microsoft's concerns over causation have more purchase in connection with the appropriate remedy issue, *i.e.*, whether the court should impose a structural remedy or merely enjoin the offensive conduct at issue. As we point out later in this opinion, divestiture is a remedy that is imposed only with great caution, in part because its long-term efficacy is rarely certain.... Absent some measure of confidence that there has been an actual loss to competition that needs to be restored, wisdom counsels against adopting radical structural relief. *See* 3 AREEDA & HOVENKAMP, ANTITRUST LAW ¶ 653b, at 91–92 ("More extensive equitable relief, particularly remedies such as divestiture designed to eliminate the monopoly altogether, raise more serious questions and require a clearer indication of a significant causal connection between the conduct and creation or maintenance of the market power."). But these queries go to questions of remedy, not liability. In short, causation affords Microsoft no defense to liability for its unlawful actions undertaken to maintain its monopoly in the operating system market.

## III. ATTEMPTED MONOPOLIZATION

Microsoft further challenges the District Court's determination of liability for "attempting to monopolize...any part of the trade or commerce among the several States." 15 U.S.C. § 2 (1997). To establish a § 2 violation for attempted monopolization, "a plaintiff must prove (1) that the defendant has engaged in predatory or anticompetitive conduct with (2) a specific intent to monopolize and (3) a dangerous probability of achieving monopoly power." *Spectrum Sports, Inc. v. McQuillan*, 506 U.S. 447, 456, 122 L. Ed. 2d 247, 113 S. Ct. 884 (1993).... Because a deficiency on any one of the three will defeat plaintiffs' claim, we look no further than plaintiffs' failure to prove a dangerous probability of achieving monopoly power in the putative browser market.

\* \* \*

The determination whether a dangerous probability of success exists is a particularly fact-intensive inquiry. The District Court determined that "the evidence supports the conclusion that Microsoft's actions did pose such a danger." *Conclusions of Law*, at 45.

\* \* \*

At the outset we note a pervasive flaw in the District Court's and plaintiffs' discussion of attempted monopolization. Simply put, plaintiffs have made the same argument under two different headings—monopoly maintenance and attempted monopolization. They have relied upon Microsoft's § 2 liability for monopolization of the operating system market as a presumptive indicator of attempted monopolization of an entirely different market. The District Court implicitly accepted this approach: It agreed with plaintiffs that the events that formed the basis for the § 2 monopolization claim "warranted *additional* liability as an illegal attempt to amass monopoly power in the browser market." (emphasis added). Thus, plaintiffs and the District Court failed to recognize the need for an analysis wholly independent of the conclusions and findings on monopoly maintenance.

To establish a dangerous probability of success, plaintiffs must as a threshold matter show that the browser market can be monopolized, *i.e.*, that a hypothetical monopolist in that market could enjoy market power. This, in turn, requires plaintiffs (1) to define the relevant market and (2) to demonstrate that substantial barriers to entry protect that market. Because plaintiffs have not carried their burden on either prong, we reverse without remand.

## A. Relevant Market

A court's evaluation of an attempted monopolization claim must include a definition of the relevant market. *See Spectrum Sports*, 506 U.S. at 455–56. Such a definition establishes a context for evaluating the defendant's actions as well as for measuring whether the challenged conduct presented a dangerous probability of monopolization. The District Court omitted this element of the *Spectrum Sports* inquiry.

Defining a market for an attempted monopolization claim involves the same steps as defining a market for a monopoly maintenance claim, namely a detailed description of the purpose of a browser—what functions may be included and what are not—and an examination of the substitutes that are part of the market and those that are not.... The District Court never engaged in such an analysis nor entered detailed findings defining what a browser is or what products might constitute substitutes.

\* \* \*

Because the determination of a relevant market is a factual question to be resolved by the District Court,... we would normally remand the case so that the District Court could formulate an appropriate definition....A remand on market definition is unnecessary, however, because the District Court's imprecision is directly traceable to plaintiffs' failure to articulate and identify evidence before the District Court as to (1) what constitutes a browser (*i.e.*, what are the technological components of or functionalities provided by a browser) and (2) why certain other products are not reasonable substitutes (*e.g.*, browser shells or viewers for individual internet extensions, such as Real Audio Player or Adobe Acrobat Reader)....Indeed, when plaintiffs in their Proposed Findings of Fact attempted to define a relevant market for the attempt claim, they pointed only to their separate products analysis for the tying claim....However, the separate products analysis for tying purposes is not a substitute for the type of market definition that *Spectrum Sports* requires.

\* \* \*

## B. Barriers to Entry

Because a firm cannot possess monopoly power in a market unless that market is also protected by significant barriers to entry...it follows that a firm cannot threaten to achieve monopoly power in a market unless that market is, or will be, similarly protected. *See Spectrum Sports*, 506 U.S. at 456 ("In order to determine whether there is a dangerous probability of monopolization, courts have found it necessary to consider...the defendant's ability to lessen or destroy competition in that market.") (citing cases). Plaintiffs have the burden of establishing barriers to entry into a properly defined relevant market....Plaintiffs must not only show that barriers to entry protect the properly defined browser market, but that those barriers are "significant." *See United States v. Baker Hughes Inc.*, 285 U.S. App. D.C. 222, 908 F.2d 981, 987 (D.C. Cir. 1990). Whether there are significant barriers to entry cannot, of course, be answered absent an appropriate market definition; thus, plaintiffs' failure on that score alone is dispositive. But even were we to assume a properly defined market, for example browsers consisting of a graphical interface plus internet protocols, plaintiffs nonetheless failed to carry their burden on barriers to entry.

Contrary to plaintiffs' contention on appeal...none of the District Court's statements constitutes a finding of barriers to entry into the web browser market....

\* \* \*

Giving plaintiffs and the District Court the benefit of the doubt, we might remand if the *possible existence* of entry barriers resulting from the *possible creation* and *exploitation* of network effects in the browser market were the only concern. That is not enough to carry the day, however, because the District Court did not make two key findings: (1) that network effects were a necessary or even probable, rather than merely possible, consequence of high market share in the browser market; and (2) that a barrier to entry resulting from network effects would be "significant" enough to confer monopoly power. Again, these deficiencies are in large part traceable to plaintiffs' own failings.... The proffered testimony contains no evidence regarding the cost of "porting" websites to different browsers or the potentially different economic incentives facing ICPs, as opposed to ISVs, in their decision to incur costs to do so. Simply invoking the phrase "network effects" without pointing to more evidence does not suffice to carry plaintiffs' burden in this respect.

Any doubt that we may have had regarding remand instead of outright reversal on the barriers to entry question was dispelled by plaintiffs' arguments on attempted monopolization before this court. Not only did plaintiffs fail to articulate a website barrier to entry *theory* in either their brief or at oral argument, they failed to point the court to evidence in the record that would support a finding that Microsoft would *likely* erect *significant* barriers to entry upon acquisition of a dominant market share.

Plaintiffs did not devote the same resources to the attempted monopolization claim as they did to the monopoly maintenance claim. But both claims require evidentiary and theoretical rigor. Because plaintiffs failed to make their case on attempted monopolization both in the District Court and before this court, there is no reason to give them a second chance to flesh out a claim that should have been fleshed out the first time around. Accordingly, we reverse the District Court's determination of §2 liability for attempted monopolization.

## IV. TYING

Microsoft also contests the District Court's determination of liability under §1 of the Sherman Act. The District Court concluded that Microsoft's contractual and technological bundling of the IE web browser (the "tied" product) with its Windows operating system ("OS") (the "tying" product) resulted in a tying arrangement that was *per se* unlawful. *Conclusions of Law,* at 47–51. We hold that the rule of reason, rather than *per se* analysis, should govern the legality of tying arrangements involving platform software products.... [T]he arrangement before us...offer[s] the first up-close look at the technological integration of added functionality into software that serves as a platform for third-party applications. There being no close parallel in prior antitrust cases, simplistic application of *per se* tying rules carries a serious risk of harm. Accordingly, we vacate the District Court's finding of a *per se* tying violation and remand the case. Plaintiffs may on remand pursue their tying claim under the rule of reason.

The facts underlying the tying allegation substantially overlap with those set forth...in connection with the §2 monopoly maintenance claim. The key District Court findings are that: (1) Microsoft required licensees of Windows 95 and 98 also to license IE as a bundle at a single price...; (2) Microsoft refused to allow OEMs to uninstall or remove IE from the Windows desktop...; (3) Microsoft designed Windows 98 in a way that withheld from consumers the ability to remove IE by use of the Add/Remove Programs utility...; and (4) Microsoft designed Windows 98 to override the user's choice of default web browser in certain circumstances....The court found that these acts constituted a *per se* tying violation....Although the District Court also found that Microsoft commingled operating system-only and browser-only routines in the same library files...it did not include this as a basis for tying liability despite plaintiffs' request that it do so....

There are four elements to a *per se* tying violation: (1) the tying and tied goods are two separate products; (2) the defendant has market power in the tying product market; (3) the defendant affords consumers no choice but to purchase the tied product from it; and (4) the tying arrangement forecloses a substantial volume of commerce. *See Eastman Kodak Co. v. Image Tech. Servs., Inc.*, 504 U.S. 451, 461–62, 119 L. Ed. 2d 265, 112 S. Ct. 2072 (1992); *Jefferson Parish Hosp. Dist. No. 2 v. Hyde*, 466 U.S. 2, 12–18, 80 L. Ed. 2d 2, 104 S. Ct. 1551 (1984).

Microsoft does not dispute that it bound Windows and IE in the four ways the District Court cited. Instead it argues that Windows (the tying good) and IE browsers (the tied good) are not "separate products,"...and that it did not substantially foreclose competing browsers from the tied product market...(Microsoft also contends that it does not have monopoly power in the tying product market...but, for reasons given in Section II.A, we uphold the District Court's finding to the contrary.)

* * *

### A. Separate-Products Inquiry Under the *Per Se* Test

The requirement that a practice involve two separate products before being condemned as an illegal tie started as a purely linguistic requirement: unless products are separate, one cannot be "tied" to the other. Indeed, the nature of the products involved in early tying cases—intuitively distinct items such as a movie projector and a film...led courts either to disregard the separate-products question...or to discuss it only in passing....It was not until *Times-Picayune Publishing Co. v. United States*, 345 U.S. 594, 97 L. Ed. 1277, 73 S. Ct. 872 (1953), that the separate-products issue became a distinct element of the test for an illegal tie. Even that case engaged in a rather cursory inquiry into whether ads sold in the morning edition of a paper were a separate product from ads sold in the evening edition.

The first case to give content to the separate-products test was *Jefferson Parish*. That case addressed a tying arrangement in which a hospital conditioned surgical care at its facility on the purchase of anesthesiological services from an affiliated medical group. The facts were a challenge for casual separate-products analysis because the tied service—anesthesia—was neither intuitively distinct from nor intuitively contained within the tying service—surgical care. A further complication was that, soon after the Court enunciated the *per se* rule for tying liability in *International Salt Co. v. United States*, 332 U.S. 392, 396, 92 L. Ed. 20, 68 S. Ct. 12 (1947), and *Northern Pacific Railway Co. v. United States*, 356 U.S. 1, 5–7, 2 L. Ed. 2d 545, 78 S. Ct. 514 (1958), new economic research began to cast doubt on the assumption, voiced by the Court when it established the rule, that "'tying agreements serve hardly any purpose beyond the suppression of competition,'" *id.* at 6 (quoting *Standard Oil of Cal. v. United States*, 337 U.S. 293, 305–6, 93 L. Ed. 1371, 69 S. Ct. 1051 (1949))....

The *Jefferson Parish* Court resolved the matter in two steps. First, it clarified that "the answer to the question whether one or two products are involved" does not turn "on the functional relation between them...." *Jefferson Parish*, 466 U.S. at 19; *see also* 466 U.S. at 19 n.30. In other words, the mere fact that two items are complements, that "one...is useless without the other," does not make them a single "product" for purposes of tying law....Second, reasoning that the "definitional question [whether two distinguishable products are involved] depends on whether the arrangement may have the type of competitive consequences addressed by the rule [against tying],"...the Court decreed that "no tying arrangement can exist unless there is a sufficient *demand* for the purchase of anesthesiological services separate from hospital services to identify a distinct product market in which it is *efficient* to offer anesthesiological services separately from hospital service[.]"

\* \* \*

The Court proceeded to examine direct and indirect evidence of consumer demand for the tied product separate from the tying product. Direct evidence addresses the question whether, when given a choice, consumers purchase the tied good from the tying good maker, or from other firms. The Court took note, for example, of testimony that patients and surgeons often requested specific anesthesiologists not associated with a hospital....Indirect evidence includes the behavior of firms without market power in the tying good market, presumably on the notion that (competitive) supply follows demand. If competitive firms always bundle the tying and tied goods, then they are a single product....Here the Court noted that only 27% of anesthesiologists in markets other than the defendant's had financial relationships with hospitals, and that, unlike radiologists and pathologists, anesthesiologists were not usually employed by hospitals, *i.e.*, bundled with hospital services....With both direct and indirect evidence concurring, the Court determined that hospital surgery and anesthesiological services were distinct goods.

To understand the logic behind the Court's consumer demand test, consider first the postulated harms from tying. The core concern is that tying prevents goods from competing directly for consumer choice on their merits, *i.e.*, being selected as a result of "buyers' independent judgment,"....With a tie, a buyer's "freedom to select the best bargain in the second market [could be] impaired by his need to purchase the tying product, and perhaps by an inability to evaluate the true cost of either product...." Direct competition on the merits of the tied product is foreclosed when the tying product either is sold only in a bundle with the tied product or, though offered separately, is sold at a bundled price, so that the buyer pays the same price whether he takes the tied product or not. In both cases, a consumer buying the tying product becomes entitled to the tied product; he will therefore likely be unwilling to buy a competitor's version of the tied product even if, making his own price/quality assessment, that is what he would prefer.

But not all ties are bad. Bundling obviously saves distribution and consumer transaction costs. 9 PHILLIP E. AREEDA, ANTITRUST LAW ¶ 1703g2, at 51–52 (1991). This is likely to be true, to take some examples from the computer industry, with the integration of math co-processors and memory into microprocessor chips and the inclusion of spell checkers in word processors....Bundling can also capitalize on certain economies of scope. A possible example is the "shared" library files that perform OS and browser functions with the very same lines of code and thus may save drive space from the clutter of redundant routines and memory when consumers use both the OS and browser simultaneously....Indeed, if there were no efficiencies from a tie (including economizing on consumer transaction costs such as the time and effort involved in choice), we would expect distinct consumer demand for each individual component of every good. In a competitive market with zero transaction costs, the computers on which this opinion was written would only be sold piecemeal—keyboard, monitor, mouse, central processing unit, disk drive, and memory all sold in separate transactions and likely by different manufacturers.

Recognizing the potential benefits from tying...the Court in *Jefferson Parish* forged a separate-products test that, like those of market power and substantial foreclosure, attempts to screen out false positives under *per se* analysis. The consumer demand test is a rough proxy for whether a tying arrangement may, on balance, be welfare-enhancing, and unsuited to *per se* condemnation. In the abstract, of course, there is always direct separate demand for products: assuming choice is available at zero cost, consumers will prefer it to no choice. Only when the efficiencies from bundling are dominated by the benefits to choice for enough consumers, however, will we actually observe consumers making independent purchases. In other words, perceptible separate demand is inversely proportional to net efficiencies. On the supply side, firms without market power will bundle two goods only when the cost savings from joint sale outweigh the value consumers place on separate choice. So bundling by all competitive firms implies strong net efficiencies. If a court finds either that there is no noticeable separate demand for the tied product or, there being no convincing direct evidence of separate demand, that the entire "competitive fringe" engages in the same behavior as the defendant…then the tying and tied products should be declared one product and *per se* liability should be rejected.

Before concluding our exegesis of *Jefferson Parish*'s separate-products test, we should clarify two things. First, *Jefferson Parish* does not endorse a direct inquiry into the efficiencies of a bundle. Rather, it proposes easy-to-administer proxies for net efficiency. In describing the separate-products test we discuss efficiencies only to explain the rationale behind the consumer demand inquiry. To allow the separate-products test to become a detailed inquiry into possible welfare consequences would turn a screening test into the very process it is expected to render unnecessary….

Second, the separate-products test is not a one-sided inquiry into the cost savings from a bundle. Although *Jefferson Parish* acknowledged that prior lower court cases looked at cost-savings to decide separate products…the Court conspicuously did not adopt that approach in its disposition of tying arrangement before it. Instead it chose proxies that balance costs savings against reduction in consumer choice.

With this background, we now turn to the separate products inquiry before us. The District Court found that many consumers, if given the option, would choose their browser separately from the OS. *Findings of Fact* ¶ 51 (noting that "corporate consumers…prefer to standardize on the same browser across different [OSs]" at the workplace). Turning to industry custom, the court found that, although all major OS vendors bundled browsers with their OSs, these companies either sold versions without a browser, or allowed OEMs or end-users either not to install the bundled browser or in any event to "uninstall" it. The court did not discuss the record evidence as to whether OS vendors other than Microsoft sold at a bundled price, with no discount for a browserless OS, perhaps because the record evidence on the issue was in conflict….

Microsoft does not dispute that many consumers demand alternative browsers. But on industry custom Microsoft contends that no other firm requires non-removal because no other firm has invested the resources to integrate web browsing as deeply into its OS as Microsoft has….(We here use the term "integrate" in the rather simple sense of converting individual goods into components of a single physical object (*e.g.*, a computer as it leaves the OEM, or a disk or sets of disks), without any normative implication that such integration is desirable or achieves special advantages. *Cf. United States v. Microsoft Corp.*, 331 U.S. App. D.C. 121, 147 F.3d 935, 950 (D.C. Cir. 1998) ("*Microsoft II*").) Microsoft contends not only that its integration of IE into Windows is innovative and beneficial but also that it requires non-removal of IE. In our discussion of monopoly maintenance we find that these claims fail the efficiency balancing applicable in that context. But the separate-products analysis is supposed to perform its function as a proxy *without* embarking on any direct analysis of efficiency. Accordingly, Microsoft's implicit argument—that in this case looking to a competitive fringe is inadequate to evaluate fully its potentially innovative technological integration, that such a comparison is between apples and oranges—poses a legitimate objection to the operation of *Jefferson Parish*'s separate-products test for the *per se* rule.

In fact there is merit to Microsoft's broader argument that *Jefferson Parish*'s consumer demand test would "chill innovation to the detriment of consumers by preventing firms from integrating into their products new functionality previously provided by standalone products—and hence, by definition, subject to separate consumer demand."...The *per se* rule's direct consumer demand and indirect industry custom inquiries are, as a general matter, backward-looking and therefore systematically poor proxies for overall efficiency in the presence of new and innovative integration.... The direct consumer demand test focuses on historic consumer behavior, likely before integration, and the indirect industry custom test looks at firms that, unlike the defendant, may not have integrated the tying and tied goods. Both tests compare incomparables— the defendant's decision to bundle in the presence of integration, on the one hand, and consumer and competitor calculations in its absence, on the other. If integration has efficiency benefits, these may be ignored by the *Jefferson Parish* proxies. Because one cannot be sure beneficial integration will be protected by the other elements of the *per se* rule, simple application of that rule's separate-products test may make consumers worse off.

In light of the monopoly maintenance section, obviously, we do not find that Microsoft's integration is welfare-enhancing that it should be absolved of tying liability. Rather, we heed Microsoft's warning that the separate-products element of the *per se* rule may not give newly integrated products a fair shake.

## B. *Per Se* Analysis Inappropriate for this Case

We now address directly the larger question as we see it: whether standard *per se* analysis should be applied "off the shelf" to evaluate the defendant's tying arrangement, one which involves software that serves as a platform for third party applications. There is no doubt that "it is far too late in the history of our antitrust jurisprudence to question the proposition that certain tying arrangements pose an unacceptable risk of stifling competition and therefore are unreasonable 'per se.'" *Jefferson Parish*, 466 U.S. at 9....But there are strong reasons to doubt that the integration of additional software functionality into an OS falls among these arrangements. Applying *per se* analysis to such an amalgamation creates undue risks of error and of deterring welfare-enhancing innovation.

The Supreme Court has warned that " 'it is only after considerable experience with certain business relationships that courts classify them as *per se* violations....'" *Broad. Music*, 441 U.S. at 9 (quoting *Topco Assocs.*, 405 U.S. at 607–8)...Yet the sort of tying arrangement attacked here is unlike any the Supreme Court has considered. The early Supreme Court cases on tying dealt with arrangements whereby the sale or lease of a patented product was conditioned on the purchase of certain unpatented products from the patentee....Later Supreme Court tying cases did not involve market power derived from patents, but continued to involve contractual ties. *See Times-Picayune*, 345 U.S. 594, 97 L. Ed. 1277, 73 S. Ct. 872 (1953) (defendant newspaper conditioned the purchase of ads in its evening edition on the purchase of ads in its morning edition); *N. Pac. Ry. v. United States*, 356 U.S. 1, 78 S. Ct. 514, 2 L. Ed. 2d

545 (1958) (defendant railroad leased land only on the condition that products manufactured on the land be shipped on its railways); *United States v. Loew's Inc.*, 371 U.S. 38, 9 L. Ed. 2d 11, 83 S. Ct. 97 (1962) (defendant distributor of copyrighted feature films conditioned the sale of desired films on the purchase of undesired films); *U.S. Steel Corp. v. Fortner Enters., Inc.*, 429 U.S. 610, 51 L. Ed. 2d 80, 97 S. Ct. 861 (1977) (*"Fortner II"*) (defendant steel company conditioned access to low interest loans on the purchase of the defendant's prefabricated homes); *Jefferson Parish*, 466 U.S. 2, 80 L. Ed. 2d 2, 104 S. Ct. 1551 (1984) (defendant hospital conditioned use of its operating rooms on the purchase of anesthesiological services from a medical group associated with the hospital); *Eastman Kodak*, 504 U.S. 451, 119 L. Ed. 2d 265, 112 S. Ct. 2072 (1992) (defendant photocopying machine manufacturer conditioned the sale of replacement parts for its machines on the use of the defendant's repair services).

In none of these cases was the tied good physically and technologically integrated with the tying good. Nor did the defendants ever argue that their tie improved the value of the tying product to users and to makers of complementary goods. In those cases where the defendant claimed that use of the tied good made the tying good more valuable to users, the Court ruled that the same result could be achieved via quality standards for substitutes of the tied good.... Here Microsoft argues that IE and Windows are an integrated physical product and that the bundling of IE APIs with Windows makes the latter a better applications platform for third-party software. It is unclear how the benefits from IE APIs could be achieved by quality standards for different browser manufacturers. We do not pass judgment on Microsoft's claims regarding the benefits from integration of its APIs. We merely note that these and other novel, purported efficiencies suggest that judicial "experience" provides little basis for believing that, "because of their pernicious effect on competition and lack of any redeeming virtue," a software firm's decisions to sell multiple functionalities as a package should be "conclusively presumed to be unreasonable and therefore illegal without elaborate inquiry as to the precise harm they have caused or the business excuse for their use." *N. Pac. Ry.*, 356 U.S. at 5 (emphasis added).

Nor have we found much insight into software integration among the decisions of lower federal courts.

\* \* \*

While the paucity of cases examining software bundling suggests a high risk that *per se* analysis may produce inaccurate results, the nature of the platform software market affirmatively suggests that *per se* rules might stunt valuable innovation. We have in mind two reasons.

First, as we explained in the previous section, the separate products test is a poor proxy for net efficiency from newly integrated products. Under *per se* analysis the first firm to merge previously distinct functionalities (*e.g.*, the inclusion of starter motors in automobiles) or to eliminate entirely the need for a second function (*e.g.*, the invention of the stain resistant carpet) risks being condemned as having tied two separate products because at the moment of integration there will appear to be a robust "distinct" market for the tied product.... Rule of reason analysis, however, affords the first mover an opportunity to demonstrate that an efficiency gain from its "tie" adequately offsets any distortion of consumer choice.

\* \* \*

The failure of the separate-products test to screen out certain cases of productive integration is particularly troubling in platform software markets such as that in which the defendant competes. Not only is integration common in such markets, but it is common among firms without market power. We have already reviewed evidence that nearly all competitive OS vendors also bundle browsers. Moreover, plaintiffs do not dispute that OS vendors can and do incorporate basic internet plumbing and other useful functionality into their OSs.... Firms without market power have no incentive to package different pieces of software together unless there are efficiency gains from doing so. The ubiquity of bundling in competitive platform software markets should give courts reason to pause before condemning such behavior in less competitive markets.

Second, because of the pervasively innovative character of platform software markets, tying in such markets may produce efficiencies that courts have not previously encountered and thus the Supreme Court had not factored into the *per se* rule as originally conceived. For example, the bundling of a browser with OSs enables an independent software developer to count on the presence of the browser's APIs, if any, on consumers' machines and thus to omit them from its own package.... It is true that software developers can bundle the browser APIs they need with their own products,... but that may force consumers to pay twice for the same API if it is bundled with two different software programs. It is also true that OEMs can include APIs with the computers they sell,... but diffusion of uniform APIs by that route may be inferior. First, many OEMs serve special subsets of Windows consumers, such as home or corporate or academic users. If just one of these OEMs decides not to bundle an API because it does not benefit enough of its clients, ISVs that use that API might have to bundle it with every copy of their program. Second, there may be a substantial lag before all OEMs bundle the same set of APIs—a lag inevitably aggravated by the first phenomenon. In a field where programs change very rapidly, delays in the spread of a necessary element (here, the APIs) may be very costly. Of course, these arguments may not justify Microsoft's decision to bundle APIs in this case, particularly because Microsoft did not merely bundle with Windows the APIs from IE, but an entire browser application (sometimes even without APIs...). A justification for bundling a component of software may not be one for bundling the entire software package, especially given the malleability of software code.... Furthermore, the interest in efficient API diffusion obviously supplies a far stronger justification for simple price-bundling than for Microsoft's contractual or technological bars to subsequent *removal* of functionality. But our qualms about redefining the boundaries of a defendant's product and the possibility of consumer gains from simplifying the work of applications developers makes us question any hard and fast approach to tying in OS software markets.

There may also be a number of efficiencies that, although very real, have been ignored in the calculations underlying the adoption of a *per se* rule for tying. We fear that these efficiencies are common in technologically dynamic markets where product development is especially unlikely to follow an easily foreseen linear pattern. * * *

These arguments all point to one conclusion.... We do not have enough empirical evidence regarding the effect of Microsoft's practice on the amount of consumer surplus created or consumer choice foreclosed by the integration of added functionality into platform software to exercise sensible judgment regarding that entire class of behavior. (For some issues we have no data.) "We need to know more than we do about the actual impact of these arrangements on competition to decide whether they... should be classified as *per se* violations of the Sherman Act." *White Motor*, 372 U.S. at 263. Until then, we will heed the wisdom that "easy labels do not always supply ready answers," *Broad. Music*, 441 U.S. at 8, and vacate the District Court's finding of *per se* tying liability under Sherman Act § 1. We remand the case for evaluation of Microsoft's tying arrangements under the rule of reason.... That rule more freely permits consideration of the benefits of bundling in software markets, particularly those for OSs, and a balancing of these benefits against the costs to consumers whose ability to make direct price/quality tradeoffs in the tied market may have been impaired.

\* \* \*

Our judgment regarding the comparative merits of the *per se* rule and the rule of reason is confined to the tying arrangement before us, where the tying product is software whose major purpose is to serve as a platform for third-party applications and the tied product is complementary software functionality. While our reasoning may at times appear to have broader force, we do not have the confidence to speak to facts outside the record, which contains scant discussion of software integration generally. Microsoft's primary justification for bundling IE APIs is that their inclusion with Windows increases the value of third-party software (and Windows) to consumers.... Because this claim applies with distinct force when the tying product is *platform* software, we have no present basis for finding the *per se* rule inapplicable to software markets generally. Nor should we be interpreted as setting a precedent for switching to the rule of reason every time a court identifies an efficiency justification for a tying arrangement. Our reading of the record suggests merely that integration of new functionality into platform software is a common practice and that wooden application of *per se* rules in this litigation may cast a cloud over platform innovation in the market for PCs, network computers and information appliances.

### C. On Remand

Should plaintiffs choose to pursue a tying claim under the rule of reason, we note the following for the benefit of the trial court:

First, on remand, plaintiffs must show that Microsoft's conduct unreasonably restrained competition. Meeting that burden "involves an inquiry into the actual effect" of Microsoft's conduct on competition in the tied good market, *Jefferson Parish*, 466 U.S. at 29, the putative market for browsers. To the extent that certain aspects of tying injury may depend on a careful definition of the tied good market and a showing of barriers to entry other than the tying arrangement itself, plaintiffs would have to establish these points.... But plaintiffs were required—and had every incentive—to provide both a definition of the browser market and barriers to entry to that market as part of their §2 attempted monopolization claim; yet they failed to do so.... Accordingly, on remand of the §1 tying claim, plaintiffs will be precluded from arguing any theory of harm that depends on a precise definition of browsers or barriers to entry (for example, network effects from Internet protocols and extensions embedded in a browser) other than what may be implicit in Microsoft's tying arrangement.

Of the harms left, plaintiffs must show that Microsoft's conduct was, on balance, anticompetitive. Microsoft may of course offer procompetitive justifications, and it is plaintiffs' burden to show that the anticompetitive effect of the conduct outweighs its benefit.

Second, the fact that we have already considered some of the behavior plaintiffs allege to constitute tying violations in the monopoly maintenance section does not resolve the §1 inquiry. The two practices that plaintiffs have most ardently claimed as tying violations are, indeed, a basis for liability under plaintiffs' §2 monopoly maintenance claim. These are Microsoft's refusal to allow OEMs to uninstall IE or remove it from the Windows desktop...and its removal of the IE entry from the Add/Remove Programs utility in Windows 98...In order for the District Court to conclude these practices also constitute § 1 tying violations, plaintiffs must demonstrate that their benefits—if any...are outweighed by the harms in the *tied product* market. *See Jefferson Parish*, 466 U.S. at 29. If the District Court is convinced of net harm, it must then consider whether any additional remedy is necessary.

[W]e also considered another alleged tying violation—the Windows 98 override of a consumer's choice of default web browser. We concluded that this behavior does not provide a distinct basis for § 2 liability because plaintiffs failed to rebut Microsoft's proffered justification by demonstrating that harms in the operating system market outweigh Microsoft's claimed benefits. On remand, however, although Microsoft may offer the same procompetitive justification for the override, plaintiffs must have a new opportunity to rebut this claim, by demonstrating that the anticompetitive effect in the *browser* market is greater than these benefits.

Finally, the District Court must also consider an alleged tying violation that we did not consider under § 2 monopoly maintenance: price bundling. First, the court must determine if Microsoft indeed price bundled—that is, was Microsoft's charge for Windows and IE higher than its charge would have been for Windows alone? This will require plaintiffs to resolve the tension between *Findings of Fact* ¶¶ 136–37, which Microsoft interprets as saying that no part of the bundled price of Windows can be attributed to IE, and *Conclusions of Law*, at 50, which says the opposite.

\* \* \*

If there is a positive price increment in Windows associated with IE (we know there is no claim of price predation), plaintiffs must demonstrate that the anticompetitive effects of Microsoft's price bundling outweigh any procompetitive justifications the company provides for it.

\* \* \*

If OS vendors without market power also sell their software bundled with a browser, the natural inference is that sale of the items as a bundle serves consumer demand and that unbundled sale would not, for otherwise a competitor could profitably offer the two products separately and capture sales of the tying good from vendors that bundle.

\* \* \*

Of course price bundling by competitive OS makers would tend to exonerate Microsoft only if the sellers in question sold their browser/OS combinations exclusively at a bundled price. If a competitive seller offers a discount for a browserless version, then—at least as to its OS and browser—the gains from bundling are outweighed by those from separate choice. The evidence on discounts appears to be in conflict....If [it] is correct that nearly all OS makers do not offer a discount, then the harm from tying—obstruction of direct consumer choice—would be theoretically created by virtually all sellers: a customer who would prefer an alternate browser is forced to pay the full price of that browser even though its value to him is only the increment in value over the bundled browser. (The result is similar to that from non-removal, which forces consumers who want the alternate browser to surrender disk space taken up by the unused, bundled browser.) If the failure to offer a price discount were universal, any impediment to direct consumer choice created by Microsoft's price-bundled sale of IE with Windows would be matched throughout the market; yet these OS suppliers on the competitive fringe would have evidently found this price bundling on balance efficient....

## V. TRIAL PROCEEDINGS AND REMEDY

*[The D.C. Circuit vacated the district court's remedial decree "for three indepen-*
*dent reasons: (1) the court failed to hold a remedies-specific evidentiary hearing*
*although facts relating to the remedy were disputed; (2) the court failed to provide*
*adequate reasons for its decreed remedies; and (3) this Court has revised the scope*
*of Microsoft's liability and it is impossible to determine to what extent that should*
*affect the remedies provisions." ]*

\* \* \*

### F. On Remand

As a general matter, a district court is afforded broad discretion to enter that relief it
calculates will best remedy the conduct it has found to be unlawful.... This is no less
true in antitrust cases.... And divestiture is a common form of relief in successful antitrust prosecutions: it is indeed "the most important of antitrust remedies." *See, e.g.,*
*United States v. E.I. du Pont de Nemours & Co.*, 366 U.S. 316, 331, 6 L. Ed. 2d 318, 81 S.
Ct. 1243 (1961).

On remand, the District Court must reconsider whether the use of the structural
remedy of divestiture is appropriate with respect to Microsoft, which argues that it is a
unitary company. By and large, cases upon which plaintiffs rely in arguing for the split of
Microsoft have involved the dissolution of entities formed by mergers and acquisitions.

\* \* \*

One apparent reason why courts have not ordered the dissolution of unitary companies is logistical difficulty. As the court explained in *United States v. ALCOA*, 91 F. Supp.
333, 416 (S.D.N.Y. 1950), a "corporation, designed to operate effectively as a single entity, cannot readily be dismembered of parts of its various operations without a marked
loss of efficiency." A corporation that has expanded by acquiring its competitors often
has preexisting internal lines of division along which it may more easily be split than a
corporation that has expanded from natural growth. Although time and corporate
modifications and developments may eventually fade those lines, at least the identifiable
entities preexisted to create a template for such division as the court might later decree.
With reference to those corporations that are not acquired by merger and acquisition,
Judge Wyzanski accurately opined in *United Shoe*:

> United conducts all machine manufacture at one plant in Beverly, with one set
> of jigs and tools, one foundry, one laboratory for machinery problems, one
> managerial staff, and one labor force. It takes no Solomon to see that this or-
> ganism cannot be cut into three equal and viable parts.

*United States v. United Shoe Machine Co.*, 110 F. Supp. 295, 348 (D. Mass. 1953).

Depending upon the evidence, the District Court may find in a remedies proceeding
that it would be no easier to split *Microsoft* in two than *United Shoe* in three. Microsoft's
Offer of Proof in response to the court's denial of an evidentiary hearing included proffered testimony from its President and CEO Steve Ballmer that the company "is, and always has been, a unified company without free-standing business units. Microsoft is not
the result of mergers or acquisitions." Microsoft further offered evidence that it is "not
organized along product lines," but rather is housed in a single corporate headquarters
and that it has

> [o]nly one sales and marketing organization which is responsible for selling all
> of the company's products, one basic research organization, one product sup-

port organization, one operations department, one information technology department, one facilities department, one purchasing department, one human resources department, one finance department, one legal department and one public relations department.

If indeed Microsoft is a unitary company, division might very well require Microsoft to reproduce each of these departments in each new entity rather than simply allocate the differing departments among them.

In devising an appropriate remedy, the District Court also should consider whether plaintiffs have established a sufficient causal connection between Microsoft's anticompetitive conduct and its dominant position in the OS market. "Mere existence of an exclusionary act does not itself justify full feasible relief against the monopolist to create maximum competition." 3 AREEDA & HOVENKAMP, ANTITRUST LAW ¶ 650a, at 67. Rather, structural relief, which is "designed to eliminate the monopoly altogether ... requires a clearer indication of a *significant causal connection* between the conduct and creation or maintenance of the market power." *Id.* ¶ 653b, at 91–92 (emphasis added). Absent such causation, the antitrust defendant's unlawful behavior should be remedied by "an injunction against continuation of that conduct."

\* \* \*

[W]e have found a causal connection between Microsoft's exclusionary conduct and its continuing position in the operating systems market only through inference.... Indeed, the District Court expressly did not adopt the position that Microsoft would have lost its position in the OS market but for its anticompetitive behavior. *Findings of Fact* ¶ 411 ("There is insufficient evidence to find that, absent Microsoft's actions, Navigator and Java already would have ignited genuine competition in the market for Intelcompatible PC operating systems."). If the court on remand is unconvinced of the causal connection between Microsoft's exclusionary conduct and the company's position in the OS market, it may well conclude that divestiture is not an appropriate remedy.

While we do not undertake to dictate to the District Court the precise form that relief should take on remand, we note again that it should be tailored to fit the wrong creating the occasion for the remedy.

## G. Conclusion

In sum, we vacate the District Court's remedies decree for three reasons. First, the District Court failed to hold an evidentiary hearing despite the presence of remedies-specific factual disputes. Second, the court did not provide adequate reasons for its decreed remedies. Finally, we have drastically altered the scope of Microsoft's liability, and it is for the District Court in the first instance to determine the propriety of a specific remedy for the limited ground of liability which we have upheld.

## VI. JUDICIAL MISCONDUCT

\* \* \*

*[The D.C. Circuit disapproved the conduct of the trial judge and disqualified him from hearing the remedial phase of the case. The disqualification was based upon Judge Jackson's public comments on the case, often in ways unfavorable to Microsoft.*

*The trial judge had reportedly given reporters secret interviews after the close of evidence but before the entry of his final judgment, on the understanding that their reporting would await the entry of his final judgment. After entering final judgement, but before ruling on the case's remedial phase, he also had spoken liberally about the case to reporters, as well as to a few groups, in ways unfavorable to Microsoft. In the appellate court's view, these actions violated Canons 2 and 3A(6) of the Code of Conduct for United States Judges which required, respectively, avoiding "impropriety and the appearance of impropriety" and refraining from "public comment on the merits" of pending cases.*

*The appellate court apologized for using media reports of the trial judge's comments (which could be hearsay) as evidence, but it saw the weight of the evidence as so strong that it would be needlessly inefficient to remand the case for fact-finding on these points.*

*For two reasons, the appellate court did not vacate all of the trial judge's findings of fact. First, "the most serious judicial misconduct occurred near or during the remedial stage." Second, Rule 52(a) of the Federal Rules of Civil Procedure, which require deference to trial courts on matters of fact, provided "no middle ground." Reasoning it would have to accept or reject all of the trial courts' findings, the court accepted all of his findings of fact and vacated only the remedial order, remanding for an evidentiary hearing on the remedy and a determination of what remedy was proper.]*

---

# The D.C. Circuit's Decision in *Microsoft III*: More Questions than Answers

1. The D.C. Circuit begins its opinion in an odd way, describing how the computer industry is special and unique. Of course antitrust analysis must take account of an industry's special economic characteristics, but does that mean that the applicable law or *principles* of antitrust analysis differ for each industry?

The traditional answer to that question has been a resounding "no." The leading case is *National Society of Professional Engineers v. United States*, 435 U.S. 679 (1978). There the government challenged a professional society's ethical rule against competitive bidding by engineers for work on construction projects. *Id.* at 682–83. The society tried to justify its rule by arguing that competitive bidding on price would de-emphasize the quality of engineering services, thereby threatening the safety and soundness of engineered structures. The Court rejected this argument in a passage that is worth quoting at length:

> The Sherman Act reflects a legislative judgment that ultimately competition will produce not only lower prices, but also better goods and services. The heart of our national economic policy long has been faith in the value of competition. The assumption that competition is the best method of allocating resources in a free market recognizes that all elements of a bargain—quality, service, safety, and durability—and not just the immediate cost, are favorably affected by the free opportunity to select among alternative offers. Even assuming occasional exceptions to the presumed consequences of competition, the statutory policy precludes inquiry into the question whether competition is good or bad.

The fact that engineers are often involved in large-scale projects significantly affecting the public safety does not alter our analysis. Exceptions to the Sherman Act for potentially dangerous goods and services would be tantamount to a repeal of the statute. In our complex economy the number of items that may cause serious harm is almost endless—automobiles, drugs, foods, aircraft components, heavy equipment, and countless others, cause serious harm to individuals or to the public at large if defectively made. The judiciary cannot indirectly protect the public against this harm by conferring monopoly privileges on the manufacturers.

*Id.* at 695–96 (citation and internal quotation marks omitted). The Court held the no-competitive-bidding rule illegal *per se*. *See id.* at 689–90.

Since *National Society*, the Supreme Court has consistently taken the position that no segment of our economy (except for baseball, for unique historical reasons) is exempt from the usual antitrust rules.

In hinting strongly that the software industry is somehow special, the court refers to the "network effects" of software, the need for software standards and the efficiencies of software integration (of which much more below). Are these things more important than the safety and soundness of structures in which people work and live, the quality of medical and dental services, and the danger of poorly made pharmaceuticals? In the cases cited above, the Supreme Court ruled or reasoned that none of these considerations trumps competition as our basic national rule of trade, precisely because competition is one of the best means to avoid the dangers of poor-quality products. Was the *Microsoft III* court bamboozled by the presumed complexity of computer software and fancy economic theory?

2. As the D.C. Circuit saw it, the personal computer industry is unique in part because of the importance of "network effects." The term "network effects" is just economic jargon for the added value and consumer benefit that a complex product or technology involving human cooperation produces as more and more people use it. As the "network" of users expands, some products (particularly those involved in communication), become more valuable to everyone.

3. Do the facts of *Microsoft III* implicate the importance of standards *per se* or the importance of how standards are made? By the time of the appellate court's decision, Microsoft's Windows operating system was thoroughly entrenched as a near-universal standard for personal computers. Microsoft had 95% of the market, which encompassed an estimated 100 million computers or more. Few would question the value, consumer benefit, and economic efficiency of having a standard operating system for so many computers, even if it is not the best.

However, was the issue in *Microsoft III* the entrenched standard of the operating system itself? Or was it whose product might become a *new* standard for Internet browsers? Netscape Communications Corp. (later acquired by AOL and then by Time-Warner) had invented the Internet browser as a widely used commercial consumer product. When Microsoft entered the browser field, Netscape had an 80% share of the browser market, and Microsoft had to play "catch-up ball." *See* Sandberg, *Sun and Netscape Are Forming Alliance Against Microsoft on Internet Standard*, WALL STREET JOURNAL, at B3 (Dec. 4, 1995) ("Netscape holds 80% of the market for Web 'browser' software used by individuals' PCs."); Sandberg and Hill, *Microsoft Probe Spurs Subpoena Tied to Internet*, WALL STREET JOURNAL, Dec. 4, 1995, at A3 ("In the estimate of Netscape and industry observers, roughly 80% of World Wide Web users, a population pegged at more than 17 million, use Netscape's software."). Was the issue whether there would *be* a standard for Internet browsers, or who would set it and how?

Normally, technological standards are set through voluntary agreement among competing manufacturers, typically through trade associations. Among the many personal-computer standards set in this way are the JPEG and TIFF graphics formats, the popular MP3 format for songs, and the 802.11b and 802.11g standards for home networks and WiFi networks, respectively. The voluntary standard-setting process is not immune from antitrust scrutiny. *See Allied Tube & Conduit Corp. v. Indian Head*, 486 U.S. 492, 496–97 (1988) (competitor who "packed" standard-setting meeting to exclude rival's product from model electrical code was not immune).

*Microsoft III*, however, involves an entirely different standard-setting "process" (if it can be called that), namely, the victory of a single party in a competitive battle between differing rival products. Microsoft had certainly won the standard-setting battle for Intel-compatible PC operating systems hands down. But the battle to set the standard for Windows-compatible Internet browsers had only just begun, with Netscape and Microsoft's Internet Explorer (which the court abbreviates as "IE") as the two leading contenders.

As first, Netscape had a solid and seemingly insurmountable lead, with its 80% market share. By the time the government's lawsuit came to appeal, however, Microsoft had forced a nearly complete reversal of positions, achieving a 75% market share. *See* Maney, *Lords of the Net Duel—But Probably Not to the Death*, U.S.A TODAY, Aug. 16. 2001, at 18 (reporting browser market shares, as of June 2001, as follows: Microsoft: 75%, Netscape 18%, other 7%). The question before the *Microsoft III* court was whether Microsoft had achieved this dramatic reversal of fortune by lawful means. Does the well-recognized economic value of standards generally bear on the answer to that question? Might not *either* Netscape or Internet Explorer have provided a useful standard for Internet browsers, as long as each was compatible with Microsoft's Windows operating system? If so, does the admitted value of standards generally really have much to do with this case?

4. The second way in which the *Microsoft III* court sees the computer industry as special is its speed of development. Although ultimately rejecting Microsoft's argument for a special standard of monopoly power, the court dwells on the computer software's status as a "technologically dynamic" market in discussing remedies. It suggests that the game of software is so fast that the referee cannot make timely calls of "foul."

But which way does/should this factor cut? Do fast-moving industries require *more* probing antitrust scrutiny for fear that anticompetitive conduct might have more devastating effects and that monopolies might become entrenched more quickly? Is basketball any less in need of referees because it is a faster-paced, more active game than baseball?

5. For our purposes, the primary value of studying *Microsoft III* is that it introduces us to the application to licensing behavior of Sherman Act §2. As discussed above, §1 focuses on so-called "concerted conduct," i.e., contracts, combinations, and conspiracies in restraint of trade. Because it involves two or more parties, any contractual restraint in a licensing agreement can fall afoul of §1 if it is unreasonably anticompetitive, either *per se* or under the rule of reason. Thus §1 is the one most commonly applied to licensing agreements generally.

Unlike § 1, Sherman Act § 2 applies to *unilateral* action by a single party (except for conspiracies to monopolize, which are relatively rare). A single party, all by itself, can monopolize or attempt to monopolize a defined market, without any contract or collusion with any other party. Microsoft's acts of tying its IE browser technologically to its operating system, as well as its threats to discontinue offering its Office product for Apple's Mac computers, were *unilateral* acts of monopolization. The leading case explaining the difference between concerted and unilateral action is *Copperweld Corp. v. Independence Tube Corp.*, 467 U.S. 752 (1984), which held that a corporation cannot conspire with its own division, employee, or wholly-owned subsidiary for purposes of § 1.

6. In one respect, monopolization and attempt-to-monopolize claims under Sherman Act § 2 are easier to prove than § 1 claims: they do not require proof of concerted action. On the other hand, § 2 claims are harder to prove in another respect: they require proof of actual or threatened monopoly power. That is, they require proof of (1) a defined product and geographic market and (2) actual or threatened monopoly power in that market. This proof in turn requires analysis of the structure and performance of the defined market, usually including the leading industry participants' market shares and relevant conditions (such as barriers to entry and excess capacity) that affect their market power.

Because § 2 claims require such detailed market analysis, they virtually never turn on upon simple categorization of behavior, such as horizontal price-fixing or division of markets. In that respect they differ starkly from § 1 claims. Although courts seldom make the point *in haec verba*, all claims under § 2 require application of the rule of reason. There is no such thing as *per se* liability under § 2. The rule of reason is appropriate for § 2 because it covers any of the myriads variant forms that attempts to quash competition on the merits can take. The absence of *per se* rules under § 2, however, has one unfortunate result: § 2 cases are costly, time-consuming, and expensive and require a great deal of preparation.

7. Section 2 cases have three elements: (1) definition of a market (product or service and geographic); (2) demonstration of monopoly power (or, for attempt cases, near monopoly power) in the defined market; and (3) proof of conduct by the defendant that suppresses competition on the merits and tends to achieve, maintain, entrench or extend a monopoly in the defined market.

What was the defined market at issue in *Microsoft III*? Do you agree with the court that Apple's Mac operating systems and such "middleware" as Java and the Internet browsers at issue in the case were not part of that defined market? What are the best factual arguments for not including them in that market, and on what legal rules for market definition are they based?

8. Under § 2, "monopoly power" is just market power that tends toward a monopoly. "Market power" is the power to raise prices and/or reduce output for a substantial period of time without rivals stealing market share. Market share is usually a good "proxy" (substitute for or measurement of) market power, but it is not conclusive. Depending upon other conditions in the defined market, a firm with a high market share may have low market power, or *vice versa*. *See* JAY DRATLER, JR., LICENSING OF INTELLECTUAL PROPERTY § 5.02[2][b][i][A] (Law Journal Press, 2002 & Supps.), LEXIS, LJLIP.

In discussing monopoly power, the *Microsoft III* court says that "monopoly power may be inferred from a firm's possession of a dominant share of a relevant market *that is protected by entry barriers*." 253 F.3d at 51 (emphasis added). This proposition implies that entry barriers are a *necessary condition* of monopoly power. For it, the *Microsoft III* court cites a single Ninth Circuit decision, *Rebel Oil Co. v. Atlantic Richfield Co.*, 51 F.3d

1421, 1434 (9th Cir. 1995). There are, however, hundreds of decisions discussing market power and monopoly power; few of them impose an absolute requirement for entry barriers as a condition of proving market or monopoly power. Moreover, the controlling precedent on attempts to monopolize does not require proof of barriers to entry; all it requires is "inquiry into the relevant product and geographic market and the defendant's *economic power in that market.*" *Spectrum Sports, Inc. v. McQuillan,* 506 U.S. 447, 456, 459 (1993) (emphasis added). For a detailed critique of the D.C. Circuit's reading of this case and other precedent, see Dratler, *supra,* 5.02[2][b][iii].

The market of interest for the attempt-to-monopolize claim was of course the market for Internet browsers—a different market than the one (for PC-compatible operating systems) that Microsoft had monopolized. The D.C. Circuit accused the government of failing even to *try* to define this secondary market. If the attempt claim failed for lack of a definition of the market that Microsoft allegedly attempted to monopolize, are the D.C. Circuit's comments on the need to prove barriers to entry into that market *dictum*?

More important, aren't barriers to entry into the browser market readily apparent from proof in the monopolization case? The D.C. Circuit seem to be looking for "structural" barriers, such as the "applications barrier to entry" into the primary (operating system) market. But barriers to entry need not be structural. Nor need they be unlawful in any way: a classic barrier to entry is a valid and lawful patent. *See generally,* Dratler, *supra,* §5.02[2][b][i][B] (citing and discussing numerous nonstructural barriers to entry recognized by courts as such).

Take a look at the "laundry list" of Microsoft's conduct in Note 10 *infra,* both conduct held unlawful and conduct not held unlawful. Do at least some of Microsoft's acts erect barriers to entry into the browser market? Don't most of them have the purpose and/or the effect of forcing third parties to use Microsoft's browser (IE) exclusively? What about Microsoft's attempt to tie its Internet browser (IE) technologically and contractually to its operating system? Doesn't that tie, coupled with Microsoft's entrenched dominance in the operating-system market, create a barrier to entry into the browser market? If so, was the D.C. Circuit willfully blind in failing to find barriers to entry into that market?

More fundamentally, does it make sense to demand proof of barriers to entry in an attempt case involving only *two* incumbent firms, where one is alleged to have attempted to monopolize by driving the other out of the market? At the time of interest in this case there was no serious commercial competition for PC-compatible browsers besides Microsoft's IE and Netscape's Navigator. (Other competitors later entered the market, but only after the settlement in this case forced Microsoft to stop demanding exclusive use of its browser.) In other words, the browser market was a two-firm market at the time. In such a case, does it make sense to demand proof of barriers to *entry* into the market when one of the only two incumbent firms is accused of attempting to monopolize the market by driving the other out of it? Does it make sense when the conduct involved in the alleged attempt had the purpose and effect of giving the defendant's product a dominant, exclusive position in that market? Does it make sense when the defendant actually succeeded in reversing the plaintiff's dominant position and achieving dominance for itself?

9. Now consider that barrier to entry. The district court found, and the appellate court affirmed, that Microsoft had a 95% share of the defined market. In addition, both courts found a significant barrier to entry, the so-called "applications barrier to entry," that further reinforced Microsoft's predominant market share.

To understand the applications barrier to entry, note that independent software vendors had developed 70,000 application programs to run on Microsoft's Windows operating systems. *See United States v. Microsoft Corp.* 253 F.3d 34, 55 (D.C. 2000). Suppose the entire personal-computer industry wanted to abandon Windows and switch to another operating system, called New OS, without losing a thing. All of the independent software vendors that produced the 70,000 application programs would have to rewrite their programs to run on New OS. This job alone would require thousands or tens of thousands of person-years of effort. But that wouldn't be all. In addition, all of the millions of users of the those 70,000 programs would have to learn or re-learn how to use them on New OS, requiring an additional substantial effort on their part.

Can you think of any other firm, either in your own experience or in the history of American industry, that enjoyed or enjoys such a monopoly? Monopolies on oil, coal, steel and aluminum rely on such things as the high capital investment required to build a new plant, patent protection, and perhaps the need to find new natural resources. Patents may be difficult to "invent around," but banks have lots of money, and scarcity of natural resources in America (oil, for example), is a relatively recent phenomenon. Did circumventing earlier monopolies ever involve the need to restructure an entire industry, requiring massive effort on the part of tens of thousands of independent vendors and millions of users? Does this analysis suggest that the danger of monopolization is stronger or weaker in the "new" economy than in the "old" economy? Is the supposed uniqueness of the "new economy" reason diffident hesitation or for more vigorous enforcement of antitrust principles?

10. The "conduct" element of a §2 claim is difficult to define or delimit in general. Firms and their employees are often ingenious and creative in devising ways to crush competition on the merits yet to make what they are doing seem innocent or even beneficial. Therefore the law has no specific definition of prohibited conduct, which in any event would quickly be circumvented.

It is black-letter law that conduct unlawful under §2 need not be illegal in itself, either under §1 or under any other law. *See* DRATLER, *supra*, §5.02[2][b][ii]. If a person with monopoly or near-monopoly power engages in conduct having the purpose or effect of suppressing or avoiding competition on the merits, that is enough to invoke §2. On this point, the language of Article 86 of the EU's Treaty of Rome, which speaks of "abuse...of...a dominant position," is more apt than the American text. The acts of abuse need not be unlawful in themselves; it is their abusive purpose or effect in crushing legitimate competition on the merits that makes them unlawful.

The conduct in which Microsoft engaged to maintain and extend its monopoly was comprehensive indeed. A number of elements are omitted from the edited opinion in *Microsoft III* above, in order to reduce its length. Here is a more complete list of what the court found unlawful and lawful:

*Unlawful conduct*: The D.C. Circuit affirmed the district court's findings that all of the following conduct of Microsoft was anticompetitive and not competitively justified and therefore violated Sherman Act §2: (1) restricting OEM licensees from adding different icons or folders from those supplied by Microsoft and from using Windows' "Active Desktop" feature to promote third-party brands; (2) tying Microsoft's browser technologically to its operating system by disabling the "Add/Remove program" utility for the browser and by commingling the browser's and operating system's code so that attempting to remove the browser would cripple the operating system; (3) granting licenses to Internet access providers providing for or encouraging exclusive use of Microsoft's browser; (4) granting licenses to independent software vendors providing for exclusive use of Microsoft's browser in exchange for informational benefits and use of a seal of approval; (5) forcing Apple computer to agree to use Microsoft's browser exclusively by threatening to discontinue developing Mac Office versions for Apple's machines; (6) entering into contracts with major independent software vendors requiring them to promote Microsoft's Java Virtual Machine exclusively; (7) deceiving Java developers about the Windows-specific nature of the Sun-incompatible Java development tools that Microsoft distributed to them; and (8) coercing Intel, through threats to cooperate with its rival, to stop helping Sun improve Java technologies. *See United States v. Microsoft Corp.*, 253 F.3d 34, 61–78 (D.C. Cir. 2001) (*Microsoft III*).

*Not Unlawful Conduct*: However, the D.C. Circuit reversed the district court's findings that the following conduct of Microsoft constituted unlawful monopolization, either finding no net adverse effect on competition or sufficient procompetitive justification: (1) restrictions in OEM licenses against launching non-Windows desktop automatically; (2) limited overriding of users' choices of default browser in certain cases; (3) giving developers free licenses to bundle Microsoft's browser with their products and to use Microsoft's development kit, as well as promotional inducements to use that browser exclusively; and (4) developing and promoting a Sun-incompatible version of Java Virtual Machine where evidence showed it had technological benefits, including faster operation. *See id.*, 253 F.3d at 63, 67, 68, 71, 75–76.

11. As the foregoing list of disapproved conduct suggests, Microsoft's effort to replace Netscape's pioneering Internet browser with its own, using all the considerable power of its operating-system monopoly, was broad and comprehensive. Ultimately, that attempt was successful, causing Microsoft's Internet Explorer nearly to change places in market share with Netscape's pioneering product in less than six years. All this occurred despite the fact that, as the district's unaltered finding stated, Microsoft's product was "not demonstrably the current 'best of breed' Web browser, nor [was] it likely to be so at any time in the immediate future." *United States v. Microsoft Corp.*, 87 F. Supp. 2d 30, 40 ("*Conclusions of Law*"), *aff'd in part and rev'd and vacated on other grounds* 253 F.3d 34 (D.C. Cir. 2001) (*Microsoft III*).

Did all this happen by accident, or did Microsoft have a carefully elaborated and assiduously implemented plan? In addressing the substance of the monopolization claims, the *Microsoft III* court de-emphasized Microsoft's intent. 253 F.3d at 59. This approach is undoubtedly correct as a matter of antitrust *liability*. Modern antitrust law de-emphasizes intent, because an intent that appears anticompetitive may be nothing more than an intent to compete vigorously but not unlawfully. In a seminal decision involving alleged predatory pricing, the Seventh Circuit put it this way:

> Firms intend to do all the business they can, to crush their rivals if they can. Intent to harm without more offers too vague a standard in a world where executives may think no further than Let's get more business.... Rivalry is harsh, and consumers gain the most when firms slash costs to the bone and pare price down to cost, all in pursuit of more business.... If courts use the vigorous, nasty pursuit of sales as evidence of a forbidden intent, they run the risk of penalizing the motive forces of competition.

*A.A. Poultry Farms, Inc. v. Rose Acre Farms, Inc.*, 881 F.2d 1396, 1401–2 (7th Cir. 1989) (internal quotation marks and citation omitted).

This approach makes eminent sense in determining whether conduct is unlawful under the antitrust laws. But what about the remedy? Once unlawfully anticompetitive conduct has been proven, should courts take the violator's intent into account in determining the appropriate remedy? Does intent at least bear on what a crusher of competition may be likely to do next? Should the remedy be the same, for example, if Microsoft had only been liable for one series of exclusive agreements, rather than for the whole laundry list of anticompetitive conduct set forth above?

12. The *Microsoft III* court also reversed the district court's decision to impose liability based upon Microsoft's entire "course of conduct." 253 F.3d at 78–80. Does that make sense as a matter of liability? The whole cannot be greater than the sum of the parts, can it? But, again, what about the remedy? Does a massive corporation like Microsoft present a greater danger to competition when proven to have engaged in a comprehensive scheme to crush competition like the one outlined above? Does/should it matter that Microsoft was reported to have $38 billion in cash to spend? *See* Steve Hamm et al., *Making the Tech Slump Pay Off*, BUSINESS WEEK, June 24, 2002, at 84.

Should courts take such matters into account in determining antitrust remedies? Should their goal be to restore a competitive market, to protect the market from further anticompetitive activity (of the same or a different sort), or just to prohibit what the violator already has done? *Cf. Zenith Radio Corp. v. Hazeltine Research*, 395 U.S. 100 (1969) ("In exercising its equitable jurisdiction, a federal court has broad power to restrain acts which are of the same type or class as unlawful acts which the court has found to have been committed or whose commission in the future, unless enjoined, may fairly be anticipated from the defendant's conduct in the past.") (citation and internal punctuation omitted).

13. The *Microsoft III* court did not attempt to prescribe the appropriate remedy. In clear *dicta*, however, it disfavored the strong medicine—splitting Microsoft up into separate operating-system and applications firms—prescribed by the district court. 253 F.3d at 105–7. It also suggested that the remedy on remand be "tailored to fit the wrong." *See id.* at 107.

The remedy that ultimately resulted was toothless. In a portion of the opinion summarized but not reproduced above, the *Microsoft III* court disqualified the trial judge for expressing strong opinions on Microsoft's conduct to reporters and others, thereby creating an appearance of bias; it therefore vacated his remedial findings and orders (while retaining his findings and conclusions on other matters) and ordered the case transferred on remand to a different judge. *See id.* at 166–77, 199.

Having had no previous experience with this mammoth case, the new trial judge pressed the parties to settle, which they ultimately did. The settlement involved a "sin no more" consent decree requiring no divestiture and no mandatory disclosure of Microsoft's source code or other intellectual property. Attorneys general from a number of states that were parties plaintiff objected to the proposed settlement on the ground that Microsoft had already ceased most of the prohibited conduct and that the settlement did little to re-establish competitive conditions in the industry. After months of haggling, the "holdout states" went back to court, only to gain a remedy that the D.C. Circuit later described as "closely parallel[ing]" the settlement with the federal government. *Massachusetts v. Microsoft Corp.*, 373 F.3d 1199, 1204 (*Microsoft IV*). Massachusetts alone, as the sole remaining "hold-out" state, appealed this litigated remedy, and the D.C. Circuit, in a remarkable and remarkably lengthy opinion, rejected every one of its many objections. *See Massachusetts v. Microsoft Corp.*, 373 F.3d 1199, 1204 (Microsoft IV) (arriving at a "final" decision on Massachusetts' objections and upholding district court's remedial decision for holdout states in its entirety). Because the holdout states' remedy closely paralleled the consent decree, the end result of the entire litigation was that Microsoft, in essence, wrote its own remedy for its many wrongs, albeit under considerable pressure in the litigation. *See* DRATLER, *supra*, § 5.02[2][b][ii][B].

With the blessed vision of hindsight, it is possible to trace this remedial debacle to flaws in the government's litigation strategy and execution. *See id.* Among other things, the government seemed to "go for broke," placing all its emphasis on the monopolization claim and the proposed "nuclear bomb" remedy of divestiture, i.e., splitting Microsoft into independent operating-system and applications businesses. *See id.* But the legal theory that the government chose—extension of Microsoft's monopoly by eliminating the threat that "middleware" would erode it—was incapable of supporting such a robust remedy. Microsoft already had one of the strongest and most entrenched monopolies in American industrial history, protected by an insurmountable barrier to entry. How much stronger could it be made by unlawfully eliminating the "middleware" threat? Since a remedy must be causally related to the wrong, the proponents of divestiture had to show how that remedy would prevent or roll back the putative strengthening of an already impregnable monopoly. Not surprisingly, no court found that the government had made such a showing convincingly.

The government's relative neglect of the other antitrust claims (especially tying and attempting to monopolize) appears to have been a major strategic error, for those claims might have demonstrated a much greater and more easily comprehensible anticompetitive effect, namely, driving Netscape from the very market it had pioneered, and with a product found no better than Netscape's. Might this litigation debacle have had something to do with the government's choice of a private, generalist "superlawyer" (David Boies) as chief trial counsel, rather than counsel (from its own ranks or outside) with solid experience in the computer industry and antitrust?

14. A few years later, a similar factual situation arose. Microsoft integrated multimedia software, called Windows Media Player, into its operating systems in an attempt to compete with independently developed multimedia software. Antitrust authorities in the United States did nothing, but European antitrust authorities included this "bundling" issue in a larger antitrust case against Microsoft, which also addressed the server market. In March 2004, the European Commission fined Microsoft 497 million Euros (612 million U.S. dollars) for antitrust violations and ordered it to offer a version of Windows without Windows Media Player. It also ordered Microsoft to disclose interface information on its server software to head off a monopoly in that separate market. *See* Paul Andrews, *EC Ruling's Big Impact is on Bundling,"* SEATTLE TIMES, Business, March 29, 2004, at C1. For a summary of the economic justification for the tougher European approach, see William Bishop & Robert Stillman, *Microsoft Got What it Deserved in Europe,* FINANCIAL TIMES (London), March 29, 2004, Comment at 21.

Numerically, the fine will hardly sting Microsoft. "The European Union's biggest fine ever against one company, about $612 million, is just slightly more than 1 percent of Microsoft's cash on hand, and is actually less than the $750 million Microsoft voluntarily agreed to pay Time Warner to settle an antitrust action over America Online." Andrews, *supra* at C1. In any event, Microsoft appealed the decision to the European Court of Justice, and the appeal is likely to take until the end of the new millennium's first decade. In the meantime, Microsoft appears to have continued to seek every business advantage for its bundled operating-system software and media player. "While the software developer ha[d] since 19 January [2005] made available a version of Windows that comes without the media player, as [the European] Commission ruling that Microsoft was acting in an uncompetitive manner by bundling the Windows Media Player with its operating system, the new version cost[] the same as the version that includes the player." DMEUROPE January 31, 2005, NEXIS, DMEURO. Will such a remedy provide a level playing field for Microsoft's competitors in the PC-compatible media-player market?

15. The question of bundling leads to the tying claim in *Microsoft III*. Tying is a § 1 offense. It involves forcing or requiring a customer to buy A in order to get B. In short, tying involves the forced "bundling" of two products or services. Although the terms "tying" and "bundling" are often used interchangeably, "bundling" is a softer, nonlegal term. It often connotes offering two products or services together without coercion, for convenience or at a discounted price.

The legal essence of tying is coercion. The seller says to the buyer, in effect, "you can't have B (the 'tying' product) unless you also take A (the 'tied' product)." In antitrust analysis, market power is generally a proxy for coercion. If the seller has market power in tying product B, then the tie can coerce the buyer to take the unwanted (tied) product A just to get desired product B. If the seller has *no* market power in B, then the buyer can get B (or an equivalent substitute) from others at a comparable price and comparable terms, so the tie does no harm.

When there is market power in the tying product B, the tie causes two types of harm. First, it coerces the buyer into buying A (instead of another seller's similar product, a different product with similar function, or no such product at all). Second, it forecloses other sellers of products like A from the market, based not on competition on the merits of product A, but on the tie. *See generally, Jefferson Parish Hosp. Dist. No. 2 v. Hyde*, 466 U.S. 2, 11–19 (1984) (discussing history and economics of § 1 tying offense).

When tying arrangements have the requisite coercive power, they are illegal *per se* under Sherman Act § 1, as well as Clayton Act § 3, 15 U.S.C. § 14, which more directly addresses tying. As the Supreme Court has said, "It is far too late in the history of our antitrust jurisprudence to question the proposition that certain tying arrangements pose an unacceptable risk of stifling competition and therefore are unreasonable '*per se*.'" *Id.*, 466 U.S. at 9. The elements of a *per se* tying offense are: (1) two separate products; (2) a contractual or other tie that bundles them; (3) appreciable economic power (or market power) in the tying product or service; and (4) an effect upon a substantial volume of commerce in the tied product. *See id.*, 466 U.S. at 20–21, 26; *Eastman Kodak Co. v. Image Technical Servs., Inc.*, 504 U.S. 451, 461–62 (1992). When a tie does not satisfy all these requirements, its analysis falls under the rule of reason. *See Jefferson Parish, supra*, 466 U.S. at 29–30.

16. Did Microsoft's tie between its browser (IE) and its Windows operating system satisfy these four requirements of the *per se* rule? After the *Microsoft III* court's analysis of monopoly power in connection with the monopolization claim, is there any doubt that Microsoft's Windows monopoly had coercive power? Microsoft's Windows operating systems enjoyed a 95% market share, reinforced by a substantial barrier to entry, as discussed above. Can you think of any more coercive combination? If a consumer didn't want IE, she could (1) buy an Apple computer at a much higher price and lose easy compatibility with Microsoft's 100-million-user network, or (2) write her own operating system and port to it the 70,000 applications programs (or as many as she wanted to use). Might those choices be enough to convince the average PC user to say "all right, I guess maybe I don't really like Netscape that much more than IE after all"? Note that tying claims require only market power, i.e., some substantial power to coerce, not power that rises to the level of a monopoly.

Was there a tie? The district court had refused to consider the technological bundling (commingling IE code with the operating system's code) as part of the tie. *See* 253 F.3d at 85. Did the court in so doing hope to avoid the difficult question whether the technological tie had technological advantages? In any event, is there any doubt, given the other listed facts, as well as all of Microsoft's illegal monopolization conduct—most of which was designed to force Internet Explorer down the throats of OEMs and computer users, among others—that there was a tie? As for an effect on a substantial volume of commerce, don't the facts suggest that? IE went from a less than 20% market share to 75% in less than six years. Doesn't that sound substantial?

17. Thus, the crux of the matter seemed to be whether there were two separate products. Netscape certainly thought there were. It had invented the product category of browsers (at least for broad consumer applications), and its separate product, marketed by a separate firm, had been widely used. Consumers, most likely, thought the same until Microsoft began offering IE, 80% of them installed or saw a separate program from a separate vendor, both called "Netscape," on their desktop.

As the *Microsoft III* court discusses at some length, the legal test for separate products is separate consumer demand, not their functional relationship. *See Jefferson Parish, supra*, 466 U.S. at 19–20 & n.30. If anesthesia is a service separate from surgery because it is offered by different doctors and billed separately, *see id.* at 22–23, isn't a browser separate from an operating system on the same rationale?

18. In refusing to find separate products for the purpose of the *per se* rule, the D.C. Circuit focuses on the question of the (presumed) efficiencies of software "integration," i.e., in this case offering an operating system and a Web browser as a single package. What are these efficiencies? Do they require that the two programs (operating system and browser) be offered by a single vendor, here Microsoft? If Netscape had maintained its originally dominant 80% market share, couldn't it also have offered the same efficiencies of software "integration"? In assuming that only Microsoft had the legal right or technical ability to offer these benefits of integration, did the *Microsoft III* court in effect assume its conclusion?

In speaking of the benefits of software integration, the court seems to focus on so-called "Application Programming Interfaces" or "APIs." They include function and subroutine calls and other technological "hooks" that independent software programmers must use to develop new programs that work with an existing program. Both the operating system (in this case Windows) and the browser (in this case either Netscape or Internet Explorer) have APIs. The court seems to think that having a standard set of APIs would provide benefits both to independent software developers and computer users. Yet, when Microsoft began its comprehensive scheme to crush Netscape, Netscape had had an 80% market share. Didn't Netscape then provide a standard set of APIs for independent software vendors and consumers to use? Does the court note any reason for assuming that Microsoft's own APIs would provide any better standard? Isn't the underlying issue not whether standards are good, but who will set them?

More fundamentally, the court seems to think that the well-established "separate demand" test for separate products is just a poor reflection of the underlying goal: economic and technological efficiency. It asserts that "[t]he *per se* rule's direct consumer demand and indirect industry custom inquiries are, as a general matter, backward-looking and therefore systematically poor proxies for overall efficiency in the presence of new and innovative integration." 253 F.3d at 89. But who is ultimately supposed to determine what is better for "overall efficiency," judges or consumers? Isn't the whole premise of antitrust law that consumers, through competition, make this decision? Isn't that what the cases cited in Note 1, *supra*, are all about?

Do antitrust judges serve as "philosopher kings and queens," sitting in judgment on the economic and technological efficiencies of various combinations of products and services? Are they competent to do so? Or do the antitrust laws simply require them to make sure that consumers get a fair choice? Is using the awesome power of Microsoft's operating-system monopoly to coerce OEMs, independent software vendors, and consumers to select Microsoft's browser rather than Netscape's giving them a fair choice?

19. From a policy perspective, the *Microsoft III* court saw itself as having to make a choice. Applying the *per se* rule in this case, it reasoned, would "chill," if not legally preclude, Microsoft's ability to provide integrated products and expand the capability of its highly popular operating system.

But is that so? If Microsoft had developed the Web browser *first* and had made it an integral part of its Windows operating system, would there be any question of its being a "separate product" for tying purposes? Didn't the very existence of the issue of "separate products" in this case arise out of the fact that Netscape had developed the product first and had marketed it as a separate add-on? Was the issue whether tying jurisprudence would ever allow Microsoft to expand its operating systems and make them better by adding new programs with new functionality? Or was it whether the law should allow Microsoft to copy the functionality of others' pioneering products and, by exerting the tremendous leverage of its operating-system monopoly, exclude them from the very market that they had pioneered and developed?

20. The court makes much of the fact that rivals to monopolists like Microsoft will still have the chance to prove ties illegal under the rule of reason, or to prove that a tie was an act or attempt of monopolization. Proving a case under the rule of reason, however, is far more difficult, time consuming, and expensive than applying a so-called *per se* rule, isn't it?

In any event, does the four-part test of *Jefferson Parish* really establish a *"per se"* rule? Most *per se* rules, like the rule against horizontal division of markets exemplified by *Topco*, involve simple categorization of behavior. In contrast, the so-called *per se* rule for tying requires an assessment of the tie's actual ability to coerce (through market power) and its effect on a substantial volume of commerce. Is that sort of rule based upon simple categorization of conduct? Or is it a shorthand application of market-based antitrust analysis, suggesting a clear and present danger to competition?

21. The *Microsoft III* did not limit its holding to the case before it. It purported broadly to hold that the rule of reason applies to any tie in which "the tying product is software whose major purpose is to serve as a platform for third-party applications and the tied product is complementary software functionality." 253 F.3d at 95.

Is this statement holding or dictum? Is it a good rule? Will it encourage independent firms to create third-party applications in the form of add-ons and tie their "me too" products to their dominant platforms? Will it encourage innovation in the software industry? Or will it encourage purveyors of dominant platforms to copy the functionality of others' innovative add-ons, thereby discouraging independent innovation?

Would a contrary rule that prohibited dominant platform purveyors from copying others' new functionality without unbundling it substantially impair their ability to make truly independent innovations? Would it hurt consumers?

22. The very software industry in which Microsoft now weighs so heavily began by unbundling a tie. In the late 1960s, IBM Corp. had nearly as dominant a share of the mar-

ket for computer hardware as Microsoft now does of the PC operating-system software market. *See* Jay Dratler, Jr., *Microsoft as an Antitrust Target: IBM in Software?*, 25 Sw. U. L. Rev. 671, 674 (1996) ("Although estimates of [IBM's] market share varied, they generally exceeded seventy percent, depending on the precise market at issue.") (footnote omitted). At that time, IBM also was nearly the sole purveyor of commercially useful software, including operating systems. The reason was that IBM had developed both the machines and the software to run them. IBM tied its software to its hardware, refusing to sell the machines separately, thereby creating a huge barrier to entry in the nascent business of writing software. In 1969, under the threat of antitrust litigation (including tying claims) from the United States government and private parties, IBM voluntarily unbundled its software from its hardware, giving birth to the software industry. *See id.* at 730–31. An important computer industry executive later described this event as "the second milestone in the history of the computer industry, the first being the change from vacuum tube to transistor technology." Martha Rounds, *IBM Saw 'Limited' Software Industry; 1969 Prediction: 'Limited But Increasing Number of Enterprises Engaged in the Development of Computer Programs for Sale*, 9 Software Mag. 37 (Mar. 15, 1989) (quoting William Norris, president of Control Data Corporation, an IBM competitor).

The software that IBM unbundled voluntarily was entirely of its own invention and design. IBM had not copied the functionality of anyone else's pioneering innovation, as Microsoft had done in the case of Netscape. Rather, IBM's employees had written the software that it unbundled in order to permit its machines to do useful work for customers. Yet by voluntarily unbundling (albeit under the pressure of antitrust litigation), IBM created the software industry, part of which Microsoft dominates today.

Is this tale just a bit of esoteric history, or does it suggest a better way to build innovative industries and avoid undue industrial concentration? Where would the software industry be today if the courts in the 1960s and 1970s, like the D.C. Circuit, had applied the rule of reason to tying software add-ons to IBM's hardware "platforms"? Would IBM have voluntarily unbundled software and created a new industry?

———————

# Chapter 10

# License Litigation and Trends in Judicial Enforcement

## I. Introduction

Disputes over license agreements are most often about the scope of licensed subject matter, amount of royalty due, term of agreement, and the meaning of various provisions that govern the conduct of the parties. Disputes can and do arise concerning validity and infringement, which, of course, are matters of federal law, but the remaining disputes are matters of contract enforcement and arise under state law.

Because both federal and state law may be applied to a license dispute, there is a continuing natural tension between federal and state law in license litigation. The parties most often express as the right to write the terms of their own bargain so long as it does not violate federal law.

Parts II and III examine that tension in the context of the doctrines of estoppel and patent misuse. In Part IV the materials illustrate, on a practical level, how state law enforces some of the more common license terms.

## II. Estoppel

### A. Patent Licensee Estoppel

#### Lear, Inc. v. Adkins
395 U.S. 653 (1969)

Opinion by Harlan, J.

\* \* \*

The progress of Adkins' effort to obtain a patent followed the typical pattern. In his initial application, the inventor made the ambitious claim that his entire method of constructing gyroscopes was sufficiently novel to merit protection. The Patent Office, however, rejected this initial claim, as well as two subsequent amendments, which progressively narrowed the scope of the invention sought to be protected. Finally, Adkins narrowed his claim drastically to assert only that the design of the apparatus used to achieve gyroscope accuracy was novel. In response, the Office issued its 1960 patent, granting a 17-year monopoly on this more modest claim.

During the long period in which Adkins was attempting to convince the Patent Office of the novelty of his ideas, however, Lear had become convinced that Adkins would never receive a patent on his invention and that it should not continue to pay substantial royalties on ideas which had not contributed substantially to the development of the art of gyroscopy. In 1957, after Adkins' patent application had been rejected twice, Lear announced that it had searched the Patent Office's files and had found a patent which it believed had fully anticipated Adkins' discovery. As a result, the company stated that it would no longer pay royalties on the large number of gyroscopes it was producing at its plant in Grand Rapids, Michigan (the Michigan gyros). Payments were continued on the smaller number of gyros produced at the company's California plant (the California gyros) for two more years until they too were terminated on April 8, 1959.

As soon as Adkins obtained his patent in 1960, he brought this lawsuit in the California Superior Court. He argued to a jury that both the Michigan and the California gyros incorporated his patented apparatus and that Lear's failure to pay royalties on these gyros was a breach both of the 1955 contract and of Lear's quasi-contractual obligations.

\* \* \*

Once again both sides appealed, this time to the California Supreme Court, which... rejected the District Court of Appeal's conclusion that the 1955 license gave Lear the right to terminate its royalty obligations in 1959. Since the 1955 agreement was still in effect, the court concluded, relying on the language we have already quoted, that the doctrine of estoppel barred Lear from questioning the propriety of the Patent Office's grant. 67 Cal. 2d [882], 907, 435 P.2d [321], 336 (1967). The court's adherence to estoppel, however, was not without qualification. After noting Lear's claim that it had developed its Michigan gyros independently, the court tested this contention by considering "whether what is being built by Lear [in Michigan] springs entirely" (emphasis supplied) from the prior art. 67 Cal. 2d at 913, 435 P. 2d at 340. Applying this test, it found that Lear had in fact "utilized the apparatus patented by Adkins throughout the period in question," 67 Cal. 2d at 915, 435 P. 2d at 341.

\* \* \*

## B.

The estoppel rule was first stringently limited in a situation in which the patentee's equities were far more compelling than those presented in the typical licensing arrangement. *Westinghouse Electric & Manufacturing Co. v. Formica Insulation Co.*, 266 U.S. 342 (1924), framed a rule to govern the recurring problem which arises when the original patent owner, after assigning his patent to another for a substantial sum, claims that the patent is worthless because it contains no new ideas. The courts of appeals had traditionally refused to permit such a defense to an infringement action on the ground that it was improper both to "sell and keep the same thing," *Faulks v. Kamp*, 3 F. 898, 902 (1880). Nevertheless, *Formica* imposed a limitation upon estoppel which was radically inconsistent with the premises upon which the "general rule" is based. The Court held that while an assignor may not directly attack the validity of a patent by reference to the prior state of the art, he could introduce such evidence to narrow the claims made in the patent. "The distinction may be a nice one but seems to be workable." 266

U.S. at 351. Workable or not, the result proved to be an anomaly: if a patent had some novelty *Formica* permitted the old owner to defend an infringement action by showing that the invention's novel aspects did not extend to the inclusion of the old owner's products; on the other hand, if a patent had no novelty at all, the old owner could not defend successfully since he would be obliged to launch the direct attack on the patent that *Formica* seemed to forbid. The incongruity of this position compelled at least one court of appeals to carry the reasoning of the *Formica* exception to its logical conclusion. In 1940 the Seventh Circuit held that a licensee could introduce evidence of the prior art to show that the licensor's claims were not novel at all and thus successfully defend an action for royalties. *Casco Products Corp. v. Sinko Tool & Manufacturing Co.,* 116 F.2d 119.

In *Scott Paper Co. v. Marcalus Manufacturing Co.,* 326 U.S. 249 (1945), this Court adopted a position similar to the Seventh Circuit's, undermining the basis of patent estoppel even more than *Formica* had done. In *Scott,* the original patent owner had attempted to defend an infringement suit brought by his assignee by proving that this product was a copy of an expired patent. The Court refused to permit the assignee to invoke an estoppel, finding that the policy of the patent laws would be frustrated if a manufacturer was required to pay for the use of information which, under the patent statutes, was the property of all. Chief Justice Stone, for the Court, did not go beyond the precise question presented by a manufacturer who asserted that he was simply copying an expired patent. Nevertheless it was impossible to limit the *Scott* doctrine to such a narrow compass. If patent policy forbids estoppel when the old owner attempts to show that he did no more than copy an expired patent, why should not the old owner also be permitted to show that the invention lacked novelty because it could be found in a technical journal or because it was obvious to one knowledgeable in the art? As Justice Frankfurter's dissent indicated, *id.* at 258–64, there were no satisfactory answers to these questions. The *Scott* exception had undermined the very basis of the "general rule."

## C.

At about the time *Scott* was decided, this Court developed yet another doctrine which was profoundly antithetic to the principles underlying estoppel. In *Sola Electric Co. v. Jefferson Electric Co.,* 317 U.S. 173 (1942), the majority refused to permit a licensor to enforce the license's price-fixing provisions without permitting the licensee to contest the validity of the underlying patent. Since the price-fixing clause was per se illegal but for the existence of a valid patent, this narrow exception could be countenanced without compromising the general estoppel principle. But the *Sola* Court went further: it held that since the patentee had sought to enforce the price-fixing clause, the licensee could also avoid paying royalties if he could show that the patent was invalid. Five years later, the "anti-trust exception" was given an even more extensive scope in the *Katzinger* and *MacGregor* cases. Here, licensors were not permitted to invoke an estoppel despite the fact that they sought only to collect their royalties. The mere existence of a price-fixing clause in the license was held to be enough to bring the validity of the patent into question. Thus in the large number of cases in which licensing agreements contained restrictions that were arguably illegal under the antitrust laws, the doctrine of estoppel was a dead letter. Justice Frankfurter, in dissent, went even further, concluding that *Katzinger* and *MacGregor* had done all but repudiate the estoppel rule: "If a doctrine that was vital law for more than ninety years will be found to have now been deprived of life, we ought at least to give it decent public burial." 329 U.S. at 416.

* * *

## III.

The uncertain status of licensee estoppel in the case law is a product of judicial efforts to accommodate the competing demands of the common law of contracts and the federal law of patents. On the one hand, the law of contracts forbids a purchaser to repudiate his promises simply because he later becomes dissatisfied with the bargain he has made. On the other hand, federal law requires that all ideas in general circulation be dedicated to the common good unless they are protected by a valid patent. *Sears, Roebuck v. Stiffel Co., supra; Compco Corp. v. Day-Brite Lighting, Inc., supra.* When faced with this basic conflict in policy, both this Court and courts throughout the land have naturally sought to develop an intermediate position which somehow would remain responsive to the radically different concerns of the two different worlds of contract and patent. The result has been a failure. Rather than creative compromise, there has been a chaos of conflicting case law, proceeding on inconsistent premises. Before renewing the search for an acceptable middle ground, we must reconsider on their own merits the arguments which may properly be advanced on both sides of the estoppel question.

### A.

It will simplify matters greatly if we first consider the most typical situation in which patent licenses are negotiated. In contrast to the present case, most manufacturers obtain a license after a patent has issued. Since the Patent Office makes an inventor's ideas public when it issues its grant of a limited monopoly, a potential licensee has access to the inventor's ideas even if he does not enter into an agreement with the patent owner. Consequently, a manufacturer gains only two benefits if he chooses to enter a licensing agreement after the patent has issued. First, by accepting a license and paying royalties for a time, the licensee may have avoided the necessity of defending an expensive infringement action during the period when he may be least able to afford one. Second, the existence of an unchallenged patent may deter others from attempting to compete with the licensee.

Under ordinary contract principles the mere fact that some benefit is received is enough to require the enforcement of the contract, regardless of the validity of the underlying patent. Nevertheless, if one tests this result by the standard of good-faith commercial dealing, it seems far from satisfactory. For the simple contract approach entirely ignores the position of the licensor who is seeking to invoke the court's assistance on his behalf. Consider, for example, the equities of the licensor who has obtained his patent through a fraud on the Patent Office. It is difficult to perceive why good faith requires that courts should permit him to recover royalties despite his licensee's attempts to show that the patent is invalid....

Even in the more typical cases, not involving conscious wrongdoing, the licensor's equities are far from compelling. A patent, in the last analysis, simply represents a legal conclusion reached by the Patent Office. Moreover, the legal conclusion is predicated on factors as to which reasonable men can differ widely. Yet the Patent Office is often obliged to reach its decision in an ex parte proceeding, without the aid of the arguments which could be advanced by parties interested in proving patent invalidity. Consequently, it does not seem to us to be unfair to require a patentee to defend the Patent Office's judgment when his licensee places the question in issue, especially since the licensor's case is buttressed by the presumption of validity which attaches to his patent. Thus, although licensee estoppel may be consistent with the letter of contractual doctrine, we cannot say that it is compelled by the spirit of contract law, which seeks to balance the claims of promisor and promisee in accord with the requirements of good faith.

Surely the equities of the licensor do not weigh very heavily when they are balanced against the important public interest in permitting full and free competition in the use of ideas which are in reality a part of the public domain. Licensees may often be the only individuals with enough economic incentive to challenge the patentability of an inventor's discovery. If they are muzzled, the public may continually be required to pay tribute to would-be monopolists without need or justification. We think it plain that the technical requirements of contract doctrine must give way before the demands of the public interest in the typical situation involving the negotiation of a license after a patent has issued.

We are satisfied that *Automatic Radio Manufacturing Co. v. Hazeltine Research, Inc., supra,* itself the product of a clouded history, should no longer be regarded as sound law with respect to its "estoppel" holding, and that holding is now overruled.

### B.

The case before us, however, presents a far more complicated estoppel problem than the one which arises in the most common licensing context. The problem arises out of the fact that Lear obtained its license in 1955, more than four years before Adkins received his 1960 patent. Indeed, from the very outset of the relationship, Lear obtained special access to Adkins' ideas in return for its promise to pay satisfactory compensation.

Thus, during the lengthy period in which Adkins was attempting to obtain a patent, Lear gained an important benefit not generally obtained by the typical licensee. For until a patent issues, a potential licensee may not learn his licensor's ideas simply by requesting the information from the Patent Office. During the time the inventor is seeking patent protection, the governing federal statute requires the Patent Office to hold an inventor's patent application in confidence. If a potential licensee hopes to use the ideas contained in a secret patent application, he must deal with the inventor himself, unless the inventor chooses to publicize his ideas to the world at large. By promising to pay Adkins royalties from the very outset of their relationship, Lear gained immediate access to ideas which it may well not have learned until the Patent Office published the details of Adkins' invention in 1960. At the core of this case, then, is the difficult question whether federal patent policy bars a State from enforcing a contract regulating access to an unpatented secret idea.

Adkins takes an extreme position on this question. The inventor does not merely argue that since Lear obtained privileged access to his ideas before 1960, the company should be required to pay royalties accruing before 1960 regardless of the validity of the patent which ultimately issued. He also argues that since Lear obtained special benefits before 1960, it should also pay royalties during the entire patent period (1960–1977), without regard to the validity of the Patent Office's grant. We cannot accept so broad an argument.

Adkins' position would permit inventors to negotiate all important licenses during the lengthy period while their applications were still pending at the Patent Office, thereby disabling entirely all those who have the strongest incentive to show that a patent is worthless. While the equities supporting Adkins' position are somewhat more appealing than those supporting the typical licensor, we cannot say that there is enough of a difference to justify such a substantial impairment of overriding federal policy.

Nor can we accept a second argument which may be advanced to support Adkins' claim to at least a portion of his post-patent royalties, regardless of the validity of the Patent Office grant. The terms of the 1955 agreement provide that royalties are to be paid until such time as the "patent...is held invalid," and the fact remains that the question of patent validity has not been finally determined in this case. Thus, it may be suggested that although Lear must be allowed to raise the question of patent validity in the present lawsuit, it must also be required to comply with its contract and continue to pay royalties until its claim is finally vindicated in the courts.

The parties' contract, however, is no more controlling on this issue than is the State's doctrine of estoppel, which is also rooted in contract principles. The decisive question is whether overriding federal policies would be significantly frustrated if licensees could be required to continue to pay royalties during the time they are challenging patent validity in the courts.

It seems to us that such a requirement would be inconsistent with the aims of federal patent policy. Enforcing this contractual provision would give the licensor an additional economic incentive to devise every conceivable dilatory tactic in an effort to postpone the day of final judicial reckoning. We can perceive no reason to encourage dilatory court tactics in this way. Moreover, the cost of prosecuting slow-moving trial proceedings and defending an inevitable appeal might well deter many licensees from attempting to prove patent invalidity in the courts. The deterrent effect would be particularly severe in the many scientific fields in which invention is proceeding at a rapid rate. In these areas, a patent may well become obsolete long before its 17-year term has expired. If a licensee has reason to believe that he will replace a patented idea with a new one in the near future, he will have little incentive to initiate lengthy court proceedings, unless he is freed from liability at least from the time he refuses to pay the contractual royalties. Lastly, enforcing this contractual provision would undermine the strong federal policy favoring the full and free use of ideas in the public domain. For all these reasons, we hold that Lear must be permitted to avoid the payment of all royalties accruing after Adkins' 1960 patent issued if Lear can prove patent invalidity.

* * *

---

## B.  Patent Assignor Estoppel

### Diamond Scientific Co. v. Ambico, Inc.

848 F.2d 1220 (Fed. Cir. 1988),
*cert. denied*, 487 U.S. 1265 (1988)

Opinion by Davis, Circuit Judge.

I.

This is the first opportunity presented to this court to examine the doctrine of assignor estoppel. Although the Supreme Court has examined this doctrine or a related doctrine—licensee estoppel—several times this century, its opinions have hardly been definite or definitive.

Beginning with *Westinghouse Electric & Manufacturing Co. v. Formica Insulation Co.*, 266 U.S. 342, 69 L. Ed. 316, 45 S. Ct. 117 (1924), the Supreme Court endorsed the rule that an assignor can be estopped from challenging the validity of the assigned patent when the assignor is sued by the assignee for infringement of the assigned patent. This estoppel bars only the assignor (and those in privity with the assignor), leaving everyone else free to try to invalidate the patent. The Court did, however, limit the estoppel by allowing the assignor to present evidence of the state of the art for the sole purpose of construing and narrowing the claims of the patent. *Id.* at 350. This accommodation permitted the assignor to defend against the infringement suit by attempting to show that the accused device fell outside the proper scope of the claims of the patent in suit, yet prevented the assignor from attacking the patent's validity.

In *Scott Paper Co. v. Marcalus Manufacturing Co.*, 326 U.S. 249, 90 L. Ed. 47, 66 S. Ct. 101 (1945), the Court sidestepped a reexamination of the merits of the assignor estoppel doctrine by once more carving an exception from the general rule. In that case, the defendant-assignor contended that the patent claimed to be infringed represented the same invention as a previously expired patent found in the prior art. The Court held that the doctrine of assignor estoppel was not available to the assignee "to foreclose the assignor of a patent from asserting the right to make use of the prior art invention of an expired patent, which anticipates that of the assigned patent...." *Id.* at 257. The Court found that the application of the doctrine in that instance was incompatible "with the patent laws which dedicate to public use the invention of an expired patent." *Id.* at 258. *Scott Paper* was a less-than-enthusiastic acknowledgment of assignor estoppel, but the Court was careful to distinguish its decision from previous applications of the doctrine: "To whatever extent that doctrine may be deemed to have survived the *Formica* decision or to be restricted by it, we think that case is not controlling here." *Id.* at 254.

*Scott Paper* is the most recent word from the Supreme Court on assignor estoppel. However, in *Lear, Inc. v. Adkins*, 395 U.S. 653, 23 L. Ed. 2d 610, 89 S. Ct. 1902 (1969), the Court addressed the somewhat analogous doctrine of licensee estoppel. Reasoning that "the equities of the licensor do not weigh very heavily when they are balanced against the important public interest in permitting full and free competition in the use of ideas which are in reality a part of the public domain[,]" the Court explicitly abolished licensee estoppel. Although *Lear* involved the licensing, rather than the assignment, of a patent, the opinion reviewed the history of "patent estoppel" in general, and indicated that the Court's previous decisions had sapped much of the vitality, if not the logic, from the assignment estoppel doctrine as well. Recalling *Scott Paper*, the Court asked, "If patent policy forbids estoppel when the old owner attempts to show that he did no more than copy an expired patent, why should not the old owner also be permitted to show that the invention lacked novelty because it could be found in a technical journal or because it was obvious to one knowledgeable in the art?...The *Scott* exception had undermined the very basis of the 'general rule.'" *Lear*, 395 U.S. at 666.

*Lear* resolved the issue of licensee estoppel by writing its obituary; but for courts wrestling with assignor estoppel it was less clear whether *Lear* had also sounded the death knell for that doctrine. Certainly, there was nothing in its holding that eliminated the doctrine. Beyond the questioning dicta in *Lear*, the Court has left assignment estoppel untouched for the past nineteen years.

## II.

The federal court cases, decided either shortly before *Lear* or since then, that discuss the doctrine of assignor estoppel reveal some uncertainty about the continued vitality of the doctrine. At least two courts have acknowledged the doctrine, although rejecting on the facts its application to the cases before them. At least five other courts have indicated their belief that assignor estoppel is no longer the prevailing rule of law. None of these courts provided much analysis of the doctrine or the reasons supporting its application in the specific circumstances, preferring instead to view the general rationale of the *Scott Paper* and *Lear* decisions as rejecting any further use of assignor estoppel. Two other courts have held that an assignee may be estopped from challenging the validity of the assigned patent. *Roberts v. Sears, Roebuck & Co.*, 573 F.2d 976, 197 USPQ 516 (7th Cir. 1978); *Coast Metals, Inc. v. Cape*, 205 USPQ 154 (D.N.J. 1979). However, the distinction between an assignor and an assignee of a patent gives those cases a distinctly different, but equally apparent, reason for application of estoppel. If an assignee of a patent were allowed to challenge the patent, it could be placed in the legally awkward position of simultaneously attacking and defending the validity of the same patent.

## III.

In examining *Lear*, one important distinction between assignors and licensees becomes apparent—a distinction that cautions against the automatic application to assignment cases of the rationale underlying *Lear* and licensees. The public policy favoring allowing a licensee to contest the validity of the patent is not present in the assignment situation. Unlike the licensee, who, without *Lear* might be forced to continue to pay for a potentially invalid patent, the assignor who would challenge the patent has already been fully paid for the patent rights.

Assignor estoppel is an equitable doctrine that prevents one who has assigned the rights to a patent (or patent application) from later contending that what was assigned is a nullity. The estoppel also operates to bar other parties in privity with the assignor, such as a corporation founded by the assignor.

## IV.

Our holding is that this is a case in which public policy calls for the application of assignor estoppel. We are, of course, not unmindful of the general public policy disfavoring the repression of competition by the enforcement of worthless patents. Yet despite the public policy encouraging people to challenge potentially invalid patents, there are still circumstances in which the equities of the contractual relationships between the parties should deprive one party (as well as others in privity with it) of the right to bring that challenge.

Appellants argue that assignor estoppel is necessarily a variation of estoppel by conduct and should be governed by the traditional elements of equitable estoppel. But the Supreme Court has never analyzed assignor estoppel by reference to the elements of equitable estoppel and has explicitly recognized assignor estoppel to be the functional equivalent of estoppel by deed. *Westinghouse*, 266 U.S. at 348–49. Estoppel by deed is a form of legal, not equitable, estoppel. *AMP, Inc. v. United States*, 182 Ct. Cl. 86, 389 F.2d 448, 452, 156 USPQ 647, 649, *cert. denied*, 391 U.S. 964, 20 L. Ed. 2d 878, 88 S. Ct. 2033 (1968). The *Westinghouse* Court did not specify whether assignor estoppel operates in precisely the same manner as estoppel by deed, which ordinarily prevents one from attacking any material fact found in the document (or deed) transferring the rights—whether assignor estoppel would prevent an assignor from attacking a material fact found in the assignment, thereby preventing the assignor's assertion of invalidity. But the extent to which the concept of an estoppel by deed may or may not shape the doctrine of assignor estoppel, though it may often play a significant role, need not confine our application of the doctrine. As noted above, we believe that the primary consideration in now applying the doctrine is the measure of unfairness and injustice that would be suffered by the assignee if the assignor were allowed to raise defenses of patent invalidity. Our analysis must be concerned mainly with the balance of equities between the parties.

We note first that Dr. Welter assigned the rights to his inventions to Diamond in exchange for valuable consideration (one dollar plus other unspecified consideration—presumably his salary over many years and other employment benefits). Dr. Welter also executed an inventor's oath, which stated his belief, inter alia, that he was the first and sole inventor, that the invention was never known or used before his invention and that it was not previously patented or described in any publication in any country. Furthermore, Dr. Welter apparently participated actively in the patent application process, including drafting the initial version of the claims and consulting on their revision.

Appellants would now defend against accusations of infringement by trying to show that the three patents in issue are invalid because the inventions either were inadequately disclosed by the specifications, lacked novelty, or would have been obvious to one of ordinary skill at the time the inventions were made. If appellants are permitted to raise these defenses and are successful in their proof, Dr. Welter will have profited both by his initial assignment of the patent applications and by his later attack on the value of the very subjects of his earlier assignment. In comparison, Diamond will have given value for the rights to Dr. Welter's inventions only to have him later deprive Diamond of the worth of those assigned rights.

We agree with the district court that the equities weigh heavily in favor of Diamond. Although the doctrine of assignor estoppel may no longer be a broad equitable device susceptible of automatic application, the case before us is appropriate for its use. When the inventor-assignor has signed the Oath, Power of Attorney and Petition, which attests to his belief in the validity of the patents, and has assigned the patent rights to another for valuable consideration, he should be estopped from defending patent infringement claims by proving that what he assigned was worthless. That is an implicit component of the assignment by Welter to Diamond which is immune from contradiction. The inventor's active participation in the prosecution and preparation of the patent applications, as is alleged here, would tilt the equities even more heavily in favor of the assignee, but consideration of this factor is not necessary to the result.

It is also irrelevant that, at the time of the assignment, Dr. Welter's patent applications were still pending and the Patent Office had not yet granted the patents. What Dr. Welter assigned were the rights to his inventions. That Diamond may have later amended the claims in the application process (a very common occurrence in patent prosecutions), with or without Dr. Welter's assistance, does not give appellants' arguments against estoppel any greater force. Our concern must be the balance of the equities. The fact is that Dr. Welter assigned the rights to his invention, irrespective of the particular language in the claims describing the inventions when the patents were ultimately granted. Appellants should not be allowed now to destroy those rights by derogating the patents' validity. Cf. AMP, Inc., 389 F.2d at 452, 156 USPQ at 649–50 (legal estoppel, in context of implied license doctrine, prevents licensor (or assignor) who has licensed (or assigned) a definable property right for valuable consideration from attempting to derogate or detract from that right). In *Westinghouse*, the Court observed that the scope of the right conveyed in the assignment of patent rights before the granting of the patent "is much less certainly defined than that of a granted patent, and the question of the extent of the estoppel against the assignor of such an inchoate right is more difficult to determine than in the case of the patent assigned after its granting." *Westinghouse*, 266 U.S. at 352–53. However, the Court merely suggested that "this difference might justify the view that the range of relevant and competent evidence in fixing the limits of the subsequent estoppel should be more liberal than in the case of an assignment of a granted patent" and found it unnecessary to decide the question. *Id.* at 353.

Nevertheless, *Westinghouse* does allow for an accommodation in such circumstances. To the extent that Diamond may have broadened the claims in the patent applications (after the assignments) beyond what could be validly claimed in light of the prior art, *Westinghouse* may allow appellants to introduce evidence of prior art to narrow the scope of the claims of the patents, which may bring their accused devices outside the scope of the claims of the patents in suit. *Id.* at 350. This exception to assignor estoppel also shows that estopping appellants from raising invalidity defenses does not necessarily prevent them from successfully defending against Diamond's infringement claims.

\* \* \*

---

# C.  Trademark Licensee Estoppel

## Seven-Up Bottling Co. v. The Seven-Up Co.
### 561 F.2d 1275 (8th Cir. 1977)

BRIGHT, Circuit Judge.

\* \* \*

Since 1929, appellee Company has sold extracts used in flavoring soft drinks and appellant Bottling has purchased the extracts from the Company, and bottled and locally distributed a soft drink made with the extract under the trademark "Seven-Up." Appellee Services was formed in 1957 to aid distributors in production and marketing of Seven-Up.

The Company secured registrations of the trademarks "Seven-Up" and "7-Up" in 1929 and 1936, for soft drinks and the syrups and extracts used in their production. From 1929 until 1939, the Company dealt with its distributors on an informal basis, with no written distributorship agreements. In 1938, this practice ended with the initiation of a franchising policy. The Company granted franchises to local bottlers who would purchase flavor extract from the Company for production and sale of soft drinks under the trademark "Seven-Up." The Company itself did not produce finished soft drinks. Franchisees were assigned territories with "the exclusive rights within said territories to prepare such soft drinks according to the formula of Company in packages bearing the trademark 'Seven-Up.'" Bottling is a party to two such agreements for territories in Missouri and Illinois, dated January 24, 1939 and January 25, 1939. These agreements contain no express term of duration.

Before 1943, the Company's licensees, such as Bottling, advertised "Seven-Up" individually in their own territories. During 1943, a national media campaign was organized by a number of licensees, including Bottling. Each licensee contributed $17.50 per gallon of flavor extract purchased from the Company to a fund administered by the Company as trustee. The Company made no contributions to this fund, but used the fund to purchase national media advertising to develop the good will of itself and its developers. This advertising fund terminated in 1950.

During 1942 and 1943, the Company applied to register the trademark "Seven-Up" along with accompanying drawings as a "collective" mark for soft drinks showing the collective mark as used on the goods "by persons duly authorized by" the Company.

Those applications state that the "collective" mark was used since 1928 by persons authorized by the Company to show the Company as the single source of "extracts or other ingredients used in compounding the beverage."

Between 1954 and 1966, the Company obtained six additional registrations showing "7-Up" in various contexts, which made claims similar to those in the 1929 and 1936 registrations. There is presently an application pending for another such registration. In 1956, Bottling and the Company entered an agreement regarding the manufacture, promotion, and sale of "pre-mix" Seven-Up. Bottling expended a large amount of money to develop the pre-mix business.

Since 1961, Bottling has manufactured and sold "post-mix" or soda fountain syrup "Seven-Up." In 1961, Bottling was offered a contract by Company covering the promotion and sale of the syrup but which would have reserved to the Company the right to make and sell syrup in Bottling's territory or to designate others to do so. Bottling rejected this offer, contending that the attempted reservation of rights would permit the Company to compete unfairly with Bottling, and would infringe beneficial rights to exclusive use of "Seven-Up" trademarks which Bottling claimed under the "collective" trademark registrations of 1942 and 1943.

Accordingly, Bottling purchased syrup from Services until later in 1961 when the parties negotiated a contract with language which Bottling claims protects its exclusive right to produce and distribute "Seven-Up" in its territory.

In 1958, Company and Services arranged for "Seven-Up" to be produced in cans. Bottling began to purchase canned "Seven-Up" from Services in 1959. These purchases continued on an informal basis until January 1968, when Bottling and the Company executed a written contract allowing Bottling to purchase "Seven-Up" in cans from sources designated by the Company as "approved packagers." More recently, the Company required Bottling to purchase "Seven-Up" in cans from Services, at prices usually higher than those of "approved packagers." Bottling sought permission from the Company to can and distribute "Seven-Up" in its territory, but in 1974 the Company refused this request except on condition that Bottling: (1) agree that the Company reserves the right to manufacture finished "Seven-Up" soft drink in Bottling's territory; (2) surrender its 1939 contract with the Company; and (3) accept a new contract with a limited term of years. Company insisted on similar conditions before it would allow Bottling to package "Seven-Up" in plastic containers. This action followed.

* * *

The establishment of an existing licensor-licensee relationship between Company and Bottling effectively constitutes an insuperable bar to recovery by Bottling with regard to its trademark claims. Under the doctrine of licensee estoppel a plaintiff-licensee is estopped from contesting the validity of its licensor's marks. *Heaton Distributing Co. v. Union Tank Car. Co.*, 387 F.2d 477, 482 (8th Cir. 1967); III CALLMAN, UNFAIR COMPETITION, TRADEMARKS AND MONOPOLIES, § 78.02, at 454 (3d ed. 1970).

* * *

In the instant case, plaintiff by judicial admission has established the existence of a present and valid licensing agreement between plaintiff and defendant. Thus becomes operative that "long settled principle of law that a licensee of a trademark or trade name may not set up any adverse claim in it as against its licensor." *Pacific Supply Cooperative v. Farmers Union Central Exchange*, 318 F.2d 894, 908–9 (9th Cir. 1963), *cert. denied,*

375 U.S. 965, 84 S. Ct. 483, 11 L. Ed. 2d 414 (1964). Plaintiff Bottling seeks cancellation of seven trademark registrations (those of 1929, 1936, 1954, 1956, 1957, 1959 and 1966) and the refusal of the trademark application of 1975 on the grounds that such are "invalid, void and of no effect" as having been fraudulently obtained or requested on the basis of materially false and fraudulent statements. The two trademark registrations of 1966 and the trademark application of 1975 are sought to be canceled for alleged inconsistency with previously registered "collective" marks. Such alleged invalidity for false and fraudulent registration statements and inconsistency with other marks as well as the plaintiff's prayer for cancellation leave little doubt but that licensor-Company's title to the marks represented by those registrations is being attacked by its licensee. Accordingly, the licensee, Bottling, is estopped to deny the validity of those trademarks.

\* \* \*

Beyond its contention that the marks licensed to it are collective marks, Bottling offers no reason why it should not be estopped from making claims to the "Seven-Up" trademarks adverse to the Company. The district court properly dismissed Bottling's trademark claims.

\* \* \*

---

# Deer Park Spring Water, Inc. v. Appalachian Mountain Spring Water Co.
### 762 F. Supp. 62 (S.D.N.Y. 1991)

LOWE, J.

\* \* \*

Plaintiff contends that the doctrine of assignor estoppel should prevent Appalachian, as a matter of law, from relying upon the fair use defense in this case. In *Diamond Scientific Co. v. Ambico, Inc.*, 848 F.2d 1220, 1224, 6 U.S.P.Q.2d (BNA) 2028 (Fed. Cir.), *cert. dismissed*, 487 U.S. 1265, 101 L. Ed. 2d 978, 109 S. Ct. 28 (1988), the Court described assignor estoppel as "an equitable doctrine that prevents one who has assigned the rights to a patent...from later contending that what was assigned is a nullity." Even assuming the doctrine applies with equal force in trademark cases, however, it does not preclude Appalachian from asserting the fair use defense in this case.

Plaintiff relies on *Shamrock Technologies, Inc. v. Medical Sterilization, Inc.*, 903 F.2d 789, 794–96, 14 U.S.P.Q.2d (BNA) 1728 (Fed. Cir. 1990), in which the Court held that assignor estoppel would bar the defendant in a patent infringement case from asserting the equitable defense of "inequitable conduct" by the patent holder. To permit use of the defense, the Court reasoned, would mean that "*Diamond Scientific* could be avoided by merely couching invalidity defenses in terms of inequitable conduct...." *Id.* at 795. In the present case, by contrast, Appalachian seeks to use the fair use defense not to attack the validity of plaintiff's trademark, but to defend its own use as reasonable and non-infringing despite the mark's validity. In other words, Appalachian does not seek to argue "that what was assigned is a nullity." *Diamond Scientific, supra.* As such, assignor estoppel does not apply.

This district has held that "the 'fair use' defense does not encompass use that will lead to consumer confusion as to the source or origin of the goods at issue." *E.g., Cull-*

*man Ventures, Inc. v. Columbian Art Works, Inc.*, 717 F. Supp. 96, 134 (S.D.N.Y. 1989). Plaintiff argues that Appalachian's use was likely to result in consumer confusion, thus barring it from relying on the fair use defense. However, as discussed above, there is a genuine dispute of fact as to the likelihood of consumer confusion resulting from Appalachian's labels. Given this dispute, we cannot say as a matter of law that Appalachian would be precluded from asserting the fair use defense. For the above reasons, plaintiff's cross-motion for summary judgment is denied.

\* \* \*

# D. Copyright Licensee Estoppel

## Twin Books Corp. v. The Walt Disney Co.
### 877 F. Supp. 496 (N.D.Cal. 1995)

WILKEN, D.J.

\* \* \*

II. Licensee estoppel

Plaintiff raises licensee estoppel as a defense to Defendants' claim that the copyright is in the public domain, asserting that as a licensee of the copyright, Disney is estopped from challenging its validity. Once again, this is an issue of first impression. Although the Supreme Court has held that licensee estoppel is inapplicable to patent licensees, *See Lear v. Adkins*, 395 U.S. 653, 23 L. Ed. 2d 610, 89 S. Ct. 1902 (1969), no court has decided whether copyright licensees are estopped. However, the Ninth Circuit holds that "where precedent in copyright cases is lacking, it is appropriate to look for guidance to patent law, 'because of the historic kinship between patent law and copyright law.'" *Harris v. Emus Records Corp.*, 734 F.2d 1329, 1333 (1984) (quoting *Sony Corp. of America v. Universal City Studios*, 464 U.S. 417, 104 S. Ct. 774, 787, 78 L. Ed. 2d 574 (1984)). *See also* 3 NIMMER Sec. 10.15[B] at 10–125 ("On the basis of Lear, which has been applied outside the patent realm to copyright cases as well, plaintiffs may no longer argue licensee estoppel.").

Plaintiff's reliance on *Saturday Evening Post Co. v. Rumbleseat Press, Inc.*, 816 F.2d 1191 (7th Cir. 1987), is unpersuasive. First, as Defendants note, in that case the court upheld an explicit no-contest clause in the copyright. license, and limited its holding to that situation: "Our case involves a negotiated clause rather than a doctrine that in effect reads a no-contest clause into every licensing agreement." *Id.* at 1200. In the dictum cited by Plaintiff, the court opined that the economic argument made by the Supreme Court in *Lear* does not apply to copyright licensees, because the "economic power conferred is much smaller." *Id.* Plaintiff's attempt to rest on this argument, given the $ 490 million in "economic power" wielded by Disney by virtue of its Bambi license, is singularly unpersuasive.

Accordingly, the Court holds that licensee estoppel does not apply in this case.

\* \* \*

# III. Patent Misuse and Hybrid Licenses

A "hybrid" is the license of one or more technologies or properties that are protectable under more than one type of intellectual property right. One of the challenges of drafting hybrid licenses is to avoid violating patent law when drafting royalty clauses, as distinguished from the patent misuse that comes into play in the antitrust setting.

Licensors naturally seek, to the extent legally possible, to maximize their return on investment. They accomplish that in a variety of ways, for example, by granting multiple licenses in separate fields and territories, minimizing reductions from gross in the calculation of net sales, and charging the highest royalty rate for the longest period possible. Because licensed patents expire long before copyrights, trademarks, and trade secrets, licensors of hybrid properties may attempt to collect royalties during the entire useful life of the licensed subject matter, regardless of the differing terms. Licensees may willingly agree to longer royalty periods in order to justify a lower rate and to spread their financial obligations over as long a period as possible.

The following cases demonstrate the legal limitations on the parties' rights when devising such compensation schemes. In *Brulotte v. Thys Co.*, *infra*, the Supreme Court declared such royalty schemes invalid *per se* if they continue after a licensed patent's expiration. As will be seen, *Brulotte v. Thys* remains the law despite criticism from both judges and commentators.

---

## Brulotte v. Thys Co.
### 379 U.S. 29 (1964)

MR. JUSTICE DOUGLAS delivered the opinion of the Court.

Respondent, owner of various patents for hop-picking, sold a machine to each of the petitioners for a flat sum and issued a license for its use. Under that license there is payable a minimum royalty of $500 for each hop-picking season or $3.33 1/3 per 200 pounds of dried hops harvested by the machine, whichever is greater. The licenses by their terms may not be assigned nor may the machines be removed from Yakima County. The licenses issued to petitioners listed 12 patents relating to hop-picking machines; but only seven were incorporated into the machines sold to and licensed for use by petitioners. Of those seven all expired on or before 1957. But the licenses issued by respondent to them continued for terms beyond that date. Petitioners refused to make royalty payments accruing both before and after the expiration of the patents. This suit followed. One defense was misuse of the patents through extension of the license agreements beyond the expiration date of the patents. The trial court rendered judgment for respondent and the Supreme Court of Washington affirmed. 62 Wash. 2d 284, 382 P. 2d 271. The case is here on a writ of certiorari. 376 U.S. 905. We conclude that the judgment below must be reversed insofar as it allows royalties to be collected which accrued after the last of the patents incorporated into the machines had expired.

The Constitution by Art. I, § 8 authorizes Congress to secure "for limited times" to inventors "the exclusive right" to their discoveries. Congress exercised that power by 35 U. S. C. § 154 which provides in part as follows: "Every patent shall contain a short title of the invention and a grant to the patentee, his heirs or assigns, for the term of seventeen years, of the right to exclude others from making, using, or selling the invention throughout the United States, referring to the specification for the particulars thereof...." The right to make, the right to sell, and the right to use "may be granted or conferred separately by the patentee." *Adams v. Burke*, 17 Wall. 453, 456. But these rights become public property once the 17-year period expires. *See Singer Mfg. Co. v. June Mfg. Co.*, 163 U.S. 169, 185; *Kellogg Co. v. National Biscuit Co.*, 305 U.S. 111, 118. As stated by Chief Justice Stone, speaking for the Court in *Scott Paper Co. v. Marcalus Co.*, 326 U.S. 249, 256:

> [A]ny attempted reservation or continuation in the patentee or those claiming under him of the patent monopoly, after the patent expires, whatever the legal device employed, runs counter to the policy and purpose of the patent laws.

The Supreme Court of Washington held that in the present case the period during which royalties were required was only "a reasonable amount of time over which to spread the payments for the use of the patent." 62 Wash. 2d, at 291, 382 P. 2d, at 275. But there is intrinsic evidence that the agreements were not designed with that limited view. As we have seen, the purchase price in each case was a flat sum, the annual payments not being part of the purchase price but royalties for use of the machine during that year. The royalty payments due for the post-expiration period are by their terms for use during that period, and are not deferred payments for use during the pre-expiration period. Nor is the case like the hypothetical ones put to us where non-patented articles are marketed at prices based on use. The machines in issue here were patented articles and the royalties exacted were the same for the post-expiration period as they were for the period of the patent. That is peculiarly significant in this case in view of other provisions of the license agreements. The license agreements prevent assignment of the machines or their removal from Yakima County after, as well as before, the expiration of the patents. Those restrictions are apt and pertinent to protection of the patent monopoly; and their applicability to the post-expiration period is a telltale sign that the licensor was using the licenses to project its monopoly beyond the patent period. They forcefully negate the suggestion that we have here a bare arrangement for a sale or a lease at an undetermined price, based on use. The sale or lease of unpatented machines on long-term payments based on a deferred purchase price or on use would present wholly different considerations. Those arrangements seldom rise to the level of a federal question. But patents are in the federal domain; and "whatever the legal device employed" (*Scott Paper Co. v. Marcalus Co., supra*, at 256) a projection of the patent monopoly after the patent expires is not enforceable. The present licenses draw no line between the term of the patent and the post-expiration period. The same provisions as respects both use and royalties are applicable to each. The contracts are, therefore, on their face a bald attempt to exact the same terms and conditions for the period after the patents have expired as they do for the monopoly period. We are, therefore, unable to conjecture what the bargaining position of the parties might have been and what resultant arrangement might have emerged had the provision for post-expiration royalties been divorced from the patent and nowise subject to its leverage. In light of those considerations, we conclude that a patentee's use of a royalty agreement that projects beyond the expiration date of the patent is unlawful per se. If that device were available to patentees, the free market visualized for the post-expiration period would be subject to monopoly influences that have no proper place there. *Automatic Radio Co. v. Hazeltine*, 339 U.S. 827, is not in point. While some of the patents under that license apparently had expired, the royalties claimed were not for a period when all of them had expired. That license covered several hundred patents and the royalty was based on the licensee's sales, even when no patents were used. The Court held that the computation of royalty payments by that formula was a convenient and reasonable device. We decline the invitation to extend it so as to project the patent monopoly beyond the 17-year period. A patent empowers the owner to exact royalties as high as he can negotiate with the leverage of that monopoly. But to use that leverage to project those royalty payments beyond the life of the patent is analogous to an effort to enlarge the monopoly of the patent by tying the sale or use of the patented article to the purchase or use of unpatented ones. *See Ethyl Gasoline Corp. v. United States*, 309 U.S. 436; *Mercoid Corp. v. Mid-Continent Inv. Co.*, 320 U.S. 661, 664–65, and cases cited. The exaction of royalties for use of a machine after the patent has expired is an assertion of monopoly power in the post-expiration period when, as we have seen, the patent has entered the public domain. We share the views of the Court of Appeals in *Ar-Tik Systems, Inc. v. Dairy Queen, Inc.*, 302 F.2d 496, 510, that after expiration of the last of the patents incorporated in the machines "the grant of patent monopoly was spent" and that an attempt to project it into another term by continuation of the licensing agreement is unenforceable.

*Reversed.*

\* \* \*

---

# Aronson v. Quick Point Pencil Co.
## 440 U.S. 257 (1979)

MR. CHIEF JUSTICE BURGER delivered the opinion of the Court.

We granted *certiorari*, 436 U.S. 943, to consider whether federal patent law preempts state contract law so as to preclude enforcement of a contract to pay royalties to a patent applicant, on sales of articles embodying the putative invention, for so long as the contracting party sells them, if a patent is not granted. In October 1955 the petitioner, Mrs. Jane Aronson, filed an application, Serial No. 542677, for a patent on a new form of keyholder. Although ingenious, the design was so simple that it readily could be copied unless it was protected by patent. In June 1956, while the patent application was pending, Mrs. Aronson negotiated a contract with the respondent, Quick Point Pencil Co., for the manufacture and sale of the keyholder. The contract was embodied in two documents. In the first, a letter from Quick Point to Mrs. Aronson, Quick Point agreed to pay Mrs. Aronson a royalty of 5% of the selling price in return for "the exclusive right to make and sell keyholders of the type shown in your application, Serial No. 542677." The letter further provided that the parties would consult one another concerning the steps to be taken "[in] the event of any infringement." The contract did not require Quick Point to manufacture the keyholder. Mrs. Aronson received a $ 750 advance on royalties and was entitled to rescind the exclusive license if Quick Point did not sell a million keyholders by the end of 1957. Quick Point retained the right to cancel the agreement whenever "the volume of sales does not meet our expectations." The duration of the agreement was not otherwise prescribed. A contemporaneous document provided that if Mrs. Aronson's patent application was "not allowed within five (5) years, Quick Point Pencil Co. [would] pay...two and one half percent (2 1/2%) of sales...so long as you [Quick Point] continue to sell same." In June 1961, when Mrs. Aronson had failed to obtain a patent on the keyholder within the five years specified in the agreement, Quick Point asserted its contractual right to reduce royalty payments to 2 1/2% of sales. In September of that year the Board of Patent Appeals issued a final rejection of the application on the ground that the keyholder was not patentable, and Mrs. Aronson did not appeal. Quick Point continued to pay reduced royalties to her for 14 years thereafter. The market was more receptive to the keyholder's novelty and utility than the Patent Office. By September 1975 Quick Point had made sales in excess of $7 million and paid Mrs. Aronson royalties totaling $203,963.84; sales were continuing to rise. However, while Quick Point was able to pre-empt the market in the earlier years and was long the only manufacturer of the Aronson keyholder, copies began to appear in the late 1960's. Quick Point's competitors, of course, were not required to pay royalties for their use of the design. Quick Point's share of the Aronson keyholder market has declined during the past decade. In November 1975 Quick Point commenced an action in the United States District Court for a declaratory judgment, pursuant to 28 U.S.C. § 2201, that the royalty agreement was unenforceable. Quick Point asserted that state law which might otherwise make the contract enforceable was pre-empted by federal patent law. This is the only issue presented to us for decision. Both parties moved for summary judgment on affidavits, exhibits, and stipulations of fact. The District Court concluded that the "language of the agreement is plain, clear and unequivocal and has no relation as to whether or not a patent is ever granted." Accordingly, it held that the agreement was valid, and that Quick Point was obliged to pay the agreed royalties pursuant to the contract for so long as it manufactured the keyholder. The Court of Appeals reversed, one judge dissenting. 567 F.2d 757. It held that since the parties contracted with reference to a pending patent application, Mrs. Aronson was estopped from denying that patent law principles governed her contract with Quick Point. Although acknowledging that this Court had never decided the precise issue, the Court of Appeals held that our prior decisions regarding patent licenses compelled the conclusion that Quick Point's contract with Mrs. Aronson became unenforceable once she failed to obtain a patent. The court held that a continuing obligation to pay royalties would be contrary to "the strong federal policy favoring the full and free use of ideas in the public domain," *Lear, Inc. v. Adkins*, 395 U.S. 653, 674 (1969). The court also observed that if Mrs. Aronson actually had obtained a patent, Quick Point would have escaped its royalty obligations either if the patent were held to be invalid, see ibid., or upon its expiration after 17 years, see *Brulotte v. Thys Co.*, 379 U.S. 29 (1964). Accordingly, it concluded that a licensee should be relieved of royalty obligations when the licensor's efforts to obtain a contemplated patent prove unsuccessful. On this record it is clear that the parties contracted with full awareness of both the pendency of a patent application and the possibility that a patent might not issue. The clause de-escalating the royalty by half in the event no patent issued within five years makes that crystal clear. Quick Point apparently placed a significant value on exploiting the basic novelty of the device, even if no patent issued; its success demonstrates that this judgment was well founded. Assuming, arguendo, that the initial letter and the commitment to pay a 5% royalty was subject to federal patent law, the provision relating to the 2 1/2% royalty was explicitly independent of federal law. The cases and principles relied on by the Court of Appeals and Quick Point do not bear on a contract that does not rely on a patent, particularly where, as here, the contracting parties agreed expressly as to alternative obligations if no patent should issue.

Commercial agreements traditionally are the domain of state law. State law is not displaced merely because the contract relates to intellectual property which may or may not be patentable; the states are free to regulate the use of such intellectual property in any manner not inconsistent with federal law. *Kewanee Oil Co. v. Bicron Corp.*, 416 U.S. 470, 479 (1974); see *Goldstein v. California*, 412 U.S. 546 (1973). In this as in other fields, the question of whether federal law pre-empts state law "involves a consideration of whether that law 'stands as an obstacle to the accomplishment and execution of the full purposes and objectives of Congress.' *Hines v. Davidowitz*, 312 U.S. 52, 67 (1941)." *Kewanee Oil Co., supra,* at 479. If it does not, state law governs. In *Kewanee Oil Co., supra,* at 480–81, we reviewed the purposes of the federal patent system. First, patent law seeks to foster and reward invention; second, it promotes disclosure of inventions to stimulate further innovation and to permit the public to practice the invention once the patent expires; third, the stringent requirements for patent protection seek to assure that ideas in the public domain remain there for the free use of the public. Enforcement of Quick Point's agreement with Mrs. Aronson is not inconsistent with any of these aims. Permitting inventors to make enforceable agreements licensing the use of their inventions in return for royalties provides an additional incentive to invention. Similarly, encouraging Mrs. Aronson to make arrangements for the manufacture of her keyholder furthers the federal policy of disclosure of inventions; these simple devices display the novel idea which they embody wherever they are seen. Quick Point argues that enforcement of such contracts conflicts with the federal policy against withdrawing ideas from the public domain and discourages recourse to the federal patent system by allowing states to extend "perpetual protection to articles too lacking in novelty to merit any patent at all under federal constitutional standards," *Sears, Roebuck & Co. v. Stiffel Co.,* 376 U.S. 225, 232 (1964). We find no merit in this contention. Enforcement of the agreement does not withdraw any idea from the public domain. The design for the keyholder was not in the public domain before Quick Point obtained its license to manufacture it. *See* Kewanee Oil Co., supra, at 484. In negotiating the agreement, Mrs. Aronson disclosed the design in confidence. Had Quick Point tried to exploit the design in breach of that confidence, it would have risked legal liability. It is equally clear that the design entered the public domain as a result of the manufacture and sale of the keyholders under the contract. Requiring Quick Point to bear the burden of royalties for the use of the design is no more inconsistent with federal patent law than any of the other costs involved in being the first to introduce a new product to the market, such as outlays for research and development, and marketing and promotional expenses. For reasons which Quick Point's experience with the Aronson keyholder demonstrate, innovative entrepreneurs have usually found such costs to be well worth paying. Finally, enforcement of this agreement does not discourage anyone from seeking a patent. Mrs. Aronson attempted to obtain a patent for over five years. It is quite true that had she succeeded, she would have received a 5% royalty only on keyholders sold during the 17-year life of the patent. Offsetting the limited terms of royalty payments, she would have received twice as much per dollar of Quick Point's sales, and both she and Quick Point could have licensed any others who produced the same keyholder. Which course would have produced the greater yield to the contracting parties is a matter of speculation; the parties resolved the uncertainties by their bargain. No decision of this Court relating to patents justifies relieving Quick Point of its contract obligations. We have held that a state may not forbid the copying of an idea in the public domain which does not meet the requirements for federal patent protection. *Compco Corp. v. Day-Brite Lighting, Inc.,* 376 U.S. 234 (1964); *Sears, Roebuck & Co. v. Stiffel Co., supra.* Enforcement of Quick Point's agreement, however, does not prevent anyone from copying the keyholder. It merely requires Quick Point to pay the consideration which it promised in return for the use of a novel device which enabled it to pre-empt the market. In *Lear, Inc. v. Adkins,* 395 U.S. 653 (1969), we held that a person licensed to use a patent may challenge the validity of the patent, and that a licensee who establishes that the patent is invalid need not pay the royalties accrued under the licensing agreement subsequent to the issuance of the patent. Both holdings relied on the desirability of encouraging licensees to challenge the validity of patents, to further the strong federal policy that only inventions which meet the rigorous requirements of patentability shall be withdrawn from the public domain. *Id.*, at 670–71, 673–74. Accordingly, neither the holding nor the rationale of *Lear* controls when no patent has issued, and no ideas have been withdrawn from public use.

Enforcement of the royalty agreement here is also consistent with the principles treated in *Brulotte v. Thys Co.*, 379 U.S. 29 (1964). There, we held that the obligation to pay royalties in return for the use of a patented device may not extend beyond the life of the patent. The principle underlying that holding was simply that the monopoly granted under a patent cannot lawfully be used to "negotiate with the leverage of that monopoly." The Court emphasized that to "use that leverage to project those royalty payments beyond the life of the patent is analogous to an effort to enlarge the monopoly of the patent...." *Id.*, at 33. Here the reduced royalty which is challenged, far from being negotiated "with the leverage" of a patent, rested on the contingency that no patent would issue within five years. No doubt a pending patent application gives the applicant some additional bargaining power for purposes of negotiating a royalty agreement. The pending application allows the inventor to hold out the hope of an exclusive right to exploit the idea, as well as the threat that the other party will be prevented from using the idea for 17 years. However, the amount of leverage arising from a patent application depends on how likely the parties consider it to be that a valid patent will issue. Here, where no patent ever issued, the record is entirely clear that the parties assigned a substantial likelihood to that contingency, since they specifically provided for a reduced royalty in the event no patent issued within five years. This case does not require us to draw the line between what constitutes abuse of a pending application and what does not. It is clear that whatever role the pending application played in the negotiation of the 5% royalty, it played no part in the contract to pay the 2 1/2% royalty indefinitely. Our holding in *Kewanee Oil Co.* puts to rest the contention that federal law pre-empts and renders unenforceable the contract made by these parties. There we held that state law forbidding the misappropriation of trade secrets was not pre-empted by federal patent law. We observed: "Certainly the patent policy of encouraging invention is not disturbed by the existence of another form of incentive to invention. In this respect the two systems [patent and trade secret law] are not and never would be in conflict." 416 U.S., at 484. Enforcement of this royalty agreement is even less offensive to federal patent policies than state law protecting trade secrets. The most commonly accepted definition of trade secrets is restricted to confidential information which is not disclosed in the normal process of exploitation. *See* RESTATEMENT OF TORTS § 757, Comment b, p. 5 (1939). Accordingly, the exploitation of trade secrets under state law may not satisfy the federal policy in favor of disclosure, whereas disclosure is inescapable in exploiting a device like the Aronson keyholder. Enforcement of these contractual obligations, freely undertaken in arm's-length negotiation and with no fixed reliance on a patent or a probable patent grant, will "encourage invention in areas where patent law does not reach, and will prompt the independent innovator to proceed with the discovery and exploitation of his invention. Competition is fostered and the public is not deprived of the use of valuable, if not quite patentable, invention." (Footnote omitted.) 416 U.S., at 485. The device which is the subject of this contract ceased to have any secrecy as soon as it was first marketed, yet when the contract was negotiated the inventiveness and novelty were sufficiently apparent to induce an experienced novelty manufacturer to agree to pay for the opportunity to be first in the market. Federal patent law is not a barrier to such a contract.

Reversed.

---

# Scheiber v. Dolby Laboratories, Inc., and Dolby Laboratories Licensing Corp.

293 F.3d 1014 (7th Cir. 2002), *cert. denied*, 537 U.S. 1109 (2003)

POSNER, Circuit Judge.

The plaintiff in a suit to enforce a patent licensing agreement appeals to us from the grant of summary judgment to the defendants, Dolby for short. Scheiber, the plaintiff, a musician turned inventor who held U.S. and Canadian patents on the audio system known as "surround sound," sued Dolby in 1983 for infringement of his patents. The parties settled the suit by agreeing that Scheiber would license his patents to Dolby in exchange for royalties. The last U.S. patent covered by the agreement was scheduled to expire in May 1993, while the last Canadian 2 No. 01-2466 patent was not scheduled to expire until September 1995. During the settlement negotiations Dolby suggested to Scheiber that in exchange for a lower royalty rate the license agreement provide that royalties on all the patents would continue until the Canadian patent expired, including, therefore, patents that had already expired. That way Dolby could, it hoped, pass on the entire royalty expense to its sublicensees without their balking at the rate. Scheiber acceded to the suggestion and the agreement was drafted accordingly, but Dolby later refused to pay royalties on any patent after it expired, precipitating this suit. Federal jurisdiction over the suit is based on diversity of citizenship, because a suit to enforce a patent licensing agreement does not arise under federal patent law. *E.g., Jim Arnold Corp. v. Hydrotech Systems, Inc.*, 109 F.3d 1567, 1575 (Fed. Cir. 1997). The presence of a federal defense (here, patent misuse) is irrelevant to jurisdiction. *Christianson v. Colt Industries Operating Corp.*, 486 U.S. 800 (1988).

\* \* \*

Dolby's principal argument is that the Supreme Court held in a decision that has never been overruled that a patent owner may not enforce a contract for the payment of patent royalties beyond the expiration date of the patent. The decision was *Brulotte v. Thys Co.*, 379 U.S. 29 (1964), dutifully followed by lower courts, including our own, in such cases as *Meehan v. PPG Industries, Inc.*, 802 F.2d 881, 883 (7th Cir. 1986); *Virginia Panel Corp. v. MAC Panel Co.*, 133 F.3d 860, 869 (Fed. Cir. 1997), and *Boggild v. Kenner Products*, 776 F.2d 1315, 1318–19 (6th Cir. 1985). *Brulotte* involved an agreement licensing patents that expired at different dates, just like this case; the two cases are indistinguishable. The decision has, it is true, been severely, and as it seems to us, with all due respect, justly, criticized, beginning with Justice Harlan's dissent, 379 U.S. at 34, and continuing with our opinion in *USM Corp. v. SPS Technologies, Inc.*, 694 F.2d 505, 510–11 (7th Cir. 1982). The Supreme Court's majority opinion reasoned that by extracting a promise to continue paying royalties after expiration of the patent, the patentee extends the patent beyond the term fixed in the patent statute and therefore in violation of the law. That is not true. After the patent expires, anyone can make the patented process or product without being guilty of patent infringement. The patent can no longer be used to exclude anybody from such production. Expiration thus accomplishes what it is supposed to accomplish. For a licensee in accordance with a provision in the license agreement to go on paying royalties after the patent expires does not extend the duration of the patent either technically or practically, because, as this case demonstrates, if the licensee agrees to continue paying royalties after the patent expires the royalty rate will be lower. The duration of the patent fixes the limit of the patentee's power to extract royalties; it is a detail whether he extracts them at a higher rate over a shorter period of time or a lower rate over a longer period of time.

This insight is not original with us. "The *Brulotte* rule incorrectly assumes that a patent license has significance after the patent terminates. When the patent term ends, the exclusive right to make, use or sell the licensed invention also ends. Because the invention is available to the world, the license in fact ceases to have value. Presumably, licensees know this when they enter into a licensing agreement. If the licensing agreement calls for royalty payments beyond the patent term, the parties base those payments o the licensees' assessment of the value of the license during the patent period. These payments, therefore, do not represent an extension in time of the patent monopoly.... Courts do not remove the obligation of the consignee to pay because payment after receipt is an extension of market power—it is simply a division of the payment-for-delivery transaction. Royalties beyond the patent term are no different. If royalties are calculated on post-patent term sales, the calculation is simply a risk-shifting credit arrangement between patentee and licensee. The arrangement can be no more than that, because the patentee at that time has nothing else to sell." Harold See & Frank M. Caprio, *The Trouble with Brulotte: the Patent Royalty Term and Patent Monopoly Extension*, 1990 UTAH L. REV. 813, 814, 851; to similar effect see Rochelle Cooper Dreyfuss, *Dethroning Lear: Licensee Estoppel and the Incentive to Innovate*, 72 VA. L. REV. 677, 709–12 (1986). "[T]he Supreme Court refused to see that typically such post-expiration royalties merely amortize the price of using patented technology." 10 PHILLIP E. AREEDA ET AL., ANTITRUST LAW §§1782c2-c3, pp. 505–11 (1996); *cf. Jahn v. 1-800-FLOWERS.com, Inc.*, 284 F.3d 807, 811–12 (7th Cir. 2002).

These criticisms might be wide of the mark if *Brulotte* had been based on the interpretation of the patent clause of the Constitution, or of the patent statute or any other statute; but it seems rather to have been a free-floating product of a misplaced fear of monopoly ("a patentee's use of a royalty agreement that projects beyond the expiration date of the patent is unlawful *per se*. If that device were available to patentees, the free market visualized for the post-expiration period would be subject to monopoly influences that have no proper place there," 379 U.S. at 32-33) that was not even tied to one of the antitrust statutes. 10 AREEDA *et al.*, *supra*, at §§1782c2, 1782c3, pp. 505, 511. The doctrinal basis of the decision was the doctrine of patent misuse, of which more later.

A patent confers a monopoly, and the longer the term of the patent the greater the monopoly. The limitation of the term of a patent, besides being commanded by the Constitution, see U.S. Const. art. I, §8, cl. 8; *Bonito Boats, Inc. v. Thunder Craft Boats, Inc.*, 489 U.S. 141, 146 (1989), and necessary to avoid impossible tracing problems (imagine if some caveman had gotten a perpetual patent on the wheel), serves to limit the monopoly power conferred on the patentee. But as we have pointed out, charging royalties beyond the term of the patent does not lengthen the patentee's monopoly; it merely alters the timing of royalty payments. This would be obvious if the license agreement between Scheiber and Dolby had become effective a month before the last patent expired. The parties could have agreed that Dolby would pay royalties for the next 100 years, but obviously the royalty rate would be minuscule because of the imminence of the patent's expiration.

However, we have no authority to overrule a Supreme Court decision no matter how dubious its reasoning strikes us, or even how out of touch with the Supreme Court's current thinking the decision seems.

* * *

Scheiber has another ground for disregarding *Brulotte* that deserves consideration.... The ground is that Dolby comes into court with "unclean hands" that should not be allowed to touch and stain the Supreme Court's decision. Scheiber points out that it was Dolby that asked him to stretch out the royalties until the last patent expired and that now seeks to get out of the obligation it not only accepted but volunteered to shoulder.

The doctrine of "unclean hands"—colorfully named, equitable in origin, and reflecting, in its name at least, the moralistic background of equity in the decrees of the clerics who filled the office of lord chancellor of England during the middle ages... nowadays just means that equitable relief will be refused if it would give the plaintiff a wrongful gain. "Today, 'unclean hands' really just means that in equity as in law the plaintiff's fault, like the defendant's, is relevant to the question of what if any remedy the plaintiff is entitled to. An obviously sensible application of this principle is to withhold an equitable remedy that would encourage or reward (and thereby encourage) illegal activity.... In what may have been the earliest application of the principle of unclean hands, a highwayman was refused an accounting against his partner in crime (and later hanged, to boot, along with the partner)." *Shondel v. McDermott, supra*, 775 F.2d at 868 (citations omitted). That is an apt description of the relief (in effect a partial rescission of the license agreement, and so equitable in character) sought by Dolby. But unfortunately for Scheiber it is an apt description of almost any case in which a party to a contract seeks relief on the basis that the contract is illegal. Dolby is in effect a private attorney general, charged by *Brulotte* with preventing Scheiber from seeking to "extend" his patent and being rewarded for this service to the law by getting out of a freely negotiated royalty obligation.

The obvious problem is that Dolby is not seeking equitable relief; it just doesn't want to pay what it owes Scheiber under their licensing agreement on the ground that the agreement, or at least so much of it as creates the duty to pay that Dolby is flouting, is unlawful and therefore unenforceable. That is how the Court put it in *Brulotte v. Thys Co., supra*, 379 U.S. at 33–34. The effect is the same as rescission but that is true in any case where the payee in a contract is allowed to refuse payment because the contract is unenforceable. Scheiber is the plaintiff, seeking damages, and Dolby is pleading the defense of illegality to contract enforcement.

* * *

What is true is that a contract that is voided on grounds of illegality—Dolby's defense to Scheiber's suit for the agreed-upon royalties—is ordinarily treated as rescinded, meaning that the parties are to be put back, so far as possible, in the positions they would have occupied had the contract never been made in the first place. *Cox v. Zale Delaware, Inc.*, 239 F.3d 910, 914 (7th Cir. 2001); *United States v. Amdahl Corp.*, 786 F.2d 387, 392–93 (Fed. Cir. 1986). For example, even if a contract is unenforceable because it violates the statute of frauds, the performing party can still claim the value of his performance, net of any payment received before the contract was rescinded, on a theory of *quantum meruit*, a type of restitution. *Cox* and *Amdahl* involved contracts that were illegal, and not just unenforceable (there is nothing remotely "wrongful" about failing to memorialize in writing a contract that is enforceable only if so memorialized), yet *quantum meruit* would still have been available had the voiding party been unduly enriched by being able to walk away from the contract. But Scheiber is not arguing that if indeed the contract is unenforceable, as we believe it is, he is entitled to some form of restitution of the benefits received by Dolby under it as a result of Dolby's being allowed to use Scheiber's patents without paying the full price that they had agreed upon. Scheiber would be entitled to such relief only if the amount of royalties that Dolby did pay was less than the fair market value of Dolby's use of the patents, which of course it may not have been. In any event he makes no claim of *quantum meruit.*

Dolby was indeed entitled to summary judgment.

---

# Notes

1. *Patent Estoppel.* Note the differences between judicial enforcement of license agreements in the various forms of estoppel, and in particular, the stark contrast between patent law, which does not recognize licensee estoppel, and trademark law, which does. What justifies this difference? *See* Neil M. Goodman, *Note: Patent Licensee Standing and the Declaratory Judgment Act,* 83 COLUM. L. REV. 186 (1938); Rochelle C. Dreyfuss, *Dethroning Lear: Licensee Estoppel and the Incentive to Innovate,* 72 VA. L. REV. 677 (1986) (broad reexamination of patents would allow patentees and licensees to share the risk of the inventive process); Nellie A. Fisher, *The Licensee's Choice: Mechanics of Successfully Challenging a Patent Under License,* 6 TEX. INTELL. PROP. L.J. 1 (1997). The answer seems to turn on the nature of the patent monopoly itself.

2. *Copyright Estoppel.* As indicated in Chapter 2, *supra,* copyright law does not prevent independent creation but strongly encourages it. Because the copyright monopoly is narrower than that of patents, less reason exists to override contract principles for the sake of avoiding invidious monopolies. *See* JAY DRATLER, JR., LICENSING OF INTELLECTUAL PROPERTY § 2.02[1][b][i] (N.Y. Publishing Co., 1994).

3. *Trademark Estoppel.* Likewise, because trademark law encourages independent development of trademarks to foster competition and because the number of alternative trade symbols for any particular use is virtually infinite, there is no special need to override contracts of equity in order to promote competition. "A competitor in principle has the ability to avoid choosing a conflicting trade symbol, and should be held to his bargain when he chooses to take a license from the true owner." DRATLER, *supra,* § 2.02[1][b][iv] (1994).

4. *Hybrid Patent and Trade Secret Licenses.* Several circuits have interpreted hybrid licensing arrangements under *Brulotte* and failed to uphold royalty payments for licensed trade secret rights after licensed patents had expired. In *Pitney Bowes v. Mestre,* 701 F.2d 1365, 1372 (11th Cir. 1983), the court noted that, as in *Brulotte,* the license failed to distinguish between exclusive licensed rights and royalties before and after expiration of the patent. The Sixth Circuit in *Boggild v. Kenner Products,* 776 F.2d 1315 (6th Cir. 1985), *cert. denied,* 477 U.S. 908, came to an identical result even though at the time of the license no patent application had been applied for. The Court held that the *Brulotte* rule of *per se* invalidity precluded enforcement of license terms that (1) the parties entered in anticipation of patent protection and (2) required royalty payments beyond the life of the patent. In reaching a similar result, *Meehan v. PPG Indus.,* 802 F.2d 881 (7th

Cir. 1986), the Court acknowledged that, even when an inventor has not yet applied for a patent, the right to apply for and obtain patent rights is valuable leverage in license negotiations, the abuse of which was the Supreme Court's concern in *Brulotte*. Finally, in *Nordion Int'l, Inc., v. Medi-Physics, Inc.*, 1995 U.S. Dist. LEXIS 12639 (N.D. Ill. 1995), the Court refused to enforce royalty payments after the patent was declared invalid, although the royalty was a fixed fee, not sales based, and the payments were to be made in the first five years of the license. The court was influenced by the fact that the agreement called the payments a royalty for use of the patent, and suggested by footnote that perhaps a payment not tied to sales is not a royalty at all. *See also, St. Regis Paper Co. v. Royal Indus.*, 552 F.2d 309 (9th Cir.), *cert. denied*, 434 U.S. 996 (1977).

The licenses in all the above cases shared two fatal drafting flaws—the licensor failed to separate the respective grants of patent and trade secret rights, and failed to charge a separate royalty for each licensed right. Apparently, no court has yet to address the post-patent validity of a royalty scheme that separately allocates royalty obligations between patent and non-patent rights. For an excellent discussion of the issues, see *Baladevon, Inc., v. Abbot Labs., Inc.*, 871 F. Supp. 89 (Dist. Mass. 1994).

What creative approaches might a licensor of multiple intellectual properties take to avoid application of the *Brulotte* rule? Consider a software license that is a hybrid because the software is copyrighted, the source code is in part a trade secret (*see* Circular 66, U.S. Copyright Office for how that is accomplished), and a patent application is pending but not issued. Should the licensor attempt to reduce its risk that the patent may not issue, or may issue considerably weakened, by writing a compensation clause that provides three separate royalty streams, one for each type of intellectual property? How would the following royalty clause fare under *Brulotte* if a patent never issues? What if the clause provides that royalties are payable for a fixed term of fifteen years? Twenty-five years? Could any single royalty rate, as described in the clause below, survive legal challenge if the patent issues and later expires, or if the court holds that it is invalid? What is the licensor's strongest argument in such a challenge?

---

# IV. Enforcing License Agreements

## A. Third Party Rights

### Rhône-Poulenc Agro, S.A. v. DeKalb Genetics Corp., v. Monsanto Co.
#### 271 F.3d 1081 (Fed. Cir. 2001)

DYK, Circuit Judge.

Rhône-Poulenc Agro, S.A. ("RPA") appeals from the decision of the United States District Court for the Middle District of North Carolina granting summary judgment of non-infringement on the ground that Monsanto Co. ("Monsanto") has a valid license to U.S. Patent No. 5,510,471, reissued on December 14, 1999 as RE 36,449 ("the '471 patent"). *Rhône-Poulenc Agro, S.A. v. Monsanto Co.*, No. 1:97CV1138, 2000 U.S. Dist. LEXIS 21330 (M.D.N.C. Feb. 8, 2000). The issue here is whether a sublicensee

(Monsanto) that acquired the sublicense from a licensee (DeKalb Genetics Corp. ("DeKalb")), that acquired the original license by fraud, may retain the sublicense by establishing that the sublicensee was a bona fide purchaser for value.

\* \* \*

Briefly the facts are these. From 1991 through 1994, RPA and DeKalb collaborated on the development of biotechnology related to specific genetic materials. During this time, a scientist at RPA, Dr. DeRose, developed an optimized transit peptide ("OTP") with a particular maize gene, which proved useful in growing herbicide resistant corn plants. The OTP is covered by the claims of the '471 patent and is the subject of RPA's patent infringement claim against Monsanto.

In 1994, RPA, DeKalb, and non-party Calgene, Inc. ("Calgene") entered into an agreement (the "1994 Agreement") that provided:

> RPA and CALGENE hereby grant to DEKALB the world-wide, paid-up right to use the RPA/CALGENE Technology and RPA/CALGENE Genetic Material in the field of use of corn. DEKALB shall have the right to grant sublicenses to the aforementioned right to use without further payment being made to RPA or CALGENE.

The RPA/CALGENE Technology and RPA/CALGENE Genetic Material included the invention claimed in the '471 patent. In 1996, DeKalb sublicensed its rights to the RPA/Calgene Technology and Genetic Material to Monsanto. At the same time Monsanto granted to DeKalb licenses to use certain intellectual property related to genetically-engineered corn. Monsanto also acquired a forty percent equity interest in DeKalb, and ten percent of DeKalb Class A (voting) stock.

On October 30, 1997, RPA filed suit against DeKalb and Monsanto, seeking, *inter alia*, to rescind the 1994 Agreement on the ground that DeKalb had procured the license (the "right to use") by fraud. RPA also alleged that DeKalb and Monsanto were infringing the '471 patent and had misappropriated RPA's trade secrets. Monsanto defended, *inter alia*, on the ground that it had a valid license to practice the invention of the patent and use the trade secrets, based on the rights owned under the 1994 Agreement that were transferred by DeKalb to Monsanto in 1996. At trial, a jury found, *inter alia*, that DeKalb had fraudulently induced RPA to enter into the 1994 Agreement. The district court ordered rescission of the 1994 Agreement. Nonetheless, Monsanto moved the district court for summary judgment that it had a valid license to the '471 patent and the right to use RPA's trade secrets because under the 1996 Agreement Monsanto was a bona fide purchaser for value of the sublicense to the patent and the trade secrets. The district court orally granted this motion and dismissed the infringement and misappropriation claims against Monsanto.

\* \* \*

The district court found that, as a sublicensee of the '471 patent and the trade secrets, Monsanto was "entitled to be considered a bona fide purchaser, because it paid value for the right to use the technology without knowledge of any wrongdoing by DeKalb." Because "Monsanto [was] a bona fide purchaser of the...technology, [it] therefore [could not] be liable as a patent infringer or a trade secret misappropriater." *Id.* at 58–59.

\* \* \*

## II

In *Rhône-Poulenc I*, we affirmed the judgment of the district court, rescinding the 1994 licensing agreement based on a jury verdict finding that DeKalb acquired its

patent license by fraud. RPA asserts that it necessarily follows that the Monsanto sublicense to the '471 patent is void, and that Monsanto can be sued for patent infringement. We agree.

* * *

III

Under some circumstances the bona fide purchaser defense in patent cases is governed by a federal statute, 35 U.S.C. §261. The statute provides that "[a]n assignment,
grant or conveyance shall be void as against any subsequent purchaser or mortgagee for
a valuable consideration, without notice, unless it is recorded in the Patent and Trademark Office within three months from its date or prior to the date of such subsequent
purchase or mortgage." 35 U.S.C. §261.

But this case does not involve a situation covered by §261. That statute is by its terms
limited to situations in which the patent owner makes inconsistent assignments, grants,
or conveyances to two entities, and the question is whether the later assignee should
prevail. Section 261 provides that a later bona fide purchaser for value without notice (a
later assignee) prevails if the earlier assignment was not timely recorded in the patent
office. This case, however, involves a different situation—the circumstance in which
the interest in the patent held by the grantor is voidable and the question is whether a
grantee may retain its interest even if the grantor's interest is voided. Section 261 does
not directly govern the resolution of this question.

Since §261 does not apply directly, we must turn to other provisions of the Patent
Act. Section 271 of the Act provides: "whoever without authority makes, uses, offers to
sell, or sells any patented invention…infringes the patent." 35 U.S.C. §271(a). We are
charged with the task of determining the meaning of the term "without authority."
Under this provision, as under other provisions of the Patent Act, the courts have developed a federal rule, where appropriate, and have deferred to state law, where that is appropriate. This issue of whether to apply state or federal law has particular importance
in this case because North Carolina state law, the law of the forum state, does not recognize a bona fide purchaser defense unless there has been a title transfer.

In general, the Supreme Court and this court have turned to state law to determine
whether there is contractual "authority" to practice the invention of a patent. Thus, the
interpretation of contracts for rights under patents is generally governed by state law.
*Aronson v. Quick Point Pencil Co.*, 440 U.S. 257, 262, 201 USPQ 1, 4 (1979); *Lear, Inc. v.
Adkins*, 395 U.S. 653, 661–62, 162 USPQ 1, 5 (1969); *Sun Studs, Inc. v. Applied Theory
Assocs., Inc.*, 772 F.2d 1557, 1561, 227 USPQ 81, 83–84 (Fed. Cir. 1985); *Studiengesellsh-
caft Kohle, M.B.H. v. Hercules, Inc.*, 105 F.3d 629, 632, 41 USPQ2d 1518, 1521 (Fed. Cir.
1997); *Gjerlov v. Schuyler Labs., Inc.*, 131 F.3d 1016, 1020, 44 USPQ2d 1881, 1885 (Fed.
Cir. 1997). Just as the interpretation of patent license contracts is generally governed by
state law, so too the consequences of fraud in the negotiation of such contracts is a matter generally governed by state law, as we have recognized in our companion case,
*Rhône-Poulenc I*, 272 F.3d at 1344, 60 USPQ2d at 1773. It may be argued that the impact of fraud upon the validity of a license as against a bona purchaser defense should
also be governed by state law. However, we confront here a unique situation in which a
federal patent statute explicitly governs the bona fide purchaser rule in some situations
but not in all situations. It would be anomalous for federal law to govern that defense in
part and for state law to govern in part. There is quite plainly a need for a uniform body
of federal law on the bona fide purchaser defense. *See Florida Prepaid Postsecondary*

*Educ. Expense Bd. v. College Savings Bank*, 527 U.S. 627, 645, 51 USPQ2d 1081, 1088 (1999) ("The need for uniformity in the construction of patent law is undoubtedly important...").

On the related question of the transferability of patent licenses, many courts have concluded that federal law must be applied. *Everex Sys, Inc. v. Cadtrak Corp. (In re CFLC, Inc.)*, 89 F.3d 673, 679, 39 USPQ2d 1518, 1523 (9th Cir. 1996); *Unarco Indus., Inc. v. Kelley Co.*, Inc., 465 F.2d 1303, 1306, 175 USPQ 199, 201 (7th Cir. 1972) (because "question of assignability of a patent license is a specific policy of federal patent law dealing with federal patent law... federal law applies to the question of the assignability of the patent license in question"), *cert. denied*, 410 U.S. 929 (1973); *PPG Indus., Inc. v. Guardian Indus. Corp.*, 597 F.2d 1090, 1093, 202 USPQ 95, 97 (6th Cir. 1979) ("Questions with respect to the assignability of a patent license are controlled by federal law."), *cert. denied*, 444 U.S. 930 (1979). In so holding, courts generally have acknowledged the need for a uniform national rule that patent licenses are personal and nontransferable in the absence of an agreement authorizing assignment, contrary to the state common law rule that contractual rights are assignable unless forbidden by an agreement.

\* \* \*

In short, because of the importance of having a uniform national rule, we hold that the bona fide purchaser defense to patent infringement is a matter of federal law. Because such a federal rule implicates an issue of patent law, the law of this circuit governs the rule. *Midwest Indus., Inc. v. Karavan Trailers, Inc.*, 175 F.3d 1356, 1359, 50 USPQ2d 1672, 1675 (Fed. Cir.) (en banc in relevant part), *cert. denied*, 528 U.S. 1019 (1999). Of course, the creation of a federal rule concerning the bona fide purchaser defense is informed by the various state common law bona fide purchaser rules as they are generally understood. *See Scaltech*, 269 F.3d at 1328, 60 USPQ2d at 1692 (looking to the Uniform Commercial Code ("U.C.C.") to develop federal rule for determining when an invalidating offer to sell under 35 U.S.C. § 102(b) occurs); *Group One*, 254 F.3d at 1047, 59 USPQ2d at 1126 (looking to the U.C.C. to inform federal law).

IV

Congress has specifically provided that patents are to be treated as personal property. 35 U.S.C. § 261. At common law, a bona fide purchaser (also known as a "good faith buyer") who acquired title to personal property was entitled to retain the property against the real owner who had lost title to the property, for example, by fraud. Generally, a bona fide purchaser is one who purchases legal title to property in good faith for valuable consideration, without notice of any other claim of interest in the property. *Malcolm v. Wilson*, 534 So. 2d 241, 242 (Ala. 1988); *Realty Portfolio, Inc. v. Hamilton (In re Hamilton)*, 125 F.3d 292, 298 (5th Cir. 1997) (applying Texas law); *Weaver v. Barden*, 49 N.Y. 286, 291–92 (1872); *Island Pond Nat'l Bank v. Lacroix*, 158 A. 684, 693 (Vt. 1932); RESTATEMENT (Restitution) § 172 and cmt. a (1937) (beneficiary of bona fide purchaser rule is one who "acquires title to property"); 77 AM. JUR. 2d § 425. The bona fide purchaser rule exists to protect innocent purchasers of property from competing equitable interests in the property because "[s]trong as a plaintiff's equity may be, it can in no case be stronger than that of a purchaser, who has put himself in peril by purchasing a title, and paying a valuable consideration, without notice of any defect in it, or adverse claim to it...." *Boone v. Chiles*, 35 U.S. 177, 210 (1836)).

At common law, however, it was quite clear that one who did not acquire title to the property could not assert the protection of the bona fide purchaser rule. Many courts have held that a party to an executory contract to purchase title, the owner of a lease, or a purchaser from a vendor who did not have title cannot benefit from the bona fide purchaser rule.

* * *

It is clear under the law of North Carolina (the state in which RPA filed suit) that "[i]n the absence of an estoppel, one is not entitled to protection as a bona fide purchaser unless he holds the legal title to the property in dispute." *Wilson v. Commercial Fin. Co.*, 79 S.E.2d 908, 914 (N.C. 1954).

* * *

Monsanto also relies on statements from various treatises on patent licensing for the proposition that a sublicense continues, even when the principal license is terminated. But the statements address the situation where the original licensee is terminated as a matter of contract law, e.g., for breach of contract. These treatises do not address the operation of the bona fide purchaser rule with respect to sublicenses and do not state or suggest that a sublicense continues even when the principal license is rescinded because it has been obtained by fraud.

* * *

Although our precedent has recognized that in some circumstances an exclusive patent license may be tantamount to an assignment of title to the patent, this is so only when "the licensee holds 'all substantial rights' under the patent." *Textile Prods., Inc. v. Mead Corp.*, 134 F.3d 1481, 1484, 45 USPQ2d 1633, 1635 (Fed. Cir.), *cert. denied*, 525 U.S. 826 (1998); *see also Intellectual Prop. Dev., Inc. v. TCI Cablevision of Cal., Inc.*, 248 F.3d 1333, 1345, 58 USPQ2d 1681, 1689 (Fed. Cir. 2001); *Prima Tek II*, 222 F.3d at 1377, 55 USPQ2d 1747; *Vaupel Textilmaschinen KG v. Meccanica Euro Italia S.P.A.*, 944 F.2d 870, 874–75, 20 USPQ2d 1045, 1048–49 (Fed. Cir. 1991). Here the license is non-exclusive, and there is no contention that the license agreement transferred "all substantial rights." Thus, an assignment did not occur, and in the absence of an "assignment, grant or conveyance," Congress contemplated that there would be no bona fide purchaser defense.

* * *

---

# PPG Industries, Inc., v. Guardian Industries Corp.
## 597 F.2d 1090 (6th Cir. 1979), *cert. denied*, 444 U.S. 930

LIVELY:

The question in this case is whether the surviving or resultant corporation in a statutory merger acquires patent license rights of the constituent corporations. [P]laintiff, PPG Industries, Inc. (PPG), appeals from a judgment of the district court dismissing its patent infringement action on the ground that the defendant, Guardian Industries, Corp. (Guardian), as licensee of the patents in suit, was not an infringer. Guardian cross-appeals from a holding by the district court that its alternate defense based on an equipment license agreement was ineffective. The district court opinion is reported at 428 F. Supp. 789 (N.D. Ohio 1977).

I

Prior to 1964 both PPG and Permaglass, Inc., were engaged in fabrication of glass products which required that sheets of glass be shaped for particular uses. Independently of each other the two fabricators developed similar processes which involved "floating glass on a bed of gas, while it was being heated and bent." This process is known in the industry as "gas hearth technology" and "air float technology"; the two terms are interchangeable. After a period of negotiations PPG and Permaglass entered into an agreement on January 1, 1964 whereby each granted rights to the other under "gas hearth system" patents already issued and in the process of prosecution. The purpose of the agreement was set forth in the preamble as follows:

> WHEREAS, PPG is desirous of acquiring from PERMAGLASS a world-wide exclusive license with right to sublicense others under PERMAGLASS Technical Data and PERMAGLASS Patent Rights, subject only to reservation by PERMAGLASS of non-exclusive rights thereunder; and

> WHEREAS, PERMAGLASS is desirous of obtaining a nonexclusive license to use Gas Hearth Systems under PPG Patent Rights, excepting in the Dominion of Canada.

This purpose was accomplished in the two sections of the agreement quoted below:

SECTION 3. GRANT FROM PERMAGLASS TO PPG

3.1 Subject to the reservation set forth in Subsection 3.3 below, PERMAGLASS hereby grants to PPG an exclusive license, with right of sublicense, to use PERMAGLASS Technical Data in Gas Hearth Systems throughout the United States of America, its territories and possessions, and all countries of the world foreign thereto.

3.2 Subject to the reservation set forth in Subsection 3.3 below, PERMAGLASS hereby grants to PPG an unlimited exclusive license, with right of sublicense, under PERMAGLASS Patent Rights.

3.3 The licenses granted to PPG under Subsections 3.1 and 3.2 above shall be subject to the reservation of a non-exclusive, non-transferable, royalty-free, world-wide right and license for the benefit and use of PERMAGLASS.

SECTION 4. GRANT FROM PPG TO PERMAGLASS

4.1 PPG hereby grants to PERMAGLASS a non-exclusive, non-transferable, royalty-free right and license to heat, bend, thermally temper and/or anneal glass using Gas Hearth Systems under PPG Patent Rights, excepting in the Dominion of Canada, and to use or sell glass articles produced thereby, but no license, express or implied, is hereby granted to PERMAGLASS under any claim of any PPG patent expressly covering any coating method, coating composition, or coated article.

Assignability of the agreement and of the license granted to Permaglass and termination of the license granted to Permaglass were covered in the following language:

SECTION 9. ASSIGNABILITY

9.1 This Agreement shall be assignable by PPG to any successor of the entire flat glass business of PPG but shall otherwise be non-assignable except with the consent of PERMAGLASS first obtained in writing.

9.2 This Agreement and the license granted by PPG to PERMAGLASS hereunder shall be personal to PERMAGLASS and non-assignable except with the consent of PPG first obtained in writing.

SECTION 11. TERMINATION

11.2 In the event that a majority of the voting stock of PERMAGLASS shall at any time become owned or controlled directly or indirectly by a manufacturer of automobiles or a manufacturer or fabricator of glass other than the present owners, the license granted to PERMAGLASS under Subsection 4.1 shall terminate forthwith.

Eleven patents are involved in this suit. Nine of them originated with Permaglass and were licensed to PPG as exclusive licensee under Section 3.2, *supra*, subject to the non-exclusive, non-transferable reservation to Permaglass set forth in Section 3.3. Two of the patents originated with PPG. Section 4.1 granted a non-exclusive, non-transferable license to Permaglass with respect to the two PPG patents. In Section 9.1 and 9.2 assignability was treated somewhat differently as between the parties, and the Section 11.2 provisions with regard to termination apply only to the license granted to Permaglass.

As of December 1969 Permaglass was merged into Guardian pursuant to applicable statutes of Ohio and Delaware. Guardian was engaged primarily in the business of fabricating and distributing windshields for automobiles and trucks. It had decided to construct a facility to manufacture raw glass and the capacity of that facility would be greater than its own requirements. Permaglass had no glass manufacturing capability and it was contemplated that its operations would utilize a large part of the excess output of the proposed Guardian facility.

The "Agreement of Merger" between Permaglass and Guardian did not refer specifically to the 1964 agreement between PPG and Permaglass. However, among Permaglass' representations in the agreement was the following:

(g) Permaglass is the owner, assignee or licensee of such patents, trademarks, trade names and copyrights as are listed and described in Exhibit "C" attached hereto. None of such patents, trademarks, trade names or copyrights is in litigation and Permaglass has not received any notice of conflict with the asserted rights of third parties relative to the use thereof.

Listed on Exhibit "C" to the merger agreement are the nine patents originally developed by Permaglass and licensed to PPG under the 1964 agreement which are involved in this infringement action.

Shortly after the merger was consummated PPG filed the present action, claiming infringement by Guardian in the use of apparatus and processes described and claimed in eleven patents which were identified by number and origin. The eleven patents were covered by the terms of the 1964 agreement. PPG asserted that it became the exclusive licensee of the nine patents which originated with Permaglass under the 1964 agreement and that the rights reserved by Permaglass were personal to it and non-transferable and non-assignable. PPG also claimed that Guardian had no rights with respect to the two patents which had originated with PPG because the license under these patents was personal to Permaglass and non-transferable and non-assignable except with the permission of PPG. In addition it claimed that the license with respect to these two patents had terminated under the provisions of Section 11.2, *supra*, by reason of the merger.

One of the defenses pled by Guardian in its answer was that it was a licensee of the patents in suit. It described the merger with Permaglass and claimed it "had succeeded to all rights, powers, ownerships, etc., of Permaglass, and as Permaglass' successor, defendant is legally entitled to operate in place of Permaglass under the January 1, 1964 agreement between Permaglass and plaintiff, free of any claim of infringement of the patents...."

After holding an evidentiary hearing the district court concluded that the parties to the 1964 agreement did not intend that the rights reserved by Permaglass in its nine patents or the rights assigned to Permaglass in the two PPG patents would not pass to a successor corporation by way of merger. The court held that there had been no assignment or transfer of the rights by Permaglass, but rather that Guardian acquired these rights by operation of law under the merger statutes of Ohio and Delaware. The provisions of the 1964 agreement making the license rights of Permaglass non-assignable and non-transferable were held not to apply because of the "continuity of interest inherent in a statutory merger that distinguishes it from the ordinary assignment or transfer case." 428 F. Supp. at 796.

With respect to the termination provision in Section 11.2 of the 1964 agreement, the district court again relied on "the nature of a statutory merger in contrast to an outright sale or acquisition of stock" in holding that a majority of the voting stock of Permaglass did not become owned or controlled by Guardian. 428 F. Supp. at 796.

II

Questions with respect to the assignability of a patent license are controlled by federal law. It has long been held by federal courts that agreements granting patent licenses are personal and not assignable unless expressly made so. *Unarco Industries, Inc. v. Kelley Company*, 465 F.2d 1303, 1306 (7th Cir. 1972), *cert. denied*, 410 U.S. 929, 93 S. Ct. 1365, 35 L. Ed. 2d 590 (1973). This has been the rule at least since 1852 when the Supreme Court decided *Troy Iron & Nail v. Corning*, 55 U.S. (14 How.) 193, 14 L. Ed. 383 (1852). *See Annotation, Assignability of Licensee's Rights Under Patent Licensing Agreement* 66 A.L.R.2d 606. The district court recognized this rule in the present case, but concluded that where patent licenses are claimed to pass by operation of law to the resultant or surviving corporation in a statutory merger there has been no assignment or transfer.

There appear to be no reported cases where the precise issue in this case has been decided. At least two treatises contain the statement that rights under a patent license owned by a constituent corporation pass to the consolidated corporation in the case of a consolidation, W. FLETCHER, CYCLOPEDIA OF THE LAW OF CORPORATIONS §7089 (revised ed. 1973); and to the new or resultant corporation in the case of a merger, A. DELLER, WALKER ON PATENTS §409 (2d ed. 1965). However, the cases cited in support of these statements by the commentators do not actually provide such support because their facts take them outside the general rule of non-assignability. Both texts rely on the decision in *Hartford-Empire Co. v. Demuth Glass Works, Inc.*, 19 F. Supp. 626 (E.D.N.Y. 1937). The agreement involved in that case specified that the patent license was assignable and its assignability was not an issue. Clearly the statement in the *Hartford-Empire* opinion that the merger conveyed to the new corporation the patent licenses owned by the old corporation results from the fact that the licenses in question were expressly made assignable, not from any general principle that such licenses pass to the resultant corporation where there is a merger. It is also noteworthy that the surviving corporation following the merger in Hartford-Empire was the original licensee, whereas in the present case the original licensee was merged into Guardian, which was the survivor. Fletcher also cites *Lightner v. Boston & A. R. Co.*, 1 Low Dec. 338, 15

Fed.Cas. No. 8,343, p. 514 (C.C.Mass.1869). In that case both of the constituent corporations had been licensed by the patent holder. Thus, the reason for the rule against assignability was not present; the patent holder had selected both as licensees. There was also language in one of the licensing agreements involved in *Lightner* which indicated to the court that a consolidation was anticipated and that use of the patented mechanism by the consolidated corporation was authorized. Again, this decision does not indicate that the general rule of non-assignability of patent licenses does not apply in merger situations.

\* \* \*

We conclude that the district court misconceived the intent of the parties to the 1964 agreement. We believe the district court put the burden on the wrong party in stating:

> Because the parties failed to provide that Permaglass' rights under the 1964 license agreement would not pass to the corporation surviving a merger, the Court finds that Guardian succeeded to Permaglass' license pursuant to 8 Del.C. § 259, and Ohio Revised Code §§ 1701.81 and 1701.83.

428 F. Supp. at 796.

The agreement provides with respect to the license which Permaglass granted to PPG that Permaglass reserved "a non-exclusive, non-transferable, royalty-free, world-wide right and license For the benefit and use of Permaglass." (emphasis added). Similarly, with respect to its own two patents, PPG granted to Permaglass "a non-exclusive, non-transferable, royalty-free right and license...." Further, the agreement provides that both it and the license granted to Permaglass "shall be personal to PERMAGLASS and non-assignable except with the consent of PPG first obtained in writing."

The quoted language from Sections 3, 4 and 9 of the 1964 agreement evinces an intent that only Permaglass was to enjoy the privileges of licensee. If the parties had intended an exception in the event of a merger, it would have been a simple matter to have so provided in the agreement. Guardian contends such an exception is not necessary since it is universally recognized that patent licenses pass from a licensee to the resultant corporation in case of a merger. This does not appear to be the case. In *Packard Instrument Co. v. ANS, Inc.*, 416 F.2d 943 (2d Cir. 1969), a license agreement provided that rights thereunder could not be transferred or assigned "except...(b) if the entire ownership and business of ANS is transferred by sale, merger, or consolidation,...." 416 F.2d at 944. Similarly, the agreement construed in *Freeman v. Seiberling Rubber Co.*, 72 F.2d 124 (6th Cir. 1934), provided that the license was not assignable except with the entire business and good will of the licensee. We conclude that if the parties had intended an exception in case of a merger to the provisions against assignment and transfer they would have included it in the agreement. It should be noted also that the district court in *Packard, supra,* held that an assignment had taken place when the licensee was merged into another corporation.

The district court also held that the patent licenses in the present case were not transferred because they passed by operation of law from Permaglass to Guardian. This conclusion is based on the theory of continuity which underlies a true merger. However, the theory of continuity relates to the fact that there is no dissolution of the constituent corporations and, even though they cease to exist, their essential corporate attributes are vested by operation of law in the surviving or resultant corporation. *Vulcan Materials Co. v. United States*, 446 F.2d 690 (5th Cir.), *cert. denied*, 404 U.S. 942, 92 S. Ct. 279, 30 L. Ed. 2d 255 (1971). It does not mean that there is no transfer of particular assets from a constituent corporation to the surviving or resultant one.

The Ohio merger statute provides that following a merger all property of a constituent corporation shall be "deemed to be Transferred to and vested in the surviving or new corporation without further act or deed...." Ohio Revised Code, (former) §1701.81(A)(4). This indicates that the transfer is by operation of law, not that there is no transfer of assets in a merger situation. The Delaware statute, which was also involved in the Permaglass-Guardian merger, provides that the property of the constituent corporations "shall be vested in the corporation surviving or resulting from such merger or consolidation,...." 8 Del.C. §259(a). The Third Circuit has construed the "shall be vested" language of the Delaware statute as follows:

> In short, the underlying property of the constituent corporations is Transferred to the resultant corporation upon the carrying out of the consolidation or merger.

*Koppers Coal & Transportation Co. v. United States*, 107 F.2d 706, 708 (3d Cir. 1939).

In his opinion in *Koppers*, Judge Biggs disposed of arguments very similar to those of Guardian in the present case, based on the theory of continuity. Terming such arguments "metaphysical" he found them completely at odds with the language of the Delaware statute. *Id.* Finally, on this point, the parties themselves provided in the merger agreement that all property of Permaglass "shall be deemed transferred to and shall vest in Guardian without further act or deed...." A transfer is no less a transfer because it takes place by operation of law rather than by a particular act of the parties. The merger was effected by the parties and the transfer was a result of their act of merging.

Thus, Sections 3, 4 and 9 of the 1964 agreement between PPG and Permaglass show an intent that the licenses held by Permaglass in the eleven patents in suit not be transferable. While this conclusion disposes of the license defense as to all eleven patents, it should be noted that Guardian's claim to licenses under the two patents which originated with PPG is also defeated by Section 11.2 of the 1964 agreement. This Section addresses a different concern from that addressed in Sections 3, 4 and 9. The restrictions on transferability and assignability in those sections prevent the patent licenses from becoming the property of third parties. The termination clause, however, provides that Permaglass' license with respect to the two PPG patents will terminate if the ownership of a majority of the voting stock of Permaglass passes from the 1964 stockholders to designated classes of persons, even though the licenses themselves might never have changed hands.

Apparently PPG was willing for Permaglass to continue as licensee under the nine patents even though ownership of its stock might change. These patents originated with Permaglass and so long as Permaglass continued to use the licenses for its own benefit a mere change in ownership of Permaglass stock would not nullify the licenses. Only a transfer or assignment would cause a termination. However, the agreement provides for termination with respect to the two original PPG patents in the event of an indirect takeover of Permaglass by a change in the ownership of a majority of its stock. The fact that PPG sought and obtained a stricter provision with respect to the two patents which it originally owned in no way indicates an intention to permit transfer of licenses under the other nine in case of a merger. None of the eleven licenses was transferable; but two of them, those involving PPG's own development in the field of gas hearth technology, were not to continue even for the benefit of the licensee if it came under the control of a manufacturer of automobiles or a competitor of PPG in the glass industry "other than the present owners" of Permaglass. A consistency among the provisions of the agreement is discernible when the different origins of the various patents are considered.

\* \* \*

---

# Verson Corp. v. Verson International Group PLC

899 F. Supp. 358 (N.D. Ill. 1995)

MORAN, Senior District Judge.

Plaintiff Verson Corporation brought this lawsuit alleging that defendants Verson International Group, Verson Wilkins Limited, and Verson International Limited violated a license agreement for intellectual property. Before us now is defendants' motion to dismiss plaintiff's amended complaint. For the reasons set forth below, the motion is denied.

### Background

Verson Corporation (Verson), the successor to Verson Allsteel Press Company (VASP) and the wholly-owned subsidiary of Allied Products Corporation, manufactures presses for the metal-forming industry. In the early 1980s VASP began experiencing financial difficulties. In order to ease through its financial downturn VASP and a group of its international managers entered into an agreement wherein the managers would buy out VASP's international operations with a newly formed independent company, Verson International Limited (collectively referred to herein, along with Verson Wilkins Limited and Verson International Limited, as "VIL"). VIL and VASP entered into a series of agreements to facilitate the management buyout (MBO), the most important for our purposes being the VASP/VIL License Agreement (license agreement). In that agreement VASP agreed to turn over to VIL its patents and non-patented trade secrets, and allowed VIL to use this know-how. The license agreement called for both parties to turn over all newly developed know-how to the other for a period of five years. The parties also agreed to a series of restrictive covenants that gave VASP the exclusive right to market its products in the United States and Canada and gave VIL the exclusive right to market its products in the rest of the world. Both territorial restrictions were to last five years.

In the first lawsuit between the parties VIL sued VASP alleging that VASP had violated the license agreement's restrictive covenants and seeking an injunction requiring Verson to turn over certain know-how. VASP argued that the territorial and durational restrictions violated state and federal antitrust laws. We enforced the restrictions only in part, finding that VIL was barred only from the use of VASP know-how in the United States and Canada, and that VASP was barred only from marketing its products in Europe. *Verson Wilkins Ltd. v. Allied Products Corp.*, 723 F. Supp. 1, 20 (N.D. Ill. 1989). We also required VASP to turn over the know-how covered under the license agreement. In 1990 the parties executed a settlement agreement disposing of the remaining disputes regarding exchange of the know-how.

Soon thereafter VIL entered into an agreement with Enprotech Mechanical Services, Inc. (Enprotech), a direct competitor of Verson in the North American market. In this agreement VIL turned over know-how it received from VASP in the 1985 license agreement and granted Enprotech the exclusive right to use this know-how to manufacture replacement parts for Verson presses. This arrangement spawned the present lawsuit. In its complaint Verson alleged that VIL violated Article 16 of the 1985 license agreement which required VIL to obtain VASP's approval before licensing the know-how to another party, by turning over VASP know-how to Enprotech. Defendants moved to dismiss the complaint, claiming that Article 16 did not survive the termination of the agreement. We granted that motion on December 30, 1994. Verson moved for reconsideration of our order and for leave to amend its complaint, arguing that the Enprotech agreement, which Verson claims is an assignment, violated the license agreement's restriction on VIL's right to assign the know-how. Although this constituted a new line of attack for Verson, we allowed it to amend its complaint to more fully make out this claim. Verson has since amended its complaint to incorporate the assignment argument. Before us now is VIL's motion to dismiss the amended complaint. VIL argues that the 1990 settlement agreement prevents Verson from maintaining this action; that it is the co-owner of the know-how, not a licensee, and thus had the right to assign it to Enprotech; that the right to assign the know-how was implicit in the 1985 licensing agreement; that a perpetual ban on assignability would be an unreasonable restraint of trade; and that its transaction with Enprotech is a sublease rather than an assignment. We will examine each of these arguments in turn.

## DISCUSSION

### A. The 1990 Settlement Agreement

VIL argues that a settlement agreement executed in connection with the earlier case involving these parties bars Verson's action here. In the first lawsuit VIL obtained an injunction requiring Verson to turn over various types of know-how related to the licensing agreement. The case was still pending, however, because the parties disputed what documents needed to be produced and who was to pay for the copying. The parties entered into a settlement in which VIL accepted some of the disputed know-how in complete satisfaction of any claim for know-how it might have had under the licensing agreement, and Verson agreed not to challenge VIL's right to use this know-how. VIL argues that this action challenging VIL's assignment (or sublease) of the know-how to Enprotech is a restriction on the use of the know-how and thus violates the settlement agreement. Verson responds that VIL's right to assign or transfer the know-how remained as it was under the licensing agreement.

We agree with Verson that the 1990 settlement agreement does not prevent it from attempting to restrict VIL's right to assign the know-how. In settlements, as in all contracts, every effort should be made to give force to the words employed by the parties and to not imply words that the parties could have used but did not. *Harris Bank Naperville v. Morse Shoe, Inc.*, 716 F. Supp. 1109, 1122 (N.D. Ill. 1989). Through the settlement Verson agreed only not to restrict VIL's use of the know-how. The word "use" does not ordinarily also include sale, transfer, or assignment. This is especially so when dealing with the right to use intellectual property. One can use know-how, trade secrets, or patents freely, but still not transfer or assign that information. The right to the know-how at issue here could easily be separated into the right to use the know-how and the right to sell, transfer, or assign the know-how, and the parties' selection of the word "use" provides support for the view that they did not intend for the settlement agreement to grant VIL a right to assign the know-how that was not already granted under the terms of the license agreement. The parties could have added "transfer or assign" to "use," and the fact that they did not is probative of the issue.

Other sections of the settlement also provide some support for that view. Under a section entitled "Reservation of Rights," both parties reserved the right to sue each other for any breach of the licensing agreement. The fact that both parties sought to preserve their rights under the licensing agreement arguably indicates that the settlement was intended only to resolve the dispute as to what know-how Verson was required to turn over and who was to pay for the copying costs. VIL's reading of the reservation-of-rights clause, that the parties intended only to prevent public disclosure of the know-how, is strained, given that the parties could have easily drafted the clause to reflect that intent but did not. Therefore, we hold that the 1990 settlement agreement was not an unambiguous waiver of Verson's right to challenge VIL's assignment of the know-how.

### B. Is VIL a Co-Owner of the Know-How Or Only a Licensee?

The premise behind Verson's complaint is that VIL is a nonexclusive licensee of the know-how. In earlier orders we expressed some doubt regarding this proposition and left open the question whether VIL is a co-owner of the know-how. *See Verson Corp. v. Verson International Group*, 1994 U.S. Dist. LEXIS 9736, No. 93 C 2996, WL 376278 at *3 (N.D.Ill. July 13, 1994). VIL seizes upon this language and presses the argument here.

The starting place for determining whether VIL is a co-owner of the know-how is the 1985 license agreement. The agreement states that "upon expiration of the term of this Agreement, subject to [confidentiality provisions], Licensee shall have the non-exclusive perpetual royalty free right to continue to exercise, use or practice the rights granted Licensee under Section 2.01 without limitation as to Territory...." As we indicated above, the use of know-how can be readily distinguished from the ownership of the know-how. Thus, one meaning of the license agreement grants VIL only the right to use the know-how to compete with Verson worldwide. The language of this provision, or the other provisions in the agreement, do not necessarily indicate the parties intended for VIL to become co-owner of the know-how at the termination of the five-year period.

Despite the lack of any express provision in the license agreement granting it co-ownership of the know-how, VIL presents four arguments to support its claim: first, that the amount it paid in connection with the MBO indicates that VIL would become co-owner of the know-how; second, that it developed some of the know-how itself; third, that the clear intent of the MBO and license agreement was to make VIL and Verson head-to-head competitors after five years; and, fourth, that VIL acquired property rights to the know-how when it acquired VASP's international operations.

We find that none of these four arguments helps VIL's cause here, even if we can entertain them in support of a motion to dismiss. First, the amount VIL paid in connection with the MBO does not by itself demonstrate anything about the parties' intent. The license agreement was just one part of a series of agreements executed in connection with the MBO. It is impossible to say as a matter of law that the consideration paid by VIL was to acquire ownership rights to the know-how after five years. VIL may be able to present evidence that the true value of what it received in the MBO could not come near the $8 million it actually paid if ownership of the know-how were not included, and in such a situation we could find the consideration paid to be probative of the parties' intent. However, we cannot make that determination on a motion to dismiss.

Second, Verson disputes VIL's claim that it developed part of the know-how at issue here. It is clear that whether or not VIL did develop this know-how is a disputed question of fact that cannot be resolved on a motion to dismiss. Such a determination must await further development by the parties.

Third, we have repeatedly recognized that the goal of the MBO in general, and the license agreement in particular, was to place VIL and Verson as head-to-head competitors at the end of five years, as VIL argues. That proposition does not, however, establish

VIL's ownership of the know-how. At the end of the agreement, VIL had every right to compete with Verson in any market in the world. In that respect the two firms were head-to-head competitors. Limiting VIL to the right to use, instead of assign, the know-how does not appear to frustrate this goal. All VIL is prevented from doing is assigning or selling the know-how to a competitor. This limitation has no effect on VIL's ability to compete with Verson in the manufacture, sale, or repair of presses.

Finally, it is not clear at this point what rights VIL acquired in the MBO when it took over VASP's international operations. Until now we have never been faced with determining exactly what rights VIL acquired in the MBO. Verson has submitted a number of the agreements involving VASP and its many subsidiaries, that purportedly demonstrate that VIL acquired only licensing rights, not ownership rights, to the know-how. VIL has not contradicted Verson's recitation of the corporate history. Accepting Verson's allegation that no ownership rights were transferred in the MBO—an allegation supported by the submitted documents—we hold that Verson has properly alleged that VIL was a mere licensee, not a co-owner, of the know-how.

## C. Implied Right of Assignability

VIL does not dispute that there is no provision in the license agreement granting it an explicit post-termination right to assign the know-how. Yet it argues that despite this lack of express authority, authority to assign its rights under the agreement must be inferred from the circumstances and the parties' conduct.

Under well-established law the holder of a nonexclusive patent license may not assign its license unless the right to assign is expressly provided for in the license agreement. *See Stenograph Corp. v. Fulkerson*, 972 F.2d 726, 729 n.2 (7th Cir. 1992) ("Patent licenses are not assignable in the absence of express language."); *Unarco Industries Inc. v. Kelley Co.*, 465 F.2d 1303, 1306 (7th Cir. 1972), *cert. denied*, 410 U.S. 929, 35 L. Ed. 2d 590, 93 S. Ct. 1365 (1973); *Gilson v. Republic of Ireland*, 252 U.S. App. D.C. 99, 787 F.2d 655, 658 (D.C. Cir. 1986); *In re CFLC, Inc.*, 174 Bankr. 119, 122 (N.D.Cal. 1994). Under this longstanding federal case law, patent licenses are treated as personal to the license holder and therefore are presumed to be not assignable. *Id.*

VIL argues that the presumption against assignability may be overcome by the circumstances and the conduct of the parties. As support, VIL cites *Farmland Irrigation Co. v. Dopplmaier*, 48 Cal. 2d 208, 308 P.2d 732 (Cal. 1957), and *Bowers v. Lake Superior Contracting & Dredging Co.*, 149 F. 983 (8th Cir. 1906). We seriously doubt whether these decisions survive the later developed line of cases refusing to imply a right of assignability of patent licenses. Even if some vestige of *Farmland* and *Bowers* remains, we cannot overlook decades of precedent to the contrary. *See Unarco Industries Inc.*, 465 F.2d at 1306. Therefore, we feel bound to require compelling evidence of the parties' intent before implying a right to assign. Such evidence is not presented here, nor may it be considered to resolve a motion to dismiss.

VIL points to two aspects of the parties' conduct to support its claim that a right of assignment should be inferred. First, it argues that the fact that the license agreement gave it broad authority to sublicense its rights without Verson's approval establishes conclusively that the parties did not believe that the patented rights were highly personable and therefore could be assigned. We disagree. VIL seeks to bootstrap its negotiated right to sublicense into a right to assign. Were VIL correct, every license granting a right to sublicense would also implicitly contain a right of assignment. That is clearly not the case. On the contrary, under the axiom of expressio unius, the presence of the provision on sublicensing indicates that the parties did not intend to allow assignments. Further, VIL cannot seriously maintain that Verson did not consider the know-how to be highly personable. The license agreement contained a strict confidentiality clause and every indication from the parties' conduct since the MBO is that the know-how is vital to successful competition in the industry. Therefore, it is clear that VIL's right to sublicense does not establish as a matter of law an intent to also allow it to assign its rights.

VIL also claims that Article 16 of the licensing agreement, which required VIL to first obtain Verson's approval before assigning its rights to a competitor, demonstrates that when the parties sought to restrict the right to assign they did so expressly, and the fact that there is no provision limiting VIL's right to assign post-termination establishes that no such limitations were intended by the parties. In addition, VIL argues that because our order of December 30, 1993, ruled that Article 16 did not survive the termination of the licensing agreement, preventing VIL from assigning its rights post-termination would mean that it had greater leeway to assign before the termination than after, which it asserts is an absurd result.

We are not persuaded that the presence of Article 16 overcomes the strong presumption against implying a right to assign licenses for intellectual property. Article 16 and a post-termination restriction on assignment are not, as VIL suggests, in hopeless conflict. It is reasonable for Verson to have allowed VIL greater leeway to assign its rights during the five-year period of the licensing agreement because VIL was prohibited by the agreement from competing with Verson in North America. After the termination of the agreement, however, VIL could compete directly with Verson in North America, which may have prompted Verson to restrict VIL's right to assign. In any event, we need not rule that this is what the parties intended. Rather, we conclude that the license agreement does not conclusively refute Verson's claim that the know-how cannot be assigned.

* * *

VIL's final argument is that its agreement with Enprotech is not an assignment at all, but rather is a sublicense, and since the license agreement granted VIL the authority to sublicense its rights, Verson's suit must fail.

Verson argues that intellectual property rights can be severed and assigned separately. That is, a patentee may assign the right to use a patent for sale of a product but retain the right to use the patent for other purposes. Support for this proposition can be found in tax cases, *see Cory v. Commissioner*, 230 F.2d 941, 944 (2d Cir.), *cert. denied*, 352 U.S. 828, 1 L. Ed. 2d 50, 77 S. Ct. 43 (1956), and in some of the cases dealing with who has standing to sue for patent infringement. *See Vaupel Textilmaschinen KG v. Meccanica Euro Italia S.P.A.*, 944 F.2d 870, 875 (Fed. Cir. 1991) (recognizing patent rights as constituting a bundle of rights). Under this view the answer depends on whether the patentee has transferred all its rights in a particular market (an assignment) or has transferred only some of those rights, retaining others for itself (a license). During the course of this litigation VIL has retreated from its earlier opposition to this principle and now seems content to argue that, even if that were the law, the Enprotech agreement still 'cannot be considered an assignment.

Verson claims that the Enprotech agreement is an assignment rather than a sublicense because VIL transferred all the rights associated with the after-market for Verson presses. Specifically, the Enprotech agreement states:

> [VIL] (i) grants and assigns to [Enprotech] (1) the exclusive (as between Licensor and Licensee), royalty free right and license to utilize the Proprietary Rights

in the Territory for the manufacture and sale of Verson Parts and for the re-building and modernization of Verson Presses and subject to the reserved rights of [VIL], the maintenance and repair of Verson Presses, and (2) the right and license to use the Trademark in connection with the manufacture and sale of Verson Parts and, subject to the review and consent of [VIL], which consent will not be unreasonably withheld, the maintenance, repair, rebuilding and modernization of Verson Presses and (ii) sells to Enprotech the Technical Information and Other Information subject to the terms and conditions of this Agreement.

The "territory" is defined to include certain countries in North America and Central America. "Proprietary rights" and "technical information" basically entail the Verson technology that VIL received under the licensing agreement. Although the parties are delineated as "Licensor" and "Licensee," and the agreement is denominated a "License," these labels are not dispositive of our inquiry here.

\* \* \*

VIL counters that it has retained sufficient rights to the after-market to render the Enprotech agreement a sublicense rather than an assignment. It identifies five such rights: (1) the right to make replacement parts in connection with the sale of new presses; (2) the exclusive right to provide service for the enhancement retrofit of Verson presses; (3) the exclusive right to provide service work for the maintenance and repair of Verson presses; (4) a fifty-year period for the agreement; and (5) a parts supply agreement requiring Enprotech to purchase spare parts from a corporation affiliated with VIL.

We can quickly dispense with VIL's argument that rights two and three render the agreement a sublicense. Those rights do not limit the agreement's grant to Enprotech of an exclusive right to manufacture replacement parts; the issue of repair service does not limit Enprotech's ability to use the know-how in the replacement parts market.

Similarly, the fifty-year period does not, as a matter of law, render the agreement a sublicense. Verson has alleged that the fifty-year period far exceeds the useful life of any of the knowhow, given the normal rate of change in technology in the industry, and thus the fifty-year period does not serve as any practical restraint on Enprotech's rights under the agreement. Since VIL has not demonstrated that this well-pleaded allegation is incorrect as a matter of law, we must accept it as being true for the purposes of this motion to dismiss.

Nor does the parts supply agreement, as a matter of law, render the Enprotech agreement a sublicense. Although Enprotech is required to purchase certain products from a VIL-affiliated corporation, the agreement states that Enprotech's failure to abide by the parts supply agreement does not affect its exclusive rights granted elsewhere in the agreement. Therefore, the parts supply agreement need not be read to limit Enprotech's right to the use the know-how in the parts market.

That leaves the Enprotech agreement's provision granting VIL the right to manufacture replacement parts in connection with the sale of new presses. It is too early at this juncture to determine as a matter of law that VIL's retention of this right limits Enprotech's interest to a mere sublicense rather than an assignment. VIL may be able to demonstrate that its retained right to provide replacement parts as part of contracts for the sale of new presses represents a sufficiently large portion of the replacement part market to make the Enprotech agreement a sublicense, but we are not in a position to make that determination here. Since VIL has failed to demonstrate that the Enprotech agreement is a license as a matter of law, we must deny its motion to dismiss. VIL is free to renew this argument at a later stage if it can present extrinsic evidence clarifying the ambiguity in the Enprotech agreement.

* * *

---

# Notes

1. RPA *and the Need for Uniformity in Patent Law*. As seen in the *RPA* case, a federal court may decline to apply state law to a contract where there is a need for a uniform body of federal law. Clearly, the federal courts will look behind the letter of patent law to policy, or perhaps legislative intent, to insure such uniformity. What, if anything, can counsel who drafted the original license agreement do to assure predictability in the choice of governing law and forum state?

2. *Protecting License Rights from Competitors.* In both the *PPG* and *Verson* cases, the licensors sought to prevent their competitors from acquiring rights to their proprietary technologies from licensees. PPG did so explicitly by causing termination of the agreement should Permaglass be acquired by a PPG competitor. In Verson, the district court's analysis was complicated by the lack of a clear intent in the agreement vis-à-vis third-party transfers and the multiple interests of the parties, which included both an intent to relieve the licensor from financial distress and the desire to "incubate" the new licensee company so that it could grow and become successful. Perhaps the licensor had a relatively weak negotiating position given that the other party was to be its financial savior. Nevertheless, the licensor was able to limit the grant to the right to "use" know how but not to transfer it to a third party. The court found that VIL could indeed become a head-to-head competitor of Verson but only directly. Many companies never license out  due to the fear of such situations, especially in markets where there are larger and more predatory competitors.

3. *Assignment or License?* The Federal Circuit held that "the term 'assignment' has a particular meaning in patent law implying formal transfer of title." *Vaupel Textilmaschinen KG v. Meccanica Euro Italia SPA*, 944 F.2d at 875 (Cal. N.C. 1991). The legal rights of the parties affected by a licensing arrangement can change based upon whether a license grant is considered exclusive, non-exclusive, or an assignment. Note that in the *Verson* case, VIL assigned Enprotech its intellectual property and sold the know-how. This language is much more consistent with an assignment than with a transfer of a license. Moreover, in the agreement, VIL warranted that it had good title to the know-how and was free to assign it. Again, this provision is more consistent with an assignment than a license.

4. *Licensees and Other Transferees.* The defendants in license agreement cases are often not the original licensees but, rather, third-parties who have acquired the license rights for a variety of business reasons. Unlike the original parties, later transferees are unfamiliar or unconcerned with the original intent of the parties. Over time commercial markets and the vicissitudes of business may also render what was once a mutually beneficial agreement into one that heavily favors one party over the other. Unsurprisingly, that later strangers to the original transaction seek to exploit such inequities by attempting to "bust" the original license restrictions.

# B.  Remedies

## Burlington Indus. v. Solutia, Inc.
### 256 F. Supp. 2d 433 (M.D.N.C. 2003)

BULLOCK, District Judge.

Plaintiff Burlington Industries, Inc. ("Plaintiff") filed this action on July 18, 2001, in Guilford County Superior Court seeking to enjoin Defendant Solutia, Inc. ("Defendant") from selling nylon yarn dyed by a certain process to carpet manufacturers for making stain resistant carpets in competition with Plaintiff.

* * *

The following material facts are undisputed. Plaintiff is a corporation involved in the carpet industry with its principal place of business in Greensboro, North Carolina. In 1995, Plaintiff sued Rossville Yarn, Inc. ("Rossville"), a Georgia corporation, in the United States District Court for the Northern District of Georgia for infringement of certain claims in two of Plaintiff's patents (the "Georgia lawsuit"). Plaintiff's patents concern dyeing processes, which Plaintiff calls its "DURACOLOR" process, in which negatively charged cationic dyeable nylon is dyed with negatively charged acid dyes. Rossville's process, called the "Prismatic" process, which was at issue in the Georgia lawsuit, involved dyeing cationic dyeable nylon (provided by Defendant) with fiber reactive acid dyes. This process was described in two patents owned by Rossville. In response to Plaintiff's claims, Rossville asserted counterclaims that Plaintiff's patents were invalid, unenforceable, and not infringed. After four years of litigation, the Georgia lawsuit was settled on January 5, 2000, through the execution of a Consent Decree, which incorporated a License Agreement and a Settlement Agreement (collectively "the Agreements") between Plaintiff and Rossville. The Consent Decree provided that Plaintiff Burlington's and Defendant Rossville's patents were valid and enforceable and would not thereafter be challenged by the other party. It further provided that the parties would execute license and settlement agreements, that all claims and counterclaims which were asserted or could be asserted were resolved, and that Rossville's antitrust lawsuit against Burlington was dismissed with prejudice. The Settlement Agreement also provided that "no implied licenses or agreements are created by the license executed by the parties." Later in January 2000, Defendant purchased the "Prismatic" patents from Rossville and from Custom Equipment Leasing, Inc., a related company.

* * *

Plaintiff seeks to enjoin Defendant from selling dyed nylon fiber which might be used by carpet manufacturers for making certain stain-resistant carpets. Plaintiff claims that it is entitled to such an injunction because Defendant is bound by the Agreements between Plaintiff and Rossville, which allegedly prohibit Rossville from selling its dyed nylon fiber for use in certain types of carpets. Consequently, Plaintiff is bringing this action against Defendant to enjoin Defendant's sale of its dyed nylon fiber to carpet manufacturers for uses "prohibited" under the Agreements.

Although it disputes that it is bound under the Agreements, Defendant primarily argues that Plaintiff cannot maintain its breach of contract claim because the Agreements do not contain the "prohibition" Plaintiff alleges. Because the License Agreement contains no "prohibition," Defendant claims that it is nothing more than a covenant not to sue Rossville under a limited patent license. Thus, if Plaintiff alleges that Defendant has sold its dyed nylon fiber for an unlicensed use, its only recourse is to sue for patent infringement. Furthermore, because Plaintiff's other causes of action are predicated on the breach of contract claim, Defendant claims that they should also be dismissed.

The issue for the court is the legal interpretation of the Agreements involved. The license grant in question states:

> Licensor hereby grants to Licensee, its licensees, successors and assigns, a non-exclusive paid-up right and license to produce nylon yarn by dyeing cationic dyeable nylon with fiber reactive dyes and a pH of no higher than pH 1.5 and applying an alkaline solution to produce covalent bonds between the dyes and the fibers in the United States of America, its territories and possessions (the "Licensed Territory"): (1) for use in making mats and rugs; and (2) for use in carpet in blends with a preponderance of acid dyeable nylon dyed with acid dyes or cationic dyeable nylon dyed with cationic dyes, but not in blends with cationic dyeable nylon dyed with acid dyes or with solution dyed (pigmented or otherwise) nylon.

\* \* \*

Plaintiff claims that this statement in the License Agreement not only granted Rossville a license to produce dyed nylon yarn for certain uses, but also prohibited it from producing its yarn for other uses. Defendant rejects this conclusion and argues that the license contains no return promise of any kind by Licensee, express or implied. As a result, Defendant claims that the License Agreement contains nothing more than a grant of a limited patent license to Rossville and a covenant not to sue by Plaintiff.

\* \* \*

Plaintiff argues that the prohibition against Rossville's "out-of-field" use is contained in the "express restriction" of the license grant beginning with the words "but not." (Pl.'s Br. Opp'n Def.'s Mot. Summ. J. at 9.) Plaintiff contends that this "but not" clause "dictates the type of carpet product which Prismatic Yarn could not be used in." Id. This reading of the wording of the license, however, is strained. Reading the words of the grant together, Plaintiff, as Licensor, is granting to Rossville, as Licensee, a "non-exclusive paid-up right and license" under its patents to produce certain types of yarn for use in certain types of mats, rugs, and carpets. The "but not" clause is simply limiting the grant of this patent license to certain defined uses.

After reviewing the License Agreement, Settlement Agreement, and Consent Decree, it is apparent that Plaintiff and Rossville entered into a patent license agreement. As the Federal Circuit has held, a patent license agreement "is in essence nothing more than a promise by the licensor not to sue the licensee" for patent infringement. *Spindelfabrik Suessen-Schurr, Stahlecker & Grill GmbH v. Schubert & Salzer Maschinenfabrik Aktiengesellschaft*, 829 F.2d 1075, 1081 (Fed. Cir. 1987).

Limiting grants of a patent license to certain uses is nothing new or unusual. In fact, "patent license agreements can be written to convey different scopes of promises not to sue, *e.g.*, a promise not to sue under a specific patent." Id. The United States Supreme Court has recognized the use of limited patent licenses as essentially a waiver of the patentee's right to sue. *General Talking Pictures Corp. v. Western Elec. Co.*, 304 U.S. 175, 181, 82 L. Ed. 1273, 58 S. Ct. 849, 1938 Dec. Comm'r Pat. 831 (1938). Subsequent cases have interpreted limited licenses consistent with this view so that a violation of the license restriction gives rise to a patent infringement suit. *See Eli Lilly and Co. v. Genetech, Inc.*, 1990 U.S. Dist. LEXIS 18619, 17 U.S.P.Q.2d 1531, 1534 (S.D. Ind. 1990). "These subsequent cases have also reasoned that violation of the license restriction does not give rise to an action for breach of contract." *Id.*

\* \* \*

---

# Sun Microsystems, Inc. v. Microsoft Corp.
## 188 F.3d 1115 (9th Cir. 1999)

SCHROEDER, Circuit Judge.

## OVERVIEW

This case illustrates how fast technology can outdistance the capacity of contract drafters to provide for the ramifications of a computer software licensing arrangement. The license in question runs from plaintiff-appellee Sun Microsystems to defendant-appellant Microsoft. It involves Java, a computer programming language Sun developed to enable the writing of programs that work on any computer operating system. The license agreement was negotiated on a rushed basis in 1996, and by 1997 both Microsoft and Sun had developed what they believed to be significant improvements to Java.

Sun filed this suit for copyright infringement, claiming that Microsoft had exceeded the scope of its license by creating an enhanced version of Java that was fully operable only on Microsoft's operating system, and further, by not adapting its implementation of Java to be compatible with Sun's addition to Java of a component known as the "Java Native Interface" ("JNI"). Sun sought an injunction barring Microsoft from including incompatible Java technology in its products. The district court granted a preliminary injunction to Sun, and Microsoft appeals. The underlying facts, the details of the negotiations, and the nature of the software involved are all more fully described in the district court's detailed opinion. *See Sun Microsystems v. Microsoft Corp.*, 21 F. Supp. 2d 1109 (N.D. Cal. 1998).

Before the district court, the parties bitterly contested the proper interpretation of the terms of the license agreement. Microsoft maintained that the agreement fully authorized all of the conduct that Sun challenged as infringing. Sun's interpretation was, of course, to the contrary. After a careful analysis of the parties' contentions, the district court held that Sun was likely to prevail on the merits of its claim that Microsoft had violated the license agreement.

The parties also disputed whether Sun's suit was properly considered as one for copyright infringement, as Sun contended, or as one for breach of contract, as Microsoft contended. The district court concluded that the claim was properly considered as an infringement action, thereby entitling Sun to a presumption of irreparable harm. *See Cadence Design Systems v. Avant! Corp.*, 125 F.3d 824, 826-27 (9th Cir. 1997), *cert. denied*, 118 S. Ct. 1795 (1998) (copyright plaintiff that demonstrates likely success on the merits entitled to a presumption of irreparable harm). The district court did not elaborate on why the case was a copyright infringement rather than a contract interpretation dispute, and it is on this point that Microsoft expends most of its ammunition on this appeal. It contends that the disputed compatibility requirements of the license agreement are affirmative covenants rather than limitations on the scope of the license, and that accordingly contractual rather than copyright remedies are appropriate if there has been any breach.

\* \* \*

## Factual Background

In March 1996, Microsoft and Sun entered into a "Technology License and Distribution Agreement" ("TLDA") for Java. Microsoft agreed to pay Sun $3.75 million a year for broad rights to use the language. In exchange, Sun granted Microsoft a non-exclusive license to "make, access, use, copy, view, display, modify, adapt, and create Derivative Works of the Technology in Source Code form" and to "make, use, import, reproduce, license, rent, lease, offer to sell, sell or otherwise distribute to end users as part of a Product…the Technology and Derivative Works thereof in binary form." *Sun Microsystems*, 21 F. Supp. 2d at 1113.

Sun had created Java so that programmers could write a single program that would work on any operating system. Because Sun wanted Java to remain cross-platform compatible, the TLDA includes compatibility requirements….In late 1997, Sun became concerned that Microsoft was distributing a "polluted" version of Java that Microsoft had modified in ways that made it incompatible with Sun's standards. Sun filed suit against Microsoft on October 7, 1997, alleging, among other things, trademark infringement, unfair competition, and breach of contract. In November 1997, Sun moved for a preliminary injunction barring Microsoft from using Sun's "Java Compatible" logo on products that failed Sun's compatibility tests. On March 24, 1998, the district court entered a preliminary injunction. *See Sun Microsystems v. Microsoft Corp.*, 999 F. Supp. 1301 (N.D. Cal. 1998). Microsoft did not appeal this injunction.

Sun then amended its complaint to add a claim for copyright infringement and filed motions for a preliminary injunction under 17 U.S.C. § 502 for copyright infringement and under California Business & Professions Code § 17200 for unfair competition. The copyright infringement motion sought an order immediately enjoining Microsoft from distributing its development kit for Java programmers, and enjoining it from distributing Internet Explorer or Windows 98 unless it could show within ninety days that those products passed Sun's compatibility tests. The unfair competition motion sought to enjoin Microsoft from abusing its dominant position in the software market by conditioning licenses for Microsoft products upon use of Microsoft's version of Java.

On November 17, 1998, the district court granted both motions. It found that Sun was likely to prevail on its claims that Microsoft had failed to comply with several of the TLDA compatibility provisions and had engaged in unfair business practices. The court entered a detailed injunction that pertained to both motions and that barred Microsoft from, among other things: (1) distributing any operating systems or internet browsers containing Java technology unless they supported JNI; (2) distributing any Java development tools unless they supported JNI and included a compiler with a default mode that disabled Microsoft's incompatible modifications; (3) incorporating any additional Microsoft keyword extensions or compiler directives into its Java software development tools; and (4) conditioning licenses to Microsoft products or the right to use the "Designed for Windows" logo on the exclusive use of either Microsoft's Java virtual machine or Microsoft's native code interfaces. *See Sun Microsystems*, 21 F. Supp. 2d at 1127–28. Microsoft appeals.

## Analysis

### I. THE COPYRIGHT INFRINGEMENT CLAIM

The standard for a preliminary injunction balances the plaintiff's likelihood of success against the relative hardships to the parties. To receive a preliminary injunction,

Sun was required to show "either a likelihood of success on the merits and the possibility of irreparable injury, or that serious questions going to the merits were raised and the balance of hardships tips sharply in its favor." *Sega Enters. v. Accolade, Inc.*, 977 F.2d 1510, 1517 (9th Cir. 1992) (citations omitted). These two alternatives represent "extremes of a single continuum," rather than two separate tests. *Benda v. Grand Lodge of Int'l Ass'n of Machinists & Aerospace Workers*, 584 F.2d 308, 315 (9th Cir. 1978). Thus, "the greater the relative hardship to the moving party, the less probability of success must be shown." *National Ctr. for Immigrants Rights v. INS*, 743 F.2d 1365, 1359 (9th Cir. 1984).

Under federal copyright law, however, a plaintiff that demonstrates a likelihood of success on the merits of a copyright infringement claim is entitled to a presumption of irreparable harm. *See Cadence Design Systems v. Avant! Corp.*, 125 F.3d 824, 826–27 (9th Cir. 1997), *cert. denied*, 118 S. Ct. 1795 (1998). That presumption means that "the balance of hardships issue cannot be accorded significant"—if any—"weight in determining whether a court should enter a preliminary injunction to prevent the use of infringing material in cases where…the plaintiff has made a strong showing of likely success on the merits." *Id.* at 830.

The district court found that Sun was likely to succeed on its contentions that Microsoft had violated the terms of the TLDA by failing to support JNI and by extending the Java language and modifying the compiler. *See Sun Microsystems*, 21 F. Supp. 2d at 1119, 1123. It therefore held that Sun was entitled to a presumption of irreparable harm. *See id.* at 1125 (citing *Johnson Controls v. Phoenix Control Sys.*, 886 F.2d 1173, 1174 (9th Cir. 1989)). The district court did not make any finding on whether there would be irreparable harm absent the copyright presumption. Finally, the district court briefly addressed hardship, stating that the potential harm to Microsoft was not "unduly burdensome" and that the requested relief would not harm the interests of third parties. *Id.* at 1126. It did not discuss the likely extent of harm to Sun if a preliminary injunction were not entered.

We address in turn the likelihood of success on the merits and the applicability of a presumption of irreparable harm. With regard to the likelihood of success, the issue is whether there is sufficient evidence to support the district court's conclusion that Sun was likely to prove that Microsoft's conduct violated the terms of the TLDA. We conclude that there is such evidence. With regard to the applicability of a presumption of irreparable harm, we agree with Microsoft that the issue turns upon whether the terms Microsoft allegedly breached were limitations on the scope of the license, which would mean that Microsoft had infringed the copyright by acting outside the scope of the license; or whether the terms were merely separate contractual covenants, which would make this a contract dispute in which the copyright presumption of irreparable harm has no application. We conclude that the district court must decide this latter issue before it decides whether Sun is entitled to a presumption of irreparable harm, and so we vacate the injunction and remand the case.

* * *

Whether this is a copyright or a contract case turns on whether the compatibility provisions help define the scope of the license. Generally, a "copyright owner who grants a nonexclusive license to use his copyrighted material waives his right to sue the licensee for copyright infringement " and can sue only for breach of contract. *Graham v. James*, 144 F.3d 229, 236 (2d Cir. 1998) (citing *Peer Int'l Corp. v. Pansa Records, Inc.*, 909 F.2d 1332, 1338–39 (9th Cir. 1990)). If, however, a license is limited in scope and the licensee acts outside the scope, the licensor can bring an action for copyright infringement. *See S.O.S., Inc. v. Payday, Inc.*, 886 F.2d 1081, 1087 (9th Cir. 1989); NIMMER ON COPYRIGHT, § 1015[A] (1999).

\* \* \*

The enforcement of a copyright license raises issues that lie at the intersection of copyright and contract law, an area of law that is not yet well developed. We must decide an issue of first impression: whether, where two sophisticated parties have negotiated a copyright license and dispute its scope, the copyright holder who has demonstrated likely success on the merits is entitled to a presumption of irreparable harm. We hold that it is, but only after the copyright holder has established that the disputed terms are limitations on the scope of the license rather than independent contractual covenants. In other words, before Sun can gain the benefits of copyright enforcement, it must definitively establish that the rights it claims were violated are copyright, not contractual, rights.

In reaching this result, we find considerable support in *Video Trip Corp. v. Lightning Video, Inc.*, 866 F.2d 50 (2d Cir. 1989), in which the Second Circuit held that preliminary contractual issues, such as the ownership of the copyright, must be resolved before the copyright presumption of irreparable harm applies. Video Trip, a company that produced copyrighted travel videotapes, had granted an exclusive license to Lightning Video to promote and distribute the tapes. When the arrangement failed to work out, the parties amended the agreement to require Lightning to dispose of its remaining inventory and furnish Video Trip with an accounting. The copyright was then to revert to Video Trip, unless Video Trip owed money under the accounting and failed to pay. The parties disagreed about the amounts owed and Lightning refused to return the tapes. Video Trip sued for an injunction against copyright infringement, claiming that the license was no longer valid; Lightning claimed it was still valid because Video Trip owed it money.

As here, the parties disputed what preliminary injunction standard should apply. The Second Circuit stated: "It is understandable why a party claiming copyright protection would prefer to ignore the contract dispute and assume the validity of the ownership of the copyright. The rules for obtaining a preliminary injunction are less onerous than in other cases." *Id.* at 52. The court held that "[s]ince the issue as to the ownership of the copyright is still to be determined, we review the order of the court below in denying the application for a preliminary injunction in light of the rule applicable in any contract case." *Id.*

The determination of whether the compatibility terms in the TLDA are covenants or limitations on the scope of the license is likewise a contractual issue, for it requires us to construe the license. We recognized this in *S.O.S., Inc. v. Payday, Inc.*, 886 F.2d 1081 (9th Cir. 1989). In *S.O.S.*, the plaintiff, which held a copyright in a computer program, had granted the defendant a license to "use" the software and had explicitly reserved all other rights. The plaintiff claimed that by modifying the software the defendant had exceeded the scope of the license and therefore infringed the copyright. The district court, using California contract law to construe the license, applied the rule that contracts should be construed against the drafter and held that the license therefore permitted any uses not explicitly forbidden. On appeal, we agreed that we should "rely on state law to provide the canons of contractual construction" provided that "such rules do not interfere with federal copyright law or policy." *Id.* at 1088.

The principles illustrated by *Video Trip* and *S.O.S.* indicate that the disputed question in this case, whether the compatibility terms in the TLDA are license restrictions or separate covenants, is a preliminary contractual issue that must be resolved under California law favorably to Sun before Sun is entitled to the copyright presumption of irreparable harm. The district court did not decide this issue. Although the parties have asked us to decide it, we conclude that it is appropriate to give the district court the first opportunity, especially given that the parties put almost no emphasis on the issue when they litigated the preliminary injunction before the district court. We therefore vacate the preliminary injunction and remand the case.

* * *

# Notes & Questions

1. *"Mini-Licenses."* Note that the entire license in the *Burlington* settlement agreement comprised only one sentence. While concise draftsmanship is an admirable quality, in this case the failure to consider the potential risk of litigation proved fatal. Would the result have been different if the license had also included a separate termination clause, under which misuse of the licensed technology would be a material breach of the agreement? One-sentence patent and copyright licenses are commonly used in a variety of contexts. In such situations where the license may be only tangential to the purpose of the agreement, the importance of careful draftsmanship can easily be overlooked.

2. *Software Licenses.* At the other end of the spectrum from *Burlington*, Sun Microsystems and Microsoft were engaged in a complex business arrangement that was entirely based upon a license agreement. Sun had granted to Microsoft a non-exclusive license to "create Derivative Works of the Technology" and to "make, use, import, reproduce, license, rent, lease, offer to sell, sell or otherwise distribute to end users as part of a Product...the Technology and Derivative Works thereof...." Elsewhere in the agreement, Sun had required that all derivative works created by Microsoft must be compatible with Sun's version of Java.

On the surface, Sun's compatibility limitation appears very similar to the field restriction in the *Burlington* case. Suppose that the agreement had included the following provision:

> Microsoft covenants and agrees to create and sell only derivative works that meet the compatibility requirements of Sun as contained herein.

At the time the agreement was drafted, Sun surely considered the risk of litigation. Did Sun have to choose between drafting for quick injunctive relief in federal court or straightforward contract damages in state court? Could it have planned better for both options? Consider the Court's aside that the case "illustrate[d] how fast technology can outdistance the capacity of contract drafters," and that the agreement was negotiated on a "rushed basis."

3. *Licensees Must Materially Breach License in Order to Bring Declaratory Judgment Actions.* If a party takes an intellectual property license to avoid a lawsuit, that party/licensee should consider that it will forgo its opportunity to later bring a declaratory judgment action against the licensor, unless the licensee first materially breaches the license. Specifically, the licensee's material breach of the license is necessary to create an "actual controversy" as required for a declaratory judgment.

Recently in *Gen-Probe Inc. v. Vysis Inc.*, 359 F.3d 1376 (Fed. Cir. 2004), the Federal Circuit revisited the issue of "actual controversies" when a license is still in effect. In this case, Gen-Probe took a patent license from Vysis as part of an overall settlement of an unrelated litigation. Gen-Probe agreed to pay royalties under protest and then filed a declaratory judgment suit for a judgment of non-infringement and invalidity in the U.S. District Court for the Southern District of California. The District Court granted Gen-Probe a judgment of non-infringement and invalidity for nonenablement and obviousness, Vysis appealed, and the Federal Circuit reversed the District Court's judgment. *Id.* at 1379.

The Federal Circuit reiterated that the Declaratory Judgment Act only supports jurisdiction in the event of an "actual controversy." 28 U.S.C. § 2201(a). The declaratory judgment plaintiff must establish an actual controversy on the "totality of the circumstances." *Id.* at 1379 (quoting *Spectronics Corp. v. H.B. Fuller Co.*, 940 F.2d 631 (Fed. Cir. 1991)). In addition, "'[t]here must be both (1) an explicit threat or other action by the patentee, which creates a reasonable apprehension on the part of the declaratory judgment plaintiff that it will face an infringement suit, and (2) present activity which could constitute infringement or concrete steps taken with the intent to conduct such activity.'" *Id.* at 1380 (quoting *BP Chems. Ltd. V. Union Carbide*, 4 F.3d 975 (Fed. Cir. 1993)).

Although the Federal Circuit had previously found that there could be apprehension of a federal infringement suit (and thus a controversy) when a license is still in effect (*Cr. Bard Inc. v. Schwartz*, 716 F.2d 874 (Fed. Cir. 1983)), in *Gen-Probe* the Federal Circuit found that the licensee, at minimum, must stop payments of the royalties and thereby materially breach the license agreement before bringing a declaratory judgment action to challenge the validity or scope of the licensed patent. *Id.* at 1382. Specifically, the court found that *Bard* was factually different, because the licensee had stopped making payments and the licensor sued for nonpayment. The court rejected Gen-Probe's argument that its payment of royalties under protest created an actual controversy, distinguishing Gen-Probe specific circumstances from an earlier "under protest" cases. *See, e.g., Altavater v. Freeman*, 319 U.S. 359 (1943) (payments made under injunction decree; court expressly refused to decide on licensee estoppel); *Aetna Life Insurance Co. v. Haworth*, 300 U.S. 227 (1937) (premium payments in a insurance disability dispute). The Federal Circuit further concluded that a material breach of the license is necessary to seek a declaratory judgment as a matter of public policy. The court reasoned that because Vysis had voluntarily relinquished its statutory right to exclude by granting Gen-Probe a non-exclusive license, and Gen-Probe could nonetheless pursue a lawsuit without materially breaching the license agreement, the licensor would "bear all the risk, while licensee would benefit from the licensee's effective cap on damages or royalties in the event of its challenge to the patent's scope of validity fails." 359 F.3d at 1381–82.

4. *Effective IP Assignment Language for To-Be-Created Intellectual Property.* In *Speedplay, Inc. v. Bebop Inc.*, the Federal Circuit distinguished between enforceable IP assignments and unenforceable "agreements to assign" IP. At issue was the enforceability of IP assignment language in a "Confidentiality and Inventions Agreement" (CIA). The CIA defined "Inventions" as any intellectual property conceived or developed by the inventor within the scope of his employment. The assignment language stated that all inventions covered by the CIA "'shall belong exclusively to [assignee] and [inventor] hereby conveys, transfers and assigns to [assignee]…all right, title and interest in and to Inventions.'" 211 F.3d 1245, 1253 (Fed. Cir. 2000).

Bebop challenges Speedplay's rights in the '894 patent on two grounds. First, Bebop contends that the CIA is merely a "promise to assign a future invention." That contention invokes this court's decision in *Arachnid, Inc. v. Merit Industries, Inc.,* 939 F.2d 1574, 1576, 19 USPQ2d 1513, 1514 (Fed.Cir.1991) in which a contractor agreed that any inventions it conceived "shall be the property of [the client], and all rights thereto *will be assigned* by the contractor to the client. Holding that the client could not bring an infringement action based on that contractual language, the Arachnid court characterized the promise as "an *agreement to assign,* not an assignment." *Id.* at 1580, 1580–81, 19 USPQ2d at 1518, 1518–19. The language in the CIA, however, differs significantly from the language at issue in *Arachnid*. It provides that inventions "shall belong" to Speedplay, and that Bryne "hereby conveys, transfers and assigns" the inventions to Speedplay. Therefore, this case is not controlled by *Arachnid,* but by *Filmtec Corp. v. Allied-Signal Inc.,* 939 F.2d 1568, 1570, 19 USPQ2d 1508, 1509 (Fed.Cir.1991), in which the contractor agreed "'to grant and does hereby grant'" to the client the rights and title to any invention, whether patentable or not. In *Filmtec* this court stated that "no further act would be required once an invention came into being; the transfer of title would occur by operation of law." *Id.* at 1573, 939 F.2d 1568, 19 USPQ2d at 1512.

*Id.* at 1253 (emphasis in original). Thus, to be effective, employee invention assignment agreements — or any agreement anticipating the assignment of IP not yet created — must contain "current" language assigning to-be-created IP (e.g., "to grant and hereby does grant" or "hereby conveys, transfers, and assigns") and must avoid mere promises of assignment.

---

# C.  Governing Law

## Texas Instruments, Inc., v. Tessera, Inc., and U.S. International Trade Commission

### 231 F.3d 1325 (Fed. Cir. 2000)

RADER, Circuit Judge.

In the United States District Court for the Central District of California, Texas Instruments Incorporated (TI) sought to enjoin Tessera, Inc. (Tessera) from continued participation in an International Trade Commission (ITC) infringement action that Tessera had initiated. The district court denied TI's motion. Because the license agreement between TI and Tessera requires any litigation, including ITC proceedings under Section 337 of the Tariff Act of 1930, to occur in the State of California, this court vacates and remands to the district court to re-entertain TI's preliminary injunction motion.

I.

On November 1, 1996, TI entered into a "Limited TCC License Agreement" with Tessera. The license agreement covers technology claimed in several of Tessera's United States patents. The technology relates to chip scale packaging, a semiconductor package with connections between the semiconductor chip and a circuit board underneath the chip, within the periphery of the chip itself. Tessera designates this type of chip package with the brand name "TCC," for Tessera Compliant Chip. TCCs occupy less space on a circuit board than conventionally packaged chips, a feature which is particularly attractive in applications such as cellular phones.

The license agreement between Tessera and TI contains a clause that governs the law and venue that applies to the agreement:

> Governing Law. This Agreement shall be governed, interpreted and construed in accordance with the laws of the State of California as if without regard to its provisions with respect to conflicts of Laws. Both parties shall use their best efforts to resolve by mutual agreement any disputes, controversies, claims or difference which may arise from, under, out of or in connection with this Agreement. If such disputes, controversies, claims or differences cannot be settled between the parties, any litigation between the parties relating to this Agreement shall take place in California. The parties hereby consent to personal jurisdiction and venue in the state and federal courts of California.

In April 1999, Tessera requested royalties for a class of TI imports known as "MicroStar BGA." Tessera sought royalties under its United States Patents Nos. 5,679,977, "Semiconductor Chip Assemblies, Methods of Making Same and Components for Same" ('997 patent); 5,852,326, "Face-Up Semiconductor Chip Assembly" ('997 patent); and 5,347,159, "Semiconductor Chip Assemblies with Face-Up Mounting and Rear-Surface Connection to Substrate." After negotiations, TI and Tessera could not agree on whether the license agreement covered the accused TI products. Therefore, on January 17, 2000, Tessera notified TI of its termination of the license agreement. In response to Tessera's notice of termination, TI filed an action for declaratory judgment of invalidity and non-infringement in the United States District Court for the Central District of California on February 1, 2000.

On March 28, 2000, Tessera filed a complaint with the ITC, under Section 337 of the Tariff Act of 1930, charging that TI's importation of the MicroStar BGA products and certain importations by others infringe the '997 and '326 patents. See 19 U.S.C. § 1337 (1994).

On April 4, 2000, TI applied for a Temporary Restraining Order (TRO) and an order requesting an expedited preliminary injunction hearing in the California district court. TI requested the court to restrain Tessera "from pursuing any disputes, controversies, claims or differences...against TI that arise from, under, out of or in connection with" the license agreement, in any place outside California. TI asserted that because the ITC tribunal is located in Washington, D.C., Tessera's ITC complaint violated the license agreement. TI further explained that the ITC determines whether to initiate an investigation within thirty days of the filing of a complaint. TI considered its request for an expedited preliminary injunction hearing warranted because Tessera could not simply withdraw its complaint once the ITC initiated an investigation. The district court denied TI's application for a TRO and set the preliminary injunction hearing date for May 1, 2000.

On April 27, 2000, the ITC instituted an investigation into the allegedly infringing imports. See, In the Matter of Certain Semiconductor Chips with Minimized Chip Package Size and Products Containing Same, Investigation No. 337-TA-432 (April 27, 2000). The ITC's Notice of Investigation named TI, Sharp Corporation, and Sharp Electronics Corporation as respondents. Id. That same day, the ITC made a motion, under Fed. R. Civ. P. 24, for leave to intervene in the preliminary injunction hearing at the district court "for the purpose of opposing [TI's] motion to enjoin [Tessera] from pursuing claims... through the ITC."

On May 2, 2000, the district court granted ITC's motion to intervene and denied TI's motion for a preliminary injunction. *See Texas Instruments Inc. v. Tessera, Inc.*, 192 F.R.D. 637 (C.D. Cal. 2000) (TII). The district court found that TI was not likely to succeed on the merits of its claim that the governing law clause covered ITC proceedings. The district court concluded that the agreement's governing law clause "is limited to 'litigation' and that [TI] has not established a likelihood of proving that [Tessera's] action before the ITC is litigation." *TI I*, at 640. In reaching this conclusion, the district court relied on the definition of "litigation" in the CAL. CODE OF CIV. PROC., section 391(a) (1994), "Vexatious Litigants." In that section, "litigation" means 'any civil action or proceeding, commenced, maintained or pending in any state or federal court.'" *TI I*, at 640 (quoting CAL. CODE CIV. PROC. § 391(a)). Based on this definition, the trial court found that the term "litigation" in the agreement "doesn't limit the parties' federal right to administrative redress." *Id.* The district court further found that enjoining Tessera's participation would be an impermissible interference with the ITC's statutorily authorized proceedings. TI appeals, invoking this court's jurisdiction of interlocutory appeals under 28 U.S.C. § 1292(c)(1) (1994).

* * *

TI's preliminary injunction motion was a request for the district court to enjoin Tessera from continued participation in an ITC proceeding. This court has exclusive appellate jurisdiction over ITC determinations made under section 337 of the Tariff Act of 1930. *See* 28 U.S.C. § 1295(a)(6) (1994). Thus, TI's appeal relates to a procedural matter arising from substantive issues in an area of law within the unique jurisdiction of this circuit. This circuit's procedural law, therefore, applies to the district court's order under review. Under Federal Circuit law, this court sustains a grant or denial of a preliminary injunction unless the district court abused its discretion, or based its decision on an erroneous legal standard or clearly erroneous findings of fact. *See Mentor Graphics Corp. v. Quickturn Design Sys., Inc.*, 150 F.3d 1374, 1377, 47 USPQ2d 1683, 1685 (Fed. Cir. 1998); *see also Hybritech Inc. v. Abbott Labs.*, 849 F.2d 1446, 1449, 7 USPQ2d 1191, 1194 (Fed. Cir. 1988).

The district court's order denying TI's motion for a preliminary injunction also presents an issue concerning interpretation of a license agreement. General contract interpretation is not within the exclusive jurisdiction of the Federal Circuit. The Supreme Court has held that "[t]he interpretation of private contracts is ordinarily a question of state law." *Volt Info. Sci., Inc. v. Bd. of Tr. of Leland Stanford Junior Univ.*, 489 U.S. 468, 474 (1989). Furthermore, the governing law clause of the license agreement requires interpretation of the agreement "in accordance with the laws of the State of California." This court will, therefore, apply California state law to interpret the license agreement. Under California state law, contracts are interpreted without deference on appeal. *Plaza Freeway Ltd. P'ship v. First Mountain Bank*, 81 Cal. Ct. App. 4th 616, 620 (2000).

* * *

The Cal. Civ. Code supplies basic rules for contract interpretation: (1) "clear and explicit" language which does not produce an absurdity will govern, Cal. Civ. Code § 1638; (2) ambiguous terms receive the meaning "which the promisor believed, at the time of making it, that the promisee understood," Cal. Civ. Code § 1649; and (3) ambiguity persisting beyond the application of the previous rule will be resolved against "the party who caused the uncertainty to exist," Cal. Civ. Code § 1654. In sum, "the mutual intention of the parties at the time the contract is formed governs interpretation." *AIU Ins. Co. v. Superior Court*, 799 P.2d 1253, 1264 (1990). When interpreting a contract provision, a court gives the contract terms their ordinary and popular meaning unless the contracting parties use them in a technical or a special sense. *Id.* at 822.

As noted above, contracts in California rely for meaning predominantly upon the mutual intention of the parties at the time of contracting. The district court did not make any findings as to the parties' understanding of the term "litigation" at the time of contracting. The license agreement at issue in this suit governs a very specific form of business arrangement, namely the licensing of patented technology. Both Tessera and TI are sophisticated corporations with experience in patent licensing. The United States Patent and Trademark Office Patent Bibliographic Database lists Tessera as the assignee of over 110 patents, TI of over 8,000 patents. These corporations necessarily regularly apply the basic tenets of patent practice. Each is well aware of available remedies for patentees and defenses for accused infringers. Thus, these contracting parties would have negotiated the clauses of the patent license agreement with knowledge of patent law, including available remedies for patent law violations.

Patent law affords a patentee several alternative remedies against a purported infringer. For alleged domestic infringement, a patentee can file an action in a district court. *See* 35 U.S.C. § 281 (1952); *see also* 28 U.S.C. § 1338 (1994). For alleged infringement through importation, a patentee can also file an action in a district court or in the ITC. *See* 19 U.S.C. § 1337. In fact, a patentee can bring suit both in a district court and in the ITC against an alleged infringer who is importing an allegedly infringing product.

The two forums offer a patentee different types of remedies. In a district court, a patentee can seek an injunction and damages. With respect to infringing imports, however, the patentee must take the additional step of requesting the U.S. Customs Service to enforce the district court judgment by seizing the offending goods. In the ITC, the patentee may not seek money damages, *Bio-Tech. Gen. Corp. v. Genetech, Inc.*, 80 F.3d 1553, 1564, 38 USPQ2d 1321, 1329 (Fed. Cir. 1996), but the ITC automatically enforces its judgment by directing the U.S. Customs Service to seize any infringing imports.

Thus, when TI and Tessera negotiated the terms of their licensing agreement, this court attributes to them adequate knowledge of the basic patent law actions and remedies available to litigants, including the available forums and venues. Both parties would have been fully aware of the forums of the district courts and the ITC for resolution of future controversies arising from the license agreement. With this in mind, this court next examines the parties' intentions in using the word "litigation" in the governing law clause of their agreement. As mentioned earlier, the district court determined the meaning of "litigation" based on the California Code of Civil Procedure Title for "Vexatious Litigants." The definition of "litigation" in that title does not govern this licensing agreement for Tessera patents. In the first place, the Cal. Code Civ. Proc., section 391, states: "*As used in this title…* 'Litigation' means…." (emphasis added). Thus, the California Code limits its definition to use in that particular title. This limitation hardly suggests that TI and Tessera would have incorporated that meaning from the California "Vexatious Litigants" section into their license agreement on patented technology.

In the field of patent law, which is more relevant to the meaning of this license, "litigation" does not exclude ITC proceedings under section 337. Section 337 proceedings are *inter partes* actions initiated by the filing of a complaint and including discovery, filing of briefs and motions, and testimony and arguments at a hearing before an administrative law judge. *See* 19 U.S.C. § 1337(c). In section 337 proceedings relevant to patent infringement, the ITC follows Title 35 of the United States Code and the case law of this court. *See* 19 U.S.C. § 1337(c). In sum, this court has consistently treated section 337 patent infringement proceedings as litigation.

\* \* \*

Indeed, the ITC itself refers to its section 337 proceedings as "litigation."

Therefore, section 337 proceedings at the ITC are recognized as litigation. As noted earlier, this court attributes knowledge of patent law and its language and usages to both parties at the time of contracting. In interpreting contracts, words are given their "clear and explicit" meaning in the field of the agreement unless it is clearly shown that the parties intended a different meaning. *See* CAL. CIV. CODE § 1638; *see also* CAL. CIV. CODE § 1649. Thus, the term "litigation" in the governing law clause of the license agreement includes section 337 proceedings at the ITC. The governing law clause, therefore, requires any litigation between the parties, including ITC proceedings, to take place in California. Because ITC actions cannot be brought in California, it follows that the parties did not agree to the ITC as a forum for litigation.

This court further notes that the governing law clause of the license agreement is not limited to license related issues such as the amount of royalty due, term of agreement, and cross-licensing. The governing law clause lists "disputes, controversies, claims or difference[s] which may *arise from, under, out of or in connection with* this Agreement." (Emphasis added.) Patent infringement disputes do arise from license agreements... Thus, the governing law clause in the present case, as in any patent license agreement, necessarily covers disputes concerning patent issues.

\* \* \*

This court reverses the district court's judgment that TI would not be likely to succeed in proving that Tessera's action before the ITC is covered by the governing law clause. This court, therefore, vacates the district court's denial of TI's preliminary injunction motion and remands to the district court to reconsider the preliminary injunction motion on the remaining preliminary injunction factors.

\* \* \*

LOURIE, Circuit Judge, dissenting.

I respectfully dissent.

Everyone familiar with patent litigation knows that ITC proceedings are considered "litigation." However, our job is to construe a particular provision of a license agreement by determining the intentions of the parties to that agreement. I conclude that ITC proceedings were not intended to be within the scope of the venue provision at issue.

Because ITC litigation is part of the patent world, as the majority clearly agrees, I believe that if the parties had intended that ITC proceedings be part of this paragraph, they would have so stated. I believe the limitation to California was intended to mean California, and not Texas or Delaware. The indication of California is a geographic limitation, not one indicating the type of forum. It did not state that litigation should be in a district court, rather than at the ITC.

Moreover, the provision relates to disputes "in connection with the agreement." Disputes in connection with a license agreement are most often disputes about the scope of licensed subject matter, amount of royalty due, term of agreement, cross-licensing, the meaning of other provisions, etc., rather than concerning the validity or infringement of the patent. The whole point of a license is not to exclude, as a patent does, but to legitimize the licensee under the patent. While obviously disputes can arise concerning validity and infringement, I believe that the language indicates that the parties meant questions most likely to arise under the contract, i.e., those that can be resolved by invoking California contract law. License agreements are construed under state law, in which case the particular venue might matter, thus supporting the idea that the parties intended one state as the venue, not another state. Moreover, the parties could not have intended that California law would govern the question of whether or not ITC proceedings are litigation, as California law has nothing relevant to offer on that issue.

* * *

---

# Notes & Questions

1. *Divining the Intent of the Parties.* In both the *TI* and *Sun v. Microsoft* cases, the courts characterized the parties as "sophisticated," meaning experienced in licensing, yet both agreements included latent ambiguities that could have been removed had counsel considered every potential eventuality. Did the majority opinion or the dissent better gauge the intent of the parties?

---

## D.  Most Favored Licensee

### Studiengesellschaft Kohle, M.B.H., v. Hercules, Inc., Himont U.S.A., and Himont, Inc.

### 105 F.3d 629 (Fed. Cir. 1997)

MAYER, Circuit Judge.

In 1986, Studiengesellschaft Kohle m.b.H. (SGK) sued Hercules, Inc.; Himont U.S.A., Inc.; and Himont, Inc. (collectively "Hercules") for patent infringement. Hercules counterclaimed, alleging that SGK had breached the most favored licensee provision of their license agreement by failing to offer Hercules a license with the same terms it offered other licensees. But for the breach, Hercules argued, it would have been licensed under the patents at issue during the period in question, thereby insulating it from infringement. The district court agreed and entered judgment for Hercules. *Studiengesellschaft Kohle m.b.H. v. Hercules, Inc.*, No. 86-566-JJF (D. Del. June 30, 1995). Because SGK has not established that the court made any clearly erroneous findings of fact or error of law, we affirm. We remand for the court to determine whether SGK is entitled to interest on its license fee.

### *Background*

SGK is the licensing arm of the Max-Planck Institute for Coal Research in Germany and the successor-in-interest to Professor Karl Ziegler, the Institute's former head, who died in 1973. For simplicity, we refer to both Professor Ziegler and SGK as SGK. Hercules manufactured and sold plastics from the 1950s through 1983, when it sold its polypropylene business to Himont U.S.A., Inc.

In the early 1950s, SGK invented a catalyst that could be used to make plastics, such as polyethylene and polypropylene. In 1954, SGK and Hercules entered a "polyolefin contract" (the "1954 contract") granting Hercules a nonexclusive license under SGK's "Patent Applications and Patents Issued Thereon." Although the United States had not issued SGK any patents at that time, the contract contemplated that Hercules would be licensed under any SGK patent issued in the future in the plastics field. The contract included a most favored licensee provision, set forth in pertinent part:

> If a license shall hereafter be granted by [SGK] to any other licensee in the United States or Canada to practice the Process or to use and sell the products of the Process under [SGK's] inventions, Patent Applications or Patents or any of them, then [SGK] shall notify Hercules promptly of the terms of such other license and if so requested by Hercules, shall make available to Hercules a copy of such other license and Hercules shall be entitled, upon demand if made three (3) months after receiving the aforementioned notice, to the benefit of any lower royalty rate or rates for its operations hereunder in the country or countries (US and Canada) in which such rates are effective, as of and after the date such more favorable rate or rates became effective under such other license but only for so long as and to the same extent and subject to the same conditions that such…lower royalty rate or rates shall be available to such other licensee; provided, however, that Hercules shall not be entitled to such more favorable rate or rates without accepting any less favorable terms that may have accompanied such more favorable rate or rates.

The contract also contained a termination clause, which granted SGK the right to terminate the agreement and the licenses upon sixty days written notice if Hercules failed to make royalty payments when due. However, Hercules had the right to cure its default by paying SGK "all sums then due under [the] Agreement," in which case the licenses would remain in full force and effect. The contract would be construed under Delaware law.

The parties amended the contract in 1962 and 1964, revising, *inter alia*, the royalty rates Hercules was to pay SGK. Both amendments contained savings provisions, stating that the 1954 contract remained effective except to the extent modified by those two amendments. SGK does not allege that these amendments modified the most favored licensee provision.

In 1972, the parties again amended the 1954 contract by granting Hercules "a fully paid-up" license through December 3, 1980, the date the '115 patent expired, under SGK's "U.S. Patent rights with respect to polypropylene…up to a limit of six hundred million pounds (600,000,000) per year sales." For sales exceeding that amount, Hercules was obligated to pay SGK royalties of one percent of its "Net Sales Price." As to SGK's patents expiring after December 3, 1980, Hercules possessed the right, upon request, to obtain "a license on terms no worse than the most favored other paying licensee of [SGK]." SGK concedes that this provision granted Hercules the "right to the most favored paying licensee's terms regardless of whether those terms had been granted before or after 1972." The amendment also provided that the terms and conditions of the 1954 contract remained in full force and effect except as modified by, or inconsistent with, this amendment. SGK concedes that "the notice provision, indeed the whole [most-favored licensee] clause, 'survived the 1972 Agreement.'"

On November 14, 1978, SGK was issued U.S. Patent No. 4,125,698 ('698 patent) for the "Polymerization of Ethylenically Unsaturated Hydrocarbons." The parties agree that under the 1972 amendment Hercules was licensed under the '698 patent, without any additional payment, through December 3, 1980. It is also undisputed that this patent is covered by the 1954 agreement, as amended.

In March 1979, SGK sent Hercules a letter terminating the 1954 contract and the licenses granted under it "for failure to account and make royalty payments" when due. In accordance with the agreement, the letter stated that the termination would become effective in sixty days unless the "breach" had been corrected and the payments made. Hercules paid SGK $339,032 within the sixty-day period, which SGK accepted. Although SGK possessed the right to question any royalty statement made by Hercules, and to have a certified public accountant audit Hercules' books to verify or determine royalties paid or payable, it did not do so.

On May 1, 1980, more than seven months before the expiration of Hercules' "paid-up" license, SGK granted Amoco Chemicals Corporation (Amoco) a nonexclusive "paid-up" license to make, use, and sell products covered by SGK's polypropylene patents in the United States. In exchange, Amoco paid SGK $1.2 million. SGK does not dispute that the '698 patent is covered by this license or that it failed to apprise Hercules of the license at the time it was granted. Hercules first learned of Amoco's license in 1987, after SGK commenced this action. It demanded an equivalent license retroactive to December 3, 1980. SGK refused, contending that: (1) Amoco was not a "paying licensee," as contemplated by the 1972 amendment; (2) Hercules' request was too late; and (3) Amoco's license was granted as part of a settlement agreement.

Prior to that time, in 1983, SGK saw a publication of industry-wide production figures, suggesting that Hercules had produced 890 million pounds of polypropylene in 1980. It asked Hercules why it had not made any royalty payment for the amount exceeding the 600 million pound royalty-free limit. Hercules claimed that while it had used or sold 747 million pounds of polypropylene, less than 600 million pounds met the definition of polypropylene requiring royalty payment. SGK argued that the excess use or sales required the payment of royalties under either the original 1954 contract or the 1972 amendment. Hercules responded that it believed it had fulfilled all of its royalty obligations.

On December 3, 1986, SGK filed suit in the United States District Court for the District of Delaware, charging Hercules with infringement of the '698 patent. Hercules counterclaimed, alleging that the 1954 license, as amended, required SGK to notify it of the Amoco agreement in 1980, the terms of which it was entitled to obtain via the most favored licensee provision of the 1954 contract, as amended. Hercules argued that it would have exercised its right to obtain a license on Amoco's terms had SGK not breached that provision. It claimed, therefore, that it was entitled to such license, retroactive to December 3, 1980, upon paying SGK $1.2 million. The court agreed and entered judgment for Hercules. This appeal followed.

## Discussion

We review the district court's factual determinations for clear error. Its legal conclusions, on the other hand, must stand unless they are incorrect as a matter of law. FED. R. CIV. P. 52(a); *King Instruments Corp. v. Perego*, 65 F.3d 941, 945, 36 USPQ2d 1129, 1131 (Fed. Cir. 1995). Central to this case is the proper construction of the parties' license agreement. This is a question of contract interpretation under Delaware law, which we review de novo. *See Cyrix Corp. v. Intel Corp.*, 77 F.3d 1381, 1384, 37 USPQ2d 1884, 1887 (Fed. Cir. 1996).

SGK first argues that the court erred in holding that it was contractually required to give Hercules notice of the terms of the Amoco license. Under Delaware law, we must "give effect to the intent of the parties as evidenced by the terms of the contract." *Burge v. Fidelity Bond and Mortgage Co.*, 648 A.2d 414, 420 (Del. 1994). We look first to the plain language. *See Ed Fine Oldsmobile, Inc. v. Diamond State Tel. Co.*, 494 A.2d 636, 638 (Del. 1985). In May 1980, SGK granted Amoco a "paid-up" license to make, use, or sell products covered by the '698 patent in exchange for $1.2 million. At that time, Hercules was also licensed under the '698 patent, but only until December 3, 1980, approximately fifteen years prior to its scheduled expiration. The most favored licensee provision of the 1954 contract, which SGK agrees survived the agreement's three subsequent amendments, provides that if SGK grants any other license in the United States or Canada to practice the process or to use or sell products under SGK's patents, including the '698 patent, then SGK "shall notify Hercules promptly of the terms of such other license."

SGK concedes that the notice provision was effective but argues that it was only obligated to provide Hercules with notice of any license with terms more favorable than Hercules' license. In 1972, Hercules obtained a "paid-up" license under SGK's patents through December 3, 1980. In 1978, the '698 patent issued. Hercules was licensed under that patent, without additional cost, by virtue of the 1972 license. Because Hercules obtained a "free" license under the '698 patent for the first 600 million pounds, no terms could be more favorable, according to SGK. So, it had no duty to apprise Hercules of the Amoco license.

SGK's interpretation does violence to the plain language of the 1954 contract. The notice clause did not condition SGK's obligation to inform Hercules of other licenses on whether such licenses were more favorable. It required SGK to notify Hercules promptly of the terms of a license granted "to any other licensee." Under SGK's construction, the power to determine whether another license was more favorable resided not with Hercules, but with SGK. That simply was not what the agreement provided. It is true that the 1954 contract granted Hercules the right, upon demand, to the benefit of any "more favorable rate or rates." However, that clause signified nothing more than the commercial reality that Hercules would opt only for a license whose terms it thought were more favorable than its own. It did not divest Hercules of the right to decide which terms were more favorable. Indeed, such a decision will not always be apparent when one considers the myriad combinations of royalty payments, lump-sum payments, and technology transfers a license can effect. Consequently, the court was correct that SGK's failure to provide notice constituted a breach of the license agreement.

SGK next says that it had no obligation to grant Hercules a license with terms equivalent to those in the Amoco license because Amoco was not a "paying licensee" within the meaning of the 1972 amendment. Again, we turn to the plain language of the license and interpret it anew. The 1972 amendment provided that for any of SGK's patents expiring after December 3, 1980, including the '698 patent, SGK would "grant Hercules, upon request, a license on terms no worse than the most favored other paying licensee of [SGK]." SGK contends that Amoco was not a "paying licensee" because it made just one lump-sum payment and no royalty payments; only licensees that make ongoing royalty payments are "paying licensee[s]."

In construing the term "paying licensee," we must give the words their ordinary meaning unless a contrary intent appears. *Citadel Holding Corp. v. Roven*, 603 A.2d 818,

824 (Del. 1992). The ordinary meaning of the term "paying licensee" is one who gives money for a license. *See* WEBSTER's II NEW RIVERSIDE UNIVERSITY DICTIONARY 863 (1984) (defining "pay" as "[t]o give money to in return for goods or services rendered"). SGK has not established that the parties intended that the term should mean something else. We see no distinction between one who makes an up-front, lump-sum payment and one who makes continuing royalty payments. Indeed, such a distinction would be doubly doubtful because a "paid-up" license presumably includes potential future royalty payments discounted to their net present value.

SGK also argues that the $1.2 million payment was in settlement of litigation; Amoco was not intended to be a "paying licensee." But the court found that Amoco paid SGK $1.2 million for a paid-up license for unlimited production under, inter alia, the '698 patent. SGK has not shown how this finding is clearly erroneous: Amoco was a "paying licensee." Our conclusion that the court did not err in finding that Amoco paid $1.2 million for its license also disposes of SGK's contention that Hercules should pay more than that amount.

Even were we to accept SGK's interpretation as reasonable, however, the provision would be ambiguous because Hercules' construction is also reasonable. See Kaiser Aluminum Corp. v. Matheson, 681 A.2d 392, 395 (Del. 1996) (contract provision is ambiguous if it is reasonably susceptible of two or more interpretations). Under such circumstances, and in the absence of any extrinsic evidence clearly establishing the parties' intent, we construe the term "paying licensee" against the drafter of the language-SGK-under the doctrine of contra proferentem. *Id.* at 398 ("It is a well-accepted principle that ambiguities in a contract should be construed against the drafter."). So, Hercules' interpretation would still prevail.

According to SGK, even if Hercules is entitled to terms equivalent to those in the Amoco license, it exercised its option too late to be effective. This argument fails because the only requirement in the 1954 contract or its amendments that limits the time in which Hercules must request a license is that it be within three months of receiving the required notice. Because SGK failed to notify Hercules of the Amoco license, that time limitation never began. The court found that Hercules first became aware of the Amoco license in 1987 through discovery in this case. Hercules demanded an equivalent license on or about March 16, 1987, so even if constructive notice could trigger the three-month limitation, Hercules met it.

\* \* \*

SGK also contends that the court erred in concluding that Hercules was entitled to a license retroactive to December 3, 1980. It argues that for six years Hercules intentionally manufactured products covered by the '698 patent, which it thought was invalid, without a license. Only after this court ruled that the patent had not been proven invalid, *see Studiengesellschaft Kohle m.b.H. v. Northern Petrochemical Co.*, 784 F.2d 351, 228 USPQ 837 (Fed. Cir. 1986), did Hercules become interested in obtaining a license. It requested a license retroactive to the date its allegedly infringing activities began, thereby insulating itself from any infringement claim. SGK argues that "nothing in Hercules' option provides for such a right."

To be sure, neither we nor the parties can know with certainty whether Hercules would have exercised its right to a license on Amoco's terms in 1980, had it received the required notice. To that extent the prospect of absolving six years of alleged infringement via a retroactive license is troubling. But the uncertainty was caused by SGK's breach, the consequences of which it must bear. The 1954 contract expressly and unambiguously provides Hercules with the right to obtain the terms of another license "effective, as of and after the date such more favorable rate or rates became effective under such other license." The agreement must stand as written. Hercules is entitled to the terms of the Amoco license effective May 1980, when the Amoco license became effective.

* * *

---

# E.  Enforcing Arbitration Clauses

## Microchip Technology, Inc. v. U.S. Phillips Corp. and Phillips Electronics North America Corp.
### 367 F.3d 1350 (Fed. Cir. 2004)

DYK, Circuit Judge.

Appellants U.S. Philips Corporation and Philips Electronics North America Corporation (collectively "Philips") appeal the decision of the United States District Court for the District of Arizona denying Philips' motion to compel arbitration. *Microchip Tech. Inc. v. U.S. Philips Corp.*, No. 01-CV-2090-PHX-PGR; 03-CV-0272-PHX-JAT (D. Ariz. June 13, 2003). Because the district court properly denied Philips' motion to compel arbitration, we affirm.

### BACKGROUND

Reduced to the essentials, the background for this case may be simply stated. Philips is the owner of U.S. Patent Nos. 4,689,740 (the "'740 patent") and 5,559,502 (the "'502 patent"), which generally relate to electronic circuits and apparatuses used to communicate between integrated circuits in a wide variety of applications, including televisions, computers and cellular phones. In October 2001, Philips sued a number of companies in the Southern District of New York (the "New York action") alleging infringement of the '740 patent. The appellee, Microchip Technology Incorporated ("Microchip"), was not one of the original defendants, but in reasonable apprehension of an infringement suit by Philips, Microchip sought a declaratory judgment in the District of Arizona (the "Arizona action") that it did not infringe and was licensed to practice the '740 patent. Subsequently, Microchip amended its complaint in the Arizona action to seek an additional declaratory judgment it did not infringe and was licensed to practice the '502 patent. Philips counterclaimed for infringement of both patents, asserting that Microchip did not have a license. Philips also added Microchip as a defendant in the New York action, alleging infringement of the '740 patent.

The license dispute centered upon a 1983 agreement (the "1983 agreement") between Philips and General Instrument Corporation ("GI"). The 1983 agreement granted GI a non-exclusive license to specified Philips' patents. Microchip claimed to be GI's successor to the 1983 agreement (and thus licensed under that agreement) because it was "spun off" from "a wholly owned subsidiary" of GI. (J.A. at 284.) Philips argued that Microchip never became a party to the 1983 agreement.

The 1983 agreement also included an arbitration clause that provided:

   All disputes arising out of or in connection with the interpretation or execution of this Agreement during its life or thereafter shall be finally settled according to the Rules of Conciliation and Arbitration of the International Chamber of Commerce by one or more arbitrators in accordance with the Rules.... The award of the Court of Arbitration shall be final and binding. (J.A. at 328.) On December 16, 2002, Philips commenced an arbitration proceeding against Microchip in the International Court of Arbitration (the "ICA") of the International Chamber of Commerce seeking resolution of the license dispute including the issue of Microchip's successorship to the 1983 agreement.

Microchip refused to arbitrate. While continuing to urge that Microchip was not a party to the 1983 agreement, Philips moved in the Arizona district court to compel Microchip to proceed with arbitration, and the ICA agreed to hold the arbitration in abeyance. Philips asserted that the issue of whether Microchip was a successor to the 1983 agreement, and other issues concerning the existence and scope of the license, were subject to arbitration. Microchip responded by filing a motion to stay the arbitration, contending that: (1) the question of whether Microchip was a party to the 1983 agreement was a gateway issue for the district court to resolve prior to referring the matter to arbitration; and (2) all of the disputed issues were for the court to decide because the arbitration clause had, by terms of the contract, expired (although the license remained in effect).

The district court denied Philips' motion to compel arbitration, but did not finally decide the issue of arbitrability, successorship or expiration of the arbitration clause. The court stated that:

> Before it can determine arbitrability, the Court must first determine if both Microchip and Philips are parties to the GI Agreement. This is admittedly in dispute and is the primary basis for declaratory relief. Making this determination would require the Court to undertake an intense factual inquiry inappropriate for a motion to dismiss. Accordingly, because the Court is unable to determine the applicability of the GI Agreement to these parties, it is unwilling to enforce the arbitration clause contained therein.

*Microchip Tech.*, slip op. at 7.

Microchip's motion to stay the arbitration was also granted. *Id.* Philips appealed from the district court's denial of its motion to compel arbitration.

\* \* \*

Turning now to the merits, the question is whether the district court was obligated to refer to arbitration questions related to the existence of an arbitration agreement between Philips and Microchip. We hold that it was not.

### A.

The obligation to arbitrate, if it exists, must arise from the 1983 agreement. The first question is whether Microchip is a successor party to the 1983 agreement originally made between Philips and GI. Microchip argues that the question of successorship is a "gateway issue" for the district court to decide because it determines whether an arbitration agreement exists between Philips and Microchip. Philips responds that there is no dispute that the agreement exists, but rather the question is whether the "arbitration clause is effective" against Microchip. Philips urges that this question is arbitrable, relying primarily on the Ninth Circuit's decision in *Teledyne, Inc. v. Kone Corp.*, 892 F.2d 1404 (9th Cir. 1989), which it argues is binding on our court.

In *Teledyne* the Ninth Circuit held that the issue of whether an agreement to arbitrate exists is arbitrable if there is no "independent challenge" to the arbitration provision separate from an attack on the contract as a whole. *Id.* at 1410. There the parties disputed whether a draft of a distribution contract had been finalized by the parties. Relying on the Supreme Court's decision in *Prima Paint Corp. v. Flood & Conklin Manufacturing Co.*, 388 U.S. 395 (1967), the Ninth Circuit held that the "court must not remove from the arbitrators consideration of a substantive challenge to a contract unless there has been an independent challenge to the making of the arbitration clause itself." *Teledyne*, 892 F.2d at 1410 (quoting *Unionmutual Stock Life Ins. Co. v. Beneficial Life Ins. Co.*, 774 F.2d 524, 529 (1st Cir. 1985)). Because there was no dispute that the draft contained an arbitration provision, the Ninth Circuit held that the existence of the contract as a whole was arbitrable absent a separate, independent challenge to the enforceability of the arbitration provision. *Id.*

The parties differ sharply over whether *Teledyne* is distinguishable under subsequent Ninth Circuit decisions. We need not resolve that dispute because we conclude that the Supreme Court has already done so. We are obligated to follow regional circuit law on questions of arbitrability that are not "intimately involved in the substance of enforcement of a patent right." *Flex-Foot*, 238 F.3d at 1365; *see also Deprenyl Animal Health v. Univ. of Toronto*, 297 F.3d 1343, 1349 (Fed. Cir. 2002). The issues of arbitrability in this case are not intimately involved in the substance of enforcement of a patent right, and we would ordinarily be obligated to follow regional circuit law. However that obligation is not unqualified. Where regional circuit authority is contrary to governing Supreme Court precedent we need not, and indeed must not, follow it. That is the situation here.

In *John Wiley & Sons, Inc. v. Livingston*, 376 U.S. 543 (1964), the Supreme Court held that the question of whether a party is bound by an agreement containing an arbitration provision is a "threshold question" for the court to decide. *Id.* at 546. There, a collective bargaining agreement containing an arbitration provision was entered into between a workers union and Interscience Publishers, Inc. ("Interscience"). *Id.* at 545. Subsequently, Interscience merged with John Wiley & Sons, Inc. ("Wiley"), and a dispute arose as to whether Wiley was bound by the collective bargaining agreement. *Id.* Wiley asserted that the merger "terminated the bargaining agreement for all purposes." *Id.* The union contended that Wiley was obligated to recognize certain "vested" rights under the agreement and sought to compel arbitration. *Id.* The Supreme Court explained that the threshold "question [wa]s whether Wiley, which did not itself sign the collective bargaining agreement on which the Union's claim to arbitration depends, is bound at all by the agreement's arbitration provision." *Id.* at 547. Because a party "cannot be compelled to arbitrate if an arbitration clause does not bind it," the Court held that there was "no doubt" that "a compulsory submission to arbitration cannot precede judicial determination that the…agreement does in fact create such a duty." *Id.* at 546–47.

Subsequent Supreme Court decisions, including decisions subsequent to the Ninth Circuit's 1989 *Teledyne* decision, have consistently reaffirmed the holding in *John Wiley*, explaining that "a gateway dispute about whether the parties are bound by a given arbitration clause [is] for a court to decide." *Howsam v. Dean Witter Reynolds, Inc.*, 537 U.S. 79, 84 (2002) (citing *John Wiley*, 376 U.S. at 546–47); *AT&T Techs., Inc. v. Communications Workers of Am.*, 475 U.S. 643, 649 (1986) ("Unless the parties clearly and unmistakably provide otherwise, the question of whether the parties agreed to arbitrate is to be decided by the court, not the arbitrator.")

\* \* \*

Contrary to the Ninth Circuit's decision in *Teledyne*, the responsibility of the judiciary to resolve the gateway dispute of whether an agreement to arbitrate exists is not limited to situations in which there is an independent challenge to the arbitration clause. *See John Wiley*, 376 U.S. at 545; *Howsam*, 537 U.S. at 84. Indeed the "threshold question" for the court in *John Wiley* was a challenge to the existence of the entire agreement. That question is essentially identical to the successorship issue in the present case, i.e., "whether [Microchip], which did not itself sign the...agreement on which [Philips'] claim to arbitration depends, is bound at all by the agreement's arbitration provision." *See John Wiley*, 376 U.S. at 547; *see also First Options*, 514 U.S. at 944 (holding the court must decide if Kaplan was bound by an agreement he did not personally sign).

Philips also argues that the present case, like *Teledyne*, is distinguishable from *John Wiley* because here the party that opposes arbitration argues (indeed urges) that it is bound by the agreement containing the arbitration provision. *See Three Valleys*, 925 F.2d at 1142 (distinguishing the decision in *Teledyne*). Again the Supreme Court has drawn no such distinction. The Court has broadly held that because a party "cannot be compelled to arbitrate if an arbitration clause does not bind it," *John Wiley*, 376 U.S. at 547, "the question of whether the parties agreed to arbitrate is to be decided by the court, not the arbitrator," *AT&T*, 475 U.S. at 649; *see Howsam*, 537 U.S. at 83; *First Options*, 514 U.S. at 944.

Therefore, we hold that the district court must determine whether Microchip was a successor party to the 1983 agreement before any issue may be referred to arbitration under that agreement. It was not error for the district court to deny Philips' motion to compel arbitration pending resolution of that question.

### B

In addition to the survivorship issue, Microchip contends that all issues in this case are for the district court to decide because the arbitration clause in the 1983 agreement has expired. The 1983 agreement provides in Article VIII that it "shall continue in force and effect" through 1987 and "[u]pon expiration...all rights, privileges and obligations...other than those specified in Articles III, IV, V, IX and X...shall terminate." (J.A. at 322.) While the license provisions (contained in Article IV) were excluded from expiration, Microchip urges that the arbitration clause (contained in Article XV) was not excepted and is no longer in effect.

Just as the question of whether an agreement to arbitrate exists between the parties is for judicial resolution, we conclude that under the Supreme Court's precedent the question of whether an arbitration agreement has expired is for the court to decide, even if this requires interpretation of the language of the agreement. Here we find no merit in Microchip's argument that the arbitration clause has expired.

It is clear on the face of the 1983 agreement's arbitration clause that the obligation to arbitrate survives expiration of the agreement's other provisions. The arbitration clause specifically provides that "[a]ll disputes arising out of or in connection with the interpretation or execution of this Agreement during its life or thereafter" are subject to arbitration. (J.A. at 328–29). In light of the unambiguous language of the arbitration clause itself, we reject Microchip's argument that the obligation to arbitrate expired prior to this dispute.

\* \* \*

# Notes

1. *Scope of Arbitration.* Arbitration clauses must be carefully drafted. *See, e.g., Tracer Research v. National Envtl. Serv. Co.*, 42 F.3d 1292 (9th Cir. 1994), *cert. dismissed*, 515 U.S. 1187 (1994). There, the Ninth Circuit carefully parsed the arbitration clause, holding that the parties should not be required to arbitrate their disputes unless they had explicitly agreed to do so. The language in question required arbitration of disputes "arising out of" the agreement, which the Court interpreted to mean disputes over contract formation or performance. On the other hand, the Court noted that language requiring arbitration of disputes "relating to" the agreement was all-inclusive, and not limited to disputes arising out of the immediate contract. *Id.* at 1295. Thus, if a client wants all matters that may arise in connection with a licensing agreement to be arbitrated, both terms should be used.

2. *Injunctive Relief in lieu of Arbitration.* What if the parties have drafted their arbitration clause to provide the sole remedy in case of dispute? May one of the parties obtain a preliminary injunction prior to commencing arbitration? In *Performance Unlimited, Inc. v. Questar Publishers, Inc.*, 52 F.3d 608 (6th Cir. 1995), the parties had agreed that arbitration "shall be the sole and exclusive remedy for resolving any disputes between the parties arising out of or involving [the] Agreement." The Plaintiff unsuccessfully sought a district court injunction that would have required the Defendant to continue paying royalties during arbitration. The license agreement contained an unusual arbitration clause:

> The Licensor...and the Publisher...agree that God, In His Word, forbids Christians to bring lawsuits against other Christians in secular courts of law... and that God desires Christians to be reconciled to one another when disputes of any nature arise between them....

> [I]n their resolution of any disputes that may arise under this Agreement, each party agrees that the provisions for mediation and arbitration set forth below shall be the sole and exclusive remedy for resolving any disputes between the parties arising out of or involving this Agreement.

> It is further agreed that the Licensor and the Publisher hereby waive whatever right they might otherwise have to maintain a lawsuit against the other in a secular court of law, on any disputes arising out of or involving this Agreement. In the event of such a dispute, the Licensor and the Publisher agree to take the following steps, in the order indicated, until such a dispute is resolved:

> (1) The Licensor and the Publisher shall meet together, pray together, and purpose to be reconciled....

> (2) The Licensor and the Publisher shall invite other witnesses, who may have knowledge of the actual facts of the dispute or whose knowledge would be helpful in resolving the dispute, to meet together with both parties, to pray together, and to purpose to be reconciled....

> (3) Both the Licensor and the Publisher shall each appoint one person as a Mediator; these two persons chosen shall then appoint a third Mediator. The three Mediators shall together determine the process of mediation, to which the Licensor and the Publisher agree to comply, and shall be free to act as Arbitrators, to whose authority the Licensor and the Publisher agree to submit. The

three Mediators shall also determine to what degree the Licensor and the Publisher shall be liable for all costs related to the mediation process.

The Federal Arbitration Act, 9 U.S.C. § 3, provides that in any suit involving an issue referable to arbitration under a written agreement, the court may "stay the trial of the action until such arbitration has been had in accordance with the terms of the agreement." The Sixth Circuit reversed the district court, holding that § 3 does not contain a clear command limiting the equitable power of the trial court, and thus a preliminary injunction could be granted to preserve the status quo pending arbitration.

Given the advantages of arbitration, which include reducing the workload of the courts and providing for speedier recoveries, there is a strong public policy interest in favor of enforcing arbitration clauses.

# Chapter 11

# International Aspects of Licensing

## I. Introduction

Today, intellectual property licensing is a global endeavor. Global markets, international treaties and a newfound adherence to have combined to make international considerations important to the license agreement.

U.S. companies routinely secure foreign patent rights well in advance of decisions on technology development[1]. U.S. patent rights are no longer considered sufficient for either product development or licensing out. Even universities are increasingly filing for foreign rights as companies expect licenses to convey worldwide rights in all fields of use.

Among the issues to be addressed in the license include U.S. export control laws, foreign government regulations, U.S. and foreign tax consequences, and exit strategies upon termination, such as dispute resolution, governing law, and bankruptcy. Consider the following.

---

### International Considerations in Licensing*
Reta J. Peery
418 PLI/Pat. 21 (1995)

* * *

### II. SPECIAL PROVISIONS TO BE INCLUDED IN LICENSES ENTERED INTO WITH LICENSEES OUTSIDE OF THE U.S.

Most provisions covered in "boilerplate" U.S. licensing agreements should be included in licensing agreements with licensees outside the U.S. The materials below ad-

---

1. The reverse is also true. In 2001, the USPTO reported that 47% of all U.S. utility patents issued went to foreign entities, a percentage which has remained remarkably stable over the last 10 years, while the total number of patents issued has almost doubled. *See* USPTO, U.S. Patent Statistics, Calendar Year 1963–2003, *at* www.uspto.gov/web/offices/ac/ido/oeip/taf/us_stat.pdf.

* Reprinted with permission, copyright 1995.

dress some of the additional provisions that should be included and/or reevaluated when entering into transactions with licensees based outside of the U.S.

(i)    *Provisions on Authorized Languages*—If the licensee is to be given rights in one or more languages, the licensing agreement should specify the authorized languages. In territories in which free trade regulations make it difficult to obligate licensees to refrain from shipping outside of their territories, limiting the authorized languages can impede undesirable exports as a practical matter.

(ii)    *Provisions on Taxes*—Many countries outside of the U.S. impose value added taxes ("VAT taxes"), and deduction of these taxes from "net sales" on which royalties are based is standard industry practice. The licensor may wish to evaluate whether it wishes to allow licensees to deduct VAT taxes from net sales, and if so, the licensor might wish to build this provision into its licensing agreements rather than waiting for the licensee to negotiate the deduction. Also, many countries outside of the U.S. impose withholding taxes against U.S. companies with respect to any sums payable by non-U.S. licensees. A sample provision contemplating the licensee's payment of this tax on the licensor's behalf is as follows; the licensor needs to ensure that appropriate documentation is procured to evidence payment of withholding taxes, as documentation is necessary to obtain credit on U.S. tax returns:

Notwithstanding the preceding provisions of this section, if: (i) any country imposes a withholding tax against Licensor with respect to any sums payable to Licensor by Licensee pursuant to this Agreement; (ii) such tax is paid by Licensee on behalf of Licensor; and (iii) such tax is an income tax with respect to which a foreign tax credit is allowable to Licensor under Section 901 of the International Revenue Code of 1986, as amended, superseded, or otherwise modified (or other applicable United States law), Licensee may deduct the amount of such withholding tax from the monies due to Licensor hereunder; provided that Licensee furnishes to Licensor, at Licensee's expense, the following information and documents with respect to the withholding tax:

(A)    an original receipt from the taxing authority with respect to the withholding tax paid (and if such receipt is in a language other than English, a certified English translation thereof); (B) a report setting forth the fees with respect to which the withholding tax was paid, the amount of withholding tax paid, the date on which the withholding tax was paid and the authority under which the withholding tax was paid, including the statutory citations and a general description of their provisions; and (C) such other information as Licensor may from time to time reasonably request to evidence Licensor's right to credit such withholding tax against its income tax liability in the United States.

(iii)    *Provisions on Blocked Currency*—The licensor should contemplate possible future difficulties in removing money from territories outside the U.S. A sample provision follows:

In the event that Licensee shall be prohibited or restricted from making payment of any monies at the time when same are due and payable to Licensor hereunder by reason of the laws or currency regulations within the Territory, Licensee shall promptly so advise Licensor in writing. Licensee shall, upon Licensor's request, deposit any such blocked funds to the credit of Licensor in a bank or banks or other depository in the Territory designated in writing by Licensor, or pay them promptly to such persons or entities as Licensor may designate in writing. Licensor shall have the right to terminate this agreement if licensee is unable to make arrangements satisfactory to Licensor for Licensor's receipt of such blocked funds.

(iv) *Exclusivity*—Many countries outside of the U.S., contain limitations on a licensor's ability to enter into "exclusive" grants. A licensor may be able to assure a licensee that the licensor will refrain from licensing any third party in the licensed territory to manufacture the goods or provide the services that are the subject of the applicable license agreement, but due to regional laws, regulations or treaties, the licensor effectively has no ability to ensure that there will be no parallel imports. In this instance, exclusivity provisions need to be carefully examined so that they are worded in an acceptable manner. All exclusivity grants should contain a caveat that the exclusivity is being granted only in accordance with or as limited by applicable law.

(v) *Provisions on Legal Standards for the Manufacture and Sale of Goods or Services Pursuant to the License*—The licensing agreement should contain provisions sufficient to provide that as between the licensor and the licensee, the licensee is responsible for ensuring that all goods or services are manufactured, sold, distributed, labeled, promoted and advertised in accordance with all applicable governmental, regulatory, professional and industry wide codes, statutes, rules and regulations. While this provision is frequently found in U.S. licensing agreements, it is of utmost importance to include it in non-U.S. agreements since the licensor generally will not be in a position to have had significant exposure to territorial, industry-specific codes.

(vi) *Provisions on Insurance*—Liability insurance and the addition of licensors as additional insureds under a licensee's liability insurance policy are commonplace in the United States, and provisions to this effect are normally included in U.S. licensing agreements. Internationally, however, these concepts may be unusual and it is economically impractical, or even impossible, for licensees to procure the types of insurance required of U.S. licensees. The licensor may wish to contemplate the licensee's inability to procure this insurance by recognizing in advance that insurance provisions will need to be addressed on a territory-by-territory basis dependent upon the licensor's analysis of the situation in a particular territory.

(vii) *Provisions Protecting the Licensor's Intellectual Property Rights*—These provisions should ensure that the licensee is obligated to cooperate fully and in good faith with the licensor for the purpose of securing and preserving the licensor's rights, including (a) cooperation on the commencement and prosecution of infringement suits (with all decisions to be made by the licensor), (b) cooperation with the licensor in undertaking the registration of any intellectual property rights in the territory in the licensor's name, and (c) where applicable, cooperation on the recordation of all documents necessary to record the licensee as a registered user of the licensed elements. In order to effectuate the latter, the licensor should find some mechanism for ensuring that licensees are indeed recorded as registered users in territories in which recordation is necessary. An identification of countries in which these registered user filings are mandatory or advisable can be obtained from intellectual property counsel or various publications.

\* \* \*

## III. TAILORING THE PROPERTY FOR CULTURAL DIFFERENCES

A. The Licensor Should Evaluate the Market to Determine Whether a Property Will Be Successful

Cultural differences mandate that a property that is wildly successful in one market may be unsuccessful in another. The licensor must assess geographical markets on a case-by-case basis to ascertain the most important territories for its focus on exploitation. In the United States, television ratings (if the property originates from a television series) and a "Q-score" are available methods of ascertaining whether a property represents a viable one for exploitation. (The Q-score is a numerical score assigned to a character by an agency which conducts survey research on how well known a character is, and how well liked a character is.) Commissioning focus groups is another alternative for market research. A combination of market research and intuition should be used to determine whether it is worthwhile to expend the time and money necessary to launch a property in a given territory.

### B. The Licensor Should Recognize that Channels of Distribution Vary From Territory to Territory

After choosing the territory and the target audience, the licensor should focus on the way that the target audience lives and shops. Retail distribution channels differ from country-to-country. The licensor should consider using international agents to gather and bring back information (as well as to attempt to locate viable licensing opportunities) but the licensor should always use the agent's information and contacts to come up with a strategic plan dictated by the licensor.

\* \* \*

# Special Concerns When Drafting International Licensing Agreements

### Patricia A. Motta

For an international licensing agreement to work, the license must consider several key issues to secure the benefits of selling intellectual property rights abroad. The form of the agreement and its substance create the context in which licensing is done and the more complete the agreement, the easier it will be to use an enforce. While no licensing agreement will completely; address every issue, a well-written agreement will be based on clear, concise, and consistent language and will consider the following issues during drafting.

### One Agreement or Several

Whether an international licensing agreement should contain one or several agreements involves looking at a myriad of concerns. Many scholars advocate that a single integrated licensing agreement is essential to ensure consistency. However, using several contracts can also be effective.

To permit the international license to hold the licensed rights effectively and without interruption, whether it is patents, trademarks, or trade secrets, the license may need to incorporate several agreements. A licensing agreement made up of one contract can be fatal, if one intellectual property right expires before another.[1]

On the other hand, separate contracts may allow parties to limit the duration of one or more rights in order to evaluate how that licensed right performs in a licensee's country. Nevertheless, parties can easily avoid using separate contracts by drafting detailed clauses that define the licensed right and expiration or termination issues in a single licensing agreement. Further, a single agreement may work to more effectively to bind

---

1. G'TZ POLLZIEN & EUGEN LANGEN, INTERNATIONAL LICENSING AGREEMENT (2d. Ed. 1973).

the relative values of the licensed rights together.[2] For example, new patent technology may be more valuable once it is disclosed to the public than an unknown trademark. However, as times goes on, the trademark may develop into unique or well-known mark. Although the patented technology is still useful, the mark's reputation and goodwill will surpass the value of other licensed rights associated with that license. Therefore, having both rights tied to one agreement allows both rights to mature in a manner beneficial to the parties, and where issues of termination and expiration are addressed consistently.

Arguably, having several contracts allows different types of intellectual property rights to be taxed accordingly. Depending on what country becomes party to an international agreement, its tax treaty, structure, and policy may differ. For example, royalties from patent and trademarks in one country may be taxed at a higher rate than royalties based on trade secret rights. In those cases, separating the industrial property rights into separate licenses enables the foreign-based parties to maximize tax treatment of each licensed right.

Lastly, one can argue that maintaining several agreements notably limits the public record in foreign countries where license registration is required. Since the value of the licensed technology and trade secret is at risk after being disclosed, parties can file separate contracts detailing only those elements of the agreement necessary for registration and recordation, rather than registering one detailed agreement.[3] Again, depending on what country becomes party to the license, foreign governments differ in registration requirements. In many cases, the details of the actual license, particularly details of remuneration are filed confidentially, and can only be reviewed through court order.[4]

Despite the above considerations, it is only in special instances that a multitude of contracts is used for an international licensing agreement. Rather, trends in international licensing favor the use of single integrated agreements.

## Dispute Resolution

In the United States, as well as many other countries throughout the world, societies regulate and manage legal issues not only through court systems, but through alternative dispute resolution mechanisms: ranging from negotiation to mediation to formal, trial-like arbitration hearings. Arbitration and mediation, remain strong and viable means for resolving disputes with respect to international license agreements. Arbitration, rather than litigation, is chosen because of its speed, flexibility, and neutrality.[5] Further, arbitration and mediation of disputes, generally has been said to be less adversarial and more confidential than litigation.[6]

Notwithstanding the advantages, dispute resolution has been riddled with many problems, including the inability to control and enforce arbitration and mediation agreements or arbitral awards.[7] Discovery generally is limited, and arguably the disputes may be more technical in nature, which may be difficult for inexperienced arbitrators or

---

2. *See* POLLZIEN & LANGEN, *supra* note 1.

3. *Id.*

4. *Id.*; *see also* Notes Section following this chapter (discussing registration of rights).

5. *See* Elmer J. Stone & Kenneth H. Slade, *Special Considerations in International Licensing Agreements* 1 TRANSNAT'L LAW 161 (1988).

6. *Id.* at 168.

7. *See generally* MARK HULEATT-JAMES & NICHOLAS GOULD, INTERNATIONAL COMMERCIAL ARBITRATION—A HANDBOOK, 1–10 (LLP Limited, Legal & Business Publishing Division, Great Britain 1996) (explaining the basic procedures and nuances in dealing with international commercial arbitration).

mediators to handle.[8] In addition, despite the commonly held belief that dispute resolution is less costly, costs can be high, especially when more complex and technical issue arise surrounding the licensed rights. Therefore, parties must discuss dispute resolution at the outset of drafting.

Generally, U.S. courts have favored arbitration in dealing with conflict across national borders and tend to view enforceability as an important component to international transactions. In *Mitsubishi Motors Copr. v. Soler Chrysler-Plymouth, Inc.*, 473 U.S. 614 (1985), the U.S. Supreme Court upheld the enforceability of arbitration provisions in an international agreement between business parties with regard to violations of U.S. antitrust law.[9] The court expressed concern and reiterated the need for predictability in solving disputes. In addition, the Supreme Court in *Scherk v. Alberto-Culver Co*, 417 U.S. 506 (1974), again upheld the enforceability of an arbitration provision in an international commerce case. This case involved fraudulent representations about the status of trademark rights. The court upheld the use of arbitration based upon a desire to ensure the "orderliness and predictability essential to any international business transaction."[10] Regardless, the key to any dispute resolution is the parties' willingness and flexibility to see litigation as a last resort.

### What Law Will Govern the Agreement?

Undoubtedly, one of the most critical components in drafting international licensing agreements is determining what parties' law will govern the agreement. In every licensing agreement the law of the jurisdiction governing the agreement should be clearly laid out. It is worthwhile to note that some jurisdictions may require local law to govern the agreement. Outside those cases, in choosing what law should govern, it is important to keep in mind the type of the licensed intellectual property and whether they are better governed by foreign intellectual property, antitrust and other public policy laws.

Further, a choice of forum may also be outlined in the agreement. However, by choosing the forum without knowing the type of dispute or how it will be handled my severely limit the parties to an inappropriate forum.

### Infringement: Protecting Intellectual Property Rights

It is the best interest of both parties to have an infringement clause in the agreement. This clause places an obligation on the licensee to notify the licensor of any infringement by third parties on the licensed rights, as well as infringement by the licensee on others.[11] Further, this clause should indicate how an infringement action should be handled, as well as issues of indemnity by the licensor.

---

## Contract Concerns in International License Agreements*

Jeffrey C. Ulin

394 PLI/Pat. 219 (1994)

The businesses of licensing entertainment software and licensing characters and trademarks for product merchandising have always been international in scope. As op-

---

8. *See* POLLZIEN & LANGEN, *supra* note 1; *see also* Klaus H. Burmeister, *International License Agreements Checklist & Drafting Suggestions* 496 PLI/Pat. 202 (1997).

9. *Mitsubishi Motors Corp. v. Soler Chrysler-Plymouth, Inc.* 723 F.2d 155 (1st Cir. 1983).

10. *Scherk v. Alberto-Culver Co.*, 417 U.S. 506 (1974).

11. *See* POLLZIEN & LANGEN, *supra* note 1.

portunities in international markets continue to grow and even overtake potential revenues from the US market, it is important to understand how standard contract provisions may need to be tailored in an international context. The range of properties which may be the subject of an international license agreement is too numerous to list, and the nuances of each deal will obviously have a significant impact on the structure of any contract. Whether the property being licensed is a multimedia product or a traditional article of merchandising, however, there are common concerns and this article will attempt to highlight some key areas which need to be carefully addressed.

While international issues can impact nearly every clause in a typical license agreement, this article will focus on the international implications with respect to the following subject matters: (1) territory implications; (2) ownership issues; (3) taxes (withholding taxes and VAT taxes); (4) royalty rate calculations; (5) accounting; and (6) governing law. This is not meant to be an exhaustive list, and no specific relevance should be attached to the order in which these items are discussed below. Also, there will be a bias in analyzing issues depending upon whether viewed from the licensee's or licensor's view, and the discussion below will assume the point of view of a US licensor ('licensor') licensing rights or properties for overseas distribution.

The descriptions and suggestions in this article are meant to be illustrative, and should not be relied upon in lieu of seeking legal counsel.

### (1) Territory Issues

Historically, contracts have been limited to a territory such as the UK or Germany. In this manner, a licensor maximizes its return on properties on the theory that the sum of the parts is greater than the whole (which obviously may or may not be true). A licensee, on the other hand, desires the broadest possible rights/territories both to maximize its own return and to hedge its bets in case projections in a particular country are not realized. There are both business and legal issues to analyze when addressing how to define rights within a territory and the boundaries of the territory itself.

Probably the most important issue is whether cross-collateralization will apply. Cross-collateralization in terms of territories means treating multiple territories as one for computing royalties. For example, a guarantee for Germany, France and Italy could be recouped from sales in all the territories. Licensors will strive to create non-cross-collateralized deals, for overages can be earned if one territory does well but another does not recoup. The following is a typical example of the benefit:

Licensee grants Licensor a minimum guarantee against royalties of $50,000 in Germany, $50,000 in France, and $50,000 in Italy against royalties for a total minimum guarantee of $150,000. If sales yield royalties of $75,000 in Germany, $60,000 in France and $10,000 in Italy (for a total of $145,000), then in a cross-collateralized deal the Licensor would only be entitled to the minimum guarantee of $150,000 (namely, royalties from all territories are used to recoup the overall guarantee). If the territories are not cross-collateralized, then the countries are looked at separately, and overages would be due Licensor in Germany ($25,000) and France ($10,000); the licensor would still be entitled to its minimum guarantee in Italy, and thus would retain a total of $185,000.

---

The concept of cross-collateralization can also apply across product categories, so that different products may be treated separately or all recoup an overall guarantee. This is typical in domestic deals, but whether to cross-collateralize multiple territories in an international license adds another level of complexity and can have a profound impact on returns.

Another territory concern is that a license agreement which grants Licensee rights in a limited territory, such as Germany, would typically also prohibit licensee from marketing product outside the territory. A European license agreement five years ago might have included a prohibition to the effect that a Licensee would only, and would require its customers to only, sell licensed products within the territory. Recent changes in European law eliminating borders between European community member states render such blanket prohibitions unenforceable. Advice from European counsel is advised when drafting language desired to comply with these laws and still preserve the integrity of territorial restrictions. Language which is generally considered acceptable is along the lines of the following:

> Subject to licensee being free to accept unsolicited orders from outside the territory but within the European economic area, Licensee shall refrain, outside the territory, from pursuing an active sales policy and shall not: (a) advertise licensed products or solicit orders for licensed products; or (b) establish branches for the sale of licensed products; or (c) maintain distribution outlets for the licensed products.

### (2) Ownership Issues

#### (a) General

Implicit in any international license agreement is the fact that a licensor owns a specific asset and is only granting limited rights to a licensee. Accordingly, license agreements will have provisions confirming that the licensor retains ownership over that asset, preventing a licensee from challenging the licensor's ownership, and vesting ownership in licensor to any derivative works based on the underlying asset. In a typical domestic license agreement, a contract would therefore include work-for-hire language together with language creating an automatic assignment in the event work is not deemed a work-for-hire. Additionally, it is common to include language whereby a licensee agrees not to attack the licensor's underlying ownership rights; related to this commitment, the Licensee would also agree not to register any of Licensor's intellectual property rights in Licensee's own name.

International laws can often add a wrinkle to common copyright notions, and even add restrictions that may render certain assignment language invalid. Article 85(1) of the Treaty of Rome ("EC Treaty") is a good example. It could be interpreted that a clause which creates an automatic assignment to a Licensor of work created by Licensee in the context of the license, is in violation of Article 85. Accordingly, clauses which state "artwork involving Licensor's property which are created by licensee shall immediately become the property of licensor" may be considered unenforceable. The roots of this conflict can in part be traced to moral rights philosophy (see below) and its edict that individual artistic rights must be strictly protected (in fact, there are certain inalienable rights apart from economic rights). Moreover, there is an implicit assumption that ones work product should not be assigned without fair consideration. This obviously presents a problem to licensors trying to tightly control their own intellectual property rights.

One way to solve this problem is to include explicit contract language that Licensor controls the design of a product/artwork by providing samples, outlines, etc. In this manner, no original work by the Licensee could be construed as Licensee's sole creation, and the Licensor should therefore be entitled to obtain/own the intellectual property rights in such new work.

If, however, there is truly 'new' work being created, then an assignment is necessary and care should be taken that the language effecting that assignment is valid. Under UK law, for example, copyright may only be transferred by an express written assignment. A problem therefore exists if the material is still to be created (not yet in existence)—this is solved by providing for a "present assignment of future copyright."

Having dealt with vesting of ownership, a contract should further limit challenges to that ownership. Again, international law may require careful wording; as an example, European cases under Article 85(1) have suggested that an obligation not to challenge the ownership of a trademark is okay, but an obligation not to challenge the validity of a trademark may be deemed anticompetitive. Again, it is such subtleties, arising from case law with which a US practitioner is unlikely familiar, which necessitates review of international agreements by foreign control.

Finally, it is also worthwhile to include a contract provision—governing registration of intellectual property in foreign territories. Depending upon circumstances, this can cut both ways. If a company is using a foreign agent that it trusts, it may want that agent's assistance in shepherding through a trademark registration locally. However, it is probably safest to use US intellectual property counsel with whom Licensor has an affiliation to coordinate and supervise foreign counsel. On the flip side of assistance in registration is the inclusion of a clause which prohibits a licensee from registering any marks related to Licensor's property. It is not uncommon for foreign companies to take a US trademark, register it in their own country, and try to force the US company to acquire the rights from them in such foreign territory. A local agent can often be useful in notifying licensor of pending registrations so that Licensor can object in time.

### (b) Moral Rights

It is critical when dealing in an international context to have a grasp of the fundamentals of the doctrine of moral rights. Moral rights legislation grants certain inalienable rights to authors of original works and it should not be taken for granted that once a work is created that its "owner" may manipulate that work any way it sees fit by virtue of owning the copyright. In fact, there may be certain prohibitions on editing and use would [that] prevent the owner from creating certain new versions.

By way of brief background, moral rights is an historically European concept, as European law draws a distinction in ownership and separately grants authors of a work the right to earn money and the right to protect their Reputation. While US copyright law focuses primarily on commercial/economic relationships, European law places greater emphasis on the right to control ones artistic or intellectual creations.

Moral rights are extremely strong in certain countries such as France, and as most countries now accept the basics of moral rights, the doctrine's impact on ownership cannot be ignored. In terms of ownership, one significant consequence of moral rights laws is that under certain European civil law, only human beings can create works; US law creates a fiction (works for hire) so that corporations can be considered the creator of, for example, an audio-visual work. A further nuance is that in certain countries the author of a work cannot contractually waive his or her moral rights (it is nevertheless worthwhile to try to obtain a moral rights waiver, irrevocable if possible, and even if limited to the maximum extent permitted under the local law); moreover, not only can such rights not be waived, but they can also be inherited. In terms of clearing rights, especially in rich content programming such as CD-ROMs where many source elements need to be cleared, this can create a significant administrative burden.

In terms of categorizing what rights may be reserved to an individual pursuant to laws/doctrines of moral rights, one should recognize that even if the copyright owner owns the economic rights in a work, the individual author may control aspects of its use. Those aspects fall into the following two main categories (the author's right of paternity and integrity) which were codified in the Berne Convention to which the United States became a signatory in 1989:

Paternity—Right to Claim Authorship/Be Identified with the Work

Right of Integrity—Right to Object to any Distortion/Derogatory Treatment Which is Prejudicial to Author's Reputation. This can be interpreted to mean any addition to, deletion from or alteration in the work.

The key relevance of moral rights is that it alters traditional notions of copyright ownership, in that certain consents may need to be obtained from third parties even though the copyright owner believed that it owned the material outright. Material changes as theoretically minor as editing to as major as colorization, will raise the issue. (An example of a court upholding an action for copyright infringement based upon tenets grounded in moral rights is *Gilliam v. American Broadcasting Companies*, 538 F.2d 14 (2nd Cir. 1976) in which the US Federal court granted relief to Monty Python; the group claimed that its scripts were edited extensively without consent prior to being shown on network television.)

### (3) Taxes

(a) Many foreign countries have withholding or similar taxes which serve to reduce a licensor's gross revenues. Such a withholding tax on royalties/license fees is usually triggered when a resident of the country makes a royalty payment to a non-resident copyright owner. Importantly, this tax is customarily deducted at the source: a licensee that has agreed to a $1M license fee and is subject to a 10% withholding tax, remits $900,000 to the licensor and 10% to the local tax authority.

To compensate for this tax, a contract should always require that the licensee tender a copy of the tax documents to the licensor, so the licensor can claim a corresponding tax credit from its own country. Assuming the tax credit can be claimed, the licensor has not lost any money; the only monetary effect is between government taxing agencies, where a foreign government would collect the sum and the US government would, in effect, lose that sum. This is all predicated, however, on the assumption that the tax credit can be utilized; depending upon a company's overall tax situation the company may not be able to avail itself of the credit and has, in fact, lost the amount of the withholding tax.

In addition to requiring that a licensee has the proper tax receipts so that a tax credit can be claimed, a contract should also require that revenues are net of taxes actually paid. In certain circumstances, if revenues are retained locally, then the tax may never have been paid and the gross amount should be accounted. Advice from foreign tax counsel is often worthwhile in structuring transactions so as to base operations in a jurisdiction with the most favorable tax treaties so as to avoid double taxation.

### (b) Value Added Taxes (VAT Taxes)

Foreign sales prices will include VAT taxes but royalties should be calculated on sales prices without VAT (i.e., invoice prices net of VAT). The importance is symmetry: if a licensor does not have VAT included in the price upon which its royalties are calculated, then the licensee should not pass along any VAT charges incurred with respect to licensed products. This is relatively simple in a pure royalty situation, but can be more complicated if the deal is on a cost basis where the parties split a percentage of profits based on an agreed formula.

### (4) Royalty Rates

All the same issues occur as in a domestic license, and specific care should be taken to define "net sales" clearly. The following is a typical definition which (a) eliminates the ambiguity of the term "sold" by referencing units actually invoiced (another wording defining "sold" would be "billed, invoiced or paid for, whichever is first"), (b) limits deductions, and (c) deals with sales to affiliates:

> Net sales means the gross invoice price billed customers less returns (but only to the extent the returns are supported by credit memos and in no event greater than % of total sales) but no deductions shall be made for cash, trade or other discounts or other uncollectible accounts. Licensed products shipped to customers but not billed shall be deemed to have the invoice price generally charged the trade by licensee. No cost incurred in the manufacture, sale, distribution or exploitation of the licensed products may be deducted from any royalties payable by licensee.

In all licenses, and especially in international contexts where the country of manufacture is likely to differ from the country of sale, it is important to focus on where the sale is made. If a sale is made F.O.B. a country of manufacture and the goods are then shipped by the purchaser to a different territory for resale, there needs to be an adjustment. Otherwise, if licensor has a 10% royalty on net sales, the royalty will be on a much lower number than perhaps contemplated. The licensor should not be worse off because his licensee sold a product F.O.B. an Asian port rather than in the country of ultimate sale. Contracts can most easily address this issue by stating different royalty rates for product actually sold in the licensed territory and for product sold F.O.B the country of manufacture (and the country of manufacture is outside the licensed territory).

### (5) Accounting Concerns

Because sales will be made in foreign currencies and likely coordinated by an agent overseas, certain business issues need to be addressed. Contracts involving international sales need to take into account the following:

- Depending upon the deal, detailed terms governing currency conversion and even treatment of blocked currency may be needed.
- Point of collection: should money paid by a licensee be paid to licensor's agent, who then deducts its fee and remits the balance to licensor, or should monies be paid directly to licensor who then pays its agent their commission? The first scenario is the most typical.

- Accountings may need to be rendered on a territory-by-territory basis; this is imperative if territories are not cross-collateralized.
- Interest should be required on late payments and audit costs should be paid by the licensee if the audit reveals significant underreporting.

### (6) Governing Law

It should go without saying that a US licensor needs to stipulate local US law. Language merely stating, for example, "The construct shall be governed by the laws of the State of California" is not sufficient because foreign laws may differ in key respects (such as moral rights rules as discussed above), the contract should also specify that conflicts of laws be resolved pursuant to local US law. Additionally, jurisdiction becomes an important concern and the agreement should require the licensee to submit to the jurisdiction of licensor's principle place of business (if the license has no US presence consideration should be given to leaving open the ability to sue locally but apply US law). The following is contract language which addresses these concerns:

> This Agreement shall be governed by and construed in accordance with the internal substantive laws of the State of _____ without reference to conflicts of law provisions. Licensee submits to the jurisdiction of the state and federal courts in the State of _____.

### (7) Summary

Structuring international licensing deals and contracts requires a sensitivity to issues which may not be of focus in a US only transaction. The examples above illustrate certain areas where a company not attentive to International concerns can forfeit revenue or potentially violate laws. By consulting with foreign counsel and focusing on these issues a company can improve its economic deals and enforce its contract terms.

---

# Notes & Questions

1. *Registration.* Most countries other than the United States require governmental approval of license agreements. Agreements must be reviewed by the governmental authority and recorded with the respective patent or trademark office. The recording requirement is commonly triggered by a licensee's payment of royalties to a licensor beyond its borders. When representing a licensor, it is good negotiating strategy to seek to place the responsibility of recording, along with its costs, on the local licensee, who is better situated to bear the burdens of recording.

Some countries also require license agreements to be registered with the central government or the license may not be valid or as exclusive as the language in the agreement dictates. *See, e.g.,* Tokkyo Ho [Japanese Patent Law], Law No. 121 of 1959, art. 98 (exclusive patent licensee must register the license with the Japanese Patent Office; if an exclusive license is not registered it is, as a matter of law, converted into a non-exclusive license regardless of what the parties intended). In 1993, Canada repealed the registered user requirements for trademark licenses. Sheldon Burshtein, *The First Five Years of the Canadian Trademark Licensing Regime,* 18 (No.10) The Licensing Journal 1 (1998).

Do registered user requirements provide the predictability and certainty intended as in Japan? Or are they merely a burden on international commerce and, therefore, should be repealed as in Canada?

2. *Culture.* To what extent should cultural differences be taken into consideration when licensing intellectual property? For example, the Chinese consider copying to be the highest form of flattery; therefore, American copyright owners should be honored to have Chinese corporations reproducing American music and movies. Is there any way to take these differences into consideration when drafting a licensing agreement where the parties do not share common cultures or rules of law?

3. *Language.* The readings above do not consider the problem of language. In many countries, even if the lawyer drafting the agreement speaks fluent English, the president or other officer of the corporation actually executing the agreement may not. If the agreement is prepared only in English, and a non-speaker of English executes it, that person will usually commission a translation of the document. Sometimes, in the translation process, nuances that were intentionally negotiated by the attorneys can be lost. Subsequently, the officer may have signed a document based on a skewed understanding of its content. Laws governing contract formation around the world are not consistent; in some countries the contract would be valid and in others it would not. Furthermore, if conflict arises in the performance of a valid contract, it is important to be able to focus the dispute on specific substantive terms of the agreement and not argue about interpretation of translated words. Therefore, a clause should also be included in international license agreements that clearly explains which language is the "original" language and which version governs the performance and enforcement of the agreement. Might technology someday overcome language differences? *See* e.g. SPL International, Free 2 Professional Translation website, *at* www.freetranslation.com (offering web-based translation services for over nine languages); www.freetranslation.com; RAY KURZWEIL, THE AGE OF SPIRITUAL MACHINES, 193 (Viking Penguin New York 1999).

4. *Royalty Rate.* The parties should structure royalty rates that are easy to calculate. Parties may have to take into account government involvement. There is a growing tendency for governments to become involved in the royalty negotiation process and to attempt to influence rates (as is the case in India, Japan, and France). Also, governments may require royalty rates not to exceed a certain percentage, or they may set other restrictions, such as limiting exporting to third countries. Carolita L. Oliveros, et al., *International Distribution Issues: Contract Materials*, SE47-ALI-ABA 917, 922 (2000) citing U.S. Department of Commerce, *Basic Guide to Exporting*, *available at* www.i-trade.com/dir01/basicgui/. If a licensee must pay royalties to a foreign licensor, a country's government may be more likely to enforce the approval/filing requirement. *Id.*

5. *Currency.* Parties to any international licensing agreement should determine the currency in which royalties will be calculated and paid. Saying "dollars" is not sufficient. There are Canadian "dollars," Australian "dollars," and even Singapore "dollars." If currency conversion will be necessary, the method by which the exchange rate is calculated should also be specified, to prevent one party from reaping a windfall from currency fluctuations. A contract may require a calculated average percentage for the royalty period rather than using the exchange rate effective on the last day of the royalty period. Oliveros, *supra*, note 4, at 923.

6. *Antitrust Laws and Licenses Involving Foreign Parties.* When a U.S. company does business with a foreign company, the license may give rise to antitrust issues both here and abroad. For example, a license to a foreign company "may be found to have a di-

rect, substantial, and reasonable foreseeable effect on U.S. foreign or domestic commerce, and be subject to U.S. antitrust law." John W. Schlicher, Licensing Intellectual Property 3 (1998) (citing 15 U.S.C. §§ 6a, 45(a)(3) (1994)); U.S. Dept. of Justice & Federal Trade Commission, *Antitrust Enforcement Guidelines for International Operations* (November 10, 1988) at 29–35. Thus the U.S. government may have a strong interest in your license with a foreign company.

The antitrust laws of the foreign country must also be considered. For example in the EU, antitrust limits come under Articles 85 and 86 of the Treaty of Rome. Article 85 prohibits agreements between two companies that restrict competition among member states. Article 86 forbids a single firm holding a dominant position from abusing power. If an agreement violates Article 85, the parties must notify the Commission of the European Communities ("Commission"), which will investigate whether the agreement fits within one of the exemptions under Article 85. Intellectual property, also, has a number of block exemptions for which the Commission automatically grants the agreement an exemption under Article 85(3). *Id.* at 105–6. Examples of these exemptions include the Franchising Regulation in 1988 (Regulation (EEC) 4087/88) and Technology Transfer Agreement Regulation (Regulation (EC) 240/96). *Id.* at 106–7.

The EU exemptions outline which agreements are acceptable and which are not. For example, Technology Transfer Block Exemption has four articles, all containing a list of "license practices or 'obligations.'" *Id.* at 112. For example, if a license meets the obligations outlined in the first Article (Article 1, the "white list") the license is then declared exempt from Article 85(1). Article 1 is concerned with parties attempting to impede parallel imports. *Id.* If a license contains the obligations listed in Article 1 and it also contains the obligations listed in Article 2 (the "whiter than white list"), the license is also exempt. Article 2 covers restrictions on competition. *Id.* at 113. If a license contains an obligation listed in Article 3 (the "black list"), the license is declared not exempt from Article 85. Article 4 (the "gray list") "says that the exemption [from Article 85] also applies to licenses that contain obligations of Article 3, if the Commission is notified of the agreement and does not oppose an exemption within four months." *Id.* at 114.

Japan has fairly detailed licensing regulation. Antitrust enforcement is governed by the Japan Fair Trade Commission (JFTC). *Id.* at 137. The most recent 1989 JFTC Guidelines are similar to that of the EU.

> The Guidelines place types of restrictions in three categories based on their expected impacts on competition. They are restrictions that (1) are not, in principle, an unfair trade practice, and listed in Article 1 [the "white list"], (2) may be an unfair trade practice, and listed in Article 2 [the "gray list"], or (3) are highly likely to be such a practice, and listed in Article 3 [the "black list"].

*Id.* at 141.

Clearly, this chapter scratches only the surface of international antitrust law and licensing regulation. It does serve, however, as a good example of how antitrust regulation of licensing in the EU and elsewhere can be complicated. Any U.S. company seeking to license with a company in the EU or elsewhere must carefully review that country's laws.

7. *Cooperative International Antitrust Enforcement Agreements.* In reviewing antitrust issues in international licensing agreements, parties must consider the effects of the recent trend of cooperative international antitrust agreements. Recently, the antitrust authorities of one country have begun to contact those of another about large international agreements. Although this may occur informally, one formal manifesta-

tion of these agreements is the U.S./E.C. cooperation agreement. C. Benjamin Crisman, Jr. and Matthew S. Barnett, *Mergers and Acquisitions: Recent Trends in Antitrust Enforcement*, 1049 PLI/CORP. 379, 416 (1988) (citing Agreement between the Government of the United States of America and the Commission of the European Communities regarding the Application of their Competition Laws, O.J. L 95/47 (April 27, 1995)). "The U.S./EC Agreement was designed to create a framework for cooperation between the competition authority of the EC (DG-IV, the EC Commission Competition Directorate) and the U.S. Federal antitrust authorities (the DOJ and the FTC)." *Id.* at 517. The concerns of both countries center on the fact that with the globalization of commerce there exists an increased chance of manipulation and anti-competitive practices that may evade review and sanction. *Id.* How do you think the U.S.'s antitrust laws will fare in a global economy?

8. *Intellectual Property in Jeopardy?* In high technology mergers and acquisitions, a company may be required to divest its right in intellectual property in the name of competition.

> The basic concern underlying cases in which [Federal Antitrust] Agencies have alleged innovation markets is that the acquiring firm will, as a result of the acquisition, have the ability as well as the incentive to reduce the level of research and development in the alleged market. Thus, the Agencies have sought to ensure that competing R&D projects remain independent competitors. Where the merger is between competitors in a high technology or "innovation" industry, such as pharmaceuticals or computer software, the government typically has required the divestiture of rights in intellectual property in order to protect competition in the relevant R&D market.

Crisman & Barnett, *supra*, at 394.

For example, the Federal Trade Commission recently allowed two Swiss companies to merge, but, according to the consent agreement, one Swiss company was required "to divest: (1) its U.S. and Canadian corn herbicide business to BASF, a German firm; and (2) its flea control business to Central Garden and Pet Supply. Although the FTC defined the relevant market as the United States, divestiture of non-U.S. assets was required to ensure the purchaser would be able to compete with the combined firm in the United States." *Id.* at 394–95. Therefore, two foreign companies entering agreements may be influenced by U.S. antitrust laws.

Interestingly, the U.S. antitrust agencies "will not consider efficiencies to be merger-specific if they could, alternatively, be achieved by divestiture and licensing instead of merger, thereby, mitigating, rather than increasing anti-competitive concerns." William T. Lifland, *Monopolies and Joint Ventures*, 1049 PLI/CORP. 151, 283 n.35 (1998).

9. *Export Laws.* International licensing agreements should also address the effect of domestic export laws on the parties. For example, U.S. export control laws place restrictions on export and re-export of U.S. goods, technology, and technical data. "Export transactions are regulated by the State Department's Office of Defense Trade Controls (which controls goods and technical data used in military applications [20 C.F.R. Part 120 *et seq.*]), the Commerce Department's Bureau of Export Administration (which regulates through the Export Administration Act of 1979, as amended, merchandise that can be used in both civilian and military applications), or the Treasury Department's Office of Foreign Asset Controls (which enforces U.S. trade embargoes)." Carole V. Aciman, *Electronic and Computer Industry Licensing*, 514 PLI/PAT. 199, 220-22 (1990) (citing Miriam A. Bishop, *Navigating the Murky Waters of U.S. Export Control Laws*, THE METROPOLITAN CORPORATE

COUNSEL, Sept. 1997). Parties should consult the export controls and licensing provisions of the newly-revised Export Administration Regulations, U.S. Dept. of Commerce, Bureau of Industry and Security, *Export Administrrration Regulations, at* www.bxa.doc.gov.

10. *Arbitration in an International Setting.* Arbitration clauses in international license agreements raise some unique concerns. The benefits of arbitration in the international setting are much the same as those discussed in Chapter 10, *supra*: expediency and inexpensiveness of dispute resolution. Most countries now have entered into some international treaty with the United States whereby they agree to recognize and enforce arbitration awards. Additionally, if a particular company may not be popular to the local population or its government, an arbitration setting may be a way to ensure a more neutral forum.

However, arbitration in the international context has disadvantages as well. Obviously, the cost of travel for the attorneys, parties, and witnesses goes up, in some cases, astronomically—for example, if the arbitration is to be held in a city such as Tokyo, Japan, one of the most expensive cities in the world. Then the perceived financial savings for including an arbitration clause in an international license agreement may be lost on travel costs of the individuals involved. It would not be unusual for an individual attorney representing a large corporation to charge it $30,000 for one week in Tokyo (including air fare, food, lodging, and attorney's fees). That figure for litigation in the United States would purchase fifty to one hundred hours (or more depending upon the billing rate of the American attorney involved) of legal time.

11. *In Anticipation of Infringement.* International license agreements must anticipate that some infringement may occur in the country where the licensee is working the license. Such agreements should state clearly that the licensee has the obligation to police the market and report to the licensor any infringing conduct it finds. The reason for this is that the licensee, and not the foreign licensor, is familiar with local market conditions, culture, advertising, etc. If infringement goes unchallenged, it may severely undercut the profits from the licensing arrangement. Costs for enforcement should be divided between the licensee and the licensor.

12. *Choice of Law.* Including a choice of law clause in an international licensing agreement has advantages and disadvantages. Clearly, if the choice of law provision is included, it facilitates a clear determination of which country's laws govern the execution, performance, and/or enforcement (all of these could be different) of the agreement. A choice of law provision also lets the foreign licensor at least attempt to have the agreement interpreted using the laws of a jurisdiction (most likely its own) with which it is most familiar. However, a choice of law clause may create issues as well. Most of these problems arise when the agreement is not clear. Sometimes an international agreement provides for a specific American state's laws as governing the agreement such as "The Laws of the State of Minnesota will govern this Agreement." Although on its face this may be clear, it ignores the fact that patent rights are created by federal statute and that trademark rights are protected by federal statute. Some have argued that no provision on choice of law should be included in an international agreement because if there are any rights in that foreign jurisdiction at all, it is because the laws of that jurisdiction provided for the creation of those intellectual property rights. As such, it is unnatural and problematic to then require a court of that state to use the laws of another country to dictate whether the licensing of such rights is valid. *See* INTERNATIONAL LICENSING AGREEMENTS (G'tz Pollzien and Eugen Langen, eds. 1973).

Certain host countries may insist that their substantive law applies regardless of the contractual choice of law provision. Therefore, the parties should review the law of the host country regarding choice of law provisions that the parties intend to include in the license agreement. "In licensing agreements with the EU, Canada, UK, Germany, Japan, and Australia, the national licensing provisions are mandatory and must be complied with regardless of whether the respective country represents the forum selected for litigation under the agreement's forum selection or choice of law provisions." Oliveros, *supra*, note 4 at 923. Further,

> In the absence of a specific clause, choice of law provisions in the governing jurisdiction would be applied. The type of license sought may also add restrictions. For instance, in the Netherlands intellectual property rights may only be transferred or assigned if there is a specific statutory grant for the transfer. These grants usually require registration of intellectual property. In many jurisdictions, such as throughout the EU countries, without a specific choice of law provision, often the law of the country "most closely connected" to the licensing agreement will govern. "Most closely connected" is defined as the locale where most characteristics of performance or principal place of business is situated.

*Id.* at 923–24, citing Dick VanEngelen, *Intellectual Property in Cross-Border Transactions*, in Patents, Copyrights, Trademarks, & Literary Property Course Handbook Series 181 (PLI 1998).

13. "*Senyoshiyoken.*" Some countries, such as Japan, have special categories of licenses. These countries divide license agreements into more than just the exclusive/non-exclusive divisions common in the West. Japan uses a special category for highly exclusive licenses or *senyoshiyoken*. Care must be given when drafting international license agreements to use the terms specifically desired by the parties. *Senyoshiyoken* gives the holder far broader rights than simply as licensee. If one simply uses the term *senyoshiyoken* thinking it is synonymous with the Anglo-American version of an exclusive licensee, you might be surprised when the holder of the *senyoshiyoken* engages in conduct you would have thought might have been beyond the scope of the original license. *See* Zentaro Kitagawa, Doing Business in Japan §6.07[2] (2004); *see also, Sunstar v. Alberto-Culver*, 2003 U.S. Dist. Lexis 17431 (N. D. Ill. 2003).

# Chapter 12

# Tax Implications in Licensing Intellectual Property

## I. Introduction

All licensing attorneys need to understand the basic tax implications of licensing from both the licensor's and licensee's perspectives. Perhaps the licensing attorney will not be providing definitive tax advice on the deal, but the attorney will be expected to recognize and avoid some common pitfalls that lead to adverse tax consequences for the client.

Although most of the case law on the taxation of licensing transactions originates in patent cases, the rules discussed below will often be applicable to other types of intellectual property. It is clear that attorneys involved in other intellectual property disciplines must draft licensing agreements to ensure that the tax treatment intended is the tax treatment that results.

The royalty paid by the licensee to the licensor is taxable income. The characterization of that income determines the type of tax and the tax rate. The Internal Revenue Code, tax regulations, and related revenue rulings are the resources from which attorneys make informed decisions regarding the tax implications of income received from royalties.

Historically it has been, and it continues to be, favorable for taxpayers to characterize income as capital gains when possible. Capital gains are taxed at rates lower than ordinary income and, when applied to large royalty payments, can save a taxpayer a considerable amount of money. Capital gains treatment is available when income is derived from the sale of a capital asset. In order to qualify for capital gains treatment, a licensor must actually transfer all *substantial rights* or an undivided interest in the intellectual property to the licensee.

## II. Substantial Rights

The cases below outline the tax treatment of license income, under 26 U.S.C. § 1235, specifically how license terms can affect whether royalties paid to a licensor will be taxed as ordinary income or capital gains. Section 1235 covers individual licensors only. The tax treatment of corporate intellectual property revenue is covered by I.R.C. §§ 1221 and 1235, among others. Whether corporate income from a licensing transaction is treated as capital gains or ordinary income involves not only the terms of the agreement, but also other gains and losses on the taxpayer's balance sheet.

---

## A.  Field of Use Limitations

### Fawick v. Commissioner of Internal Revenue
436 F.2d 655 (6th Cir. 1971)

PHILLIPS, Chief Judge.

This case involves the issue of how income received from exploitation of a patent should be treated under the Federal income tax laws. Specifically, the issue on this appeal is whether or not an exclusive patent license having a field-of-use restriction is a transfer of "property consisting of all substantial rights to a patent" within the meaning of § 1235 of the Internal Revenue Code of 1954, 26 U.S.C. § 1235.

The Tax Court held that the exclusive license containing a field-of-use restriction in this case was a transfer of such property and that the income received thereunder was entitled to capital gains treatment pursuant to the provisions of § 1235. The Commissioner appeals. We reverse.

Our summary of the facts will be limited to those necessary for an understanding of the contentions raised by the parties and the disposition that we make of the issue presented. A complete statement of the facts appears in the opinion of the Tax Court reported at 52 T.C. 104. Reference may be had to that opinion for a more detailed factual recitation.

Mr. Fawick (the taxpayer) has been an inventor since sometime before 1926 and has been issued some 200 patents during his lifetime. His normal practice has been to exploit his inventions on his own rather than to license others to develop and market them.

Prior to 1928 the taxpayer was engaged in the business of manufacturing clutches in Racine, Wisconsin. He sold this business and moved to Akron, Ohio. While in Akron he visited various rubber plants and began to conceive the idea of a flexible brake, coupling and clutch with certain of the moving parts made of rubber. About 1936 he completed these inventions and made test models of his flexible coupling and clutch, utilizing the principle of a rubber gland inflated with air. Patent applications were filed on this invention and on February 23, 1937, the taxpayer entered into a license agreement with the Falk Corporation covering the inventions described in the applications. The agreement contained the following provisions:

\* \* \*

"(1)  Fawick hereby grants to Falk an *exclusive* license to make, to use, and to sell in the United States, its territories and possessions, and in the Dominion of Canada, *flexible couplings*, as distinguished from driving clutches and other forms of power transmissions, embodying any of the inventions of the above identified patent applications or any improvement thereon that may be owned, controlled, or subject to licensing by Fawick.

"(2)  Fawick hereby grants to Falk an *exclusive* license to make, to use, and to sell in the United States, its territories and possessions, and in the Dominion of Canada, *but only for marine service*, one-to-one *driving clutches* embodying any invention of the above identified patent applications or any improvement thereon that may be owned, controlled, or subject to licensing by Fawick; and also *a non-exclusive* license to make, to use, and to sell such embodiments in the United States, its territories and possessions, and in the Dominion of Canada, but only as a part of *complete geared power transmission units* of Falk's manufacture.

"(3)  Falk agrees to pay to Fawick Twenty-five Thousand Dollars ($25,000) upon the signing hereof and, in addition thereto on or before the 15th day of January, April, July, and October of each year, Falk shall pay to Fawick upon all flexible couplings made hereunder, and installed for use by Falk or delivered to the customer during the next preceding three calendar months, and embodying any invention of the above identified patent applications as defined by any pending claim thereof or by a claim or claims of letters patent issued upon any of them, a royalty of five percent (5%) of the amount of the net sales price of the couplings after trade discounts but before cash discounts; and upon all driving clutches made hereunder, and installed for use by Falk or delivered to the customer during the next preceding three calendar months, a royalty of seven percent (7%) of the amount of the net sales price of the clutches after trade discounts but before cash discounts." (Emphasis supplied.)

\* \* \*

Rights under these patents also were granted to another corporation created by the taxpayer. In 1938 the taxpayer organized Fawick Corporation under the laws of Indiana to engage in the manufacture and sale of these clutches for other than marine use. As of December 30, 1938, he assigned to Fawick Corporation his rights in the patents, excluding the rights previously assigned to Falk Corporation in the above-quoted agreement and also excluding certain rights which he reserved to himself. In return for this assignment the taxpayer received all the stock of Fawick Corporation. Later, Fawick Corporation became publicly held, with its stock listed on the New York Stock Exchange. As of 1963, however, the taxpayer and his family owned slightly over fifty per cent of the stock of Fawick Corporation. During the years here in issue and prior thereto, Fawick Corporation manufactured clutches for industrial use in substantial quantities. Many thousands of flexible clutches were manufactured by Fawick Corporation under the taxpayer's patents for various industrial uses, including oil field equipment and heavy metal stamping equipment. Neither the taxpayer nor Fawick Corporation ever manufactured any flexible clutches for marine use except that Fawick Corporation did some manufacturing by agreement with Falk during World War II, when Falk was unable to supply the defense demand for such clutches.

Returning to the above-quoted agreement between the taxpayer and Falk Corporation, we construe this document as granting to Falk:

(1)  An exclusive license for the flexible couplings,
(2)  An exclusive license for driving clutches but *limited* to *marine service only*, and
(3)  A non-exclusive license for the complete geared-power transmission units.

The agreement also provided that patents covering improvements on the couplings and clutches were to be covered by the license. One such improvement patent (U.S. Letters Patent No. 2,662,625) was issued to the taxpayer on December 15, 1953. The improvement embodied in this patent was used by the Falk Corporation during the tax years here in question (1961–63) with royalties thereon paid to the taxpayer under the agreement. The royalties paid during the pertinent period for manufacture of the various devices are as follows:

| Year | Couplings | Marine Clutches |
|------|-----------|-----------------|
| 1961 | $2,167.40 | $5,386.66 |
| 1962 | 2,283.90 | 5,526.67 |
| 1963 | 2,383.43 | 4,295.69 |

The 1961 royalties paid for the manufacture of both couplings and clutches were reported by taxpayer and his wife on their joint income tax return as ordinary income. On their joint return for 1962 they reported all the royalties as long term capital gains. The Commissioner determined that the 1962 royalties paid for manufacturing marine clutches was ordinary income but did not change the method of reporting the royalties paid for manufacturing the couplings. The 1963 royalties paid were reported on the joint return as both ordinary income (that paid with respect to marine clutches) and long term capital gain (that paid with respect to couplings).

All the clutches manufactured by Falk Corporation during 1961–63 were incorporated as a part of a complete geared-power transmission unit and all such units were manufactured for marine service only.

The present controversy arose when the taxpayer petitioned for a redetermination of deficiencies as set forth by the Commissioner in his notice of deficiencies dated November 22, 1966. The deficiencies found by the Commissioner were a result of the treatment as long term capital gain of the royalties paid by Falk Corporation to taxpayer for the production of the marine clutches.

The Commissioner did not determine any deficiencies as a result of the long term capital gain treatment of the royalties paid for manufacture of the couplings. The taxpayer urges that by not finding a deficiency as a result of the capital gain treatment of royalties paid for manufacturing of the couplings, the Commissioner has taken a position inconsistent with that taken with respect to the royalties for manufacturing of the clutches. The taxpayer argues that the two should be treated the same (since the patent in question covers a number of articles in addition to couplings) and that by failing to claim a deficiency for the couplings, the Commissioner has recognized the right of the taxpayer to capital gain treatment for the clutches. On this appeal we are concerned only with the correctness of the challenged deficiencies, which involve royalties for the clutches. We express no opinion as to the tax treatment of royalties from the couplings.

The taxpayer's claim for redetermination was based on § 1235. His argument before the Tax Court was to the effect that (1) the royalties were paid under the exclusive, for-marine-service-only clause of the license and that (2) this clause was a transfer of "property consisting of all substantial rights to a patent," thus entitling the income generated thereunder to long term capital gain treatment. The Commissioner contested both these arguments, contending that (1) the royalties were paid under the non-exclusive, complete-geared-power-transmission-unit clause of the license, and that (2) even if the royalties were paid under the exclusive, for-marine-service-only clause, this clause did not effect a transfer of all substantial rights to a patent within the meaning and intent of the statute.

The Tax Court ruled in favor of the taxpayer on both points, and on this appeal the Commissioner alleges error in both instances. Because of the decision we make on the second of these points, we do not find it necessary to consider the first.

The determinative issue on this appeal is whether a patent license containing a field-of-use restriction is a transfer of "property consisting of all substantial rights to a patent" within the meaning of § 1235 of the Code. Section 1235 provides:

(a) General.—A transfer (other than by gift, inheritance, or devise) of property consisting of all substantial rights to a patent, or an undivided interest therein which includes a part of all such rights, by any holder shall be considered the sale or exchange of a capital asset held for more than 6 months, regardless of whether or not payments in consideration of such transfer are—

(1) payable periodically over a period generally coterminous with the transferee's use of the patent, or

(2) contingent on the productivity, use, or disposition of the property transferred.

### 1) Background of the 1954 Statute

A resolution of the issue presented on this appeal requires a consideration of the state of the law as it existed prior to the enactment of the 1954 Code. Before 1954 there was no I.R.C. section corresponding to the present § 1235. Prior to 1954 the only way an inventor could get capital gain treatment for income received from exploitation of a patent was by qualifying under the sections corresponding to the present §§ 1202, 1221 and 1222. To qualify, the inventor must have been an "amateur" rather than a "professional." Otherwise, the sale would have been of property held primarily for sale in the ordinary course of his business and taxed as ordinary income. As a further qualification, some courts held that the payment had to be on a lump sum basis. Although a majority of the decisions did not adopt and apply this second requirement, some accepted it at the insistence of the Commissioner. It was the Commission's position prior to the enactment of § 1235 that the capital gain provisions of the Code were designed to lessen the tax burden on persons selling property for a gain, the gain having been produced over a period of years but realized in a single tax year, and that to qualify for the more favorable capital gain treatment now allowed under § 1235, the income would have to be realized in a single tax year, not over a period of several years as in the usual patent royalty situation. For a clear statement of the Commissioner's argument and the reasons for rejecting it, see *Dreymann v. Commissioner*, 11 T.C. 153, 162–63, where the Court said:

> We do not agree with respondent's contention that to apply the benefits of the long term capital gain provisions to the amounts received from Grant in the years here involved would be repugnant to the 'underlying theory of the capital gains limitations.' He argues that the purpose of the capital gains limitations is to lessen the impact of the Federal income tax 'on the realization in one lump sum in one taxable year of an increment in value which had taken place over a number of years.' Since petitioner here did not sell the process for one lump sum, he concludes, the application of the capital gains limitations in the case at bar would defeat the intent and purpose of Congress. In the first place, section 117 of the Revenue Act of 1934 did not contain any provision to the effect that payment from the sale of a capital asset must be in one lump sum. Respondent supports his position, however, by pointing to House Report No. 350, 67th Cong., 1st sess. (C.B. 1939-1 (Part 2), p. 176). That report accompanied the Revenue Act of 1921, which first introduced the capital gains provision into our taxing statute. It reads in part as follows:

> Section 206: The sale of farms, mineral properties, and other capital assets is now seriously retarded by the fact that gains and profits earned over a series of years are under the present law taxed as a lump sum (and the amount of surtax greatly enhanced thereby) in the year in which the profit is realized.

* * *

*See also* C.B. 1939-1 (Part 2), p. 189, and S. Rept. No. 275, sec. 206.

There is nothing in the House report or in the Senate report which supports respondent's assertion that a taxpayer, in order to have the tax benefit of the capital gains provisions must sell his asset for one lump sum. As a matter of fact, this and other courts have held that where, as here, the consideration for the sale of a capital asset was in the form of periodic payments based on a percentage of the gross sales made during the year, the taxpayer was entitled to a capital gains limitation on the sums received in each year. *See Commissioner v. Celanese Corporation*, [78 U.S. App. D.C. 292, 140 F.2d 339 (1994)] *supra*; *George James Nicholson*, 3 T.C. 596, and cases cited therein. We can find no valid reason for holding otherwise in this case.

In *Myers v. Commissioner*, 6 T.C. 258, the Tax Court held in 1946 that an "amateur" inventor was entitled to capital gain treatment of royalty income even though the payments were contingent on production, i.e., in the form of royalties. The Commissioner published a non-acquiescence in that decision. The report of the Senate Finance Committee, 1954 U.S. Code Cong. & Ad. News 5080, 5082, contained the following:

> In 1950 the prospect of continued litigation was engendered in this area by the issuance of Mimeograph 6490 (1950-1 CB 9), in which the Commissioner of Internal Revenue announced that he would thereafter regard such assignments or licenses as 'providing for the payment of royalties taxable as ordinary income' if payment is measured by the production, sale, or use of the property transferred or if it is payable periodically over a period generally coterminous with the transferee's use of the patent. To obviate the uncertainty caused by this mimeograph and to provide an incentive to inventors to contribute to the welfare of the Nation, your committee intends, in subsection (a), to give statutory assurance to certain patent holders that the sale of a patent (whether as an 'assignment' or 'exclusive license') shall not be deemed not to constitute a 'sale or exchange' for tax purposes solely on account of the mode of payment.

2) Purpose of § 1235

From this review of the germination of Sect. 1235, we conclude that the section was intended to assure inventors that their license royalties would be afforded capital gain treatment "regardless of whether or not payments in consideration of such transfer are—

(1) payable periodically over a period generally coterminous with the transferee's use of the patent, or

(2) contingent on the productivity, use, or disposition of the property transferred.

This preferred capital gain treatment is conditioned, however, upon the holder transferring property consisting of all substantial rights to the patent. The emphasis of the section, as we read it, is on the tax consequence of the "sale of a patent" where the consideration is in the form of contingent royalty payments and not on providing some special treatment as a result of the transfer of property consisting of all substantial rights to a patent. The "incentive to inventors to contribute to the welfare of the Nation" resulted when capital gain treatment was provided under § 1235 for "professional" as well as "amateur" inventors otherwise qualifying under the statute. Thus, the twofold purpose of the section (i.e., to negate the effect of Mimeograph 6490 and to provide an incentive to inventors) does not point to the interpretation urged by the tax-payer, viz.: that the section was designed to permit capital gain treatment of income from transfers having a field-of-use restriction.

For tax purposes the normal business exploitation of patent property can be analogized to the business exploitation of any other capital assets. If a taxpayer rents a capital asset, the law treats the rental income as ordinary income, whereas, if he sells the asset and otherwise meets the statutory requirements, he gets capital gain treatment.

The reason for § 1235 is that even when patents are sold, the normal transaction involves periodic payments of the sale price "contingent on the productivity, use or disposition of the property transferred." This form of payment is so much like rental payments in the commonplace transactions involving other capital assets that Congress found it necessary to declare specifically that such transfers are entitled to capital gain treatment irrespective of the mode of payment.

### 3) What is "Property consisting of all substantial rights to a patent?"

Apparently Congress, in drafting § 1235, chose the phrase "transfer...of property consisting of all substantial rights to a patent" rather than "sale of a patent," since, due to the special character of a patent, the transferor must maintain some control over the property in order to get his maximum sale price from the transferee. Hence, Congress required only that the holder transfer "all substantial rights" to a patent rather than make a complete divestiture of title to the property.

The report of the Senate Finance Committee makes it clear, however, that the preferred treatment should be limited to transfers in the nature of a sale, in the sense that the transferor must release to the transferee all substantial rights evidenced by the patent, and that interpretation should prevail regardless of whether the transaction is termed an "assignment" or an "exclusive license."

> "The section does not detail precisely what constitutes the formal components of a sale or exchange of patent rights beyond requiring that all substantial rights evidenced by the patent (other than the right to such periodic or contingent payments) should be transferred to the transferee for consideration. This requirement recognizes the basic criteria of a 'sale or exchange' under existing law, with the exception noted relating to contingent payments, which exception is justified in the patent area for 'holders' as herein defined. To illustrate, exclusive licenses to manufacture, use, and sell for the life of the patent, are considered to be 'sales or exchanges' because, in substantive effect, all 'right, title, and interest' in the patent property is transferred (irrespective of the location of legal title or other formalities of language contained in the license agreement). Moreover, the courts have recognized that an exclusive license agreement in some instances may constitute a sale for tax purposes even where the right to 'use' the invention has not been conveyed to the licensee, if it is shown that such failure did not represent the retention of a substantial right under the patent by the licensor. It is the intention of your committee to continue this realistic test, whereby the entire transaction, regardless of formalities, should be examined in its factual context *to determine whether or not substantially all rights of the owner in the patent property have been released to the transferee*, rather than recognizing less relevant verbal touchstones. The word 'title' is not employed because the retention of bare legal title in a transaction involving an exclusive license may not represent the retention of a substan-

tial right in the patent property by the transferor. Furthermore, retention by the transferor of rights in the property which are not of the nature of rights evidenced by the patent and which are not inconsistent with the passage of ownership, such as a security interest (e. g., a vendor's lien) or a reservation in the nature of a condition subsequent (e. g., a forfeiture on account of nonperformance) are not to be considered as such a retention as will defeat the applicability of this section. On the other hand, a transfer terminable at will by the transferor would not qualify.

1954 U.S. Code Cong. & Ad. News pp. 5082–883. [Emphasis added.]

With the above cited legislative history as background, it is our opinion that a two prong inquiry is necessary to determine if a transaction qualifies for special treatment under § 1235. The initial inquiry for determining whether or not there has been a transfer by the holder of "property consisting of all substantial rights to a patent" requires consideration of what the holder has left after the transfer. If he retains any substantial rights to the patent, then he has not transferred the property that comprises all those rights.

If the taxpayer can show that he has no substantial rights in the patent after the transfer, as a second inquiry we must look at what he actually relinquished to the transferee. It is our opinion that the phrase "all substantial rights to a patent" is a reference to the monopoly right for which the patent stands. The monopoly right granted by the patent is the right to exclude others from making, using, or selling the invention. This necessarily encompasses the right to exclude others from any particular industrial field in which those others might choose to use the invention. This is the right that must be sold to the transferee, and the transfer must cover all practical fields-of-use for the invention.

Realistic use of the approach we have outlined will meet the objectives of the section. For example, a field-of-use restriction in a license may not prevent the transfer from being one of property consisting of all substantial rights to a patent, where the field-of-use to which the licensee is restricted is the only field in which the invention has value. *See, e.g., United States v. Carruthers*, 219 F.2d 21 (9th Cir. [1955]), involving a transfer limited to the tuna industry, but "the patents had no established value for any purpose other than processing tuna fish." The right to exclude others from making, using or selling the invention in all practical fields-of-use is a part of the grant which gives existence to and defines the property.

While we have discussed the monopoly right of a patent in the technically correct language of the right to exclude we recognize that most patent transfers are written in terms of the right to make, use and sell rather than the right to exclude others from making, using or selling the patented invention. Where such a transfer is involved we hold that in order for the income from the transfer to qualify for § 1235 treatment, the transfer must cover all practical fields-of-use.

Our approach does not affect the right of the holder to retain legal title to the patent or the right to veto sublicenses, since these powers are designed to protect the transferor's interest in the continuance of the purchase payments and do not interfere with the full use by the transferee of the monopoly right in the patent. *See generally*, DELLER'S WALKER ON PATENTS, § 221 (1965).

Applying the approach that we outline to the present controversy, we find that the record establishes that the Fawick patents had known value outside the marine service industry at the time of the license, as demonstrated by the licensing arrangement with

Fawick Corporation described above. The transaction therefore fails to qualify under § 1235 for capital gain treatment.

In *E.I. duPont de Nemours & Co. v. United States*, 432 F.2d 1052 (3rd Cir. 1970), Judge Fullam speaking for the Third Circuit on substantially the same issue as is before this Court said:

> To determine whether the taxpayer did transfer all of the substantial rights in the patents in question, the key question is whether the transferor retained any rights which, in the aggregate, have substantial value.

The test adopted by the Third Circuit is consistent with our initial inquiry outlined above, although the present case differs in outcome from the *du Pont* case because of the facts to which the test is applied. As was said in *du Pont*:

> After analyzing each of the [retained] rights individually, and finding it value-less, the District Court concluded that the taxpayer had not retained substantial rights in the patents, and that the transfer qualified for capital gains treatment. Indeed, at the conclusion of this discussion of the various retained rights, Chief Judge Wright expressly stated:

> No substantial rights in the eight patents transferred having been retained, the 1954 transactions constituted a sale of those patents, the proceeds of which are entitled to capital gains treatment. (244a).

Accordingly, the only issue before this Court is whether the District Court findings are clearly erroneous. We have concluded that the record adequately supports the findings of the District Court.

One further point raised by the taxpayer merits discussion. He correctly points to the fact that the statute speaks in terms of transfers of "property consisting of all substantial rights to a patent" rather than merely transfers of "all substantial rights to a patent." He then contends that the phrase "all substantial rights to a patent" is a reference to the right to make, use or sell the invention, and that a license to make, use and sell the invention for a given field-of-use is a transfer of property consisting of all those substantial rights.

We reject this argument for two reasons. First, if the section were applicable to all transfers that included the right to make, use and sell the invention, then practically all licensing arrangements would generate capital gain since "property" of that character is transferred even in a non-exclusive license. We do not construe taxpayer's argument to suggest that the section goes that far. Second, in our opinion, Congress used the term "property" in the phrase "property consisting of all substantial rights to a patent" to assure that the section would apply to transfers that take place both before and after the patent is granted, or for that matter, before the patent application is filed. The right to a patent comes into existence at the time the invention is reduced to practice, and when that right is transferred, the "property" consisting of all substantial rights to a patent has been transferred. Section 1235 is applicable even though the patent is not in existence. If the term "property" had been left out of the section, then the section would have applied only to transfers taking place after the patent was issued.

> The section does not apply to a property right in an invention differing from the monopoly rights evidenced by a patent. However, since the inventor possesses an exclusive inchoate right to obtain a patent, he may transfer his interest, whatever it may be, in any subsequently issued patent before its issuance and before as well as after he has made application for such patent.

1954 U.S. Code Cong. & Ad. News p. 5082.

### 4) The Regulations

In 1965 the Commissioner promulgated Treasury Regulation 1.1235-2, as follows:

Sec. 1.1235-2. Definition of terms.

* * *

(b) *All substantial rights to a patent.* (1) The term 'all substantial rights to a patent' means all rights (whether or not then held by the grantor) which are of value at the time the rights to the patent (or an undivided interest therein) are transferred. The term 'all substantial rights to a patent' does not include a grant of rights to a patent -

* * *

(iii). Which grants right to the grantee, in fields of use within trades or industries, which are less than all the rights covered by the patent, which exist and have value at the time of the grant; or

* * *

(c) *Undivided interest.* A person owns an 'undivided interest' in all substantial rights to a patent when he owns the same fractional share of each and every substantial right to the patent. It does not include, for example, a right to the income from a patent, or a license limited geographically, or a license which covers some, but not all, of the valuable claims or uses covered by the patent. A transfer limited in duration by the terms of the instrument to a period less than the remaining life of the patent is not a transfer of an undivided interest in all substantial rights to a patent.

* * *

In our opinion the regulation above quoted embodies the proper interpretation of § 1235. We agree with the reasoning of *Redler Conveyor Co. v. Commissioner of Internal Revenue*, 303 F.2d 567 (1st Cir.), interpreting § 1235 before promulgation of the regulation.

We find nothing in the opinion in *Rodgers* to convince us that the taxpayer here is entitled to capital gain treatment under § 1235.

* * *

---

# Mros v. Commissioner of Internal Revenue
## 493 F.2d 813 (9th Cir. 1974)

PER CURIUM

This appeal from the Tax Court of the United States involves disputed federal income taxes for the year 1966. The legal issue presented by this case is whether a transfer of patent rights by taxpayer subject to a field of use restriction was a transfer of "all substantial rights" to a patent within the meaning of Section 1235 of the Internal Revenue Code of 1954, and thus a capital transaction, even though the taxpayer retained rights in his patent property to license to others outside the fields of use already granted.

This case was submitted to the Tax Court on a stipulation of facts, exhibits, and testimony of the taxpayer. The material facts as found by the Tax Court are summarized as follows:

Taxpayer invented and patented a "Combined Gear Reduction and Clutch Mechanism." The gear reduction device had a much higher reduction ratio and a greater load-carrying capacity than other types of gear reduction mechanism of comparable size, and had potential applicability to virtually any equipment that might require some kind of gear reduction.

In 1966, the taxpayer entered into an agreement with Serka Industries, Inc. (hereinafter "Serka"), whereby Serka was granted—

"The sole and exclusive right, license, and privilege under the Mros Patent Rights to manufacture, use and sell and to sublicense others their right to manufacture and sell any invention within the Field of Agreement." The "Field of Agreement" referred to was limited to—"hoists, winches, boat accessory devices and air motor power drives, and methods and processes for manufacture or use thereof."

Serka agreed to pay the taxpayer advance royalties of $1000 upon the execution of the agreement and $100 per week for the full term of the patent. Advance royalties were to be credited against earned royalties, which were to be computed on the basis of 5 percent of the net selling price of each item made and sold by Serka. In 1966, the taxpayer received advance royalty payments of $4500 from Serka. This amount was not reported on taxpayer's 1966 return. Taxpayer later agreed that the advance royalty was taxable, but then claimed that the payment was subject to capital gain treatment.

Subsequent to concluding the 1966 agreement with Serka, the taxpayer unsuccessfully endeavored to interest other parties in utilizing the patents in fields other than those to which Serka had been given exclusive rights. In 1970, however, the taxpayer and Serka renegotiated their 1966 contract to extend Serka's rights to all possible commercial applications of the patent, in consideration of increased payments to taxpayer.

The Commissioner determined that the royalties were not entitled to capital gain treatment, and therefore determined a deficiency of $707.01 plus an addition to tax under Code Section 6653(a).

The Tax Court held that the advance royalty payments received by the taxpayer 1966 were subject to capital gain treatment, on the ground that a grant of the exclusive right to a patented invention in a particular field of use qualifies as a transfer of "all substantial rights" under Code Section 1235. In so holding, it held invalid Section 1.1235-2(b)(1)(iii) of the Treasury Regulations, which excludes from the benefits of Section 1235 a grant of rights "in fields of use within trades or industries, which are less than all the rights covered by the patent, which exist and have value at the time of the grant." The Commissioner timely filed notice of appeal. We reverse.

I

Section 1235 of the Internal Revenue Code (1954) reads as follows:

Sale or Exchange of Patents.

(a) General—A transfer (other than by gift, inheritance, or devise) of property consisting of all substantial rights to a patent, or an undivided interest therein which includes a part of all such rights, by any holder shall be considered the sale or exchange of a capital asset held for more than 6 months, regardless of whether or not payments in consideration of such transfer are—

(1) payable periodically over a period generally coterminous with the transferee's use of the patent, or

(2) contingent on the productivity, use or disposition of the property transferred.

The relevant Treasury Regulations (1954 Code) read as follows:

§ 1.1235-2. Definition of terms.

(b) All substantial rights to a patent.

(1) The term "all substantial rights to a patent" means all rights (whether or not then held by the grantor) which are of value at the time the rights to the patent (or an undivided interest therein) are transferred. The term "all substantial rights to a patent" does not include a grant of rights to a patent—

\* \* \*

(iii) Which grants rights to the grantee, in fields of use within trades or industries, which are less than all the rights covered by the patent, which exist and have value at the time of the grant;

\* \* \*

(c) Undivided interest. A person owns an "undivided interest" in all substantial rights to a patent when he owns the same fractional share of each and every substantial right to the patent. It does not include, for example, a right to the income from a patent, or a license limited geographically, or a license which covers some, but not all, of the valuable claims or uses covered by the patent. A transfer limited in duration by the terms of the instrument to a period less than the remaining life of the patent is not a transfer of an undivided interest in all substantial rights of a patent.

\* \* \*

Appellant argues that the taxpayer did not transfer "all substantial rights" to his gear reduction and clutch patents within the meaning of Section 1235 of the I.R.C., as properly interpreted by Section 1.1235-2(b) (1) (iii) of the Treasury Regulations. Such regulations exclude from the phrase "all substantial rights of a patent" the transfer of rights "in fields of use within trades or industries which are less than all the rights covered by the patent, which exist and have value at the time of the grant." Thus, since the 1966 agreement between the taxpayer and Serka contained a field of use restriction which limited applications of taxpayer's invention to hoists, winches, boat accessories, and air motor power drives, and since the record established that taxpayer's invention had other valuable uses (clear evidence of this is the new contract made with Serka in 1970 which extended Serka's rights to all possible commercial applications of the patent in consideration of increased payments to the taxpayer), the royalties from the 1966 contract are not entitled to capital gain treatment.

## II

The limited case authority and congressional history available does support the position of the Commissioner.

The only case to date cited by either party in which an appellate court has dealt with the foregoing field-of-use regulation is *Fawick v. Commissioner*, 52 T.C. 104 (1969), *rev'd*, 436 F.2d 655 (6th Cir. 1971), wherein the Sixth Circuit reversed the Tax Court, and held that the regulation was a valid implementation of Section 1235 and the underlying Congressional intent, and that it was consistent with the longstanding principle of patent law that a sale is not accomplished unless the "whole patent" is transferred.

The analysis suggested by the Sixth Circuit to determine whether the taxpayer is entitled to Section 1235 benefits is a two-fold test, outlined as follows: (1) What did the taxpayer actually *give up* by the transfer; that is, was there an actual transfer of the monopoly rights in a patent; and (2) what did the taxpayer *retain* after the transfer; that is, are any substantial rights retained.

Applying this two-fold test, the Sixth Circuit determined that since the record established that the *Fawick* patents had known value outside the marine service industry (the limited field of use license) at the time of the license, the transaction failed to qualify for capital gain treatment under Section 1235.

Applying this analysis (which we believe to be the correct one) to the present case, it is clear that the Mros patent transaction likewise cannot qualify for capital gain treatment. The record clearly establishes that the Mros patent had potential value in fields other than the limited field of use which was the subject of the 1966 agreement with Serka. The latter agreement in 1970 whereby *all* rights to the Mros patent in any field were transferred to Serka for increased payments is sufficient evidence of this. There is, in addition, the taxpayer's own statement at trial that his patent had potential applicability for a variety of fields.

A similar test to that of the Sixth Circuit was adopted by the Third Circuit *in E.I. duPont de Nemours & Co. v. United States*, 432 F.2d 1052 (3rd Cir. 1970); however, under the facts of the *duPont* case (the District Court found that the rights reserved were valueless), the result was different.

Support for the position argued by the Commissioner is also found in the First Circuit's decision in *Redler Conveyor Co. v. Commissioner of Internal Revenue*, 303 F.2d 567 (1st Cir. 1962). Both *Redler Conveyor* and *duPont* were cited with approval by the court in *Fawick* even though neither of these cases dealt with either Section 1235 or the Treasury Regulation at issue in *Fawick* and in this present case.

With regard to the Treasury Regulation 1.1235-2, the Sixth Circuit in *Fawick* pointed out that such regulation was promulgated in 1965 (Section 1235 itself was enacted in 1954), after a number of courts which had considered the issue involved had come to arguably different conclusions. With regard to the validity of Treasury Regulations, the language of the United States Supreme Court in *Commissioner v. South Texas Co.*, 333 U.S. 496, 92 L. Ed. 831, 68 S. Ct. 695 (1948), is particularly instructive:

> This Court has many times declared that Treasury regulations must be sustained unless unreasonable and plainly inconsistent with the revenue statutes...(and) should not be overruled except for weighty reasons.

*Id*. at 501.

The Sixth Circuit in *Fawick* found that the regulation embodied the proper interpretation of Section 1235. We agree. The statute itself does not specifically determine whether a transfer for a limited field of use is entitled to be considered in a Section 1235 transfer. However, the statute does require that a transfer be a transfer of "all substantial rights" to a patent to be entitled to such preferential capital gain treatment. Thus, it would seem that the regulation is certainly not unreasonable and plainly inconsistent with the language of the statute.

A careful reading of the legislative history of Section 1235 likewise convinces us that a limited transfer of patent rights would not qualify for the preferred capital gain treatment. The following language from the Senate Report is particularly instructive:

> It is the intention of your committee to continue this realistic test, whereby the entire transaction, regardless of formalities, should be examined in its factual context to determine whether or not substantially all rights of the owner in the patent property have been released to the transferee, rather than recognizing less relevant verbal touchstones.... Furthermore, retention by the transferor of rights in the *property which are not of the nature of rights evidenced by the patent* and which are not inconsistent with the passage of ownership, such as a security interest (e.g., a vendor's lien) or a reservation in the nature of a condition subsequent (e.g., a forfeiture on account of nonperformance) are not to be considered as such a retention as will defeat the applicability of this section.

3 U.S.C. Cong. & Adm. News (1954) 5083 (emphasis added.)

In the instant case, the 1966 agreement between taxpayer and Serka clearly involved a transfer of rights to the patent for a limited field-of-use. The rights retained by the taxpayer in his patent were not in the nature of a security interest, but rather, were of the nature of rights evidenced by the patent. Thus, the congressional history available leads to the conclusion that such a limited transfer would not qualify for capital gain treatment, and that the Treasury regulation barring such treatment to a limited field-of-use transfer is valid. Any allowance of such preferential tax treatment to such a limited transfer of patent rights should have to come from Congress and not from this Court by an unwarranted extension of the literal mandate of Congress that "all substantial rights" to a patent must be transferred before capital gain treatment is allowed.

Accordingly, the decision of the Tax Court is reversed, and the case is remanded to that Court for further proceedings not inconsistent with this opinion.

---

## B.  In the University Setting

### IRS Technical Advice Memorandum
TAM 200249002
August 8, 2002

#### ISSUE(S):

Whether Taxpayer is entitled to capital gains treatment under § 1235 of the Internal Revenue Code for royalties received from University.

#### CONCLUSION:

Taxpayer is entitled to capital gains treatment under § 1235 for royalties received from University, which are in exchange for all substantial rights in the patent to Invention.

#### FACTS:

Taxpayer has been a professor at University since Date. University is part of the State University System. Taxpayer's responsibilities have involved teaching, conducting research, and administrative tasks in varying degrees, with between fifty and one hundred percent of Taxpayer's efforts devoted to research during any given academic term. Taxpayer receives a salary for Taxpayer's employment with University.

The collective bargaining agreement, to which Taxpayer is a party, incorporates State's Administrative Code provisions relating to inventions by University employees. The State Administrative Code provides, in part, that an invention which is made in the field or discipline in which the employee is employed by University, or by using University support, is the property of University and the employee shall share in the proceeds therefrom. It further directs the University Vice President to conduct an investigation which assesses the respective equities of the inventor and University in the invention, and determines its importance and the extent to which University should be involved in its protection, development and promotion. The Vice President will then inform the inventor of University's decision on whether or not to assert rights in the invention. If University wishes to own the invention, the division, between University and the inventor, of proceeds generated by the licensing or assignment of patent rights or trade secrets, will be set out in a written contract between University and the inventor. If University decides to not exercise its rights, the invention becomes the sole property of the employee.

In the course of Taxpayer's research, Taxpayer developed Invention. Taxpayer filed patent applications for Invention. Taxpayer then executed assignment agreements which assigned Taxpayer's interest in the patent applications to University. Taxpayer also entered into a royalty distribution agreement with University regarding Invention. The royalty agreement provided that Taxpayer would receive $x$ percent of the first $\$y$ in royalties resulting from University's licensing of the patents, and $z$ percent of royalties in excess of $\$y$. University licensed the patents to Manufacturer, who has produced Invention for sale. Taxpayer's share of the royalties paid by Manufacturer for the years in question amounts to $\$a$, $\$b$ and $\$c$, respectively. University has treated these amounts as royalty payments, and not as part of Taxpayer's salary.

## LAW AND ANALYSIS:

Section 1235(a) provides that a transfer (other than by gift, inheritance, or devise) of property consisting of all substantial rights to a patent, or an undivided interest therein which includes a part of all such rights, by any holder shall be considered the sale or exchange of a capital asset held for more than 1 year, regardless of whether or not payments in consideration of such transfer are—(1) payable periodically over a period generally coterminous with the transferee's use of the patent, or (2) contingent on the productivity, use, or disposition of the property transferred.

Section 1235(b) defines a "holder" as: (1) any individual whose efforts created such property; or (2) any other individual who has acquired his interest in such property in exchange for consideration in money or money's worth paid to such creator prior to actual reduction to practice of the invention covered by the patent, if such individual is neither—(A) the employer of such creator, nor (B) related to such creator (within the meaning of § 1235(d)).

Section 1.1235-1(c)(2) of the Income Tax Regulations provides that payments received by an employee as compensation for services rendered as an employee under an employment contract requiring the employee to transfer to the employer the rights to any invention by such employee are not attributable to a transfer to which § 1235 applies. However, whether payments received by an employee from his employer (under an employment contract or otherwise) are attributable to the transfer by the employee of all substantial rights to a patent (or an undivided interest therein) or are compensation for services rendered the employer by the employee is a question of fact. In determining which is the case, consideration shall be given not only to all the facts and circumstances of the employment relationship but also to whether the amount of such payments depends upon the production, sale, or use by, or the value to, the employer of the patent rights transferred by the employee. If it is determined that payments are attributable to the transfer of patent rights, and all other requirements under § 1235 are met, such payments shall be treated as proceeds derived from the sale of a patent.

Section 1.1235-2(a) states that the term "patent" means a patent granted under the provisions of Title 35 of the United States Code, or any foreign patent granting rights generally similar to those under a United States patent. It is not necessary that the patent or patent application for the invention be in existence if the requirements of § 1235 are otherwise met.

Initially, it appears that Taxpayer is entitled to § 1235 treatment. Section 1235(a) allows long term capital gains treatment for payments received for the transfer, by a holder, of all substantial rights to a patent. It is undisputed that Taxpayer qualifies as a holder under § 1235(b), as it was Taxpayer's efforts that created Invention. However, because Invention arose from Taxpayer's employment with University, the requirements of § 1.1235-1(c)(2) must be satisfied. All of the facts and circumstances of the employment relationship must be considered to determine whether payments to Taxpayer were compensation for services or payment for the transfer of Taxpayer's patent rights. Also, whether the amount of payments depends on the production, sale, use or value of the patent must be considered.

In *Chilton v. Commissioner*, 40 T.C. 552 (1963), the taxpayer was employed as an engineer, responsible for the design of aircraft engines. His employment contract stated that, if the taxpayer invented anything related to aircraft engines or accessories, "all said inventions and improvements shall belong to and be the sole and exclusive property of [employer] in and for all countries of the world." *Id.* at 556. The taxpayer invented several things, many of which his employer selected to have assigned to it. *Id.* at 556–57. The taxpayer patented these inventions, assigned them to his employer, and received various additional payments. *Id.* His employer treated these additional amounts as royalties, rather than including them in with the taxpayer's regular salary. *Id.* at 563. The Tax Court rejected the Commissioner's argument that, because of the quoted language in the taxpayer's employment contract, the taxpayer never owned any substantial rights to transfer. *Id.* at 561. Further, the taxpayer was not "hired to invent," because he was hired to apply his inventive ability, rather than to invent a specific product, and was therefore permitted to treat the royalty payments as long term capital gains under § 1235. *Id.* at 563.

In *McClain v. Commissioner*, 40 T.C. 841 (1963), the taxpayer also was employed as a design engineer for an aircraft company. The taxpayer's employment contract contained similar language as in *Chilton* about inventions. The Tax Court found no substantial difference between *McClain* and *Chilton*, stating that the taxpayer had an even better claim under § 1235, because the taxpayer in *Chilton* had been hired to improve engine designs and develop new ones. In contrast, the Tax Court rejected the taxpayer's § 1235 argument in *Beausoleil v. Commissioner*, 66 T.C. 244 (1976). *Beausoleil* involved an invention incentive program, in which employee inventions earned points toward reward plateaus. The Tax Court found that there was no connection between the eventual achievement award money and the assignments of the rights to individual inventions. *Id.* at 249. Further, the employer treated these awards as salary. *Id.* The payments also bore no relation to the usefulness of the invention. *Id.* at 250. The payments were given ordinary income treatment. *Id.* The U.S. Court of Appeals for the Second Circuit, in applying these cases, also stressed that an important factor to consider in receiving § 1235 treatment is whether the payments would continue beyond the employment relationship, for the entire life of the patent. *See Lehman v. Commissioner*, 835 F.2d 431, 436 (2d Cir. 1987).

The facts of Taxpayer's case are essentially equivalent to the facts of *Chilton* and *McClain*. Looking to the facts and circumstances of the employment relationship, the payments in question are connected to the transfer of the rights to Invention, rather than compensation for services. The compensation received for the rights to Invention are in addition to and separate from Taxpayer's salary, pursuant to a separate agreement with University. Taxpayer executed a separate assignment of rights document as well. University treats the payments as royalties, and not as salary. It appears that the right to continued receipt of these payments is not contingent on continued employment with University. The amount of the payments received by Taxpayer are dependent on the use or value of the licensing of the patent. The royalty agreement provides that the amount of the payment is a percentage of what University receives in royalties from its licensing of the patent. The amount received varied substantially during the years in question.

There is a question of whether the provisions of the State Administrative Code pertaining to research at University preclude Taxpayer from ever having acquired any interest in Invention. If this were so, § 1235 treatment would be precluded, because Taxpayer would have no rights to transfer. The well established principle is that initial patent rights vest with the inventor. *See* 35 U.S.C. § 111; *Beech Aircraft Corp. v. EDO Corp.*, 990 F.2d 1237, 1248 (Fed. Cir. 1993); *Teets v. Chromalloy Gas Turbine Corp.*, 83 F.3d 403, 407 (Fed. Cir. 1996)("…an invention presumptively belongs to its creator"). "The federal Patent Act leaves no room for states to supplement the national standard for inventorship." *See University of Colorado Foundation, Inc. v. American Cyanamid Co.*, 196 F.3d 1366, 1372 (Fed. Cir. 1999). "Therefore, the field of federal patent law preempts any state law that purports to define rights based on inventorship." *Id.* State contract and property law may govern with respect to determining who has acquired rights from the inventor, but it cannot supplant the creation of such rights under federal law. There is no dispute that University acquired a property interest in Invention from Taxpayer, but state statutes cannot operate to extinguish inventorship.

The provisions in the State Administrative Code should be read as having the same effect as similar contract provisions in the cases cited above. Any other reading would leave the statute preempted. This reading is consistent with the reading of the Administrative Code itself, which acts as a handbook of University policy. Because University is an organ of State, the policies of University have been codified, along with the policies of all the schools in the State university system. The State Administrative Code has been included in the collective bargaining agreement between University professors and University. The State Administrative Code sections themselves do not appear to attempt to abrogate the inventor's initial property rights. The provisions are contractual in nature, calling for the assignment of rights in order to share in the proceeds. University must exercise its rights if it wishes to take full ownership of a particular invention. In situations in which University decides not to obtain a particular invention, the employee may keep it. This reading is consistent with the submitted opinion of the University Office of General Counsel. Thus, even if state law could extinguish any possible rights an employee may acquire through creation of an invention, this statute does not do that.

It is of no concern that the transfer of rights to future inventions took place in the adoption of Taxpayer's employment contract. Section 1.1235-2(a) states that the patent need not be in existence at the time of the transfer for § 1235 to apply. In an analogous case regarding an independent contractor, the Tax Court explained the relating back concept. *See Gilson v. Commissioner*, T.C. Memo 1984-447 (1984). "[T]he taxpayer's obligation from the outset to assign his invention to the other party does not render unavailable the benefits of section 1235—it is unimportant whether the contract to assign is viewed as executory, so that no 'transfer' occurs until formal assignment and payment, or whether the payment is viewed as relating back to the previous transfer of patent rights." *Id.* It is irrelevant for the purposes of § 1235 whether the substantial rights are viewed as having been transferred in the original employment contract, or in the later assignment document.

For the foregoing reasons, we conclude that Taxpayer is entitled to capital gains treatment under § 1235 for royalty payments received in exchange for all substantial rights to the patents for Invention.

---

## C. Licensor in Control

### Eickmeyer v. Commissioner of Internal Revenue
#### 580 F.2d 395 (10th Cir. 1978)

DOYLE, Circuit Judge.

This is an appeal by the Commissioner of Internal Revenue from an unfavorable ruling by the United States Tax Court. The Commissioner determined deficiencies in the taxpayer's federal income tax for the years 1968, 1969 and 1970, amounting to $48,143.43, $115,363.38 and $92,842.58. The Tax Court reversed and redetermined the deficiencies in the amounts of $1,666.25 for 1968, $1,633.49 for 1969, and $1,588.74 for 1970.

The question for decision is whether the interests assigned are of such a character so as to be taxed as ordinary income as opposed to capital gains. The income is derived from payments made by unrelated third parties to the taxpayer Allen G. Eickmeyer for use of a patented process.

During the period January 1, 1960 through December 31, 1970, Eickmeyer entered into 12 separate agreements for the use of the so-called Catacarb process, which process was patented and has wide application in the oil refining, petrochemical, and fertilizer processing industries. The patent was not issued until November 26, 1974, and Eickmeyer is the only record holder of an interest in the several applications that were made and is the only record owner in the patent as well.

During the 1960s, the period mentioned above, Eickmeyer entered into 12 separate agreements, and during the three years in question he received payments pursuant to eight of those agreements.

There were three agreements which were entered into before 1968. Each of these granted the transferee an "exclusive license" in the process. The contracts with Bechtel Corporation and Sun Oil Company defined "exclusive license" as "the sale and transfer of an irrevocable, undivided interest in the complete Catacarb Process and the Patent Rights covering said Process, the size and/or capacity of said interest defined by the purchase price or royalty paid." In the Atlantic Richfield Company contract, the term "exclusive license" was defined as "the sale and transfer of an irrevocable undivided interest to make, use and sell the complete process."

Each of the mentioned contracts transfers the patent rights for ten years or for the life of the patent, whichever is longer. There is no provision in any one of them giving to Eickmeyer any right of termination. Bechtel is authorized to sublicense provided it promptly notifies Eickmeyer and pays to Eickmeyer "all royalties herein provided." There is provision in the Atlantic Richfield agreement which prohibits assignments without Eickmeyer's consent, but does not mention sublicensing. Nor does the Sun Oil agreement have any provision providing for sublicensing or assignment.

There were five other agreements made during the period from 1968 to 1970. Contracting parties were Chemical Construction Corporation, Dawood Hercules Chemicals Limited, J.F. Pritchard & Company, M.W. Kellogg Company and Tenneco Oil Company. Each of these agreements contains a provision purporting to grant "an undivided 1% interest in the Patent Rights." The Dawood Hercules contract grants this interest in Pakistani patents. The Kellogg agreement grants an interest in all United States and foreign patents. The other agreements grant interests in United States patents. With the exception of Dawood Hercules, the agreements all provide for sublicensing or subassignment. The Dawood Hercules agreement has no contrary provision. All except the Tenneco contract authorize Eickmeyer to terminate on default of the transferees. The Kellogg and Pritchard agreements only authorize the transferee to sue for infringement in its own name. All agreements continue during the life of the patent.

Provisions are made in all of the agreements for the payment of royalties measured by the amount of use made of the patent. None of the agreements restricts the rights geographically or according to fields of use, and none of them reserves to Eickmeyer the right to sue for infringement.

The most significant and revealing fact is that which purports to give the assignees of the patent the right to transfer a similar interest to other parties. Coupled with this is the requirement that the compensation measured by the extended use of the patent by these subassignees must flow to Eickmeyer.

The crucial provision of the code, I.R.C. § 1235(a), applicable to the taxable years here in question, provides in essence that a transfer of property consisting of all substantial rights to a patent, or an undivided interest therein which includes a part of all such rights, by any holder shall be considered the sale or exchange of a capital asset held for more than 6 months (now 1 year), regardless of whether or not payments in consideration of such transfer are—

(1) payable periodically over a period generally coterminous with the transferee's use of the patent, or
(2) contingent on the productivity, use, or disposition of the property transferred.

The area of dispute is whether there has been a transfer of "an undivided interest" in "all substantial rights" to the patents. The term "undivided interest" is defined in Treas. Reg. § 1235-2(c) (1965) as follows:

A person owns an "undivided interest" in all substantial rights to a patent when he owns the same fractional share of each and every substantial right to the patent. It does not include, for example, a right to the income from a patent, or a license limited geographically, or a license which covers some, but not all, of the valuable claims or uses covered by the patent. A transfer limited in duration by the terms of the instrument to a period less than the remaining life of the patent is not a transfer of an undivided interest in all substantial rights to a patent.

The Treasury Regulation thus considers ownership of the same fractional share of each and every substantial right to the patent to be the important quality of an undivided interest. Excluded is the right to income from a patent or a license limited geographically or right to the income of a license which covers some but not all of the valuable claims or uses covered by the patent.

Although the taxpayer sought capital gain treatment of the royalty income received from all of the above-mentioned assignments, the Commissioner ruled that because he had retained substantial rights in the patent and had not sold undivided interests in it, he was not entitled to such treatment because § 1235 was not applicable.

On the other hand, the Tax Court ruling was that all of the assignments were transfers of undivided interests and that § 1235 applied and operated so as to give the taxpayer capital gain treatment.

We conclude that the Commissioner correctly concluded that Eickmeyer retained significant interest in the patent and that the transfers or assignments here considered do not meet the standards which are set forth in § 1235(a), *supra*.

I

The starting point is I.R.C. § 1235(a), which sets forth the terms under which there can be a transfer of a patent or an interest in the patent which can be considered the sale or exchange of a capital asset even though the payments are measured by the use of the patent. The fundamental statutory requirement is that there be a transfer "of property consisting of all substantial rights to a patent, or an undivided interest therein which includes a part of all such rights" (emphasis supplied). It is fundamental, therefore, that although the percentage of ownership or quantity of ownership need not be the same as that of the transferor, the character of the right of transfer must be the same. Each element in the title must be present in that which is transferred. That is where the interest with which we are here concerned falls short of being taxable as a capital gain.

The date of the enactment of § 1235, *supra*, was 1954. Prior to that capital gain treatment was available if it were determined that there had been a sale of all substantial rights in the patent as opposed to a mere licensing arrangement. *See* 3B J. MERTENS, THE LAW OF FEDERAL INCOME TAXATION §§ 22.133–34 (1973). That author states that in order to get a capital gain both before § 1235 and thereafter, there must be a sale of an interest in all of the rights which the transferor has in the patent. It must be a sale or exchange of the patent or invention. Mertens further states that a flexible test which has been used by some courts is "whether rights amounting to full and complete control were relinquished." It is, of course, recognized that a sale of the entire patent is not necessary. The quantity or percentage sold is not controlling. *See, e.g., Dairy Queen, Inc. v. Commissioner*, 250 F.2d 503 (10th Cir. 1957). Although *Dairy Queen* was a pre-§ 1235 case, the statute does not alter this principle. The statute was designed to give capital gain treatment regardless of whether payment is measured by use of the property transferred or payable over a period equal to the life of the patent. *See* S. Rep. No. 1622, 83d Cong., 2d Sess., *reprinted in* [1954] U.S. Code Cong. & Ad. News 4621, 4747, 5081–84.

On the issue as to what property a patentee has for purposes of assignment, the Supreme Court in a non-tax case, *Waterman v. Mackenzie*, 138 U.S. 252, 255, 34 L. Ed. 923, 11 S. Ct. 334 (1891), has utilized three kinds of interest which are available:

> The patentee or his assigns may, by instrument in writing, assign, grant and convey, either, 1st, the whole patent, comprising the exclusive right to make, use and vend the invention throughout the United States; or, 2d, an undivided part or share of that exclusive right; or, 3d, the exclusive right under the patent within and throughout a specified part of the United States.

138 U.S. at 255.

The opinion of the Court adds the following significant statement:

> Any assignment or transfer, short of one of these, is a mere license, giving the licensee no title in the patent, and no right to sue at law in his own name for an infringement. Rev. Stat. sec. 4919; *Gayler v. Wilder*, 51 U.S. (10 How.) 477, 494, 495, 13 L. Ed. 504 ; *Moore v. Marsh*, 74 U.S. (7 Wall.) 515, [19 L. Ed. 37]. In equity, as at law, when the transfer amounts to a license only, the title remains in the owner of the patent; and suit must be brought in his name, and never in the name of the licensee alone, unless that is necessary to prevent an absolute failure of justice; as where the patentee is the infringer, and cannot sue himself.

138 U.S. at 255.

Granted that *Waterman* is not a tax case, nevertheless, the taxing statute does not seek to change *Waterman's* definition of property interests present in a patent and available for a transfer. Eickmeyer argues that while he has retained the power to create additional interests by making additional assignments, this right is shared with the other transferees, who also have the right to sublicense or subassign. Like Eickmeyer, it is said that they can extend the use of the patent at will. If they, in reality, shared this right, the argument that Sect. 1235 applies to authorize a capital gain would have some persuasiveness. The right of the transferee here to sublicense or subassign is, however, only an appearance of a right. Analysis shows that even though a transferee were to grant a sublicense or sub-assignment, he would be doing it only on behalf of Eickmeyer, for in the event of such a transfer the royalties would inevitably be paid to Eickmeyer by either his transferee or the subtransferee. These payments are always measured by the use of the patent. If Eick-meyer's transferee were to charge a higher royalty rate, Eickmeyer could license the subli-censees at the lower rate. Thus the presence of this terminology in the agreement is not significant in view of the legal and practical consequences which are mentioned above and this, of course, has to be confronted because substance rather than form prevails. The fact then that each of the contracts purports to convey an undivided interest is not con-trolling. We must consider the consequences which flow from this "undivided interest."

## II.

Also supportive of the conclusion we reach is 35 U.S.C. Sect. 262, which provides that "In the absence of any agreement to the contrary, each of the joint owners of a patent may make, use or sell the patented invention without the consent of and without accounting to the other owners." This helps to prove that if the transferee is indeed an owner, he would not have to account to the other owners. But here, of course, account-ing to the owner is the essential part. Eickmeyer is shown to have retained the all-im-portant right to collect for all uses of the patent whether by the original transferee or subsequent ones. Furthermore, in genuine owner situations each of the owners can grant a license, assign his share of the patent, and sue for infringement or for royalties. *See Willingham v. Star Cutter Co.*, 555 F.2d 1340, 1344 (6th Cir. 1977).

### III.

The practical effect of Eickmeyer's assignment is to grant non-exclusive licenses to each of the transferees. Each of the transferees remains under the control of Eickmeyer. *Cf. Walen v. United States*, 273 F.2d 599 (1st Cir. 1959), wherein the possibility of selling a partial interest in a patent and obtaining capital gain treatment was recognized prior to the enactment of § 1235. The First Circuit said that "to do so it should be a transfer of a measurable, identifiable share, and not of an undefined one of elastic proportions dependent upon how many subsequent 'shares' the grantor might elect to create." *Id.* at 602 n.3.

The unlimited power enjoyed by Eickmeyer to create new licenses or owners also serves to reveal the true character of his property interest. By reason of this it differs from *Kavanagh v. Evans*, 188 F.2d 234 (6th Cir. 1951). In that case the transferor of a patent retained only a license together with the right to transfer it to one other person in case he did not exercise the license himself.

\* \* \*

We have one final observation. The assignments by Eickmeyer of purported interests withheld in each instance the right to exclude others from use of the patent. Failure to transfer this also shows that no substantial interest in the patent was granted.

\* \* \*

In summary:

1.    The term "undivided interest" contemplates a fractional interest in all of the rights which are part of ownership of the patent.

2.    The taxpayer retained the power to create additional interests by making additional assignments and retained the right to payments or royalties based upon use, including not only payments by his assignees or transferees, but also subassignees.

3.    The transferees in this instance are not owners because, among other indications, they are accountable to Eickmeyer.

4.    Each of the transferees remains under the control of Eickmeyer. These transferees are nothing more than licensees. Accordingly, Eickmeyer is not entitled to have capital gain treatment for the royalty income.

Accordingly, the judgment of the Tax Court is reversed. The cause is remanded for redetermination of the taxpayer's deficiency consistent with the opinion of this court.

---

## D.  Territorial Limitations

### Kueneman v. Commissioner of Internal Revenue
628 F.2d 1196 (9th Cir. 1980)

POOLE, Cir. J.

This is an appeal by five taxpayers from a decision of the United States Tax Court determining deficiencies in their federal income taxes for the years 1971 and 1972. During these years, appellants Don and Irene Kueneman, John Kueneman, and Edmund and Ella Harrell reported royalty payments received from an exclusive transfer of patent rights within a specified geographical area as long-term capital gains on their federal income tax returns. The Tax Court held that this did not constitute a transfer of "all substantial rights" to the patent within the meaning of Section 1235 of the Internal Revenue Code of 1954, and that appellants could not report royalty payments as long-term capital gains. Notice of appeal was timely filed. Our jurisdiction rests on 26 U.S.C. Sect. 7482. We affirm.

This case was submitted to the Tax Court on stipulated facts which may be summarized as follows:

Taxpayers Don Kueneman and John Kueneman were the principal investors of a type of rock-crushing machine for which they obtained patents in the 1940s. In 1946, they entered into an agreement which altered the ownership of the patents so that John Kueneman, Don Kueneman, Alma Harrell, and Cyril Kenville, held specified undivided ownership interests. In November, 1948, John Kueneman, who was authorized to act on behalf of the others, entered into a licensing agreement with Pennsylvania Crusher Co., (Crusher), a New York corporation. In return for specified royalty payments, the license granted Crusher the exclusive right to make, vend, and use the patented machinery throughout Puerto Rico, eastern Canada, and all of the United States east of North Dakota, South Dakota, Nebraska, Kansas, Oklahoma, and Texas, during the lives of the patents.

In 1971 and 1972 Don and Irene Kueneman and Edmund and Ella Harrell filed joint federal income tax returns while John Kueneman filed individual tax returns. All reported receipt of royalty payments from Crusher, which they treated as long-term capital gains. Relying upon Sect. 1235 as interpreted by Treasury Regulation 1.1235-2(b)(1)(I), the Commissioner of the Internal Revenue Service determined that the royalty income was ordinary income and assessed substantial deficiencies against the taxpayers.

The taxpayers filed a petition in the Tax Court for redetermination of the deficiencies on the basis of two Tax Court decisions which had held that an exclusive geographical patent transfer automatically disposed of all substantial rights to the patent and qualified for capital gain treatment under § 1235. See Estate of Klein v. Commissioner, 61 T.C. 332 (1973), rev'd. 507 F.2d 617 (7th Cir. 1974), cert. denied, 421 U.S. 991, 95 S. Ct. 1998, 44 L. Ed. 2d 482 (1975); Rodgers v. Commissioner, 51 T.C. 927 (1969). The Tax Court then re-examined its interpretation of Sect. 1235 because of the general appellate criticism of these precedents. See Estate of Klein, supra; Mros v. Commissioner, 493 F.2d 813 (9th Cir. 1974) (patent transfer subject to field-of-use restriction does not dispose of all substantial rights under Sect. 1235); Fawick v. Commissioner, 436 F.2d 655 (6th Cir. 1971) (same) rev'g. 52 T.C. 104 (1969). It held that taxpayers' exclusive geographical transfer did not automatically dispose of "all substantial rights" in their patent under § 1235. This holding overruled Estate of Klein and Rodgers v. Commissioner to the extent they had held to the contrary. Finding that the taxpayers' retained patent rights were substantial, the Tax Court ruled that their royalty income was taxable as ordinary income. Kueneman v. Commissioner, 68 T.C. 609 (1977).

The sole issue is whether appellants' exclusive transfer of their patent rights within a specified geographical area was a transfer of "all substantial rights" to the patent within the meaning of § 1235. If so they are entitled to treat royalty payments as long-term capital gains. We conclude that it was not such a transfer.

Section 1235(a) provides:

Sect. 1235. Sale or exchange of patents.

(a) General. a transfer (other than by gift, inheritance, or devise) of property consisting of all substantial rights to a patent, or an undivided interest therein which includes a part of all such rights, by any holder shall be considered the sale or exchange of a capital asset held for more than 6 months, regardless of whether or not payments in consideration of such transfer are

(1) payable periodically over a period generally coterminous with the transferee's use of the patent, or

(2) contingent on the productivity, use, or disposition of the property transferred.

The relevant Treasury Regulations, § 1.1235-2, as amended by T.D. 6852, October 1, 1965, provide in pertinent part:

§ 1.1235-2. Definition of terms.

"(b) All substantial rights to a patent. (1) The term "all substantial rights to a patent" means all rights (whether or not then held by the grantor) which are of value at the time the rights to the patent (or an undivided interest therein) are transferred. *The term "all substantial rights to a patent" does not include a grant of rights to a patent—*

"(i) *Which is limited geographically within the country of issuance* ;

"(c) Undivided interest. A person owns an'*undivided interest*' in all substantial rights to a patent when he owns the same fractional share of each and every substantial right to the patent. It *does not include*, for example...*a license limited geographically,....*"

(Emphasis added)

Appellants argue that their transfer disposed of "all substantial rights" to their patents under § 1235, reasoning that they thereby relinquished the monopoly right conferred by the patents to make, use, and sell the patented invention within the specified geographic area. They assert that the Tax Court misconstrued the legislative history and cases involving field-of-use restrictions. Their position is that Congress intended for an exclusive geographic transfer of patent rights to qualify for capital gains treatment under § 1235. Conceding that a patent transfer subject to a field-of-use restriction does not constitute the sale of a capital asset, *see Mros v. Commissioners, supra; Fawick v. Commissioner, supra*, they argue that the rationales of these cases are inapplicable to an exclusive geographic transfer.

The Seventh Circuit appears to be the only appellate court which has considered the tax consequences of a geographically limited transfer of patent rights and the validity of Treasury Regulation § 1.1235-2(b)(I). *Estate of Klein v. Commissioner*, 507 F.2d 617, 621 (7th Cir. 1974), reversed the Tax Court and held that an exclusive transfer of a patented process for the production of organic compost in certain eastern states did not relinquish "all substantial rights" to the patent within the meaning of § 1235. The Court said that the statutory requirement that "all substantial rights" be transferred indicated Congress' intent that a transfer of a part only of the patent rights should not be considered a sale or exchange of a capital asset. It found support for this conclusion in the Senate Committee Report excluding geographically limited transfers from consideration under Sect. 1235 as an "undivided interest." *See* 3 U.S. Code Cong. & Admin.News, pp. 4025,

5082 (1954); p. 1201, *infra*. Treasury Regulation Sect. 1.1235-2(b)(I) was seen as consistent with the statutory language and underlying Congressional intent.

The Seventh Circuit also found support in our decision in *Mros v. Commissioner, supra*. In *Mros*, we reversed the Tax Court and held that the transfer of patent rights to a gear reduction device for a limited industrial field-of-use did not transfer "all substantial rights" in the patent under § 1235. Relying upon the analysis suggested by the Sixth Circuit's decision in *Fawick v. Commissioner, supra*, 436 F.2d at 662–63, that a patent transfer subject to a field-of-use restriction did not qualify for capital gains treatment under § 1235, we adopted a two-prong test to determine whether a taxpayer is entitled to § 1235 benefits:

(1)  What did the taxpayer actually give up by the transfer; that is, was there an actual transfer of the monopoly rights in a patent; and (2) what did the taxpayer retain after the transfer; that is, are any substantial rights retained. [Citations omitted] Since the patent in *Mros* had potential value in fields-of-use other than the field that was the subject of the transfer, we concluded that such a transaction could not qualify for capital gains treatment. The legislative history supported this conclusion, and we also upheld Treasury Regulation 1.235-2(b)(I) as a valid implementation of § 1235.

Appellants argue that geographic divisions are fundamentally distinguishable from field-of-use divisions. We agree and recognize that *Mros* is not controlling in this case. The separate Treasury regulations and body of case law concerning field-of-use transfers and geographical area transfers reflect their separate and distinct nature. But this is not to say that the approach used in *Mros* is inapposite to a transfer subject to a geographical restriction. The *Mros* analysis embodies the language of § 1235 and its underlying legislative history. Field-of-use and geographical divisions must both comply with § 1235 as construed in accordance with the legislative history in order to qualify for capital gains. Accordingly, we conclude that the standard embraced in *Mros* in the context of a field-of-use transfer for determining whether a taxpayer is entitled to § 1235 benefits applies also to an exclusive geographical transfer. *See Estate of Klein v. Commissioner, supra*, 507 F.2d at 622 (no difference in principle under § 1235 between field-of-use transfers and geographic transfer).

Thus, applying our two-prong analysis, it is clear that appellants' geographically limited transfer does not entitle them to capital gains treatment under § 1235. A patent gives the patent holder the monopoly right to make, use, and sell the patented invention throughout the United States during the life of the patent, see 35 U.S.C. Sect. 271(a), and to exclude others from doing so. To qualify for the capital gains advantage it is this right that must be transferred, and in the context of a geographical transfer it must include all areas of the United States in which the patented invention has potential value. Appellants relinquished their monopoly rights in the patented rock-crushing machine only in the eastern portion of the United States. They transferred less than all the monopoly rights represented by the patent, retaining the exclusive rights to make, use, and vend the patented machine in the western portion of the United States. The record does not indicate that these retained monopoly rights were not substantial. Consequently, we find that appellants have failed to establish that their exclusive geographical transfer disposed of "all substantial rights" to their patents within the meaning of § 1235.

We have carefully reviewed the legislative history of § 1235 and are convinced that its supports our analysis. Congress enacted § 1235 as an incentive to investors and to assure them that their license royalties would be afforded capital gains treatment whether payments were payable periodically or contingent on the use of the property transferred. *See* U.S. Code Cong. & Admin. News at 5082 (1954); *Fawick v. Commissioner, supra,* 436 F.2d at 660–61. This was, however, conditioned on the transfer by the patent holder of property consisting of all substantial rights to a patent. A transfer of patent rights limited to geographical area is not a transfer of "all substantial rights." In *Mros, supra,* 493 F.2d at 817, we found this instructive language from the Senate Report:

> It is the intention of your committee to continue this realistic test, whereby the entire transaction, regardless of formalities, should be examined in its factual context to determine whether or not substantially all rights of the owner in the patent property have been released to the transferee, rather than recognizing less relevant verbal touchstones.... Furthermore, retention by the transferor of rights in the property which are not of the nature of rights evidenced by the patent and which are not inconsistent with the passage of ownership, such as a security interest (e.g., a vendor's lien) or a reservation in the nature of a condition subsequent (e.g., a forfeiture on account of non-performance) are not to be considered as such a retention as will defeat the applicability of this section.

3 U.S.Code Cong. & Admin. News (1954) p. 5083.

We believe Congress used the phrase "all substantial rights to the patent property" to refer to the monopoly rights represented by the patent throughout the United States. *See Fawick v. Commissioner, supra,* 436 F.2d at 662. This conclusion is fortified by the legislative history which explains the language of § 1235 providing that capital gain treatment is proper where a patent owner transfers "an undivided interest." The Senate Committee Report states:

> By "undivided interest" a part of each property right represented by the patent (constituting a fractional share of the whole patent) is meant (and not, for example, a lesser interest such as a right to income, or a license limited geographically, or a license which conveys some, but not all, of the claims or uses covered by the patent).

3 U.S.Code Cong. & Admin.News, p. 5082 (1954).

A transfer limited geographically was to be excluded from consideration as an "undivided interest" because it does not convey a "fractional share of each property right represented by the patent." Therefore, transfer of such a "lesser interest" does not transfer "all substantial rights" to the patent the entirety of each property right evidenced by the patent.

The Secretary has broad authority to promulgate reasonable regulations to implement the revenue laws, under § 7805(a) of the Internal Revenue Code of 1954, and to amend the regulations when he deems it appropriate. The Supreme Court has instructed that "Treasury regulations must be sustained unless unreasonable and plainly inconsistent with the revenue statutes...(and) should not be overruled except for weighty reasons." *Commissioner v. South Texas Co.,* 333 U.S. 496, 566, 68 S. Ct. 695, 698, 92 L. Ed. 831 (1948).

We conclude, as did the Seventh Circuit, that this regulation represents the proper interpretation of § 1235. *See Estate of Klein v. Commissioner, supra,* 507 F.2d at 621–22. We therefore determine that § 1.1235-2 of the Regulations as amended by T.D. 6852 is neither unreasonable or plainly inconsistent with § 1235.

AFFIRMED.

# E.  Retained Right to Income

## Kirby v. United States
191 F. Supp. 571 (S.D. Tex. 1960)

INGRAHAM, J.

This is an action for recovery of income taxes for the year 1953 amounting to $4,977.87, plus statutory interest, and for the year 1954 amounting to $8,502.87, plus statutory interest. Haysel Kirby is a party to this suit by virtue of the fact that she was the wife of plaintiff, John H. Kirby II, and filed a joint return with him in 1953 and 1954. The evidence was garnered and the case heard through stipulations, answers to interrogatories, requests for admissions, and undisputed testimony. The parties have submitted thorough briefs.

Plaintiff Kirby was issued a patent on a magnetic fishing tool device in 1951. This device is used to recover metallic fragments from oil wells. On May 9, 1952, he entered into an agreement with K & G Oil Tool & Service Co., Inc. (hereinafter K & G), concerning this patent and tool. The agreement (plaintiff's Exhibit 4) reads in part:

"Licensor hereby grants and conveys to Licensee the sole and exclusive right to manufacture, lease and let throughout the United States and the Dominion of Canada, the Magnetic Fishing Tool or improvements thereto."

\* \* \*

Licensor, plaintiff Kirby, was to be paid by licensee, K & G, a percentage of gross rentals as defined by the agreement. Licensee could not sell but was to rent or lease the equipment. Licensee was given the right to sue for infringement at its own expense and for its own account. The contract is to continue in force for the life of the main patent with an option in licensee to extend at the end of the term if there are patents then in existence, such as patents on improvements in the tool, and plaintiff has been issued additional patents covering improvements in the fishing tool.

Thus it is seen that by the terms of the contract licensee had the exclusive right to manufacture, lease, and let the tool within the United States and Canada. Licensee was not granted the right to "use" the tool in so many words, but a grant of such right is implicit in the agreement. K & G is a service company, owns no wells or drilling equipment as such, and consequently did not desire to "use" the equipment other than in providing its service to drillers and others who might need it. Licensee had, by the terms of the contract, no right to sell the equipment. Licensor, taxpayer, had the right to sell the device outside the United States and Canada. It might be well to observe here that it is customary in the industry to lease or rent these service tools, usually with operators. The reason for renting rather than selling being that it is more practicable and profitable for all parties concerned for a service company such as K & G to own and operate than for drillers to attempt to own, operate, and maintain a complete set of the tools.

Licensor, taxpayer, had a number of these devices manufactured in the United States, not by K & G, and sold them outside the United States and Canada, with all of the sales but one being consummated in the United States. The evidence shows that the taxpayer's income from the foreign sales almost equaled his royalty payments in 1955 and exceeded the royalties in 1956, 1957, and 1958. Under the contract, taxpayer was paid by K & G in 1953 the sum of $16,587.15 and in 1954 the sum of $26,429.78, which was the royalty equivalent to 5% Of the gross rental of the tools for each of these years.

Taxpayers duly filed their joint return for 1953 and reported the royalty of $16,587.15 as ordinary income, and income taxes were paid on that basis. After the 1954 Internal Revenue Act clarified the tax treatment of patent royalties, taxpayers timely filed claim for refund of $4,977.87 with interest, contending that the amount of $16,587.15 represented consideration for the sale of his patent and that such amount was long term capital gain rather than ordinary income.

Taxpayers duly filed their joint return for 1954 and reported the royalty received of $26,429.78 and calculated and paid the tax on a capital gains basis. The Commissioner of Internal Revenue found and assessed a deficiency in tax of $8,502.87 which taxpayers paid. Taxpayers timely filed a claim for refund of $8,502.87, with interest, contending that the amount of $26,429.78 represented consideration for the sale of his patent and that such sum was a long term capital gain, not ordinary income. Plaintiffs sue here after exhaustion of administrative remedies.

The pertinent statutory provision is Internal Revenue Code of 1939:

> Sec. 117(q) (As added by Sec. 1 of the Act of June 29, 1956, c. 464, 70 Stat. 404) Transfer of patent rights.

> (1) General rule.—A transfer (other than by gift, inheritance, or devise) of property consisting of all substantial rights to a patent, or an undivided interest therein which includes a part of all such rights, by any holder shall be considered the sale or exchange of a capital asset held for more than 6 months, regardless of whether or not payments in consideration of such transfer are

> (A) payable periodically over a period generally coterminous with the transferee's use of the patent, or

> (B) contingent on the productivity, use, or disposition of the property transferred.

26 U.S.C.A. Sect. 117(q).

Internal Revenue Code of 1939, Sec. 117(q), supra, governs the year 1953. Internal Revenue Code of 1954, Sec. 1235, 26 U.S.C.A. § 1235, governs 1954 but is not reproduced here, because it is essentially the same as Internal Revenue Code of 1939, Sec. 117(q).

Treas. Reg. Sec. 1.1235-2 (1954 Code) provides:

> (b) All substantial rights to a patent. (1) The term 'all substantial rights to a patent' means all rights which are of value at the time the rights to the patent (or an undivided interest therein) are transferred. The circumstances of the whole transaction, rather than the particular terminology used in the instrument of transfer, shall be considered in determining whether or not all substantial rights to a patent are transferred in a transaction.

* * *

The position of taxpayer, as I conceive it, is that the licensee was granted exclusive right to manufacture, lease, let, and use the tool. That the only right not granted to licensee was the right to sell the tool in the United States or Canada. The court is told that the right to sell this particular tool is not a 'substantial' right under the statutes or the authorities hereinafter cited and discussed. That even though K & G was not granted the right to sell, in fact was prohibited from selling in the United States and Canada, taxpayer did not retain any right to sell machines manufactured in the United

States because he had no right to manufacture them in the United States or Canada. Plaintiff says that taxpayer did not 'retain' any right to manufacture and sell abroad because such right was open to all. Finally, it is taxpayer's position that I cannot look to acts transpiring in 1955 and subsequently because the contract is, they say, unambiguous in its terms.

On the other hand, the position of the government seems to be, the contract as it may, that taxpayer did manufacture or have manufactured in the United States some of these tools, that he did sell them abroad, that most of the sales were consummated in the United States, and that he did profit more by them than he did by the contract with K & G in 1956 and subsequent years. The government's position, simply stated, is that they are unable to see how rights which are demonstrably so valuable monetarily can be said to be other than 'substantial.'

The issue is whether taxpayer transferred 'all substantial rights' (Int.Rev.Code of 1939, Sec. 117(q); Int. Rev. Code of 1954, Sec. 1235) in this patent or these patents so as to qualify under these statutes for capital gains treatment.

\* \* \*

Taxpayer places considerable reliance on *Lawrence v. United States*, 5 Cir., 1957, 242 F.2d 542, a case much like the one under consideration but with important differences. The case was not reported in the district court, but apparently there were no foreign sales by the licensor such as we have here. The only right retained by the licensor in *Lawrence* was the right to sell the invention in the United States. Accordingly, the only question raised was whether the retention of that right was the retention of a substantial right. All that *Lawrence* held was that it could not be said as a matter of law that the failure of the licensor to grant to the licensee the right to sell the device involved there in the United States amounted to a failure of the licensor to transfer 'all substantial rights' to the licensee. *Lawrence* also said that "what is 'substantial' often becomes a factual question to be decided according to the facts and circumstances of each case and the peculiarities inherent in each patent." 242 F.2d 542, at 545. The substantiality of the right to manufacture for foreign sales was not determined there, nor was the right to make foreign sales treated.

I think that plaintiff might agree that had he retained the right, on the face of the contract, to manufacture this tool in the United States for sale abroad that this retention would be the retention of a "substantial right" in the patent, thus disqualifying him for capital gains treatment. But plaintiff insists that I cannot look at the actual manufacture here, for sale abroad, to get at the meaning of an unambiguous contract entered into long before. Plaintiff cites a number of authorities to the effect that subsequent events are not competent to determine whether taxpayer retained any substantial rights under his contract of May 1952. Plaintiff misconceives the relevance of the manufacture here with sales abroad. I consider these sales abroad solely to arrive at whether the rights retained by licensor-taxpayer are "substantial rights" within the meaning of Internal Revenue Code of 1939, Sec. 117(q), and Internal Revenue Code of 1954, Sec. 1235. I think they are. As pointed out above the terms of the contract seem to preclude the manufacture of the tools in this country by the taxpayer, and plaintiff says the contract is unambiguous. But surely plaintiff would not insist that taxpayer might have manufactured and sold the tools in the United States under this contract and then said to the government that he should get capital gain treatment on the royalties from K & G because the contract said he could not manufacture and sell the tools in the United States. The court is not varying the terms of the contract, but is simply looking at what taxpayer actually retained, and it sees that he retained "substantial rights."

On this point, looking to subsequent acts of the parties to arrive at what rights were in actuality transferred and what retained, taxpayer relies very heavily on *Wing v. C.I.R.*, 8 Cir., 1960, 278 F.2d 656. Taxpayer quoted the following from that opinion at page 661:

> It seems to be the contention of the Commissioner that subsequent acts of the parties in granting limited license agreements to various parties had the effect of transforming the assignment from Wing to Parker into a license. By no subsequent act was there reinvested in Wing any substantial right in the patents and Wing's joining with Parker in these sublicenses, whether required by the sublicensee or by Parker, was not inconsistent with his contract assigning all substantial rights in his patents to Parker. The payment of royalties, as pointed out in *Watson v. United States, supra,* was a part of the compensation received by Wing for assigning all his substantial rights in the patents to Parker.

A complete reading and understanding of the quoted passage and the whole case will demonstrate that taxpayer's reliance is misplaced. The gist of the passage is that in *Wing* the subsequent acts did not transform a sale by contract into a license; neither the passage quoted nor the case said that subsequent acts could not transform a sale into a license. In fact the case and passage seem to demonstrate very clearly just what taxpayer says is not true, and that is, that I may look to subsequent acts of the parties to ascertain just what rights were actually retained. Further as to *Wing* the court states in the passage quoted that licensor's joining with licensee in the sublicenses 'was not inconsistent with his contract.' The acts of Kirby, manufacturing the tools in the United States and selling them abroad, were, it seems to me, inconsistent with his contract.

Taxpayer says that Congress has indicated that the substance of each transaction should be looked to rather than the form in arriving at whether all substantial rights have been transferred. S.Rep.No. 1622, 83d Cong., 2d Sess. 439–40 (1954). I agree. Taxpayer then says that the court cannot look to the foreign sales in arriving at whether all substantial rights were transferred. I do not agree. Taxpayer says that this legislation is to be liberally construed and cites cases which say just that. However liberally construed, this statute says that the patentee must transfer all substantial rights to be eligible for capital gain treatment. What is substantial is often a question of fact as here. *Lawrence v. United States, supra.* It would seem that had Congress meant for all transfer of interests in patents to receive capital gain treatment, they would have said so. So, the court is still faced with deciding in each case whether all substantial rights were transferred. The right which gives us trouble here is the right of licensor to manufacture the patented device in the United States, or have it manufactured, and sell it abroad; a right he most certainly exercised whether he retained it on the face of the contract or not. As the figures in footnote one demonstrate, taxpayer's net profit from foreign sales in the period from 1955–1958 was $121,372.41. How such monetary gain can be labeled other than 'substantial' is beyond the court's understanding. Taxpayer's manufacturing and selling abroad was by the standard of pecuniary return plainly a "substantial right." I so find it to be substantial within the meaning of Internal Revenue Code of 1939, Sec. 117(q), and Internal Revenue Code of 1954, Sec. 1235. Although not precisely in point factually, yet the rationale of *American Chemical Paint Co. v. Smith*, D.C.E.D. Pa. 1955, 131 F. Supp. 734, supports this result. It is believed that an examination of the entire transaction, irrespective of verbal touchstones in the May 1952 contract, compels this conclusion; such a realistic test, buttressed on acts, is called for by S. Rep. No. 1622, 83d Cong. 2d Sess. 439–40 (1954). Had taxpayer Kirby, like Lawrence, in fact divested himself of the right to manufacture for sale abroad, the two cases would be almost identical on their facts. But Kirby manufactured, or had manufactured, in the United States these devices, and he sold them in foreign countries. Therein the facts of the cases are different and reach a different result.

It follows that plaintiffs are not entitled to recover. Judgment will be entered for defendant with costs. The clerk will notify counsel to draft and submit judgment accordingly.

---

# F.   Application of Tax Rules in Technology Transfers

## Federal Taxation of Software Technology Transfers (Part I)*

Marc Gordon Blatt

12 No. 7 COMPUTER LAW. 1 (1995)

* * *

### Characterizing Transfers of Intellectual Property Rights

Determining whether compensation received for the transfer of an intellectual property right will be taxed as ordinary income or as capital gain generally depends upon resolution of the following issues: (1) whether the intellectual property right constitutes a capital asset or Sec. 1231 asset (generally, this section provides capital gains treatment for recognized gains on transfers of certain property used in a trade or business if Sec.1231 gains exceed Sec. 1231 losses in a taxable year and ordinary loss treatment if Sec. 1231 losses exceed Sec. 1231 gains); (2) whether the transferred right was sold or merely licensed; and (3) whether the intellectual property was held for a period of more than one year prior to the transfer. The sale of a capital asset or Sec. 1231 asset, held by the taxpayer for over one year prior to the transfer, will ordinarily qualify for the more generous capital gains rates under Sec. 1(h).

Patents, copyrights, and trade secrets each constitute transferable property rights. However, as discussed below, various Code provisions come into play when determining whether long-term capital gains treatment is available for transfers of intellectual property. The focus, for characterization purposes, is on the intentions of the parties as evidenced by the terms and conditions of the contractual agreement. This analysis requires consideration of the contract's language in its entirety. The courts and the Internal Revenue Service (hereinafter the Service) consider the federal tax treatment of both copyrights and trade secrets to be similar in most respects to patents for characterization purposes. Therefore, the rules for determining whether a patent constitutes a capital asset provide the logical starting point for purposes of this analysis. However, the practitioner should keep in mind that each asset to be transferred in the transaction must be characterized separately for tax purposes.

### Characterizing Patent Transfers Under Sec. 1235

The analysis for determining whether a patent transfer will be characterized as a capital gain should begin with Sec. 1235 (generally, this section provides a safe-harbor capital asset characterization for patent transferors). A patent, for purposes of this section, "means a patent granted under the provisions of Title 35 of the United States

---

* Reprinted with permission of the publisher, copyright 1995.

Code, or any foreign patent granting rights generally similar to those under a United States patent." The requirements for Sec. 1235 capital asset characterization are set out as follows:

(a) General-A transfer (other than by gift, inheritance, or devise) of property consisting of all substantial rights to a patent, or an undivided interest therein which includes a part of all such rights, by any holder shall be considered the sale or exchange of a capital asset held for more than 1 year, regardless of whether or not payments in consideration of such transfer are

(1) payable periodically over a period generally coterminous with the transferee's use of the patent, or

(2) contingent on the productivity, use, or disposition of the property transferred....

Thus, a transfer by a patent "holder," satisfying all other requirements under Sec. 1235, will receive capital gains treatment regardless of whether the patent's holding period exceeds one year and irrespective of the method of payment employed or consideration to be received. Section 1235's applicability depends upon whether: (1) the transferor satisfies the "holder" requirement; and, if so, (2) whether a transfer of "all substantial rights" to the patent, or an "undivided interest" of all such rights, has transpired.

### The Sec. 1235 "Holder" Requirement

Qualification as a Sec. 1235 "holder" is restricted solely to individuals. Section 1235(b)(1) defines a "holder" as "any individual whose efforts created" the patentable invention. The original creator of a patented invention will always satisfy this requirement since individuals invent, not companies or employers. Individual inventors will satisfy this requirement irrespective of their status as professional inventors. Additionally, Sec. 1235(b)(2) extends the definition of a "holder" to include, subject to certain limitations, any individual who has acquired a complete or undivided interest in a patent for "money or money's worth paid to" the inventor. Employers who purchase patentable inventions from their employees may or may not qualify as a "holder" depending upon the facts and circumstances surrounding both the employment and the transfer of the invention. On the other hand, neither the Internal Revenue Code nor the treasury regulations restrict a transferee, having received patents created pursuant to an independent contractor relationship, from qualifying as a Sec. 1235 "holder."

Employers who compensate the original inventor, under an "employment to invent" agreement, are barred from Sec. 1235 "holder" status. However, payments made by an employer to an employee that "are attributable to the transfer of patent rights, [unrelated to employment services and having satisfied] all other...section 1235...[requirements, will] be treated [by the Service] as proceeds derived from the sale of a patent." This raises the issue as to whether an employer, possessing a "shop-right" in the employee's invention, will qualify as a "holder" upon subsequent acquisition of a complete or an undivided interest in the invention.

The regulations under Sec. 1235 state that determination of "whether payments... [by an employer to] an employee...are attributable to...[an employee's] transfer...of all substantial rights to a patent or are compensation for services rendered is a question of fact." Therefore, an employer's subsequent purchase of the patent's exclusive rights should qualify the employer as a "holder" so long as the transfer was not contemplated under the terms of the employment agreement or as part of any other agreement involving services between the employer and his employee.

Additionally, "holder" status under Sec. 1235(b)(2) requires satisfaction of the following: (1) the acquisition must occur prior to the patentable invention's "actual reduction to practice"; and (2) the acquiring individual cannot be "related" to the inventor. The term "actual reduction to practice" has the same meaning as it does under Sec. 35 U.S.C.A. 102(g).

Generally, an invention is reduced to practice when it has been tested and operated successfully under operating conditions. This may occur either before or after application for a patent but cannot occur later than the earliest time that...commercial exploitation of the invention occur. In relation to software development, whether a patentable process has been reduced to actual practice should focus upon the debugging, compiling, and final state of the program—i.e., the program's intended interactive purpose and contemplated storage medium. For example, a software patent, involving a program intended to be utilized as firmware within a computer, having successfully been debugged, compiled, and run from the computer's hard drive, should not be considered to have actually been reduced to practice since the "mask work" process has not been completed—i.e., the "mask work" procedure may result in errors or reduction in the efficiency required for successful operation of the entire process. Upon qualifying as a "holder" for Sec. 1235 purposes, the final step is to determine whether the transfer satisfies the "all substantial rights of value" requirement.

### Interpreting 'All Substantial Rights of Value'

In order for a patent transaction to be considered a transfer of "all substantial rights of value" the transferor must transfer all valuable rights granted to the patent holder by law and must not have retained any rights of value. A transfer of an equal and undivided fractional interest in all substantial rights to a patent will also satisfy this requirement. When drafting a proposed patent transfer under Sec. 1235, the practitioner must take great care to avoid the retention of valuable rights. However, a transferor's reservation of rights, having no practical or material value, in the aggregate, at the time of entering into the agreement, will not defeat the transaction's characterization as a sale.

The principal rights granted under patent law are the right to exclude others from manufacturing, using, or selling the patent's subject matter. An exclusive license of all principal rights granted for an entire patent, without reservation, satisfies this requirement. However, any agreement that reserves for the transferor the right to terminate the transfer "at will" is considered the retention of a substantial right of value. Examples of rights that may be retained by the transferor are: (1) "the retention...of legal title for purposes of securing performance or payment by the transferee in a transaction involving [an] exclusive license" of the patent's principal rights over its lifetime; and (2) the transferor's "retention...of rights in the property...not inconsistent with the passage of ownership, such as the retention of a security interest ([e.g.,] a vendor's lien), or by a reservation of a condition subsequent ([e.g.,] a provision for forfeiture on account of nonperformance)." Additionally, "shop-rights" have been determined not "to dilute the [inventor's] 'substantial rights of value' within the meaning of [Sec. 1235]."

Transfers that are limited geographically within an area constituting less than the patent's entire country of issuance, or restricted to specific fields-of-use (where the transferor retains, at the time of the transfer, other valuable fields protected under the same patent), or limited to less than the remaining statutory life of the patent are not considered to be transfers of all substantial rights of value. Therefore, an attempt to restrict a transfer in any of the above-described methods will defeat Sec. 1235 capital asset status.

Finally, absolute rights to prohibit a transferee's sublicensing or subassignment of the patent or "failure to convey the right to use or sell the patent…" to the transferee, depending upon the overall facts and circumstances of the transaction, may or may not prevent qualification as a transfer of all substantial rights of value. A transfer of "all substantial rights of value" by a Sec. 1235 "holder" will qualify the patent transfer as a Sec. 1235 capital asset. However, failure to satisfy the requirements under Sec. 1235 does not preclude the possibility of capital gains treatment under Secs. 1221 and 1231.

### Characterizing Patent Transfers Under Secs. 1221 and 1231

Section 1221 defines the term "Capital Asset." In general, a patent may, subject to certain limitations, qualify as a capital asset under Sec. 1221. Akin to Sec. 1235, qualification for capital asset treatment is not dependent upon the transfer's method of payment—i.e., royalties based upon the productivity of the patent may still qualify as a "sale or exchange." However, Sec. 1221 specifically excludes property used in a taxpayer's trade or business if such property is includable in the taxpayer's inventory or depreciable under Sec. 167. On the other hand, non-inventory related, depreciable patents of a trade or business may still qualify as Sec. 1231 assets (generally, this section provides capital gains treatment for recognized gains on transfers of certain property used in a trade or business if Sec. 1231 gains exceed Sec. 1231 losses in a taxable year and ordinary loss treatment if Sec. 1231 losses exceed Sec. 1231 gains).

Section 167(a) permits depreciation, subject to the restrictions discussed below, for computer software that is either used in a trade or business or held for the production of income. Since Sec. 1231 asset status does not apply to property held for income production, this analysis will focus upon software used in a trade or business. Software that satisfies the conditions of Sec. 167 may be straight-line depreciated over a useful-life term of 36 months. However, not all software applications will qualify for depreciation.

Depreciable computer software generally includes programs that are "designed to cause a computer to perform a desired function." This definition, for purposes of Secs. 167 and 197, specifically excludes database type programs unless the database itself has fallen into the public domain and is incidental to the program's operation. Only noncustomized "shrink-wrap" software and "computer software that was not acquired in a transaction (or a series of related transactions) involving the acquisition of a trade or business or a substantial portion thereof," will qualify as depreciable property under Sec. 167. However, although amortizable software under Sec. 197 is excluded under Sec. 167, "amortizable section 197 intangibles…[are characterized] as property subject to the allowance for depreciation provided in section 167." Therefore, except for the above-described database programs, non-inventory software that is used in the transferor's trade or business may qualify for Sec. 1231 asset status.

As contrasted with treatment under Sec. 1235, corporations are not precluded from capital gains treatment under Secs. 1221 or 1231. On the other hand, taxpayers who are actively involved in the trade or business of selling patent rights, which quite clearly includes professional inventors, typically qualify for capital gains treatment solely under Sec. 1235 since patents will usually constitute inventory. Patents that are held by an individual or corporate taxpayer for the production of income, not used as part of its trade or business activities, may qualify as a Sec. 1221 capital asset. Additionally, Sec. 1221 capital assets and Sec. 1231 assets, as distinguished from assets treated under Sec. 1235, must be held for a period of over one year. Therefore, patents held for more than one year by amateur inventors, by investors holding patents not otherwise utilized as part of their trade or business, or by a trade or business as a non-inventory-related asset, may qualify for capital gains treatment under Secs. 1221 or 1231 upon satisfaction of the "sale or exchange" requirement.

The "sale or exchange" requirement for either of these sections is satisfied if "all substantial rights of value" to the patent have been transferred. As with Sec. 1235, the focus on "the value of the rights retained or transferred [is on] the date of the transfer" and the intent of the parties to the agreement. This analysis mirrors the "all substantial rights of value" discussion of Sec. 1235, *supra*, subject to two exceptions: (1) a transfer of an exclusive and undivided interest in a patent may be limited geographically to specific regions within the country for which the transferred patent rights exist; and (2) a transfer of an exclusive and undivided interest restricted to a patent's limited field-of-use is arguably a transfer satisfying the "sale or exchange" requirement.

The versatility of Sec. 1221 capital assets and Sec. 1231 assets, based upon their geographic divisibility, arguable field-of-use divisibility, and availability to corporations, cause Sec. 1235 to be far less desirable from a transactional perspective. An issue worth considering is whether a professional inventor will be able to successfully avoid Sec. 1235 capital gains treatment by transferring patents in a Sec. 351 non-recognition exchange and then qualify for capital gains treatment under Secs. 1221 or 1231. Failure to satisfy Secs. 1221, 1231, 1235, or 351 for software patent transfers results in characterization as a license agreement, taxable as ordinary income. However, the characterization of a patent will typically not affect the treatment of trade secrets or copyrights.

## Characterizing Transfers of Trade Secrets

Transactions involving unpatented know-how and trade secrets are not specifically covered under the Code or its regulations. However, this subject matter constitutes salable property rights and tax consequences are determined under the same rationale as patents. Although Sec. 1235 specifically addresses patents, a trade secret that is otherwise patentable may qualify as a capital asset under this provision. Additionally, know-how that is incidental to a patent takes on the characterization of the patent—especially when the patent and the trade secret are transferred within the same or related agreements and "closely interrelated as a bundle of rights." If Sec. 1235 capital asset characterization is unavailable, the next step is to analyze Secs. 1221 and 1231 to determine whether the trade secret (or know-how incident to a patent) satisfies the asset characterization requirements, the requisite holding period, and the "sale or exchange" requirement. For each of these provisions, the principle issue that must be addressed is what constitutes a transfer of "all substantial rights of value" regarding trade secret technology.

In order for a transaction involving the transfer of trade secrets to be considered a sale or exchange, the transferor must convey "the [exclusive] right to use the secret and in addition convey his most important remaining right, the right to prevent unauthorized disclosure (and effectively the right to prevent further use of the trade secret by others)." Additionally, the transferee must retain these rights for the entire economic useful life of the trade secret. A failure to establish that a trade secret will have absolutely no practical or material value upon the agreement's termination date will give rise to the presumption that a substantial right of value has been retained. Moreover, the fact that it is impossible to erase these secrets from the transferee's knowledge does not alter this conclusion since a reversionary right incorporated into an agreement will implicitly impose a legally binding duty of non-disclosure upon the transferee. Therefore, the safest approach for protecting the transaction's characterization will be to expressly transfer the trade secret in perpetuity to the transferee conditioned upon the transferee's agreement not to disclose such trade secrets except as necessary for utilization of such processes.

As with patents, transfers of trade secrets that are limited to certain geographic regions, and most probably field-of-use restrictions, may qualify for capital asset or Sec. 1231 asset treatment, but will not qualify for Sec. 1235 "capital asset" treatment. Moreover, all trade secret transfers, including those involving geographic and, most probably, field-of-use limitations, will be considered a transfer of all substantial rights of value notwithstanding the imposition of the following restrictions within the agreement: (1) a provision restricting the transferee's disclosure of the trade secret except for the purpose of manufacturing, using, selling, and licensing others within its exclusive territory so long as the transferor's purpose is to protect his own retained territorial or field-of-use rights; (2) a provision restricting a total or partial substitution of the parties to the agreement without first obtaining the transferor's consent; and (3) a condition subsequent, including force majeure clauses, calling for reversion of the subject matter upon the happening of an event beyond the transferor's control.

With regard to the transfer of trade secrets in a Sec. 351 non-recognition exchange, the Service's position is that the unqualified transfer in perpetuity of the exclusive right to use a secret process or other similar secret information qualifying as property within all the territory of a country, or the unqualified transfer in perpetuity of the exclusive right to make, use and sell an unpatented but secret product within all the territory of a country, will be treated as the transfer of all substantial rights.

However, it seems unlikely that the Service's restriction of Sec. 351 exchanges solely to transfers of secret process licenses exclusively for entire countries will withstand judicial scrutiny. In *E.I. Du Pont de Nemours v. United States*, the U.S. Court of Claims, in a case involving the transfer of non-exclusive licenses for French patents to its wholly-owned French subsidiary in exchange for stock, ruled that a valid Sec. 351 exchange may involve "dispositions [of intangible property] which are less than substantially complete...so long as control is maintained over what is transferred through the receipt of the transferee's stock." The *Du Pont* court's analysis strongly disfavors the Service's position relative to secret processes since trade secret and know-how transfers have generally been treated as akin to patents under the Code. Nevertheless, if the trade secret was developed specifically for the transferee, the Service may reasonably contend that the payments, or stock received in an attempted Sec. 351 exchange, were for services rendered and thus taxable as ordinary income. In any event, it cannot be over-emphasized that a failure to satisfy Secs. 1221, 1231, 1235, or 351 for transfers involving trade secrets results in characterization as a license taxable as ordinary income.

## Characterizing Transfers Involving Copyrights

Unlike patents and trade secrets, copyright capital asset treatment is determined solely under Secs. 1221 and 1231. Whether a copyright will qualify as "property" for the purposes of these sections depends upon the transferor's ownership interest. Sections 1221 and 1231 each preclude capital gains treatment for transferors who created the copyrighted work. The regulations provide that a taxpayer who personally "performs creative or productive work affirmatively contribut[ing] to the [copyright's] creation" in whole or in part, is deemed a creator (the "Creator" Test). Thus, individual joint work and collective work authors are denied capital gains treatment since, under copyright law, each author would be required to have contributed protectable subject matter to the work.

The regulations further exclude capital gains treatment for taxpayers who "direct[ed] and guide[ed] others in" the creation of the copyrighted work (the "Direction and Guidance" Test). This entirely eliminates Sec. 1221 and Sec. 1231 capital asset characterization for copyrights created as works made for hire. Apparently, even works held by a taxpayer, originally purchased from an independent contractor who created the work, could potentially be precluded under this restriction if the taxpayer is determined to have directed and guided the work's creation. There are no factors or "safe-harbor" rules set out in the regulations for determining how much direction or guidance is necessary to fall under this exclusion. The only transferors who will clearly fall outside this restriction will be those investors, trades, or businesses who purchased copyrights issued for software without any input regarding its development.

For those transferors whose copyrights have been held for over one year and satisfy the "property" requirements of Sec. 1221 or Sec. 1231, the transfer must also constitute a "sale or exchange." This requirement is tested under the "all substantial rights of value" standard. Except for the following discussion of copyright divisibility, the analysis discussed under patent transfers is applicable.

In *Herwig v. United States*, the United States Court of Claims ruled that the transfer of an "exclusive and perpetual grant of any one of the 'bundle of rights' which go to make up a copyright [may qualify] as a 'sale' of personal property rather than a mere license." Subsequent to the *Herwig* decision, the Service issued its own analysis of copyright divisibility based upon its understanding of the case. The Service concluded that "consideration received by a proprietor of a copyright for a grant transferring the exclusive right to exploit the copyrighted work in a medium of publication throughout the life of the copyright shall be treated as the proceeds from a sale of property" irrespective of the method of payment employed. However, this analysis is inconsistent with the copyright law and the *Herwig* decision.

The five exclusive rights granted to an owner of a copyright are not based upon the medium of publication as the Service implies in its revenue ruling. Moreover, the right to create a derivative work is not the sole right which may be severed from the other existing rights. Each of the exclusive rights granted under 17 U.S.C.A. Sec. 106 may be transferred, subdivided, owned, and enforced independent of the other. These are the rights that the court referred to as the "bundle of rights" which make up a copyright. The Service misinterpreted this language to mean that it is the authorization to create a derivative work for a specified copyright medium of publication that will constitute a sale. Although the court did state that the exclusive rights "can be exercised or purchased by...a variety of industries such as the...motion picture industry," it did not conclude that the authorized medium was the key to divisibility. The language of the *Herwig* decision specifically determined that the transfer of an exclusive right, independent of the other rights, may constitute the sale of a capital asset.

Finally, it should be noted that a transfer of a copyright interest, having failed to qualify for capital gains treatment due to the restrictions imposed under Secs. 1221(3) or 1231(b)(1), will retain its ordinary income character even if transferred under a non-recognition provision of the Code (e.g., Sec. 351). After determining the character of each intellectual property interest, the practitioner must then allocate the transaction's total consideration to each asset, tangible and intangible, to be transferred.

## Valuation of Transferred Assets

The consideration to be received by the transferor under the agreement must be allocated to each asset, tangible and intangible, separately. This allocation should be based upon objective valuations determined by an independent accounting firm, experienced in the valuation of high-technology intellectual property assets, or an intellectual property attorney's opinion, weighting each intellectual property asset, in non-dollar percentiles, in relation to the other tangible and intangible interests in the software. By comparing and weighting each asset's value to the software's overall value, each asset, tangible and intangible, can then be allocated its percentage of the total consideration received. The best method for supporting an allocation is the retention of the documentation created throughout the course of the software's life. Documentation procedures can be economically feasible if developed to focus upon the most valuable intellectual property protections available. The project plan should require the retention of the following types of developmental records: (1) flowcharts and other working papers; (2) plans; (3) surveys and test results; (4) commercial feasibility studies; and (5) copyright and patent information (including prior art validity searches). Documentation "should be maintained in such a way as to qualify as business records under... [Rule 803(6) of the Federal Rules of Evidence]." Moreover, besides creating the foundation for valuation and allocation, proper documentation during the life of the software is tantamount to preserving the client's legal rights against infringement.

The taxpayer has the burden of proof that an allocation to a capital asset was proper. Additionally, a transaction involving both software and technical services requires the value of the services to be separately allocated unless they are determined to be "ancillary and subsidiary" to the intellectual property rights being transferred. Services deemed to be "ancillary and subsidiary" to assignments of intellectual property take on the character of the transferred rights—i.e., the "sale or exchange" of a capital asset or a license.

"Start-up" services rendered to assist a transferee in sophisticated technology will most probably be considered "ancillary and subsidiary." The more sophisticated the technology, the more likely services will be characterized as "ancillary and subsidiary" to the technology; whereas, payment for "[c]ontinuing technical assistance after start-up" will ordinarily be treated as compensation for professional services and therefore, allocated separately as services income. However, technical services after start-up, determined to be insignificant in value, take on the nature of the transferred technology and are not required to be separately allocated.

The practitioner should always bear in mind that a substantial valuation misstatement may cause the client to be liable for the "Accuracy Related" penalty under I.R.C. Sec. 6662 in addition to the understated tax obligation. Moreover, the practitioner, appraiser, and tax preparer may each be subject to a penalty for "aiding and abetting" understatements of tax liability if the valuation and allocation was knowingly calculated to result in the understatement of the client's tax liability.

---

# Federal Taxation of Software Technology Transfers (Part II)*

Marc Gordon Blatt

12 No. 8 COMPUTER LAW. 17 (1995)

\* \* \*

---

\* Reprinted with permission of the publisher, copyright 1995.

## International Tax Considerations

International transactions involving computer software have become quite common due to the ever-expanding international high technology community. In addition to characterization, valuation, and allocation issues which are relevant when addressing U.S. domestic and U.S. international tax laws, specific tax provisions must further be assessed when evaluating an international software transaction. The following discussion will first focus upon the "source of income" rules relating to United States taxation of foreign persons and the availability of "foreign tax credits" (hereinafter FTCs) for U.S. taxpayers. Next, the issue as to whether foreign software transferors will be subject to United States taxation will be discussed. Finally, the availability of FTCs to U.S. taxpayers for foreign taxes imposed upon international software transactions will be evaluated. Although an in-depth analysis of U.S. Tax Treaties is beyond the scope of this article, the practitioner should always determine whether a tax convention is in effect since nonresident tax consequences (including withholding requirements) may be reduced and the availability of FTCs may be precluded.

## Sourcing Income from International Transactions

The general rule for sourcing sales of personal property, including intangibles, is that income shall be sourced in the seller's country of residence. The definition of an intangible includes patents, copyrights, and trade secrets. Payments in consideration for the "sale or exchange" of technology, not contingent upon the productivity, use, or disposition of the computer software, are sourced under the general rule. However, "to the extent such payments are so contingent, the source of such payments shall be determined...as if [they] were royalties." Therefore, a software transaction may still be sourced, in whole or in part, as a royalty notwithstanding the characterization of the transfer as a "sale or exchange" of capital assets.

Royalties are sourced in the country where the intellectual property protections exist. Thus, foreign technology is sourced outside the United States under Sec. 862(a)(4); whereas, United States technology is sourced within the United States under Sec. 861(a)(4). It should be noted that a computer software transaction may still constitute a royalty, notwithstanding a "lump-sum" payment, if it is determined that the payment was based upon the software's productivity, use, or disposition. Additionally, technical assistance services income, unless ancillary to the technology transfer, will be sourced in the country where performed.

The allocations for the sale of the computer software, including both tangible property and its related technology, must each be sourced separately.

Additionally, gain from the sale of an intangible which is attributable to depreciation is to be proportionately allocated between the amount depreciated under U.S. and foreign tax law(s) under Sec. 865(c)(1), but gain in excess of depreciation is not to be sourced as inventory under Sec. 865(c)(2). In light of the rules for determining the source of income for intangibles, the U.S. tax consequences for nonresident aliens as transferor's of computer software may now be addressed.

## U.S. Tax Consequences for Nonresident Aliens

Generally, a nonresident alien or foreign corporation, not engaged in a U.S. trade or business, is subject to a thirty percent tax on gross income derived from all "fixed or determinable annual or periodical" income (commonly referred to as FDAP income). A nonresident alien is a foreign corporation or an individual who is neither a U.S. citizen nor a U.S. resident. However, a nonresident alien individual may elect to be taxed as a U.S. resident.

U.S. citizens and U.S. residents are generally taxed upon their worldwide income. If a nonresident has an office or is otherwise engaged in a U.S. trade or business to which the income received under the technology transfer is "effectively connected," then U.S. resident tax treatment may result for all U.S.-sourced income, including FDAP income, sales or exchanges of capital assets, and any other income, gain, or loss from sources within the United States. Additionally, software royalties sourced outside the United States may be taxable to a nonresident alien if the alien has an office or other fixed place of business within the United States to which that income is attributable.

Focusing on nonresidents not otherwise actively engaged in a U.S. trade or business, FDAP income does not generally include gains from the sale or exchange of capital assets. However, transfers involving U.S. patents, copyrights, or trade secrets not otherwise taxable as "effectively connected income" under Sec. 864(c)(1) are subject to a 30 percent tax to the extent gains are contingent upon the productivity, use, or disposition of the technology—i.e., U.S.-source "royalties." "[I]f more than 50 percent of the gain...for any taxable year...is [attributable to such] payments, [the entire] gain...from the sale or exchange of such property or interest" thereof, is taxable as FDAP income. Therefore, the practitioner must take great care in advising a client of the potential characterization consequences for U.S.-sourced technology when determining whether payments should be based upon the technology's productivity, use, or disposition.

The mechanisms for assuring recovery of income taxes are the withholding provisions set out in Secs. 1441 and 1442. Typically, the transferee, whether an individual or corporation, will be required to deduct and withhold a flat tax of 30 percent of the gross amount paid for the technology. This requirement can be substantially burdensome upon the transferor since the amount withheld may far exceed the tax owed. Moreover, the withholding requirement may significantly reduce the availability of the cash resources necessary to maintain a competitive edge in developing future software technology.

Apparently, only four realistic alternatives are available for avoiding the withholding requirements: (1) satisfy the requirements for U.S. resident status and be subject to worldwide taxation; (2) operate a U.S. branch which actively and independently negotiates the technology transfer; (3) create a wholly-owned U.S. subsidiary corporation which actively and independently negotiates the technology transfer; or (4) base the consideration received under the transaction upon a fixed valuation of the software's intellectual property rights, not upon the productivity, use, or disposition of the technology. Alternative four is the only solution that does not involve external considerations.

Alternative one requires an analysis of whether the deductions and credits available to the nonresident would sufficiently offset U.S. taxation of its worldwide income. Both alternatives two and three require a business and tax analysis as to whether it is economically feasible and practicable to expand the client's business operations into the United States. However, alternative four sources the transaction outside the United States and therefore, absent the prior existence of alternatives one, two, or three, no U.S. tax or withholding will be imposed. For transactions that cannot be structured under alternative four, either of the three other alternatives discussed may provide for the availability of an FTC for purposes of offsetting U.S. taxable dollars.

## Foreign Tax Credits for U.S. Taxpayers

In the absence of an applicable U.S. tax treaty that eliminates the foreign tax, an FTC may be available as a method of reducing or eliminating the double taxation of a U.S. taxpayer's income—i.e., taxation by both the United States and a foreign country. This credit may be available, upon election, to U.S. citizens, U.S. corporations, U.S. residents, and certain qualified nonresident alien taxpayers. FTCs will be denied for taxes imposed by any foreign country to which the U.S. government has severed relations for political, economic, or military defense purposes.

The total number of FTCs available for offsetting U.S. taxes are limited to the extent the taxpayer's proportionate share of foreign source taxable income bears to his entire worldwide taxable income. Moreover, eight specific categories of income must be separated and segregated from each of the other categories and from all other income not specifically addressed under Sec. 904(d). This process is commonly referred to as "basketing." FTCs generated in one basket can typically only be used to offset taxes generated from income in that particular basket. All income not falling into one of the specifically listed categories is placed into the residual "general limitation" basket—this ninth basket includes foreign active trade or business income. The relevant baskets for the purposes of this discussion are the "passive income" and "general limitation" baskets. The FTC limitation calculation, which must be calculated separately for each basket, is determined by multiplying the total U.S. income tax owed, based upon the taxpayer's worldwide taxable income, by the product of the total foreign sourced taxable income allocated to a specific basket over the taxpayer's worldwide taxable income. Additionally, special mechanical rules regarding personal exemptions and capital gains must be followed when determining the taxpayer's Sec. 904(a) worldwide and foreign sourced "taxable income."

"Passive income" is defined as any income which, subject to certain exceptions, qualifies as "foreign personal holding company" income under the rules for controlled foreign corporations. Foreign sourced royalties and net capital gains, not otherwise derived from the taxpayer's active trade or business, must be placed in the "passive income" basket unless subject to the "high-tax kick-out" exception discussed below. Any income derived from the taxpayer's active trade or business, not involving a related person, is placed into the general limitation basket. Specifically, transfers of technology characterized as Sec. 1231 assets or royalties based upon technology that the taxpayer "has developed, created, or produced, or has acquired and added substantial value to," under circumstances where the taxpayer is regularly engaged in these activities, are considered to be derived from the active trade or business of the taxpayer. The importance of the general limitation basket FTC cannot be overemphasized—e.g., FTCs generated under the general limitation basket may be used to offset the taxpayer's entire U.S. taxable income on a dollar-for-dollar basis; whereas FTCs generated under the passive limitation basket may only be used to offset the taxpayer's passive U.S. taxable income.

The "high-tax kick-out" exception places any foreign sourced "passive income" into the "general limitation" basket if such income was subject to foreign income taxes in excess of "the highest rate of tax specified in section 1 or 11 (whichever applies) multiplied by the amount of such income (determined with regard to section 78)."

Upon basketing each separate component of the foreign sourced technology (i.e., copyrights, patents, and trade secrets) and calculating their respective FTCs, the taxpayer may then use the available FTCs under each basket to offset its respective U.S. taxes on a dollar-for-dollar basis. Prior to concluding this discussion, there is one potential trap for the unwary that must now be factored into the tax analysis regarding software technology transactions—the Sec. 1253 "franchise" dilemma.

### "Franchise" Characterization of Software Transfers

In June of 1994, the U.S. Court of Federal Claims unleashed a "Pandora's box" upon software technology transferors when it decided *SyncSort, Inc. v. The United States* [31 Fed. CI. 545 (June 24, 1994)]. SyncSort, from 1979 through 1985, was a software company "principally...engaged in the business of marketing and leasing or licensing" a computer database "sort" program in the U.S. domestic market. Upon being approached by four foreign computer consulting firms, SyncSort entered into licensing agreements with all four firms. In general, the agreements "granted each of the four licensees, *inter alia*, an exclusive license within a specified geographic area to promote, advertise, duplicate, use, sublicense, and sublease the...Program." Additionally, rights involving trade secrets, "licensed technology," and the "SyncSort" trademark were transferred in each license agreement. Payments received in consideration for each license were to be calculated based upon a fixed royalty ranging from 25 to 50 percent of the licensee's gross revenues. For each of the challenged tax years (1979 through 1985), SyncSort claimed "long-term capital gains" for payments received under the agreements. The Service disputed the characterization and claimed, quite possibly enlightened by the taxpayer's filings, that the payments were ordinary income based on Sec. 1253.

The Claims Court determined that Sec. 1253 requires the following bifurcated analysis: (1) the court must determine whether a transfer of a franchise is involved[;] and [if so,] (2) whether the [transferor] maintained the requisite 'power, right, or continuing interest with respect to the subject matter of the franchise.' Section 1253(b)(1) defines a "franchise" as follows:

> The term "franchise" includes an agreement which gives one of the parties to the agreement the right to distribute, sell, or provide goods, services, or facilities, within a specified area.

Clearly, as the court quickly determined, an exclusive license for a specific geographic area to distribute the program falls within this liberal definition. Moreover, it is difficult to imagine any exclusive license, sale, or exchange agreement involving geographically restricted technology transfers that would not satisfy these requirements. It is the second requirement (the "Significant Power" test) that imposes some restraint upon this characterization.

A transferor, under Sec. 1253(b)(2), will have retained a "significant power, right, or continuing interest" upon the existence of, but not limited to, the following rights:

(A) A right to disapprove any assignment of such interest, or any part thereof.

(B) A right to terminate at will.

(C) A right to prescribe the standards of quality of products used or sold, or of services furnished, and of the equipment and facilities used to promote such products or services.

(D) A right to require that the transferee sell or advertise only products or services of the transferor.

(E) A right to require that the transferee purchase substantially all of his supplies and equipment from the transferor.

(F) A right to payments contingent upon the productivity, use, or disposition of the subject matter...transferred, if such payments constitute a substantial element under the transfer agreement.

The *SyncSort* court ruled that the taxpayer had retained significant rights based upon its determination that each license agreement specifically retained the rights described in subsections (A), (C), (D), and (F) of Sec. 1253(b)(2). Furthermore, the court refused to segregate and separately allocate the program, licensed technology, and trade secrets as capital assets. It ruled that, based upon Sec. 1253's legislative history and the specific treatment of patents under Sec. 1235, only trademarks, trade names, and "Sec. 1235" patents were to be excluded from the "transfer of a franchise" language. However, neither the legislative history of Sec. 1253 nor any specific statute under Title 26 require the exclusion of other types of intangible assets that are otherwise connected with the "transfer of a franchise." The court then proceeded to grant summary judgment in favor of the Service and ruled that all of the payments received by SyncSort were taxable as ordinary income.

Although the *SyncSort* case and the Code itself provide little guidance as to how the "Significant Power" test should be evaluated when drafting a technology transfer, it is clearly in the client's best interest, based upon the language and legislative history of Sec. 1253, to treat the retention of any of the listed rights as the retention of a "significant power." More importantly, the court's determination that copyrights, non-Sec. 1235 patents, and non-Sec. 1235 trade secrets are not severable from Sec. 1253 emphasizes the necessity for structuring the transaction in this manner. The practitioner should advise his client that, due to the uncertainty of the law as to proper application of this section to technology transfers, no guarantee regarding a favorable ruling by the Service or the courts is possible. Absent the issuance of new Sec. 1253 regulations (or case law) specifically addressing the application of the "significant power" test to technology transfers, Sec. 1253 represents a quagmire for the knowledgeable practitioner, but more importantly, a potentially devastating trap for the unwary.

\* \* \*

# III. Intellectual Property Holding Companies[1]

## A.  Introduction

The topic of intercompany licensing of intellectual property ("IP") is one of the most debated areas among multinational corporations, transfer pricing economists, tax advisors, and tax authorities worldwide. Initially, it may seem strange that there is so much controversy surrounding intercompany licensing since IP is essentially being licensed between related companies. However, the main driver of scrutiny stems from a company's ability to move intercompany profits (through intercompany licensing of IP) to another country or state, which can influence their overall state and federal effective tax

---

1. This sub-section was drafted by Christopher Desmond at Ceteris, Inc. in Chicago, IL. The editors are deeply grateful for this contribution.

rate and corresponding payments. In some instances, a slight change in the intercompany license can mean millions of dollars in savings though tax rate arbitrage. As a result, tax authorities in the U.S., foreign, and state jurisdictions have assembled laws and guidelines to regulate intercompany licensing of IP. This section will focus on the core components of intercompany pricing for the licensing of IP as well as an overview of the implications that may arise in the U.S. federal and state levels.

### How is intercompany IP defined?

IP, by its very nature, is unique and thus causes controversy among taxpayers and tax authorities relative to its evaluation. Because these complexities multiply when IP is examined on an intercompany basis, it is important to define what "IP" is from an intercompany licensing perspective. The U.S. Treasury Regulations under Section 1.482 ("Section 482") were created as guidance on the federal level to determine if intercompany transfers (including licensing of IP) are being charged at as arm's length (i.e., what an unrelated party would have paid under similar circumstances). Within Section 1.482(b), the usual examples of IP are identified to include: patents, copyrights, trademarks, brand names, formulae, franchises, etc. Within Section 482, other examples of IP are touched upon such as managerial know-how, a supply or distribution network, or a well executed internal process. An additional source of intercompany IP identification stems from Internal Revenue Code Section 936 (h)(3) B-C. Under this section the usual suspects are also discussed, but also include other types of IP such as a franchise, contract, method, program, system, procedure, campaign, survey, study, forecast, estimate, customer list, and technical data. Both lists are not exhaustive and are open to interpretation. In fact, Section 482 states that an intangible is something that "derives its value not from its physical attributes but from its intellectual content or intangible properties."

### Where is IP within a company?

Once IP is defined, a common question is how one identifies IP within a company. There are typical places within a company where IP resides. A good starting point would be within a company's legal department. Often, this group already has a detail catalogue of the trademarks, patents, and other core IP. Once this is complete, the real investigative work begins relative to uncommon IP (e.g., methods, systems and procedures) that adds to a company's bottom line and perhaps drives profits. To help identify the non-typical IP, interviewing management in functions typically associated with IP-creating activities such as manufacturing, R&D, engineering, marketing, and IT are a great source. These interviews will typically lead to much of the core IP within a company.

An investigation must be extensive in order to minimize risk. There have been many disputes when a tax authority claims the existence of IP that the taxpayer either ignored or felt was of insignificant value. At a minimum, a company has to keep informal records of the IP they feel is significant, otherwise dispute and tax penalties may arise.

### What is the value of the IP?

After the IP is identified, the next logical question is the value of the intercompany IP. Under Section 482, there are several specified methods for valuing intangibles: the comparable uncontrolled transaction (CUT) method, the comparable profits method (CPM), and the profit split method (which allows for either a comparable profit split method or residual profit split method). Most practitioners that value intercompany IP would agree that the best method usually involves internal CUTs (comparable agreements that the company has with third parties for the same IP) or external CUTs (publicly available license agreements between two unrelated parties for similar IP). Practitioners utilize one or more of these methods to determine arm's length consideration for the intercompany licensing of IP.

Typically, intercompany licensing agreements are structured in a manner whereby the licensee pays one royalty rate as a percentage of net sales. However, sometimes a company will not assemble the agreement to account for variances in net sales, units of production, or some other measure of business activity changes. While this fact is often overlooked when developing intercompany royalties, it may have important tax ramifications over time. For instance, an economic downturn within an industry may depress a licensee's operating margins and create post-royalty losses if a constant royalty rate is administered. On the other hand, if the royalty was implemented using a step-royalty based upon sales or units produced, these losses may be avoided. This type of royalty rate structure often reduces problems for a company as their business changes over time.

It is also important to note that when a third-party negotiates a royalty rate, it is typically based upon an anticipated dollar amount of expected sales or volumes rather than a market-based royalty rate. One exception to this is franchise arrangements which often provide a royalty rate that does not consider the sales of an individual franchisee or their ability to pay. However, franchisor will often waive or defer payment of royalties until a franchisee is able to establish positive cash flows.

Even after a thorough analysis has been completed, many disputes still arise. For example, an individual patent may not have as much value compared to a portfolio of patents. By having patents groped together as a portfolio, this may prevent a competitor within a certain geographic market from "inventing around" the process to enter the market. As a result, the portfolio of patents may generate greater value than any one individual patent. For practitioners valuing intercompany IP, this is extremely important to realize because the value of a patent within a portfolio may be vastly different than individual patent found in the public record.

*How is the IP Licensed?*

Finally, it is important to determine the various options when intercompany IP is licensed. Typically there are two major categories: licensing and cost sharing. When determining the intercompany licensing structure, it is important to design and implement an appropriate strategy that incorporates the benefits and risks from both a tax and operational perspective.

The first, and most common, option is intercompany licensing by a single owner of IP. In this situation, the royalties can be collected by the one owner from the entities using the IP. For example, a company may develop a trademark within a certain geographic area and then decided to market the same trademark to other markets at a later date. The company may then charge a royalty for the intercompany license of that trademark to the licensees in other countries.

The second option is cost sharing. Under the principals of cost sharing, two or more parties agree to share in the costs of development and managing one or more intangibles in proportion to their shares of anticipated benefits. There are several concerns that companies often voice about U.S. rules related to cost sharing.

One concern is a look-back provision that compares the level of actual benefits in any year relative to the projected benefit. If, upon examination, there were no extraordinary events that could account for the differences, the Department of Treasury can make an adjustment if the divergence for a controlled participant is greater than 20 percent. Any participants outside the U.S. are treated as one controlled group under the U.S. rules. As a result, taxpayers must put in place a mechanism review the actual benefits versus the projected benefits.

Another concern is the cost base that is shared among the participants. For example, currently there is a heated court case between Xilinx Inc. and the IRS concerning whether stock option expenses should be included in the cost base. In this case, Xilinx is arguing that the IRS should bear the burden of proof concerning the cost sharing of employee stock options because it abandoned its original deficiency notice position by drastically changing both its theory and amounts at issue.[2]

Another significant component to a cost sharing agreement is a buy-in payment. A buy-in payment is typically used for the right to use pre- existing intangibles. A significant issue that must be dealt with in calculating a buy-in payment often involves the economic life, an appropriate discount rate, and its expected amortization rate (as determined using economic versus accounting conventions).

Finally, the Department of the Treasury is expected to issue newly proposed cost sharing regulations to deal with valuation issues of cost sharing.

Now that the "how," "what," and "why" of intercompany licensing of IP have been discussed, its ramifications in the U.S. are covered. There are two main areas where intercompany licensing is challenged in the U.S. from a tax perspective. The first is on the federal level and the second is on the state level. The implications of each are discussed in more detail below.

# B.  Federal Tax Implications

From the federal perspective, the aforementioned Section 482 regulations were established as a means to determine arm's length consideration for intercompany licensing of IP and other intercompany transactions. In 1994, the U.S. also issued penalties for noncompliance under the U.S. Treasury Regulations Section 1.6662 ("Section 6662"). Under Section 6662, a 20 percent penalty is imposed for net Section 482 adjustments of $5.0 million or 10 percent in net proceeds. The penalty increases to 40 percent for net Section 482 adjustments of $10.0 million or 20 percent of net proceeds. Taxpayers also are subject to a Section 6662 penalty if their transfer price is 200 percent or more or 50 percent or less of a correct transfer price.[3] "Taxpayers, however, can avoid the accuracy-related penalty if they can establish, among other things, that there was reasonable cause for the underpayment and that they acted in good faith within the meaning of section 6664(c)."[4]

In 2004, Section 482 transfer pricing allocations by the IRS totaled $8.4 billion—four times the highest level of disputed allocations filed in any single year since 1993.[5] The biggest case involved the U.S. subsidiary of GlaxoSmithKline PLC that submitted a tax court petition protesting a record-setting $7.8 billion in Section 482 adjustments by the IRS.[6] In this adjustment, the main issue was the value that marketing IP played in the promotion of drugs in the U.S. From the IRS' perspective,

---

2. *Xilinx Inc. v. Comm'r*, T.C., Nos. 4142-01 and 702-03, briefs on burden of proof filed Sept. 8, 2004.

3. The final Section 6662 regulations released 1996.

4. U.S. Treasury Regulations Section 1.6662 and Section 1.6664.

5. BNA Tax Management, Volume 13 Number 17, Wednesday, January 19, 2005.

6. *GlaxoSmithKline PLC v. Comm'r*, No. 5750-04.

GlaxoSmithKline PLC undervalued the importance of marketing in the success of the drugs in the U.S. and overstated the importance of R&D and marketing IP performed in the UK.

Recently, the Department of Treasury issued Proposed Section 482 Rules on Services and Intangibles. One of the primary concerns of these proposed regulations is that it may allow the Department of Treasury to impute legal ownership based upon the perceived control of IP. While this presumably allows for the ability to more easily separate the value of legal versus economic ownership of intangibles, the Department of Treasury may be able to impute the contractual terms between parties. As a precaution, many companies are implementing intercompany agreements and documentation for their intercompany IP transactions.

## C. State Tax Implications

From the state perspective, one of the hottest trends during the 1990's was the creation of an IP holding company (sometimes referred to as an intangible holding company "IHC"). In forming an IP holding company, the parent corporation drops down a wholly-owned subsidiary, typically incorporated in a tax-favorable state other than the state of incorporation of the parent, and assigns all the rights of its intellectual property to the newly formed entity. The operating divisions, as well as third-party licensees, pay royalties to the wholly-owned subsidiary for use of the intellectual property. The company then deducts from its state income tax the royalties paid to the IP holding company by the operating divisions, and does not report in its state income tax return the income received by the IP holding company because it was received in a different taxing jurisdiction. Moreover some states, such as Delaware, do not tax royalty income.

States such as New York, North Carolina, and Arkansas have recently enacted legislation that essentially disallows royalty expenses as a deduction within their state. In these states, taxpayers are required to add back certain royalty expenses from a related member or members pursuant to their new laws. Within each state's law, there is usually exceptions-to-the-rule where the state add-back does not apply. In fact, in certain situations, an IP holding company it is still a viable option. The article below discusses evolution of the IP holding company (referred to as an intangible property holding company ("IHC") in the article) and how, if effectively managed, can still work in the state and local level.

---

## The Intangible Holding Company: Effectively Managing Intangible Property*

Christopher Desmond & Wesley Cornwell
2004 STT 21-8
(This article originally was published in State Tax
Notes, Tax Analysts, January 29, 2004.)

Since the late 1980s, companies have increasingly sought to manage and protect their corporate intangible property through the use of an intangible property holding company (IHC). In the IHC model, some or all of a company's intangible property—for

---

* Reprinted with permission of PricewaterhouseCooper, copyright 2004.

example, trademarks and patents—regardless of which division or operating unit in which it resides, are typically transferred into a new legal entity, the IHC. The operating units, and possibly third-party licensees, then pay royalties to the IHC for the right to use the intangible property.

Increasingly, IHCs are being challenged by state taxing authorities on the ground that they have no valid business purpose and that the payments made to IHCs lack economic substance or are not arm's length. When taxpayers have been challenged in the state courts, many judgments have been against the taxpayer.

### States Challenge IHCs on Three Main Grounds

States, in their growing need for revenue, have typically attacked the IHC structure on three grounds.

First, they have argued that IHCs have no valid business purpose (a purpose other than that of reducing the company's tax liability) and that the economic substance of intercompany royalty payments is not supportable.

Second, they have argued that royalty payments are higher than those that would have been paid in arm's length transactions between unrelated corporate entities.

Finally, they have argued that even though the IHC may be based in another state and has no physical presence in the state making the claim, by collecting a royalty from a parent company or sibling operating unit that does operate within the state, the IHC has a taxable nexus to the state making the tax claim.

Few states have asserted the third ground of economic nexus; most controversies around IHCs and their tax liability focus on the first two grounds—whether there are valid business purposes and supportable economic substance for the IHC's existence, or if the intercompany royalties paid have economic substance with the arm's length standard using the guidance of Treasury Reg. section 1.482 (section 482).

### Valid Business Purpose and Economic Substance

States attacking the business purpose of IHCs argue that the transaction involving one related affiliate paying royalties to an IHC for the right to use some intangible property is a sham and has no economic substance beyond the artificial reduction of taxes by moving income from a state that imposes tax on the activity carried out in that state (production, marketing, or sales) to a state that imposes no tax (or imposes tax at a substantially reduced rate) on the activity carried out in that state (holding the intangible property).

Many state taxing authorities have made this argument, and they have often prevailed in their state courts (for example, *Syms Corp. v. Commissioner of Revenue*, Mass. App. Tax Bd., Sept. 14, 2000; *Comptroller v. SYL Inc.* and *Comptroller of the Treasury v. Crown Cork & Seal Company (Delaware) Inc.*, U.S., No. 03-566, *cert. denied* Dec. 15, 2003) Nos. 76 & 80 Md. Ct. App., June 9, 2003). State court rulings have demonstrated, however, that companies can be successful in establishing and maintaining an IHC as long as proper implementation and transfer pricing documentation has been performed. The key is showing that the IHC, in the words of the Supreme Judicial Court of Massachusetts in *Sherwin-Williams Co. v. Commissioner of Revenue* (SJC-08516, Sept. 10, 2001 to Oct. 31, 2002), is "a viable business entity…formed for a substantial business purpose or actually engaged in substantive business activity."

In dealing with Sherwin-Williams's IHC, based on the same set of facts under which the Massachusetts Supreme Judicial Court upheld the Sherwin-Williams royalty payments to its Delaware-based IHC subsidiaries, the New York State Tax Appeals Tribunal sided with the state's Division of Taxation in disallowing the arrangement and forcing Sherwin-Williams to report on a combined basis (*In the Matter of the Petition of the Sherwin-Williams Co.*, decision DTA No. 816712).

What states complain about," said Boston-based Irving H. Plotkin, an economist and the managing director of PricewaterhouseCoopers LLP's Tax and Economic Controversy Practice, "is that companies often create an intangible holding company, place the company's trade name in the holding company, then the IHC makes the company rent back the name, and that this is the only transaction that takes place. Business purpose and economic substance, a company uses the IHC for purposes other than just moving money; it should have people in the IHC specifically charged with the management of the intangible assets, engaging in third-party licensing, monitoring and fighting infringements of the intangible property, guarding against free-riding on the intangible property, etc."

### Using the Arm's-Length Standard for an IHC

Several tests have been used by taxing authorities and corporations on opposite sides of the argument to determine whether a royalty payment is arm's length based on the transfer pricing principles and methods under section 482. Some analyses focus on whether the payment being made in the intercompany transfer is comparable to payments that would have been paid by two unrelated companies through license agreements of similar intangible property, while most analyses focus on benchmarking one of the taxpayer's companies (typically not the IHC) against similar companies within the same industry. The latter analyses typically use comparables and base their suggested royalty rate on an analysis that is fundamentally argument by analogy.

Plotkin, however, has successfully used sophisticated econometric models and rate-return-analyses for establishing the propriety of intercompany royalty payments to IHCs.

"The central question," Plotkin said, "is whether it is reasonable for the entity paying the royalty to have made that payment. I'm not smart enough to know if the price (royalty rate) is right, so I ask whether the result is appropriate. This is the essential teaching of the section 482 regulations and the 'commensurate with income' legislative and regulatory standards."

In one of the most recent state decisions, *Cambridge Brands v. Massachusetts Commissioner of Revenue* (Commonwealth of Massachusetts Appellate Tax Board, July 16, 2003), Plotkin's analysis helped substantiate the business purpose and economic substance of Charm's Marketing, the trademark manager for Tootsie Roll Inc., as well as the arm's length nature of royalty payments made by Cambridge Brands, the Massachusetts manufacturer, to Charm's Marketing.

Plotkin demonstrated that Cambridge Brands earned postroyalty returns in excess of 95 percent of American industries. This convinced the Massachusetts Appellate Tax Board that economic substance existed and that the royalty rate was not excessive; Cambridge Brands' tax filing position was upheld and its intercompany royalty payment and corporate structure were respected.

### Helping Protect Your IHC

If properly structured and managed, an IHC can be a powerful tool for deriving value from intellectual property.

"The intangible property a company owns is often its most valuable asset," Plotkin said. "But state taxing authorities are becoming increasingly aggressive in seeking revenue and are loath to recognize IHCs in general, and especially those that seem to be established solely for the purpose of reducing taxes in the state."

"In the case of Cambridge Brands and Charm's Marketing, the facts were powerful. Cambridge Brands was a simple factory, with no intangibles of its own. It licensed profitable names, like Junior Mints, and the price it paid to license the names of the products it produced elevated its profitability. Finally, the names of the products were never owned by, nor promoted by, the factory itself; it was, for all intents and purposes, merely a contract manufacturer for the intangible property owner."

For companies looking to establish an IHC today or to determine if its IHC will stand up to state tax authorities' scrutiny, Plotkin believes it is possible to evaluate an IHC's status to determine whether it is performing the functions it should be in managing intellectual property and properly charging for the use of its intangibles or services. Among the points the review should focus on are:

- registration of copyrights, trademarks, patents, and other intellectual property;
- establishment of intercompany agreements;
- active participation by the IHC in protection of the intellectual property from infringement or impairment by third parties, either directly or by hiring contract services from a law or accounting firm;
- active policing by the IHC of use of the intellectual property by the related entities (for example, advertising, signage, trade dress, and store operations) as they might hurt the value of the intellectual property;
- active involvement by the IHC in licensing the intellectual property to third parties and to foreign subsidiaries;
- test the economic reasonableness of the related-party royalty charges against the arm's length standard; this is best done by observing the economics of the licensee; and
- ensure rights and costs for research and development and strategic marketing efforts attributed to the IHC are properly borne by the IHC.

With these points and contemporaneous transfer pricing documentation, a taxpayer will improve the chances of its success in operating an IHC.

---

While in certain situations it may be reasonable to implement an IHC structure, many transfer pricing and tax practitioners are implementing alternative strategies. For example, instead of licensing the IP on a stand alone basis, the IP value may be embedded within the actual intercompany sale of tangible property, or may be embedded in intercompany services provided. These structures minimize any intercompany licenses and state add-backs and are often more directly aligned with actual operational activities of the corporation and legal entities involved.

# D. Conclusion

Regardless of the ultimate determination of the value of IP, it is important to note that there are no universal conclusions among transfer pricing and tax practitioners as well as the tax authorities. Intercompany licensing of IP is case-specific, and varies across industries, companies, and time. As a result, it is important to develop an approach to identify, value, and document intercompany IP appropriately to mitigate challenges by tax authorities.

---

# E.  Recent Judicial Activity

## The Sherwin-Williams Company v. Commissioner of Revenue
### 778 N.E.2d 504 (Mass. 2002)

CORDY, J.

The Sherwin-Williams Company (Sherwin-Williams) appealed from a decision of the Appellate Tax Board (board) upholding the denial by the Commissioner of Revenue (commissioner) of its request to abate $59,445.40 in corporate excise taxes assessed for tax year 1991 and we transferred the case to this court on our own motion. The contested assessment was the result of the commissioner's disallowance of approximately $47 million that Sherwin-Williams had deducted from its taxable income for royalty payments to two wholly owned subsidiaries, Sherwin-Williams Investment Management Company, Inc. (SWIMC), and Dupli-Color Investment Management Company, Inc. (DIMC) (collectively referred to as the subsidiaries), for the use of certain trade names, trademarks, and service marks (marks), that Sherwin-Williams had transferred to the subsidiaries and licensed back as part of a corporate reorganization of its intangible assets in January, 1991. The commissioner also disallowed $80,000 that Sherwin-Williams had deducted for interest payments to SWIMC, in connection with a $7 million loan made to it by SWIMC in the fourth quarter of 1991, which was repaid in the first quarter of 1992.

After a protracted evidentiary hearing, the board found that Sherwin-Williams had not sustained its burden of establishing its entitlement to an abatement, and that the commissioner had properly disallowed the deductions on three alternative grounds: (1) the transfer and license back of the marks was a sham and could be disregarded under the "sham transaction doctrine"; (2) the royalty payments were not deductible as ordinary and necessary business expenses when there was no valid business purpose justifying the expense; and (3) G.L. c. 63, § 39A, permitted the commissioner to adjust the taxable income of Sherwin-Williams by eliminating the royalty payments because they were not made at arm's length and distorted the actual income of Sherwin-Williams. The board also affirmed the elimination of the interest expense deduction based on the commissioner's contention that Sherwin-Williams should never have paid the royalties that generated both the need to borrow money from SWIMC, and the source of the funds loaned to it.

We conclude that the board erred when it found that the transfer and licensing back transactions between Sherwin-Williams and its subsidiaries were without economic substance and therefore a sham. We also conclude that: the payment of royalties and interest to SWIMC and DIMC were properly deductible by Sherwin-Williams because obtaining licenses to use the marks was necessary to the conduct of its business; even assuming G.L. c. 63, § 39A, empowers the commissioner to eliminate payments made between a foreign parent corporation and its subsidiaries, it does so only to the extent that such payments are in excess of fair value, and in light of the substantial evidence that the royalties paid by Sherwin-Williams reflected fair value, there is no basis to support the elimination of these payments; and, because the transactions were not a sham, and the loan between SWIMC and Sherwin-Williams was genuine, interest was properly chargeable to Sherwin-Williams when it borrowed the funds and was, accordingly, properly deductible.

1. *Background.* From the uncontested evidence presented at the evidentiary hearing, we set forth the following backdrop to the issues presented for decision. Sherwin-Williams is a corporation that has manufactured, distributed, and sold paints and related products for more than 125 years. It was incorporated under the laws of the State of Ohio, and has its principal place of business in Cleveland. It manufactures and sells its products under many brand names, including its own signature brand, "Sherwin-Williams," and other brands, including "Dutch Boy," "Martin-Senour," "Kem-Tone," "Dupli-Color," and "Krylon." Sherwin-Williams also uses hundreds of marks, including the "Sherwin-Williams" trademark, several "Dutch Boy" trademarks, and "The Look that Gets the Look" slogan.

In June, 1990, one of Sherwin-Williams's attorneys suggested to Robert E. McDonald, Sherwin-Williams's senior corporate counsel for patents and trademarks, the idea of forming two subsidiary companies to hold and manage the Sherwin-Williams marks and to invest and manage royalty proceeds earned therefrom. McDonald discussed this idea with other senior corporate officials, who asked him to evaluate the potential benefits and risks of establishing such subsidiaries and transferring the Sherwin-Williams marks to them. After concluding that the potential benefits would be substantial, McDonald traveled to Delaware, along with another Sherwin-Williams employee, to meet with individuals who had experience in the management of intangible asset holding companies there. They met with lawyers, bankers, and investment managers, including Donald J. Puglisi.

Puglisi was a professor of business and finance at the University of Delaware, the founder and owner of an investment management and services firm (Puglisi and Associates), and a member of the board of directors of many investment companies and Delaware subsidiaries of foreign corporations. His expertise was principally in business management, portfolio management, and corporate finance. Puglisi and McDonald discussed how intangible asset subsidiaries might be created in Delaware to manage and protect Sherwin-Williams's marks, increase their value, and maximize the investment of royalty income. They also discussed Puglisi's expertise and interest in assisting the companies if Sherwin-Williams decided to create the Delaware subsidiaries.

Delaware was a jurisdiction with which Sherwin-Williams was very familiar, having previously established a number of corporate subsidiaries there. It afforded significant legal and tax advantages to corporations that confined their activities to holding, maintaining, and managing intangible assets. In particular, under Delaware law, royalties and other income earned by such corporations were exempt from State taxation. Del. Code Ann. tit. 30, § 1902(b)(8) (1997). These advantages were known and considered by McDonald and Sherwin-Williams in evaluating the trademark subsidiary plan.

On his return from Delaware, McDonald had further meetings with senior corporate officials, including Sherwin-Williams's chief financial officer and its general counsel, to discuss and evaluate the benefits of transferring the company's marks into separate corporations. McDonald also assessed the legal risks attendant to the transfer of the marks to ensure that it could be done without jeopardizing their continued validity. He further directed an effort to fully identify, catalogue, and document properly the hundreds of marks that Sherwin-Williams had developed or acquired during its many years of operation, including common-law trademarks that had never been recorded with the United States Patent and Trademark Office. These efforts continued over many months, culminating in the preparation by McDonald and others of a business plan for consideration by senior management, and ultimately the Sherwin-Williams board of directors, in January, 1991.

On January 23, 1991, the Sherwin-Williams board of directors voted to form SWIMC and DIMC under Delaware law, and to transfer to them all of Sherwin-Williams's domestic marks. The minutes of the January 23, 1991, board meeting set forth the reasons for the board vote, including:

(1) improvement of quality control oversight and increased efficiencies with regard to the marks by virtue of having profit centers separate from Sherwin-Williams;

(2) easier profit analysis of Sherwin-Williams by having profit centers for the marks that were separate from it;

(3) enhanced ability to enter into third-party licensing arrangements at advantageous royalty rates;

(4) increased over-all profitability because of the availability of Delaware's corporate income tax exemption for investment management and trademark holding companies;

(5) maximized investment returns associated with the marks due to separate and centralized investment management;

(6) enhanced borrowing capabilities;

(7) subsidiaries could be used in certain instances to acquire businesses;

(8) provided ability to take advantage of the well-developed body of corporate law and expeditious legal system in Delaware;

(9) insulated the marks from Sherwin-Williams's liabilities;

(10) provided flexibility in preventing a hostile takeover; and

(11) increased liquidity.

Under the board-approved plan, all of the marks affiliated with aerosol products were assigned to DIMC, and all of the marks affiliated with nonaerosol products were assigned to SWIMC. These assignments were recorded in the United States Patent and Trademark Office, and SWIMC and DIMC became the owners of the marks. Sherwin-Williams also contributed $50,000 and $42,000 respectively to SWIMC and DIMC to help finance the startup of the companies. In return, Sherwin-Williams and another of its subsidiaries, Dupli-Color Products Company, received one hundred per cent of the stock of both subsidiaries, and agreements that licensed most, but not all, of the marks back to Sherwin-Williams for ten-year terms on a nonexclusive basis. Under the licensing agreements Sherwin-Williams agreed to pay royalties to the subsidiaries quarterly, based on a percentage of the sales of the products bearing those marks. The value of the marks transferred to the subsidiaries, and fair market royalty rates, were to be determined by an independent appraisal company.

SWIMC and DIMC were incorporated in Delaware seven days after the January 23 vote. Their boards of directors first met on February 1, 1991, in Delaware. The original boards of directors of each subsidiary were comprised of the same three individuals. John Ault, the controller of Sherwin-Williams, served as chairman of both boards. Conway Ivy, a vice-president and then treasurer of Sherwin-Williams, served as the second board member. Donald Puglisi, who was not affiliated with Sherwin-Williams, served as the third member. Puglisi was elected president and treasurer. Gordon Stewart, a partner in the Delaware office of Duane, Morris, & Heckscher (who had been retained as corporate counsel to the subsidiaries), was elected secretary of both companies. At their second set of board meetings in the spring of 1991, Stewart was elected to each of the boards of directors as a fourth member. SWIMC and DIMC each agreed to pay Puglisi a salary of $18,000 annually, and each agreed to pay Stewart $500 annually. The subsidiaries had no other employees during 1991.

SWIMC and DIMC jointly executed a lease agreement with the Bank of Delaware for an office that the subsidiaries used to store records. Puglisi conducted his work as president of the subsidiaries, as well as work in connection with his other businesses, from his own office in Newark, Delaware. Puglisi and Associates charged rent to each subsidiary for the use of his office. The subsidiaries each opened bank accounts with the Bank of Delaware, and arranged for the bank to take physical custody of the marks on transfer from Sherwin- Williams. In addition to retaining independent corporate legal counsel (Stewart), the subsidiaries also retained an independent auditing firm. Routine accounting work was done by Puglisi and Associates.

The articles of organization of both SWIMC and DIMC provided that their activities would "be confined to the maintenance and management of its intangible investments." The articles also placed restrictions and prohibitions on the subsidiaries, providing that neither SWIMC nor DIMC could "lease, sell, exchange, transfer, license, assign (except to affiliates), or dispose of any of the assets of the Corporation (except for assets having a value under $2,000)," in the absence of approval by the holder of the majority of shares. In addition, neither subsidiary could pledge any of its assets without the approval of a majority of stockholders. These restrictions were reiterated in the bylaws for both corporations. The articles and bylaws were subsequently amended to eliminate stockholder approval for the licensing of the marks to conform with the subsidiaries' practice of entering license agreements without securing stockholder approval.

Once the subsidiaries had been formed, Sherwin-Williams engaged American Appraisal Associates (AAA) to appraise the value of the marks that it was transferring to the subsidiaries in exchange for their stock, and to help establish an arm's-length royalty rate for the license back of the marks it intended to use. AAA appraised the value of the marks to be $328,000,000, and recommended royalty rates ranging from one per cent to four and one-half per cent for each of Sherwin-Williams's product divisions.

After their formation SWIMC and DIMC operated as ongoing businesses, entering into nonexclusive licensing agreements with Sherwin-Williams and other unrelated licensees, receiving substantial royalty payments (principally from Sherwin-Williams), setting their own investment policies, investing their royalty income and earning a return on those investments greater than that earned on comparable funds by their parent, paying taxes, and hiring and paying professionals to audit the companies and to perform occasional quality control testing on Sherwin-Williams's products. They also hired and paid their own lawyers to represent them in multiple trademark proceedings. To assist them with the filings necessary to maintain the marks, both companies contracted with Sherwin-Williams and paid market rates on periodic invoices for the services they received. All corporate formalities were meticulously observed.

Sherwin-Williams's senior management had concerns dating as far back as 1983 regarding the maintenance and effective management of its marks because one of its marks, the "Canada Paint Company," which was to be used in a Canadian joint venture had been lost. The corporate official who had been most vocal in expressing these concerns, Conway Ivy, was put on the boards of SWIMC and DIMC when they were formed in 1991. The testimony of senior corporate managers further established that before 1991, the multiple divisions of Sherwin-Williams, its decentralized management and culture, and the use of many of the marks across divisions, created uncertain authority and diffuse decision-making regarding the maintenance and exploitation of the marks, contributing to their ineffective and inadequate management as a company asset. Finally, board members of SWIMC and DIMC and Sherwin-Williams's associate general counsel for patents and trademarks testified that these concerns had been effectively addressed by the transfer of the marks to the subsidiaries whose sole focus was on their maintenance and management.

In the proceedings before the board, the commissioner offered evidence from several experts who testified that the many nontax business reasons proffered by Sherwin-Williams for the transfer and licensing back of the marks were either illusory, unrealistic, contradictory, not achievable, or could have been better achieved by internal business adjustments rather than by creating subsidiaries and transferring valuable assets to them to be licensed back. Sherwin-Williams contested the testimony of the commissioner's experts through the testimony of its own experts. None of the commissioner's experts contended that the subsidiaries were not ongoing, profit-making businesses, engaged in business activities including and apart from the licensing of their marks to Sherwin-Williams, or that the royalty rates paid by Sherwin-Williams were outside the range of royalties that would be paid by parties acting at arm's length.

2. *Sham transaction.* Massachusetts recognizes the "sham transaction doctrine" that gives the commissioner the authority "to disregard, for taxing purposes, transactions that have no economic substance or business purpose other than tax avoidance." *Syms Corp. v. Commissioner of Revenue*, 436 Mass. 505, 509–10 (2002) (*Syms*). The doctrine generally "works to prevent taxpayers from claiming the tax benefits of transactions that, although within the language of the tax code, are not the type of transactions the law intended to favor with the benefit." *Id.* at 510, citing *Horn v. Commissioner of Internal Revenue*, 968 F.2d 1229, 1236–37 (D.C. Cir. 1992).

"The question whether or not a transaction is a sham for purposes of the application of the doctrine is, of necessity, primarily a factual one, on which the taxpayer bears the burden of proof in the abatement process." *Syms, supra* at 511. Our review of the board's factual findings is limited to whether, as a matter of law, the evidence is sufficient to support them. *Olympic & York State St. Co. v. Assessors of Boston*, 428 Mass. 236, 240 (1998). If supported by sufficient evidence, we will not reverse a decision of the board unless it is based on an incorrect application of the law. *Koch v. Commissioner of Revenue*, 416 Mass. 540, 555 (1993).

In *Syms,* we upheld a finding of the board that a transfer and licensing back of trademarks between a parent and its newly formed subsidiary was a sham transaction for taxing purposes. There, the evidence that the transaction was specifically designed as a tax avoidance scheme; royalties were paid to the subsidiary once a year and quickly returned to the parent company as dividends; the subsidiary did not do business other than to act as a conduit for the circular flow of royalty money; and the parent continued to pay all of the expenses of maintaining and defending the trademarks it had transferred to the subsidiary, fully supported the board's findings that the transaction had no practical economic effect other than the creation of a tax benefit and that tax avoidance was its motivating factor and only purpose.

The facts of the present case are substantially different. There is no evidence that the transfer of the marks to the subsidiary corporations and their licensing back to Sherwin-Williams was specifically devised as a tax avoidance scheme. The revenue earned by the subsidiaries, including the proceeds from the royalty payments made by Sherwin-Williams, was not returned to Sherwin-Williams as a dividend but, rather, was retained and invested as part of their ongoing business operations, earning significant additional income. The subsidiaries entered into nonexclusive license agreements not only with Sherwin-Williams, but also with unrelated parties. The subsidiaries assumed and paid the expenses of maintaining and defending their trademark assets. Whether the board properly applied the sham transaction doctrine to these facts requires a more rigorous analysis of the origin and purposes of that doctrine than was necessary in *Syms*.

We start with two principles first articulated by Judge Learned Hand in *Helvering v. Gregory*, 69 F.2d 809 (2d Cir.1934), the seminal case establishing the sham transaction doctrine. The first principle is: "Any one may so arrange his affairs that his taxes shall be as low as possible; he is not bound to choose the pattern which will best pay the Treasury; there is not even a patriotic duty to increase one's taxes." *Id.* at 810. Or, as stated by the United States Supreme Court in its affirmance of Judge Hand's decision: "The legal right of a taxpayer to decrease the amount of what otherwise would be his taxes, or altogether avoid them, by means which the law permits, cannot be doubted." *Gregory v. Helvering*, 293 U.S. 465, 469 (1935) (*Gregory* ). *See Knetsch v. United States*, 364 U.S. 361, 365 (1960), quoting *Gregory, supra*; *Yosha v. Commissioner of Internal Revenue*, 861 F.2d 494, 497 (7th Cir.1988) ("There is no rule against taking advantage of opportunities created by [the Legislature or revenue service] for beating taxes"). The second principle is that a transaction "does not lose its [tax] immunity, because it is actuated by a desire to avoid, or, if one chooses, evade, taxation." *Helvering v. Gregory, supra* at 810. In other words, our tax system is a rule-based system, objective in nature, that places principal importance on what taxpayers do and the economic consequences attached to those actions, not on what may have subjectively motivated them to act in the first place.

Based on these two principles, Sherwin-Williams, on initially going into business, could have organized itself in such a way that its intangible assets (e.g., its marks) were held in a corporation separate from the corporations holding its production facilities and sales operations; the corporation owning the marks could have licensed those marks to its sister corporations; and this arrangement would have been respected by taxing authorities even if the structure were motivated entirely by a desire to minimize Sherwin-Williams's over-all tax burdens. Although motivated by tax considerations, such a structure would not have been an uncommon way of doing business nor an artificial construct whose only possible effect was the avoidance of taxes. Against this backdrop, we decide what an established business enterprise must prove when it undertakes to reorganize itself to effectuate a more efficient tax structure in order that the taxing authorities recognize the reorganization for tax purposes, rather than disregard it as a sham.

The facts and holding in the *Gregory* decision are instructive on this question. In that case, the taxpayer owned all the stock of a corporation, which in turn owned 1,000 shares of a second corporation. *Gregory, supra* at 467. "For the sole purpose of procuring a transfer of these shares to herself in order to sell them for her individual profit, and, at the same time, diminish the amount of income tax which would result from a direct transfer [of the stock] by way of dividend," the taxpayer sought to bring about a business "reorganization" under the tax code. *Id.* To that end, the corporation set up a subsidiary to which the 1,000 shares of stock were transferred. All of the stock of the subsidiary were then transferred to the taxpayer on a tax free basis. Three days later, the taxpayer dissolved the subsidiary and distributed the 1,000 shares to herself on a reduced tax basis. *Id.* As the Supreme Court noted, "[n]o other business was ever transacted, or intended to be transacted, by [the subsidiary]." *Id.*

In setting aside the transaction as a sham for taxing purposes, the United States Court of Appeals for the Second Circuit and subsequently the Supreme Court disregarded the question of taxpayer's motive, focusing instead on whether the transactions were a business reorganization as contemplated by the reorganization statute or "an elaborate and devious form of conveyance masquerading as a corporate reorganization, and nothing else." *Id.* at 470. Both courts concluded that it was the latter. Although the transactions met the technical requirements of the reorganization statute, the evidence demonstrated that there was "no business or corporate purpose," and that the "sole object and accomplishment...was the consummation of a preconceived plan, not to reorganize a business or any part of a business, but to transfer a parcel of corporate shares to the petitioner." *Id.* at 469. Consequently, "the transaction upon its face [lay] outside the plain intent of the [reorganization] statute," and did not qualify for the favorable tax treatment available to such reorganizations under the statute. *Id.* at 470.

The Supreme Court further elaborated on the sham transaction doctrine in *Frank Lyon Co. v. United States*, 435 U.S. 561 (1978) (*Lyon*), in which it concluded that a sale and leaseback of real property needed to be respected for tax purposes. In *Lyon*, a bank sold a building that it was constructing to the Frank Lyon Company (company), which simultaneously leased the building back to the bank for its own use. *Id.* at 566. After the purchase and completion of construction, the company became liable on the permanent financing loan for the building, which was secured by an assignment of the bank's lease. *Id.* at 568. The company took various tax deductions and depreciation allowances premised on its ownership of the building. *Id.* The Commissioner of Internal Revenue challenged the company's right to those deductions and allowances, asserting, *inter alia*, that the bank was the owner of the building and the sale and leaseback should be disregarded as a sham for taxing purposes. *Id.* at 568–69. The Supreme Court concluded that the sale and leaseback had economic substance and was therefore not a sham because the obligation to repay the loan fell squarely on the company, and that "so long as the lessor retains significant and genuine attributes of the traditional lessor status, the form of the transaction adopted by the parties governs for tax purposes." *Id.* at 583–84.

Taken together, the *Gregory* and *Lyon* decisions suggest that for a business reorganization that results in tax advantages to be respected for taxing purposes, the taxpayer must demonstrate that the reorganization is "real" or "genuine," and not just form without substance. Stated otherwise, the taxpayer must demonstrate that the reorganization results in "a viable business entity," that is one which is "formed for a substantial business purpose or actually engage[s] in substantive business activity." *Northern Ind. Pub. Serv. Co. v. Commissioner of Internal Revenue*, 115 F.3d 506, 511 (7th Cir.1997), quoting *Bass v. Commissioner of Internal Revenue*, 50 T.C. 595, 600 (1968).

Sham transaction cases most often involve discrete transactions by businesses or individuals rather than business reorganizations. In determining whether a transaction is real or just form over substance, a number of Federal courts have adopted a "two prong" sham transaction inquiry. *Rice's Toyota World, Inc. v. Commissioner of Internal Revenue*, 752 F.2d 89 (4th Cir.1985) (*Rice's Toyota*). The first prong of the inquiry examines whether the transaction has economic substance other than the creation of a tax benefit, which has been labeled the "objective" economic substance test. The second prong examines whether the transaction was motivated by any business purpose other than obtaining a tax benefit, which has been labeled the "subjective" business purpose test. While often using similar language, courts have applied this "two prong" inquiry in different ways. In *Rice's Toyota, supra* at 91, the court concluded that "[t]o treat a transaction as a sham, the court must find that the taxpayer was motivated by no business purposes other than obtaining tax benefits in entering the transaction, *and* that the transaction has no economic substance because no reasonable possibility of a profit exists" (emphasis added). According to *Rice's Toyota* and its progeny, if a taxpayer's transaction satisfies the requirements of *either* prong of the test it must be respected for taxing purposes. *See Horn v. Commissioner of Internal Revenue,* 968 F.2d 1229 (D.C. Cir. 1992); *United States v. Wexler,* 31 F.3d 117 (3d Cir. 1994); *Boca Investerings Partnership v. United States,* 167 F.Supp.2d 298 (D.D.C. 2001).

Other courts have rejected a rigid two-step analysis, opting instead to treat economic substance and business purpose as "more precise factors to consider in the application of [the] traditional sham analysis; that is, whether the transaction had any practical economic effects other than the creation of income tax losses." *Sochin v. Commissioner of Internal Revenue,* 843 F.2d 351, 354 (9th Cir.), *cert. denied,* 488 U.S. 824 (1988). *See ACM Partnership v. Commissioner of Internal Revenue,* 157 F.3d 231 (3d Cir. 1998); *Casebeer v. Commissioner of Internal Revenue,* 909 F.2d 1360, 1363 (9th Cir. 1990); *James v. Commissioner of Internal Revenue,* 899 F.2d 905 (10th Cir. 1990); *Shriver v. Commissioner of Internal Revenue,* 899 F.2d 724, 726 (8th Cir. 1990); *Rose v. Commissioner of Internal Revenue,* 868 F.2d 851, 854 (6th Cir. 1989). *See also Bergman v. United States,* 174 F.3d 928, 932 (8th Cir. 1999) ("a transaction must have a purpose, substance, or utility beyond creating a tax deduction for it to have...effect").

We agree with those courts that have concluded that whether a transaction that results in tax benefits is real, such that it ought to be respected for taxing purposes, depends on whether it has had practical economic effects beyond the creation of those tax benefits. In the context of a business reorganization resulting in new corporate entities owning or carrying on a portion of the business previously held or conducted by the taxpayer, this requires inquiry into whether the new entities are "viable," that is, "formed for a substantial business purpose or actually engag[ing] in substantive business activity." *Northern Ind. Pub. Serv. v. Commissioner of Internal Revenue, supra* at 511. In making this inquiry, consideration of the often interrelated factors of economic substance and business purpose, is appropriate.

We turn now to the questioned transactions in this case. The board found that none of the transactions at issue, however defined, had either economic substance or business purpose other than tax avoidance. The board also found that, even if the transactions had had a business purpose other than tax avoidance, their lack of economic substance was fatal to Sherwin-Williams's claim. We disagree. These transactions (the transfer and license back of property) are a product and intended part of a business reorganization, and their economic substance and business purpose must be assessed not in the narrow confines of the specific transactions between the parent and the subsidiaries, but in the broader context of the operation of the resultant businesses. *See Northern Ind. Pub. Serv. Co. v. Commissioner of Internal Revenue, supra* at 512 (newly created subsidiary's existence, transactions with parent, and other economic activities all relevant to sham transaction analysis). After applying the proper legal standards to the evidence, we conclude that the reorganization, including the transfer and licensing back of the marks, had economic substance in that it resulted in the creation of viable business entities engaging in substantive business activity.

The evidence of economic substance, or substantive business activity, beyond the creation of tax benefits for Sherwin-Williams, was substantial. Legal title and physical possession of the marks passed from Sherwin-Williams to the subsidiaries, as did the benefits and burdens of owning the marks. The subsidiaries entered into genuine obligations with unrelated third parties for use of the marks. The subsidiaries received royalties, which they invested with unrelated third parties to earn additional income for their businesses. The subsidiaries incurred and paid substantial liabilities to unrelated third parties and Sherwin-Williams to maintain, manage, and defend the marks. In sum, the subsidiaries became viable, ongoing business enterprises within the family of Sherwin-Williams companies, and not businesses in form only, to be "put to death" after exercising the limited function of creating a tax benefit. *Gregory v. Helvering*, 293 U.S. 465, 470 (1935). *See Bass v. Commissioner of Internal Revenue*, 50 T.C. 595, 600 (1968) (taxpayers' newly formed subsidiary engaged in "substantive business activity" when it held title to working interests in oil and gas leaseholds; assumed and paid its share of expenses for the operation of those leaseholds; collected income from the leaseholds and invested its excess funds; signed contracts regarding the management of the properties; and filed income tax returns).

In the face of this substantial evidence, the board rested its finding that the reorganization and consequent transactions were without economic substance, principally on subsidiary findings that after the reorganization: (1) Sherwin- Williams owned the stock of, and therefore controlled, the subsidiaries; (2) Sherwin-Williams (and not the subsidiaries) expended the money to advertise the products that carried the marks; and (3) Sherwin-Williams's employees continued to provide the services necessary to maintain the marks. While these subsidiary findings are supported in the record, they do not support the board's ultimate finding that the reorganization was without economic substance or effect and therefore a sham.

The separate corporate identities of Sherwin-Williams and the subsidiaries must be respected for tax purposes (where they conduct equivalent of business activity), *see Moline Props. v. Commissioner of Internal Revenue*, 319 U.S. 436, 438–39 (1943), regardless of their stock ownership. While transactions that occur between related companies require close scrutiny to ensure that they have substance as well as form (and that they are valued at levels neither artificially inflated nor deflated because of the interrelated nature of their ownership), the fact that Sherwin-Williams owned the stock of the subsidiaries does not mean that the reorganization had no economic substance or effect on its business. It no longer owned the marks. Instead, it owned stock in the companies that do. It no longer had the exclusive right to use the marks. Instead, it had nonexclusive and time-limited licenses to most but not all of them. The new owners of the marks were free, under their amended bylaws, to enter into licensing agreements with companies other than Sherwin-Williams without shareholder approval, and the subsidiaries did so. In addition, Sherwin-Williams relinquished control over monies it previously retained but now paid to the subsidiaries as royalties. These monies were not returned to it as dividends. They were invested (and therefore placed at risk) by the subsidiaries, under their own investment guidelines and with third parties outside of Sherwin-Williams's control. These changes resulted from the reorganization and have legal, practical, and economic effects on Sherwin-Williams regardless of its stock ownership position. More importantly, they are ample evidence of a reorganization that has resulted in the creation of new, viable business enterprises.

Sherwin-Williams incurred advertising expenses to sell its products not to promote or strengthen the marks. While the marks undoubtedly benefited from the advertising and sale of Sherwin-Williams products bearing their names, such benefits are secondary to the principal purpose of the expenditures. Sherwin-Williams properly expended and expensed these advertising costs against its sales. In this regard, the board's finding that Sherwin-Williams and not the subsidiaries incurred the costs of advertising its products is inconsequential to the ultimate question whether the reorganization was real.

Finally, that the subsidiaries contracted with Sherwin-Williams for professional services necessary to maintain the marks bears little relationship to whether the reorganization had economic substance. What is relevant is whether the subsidiaries paid the expenses of running their businesses (with whomever they may have contracted) or whether those expenses continued to be paid by the parent company, as they were in the *Syms* case. Here, those expenses were paid by the subsidiaries to Sherwin-Williams and, in significantly greater amounts, to other unrelated professionals.

We turn next to the board's assessment of business purpose about which there was a great deal of contested evidence. Applying our limited scope of review to the evidence before the board, we conclude that there was sufficient evidence to support the board's finding that Sherwin-Williams failed to prove that it undertook the reorganization for any of the reasons adopted by its board of directors on January 23, 1991, other than reducing its State tax burden. This finding is of course not conclusive on the ultimate question whether the reorganization was real. Indeed, the board found that, even if the reorganization and the consequent transfer and licensing transactions had been motivated by nontax reasons, or served other business purposes, they would still be a sham because they lacked economic substance beyond the creation of tax benefits.

We embrace the reasoning of courts that have concluded that tax motivation is irrelevant where a business reorganization results in the creation of a viable business entity engaged in substantive business activity rather than in a "bald and mischievous fiction." *Moline Props. v. Commissioner of Internal Revenue, supra* at 439. *See Northern Ind. Pub. Serv. Co. v. Commissioner of Revenue,* 115 F.3d 506, 512 (7th Cir. 1997) (public utility's formation of wholly owned Netherlands subsidiary to borrow money for parent overseas without triggering Federal withholding tax requirement not a sham, in spite of tax avoidance motive, where subsidiary engaged in substantive business activity); *Stearns Magnetic Mfg. Co. v. Commissioner of Internal Revenue,* 208 F.2d 849, 852 (7th Cir. 1954) (corporate taxpayer who transferred patents to stockholder partnership as dividend and licensed them back, may convert form of business as it wishes, even though motive is to reduce taxes; conversion must be accorded recognition unless it is a change in form only, without substance); *Bass v. Commissioner of Internal Revenue,* 50 T.C. 595, 600 (1968) (tax avoidance purpose for reorganizing business into foreign corporate form irrelevant where form adopted was viable business entity, i.e., one which "actually engaged in substantive business activity"). Because the record in this case establishes that the reorganization and subsequent transfer and licensing transactions were genuine, creating viable businesses engaged in substantive economic activities apart from the creation of tax benefits for Sherwin-Williams, they cannot be disregarded by the commissioner as a sham regardless of their tax-motivated purpose.

3. *Ordinary and necessary business expenses.* General Laws c. 63, § 1 ("[n]et income"), provides that corporations may take such deductions as are allowable under the Internal Revenue Code (IRC). *See* G.L. c. 63, § 1. Under the IRC, only "ordinary and necessary" business expenses are allowable deductions. 26 U.S.C. § 162 (2000). The determination whether an expenditure satisfies the requirements for deductibility under § 162 is a question of fact. *See Commissioner of Internal Revenue v. Heininger,* 320 U.S. 467, 475 (1943).

To qualify as an allowable deduction under § 162, a taxpayer must demonstrate that an expenditure satisfies five requirements: (1) it was paid or incurred during the taxable year, (2) it was used to carry on a trade or business, (3) it was an expense, (4) it was a necessary expense, and (5) it was an ordinary expense. *See Commissioner of Internal Revenue v. Lincoln Sav. & Loan Ass'n*, 403 U.S. 345, 352 (1971). The issue here is whether the royalty payments for the use of the marks were ordinary and necessary business expenses.

Exactly what constitutes an "ordinary and necessary" business expense has been the subject of much discussion over the years. In *Welch v. Helvering*, 290 U.S. 111, 115 (1933), United States Supreme Court Justice Cardozo noted: "The standard set up by the statute is not a rule of law; it is rather a way of life. Life in all its fullness must supply the answer to the riddle." In *Deputy v. DuPont*, 308 U.S. 488, 495–96 (1940), Justice Douglas emphasized that "ordinary has the connotation of normal, usual, or customary," and that each case "turns on its special facts." And in *Commissioner of Internal Revenue v. Tellier*, 383 U.S. 687 (1966), Justice Stewart observed: "Our decisions have consistently construed the term 'necessary' as imposing only the minimal requirement that the expense be 'appropriate and helpful' for 'the development of the [taxpayer's] business.'" *Id.* at 689, quoting *Welch v. Helvering*, 290 U.S. 111, 113 (1933).

As an alternative ground for the disallowance of Sherwin-Williams's deduction of royalty payments, the board concluded that Sherwin-Williams's payment of royalties to its wholly owned subsidiaries was not deductible as an ordinary and necessary business expense because "the transfer and license-back transactions between Sherwin-Williams and its subsidiaries should have been royalty-free." It based this conclusion on its findings that Sherwin-Williams maintained the value of the marks after the transfer (by way of advertising and services), and that the subsidiaries "had not developed the [m]arks in any way, or built any goodwill, or created anything of value that could be licensed back to the parent."

We disagree with the board's analysis. As noted earlier, advertising costs were incurred for the purpose of selling products not maintaining the value of the marks, and any services provided by Sherwin-Williams to maintain the marks were paid for by the subsidiaries. More fundamentally, however, the board misconstrues the nature of the reorganization. While Sherwin-Williams may have voluntarily conveyed the marks to its newly formed subsidiaries, it received full consideration for the conveyance, i.e., one hundred per cent of their stock. The relevant question is not who created the value in the marks, but who had the right to that value, at the time the royalty payments were made. Once conveyed, Sherwin-Williams had no legal right or claim to the marks absent licensing agreements. Moreover, the subsidiaries were not required to add value to what they had acquired from Sherwin-Williams in order to get fair market royalty rates from it or from the unrelated third-party licensees with whom they did business. If the subsidiaries had used some of their stock (or cash) to acquire marks from another company and in turn licensed them to Sherwin-Williams, there would be no need for them to "add value" in order properly to demand the payment of royalty fees, and none is required in these circumstances. As the commissioner's expert, Professor Alan L. Feld, conceded on cross-examination, "In the corporate world…a company does have the right to make a bona fide complete transfer of a tree…and then whoever owns the tree, they get the fruit."

Because we have concluded that the reorganization of Sherwin-Williams's intangible assets was not a sham, the answer to the question who had the right to the value of the marks, as a matter of law and substance, is the subsidiaries. The deductibility of the royalty payments between Sherwin-Williams and the subsidiaries must therefore be treated as the deductibility of any other expense incurred in a bona fide transaction between related entities.

The payment of the royalties was a necessary expense because Sherwin-Williams had "irrevocably divested itself of all title [to the marks] and had a right to enjoy the property thereafter only upon payment of reasonable rental." *Stearns Magnetic Mfg. Co. v. Commissioner of Internal Revenue*, 208 F.2d 849, 853 (7th Cir. 1954). Once the marks had been transferred to the subsidiaries, the royalty payments were necessary so that Sherwin-Williams could use the marks to advertise and sell its products. One of the commissioner's experts testified about the importance of the marks: "I think the trademarks at Sherwin-Williams are very important to its business.... Their trademarks are very intertwined with the rest of their business." We agree, and conclude that the royalty payments were "'appropriate and helpful' for 'the development of [Sherwin-Williams's] business.'" *Commissioner of Internal Revenue v. Tellier, supra* at 689, quoting *Welch v. Helvering, supra* at 113.

The payment of royalties was also an ordinary expense. "Ordinary has the connotation of normal, usual, or customary." *Deputy v. DuPont, supra* at 495. Although "the transaction which gives rise to [the expense] must be of common or frequent occurrence in the type of business involved...the fact that a particular expense would be an ordinary or common one in the course of one business and so deductible...does not necessarily make it such in connection with another business." *Id.* In finding that the expense was not "ordinary," the board credited and relied on the testimony of one of the commissioner's witnesses who testified in general terms, and without specifics, that license back arrangements between parent and subsidiary corporations are quite typically "royalty free." He also testified, however, that he was personally aware of instances where companies licensed intangible assets to affiliates and charged them royalties for their use. Puglisi testified that when Sherwin-Williams once asked him for a royalty-free license, he turned them down. Based on the particular facts of this case in all their fullness, we conclude that there was not substantial evidence before the board to support its finding that the royalty payments were not ordinary expenses.

4. *Reasonableness of the royalty payments.* Although we have concluded that the royalty payments that Sherwin-Williams made to the subsidiaries were ordinary and necessary expenses, we must also consider whether the amount of the royalty payments was reasonable. "Inherent in section 162(a)'s concept of 'ordinary and necessary' expenses is the requirement that any payment asserted to be allowable as a deduction...be reasonable in relation to its purpose. 'An expenditure may be, by its nature, ordinary and necessary, but at the same time it may be unreasonable in amount.'" *Audano v. United States*, 428 F.2d 251, 256 (5th Cir. 1970), quoting *United States v. Haskel Eng'g & Supply Co.*, 380 F.2d 786, 788 (9th Cir. 1967).

The agreements under which payments are made will be given effect "if the arrangement is fair and reasonable, judged by the standards of a transaction entered into by parties dealing at arm's length." *Stearns Magnetic Mfg. Co. v. Commissioner of Internal Revenue*, 208 F.2d 849, 852 (7th Cir. 1954). See *Audano v. United States, supra* at 256 (if agreement was such as "reasonable men dealing at arm's length" would have made, it should be valid for tax purposes). A common method for establishing reasonableness is the use of professional appraisers who can look broadly at related industries and practices and estimate a proper royalty rate. The AAA report appraised the value of the marks and recommended royalty rates ranging from one per cent to four and one-half per cent for each of Sherwin-Williams's product divisions. We are satisfied from our review of the record that this report established royalty rates that represented arm's-length transactions, and the commissioner's experts did not testify otherwise.

5. *General Laws c. 63, § 39A.* General Laws c. 63, § 39A, provides that the commissioner may determine the "net income of a foreign corporation which is a subsidiary of another corporation or closely affiliated therewith by stock ownership" by "eliminating all payments to the parent corporation or affiliated corporations in excess of fair value." The purpose of the statute is to give the commissioner the "authority to make adjustments to correct the effect of less than arm's length transactions," between closely affiliated companies, *Commissioner of Revenue v. AMIWoodbroke, Inc.,* 418 Mass. 92, 97 (1994), quoting *Polaroid Corp. v. Commissioner of Revenue,* 393 Mass. 490, 500 (1984) and thereby address concerns that "tax evasion by means of intercorporate transactions…would depress the…income of corporations subject to taxation in Massachusetts." *Id.*

The board found that the transfer and license back of the marks in exchange for royalty payments were not arm's-length transactions because Sherwin-Williams controlled the subsidiaries and there was never a question that the marks would be licensed back to Sherwin-Williams because its existence depended on their use. It further found that the royalty payments had no economic purpose because Sherwin-Williams had itself created the obligation by transferring the marks, and the subsidiaries did nothing to add value to them which would justify such payments. Consequently, it concluded that any payments were in excess of fair market value.

Sherwin-Williams contends that § 39A does not apply to it because it is a parent corporation, not a subsidiary. It also contended that the royalty payments reflected fair value and arm's-length rates as evidenced by the AAA appraisal report, the testimony of its own witnesses, and the testimony of the commissioner's experts. Consequently, there were no payments to eliminate.

Although we agree with the board that the transactions were not entered into at arm's length, the relevant inquiries are whether the transfers were bona fide (which we have concluded they were) and if so, whether the royalty rates paid were in excess of fair market value (which we have concluded they were not).

Assuming that § 39A, construed to give effect to its broad remedial purpose, permits the commissioner to eliminate payments made by a parent to a subsidiary corporation, it does so only to the extent that those payments are in excess of fair value. Having concluded that the board was in error in concluding that the payments were in excess of fair value, we hold that the commissioner's adjustment to Sherwin-Williams's income could not have been made pursuant to § 39A.

6. *Interest expense.* The commissioner disallowed a deduction for interest that Sherwin-Williams paid SWIMC in connection with a short-term loan of $7 million. The rationale for the disallowance was that, because the royalty payments from Sherwin-Williams to SWIMC were unnecessary, the loan back to Sherwin-Williams and the interest on that loan were also unnecessary. The board affirmed the disallowance. We reverse. Because we have concluded that the transfer and license back of the marks was not a sham and the royalty payments were necessary and ordinary expenses of Sherwin-Williams, and because there is no dispute that the loan was actually made, the interest paid to secure it was deductible.

7. *Conclusion.* The decision of the Appellate Tax Board is reversed.

*So ordered.*

# Massachusetts Legislature Paints Over Sherwin-Williams, Modifies State Tax Treatment of IP Holding Companies*

Richard W. Giuliani & Michael J. Nathanson
10 INTELL. PROP. TODAY 38 (July 2003)

Intellectual property holding companies have long been an integral part of business plans for companies that own valuable intellectual property. In general, IP holding companies are created and used under the following circumstances. A company with valuable intellectual property ("Parent") operating in a high-tax state that taxes royalty income ("State P") identifies a state that does not tax holding companies—or that taxes them at a low rate—on royalty income ("State S"). Parent then creates a subsidiary or, in some cases, utilizes an existing subsidiary ("Sub") to operate in State S. Parent transfers some or all of its intellectual property to Sub, which, in turn, attempts to establish and maintain an independent presence, including its own offices, in State S. Sub then licenses the intellectual property to Parent and, in some cases, to third parties as part of its business of maintaining and managing its holdings.

Among the state tax benefits that potentially can be achieved through the use of an IP holding company are that:

- Parent may deduct against its State P income (and its income attributable to other high-tax jurisdictions) the royalties that it pays to Sub;
- parent may be able to mitigate the effect of any net worth taxes imposed by State P; and
- for State S tax purposes, Sub will not be required to pay tax—or it will be required to pay relatively little tax—on its receipt of royalties from Parent and other licensees.

Moreover, Parent typically can access the cash received by Sub through loans, dividends, payments for administrative services, or other conventions, depending on what is most tax-efficient. Where Sub makes loans to Parent, Parent may further be able to deduct interest that it pays to Sub.

Among the non-tax benefits that can be achieved through the use of an IP holding company are that:

- it may be easier to contract for, maintain, and account for intellectual property and licenses to third parties if the intellectual property is located in a separate corporation, the primary or sole business of which is licensing;
- it ultimately may be easier to sell intellectual property that has been isolated within a saleable subsidiary; and
- the establishment of terms for a license to Parent may provide helpful information about the market value of the intellectual property, which, in turn, may be useful to third parties and for tax and financial accounting purposes.

In an effort to preserve their shrinking tax bases, however, high-tax states have aggressively pursued and challenged companies that establish IP and other holding companies. Among the most common grounds asserted by states that seek to deny the above tax benefits are that:

- Sub has no substance, is a sham, and/or is merely the alter ego of Parent, and should therefore be ignored for state tax purposes;

---

* Reprinted with permission of the authors, copyright 2003.

- taxing nexus exists between Sub and the states from which royalties are paid; and
- royalties paid by Parent should be reallocated to Parent based on transfer-pricing or similar principles.

In order to maximize Parent's chances for realizing the above state tax benefits and for successfully defending itself against any challenges, Parent typically endeavors to ensure that Sub establishes and maintains a substantive, independent, business-like presence in State S. In this regard, Sub typically seeks to have:

- a State S telephone number and office address, which is used for all correspondence and for filing all tax returns;
- its own State S bank and investment accounts; its books and records stored and maintained in State S;
- directors that hold their meetings in State S;
- officers and employees that perform their duties for Sub in State S; and
- if possible, at least some directors and officers that are not also directors and officers of Parent.

In sum, Parent and Sub attempt to justify Sub's existence with non-tax business purposes, and all corporate formalities—including those necessary to effect and sustain the transfer of intellectual property from Parent to Sub—are strictly observed so as to preserve the separate identity of Sub and its assets on the one hand from Parent and its assets on the other.

## RECENT JUDICIAL ACTIVITY

States have litigated the above issues, often successfully, particularly where they believe they can establish that Sub has no substance, is a sham, and/or is merely the alter ego of Parent. States have been less successful where Sub has a substantive, independent, business-like presence in State S. *Compare, e.g., Syms Corp. v. Commissioner of Revenue,* 436 Mass. 505 (2002) *with Sherwin-Williams Company v. Commissioner of Revenue,* 438 Mass. 71 (2002).

In Massachusetts, the *Sherwin-Williams* case is the most recent example of such litigation. In *Sherwin-Williams,* the Massachusetts Appellate Tax Board had concluded that the Commissioner of Revenue had properly disallowed deductions for royalties on three alternative grounds:

- the transfer and license back of intangible assets was a sham and should be disregarded under the "sham transaction doctrine";
- the royalty payments were not deductible as ordinary and necessary business expenses as there was no valid business purpose justifying such expense; and
- Massachusetts law permitted the Commissioner to adjust the taxable income of Sherwin-Williams by eliminating the royalty payments because they were not made at arm's-length and distorted the actual income of Sherwin-Williams.

The Massachusetts Supreme Judicial Court systematically addressed and dismantled each of the bases of the Appellate Tax Board decision. With respect to the sham transaction finding, the Court concluded that the record in the case established that the reorganization and subsequent transfer and licensing transactions were genuine, creating viable businesses engaged in substantive economic activities apart from the creation of tax benefits for Sherwin-Williams, and, accordingly, they could not be disregarded by the Commissioner as a sham—regardless of their tax-motivated purpose. The Court embraced "the reasoning of courts that have concluded that tax motivation is irrelevant where a business reorganization results in the creation of a viable business entity engaged in substantive business activity rather than a 'bald and mischievous fiction.'"

The Court distinguished the *Syms* case, noting that the evidence in that case showed that the transaction was specifically designed as a tax-avoidance scheme; that royalties were paid to the subsidiary once a year and quickly returned to the parent company as dividends; that the subsidiary did not do business other than to act as a conduit for the circular flow of royalty money; and that the parent continued to pay all the expenses of maintaining and defending the trademarks it had transferred to the subsidiary.

The Court then addressed the question of whether the royalties paid by Sherwin-Williams were ordinary and necessary business expenses. The Appellate Tax Board had concluded that the Sherwin-Williams payments of royalties were not deductible as a necessary and ordinary business expense because "the transfer and license-back transactions between Sherwin-Williams and its subsidiaries should have been royalty-free." The Board had based its conclusion on its findings that Sherwin-Williams maintained the value of the marks after the transfer (by way of advertising and services) and that the subsidiaries had not developed the marks in any way, built up goodwill, or created anything of value that could be licensed back to the parent.

The Court properly disagreed with the Board's analysis, noting that the Board misconstrued the nature of the reorganization, and the Court made the common tax-sense observation that while Sherwin-Williams may have voluntarily conveyed its marks to its newly formed subsidiaries, it received full consideration for the conveyance, i.e., 100% of their stock. For the Court, the relevant question was not who created the value in the marks but who had a right to that value at the time the royalty payments were made. The Court quoted one of the Commissioner's experts who conceded on a cross-examination that "in the corporate world…a company does not have the right to make a bona fide complete transfer of a tree…and then whoever owns the tree, they get the fruit."

Since the reorganization was not a sham and the subsidiaries clearly had a right to the marks, the deduction of the royalty payments had to be treated like the deduction of any other expense incurred in a bona fide transaction between related entities. It was a necessary expense because Sherwin-Williams had irrevocably divested itself of all title to the marks and had a right to enjoy the property thereafter only upon payment of a reasonable royalty.

The court also concluded that the royalties constituted an ordinary expense. The Board had concluded that the expense was not ordinary because, in reliance on testimony of one of the Commissioner's witnesses, the Board determined that license-back arrangements between parent and subsidiary corporations quite typically are royalty-free. Based on the particular facts in this case, the Court concluded that there was not substantial evidence before the Board to support the finding that the royalty payments were not ordinary expenses.

The Court next concluded that the royalty payments were reasonable in light of the uncontradicted appraisal report submitted by the taxpayer. For the same reason, the Court concluded that the Commissioner could not reallocate or disallow the deductions under Massachusetts law, which permitted the Commissioner to determine the net income of a foreign corporation that is a subsidiary of another corporation or closely affiliated therewith by stock ownership by eliminating any payments to the parent corporation or affiliated corporation in excess of their value. The Board had concluded that the payments were not arm's-length because Sherwin-Williams had controlled the subsidiaries. The court correctly noted that the question was not a question of relationship but a question of whether the transfers were bona fide and, if so, whether royalties paid were in excess of fair market value, and the Court concluded they were not.

In sum, it appears that the key to victory for Sherwin-Williams was convincing the Court that its holding companies were "viable business entities engaging in substantive business activities." In particular, it appears that the Court was impressed with the following specific facts.

- The subsidiaries were owners of the trademarks and were free, subject to their amended bylaws, to enter into licensing agreements with companies other than Sherwin-Williams without shareholder approval (and they did enter such agreements).
- Sherwin-Williams paid royalties to its subsidiaries and, unlike the Syms subsidiary, the royalties were retained by the subsidiaries and were not returned to Sherwin-Williams as dividends.
- The royalty income was invested by the Sherwin-Williams subsidiaries (and therefore placed at risk) under their own investment guidelines and with third parties outside of Sherwin-Williams' control.
- Although the subsidiaries contracted with Sherwin-Williams for professional services necessary to maintain the marks, they paid arm's-length fees to Sherwin-Williams and also engaged other unrelated professionals.

## THE LEGISLATURE'S "BROAD BRUSH"

On March 5, 2003, before the paint was dry on the Court's decision in *Sherwin-Williams*, the Governor of Massachusetts signed legislation that effectively repeals the *Sherwin-Williams* case. In particular, this legislation adds the following new provision to the Massachusetts General Laws:

> In applying the statutes referred to in [the corporate tax provisions], the commissioner may, in his discretion, disallow the asserted tax consequences of a transaction by asserting the application of the sham transaction doctrine or any other related tax doctrine, in which case the taxpayer shall have the burden of demonstrating by clear and convincing evidence as determined by the commissioner that the transaction possessed both: (i) a valid, good-faith business purpose other than tax avoidance; and (ii) economic substance apart from the asserted tax benefit. In all such cases, the taxpayer shall have also the burden of demonstrating by clear and convincing evidence as determined by the commissioner that the asserted nontax business purpose is commensurate with the tax benefit claimed. Nothing in this section shall be construed to limit or negate the commissioner's authority to make tax adjustments as otherwise permitted by law.

This Section, which is effective for tax years beginning on or after January 1, 2002, and to which the Legislature refers as a "clarification," appears to give the Commissioner broad powers to disallow the tax consequences of any transaction that the Commissioner determines to be a sham transaction and requires the taxpayer to demonstrate by clear and convincing evidence that the transaction at issue has both a valid good-faith business purpose other than tax avoidance and economic substance apart from the asserted tax benefit.

In perhaps an even more direct assault on the *Sherwin-Williams* case, the above legislation also amends the corporate tax statute to provide, in pertinent part, that:

For purposes of computing its net income under this chapter, a taxpayer shall add back otherwise deductible interest expenses and costs and intangible expenses and costs directly or indirectly paid, accrued or incurred to, or in connection directly or indirectly with one or more direct or indirect transactions with, one or more related members.

The adjustments required in [this provision] shall not apply if: (A) the taxpayer establishes by clear and convincing evidence, as determined by the commissioner, that the adjustments are unreasonable; or (B) the taxpayer and the commissioner agree in writing to the application or use of an alternative method of apportionment.... Nothing in this subsection shall be construed to limit or negate the commissioner's authority to otherwise enter into agreements and compromises otherwise allowed by law.

The clear intent of these provisions is to disallow any expenses relating to intangible property when such expenses are paid to a related party, except in certain limited circumstances. In order to avoid this result, a taxpayer must establish "by clear and convincing evidence" that the adjustments proposed by the Commissioner are unreasonable, or the taxpayer and the Commissioner must agree in writing to the application or use of an alternative method of apportionment. Again, these provisions are effective for tax years beginning on or after January 1, 2002, and are referred to as a "clarification."

## CONCLUSION

In all likelihood, the above legislation will be challenged as being unconstitutional, but its constitutionality, while questionable, may ultimately be upheld. As to the *Sherwin-Williams* case, the Commonwealth petitioned the Supreme Judicial Court for a re-hearing, but its petition was denied. In any event, at this point, companies seeking to establish holding companies, and even companies that already have them, must brace themselves, and begin preparations for, attacks under the new legislation and, ultimately, litigation.

---

# Notes & Questions

1. *Kirby and the Relevance of Sales Income.* The judge in *Kirby* stated that the amount of income received by the licensor from overseas sales was "substantial" and represented the reservation of a substantial right. What if the sales had been minimal? Could one come to the same conclusion? Should the potential economic value of the licensor's retained rights be the determining factor in whether income is ordinary income or capital gains? How else could the judge in *Kirby* have reached the same conclusion?

2. *Geographic Limitations.* License grants that are limited to geographic territories, rather than worldwide, circumscribe the licensee's exploitation of patent rights. As seen in this chapter's cases, individual licensors do so at their peril. Would it make sense for § 1235 purposes to grant a worldwide license to assure capital gains tax treatment, even if the licensee will commercialize in only limited fields or territories? What if there is little likelihood that the licensor will be able to find suitable licensees for other markets?

3. *IRC Requirements.* In order to obtain capital gains treatment under § 117(q) of the Internal Revenue Code of 1939, a transfer of a patent must be considered a sale or ex-

change of a capital asset held for more than six months where the following conditions are met:

(a)  transfer is made other than by gift, inheritance, or devise;

(b)  transfer is of all substantial rights to patent or invention, or undivided interest therein; and

(c)  transfer is made by taxpayer who qualifies as 'holder.'

The dispute in the *Kirby* case was over (b). Indeed, most disputes of this nature are over whether the transfer is of all substantial rights. If the licensor transfers all substantial rights, who is the appropriate party plaintiff in the event a third party infringes the patent? The licensor or the licensee? Or are both necessary parties? What if the licensee has acquiesced to the infringement but the licensor has not?

4. *IRS Considerations.* While the language of the license agreement sets out the duties and obligations of the parties, it does not control the characterization of income. The IRS will look at the circumstances surrounding the entire transaction in determining income characterization. Thus, counsel for the licensor should examine the license agreement carefully to assure it will withstand IRS scrutiny. For example, lack of holder status (e.g. holders who transfer patents to a related party), or failure to hold the property for longer than one year prior to transfer will force the income to be treated as ordinary.

Transfers which do not meet requirements of § 1235 should be examined to determine whether they fall within the definition of a capital asset under §§ 1221 or 1231. Either section will allow treatment of income as capital gains within certain prescribed conditions.

Trademark and franchise transfers are covered by § 1253. Again, income from a transaction determined to be a license will be treated as ordinary income and any payments received will be deductible. A transaction constituting a sale will be allowed capital gains treatment. Reservations of control with respect to a trademark or franchise transfer must be analyzed to determine whether they constitute retention of sufficient rights to result in a mere license. Examples of significant rights include, but are not limited to, control over assignment or transfers of the interest, restrictions on the purchase of supporting products to the licensor's supplies, restrictions on what other products or services can be sold or advertised by the licensee, the right to terminate at will, and substantial business control.

5. *Franchise Laws.* Some trademark licenses can run afoul of franchise law. Licensors must carefully consider how much control will be exercised over the licensee's business operations. If the control level is eventually found "significant," the license can be construed as a franchise agreement. The following license terms may be evidence of significant control:

(i)   The licensee is required to sell a certain type or quality of product;

(ii)  The licensee is required to utilize training manuals provided by licensor or follow specific operating procedures;

(iii) The licensee is required to purchase ingredients or products from designated suppliers; or

(iv)  The licensee is required to advertise or promote its goods and/or services in a specified manner.

Susan Progoff, *Trademark Licensing*, 534 PLI/PAT. 9, 11 (1998).

Thus, the licensor will be subject to strict state and federal franchise rules and heavy penalties for noncompliance. The federal law regulating franchise operations is found in the Federal Trade Commission Franchise Rule, 16 C.F.R. § 436.

State franchise laws may treat trademark licenses that include quality control and enforcement of business plans as franchise agreements. Thus, the parties may be required to register as a franchise in all or many states in which they intend to do business. Even where the parties include a clause in the contract specifically stating the license is not a franchise, states will generally look to all the business terms of the agreement to determine whether it is a license or a franchise.

6. *Intangible Holding Companies.* States are becoming increasingly active in eliminating the IHC "loophole" in their tax systems. On January 28, 2004, the Missouri House approved HB 969, which is intended to prevent corporations from avoiding state income taxes. The bill's sponsor, Rep. Shannon Cooper (R) commented that the legislation will enable the Missouri Department of Revenue to prosecute companies that make excessive expense and interest payments to Delaware holding companies. The approval of HB 969 is a result of the *Acme Royalty Co. v. Director of Revenue*, 96 S.W.3d 72 (Mo. 2002), in which the Missouri Supreme Court held that two Delaware holding companies could not be required to pay Missouri state income tax because Missouri state law was ambiguous on the point. HB 969 sets forth five criteria for the "arm's length test":

- the corporation has no rights of use or ownership of the intangible property except those rights granted by the related entity;
- the related entity is engaged in a profit-making business;
- net income from the intangible expenses and costs or interest expenses and costs is retained and invested by the related entity for the benefit of the stockholders of the related entity;
- expenses of maintaining, managing, and defending the property of the related entity are paid for by the related entity, and if such services are provided by the corporation, the related entity pays for such services at an arm's-length rate as determined by an independent appraisal or other evidence; or
- the related entity holds separate board meetings, maintains separate assets, executes separate contracts, maintains separate offices, and has employees separate from the corporation.

The controversy is not over. There is much opposition to HB 969 in particular by the Missouri Department of Revenue because the newly approved bill shifts the burden of proof to it in seeking to disallow deductions. In response, Representative Cooper stated "I think the taxpayer should always be innocent until proven guilty." Karen Setze, *Missouri House OK's Limitation on Delaware Holding Company Deduction,* 2004 STT 21–23 (January 30, 2004).

---

# Chapter 13

# Bankruptcy and Security Interests in Licensing

## I. Introduction

While the prospect of bankruptcy is rarely in the minds of the parties negotiating an intellectual property license, counsel must address the possibility of bankruptcy in the agreement or risk unintended or even devastating consequences under the Bankruptcy Code. Inclusion of appropriate language can often save a licensee's rights in intellectual property from the bankruptcy court as well as from creditors.

From a negotiating standpoint the conflict between the optimism inherent in a new license relationship and the harsh realities of a later bankruptcy filing by one of the parties provides one tactical advantage. It is often relatively easy to convince the other side to allow your client to insert appropriate language dealing with the contingency of bankruptcy. If there is an objection to the insertion, the other side risks suggesting that its own bankruptcy is a serious enough possibility to warrant the objection. If the playing field for the negotiations is relatively level, neither party will typically wish to raise suspicions about its own future financial stability.

The most important change in the Bankruptcy Code pertaining to intellectual property licenses took place in response to the Fourth Circuit's 1985 *Lubrizol* decision, which highlighted the then Bankruptcy Code's harsh treatment of licensees.

---

# II. Are License Agreements Executory Contracts?

## Lubrizol Enterprises, Inc. v. Richmond Metal Finishers, Inc.
### 756 F.2d 1043 (4th Cir. 1985), *cert. denied*, 475 U.S. 1057 (1985)

JAMES DICKSON PHILLIPS, Circuit Judge:

The question is whether Richmond Metal Finishers (RMF), a bankrupt debtor in possession, should have been allowed to reject as executory a technology licensing agreement with Lubrizol Enterprises (Lubrizol) as licensee.

\* \* \*

### I

In July of 1982, RMF entered into the contract with Lubrizol that granted Lubrizol a nonexclusive license to utilize a metal coating process technology owned by RMF. RMF owed the following duties to Lubrizol under the agreement: (1) to notify Lubrizol of any patent infringement suit and to defend in such suit; (2) to notify Lubrizol of any other use or licensing of the process, and to reduce royalty payments if a lower royalty rate agreement was reached with another licensee; and (3) to indemnify Lubrizol for losses arising out of any misrepresentation or breach of warranty by RMF. Lubrizol owed RMF reciprocal duties of accounting for and paying royalties for use of the process and of canceling certain existing indebtedness. The contract provided that Lubrizol would defer use of the process until May 1, 1983, and in fact, Lubrizol has never used the RMF technology.

RMF filed a petition for bankruptcy pursuant to Chapter 11 of the Bankruptcy Code on August 16, 1983. As part of its plan to emerge from bankruptcy, RMF sought, pursuant to Sec. 365(a), to reject the contract with Lubrizol in order to facilitate sale or licensing of the technology unhindered by restrictive provisions in the Lubrizol agreement. On RMF's motion for approval of the rejection, the bankruptcy court properly interpreted Sec. 365 as requiring it to undertake a two-step inquiry to determine the propriety of rejection: first, whether the contract is executory; next, if so, whether its rejection would be advantageous to the bankrupt.

Making that inquiry, the bankruptcy court determined that both tests were satisfied and approved the rejection. But, as indicated, the district court then reversed that determination on the basis that neither test was satisfied and disallowed the rejection. This appeal followed.

### II

We conclude initially that, as the bankruptcy court ruled, the technology licensing agreement in this case was an executory contract, within contemplation of 11 U.S.C. Sec. 365(a). Under that provision a contract is executory if performance is due to some extent on both sides. *NLRB v. Bildisco and Bildisco*, [465] U.S. [513], [522], 104 S. Ct. 1188, 1194 n. 6, 79 L. Ed.2d 482 (1984). This court has recently adopted Professor Countryman's more specific test for determining whether a contract is "executory" in the required sense. By that test, a contract is executory if the "'obligations of both the bankrupt and the other party to the contract are so far unperformed that the failure of either to complete the performance would constitute a material breach excusing the performance of the other.'" *Gloria Manufacturing Corp. v. International Ladies' Garment Workers' Union*, 734 F.2d 1020, 1022 (4th Cir. 1984) (quoting Countryman, *Executory Contracts in Bankruptcy: Part I*, 57 MINN.L.REV. 439, 460 (1973). This issue is one of law that may be freely reviewed by successive courts.

Applying that test here, we conclude that the licensing agreement was at the critical time executory. RMF owed Lubrizol the continuing duties of notifying Lubrizol of further licensing of the process and of reducing Lubrizol's royalty rate to meet any more favorable rates granted to subsequent licensees. By their terms, RMF's obligations to give notice and to restrict its right to license its process at royalty rates it desired without lowering Lubrizol's royalty rate extended over the life of the agreement, and remained unperformed. Moreover, RMF owed Lubrizol additional contingent duties of notifying it of suits, defending suits and indemnifying it for certain losses.

The unperformed, continuing core obligations of notice and forbearance in licensing made the contract executory as to RMF. In *Fenix Cattle Co. v. Silver (In re Select-A-Seat Corp.)*, 625 F.2d 290, 292 (9th Cir. 1980), the court found that an obligation of a debtor to refrain from selling software packages under an exclusive licensing agreement made a contract executory as to the debtor notwithstanding the continuing obligation was only one of forbearance. Although the license to Lubrizol was not exclusive, RMF owed the same type of unperformed continuing duty of forbearance arising out of the most favored licensee clause running in favor of Lubrizol. Breach of that duty would clearly constitute a material breach of the agreement.

Moreover, the contract was further executory as to RMF because of the contingent duties that RMF owed of giving notice of and defending infringement suits and of indemnifying Lubrizol for certain losses arising out of the use of the technology. Contingency of an obligation does not prevent its being executory under Sec. 365. *See In re Smith Jones, Inc.*, 26 B.R. 289, 292 (Bankr. D. Minn.1982) (warranty obligations executory as to promissor*); In re O.P.M. Leasing Services, Inc.*, 23 B.R. 104, 117 (Bankr. S.D.N.Y. 1982) (obligation to defend infringement suits makes contract executory as to promissor). Until the time has expired during which an event triggering a contingent duty may occur, the contingent obligation represents a continuing duty to stand ready to perform if the contingency occurs. A breach of that duty once it was triggered by the contingency (or presumably, by anticipatory repudiation) would have been material.

Because a contract is not executory within the meaning of Sec. 365(a) unless it is executory as to both parties, it is also necessary to determine whether the licensing agreement was executory as to Lubrizol. *See Bildisco*, 465 U.S. at [513], 104 S. Ct. at 1194 n. 6. We conclude that it was.

Lubrizol owed RMF the unperformed and continuing duty of accounting for and paying royalties for the life of the agreement. It is true that a contract is not executory as to a party simply because the party is obligated to make payments of money to the other party. *See Smith Jones*, 26 B.R. at 292; H.Rep. No. 95-595, 95th Cong., 2d Sess. 347, *reprinted in* 1978 U.S. Code Cong. & Ad. News 5787, 5963, 6303-04. Therefore, if Lubrizol had owed RMF nothing more than a duty to make fixed payments or cancel specified indebtedness under the agreement, the agreement would not be executory as to Lubrizol. However, the promise to account for and pay royalties required that Lubrizol deliver written quarterly sales reports and keep books of account subject to inspection by an independent Certified Public Accountant. This promise goes beyond a mere debt, or promise to pay money, and was at the critical time executory. *See Fenix Cattle*, 625 F.2d at 292. Additionally, subject to certain exceptions, Lubrizol was obligated to keep all license technology in confidence for a number of years.

Since the licensing agreement is executory as to each party, it is executory within the meaning of Sec. 365(a), and the district court erred as a matter of law in reaching a contrary conclusion.

### III

There remains the question whether rejection of the executory contract would be advantageous to the bankrupt. *See Borman's, Inc. v. Allied Supermarkets, Inc.*, 706 F.2d 187, 189 (6th Cir. 1983). Courts addressing that question must start with the proposition that the bankrupt's decision upon it is to be accorded the deference mandated by the sound business judgment rule as generally applied by courts to discretionary actions or decisions of corporate directors. [Citations omitted.]

As generally formulated and applied in corporate litigation the rule is that courts should defer to—should not interfere with—decisions of corporate directors upon matters entrusted to their business judgment except upon a finding of bad faith or gross abuse of their "business discretion." *See, e.g., Lewis v. Anderson*, 615 F.2d 778, 782 (9th Cir. 1979); *Polin v. Conductron Corp.*, 552 F.2d 797, 809 (8th Cir. 1977). Transposed to the bankruptcy context, the rule as applied to a bankrupt's decision to reject an executory contract because of perceived business advantage requires that the decision be accepted by courts unless it is shown that the bankrupt's decision was one taken in bad faith or in gross abuse of the bankrupt's retained business discretion.

In bankruptcy litigation the issue is of course first presented for judicial determination when a debtor, having decided that rejection will be beneficial within contemplation of Sec. 365(a), moves for approval of the rejection. The issue thereby presented for first instance judicial determination by the bankruptcy court is whether the decision of the debtor that rejection will be advantageous is so manifestly unreasonable that it could not be based on sound business judgment, but only on bad faith, or whim or caprice. That issue is one of fact to be decided as such by the bankruptcy court by the normal processes of fact adjudication. And the resulting fact determination by the bankruptcy court is perforce then reviewable up the line under the clearly erroneous standard. *See Minges*, 602 F.2d at 43; *see generally* 1 COLLIER ON BANKRUPTCY 3.03(8)(b) (L. King 15th ed. 1984).

Here, the bankruptcy judge had before him evidence not rebutted by Lubrizol that the metal coating process subject to the licensing agreement is RMF's principal asset and that sale or licensing of the technology represented the primary potential source of funds by which RMF might emerge from bankruptcy. The testimony of RMF's president, also factually uncontested by Lubrizol, indicated that sale or further licensing of the technology would be facilitated by stripping Lubrizol of its rights in the process and that, correspondingly, continued obligation to Lubrizol under the agreement would hinder RMF's capability to sell or license the technology on more advantageous terms to other potential licensees. On the basis of this evidence the bankruptcy court determined that the debtor's decision to reject was based upon sound business judgment and approved it.

On appeal the district court simply found to the contrary that the debtor's decision to reject did not represent a sound business judgment. The district court's determination rested essentially on two grounds: that RMF's purely contingent obligations under the agreement were not sufficiently onerous that relief from them would constitute a substantial benefit to RMF; and that because rejection could not deprive Lubrizol of all its rights to the technology, rejection could not reasonably be found beneficial. We conclude that in both of these respects the district court's factual findings, at odds with those of the bankruptcy court, were clearly erroneous and cannot stand.

## A

In finding that the debtor's contingent obligations were not sufficiently onerous that relief from them would be beneficial, the district court could only have been substituting its business judgment for that of the debtor. There is nothing in the record from which it could be concluded that the debtor's decision on that point could not have been reached by the exercise of sound (though possibly faulty) business judgment in the normal process of evaluating alternative courses of action. If that could not be concluded, then the business judgment rule required that the debtor's factual evaluation be accepted by the court, as it had been by the bankruptcy court. *See Schein v. Caesar's World, Inc.,* 491 F.2d 17, 20 (5th Cir. 1974).

## B

On the second point, we can only conclude that the district court was under a misapprehension of controlling law in thinking that by rejecting the agreement the debtor could not deprive Lubrizol of all rights to the process. Under 11 U.S.C. Sec. 365(g), Lubrizol would be entitled to treat rejection as a breach and seek a money damages remedy; however, it could not seek to retain its contract rights in the technology by specific performance even if that remedy would ordinarily be available upon breach of this type of contract. *See In re Waldron,* 36 B.R. 633, 642 n. 4 (Bankr. S.D. Fla. 1984). Even though Sec. 365(g) treats rejection as a breach, the legislative history of Sec. 365(g) makes clear that the purpose of the provision is to provide only a damages remedy for the non-bankrupt party. H.Rep. No. 95-595, 95th Cong., 2d Sess. 349, reprinted in 1978 U.S.Code Cong. & Ad.News 5963, 6305. For the same reason, Lubrizol cannot rely on provisions within its agreement with RMF for continued use of the technology by Lubrizol upon breach by RMF. Here again, the statutory "breach" contemplated by Sec. 365(g) controls, and provides only a money damages remedy for the non-bankrupt party. Allowing specific performance would obviously undercut the core purpose of rejection under Sec. 365(a), and that consequence cannot therefore be read into congressional intent.

## IV

Lubrizol strongly urges upon us policy concerns in support of the district court's refusal to defer to the debtor's decision to reject or, preliminarily, to treat the contract as executory for Sec. 365(a) purposes. We understand the concerns, but think they cannot control decision here.

It cannot be gainsaid that allowing rejection of such contracts as executory imposes serious burdens upon contracting parties such as Lubrizol. Nor can it be doubted that allowing rejection in this and comparable cases could have a general chilling effect upon the willingness of such parties to contract at all with businesses in possible financial difficulty. But under bankruptcy law such equitable considerations may not be indulged by courts in respect of the type of contract here in issue. Congress has plainly provided for the rejection of executory contracts, notwithstanding the obvious adverse consequences for contracting parties thereby made inevitable. Awareness by Congress of those consequences is indeed specifically reflected in the special treatment accorded to union members under collective bargaining contracts, *see Bildisco*, 465 U.S. at [513], 104 S. Ct. at 1193–96, and to lessees of real property, *see* 11 U.S.C. Sec. 365(h). But no comparable special treatment is provided for technology licensees such as Lubrizol. They share the general hazards created by sec. 365 for all business entities dealing with potential bankrupts in the respects at issue here.

The judgment of the district court is reversed and the case is remanded for entry of judgment in conformity with that entered by the bankruptcy court.

REVERSED AND REMANDED.

————————

# III. Post-*Lubrizol* Legislative Developments

The *Lubrizol* decision sent tremors through the business world, particularly among licensees whose businesses were highly dependent on licensed technology. Under the rule in *Lubrizol*, even software escrow agreements, designed to place licensed source code in the possession of a third party and beyond the control of the licensor, would be useless in the face of a Section 365 rejection, which completely cuts off a licensee's right to use the property, even if the property is not in the bankrupt licensor's possession or control. In response to the concerns of licensees, Congress amended the Bankruptcy Code to afford "special treatment" to licensees of technology.

————————

## Structuring License Agreements with Companies in Financial Difficulty Section 365(n) — Divining Rod or Obstacle Course?*

Marjorie F. Chertok
65 St. John's L. Rev. 1045, 1053–75 (1991)

\* \* \*

II.   CONGRESSIONAL REACTION TO THE CONFLICTING TREATMENT OF LICENSE AGREEMENTS UNDER SECTION 365(a)

In 1988, *Lubrizol* and its progeny were brought to the attention of the judiciary committees of the House and Senate. After hearings attended by members of the bankruptcy bar and technical community, Congress concluded that the then-existing precedents were insufficient to protect and foster the development of intellectual property. Accordingly, Congress accepted the recommendation of the *Lubrizol* court and enacted legislation designed to protect licensees and thereby encourage technological innovation.

A review of the legislative history indicates a Congressional awareness that the tension between the federal policies underlying the Bankruptcy Code, and those behind the Patent Code and Copyright Act, necessitated modification of the Code. For example, one of the policies behind the copyright and patent laws is encouragement of ac-

————

\* Reprinted with permission of the publisher, copyright 1991.

cess to intellectual properties through the payment of royalties. Absent legislation, the right to reject a license agreement would give debtor-licensors a stronger monopoly than the drafters of the patent or copyright laws had ever intended because it would allow the licensee the unilateral right to withhold its technology from the marketplace.

Consequently, the drafters limited the traditional powers of debtors to obtain relief from onerous contracts, acknowledging that although it is important to protect debtors from onerous contracts, it is equally important for Congress to promote technological development and innovation by protecting the rights of nonbankrupt licensees.

## A. The Economic and Public Policy Issues Addressed Under the Act

In enacting section 365(n), Congress recognized that technological development and innovation are advanced by encouraging solvent licensees to invest in start-up companies. Indeed, the economic reality is that intellectual property is often developed by undercapitalized companies relying on the financial support of solvent licensees to provide "venture capital" for development. To encourage investment in intellectual property and to protect the rights of the licensees who contribute financing, research, development, manufacturing, or marketing skills, Congress limited the power of debtor-licensors to "reject" licenses as executory contracts.

As the judiciary committees observed, it would be inequitable if a licensee who funded the development of the intellectual property, or who invested substantial monies in anticipation of using or marketing the technology, were denied the benefit of its bargain. It would also be unjust if the debtor or creditors' committee could unilaterally disclose jointly developed trade secrets, patents, or copyrightable information. Such disclosures would have a devastating effect on the licensee's business, possibly even causing its bankruptcy. The judiciary committees compared the licensee's predicament to that of a lessee of real property because in both instances the consequences of the debtor's breach is not compensable in monetary damages.

## B. The Congressional Reaction

To prevent these consequences and encourage public investment in intellectual property, Congress modified section 365 of the Code to enable the licensee to structure agreements protecting its right to use and control distribution of intellectual property in the event that the licensor files for bankruptcy protection. This modification of section 365 of the Code in essence allowed for pre-bankruptcy planning on the part of licensees.

The drafters observed that the modification of section 365 represented a substantial curtailment of the policy of protecting debtors in favor of the policy encouraging technological innovation. Importantly, in the legislative history of the Act, Congress advises the bankruptcy courts to recognize agreements that foster the development of intellectual property, even if these agreements technically contravene accepted principles of bankruptcy law.

Consistent with the public policy of encouraging technological innovation, the drafters enacted a broad definition of intellectual property. This definition covers a wide range of licensing arrangements and variants of intellectual property, including the following: (a) trade secrets; (b) inventions, processes, designs, or plants protected under title 35; (c) patent applications; (d) plant variety; (e) works of authorship protected under title 17 (Copyright Act); and (f) mask works protected under chapter 9 of title 17, "to the extent protected by applicable non-bankruptcy law." Not all intellectual property is covered under the Act. For example, trade names and trade marks are explicitly omitted from protection under the Act. Moreover, although the Act provides substantial incentives and protections to licensees, it does not provide any specific protections for (1) venture capital invested by licensors in high technology companies, (2) licenses entered into between debtor-licensees and solvent licensors, or (3) licenses of intellectual property that are assumed and assigned to third parties. For example, the drafters did not propose to protect a venture capital licensee's investment by treating the licensee as a secured creditor, nor did Congress attempt to examine the effect that a licensee's vested right to the technology would have on the rights of secured creditors. In addition, the drafters failed to address the situation in which the debtor-licensor owns the original intellectual property, and the licensee owns updates or supplements to the technology that are essential to the debtor's use of the product. Finally, the Act is silent about the degree of adequate protection that must be provided to the licensee so as to permit assignment of the license to third parties. In these instances, the provisions of the Act may deviate from the judiciary committees' stated purpose of protecting technological innovation.

### III. THE PROTECTIONS OFFERED LICENSEES UNDER SECTION 365(n)(1)

Section 365(n), unlike most other Code provisions, was drafted with the expectation that licensees will engage in pre-bankruptcy planning. Indeed, section 365(n) explicitly allows licensees to modify contractual rights given to debtors and creditors under the Code. These rights, addressed in the following subsections, include the debtor's right to (1) reject onerous executory contracts, (2) enforce the protections of the automatic stay, (3) require notice and a hearing before property is removed from the estate, and (4) avoid adherence to ipso facto clauses. Although these rights are broad, the Act places the onus of drafting on licensees. If the right is not retained in the license, the non-Act provisions of the Code will undoubtedly be applied to the license agreement.

### A. Section 365(n)(1) — The Licensee's Right to Retain Its Vested Rights Under the License Agreement

Section 365(n)(1) provides that if the trustee or debtor rejects an executory license agreement covering intellectual property, the licensee may elect either one of the following courses of conduct:

(A) to treat [the] contract as terminated…or (B) to retain its rights (including a right to enforce any exclusivity provision of such contract, but excluding any other right under applicable nonbankruptcy law to specific performance of such contract) under such contract and under any agreement supplementary to such contract…as such rights existed immediately before the case commenced, for—(i) the duration of such contract; and (ii) any period for which such contract may be extended by the licensee as of right under applicable nonbankruptcy law. According to the legislative history of section 365(n)(1), in the event that the license agreement is rejected, the licensor may retain the following rights under the terms of the agreement:

(a) Protection of trade secrets, copyrights, patents and confidential information against all persons including creditors;

(b) Continued exclusive use and distribution of the intellectual property for the length of the license as well as any extensions provided under the license or applicable law; and

(c) Enforcement of non-compete clauses against the debtor and any successor entity.

The drafters recognized that the term of license agreements is often contingent upon the occurrence of certain triggering events, such as the approval of a patent application.

Accordingly, the scope of section 365(n)(1) is not limited to contracts that have commenced as of the filing date. Rather, "[t]he benefits of the bill are intended to extend to such license agreements [that commence upon a 'triggering event'], consistent with the limitation that the licensee's rights are only in the underlying intellectual property as it existed at the time of the filing."

Section 365(n)(1) does not, however, protect the licensee's right to property that is not fully developed, nor does it provide for reduction of royalty payments for use of such partially developed property. Therefore, although section 365(n)(1) provides a degree of prospective relief generally unavailable to parties to executory contracts, it ignores the economic reality that the licensor may file a bankruptcy petition before it completes development of the intellectual property. In that event, the contractual expectations of the licensee will be frustrated because the licensee will have the right to use the technology only in the form that existed as of the filing date, despite the fact that the parties contemplated that the licensee would benefit from the licensor's development of the technology into a more sophisticated form.

---

# IV. Judicial Interpretation of Section 365(n)

Following the enactment of the Intellectual Property Bankruptcy Protection Act (IPBPA) in 1988, creating Section 365(n), the judiciary went to work interpreting the statutory language. This judicial gloss has had a significant impact on the application of 365(n). For instance, the term "royalties" in 365(n) has been clarified by the courts in cases such as the following.

---

## In Re Prize Frize Inc.
### 32 F.3d 426 (9th Cir. 1994)

PERRIS, J.

This case, of first impression in any circuit, turns on whether license fees, paid by a licensee for the use of technology, patents, and proprietary rights, are "royalties" within the meaning of 11 U.S.C. Section 365(n)(2)(B) and, as such, must continue to be paid after the licensor in bankruptcy has exercised its statutory right to reject the contract.

### FACTS

The debtor, Prize Frize, Inc., is the owner and licensor of all technology, patents, proprietary rights and related rights used in the manufacture and sale of a french fry vending machine. On March 6, 1991, the debtor entered into a License Agreement granting an exclusive license to utilize the proprietary rights and to manufacture, use and sell the vending machine. In consideration for the license to use the proprietary information and related rights, the licensee agreed to pay the debtor a $1,250,000 license fee—$300,000 to be paid within ten days of execution of the agreement with the balance due in $50,000 monthly payments. The licensee also agreed to pay royalty payments based on a percentage of franchise fees, of net marketing revenues and of any sales of the machines or certain related products. The license agreement also provided that if there was a failure of design and/or components of the machines to the extent that they were not fit for their intended use and were withdrawn from service, then the licensee's obligations would be suspended for a period of 180 days, during which time the debtor was entitled to cure any defect. Encino Business Management, Inc. (EBM) is the successor licensee under this license.

The debtor filed its Chapter 11 petition on March 12, 1991. In September of 1991, EBM, which had become the licensee, stopped making the $50,000 per month license fee payments and has made no payments since. EBM contends that there is a design defect in the machines which caused the machines to be withdrawn from service and which allowed the suspension of its obligation to pay the debtor.

The debtor subsequently filed a motion to reject the license agreement with EBM and to compel EBM to elect whether it wished to retain its rights under section 365(n)(1). EBM did not file a written response to the motion. At the hearing, EBM's counsel indicated that he did not oppose rejection. He disputed, however, that EBM should be required to immediately pay $350,000 in past due license fee payments, contending that the obligation to make such payments was suspended because of the purported design defect.

The bankruptcy court entered an order indicating that the debtor might reject the agreement, that EBM might elect whether to retain its rights under the agreement pursuant to section 365(n)(1) and that if EBM elected to retain its rights under the agreement it must do the following: (1) make all license fee payments presently due in the amount of $350,000 within seven days of its election; (2) pay the $400,000 balance of the license fee in monthly installments of $50,000; and (3) waive any and all rights of setoff with respect to the contract and applicable non-bankruptcy law and any claim under section 503(b) arising from performance under the agreement. The court's order also stated that assuming, arguendo, that EBM's payment obligations were properly suspended, the 180-day suspension period had ended and the September to March monthly payments were now due.

EBM appealed. The BAP held that the license fees were "royalty payments" within the meaning of 11 U.S.C. Section 365(n)(1)(B). The BAP also noted that EBM had submitted no evidence of a design defect justifying it in suspending the payments. The BAP affirmed the order of the bankruptcy court. EBM appeals.

## ANALYSIS

No evidence has been presented by EBM of design defect, and so we do not consider this basis for EBM's appeal but proceed to its principal contention.

Section 365 of the Bankruptcy Code is an intricate statutory scheme governing the treatment by the trustee in bankruptcy or the debtor-in-possession of the executory contracts of the debtor. There is no dispute that the license agreement between EBM and the debtor was executory, i.e. there were obligations on both sides which to some extent were unperformed. *See In re Frontier Properties, Inc.*, 979 F.2d 1358, 1364 (9th Cir. 1992); *In re Quintex Entertainment, Inc.*, 950 F.2d 1492, 1495–96 (9th Cir. 1991). Consequently, the debtor had the right to reject the contract. However, section 365(n)(1) qualifies this right when the debtor is "a licensor of a right to intellectual property." There is no dispute that the debtor is such a licensor. *See* 11 U.S.C. Section 101(56) defining intellectual property). Consequently, EBM as "the licensee under such contract" could make an election. Section 365(n)(1). EBM could either treat the contract as terminated as provided by (n)(1)(A), or EBM could retain its rights to the intellectual property for the duration of the contract and any period for which the contract might be extended by the licensee as of right under applicable nonbankruptcy law. *Id.* at (n)(1)(B).

EBM elected to retain its rights. It was then obligated to "make all royalty payments due under such contract." *Id.* at (n)(2)(B). By the terms of the statute EBM was also "deemed to waive any right of setoff it may have with respect to such contract under this title or applicable nonbankruptcy law." *Id.* at (n)(2)(C)(i).

Section 365(n) has struck a fair balance between the interests of the bankrupt and the interests of a licensee of the bankrupt's intellectual property. The bankrupt cannot terminate and strip the licensee of rights the licensee had bargained for. The licensee cannot retain the use able of those rights without paying for them. It is essential to the balance struck that the payments due for the use of the intellectual property should be analyzed as "royalties," required by the statute itself to be met by the licensee who is enjoying the benefit of the bankrupt's patents, proprietary property, and technology. As the BAP observed, the legislative history buttresses this commonsense interpretation of "royalties" in the statute. *See* H.R. Rep. No. 1012, 100th Cong., 2d Sess., at 9 (1988).

EBM's principal argument is that the licensing agreement itself makes a distinction between what the agreement calls "license fees" and what the agreement calls "royalty payments." The "royalty payments" in the agreement are percentages payable on the retail sales price of each machine sold by EBM; the "license fees" in the agreement are the sums here in dispute, which were to be paid for the license to manufacture and sell the vending machine. EBM's argument is not frivolous. Nonetheless the parties by their choice of names cannot alter the underlying reality nor change the balance that the Bankruptcy Code has struck. Despite the nomenclature used in the agreement, the license fees to be paid by EBM are royalties in the sense of section 365(n). Section 365(n) speaks repeatedly of "licensor" and "licensee" with the clear implication that payments by licensee to licensor for the use of intellectual property are, indifferently, "licensing fees" or "royalties," and, as royalties, must be paid by the licensee who elects to keep its license after the licensor's bankruptcy. The same indifference to nomenclature in referring to a licensee's lump sum or percentage-of-sales payments as royalties is apparent in patent cases. *Zenith Radio Corp. v. Hazeltine Research, Inc.,* 395 U.S. 100, 138–39 (1969); *Automatic Radio Manufacturing Co., Inc. v. Hazeltine Research, Inc.,* 339 U.S. 827 (1950).

EBM's fallback position on appeal is that the debtor has been freed by its rejection of the contract from the obligations assumed by the debtor under Article V ("Representations, Warranties and Covenants by PFI") of the agreement. These obligations included the debtor's agreement to hold EBM harmless from any claim arising out of events preceding the agreement, to defend any infringement suit relating to technology or design included in the machine, and to prosecute at its own expense any infringers of the rights granted by the agreement. The debtor also represented that the design of the Stand-Alone Machine was free from material defects. These obligations raise the question whether it is proper to consider all of the license fees as royalties or whether some portion of the fees should be allocated to payment for the obligations assumed by the debtor. Neither the bankruptcy court nor the BAP addressed this possibility. They did not because EBM did not present this question to them. It is consequently too late to raise it here. EBM still has its unsecured claim for breach of the entire license agreement that section 365(g) accords it. As its appeal was non-frivolous, no attorney's fees are awarded.

As what the licensing agreement denominates "license fees" must be regarded as "royalty payments" for purposes of Section 365(n)(1)(B), the judgment of the BAP is

AFFIRMED.

---

# V. Effect of IPBPA on Licensing Intellectual Property

While most agree that the IPBPA brought needed reform, many commentators believe that licensees, especially trademark licensees, should receive additional protections.

## The Effect of Bankruptcy on the Licensing of Intellectual Property Rights[*]

Anthony Giaccio

2 ALBANY L. J. OF SCIENCE & TECH. 93 (1992)

\* \* \*

### IV. THE DIFFICULTIES CREATED BY THE DEFINITION OF INTELLECTUAL PROPERTY: PURPOSE AND EFFECT

A problem arises when protected rights are granted in conjunction with rights that are excluded from the definition of intellectual property. Excluding some of the rights from protection may deprive a licensee of the overall value of the section 365(n) right of election. An illustration of this situation occurs when a licensor grants an ancillary trade right, such as a trade name or another state law based intellectual property right, in connection with patent or copyright. Since the licensee's right of election does not cover the entire bundle of intellectual property rights required in order to market the ultimate product, the licensee's benefit is greatly reduced.

### A. Why Are Certain Forms of Intellectual Property Excluded?

#### 1. A Review of the Legislative History

It is helpful to review the statute's legislative history in trying to assess why Congress included some but not all intellectual property rights in section 101(56). Early versions of section 101(56) included the term intellectual property without defining it. As hearings before the House Subcommittee on Monopolies and Commercial Law and the Senate Subcommittee on Courts and Administrate Practice progressed, concern was raised regarding the scope of the application of the statute to intellectual property. In order that the statute not be read to exclude major forms of intellectual property, Congress decided to detail the scope of the term. However, in order to frame a broad definition, Congress actually narrowed the term to encompass only those rights mentioned in section 101(56).

One substantial body of federal and state intellectual property law that is not covered by the definition is trademark law. Trademarks, like the other forms of intellectual property, are unique and deserving of independent protection. However, opponents of

---

[*] Reprinted with permission of the publisher, copyright 1992.

including trademarks in the definition of intellectual property feared that their inclusion would extend the application of section 365(n) too liberally by granting a right of election to every retail franchise that owned a trademark. The scope of section 365(n) should and does create an exemption to section 365(a) with regard to the intellectual property elements of a contract. An element of intellectual property does not run with the owner to all contracts. The statute states that the contract must be one dealing specifically with intellectual property in order for the exemption to apply at all. Section 101 does not include trademarks for another reason: In order to retain a protected interest, the trademark licensor is obligated to monitor the use of the mark in order to ensure its integrity, thereby requiring a continuing obligation on the part of the licensor. Though there was concern about the continued impact of the Lubrizol decision on the licensee, Congress was reluctant to change the law with respect to trademarks without further study.

The concerns of Congress are inapposite for several reasons. First, although a trustee may not be qualified to maintain the integrity of the mark, a debtor in possession is certainly capable of performing that function. Second, the purpose of rejecting the contract is to re-license the trademark to another licensee at a better rate in order to increase the source of income needed to repay general creditors. In such a situation, a trustee may be managing the estate, thereby raising the identical issue of whether the trustee is capable of adequately monitoring the use of the mark. Lastly, if the trustee retains the mark without re-licensing it after rejecting the contract, then the trustee will still be obliged to maintain the mark. Failure to use the mark at all by anyone may also constitute a loss of protection for the mark, a detriment to the unsecured creditors. All of these consequences can be avoided by allowing the original licensee to elect to retain the trademark rights under the contract thereby guaranteeing the continuing obligation to pay royalties to the debtor and to protect the integrity of the trademark. This alternative makes more sense since the licensee has an economic incentive—the success of the product or service covered by the trademark—to maintain the integrity of the mark.

### 2. A Look at the Constitutional Basis for Congressional Legislation

The conceptual basis for the 1988 amendment can be found in two areas of the Constitution. First, under Article I, Section 8, Clause 4, laws may be made that are designed to "[t]o keep secure the rights of intellectual property licensors and licensees which come under protection of title 11 of United States Code, the bankruptcy code." Second, under Article I, Section 8, Clause 8, Congress is empowered to draft laws that "promote the Progress of Science and useful Arts, by securing for limited Times to Authors and Inventors the exclusive Right to their respective Writings and Discoveries."

It may be asserted that not all forms of intellectual property rights are included in the statutory definition because the conceptual foundation and the constitutional basis are limited to forms of federally protected rights. Any extension to state law based rights would exceed the constitutional basis of the legislation. There are, however, several flaws with this analysis. First, section 101(56) includes trade secret law as a form of intellectual property. Trade secret law, although by its nature uniformly protected by secrecy, is a state law based right that varies from jurisdiction to jurisdiction. Second, while it is true that trademarks, trade names, and service marks, which are excluded from section 101(56), are not derived from either of the clauses mentioned above, Congress has the authority to protect these rights under the Commerce Clause. Congress may, therefore, protect those marks that affect interstate commerce. The current lack of uniform application of section 365(n) creates inequities because it fails to balance the competing interests of both bankruptcy and intellectual property law.

## B. The Effect: The Intended Result Is Frustrated
### When a License Includes Multiple Types of Rights

Although Congress intended to keep the definition of intellectual property broad, it did not reach the entire scope of the subject matter. Intellectual property is a fluid body of law. There are many instances when the value of the ultimate product depends upon the combination of several different forms of intellectual property rights. If the power to elect among these rights does not apply to all of the forms embodied in the final product, the value of retaining any single right is severely diminished. A prominent example arises in the computer software industry. A licensor of a computer software program may license both a copyrighted program and the trademark of the program to a licensee. Pursuant to the contract, the licensee may make, use, and sell the program to the public. The licensee will market the final product to the public. If the licensor files for bankruptcy, it may reject the contract as executory when rejection is to the advantage of its unsecured creditors. The licensee then has the right to elect to retain some rights to the program. The licensee may retain the right to make, use, and sell the computer software program, but since trademarks are not covered under the statute as intellectual property, the licensee may not market the product under the trade name. The licensor retains the trademark rights and may license those rights to a third party.

This bifurcation of intellectual property rights is not a sound policy. Under section 365(g), the licensee is left with a money damage claim for the breach of contract, not injunctive relief. Money damages are often inadequate because the value of the license is lost since the licensee's product must now be marketed under a new trademark and another manufacturer may use the prior trademark. Moreover, the licensor would not have rejected the contract if it were not advantageous when balanced against the money damage claim.

As a matter of public policy this is not a favorable situation. The value of the trademark may be a result of the licensee's use of the mark. The result, marketing of an alternative and potentially inferior product under the trade name made valuable by the former licensor, runs contrary to a basic tenet of trademark law—to avoid confusion as to the source of the product. The intended result of section 365(n), to secure the rights of licensors and licensees of intellectual property, is frustrated because the commercial value of the right of election is lost.

## V. THE DIFFICULTIES WITH THE EXISTING MECHANISM

### A. It Does Not Satisfy the Fundamental Policy Objectives of Either Body of Law

One of the central problems of the overlap of bankruptcy and intellectual property protection is that the two bodies of law have inconsistent fundamental policy objectives. The application of a rigid test, such as that used in *Lubrizol* and embodied in the amended section 365(n), does not assure the proper balance between the two bodies of law.

### 1. Bankruptcy Law Policy

The primary purpose of section 365(a) is to relieve the bankrupt estate from burdensome obligations. One theme of the bankruptcy process is to give the debtor a fresh start. In *NLRB v. Bildisco and Bildisco*, a collective bargaining agreement case, the Supreme Court stated that the "policy of Chapter 11 is to permit the successful rehabilitation of debtors." The second purpose of section 365(a) is to provide a maximum distribution of the remaining assets to the general unsecured creditors. This objective is guided by the fact that there will not be enough money to pay all of the creditors in full. Accordingly, it is the responsibility of the representative to gather as much of the debtor's assets as possible and distribute them to creditors. Section 365(a) fulfills this goal by allowing the representative to reject any burdensome contracts thereby permitting the debtor to re-license the subject matter of the license at a higher royalty rate.

Generally, this is an effective policy. The debtor may renegotiate with existing licensees or attract new licensees who may be willing to pay higher royalty rates. In exchange, the rejected licensee retains a money damage cause of action for breach of contract. Ordinarily, the injury to the licensee is not deleterious since there is usually an alternative source of supply of the subject matter of the license, and the money award acts as cover. In special circumstances, however, the application of section 365(a) is not equitable due to the nature of the subject matter involved. In such instances, exemptions have been made to this mechanism permitting the sale, lease, or time-share of real property, collective bargaining agreements, and intellectual property licenses.

### 2. Intellectual Property Law Policy

The principal purpose of intellectual property licensing is the need for a reliable mechanism for the protection and dissemination of technological innovation and creativity. Licensing is one of the most effective tools for promoting this policy since it allows the creator to establish and expand commercial applications of the subject matter. It is also a flexible tool for granting others the exclusive or non-exclusive right to make, use, or sell the underlying protected interest. The inventor retains an ownership interest in the subject matter and may grant ownership rights to others. The licensor may license the entire right to several individuals in different geographic areas for different lengths of time, or may license parts of the entire right. The inventor may also limit the rights granted to certain applications or industries.

Licensing also promotes the efficient dissemination of technology from the stage of creation and innovation to the stage of application and production. While a sale grants rights to one entity, with licensing a larger number of entities may actually be using the technology. Absent licensing, a licensee would be required to purchase the technology outright and may not be willing to compensate a licensor at a high rate because the value of the license at that point will be quite speculative. The licensing scheme creates an innovation incentive for by small, start-up companies to license technology by relying on otherwise unavailable seed money that is needed to recoup research and development costs. In addition, the public at large and the national economy benefit by the efficient transfer of technology from the inventor to the work place.

An intellectual property license by definition involves unique rights. The grant is an inherently powerful tool because of its exclusive nature and the resulting lack of alternative supply. On a scientific level, alternative methods could be developed, but further development may be economically prohibitive. When a licensee is denied an exclusive right, the licensee has effectively lost the ability to utilize that product or process absent infringement for a period of time.

## B. The Rigid Application of Section 365 Frustrates the Policy Objectives

The rigid application of section 365(n) frustrates policy objectives behind bankruptcy and intellectual property law. To illustrate how continued inequities will result under the rigid mechanism, the facts in Lubrizol will be reviewed as if decided under the new section 365(n) mechanism.

In *Lubrizol*, the court of appeals held that the non-exclusive contract between the parties was executory and properly rejected by the debtor in possession. Under the new section 365(n), the licensee would then have the right to elect to retain specified rights to the technology under the rejected contract.

In terms of bankruptcy law, the changed outcome may still be inequitable because a licensee may never have used or relied upon the technology granted in the license; therefore, the bankrupt licensor would be required to retain obligations under a contract when rejection would not harm the licensee. Such was the fact situation in *Lubrizol*. Nonetheless, the licensee may still elect to retain the rights to the technology. The resulting situation is inequitable because the debtor's interest in rehabilitation and maximizing the funds available to unsecured creditors would outweigh the licensee's injury flowing from the rejection of the contract. A flexible balancing test, including this factor in the decision of whether or not to allow the licensor to reject the contract, would be more equitable.

Permitting the licensee to elect to retain rights under the new section 365(n) mechanism is also inequitable because the licensee does not receive the full bundle of bargained-for rights under the right of election. The rights retained under section 365(n) are limited to the technology developed at the time of the bankruptcy filing and are not defined by the terms of the contract. In addition, the licensee may demand only embodiments or derivative works of technology in existence prior to the petition filing date and pursuant to a pre-petition agreement. Absent the section 365(n) statutory mechanism, the debtor would assume the contract and the parties continue to perform under its terms.

The creation of a restrictive, where a licensor may reject the contract without regard to the effect on the licensee and the licensee may elect to retain rights under the contract without regard to the effect on the licensor, is inequitable. Moreover, it fails to give the bankruptcy court enough flexibility to balance both the fundamental policy objectives of each body of law and the equitable factors that arise in a particular case.

---

# VI. Unexpected Judicial Results

## Institut Pasteur v. Cambridge Biotech Corp.
### 104 F.3d 489 (1st Cir. 1997)

CYR, J.

Unsuccessful in their intermediate appeal to the district court, Institut Pasteur and Pasteur Sanofi Diagnostics (collectively: "Pasteur") again appeal from the bankruptcy court order which confirmed the chapter 11 reorganization plan ("Plan") proposed by debtor-in-possession Cambridge Biotech Corporation ("CBC"), the holder of two licenses to utilize Pasteur patents. The Plan provision central to the present dispute calls for the sale of all CBC stock to a subsidiary of bioMerieux Vitek, Inc. ("bioMerieux"), a major competitor of appellant Pasteur. Finding no error, we affirm.

I

BACKGROUND

CBC manufactures and sells retroviral diagnostic tests for detecting the human immunodeficiency virus (HIV) associated with AIDS. Its HIV diagnostics division annually generates approximately $14 million in revenues. Institut Pasteur, a nonprofit French foundation engaged in AIDS-related research and development, owns various patented procedures for diagnosing HIV Virus Type 2 ("HIV2 procedures"). Pasteur Sanofi Diagnostics holds the exclusive right to use and sublicense Institut Pasteur's patents.

In October 1989, CBC and Pasteur entered into mutual cross-license agreements, whereby each acquired a nonexclusive perpetual license to use some of the technology patented or licensed by the other. Specifically, CBC acquired the right to incorporate Pasteur's HIV2 procedures into any diagnostic kits sold by CBC in the United States, Canada, Mexico, Australia, New Zealand and elsewhere.

Each cross-license broadly prohibits the licensee from assigning or sublicensing to others. *See* Royalty-Free Cross-License, at Section 7.1; Royalty-Bearing Cross-License, at Section 8.1 (" [N]o other person shall acquire or have any right under or by virtue of this Agreement."). Nevertheless, either Pasteur or CBC was authorized to "extend to its Affiliated Companies the benefits of this Agreement so that such party shall remain responsible with regard [to] all [license] obligations." *Id.* Section 1.4. "Affiliated Company" is defined as "an organization that controls or is controlled by a party or an organization that is under common control with a party." *Id.*

CBC filed its chapter 11 petition on July 7, 1994, and thereafter continued to operate its retroviral diagnostic testing business as debtor-in-possession. Its reorganization plan proposed that CBC assume both cross-licenses, see 11 U.S.C. Section 365 (executory contracts), continue to operate its retroviral diagnostics division utilizing Pasteur's patented HIV2 procedures, and sell all CBC stock to a subsidiary of bioMerieux, a giant French biotechnology corporation and Pasteur's direct competitor in international biotechnology sales. Pasteur previously had licensed bioMerieux to use its HIV2 procedures, but the earlier license related to a single product manufactured by bioMerieux (i.e., bioMerieux's VIDAS automated immunoassay test system), and applied only to VIDAS sales in markets other than the United States, Canada, Mexico, Australia, and New Zealand, markets expressly encompassed within the CBC cross-licenses.

Not surprisingly, in due course Pasteur objected to the Plan. Citing Bankruptcy Code Section 365(c), 11 U.S.C. Section 365(c), it contended that the proposed sale of CBC's stock to bioMerieux amounted to CBC's assumption of the patent cross-licenses and their de facto "assignment" to a third party in contravention of the presumption of nonassignability ordained by the federal common law of patents, as well as the explicit nonassignability provision contained in the cross-licenses. Isabelle Bressac, Pasteur's licensing director, attested that Pasteur would not have granted its competitor, bioMerieux, or a subsidiary, a patent license under the terms allowed CBC.

The bankruptcy court authorized CBC to assume the cross-licenses over Pasteur's objection. It ruled that the proposed sale of CBC stock to bioMerieux did not constitute a de facto "assignment" of the cross-licenses to bioMerieux, but merely an assumption of the cross-licenses by the reorganized debtor under new owner ship, and that Bankruptcy Code Section 365(c) enabled CBC to assume the cross-licenses as debtor-in-possession because the prepetition licensing relationship between Pasteur and CBC was neither "unique" nor "something in the category of a personal services contract." *In re Cambridge Biotech Corp.*, No. 94- 43054, slip op. at 17–18, 24 (Bankr. D. Mass. Sept. 18, 1996). The district court upheld the bankruptcy court ruling on intermediate appeal.

II

DISCUSSION

* * *

B.The Merits

Pasteur argues that the CBC Plan effects a de facto assignment of its two cross-licenses to bioMerieux, contrary to Bankruptcy Code Section 365(c)(1) which provides as follows:

> The trustee [*viz.*, CBC] may not assume or assign any executory contract... whether or not such contract...prohibits or restricts assignment of rights or delegation of duties, if—
>
> (1) (A) applicable law excuses a party[ ] other than the debtor [ ] [ *viz.*, Pasteur] to such contract...from accepting performance from or rendering performance to an entity other than the debtor or the debtor in possession, whether or not such contract...prohibits or restricts assumption or assignment; and
>
> (B)such party [ *viz.*, Pasteur] does not consent to such assumption or assignment....

11 U.S.C. Section 365(c)(1).

Pasteur argues that in order to encourage optimum product innovation the federal common law of patents presumes that patent licensees, such as CBC, may not sublicense to third parties absent the patent holder's consent. This federal common law rule of presumptive nonassignability thus qualifies as an "applicable law," within the meaning of Bankruptcy Code Section 365(c)(1)(A), which precludes Pasteur from being compelled to accept performance from any entity other than CBC e.g., bioMerieux's subsidiary and therefore prevents CBC from either assuming or assigning these cross-licenses. *See Everex Sys., Inc. v. Cadtrak Corp. (In re CFLC, Inc.)*, 89 F.3d 673, 679–80 (9th Cir. 1996) (federal patent law of nonassignability preempts state law relating to patent license assignability). Further, says Pasteur, even assuming that section 365(c) might allow a debtor simply to assume the cross-licenses without a subsequent assignment to a third party, CBC formally structured this Plan transaction as an assumption by the debtor-in-possession, whereas in substance it was an assignment of the cross-licenses to bioMerieux, a complete stranger to the original cross-licensing agreements.

These contentions are foreclosed by our decision in *Summit Inv. & Dev. Corp. v. Leroux (In re Leroux)*, 69 F.3d 608 (1st Cir. 1995), which analyzed and interpreted companion Bankruptcy Code subsections 365(c) and (e) and their relevant legislative history. As in the present case, in *Leroux* we were urged to interpret subsections 365(c) and (e) as mandating a "hypothetical test." Under such an approach, the chapter 11 debtor would lose its option to assume the contract, even though it never intended to assign the contract to another entity, if either the particular executory contract or the applicable nonbankruptcy law purported to terminate the contract automatically upon the filing of the chapter 11 petition or to preclude its assignment to an entity not a party to the contract. *Id.* at 612.

We rejected the proposed hypothetical test in *Leroux*, holding instead that subsections 365(c) and (e) contemplate a case-by-case inquiry into whether the nondebtor party (viz., Pasteur) actually was being "forced to accept performance under its executory contract from someone other than the debtor party with whom it originally contracted." *Id.* Where the particular transaction envisions that the debtor-in-possession would assume and continue to perform under an executory contract, the bankruptcy court cannot simply presume as a matter of law that the debtor-in-possession is a legal entity materially distinct from the prepetition debtor with whom the nondebtor party (viz., Pasteur) contracted. *Id.* at 613–14 (citing H.R. Rep. No. 1195, 96th Cong., 2d Sess. Section 27(b) (1980); *NLRB v. Bildisco & Bildisco*, 465 U.S. 513, 528 (1984)). Rather, "sensitive to the rights of the nondebtor party (viz., Pasteur)," the bankruptcy court must focus on the performance actually to be rendered by the debtor-in-possession with a view to ensuring that the nondebtor party (viz., Pasteur) will receive "the full benefit of [its] bargain." *Id.* at 612–13 (citing S. Rep. No. 989, 95th Cong., 2d Sess. 59 (1978), *reprinted in* 1980 U.S.C.C.A.N. 5787, 5845).

Given the pragmatic "actual performance" test adopted in *Leroux*, the ultimate findings of fact and conclusions of law made by the bankruptcy court below did not constitute error. CBC simply does not occupy the same position as the debtor in *CFLC, Inc.*, 89 F.3d 673 (9th Cir. 1996), upon which Pasteur relies most heavily. The Plan in *CFLC, Inc.* unmistakably provided for an outright assignment of the debtor's patent license to an entirely different corporation with which the patent holder Cadtrak Corporation had never contracted. *Id.* at 679–80. By contrast, CBC all along has conducted, and proposes to continue, its retroviral diagnostic enterprise as the same corporate entity which functioned prepetition, while utilizing Pasteur's HIV2 procedures in that same prepetition endeavor.

Pasteur nonetheless insists that the reorganized CBC is different than the prepetition entity, not due merely to its Chapter 11 filing but because it is now owned by a different legal entity than before namely, bioMerieux's subsidiary qua CBC shareholder. Pasteur's contention finds no support, however, either in Massachusetts law...or in the cross-license provisions it negotiated.

Stock sales are not mergers whereby outright title and ownership of the licensee-corporation's assets (including its patent licenses) pass to the acquiring corporation. Rather, as a corporation, CBC "is a legal entity distinct from its shareholders." *Seagram Distillers Co. v. Alcoholic Beverages Control Comm'n*, 519 N.E.2d 276, 281 (Mass. 1988) (citing 6 William M. Fletcher, Cyclopedia of Corporations § 2456 (1979 & Supp. 1986)). Absent compelling grounds for disregarding its corporate form, therefore, CBC's separate legal identity, and its ownership of the patent cross-licenses, survive without interruption notwithstanding repeated and even drastic changes in its ownership. *See id.* (holding that corporation's sale of all its capital stock does not alter its identity, nor effect a transfer of the corporation's executory contracts or licenses); *see also PPG Indus. v. Guardian Indus. Corp.*, 597 F.2d 1090, 1096 (6th Cir.), *cert. denied*, 444 U.S. 930 (1979) (same; distinguishing mere sale of stock from a transfer of patent license as part of corporate merger wherein merging licensee ends its corporate existence). Pasteur cites no apposite authority to the contrary.

Furthermore, Pasteur's position finds no support in the negotiated terms of its cross-licenses. As the patent holder and given CBC's corporate form and the governing Massachusetts law, *supra*, Pasteur was free to negotiate restrictions on CBC's continuing rights under the cross-licenses based on changes in its stock ownership or corporate control. *See id.* at 1095 (parties may override law of merger by negotiating express patent license provision); *see also Seagram*, 519 N.E.2d at 280–81. Nevertheless, these cross-licenses contain no provision either limiting or terminating CBC's rights in the event its stock ownership were to change hands. The generic nonassignability provisions found in these cross-licenses, see, e.g., Royalty-Free Cross-License, at Section 7.1 ("This Agreement...has been made solely for the benefit of the parties hereto" and "no other person shall acquire or have any right under or by virtue of this Agreement."), plainly do not address the circumstance presented here. Rather, these nonassignability provisions simply beg the essential question, which is whether bioMerieux's subsidiary, by virtue of its acquisition of CBC stock, terminated CBC's rights under the cross-licenses. Interpreted as Pasteur proposes, CBC's own rights under the cross-licenses would terminate with any change in the identity of any CBC stockholder.

Other cross-license provisions directly undercut Pasteur's interpretation as well. *See Willitts v. Roman Catholic Archbishop of Boston*, 581 N.E.2d 475, 478 (Mass. 1991) (noting that a contract must be interpreted as a whole). These cross-licenses explicitly authorize CBC to share its license rights with any "affiliated company," which on its face presumably encompasses a parent corporation such as bioMerieux's subsidiary. Cross-Licenses, at Section 1.4 (defining "Affiliated Company" as "an organization which controls...a party or an organization which is under common control with a party"); *see, supra,* Section I. Yet more importantly, CBC insisted upon a provision which would afford it the unilateral right to terminate any sublicense Pasteur might extend to a company called Genetic Systems "if control of Genetic Systems shall...be acquired, directly or indirectly, by any person or group of connected persons or company not having such control at the date hereof, by reconstruction, amalgamation, acquisition of shares or assets or otherwise." Royalty-Free-Cross-license, at Section 2.3 (emphasis added); *see PPG Indus.*, 597 F.2d at 1096 (noting that patent holder's express reservation of change-of-stock-ownership condition in two patent licenses suggested its intention not to reserve condition in nine other patent licenses); *see also Plumbers & Steamfitters Local 150 v. Vertex Constr. Co.*, 932 F.2d 1443, 1449 (11th Cir. 1991) ("[T]he doctrine of *expressio unius est exclusio alterius* instructs that when certain matters are mentioned in a contract, other similar matters not mentioned were intended to be excluded."). Taken together, these provisions persuade us that Pasteur foresaw, or reasonably should have foreseen, that CBC might undergo changes of stock ownership that would not alter its corporate legal identity, but nonetheless chose not to condition the continued viability of its cross-licenses accordingly.

## III

## CONCLUSION

As CBC remains in all material respects the legal entity with which Pasteur freely contracted, Pasteur has not made the required individualized showing that it is or will be deprived of "the full benefit of [its] bargain," *Leroux*, 69 F.3d at 612–13, under the ruling challenged on appeal. Accordingly, the district court judgment is affirmed and costs are awarded to appellee. So ordered.

# In re Catapult Entertainment, Inc., v.
# Catapult Entertainment, Inc.

### 165 F.3d 747 (9th Cir. 1999)

FLETCHER, Circuit Judge:

Appellant Stephen Perlman ("Perlman") licensed certain patents to appellee Catapult Entertainment, Inc. ("Catapult"). He now seeks to bar Catapult, which has since become a Chapter 11 debtor in possession, from assuming the patent licenses as part of its reorganization plan. Notwithstanding Perlman's objections, the bankruptcy court approved the assumption of the licenses and confirmed the reorganization plan. The district court affirmed the bankruptcy court on intermediate appeal. Perlman appeals that decision. We are called upon to determine whether, in light of § 365(c)(1) of the Bankruptcy Code, a Chapter 11 debtor in possession may assume certain nonexclusive patent licenses over a licensor's objection. We conclude that the bankruptcy court erred in permitting the debtor in possession to assume the patent licenses in question.

## I.

Catapult, a California corporation, was formed in 1994 to create an online gaming network for 16-bit console videogames. That same year, Catapult entered into two license agreements with Perlman, wherein Perlman granted to Catapult the right to exploit certain relevant technologies, including patents and patent applications.

In October 1996, Catapult filed for reorganization under Chapter 11 of the Bankruptcy Code. Shortly before the filing of the bankruptcy petition, Catapult entered into a merger agreement with Mpath Interactive, Inc. ("Mpath"). This agreement contemplated the filing of the bankruptcy petition, followed by a reorganization via a "reverse triangular merger" involving Mpath, MPCAT Acquisition Corporation ("MPCAT"), and Catapult. Under the terms of the merger agreement, MPCAT (a wholly-owned subsidiary of Mpath created for this transaction) would merge into Catapult, leaving Catapult as the surviving entity. When the dust cleared, Catapult's creditors and equity holders would have received approximately $14 million in cash, notes, and securities; Catapult, in turn, would have become a wholly-owned subsidiary of Mpath. The relevant third party creditors and equity holders accepted Catapult's reorganization plan by the majorities required by the Bankruptcy Code.

On October 24, 1996, as part of the reorganization plan, Catapult filed a motion with the bankruptcy court seeking to assume some 140 executory contracts and leases, including the Perlman licenses. Over Perlman's objection, the bankruptcy court granted Catapult's motion and approved the reorganization plan. The district court subsequently affirmed the bankruptcy court. This appeal followed. We have jurisdiction pursuant to 28 U.S.C. § 158(d) and, because the relevant facts are undisputed, review the orders below *de novo. See Everex Sys. v. Cadtrak Corp. (In re CFLC, Inc.),* 89 F.3d 673, 675 (9th Cir. 1996).

## II.

Section 365 of the Bankruptcy Code gives a trustee in bankruptcy (or, in a Chapter 11 case, the debtor in possession) the authority to assume, assign, or reject the executory contracts and unexpired leases of the debtor, notwithstanding any contrary provisions appearing in such contracts or leases. *See* 11 U.S.C. § 365(a) & (f). This extraordinary authority, however, is not absolute. Section 365(c)(1) provides that, notwithstanding the general policy set out in § 365(a):

(c) The trustee may not assume or assign any executory contract or unexpired lease of the debtor, whether or not such contract or lease prohibits or restricts assignment of rights or delegation of duties, if

(1)(A) applicable law excuses a party, other than the debtor, to such contract or lease from accepting performance from or rendering performance to an entity other than the debtor or the debtor in possession, whether or not such contract or lease prohibits or restricts assignment of rights or delegation of duties; and

(B) such party does not consent to such assumption or assignment....

11 U.S.C. § 365(c). Our task, simply put, is to apply this statutory language to the facts at hand and determine whether it prohibits Catapult, as the debtor in possession, from assuming the Perlman licenses without Perlman's consent.

*  *  *

### III.

We begin, as we must, with the statutory language.... Before applying the statutory language to the case at hand, we first resolve a number of preliminary issues that are either not disputed by the parties, or are so clearly established as to deserve no more than passing reference.

[Having] cleared away these preliminary matters, application of the statute to the facts of this case becomes relatively straightforward:

(c) *Catapult* may not assume... *the Perlman licenses,*... if

(1)(A) *federal patent law* excuses *Perlman* from accepting performance from or rendering performance to an entity other than *Catapult*...; and

(B) *Perlman* does not consent to such assumption....

11 U.S.C. § 365(c) (substitutions in italics). Since federal patent law makes nonexclusive patent licenses personal and nondelegable, § 365(c)(1)(A) is satisfied. Perlman has withheld his consent, thus satisfying § 365(c)(1)(B). Accordingly, the plain language of § 365(c)(1) bars Catapult from assuming the Perlman licenses.

### V.

Because the statute speaks clearly, and its plain language does not produce a patently absurd result or contravene any clear legislative history, we must "hold Congress to its words." *Brooker,* 947 F.2d at 414–15. Accordingly, we hold that, where applicable non-bankruptcy law makes an executory contract nonassignable because the identity of the nondebtor party is material, a debtor in possession may not assume the contract absent consent of the nondebtor party. A straightforward application of § 365(c)(1) to the circumstances of this case precludes Catapult from assuming the Perlman licenses over Perlman's objection. Consequently, the bankruptcy court erred when it approved Catapult's motion to assume the Perlman licenses, and the district court erred in affirming the bankruptcy court.

REVERSED.

# VII. Strategies for Protecting Clients in Potential Bankruptcy Settings

Despite its shortcomings, the current Bankruptcy Code is a reality that practitioners must deal with in drafting license agreements. Commentators have proposed several strategies for protecting a client's rights in anticipation of a possible bankruptcy filing. Some of the better and/or more provocative ones follow.

## Intellectual Property Issues in Chapter 11 Bankruptcy Reorganization Cases*

### David S. Kupetz
### 35 IDEA 383 (1995)

* * *

#### C. Drafting Suggestions Designed to Maximize the Protections Available Under Section 365(n) for Intellectual Property Licensees

As discussed above, in order for a licensee to be entitled to the protections of 11 U.S.C. section 365(n), the license agreement must: (1) involve a license of "intellectual property" as defined in 11 U.S.C. section 101(56); and (2) the agreement must be an executory contract. One way to completely avoid the risk of rejection of an executory contract for the intellectual property licensee in a bankruptcy case is for that party, if possible, to purchase the technology outright instead of merely taking it under a license agreement. When addressing the issues presented by a possible future bankruptcy and rejection of the license agreement under 11 U.S.C. section 365(n), the licensee should seek both to create disincentives for rejection of the agreement as an executory contract and to create protections in the event of rejection.

#### D. Make Section 365(n) Explicitly Apply

The addition of section 365(n) to the Bankruptcy Code was designed to increase the likelihood that an intellectual property licensee would receive the benefit of its bargain following the bankruptcy of a licensor it had contracted with. Because the definition of "intellectual property" set forth in 11 U.S.C. section 101(56) is limited and restrictive in scope, the licensee should attempt to characterize the property which will be the subject matter of the agreement in the terms expressly set forth in 11 U.S.C. section 101(56). The licensee should require that the license agreement expressly provide that the parties agree that the licensed property is "intellectual property" as defined in 11 U.S.C. section 101(56) and that the license agreement is governed by 11 U.S.C. section 365(n) in the event that the licensor commences a case under the Bankruptcy Code. Although these provisions may have questionable validity in a later bankruptcy case by the licensor, at a minimum, they should be of value in establishing the parties' intent at the time the agreement was negotiated and may serve as an admission in a future bankruptcy case.

Further, as discussed above, executory contracts for bankruptcy purposes involve situations where unperformed obligations remain on both sides of the agreement as of the

---

date of the commencement of a bankruptcy case. In drafting a license agreement the licensee should see that the agreement itself delineates, in significant detail, the scope and nature of the continuing obligations of both the licensor and the licensee over the life of the contract. In the event the licensor later commences a bankruptcy case, this should increase the likelihood that the agreement will be found to be an executory contract.

## E. Royalty Provisions

When a debtor/licensor rejects an intellectual property license and the licensee elects to continue to use the property, the licensee is required to continue to make "royalty payments" to the licensor. However, while the licensor's rejection of the license agreement does not interfere with the licensee's continued use of the property, rejection permits the licensor to avoid its continuing affirmative obligations under the agreement which might include, for example, any obligation to train the licensee's personnel, to provide marketing service functions, product service, technical service, maintenance functions, defend against infringement, or the like. Thus, when drafting the license agreement, the licensee should specify the payments ("royalty payments") related to the use of the technology and segregate out those payments attributable to the performance of collateral obligations or services such as maintenance, training, marketing or other service. If the payments are lumped into one royalty payment, upon rejection by the debtor/licensor under 11 U.S.C. section 365(n), the licensee could be required to pay the full price for the collateral obligations even if they are not being performed. Thus, if the license is rejected, and the licensor discontinues performing collateral services such as maintenance, training, or marketing or other functions, if the licensee uses adequate care in drafting the agreement, it should not be obligated to make those payments attributable to such unperformed services. The licensee should only have to make the payments related to the use of the intellectual property itself.

An alternative provision could provide for a royalty rate reduction which could explicitly provide that to the extent that a royalty payment for intellectual property is attributable to the licensor's performance of collateral obligations or services, the royalty shall be reduced a defined amount if the collateral obligations are not being performed. Another option would be to structure a forfeiture of the royalty upon a defined event of material breach (other than insolvency or bankruptcy). However, this drastic remedy is likely to be viewed as unenforceable even if not found to be an ipso facto provision.

## F. Assignment Provisions

Section 365(n) of the Bankruptcy Code governs the rejection of an intellectual property license agreement. However, this section does not provide for the assumption or assignment of such an executory contract. Under 11 U.S.C. section 365(f), notwithstanding any provision in the contract to the contrary, the debtor in possession may assign to a third party an executory contract if such contract is assumed and if "adequate assurance of future performance" by the assignee of such contract is provided. With the exception of shopping center leases, what constitutes "adequate assurance of future performance" is not defined in the Bankruptcy Code. In preparing a license agreement, the licensee should attempt to define what constitutes adequate assurance of future performance if the license is ultimately assigned to a third party in a bankruptcy case. For example, it could be explicitly stated that any such assignee must affirmatively assume all of the debtor/licensor's obligations under the agreement and/or that certain net worth or capital requirements must be met by the licensee to ensure that the service, maintenance, marketing, research and development obligations originally bargained for can be fulfilled. While these kinds of provisions in pre- bankruptcy agreements may not be enforceable in the event of a future bankruptcy filing by the licensor, they may provide evidence of the intent of the parties and may serve to help guide the Bankruptcy Court in addressing this issue if it ultimately arises.

### G. Define Events of Material Breach

As stated above, ipso facto clauses that trigger a default or remedy under the contract as a result of the debtor/licensor's insolvency or commencement of a bankruptcy case are unenforceable. Thus, the contractual language should refer to other events of default and remedies. The events, which constitute a breach, should be important to the licensee such as a failure to perform a significant collateral obligation or an ancillary agreement. All such events should be specifically set forth in the contract.

* * *

### H. Perfecting Security Interests in Intellectual Property

As we've seen, one of the recommended strategies for a licensee is to obtain a security interest in the subject matter of the license, so as to position itself as a secured creditor in the event of the licensor's bankruptcy. The greatest challenge here is often perfecting the security interest appropriately. Filings that comply with the typical UCC requirements for perfecting a security interest in other forms of property are not always effective for perfecting security interests in intellectual properties. The proper procedure will vary with the type of intellectual property being licensed, and the same hybrid license will result in several different filings in order to adequately perfect security interests in each of the licensed properties.

---

# VIII. Perfecting Security Interests in Intellectual Property

## A. Perfecting Security Interests in Copyrights

### In re Peregrine Entertainment, Ltd.
### 116 B.R. 194 (C.D. Ca. 1990)

KOZINSKI, Circuit Judge.

This appeal from a decision of the bankruptcy court raises an issue never before confronted by a federal court in a published opinion: Is a security interest in a copyright perfected by an appropriate filing with the United States Copyright Office or by a UCC-1 financing statement filed with the relevant secretary of state?

I

National Peregrine, Inc. (NPI) is a Chapter 11 debtor in possession whose principal assets are a library of copyrights, distribution rights and licenses to approximately 145 films, and accounts receivable arising from the licensing of these films to various programmers. NPI claims to have an outright assignment of some of the copyrights; as for the others, NPI claims it has an exclusive license to distribute in a certain territory, or for a certain period of time....

In June 1985, Capitol Federal Savings and Loan Association of Denver (Cap Fed) extended to American National Enterprises, Inc., NPI's predecessor by merger, a six million dollar line of credit secured by what is now NPI's film library. Both the security agreement and the UCC-1 financing statements filed by Cap Fed describe the collateral as "[a]ll inventory consisting of films and all accounts, contract rights, chattel paper, general intangibles, instruments, equipment, and documents related to such inventory, now owned or hereafter acquired by the Debtor." Although Cap Fed filed its UCC-1 financing statements in California, Colorado and Utah, it did not record its security interest in the United States Copyright Office.

\* \* \*

## II

### A. Where to File

The Copyright Act provides that "[a]ny transfer of copyright ownership or other document pertaining to a copyright" may be recorded in the United States Copyright Office. 17 U.S.C. § 205(a); *see* Copyright Office Circular 12: *Recordation of Transfers and Other Documents* (*reprinted in* 1 Copyright L.Rep. (CCH) P 15,015) [hereinafter "Circular 12"]. A "transfer" under the Act includes any "mortgage" or "hypothecation of a copyright," whether "in whole or in part" and "by any means of conveyance or by operation of law." 17 U.S.C. §§ 101, 201(d)(1); *see* 3 NIMMER ON COPYRIGHT § 10.05[A], at 10-43 — 10-45 (1989). The terms "mortgage" and "hypothecation" include a pledge of property as security or collateral for a debt. *See* BLACK'S LAW DICTIONARY 669 (5th ed., 1979). In addition, the Copyright Office has defined a "document pertaining to a copyright" as one that has a direct or indirect relationship to the existence, scope, duration, or identification of a copyright, or to the ownership, division, allocation, licensing, transfer, or exercise of rights under a copyright. That relationship may be past, present, future, or potential. 37 C.F.R. § 201.4(a)(2); *see also* Compendium of Copyright Office Practices II PP 1602-1603 (identifying which documents the Copyright Office will accept for filing).

It is clear from the preceding that an agreement granting a creditor a security interest in a copyright may be recorded in the Copyright Office. *See* G. GILMORE, SECURITY INTERESTS IN PERSONAL PROPERTY § 17.3, 545 (1965). Likewise, because a copyright entitles the holder to receive all income derived from the display of the creative work, *see* 17 U.S.C. Section 106, an agreement creating a security interest in the receivables generated by a copyright may also be recorded in the Copyright Office. Thus, Cap Fed's security interest could have been recorded in the Copyright Office; the parties seem to agree on this much. The question is does the UCC provide a parallel method of perfecting a security interest in a copyright? One can answer this question by reference to either federal or state law; both inquiries lead to the same conclusion.

1. Even in the absence of express language, federal regulation will preempt state law if it is so pervasive as to indicate that "Congress left no room for supplementary state regulation," or if "the federal interest is so dominant that the federal system will be assumed to preclude enforcement of state laws on the same subject." *Hillsborough*

*County v. Automated Medical Laboratories, Inc.*, 471 U.S. 707, 713, 105 S. Ct. 2371, 2375, 85 L. Ed.2d 714 (1985) (internal quotations omitted). Here, the comprehensive scope of the federal Copyright Act's recording provisions, along with the unique federal interests they implicate, support the view that federal law preempts state methods of perfecting security interests in copyrights and related accounts receivable.

The federal copyright laws ensure "predictability and certainty of copyright owner-ship," "promote national uniformity" and "avoid the practical difficulties of determin-ing and enforcing an author's rights under the differing laws and in the separate courts of the various States." *Community for Creative Non-Violence v. Reid*, 490 U.S. 730, 109 S. Ct. 2166, 2177, 104 L. Ed. 2d 811 (1989); H.R. Rep. No. 1476, 94th Cong., 2d Sess. 129 (1976), U.S.Code Cong. & Admin.News 1976, p. 5659. As discussed above, section 205(a) of the Copyright Act establishes a uniform method for recording security inter-ests in copyrights. A secured creditor need only file in the Copyright Office in order to give "all persons constructive notice of the facts stated in the recorded document." 17 U.S.C. § 205(c).

Likewise, an interested third party need only search the indices maintained by the Copyright Office to determine whether a particular copyright is encumbered. *See Northern Songs, Ltd. v. Distinguished Productions, Inc.*, 581 F. Supp. 638, 640–41 (S.D.N.Y. 1984); Circular 12, at 8035-4.

A recording system works by virtue of the fact that interested parties have a specific place to look in order to discover with certainty whether a particular interest has been transferred or encumbered. To the extent there are competing recordation schemes, this lessens the utility of each; when records are scattered in several filing units, potential creditors must conduct several searches before they can be sure that the property is not encumbered. It is for that reason that parallel recordation schemes for the same types of property are scarce as hens' teeth; the court is aware of no others, and the parties have cited none. No useful purposes would be served—indeed, much confusion would re-sult—if creditors were permitted to perfect security interests by filing with either the Copyright Office or state offices.

If state methods of perfection were valid, a third party (such as a potential purchaser of the copyright) who wanted to learn of any encumbrances thereon would have to check not merely the indices of the U.S. Copyright Office, but also the indices of any relevant secretary of state. Because copyrights are incorporeal—they have no fixed situs—a number of state authorities could be relevant.... Thus, interested third parties could never be entirely sure that all relevant jurisdictions have been searched. This pos-sibility, together with the expense and delay of conducting searches in a variety of juris-dictions, could hinder the purchase and sale of copyrights, frustrating Congress's policy that copyrights be readily transferable in commerce.

This is the reasoning adopted by the Ninth Circuit in *Danning v. Pacific Propeller*. *Danning* held that 49 U.S.C.A. § 1403(a), the Federal Aviation Act's provision for recording conveyances and the creation of liens and security interests in civil aircraft, preempts state filing provisions. 620 F.2d at 735–36. According to Danning, "[t]he pre-dominant purpose of the statute was to provide one central place for the filing of [liens on aircraft] and thus eliminate the need, given the highly mobile nature of aircraft and their appurtenances, for the examination of State and County records." 620 F.2d at 735–36. Copyrights, even more than aircraft, lack a clear situs; tangible, movable goods such as airplanes must always exist at some physical location; they may have a home base from which they operate or where they receive regular maintenance. The same cannot be said of intangibles. As noted above, this lack of an identifiable situs militates against individual state filings and in favor of a single, national registration scheme.

Moreover...the Copyright Act establishes its own scheme for determining priority between conflicting transferees, one that differs in certain respects from that of Article Nine. Under Article Nine, priority between holders of conflicting security interests in intangibles is generally determined by who perfected his interest first. UCC § 9312(5). By contrast, section 205(d) of the Copyright Act provides: "As between two conflicting transfers, the one executed first prevails if it is recorded, in the manner required to give constructive notice under subsection (c), within one month after its execution in the United States or within two months after its execution outside the United States, or at any time before recordation in such manner of the later transfer...." 17 U.S.C. § 205(d)....Thus, unlike Article Nine, the Copyright Act permits the effect of recording with the Copyright Office to relate back as far as two months.

Because the Copyright Act and Article Nine create different priority schemes, there will be occasions when different results will be reached depending on which scheme was employed. The availability of filing under the UCC would thus undermine the priority scheme established by Congress with respect to copyrights. This type of direct interference with the operation of federal law weighs heavily in favor of preemption. *See generally Bonito Boats, Inc. v. Thunder Craft Boats, Inc.*, 489 U.S. 141, 109 S. Ct. 971, 103 L. Ed. 2d 118 (1989).

The bankruptcy court below nevertheless concluded that security interests in copyrights could be perfected by filing either with the copyright office or with the secretary of state under the UCC, making a tongue-in-cheek analogy to the use of a belt and suspenders to hold up a pair of pants. According to the bankruptcy court, because either device is equally useful, one should be free to choose which one to wear. With all due respect, this court finds the analogy inapt. There is no legitimate reason why pants should be held up in only one particular manner: Individuals and public modesty are equally served by either device, or even by a safety pin or a piece of rope; all that really matters is that the job gets done. Registration schemes are different in that the way notice is given is precisely what matters. To the extent interested parties are confused as to which system is being employed, this increases the level of uncertainty and multiplies the risk of error, exposing creditors to the possibility that they might get caught with their pants down.

A recordation scheme best serves its purpose where interested parties can obtain notice of all encumbrances by referring to a single, precisely defined recordation system. The availability of parallel state recordation systems that could put parties on constructive notice as to encumbrances on copyrights would surely interfere with the effectiveness of the federal recordation scheme. Given the virtual absence of dual recordation schemes in our legal system, Congress cannot be presumed to have contemplated such a result. The court therefore concludes that any state recordation system pertaining to interests in copyrights would be preempted by the Copyright Act.

2.     *State law leads to the same conclusion.* Article Nine of the Uniform Commercial Code establishes a comprehensive scheme for the regulation of security interests in personal property and fixtures. By superseding a multitude of pre-Code security devices, it provides "a simple and unified structure within which the immense variety of present-day secured financing transactions can go forward with less cost and greater certainty." UCC § 9101, Official Comment. However, Article Nine is not all encompassing; under the "step back" provision of UCC section 9104, Article Nine does not apply

"[t]o a security interest subject to any statute of the United States to the extent that such statute governs the rights of parties to and third parties affected by transactions in particular types of property."

For most items of personal property, Article Nine provides that security interests must be perfected by filing with the office of the secretary of state in which the debtor is located. *See* UCC §§ 9302(1), 9401(1)(c). Such filing, however, is not "necessary or effective to perfect a security interest in property subject to . . . [a] statute or treaty of the United States which provides for a national or international registration . . . or which specifies a place of filing different from that specified in [Article Nine] for filing of the security interest." UCC § 9302(3)(a). When a national system for recording security interests exists, the Code treats compliance with that system as "equivalent to the filing of a financing statement under [Article Nine,] and a security interest in property subject to the statute or treaty can be perfected only by compliance therewith. . . ." UCC § 9302(4).

As discussed above, section 205(a) of the Copyright Act clearly does establish a national system for recording transfers of copyright interests, and it specifies a place of filing different from that provided in Article Nine. Recording in the Copyright Office gives nationwide, constructive notice to third parties of the recorded encumbrance. Except for the fact that the Copyright Office's indices are organized on the basis of the title and registration number, rather than by reference to the identity of the debtor, this system is nearly identical to that which Article Nine generally provides on a statewide basis. And, lest there be any doubt, the drafters of the UCC specifically identified the Copyright Act as establishing the type of national registration system that would trigger the section 9302(3) and (4) step back provisions.

\* \* \*

The court therefore concludes that the Copyright Act provides for national registration and "specifies a place of filing different from that specified in [Article Nine] for filing of the security interest." UCC § 9302(3)(a). Recording in the U.S. Copyright Office, rather than filing a financing statement under Article Nine, is the proper method for perfecting a security interest in a copyright.

In reaching this conclusion, the court rejects *City Bank & Trust Co. v. Otto Fabric, Inc.,* 83 B.R. 780 (D. Kan. 1988), and *In re Transportation Design & Technology Inc.,* 48 B.R. 635 (Bankr. S.D. Cal. 1985), insofar as they are germane to the issues presented here. Both cases held that, under the UCC, security interests in patents need not be recorded in the U.S. Patent and Trademark Office to be perfected as against lien creditors because the federal statute governing patent assignments does not specifically provide for liens:

> Applications for patent, patents, or any interest therein, shall be assignable in law by an instrument in writing. The applicant, patentee, or his assigns or legal representatives may in like manner grant and convey an exclusive right under his application for patent, or patents, to the whole or any specified part of the United States.

\* \* \*

"An assignment, grant or conveyance shall be void as against *any subsequent purchaser or mortgagee* for a valuable consideration, without notice, unless it is recorded in the Patent and Trademark Office within three months from its date or prior to the date of such subsequent purchase or mortgage." 35 U.S.C. § 261 (*emphasis added*).

According to *In re Transportation,* because section 261's priority scheme only provides for a "subsequent purchaser or mortgagee for valuable consideration," it does not require recording in the Patent and Trademark Office to perfect against lien creditors. *See* 48 B.R. at 639.

Likewise, *City Bank* held that "the failure of the statute to mention protection against lien creditors suggests that it is unnecessary to record an assignment or other conveyance with the Patent Office to protect the appellant's security interest against the trustee." 83 B.R. at 782.

These cases misconstrue the plain language of UCC section 9104, which provides for the voluntary step back of Article Nine's provisions "*to the extent* [federal law] governs the rights of [the] parties." UCC § 9104(a) (emphasis added). Thus, when a federal statute provides for a national system of recordation or specifies a place of filing different from that in Article Nine, the methods of perfection specified in Article Nine are supplanted by that national system; compliance with a national system of recordation is equivalent to the filing of a financing statement under Article Nine. UCC § 9302(4). Whether the federal statute also provides a priority scheme different from that in Article Nine is a separate issue, addressed below....Compliance with a national registration scheme is necessary for perfection regardless of whether federal law governs priorities. Cap Fed's security interest in the copyrights of the films in NPI's library and the receivables they have generated therefore is unperfected.

### B. Effect of Failing to Record with the Copyright Office

Having concluded that Cap Fed should have, but did not, record its security interest with the Copyright Office, the court must next determine whether NPI as a debtor in possession can subordinate Cap Fed's interest and recover it for the benefit of the bankruptcy estate. As a debtor in possession, NPI has nearly all of the powers of a bankruptcy trustee, *see* 11 U.S.C. section 1107(a), including the authority to set aside preferential or fraudulent transfers, as well as transfers otherwise voidable under applicable state or federal law. *See* 11 U.S.C. §§ 544, 547, 548.

Particularly relevant is the "strong arm clause" of 11 U.S.C. section 544(a)(1), which, in respect to personal property in the bankruptcy estate, gives the debtor in possession every right and power state law confers upon one who has acquired a lien by legal or equitable proceedings. If, under the applicable law, a judicial lien creditor would prevail over an adverse claimant, the debtor in possession prevails; if not, not. *Wind Power Systems, Inc. v. Cannon Financial Group*, Inc. (*In re Wind Power Systems, Inc.*), 841 F.2d 288, 293 (9th Cir. 1988); *Angeles Real Estate Co. v. Kerxton (In re Construction General Inc.)*, 737 F.2d 416, 418 (4th Cir. 1984). A lien creditor generally takes priority over unperfected security interests in estate property because, under Article Nine, "an unperfected security interest is subordinate to the rights of... [a] person who becomes a lien creditor before the security interest is perfected." UCC § 9301(1)(b). But, as discussed previously, the UCC does not apply to the extent a federal statute "governs the rights of parties to and third parties affected by transactions in particular types of property." UCC § 9104. Section 205(d) of the Copyright Act is such a statute, establishing a priority scheme between conflicting transfers of interests in a copyright:

> As between two conflicting transfers, the one executed first prevails if it is recorded, in the manner required to give constructive notice under subsection (c), within one month after its execution in the United States or within two months after its execution outside the United States, or at any time before recordation in such manner of the later transfer. Otherwise, the later transfer prevails if recorded first in such manner, and if taken in good faith, for valu-

able consideration or on the basis of a binding promise to pay royalties, and without notice of the earlier transfer.

17 U.S.C. § 205(d).

For the reasons discussed above...the federal priority scheme preempts the state priority scheme.

Section 205(d) does not expressly address the rights of lien creditors, speaking only in terms of competing transfers of copyright interests. To determine whether NPI, as a hypothetical lien creditor, may avoid Cap Fed's unperfected security interest, the court must therefore consider whether a judicial lien is a transfer as that term is used in the Copyright Act.

\* \* \*

[T]he Copyright Act recognizes transfers of copyright ownership "in whole or in part by any means of conveyance or by operation of law." 17 U.S.C. § 201(d)(1). Transfer is defined broadly to include any "assignment, mortgage, exclusive license, or any other conveyance, alienation, or hypothecation of a copyright...whether or not it is limited in time or place of effect." 17 U.S.C. § 101. A judicial lien creditor is a creditor who has obtained a lien "by judgment, levy, sequestration, or other legal or equitable process or proceeding." 11 U.S.C. § 101(32). Such a creditor typically has the power to seize and sell property held by the debtor at the time of the creation of the lien in order to satisfy the judgment or, in the case of general intangibles such as copyrights, to collect the revenues generated by the intangible as they come due. *See, e.g.*, Cal. Civ. P. Code §§ 701.510, 701.520, 701.640. Thus, while the creation of a lien on a copyright may not give a creditor an immediate right to control the copyright, it amounts to a sufficient transfer of rights to come within the broad definition of transfer under the Copyright Act. *See Phoenix Bond & Indemnity Co. v. Shamblin (In re Shamblin)*, 890 F.2d 123, 127 n.7 (9th Cir. 1989) (under the Bankruptcy Code, "[t]his court has consistently treated the creation of liens on the debtor's property as a transfer").

Cap Fed contends that, in order to prevail under 17 U.S.C. section 205(d), NPI must have the status of a bona fide purchaser, rather than that of a judicial lien creditor. *See Pistole v. Mellor (In re Mellor)*, 734 F.2d 1396, 1401 n.4 (9th Cir. 1984) (judicial lien creditor does not have the same rights as a bona fide purchaser); *cf.* 11 U.S.C. § 544(a)(3) (for real estate in the bankruptcy estate, debtor in possession has the rights of a bona fide purchaser). Cap Fed, in essence, is arguing that the term transfer in section 205(d) refers only to consensual transfers. For the reasons expressed above, the court rejects this argument. The Copyright Act's definition of transfer is very broad and specifically includes transfers by operation of law. 17 U.S.C. § 201(d)(1). The term is broad enough to encompass not merely purchasers, but lien creditors as well. NPI therefore is entitled to priority if it meets the statutory good faith, notice, consideration and recording requirements of section 205(a). As the hypothetical lien creditor, NPI is deemed to have taken in good faith and without notice. *See* 11 U.S.C. § 544(a).

\* \* \*

## CONCLUSION

The judgment of the bankruptcy court is reversed. The case is ordered remanded for a determination of which movies in NPI's library are the subject of valid copyrights. The court shall then determine the status of Cap Fed's security interest in the movies and the debtor's other property. To the extent that interest is unperfected, the court shall permit NPI to exercise its avoidance powers under the Bankruptcy Code.

IT IS SO ORDERED.

---

# B.  Perfecting Security Interests in Trademarks

## In re 199Z, Inc.

137 B.R. 778 (C.D. Ca. 1992)

RYAN, Bankruptcy Judge.

### I. INTRODUCTION

#### A. Factual Background and Procedural History

199Z, Inc., a California corporation ("199Z" or "Debtor") entered into an asset purchase agreement dated as of February 5, 1990, with 1200 Valencia, Inc., a California corporation ("Valencia"), Ocean Pacific Sunwear, Ltd., a California limited partnership ("OP") (collectively, "Defendants"), and Republic Factors Corp., a California corporation ("Republic"). Valencia is the general partner of OP. Pursuant to this asset purchase agreement, Defendants sold and 199Z purchased assets associated with the trademarks "JIMMY'Z" and "WOODY LOGO" ("Trademark Assets"). In exchange for the Trademark Assets, 199Z gave Defendants a total purchase price of $6,346,183.00, consisting of $500,000.00 cash and promissory notes for $2,300,000.00 and $3,346,183.00. As security for the promissory notes, 199Z executed a security agreement in favor of OP encumbering all of 199Z's business, goodwill, trademarks and assets ("Security Agreement").

To perfect this security interest, 199Z (1) recorded a Memorandum of Security Agreement in the U.S. Patent & Trademark Office (the "Patent Office") on April 2, 1990; and (2) filed a UCC-1 Financing Statement in the Office of the Secretary of State of California on June 4, 1990 ("June UCC-1"); and (3) filed an amended UCC-1 Financing Statement in the Office of the Secretary of State of California on November 1, 1990, including a UCC-2 amendment to the June UCC-1 ("November UCC-2").

The November UCC-2 resulted from the discovery of an error in the June UCC-1. The June UCC-1, in the section describing the property covered by the UCC-1, states "See Attachment A hereto." Attachment A states:

*Exhibit A*

The personal property in which [OP] as Debtor, grants a security interest to Republic Factors Corp., as Secured Party, includes, but is not limited to, all of the following, whether now owned or hereafter acquired:

1.  Trademarks. Any and all trademarks, trade names or trade styles, registered or recognized in the United States of America or in any state or territory therein or in any foreign country, excluding the trademark, tradename [sic] and trade styles of "JIMMY'Z" and "WOODY LOGO"; and

2. Property. All of debtor's presently existing and hereafter acquired goodwill (whether associated with and identified by the Trademarks or not)...."

Obviously, "Exhibit A" refers to an agreement between OP and Republic, and not to the Security Agreement between Debtor and Defendants. The corrected exhibit to the November UCC-2 states:

*Personal Property*

The personal property in which 199Z, Inc., as Debtor, grants a security interest to [OP], as Secured Party, includes, but is not limited to, all of the following, whether now owned or hereafter acquired:

1. Trademarks. Any and all trademarks, trade names or trade styles, registered or recognized in the United States of America or in any state or territory therein or in any foreign country; and
2. Property. All of debtor's presently existing and hereafter acquired goodwill associated with and identified by the Trademarks, business...."

On November 10, 1990, OP declared that all sums due to it under the asset purchase agreement were immediately payable. A foreclosure sale was noticed and held, at which OP purchased the assets encumbered by the Security Agreement through a $1,000,000.00 credit bid.

An involuntary petition under Chapter 7 of the Bankruptcy Code was filed against 199Z on December 6, 1990. On January 14, 1991, Debtor filed a Notice of Consent to Entry of Order for Relief and Election to Convert to Case Under Chapter 11. This Court entered an order converting the case to a case under Chapter 11 on January 24, 1991. On Debtor's motion, this Court entered an order converting the case to a case under Chapter 7 on April 16, 1991. James J. Joseph ("Trustee") was appointed as the acting Chapter 7 Trustee for the estate of 199Z on May 10, 1991.

\* \* \*

### B. Analysis

Federal Bankruptcy Rules of Procedure Rule 7056 incorporates Federal Rules of Civil Procedure Rule 56 by reference in adversary actions. Rule 56 states that the Court shall grant summary judgment or summary adjudication of issues where the evidence presented demonstrates that no genuine issue of material fact exists and that the moving party is entitled to judgment as a matter of law. (*See Anderson v. Liberty Lobby*, 477 U.S. 242, 247–48, 106 S. Ct. 2505, 2509–10, 91 L. Ed. 2d 202 (1986).)

The dispositive legal issues, which Defendants present for decision, are more coherently stated:

(1) How is a security interest in trademarks, trade names and trade style properly perfected?
(2) Do Defendants have a perfected security in the Trademark Assets?
(3) Perfection of Security Interest in Trademark Assets: Federal Law

The Uniform Commercial Code provides for perfection of a security interest through filing a financing statement conforming with its requirements with the appropriate Secretary of State. In this manner, a security interest in "general intangibles" can be perfected. The Uniform Commercial Code Official Comment to Section 9-106 ("Definitions: 'Account;' 'General Intangibles'") states:

The term "general intangibles" brings under this Article miscellaneous types of contractual rights and other personal property, which are used or may become customarily used as commercial security. Examples are goodwill, literary rights and rights to performance. Other examples are copyrights, trademarks and patents, except to the extent that they may be excluded by Section 9-104(a).

*Id.* …

In turn, section 9-104 provides:

This Article does not apply

(a)  to a security interest subject to any statute of the United States, to the extent that such statute governs the rights of parties to and third parties affected by transactions in particular types of property;

*Id.*

Further, section 9-302(3)(a) states that a filing under that section is not necessary or effective to perfect a security interest subject to

[a] statute or treaty of the United States which provides for a national or international registration…or which specifies a place of filing different from that specified in [Article Nine] for filing of the security interest.

*Id.*

Defendants argue that, regardless of the sufficiency of either the June UCC-1 or the November UCC-2, their claimed security interest should be deemed perfected through their filing with the Patent Office. As authority for this proposition, Defendants direct the attention of the Court to *National Peregrine, Inc. v. Capitol Federal Savings & Loan of Denver (In re Peregrine Entertainment, Ltd.)*, 116 B.R. 194 (C.D. Cal. 1990) ("*Peregrine*"). In *Peregrine*, Judge Kozinski held that the Copyright Act preempted state law provisions with respect to the perfection of security interests in copyrights, and that a creditor seeking to perfect a security interest in copyrights must file the appropriate documents with the U.S. Copyright Office and not with the Secretary of State. While many of the characteristics of copyright supporting federal preemption of state law, as outlined by Judge Kozinski, are equally applicable to trademarks (such as a unique federal interest in the subject matter as shown through comprehensive federal legislation, promotion of uniformity, and lack of situs of the personal property because of its incorporeal nature), one critical distinction exists between the federal legislation at issue in *Peregrine* and the Lanham Act trademark legislation. The Copyright Act provides expressly for the filing of any "mortgage" or "hypothecation" of a copyright, including a pledge of the copyright as security or collateral for a debt. *Peregrine*, 116 B.R. at 198–99. The Lanham Act, however, provides expressly only for the filing of an assignment of a trademark, and the definition of "assignment" does not include pledges, mortgages or hypothecations of trademarks.

Trademark cases distinguish between security interests and assignments. An "assignment" of a trademark is an absolute transfer of the entire right, title and interest to the trademark. The grant of a security interest is not such a transfer. It is merely what the term suggests—a device to secure an indebtedness. It is a mere agreement to assign in the event of default by the debtor. Since a security interest in a trademark is not equivalent to an assignment, the filing of a security interest is not covered by the Lanham Act.…Had Congress intended that security interests in trademarks be perfected by filing with the Patent Office, it could have expressly provided for such a filing, as it did in the Copyright Act.... This Court finds this distinction dispositive. Although there is no reported appellate decision precisely on point, this Court cannot find as a matter of law that the federal preemption for the purposes of perfecting security interest in copyrights set forth in *Peregrine* applies equally to the perfection of security interests in trademarks. This conclusion is harmonious with those reached in the reported decisions of other bankruptcy courts. Accordingly, the recordation of the Memorandum of Security Agreement in the Patent Office did not perfect Defendants' security interest in the Trademark Assets.

[*The court then went on to conclude that in order to perfect security interests in Trademark Assets, a general UCC-1 form must be filed in the appropriate jurisdiction.*]

---

## C.  Perfecting Security Interests in Patents

### In re Cybernetic Services, Inc.
### 252 F.3d 1039 (9th Cir. 2001)

GRABER, Circuit Judge:

As is often true in the field of intellectual property, we must apply an antiquated statute in a modern context. The question that we decide today is whether 35 U.S.C. § 261 of the Patent Act, or Article 9 of the Uniform Commercial Code (UCC), as adopted in California, requires the holder of a security interest in a patent to record that interest with the federal Patent and Trademark Office (PTO) in order to perfect the interest as against a subsequent lien creditor. We answer "no"; neither the Patent Act nor Article 9 so requires. We therefore affirm the decision of the Bankruptcy Appellate Panel (BAP).

#### FACTUAL AND PROCEDURAL BACKGROUND

The parties stipulated to the relevant facts: Matsco, Inc., and Matsco Financial Corporation (Petitioners) have a security interest in a patent developed by Cybernetic Services, Inc. (Debtor)....

Petitioners' security interest in the patent was "properly prepared, executed by the Debtor and timely filed with the Secretary of State of the State of California," in accordance with the California Commercial Code. Petitioners did not record their interest with the PTO.

After Petitioners had recorded their security interest with the State of California, certain creditors filed an involuntary Chapter 7 petition against Debtor, and an order of relief was granted. The primary asset of Debtor's estate is the patent. Petitioners then filed a motion for relief from the automatic stay so that they could foreclose on their interest in the patent. The bankruptcy Trustee opposed the motion, arguing that Petitioners had failed to perfect their interest because they did not record it with the PTO.

The bankruptcy court ruled that Petitioners had properly perfected their security interest in the patent by following the provisions of Article 9. Furthermore, the court reasoned, because Petitioners had perfected their security interest before the filing of the bankruptcy petition, Petitioners had priority over the Trustee's claim in the patent and deserved relief from the stay. Accordingly, the bankruptcy court granted Petitioners' motion. The BAP affirmed.

Petitioners then filed this timely appeal.

## DISCUSSION

Article 9 of the UCC, as adopted in California, governs the method for perfecting a security interest in personal property. Article 9 applies to "general intangibles," a term that includes intellectual property. CAL. COM.CODE § 9106. The parties do not dispute that Petitioners complied with Article 9's general filing requirements and, in the case of most types of property, would have priority over a subsequent lien creditor. The narrower question in this case is whether Petitioners' actions were sufficient to perfect their interest when the "general intangible" to which the lien attached is a patent. The parties also do not dispute that, if Petitioners were required to file notice of their security interest in the patent with the PTO, then the Trustee, as a hypothetical lien creditor under 11 U.S.C. § 544(a)(1), has a superior right to the patent.

The Trustee makes two arguments. First, the Trustee contends that the Patent Act preempts Article 9's filing requirements. Second, the Trustee argues that Article 9 itself provides that a security interest in a patent can be perfected only by filing it with the PTO. We discuss each argument in turn.

### A. Preemption

#### 1. The Analytical Framework

"[T]he Supremacy Clause, U.S. Const., Art. VI, cl. 2, invalidates state laws that 'interfere with, or are contrary to,' federal law." *Hillsborough County, Fla. v. Automated Med. Labs., Inc.*, 471 U.S. 707, 712, 105 S. Ct. 2371, 85 L. Ed. 2d 714 (1985) (*quoting Gibbons v. Ogden*, 22 U.S. (9 Wheat.) 1, 92, 6 L. Ed. 23 (1824)). Congress may preempt state law in several different ways. Congress may do so expressly (express preemption). *Id.* at 713, 105 S. Ct. 2371. Even in the absence of express preemptive text, Congress' intent to preempt an entire field of state law may be inferred "where the scheme of federal regulation is sufficiently comprehensive to make reasonable the inference that Congress 'left no room' for supplementary state regulation" (field preemption). *Id.* (quoting *Rice v. Santa Fe Elevator Corp.*, 331 U.S. 218, 230, 67 S. Ct. 1146, 91 L .Ed. 1447 (1947)). State law also is preempted "when compliance with both state and federal law is impossible," or if the operation of state law " 'stands as an obstacle to the accomplishment and execution of the full purposes and objectives of Congress'" (conflict preemption). *G.S. Rasmussen & Assocs. v. Kalitta Flying Serv., Inc.*, 958 F.2d 896, 903–4 (9th Cir. 1992) (quoting *Kewanee Oil Co. v. Bicron Corp.*, 416 U.S. 470, 479, 94 S. Ct. 1879, 40 L. Ed. 2d 315 (1974)). In all cases, "[c]ongressional intent to preempt state law must be clear and manifest." *Indus. Truck Ass'n v. Henry*, 125 F.3d 1305, 1309 (9th Cir. 1997).

The Patent Act does not contain preemptive text, so express preemption is not an issue here. Concerning field and conflict preemption, the Supreme Court has adopted a "pragmatic" approach to deciding whether the Patent Act preempts a particular state law. *Bonito Boats, Inc. v. Thunder Craft Boats, Inc.*, 489 U.S. 141, 156, 109 S. Ct. 971, 103 L. Ed. 2d 118 (1989). Congress, in the Patent Act, "has balanced innovation incentives against promoting free competition, and state laws upsetting that balance are preempted." *G.S. Rasmussen*, 958 F.2d at 904. "[S]tate regulation of intellectual property must yield *to the extent that it clashes* with the balance struck by Congress" in the Patent Act. *Bonito Boats*, 489 U.S. at 152, 109 S. Ct. 971 (emphasis added).

Using this form of analysis, the Supreme Court has held, on numerous occasions, that the Patent Act preempts a state law that grants patent-like protection to a product. *See, e.g., id.; Sears, Roebuck & Co. v. Stiffel Co.*, 376 U.S. 225, 231, 84 S. Ct. 784, 11 L. Ed. 2d 661 (1964); *Compco Corp. v. Day-Brite Lighting, Inc.*, 376 U.S. 234, 237, 84 S. Ct. 779, 11 L. Ed. 2d 669 (1964). Those cases do not control, however, because we are confronted not with a state law that grants patent-like protection to a product but, rather, with a state commercial law that provides a method for perfecting a security interest in a federally protected patent.

That distinction is key because the Supreme Court has instructed clearly that the Patent Act does not preempt every state commercial law that touches on intellectual property. For example, in *Aronson v. Quick Point Pencil Co.*, 440 U.S. 257, 262, 99 S. Ct. 1096, 59 L. Ed. 2d 296 (1979), the Supreme Court observed that commercial agreements "traditionally are the domain of state law. State law is not displaced merely because the contract relates to intellectual property which may or may not be patentable; the states are free to regulate the use of such intellectual property in any manner not inconsistent with federal law."

The Court also has held that the Patent Act does not preempt a state's trade secret law even though the practical effect of the state law is to prohibit the public dissemination of information that, under the Patent Act, is not eligible for protection. *Kewanee Oil*, 416 U.S. at 474, 94 S. Ct. 1879.

It is within this framework that we evaluate the Trustee's claim. The Trustee argues that the recording provision found in 35 U.S.C. § 261 requires that the holder of a security interest in a patent record that interest with the PTO in order to perfect as to a subsequent lien creditor. Section 261 provides:

§ 261 Ownership; assignment

Subject to the provisions of this title, patents shall have the attributes of personal property.

Applications for patent, patents, or any interest therein, shall be assignable in law by an instrument in writing. The applicant, patentee, or his assigns or legal representatives may in like manner grant and convey an exclusive right under his application for patent, or patents, to the whole or any specified part of the United States.

A certificate of acknowledgment under the hand and official seal of a person authorized to administer oaths within the United States, or, in a foreign country, of a diplomatic or consular officer of the United States or an officer authorized to administer oaths whose authority is proved by a certificate of a diplomatic or consular officer of the United States, or apostle of an official designated by a foreign country which, by treaty or convention, accords like effect to apostles of designated officials in the United States, shall be prima facie evidence of the execution of an assignment, grant or conveyance of a patent or application for patent.

An assignment, grant or conveyance shall be void as against any subsequent purchaser or mortgagee for a valuable consideration, without notice, unless it is recorded in the Patent and Trademark Office within three months from its date or prior to the date of such subsequent purchase or mortgage.

If the Trustee's reading of the relevant portion of § 261 is correct, then to the extent that Article 9 allows a different method of perfection, it would be preempted under either a "field" or "conflict" preemption theory. That is because recording systems increase a patent's marketability and thus play an integral role in the incentive scheme created by Congress. Recording systems provide notice and certainty to present and future parties to a transaction; they work "by virtue of the fact that interested parties have a specific place to look in order to discover with certainty whether a particular interest has been transferred." *Nat'l Peregrine, Inc. v. Capitol Fed. Savs. & Loan Ass'n (In re Peregrine Entm't, Ltd.)*, 116 B.R. 194, 200 (C.D. Cal. 1990); *see also Littlefield v. Perry*, 21 Wall. 205, 88 U.S. 205, 221, 22 L. Ed. 577 (1874) (noting that the Patent Act's recording system "is intended for the benefit of the public" and that "[b]ona fide purchasers look to it for their protection").

If, as the Trustee argues, the Patent Act expressly delineates the place where a party must go to acquire notice and certainty about liens on patents, then a state law that requires the public to look elsewhere unquestionably would undercut the value of the Patent Act's recording scheme. If, on the other hand, § 261 does not cover liens on patents, then Article 9's filing requirements do not conflict with any policies inherent in the Patent Act's recording scheme....

As noted, the Trustee argues that § 261 required Petitioners to record their interest with the PTO. If that is true, then the Trustee has priority to the patent's proceeds, either because there is a clear conflict between the state and federal schemes and the state scheme is preempted, or because the Patent Act "governs the rights of parties" to the transaction and § 9104(a) operates to nullify Article 9's filing requirements. We turn to that issue now.

### 2. The Patent Act Requires Parties to Record with the PTO Only Ownership Interest in Patents.

As noted, the Patent Act's recording provision provides that an "assignment, grant or conveyance shall be void as against any subsequent purchaser or mortgagee for a valuable consideration, without notice, unless it is recorded in the [PTO]." 35 U.S.C. § 261. In order to determine whether Congress intended for parties to record with the PTO the type of interest that is at issue in this case, we must give the words of the statute the meaning that they had in 1870, the year in which the current version of § 261 was enacted.

The first phrase in § 261's recording provision—"assignment, grant or conveyance"—refers to different types of transactions. The neighboring clause—"shall be void as against any subsequent purchaser or mortgagee"—refers to the status of the party that receives an interest in the patent. Therefore, for the Trustee to prevail in this case, (1) Petitioners' transaction with Debtor must have been the type of "assignment, grant or conveyance" referred to in § 261, and (2) the Trustee, who has the status of a hypothetical lien creditor, must be a "subsequent purchaser or mortgagee." We hold that neither condition is met.

\* \* \*

### a. The Phrase "Assignment, Grant or Conveyance" Concerns Transfers of Ownership Interests Only.

The historical meanings of the terms "assignment, grant or conveyance" all involved the transfer of an ownership interest. A patent "assignment" referred to a transaction that transferred specific rights in the patent, all involving the patent's title.

A "grant," historically, also referred to a transfer of an ownership interest in a patent, but only as to a specific geographic area.

Although older cases defining the term "conveyance" in the context of intangible property are sparse, and its historic meaning tended to vary, the common contemporaneous definition was "to transfer the legal title...from the present owner to another." *Abendroth v. Town of Greenwich*, 29 Conn. 356 (1860); *see also, e.g., Frame v. Bivens*, 189 F. 785, 789 (C.C.E.D. Okla.1909) ("A conveyance is the transfer of the title of land from one person or class of persons to another."); I BOUVIER'S LAW DICTIONARY 361 (14th ed. 1874) (defining "conveyance" as the "transfer of the title of land from one person or class of persons to another"); I BURRILL'S LAW DICTIONARY 375 (2d ed. 1871) (defining "conveyance" as an "instrument in writing, by which property or the title to property is transferred from one person to another"); BLACK'S LAW DICTIONARY 431 (3d ed. 1933) ("In the strict legal sense, a transfer of legal title to land.").

That Congress intended to incorporate the common, contemporaneous meanings of the words "assignment," "grant," and "conveyance" into the Patent Act's recording provision can be seen when § 261 is examined in its entirety. The first clue is the provision's title: "Ownership; assignment." *See United States v. Kaluna*, 192 F.3d 1188, 1195 (9th Cir. 1999) (instructing that a statute's title is a tool for interpreting the statute's meaning). By using the unambiguous words "ownership; assignment," Congress must have intended to introduce the subject that was to follow: the ownership of patents and the assignment thereof.

Continuing through § 261, the second paragraph states that patents shall be assignable by an instrument in writing. That paragraph goes on to provide that the patentee or the patentee's assigns "may in like manner *grant and convey an exclusive right* under his application for patent...to the whole or any specified part of the United States." (Emphasis added.) The types of transactions referred to in § 261's second paragraph—(1) the assignment of a patent, and (2) the grant or conveyance of an exclusive right in a patent in the whole or part of the United States—track the historical definitions of assignment, grant, and conveyance that we just discussed—transactions that all involve the transfer of an ownership interest in a patent.

Moreover, we presume that words used more than once in the same statute have the same meaning throughout. *Boise Cascade Corp. v. EPA*, 942 F.2d 1427, 1432 (9th Cir. 1991). Here, the second paragraph of § 261 uses the words "grant and convey" to signify the transfer of an "exclusive right [in a patent]...to the whole or any specified part of the United States." We presume, then, that when Congress used the words "grant or conveyance" two paragraphs later in the same statute, Congress still intended to refer to ownership interests only. Supreme Court precedent supports our view that the terms "assignment, grant or conveyance" refer to ownership interests only. In *Waterman [v. Mackenzie,* 138 U.S. 252 (1891)], the Supreme Court analyzed the nature of a patent "assignment" and "mortgage." The plaintiff in *Waterman* assigned to his wife a patent for an improvement in fountain pens. The plaintiff's wife then granted back to the plaintiff a license to use the patent. That license was never recorded. The wife then assigned the patent to a third party as collateral for a debt; the document concerning this arrangement was filed with the PTO. Finally, the wife assigned the patent back to the plaintiff. The question for the Court was whether the plaintiff had standing to bring an action for infringement of the patent. The Court held that only the third party had standing. 138 U.S. at 261, 11 S. Ct. 334.

In resolving the matter, the Court noted that a patent's owner may convey, assign, or grant one of three interests:

> [1] the whole patent, comprising the exclusive right to make, use and vend the invention throughout the United States; or
>
> [2] an undivided part or share of that exclusive right; or
>
> [3] the exclusive right under the patent within and throughout a specified part of the United States. A transfer of either of these three kinds of interests is an *assignment*, properly speaking, and vests in the assignee a *title* in so much of the patent itself, with a right to sue infringers.... Any assignment or transfer, short of one of these, is a *mere license*, giving the licensee no title in the patent, and no right to sue at law in his own name for an infringement.

*Id.* at 255, 11 S. Ct. 334 (emphasis added) (citation omitted). Whether a particular conveyance qualifies as an assignment or a license "does not depend upon the name by which it calls itself, but upon the legal effect of its provisions," *Id.* at 256, 11 S. Ct. 334; that is, whether title is passed depends on the rights that were transferred by the contracting parties. Only the holder of an ownership interest in the patent had standing to sue.

*Waterman* contains no explicit holding that 35 U.S.C. § 261 applies only to a secured transaction that effects a transfer of ownership, but it does imply as much. The Court in *Waterman* expressly differentiated between three kinds of transfers of ownership interests — all of which it labeled as versions of "assignments" — and everything else, which it referred to as "mere licenses." The Court did not discuss "grants" or "conveyances" separately, but (1) as a matter of logic, they must fall into one of the two overarching and mutually exclusive categories that the Court created: assignments (ownership interests) or licenses (less than ownership interests); and (2) the kinds of transfers of ownership interests discussed by the Court (and labeled "assignments") correspond neatly to the historical definitions of the transactions delineated in the statute. *See Hillman* at 2–19 to 2–20 (observing that the Patent Act "distinguishes 'assignments' of patents (of which 'grants' and 'conveyances' are specific types) from all other transfers (which are called 'licenses')"). It is clear, then, that the transactions that the Court referred to as effecting a transfer of ownership are the same transactions that Congress referred to as an "assignment, grant or conveyance."

\* \* \*

In summary, the statute's text, context, and structure, when read in the light of Supreme Court precedent, compel the conclusion that a security interest in a patent that does not involve a transfer of the rights of ownership is a "mere license" and is not an "assignment, grant or conveyance" within the meaning of 35 U.S.C. § 261. And because § 261 provides that only an "assignment, grant or conveyance shall be void" as against subsequent purchasers and mortgagees, only transfers of ownership interests need to be recorded with the PTO. *See Moraine Prods. v. ICI Am., Inc.*, 538 F.2d 134, 143 (7th Cir. 1976) ("'Patent licenses are not governed by the Patent Act, Section 261 being inapplicable to licensees.'" (quoting P. ROSENBERG, PATENT LAW FUNDAMENTALS 264 (1975))); *Keystone Type Foundry v. Fastpress Co.*, 272 F. 242, 245 (2d Cir. 1921) ("[I]t had long passed into the text-books that...an assignee acquired title subject to prior licenses of which the assignee must inform himself as best he can, and at his own risk."); *Jones v. Berger*, 58 F. 1006, 1007 (C.C.D. Md. 1893) ("There would seem to be no doubt that a license to use a patent not exclusive of others need not be recorded....A subsequent assignee takes title to the patent subject to such licenses, of which he must inform himself as best he can at his own risk." (citations omitted)); *Sanofi, S.A. v. Med-Tech*

*Veterinarian Prods., Inc.*, 565 F. Supp. 931, 939 (D.N.J. 1983) (holding that "there is no obligation to record a license" with the PTO); 2 ROBINSON § 817, at 602 ("A license is not such a conveyance of an interest in the patented invention as to affect its ownership, and hence is not required to be recorded.").

In the present case, the parties do not dispute that the transaction that gave Petitioners their interest in the patent did not involve a transfer of an ownership interest in the patent. Petitioners held a "mere license," which did not have to be recorded with the PTO.

### b. The Phrase "Subsequent Purchaser or Mortgagee" does not Include Subsequent Lien Creditors.

The Trustee's argument fails not only because a security interest that does not transfer ownership is not an "assignment, grant or conveyance," but also because he is not a subsequent "purchaser or mortgagee." Congress intended for parties to record their ownership interests in a patent so as to provide constructive notice only to subsequent holders of an ownership interest. Again, we derive our conclusion from the historical definitions of the words, from the context and structure of § 261, and from Supreme Court precedent.

The historical meaning of "purchaser or mortgagee" proves that Congress intended for the recording provision to give constructive notice only to subsequent holders of an ownership interest. For the sake of convenience, we begin with the definition of "mortgagee."

Historically, a "mortgagee" was someone who obtained title to property used to secure a debt. *See* JAMES SCHOULER, PERSONAL PROPERTY § 416, at 622 (5th ed.1918) (noting that "[m]ortages of chattels, then, are to be distinguished at common law from liens and pledges in this sort of out-and-out transfer of the title conditionally which is carried by the original transaction"). A "mortgage" must be differentiated from a "pledge," a term that is absent from the Patent Act. Professor Gilmore, in his treatise, Security Interests in PERSONAL PROPERTY § 1.1, at 8, notes that the historical distinction between a pledge and a mortgage was that "the mortgagee got title or an estate whereas the pledgee got merely possession with a right to foreclose on default." Similarly, Judge Learned Hand wrote, in 1922, that it "is everywhere agreed that the significant distinction between a pledge and a mortgage is that in the first the creditor gets no title,... while in the second he does." *Ex parte Crombie & La Mothe, Inc.* (*In re German Publ'n Soc'y*), 289 F. 509, 509 (S.D.N.Y. 1922); *see also* LEONARD A. JONES, A TREATISE ON THE LAW OF COLLATERAL SECURITIES AND PLEDGES § 2, at 4 (Edward M. White rev., 3d ed. 1912) (defining a "pledge" as "something more than a mere lien and something less than a mortgage"), *cited in* BLACK'S LAW DICTIONARY 1175 (7th ed. 1999).

That the Patent Act refers to securing a patent through a "mortgage" but not through a "pledge" is significant, for both were common methods of using a patent as collateral. *See* SCHOULER § 395, at 589 (noting that patent rights "are constantly interchanged in our business community for the purpose of pledge"); *cf.* GILMORE § 1.2, at 9–10 ("If it ever was true that only tangible chattels could be pledged, it is well over a century since that proposition had any vitality."). Generally, the inclusion of certain terms in a statute implies the exclusion of others. *United States v. Kakatin*, 214 F.3d 1049, 1051 (9th Cir. 2000). It seems then, that by using the term "mortgagee," but not "lien" or "pledge," Congress intended in 1870 for the Patent Act's recording provision to protect only those who obtained title to a patent.

The term "purchaser" does not detract from this conclusion. Section 261 instructs that an unrecorded "assignment, grant or conveyance" shall be void as against a subsequent "purchaser...for a valuable consideration, without notice." The historical definition of a "purchaser for value and without notice" was a "bona fide purchaser. A purchaser...who takes a conveyance purporting to pass the entire title, legal and equitable," who pays value and does not have notice of the rights of others to the property. BOUVIER'S LAW DICTIONARY 1005 (Baldwin's Century ed. 1926). The Supreme Court seems to have accepted this definition as well. *See Littlefield*, 88 U.S. at 221 (noting that "[b]ona fide purchasers look to [the Patent Act's recording provision] for their protection").

Congress, by stating that certain transactions shall be void as against a subsequent "purchaser or mortgagee" intended for the words to be read together: A "purchaser" is one who buys an ownership interest in the patent, while a "mortgagee" is one who obtains an ownership interest in a patent as collateral for a debt. Our previous comments about the context and structure of § 261 support our conclusion that Congress intended to protect only subsequent holders of an ownership interest. As noted, the title of § 261 is "Ownership; assignment," which suggests that the recording provision is concerned only with ownership interests.

Similarly, the second paragraph delineates the types of transactions that § 261 covers—(1) the assignment of a patent, and (2) the grant or conveyance of an exclusive right in the patent to the whole or any specified part of the United States—each involving the transfer of an ownership interest in a patent. It follows that, when Congress referred to a "subsequent purchaser or mortgagee," it was simply describing the future recipients of those transactions. In one case the recipient bought the interest (purchaser), while in the other the recipient loaned money and received the interest as collateral (mortgagee). In either case, an ownership interest was transferred.

Precedent confirms our reading of the statute. The Supreme Court has endorsed the view that Congress intended to provide constructive notice only to subsequent recipients of an ownership interest in a patent. In *Waterman*, the Court observed, as we do, that the Patent Act refers to a "mortgage" but not to a "pledge." The Court noted that, when a party has the status of a mortgagee, it is not merely the possession or a special property that passes; but, both at law and in equity, *the whole title is transferred to the mortgagee, as security for the debt*, subject only to be defeated by performance of the condition...and the right of possession, when there is no express stipulation to the contrary, goes with the right of property. 138 U.S. at 258, 11 S. Ct. 334 (emphasis added). Moreover, with title or possession of the property came certain rights in the mortgagee. *Id.* at 258–59, 11 S. Ct. 334. But a patent right "is incorporeal property, not susceptible of actual delivery or possession." *Id.* at 260, 11 S. Ct. 334. Therefore, when "it is provided by statute that a mortgage of personal property shall not be valid against third persons, unless the mortgage is recorded, *a recording of the mortgage is a substitute for, and...equivalent to, a delivery of possession, and makes the title and the possession of the mortgagee good against all the world."* *Id.* at 260, 11 S. Ct. 334 (emphasis added).

The Court then observed that, once a mortgagee has recorded the transaction, that party is "entitled to grant licenses, to receive license fees and royalties, and to have an account of profits or an award of damages against infringers." *Id.* Because the Court had already noted that only the holder of an ownership interest in a patent could sue for damages against infringers, it is clear that the Court read the term "mortgagee" to refer to a party who held an ownership interest in the patent.

In summary, the historical definitions of the terms "purchaser or mortgagee," taken in context and read in the light of Supreme Court precedent, establish that Congress was concerned only with providing constructive notice to subsequent parties who take an ownership interest in the patent in question. *See In re Transp. Design & Tech., Inc.*, 48

B.R. 635, 639–40 (1985) (interpreting *Waterman* as holding that the Patent Act is concerned only with transactions that transfer title); *City Bank & Trust Co. v. Otto Fabric, Inc.*, 83 B.R. 780, 782–83 (D.Kan. 1988) (same).

The Trustee is not a subsequent "mortgagee," as that term is used in 35 U.S.C. § 261, because the holder of a patent mortgage holds title to the patent itself. *Waterman*, 138 U.S. at 258, 11 S. Ct. 334. Instead, the Trustee is a hypothetical lien creditor. The Patent Act does not require parties to record documents in order to provide constructive notice to subsequent lien creditors who do not hold title to the patent.

* * *

### 4. Cases Interpreting the Copyright Act do not Control.

The Trustee's final argument is that this court should follow Peregrine, in which a district court held that the Copyright Act preempts state methods of perfecting security interests in copyrights. The court in *Peregrine* observed that the "federal copyright laws ensure predictability and certainty of copyright ownership, promote national uniformity and avoid the practical difficulties of determining and enforcing an author's rights under the differing laws and in the separate courts of the various States." 116 B.R. at 199 (internal quotation marks omitted). The court reasoned that allowing state methods to stand would conflict with those goals. *Id. But see* 4 WHITE & SUMMERS § 30-12, at 86 (referring to *Peregrine* as "misguided").

Of course, *Peregrine* is not binding on this court although, in the present case, we have no occasion to pass on its correctness as an interpretation of the Copyright Act. We note, however, that the Copyright Act, by its terms, governs security interests. The Copyright Act governs any "transfer" of ownership, which is defined by statute to include any "hypothecation." 17 U.S.C. §§ 101, 201(d)(1). A "hypothecation" is the "pledging of something as security without delivery of title or possession." BLACK'S LAW DICTIONARY 747 (7th ed. 1999); *see also* DOUGLAS J. WHALEY, PROBLEMS AND MATERIALS ON SECURED TRANSACTIONS 10 n. 3 (4th ed. 1997) (noting that a "pledge is sometimes called a hypothecation").

By contrast, the Patent Act does not refer to a "hypothecation" and, as we have demonstrated, does not refer to security interests at all. The fact that one federal intellectual property statute with a recording provision expressly refers to security interests (the Copyright Act), while another does not (the Patent Act), is more evidence that security interests are outside the scope of 35 U.S.C. § 261. *See S. Cal. Bank v. Zimmerman (In re Hilde)*, 120 F.3d 950, 955 (9th Cir. 1997) (noting that, when "a statute omits a specific matter from its coverage, the inclusion of such a matter in another statute on a related subject demonstrates an intent to omit the matter from the coverage of the statute in which it is not mentioned") (quoting *Cal. Coastal Comm'n v. Quanta Inv. Corp.*, 113 Cal. App.3d 579, 599, 170 Cal. Rptr. 263 (1980)).

### 5. PTO Regulations Require Only the Recording of Documents that Transfer Ownership in a Patent.

It is worthy of mention that the applicable PTO regulations parallel our interpretation of 35 U.S.C. § 261. Title 37 C.F.R. § 3.11(a) provides that "assignments" must be recorded in the PTO. That regulation also states that "[o]ther documents *affecting title* to applications, patents, or registrations, will be recorded at the discretion of the Commissioner" of Patents and Trademarks. (*Emphasis added.*) Section 313 of the Manual of Patent Examining Procedure (7th ed. 1998) explains that "[o]ther documents" that may be filed include "agreements which convey a security interest. Such documents are recorded in the public interest in order to give third parties notification of equitable interests...."

Title 37 C.F.R. §3.11 is illuminating because it shows that the PTO does not consider security interests to be "assignments, grants or conveyances." Under 35 U.S.C. §261, certain conveyances—those that transfer an ownership interest—must be recorded to be effective as against a subsequent purchaser or mortgagee. If security interests were "assignments, grants or conveyances," then they would have to be filed to provide constructive notice to a subsequent purchaser or mortgagee, consistent with the Patent Act. As a matter of law and logic, the Commissioner would not have the "discretion" to reject federal filing.

The PTO consistently has interpreted 35 U.S.C. §261 in this way. An earlier version of the regulation, 37 C.F.R. §1.331, which was originally enacted in 1959, allowed for the federal filing of "[o]ther instruments affecting title to a patent... *even though the recording thereof may not serve as constructive notice under 35 U.S.C. 261.*" 37 C.F.R. §1.331(a) (emphasis added). Similarly, 37 C.F.R. §7, also originally enacted in 1959, distinguished between "assignments" and "licenses," much as Waterman had. "Assignment" meant any "instrument which conveys to the Government only the title to a patent." 37 C.F.R. §7.2 (removed and reserved Oct. 10, 1997). "Licenses" were any instruments other than assignments. 37 C.F.R. §7.3 (removed and reserved Oct. 10, 1997).

We acknowledge that the issue in this case "is a pure question of statutory construction for the courts to decide" and that the PTO's interpretation is not entitled to any particular deference. *INS v. Cardoza-Fonseca*, 480 U.S. 421, 446, 107 S. Ct. 1207, 94 L. Ed. 2d 434 (1987); *see also Chevron U.S.A., Inc. v. Natural Res. Def. Council, Inc.*, 467 U.S. 837, 843 n. 9, 104 S. Ct. 2778, 81 L. Ed. 2d 694 (1984) (noting that the "judiciary is the final authority on issues of statutory construction"). Although the statute is ambiguous now, it seems not to have been in 1870. Moreover, we do not believe that 35 U.S.C. §261 contains within it a delegation of authority, either explicit or implicit, that would enable the PTO to broaden or narrow the reach of the Patent Act's recording provision. *See id.* at 844, 104 S. Ct. 2778 (noting that deference is appropriate only when Congress has delegated the authority to an administrative agency to fill a statutory gap or interpret an ambiguous provision.)

However, when we must interpret an archaic statute, the historic practice of the agency that was created to help implement that statute can shed light on its meaning. *Cf. Mesa Verde Constr. Co. v. N. Cal. Dist. Council of Laborers*, 861 F.2d 1124, 1130 n. 5 (9th Cir. 1988) (stating that "[w]e have long recognized that considerable weight should be accorded to an executive department's construction of a statutory scheme it is entrusted to administer"). Under 37 C.F.R. §3.1l, Petitioners were not required to record with the PTO their security interest in order to perfect as to the Trustee.

### 6. There is no Conflict Between the Patent Act and Article 9 in this Case.

Because the Patent Act does not cover security interests or lien creditors at all, there is no conflict between 35 U.S.C. §261 and Article 9. Petitioners did not have to file with the PTO to perfect their security interest as to a subsequent lien creditor.

### B. Article 9's Step-Back Provision

The Trustee's second major argument is that Article 9 itself requires that a creditor file notice of a secured transaction with the PTO in order to perfect a security interest. California Commercial Code §9302(3)(a) states that the filing of a financing statement pursuant to Article 9 "is not necessary or effective to perfect a security interest in property subject to... [a] statute... which provides for a national or international registration…or which specifies a place of filing different from that specified in" Article 9. If §9302(3)(a) applies, then a party must utilize the federal registration system in order to perfect its security interest. CAL. COM. CODE §9302(4).

The question, then, is whether the Patent Act is "[a] statute…which provides for a national or international registration…or which specifies a place of filing different from that specified in" Article 9. CAL. COM. CODE §9302(3)(a). The Patent Act is clearly a statute that provides for a national registration. But that begs the more focused question: a national registration of what? Courts have tended to use the context of the statute to amplify the bare text and to answer the focused question: a national registration of security interests.

For example, in *Aerocon Engineering, Inc. v. Silicon Valley Bank* (*In re World Auxiliary Power Co.*), 244 B.R. 149, 155 (1999), the bankruptcy court observed that §9302(3)(a), if read literally, would be absurd. It would provide that, whenever a particular type of collateral may be registered nationally, regardless of whether the federal statute specifies a place for filing a security interest different than that provided by the UCC, filing a UCC-1 financing statement would be neither necessary nor effective to perfect a security interest in the collateral.

Courts have thus read §9302(3)(a) as providing that federal filing is necessary only when there is a statute that "provides for" a national registration of security interests. *See, e.g., Trimarchi v. Together Dev. Corp.*, 255 B.R. 606, 610 (D.Mass. 2000) (holding that §9302(3)(a) did not require the federal filing of a trademark because the Lanham Act does not provide for a national recording system of security interests). We agree with that interpretation.

Under that more restrictive definition, it is clear that the Patent Act is outside the scope of §9302(3)(a). As we have explained, a transaction that grants a party a security interest in a patent but does not effect a transfer of title is not the type of "assignment, grant or conveyance" that is referred to in 35 U.S.C. §261. The transaction in this case did not transfer an ownership interest. Therefore, §9302(3)(a) did not require that Petitioners record their security interest with the PTO.

The Comments to Article 9 of the UCC support this view. Comment 8 states that §9302(3) exempts from the filing provisions of this Article transactions as to which an adequate system of filing, state or federal, has been set up outside this Article and subsection (4) makes clear that when such a system exists perfection of a relevant security interest can be had only through compliance with that system.

The Comments instruct that "17 U.S.C. §§28, 30 (copyrights), 49 U.S.C. §1403 (aircraft), [and] 49 U.S.C. §20(c) (railroads)" are examples of the "type of federal statutes" referred to in §9302(3). Each of the statutes listed in the Comments refers expressly to security interests. *See* 17 U.S.C. §101; 49 U.S.C. §44107; 49 U.S.C. §11301. The Patent Act is not among them.

## C. Conclusion

Because 35 U.S.C. §261 concerns only transactions that effect a transfer of an ownership interest in a patent, the Patent Act does not preempt Article 9, and neither California Commercial Code §9104(a) nor §9302(3) applies. Consequently, Petitioners perfected their security interest in Debtor's patent by recording it with the California Secretary of State. They have priority over the Trustee's claim because they recorded their interest before the filing of the bankruptcy petition.

AFFIRMED.

---

# Notes & Questions

1. Congress enacted the Bankruptcy Code in 1978 under the 1978 Bankruptcy Reform Act. Bankruptcy can be filed under one of five distinctly different chapters of the Bankruptcy Code. Chapters 12 and 9 are specialized provisions pertaining only to bankruptcy proceedings for family farms and municipal debts, respectively. *See* 11 U.S.C. §§ 1201–1239; 11 U.S.C. §§ 901–946. Chapter 7, or liquidation bankruptcy, involves the process of collecting the debtor's assets, reducing them to cash, and distributing pro rata shares of the liquidated assets to the creditors. Distribution of the debtor's liquidated assets may be subject to the rights of the debtor in certain exempt property. The distribution may also be subject to the rights of secured creditors in the collateral held against the debtor's assets. *See* 11 U.S.C. §§ 701–766.

Chapter 11, or debtor in possession bankruptcy, involves business reorganization and rehabilitation. Debtors are allowed to remain in control of their businesses while repaying creditors through an acceptable plan of reorganization. The reorganization plan is subject to approval by the creditors. Because the debtor is allowed to retain possession of the business and associated assets, intellectual property licensing issues generally occur in Chapter 11 bankruptcy proceedings, the focus of this chapter. *See* 11 U.S.C. §§ 1101–1174.

Chapter 13, or individual debt repayment bankruptcy, provides individuals or small businesses the opportunity to repay all or some portion of their indebtedness over time provided that they still have a regular income source. Chapter 13 is similar to Chapter 11 in that the debtor is required to propose a restructuring and repayment plan that is subject to approval by the creditors. Chapter 13 is different than Chapter 11, however, in that an appointed trustee supervises the debtor's performance under the plan. In addition, Chapter 13 only applies to individuals or small businesses that owe unsecured debts of less than $290,525 and secured debts of less than $871,550 at the date of filing a bankruptcy petition. *See* 11 U.S.C. §§ 1301–1330.

The intellectual property concerns of protecting original expression and preventing consumer confusion are of secondary importance in bankruptcy proceedings. The Bankruptcy Code is concerned with rehabilitating the debtor to provide it with a fresh start and enlarge the bankruptcy estate as much as possible to maximize payments to creditors. These interests may clash with the interests behind some bankruptcy proceedings, particularly those involving intellectual property assets. In addition the debtor, either as licensee or licensor, has an advantage in that the bankruptcy court is the exclusive forum for determining disputes with debtors. The bankruptcy court applies the rules and underlying policies of the Bankruptcy Code rather than those of intellectual property law. *See* Stuart M. Riback, *Intellectual Property Licenses: The Impact of Bankruptcy*, 762 PLI/PAT. 1093, 1096 (2000).

2. *The Application of 365(n) and Its Results.* The mechanics of applying section 365(n) are sometimes confusing. The following is a brief overview:

    a.   Rejection of Executory Contract by Licensor

The protections under Section 365(n) are only triggered when the trustee has rejected an executory contract under which the debtor is a licensor of a right to intellectual property. 11 U.S.C. § 365(n)(1). Like § 365(a), rejection is subject to court approval based on an evaluation of whether the decision is within sound business judgment for the state. *See In re Ron Matusalem*, 158 B.R. 514, 515, 522 (Bankr. S.D. Fla. 1993) (court refused to authorize rejection based in a finding of the debtor's bad faith and lack of a justified business purpose for seeking rejection).

b.  Protections to License Before Rejection

Under Section 365(n)(4), the licensee of intellectual property rights (as defined by the statute) is provided protection over its licensed rights before rejection. First, unless and until the trustee rejects a license agreement and upon written request by the licensee, the trustee might perform all obligations under the license agreement, or provide the licensee with the intellectual property and any embodiment of the intellectual property as provided for in the licensee agreement or supplementary agreement. 11 U.S.C. § 365(n)(4)(A)(i)(ii). The intellectual property and embodiment must be in existence at time of the bankruptcy petition. S. Rep. No. 100-105, at 14.

Second, upon written request from the licensee, the trustee must not interfere with the rights of the licensee as provided in the license agreement or supplementary agreement including any right of the licensee to obtain the intellectual property from the third party. 11 U.S.C. § 365(n)(4)(B).

c.  Elections by the Licensee

(i)  Election to Claim of Damages 365(n)(1)(A)

After the debtor-licensor has rejected the license agreement, the licensee has one of two options. First, the licensee may elect to treat the license agreement as breached. 11 U.S.C. § 365(n)(1)(A). In such case, the license is terminated and licensee has a pre-petition claim for damages resulting from the breach, and has the same rights as he would have had before 365(n) was enacted.

(ii)  Election to Maintain Rights to Intellectual Property 365(n)(1)(B)

In the alternative, the licensee can elect to retain its rights under the license agreement, as such rights existed immediately before the petition for bankruptcy. A licensee must make an affirmative election of its rights under § 365(n)(1)(B).

(iii) Rights Protected Under 365(n)(1)(B)

The licensee is entitled to certain rights as they existed immediately before the petition for bankruptcy as they are provided for in the license agreement, including enforcement of any exclusivity provision in the license agreement; however, the licensee is not entitled to any right under the license agreement which requires specific performance on the part of the trustee-licensor. However, covenants that impose no burden on the estate and require no action by the trustee will be enforced.

Moreover, the licensee is entitled to any embodiment of the intellectual property, to the extent in existence at the time of filing, to which the licensor and licensee have contracted for in the license agreement. For example, if the license agreement provided that the licensor must deliver the prototype to the extent it is complete at time of the petition.

Lastly, the licensee is not only entitled to rights specified in the license agreement, but also to the rights in any agreement supplementary to such license agreement whether or not the supplementary agreement was rejected by the trustee. For example, if a licensor, licensee, and escrow agent entered into an escrow agreement supplementary to the license agreement which provided for certain license-related information to be held by the escrow agent until the triggering of some event, then the licensee can also enforce its rights under the escrow agreement. S. Rep. No. 100, 505, at 12.

(iv) Duration of Protection

The licensee's rights to the intellectual property under § 365(n)(1)(B) continue for the duration of the term of the license agreement and any period for which the license agreement may be extended by the licensee has a right under the applicable non-bankruptcy law.

Jeffery W. Levitan, *Bankruptcy Issues in Intellectual Property Transactions*, 519 PLI/Pat 189, 219-22 (1998).

The application of 365(n) has led to varying results. In *In re EI International*, 18 U.S.P.Q. 2d 2045 (B.C.D. Id., 1991), the court concluded that the licensee, by not formally choosing either to retain or terminate its rights under § 365(n), elected to terminate all rights pursuant to § 365(n)(1)(A). "Since [Licensee] has not opted to 'retain its benefits' under the rejected agreement as followed by 365(n)(1)(B), the extent of its claim will be determined as if the contract had been rejected under 365(n)(1)(A). This analysis results in [licensee's] claim receiving the same treatment as any other claim resulting from a rejected executory contract under Section 365." *EI Int'l*, 18 U.S.P.Q. 2d at 2047.

Although the licensee could still recover, the *EI International* court unilaterally severed the licensee's right to elect to retain the intellectual property allowed under § 365(n)(1)(B). Even though the licensee wished to retain the intellectual property, the court decided that the licensee's inaction resulted in an election to terminate the licensing agreement. Thus, the court essentially deprived the licensee of its option to maintain its rights, as they existed immediately before the debtor's Chapter 11 filing. Patrick Law, *Intellectual Property Licenses and Bankruptcy—Has the IPLBA Thawed the "Chilling Effects" of Lubrizol v. Richmond Metal Finishers?*, 99 Com. L.J. 261, 269–70 (1994).

However, the results differ in *Encino Business Management v. Prize Frize, Inc.*, 150 B.R. 456, 460 (9th Cir. BAP 1993), *aff'd* 32 F.3d 426 (9th Cir. 1994). The debtor/licensor, similarly, invoked § 365(n) in *Encino* to compel the licensee to make the election under Subsection (1)(B) and in turn, to make payments required under Subsection (2). However, the Appellate Panel affirmed an order prescribing: (1) the licensee elect to retain its rights and make the election under Subsection (1)(B); and (2) in turn, pay the requisite royalties. *Supra*, at 460–61.

*Encino*, the previous cases demonstrate that although Congress adopted 365(n) to: (1) lessen hardships on licensees from the rejection of intellectual property licenses; and (2) lessen the potential chilling effect of *Lubrizol*, it may be used by debtor/licensor "as a sword, resulting in a less desirable outcome for the licensee, notwithstanding that the statute was strictly applied." Law, *supra*, at 271.

3. *Problems with the IPLBA.* Some notable problems with the IPLBA are: (1) the IPLBA does not extend to trademark protection; (2) the licensor rejection of improvements clauses; and (3) the assignment of an intellectual property license to a third party by the licensor under Section 365(f). *Id.* at 270–71.

a. *The IPLBA's omission of trademark license protection.* Congress chose to omit trademarks from the IPLBA because: (1) the main concern was with encouraging development of patents; (2) trademarks depend on the quality control of the licensee; and (3) further study was needed to address trademarks. *Id.* at 271. Do you think this has a "chilling effect" on trademark licenses? What about protection for trademark licenses that often accompany technology? Do you think allowing trademark licenses protection under the IPLBA would undermine the quality of products made under those licenses? *See generally*, Law, supra, at 271.

b. *Licensor rejection of improvement clauses.* Section 365(n) protects a licensee's right to an intellectual property at the time the bankruptcy suit is filed. "Even though the parties agreed that the licensee would be the recipient of future developments, the IPLBA is unclear as to what rights the licensee retains in the licensor's development of the technology after the filing of bankruptcy." *Id.* at 371. If the IPLBA allows a licensor to avoid future commitments, this too will have a chilling effect on intellectual property licenses. No case law has yet interpreted whether or not the licensee's rights under the IPLBA will apply to future improvements after the licensor's bankruptcy filing.

c. *Licensor assignment of licenses to third parties.* Section 365(f) allows debtor/licensors and trustees to assign licenses to a third party, despite a provision to the contrary, if the contract "includes an adequate assurance of future performance" by the assignee. *Id.* at 273–74 (citing 11 U.S.C. § 365(f)). Section 365(n) makes no specific references to or prohibitions against this type of assignment. However, intellectual property licenses are often unique and it is not always clear that an assignee may be able to render the same performance contract as the licensor. Could this have a "chilling effect" on intellectual property licenses?

4. *The Writing Requirement.* Section 523(a)(2)(B) of the Bankruptcy Code requires a showing that a materially false statement is a "statement in writing." 11 U.S.C. § 523(a)(2)(B)(1993). In the recent case of *In re Kaspar, Bellso First Fed. Credit Union v. Kaspar (In re Kaspar),* 125 F.3d 1358 (10th Cir. 1997), the court held that a computer-generated record is not a writing for bankruptcy purposes.

In *In re Kaspar* debtors applied for a line of credit and a credit card over the telephone. In response to questions asked by the creditor's employee, they provided financial information that the creditor's employee entered into the computer. The debtors never saw the computer-generated summary of information. The creditor then issued the line of credit and the credit card. When the debtors filed for bankruptcy, the creditor sought an order declaring its debts nondischargeable based on misrepresentations made to it by the debtors. The bankruptcy court denied the order and found that the creditor had failed to meet its requirement of showing that the materially false statement was a "statement in writing" as required by § 523(a)(2)(B) of the Bankruptcy Code. The court framed the question and its answer in this fashion:

> This appeal presents the question of whether modern technology and business practices grounded in convenience will prevail over the strict language of statutory law. In particular, we address whether a computer generated statement of financial condition given in an application for credit neither seen nor signed by the debtor constitutes "a writing" under § 523(a)(2)(B) of the Bankruptcy

Code....We believe the statute must be literally interpreted, and the oral statements made by the debtor which led to the computer equivalent of "a writing" within the meaning of § 523(a)(2)(B).

*Kaspar*, 125 F.3d at 1359.

The court based its decision on a number of considerations. First, the court cited authority that the writing had to be prepared by the bankrupt, signed by the bankrupt, or written by someone else, but adopted and used by the debtor. Second, the court noted the ordinary rule that exceptions to discharge should be narrowly construed. Third, the court noted that "giving a statement of financial condition is a solemn part of significant credit transactions; therefore, it is only natural that solemnity be sanctified by a document which the debtor prepares or sees and adopts. R.J. Robertson, *Electronic Commerce on the Internet and the Statute of Frauds*, 49 S.C. L. Rev. 787, 805–6 (1998).

What does this mean for "click-wrap" and other electronic licenses that are created over computer networks like the Internet? *See* Chapter 8, *supra*.

5. The court in *In re Peregrine Entertainment* criticized earlier cases that held that the Patent Act did not preempt the UCC. *In re Peregrine Entm't, Ltd.*, 116 B.R. 194, 203–4 (C.D. Cal. 1990). The court's broad language would seem to extend to the Lanham Act as well. In *In re Peregrine*, the court held that "when a federal statute provides for a national system of recordation or specifies a place of filing different from that in Article Nine, the methods of perfection specified in Article Nine are supplanted by that national system...." *Id.* at 204. The court reasoned that the decisions interpreting the Patent Act erroneously focused on the priority scheme of the Patent Act in judging perfection preemption, stating '[c]ompliance with a national registration scheme is necessary for perfection regardless of whether federal law governs priorities." G. Larry Engel, *Intellectual Property and Related Asset Considerations in Bankruptcy Cases: Recent Developments Illustrate a Future Trend of Dysfunctional Conflicts Among Competing IP and Commercial Laws in Need of Reconciliation for Good Business*, 767 PLI/Comm. 1009, 1015–16 (1998) (citing *In re Peregrine Entm't, Ltd.*,116 B.R. 194, 204 (C.D. Cal. 1990)). Engel succinctly summarizes the problem as follows:

It is hard to imagine a more provocative doctrine for IP law than the erroneous and unprecedented conclusion some aggressive trustees in bankruptcy now assert based upon *In re Avalon Software, Inc.*, 209 B.R. 517 (Bankr. D. Ariz. 1997): the legal consequences of the failure to register copyrights and thereafter to perfect security interests therein with appropriate Copyright Office filings means that the trustee in bankruptcy may defeat any competing security interests in the software and its "proceeds," including those perfected security interests in patents, trademarks, trade secrets, and general intangibles and accounts receivables from cases the court may find allocation of such software and proceeds among the different IP and UCC categories extraordinarily difficult or impractical, there is no meritorious legal or policy basis for subordinating or negating patents, trade secrets, and trademarks in favor of unregistered copyrights or for ignoring the role of patents, trade secrets and trademarks in software products or licenses. While some IP and commercial lawyers dismiss *Avalon Software* as merely an incorrectly decided aberration, many trustees in bankruptcy continue to cite that decision with passion as supporting many dubious IP principles.

Engel, *supra*, at 1015–16.

6. *What happens when an intellectual property licensee claims bankruptcy?* The IPBPH does not apply when the licensee is the debtor. If an intellectual property contract is determined to be executory, the trustee can take one of three actions under Section 365: the trustee can reject the contract; the trustee can assume the contract; or the trustee can assume and assign the contract. William M. Goldman, *The Treatment of Intellectual Property in Bankruptcy*, 670 PLI/PAT 297, 320 (2001) (citing *In re Norquist*, 43 B.R. 224, 225 (Bankr. E.D. Wash 1984)). The Bankruptcy Code allows the trustee to ignore anti-assignment clauses (clauses that restrict the licensee's ability to assign a contract to a third party) and *ipso facto* clauses (clauses that terminate the contract or create a default upon the insolvency or commencement of a bankruptcy case). Goldman, *supra*, at 324 (citing Bankruptcy Code § 365 (e)(1)). However, Bankruptcy Code § 365 (e)(2) states that *ipso facto* clauses can be enforced if "applicable law" excuses the non debtor party to the contract "from accepting performance from or rendering performance to the trustee or to an assignee of such contract or lease, whether or not such contract or lease prohibits or restricts assignment of rights and delegation of duties."

Further, "Section 362(a) of the Bankruptcy Code creates an 'automatic stay' against, *inter alia*, any action to exercise control over property of the debtor's estate. Consequently, the automatic stay will impair the licensor's exercise of its duty to control the licensee's use of its property." Goldman, at 328.

A licensor in this position should consider whether its executory contract is of a type that cannot be assigned or assumed. Most important to licensors are contracts that are *non-assignable* under non-bankruptcy law. For example, non-exclusive patent licenses are not assignable. In *Everex Systems, Inc. v. Cadtrack Corporation*, 89 F.3d 673 (9th Cir. 1996), the Ninth Circuit sustained a licensor's objection to a debtor assigning its rights under a non-exclusive patent license. The Ninth Circuit's decision followed Bankruptcy Code § 365 (c)(1)(A) that "limits a trustee's right to assign an executory contract when applicable law excuses the non-debtor party from accepting performance from an assignee. The relevant applicable law was the Federal common law principle that non-exclusive patent licenses contain an implied term restricting assignment." WILLIAM L. NORTON, JR., 6A NORTON BANKR. L. & PRAC. 2d § 151:30 (2002 Update) (citing *C.I.R. v. Sunnen*, 333 U.S. 591 609 (1948)); *see also In re Catapult Entm't, Inc.*, 165 F.3d 747 (9th Cir. 1999) (non-exclusive patent license is personal and may only be assumed and assigned with consent of licensor).

Non-exclusive copyright licenses are also considered non-assignable under the same rationale. Goldman at 322 (citing *In re Patient Educ. Media, Inc.*, 210 B.R. 237, 242 (Bankr. S.D.N.Y. 1997) (non-exclusive copyright license non-assignable)).

As seen in Section VII, courts are divided on whether restrictions on assignment by a debtor also extend to assumption by a debtor. Section 365(n) states, "the trustee may not assume or assign any executory contract or unexpired lease of the debtor...." 11 U.S.C. § 365(c). As you read earlier, the First Circuit adopted a different, "actual test" holding that § 365(c) restricts assumption only when the trustee actually intends to assign the contract after assumption. *Institut Pasteur v. Cambridge Biotech Corp.*, 104 F.3d 489 (1st Cir. 1997) (under actual test, court allowed the debtor company to assume licensee rights under a patent license and then transfer its entire shareholdings to a third party). In contrast, the Ninth Circuit adopted a "hypothetical test" for interpreting the language in § 365(c), holding that the Section restricts assumption of an executory contract when a hypothetical assignment would be prohibited. *In re Catapult Entm't, Inc.*,

165 F. 3d 747 (9th Cir. 1999), *cert. dismissed*, 528 U.S. 924 (1999) (under the hypothetical test debtor could not assume rights under a non-exclusive patent license if the licensor objected).

Another option for the licensor is to petition the court to lift the automatic stay so that the licensor can terminate the license. Goldman, at 328 (citing *In re Tudor Motor Lodge Assocs.*, 102 B.R. 936, 955 (Bankr. D.N.J. 1989). A licensor can also ask the court for an order directing the licensee to assume or reject the contract within a specified time period. Bankruptcy Code § 365(d)(2). The licensor will, however, need to provide a compelling reason why the decision must be expedited. Courts are generally reluctant to force a trustee to decide quickly. Goldman, *supra*, at 329 (citing *In re Gunter Hotel Assocs.*, 96 B.R. 696 (Bankr. W.D. Tex. 1988). If the licensee rejects the contract, the automatic stay is lifted with respect to that contract. Bankruptcy Code § 362 (c)(1).

Trademark licenses do not fall within the category of non-assignable executory licenses. The Lanham Act requires trademark licensors to control "the nature and quality of the goods and services" sold by licensee. What happens if the trustee, or the trustee's assignee, cannot, or does not want, to incur these added expenses? In the case of Chapter 11, the trustee may find that the cost to maintain the quality of the goods produced under a license outweighs the benefits received from assumption. In the case of Chapter 7, without obtaining court approval, the trustee cannot operate debtor's business. The trustee therefore may be unable to fulfill the Lanham Act obligation. Goldman at 338–39. Is the trademark licensor's only recourse the costly and speculative "stop-assumption and assignment" provisions listed earlier in this note? What other measures can a licensor take to protect its trademark and goodwill in the face of a licensee's bankruptcy?

7. *Bankruptcy and Privacy Policies.* A company should carefully consider the terms of its website privacy policies, as these terms may become relevant if the company must later file for bankruptcy. For example, Toysmart.com was a company that offered toys for sale via a website. Toysmart.com collected personal information from its customers. Toysmart.com's privacy policy terms expressly stated that this information would *never* be shared with third parties. Toysmart.com later ran into financial difficulty and attempted to sell its assets, including its customer lists and corresponding information. The FTC filed a lawsuit in the U.S. District Court for the District of Massachusetts against Toysmart to prevent the sale of the customer information charging that the company violated Section 5 of the FTC Act by misrepresenting to consumers that personal information would *never* be shared with third parties. The FTC ultimately settled with Toysmart under an agreement that forbids the sale of customer information governed by that privacy policy except under very limited circumstances. *See* News Release, Federal Trade Commission, FTC Announces Settlement with Bankrupt Website, Toysmart.com, Regarding Alleged Privacy Violations (July 21, 2000), *available at* http://www.ftc.gov/opa /2000/07/toysmart2.htm.

Further, drafters of privacy policies should be careful to consider the difficulties in later amending that policy. The customer information collected under the first version of the policy must be kept separate from later-collected information governed by a later draft of the policy. The company must then bear the administrative burden of treating each set of information under the terms of the applicable policy.

8. While the holding in *In re Peregine* resolved the issue of perfecting security interests in registered copyrights, the Ninth Circuit left open the issue of perfecting security interests in *unregistered* copyrights. Following *Peregrine*, the court in *In re Avalon Software Inc.*, 209 B.R. 517 (Bankr. D. Ariz. 1997) held that a security interest in an unregistered

copyright was governed by the Copyright Act and, thus, could only be perfected by filing in the Copyright Office. The court also found that unregistered copyrights could not be perfected at all. However, one of the most common provisions in a security agreement is a provision for after-acquired property of the same type. If as the *Avalon* court found, security interests can only be filed in registered copyrights, any "after-acquired property" would have to be registered first and a new security interest filed in the Copyright Office. This would be especially burdensome for software development companies that routinely update versions of their software without registering the copyright.

The Ninth Circuit in *Aerocon Engineering v. Silicon Valley Bank (In re World Auxiliary Power Co.)*, 303 F.3d 1120 (9th Cir. 2002), addressed the issue of whether federal or state law governs the priority of security interest in unregistered copyrights head on and held that unregistered copyrighted works can be perfected by filing a UCC financing statement. The court reasoned that because the Copyright Act does not provide a means for perfecting an interest in an unregistered copyright, it does not preempt the scheme of perfection under the UCC. The Ninth Circuit observed that Congress must have contemplated that most copyrights would be unregistered and despite this fact, only provided for protection in registered copyrights. Nevertheless, "[t]here is no reason to infer from Congress's silence as to unregistered copyrights an intent to make such copyrights useless as collateral by preempting state law but not providing any federal priority scheme for unregistered copyrights." The court reasoned that if copyright registration were a prerequisite to perfection, it would mean that congress intended to make unregistered copyrights useless as collateral amounting to a presumption in favor of federal preemption. The Ninth Circuit concluded that the "only reasonable inference to draw is that Congress chose not to create a federal scheme for security interests in unregistered copyrights, but left the matter to States, which have traditionally governed security interests." *Id.* at 1131.

# Chapter 14

# Biotechnology Licensing

## I. Introduction

At the dawn of the twenty-first century, two fields of technology dominate everyone's short list of those likely to have the greatest long-run economic and social impact. One is computer technology, including software, the Internet, and the convergence of media. The other is biotechnology.

Perhaps even more likely than instantaneous worldwide multimedia communication, biotechnology is likely to have a profound effect on human life generally. Not only does it promise to alleviate, if not prevent or cure, many of the ills and infirmities that have seemed to be an inextricable part of "the human condition" since prehistoric times. More fundamentally, it promises to reorder our understanding of ourselves as living organisms and our place in the universe. What does it mean to be "alive"? Is each individual's genetic makeup fortuitous and immutable, or can we change it, before or after birth? In the long run, answers to these questions, now being developed, are likely to affect our views of our world and ourselves more profoundly than any technology in human history.

Yet biotechnology is also different in other, less "political" ways. As the Supreme Court itself has recognized, research in biotechnology is subject to considerably greater uncertainty than research in most other fields of modern technology.[1] We can now design complex computer chips, computer programs, and even airplanes on the basis of applied scientific theory, using specialized simulators and automated design tools. For example, both competing versions of the so-called "Joint Strike Fighter," one of the most advanced airplanes ever developed, flew properly on their first test flights. Modern computer simulation and computerized design, coupled with the advanced state of aerodynamic theory and materials science, allowed these planes to be developed without the nasty and sometimes fatal accidents that used to attend flight testing of virtually all new aerospace products.

In contrast, nearly every new drug requires years of clinical testing, typically with hundreds or thousands of human subjects, just to determine whether its clinical benefits outweigh its risks. Imagine how much slower progress in the electronics or transportation industry would be if every new computer, automobile, or airframe required years of "clinical" testing with thousands of different users, drivers, or pilots. Although it has many sources, the well-recognized special uncertainty and unpre-

---

1. See Brenner v. Manson, 383 U.S. 519 (1966).

773

dictability of biotechnology stems in part from unknown and perhaps unknowable genetic variations from individual to individual that exist in every species, including humans.

This uncertainty has several important practical consequences. First, research and development in biotechnology is nearly always expensive and risky. A 2001 study of drug development in the private sector put the cost of developing a *single* new pharmaceutical (including the cost of failures) at $800 million, including clinical testing.[2] Another study estimated the chances of success of a drug *even after proof in the laboratory* at one in five.[3] According to the *Wall Street Journal*, the biotechnology industry, since its inception, has collectively generated losses of more than $40 billion. That paper described the industry as "a casino that sends capital to otherwise neglected high-risk corners of research—and rewards a very few with huge payments."[4]

With this sort of high cost and risk, only a patent can provide sufficient certainty of financial return to justify private-sector investment in research and development. Like the pharmaceutical industry of which it is a part, biotechnology is therefore a classic patent-driven industry.

Patents are not the only kind of intellectual property relevant to biotechnology. Trade-secret protection has its place, for example, for production and other processes that can be used in secret and during the development stage of both processes and products. Yet besides trade secrets, other fields of intellectual property have little relevance to what makes biotechnology unique. There has been some speculation that long genetic sequences may some day be treated like DNA "messages" written in the genetic alphabet (A, G, C, and T) and therefore might be subject to copyright protection. So far, however, no court has addressed this speculation, and no private investor has relied on it. The great cost, risk, and uncertainty involved in biotechnology research makes patents the overwhelming favorite for protecting investment in this industry.

A second consequence of the uncertainty of biotechnology is the importance of tangible results. In other fields, the results of research and development often appear in abstract, intangible form. For example, a listing of source code for a computer program,

---

2. *See* News Release, Tufts Center for the Study of Drug Development, Tufts Center for the Study of Drug Development Pegs Cost of a New Prescription Medicine at $802 Million (Nov. 30, 2001), available at http://csdd.tufts.edu/NewsEvents/RecentNews.asp?newsid=6 (visited May 19, 2004).

3. *See* Henry Grabowski, *Patents and New Product Development in the Pharmaceutical and Biotechnology Industries*, 8 GEO. PUBLIC POL'Y REV. 7, 9 (2003), citing Joseph A. DiMasi, *Success Rates for New Drugs Entering Clinical Testing in the United States* 58 J. CLINICAL PHARMACOLOGY AND THERAPEUTICS 1–14 (1995) ("Typically, many thousands of compounds are examined in the pre-clinical period for every one that makes it into human testing. Only 20 percent of the compounds entering clinical trials survive the development process and gain FDA approval.").

4. David P. Hamilton, *Dose of Reality—Biotech's Dismal Bottom Line: More Than $40 Billion in Losses*, WALL ST. J., May 20, 2004, at A1.

This report distinguished firms in the "biotechnology industry" from traditional (and usually larger) pharmaceutical companies by the former's use of recombinant DNA technology or "genetic engineering" to develop drugs and other health-related products. *See id.* It measured the biotechnology's industry's lifetime from the initial public offering of the first such firm (Amgen) to "go public" in 1983. *See id.* It also reported other interesting statistics:

> Biotechnology research spending now consumes roughly $18 billion a year, more than the federal National Institutes of Health spends on heart disease, cancer and infectious disease, and close to two-thirds of the pharmaceutical industry's research spending. Taxpayers fund the NIH, while buyers of profitable prescription drugs pay for the billions that [pharmaceutical] companies such as Merck & Co. and Pfizer Inc. plow into research.

or a series of blueprints for an airframe, often contains enough information for skilled programmers or mechanics to reproduce the end result (the program or the airplane) from raw materials. Not so in biotechnology. Successive attempts to use the very same techniques to splice genetic sequences, or to implant a gene into a living cell, may produce entirely different results for unknown reasons, including genetic variations in the cells or biological materials used. Consequently, the *tangible* results of a successful experiment—a cell culture, a self-replicating cell "line," or a genetically modified organism—may assume special importance in biotechnology. Often contractual terms governing the physical transfer, possession, use, safekeeping, and return of these tangible materials are among the most important provisions of biotechnology licensing agreements. Indeed, tangible materials have become so important in biotechnology licensing that they have led to a renaissance of interest in the old common law of "bailment," i.e., the old common law governing the lending or borrowing of tangible materials without transfer of title.

A third consequence of uncertainty in biotechnology derives directly from the first two. The uncertainty of research in biotechnology makes tangible materials with desired genetic or other biological characteristics extremely important. But what if those tangible materials are derived from a human being, such as a test subject? What legal rights, if any, does a person whose body, cells, or body fluids are used to produce vital materials have in them? As we will see, questions like this implicate ethical and moral issues as well as the law.

Ethical and moral factors also raise a whole host of other considerations, which further differentiate biotechnology from other patent-driven technologies. The primary application of biotechnology is of course in human health care. Already, seemingly miraculous discoveries have shown great promise in preventing and curing disease, extending life, and relieving human suffering.

Sometimes the application of these discoveries is a matter of life or death. In that case, their practical, human importance may challenge traditional economic and legal approaches. An injunction, for example, is generally the standard remedy for proven patent infringement. But suppose an injunction to avoid infringing a patent would preclude the manufacture and sale of unique material needed to diagnose, prevent or cure disease. Should a court issue the injunction and trust to the marketplace to provide the vitally needed products? Should it do so even if there is some risk that people may suffer or die as a result? Or should the court deny the injunction until the patentee arranges to satisfy market demand and prevent needless harm or suffering?

Similar issues arise with respect to patented pharmaceuticals that some people need to survive. A classic example, discussed in the Notes to Chapter 4, is retroviral drugs used to prevent HIV infections from developing into full-blown AIDS. If people who need those drugs to survive, here and abroad, are too poor to afford them, should the law require compulsory patent licensing, or compulsory production, on humanitarian grounds? If it does so, how will the law encourage the massive investment necessary to develop *succeeding* generations of similar drugs in the face of the formidable investment risks discussed above? Questions of this sort, which implicate law, economics, morals and ethics, will never go away. Rather, they will become more acute as the curative power of biotechnology increases, and with it the expense, difficulty and uncertainty of obtaining further positive results.

As discussed below, the Bayh-Dole Act gives the federal government statutory "march-in" rights, that is, the rights to exploit (or to license exploitation of) government-sponsored technology, despite exclusive licenses, if private exploitation is insufficient to meet demand. While the relevant statutory provisions are by no means limited to biotechnology, their principal use is likely to be in biotechnology, for inventions in that field present the greatest danger to the public welfare in the event of "nonworking" or under-use of potentially beneficial technology. The government's march-in rights, however, are only a partial solution to the general problem. They apply only to federally sponsored research, not to private research, and they make no provision for humanitarian exploitation of biotechnology's "miracles" outside the United States, where problems of poverty and adequate compensation may be most acute.

As this brief introduction shows, biotechnology differs from other fields of advanced technology in many important respects. Its impact on moral, ethical, religious and therefore political issues is incomparably more direct and profound. Its inherent uncertainty makes it a paradigmatic patent-driven field of industry, yet that very same uncertainty makes patents harder to get and the tangible results of experiments more important. And its practical, moral and ethical importance promises only more hard choices in balancing financial incentives for research and development against humanitarian aid to all who may need the resulting "miracles." As a result, biotechnology development and licensing portend a host of controversies not only for intellectual property and licensing lawyers, but for judges, legislators, and policy makers as well.

---

# II. On the Frontiers of Science and Patent Law

## Re-Engineering Patent Law:
## The Challenge of New Technologies*

C. Long

2 WASH. U. J.L. & POL'Y 229 (2000)

Excerpt from Patent Law and Policy Symposium: Re-Engineering Patent Law:
Part II: Judicial Issues: Patents and Cumulative Innovation

\* \* \*

An entire industry has sprung up surrounding the creation of genomic information. The creation of massive quantities of raw data and information about genes and protein sequences, on an almost daily basis, has created information bottlenecks in the lab and in the market. No single lab or firm can absorb even a small part of this expanding information. Having compiled masses of genomic information, scientists now find themselves asking the next question: exactly what do the products of these genes do? The answer, at least as far as investors are concerned, is that it may not matter: genomic information has become a key strategic and competitive asset independent of applied products. This explosion of genomics data and the proliferation of new information-based research approaches call into question many long-held beliefs

---

*Reprinted with permission of the publisher, copyright 2000.

and assumptions about the role of intellectual property rights as incentives for research discovery, incentives for technology innovation, and incentives for the diffusion of both.

As Walter Gilbert first predicted in 1991, burgeoning genetic knowledge was destined to change the paradigm of biomedical research—and he easily could have included the accepted paths for pharmaceutical industry innovation. Traditionally, rapid imitation of new products in the pharmaceutical industry was difficult because patents provided solid protection, for the most part, against imitation. Because pharmaceutical products are very specific, small variations in molecular structure can have disproportionate effects on the drug's pharmacological properties. With a few exceptions, this made it difficult for a competitor to invent around a patent on a molecular compound or class of compounds by making small changes to the drug's structure. Thus, although pharmaceutical innovation was a capital-intensive, high-risk process, relatively strong patent protection on the product that finally emerged at the end of the research pipeline allowed firms to recoup their investment.

Biomedical research, particularly that pertaining to genomics, departs from this model. Most significantly, genomic information and research tools based on information technologies—not only the products derived from their use—have themselves become marketable. The core business of an increasing number of new market entrants is information about the genetic codes of various organisms, not the sale of drugs or diagnostics. For example, Celera, a private sector firm, announced that it derives its revenues primarily from subscription fees from database customers, rather than from licensing intellectual property rights or selling products.

Biomedical research requires ongoing access to the state of the art. Drug discovery, diagnostic discovery, and innovation have become progressively more dependent on access to a common pool of accumulated scientific knowledge. Continued product discoveries and innovations also rely increasingly on the knowledge gleaned from preceding ones and on generally available techniques that have made the process of innovation more predictable. The process of innovation and invention for new drugs and diagnostics is beginning to reflect the thrust of entirely new conceptual approaches, a broad range of new market entrants in new niche markets, product lifecycles that are shortening dramatically, and the growing importance of basic research and its results to the trajectory of new product innovation.

New investment in basic biomedical research is frequently oriented "to securing ownership of research and developing it toward markets." John Hodgson, *Biotechnology in a Year of Living Prosperously*, 15 NATURE BIOTECHNOLOGY 227–30 (1997). New entrants in the upstream market for genomic information are less capital intensive, exhibit much faster time to market, and offer different risk-reward models for investors than the traditional pharmaceutical companies. The marked trend to strategic alliances reflects the importance of preemptively acquiring ownership of research. Genomic database networks have stimulated the formation of strategic alliances among pharmaceutical, biotech, genomic, and information technology companies in an attempt to gain control of a package of genomic information and data to sell or license to users.

Even if the information generated by new market entrants is not always patentable, the question of who owns it is becoming more porous. New biomedical research approaches and the increasing value of genomic information are creating a new "food chain" or "discovery pipeline" that undermines the traditional market structure in which nonprofit institutions, first generation biotechnology firms, and integrated drug companies play clearly defined roles shepherding research from the basic to the applied end of the discovery pipeline. Instead, both ends of the spectrum are coming together as pharmaceutical producers enter into strategic alliances with, or acquire outright, small firms specializing in the production of genetic information. New risk-sharing collaborative arrangements such as strategic alliances consortia, and mergers and acquisitions also introduce significant changes in the status quo.

The enhanced role of ideas and discoveries in value and wealth creation means larger firms must become research portfolio managers, both internally and externally. Once a research finding or technology appears promising, there are incentives to acquire rights to it. Once it shows sufficient value in enabling product development, integrated firms often buy the owner. For the bulk of research, however, there is a growing need to broker uncertainty and risk, including the ownership of rights, which creates an environment in which strategic alliances and brokerage functions dominate.

The link between scientific breakthroughs and marketable innovations continues to shorten and tighten. The compression of the time involved in this research and innovation makes the linkage even stronger as new complementary relationships must be forged to meet the competitive pressures of basic biomedical research in universities and in the marketplace. The initial evidence suggests that, as occurred in the electronics industry when product life-cycles shortened dramatically, innovation rewards increasingly will come from so-called "first mover" advantages in being the first to market rather than from patent rights alone. For example, Celera has announced that its competitive strategy is to "promote use of [its] information by a wide variety of users...to ensure access to valuable sequencing data by the entire biomedical and agricultural research community."

The sheer quantities of information created by the Human Genome Project and other genomics research ventures have focused attention away from defining information possession, the raison d'etre of the intellectual property system, to optimizing information management—an area in which the intellectual property system is decidedly deficient. While the scientific community is faced with the fundamental questions of how to cope with this information explosion, and how to apply it to key areas, the intellectual property system is challenged by the fact that it simply was not designed to handle the realities of information production and management that are occurring in the field of genetic research today. This is creating a number of crosscurrents that are forcing a reexamination of the scope and nature of rights needed to maintain discovery and innovation.

* * *

Current models of intellectual property protection fail to account for the nuances of a research and development process in which patents can be granted at multiple stages. The information-intensive qualities of scientific innovations, combined with the cumulative nature of scientific research, suggest that current models of proprietary rights protection are insufficient. Neither a model that grants broad rights to all initial inventors nor a model that reserves excessive protection for subsequent innovators should be applied across the entire range of basic research results....

One concern is that biomedical research is an area in which overbroad patents to initial innovators will enervate the incentives for downstream research. One commentator has argued that "excessive protection for first generation innovation can impede later stages, thereby undermining some of the salutary effects of strong intellectual property protection." [Peter Menell, *The Challenges of Reforming Intellectual Property Protection for Computer Software*, 97 COLUM. L. REV. 2644, 2646 (1994)].

Under some circumstances, strong protection for certain discoveries too early in their evolution will retard further development or redirect research in less beneficial directions. For example, the semiconductor industry in its formative years was marked by rapid, multidirectional progress in both the underlying basic research and the cumulative technology that grew out of it. This highly beneficial burst of scientific, technological, and economic advancement had broad social consequences, only partially glimpsed at the time, that would not have been possible in a legal regime that strongly protected intellectual property rights in many of the early innovations.

Other industries, however, rely heavily on strong patent protection. One study shows that eighty percent of firms surveyed in the chemical, transportation equipment, electrical equipment, food, metals, and machinery industries indicated that the strength of intellectual property protection had a "major effect" in their willingness to invest in research and development facilities abroad. There are significant differences, however, between sectors in research and development, investment, and innovative performance. The impact of patent protection on market behavior depends on the character of technology in a field, the nature of the industry involved, and the way in which research is conducted. It is unclear whether conclusions gleaned from industries characterized by tangible commercial products can be extrapolated to biomedical research generally. It is certain that such conclusions cannot be extended to patents on biomedical research results that are so far upstream that no commercial product currently exists.

Strong protection for upstream innovation can significantly affect the incentive to conduct follow-on research, but commentators disagree on precisely how. While one model of intellectual property protection argues that early allocation of patent rights can make downstream research allocations more efficient, other models suggest that upstream protection steers research away from incremental improvements over existing inventions. When innovation in a field of scientific endeavor, such as biomedical research, is cumulative and characterized by information-intensive inputs, I do not presume that granting a broad scope of protection induces efficient downstream innovation. Instead, I regard this as an unsettled issue in need of more research. If biomedical research is an area in which proprietary rights at early stages of innovation determine the outcomes of later stages, it would be helpful to know what factors cause proprietary rights at early stages to hinder or help downstream research.

Analysis is complicated by the fact that patentability standards have proven to be very dynamic over the past twenty years. Over time, patentable subject matter has crept ever closer to the basic end of the biomedical research spectrum. Today, the scope of protection for biomedical inventions can be very broad and may cover very basic research. For example, patents have issued on such inventions as any "non-human mammal" all of the cells of which contain an introduced cancer-inducing DNA sequence, stem cells, and partial gene fragments so small that they comprised, on average, less than 0.000005% of the human genome. Each of these inventions has been, or is anticipated to be, the source from which further research and discoveries will spring.

\* \* \*

# Bioinformatics and Intellectual Property Protection*
M. Scott McBride
17 BERKELEY TECH. L.J. 1331 (Fall, 2002)

### Introduction

Advances in biotechnological techniques, such as DNA, RNA, and protein sequencing, and more widespread application of these techniques, have led to a huge accumulation of information in the past two decades. The DNA of the human genome has now been sequenced, and the entire human genome will likely be assembled and determined in the near future. Much of this information is in "raw form" and must be analyzed, organized, and stored. Bioinformatics is the "research, development, or application of computational tools and approaches for expanding the use of biological, medical, behavioral or health data." It is an amalgamation of biology and information technology.

\* \* \*

Before one can understand intellectual property protection for bioinformatics, it is necessary to understand the nature of the various components that comprise the field of bioinformatics. Bioinformatics involves the acquisition, organization, storage, analysis, and visualization of information contained within biological molecules. For the purposes of this article, bioinformatics is analyzed according to the following categories: (A) biological sequences such as DNA, RNA, and protein sequences; (B) databases in which these sequences are organized; and (C) software and hardware designed to create, access, organize, and analyze information contained within these sequences and databases.

### A. DNA, RNA, and Protein Sequences

Scientists classify biological molecules into four general classes that include nucleic acids (which comprise DNA and RNA), proteins, lipids, and carbohydrates. Bioinformatics is currently focused on the biology of DNA, RNA, and protein. DNA is the material whereby genetic traits are transmitted from one generation to the next. Genes are comprised of DNA. Before DNA is "expressed," i.e., effects a genetic trait, DNA serves as a "template" to create an RNA molecule. The information within this RNA molecule is then interpreted by cellular machinery to create a protein. As such, RNA is an intermediary molecule within the process of genetic expression. The protein created from the RNA molecule is typically the final effecter of the genetic trait. Based on the information within the DNA molecule, a protein folds into a three-dimensional structure, which ultimately determines its function. For example, most enzymes are composed of protein, and many diseases, e.g., lactose intolerance, are the result of defective enzymes created from a mutated DNA. In conclusion, the central dogma of molecular biology is described by the expression:

### DNA a RNA a Protein

Each of these three molecules are described using a fairly simple code: DNA by A,C,G,T; RNA by A,C,G,U; and protein by twenty different amino acids. DNA, or deoxyribonucleic acid, is a large molecule comprised of four different repeating units called nucleotides. DNA nucleotides contain one of four nitrogenous bases (adenine ("A"), gua-

---

nine ("G"), cytosine ("C"), or thymine ("T")), and the sequence of a particular DNA is typically described by using the single-letter designation of the nucleotides within the DNA sequence, e.g., ATTGGCATGGA. RNA, like DNA, is comprised of a chain of nucleotide molecules. However, RNA differs from DNA because it contains RNA nucleotides, rather than DNA nucleotides. RNA nucleotides, like DNA nucleotides, may contain adenine, guanine, or cytosine, but unlike DNA nucleotides, RNA nucleotides use uracil ("U") instead of thymine. In a simplistic way, an RNA molecule is a copy of the DNA where "T" is replaced with "U." Therefore, a DNA molecule with the sequence "ATTGGCATGGA," would have a corresponding RNA molecule with the sequence "AUUGGCAUGGA." This RNA molecule is used as a template to synthesize the encoded protein.

Proteins are comprised of twenty different amino acids described by the single letter designations A, C, D, E, F, G, H, I, K, L, M, N, P, Q, R, S, T, V, W, Y, and a protein molecule contains a sequence of any combination of these twenty amino acids, e.g., P-A-T-E-N-T-L-A-W-I-S-G-R-E-A-T. Each of these twenty amino acids is specified by three nucleotides of RNA, e.g., AUG corresponds to methionine or "M." Such triplets comprise codons. Because there are sixty-four different combinations of nucleotide triplets, i.e., $4[su'3'] = 64$, and there are only twenty amino acids, there are more codons than necessary to code for the twenty amino acids. As such, more than one codon can code for a particular amino acid, thereby leading to redundancy in the genetic code. Because of this redundancy, it is not always possible to determine the correct codon sequence for a given amino acid, while it is always possible to determine the correct amino acid for a given codon sequence.

Gene expression, or the route from gene to protein, is regulated within cells. Thus, two genetically identical cells, such as a skin cell and a nerve cell, may express a different complement of proteins and hence exhibit different traits. One aspect of bioinformatics is the study of gene expression through functional genomics (e.g., studying the expression of genes at the mRNA level), and functional proteomics (e.g., studying the expression of genes at the protein level).

In summary, DNA, RNA, and protein are large molecules comprised of repeating units of DNA nucleotides, RNA nucleotides, and amino acids, respectively. DNA, RNA, and protein can be described by the sequence of these repeating units, and the sequence of these repeating units ultimately determines the function of the DNA, RNA, or protein. Therefore, the sequence of the DNA, RNA, or protein contains functional information.

## B. Biological Databases

As more DNA, RNA, and protein sequences are reported, scientists are developing biological databases to catalog and store the sequence information. These databases are valuable if the stored information can be readily searched, accessed, and analyzed. For instance, scientists can use these databases to compare and assign biological functions to particular or characteristic sequences (i.e., "motifs"). Then, when a scientist obtains a sequence from an unknown DNA, RNA, or protein molecule, the scientist can use these databases to identify the unknown molecule and determine its function. Scientists are encouraged to contribute to these databases. For instance, most scientific journals expect the scientist to submit the sequence of a novel biological molecule to a public database prior to publication. Failure to submit a sequence may result in the scientist being denied the opportunity to publish the article.

Although several databases are available to the general public, private companies are not required to make their databases freely available. For example, one company working on sequencing the human genome, Celera, generally charges for access to its database, although it provides free access to "qualified academic users." Celera claims that its database is subject to patent and copyright protection, an issue disputed by Celera's noncommercial competitor, the IHGSC. Celera's case exemplifies the necessity of analyzing whether databases such as Celera's should be subject to IP protection.

## C. Bioinformatic Software and Hardware

To utilize information contained in these databases, software developers have developed bioinformatic programs to organize, access, analyze, and view sequence information. One such program, BLAST® ("Basic Local Alignment Search Tool"), compares sequences for similarity by first aligning the two sequences at areas of local identity or similarity and then calculating a "similarity score." Such algorithms can be designed to incorporate scientific principles based on the molecular biology of DNA, RNA, and protein. For example, an algorithm may be created to compare two nucleotides or amino acids that are not identical but function similarly based on their molecular biology. Such programs are useful in predicting the function of an unknown gene or protein, or to draw evolutionary relationships.

Engineers have also developed computer hardware and machines that facilitate the acquisition and storage of biological information. For example, machines called "thermocyclers" amplify small amounts of DNA or RNA to provide a scientist with a workable amount for sequencing. Other machines rapidly determine the sequence of DNA, RNA, or protein molecules. One of the most promising recent inventions is the "gene chip." A gene chip contains many different DNA sequences organized in a grid or microarray on the chip. By exposing the chip to a test sample of DNA, a scientist determines whether the test sample corresponds to any of the sequences on the chip through a process called "hybridization." The gene chip is advantageous because it is a "high throughput device," meaning that a scientist can obtain a large amount of information from a single input or experiment, and furthermore, the gene chip is suitable for automation.

\* \* \*

## Patent Protection for DNA, RNA, and Protein Sequences

Section 101 permits the patentability of "compositions of matter." Courts have held this as including "all compositions of two or more substances and...all composite articles, whether they be the results of chemical union, or of mechanical mixture, or whether they be gases, fluids, powders or solids." The USPTO has specifically interpreted this to include DNA, RNA, and protein compositions because they are composed of two or more substances—DNA and RNA are composed of nucleotides while proteins are made up of amino acids. Indeed, many DNA, RNA, and protein molecules have been patented as compositions.

However, it was not always clear that biological molecules were patentable subject matter. Only after the Supreme Court's decision in *Diamond v. Chakrabarty* did patents on biological molecules become widespread. Writing for the majority, Chief Justice Burger concluded that 101 permitted the patenting of genetically modified bacteria, stating, "Congress intended statutory subject matter to 'include anything under the sun that is made by man.'" Since then, the USPTO has permitted the patenting of biological molecules under the premise that a biological molecule is a "composition made by man," where the biological molecule has been isolated and purified from its natural setting.

While biological molecules are themselves patentable as compositions, the information within the composition, i.e., the abstract biological sequence itself, arguably is not patentable subject matter. Based on the Supreme Court's holding in *Diamond v. Diehr*, to qualify as patentable subject matter the biological sequence would have to be categorized as a process, machine, apparatus, or composition, and do more than describe a "natural phenomenon." The *Diehr* Court also excluded "laws of nature...and abstract ideas" from patent protection. "An idea of itself is not patentable," and neither is "[a] principle, in the abstract[,] a fundamental truth[,] an original cause[, or] a motive." As "Einstein could not patent his celebrated law that "E = mc²" [and] Newton [could not] have patented the law of gravity," it is unlikely that one could patent a biological sequence since it may be characterized as a natural phenomenon. Therefore, patent protection for DNA, RNA, or protein extends only to the physical/biological composition, and not to the abstract biological sequence information that describes the composition. Thus, a patentee could only prevent another from using the composition itself and not the information within the molecule.

* * *

### Copyright Protection for DNA, RNA, and Protein Sequences

Arguably, the originator(s) of the DNA code nomenclature (who used A, G, C, and T to describe a DNA's sequence), the RNA code nomenclature (who used A, G, C, and U to describe an RNA's sequence), and the protein code nomenclature (who used A, C, D, E, F, G, H, I, K, L, M, N, P, Q, R, S, T, V, W, Y to describe a protein's sequence) may have had a legitimate claim to copyright protection for their original expression. However, as the law now stands "the Copyright Office has unofficially stated that it will not grant copyright registration to gene sequences or DNA molecules because they are not copyrightable subject matter." Furthermore, a contemporary scientist discovering a biological molecule probably would not be entitled to copyright protection for the sequence of the newly discovered molecule or information contained therein for several reasons.

First, the scientist is not the original author of the biological code nomenclatures. Although the scientist is the first to report the sequence of the novel molecule and the reported sequence may therefore comprise "original expression" under copyright law, the originality of his expression is minimal because the biological codes have been used for decades to report sequences. Second, the sequence or information that the scientist seeks to protect is a "discovery" or "idea," neither of which is entitled to copyright protection. Third, because of the limited ways to express a DNA, RNA, or protein sequence, these biological codes have become standard techniques for describing molecules and are therefore not "creative expression." Under the doctrine of scenes a faire, "when similar features...are 'as a practical matter indispensable, or at least standard in the treatment of a given [idea], they are treated like ideas and are therefore not protected by copyright.'" Where there is simply no other way to describe a natural phenomenon, there is no room for "creative expression."

Even if the scientist were to obtain copyright protection for the sequence of a discovered biological molecule, an accused infringer might assert the defense of "fair use" under 107. In determining "fair use," courts use four balancing factors including (1) "the purpose and character of the use," e.g., commercial versus not-for-profit, (2) "the nature of the copyrighted work," e.g., fiction versus nonfiction compilation, (3) "amount and substantiality of the portion used," e.g., an entire work versus a small portion of a large work, and (4) "effect of the use upon the potential market." For example, "fair use" would arguably exist where the accused infringer shows that he used the sequence of a single gene from a large copyrighted compilation (assuming that the compilation is copyrightable where his purpose was "criticism, comment, news reporting, teaching, scholarship, or research" in a not-for-profit, academic setting. In this regard, many critics of IP protection for bioinformatics have been academic researchers, for whom the "fair use" is more likely to apply. In summary, copyright protection for biological sequences is probably unavailable, and were it to become available, it might be evaded by some of its strongest critics under the "fair use" exception.

### Copyright Protection for Biological Databases

The Copyright Act of 1976 specifically describes compilations as copyrightable subject matter; therefore if a database is described as a compilation, it may qualify for copyright protection. The Supreme Court explored the boundaries of copyright protection for compilations in *Feist Publications, Inc. v. Rural Telephone Service Co.* In *Feist* the work at issue was a telephone book, for which the creator sought copyright protection. Justice O'Connor, writing for the majority, described the issue in the case: "Facts are not copyrightable [but] compilations of facts generally are." However, the compilation must be sufficiently original, e.g., in selection or arrangement of the compiled facts. Where a compilation is copyrighted, copyright protection does not extend to every element of the work. "Originality is the sine qua non of copyright [and] copyright protection may extend only to those components of a work that are original to the author."

Applying *Feist's* principles, biological databases are copyrightable, provided they contain the requisite originality. For example, a scientist might obtain copyright protection if he chooses an original set of genes or proteins for a database or arranges the database in an original way. However, the copyright protection would not extend to all the genes or proteins in the database. Rather, copyright protection would extend only to his original selection or arrangement. Thus, a competitor who creates his own database using individual elements of the scientist's copyrighted database would not infringe the scientist's copyright so long as the competitor does not use the same selection or arrangement as the scientist's copyrighted database. Therefore, copyright protection for databases is limited.

Certain databases might have qualified for sui generis protection under bills that were debated in the U.S. House of Representatives in 1998 and 1999. These bills contemplated *sui generis* protection for databases and borrowed elements from the Patent Act, e.g., a short defined term, and elements from the Copyright Act, e.g., a research exception comparable to "fair use." To date, this legislation has not been enacted. However, because some members of the European Union have enacted sui generis protection for databases under an E.C. Directive, Congress may feel pressure to harmonize U.S. law and enact some form of database protection in the future.

### Trade Secret Protection for Biological Databases

Trade secret protection is also available for databases if the database can be shown to derive "independent economic value…from not being generally known." If the owner of a database wishes to commercialize it by selling access or even the database itself, the creator runs the risk that the information within the database will be disclosed and released to the public domain. To avoid such a risk, the owner might engineer or acquire security devices that allow access to the database without revealing the entire contents. Nevertheless, these devices can be circumvented and the database content released into the public domain, thereby forever destroying the trade secret status of the information. Notwithstanding such risks, some databases owners have attempted to "exploit [their] databases commercially by controlling access to them, in effect using contracts and trade secrecy to protect their intellectual property." Even where database owners have controlled access and secrecy through contracts, third party release of independently acquired information into the public domain has hampered efforts to commercialize these databases. For instance, as part of its policy, the Wellcome Trust, called the "world's largest medical charity," releases the DNA sequence information that it gathers from the human genome into the public domain. Likewise, pharmaceutical giant Merck sponsored human DNA sequencing research by Washington University for "instantaneous dedication [of the results] to the public domain." This policy increases the amount of information that is freely available and, therefore, may diminish the value of fee-based databases. Merck nonetheless believes that release of such information into the public domain will benefit its own development efforts in the long run. Data released by the Wellcome Trust or companies like Merck may be incorporated into the free databases offered by the NIH. Therefore, if the owner of a database wishes to maintain the database as a trade secret, the owner must protect against not only unlicensed access, but also erosion of the database's value through third party disclosures and the growth in the number of free databases.

\* \* \*

# III. The Regime for Licensing Federally Sponsored Research

The Bayh-Dole Act of 1980, 35 U.S.C. §§ 200–212, set the stage for the biotech revolution by granting non-profit universities and hospitals the right to patent and license inventions created with the support of federal funding. Universities receive 80–90% of their external research support from the federal government. Since Bayh-Dole, university research has helped spur the biotechnology revolution through the development of platform technologies like the Cohen-Boyer patents and licenses on techniques for recombinant DNA PCR in the 1980's, and since then, a host of new pharmaceuticals and biotechnologies, among them the cancer drug Taxol, the Cox-II inhibitors like Celebrex, Rogaine and the nicotine patch. In 2000, universities and non-profits received more than $1 billion in royalties (compared to $862 million in the previous year), filed 6,375 new U.S. patent applications, and executed 4,362 new licenses and options, of which more than 450 were to startup companies. (<www.autm.net/surveys/2000/summary-noe.pdf>).

## A. The Bayh-Dole Act

The Bayh-Dole Act permits any small business or nonprofit to elect to retain title to any invention made during a research project sponsored by the federal government. To qualify to retain title, the inventing entity must disclose the invention to the funding agency, file a patent application prior to any statutory bar date, acknowledge the government's support in the patent application, and grant a non-exclusive, non-transferable, irrevocable paid-up license to the funding agency to practice the invention for on behalf of the U.S. government throughout the world. With such title in hand, the inventing entity is free to license the patent rights for commercial purposes, so long as all products embodying the subject invention (or produced through the use of the invention) are manufactured substantially in the United States.

The regulations implementing the Bayh-Dole Act are set out at 37 C.F.R. § 401, and provide a standard inventions rights clause (to be tailored for each Federal agency's use) having certain basic provisions which track the provisions of the Act summarized above in all funding contracts. There are provisions for modification of those basic provisions, set out in 37 C.F.R. Section 401.3(a), the most important being the "exceptional circumstances" provision of Section 401.3(a)(2), which allows modification when the funding agency determines that it "will better promote the policy and objectives of Chapter 18 of Title 35 of the United States Code."

# B.  "March-in" Rights and Compulsory Licensing

Section 203 of the Patent Act of 1952, as amended by the Bayh-Dole Act of 1980, gives the federal government so-called "march-in rights" with respect to inventions derived from federally sponsored research. In essence, "march-in rights" are the rights of the government to require the licensing for the public benefit of inventions developed under federal sponsorship, or itself to license those inventions if the contractor that developed them does not do so.

A moment's thought reveals that such disputes, if they arise, are likely to draw courts into matters of scientific, technical and business judgment. In what fields of use might the invention at issue be valuable? How should it be exploited? What auxiliary inventions or technologies may be necessary to utilize it? Do the contractor's answers to these questions serve the public interest, and do they do so with reasonable speed? Ordinarily, these questions are left to private business judgment and the private marketplace. If a dispute over march-in rights develops, however, the contractor who developed the invention and another private party that wants to use it will be in court, each arguing that its plan for exploiting the invention in the public interest is better.

How should courts resolve such disputes? Can they do so without second-guessing the parties' scientific, technical, and business judgment? If not, to whom should they give the benefit of any doubt? Should courts favor the contractor because it developed the invention and presumably knows more about it, or should they favor the putative compulsory licensee on the ground that the government already has decided, pursuant to statutory authority, that the contractor has not done enough? What if a would-be compulsory licensee seeks to force the government to grant such a compulsory license, even before it has independently decided that such a license is necessary for the public welfare? The following case illustrates how difficult such judgments can be.

The first case in which a federal agency was petitioned to invoke march-in rights involved a drug that was exclusively licensed by Johns Hopkins University to Baxter Healthcare Corporation. The petitioner, CellPro, Inc., sought to obtain a license from the National Institutes of Health, which had funded the original research, after it was unable to negotiate a license from Baxter. At the same time, CellPro was trying to market a similar drug, for which it was being sued by Baxter for patent infringement. The proceeding was heard by the Director of NIH. His opinion follows.

---

# Determination in the Case of Petition of CellPro, Inc.

### National Institutes of Health Office of the Director
*at* www.nih.gov/news/pr/aug97/nihb-01.htm

The National Institutes of Health (NIH) has determined that the initiation of march-in procedures, as requested under the petition outlined below, is not warranted at this time. NIH retains jurisdiction over the instant proceedings until such time as a comparable alternative product becomes available for sale in the United States.

## The CellPro Petition

On March 3, 1997, CellPro, Incorporated (CellPro) filed a petition with the Secretary of Health and Human Services (Secretary) requesting that the Government exercise march-in rights under the Bayh Dole Act (Act), 35 U.S.C. §§ 202–212, in connection with certain patents owned by The Johns Hopkins University (Hopkins) and licensed first to Becton-Dickinson and then to Baxter Healthcare Corporation (Baxter). As discussed in greater detail below, the march-in provision of the Act authorizes the Government, in certain circumstances, to require the contractor (or grantee) or its exclusive licensee to license a Federally-funded invention to a responsible applicant on reasonable terms, or to grant such a license itself. CellPro asserts that such action is necessary to alleviate health or safety needs that have arisen because the United States District Court for the District of Delaware (Court) has found the stem cell separation device developed by CellPro, the Ceprate SC, to infringe two of the patents in question and has enjoined its sale. Alternatively, CellPro asserts that march-in is warranted because Hopkins and Baxter have failed to take reasonable steps to commercialize the technology. At the present time, CellPro is the only company that has an FDA-approved device commercially available.

\* \* \*

## Statutory Background and Criteria

The stated policy and objective of the Bayh-Dole Act is:

> [T]o use the patent system to promote the utilization of inventions arising from federally supported research or development; to encourage maximum participation of small business firms in federally supported research and development efforts; to promote collaboration between commercial concerns and nonprofit organizations, including universities; to ensure that inventions made by nonprofit organizations and small business firms are used in a manner to promote free competition and enterprise; to promote the commercialization and public availability of inventions made in the United States by United States industry and labor; to ensure that the Government obtains sufficient rights in federally supported inventions to meet the needs of the Government and protect the public against nonuse or unreasonable use of inventions; and to minimize the costs of administering policies in this area.

Act at § 200.

\* \* \*

In giving contractors the right to elect title to inventions made with Federal funding, the Act also includes various safeguards on the public investment in the research. For example, the Federal agency retains a nonexclusive, nontransferable, irrevocable, paid-up license to practice or have practiced for or on behalf of the United States any subject invention throughout the world. 35 U.S.C. § 202(c)(4). In addition, the Act includes march-in rights, which provide a Federal agency with the authority in certain, very limited circumstances, to make sure that a federally funded invention is available to the public. Section 203(1) states:

> With respect to any subject invention in which a small business firm or non-profit organization has acquired title under this chapter, the Federal agency under whose funding agreement the subject invention was made shall have the right, in accordance with such procedures as are provided in regulations promulgated hereunder to require the contractor, an assignee or exclusive licensee of a subject invention to grant a nonexclusive, partially exclusive, or exclusive license in any field of use to a responsible applicant or applicants, upon terms that are reasonable under the circumstances, and if the contractor, assignee or exclusive licensee refuses such request, to grant such a license itself, if the Federal agency determines that such —
>
> (a) action is necessary because the contractor or assignee has not taken, or is not expected to take within a reasonable time, effective steps to achieve practical application of the subject invention in such field of use;
>
> (b) action is necessary to alleviate health or safety needs which are not reasonably satisfied by the contractor, assignee, or their licensees;
>
> (c) action is necessary to meet requirements for public use specified by Federal regulations and such requirements are not reasonably satisfied by the contractor, assignee, or licensees; or
>
> (d) action is necessary because the agreement required by section 204 has not been obtained or waived or because a licensee of the exclusive right to use or sell any subject invention in the United States is in breach of its agreement obtained pursuant to section 204.5.

* * *

## Decision

The NIH has evaluated the administrative record with regard to two prongs of the statutory criteria, 35 U.S.C. § 203(1)(a) and (b). The NIH has examined whether: (1) Baxter has failed to take, or is not expected to take within a reasonable time, effective steps to achieve practical application of the subject inventions; and (2) there exists a health or safety need which is not reasonably satisfied by Hopkins or Baxter. Based on these criteria and the available information, march-in is not warranted at this time.

## Practical Application of the Subject Inventions

Practical application is defined under 37 C.F.R. § 404.3(d) as "to manufacture in the case of a composition or product, to practice in the case of a process or method, or to operate in the case of a machine or system; and, in each case, under such conditions as to establish that the invention is being utilized and that its benefits are to the extent permitted by law or Government regulations available to the public on reasonable terms." The administrative record demonstrates that Hopkins and Baxter have clearly met this standard.

This technology was originally developed in the laboratory of Dr. Curt Civin at Hopkins and first published in 1984. Hopkins filed for patent protection and was awarded four patents, the first of which issued in 1987. The technology was first exclusively licensed to Becton-Dickinson & Co. (BD). BD began marketing the first anti-CD34 antibody in 1985 and has sold anti-CD34 antibodies worldwide ever since. Since BD was only interested in the diagnostic applications, the company exclusively sublicensed therapeutic rights to Baxter. Baxter began development of a therapeutic system and sublicensed rights to Applied Immune Sciences (now part of RPR Gencell) and Systemix (now part of Novartis). Baxter also held licensing discussions with CellPro, but no license agreement was signed.

By late 1991, Baxter had developed a prototype stem cell selection device. In 1992, Dr. Civin began clinical trials with the device, and Baxter started its own clinical trials in 1993. In January 1995, Baxter's Isolex 300 System received regulatory approval in Europe (CE Mark of Conformity for Medical Devices). In the United States, Baxter's systems have been installed in numerous transplant centers over the past three years; the Baxter device has been used in clinical trials to process peripheral blood and bone marrow for hematopoietic reconstitution in patients. On February 24, 1997, Baxter filed for Pre-market Approval (PMA) of its Isolex 300SA System. In addition to effectively licensing and developing the technology, Hopkins, BD and Baxter have aggressively defended the patents in court. In 1994, the three parties joined in a suit against CellPro for infringement of the Civin patents.

Accordingly, NIH concludes that Hopkins and Baxter have taken effective steps to achieve practical application, as demonstrated by Hopkins' licensing, Baxter's manufacture, practice, and operation of the Isolex 300, and the device's availability to and use by the public to the extent permitted at this time under applicable law (i.e., foreign sales as well as widespread clinical research use in the U.S.). With regard to FDA approval and commercial sale of the Baxter Isolex 300 in the United States, the administrative record indicates that Baxter is vigorously pursuing an active application. Based on these facts, we conclude that Hopkins and Baxter have met the statutory and regulatory standard for practical application.

### Health or Safety Needs

The question of whether the CellPro Ceprate SC fulfills health or safety needs not reasonably satisfied by the Baxter Isolex 300 has been the central inquiry and priority of the NIH in evaluating CellPro's petition for march-in. In this regard, we note the considerable debate among scientists and clinicians as to whether immunoselection of stem cells with selection devices prior to transplantation provides a clinically significant benefit to patients over standard hematopoietic transplantation techniques. The clinical benefit upon which the CellPro Ceprate SC device was approved by FDA consisted of a reduction of infusional toxicity associated with the administration of bone marrow prepared with standard techniques. To date, neither party has presented to the Biological Response Modifiers Advisory Committee any studies documenting that cell separation devices improve stem cell engraftment, disease-free survival, or overall survival. Thus, it is premature for either Baxter or CellPro to claim patient benefits (other than a decrease in infusional toxicities) from stem cell isolation and purification, T-cell, lymphocyte, and tumor cell purging, or other claimed uses.

It is equally premature, and inappropriate, for NIH to substitute its judgment for that of clinicians and patients seeking to avail themselves of an FDA-approved medical device. The FDA has determined that the Ceprate SC is safe and effective for selecting stem cells from autologous bone marrow for hematopoietic reconstitution. Thus, to the extent that the Ceprate SC is the only device that is available for sale in the United States for this purpose, it fulfills a health need for those who wish to use it, until such time as a comparable alternative product becomes available for sale.

As explained more fully below, the administrative record demonstrates that Hopkins and Baxter have taken appropriate steps to reasonably satisfy this need. First, they have refrained from enforcing patent rights to the full extent of the law in order to allow the continuing sale of the Ceprate SC until the Baxter product is approved for sale by the FDA. Second, they have pledged to ensure that the Baxter product is as widely available as possible through clinical trials, and to ensure patient access to the fullest extent possible.

### (1) Continuing Sale of CellPro Device

In deference to the health need fulfilled by the CellPro device in the absence of an FDA-approved alternative, Hopkins and Baxter have refrained from enforcing their patent rights to the full extent of the law. Specifically, they modified a proposed order of injunction filed for consideration in the patent litigation in Federal District Court. The Order issued by the Court on July 24, 1997 states, in pertinent part:

> CellPro may continue to make, have made, use and sell SC Systems and disposable products (including the 12.8 antibody) for use with SC Systems, within the United States, until such time as an alternative stem cell concentration device, manufactured under a license under the '204 and '680 patents, is approved for therapeutic use in the United States by the United States Food and Drug Administration...and for a period of three months thereafter....In addition, certain price and volume restrictions contained in the Court's Order specifically do not apply to the provision of products solely for use in clinical trials....

CellPro argues vigorously, however, in documents filed prior to the entry of the Court's Order, that the terms of the proposed order, most specifically the requirement of payments to Baxter for sales of CellPro product, would force CellPro out of business and result in the loss of availability of the CellPro device.

First, we rely on the Court's finding that it is unlikely that the terms of the Order will result in the loss of availability of the CellPro product. This issue was specifically before the Court, supported by an exhaustive factual record resulting from years of litigation. Although NIH is determining whether to open a fact-finding proceeding, as opposed to conducting one, we also found no convincing evidence that CellPro will be unable to supply patients with its product under the terms of the Court Order. The terms of the Order may be unpalatable to CellPro, but CellPro need only operate under those constraints pending a decision on its appeal of the Court's adverse verdict on infringement. The Court specifically found that CellPro "possesses adequate cash reserves to allow it to continue operations during the pendency of its appeal," Memorandum Opinion at p. 24, and determined that it would most likely be in CellPro's interest to continue operations pending the outcome of the appeal. Moreover, the Court has retained jurisdiction and invited the parties to apply to the Court for modification of the terms of the injunction, specifically, the payment of incremental profits to Baxter, if the amount determined by the Court "either provides inadequate relief or works an injustice inconsistent with equitable principles." *Id.*

Second, the loss of availability of the CellPro product is relevant to the "health need" criteria only during the period prior to FDA approval and availability for sale of a comparable alternative product. In petitioning NIH to open a separate proceeding on this matter, CellPro argues that its continuing viability and success, even beyond FDA approval of a comparable alternative, should be a matter of concern to the NIH because CellPro has developed and is marketing an important health care product. Invoking our prior caveat as to the investigational nature of these devices, we concur that, as a general matter, NIH supports the development and success of the biotechnology industry. It is indeed very important to the NIH that biotechnology and pharmaceutical companies thrive and compete in order to bring new health care products to the public. Developing and commercializing such products out of federally-funded research is the foundation and essence of the Bayh-Dole Act.

We are wary, however, of forced attempts to influence the marketplace for the benefit of a single company, particularly when such actions may have far-reaching repercussions on many companies' and investors' future willingness to invest in federally funded medical technologies. The patent system, with its resultant predictability for investment and commercial development, is the means chosen by Congress for ensuring the development and dissemination of new and useful technologies. It has proven to be an effective means for the development of health care technologies. In exercising its authorities under the Bayh-Dole Act, NIH is mindful of the broader public health implications of a march-in proceeding, including the potential loss of new health care products yet to be developed from federally funded research.

On balance, we believe it is inappropriate for the NIH to intercede in this matter to ensure CellPro's commercial future. Viability and success in the private sector is appropriately governed by the marketplace, and significantly influenced by management practices and decisions. CellPro had the opportunity to license the invention from Baxter but decided against doing so, and instead risked patent infringement litigation. It would be inappropriate for the NIH, a public health agency, to exercise its authorities under the Bayh-Dole Act to procure for CellPro more favorable commercial terms than it can otherwise obtain from the Court or from the patent owners. CellPro's commercial viability is best left to CellPro's management and the marketplace.

## (2) Reasonable Steps to Ensure Widespread Availability of Baxter's Product

Hopkins and Baxter have also pledged to reasonably satisfy any health need created by the loss of the CellPro product in the unlikely event that patient access to this technology is restricted before a comparable alternative product is approved by the FDA and becomes available for sale.

In several of its submissions to NIH...Baxter committed to ensuring there would be no gap in patient access to stem cell separation technology. Baxter committed to installing its device free of charge at any site from which CellPro might withdraw, and to provide that site with the same level of support on the same terms as CellPro. Baxter also committed to obtaining all clinical and regulatory approvals necessary to place the Isolex system into operation as soon as possible.

CellPro asserted that Baxter is unable to fulfill this pledge; however, neither party submitted evidence sufficient for a definitive determination, and it would be premature for the NIH to act based on Baxter's failure to accomplish what events have not yet required it to do. In any event, we believe the likelihood of Baxter having to substitute devices in order to ensure patient access is remote, as discussed above. Nevertheless, pending FDA approval and availability for sale of a comparable alternative product, NIH will continue to monitor the situation and will retain jurisdiction to initiate march-in without the filing of a new request, in the event that health needs are not being reasonably satisfied.

Conclusion

The NIH has determined not to initiate proceedings to pursue march-in rights on the basis of the available information. NIH has examined the criteria of 35 U.S.C. § 203(1)(a) and (b) and found that march-in is not warranted under either criteria. Specifically, the NIH has determined that Hopkins and Baxter have taken, or are expected to take within a reasonable time, effective steps to achieve practical application of the applicable patents, as demonstrated by Hopkins' licensing activities and Baxter's manufacture, practice, and operation of the Isolex 300, as well as the pending applications for FDA approval. NIH also finds that the available information fails to demonstrate an unmet health need that is not reasonably satisfied by Hopkins and Baxter.

The NIH will continue to monitor issues related to patient access to the CellPro or Baxter devices during the period prior to FDA approval and availability for sale of a comparable alternative device.

---

# Notes & Questions

1. *CellPro — The Rest of the Story.* Dr. Varmus noted that the "central inquiry and priority" of NIH in the march-in rights proceeding was "the question of whether the CellPro Ceprate SC fulfills health or safety needs not reasonably satisfied by the Baxter Isolex 300." Is the NIH an appropriate forum in which to determine the intellectual property rights of the parties? Can a limited proceeding designed only to effectuate national health policy ever be an engine for the full and frank examination of the facts? Would a contrary decision by Dr. Varmus have resulted in legalized patent infringement for the sake of public health needs?

As far back as 1991, Johns Hopkins attempted on three separate occasions to license the technology to CellPro only to be refused. Christoher E. Bush, *Medical Patent Battle Leads to Bayh-Dole Act Test Case*, CORPORATE LEGAL TIMES, Jan. 1998, at 8. For what reasons might CellPro have refused a license?

2. *Other Types of Compulsory Licensing.* The government march-in sought in the CellPro matter, *supra*, is just one example of the growing field of compulsory licensing of intellectual properties. Compulsory licenses are becoming a powerful, but controversial, tool that allows government to intervene in private markets and the courts to implement remedies in antitrust and eminent domain cases. Its proponents see compulsory licensing as a valuable weapon to combat increasingly broad claims in patents issued to pharmaceutical companies. *See Anticipating the 21st Century: Competition Policy in the New High-Tech, Global Marketplace*, Report by the Federal Trade Commission Staff, Vol. 1, May 1996, Chapter 8, pages 13–15, *at* www.ftc.gov/opp/global.htm. Specific U.S. statutes, in addition to Bayh-Dole, that authorize government-issued compulsory licenses include:

     a.    17 U.S.C. Sec. 111(d), compulsory licensing of secondary transmissions by cable broadcasters.

     b.    17 U.S.C. Sec. 115, compulsory licensing of rights in non-dramatic musical works to make and distribute phono-records.

     c.    42 U.S.C. § 7608, mandatory licensing of air pollution prevention inventions (Clean Air Act).

d. 28 U.S.C. § 1498, a suit against the government in the U.S. Court of Federal Claims is the exclusive remedy by a patent holder who alleges his or her patented invention has been infringed by the U.S. government or by one acting for the government. The statute protects and relieves contractors from any liability for infringement to the owner when an invention is used by or manufactured for the United States. Unlike a private party, the government cannot commit the tort of "patent infringement." Governmental use of a patented invention is viewed as an eminent domain taking of a license under the patent and not as a tort. *See Hughes Aircraft Co. v. United States,* 86 F.3d 156 (Fed. Cir. 1996)., page __ herein.

e. 42 U.S.C. Sec. 2183, mandatory licensing of patents "affected with the public interest" in the field of production or utilization of special nuclear material or atomic energy.

One author has suggested that compulsory licensing in the copyright field has allowed new technologies to flourish without harming the original works:

> Whenever we have discovered or enacted a copyright exception, an industry has grown up within its shelter. Player piano rolls became ubiquitous after courts ruled that they did not infringe the copyright in the underlying musical composition. Phonograph records superseded both piano rolls and sheet music with the aid of the compulsory license for mechanical reproductions; the jukebox industry arose to take advantage of the copyright exemption accorded to "the reproduction or rendition of a musical composition by or upon coin-operated machines." Composers continued to write music, and found ways to exploit these new media for their works....

*See* Jessica Litman, *The Exclusive Right to Read,* 13 CARDOZO ARTS & ENT. L.J. 29 (1994). Is this argument persuasive? Does it apply equally well in the field of patent licenses?

---

# IV. Novel Licensing Solutions in the Public Interest — Embryonic Stem Cells

When President Bush banned the use of federal funds for the creation of new embryonic stem cell lines in 2001, Fact Sheet, The White House, Embryonic Stem Cell Research (Aug. 9, 2001), *available at* www.whitehouse.gov/news/releases/2001/08/20010809-1.html), a huge commercial opportunity was created for the Wisconsin Alumni Research Foundation (WARF), the technology transfer arm of the University of Wisconsin. WARF owned a number of existing cell lines exempt from the ban, and perhaps more importantly, several pending and issued patents that purport to cover both cloning methods and certain cells created at the University of Wisconsin. As a result, WARF created a new company, WiCell, to commercialize the Wisconsin stem cell technologies. WARF had already exclusively licensed its stem cell patents to Geron Corporation. Using WARF's retained patent rights, WiCell began supplying embryonic stem cells under non-exclusive licenses to university, government and industry labs. Because stem cells are self-replicating, WiCell has an inexhaustible supply of licensable materials so long as its patent monopoly holds.

---

# A Call to Legal Arms: Bringing Embryonic Stem Cells Therapies to Market*

John C. Miller

13 Alb. L.J. Sci. & Tech. 555 (2003)

\* \* \*

## The Science

Stem cells are defined as cells that have the abilities to perpetuate themselves through division for indefinite periods and to become the cells of a particular tissue through differentiation. There are three general types of stem cells: totipotent stem cells, pluripotent stem cells, and multipotent stem cells. The zygote, formed when a sperm fertilizes an egg, is a totipotent stem cell-it can give rise to any cell necessary for fetal development. The zygote divides into identical totipotent cells. Approximately four days after fertilization and after several cycles of cell division, the totipotent cells form the blastocyst, a hollow sphere of cells. The blastocyst is comprised of an outer layer of cells and an inner cell mass. The cells in the inner cell mass are pluripotent, meaning that they can give rise to almost every type of cell in the human body. The pluripotent cells yield multipotent cells, also known as adult stem cells. Examples of multipotent stem cells are haematopoietic stem cells, which are responsible for generating blood and immune cells.

Human pluripotent cell lines have been isolated from two sources. James Thomson, a researcher at the University of Wisconsin, was the first to isolate pluripotent stem cells from the inner cell mass of the human embryo at the blastocyst stage. Cell lines derived from this source have been termed embryonic stem cells. Second, John Gearhart, a researcher at The Johns Hopkins University School of Medicine, isolated pluripotent stem cells from fetal tissue that was destined to develop into reproductive organs. These cells are referred to as embryonic germ cells. Researchers continue to explore and debate the similarities and differences between embryonic stem cells and embryonic germ cells.

## Potential Applications

Pluripotent stem cells promise to transform medicine in several ways. First, research with pluripotent stem cells could shed light on complex cellular events. Serious medical conditions, such as cancer and birth defects, are caused by errors during cell specialization and cell division. A better understanding of cellular events will allow scientists "to further delineate the fundamental errors that cause these often deadly illnesses."

Second, pluripotent stem cells could be used to increase the efficacy of drug development. New drug candidates could be tested on different types of cells derived from stem cells.

Third, stem cell research can enhance tissue engineering and cell therapy. Tissue engineering and cell therapy involve the use of living cells and other natural or synthetic compounds to develop implantable parts for the restoration, maintenance, or replacement of body tissues and organs. Three of the most promising and urgently needed applications of ESCs are in the fields of cardiology, neurology, and diabetes. Heart disease

---

*Reprinted with permission of the publisher, copyright 2003

and stroke are the primary causes of death in the United States, millions suffer from neurodegenerative disorders, and approximately one million Americans cope with Type 1 diabetes. Early studies suggest that embryonic stem cells can be induced to differentiate into cardiomyocytes, neural cells, and pancreatic islet cells. These cells can be implanted into diseased patients to replace damaged cells and restore function.

## The Patent

Embryonic stem cells were first isolated from mice in 1981. Two decades of research culminated in the isolation of embryonic stem cells from rhesus monkeys in 1995. The Wisconsin Alumni Research Foundation (WARF), an entity at the University of Wisconsin that owned the rights to the invention, filed for a patent on a "purified preparation of primate embryonic stem cells" and a "method for isolating" them in 1996. While the patent application was still pending in the spring of 1998, Thomson derived embryonic stem cells in humans. Thereafter, WARF filed a divisional application claiming a "purified preparation of pluripotent human embryonic stem cells" and a "method for isolating" them. Patent 5,843,780 issued on December 1, 1998, and patent 6,200,806 issued on March 13, 2001. Patent 6,200,80 allows WARF to exclude others from making, using, selling, or importing human embryonic stem cells throughout the United States. WARF has also filed for patents in other countries.

## Geron's Rights

Because federal regulations prohibited funding for research involving human embryos, Wisconsin researchers obtained private funding for their research. They found support in the Geron Corporation, which channeled approximately one million dollars into the research. After Thomson's successful isolation of ESCs, Geron signed a licensing agreement with WARF. The foundation granted Geron exclusive rights to develop embryonic stem cells into six cell types: neural, cardiomyocyte, pancreatic islet, hematopoietic, chondrocyte, and osteoblast cells. Ambiguities in the agreement also enabled Geron to assert that it had options to gain exclusive rights to additional cell types.

In August 2001, in response to Geron's assertion that it was entitled to exclusive rights to additional cell types, the foundation filed a lawsuit against Geron. The parties reached a settlement agreement in January 2002, which provides Geron with exclusive rights to neural, cardiomyocyte, and pancreatic islet cells, and nonexclusive rights to hematopoietic, chondrocyte, and osteoblast cells. Under the agreement, WARF can license development of the remaining two hundred cells to other companies. In addition, Geron maintains nonexclusive rights to develop non-therapeutic research products, such as drug-screening tests, in certain cell types. Finally, the agreement promises academic and government scientists that they can perform non-commercial research on stem cells without being charged.

## WARF's Licensing Policy

In the aftermath of isolating the stem cells, WARF established the WiCell Research Institute, a separate subsidiary, to grant licenses for stem cell use. The terms of each license depend on whether the licensee is a non-profit researcher or a private corporation. Academic and government researchers can obtain stem cells from the institute for the cost of production of the cells. The license agreement requires the researchers to follow certain ethical guidelines and other policies. Researchers making discoveries arising from cell research can publish their results, or even obtain patents, without consulting the foundation. However, if scientists wish to commercialize the invention, they must negotiate licensing terms with the foundation. Although many researchers have applauded the licensing arrangement as fair, some have criticized it and refused to agree to its terms. While stem cells are widely available to non-profit researchers nearly free of charge, private companies must negotiate licensing terms with WARF. Because WARF licenses are confidential, the number of firms that have concluded commercial licenses with the foundation is uncertain.

\* \* \*

Although the first shot has not been fired, legal soldiers may be on the brink of an intellectual property battle over ESCs. WARF ardently maintains that its patent extends to all embryonic stem cells — regardless of how they are produced and where they are from. The foundation has assembled an impressive legal battalion to monitor and enforce its intellectual property rights. At the same time, companies across the globe are challenging WARF's position by questioning the validity of the patent and declaring that they have derived embryonic stem cells through different methods. For example, BresaGen has intimated that it has or will be able to derive ESCs from the primitive ectoderm of embryoid bodies — a stage occurring slightly after the formation of the inner cell mass. Additionally, Reliance Life Sciences, ES Cell International, and CyThera Inc. all maintain that they use novel processes for isolation and purification of ESCs.

The patent wars could be ignited in several different ways. First, at least one group of researchers has reported that it shipped ESCs to the United States without a license. If the foundation cannot extract license agreements from groups importing stem cells, it may launch a lawsuit to enforce its patent rights. Second, patent applications have been filed for alternative methods for deriving ESCs. Assuming these patents are rejected by the Patent and Trademark Office (PTO), the patentees could seek recourse in court. Finally, in the long term, any attempts at commercialization of any product based on embryonic stem cells without WARF's consent would certainly spark a lawsuit. A court will then be forced to decide the validity of the Thomson patent and whether there is infringement.

\* \* \*

Advocates of the validity of the claim to ESCs can argue that the monopoly regime governed by WARF will not restrict others from researching and developing stem cell technologies. WARF has relentlessly expressed its desire to "make this technology as accessible as possible." The foundation distributes the cells to academic and government scientists for the costs of production, and it does not demand ownership rights of any discoveries produced using the cells. Furthermore, WARF has granted non-exclusive commercial licenses, on reasonable terms, to several companies. Supporters of a broad patent can draw analogies between the Thomson patent and the Cohen-Boyer patent on techniques for recombinant DNA. Just as Stanford University's licensing of the Cohen-Boyer patent at reasonable rates fueled the development of the early biotechnology industry, WARF's strategy will cultivate stem cell therapies.

While WARF's efforts to facilitate distribution and licensing of stem cells are laudable, the contention that such efforts justify a broad patent fails in light of Geron's exclusive license. Geron's right to exclude others from researching, developing, and marketing cardiac, pancreatic, and neural stem cell therapies will deter firms and academic researchers from engaging in research and development.

In order for firms and researchers to invest in developing these cell therapies, they must be able to obtain a license on commercially reasonable terms before conducting the research, or at least have confidence in obtaining a commercially reasonable license if a marketable therapy is produced. Although Geron maintains that it is willing to engage in licensing negotiations, it will be extremely difficult to conclude license agreements before investing in product development. Licensees are unlikely to disclose sensitive information related to their plans for a commercial product. In addition, Geron is likely to be reluctant to establish fixed royalties for undeveloped, downstream products with uncertain commercial value. Indeed, an executive at one stem cell company notes that "it would be a waste of time to try to get a reasonable license from Geron...." The high transaction costs associated with such negotiations, combined with the expectation that there is a low likelihood of concluding a reasonable agreement, will deter firms from attempting to obtain licenses ex ante. Firms are also unlikely to initiate such research in reliance on obtaining a license agreement *ex post*. A negotiation occurring after the development of a commercial product would place Geron in a strategic bargaining advantage. The company could demand any royalty it desired, and the license seeker would have to relent. With no guarantees that firms will be able to reap a substantial portion of a new product's market value, firms are unlikely to embark on the commercial development of cardiac, pancreatic, or neural stem cell therapies.

* * *

# V. Patenting and Licensing Tangible Biological Materials

As noted in the introduction of this chapter, the inherent uncertainty and unpredictability of biological research gives the tangible results of research and experiment particular importance. Experiments in biology are not as reproducible as experiments in the "harder" sciences. Attempts to clone an organism or insert a gene or gene segment in a living cell may fail ten times and, for unknown or poorly understood reasons, succeed on the eleventh try. This uncertainty and unpredictability makes the results of successful experiments very valuable, whether they are gene segments, cell lines, or genetically modified living organisms. The recent history of biotechnology is replete with stories of particular living matter, whose progeny have been shared around the world and have been used in hundreds of experiments and research projects.

The relationship between intellectual property and the tangible results of successful research can be both troubling and exasperating. A biotechnology process patent, for example, may be valid, as demonstrated by self-replicating life forms resulting from successful application of the process. Without access to those life forms, however, a researcher may have to spend a great deal of time and trouble in trial-and-error experiment in order to reproduce the successful results. This is one reason why both United States and international regulations provide for official centralized depositories for biological materials needed to realize patented biotechnology inventions;[13] deposits in

---

13. *See* JAY DRATLER, JR., INTELLECTUAL PROPERTY LAW: COMMERICAL, CREATIVE, AND INDUSTRIAL PROPERTY § 2.04[1][e] (Law Journal Press 1991).

these institutions can substitute for the abstract, intangible "enabling disclosure" that allows the public to practice patented inventions in other, less uncertain fields.[14]

Because of the uncertainty inherent in biotechnology research, an abstract, intangible disclosure of information may not be enough to make practical use of a biotechnology invention. Rather, access to tangible biological materials, either from the patentee or from a patent depository, may be necessary for commercial use and exploitation. If so, provisions in licensing agreements for access to and use of such materials may be as important as technology-transfer and technical assistance provisions in licensing agreements involving patents in the "harder" sciences.

The fact that biological materials are a separate and distinct focus of both practical and legal concern raises a number of questions that do not often arise in other patent-driven industries, in which abstract information alone is sufficient to use and reproduce patented inventions and other licensed technology. One of the most important questions involves ownership and possession of tangible biological materials. The following case raises the question whether a medical patient whose body produced the materials, or materials of which they are progeny, has rights in the materials and, by extension, the research in which they are used.

---

# Moore v. Regents of the University of California

### 793 P.2d 479 (Cal. 1990), *cert. denied*, 499 U.S 936 (1991)

PANELLI, Justice.

We granted review in this case to determine whether plaintiff has stated a cause of action against his physician and other defendants for using his cells in potentially lucrative medical research without his permission. Plaintiff alleges that his physician failed to disclose preexisting research and economic interests in the cells before obtaining consent to the medical procedures by which they were extracted. The superior court sustained all defendants' demurrers to the third amended complaint, and the Court of Appeal reversed. We hold that the complaint states a cause of action for breach of the physician's disclosure obligations, but not for conversion.

\* \* \*

The plaintiff is John Moore (Moore), who underwent treatment for hairy-cell leukemia at the Medical Center of the University of California at Los Angeles (UCLA Medical Center). The five defendants are: (1) Dr. David W. Golde (Golde), a physician who attended Moore at UCLA Medical Center; (2) the Regents of the University of California (Regents), who own and operate the university; (3) Shirley G. Quan, a researcher employed by the Regents; (4) Genetics Institute, Inc. (Genetics Institute); and (5) Sandoz Pharmaceuticals Corporation and related entities (collectively Sandoz).

Moore first visited UCLA Medical Center on October 5, 1976, shortly after he learned that he had hairy-cell leukemia. After hospitalizing Moore and "withdr[awing] extensive amounts of blood, bone marrow aspirate, and other bodily

---

14. See: 35 U.S.C. §112, ¶1 ("The [patent] specification shall contain a written description of the invention, and of the manner and process of making and using it, in such full, clear, concise, and exact terms as to enable any person skilled in the art to which it pertains, or with which it is most nearly connected, to make and use the same."); Dratler, *supra* §2.04[1][a].

substances," Golde confirmed that diagnosis. At this time all defendants, including Golde, were aware that "certain blood products and blood components were of great value in a number of commercial and scientific efforts" and that access to a patient whose blood contained these substances would provide "competitive, commercial, and scientific advantages."

On October 8, 1976, Golde recommended that Moore's spleen be removed. Golde informed Moore "that he had reason to fear for his life, and that the proposed splenectomy operation...was necessary to slow down the progress of his disease." Based upon Golde's representations, Moore signed a written consent form authorizing the splenectomy.

Before the operation, Golde and Quan "formed the intent and made arrangements to obtain portions of [Moore's] spleen following its removal" and to take them to a separate research unit. Golde gave written instructions to this effect on October 18 and 19, 1976. These research activities "were not intended to have...any relation to [Moore's] medical...care." However, neither Golde nor Quan informed Moore of their plans to conduct this research or requested his permission. Surgeons at UCLA Medical Center, whom the complaint does not name as defendants, removed Moore's spleen on October 20, 1976.

Moore returned to the UCLA Medical Center several times between November 1976 and September 1983. He did so at Golde's direction and based upon representations "that such visits were necessary and required for his health and well-being, and based upon the trust inherent in and by virtue of the physician-patient relationship...." On each of these visits Golde withdrew additional samples of "blood, blood serum, skin, bone marrow aspirate, and sperm." On each occasion Moore travelled to the UCLA Medical Center from his home in Seattle because he had been told that the procedures were to be performed only there and only under Golde's direction.

In fact, [however,] throughout the period of time that [Moore] was under [Golde's] care and treatment,...the defendants were actively involved in a number of activities which they concealed from [Moore]...." Specifically, defendants were conducting research on Moore's cells and planned to "benefit financially and competitively...[by exploiting the cells] and [their] exclusive access to [the cells] by virtue of [Golde's] ongoing physician-patient relationship...."

Sometime before August 1979, Golde established a cell line from Moore's T-lymphocytes. On January 30, 1981, the Regents applied for a patent on the cell line, listing Golde and Quan as inventors. "[B]y virtue of an established policy..., [the] Regents, Golde, and Quan would share in any royalties or profits...arising out of [the] patent." The patent issued on March 20, 1984, naming Golde and Quan as the inventors of the cell line and the Regents as the assignee of the patent. (U.S. Patent No. 4,438,032 (Mar. 20, 1984).)

The Regent's patent also covers various methods for using the cell line to produce lymphokines. Moore admits in his complaint that "the true clinical potential of each of the lymphokines...[is] difficult to predict, [but]...competing commercial firms in these relevant fields have published reports in biotechnology industry periodicals predicting a potential market of approximately $3.01 Billion Dollars by the year 1990 for a whole range of [such lymphokines]...."

With the Regents' assistance, Golde negotiated agreements for commercial development of the cell line and products to be derived from it. Under an agreement with Genetics Institute, Golde "became a paid consultant" and "acquired the rights to 75,000 shares of common stock." Genetics Institute also agreed to pay Golde and the Regents "at least $330,000 over three years, including a pro-rata share of [Golde's] salary and fringe benefits, in exchange for...exclusive access to the materials and research performed" on the cell line and products derived from it. On June 4, 1982, Sandoz "was added to the agreement," and compensation payable to Golde and the Regents was increased by $110,000.

\* \* \*

## B. Conversion

Moore also attempts to characterize the invasion of his rights as a conversion—a tort that protects against interference with possessory and ownership interests in personal property. He theorizes that he continued to own his cells following their removal from his body, at least for the purpose of directing their use, and that he never consented to their use in potentially lucrative medical research. Thus, to complete Moore's argument, defendants' unauthorized use of his cells constitutes a conversion. As a result of the alleged conversion, Moore claims a proprietary interest in each of the products that any of the defendants might ever create from his cells or the patented cell line.

No court, however, has ever in a reported decision imposed conversion liability for the use of human cells in medical research. While that fact does not end our inquiry, it raises a flag of caution. In effect, what Moore is asking us to do is to impose a tort duty on scientists to investigate the consensual pedigree of each human cell sample used in research. To impose such a duty, which would affect medical research of importance to all of society, implicates policy concerns far removed from the traditional, two-party ownership disputes in which the law of conversion arose, invoking a tort theory originally used to determine whether the loser or the finder of a horse had the better title, Moore claims ownership of the results of socially important medical research, including the genetic code for chemicals that regulate the functions of every human being's immune system.

\* \* \*

Accordingly, we first consider whether the tort of conversion clearly gives Moore a cause of action under existing law. We do not believe it does. Because of the novelty of Moore's claim to own the biological materials at issue, to apply the theory of conversion in this context would frankly have to be recognized as an extension of the theory. Therefore, we consider next whether it is advisable to extend the tort to this context.

### 1. Moore's Claim Under Existing Law

"To establish a conversion, plaintiff must establish an actual interference with his ownership or right of possession....Where plaintiff neither has title to the property alleged to have been converted, nor possession thereof, he cannot maintain an action for conversion." (*Del E. Webb Corp. v. Structural Materials Co.* (1981) 123 Cal. App. 3d 593, 610–11 [176 Cal. Rptr. 824]. *See also General Motors A. Corp. v. Dallas* (1926) 198 Cal. 365, 370 [245 P. 184].)

Since Moore clearly did not expect to retain possession of his cells following their removal, to sue for their conversion he must have retained an ownership interest in them. But there are several reasons to doubt that he did retain any such interest. First, no reported judicial decision supports Moore's claim, either directly or by close analogy. Second, California statutory law drastically limits any continuing interest of a patient in excised cells. Third, the subject matters of the Regents' patent—the patented cell line and the products derived from it—cannot be Moore's property.

Neither the Court of Appeal's opinion, the parties' briefs, nor our research discloses a case holding that a person retains a sufficient interest in excised cells to support a cause of action for conversion. We do not find this surprising, since the laws governing such things as human tissues, transplantable organs, blood, fetuses, pituitary glands, corneal tissue, and dead bodies deal with human biological materials as objects sui generis, regulating their disposition to achieve policy goals rather than abandoning them to the general law of personal property. It is these specialized statutes, not the law of conversion, to which courts ordinarily should and do look for guidance on the disposition of human biological materials.

Lacking direct authority for importing the law of conversion into this context, Moore relies, as did the Court of Appeal, primarily on decisions addressing privacy rights. One line of cases involves unwanted publicity. (*Lugosi v. Universal Pictures* (1979) 25 Cal. 3d 813 [160 Cal. Rptr. 323, 603 P.2d 425, 10 A.L.R.4th 1150]; *Motschenbacher v. R. J. Reynolds Tobacco Company* (9th Cir. 1974) 498 F.2d 821 [interpreting Cal. law].) These opinions hold that every person has a proprietary interest in his own likeness and that unauthorized, business use of a likeness is redressible as a tort. But in neither opinion did the authoring court expressly base its holding on property law. (*Lugosi v. Universal Pictures*, *supra*, 25 Cal. 3d at pp. 819, 823–26; *Motschenbacher v. R. J. Reynolds Tobacco Company*, *supra*, 498 F.2d at pp. 825–26.) Each court stated, following Prosser, that it was "pointless" to debate the proper characterization of the proprietary interest in a likeness. (*Motschenbacher v. R. J. Reynolds Tobacco Company*, *supra*, 498 F.2d at p. 825, quoting PROSSER, LAW OF TORTS (4th ed. 1971) at p. 807; *Lugosi v. Universal Pictures*, *supra*, 25 Cal. 3d at pp. 819, 824.) For purposes of determining whether the tort of conversion lies, however, the characterization of the right in question is far from pointless. Only property can be converted.

Not only are the wrongful-publicity cases irrelevant to the issue of conversion, but the analogy to them seriously misconceives the nature of the genetic materials and research involved in this case. Moore, adopting the analogy originally advanced by the Court of Appeal, argues that "[i]f the courts have found a sufficient proprietary interest in one's persona, how could one not have a right in one's own genetic material, something far more profoundly the essence of one's human uniqueness than a name or a face?" However, as the defendants' patent makes clear — and the complaint, too, if read with an understanding of the scientific terms which it has borrowed from the patent — the goal and result of defendants' efforts has been to manufacture lymphokines. Lymphokines, unlike a name or a face, have the same molecular structure in every human being and the same, important functions in every human being's immune system. Moreover, the particular genetic material which is responsible for the natural production of lymphokines, and which defendants use to manufacture lymphokines in the laboratory, is also the same in every person; it is no more unique to Moore than the number of vertebrae in the spine or the chemical formula of hemoglobin.

Another privacy case offered by analogy to support Moore's claim establishes only that patients have a right to refuse medical treatment. (*Bouvia v. Superior Court* (1986) 179 Cal. App. 3d 1127 [225 Cal. Rptr. 297].) In this context the court in Bouvia wrote that "'[e]very human being of adult years and sound mind has a right to determine what shall be done with his own body....'" (*Id.*, at p. 1139, *quoting from Schloendorff v. New York Hospital*, *supra*, 211 N.Y. 125 [105 N.E. 92, 93].) Relying on this language to support the proposition that a patient has a continuing right to control the use of excised cells, the Court of Appeal in this case concluded that "[a] patient must have the ultimate power to control what becomes of his or her tissues. To hold otherwise would open the door to a massive invasion of human privacy and dignity in the name of medical progress." Yet one may earnestly wish to protect privacy and dignity without accepting the extremely problematic conclusion that interference with those interests amounts to a conversion of personal property. Nor is it necessary to force the round pegs of "privacy" and "dignity" into the square hole of "property" in order to protect the patient, since the fiduciary-duty and informed-consent theories protect these interests directly by requiring full disclosure.

The next consideration that makes Moore's claim of ownership problematic is California statutory law, which drastically limits a patient's control over excised cells. Pursuant to Health and Safety Code section 7054.4, "[n]otwithstanding any other provision of law, recognizable anatomical parts, human tissues, anatomical human remains, or infectious waste following conclusion of scientific use shall be disposed of by interment, incineration, or any other method determined by the state department [of health services] to protect the public health and safety." Clearly the Legislature did not specifically intend this statute to resolve the question of whether a patient is entitled to compensation for the nonconsensual use of excised cells. A primary object of the statute is to ensure the safe handling of potentially hazardous biological waste materials. Yet one cannot escape the conclusion that the statute's practical effect is to limit, drastically, a patient's control over excised cells. By restricting how excised cells may be used and requiring their eventual destruction, the statute eliminates so many of the rights ordinarily attached to property that one cannot simply assume that what is left amounts to "property" or "ownership" for purposes of conversion law.

It may be that some limited right to control the use of excised cells does survive the operation of this statute. There is, for example, no need to read the statute to permit "scientific use" contrary to the patient's expressed wish. A fully informed patient may always withhold consent to treatment by a physician whose research plans the patient does not approve. That right, however, as already discussed, is protected by the fiduciary-duty and informed-consent theories.

Finally, the subject matter of the Regents' patent—the patented cell line and the products derived from it—cannot be Moore's property. This is because the patented cell line is both factually and legally distinct from the cells taken from Moore's body. Federal law permits the patenting of organisms that represent the product of "human ingenuity," but not naturally occurring organisms. (*Diamond v. Chakrabarty* (1980) 447 U.S. 303, 309–10 [65 L. Ed. 2d 144, 150, 100 S. Ct. 2204].) Human cell lines are patentable because "[l]ong-term adaptation and growth of human tissues and cells in culture is difficult—often considered an art...," and the probability of success is low. (OTA Rep., *supra*, at p. 33; see fn. 2, ante.) It is this inventive effort that patent law rewards, not the discovery of naturally occurring raw materials. Thus, Moore's allegations that he owns the cell line and the products derived from it are inconsistent with the patent, which constitutes an authoritative determination that the cell line is the product of invention. Since such allegations are nothing more than arguments or conclusions of law, they of course do not bind us. (*Daar v. Yellow Cab Co.*, *supra*, 67 Cal. 2d at p. 713.)

## 2. Should Conversion Liability Be Extended?

As we have discussed, Moore's novel claim to own the biological materials at issue in this case is problematic, at best. Accordingly, his attempt to apply the theory of conversion within this context must frankly be recognized as a request to extend that theory. While we do not purport to hold that excised cells can never be property for any purpose whatsoever, the novelty of Moore's claim demands express consideration of the policies to be served by extending liability (*cf. Nally v. Grace Community Church*, *supra*, 47 Cal. 3d at pp. 291–300; *Foley v. Interactive Data Corp.*, *supra*, 47 Cal. 3d at pp.

694–700; *Brown v. Superior Court, supra,* 44 Cal. 3d at pp. 1061–66) rather than blind deference to a complaint alleging as a legal conclusion the existence of a cause of action.

There are three reasons why it is inappropriate to impose liability for conversion based upon the allegations of Moore's complaint. First, a fair balancing of the relevant policy considerations counsels against extending the tort. Second, problems in this area are better suited to legislative resolution. Third, the tort of conversion is not necessary to protect patients' rights. For these reasons, we conclude that the use of excised human cells in medical research does not amount to a conversion.

Of the relevant policy considerations, two are of overriding importance. The first is protection of a competent patient's right to make autonomous medical decisions. That right, as already discussed, is grounded in well-recognized and long-standing principles of fiduciary duty and informed consent. This policy weighs in favor of providing a remedy to patients when physicians act with undisclosed motives that may affect their professional judgment. The second important policy consideration is that we not threaten with disabling civil liability innocent parties who are engaged in socially useful activities, such as researchers who have no reason to believe that their use of a particular cell sample is, or may be, against a donor's wishes.

To reach an appropriate balance of these policy considerations is extremely important. In its report to Congress (*see* fn. 2, *ante*), the Office of Technology Assessment emphasized that "[u]ncertainty about how courts will resolve disputes between specimen sources and specimen users could be detrimental to both academic researchers and the infant biotechnology industry, particularly when the rights are asserted long after the specimen was obtained. The assertion of rights by sources would affect not only the researcher who obtained the original specimen, but perhaps other researchers as well.

"Biological materials are routinely distributed to other researchers for experimental purposes, and scientists who obtain cell lines or other specimen-derived products, such as gene clones, from the original researcher could also be sued under certain legal theories [such as conversion]. Furthermore, the uncertainty could affect product developments as well as research. Since inventions containing human tissues and cells may be patented and licensed for commercial use, companies are unlikely to invest heavily in developing, manufacturing, or marketing a product when uncertainty about clear title exists." (OTA Rep., *supra,* at p. 27.)

Indeed, so significant is the potential obstacle to research stemming from uncertainty about legal title to biological materials that the Office of Technology Assessment reached this striking conclusion: "[R]egardless of the merit of claims by the different interested parties, resolving the current uncertainty may be more important to the future of biotechnology than resolving it in any particular way." (OTA Rep., *supra,* at p. 27.)

We need not, however, make an arbitrary choice between liability and nonliability. Instead, an examination of the relevant policy considerations suggests an appropriate balance: Liability based upon existing disclosure obligations, rather than an unprecedented extension of the conversion theory, protects patients' rights of privacy and autonomy without unnecessarily hindering research.

To be sure, the threat of liability for conversion might help to enforce patients' rights indirectly. This is because physicians might be able to avoid liability by obtaining patients' consent, in the broadest possible terms, to any conceivable subsequent research use of excised cells. Unfortunately, to extend the conversion theory would utterly sacrifice the other goal of protecting innocent parties. Since conversion is a strict liability tort, it would impose liability on all those into whose hands the cells come, whether or not the particular defendant participated in, or knew of, the inadequate disclosures that violated the patient's right to make an informed decision. In contrast to the conversion theory, the fiduciary-duty and informed-consent theories protect the patient directly, without punishing innocent parties or creating disincentives to the conduct of socially beneficial research.

Research on human cells plays a critical role in medical research. This is so because researchers are increasingly able to isolate naturally occurring, medically useful biological substances and to produce useful quantities of such substances through genetic engineering. These efforts are beginning to bear fruit. Products developed through biotechnology that have already been approved for marketing in this country include treatments and tests for leukemia, cancer, diabetes, dwarfism, hepatitis-B, kidney transplant rejection, emphysema, osteoporosis, ulcers, anemia, infertility, and gynecological tumors, to name but a few. (Note, *Source Compensation for Tissues and Cells Used in Biotechnical Research: Why a Source Shouldn't Share in the Profits* (1989) 64 Notre Dame L. Rev. 628 & fn. 1 (hereafter Note, *Source Compensation*); *see also* OTA Rep., *supra*, at pp. 58–59.)

The extension of conversion law into this area will hinder research by restricting access to the necessary raw materials. Thousands of human cell lines already exist in tissue repositories, such as the American Type Culture Collection and those operated by the National Institutes of Health and the American Cancer Society. These repositories respond to tens of thousands of requests for samples annually. Since the patent office requires the holders of patents on cell lines to make samples available to anyone, many patent holders place their cell lines in repositories to avoid the administrative burden of responding to requests. (OTA Rep., *supra*, at p. 53.) At present, human cell lines are routinely copied and distributed to other researchers for experimental purposes, usually free of charge. This exchange of scientific materials, which still is relatively free and efficient, will surely be compromised if each cell sample becomes the potential subject matter of a lawsuit. (OTA Rep., *supra*, at p. 52.)

To expand liability by extending conversion law into this area would have a broad impact. The House Committee on Science and Technology of the United States Congress found that "49 percent of the researchers at medical institutions surveyed used human tissues or cells in their research." Many receive grants from the National Institute of Health for this work. (OTA Rep., *supra*, at p. 52.) In addition, "there are nearly 350 commercial biotechnology firms in the United States actively engaged in biotechnology research and commercial product development and approximately 25 to 30 percent appear to be engaged in research to develop a human therapeutic or diagnostic reagent....Most, but not all, of the human therapeutic products are derived from human tissues and cells, or human cell lines or cloned genes." (*Id.*, at p. 56.)

In deciding whether to create new tort duties we have in the past considered the impact that expanded liability would have on activities that are important to society, such as research. For example, in *Brown v. Superior Court*, *supra*, 44 Cal. 3d 1049, the fear that strict product liability would frustrate pharmaceutical research led us to hold that a drug manufacturer's liability should not be measured by those standards. We wrote that, "[i]f drug manufacturers were subject to strict liability, they might be reluctant to undertake research programs to develop some pharmaceuticals that would prove beneficial or to distribute others that are available to be marketed, because of the fear of large adverse monetary judgments." (*Id.*, at p. 1063.)

As in *Brown*, the theory of liability that Moore urges us to endorse threatens to destroy the economic incentive to conduct important medical research. If the use of cells in research is a conversion, then with every cell sample a researcher purchases a ticket in a litigation lottery. Because liability for conversion is predicated on a continuing ownership interest, "companies are unlikely to invest heavily in developing, manufacturing, or marketing a product when uncertainty about clear title exists." (OTA Rep., *supra*, at p. 27.) In our view, borrowing again from *Brown*, "[i]t is not unreasonable to conclude in these circumstances that the imposition of a harsher test for liability would not further the public interest in the development and availability of these important products." (*Brown v. Superior Court*, *supra*, 44 Cal. 3d at p. 1065.)

\* \* \*

If the scientific users of human cells are to be held liable for failing to investigate the consensual pedigree of their raw materials, we believe the Legislature should make that decision. Complex policy choices affecting all society are involved, and "[l]egislatures, in making such policy decisions, have the ability to gather empirical evidence, solicit the advice of experts, and hold hearings at which all interested parties present evidence and express their views...." (*Foley v. Interactive Data Corp.*, *supra*, 47 Cal. 3d at p. 694, fn. 31.) Legislative competence to act in this area is demonstrated by the existing statutes governing the use and disposition of human biological materials. Legislative interest is demonstrated by the extensive study recently commissioned by the United States Congress. (OTA Rep., *supra*.) Commentators are also recommending legislative solutions. (*See* Danforth, *Cells, Sales, and Royalties: The Patient's Right to a Portion of the Profits* (1988) 6 Yale L. & Pol'y Rev. 179, 198–201; Note, *Source Compensation*, *supra*, 64 Notre Dame L. Rev. at pp. 643–45.)

\* \* \*

For these reasons, we hold that the allegations of Moore's third amended complaint state a cause of action for breach of fiduciary duty or lack of informed consent, but not conversion.

---

# Notes & Questions

1. In this important case of first impression, the *Moore* court tried to balance the legitimate rights of patients against the need for flexibility and spontaneity in medical research. The decision's importance is magnified by the fact that California has nearly one-half of the nation's biotechnology research capacity.

Did this decision achieve a proper balance? Try to articulate precisely what rights patients and medical researchers in California have in patients' cells and body fluids after this decision. On what legal theories is each party's rights based? Do the rights of medical researchers to do their research depend upon patients' informed consent, or is that consent a separate issue, which "decouples" property rights in bodily products from the question of proper legal procedure in the hospital?

2. What does this decision say about the legal status of a patient's cells and body fluids once removed from his or her body? Are they "property"? If so, to whom do they belong?

The court cites and quotes a number of California statutes imposing rights, duties and obligations with respect to these bodily products that appear inconsistent with ordinary concepts of tangible personal property. What conclusion can one draw from these citations? Are these bodily products the property of the doctor or hospital that extracted them? Or are they "*res nullia*," no one's property? If the latter, is possession not just the proverbial nine-tenths of the law, but all of it?

In reaching its conclusion that Moore had no relevant property rights, the court also emphasizes the fact that human lymphokines—the object of the defendant's patent—vary little from individual to individual. But what about other bodily products? It is well known that individual variations in genetic structure are common. Indeed, many scientists believe that they are largely responsible for individual differences in susceptibility to disease and responses to therapy. Suppose Moore could prove that his bodily product at issue contained important genetic variations unique to him as an individual. Would the court then reach a different conclusion and grant him property rights?

3. What was the central basis for this decision? Was it the weight of the many California statutes dealing with bodily products in ways inconsistent with traditional property rights? Was it the non-uniqueness of the human lymphokines that the defendants sought to patent? Or was it policy? Precisely what policies did this decision purport to vindicate, and how? Was the decision driven by legal doctrine or by these policies?

4. The *Moore* decision certainly facilitated biomedical research. It did so in three ways. First, it avoided the administrative difficulty and expense of scientists having to trace the origins of, and putative property rights in, all the myriad body fluids, cells, cell lines, proteins and gene segments that they use in their research. As the court notes, biotechnology scientists—especially those working in universities and nonprofit research laboratories—have the custom of sharing and exchanging biological materials on request. Materials related to patents are available upon request from legally mandated depositories. Imagine the increased difficulty in administering both these depositories and research in general if scientists had to consider the property rights of each patient whose treatment might have contributed to the development of particular biological materials.

Second, the simple notion of a property right in chattels would be difficult, if not impossible, to adapt to biological materials. The very essence of those materials is their transformation into other things. Through reproduction, mutation, recombinant DNA technology, chemical synthesis and other means, scientists constantly to transform biological materials derived from patients into purer, simpler, safer and more effective materials for use in diagnosis and treatment. How would property rights apply to the results of such transformation? Suppose particular biological materials derived from the body fluids of three patients are transformed through a recombinant process into genetically modified living cells, which, during reproduction, spontaneously mutate into a cell line highly useful in research. Who would "own" that cell line—the patients or the many scientists whose work contributed to its production—and in what proportions? Entire new theories of property rights and co-ownership would have to be developed to resolve these questions. In the meantime, legal rights, and therefore investment in biotechnology, would be subject to debilitating uncertainty.

Finally, the result in *Moore* spared courts from making the Solomonic decisions necessary to "weigh" a patient's contribution in suffering and anxiety against the more focused contributions of scientists and their investment backers in producing new matter useful in human health care. Who contributed more to the defendant's patented lymphokines, Moore, whose body products helped develop them, or the scientists whose years of research and study made those body products useful? And how should Moore's "contribution" be weighed? Should it depend upon how successful was his treatment? whether and how much he suffered as a result? whether his blood was drawn while he was alive? The result in *Moore* spared both scientists and courts the moral impossibility of making these "apples and oranges" comparisons in a reasonably consistent way.

5. A ruling that *patients* have no property rights in biological materials derived from their body products once they are removed from their body does not necessarily mean that no property rights exist. How should the results and reasoning of *Moore* be applied to property claims *by others* in biological materials? Should the developers of particular materials have property rights in them? If so, who should have property rights in related materials in which those materials are transformed by genetic engineering, mutation, or simple reproduction? If a group of scientists develop a cell line with unique properties, for example, should they collectively own all progeny and "natural" mutations of that cell line? all recombinant variations of it?

If answering these questions is left to case-by-case development of the common law, it may take decades for the courts to produce stable, sensible and comprehensible answers on which business and investors can rely. But what about contract? Can contractual provisions in licensing or other agreements provide answers to these questions that court would or should respect?

Suppose, for example, that Firm A has developed a unique cell line, with unique genetic sequences and medical properties, that is highly useful in biomedical research. Let us call it Cell Line X. Firm B wishes to use that cell line in research and so signs an agreement containing the following clause:

> Firm B agrees that Cell Line X, and anything derived from Cell Line X, will be the sole and exclusive property of Firm A, whether derived by physical or chemical transformation, genetic engineering, combination or recombination, reproduction, hybridization, cloning, natural or induced mutation, or any other natural or artificial technique or process now known or later developed (collectively, 'Derived Products'). Firm B agrees to acknowledge and respect Firm A's property rights in any and all Derived Products, to return any Derived Product to Firm A promptly on Firm A's request, and not to grant any third party possession of any Derived Product without Firm A's prior written consent.

Should a court enforce this clause? Would doing so be consistent with the public policies enunciated in *Moore*? Would failing to enforce it render rights in the results of biomedical research uncertain and hence discourage investment in that research? What lines, if any, should courts draw with respect to the lawful reach of such contractual provisions?

What if the foregoing clause, in addition to asserting property rights in anything derived from Cell Line X, attempted to assert co-ownership in any patent relating to research using Cell Line X. Should the courts enforce that type of provision? Would it be consistent with the policies underlying patent law and the patent statute's requirement that patents issue only to inventors (*see* 35 U.S.C. § 102(f))? Would it be consistent with public policy as expressed in the *Moore* decision?

6. The *Moore* court tried to simplify the law governing property rights in biological materials. It did so, however, by excluding only one class of persons—patients not participating in research other than by donating their bodily matter—from only one set of legal rights—tangible personal property rights in the donated bodily matter. There are

many other classes of persons who might have interests in the results of biomedical re-search. They include subjects of clinical trials, transplant donors (or their heirs) and transplant recipients, co-workers, and the developers of biological materials used in others' research. There are also many other classes of legal issues, including the right to possession or access (as distinguished from "ownership"), the right to credit for the re-sults of the research, ownership or co-ownership of any resulting intellectual property (typically patents or trade secrets), and the rights to an exclusive or nonexclusive license under any resulting intellectual property.

Should the same result in *Moore* apply to all these different claims? Should the common-law and the policies enunciated in *Moore* govern them? Should contract? Should absolute freedom of contract prevail, or should the law impose limits on the extent to which these claims can be enhanced or disclaimed by contract, for example, in licensing agreements? These questions are of interest not just to observers of the biotechnology industry. They are of vital interest to licensing lawyers as well, for lawyers' sense of what is reasonable, and their corresponding predictions as to how courts might rule, may make the difference between valid and invalid contractual provisions.

\* \* \*

# VI. Tangible Biological Materials as Tools of Invention

The development of life science "tools" made from biological materials like cell lines, proteins, monoclonal antibodies, genes, DNA, etc., has led to a thriving market in such materials among university and industry labs. A sort of "life science software," many bi-ological materials are self-replicating or easily reproduced, and can be easily distributed. They are called tools, because they can be used in combination with other materials and techniques to create wholly new, patentable inventions.

However, what if instead of given away or sold, the tools were licensed? Then per-haps the owners could theoretically "reach through" a license to obtain rights in any new inventions made by the licensee using the tools, in the same way that the manufac-turer of scientific instruments might assert intellectual property rights in a new inven-tion developed with the help of the instrument.

That is exactly what has happened. Such transfers are legally accomplished using a ma-terial transfer agreement (MTA). Formerly, MTAs were simple one-page agreements, however, it is now common practice for biotech and pharmaceutical companies to make research tools available only under onerous MTAs that require the recipient to either as-sign to the provider all inventions made using the provider's material, or grant to the provider non-exclusive, paid up licenses to use any resulting inventions. Additionally, these MTAs often add additional burdensome liability requirements. Concerned about the chilling affect of such agreements on the dissemination of federally funded research, the NIH in 1998 published guidelines for the use of biological materials in federally funded research.

# Sharing Biomedical Research Resources: Principles and Guidelines for Recipients of NIH Research Grants and Contracts

64 FR 72090 (December 23, 1999)

\* \* \*

## Appendix

### GUIDELINES FOR IMPLEMENTATION

The following Guidelines provide specific information, strategies, and model language for patent and license professionals and sponsored research administrators at Recipient institutions to assist in implementing the Principles on Obtaining and Disseminating Biomedical Resources. Recipients are encouraged to use the strategies below, other strategies developed at their own institutions, or any other appropriate means of achieving the Principles.

Guidelines for Disseminating Research Resources Arising Out of NIH-Funded Research

### Definition of Research Tools

The definition of research tools is necessarily broad, and it is acknowledged that the same material can have different uses, being a research tool in some contexts and a product in others. In determining how an NIH-funded resource that falls within the definition should be handled, Recipients should determine whether: 1) the primary usefulness of the resource is as a tool for discovery rather than an FDA-approved product or integral component of such a product; 2) the resource is a broad, enabling invention that will be useful to many scientists (or multiple companies in developing multiple products), rather than a project or product-specific resource; and 3) the resource is readily useable or distributable as a tool rather than the situation where private sector involvement is necessary or the most expedient means for developing or distributing the resource. Recipients should ensure that their intellectual property strategy for resources fitting one or more of the above criteria enhances rather than restricts the ultimate availability of the resource. If Recipient believes private sector involvement is desirable to achieve this goal, Recipient should strategically license the invention under terms commensurate with the goal.

### Use of Simple Letter Agreement

Recipients are expected to ensure that unique research resources arising from NIH-funded research are made available to the scientific research community. The majority of transfers to not-for-profit entities should be implemented under terms no more restrictive than the UBMTA. In particular, Recipients are expected to use the Simple Letter Agreement provided below, or another document with no more restrictive terms, to readily transfer unpatented tools developed with NIH funds to other Recipients for use in NIH-funded projects. If the materials are patented or licensed to an exclusive provider, other arrangements may be used, but commercialization option rights, royalty reach-through, or product reach-through rights back to the provider are inappropriate.

Similarly, when for-profit entities are seeking access to NIH-funded tools for internal use purposes, Recipients should ensure that the tools are transferred with the fewest encumbrances possible. The Simple Letter Agreement may be expanded for use in transferring tools to for-profit entities, or simple internal use license agreements with execution or annual use fees may be appropriate.

### Simple Letter Agreement for the Transfer of Materials

In response to the RECIPIENT's request for the MATERIAL [insert description] the PROVIDER asks that the RECIPIENT and the RECIPIENT SCIENTIST agree to the following before the RECIPIENT receives the MATERIAL:

1. The above MATERIAL is the property of the PROVIDER and is made available as a service to the research community.

2. THIS MATERIAL IS NOT FOR USE IN HUMAN SUBJECTS.

3. The MATERIAL will be used for teaching or not-for-profit research purposes only.

4. The MATERIAL will not be further distributed to others without the PROVIDER's written consent. The RECIPIENT shall refer any request for the MATERIAL to the PROVIDER. To the extent supplies are available, the PROVIDER or the PROVIDER SCIENTIST agree to make the MATERIAL available, under a separate Simple Letter Agreement to other scientists for teaching or not-for-profit research purposes only.

5. The RECIPIENT agrees to acknowledge the source of the MATERIAL in any publications reporting use of it.

6. Any MATERIAL delivered pursuant to this Agreement is understood to be experimental in nature and may have hazardous properties. THE PROVIDER MAKES NO REPRESENTATIONS AND EXTENDS NO WARRANTIES OF ANY KIND, EITHER EXPRESSED OR IMPLIED. THERE ARE NO EXPRESS OR IMPLIED WARRANTIES OF MERCHANTABILITY OR FITNESS FOR A PARTICULAR PURPOSE, OR THAT THE USE OF THE MATERIAL WILL NOT INFRINGE ANY PATENT, COPYRIGHT, TRADEMARK, OR OTHER PROPRIETARY RIGHTS. Unless prohibited by law, Recipient assumes all liability for claims for damages against it by third parties which may arise from the use, storage or disposal of the Material except that, to the extent permitted by law, the Provider shall be liable to the Recipient when the damage is caused by the gross negligence or willful misconduct of the Provider.

7. The RECIPIENT agrees to use the MATERIAL in compliance with all applicable statutes and regulations.

8. The MATERIAL is provided at no cost, or with an optional transmittal fee solely to reimburse the PROVIDER for its preparation and distribution costs. If a fee is requested, the amount will be indicated here: [insert fee].

* * *

———————

# VII. Limiting Exclusive Licenses to Appropriate Field of Use

Exclusive licenses for research tools (where no further research and development is needed to realize the invention's usefulness as a tool) should generally be avoided except in cases where the licensee undertakes to make the research tool widely available to researchers through unrestricted sale, or the licensor retains rights to make the research tool widely available. When an exclusive license is necessary to promote investment in commercial applications of a subject invention that is also a research tool, the recipient should ordinarily limit the exclusive license to the commercial field of use, retaining rights regarding use and distribution as a research tool.

Examples of possible language include the following:

"'Research License' means a nontransferable, nonexclusive license to make and to use the Licensed Products or Licensed Processes as defined by the Licensed Patent Rights for purposes of research and not for purposes of commercial manufacture, distribution, or provision of services, or in lieu of purchase, or for developing a directly related secondary product that can be sold. Licensor reserves the right to grant such nonexclusive Research Licenses directly or to require Licensee to grant nonexclusive Research Licenses on reasonable terms. The purpose of this Research License is to encourage basic research, whether conducted at an academic or corporate facility. In order to safeguard the Licensed Patent Rights, however, Licensor shall consult with Licensee before granting to commercial entities a Research License or providing to them research samples of the materials."

"Licensor reserves the right to provide the Biological Materials and to grant licenses under Patent Rights to not-for-profit and governmental institutions for their internal research and scholarly use."

"Notwithstanding anything to the contrary in this agreement, Licensor shall retain a paid-up, nonexclusive, irrevocable license to practice, and to sublicense other not-for-profit research organizations to practice, the Patent Rights for internal research use."

"The grant of rights provided herein is subject to the rights of the United States government pursuant to the Bayh-Dole Act and is limited by the right of the Licensor to use Patent Rights for its own research and educational purposes and to freely distribute Materials to not-for-profit entities for internal research purposes."

"Licensor reserves the right to supply any or all of the Biological Materials to academic research scientists, subject to limitation of use by such scientists for research purposes and restriction from further distribution."

"Licensor reserves the right to practice under the Patent Rights and to use and distribute to third parties the Tangible Property for Licensor's own internal research purposes."

\* \* \*

# University of Rochester v. G.D. Searle & Co., Inc.
## 358 F.3d 916 (Fed. Cir. 2004)

LOURIE, Circuit Judge.

The University of Rochester ("Rochester") appeals from the decision of the United States District Court for the Western District of New York granting summary judgment that United States Patent 6,048,850 is invalid. *Univ. of Rochester v. G.D. Searle & Co.*, 249 F. Supp. 2d 216 (W.D.N.Y. 2003). Because we conclude that the court did not err in holding the '850 patent invalid for failing to comply with the written description requirement of 35 U.S.C. § 112, ¶ 1, and in granting summary judgment on that ground, we affirm.

## BACKGROUND

Traditional non-steroidal anti-inflammatory drugs ("NSAIDs") such as aspirin, ibuprofen, ketoprofen, and naproxen are believed to function by inhibiting the activity of enzymes called cyclooxygenases. Cyclooxygenases catalyze the production of a molecule called prostaglandin H[2], which is a precursor for other prostaglandins that perform various functions in the human body. *Id.* at 219.

In the early 1990s, scientists discovered the existence and separate functions of two distinct cyclooxygenases, referred to as "COX-1" and "COX-2." COX-1 is expressed (i.e., produced biologically) in the gastrointestinal tract, where it is involved in the production of prostaglandins that serve a beneficial role by, for example, providing protection for the stomach lining. *Id.* COX-2 is expressed in response to inflammatory stimuli, and is thought to be responsible for the inflammation associated with diseases such as arthritis. *Id.* It is now known that the traditional NSAIDs inhibit both COX-1 and COX-2, and as a result they not only reduce inflammation, but also can cause undesirable side effects such as stomach upset, irritation, ulcers, and bleeding. *Id.*

After the separate functions of COX-1 and COX-2 were discovered, it was hypothesized that it would be possible to reduce inflammation without gastrointestinal side effects if a method could be found for selectively inhibiting the activity of COX-2 (i.e., inhibiting the activity of COX-2 without inhibiting COX-1 activity). *Id.* To that end, Rochester scientists developed a screening assay for use in determining whether a particular drug displayed such selectivity, and filed a U.S. patent application directed to their developments in 1992. After filing a series of continuation, continuation-in-part, and divisional applications derived from that 1992 application, the scientists eventually received United States Patent 5,837,479 in 1998, covering methods "for identifying a compound that inhibits prostaglandin synthesis catalyzed by mammalian prostaglandin H synthase-2 (PGHS-2)."

From a division of the application that led to the '479 patent, the scientists also obtained, on April 11, 2000, the '850 patent. The '850 patent contains three independent claims and five dependent claims. The three independent claims read as follows:

1. A method for selectively inhibiting PGHS-2 activity in a human host, comprising administering a non-steroidal compound that selectively inhibits activity of the PGHS-2 gene product to a human host in need of such treatment.
2. A method for selectively inhibiting PGHS-2 activity in a human host, comprising administering a non-steroidal compound that selectively inhibits activity of the PGHS-2 gene product in a human host in need of such treatment, wherein the activity of the non-steroidal compound does not result in significant toxic side effects in the human host.

3.  A method for selectively inhibiting PGHS-2 activity in a human host, comprising administering a non-steroidal compound that selectively inhibits activity of the PGHS-2 gene product in a human host in need of such treatment, wherein the ability of the non-steroidal compound to selectively inhibit the activity of the PGHS-2 gene product is determined by:

    a)  contacting a genetically engineered cell that expresses human PGHS-2, and not human PGHS-1, with the compound for 30 minutes, and exposing the cell to a pre-determined-amount of arachidonic acid;

    b)  contacting a genetically engineered cell that expresses human PGHS-1, and not human PGHS-2, with the compound for 30 minutes, and exposing the cell to a pre-determined amount of arachidonic acid;

    c)  measuring the conversion of arachidonic acid to its prostaglandin metabolite; and

    d)  comparing the amount of the converted arachidonic acid converted by each cell exposed to the compound to the amount of the arachidonic acid converted by control cells that were not exposed to the compound, so that the compounds that inhibit PGHS-2 and not PGHS-1 activity are identified.

'850 patent, col. 71, l. 36 – col. 72, l. 51. Thus, all eight claims are directed to methods "for selectively inhibiting PGHS-2 activity in a human host" by "administering a non-steroidal compound that selectively inhibits activity of the PGHS-2 gene product to [or in] a human host in need of such treatment."

On the day the '850 patent issued, Rochester sued G.D. Searle & Co., Inc., Monsanto Co., Pharmacia Corp., and Pfizer Inc. (collectively, "Pfizer"), alleging that Pfizer's sale of its COX-2 inhibitors Celebrex(r) and Bextra(r) for treatment of inflammation infringed the '850 patent, and seeking injunctive and monetary relief. *Univ. of Rochester*, 249 F. Supp. 2d at 220. In May 2002, Pfizer moved for summary judgment of invalidity of the '850 patent for failure to comply with the written description and enablement requirements of 35 U.S.C. § 112, ¶ 1. Rochester opposed the motion and filed a cross-motion for summary judgment with respect to the written description issue. *Id.*

In evaluating the parties' motions, the district court found that, although all of the claims require the use of a "non-steroidal compound that selectively inhibits activity of the PGHS-2 gene," the '850 patent neither discloses any such compound nor provides any suggestion as to how such a compound could be made or otherwise obtained other than by trial-and-error research. *Id.* at 224–25, 228–29. Indeed, the court found no evidence in the '850 patent that the inventors themselves knew of any such compound at the time their patent application was filed. *Id.* at 228. Accordingly, the court concluded that the patent's claims are invalid for lack of written description. *Id.* at 224.

The district court also found that practice of the claimed methods would require "a person of ordinary skill in the art…to engage in undue experimentation, with no assurance of success," and on that basis concluded that the claims are also invalid for lack of enablement. *Id.* at 232. The court considered, but rejected as conclusory, Rochester's experts' opinions that one of skill in the art would have known to start with existing NSAIDs and would have used routine methods to make structural changes to lead compounds to optimize them, citing a general failure to point to any language in the patent supporting those opinions. *Id.* at 233.

Finding no genuine issue of material fact concerning either written description or enablement, the district court accordingly granted Pfizer's motions for summary judgment of invalidity of the '850 patent for failure to meet the written description and enablement requirements, denied Rochester's cross-motion, and dismissed the complaint. *Id.* at 235–36.

Rochester now appeals. We have jurisdiction pursuant to 28 U.S.C. § 1295(a)(1).

* * *

In its first argument, Rochester asserts that the district court effectively—but erroneously—held that a patent claiming a method of obtaining a biological effect in a human by administering a compound cannot, as a matter of law, satisfy the written description requirement without disclosing the identity of any such compound. Indeed, Rochester contends that "no written description requirement exists independent of enablement." In any event, Rochester argues that its patent met the requirements of § 112 and is not invalid.

Pfizer responds to Rochester's argument by pointing out that we have "interpreted § 112 'as requiring a "written description" of an invention separate from enablement,'" (citing *Enzo Biochem, Inc. v. Gen-Probe Inc.*, 323 F.3d 956, 963 (Fed. Cir. 2002)), and that "the many prior precedential decisions" contrary to Rochester's position "cannot be overruled except by an en banc decision." Pfizer also cites *Vas-Cath Inc. v. Mahurkar*, 935 F.2d 1555 (Fed. Cir. 1991), in which we explained that "the purpose of the written description requirement is broader than to merely explain how to 'make and use' [the invention]," *id.* at 1563; and *Reiffin v. Microsoft Corp.*, 214 F.3d 1342 (Fed. Cir. 2000), in which we stated that the purpose of the written description requirement is to "ensure that the scope of the right to exclude, as set forth in the claims, does not overreach the scope of the inventor's contribution to the field of art as described in the patent specification," *id.* at 1345. Pfizer asserts that a patent fails to satisfy the written description requirement if it claims a method of achieving a biological effect, but discloses no compounds that can accomplish that result. It maintains that the district court correctly invalidated Rochester's '850 patent.

We agree with Pfizer that our precedent recognizes a written description requirement and that the '850 patent does not satisfy that requirement. As in any case involving statutory interpretation, we begin with the language of the statute itself. *Consumer Prod. Safety Comm'n v. GTE Sylvania, Inc.*, 447 U.S. 102, 108, 64 L. Ed. 2d 766, 100 S. Ct. 2051 (1980). Section 112 provides, in relevant part, that:

> The specification shall contain a written description of the invention, and of the manner and process of making and using it, in such full, clear, concise, and exact terms as to enable any person skilled in the art to which it pertains, or with which it is most nearly connected, to make and use the same, and shall set forth the best mode contemplated by the inventor of carrying out his invention.

35 U.S.C. § 112, P 1 (2000). Three separate requirements are contained in that provision: (1) "the specification shall contain a written description of the invention"; (2) "the specification shall contain a written description... of the manner and process of making and using it [i.e., the invention] in such full, clear, concise, and exact terms as to enable any person skilled in the art to which it pertains, or with which it is most nearly connected, to make and use the same"; and (3) "the specification... shall set forth the best mode contemplated by the inventor of carrying out his invention."

In common parlance, as well as in our and our predecessor court's case law, those three requirements are referred to as the "written description requirement," the "enablement requirement," and the "best mode requirement," respectively. *See In re Moore*, 58 C.C.P.A. 1042, 439 F.2d 1232, 1235 (CCPA 1971) ("Robert Moore") ("This first paragraph analysis in itself contains several inquiries. Considering the language of the statute, it should be evident that these inquiries include determining whether the subject matter defined in the claims is described in the specification, whether the specification disclosure as a whole is such as to enable one skilled in the art to make and use the claimed invention, and whether the best mode contemplated by the inventor of carrying out that invention is set forth."). The United States Supreme Court also recently acknowledged written description as a statutory requirement distinct not only from the best mode requirement, but also from enablement. *See Festo Corp. v. Shoketsu Kinzoku Kogyo Kabushiki Co.*, 535 U.S. 722, 736, 152 L. Ed. 2d 944, 122 S. Ct. 1831 (2002) ("[A] number of statutory requirements must be satisfied before a patent can issue. The claimed subject matter must be useful, novel, and not obvious. 35 U.S.C. §§ 101–103 (1994 ed. and Supp. V). In addition, the patent application must describe, enable, and set forth the best mode of carrying out the invention. *Id.* at § 112 (1994 ed.). These latter requirements must be satisfied before issuance of the patent, for exclusive patent rights are given in exchange for disclosing the invention to the public." Although there is often significant overlap between the three requirements, they are nonetheless independent of each other. *In re Alton*, 76 F.3d 1168, 1172 (Fed. Cir. 1996). Thus, an invention may be described without an enabling disclosure of how to make and use it. A description of a chemical compound without a description of how to make and use it, unless within the skill of one of ordinary skill in the art, is an example. Moreover, an invention may be enabled even though it has not been described.

The "written description" requirement serves a teaching function, as a "quid pro quo" in which the public is given "meaningful disclosure in exchange for being excluded from practicing the invention for a limited period of time." *Enzo*, 323 F.3d at 970. Rochester argues, however, that this teaching, or "public notice," function, although "virtually unchanged since the 1793 Patent Act," in fact "became redundant with the advent of claims in 1870." We disagree. Statutory language does not become redundant unless repealed by Congress, in which case it no longer exists.

In addition, and most significantly, our precedent clearly recognizes a separate written description requirement. In *In re Ruschig*, 54 C.C.P.A. 1551, 379 F.2d 990 (CCPA 1967), our predecessor court affirmed a rejection under 35 U.S.C. § 112 of a claim that was added to a patent application during prosecution to provoke an interference. That application had originally included a claim directed to a genus of chemical compounds, all having a central benzenesulphonylurea structure and two variable substituents attached at specified sites on that structure. *Id.* at 994. As a result of the way in which those substituents were defined in the claim, the genus defined by the claim included thousands of compounds, corresponding to all the possible permutations of the substituents. *Id.* at 993–94. The added claim, in contrast, was directed to a single member of that genus, N-(p-chlorobenzesulfonyl)-N-propylurea. *Id.* at 991. Although that compound was within the literal scope of the originally filed claim, it was never "named or otherwise exemplified" in the appellants' original patent application. *Id.* at 992. The examiner rejected the added claim on the basis that the specific compound was not adequately supported by the specification as filed. *Id.*

The Patent Office Board of Appeals, and subsequently the Court of Customs and Patent Appeals, affirmed that rejection. In reaching its decision, the court observed that the claimed compound was not described in the specification and would not "convey clearly to those skilled in the art, to whom it is addressed, in any way, the information that appellants invented that specific compound." *Id.* at 996. It did not teach the specific compound. Although the appellants had argued that the rejection was improper because one skilled in the art would be enabled by the specification to make the specific compound, the court explained that it was "doubtful that the rejection [was] truly based on section 112, at least on the parts relied on by appellants [i.e., the 'language therein about enabling one skilled in the art to make the invention']. If based on section 112, it is on the requirement thereof that 'The specification shall contain a written description of the invention.'" *Id.* at 995–96.

While it is true that this court and its predecessor have repeatedly held that claimed subject matter "need not be described in haec verba" in the specification to satisfy the written description requirement, e.g., *In re Smith*, 481 F.2d 910, 914 (CCPA 1973), it is also true that the requirement must still be met in some way so as to "describe the claimed invention so that one skilled in the art can recognize what is claimed." *Enzo*, 323 F.3d at 968. We have further explained that:

> The appearance of mere indistinct words in a specification or a claim, even an original claim, does not necessarily satisfy that requirement....A description of an anti-inflammatory steroid, i.e., a steroid (a generic structural term) described even in terms of its function of lessening inflammation of tissues fails to distinguish any steroid from others having the same activity or function. A description of what a material does, rather than of what it is, usually does not suffice. [*Regents of the Univ. of Cal. v.*] *Eli Lilly* [*& Co., Inc.*], 119 F.3d [1559,] 1568 [(Fed. Cir. 1997) ("*Lilly*")]....The disclosure must allow one skilled in the art to visualize or recognize the identity of the subject matter purportedly described. *Id.*

*Enzo*, 323 F.3d at 968. Similarly, for example, in the nineteenth century, use of the word "automobile" would not have sufficed to describe a newly invented automobile; an inventor would need to describe what an automobile is, viz., a chassis, an engine, seats, wheels on axles, etc. Thus, generalized language may not suffice if it does not convey the detailed identity of an invention. In this case, there is no language here, generalized or otherwise, that describes compounds that achieve the claimed effect.

Rochester is also factually incorrect in its assertion that a written description requirement separate from the enablement requirement was not recognized prior to *Ruschig* in 1967. For example, in *Jepson v. Coleman*, 50 C.C.P.A. 1051, 314 F.2d 533, 1963 Dec. Comm'r Pat. 304 (CCPA 1963), our predecessor court explicitly rejected the notion that an enabling disclosure necessarily satisfies the written description requirement: "It is not a question whether one skilled in the art might be able to construct the patentee's device from the teachings of the disclosure of the application. Rather, it is a question whether the application necessarily discloses that particular device." *Id.*at 536. Still earlier, that court affirmed a decision of the Board of Appeals of the Patent Office affirming the rejection of an applicant's claims on the basis that those claims were "broader than the disclosure in appellant's application and...were properly rejected for that reason." *In re Moore*, 33 C.C.P.A. 1083, 155 F.2d 379, 382, 1946 Dec. Comm'r Pat. 421 (CCPA 1946) ("*Wm. Moore*"). The court stated that it "is well settled that claims in an application which are broader than the applicant's disclosure are not allowable." *Id.*

Similarly, in 1962 the court affirmed the Board's rejection of the original claims in a patent application, based on, *inter alia*, the rejected claims' "failure to meet the requirements of 35 U.S.C. § 112 in that they are broader than the invention described in the written description thereof as set forth in the specification." *In re Sus*, 49 C.C.P.A. 1301, 306 F.2d 494, 497, 1962 Dec. Comm'r Pat. 486 (CCPA 1962). In that case, the court specifically identified the "pertinent portions of 35 U.S.C. § 112 to be here considered" as the following: " 'The specification shall contain a written description of the invention....The specification shall conclude with one or more claims particularly pointing out and distinctly claiming the subject matter which the applicant regards as his invention.' " *Id.* at 494. According to the court, "one skilled in this art would not be taught by the written description of the invention in the specification that any 'aryl or substituted aryl radical' would be suitable for the purposes of the invention but rather that only certain aryl radicals and certain specifically substituted aryl radicals would be suitable for such purposes." *Id.* at 504. The issues in *Jepson, Wm. Moore,* and *Sus* were clearly not confined to a determination whether the enablement requirement was met. They were independent written description issues.

Rochester's suggestion in its brief that *Lilly* "compounded *Ruschig's* error" by "invoking the written description requirement in a case without priority issues" is similarly deficient. Neither *Wm. Moore* nor *Sus,* for example, involved any priority issues. Moreover, even if the court had never had occasion to apply the written description requirement to original claims prior to the 1987 *Lilly* decision, that requirement was nonetheless always present. As explained in *Enzo:*

> It is said that applying the written description requirement outside of the priority context was novel until several years ago. Maybe so, maybe not; certainly such a holding was not precluded by statute or precedent. New interpretations of old statutes in light of new fact situations occur all the time....

> As for the lack of earlier cases on this issue, it regularly happens in adjudication that issues do not arise until counsel raise them, and, when that occurs, courts are then required to decide them.

323 F.3d at 971–72 (Lourie, J., concurring in Denial of Petition for Rehearing En Banc). In any event, the basic requirement of a written description of an invention exists whether a question of priority has arisen or not. The statute does not limit the requirement to cases in which a priority question arises.

Indeed, as early as 1822 the Supreme Court recognized the existence of separate written description and enablement requirements:

> The patent act requires...that the party [i.e., the inventor] "shall deliver a written description of his invention, in such full, clear, and exact terms, as to distinguish the same from all other things before known, and to enable any person skilled in the art or science, &c. &c. to make, compound, and use the same." The specification, then has two objects: one is to make known the manner of constructing the machine (if the invention is of a machine) so as to enable not to be patented.

*Evans v. Eaton,* 20 U.S. (7 Wheat.) 356, 433–34, 5 L. Ed. 472 (1822). The Patent Act of 1793, 1 Stat. 318, which was in force at the time Evans was decided, required, in relevant part, that every inventor "deliver a written description of his invention, and of the manner of using, or process of compounding the same, in such full, clear, and exact terms, as to distinguish the same from all other things before known, and to enable any person skilled in the art or science...to make, compound, and use the same...." *In re Barker,* 559 F.2d 588, 592 (CCPA 1977) (ellipses in original). Although the patent statutes have been extensively revised since 1822, most notably in the addition of the requirement of claims, the language of the present statute is not very different in its articulation of the written description requirement. *Id.* at 592–94.

Rochester also argues that *Fiers v. Revel,* 984 F.2d 1164 (Fed. Cir. 1993), *Lilly,* and *Enzo* are all distinguishable because they were limited to DNA-based inventions.

Rochester asserts that undisputed evidence shows that, based on the '850 patent's teachings, skilled artisans would be able to recognize COX-2-selective inhibitors.

We agree with Rochester that *Fiers*, *Lilly*, and *Enzo* differ from this case in that they all related to genetic material whereas this case does not, but we find that distinction to be unhelpful to Rochester's position. It is irrelevant; the statute applies to all types of inventions. We see no reason for the rule to be any different when non-genetic materials are at issue; in fact, where there might be some basis for finding a written description requirement to be satisfied in a genetics case based on the complementariness of a nucleic acid and, for example, a protein, that correspondence might be less clear in a non-genetic situation. In *Enzo*, we explained that functional descriptions of genetic material can, in some cases, meet the written description requirement if those functional characteristics are "coupled with a known or disclosed correlation between function and structure, or some combination of such characteristics." 323 F.3d at 964 (quoting from the PTO's *Guidelines for Examination of Patent Applications Under the 35 U.S.C. 112, P1, "Written Description" Requirement*, 66 Fed. Reg. 1099, 1106). DNA and RNA are each made up of just four building blocks that interact with each other in a highly predictable manner. Each of those building blocks, or "nucleotides," is characterized by a unique "base": In the case of DNA, the four nucleotides include the bases adenine, thymine, cytosine, and guanine; RNA also includes adenine, cytosine, and guanine, but contains the base uracil in place of thymine. Adenine on one strand of DNA binds, or "hybridizes," to thymine on the other; in RNA, adenine binds to uracil; and in either DNA or RNA, cytosine binds to guanine. Given the sequence of a single strand of DNA or RNA, it may therefore have become a routine matter to envision the precise sequence of a "complementary" strand that will bind to it. Therefore, disclosure of a DNA sequence might support a claim to the complementary molecules that can hybridize to it.

The same is not necessarily true in the chemical arts more generally. Even with the three-dimensional structures of enzymes such as COX-1 and COX-2 in hand, it may even now not be within the ordinary skill in the art to predict what compounds might bind to and inhibit them, let alone have been within the purview of one of ordinary skill in the art in the 1993–1995 period in which the applications that led to the '850 patent were filed. Rochester and its experts do not offer any persuasive evidence to the contrary. As the district court pointed out:

> Tellingly,…what plaintiff's experts do not say is that one of skill in the art would, from reading the patent, understand what compound or compounds— which, as the patent makes clear, are necessary to practice the claimed method—would be suitable, nor would one know how to find such a compound except through trial and error.…Plaintiff's experts opine that a person of ordinary skill in the art would understand from reading the '850 patent what method is claimed, but it is clear from reading the patent that one critical aspect of the method—a compound that selectively inhibits PGHS-2 activity—was hypothetical, for it is clear that the inventors had neither possession nor knowledge of such a compound.

*Univ. of Rochester*, 249 F. Supp. 2d at 229.

Rochester also attempts to distinguish *Fiers*, *Lilly*, and *Enzo* by suggesting that the holdings in those cases were limited to composition of matter claims, whereas the '850 patent is directed to a method. We agree with the district court that that is "a semantic distinction without a difference." *Univ. of Rochester*, 249 F. Supp. 2d at 228. Regardless whether a compound is claimed *per se* or a method is claimed that entails the use of the compound, the inventor cannot lay claim to that subject matter unless he can provide a description of the compound sufficient to distinguish infringing compounds from non-infringing compounds, or infringing methods from non-infringing methods. As the district court observed, "the claimed method depends upon finding a compound that selectively inhibits PGHS-2 activity. Without such a compound, it is impossible to practice the claimed method of treatment." *Id.*

We of course do not mean to suggest that the written description requirement can be satisfied only by providing a description of an actual reduction to practice. Constructive reduction to practice is an established method of disclosure, but the application must nonetheless "describe the claimed subject matter in terms that establish that [the applicant] was in possession of the...claimed invention, including all of the elements and limitations." *Hyatt v. Boone*, 146 F.3d 1348, 1353 (Fed. Cir. 1998). *But see Enzo*, 323 F.3d at 969 ("Application of the written description requirement, however, is not subsumed by the 'possession' inquiry. A showing of 'possession' is ancillary to the statutory mandate that 'the specification shall contain a written description of the invention,' and that requirement is not met if, despite a showing of possession, the specification does not adequately describe the invention."). The specification must teach the invention by describing it.

Rochester also contends that "the patent-in-suit cannot be *per se* invalid," because written description is a question of fact. Rochester further argues that:

Consistent with written description's fact-intensive nature, this Court has recognized diverse forms of description, including description primarily (if not entirely) based on functional characteristics. *In Union Oil [Co. v. Atlantic Richfield Co.*, 208 F.3d 989 (Fed. Cir. 2000) ("*Unocal*")], for example, the Court rejected the argument that the patent-in-suit was invalid because it described claimed gasoline mixtures by their "desired characteristics," rather than by their "exact chemical components."

In response, Pfizer argues that the district court did not apply a *per se* rule, and that written description of a method of selectively inhibiting the activity of an enzyme by administering a chemical compound is insufficient unless a skilled artisan can recognize the identity of the compound, and the description must convey what the compound is, not just what it does. Pfizer points out that the district court found that the '850 patent does not disclose the structure or physical properties of any of the compounds required to practice the claimed methods, and that the structure of such compounds cannot be deduced from any known structure-function correlation. Pfizer agrees with the district court that the '850 patent discloses nothing more than a hoped-for function for an as-yet-to-be-discovered compound, and a research plan for trying to find it.

We agree with Pfizer that the '850 patent is deficient in failing to adequately describe the claimed invention. First, although compliance with the written description requirement is a question of fact, *Vas-Cath*, 935 F.2d at 1561, Rochester's argument that a patent may not be held invalid on its face is contrary to our case law. *In PIN/NIP, Inc. v. Platte Chemical Co.*, 304 F.3d 1235 (Fed. Cir. 2002), for example, we held that a patent can be held invalid for failure to meet the written description requirement, based solely on the language of the patent specification. After all, it is in the patent specification where the written description requirement must be met. Similarly, in *TurboCare Division of Demag Delaval Turbomachinery Corp. v. General Electric Co.*, 264 F.3d 1111 (Fed. Cir. 2001), we held that "no reasonable juror could find that [an appellant's] original disclosure was sufficiently detailed to enable one of skill in the art to recognize that [the appellant] invented what is claimed," and accordingly upheld a grant of summary judgment. *Id.* at 1119.

Second, it is undisputed that the '850 patent does not disclose any compounds that can be used in its claimed methods. The claimed methods thus cannot be practiced based on the patent's specification, even considering the knowledge of one skilled in the art. No compounds that will perform the claimed method are disclosed, nor has any evidence been shown that such a compound was known. The '850 patent does contain substantial description of the cyclooxygenases, including the nucleotide sequences of coding and promoter regions of the genes that encode human COX-1 and COX-2 and a comparison of those sequences. *See, e.g.,* '850 patent, figs. 6A-6B, 10A-10D, and 11A-11C. The patent also describes in detail how to make cells that express either COX-1 or COX-2, but not both, *id.* § 5.2, at cols. 8–20, as well as "assays for screening compounds, including peptides, polynucleotides, and small organic molecules to identify those that inhibit the expression or activity of the PGHS-2 gene product; and methods of treating diseases characterized by aberrant PGHS-2 activity using such compounds," id. At col. 8, ll. 2-7; *see also id.* § 5.6, at cols. 24–25. Such assay methods are in fact claimed in the '479 patent, i.e., Rochester's *other* patent based on the same disclosure. The '850 patent specification also describes what can be done with any compounds that may potentially be identified through those assays, including formulation into pharmaceuticals, routes of administration, estimation of effective dosage, and suitable dosage forms. *Id.* § 5.8, at cols. 27–34. As pointed out by the district court, however, the '850 patent does not disclose just "*which* 'peptides, polynucleotides, and small organic molecules' have the desired characteristic of selectively inhibiting PGHS-2." *Univ. of Rochester*, 249 F. Supp. 2d at 224. Without such disclosure, the claimed methods cannot be said to have been described. As we held in *Lilly*, "an adequate written description of a DNA…'requires a precise definition, such as by structure, formula, chemical name, or physical properties,' not a mere wish or plan for obtaining the claimed chemical invention." 119 F.3d at 1566 (quoting *Fiers*, 984 F.2d at 1171). For reasons stated above, that requirement applies just as well to non-DNA (or -RNA) chemical inventions.

Third, Rochester's reliance on *Unocal* is unavailing Although we held in that case that a "description of the exact chemical component of each combination that falls within the range claims of the…patent" is not necessary to comply with § 112, we explained that the patentee is nonetheless required to provide sufficient description to show one of skill in the art that the inventor possessed the claimed invention at the time of filing. *Unocal*, 208 F.3d at 997. Evidence was adduced in that case that artisans skilled in petroleum refining were aware of the properties of raw petroleum sources and knew how to mix streams of such sources to achieve a final product with desired characteristics. Accordingly, we held that the written description requirement was satisfied in that case by specifying the ranges of properties of the claimed gasolines, reflecting the way that oil refiners actually formulate gasoline, such that one skilled in the art could recognize what was being claimed. *Id.* at 992. The present case is not analogous. Rochester did not present any evidence that the ordinarily skilled artisan would be able to identify any compound based on its vague functional description as "a non-steroidal compound that selectively inhibits activity of the PGHS-2 gene product."

Rochester also cites *In re Edwards*, 568 F.2d 1349 (CCPA 1978), and *In re Herschler*, 591 F.2d 693 (CCPA 1979), in support of its arguments. Those cases are also inapposite. In *Edwards*, the court held that the written description requirement was satisfied by a specification that described a claimed compound by the process by which it was made, rather than by its structure, because the court found that Edwards' application, "taken as a whole, reasonably leads persons skilled in the art to the [recited reactions] and, concomitantly, to the claimed compound." 568 F.2d at 1354. In marked contrast to the *Edwards* application, the specification of the '850 patent contains no disclosure of any method for making even a single "non-steroidal compound that selectively inhibits activity of the PGHS-2 gene product." In *Herschler*, the court found adequate written description support for broad claims to processes for topically administering a physiologically active steroidal agent to a human or animal by concurrently administering the steroidal agent and dimethyl sulfoxide ("DMSO"), even though the specification disclosed only one example of a "physiologically active steroidal agent." Critically, however, there was no question in that case that, unlike "non-steroidal compounds that selectively inhibit[ ] activity of the PGHS-2 gene product," numerous physiologically active steroidal agents were known to those of ordinary skill in the art. As the court there noted, "were this application drawn to novel 'steroidal agents,' a different question would be posed." 591 F.2d at 701. The novelty in that invention was the DMSO solvent, not the steroids.

* * *

Rochester argues that "the appealed decision vitiates universities' ability to bring pioneering innovations to the public," and that:

> Congress has determined that licensing of academia's inventions to industry is the best way to bring groundbreaking inventions to the public. *See* 35 U.S.C. § 200. By vesting in universities the patent rights to their federally funded research, the Bayh-Dole Act of 1980 encouraged "private industry to utilize government funded inventions through the commitment of the risk capital necessary to develop such inventions to the point of commercial application." H.R. Rep. No. 96-1307, pt. 1, at 3 (1980).

Further, *amici* the University of California and the University of Texas assert that "this Court's decision will have a significant impact on the continuing viability of technology transfer programs at universities and on the equitable allocation of intellectual property rights between universities and the private sector."

That argument is unsound. The Bayh-Dole Act was intended to enable universities to profit from their federally-funded research. It was not intended to relax the statutory requirements for patentability. As pointed out by *amicus* Eli Lilly, "no connection exists between the Bayh-Dole Act and the legal standards that courts employ to assess patentability. Furthermore, none of the eight policy objectives of the Bayh-Dole Act encourages or condones less stringent application of the patent laws to universities than to other entities. See 35 U.S.C. § 200."

In sum, because the '850 patent does not provide any guidance that would steer the skilled practitioner toward compounds that can be used to carry out the claimed methods — an essential element of every claim of that patent — and has not provided evidence that any such compounds were otherwise within the knowledge of a person of ordinary skill in the art at the relevant time, Rochester has failed to raise any question of material fact whether the named inventors disclosed the claimed invention. Accordingly, we affirm the district court's grant of Pfizer's motion for summary judgment.

* * *

# Notes & Questions

1. *Reach Through Infringement.* While the University of Rochester's patent encompassed methods of treatment employing *any* PGHS-2 inhibitor, the Court noted that the '850 patent failed to disclose any such compound nor provided any suggestion as to how such a compound could be made or otherwise obtained other than by trial-and-error research. Indeed, the court found no evidence in the '850 patent that the inventors themselves knew of any such compound at the time their patent application was filed. This case illustrates how the emergence of powerful biological research tools has spurred universities and the biotech and pharmaceutical industries to explore ways to patent or otherwise protect their intellectual property rights in tool technologies. Given the result, are there any other viable patent and license strategies the University could have pursued to commercialize its rights in the PGHS-2 assay?

2. *Reach Through Royalties.* Could the University have licensed the assay to the defendants as a trade secret, and collected downstream royalties on the sale of any drug developed from an inhibitor discovered by using the assay? Because of limitations in NIH regulations on Bayh-Dole, the licensed technology could remain a viable trade secret only if it was developed using private funding.

Reach through licensing solves the problem of valuing basic research itself. By permitting the licensee to pay for use of the assay through royalties on sales of downstream products, both parties have an economic incentive to do a license. What factors would come into play when negotiating a fair royalty? The licensee could argue that the tool is not only a very small part of the drug development process, but also offers no guarantee that its use would result in the discovery of a commercial product. Wouldn't the University counter that, but for the tool, the prospective licensee might never discover the desired compound?

3. *Reach Through Licensing and the NIH.* Reach through licensing has been strongly criticized by the NIH. (*See, Guidelines for Sharing Biomedical Resources, supra*). The NIH is opposed to such licenses of research tools because they remove valuable technology from the public domain. When the NIH first solicited comment on a proposal to create a rule or guide for research tools, universities were strongly opposed. Universities are both licensors and licensees of research tools, and much federally sponsored research is conducted using research tools acquired under material transfer agreements from the private sector. It was unclear what the overall impact would be on the market for research tools. The Guidelines eventually appeared in the Federal Register as suggestions only.

Licensor reserves the right to provide the Biological Materials and to grant licenses under Patent Rights to not-for-profit and governmental institutions for their internal research and scholarly use.

4. *Patenting and Academic Publishing.* Consider the possibility that the inventors may have wanted to publish their early results, rather than wait for the possibility of discovering a commercial quality inhibitor. Publishing pressures result in the research lab when research faculty, and graduate and postdoctoral research assistants desire to publish in order to advance their careers. Provisional patents prior to conference presentations can be risky, given their limitations.

# VIII. Modulating Injunctive Relief

The effect of patent rights on public health and welfare is not limited to government-sponsored inventions. Any patent on an invention that implicates public health can have a similar effect. It is black-letter law that a permanent injunction against the use, manufacture and sale of a patented invention is a proper—if not the standard—remedy in a fully-tried case of patent infringement.[11] (The rule is different for *preliminary* injunctions—those granted before a full trial on the merits—because the judge must balance the risk or error before trial against the risk of harm to the parties in the interim.[12]) A permanent injunction against infringement of a patent with health and safety implications, however, can have the same effect as the neglect, suppression, abandonment, etc., that march-in rights were intended to alleviate.

Under what circumstances should a court refuse to grant such an injunction, thereby in part subverting the economic regime of exclusivity in patented inventions, because granting the injunction might adversely affect the public interest in health or safety? The following case addresses this difficult question in the context of an invention of anti-pollution technology.

## City of Milwaukee v. Activated Sludge, Inc.
69 F.2d 577 (7th Cir.), *cert. denied* 293 U.S. 576 (1934)

SPARKS, Circuit Judge.

This is an appeal from a decree of the District Court holding [certain] United States patents issued to Walter Jones valid, and that appellant has infringed [certain] enumerated claims[.]

* * *

All of the patents pertain to the treatment of sewage by aeration. No. 587 relates to apparatus, and the others relate to process. [Certain of them] pertain to and depend upon the "Activated Sludge Process."

* * *

Prior to 1912 bio-chemists generally understood certain processes of nature which are collectively designated as the "nitrogen cycle." In order to comprehend the subject matter before us, and the contentions of the parties with respect to the claims in suit, it

---

11. *See* Jay Dratler, Jr., Intellectual Property Law: Commercial, Creative and Industrial Property § 13.01[2] (Law Journal Press 1991).
12. *See id.*, § 13.01[1].

is necessary to describe that cycle in a general way, for it was by consideration of the natural laws therein involved that the successful disposal of sewage was attained.

Plant life grows by absorbing carbon dioxide from the air and food from the earth. That food must include certain simple nitrogenous compounds, such as nitrates and nitrites, which in turn are converted by the plants into more complex nitrogenous compounds. Plants become the food of animals whose life and digestive processes convert the nitrogenous compounds of the plants into still more complex nitrogenous compounds. When an animal dies, a process of putrefaction sets in, converting the most complex nitrogenous compounds of animal tissue into simpler ones, more or less soluble in water. Those compounds in solution are carried by the water into the earth where they are further reduced and converted into nitrates and nitrites ready again to become the food of plants. Of course much plant life dies and decays without ever being used as animal food, and in that case its nitrogenous compounds are more directly reduced.

Again, animal life does not necessarily have to die in order to start the process of conversion. The animal's excreta during life immediately become the subject of putrefaction, degradation, and conversion to the simpler nitrogenous compounds. The intermediate products of putrefaction are inimical to the existence of both plants and animals, hence it is essential that the putrefaction of both animal and vegetable life be followed by a process of purification by which it may be converted into the simple and wholesome compounds. Purification is largely a matter of oxidation which may be effected in time by exposure to air, or to running water which contains air, but oxidation by mere exposure to air is a very slow and offensive process.

For many years prior to the disclosures of the patents in suit it was known that bacteria performed an essential part in nature's processes of putrefaction and purification. It was known that anaerobic bacteria, those which live out of contact with air, attack animal bodies soon after their death, and promote the putrefactive processes which result in the conversion of the very complex nitrogenous compounds into the simpler and more soluble ones such as ammonias, amidos, and aminos. These in turn are acted upon through processes of purification by aerobic bacteria, which thrive in the presence of air, and are converted into the nitrates and nitrites to be used again as plant food. It was also known that the absence of air was inimical to the life processes of aerobic bacteria, while the presence of it was inimical to the anaerobic.

Appellee correctly defines purification of sewage as the conversion of the putrescent and putrescible, and perhaps other more or less complex nitrogenous, carbonaceous and sulphurous compounds into simpler compounds which are wholesome and inoffensive. This action involves ultimately the oxidation of the compounds, and a sufficient degree of oxidation means adequate purification. When all or a great proportion of the total nitrogen is reduced to nitrates and nitrites it is said that a sufficiently complete purification has been effected. This is not because the nitrogenous compounds are the only ones which require oxidation, but because they are the most difficult to oxidize, and when that is accomplished the carbonaceous and sulphurous compounds will of necessity have been sufficiently oxidized.

Nature's process of purifying sewage involved the reduction of dead animal or plant life by putrefaction from its complex forms to the soluble compounds such as the ammonias, amidos and aminos. In these forms they could be dissolved in rain or other water and thus seeped into the earth or flowed over its surface into streams. Here these intermediate compounds came into contact with the aerobic bacteria contained in the surface soil and also upon the surfaces of stones and rocks in running streams. In streams, these aerobic bacteria grew on certain slimy, gelatinous substances adhering to the stones and rocks, and absorbed the air contained in the running water. As a result of the contact between these bacteria and the intermediate nitrogenous compounds, the latter were further reduced to the simpler and more oxidized compounds such as nitrates and nitrites, and in this state, they had attained purification. These natural processes, although extremely slow, were quite adequate to effect requisite purification of a reasonable amount of pollution, but they were much too slow to effect or maintain the purification of streams and lakes into which the sewage of large cities was poured.

How to dispose of abnormal amounts of sewage, caused by the growth of population and industry was a question that confronted the scientist and inventor from very early years, and it was never answered successfully prior to the disclosures out of which this controversy arises. Several methods of artificial sewage disposal were tried such as flowing over large areas of land, and contact filters, which include the trickling and sprinkling systems, through such media as tanks of rock, stone, cork, and sand. All such methods were very slow and expensive and proved to be quite unsatisfactory. Efforts were made to accomplish the desired result by chemical precipitation, but that method was likewise expensive and for that reason its extensive use was prohibited. No bacterial action was involved in it. In all those processes, except precipitation, nature's process was followed or approximated, and in each there remained after aeration and running off the liquid a sludge-like residuum of which no use was made. At the time the patents were issued it was known that this sludge contained both aerobic and anaerobic bacteria, and if permitted to lie dormant it would become septic and fetid because of the activity of the anaerobic bacteria in the absence of air, but if kept in an active state it would become purified by reason of the activity of the aerobic bacteria in the presence of air. Thus the idea of activation of the sludge formed the basis of further experimentation which resulted in the solution of the troublesome question. Its success was found to be dependent upon the fact that all sludge should be kept in active but gentle circulation with the sewage by the introduction of a continuous flow of air.

The patents in suit do not purport to cover the discovery of the bacteria, nor their characteristic activities, but they do claim the method and apparatus by virtue of which conditions are provided under which the aerobic bacteria are permitted to function to the best advantage....

\* \* \*

...[T]he method which appellee claims was disclosed for the first time by the Jones patents,...is admitted by both parties was invention and of revolutionary benefit to mankind....

\* \* \*

We are convinced that the trial court correctly held that Jones was the original, first, and sole inventor of the patents in suit; that the claims charged to be infringed are valid claims; and that the patents in suit are entitled to effective filing dates as of the filing dates of the British patents upon which the American patents are respectively alleged to be based....

\* \* \*

[*The court held that the appellant City of Milwaukee had infringed various claims of the patents in suit, had been properly named as a party and had been properly notified.*]

Included in appellant's answer to the bill is a counter-claim for damages arising out of alleged threats of infringement suits by appellee and its agents against public corporations and municipalities including appellant. The record discloses no factual basis to support this counter-claim.

\* \* \*

The decree in this case enjoins appellant from operating its plant. Ordinarily courts will protect patent rights by injunctive process. In determining whether that process shall be made permanent, the equities of all parties concerned should be considered. In the instant case both parties have strong equities, and there are many others who are indirectly concerned whose equities are even stronger than those of the parties. The damages of appellee may be compensated by a money judgment, and yet it has been subjected to great delay, and perhaps may yet suffer further delay, and greater than it otherwise would if the injunction were made permanent. It is only fair to say that these delays have been caused by the enormous amount of work necessarily occasioned by the issues involved. If, however, the injunction ordered by the trial court is made permanent in this case, it would close the sewage plant, leaving the entire community without any means for the disposal of raw sewage other than running it into Lake Michigan, thereby polluting its waters and endangering the health and lives of that and other adjoining communities. It is suggested that such harmful effect could be counteracted by chemical treatment of the sewage, but where, as here, the health and the lives of more than half a million people are involved, we think no risk should be taken, and we feel impelled to deny appellee's contention in this respect. This view is sustained by the group of cases to which appellant has called our attention in which injunctive relief was denied on the ground that it was not absolutely essential to preserve the rights of the patentee, and would cause the infringer irreparable damage. In none of those cases were the facts as serious or might the results have been as dangerous as in the case at bar....

The decree is affirmed except as to the injunction, and as to it the decree is reversed. The costs of this appeal are adjudged one-fourth against appellee, and three-fourths against appellant, and the cause is remanded with instructions to dissolve the injunction, and for further proceedings not inconsistent with this opinion.

\* \* \*

# Notes & Questions

1. What was the ultimate result in *Activated Sludge*? Did the Seventh Circuit deny the patentee all relief, or just injunctive relief? If the latter, was there any substantial *economic* difference between the court did and what if might have done if it had granted the City of Milwaukee a compulsory licenses to use the patented sewage-treatment technology without any voluntary agreement on the patentee's part? If you can analogize the result in this case to a hypothetical compulsory license of the patented technology, who determines the terms of the license and, in particular, the royalty rate?

2. Was the Seventh Circuit's decision in *Activated Sludge* correct? Did it realistically have any other choice? Would an injunction that would have polluted Lake Michigan been an appropriate use of judicial power, just to preserve the patentee's statutory exclusive rights?

Now suppose that Jones' technology was not the only way to purify sewage sludge through aeration and the consequent activation of aerobic bacteria. Suppose that Firm B had an alternative patented technology to accomplish the same end, which did not infringe any of Jones' patents. In that case, should the court have refused to grant an injunction to stop the infringement of Jones' patent? Should the answer depend upon the time and money needed to convert Milwaukee's sewage treatment plant from Jones' patented technology to Firm B's? Should it depend upon the City's ability to enter into a licensing agreement with Firm B? If the court granted an injunction against using Jones' technology, wouldn't that give Firm B a great deal of leverage in licensing negotiations?

3. In *CellPro*, the NIH refused to exercise its march-in rights to grant a compulsory license of patented technology to a contending firm other than the contractor that had developed the technology and owned the patent. In *Activated Sludge*, the court in effect granted the City of Milwaukee a compulsory license by denying injunctive relief but awarding damages. Try to articulate, as precisely as possible, the reasons for the differing result in the two cases. Were the differences matters of law or applicable legal standards? matters of fact? matters of policy? Does good policy support the result in each case?

4. *Activated Sludge* was an unusual case. It involved a request for a permanent injunction to prevent further patent infringement, made after a complete trial on the merits had found the patent valid and infringed. Very few courts have denied injunctive relief under such circumstances. *See* Jay Dratler, Jr., Intellectual Property Law: Commercial, Creative and Industrial Property § 13.01[2] (Law Journal Press 1991). Can you think of economic or policy reasons why? What would happen to the incentives to invent and to disclose inventions that patent law creates if courts made close judgments, in every case, whether a permanent injunction was an appropriate remedy for adjudicated infringement?

5. Request for *preliminary* injunctions, made before a full trial on the merits, are different. Black-letter law requires a balancing test in such cases, which weighs the likelihood of success of the patent-infringement claim at trial against the harm that an erroneous preliminary decision before trial might cause either party. *See* Dratler, *supra*, § 13.01[1] (Law Journal Press 1991). The most well-established test weights four factors in such cases: (1) the plaintiff-patentee's likelihood of success on the merits at trial; (2) the irreparable harm to the patentee that might occur if an preliminary injunction is denied; (3) the "balance of harms," i.e., whether the patentee will be hurt more if a preliminary injunction is erroneously denied than that defendant will be hurt if one is erroneously granted; and (4) the public interest. *See id.* Although the public interest is just one of the four traditional factors, it does give courts the power to consider such things as the pollution of Lake Michigan before granting preliminary injunctive relief.

6. *Activated Sludge* may have been an extreme case. It involved no alternative technology and no party claiming an alternative way of reaching the same desirable end — purifying sewage before dumping it into Lake Michigan. Cases involving such alternatives may present much closer questions.

Suppose, for example, that Firm A and Firm B both intend to market advanced "kits" for diagnosing a serious and potentially life-threatening diseases. Suppose further that Firm A owns a patent that covers the kits' technology, but that Firm B is further along in exploiting the patented technology and getting actual useful kits on the market. Firm A sues Firm B for patent infringement, asks for a preliminary injunction against the marketing and sale of Firm B's kits and makes a prima facie showing that Firm A's patents are valid and infringed by Firm B's kits. Should the court grant a preliminary injunction against the sale of Firm B's kits? *See Hybritech, Inc. v. Abbott Labs.*, 849 F.2d 1446,

1455–58 (Fed. Cir. 1988). What difference would it make if the same matters arose after a full trial on the merits, in which the court found Firm A's patents valid and infringed?

7. Patents with healthcare implications are by no means new. The explosion of research in biotechnology, however, may have increased both their number and the importance of their impact on public health. If so, courts can expect to see more cases like *CellPro*, *Activated Sludge*, and *Hybritech* in which self-interested parties cite the public interest — with some justification — as ground for compulsory licensing of patents in their favor.

How should these apparent changes affect your work as a licensing attorney representing a patentee with valuable health-related biotechnology? Should you be more accommodating in licensing negotiations, for fear that a compulsory license may follow if you are not? Should these legal developments make you more likely to recommend licensing competitors of your client? Can you think of any strategies in negotiation and licensing that might minimize the risk that a competitor could claim a compulsory license, either under the government's march-in rules or in infringement litigation?

# Table of Cases

# Index